Fundamentals of
Cost Accounting

Seventh Edition

T.R. Sikka
(M.Com., Ph.D., F.C.S.,)
Formerly Senior Lecturer, D.A.V. College,
Amritsar
Formerly Head, Department of Management Studies,
Amritsar College of Engineering and Technology,
Amritsar

Viva Books

New Delhi | Mumbai | Chennai | Kolkata | Bengaluru | Hyderabad | Kochi | Guwahati

Publisher's note

Every possible effort has been made to ensure that the information contained in this book is accurate at the time of going to press, and the publisher and author cannot accept responsibility for any errors or omissions, however caused. No responsibility for loss or damage occasioned to any person acting, or refraining from action, as a result of the material in this publication can be accepted by the editor, the publisher or the author.

Every effort has been made to trace the owners of copyright material used in this book. The author and the publisher will be grateful for any omission brought to their notice for acknowledgment in the future editions of the book.

First Published 2003
Reprinted 2005, 2007
Seventh Edition 2012

Viva Books Private Limited

- 4737/23, Ansari Road, Daryaganj, New Delhi 110 002
  Tel. 42242200, 23258325, 23283121, Email: vivadelhi@vivagroupindia.net
- 76, Service Industries, Shirvane, Sector 1, Nerul, Navi Mumbai 400 706
  Tel. 27721273, 27721274, Email: vivamumbai@vivagroupindia.net
- Jamals Fazal Chambers, 26 Greams Road, Chennai 600 006
  Tel. 28294241, 28290304, Email: vivachennai@vivagroupindia.net
- B-103, Jindal Towers, 21/1A/3 Darga Road, Kolkata 700 017
  Tel. 22816713, Email: vivakolkata@vivagroupindia.net
- 7, GF, Sovereign Park Aptts., 56-58, K. R. Road, Basavanagudi, Bengaluru 560 004
  Tel. 26607409, Email: vivabangalore@vivagroupindia.net
- 101-102, Moghal Marc Apartments, 3-4-637 to 641, Narayanguda, Hyderabad 500 029
  Tel. 27564481, Email: vivahyderabad@vivagroupindia.net
- First Floor, Beevi Towers, SRM Road, Kaloor, Kochi 682 018
  Tel. 0484-2403055, 2403056, Email: vivakochi@vivagroupindia.net
- 232, GNB Road, Beside UCO Bank, Silpukhuri, Guwahati 781 003
  Tel. 0361-2666386, Email: vivaguwahati@vivagroupindia.net

www.vivagroupindia.com

ISBN: 978-81-309-1870-9

Published by Vinod Vasishtha for Viva Books Private Limited, 4737/23 Ansari Road, Daryaganj, New Delhi 110 002.

Printed & bound by Raj Press, R-3, Inderpuri, New Delhi 110 012.

M0230

Fundamentals of Cost Accounting

Contents

Foreword

Cost Accounting is a highly specialized subject and is an integral part of Commerce education. There has been a dearth of good standard textbooks on the subject that explain the theory and practice of the subject. I congratulate Dr. T.R. Sikka for writing this book titled *Fundamentals of Cost Accounting*, which deals with both, the theoretical and practical aspects of the subject and hope that it will fill the void that exists in this field. This book is an outcome of over three decades of experience of the author teaching this subject.

I genuinely feel that the book provides a precise and lucid treatment of the basic principles of Cost Accounting supported by a number of objective type questions and practical exercises at the end of each chapter to assist the students in understanding the various topics properly. The book is fairly comprehensive and covers almost all areas on the subject.

I am confident that the book shall prove to be useful to the students of B.Com., B.B.A., M.B.A., M.Com., C.A. and I.C.W.A.

Dr. Subhash Chander,
Prof. and Head, Department of Commerce
and Business Management,
Guru Nanak Dev University, Amritsar

Preface

It gives me immense pleasure in presenting this book on Cost Accounting to my colleagues and students. Cost Accounting is a highly specialized subject requiring indepth understanding of its complicated concepts and techniques. This book is intended to serve as a textbook for the students of B.Com., B.B.A., B.C.A., M.B.A., M.Com., Institute of Chartered Accountants of India, the Institute of Cost and Works Accountants of India, the Institute of Company Secretaries of India and various other bodies and Management Associations. Each topic in the book has been treated in an easy and lucid style. The book contains a sufficient number of worked-out problems. A good number of objective type questions, short answer type questions, long answer type questions, and exercises have been given at the end of each chapter.

My gratefulness is unlimited to a large number of distinguished scholars and teachers including friends and colleagues, who have helped and encouraged me in a number of ways in writing this book.

My sincere thanks are also due to my publishers, Viva Books, New Delhi, for taking very nice and tender care of the book while in press.

Constructive suggestions for the improvement of the book will be gratefully acknowledged and incorporated in the next edition.

T.R. Sikka

1

Cost Accounting – An Overview

The present age is the age of competition and it is noted that there is a struggle for existence in every field and more particularly in the field of business (which comprises trade, commerce, industry and direct services). It is necessary for every business concern to carry on its activities with utmost efficiency so as to ensure the optimum utilisation of the limited resources lying at its disposal. Accounting plays an important role in the efficient and successful running of any business. Actually speaking, the planned development of any business concern is possible only if we collect and analyse the financial data in a systematic manner. It is possible only if a good system of accounting has been in use. Accounting has three main branches:

(*i*) Financial Accounting,
(*ii*) Cost Accounting, and
(*iii*) Management Accounting.

Financial Accounting is the art or process of recording, classifying and summarising the transactions of financial nature in a systematic manner and interpreting the results thereof. Financial accounting is the traditional form of accounting which is mainly concerned with the recording of day-to-day transactions of the business in the proper books of account with the object of enabling the preparation of Profit and Loss Account and Balance Sheet. Profit and Loss Account discloses the net profit or the net loss of the business for some specified period while the Balance Sheet shows the financial position of the business at a certain date.

Cost Accounting is the art or process of recording, analysing and classifying of expenditure for the purpose of product costing or service costing, ascertainment of profitability, operational planning and cost control. Cost accounting is a forward looking approach which is related to the recording, analysing and classifying of expenditure with the object of ascertaining the total and per unit cost of a product or service. Cost accounting is an internal aspect of the organisation which measures the operational efficiency of an enterprise and assists the management to maintain costs at the lowest point consistent with the efficient operating conditions. Standard costing, budgetary control and marginal costing are some of the dynamic techniques of cost accounting which are widely used now-a-days.

Management Accounting is the presentation of accounting information in such a way as to assist the management in the creation of policy and in the day-to-day operations of an undertaking. Management accounting relates to the use of financial and cost data for the purposes of evaluating the performance of the business as a whole and the various departments comprising it in relation to pre-determined targets. It also assists in reviewing existing policies or making decisions about new policies and in forward planning.

NEED FOR COST ACCOUNTING (OR LIMITATIONS OF FINANCIAL ACCOUNTING)

Financial accounting, which is historical in nature, is mainly concerned with the recording of day-to-day business transactions. It is simply a post-mortem of the past events. Under financial accounting, business transactions are first recorded in the books of original entry, then classified into ledger and finally summarised by preparing Trial Balance. From trial balance, the Profit and Loss Account or Income Statement is prepared to ascertain the periodic profit or loss and Balance Sheet or Position Statement is prepared to ascertain the financial position of the business as at the end of the accounting period. Financial accounting gives only a general idea about the working of the business and permits the management to control, in a general way, the major functions of the business viz., finance, production, administration and distribution. But it does not give details regarding the operating efficiency of these divisions. Financial accounting suffers from the following limitations or deficiencies:

1. **No provision for material control:** Financial accounts do not contain detailed particulars of materials consumed in a manufacturing concern. Although, the financial accounts record the value of opening and closing stocks and the cost of raw materials purchased, they are silent as to the quantity of the various items of raw material issued to different departments or jobs and the price at which they have been issued. Therefore, the cost of raw material consumed for the manufacture of a particular unit of output cannot be ascertained from financial accounts.
2. **Non-availability of detailed particulars about labour cost:** Financial accounts contain the record of the total wages paid to the workers during a specified period but they are silent as to number of workers employed, number of workers engaged on different jobs or in different departments, number of hours worked by each worker, rate of wages, total wages paid job-wise, product-wise or department-wise etc. Financial accounts also do not contain separate records for direct and indirect wages. Further, no distinction is made between the wages of efficient and inefficient workers.

As such it becomes difficult to ascertain as to whether the increase in the wage rates of workers or increase in the number of workers has led to a corresponding increase in the quantity of output or not.

3. **Classification of accounts in a general manner:** Under financial accounting system, accounts to be prepared are classified into personal, real and nominal accounts. Such a classification of accounts does not help in ascertaining the cost of production product-wise, job-wise, department-wise, work-order-wise etc.
4. **No classification of costs into direct and indirect items:** In financial accounts prepared under the financial accounting system, costs are not classified as to direct and indirect items and are not assigned or allocated to each product at each stage of production or to each department or process.
5. **Ascertainment of true cost of production not possible:** Financial accounts keep a record of all the expenses of the business whether or not these are relevant to cost of production. As such, the exact or true cost of a product, job, work-order or process cannot be ascertained from financial accounts nor can we decide as to whether or not all the relevant items of cost have been considered in ascertaining the total cost.
6. **No provision for a system of standards:** In a manufacturing concern carrying on production on large scale basis, its manager generally finds himself unable to supervise personally each and every activity involved in the manufacturing of goods. As such standards and targets have to be fixed in advance for various activities of the manufacturing concern. The actual performance is to be compared with the pre-determined standards in order to find out the differences and to provide for their analysis and remedial action, in case the performance is below standard. Financial accounting system has no provision for such a system of standards.
7. **No records for wastages:** Under financial accounting system, no records are kept in respect of the wastage of materials, man-hours and machine-hours taking place during the course of production. As such, no steps can be taken to eliminate or to minimise the various types of wastages.
8. **No assistance in fixation of selling price and calculation of tender price:** Financial accounting system fails to supply data regarding the true or exact cost of production on account of which the manufacturer finds himself unable to fix a competitive selling price for his products. Many a times, a manufacturer or a contractor has to submit quotations or tender to a prospective customer for the supply of a large quantity of a product at some future date or for the execution of a contract. The quotation price or the tender price should be competitive. A competitive quotation price or tender price can be determined with reference to the past cost data and changes anticipated over the previous cost levels. Since

financial accounting system does not supply data relating to true cost of production, the preparation of tenders and quotations becomes a difficult job.

9. **No assistance in cost control:** Financial accounting system does not help the management in controlling costs since it does not provide for a system of cost control. This limitation arises on account of the following reasons:
   (*a*) In financial accounts costs and expenses are recorded only after these have been actually incurred or spent. Hence, financial accounts do not leave any room for taking corrective action.
   (*b*) Financial accounts do not have any technique to check the reasonableness of any cost or expenditure.
   (*c*) Financial accounts do not help in fixing the responsibility on any individual for any wastage or excessive cost.
10. **Financial accounts deal only with the over-all profitability of the business concern:** Financial accounts of a business concern are so designed as to disclose the overall profit or loss of that business concern for a specified period. Financial accounts do not deal with the product-wise, job-wise, process-wise, department-wise profitability of the business. Hence, the unprofitable activities of the business are not disclosed and the necessary steps cannot be taken to make them profitable or to discontinue them.
11. **No provision for comparison of costs:** Financial accounts do not provide data for the comparison of the costing results of a particular period with that of other periods of operation of the same business concern or with that of other concerns in the same line of industry.
12. **No assistance in planning and decision-making:** Financial accounting system does not provide any guidance and assistance to the management in taking various important decisions relating to the operations of an undertaking. The management may require information for the following purposes:
   (*a*) Evaluation of the profitability of the alternative methods of production
   (*b*) Selection of the most profitable product-mix or sales-mix
   (*c*) Manufacture or buy decision
   (*d*) Operate or shut-down decision
   (*e*) Determination of sales required to earn desired profits
   (*f*) Ascertainment of the effect of changes in selling price on profits
   (*g*) Determination of the Break-even Point, Margin of Safety etc.

Financial accounting system does not provide the required data and assistance for the purpose of making decisions on the above mentioned matters.

All these limitations of financial accounting system have led to the development of cost accounting system.

DEFINITION OF COST ACCOUNTANCY

The Institute of Cost and Management Accountants, London, in its Costing Terminology, has defined the term 'Cost Accountancy' as "the application of costing and cost accounting principles, methods and techniques to the science, art and practice of cost control and the ascertainment of profitability. It includes the presentation of information derived therefrom for the purpose of managerial decision making."

In the above definition, two main terms 'Costing' and 'Cost Accounting' have been used. The term 'Costing' has been defined by the Institute of Cost and Management Accountants as "the techniques and processes of ascertaining costs." Costing involves systems, methods and techniques of accumulation, classification and analysis of costs or expenditure incurred in respect of a product manufactured or service rendered. The term 'Cost Accounting' has been defined by the Institute of Cost and Management Accountants as "the process of accounting for cost from the point at which expenditure is incurred or committed to the establishment of its ultimate relationship with cost centres and cost units. In its widest usage, it embraces the preparation of statistical data, the application of cost control methods and the ascertainment of the profitability of activities carried out or planned." Cost accounting involves the recording of costs for the purpose of ascertaining and controlling the costs of products and services. Cost accounting is systematic process of recording the costs of operating a business concern in order to ascertain the total and per unit cost of products and services. Cost accounting system provides data and information for the assistance and guidance of the management in cost control.

According to Harold J. Wheldon — "Costing is the classifying, recording, and appropriate allocation of expenditure for the determination of the cost of products or services and for the presentation of suitably arranged data for purposes of control and guidance of the management. It includes the ascertainment of the cost of every order, job, contract, process, service or unit as may be appropriate. It deals with the costs of production, selling and distribution." This definition emphasises the allocation of costs relating to production and sale with a view to ascertaining the cost of every job, process, contract, service or unit. Thus, this definition is very exhaustive but too lengthy.

R.N. Carter defines "cost accounting"* as "a system of recording in accounts the materials used and labour employed in the manufacture of a certain

* Although strictly speaking, the terms 'Costing', 'Cost Accounting' and 'Cost Accountancy' are distinct from each other, these are used interchangeably by various authorities on accountancy.

commodity or on a particular job." This definition is comparatively smaller but does not bring out the main essentials of cost accounting system. It will be readily agreed that mere record keeping of materials and labour cannot be called cost accounting. Further, this definition emphasises the ascertainment of the cost of commodities manufactured or jobs performed as the main object of cost accounting system and ignores the ascertainment of the cost of services rendered by a business concern.

According to Horton and Mason, Cost Accounting is "the method of recording accurately the facts of manufacture or other undertakings in such a way, that necessary information thereon may be available in the form required at the earliest possible moment." This definition emphasises the importance of accurate recording, disclosure of necessary information, useful form and prompt reference. All these are certainly the important features of a system of cost accounting but the definition need not to include them.

According to Gordon Shillinglaw, Cost Accounting is defined as "the body of concepts, methods and procedures used to measure, analyse, or estimate the costs, profitability and performance of individual products, departments, and other segments of a company's operations, for either internal or external use or both, and to report on these questions to the interested parties." This definition is simple as well as exhaustive and covers all the important features of the cost accounting system.

After discussing the above definitions, it can be asserted that cost accountancy is the science, art and practice of a cost accountant. Cost accountancy is a science in the sense that it includes the systematic knowledge which a cost accountant should possess for discharging his duties properly. It is an art in the sense that it includes the ability and skill with which a cost accountant is in a position to apply his knowledge of the principles of cost accountancy to various managerial problems such as ascertainment of profitability, introduction of a new product, selection of the most profitable sales-mix, whether to make or to buy, to operate or shut-down etc. Practice refers to the continuous efforts of a cost accountant in the field of cost accountancy.

FEATURES OF COST ACCOUNTANCY

The main features of cost accountancy may be given as follows:

1. Cost accountancy is a special branch of accountancy dealing with the ascertainment of cost of products and services.
2. Cost accountancy is both a science and an art.
3. It follows the same double entry system as in financial accounting.
4. It involves the processes of accumulation, classification, analysis, recording and ascertainment of costs.

5. It determines the total and per unit cost of products and services.
6. It provides data for fixing the selling price of products and services and for determining the quotation price or tender price.
7. It provides data to the management for exercising effective control over costs.
8. It provides data to the management for use in forward planning and decision-making process.

SCOPE OF COST ACCOUNTANCY

Expanding the ideas contained in the definition of "Cost Accountancy" as given the Terminology of Cost Accountancy of the Institute of Cost and Management Accountants (London), it may be said that cost accountancy includes the following subjects:

(*i*) **Costing:** Costing refers to the techniques and processes of ascertaining costs. It involves systems, methods and techniques of accumulation, classification, analysis and appropriate allocation of expenditure incurred in respect of a product or service. Thus costing consists of the principles, rules and methods which are used for determining the costs of products and services.

(*ii*) **Cost Accounting:** Cost accounting is the science which records and determines scientifically the accurate cost of manufacture or service per unit and controls and guides the persons involved in the organisation of production. Thus, cost accounting is the formal mechanism by which cost data are provided for ascertaining and controlling the costs of products or services.

(*iii*) **Cost Control:** Cost control is the guidance and regulation, by executive action, of the costs of operating an undertaking. It guides the organisation to achieve the target of the undertaking for a given period. Cost control involves the setting up of targets for expenses and production performances, measurement of the actuals, comparison of actuals with targets to ascertain the variances, analysis of variances and taking corrective action to eliminate variances.

The guidance and regulation is done through an action by the executive who is responsible for the incurring of the expenditure.

(*iv*) **Budgetary Control:** Budgetary control is a system whereby the budgets are used as a means of planning and controlling costs. Budgetary control is the establishment of budgets relating to the responsibilities of executives to the requirements of a policy, and the continuous comparison of actual with budgeted results, either to secure by individual action the objective of that policy or to provide a basis for its revision. Budgetary control involves the establishment of budgets for each section of the organisation, measurement of the actual performances and their comparison with budgeted performances to determine the deviations, the ascertainment of reasons for such deviations and taking suitable actions to remedy the defects.

(*v*) **Cost Audit:** Cost audit is the verification of the correctness of cost accounts and a check on the adherence to the cost accounting plan. The purpose of the cost audit is to ensure that the figures as shown by cost accounts are correct and that cost accounts, cost centres and cost units have been properly charged.

OBJECTS OF COST ACCOUNTING

The primary or ostensible object of cost accounting is to find out the cost of unit production of a commodity or service. According to J.R. Batliboi – "The main object of cost accounts, irrespective of the branch of industry to which they are applied should always be to express faithfully and accurately the true costs."* The objects of cost accounting may be summarised as follows:

1. To study, analyse and classify the cost of production.
2. To ascertain the total and per unit cost of the commodity produced, work performed and service rendered.
3. To ascertain the profitability of different products, jobs or work-orders.
4. To exercise effective control over wastage and loss of materials during production.
5. To provide means to measure the efficiency of labour.
6. To exercise effective control on the total cost of labour engaged in each department of the business.
7. To exercise effective control on the idle time of workers and machines.
8. To enable the manufacturers to study comparative costs of different periods and to throw light on the extent and causes of variation.
9. To provide statistical data for the purpose of submitting quotations or tenders.
10. To provide reliable information and statistical data for framing the future policy of the manufacturing concern.
11. To collect data for the preparation of cost accounts.
12. To provide for cost control through budgetary control and standard costing systems.

COSTING, ESTIMATING AND PRICING

Sometimes there may arise confusion as regards the exact meaning of the terms 'Costing', 'Estimating' and 'Pricing', which are used in connection with cost

* Works Organisation, Management and Cost Control – J.R. Batliboli, page 427.

accounts. The exact meaning of these terms should be understood at this stage.

'Costing' means ascertaining actual cost. It can be defined as ascertaining the actual cost of an article that has already been produced or of a service that has already been rendered.

'Estimating', on the other hand, refers to ascertaining in advance of the probable cost of manufacturing an article or of completing a contract or of executing a process in near future. Estimating is based on past (recorded) experience. Estimating necessarily involves some guess but such guess should be as close to facts as possible. One of the advantage of cost accounting system is that it provides reliable data on the basis of which estimates or tenders for future work can be prepared much more accurately than can be possible without them. In this way, the margin of error in estimating cost is reduced and the businessman can quote a competitive price. While estimating cost on the basis of past cost data, the anticipated changes in relevant costs must be taken into account otherwise the estimates may not be correct.

'Pricing'means fixing the selling price of an article. Pricing of an article already produced should be preceded by and based on costing though some other factors are also taken into account i.e., price of competitive articles, future trend of prices, etc. In cases where pricing of an article has to be done before its actual production, it is preceded by estimating rather than costing and has to be based on it. But in such cases, the estimating itself must be based on actual cost data adjusted to anticipated changes in the relevant items of cost.

COST ACCOUNTING AND FINANCIAL ACCOUNTING – A COMPARATIVE STUDY

Cost accounting is very closely related to financial accounting. It is generally said that cost accounting system is complimentary to the financial accounting system. According to L.W. Hawkins—"the ordinary trading account is a locked warehouse of most valuable information, to which the cost system is the key." The Trading and Profit and Loss Account or the financial accounts disclose the overall profit and losses of a business for a specified period. Cost accounts throw light upon the particular factors which have brought about the profits or losses, as the case may be. This fact can be understood with the help of the following illustration:

P.D. Company is engaged in the manufacture of three products 'A' 'B' and 'C'. The financial books of the company give the following information:

Trading and Profit and Loss Account for the year ended...

	Rs.		Rs.
To Materials consumed	40,000	By Sales	1,50,000
To Direct Wages	32,000		
To Direct Expenses	5,000		
To Manufacturing Expenses	25,000		
To Gross Profit c/d	48,000		
	1,50,000		1,50,000
To Office and Administrative Expenses	6,000	By Gross Profit b/d	48,000
To Selling and Distribution Expenses	12,000		
To Net Profit	30,000		
	48,000		48,000

The cost accountant of the company (under the cost accounting system) will present the above data in the following form:

Statement of Cost and Profit

Items	Total	Product A	Product B	Product C
	Rs.	Rs.	Rs.	Rs.
Direct Materials	40,000	16,000	16,000	8,000
Direct Wages	32,000	12,000	16,000	4,000
Direct Expenses	5,000	2,000	2,000	1,000
Prime Cost	77,000	30,000	34,000	13,000
Factory Expenses	25,000	8,000	14,000	3,000
Factory Cost	1,02,000	38,000	48,000	16,000
Office and Administrative Expenses	6,000	3,000	1,000	2,000
Cost of Production	1,08,000	41,000	49,000	18,000
Selling and Distribution Expenses	12,000	5,000	5,000	2,000
Total Cost	1,20,000	46,000	54,000	20,000
Sales	1,50,000	76,000	40,000	34,000
Profit/Loss	30,000	30,000	(–) 14,000	14,000
% of Profit on Sales	20%	39.47%	(–) 35%	41.18%

Financial accounting records show an overall profitability of 20% on sales while cost accounting records show a profit of 39.47% and 41.18% on products 'A' and 'C' respectively while there is a loss of Rs. 14,000 (35%) on product 'B'. The cost records make it clear that a big part of the profits is being eaten away by product 'B'. If complete details are known to the management, it may take necessary steps to make the product 'B' a profitable one. If it is not possible, the production of product 'B' may be stopped.

Thus, while financial accounts enable the businessman to ascertain the total profits or losses of the business concern, cost accounts with their analytical approach, disclose the detailed analysis of the factors leading to such profits or losses. Cost accounts, by disclosing the factors which have led to a loss to the business concern, also enable the businessman or management to take steps necessary for eliminating such loss in future. Further, financial accounts consist of the figures of costs and expenses in a summarised form whereas the cost accounts present the information about these expenses in a scientifically analysed and classified form for assisting the management in the ascertainment of costs, ascertainment of profitability, fixation of selling price, operational planning and cost control.

Therefore, it can rightly be said that the ordinary Trading and Profit and Loss Account (Financial accounts) contain very useful data and the cost accounts supply useful details of the data contained in the financial accounts.

SIMILARITIES BETWEEN COST ACCOUNTING AND FINANCIAL ACCOUNTING

Cost accounts and Financial accounts which are kept quite separate in a business concern, are similar in certain respects while in some other respects these differ from each other. The various similarities between cost accounts and financial accounts may be given as follows:

(*i*) Both cost accounts and financial accounts are maintained on the basis of Double Entry System of Accounting.

(*ii*) Recording of transactions, both under cost accounting system and financial accounting system, is made on the basis of common vouchers, invoices and documents.

(*iii*) Both cost accounts and financial accounts disclose the profit or loss of the business.

(*iv*) Both cost accounts and financial accounts involve the process of matching the costs and revenues of the related activity for the current period.

(v) Both the accounting systems contain the record of direct costs and indirect costs.

(*vi*) Both the accounting systems enable the business concern to compare and reconcile the trading results.

(*vii*) Both the accounting systems assist the management in formulating the future business policy and making various managerial decisions.

DIFFERENCES BETWEEN COST AND FINANCIAL ACCOUNTS

Although, both cost accounts and financial accounts are prepared on the basis of common principles and common vouchers and documents, they differ from each other on the following points:

(*i*) Financial accounts are very comprehensive in nature and cover all business transanctions while cost accounts cover only the transanctions relating to the manufacturing and sale of products and services.

(*ii*) Financial accounts deal with all items of expenses, losses, income and gains but cost accounts deal with only those items of expenses which enter into the cost of production.

(*iii*) Financial accounts do not contain analysis of expenditure according to elements, functions, behaviour, departments or products. Cost accounts record expenses by elements, functions, variability, departments etc., to study them analytically,

(*iv*) Financial accounts do not present the accounting information in a well-classified and analysed form so as to disclose the cost per unit at all stages. Cost accounts present well-classified and analysed details of expenses to disclose per unit cost at all stages of production.

(*v*) Financial accounts disclose the overall profitability of the business whereas cost accounts deal with product-wise, job-wise, department-wise and process- wise profitability.

(*vi*) Financial accounts deal with facts or actual figures alone. Cost accounts deal with facts as well as estimates as a result of which the results of cost accounts do not always tally with those of financial accounts.

(*vii*) Financial accounts do not disclose information relating to wastage of materials and the loss of man-hours and machine-hours. Cost accounts, on the other hand, contain full information relating to all types of wastage incurred during production.

(*viii*) The maintenance of financial accounts is compulsory in a business while cost accounts, though important and advantageous, need not be maintained compulsorily.

(*xi*) Financial accounts cannot be incorporated in cost accounts whereas cost accounts may be incorporated in financial accounts.

(*x*) Financial accounts do not provide any means to measure the efficiency and to exercise control over costs. Cost accounts develop standard costs against which actual costs can be compared and reasons for variances may be enquired into for taking corrective action.

(*xi*) Financial accounts fail to guide the businessman in the fixation of selling prices and calculation of estimates. Cost accounts furnish detailed cost information at different levels of production which forms basis for determining selling prices and calculating the tender price.

ADVANTAGES OF COST ACCOUNTING

Cost accounting system renders invaluable services to the manufacturers, management, employees, investors, consumers and Government. These services or advantages may be summarised as follows:

(A) ADVANTAGES TO MANUFACTURERS AND MANAGEMENT

The main advantages of a sound cost accounting system to the manufacturers and management are:

1. **Ascertainment of cost:** The principal object of cost accounting system is to ascertain scientifically the cost of production and this is also the main advantage of the cost accounting system. The cost accounting system enables the manufacturer to ascertain exact cost per unit, per job or per contract not only at the final stage of completion but also at the various stages of production or execution. Further, cost accounting system also discloses the extent to which each element of expenditure contributes to the total cost.
2. **Disclosure of profitable and unprofitable activities:** Cost accounting system discloses the profitable and unprofitable activities of a business and thus affords valuable suggestion for a contraction or elimination of those which are less profitable or completely unprofitable, and for an expansion or adoption of those which are profitable. In case of non-availability of costing data, the profits of one department or product may be eaten away by the losses incurred in some other department or in respect of some other product and the businessman may have no idea that by closing down or improving the latter, his business can become highly profitable.
3. **Provision of basis for determination of selling price:** By disclosing actual cost of production, cost accounting system provides the businessman with a reliable basis for fixing selling prices of his products. Thus it saves the manufacturer from losses which may arise due to injudicious fixation of prices without actually looking to the cost of production.
4. **Calculation of tender price or quotation price:** Cost accounting system provides a reliable basis for preparing tenders or quotations at which the manufacturer agrees to supply goods to a prospective customer at some future date. If the tenders are based on actual cost data, they are bound to be competitive and sure to be accepted by the prospective customer.
5. **Disclosure of the constitution of cost:** Cost accounting system reveals as to what proportion do material cost, labour cost and overhead bear to the total cost. Thus, it assists the manufacturer in ascertaining the importance of each element of cost and in determining where there is greater scope for economy.
6. **Comparison of cost:** Cost accounting system furnishes reliable data for comparing costs in different periods, for different volumes of output, in different departments or processes and in different establishments.
7. **Control of costs:** Cost accounting system serves as a means of controlling costs through–
   (*i*) an efficient system of material control which provides for proper checks on purchasing, receiving, storage and issue of materials and also prevents wastages, leakages, pilferage and overstocking of materials by fixing stock levels;

(*ii*) an efficient system of labour control which provides for proper control over the arrival and departure of workers, analysis of the time of the workers and the payment of wages;

(*iii*) ensuring optimum utilisation of plant capacity. Cost accounting system also develops standard costs of each element of cost to serve as a yardstick to measure the efficiency of actual operations. In case of variances, it gives rise to thorough enquiry into their causes so as to enable the manufacturer to take corrective action to eliminate the same.

8. **Helpful in planning and decision-making:** The various cost records maintained under the cost accounting system provide valuable information for the purpose of future planning and for decision-making. The costing records assist the management in making the following decisions:
   (*i*) Manufacture or buy decisions;
   (*ii*) Selection of the profitable product-mix;
   (*iii*) Operate or shut-down decision;
   (*iv*) Selection of the profitable method of production;
   (*v*) Fixation of the selling price.
9. **Check on the accuracy of financial accounts:** Cost accounting system provides an independent and most reliable check on the accuracy of financial accounts by means of the reconciliation of profits as shown by cost accounts and financial accounts.

(B) ADVANTAGES TO INVESTORS AND FINANCIAL INSTITUTIONS

Investors and financial institutions are always interested in making investment in and granting loans to those industrial concerns which have good profitability and sound financial position. Manufacturing concerns adopting cost accounting exercise cost control which, in its own turn, ensures higher profitability and sound financial position.

(C) ADVANTAGES TO WORKERS

Cost accounting system aims at utilising the labour force in the most efficient manner and does not involve the exploitation of workers. Cost accounting system stresses the classification of workers according to their efficiency and formulates plan of wage payment under which efficient workers get proper reward for their work and less efficient workers get an incentive to increase their efficiency. Thus, cost accounting system helps in increasing the efficiency of the workers of the business undertakings.

A good system of costing helps in maximising the profits of any business concern, thus giving it a long and prosperous life. This factor is helpful in ensuring permanency of employment and fair reward for work to the workers.

Cost accounting system also helps in minimising the possibilities of mis-understanding between workers and employers on the questions of fairness of profits and rate of wages. Thus, it minimises the chances of labour disputes in business concerns.

(D) ADVANTAGES TO CONSUMERS AND GENERAL PUBLIC

Cost accounting system provides for cost control through the utilisation of the various factors of production in the most efficient manner. Cost control leads to a reduction in the cost of products and services. As a result of it, the various products and services are offered to the consumers at a lower price. Thus, the consumers are in a position to enjoy quality goods and services at the most reasonable price. Further, permanency of the existence of business concerns due to high profitability as a result of cost control, ensures un-interrupted supply of goods to consumers and general public. Thus, the consumers are protected against the evils of hoarding and black-marketing.

(E) ADVANTAGES TO NATIONAL ECONOMY

Present age is the age of planning. To bring about planned economic development, the Government of every country prepares economic plans. For proper economic and industrial development, the Government requires data relating to cost of production in various industries so as to decide about the various economic incentives and financial assistance to be given to them. The Government also requires these data for use in framing its various economic policies e.g., Business Policy, Industrial Policy, Import and Export Policy, Taxation Policy etc.

Further, the Government has also to take into account the total cost involved in any economic and industrial plan before it is implemented. It is possible only through cost accounting system.

Objections to Cost Accounting

Sometimes certain objections are raised against cost accounting system and some disadvantages thereof pointed out. But the fact remains that there are no real disadvantages of the system itself. The disadvantages of the cost accounting system arise only if the system is not applied with caution and care. The main objections against cost accounting system are as follows:

1. **Cost accounting is unnecessary:** It is generally agrued that maintenance of the costing records for the purpose of operating the cost accounting system, is unnecessary and involves duplication of accounting work. But this argument cannot be treated as valid in this present age of cut throat competition. The management of any manufacturing concern, in order to face competition, should know not only the exact cost of its products but also the constitution of cost or its various elements. Cost accounting system renders invaluable services to the management in the following ways:

(*a*) It helps the management in ascertaining the accurate cost of products of the manufacturing concern and how it has been made up.

(*b*) It provides a reliable basis to the management for fixing a reasonable and competitive selling price and quotation price.

(*c*) It assists in controlling the costs of material, labour and overhead by eliminating or mininising all types of wastages, leakages and inefficiencies.

(*d*) It helps the management in exercising cost control and maximising profits through the techniques of standard costing and budgetary control.

(*e*) It provides invaluable data for the assistance and guidance of the management in the decision-making process.

Keeping in view the above mentioned advantages of the cost accounting system, it can be said that cost accounting is not unnecessary.

2. **Cost accounting system cannot be adopted by small business concerns:** It is generally said that the adoption of cost accounting system is costly and hence the small business concerns are unable to adopt it and to enjoy its advantages. But it should be remembered that costing system should be adopted not as a matter of fashion but as a matter of necessity. If a small business concern needs the costing system, the system should be so designed that it is within the financial capacity of that business. The practical importance of the objection is, therefore, negligible.
3. **Cost accounting system is very costly:** The third disadvantage of the cost accounting system is that its installation and subsequent operation involves additional expenditure which leads to an increase in the cost of production and reduces the profitability of the business concern. But cost accounting system being costly in itself is no disadvantage provided the system is a profitable investment for any business concern. The cost accounting system should be economical and the cost of its operation should be commensurate with the advantages accruing from it. If this principle is faithfully observed, there is no possibility of the cost accounting system being costly.
4. **Costing results are misleading:** It is generally said that cost accounting system involves the use of the estimated figures and costing results may be misleading if errors somehow creep in. But it may happen only in case of wrong application of the system by the persons who are not well-trained in cost accounting principles. Thus, the fault lies with the man and not with the cost accounting system.

Practical difficulties in the installation of costing system:

The management, while installing a costing system, apart from technical costing problems, has to face certain practical difficulties which are:

(*i*) Suspicion of employees and lack of co-operation from other executives.

(*ii*) Lack of interest in cost reduction due to absence of cost-consciousness among executives.

(*iii*) Improper and inefficient completion of forms and their submission as such to the cost office.

In order to overcome these difficulties, the management should make efforts to win the confidence of the workers by educating them about the advantages of the costing system before introducing the same. Regular meetings of executives and supervisory staff should be convened so as to educate them as to how the costing system is going to assist them in discharging their duties properly. After installing the costing system, continuous check over the progress of the system should be kept. Only the continuous efforts on the part of management and cost accountant can ensure the success of costing system.

Essential Factors to be Considered for Designing a Cost Accounting System: For ensuring the efficient and successful operation of the cost accounting system, certain factors are to be given due consideration while designing such a system. These factors may be given as follows:

(*i*) **Technical Details of the Business:** All the technical details of the business concern, its organisational structure, manufacturing procedure and process, selling and distribution procedure and type of cost information should be thoroughly understood.

(*ii*) **Selection of the Suitable Costing Technique:** A suitable technique for the ascertainment of cost of products should be selected. Cost can be ascertained by the techniques of standard costing or actual costing, marginal costing or absorption costing.

(*iii*) **Suitable Method of Pricing out Materials:** For the purpose of ascertaining the true cost of materials consumed in the manufacturing process, there should be a suitable method of pricing out materials issued to production e.g., Actual Cost Price Method (First-in-First-Out or Last-in-First-Out) Average Cost Method, Market Price Method etc.

(*iv*) **Selection of the Method of Wage Payment and the Method of Time-booking:** A suitable method of wage payment keeping in view the nature of the product should be devised. Wages may be paid on the basis of Time Rate System, Piece Rate System or Incentive Plans. Further, a suitable method for the analysis of the time of the direct labour on various jobs, work-orders etc., should be devised so that true labour cost of each job, work-order etc., may be ascertained.

(*v*) **Method of Overhead Accounting:** The total cost of a product or service not only comprises direct costs but also a part of the indirect costs. For the purpose of ascertaining the proper share of a product in the total amount of overhead, a sound plan for the collection, allocation, apportionment and absorption of overhead should be devised.

(*vi*) **Methods of Treatment of Wastage, Scrap and Idle Time:** Manufacturing process in a busines concern may involve wastage or loss of materials, scrap of materials and idle time of men and machines. The management should decide the ways in which the cost of wastage of materials, cost of materials scrapped and the cost of idle time are to the treated.

(*vii*) **Designing Suitable Forms:** Cost accounting system involves the collection and dissemination of cost data. For efficiency and accuracy in the collection and dissemination of cost data, use of printed forms is made. These forms have to be suitably designed keeping in view the requirements of the business concern.

(*viii*) **Introduction of Budgetary Control Technique:** From the view point of measuring the efficiency of performance, technique of budgetary control is introduced so that actual performance may be compared with budgetary figures.

Installation of a Costing System:

Broadly speaking, the objective of any costing system should be to collect statistical data for significant operations of the undertaking, to analyse it and to make it available to the management in a suitable form with a view to assisting it in taking managerial decisions. Hence the costing system should primarily be set up for the benefit of the undertaking. Accordingly, the following general matters and conditions should be considered while introducing a costing system:

1. **Objectives of Costing System:** First of all, the objectives of installing the costing system in the business concern and the expectations of the management from the system, should be determined in clear terms. The costing system may be introduced for fixing prices or for instituting a system of cost control.
2. **Consideration of the Significant Variables:** It is necessary to ascertain the significant variables of the manufacturing unit which are amenable to control and affect the business unit. In some of the manufacturing units, material cost is the dominant factor. In such a case, the costing system should devote greater attention to control material cost. It can be done through effective supervision over purchasing, receiving, storing, issuing, pricing and utilising the materials. If labour cost is the dominant factor, elaborate system has to be devised to effectively control the recruitment, preparation of labour records, and payment of wages.
3. **Suitability to the Product:** The costing system to be installed must be according to the nature of the product or the manufacturing process involved.
4. **Suitability to General Organisation:** The costing system should be organised in such a way that it suits the general organisation of the undertaking. Costing system should be introduced without unduly altering or extending the present organisation.

5. **Consideration of the Technical Details of the Business:** The technical aspects of the working of the business should be taken into consideration and an attempt should be made to win the sympathetic assistance or support of the principal members of the supervisory staff.
6. **Use of Standard Forms:** Printed forms should be used to record the cost data so as to reduce the clerical work and to minimise the possibility of errors.
7. **Details of Cost Records:** The details in which records are to be kept should be minimum according to the requirements of the management.
8. **Prompt Availability of Costing Information:** Arrangements should be made to make the costing results available to the management regularly and promptly as they are of immense help to the management in taking timely actions.
9. **Degree of Accuracy Desired:** The degree of accuracy of cost data desired and the manner in which such accuracy may be verified should be determined.
10. **Reconciliation of Results:** Both cost accounts and financial accounts should be inter-locked into a single accounting system or the results of separate sets of accounts, cost and financial, should be capable of reconciliation.

Characteristics of an Ideal System of Cost Accounting:

A good system of cost accounting is that which achieves the objects of costing in the best possible way and brings to the business, advantages which have already been discussed. An ideal system of costing should possess the following characteristics:

1. **Simplicity.** Costing system should be simple to operate and easy to understand. The facts, figures and other informations revealed by cost accounts should be so presented as to make them easily graspable. As such the needless elaboration of costing records should be avoided.
2. **Suitability to the Business.** A costing system should be so devised as to suit the conditions, requirements, nature and size of the business. A costing system which serves the purposes of the business and supplies necessary information for running the business successfully is an ideal system for that business.
3. **Economy.** In order that the system of costing may become a profitable investment of the business, the cost of installing and operating the system must be within the financial capacity of the business.
4. **Elasticity.** The system of costing should be elastic and capable of adapting itself to altered conditions and must not be rigid. It should, in particular, be suitable to handle a large volume of work as also to deal with changes in the nature of business.

5. **Accuracy.** An ideal system of costing is that which ensures accuracy of the records to be maintained. If the costing records maintained are not correct and accurate, the results or conclusions drawn therefrom are bound to be inaccurate and misleading.
6. **Comparability.** The costing records must be presented in a scientifically classified form so that a comparative study of costing results of different periods can be made.
7. **Promptness.** An ideal system of costing is one in which informations necessary for its functioning are promptly, easily and punctually available. Promptness can be ensured if arrangements are made for the prompt supply of records by the various departments relating to materials, labour, overhead etc., to the costing office and the data obtained are promptly analysed and recorded.
8. **Reconciliation of Results.** The costing system should be so maintained as to make reconciliation of cost accounts with financial accounts easy and simple. This reconciliation is very essential for checking the accuracy of cost accounts as also for measuring the efficiency of costing system.

METHODS OF COSTING

Different methods of costing are applied for ascertaining unit cost in different industries based on the nature of operation and unit of finished product involved. All these methods have the same general principles but they differ in so far as the methods used in collecting and presenting cost data are concerned. Basically, there are two methods of costing viz., Job Costing and Process Costing. Job costing is applied to special order type of industry which is devoted to the execution of specific orders such as printing press, ship building, house building, road construction, bridge construction etc. The main object of job costing is to ascertain the cost and profit or loss in respect of each job, contract or project undertaken. Process costing is applied to mass production type of industry engaged in the continuous production of uniform standard products such as chemicals, oil, cement, cloth, yarn, mining, colliery etc. The main object of process costing is to ascertain the cost of process or operation involved in converting raw materials into finished products. The different methods of costing, which represent finer divisions of these two basic methods, may be enumerated as follows:

1. Single Costing or Unit Costing:

This method of costing is applied to ascertain the total and per unit cost of standard product turned out in a manufacturing concern. This method of costing is generally applied to industries where the following features are present:

(*a*) The output or production is continuous.

(*b*) The units of output are identical.

(*c*) The units of output are natural.

(*d*) It is desirable to ascertain the cost per unit of output *e.g.*, per tonne, per kilogram, per metre etc.

The above mentioned features are present in industries like collieries, brick works, flour mills, quarries, cement mills, paper mills, iron and steel mills, sugar mills etc., which are engaged in producing only one type of product or a few grades of the same product.

This method of costing is adopted with a view to ascertain the total cost and also the per unit cost by making a detailed analysis of different elements of cost (*e.g.*, direct material cost, direct labour cost, direct expenses and overhead) under various heads *e.g.*, Prime Cost, Works Cost, Office Cost and Total Cost. This method does not require a detailed apportionment of overhead since all overhead are incurred on identical units but the production of few grades or various sizes of the same commodity shall require a careful apportionment of overhead to these grades and sizes. The analysis of cost may be presented periodically in the form of a statement (known as Cost Sheet or Statement of Cost) or an account (known as Production Account).

2. Process Costing:

This method of costing is employed to ascertain the cost of production in industries where a product passes through different processes or stages, each distinct and well-defined, before its completion. Under process costing, there is a finished product at each stage or process (which becomes the raw material of the subsequent process till it reaches the final stage of completion) and this renders it necessary to know the cost of production at each stage. Process costing method is generally applied to industries where:

(*a*) the production is continuous and is carried on for own stock.

(*b*) the finished product, before completion, has to pass through various processes or stages, each being separate and well-defined.

(*c*) the order or the sequence of processes is specific and pre-determined.

(*d*) the units manufactured are uniform and standardised.

(*e*) the finished product of each process becomes the raw material of the next process except that of the last process which is transferred to the Finished Stock Account.

This method is generally employed in industries like chemical works, distilleries, refineries, edible oils, soap making, food products, paints making etc. Under this method, a separate account is opened for each process and costing information is presented in the form of Process Account which is debited with the costs incurred thereon.

3. Job Costing:

Job costing is the method of costing which is applied to ascertain the costs of specific jobs or work-orders which are treated as contracts of small size. These jobs are generally dissimilar, of non-repetitive nature and may not be comparable with each other. This method is also known as 'Job Lot Costing' or 'Lot Costing' and has the following main features:

(*a*) Under job costing, production is carried on by a manufacturer against customer's order and not for own stock.
(*b*) Each job or work-order is of a separate nature.
(*c*) The jobs or work-orders are generally executed in factories, work-shops and repair-shops. But sometimes the job work is also done outside the factory or work-shop *e.g.,* plumbering job, sewerage work etc.
(*d*) The unit of costing, under this method, is a job or specific work-order.
(*e*) Under this method, the production and its requirement are determined first and then the expenses are ascertained in relation to it.

Job costing method is most suitable to such activities as printing press, painting and decorating, automobile garages, repair shops, electrical fittings, engineering works, plumbering works etc., where work is done according to the customer's specifications.

4. Contract Costing:

This method of costing is applied in a business where separate contracts of non-repetitive nature are undertaken. A contract is a job of large size which may extend even beyond one accounting period. The person executing the contract is known as 'Contractor' and the person for whom it is executed is known as 'Contractee'. The main features of contract costing may be summarised as follows:

(*a*) Contracts are executed at contract site away from contractor's premises.
(*b*) Contracts are jobs of large size and may continue over more than one accounting period.
(*c*) Each contract is treated as a separate unit of cost for the purpose of cost ascertainment.
(*d*) The contracts are executed as per the specifications given by the contractee.
(*e*) Since the work is executed at the contract site, most of the items of cost to be incurred are direct in nature.
(*f*) The contract is executed by the contractor for some agreed amount of consideration known as 'Contract Price'.
(*g*) The payments by the contractee are made to the conctractor in instalments on the basis of the extent of the work already completed by him and certified as complete by contractee's engineer or architect.

Contract costing is most suitable to ship-building, road construction, building construction, civil engineering works etc. The presentation of costing information relating to contracts is made in the form of a separate contract account opened for each contract.

5. Batch Costing:

It is a part of job costing and is applied to ascertain the cost of production in industries where production is carried on in batches. A batch may be defined as a group of specified number of similar products. Under this method, a batch is treated as one job and the cost of this complete batch is ascertained. This method is generally applied in those industries where the following features are present:

(*a*) The production is carried on in batches and each batch consists of a specified number of similar products.

(*b*) The production is done for own stock to be sold to customers.

(*c*) The total cost of the batch is divided by the total number of units in the batch to find out the cost per unit.

(*d*) Each batch is assigned a specified number or code which is mentioned on the products.

Batch costing is generally employed in industries engaged in biscuit manufacture, toy making, spare parts manufacture, canned products, ready-made garments, spare parts of complex products like motor cars, scooters, radios, watches etc.

6. Operating Costing:

Operating costing is the method of costing applied to ascertain the cost of providing or operating a service. This method of costing is employed in those undertakings which are engaged in operating or providing services rather than in manufacturing tangible products. The undertakings, adopting operating costing, generally have the following features:

(*a*) These undertakings are engaged in rendering services of unique nature to their customers.

(*b*) These undertakings are required to invest a large proportion of their total capital in fixed assets *e.g.*, buses, trucks, motor lorries, ships, aircrafts, railway engines, wagons, railway lines etc.

(*c*) The amount of working capital required to meet out the day-to-day expenses, is comparatively less.

This method is applicable to road transport undertakings, railways, tramways, airways, shipping companies, electricity companies, gas companies, hospitals, cinemas, hotels, canteens, water works etc. The presentation of costing information is made in the form of a statement known as "Operating Cost Sheet."

7. Operation Costing:

Operation costing represents a refinement of process costing. Under this method, the cost of each operation in each process or stage of production is ascertained separately. Operation cost generally refers to 'conversion cost', *i.e.*, cost of labour and overhead. At the end of each operation, unit operation cost is ascertained by dividing the conversion cost by output. Thereafter, the cost of finished unit is determined by adding the material cost and the cost of various operations through which it passes.

This method is employed in industries where mass or repetitive production is carried out or where articles or components have to be stocked in semi-finished stage, to facilitate the execution of special orders, or for convenience of issue for later operations.

8. Multiple or Composite Costing:

Multiple or composite costing is applied to ascertain the cost of complex products manufactured by a manufacturing concern where no single method of costing is applicable. Under this method, the total cost is ascertained by aggregating component costs which are collected by both job costing and process costing.

Multiple costing is applied to industries engaged in the production of bi-cycles, motor cycles, scooters, motor cars, radios, televisions, typewriters, accounting machines, engines and other complex products.

9. Departmental Costing:

This method of costing is adopted where the factory is divided into several departments and it is desired to ascertain the cost of production of each department rather than the cost of each article produced. Under this method, the costs are first allocated to the various departments of the manufacturing concern and then to the different products manufactured in a particular department.

Types of Costing: Types of costing refer to various systems used for ascertaining and analysing costs. The various types of costing are as follows:

1. **Historical Costing:** The ascertainment and recording of costs after they have been incurred is known as historical costing. It provides the management with a record of what has happened and is thus a post-mortem of the actual costs. Since, it is conventional in nature, it is known as 'Conventional Costing' or 'Actual Costing'. Actual costs can be ascertained in two ways: (*i*) Post costing, and (*ii*) Concurrent or continuous costing.

   Post costing: Under this system, cost is ascertained after production is completed, by analysing financial data in such a way as will disclose the cost of the units which have been produced. The main advantage of this procedure is that the figures analysed are the actuals and hence the cost arrived at is correct. But the serious drawback of this procedure is that it is historical in nature since the information is obtained after the event has taken place. As such this procedure does not enable the manufacturer to take corrective action in time.

   Continuous costing: Under this system, cost is ascertained by recording expenditure and allocating it to production as and when the same is incurred, with the result that cost is ascertained as soon the job is completed or even when the job is in progress. This necessarily involves the use of estimates, specially in respect of overhead. Hence the figures of cost ascertained may not be exact. But since this method makes available the costing information promptly, it enables the management to take the necessary corrective action. But this system does not provide any standard for judging the efficiency of the current operations and does not disclose, what the cost of the job ought to have been.

2. **Standard Costing:** According to the Terminology of Cost Accountancy of the Institute of Cost and Management Accountants, 'Standard Costing' refers to "the preparation and use of standard costs, their comparison with actual costs and the analysis of variances to their causes and points of incidence". Under standard costing, costs are computed in advance on the basis of normal or probable expectation. The costs so computed are known as 'standards' or 'standard costs' and these are compared with actual costs, when incurred, so as to ascertain the variances or differences. These variances or differences are later on analysed to their causes so as to enable the management to take corrective action where necessary.
3. **Marginal Costing:** Marginal Costing (also known as Variable Costing) refers to "the ascertainment of marginal costs and of the effect on profit of changes in volume or type of output by differentiating between fixed costs and variable costs". Under marginal costing, all costs are segregated into fixed costs and variable costs. Fixed costs refer to costs which tend to remain fixed or constant in total with changes in volume of output. Variable costs refer to costs which tend to vary or change in total directly in proportion to changes in the volume of output. The main object of marginal costing is to deal with the effects of changes in the volume or range of output on the costs or profit of a business concern.
4. **Direct Costing:** According to the 'Terminology of Cost Accountancy' of the Institute of Cost and Management Accountants, 'direct costing' means "the practice of charging of all direct costs to operations, processes or products, leaving all indirect costs to be written off against profits in the period in which they arise". This differs from marginal costing in that some fixed costs could be considered to be direct costs in appropriate circumstances.
5. **Absorption Costing:** It has been defined by the Institute of Cost and Management Accountants as "the practice of charging all costs, both variable and fixed, to operations, processes or products." Under absorption costing, no distinction is made between fixed costs and variable costs and all costs, whether fixed or variable, are taken into account for ascertaining the cost of production. Absorption costing is also known as 'Full Costing'.

6. **Uniform Costing:** It has been defined by the Institute of Cost and Management Accountants as "the use by several undertakings of the same costing principles and/or practices". Thus, when a number of undertakings, whether under the same management or otherwise, decide to adhere to one set of accepted costing principles particularly in matters where there can be two opinions, they are said to be following uniform costing. It attempts to establish uniform costing methods so that comparison of performances in various undertakings can be made to the common advantage of all the participating undertakings.

'Cost Centre' and 'Cost Unit':

In cost accounting, costs are ascertained by cost centres and cost units. As such, it is necessary to know the meaning of these two terms.

Cost Centre: Cost centre may be defined as any location, person or item of equipment (or a group of these) for which costs may be ascertained and used for the purposes of cost control. Cost centre refers to any place, person, machine, section, part, activity or function within an organisation or undertaking, by which costs are collected or accumulated, and to which costs are allocated. Cost centre is, thus, a natural division of an undertaking for purposes of measuring cost of a particular operation and for applying this cost to product. Cost centre in an organisation is formed keeping in view the convenience of cost accumulation, comparability and control of costs. If costs are accumulated for a person or by a department or for a machine, such person, department or machine will be treated as a cost centre.

In an undertaking, cost centres may be divided into two parts:

(*i*) Production cost centres, and

(*ii*) Service cost centres.

A production cost centre refers to a cost centre which is engaged on regular production *i.e.*, in converting raw materials into finished products. A service cost centre is a centre which is not engaged on regular production but which assists the production cost centres in carrying on their activities *e.g.*, stores department, personnel department, maintenance department etc.

Cost centres may also be divided into operation cost centres and process cost centres; personal cost centres and impersonal cost centres. Operation cost centre refers to a cost centre which consists of those machines and/or persons carrying out similar operations while a process cost centre is one which consists of a specific process or a continuous sequence of operations.

A personal cost centre is a cost centre which consists of a person or group of persons *e.g.*, departmental foreman, salesman, supervisor, factory manager etc. An impersonal cost centre refers to a cost centre which consists of a location or item of equipment or a group of these *e.g.*, machines, departments, vehicles etc.

Cost Unit:

After costs have been ascertained, accumulated, classified and recorded, these have to be related to a convenient measure of the quantity of the product or service. This measure of quantity of product or service is known as 'cost unit'. A cost unit is defined as "a unit of quantity of product, service or time (or a combination of these) in relation to which costs may be ascertained or expressed". In other words, a cost unit is a standard or unit of measurement of the goods manufactured or service rendered. Cost unit may be in terms of number, length, area, weight, volume, time and value. A unit of cost must possess the following characteristics:

(*i*) It must be one with which expenditure can be conveniently associated.
(*ii*) It must be appropriate or natural to business operations and the product.
(*iii*) It must be certain or definite and not changing from time to time.
(*iv*) It must be simple to understand and to quote.
(*v*) It must have a universal acceptability.

Types of Cost Units:

Cost units may be divided into two parts:

(*a*) Simple Unit: It involves the use of a single standard or unit of measurement of the goods manufactured *e.g.*, per piece, per kilogram, per quintal, per tonne, per gallon, per metre etc.

(*b*) Composite Unit or Complex Unit: It is a combination of two simple units *e.g.*, per passenger-kilometre, per tonne-kilometre, per kilowatt-hour etc.

Examples of cost units:

Following are the cost units which are commonly used in different industries:

Name of Industry	Product/Service	Cost Unit
Collieries	Coal	Per tonne coal
Mining	Minerals	Per tonne mineral
Iron and Steel Mills	Iron and Steel	Per tonne steel
Sugar Mills	Sugar	Per quintal sugar
Flour Mills	Flour	Per quintal flour
Paper Mills	Paper	Per kilogram paper
Cement mills	Cement	Per tonne cement
Chemical Factories	Chemicals	Per litre/per gallon
Pencil Manufacturing	Pencils	Per gross/per dozen
Oil Mills	Oil	Per litre/per gallon
Textile Mills		
(*a*) Spinning Mills	Yarn	Per kilogram yarn
(*b*) Weaving Mills	Cloth	Per metre cloth
Automobile Factories	Scooters	Per scooter

	Motor car	Per motor car
Contract Business	Contract/Job	Per contract/per job.
Brick works	Bricks	Per thousand bricks
Water Works	Water	Per thousand gallons
Power House	Electricity	Per kilowatt-hour
Transport Business	Carrying goods	Per tonne-kilometre
	Carrying passenger	Per passenger-kilometre
Cinema Houses	Film show	Per man-show
Hotel	Night-stay	Per man-room

Difference between Cost Centre and Cost Unit:

The main points of difference between cost centre and cost unit may be given as follows:

(*i*) Costs are accumulated by cost centres, whereas these are measured and expressed in terms of cost units.

(*ii*) Costs centres may be used as basis of classifying costs. But cost units do not serve as basis of classification of costs.

(*iii*) Different cost centres may be involved in the production of a product, whereas a product will have only one cost unit in which its costs are expressed.

(*iv*) Formulation of cost centres depends upon the nature and techniques of production processes, size of the organisation and the nature of the organisational structure. Determination of cost units depends upon the nature of the final product or final output and the prevailing practices of trade.

(*v*) Cost centres are created for assisting the management in the functions of budgeting and controlling. But it is not so with cost units.

OBJECTIVE TYPE QUESTIONS

A. Multiple Choice Questions:

Select the correct answer in each of the following:

(*a*) Financial accounting is concerned with the:
  (*i*) recording of business expenses and revenues
  (*ii*) recording of cost of products and services
  (*iii*) recording of day-to-day business transactions
  (*iv*) none of the above three.

(*b*) The nature of financial accounting is:
  (*i*) historical
  (*ii*) forward-looking
  (*iii*) analytical
  (*iv*) social.

(*c*) The main object of cost accounting is:
   (*i*) to record day-to-day transactions of the business
   (*ii*) to reveal managerial efficiency
   (*iii*) to ascertain true cost of products and services
   (*iv*) to determine tender price.

(*d*) Cost Accounting emerged mainly on account of:
   (*i*) Statutory requirements
   (*ii*) Competition in the market
   (*iii*) Labour unrest
   (*iv*) Limitations of financial accounting.

(*e*) Advantages of cost accounting system accrue:
   (*i*) only to workers
   (*ii*) only to Government
   (*iii*) only to consumers
   (*iv*) to management, workers, consumers and Government.

(*f*) Cost accounting is applied to
   (*i*) Public undertakings only
   (*ii*) Large business enterprises only
   (*iii*) Small business concerns only
   (*iv*) Manufacturing and service concerns.

(*g*) A colliery company employs:
   (*i*) Contract costing
   (*ii*) Batch costing
   (*iii*) Operating costing
   (*iv*) Single costing.

(*h*) Marginal costing is concerned with:
   (*i*) Fixed costs.
   (*ii*) Variable costs.
   (*iii*) Semi-fixed costs
   (*iv*) None of the above three.

(*i*) A Biscuit manufacturing concern employs:
   (*i*) Operating costing
   (*ii*) Departmental costing
   (*iii*) Batch costing
   (*iv*) Contract costing.

[**Ans.** (*a*) (*iii*); (*b*) (*i*); (*c*) (*iii*); (*d*) (*iv*); (*e*) (*iv*); (*f*) (*iv*); (*g*) (*iv*); (*h*) (*ii*); (*i*) (*iii*)]

B. True/False statements:

Indicate whether the following statements are 'True' or 'False':

(*a*) Cost accounting system is traditional in nature.

(*b*) Financial accounting is historical in nature.

(*c*) Financial accounting helps in exercising cost control.

(*d*) Cost accounting is a valuable aid to management in decision-making.

(*e*) Contract costing is applied by transport undertakings.

(*f*) While financial accounting leads to external reporting, cost accounting restricts itself to internal reporting.

(*g*) A colliery company employs single costing.

(*h*) Cost accounting concepts include planning, controlling, and product-costing but not profit-sharing.

[**Ans.** (*a*) False; (*b*) True; (*c*) False; (*d*) True; (*e*) False; (*f*) True; (*g*) True; (*h*) True.]

C. Filling the blanks:

Fill in the blanks with appropriate words.

(*i*) Financial accounting is .... in nature.

(*ii*) .... refers to the techniques and processes of ascertaining costs.

(*iii*) Cost Audit is the .... of the correctness of cost accounts.

(*iv*) .... control is a system where by budgets are used as a means of planning and .... costs.

(*v*) .... is the method employed to ascertain the cost and profitability of contracts undertaken by contractors.

(*vi*) Cost centre is a ......, person or item of .... (or a group of these) for which costs may be ascertained and used for the purposes of ....

(*vii*) .... means fixing the selling price of article.

[**Ans.** (*i*) historical (*ii*) costing (*iii*) verification (*iv*) Budgetary, controlling (*v*) contract costing (*vi*) location, equipment, cost control (*vii*) Pricing.]

SHORT ANSWER TYPE OUESTIONS

1. Give three limitations of financial accounting.

2. What is Cost Accounting?

3. Give the basic difference between cost accounting and financial accounting.

4. How is cost accounting beneficial to management?

5. How is cost accounting useful to workers?

6. Give any two limitations of cost accounting.

7. Is it correct to say that cost accounting is unnecessary?

8. Do you agree that cost accounting is expensive?

9. What is meant by 'Pricing'?

10. What is meant by 'Estimating'?

11. What is meant by 'Cost Centre'?

12. Define 'Cost Unit'.

13. What is the difference between production cost centre and service cost centre?

14. What is Batch costing?

15. Give any four features of Contract Costing.

16. What is Operating Costing?

17. What is Post Costing?

18. Briefly discuss the scope of Cost Accountancy.

19. What is Continuous Costing?

20. What is meant by Operation Costing?

21. Distinguish between 'Costing' and 'Pricing'?

LONG ANSWER TYPE QUESTIONS

1. Discuss the limitations and deficiencies of financial accounts.

2. What is meant by 'Costing', 'Cost Accounting' and 'Cost Accountancy'?
(*Punjabi, B.Com., 1982*)

3. What is Cost Accounting? Explain briefly the objects and advantages of Cost Accounting.

4. What is Cost Accounting? In what respects does it differ from Financial Accounting?
(*M.D.U., B.Com., 1993 Andhra, B.Com., 1983*)

5. It is said – "Cost Accounting is a system of foresight and not a post-mortem examination, it turns losses into profits, speeds up activities and eliminates waste." Discuss in detail this statement.
(*G.N.D.U., B.Com., 1995*)
(*M.D.U., B.Com., 1984, I.C.W.A. Final*)

6. Explain the terms 'Costing', 'Cost Accounting' and 'Cost Accountancy'. What are the functions of Cost Accounting?
(*G.N.D.U., B.Com., 1996*)

7. "Cost Accounting is an indispensable tool of modern management". Discuss this statement and bring out the nature and scope of Cost Accounting. (*G.N.D.U., B.Com., 2004*)

8. "A good system of costing serves and helps to secure economy in manufacture". Discuss the statement to show the objects and functions of Cost Accounting.

(*Himachal B. Com., 1980, M.D.U., B.Com., 1984*)
(*Punjab, B.Com., 1991*)
(*Mysore B.B.M.*)
(*Delhi, B.Com. Hons.*)

9. Cost Accounting assists (*a*) in controlling efficiency, (*b*) in pricing products, (*c*) in providing a basis for operating policy. Elucidate with reasons.

10. "The ordinary trading account is a locked store-house of most valuable information, to which the cost system is the key." Elucidate the above statement and explain the difference between cost and financial accounts.

(*G.N.D.U.; B.Com., 1972, 1979; 1983*)

11. Explain the advantages of introducing a costing system in an industrial organisation. (*Meerut B.Com.*)

12. "Cost system has become an essential tool in the hands of management." Comment. (*M.Com., Kerala*)

13. "Cost Accounting is a tool of managerial planning and control". Explain (*Delhi, B.Com. Hons.*)

14. Examine critically the drawbacks of conventional financial accounting. Do you think that these limitations have been overcome by the introduction of cost accounting?

15. Which method of costing would you recommend for the following industries? Give reasons:

(*i*) Ship Building (*ii*) Automobile Manufacturing (*iii*) Cement (*iv*) Chemicals (*v*) Transport.

(*M.D.U., B.Com., 1993*) (*Punjab B.Com., 1983*)

16. Differentiate between:

(*i*) Job Costing and Operating Costing
(*ii*) Operation Costing and Operating Costing

(*M.D.U., B.Com., 1993*)
(*Punjab, B.Com., 1983*)

17. What are the different methods of costing? State the applicability of these methods.

18. What methods of costing would you recommend for the following industries? Give reasons

(*i*) Ship building (*iii*) Oil Refinery

(*ii*) Toy Making (*iv*) Sugar
(*v*) Radio Receivers.

(*I.C.W.A. Inter*).

19. What are the main essentials of an ideal system of cost accounting?

20. What is costing? What are its objects? State its merits.

(*Punjabi, B.Com., 1985*)

21. "Costing is the classification, recording and appropriate allocation of expenditure for determination of costs of products and services." Explain the statement and state the principles of cost accountancy.

(*G.N.D.U., B.Com., 1979*)

22. What is Cost Accounting? What are its objectives? How do cost accounting records help in the planning and control of operations of a business enterprise?

(*Delhi, B.Com. 1982, G.N.D.U, B.Com., 1984*)

23. Cost accounting is a branch of accounting and it has been evolved to do away the limitations of financial accounting and to meet the needs of management." Discuss. (*Himachal, B.Com., 1996*)

24. "Cost is an instrument of management control". Give your comments.

(*Himachal, B.Com., 1994*)

25. "Costing is a technique, entirely separate from the procedure of financial accounting." (*Himachal, B.Com., 1994 Sept*)

26. What is meant by Cost Accounting? How does Cost Accounting differ in technique and procedure from financial accounting?

(*Himachal B.Com., 1995*)

27. What is meant by 'Cost centre' and 'Cost unit'? What are their types? What is the difference between 'Cost centre' and 'Cost unit'?

28. What are the factors which are to be taken into account for installing a Cost Accounting system in a manufacturing concern?

29. Discuss the various objections to the installation of cost accounting system. (*G.N.D.U., B.Com., 2001*)

30. Define a 'Cost centre'. How would you classify cost centres? Distinguish between 'Cost centre' and 'Cost unit'.

31. Write notes on:

(*i*) Costing, Estimating and Pricing
(*ii*) Cost unit
(*iii*) Cost centre.

32. (*a*) What are the essentials of a good Cost Accounting System?

(*b*) Narrate the essential factors to be considered while designing and installing a Cost Accounting System. (*C.A. Inter 1996*)

33. 'Money spent on installing a Cost Accounting System is not an expense but an investment." Give your views.

34. You have been asked to install a costing system in a manufacturing concern. Apart from technical costing problems, what practical difficulties would you expect to meet and how would you propose to obviate or overcome them? (*I.C.WA.*)

35. Define Cost Accounting, Discuss the nature and scope of Cost Accounting. (*Pbi. Univ. B.Com., 2008*)

36. "Cost Accounting is an indispensable tool of modern management." Discuss the importance of Cost Accounting in the light of this statement. (*G.N.D.U., B.Com., 2008*)

37. Define Cost Accounting. Also give points of difference between Cost Accounting and Financial Accounting. (*H.P.U., B.Com., 2008*)

38. "Cost Accounting is an unnecessary luxury for business establishments." Do you agree? (*G.N.D.U., B.Com., 2002*)

2

Elements and Components of Cost

In the Oxford Dictionary 'cost' means 'the price paid for something'. But in the management terminology, 'cost' refers to expenditure and not to price. 'Cost' represents a sacrifice, a foregoing or a release of something of value. The Institute of Cost and Management Accountants, London, has defined cost as "the amount of expenditure (actual or notional) incurred on or attributable to a given thing." For manufacturing of cotton fabrics, the expenditure incurred on the purchase of cotton yarn, wages paid to weavers, salary paid to factory foreman, depreciation on machinery used in the manufacture of fabrics, notional rent of owned factory building etc., are the items of cost.

One of the main objects of cost accounting is to present the analysis of the total cost of production in such a manner as to provide the maximum information useful to the business. The analysis and classification of costs is basically made with reference to factors on which expenditure is incurred. These factors are known as 'elements of cost'. 'Element' may also be defined as a group name of smaller costs of identical nature. The various elements of cost are:

1. Material cost
2. Labour cost or wages
3. Expenses.

MATERIAL COST

'Material cost' refers to the cost of commodities supplied to an undertaking *e.g.*, cost of yarn and dyes supplied to an undertaking engaged in the manufacture of cloth, cost of leather, thread, nails and shoe polish supplied to an undertaking engaged in the manufacture of shoes etc. Material cost may be further sub-divided into:

(*a*) Direct Material Cost: Direct material cost means the cost of materials which can be identified with and allocated to cost centres or cost units e.g., cost of wood in case of furniture, cost of cotton in case of cotton yarn, cost of yarn in case of cloth, cost of iron in case of machinery etc. The main feature of direct materials is that these enter into and form part of the finished product.

(b) Indirect Material Cost: It refers to the material cost which cannot be allocated but can be apportioned to or absorbed by cost centres or cost units. These are the materials which cannot be traced as part of the product and their cost is distributed among the various cost centres or cost units on some equitable basis. Examples of indirect materials are coal and fuel for generating power, cotton waste, lubricating oil and grease used in maintaining the machinery, materials consumed for repair and maintenance work, dusters and brooms used for cleaning the factory etc.

LABOUR COST (OR WAGES)

Labour cost refers to the cost of remuneration of the employees of an undertaking *e.g.*, wages, salaries, commission etc. Labour cost may be sub-divided into:

(a) Direct Labour Cost (or Direct Wages): It refers to labour cost which can be identified with and allocated to cost centres or cost units. It includes the remuneration paid for converting the raw material into finished products or for altering the construction, composition or condition of the product manufactured by an undertaking *e.g.*, wages paid for spinning yarn in case of spinning mill, wages paid for weaving cloth in case of cloth mill, wages paid to a mason for construction of building by a building contractor etc. In case of a service concern, direct labour cost refers to the wages paid to those who directly carry out or operate the service e.g., wages paid to the driver and conductor of a bus in case of the transport business.

(b) Indirect Labour Cost (or Indirect Wages): It refers to the labour cost or wages which cannot be allocated but can be apportioned to or absorbed by cost centres or cost units e.g., salary paid to factory manager, salary paid to factory supervisor or foreman, salary paid to general manager or sales manager etc.

EXPENSES

Expenses refer to the cost of services provided to an undertaking and the notional cost of the use of owned assets (i.e., depreciation of owned factory building, depreciation of office building, depreciation of show-room building, depreciation of plant and machinery etc.). Expenses are sub-divided into:

(a) Direct Expenses (or Chargeable Expenses): These are the expenses (other than direct material cost and direct labour cost) which can be identified with and allocated to cost centres or cost units e.g., royalties paid on the basis of output, hire charges of special plant or machinery, carriage and freight on direct materials purchased if such carriage and freight have not been added to the cost of materials, import duty and octroi paid on the purchases of imported direct materials (if not added to their purchase price).

(*b*) Indirect Expenses: Expenses which cannot be allocated but can be apportioned to or absorbed by cost centres or cost units e.g., rent, rates, taxes and insurance of factory building, factory lighting, repairs to factory building, depreciation of plant and machinery, repairs to machinery, depreciation and insurance of office building, depreciation and insurance of show-room building etc., are known as indirect expenses.

The aggregate of direct material cost, direct labour cost and direct expenses is known as 'Direct Cost' whereas the aggregate of indirect material cost, indirect labour cost and indirect expenses is known as 'Indirect Cost' or 'Overhead'. Indirect cost or overhead may again be classified on the basis of functions as follows:

(*i*) **Factory Overhead or Works Overhead:** Factory overhead includes all the indirect costs incurred in the factory in connection with manufacturing operations. Factory overhead comprises the cost of indirect materials, cost of indirect labour and all other indirect expenses which are incurred in the running of the factory or works e.g., lubricating oil, cotton waste for cleaning the machinery, coal, gas and fuel, wages of store-keeper, wages of time-keeper, salaries of foremen and factory supervisors, factory rent, factory rates and insurance, repairs to factory building, depreciation of factory plant and machinery, depreciation of owned factory building etc.

(*ii*) **Office and Administration Overhead:** These include all indirect costs relating to the direction, control and administration of an undertaking. In other words, office and administration overhead refers to general office expenses and expenses of administration and control of business *e.g.*, office rent, office rates and insurance, depreciation of owned office building, office lighting, depreciation of office furniture, office stationery, audit fee, directors' remuneration, salary of general manager, salaries of general clerical staff, bank charges etc.

(*iii*) **Selling and Distribution Overhead:** These include all indirect costs which are incurred for promoting sales and retaining the customers and for delivering the goods after their manufacture to the consumers *e.g.*, cost of advertisement, rent, rates, taxes and insurance of show-room building, depreciation of owned show-room building, show-room lighting, salary of sales manager, salaries of salesmen, commission on sales, carriage on sales, packing charges, rent or depreciation of warehouse, salary of warehouse-keeper, running and maintenance of delivery vans etc.

COMPONENTS OF COST

A 'component of cost' may be defined as the cumulative or aggregate of different elements of cost. By aggregating or grouping the various elements of cost, the following components or types of cost are obtained:

(*a*) **Prime Cost:** Prime cost is the aggregate of direct material cost, direct labour cost and direct expenses. Prime Cost is also known as 'Flat Cost', 'First Cost' or 'Direct Cost'

(*b*) **Factory Cost:** Prime cost plus factory overhead (or works overhead) is known as factory cost. Thus, factory cost is the aggregate of direct material cost, direct labour cost, direct expenses and factory overhead. Factory cost is also known as 'Works Cost', 'Production Cost' or 'Manufacturing Cost'.

(*c*) **Office Cost:** Factory cost plus office and administrative overhead is known as 'Office Cost'. Office cost is also known as 'Gross Cost' or 'Cost of Production'.

(*d*) **Total Cost:** Total cost is made up of cost of production plus selling and distribution overhead. Thus, total cost includes all the elements of cost or all the items of expenditure till the commodity has been finally sold. Total cost is also known as 'Selling Cost' or 'Cost of Sales'.

SELLING PRICE

Selling price is not the same thing as selling cost. Selling price is the Selling Cost (or Total Cost or Cost of Sales) plus profit.

The various components of cost can be shown by means of the following diagram:

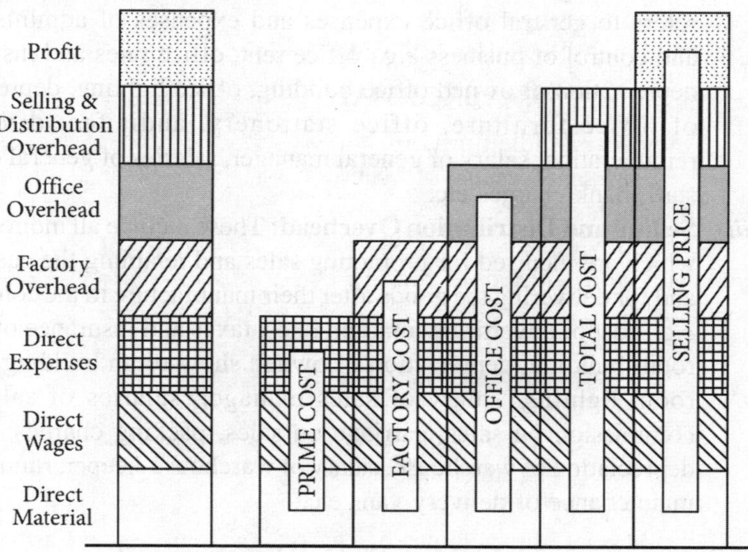

EXPLANATION

(*a*) Direct Material Cost + Direct Wages + Direct Expenses = Prime Cost.
(*b*) Prime Cost + Factory Overhead = Factory Cost.
(*c*) Factory Cost + Office and Administration Overhead = Office Cost.
(*d*) Office Cost + Selling and Distribution Overhead = Total Cost.
(*e*) Total Cost + Profit = Selling Price.

ITEMS EXCLUDED FROM COST ACCOUNTS

The following items which are included in the financial accounts of a manufacturing concern, shall not be included in cost accounts since they are not related to cost of production:

1. ITEMS OF APPROPRIATION OF PROFIT

(*a*) Income tax paid and legal expenses incurred in connection with assessment of income tax.
(*b*) Transfer to reserves.
(*c*) Dividends on shares paid by a company.
(*d*) Amount written off — goodwill, preliminary expenses, underwriting commission, discount allowed on shares or debentures.
(*e*) Bonus paid to the employees of the undertaking, if such payment is based on profits.

2. ITEMS OF PURE FINANCE

(*a*) Interest and dividends received on investments.
(*b*) Rent received.
(*c*) Profit or loss on sale of investments, fixed assets etc.
(*d*) Expenses on raising capital.
(*e*) Cash discount allowed or received.

3. ABNORMAL ITEMS

(*a*) Cost of abnormal idle time.
(*b*) Cost of abnormal wastage of materials.
(*c*) Exceptional bad debts.
(*d*) Abnormal saving.
(*e*) Penalties and fines paid for the infringement of Govt. rules and regulations.

PREPARATION OF COST SHEET

The calculation of cost of production at various stages can be shown by means of a statement called 'Cost Sheet'. Cost Sheet is an analytical presentation of the cost of the product in the form of a statement and shows the various elements and components of cost. The specimen of a Cost Sheet may be given as follows:

COST SHEET

Period .... Output ....

Particulars of items	Total Rs. P.	Per Unit Rs. P.
Direct Materials Consumed	–	–
Direct Wages	–	–
Direct Expenses	–	–
Prime Cost	–	–
Factory Overhead	–	–
Factory Cost (Works Cost)	–	–
Office and Administration Overhead	–	–
Cost of Production	–	–
Selling and Distribution Overhead	–	–
Total Cost	–	–

Illustration 1

From the following particulars, calculate (*a*) Prime Cost, (*b*) Factory Cost, (*c*) Cost of Production and (*d*) Total Cost:

	Rs.
Direct Materials Consumed	75,000
Direct Wages	1,20,000
Direct Expenses	30,000
Factory Overhead	50,000
Office and Administration Overhead	35,000
Selling and Distribution Overhead	45,000

No. of Units Manufactured: 2,000.

Solution

COST SHEET

Period .... Output: 2,000 Units.

Particulars	Total	Per Unit
	Rs.	Rs.
Direct Materials Consumed	75,000	37.50
Direct Wages	1,20,000	60.00
Direct Expenses	30,000	15.00
Prime Cost	2,25,000	112.50
Factory Overhead	50,000	25.00
Factory Cost	2,75,000	137.50
Office and Administration Overhead	35,000	17.50
Cost of Production	3,10,000	155.00
Selling and Distribution Overhead	45,000	22.50
Total Cost	**3,55,000**	**177.50**

Illustration 2

From the following particulars, prepare a cost sheet showing the total and per ton cost for the month of January, 2009:

	Rs.		Rs.
Raw Materials	66,000	Direct Wages	70,000
Indirect Wages	21,000	Factory Rent	15,000
Factory Lighting	4,400	Factory Heating	3,000
Motive Power	8,800	Haulage	6,000
Directors' Fees (Works)	2,000	Directors' Fees (Office)	4,000
Factory Cleaning	1,000	Sundry Office Expenses	400
Factory Stationery	1,500	Office Stationery	1,800
Loose Tools Written off	1,200	Office Rent and Taxes	1,000
Water Supply	2,400	Factory Insurance	2,200
Legal Expenses	800	Direct Expenses	6,000
Rent of warehouse	4,000	Depreciation of Machinery	4,000
Depreciation of office buildings	2,000	Depreciation of Delivery Vans	400
Bad Debts	200	Advertising	600
Sales Department Salaries	3,000	Upkeep of Delivery Vans	1,400
Commission on Sales	3,000	Bank Charges	100

The total output for the period has been 10,000 tons.

Solution

COST SHEET

Period: January, 2009 Output: 10,000 Tons.

Particulars		Total Rs. P.	Per ton. Rs. P.
Raw Materials		66,000	6.60
Direct Wages		70,000	7.00
Direct Expenses		6,000	0.60
Prime Cost		**1,42,000**	**14.20**
Factory Overhead:			
Indirect Wages	21,000		
Factory Rent	15,000		
Factory Lighting	4,400		
Factory Heating	3,000		
Motive Power	8,800		
Haulage	6,000		
Directors' Fees (Works)	2,000		
Factory Cleaning	1,000		
Factory Stationery	1,500		
Loose Tools Written off	1,200		
Water Supply	2,400		
Factory Insurance	2,200		
Depreciation of Machinery	4,000		
		72,500	**7.25**
	Factory Cost	**2,14,500**	**21.45**

Office Overhead:			
Directors' Fees (Office)	4,000		
Sundry Office Expenses	400		
Office Stationery	1,800		
Office Rent and Taxes	1,000		
Legal Expenses	800		
Depreciation of Office Buildings	2,000		
Bank Charges	100		
		10,100	**1.01**
Cost of Production		**2,24,600**	**22.46**
Selling and Distribution Overhead:			
Rent of Warehouse	4,000		
Bad Debts	200		
Sales Department Salaries	3,000		
Commission on Sales	3,000		
Depreciation of Delivery Vans	400		
Advertising	600		
Upkeep of Deliver Vans	1,400		
		12,600	**1.26**
Total Cost		**2,37,200**	**23.72**

Illustration 3

Satyam Products Ltd. supplies you the following information relating to product 'X' for the month of October, 2009:

Raw materials consumed	Rs. 60,000
Direct Wages	Rs. 36,000
No. of machine hours worked.	500
Machine Hour Rate	Rs. 20
Office overhead	20% on Works Cost
Selling overhead	Rs. 2 per unit sold
No. of units manufactured:	5,000
No. of units sold	4,000 @ Rs. 35 per unit

You are required to prepare a Cost Sheet in respect of the above showing cost and profit per unit.

Solution

COST SHEET

Period: Oct., 2009 — Output: 5,000 Units

Particulars	Total	Per Unit
	Rs. P.	**Rs. P.**
Raw Materials Consumed	60,000	12.00
Direct Wages.	36,000	7.20
Prime Cost	**96,000**	**19.20**
Factory Overhead @ Rs. 20 per machine hour for 500 hours	10,000	2.00
Works Cost	**1,06,000**	**21.20**
Office Overhead @ 20% on Works Cost	21,200	4.24
Cost of Production	**1,27,200**	**25.44**
Less Closing Stock of finished goods (1,000 units @ Rs. 25.44 per unit)	25,440	–

Cost of Goods Sold	**1,01,760**	**25.44**
Selling Overhead @ Rs. 2 per unit sold	8,000	2.00
Cost of Sales	**1,09,760**	**27.44**
Profit	**30,240**	**7.56**
Sales (4,000 units @ Rs. 35 per unit)	**1,40,000**	**35.00**

Illustration 4

The following particulars relating to the year 2008-09 have been taken from the books of a Chemical Works manufacturing and selling a chemical mixture:

		Rs.
Stock on 1-4—2008:		
Raw Materials	2,000 kgs.	2,000
Finished Mixture	500 kgs.	1,750
Factory Stores		7,250
Purchases:		
Raw Materials	1,60,000 kgs.	1,80,000
Factory Stores		24,250
Sales:		
Finished Mixture	1,53,050 kgs.	9,18,000
Factory Scrap	500 kgs.	8,170
Factory wages		1,78,650
Power		30,400
Depreciation of Machinery		18,000
Salaries:		
Factory		72,200
Office		37,200
Selling		41,500
Expenses:		
Direct		18,500
Office		18,200
Selling		18,000
Stock as on 31-3-2009:		
Raw Material	1,200 kgs.	
Finished Mixture	450 kgs.	
Factory Stores		5,500

The stock of finished mixture at the end of the year is to the valued at the factory cost of the mixture for that your. The purchase price of raw material remained unchanged throughout 2008-09. Prepare a statement giving the maximum possible information about cost and its break up for the year 2008-09.

(B.Com. Delhi)

Solution

COST SHEET

Period: .... Output: 1,53,000 kgs. Mixture

Particulars			Rs.
Raw Materials Consumed:	**Kgs.**	**Rs.**	
Opening Stock of R.M.	2,000	2,000	
Add Purchases of R.M.	1,60,000	1,80,000	
	1,62,000	**1,82,000**	
Less Closing Stock of R.M.	1,200	1,350	
Rs. 1,80,000/1,60,000 kgs. × 1,200 kgs.	**1,60,800**	**1,80,650**	**1,80,650**
Factory Wages			1,78,650
Direct Expenses			18,500
Prime Cost			**3,77,800**
Factory Overhead	**Rs.**		
Factory stores used (Rs. 7,250 + 24,250 – 5,500)	25,950		
Power	30,400		
Depreciation of machinery	18,000		
Factory Salaries	72,220		
	1,46,570		
Less Sale of Factory Scrap	8,170		1,38,400
Factory Cost (1,53,000 kgs.)			**5,16,200**
Office Overhead:	**Rs.**		
Office Salaries		37,220	
Office Expenses	18,200		55,420
Cost of Production (1,53,000 kgs.)			**5,71,620**
Add Opening Stock of Finished Mixture (500 kgs.)			1,750
			5,73,370
Less Closing Stock of Finished Mixture (450 kgs. At Factory Cost)			1,518
Cost of Production of finished mixture sold (1,53,050 kgs.)			5,71,852
Selling Overhead:			
Salaries	41,500		
Expenses	18,000		
			59,500
	Cost of Sales		6,31,352
	Profit		2,86,648
Sales (1,53,050 kgs.)			**9,18,000**

Notes:

(*i*) Calculation of Output:

Finished Mixture Sold	1,53,050 kgs.
Add Closing Stock of Finished Mixture	450 kgs.
	1,53,500 kgs.
Less Opening Stock of Finished Mixture	500 kgs.
Output	1,53,000 kgs.

(*ii*) Calculation of the Value of Closing Stock of Finished Mixture at Factory Cost:

$$= \frac{\text{Factory Cost}}{\text{Output}} \times \text{Units of Closing Stock}$$

$$= \frac{\text{Rs. } 5{,}16{,}200}{1{,}53{,}000 \text{ kgs.}} \times 450 \text{ kgs.} \quad = \text{Rs. } 1{,}518.$$

Illustration 5

Prepare a Cost Sheet from the following:

Direct Labour Cost (160% of Factory overhead)		Rs. 16,000
Cost of Goods Sold		Rs. 56,000
	Opening Rs.	**Closing Rs.**
Raw Materials	8,000	8,600
Work-in-Progress	8,000	12,000
Finished Goods	14,000	18,000
Other data:		
Selling Expenses		3,400
General and Administrative Expenses		2,600
Sales for the month		75,000

(*C.A. Inter, Punjab Univ., B.Com. 1985, Punjabi Univ., 1988*)

Solution

Calculation of Cost of Raw Materials Purchased (by Reversal Method)

	Rs.
Cost of Goods Sold	56,000
Add Closing Stock of Finished Goods	18,000
	74,000
Less Opening Stock of Finished Goods	14,000
Cost of Production	**60,000**
Less General and Administrative Expenses	2,600
Factory Cost	**57,400**
Add Closing Stock of Work-in-Progress	12,000
	69,400
Less Opening Stock of Work-in-Progress	8,000
	61,400
Less Factory Overhead $\left(16{,}000 \times \frac{100}{160}\right)$	10,000
Prime Cost	**51,400**
Less Direct Wages	16,000
Cost of Raw Materials Consumed	**35,400**
Add Closing Stock of Raw Materials	8,600
	44,000
Lass Opening Stock of Raw Materials	8,000
Cost of Raw Materials Purchased	**36,000**

After ascertaining the cost of raw materials purchased, the cost sheet can be presented as follows:

COST SHEET

Period: .... Output: ....

		Rs.
Cost of Raw Materials Consumed		
Opening Stock of Raw Materials	8,000	
Add Purchases of Raw Materials	36,000	
	44,000	
Less Closing Stock of Raw Materials	8,600	
		35,400
Direct Labour Cost		16,000
Prime Cost		**51,400**
Factory Overhead		10,000
		61,400
Add Opening Stock of Work-in-Progress		8,000
		69,400
Less Closing Stock of Work-in-Progress		12,000
Factory Cost		**57,400**
General and Administrative Expenses		2,600
Cost of Production		**60,000**
Add Opening Stock of Finished Goods		14,000
		74,000
Less Closing Stock of Finished Goods		18,000
Cost of goods sold		**56,000**
Selling Expenses		3,400
Cost of Sales		**59,400**
Profit		**15,600**
Sales		**75,000**

Illustration 6

The following figures are extracted from the books of Bhola Sweets for the year ended 31st March, 2003:

	Stocks 1/04/02 Rs.	Purchases Rs.	Stocks 31/03/03 Rs.
Sugar and Glucose	13,600	70,340	16,200
Milk and Fats	6,200	53,000	5,800
Essences & Flavours	400	4,800	800
Containers & wrappings	18,400	93,000	16,800
Finished Goods	12,000	—	14,000

	Rs.
Direct wages	36,800
Factory Supervision	8,000
Machinery maintenance	7,000
Depreciation: Machinery	600

Building (5/6 Factory, 1/6 Office)	720
Directors' Remuneration (Rs. 7,500 chargeable to factory)	24,000
Rates & Insurance (7/8 Factory, 1/8 Office)	1,200
Heating & Lighting — Factory	750
— Office	240
Power	3,500
Sundry Factory expenses	2,780
Office expenses	8,860
Selling expenses	28,500
Sales	4,23,750

Sweets produced: 1,30,000 kgs.

Calculate cost per tonne and also total profit.

Solution

COST SHEET

				Total 1,30,000 Kgs. or 130 Tonnes	Per Tonne
				Rs.	Rs.
Raw Materials Consumed:					
	Opening stock Rs.	Purchases Rs.	Closing stock Rs.		
Sugar & Glucose	13,600 +	70,340 –	16,200	67,740	521.08
Milk & Fats	6,200 +	53,000 –	5,800	53,400	410.76
Essences & Flavours	400 +	4,800 –	800	4,400	33.85
Containers & Wrapping	18,400 +	93,000 –	16,800	94,600	727.69
				2,20,140	1,693.38
Direct wages				36,800	283.08
Prime Cost				2,56,940	1,976.46
Factory Overhead:					
Factory Supervision		8,000			
Machinery Maintenance		7,000			
Depreciation of Machinery		600			
Depreciation on Building (5/6)		600			
Directors' Remuneration		7,500			
Rates & Insurance		1,050			
Factory Heating & Lighting		750			
Power		3,500			
Sundry Factory Expenses		2,780		31,780	244.46
		Factory Cost		2,88,720	2,220.92
Office Overhead:					
Depreciation of Building		120			
Director's Remuneration		16,500			
Rates & Insurance		150			
Heating & Lighting		240			
Office Expenses		8,860		25,870	199.00
			Cost of Production	3,14,590	2,419.92
Selling Overhead				28,500	219.23
			Total Cost	3,43,090	2,639.15
			Profit	80,660	
			Sales	4,23,750	

OBJECTIVE TYPE QUESTIONS

1. State which of the following items should be grouped under Factory Overhead:

(*i*) Salary of Time-keeper
(*ii*) Salary of store-keeper
(*iii*) Counting office salaries
(*iv*) Drawing office salaries
(*v*) Salary of general manager
(*vi*) Salary of sales manager
(*vii*) Salary of Chief Engineer
(*viii*) Salary of warehouse-keeper

[**Ans.** (*i*), (*ii*), (*iv*), (*vii*)]

2. State which of the following items should be grouped under office overhead:

(*i*) Factory Manager's salary
(*ii*) General manager's salary
(*iii*) Factory power
(*iv*) Repairs to office building
(*v*) Depreciation of office furniture
(*vi*) Directors' fees
(*vii*) Postage and stationery
(*viii*) General Expenses.

[**Ans.** (*ii*), (*iv*), (*v*), (*vi*), (*vii*), (*viii*)]

3. State which of the following items should be grouped under Selling and Distribution Overhead:

(*i*) Factory Rent
(*ii*) Commission on sales
(*iii*) Carriage outward
(*iv*) Office Rent
(*v*) Rent of warehouse
(*vi*) Packing Expenses
(*vii*) Bad Debts
(*viii*) Factory manager's salary

[**Ans.** (*ii*), (*iii*), (*v*), (*vi*), (*vii*)]

4. Fill in the blanks:

(*a*) .... + Purchases of Raw Materials (Net) + Carriage on Raw Materials – Closing Stock of Raw Materials = Cost of Raw Materials Consumed.

(*b*) Direct Materials + ... + Direct Expenses = Prime Cost

(*c*) Prime Cost + Works Overhead = ...

(*d*) .... + Works Overhead + Office Overhead = Cost of Production.

(*e*) Cost of Production + ... – Closing Stock of Finished Goods = Cost of Goods Sold.

(*f*) Cost of Goods Sold + Selling and Distribution Overhead = ...

(*g*) .... + Profit = Sales.

[**Ans.** (*a*) Opening Stock of Raw materials (*b*) Direct Wages (*c*) Works Cost (*d*) Prime Cost (*e*) Prime Cost (*f*) Opening Stock of Finished Goods (*g*) Cost of Sales.]

5. State whether the following statements are 'True' or 'False':

(*a*) Aggregate of direct materials cost, direct wages and direct expenses is known as 'Prime Cost'.

(*b*) Aggregate of Prime Cost and Factory Overhead is known as 'Office Cost'.

(*c*) Direct wages is the part of factory overhead.

(*d*) Chargeable expenses is an item of Prime Cost.

(*e*) Royalties paid on the basis of sales is an item of selling and distribution overhead.

(*f*) Drawing office salaries is an item of factory overhead.

(*g*) Depreciation on plant and machinery is an item of office overhead.

[**Ans.** True (*a*), (*d*), (*e*), (*f*) False (*b*), (*c*), (*g*)]

6. Multiple Choice Questions:
Give the correct answer to the following questions:

(*a*) Aggregate of direct costs is known as:

(*i*) Direct Material Cost (*ii*) Direct Wages
(*iii*) Direct Expenses (*iv*) Prime Cost.

(*b*) All costs other than direct materials cost, direct labour cost and direct expenses are known as:

(*i*) Indirect Material Cost (*ii*) Overhead
(*iii*) Indirect Labour Cost (*iv*) Indirect Expenses.

(*c*) Aggregate of Prime Cost and Factory Overhead is known as:

(*i*) Works oncost (*ii*) Works Cost
(*iii*) Cost of Production (*iv*) Direct Cost.

(*d*) Salary paid to factory manager is an item of

(*i*) Prime Cost (*ii*) Factory Overhead
(*iii*) Selling Overhead (*iv*) Office Overhead.

(*e*) Aggregate of Cost of Goods Sold and Selling and Distribution Overhead is known as

(*i*) Total Cost (*iii*) Cost of Sales
(*ii*) Office Cost (*iv*) Selling Overhead.

[**Ans.** (*a*) (*iv*), (*b*) (*ii*), (*c*) (*ii*), (*d*) (*ii*), (*e*) (*iii*)]

SHORT ANSWER TYPE QUESTIONS

1. What is meant by 'elements' of cost?

2. What is the difference between 'elements' and 'components' of cost?

3. Discuss the meaning of direct material cost.

4. What is direct labour cost? How does it differ from indirect labour cost?

5. What is meant by direct expenses? Give any five items of direct expenses.
6. What is 'Cost Sheet'? Give the specimen of a Cost Sheet.
7. What do you understand by:
   (*i*) Indirect material cost
   (*ii*) Factory overhead
   (*iii*) Office and administration overhead
8. What is meant by Factory Cost?
9. What is meant by Cost of Sales?
10. What is 'Overhead'? Give their classification according to functions.

LONG ANSWER TYPE QUESTIONS

1. What do you mean by elements of cost? Give the main components of cost and explain them with the help of a diagram.
2. Distinguish between 'Direct costs' and 'Indirect costs'. What types of costs are included in direct costs?
3. Explain the term 'Overhead'. How do you classify overhead with reference to functions ? Give examples.
4. What are the various items which are not included in cost accounts?

EXERCISES

1. From the following particulars, prepare a Cost Sheet for three months ending on 31st March 2009:

	Rs.
Raw Materials consumed	3,00,000
Direct Wages	4,50,000
Direct Expenses	75,000
Factory Overhead	2,25,000
Office Overhead	1,20,000
Selling Overhead	1,05,000
Total Output:	**1,000 Units.**

[**Ans.** Prime Cost: Rs. 8,25,000; Factory Cost: Rs. 10,50,000; Cost of Production: Rs. 11,70,000; Total Cost: Rs 12,75,000]

2. From the following particulars, prepare a Cost Sheet for the period ended 31st March, 2009.

	Rs.
Raw Materials	33,000
Productive Wages	35,000
Unproductive Wages	10,500
Factory Rent and taxes	7,500
Factory Lighting	2,200
Factory Heating	1,500
Motive Power	4,400
Directors' Fees	4,000
Factory Cleaning	2,000
Sundry Office Expenses	2,500
Factory Stationery	200
Office Stationery	750
Loose Tools written off	900
Office Rent	3,600
Haulage	1,000
Water Supply	1,500
Factory Insurance	800
Office Insurance	500
Legal Expenses	400
Direct Expenses	3,000
Rent of warehouse	300
Depreciation of Plant and Machinery	2,000
Depreciation of Office Building	300
Bad Debts	200
Advertising	500
Sales Department Salaries	1,500
Upkeep of delivery vans	700
Commission on sales	1,500
Total Output	**15,000 Tons.**

[**Ans.** Prime Cost: Rs. 71,000; Works Cost: Rs. 1,05,500; Office Cost: Rs 1,17,550; Total Cost: Rs. 1,22,250]

3. The following informations have been taken from the books of H.K. Manufacturing Co. Prepare a Cost Sheet of the manufacturer:

	Rs.
Direct materials used	1,50,000
Direct wages	1,30,000
Depreciation of Factory Buildings	5,000
Insurance: Staff Car	1,000
Office Building	800
Factory Building	700
Expenses of delivery vans	1,500
Depreciation: Office Building	2,000
Staff car	500
Salaries: Sales manager	10,000
Chief Engineer	11,000
Others	25,000
Warehouse Expenses	2,500
Electricity (Including Rs. 2,000 for office and Rs. 500 for show-room)	8,000
Show-room Expenses	3,500
Cost of Printing of Price Lists'	1,000
Advertisement	2,700
Sundry Factory Expenses	20,000
Sales Promotion Expenses	2,000
Expenses for participation in Industrial Exhibition	5,000
Opening Stock of Finished Goods (800 units)	40,000
Closing Stock of Finished Goods (500 Units)	25,000
Sales	5,00,000

(No. of Units Produced: 7,000)

[**Ans.** Prime Cost: Rs, 2,80,000; Works Cost: Rs. 3,22,200; Cost of Production: Rs. 3,53,500; Cost of Goods sold: Rs. 3,68,500; Cost of sales: Rs. 3,97,200; Net Profit: Rs.1,02,800]

4. From the following particulars, prepare the Cost Sheet of a manufacturer for the month of Oct., 2009:

	Rs.
Materials Consumed	2,00,000
Direct Labour	3,00,000
Chargeable Expenses	50,000
Factory Rent, Rates and Taxes	60,000
Depreciation on machinery	80,000
General Expenses	44,000
Light and Water	34,000
Indirect Material	18,000
Factory Supervision	42,000
Total Output:	**10,000 Tonnes**

[**Ans.** Prime Cost: Rs.5,50,000; Factory Cost: Rs. 7,84,000;
Cost of Production : Rs. 8,28,000]

5. The following data relate to the manufacture of a standard product during 4 weeks ending 30th June, 2009:

Raw Material consumed	Rs. 40,000
Direct wages	Rs. 24,000
Machine Hours worked	190 Hours
Machine Hour Rate	Rs. 20
Office overhead	15% on Factory cost
Selling overhead	75 paise per unit sold
No. of Units produced	20,000
No. of Units sold (@Rs. 5 each)	18,000

You are required to prepare a Cost Sheet for the above.

[**Ans.** Prime Cost : Rs.64,000 ; Works Cost : Rs.67,800;
Cost of Production: Rs. 77,970;
Cost of Goods Sold: Rs. 70,173;
Cost of Sales : Rs. 83,673
Profit : Rs. 6,327]

6. The books and records of the Dixcy Creation Ltd., present the following data for the month of August, 2009:

Direct Labour Cost (160% of factory overhead)	Rs. 40,000
Cost of Goods Sold	Rs. 1,40,000

Inventory accounts showed these opening and closing balances:

	August 1	**August 31**
Raw Materials	20,000	21,500
Work-in-Progress	20,000	30,000
Finished Goods	35,000	45,000
Other data:		
Selling Expenses		8,500
General and Administration Expenses		6,500
Sales for the month		1,87,500

You are required to prepare a statement showing cost of goods manufactured and sold and profit earned

[**Ans.** Cost of Raw Materials Purchased: Rs. 90,000; Prime Cost: Rs. 1,28,500; Factory Cost: Rs. 1,43,500; Cost of Production Rs. 1,50,000; Cost of Sales: Rs. 1,48,500; Profit: Rs. 39,000]

7. The books of Adarsh Manufacturing Company present the following data for the month of April, 2009. Direct labour cost Rs. 17,500 being 175% of the works overhead. Cost of goods sold excluding administration expenses Rs. 56,000

Inventory accounts showed the following opening and closing balances:

	April 1	**April 30**
	Rs.	**Rs.**
Raw Materials	8,000	10,600
Work-in-progress	10,500	14,500
Finished Goods	17,600	19,000

Other data are:

	Rs.
Selling Expenses	3,500
General and administration expenses	2,500
Sales for the month	75,000

You are required to:

(*i*) Compute the value of materials purchased.

(*ii*) Prepare a cost statement showing the various elements of cost and also the profit.

(C.A. Inter, May 1992 Year Changed)

[**Ans.** (*i*) Rs. 36,500 (*ii*) Prime Cost Rs. 51,400; Works Cost Rs. 61,400; Cost of goods manufactured Rs. 57,400; Cost of Sales Rs. 62,000; Profit Rs. 13,000]

8. The following data relate to the manufacture of a standard product during the four weeks ended 18th Oct., 2009:

Raw materials consumed	Rs. 30,000
Direct wages	Rs. 19,600
Machine hours worked	Rs. 2,300
Machine hour rate	Re. 1
Office oncost	10% of works cost
Selling oncost	20 Paise per unit
No. of units produced	19,030
Units sold	11,418@Rs.4 each

You are required to prepare a Cost Sheet in respect of the above showing: (*a*) cost per unit and (*b*) profit for the period.

[**Ans.** (*a*) Rs. 3.20 (*b*) Rs. 9,134.40J

9. Dunkel Ltd. started a factory in Navi Mumbai on 1st April, 2008. Following details are furnished about its activity during the year ended 31st March, 2009:

Raw materials consumed	40,000 units 7 per unit
Direct wages:	
(*a*) Skilled worker	Rs. 9 per unit
(*b*) Unskilled worker	Rs. 6 per unit
Royalty (on Raw Material consumed)	Rs. 3 per unit
Works overhead	@ Rs. 8 per machine hour
Machine Hours worked	25,000
Office overheads	1/3rd of works cost
Sales Commission	Rs. 4 per unit
Units produced	40,000
Stock of units at the end	4,000 units to be valued at cost of production per unit
Sale price per unit	Rs. 50 per unit

Prepare Cost Sheet.

[**Ans.** Cost of Sales per unit Rs. 44; Total Profit 2,16,000]

10. The following details are given to you by M/s Austin Car Mfg. Co. for the year 2009. Prepare a statement showing cost and profit per car sold:

	Luxury Car	Janta Car
	Rs.	Rs.
(*a*) Materials	2,40,000	3,23,200
(*b*) Direct wages	4,56,000	5,65,600

(c) Works overhead 100% on direct wages

(*d*) Office overhead 25% on works oncost

(*e*) 60 Luxury cars and 101 Janta cars were sold @ Rs. 30,000 and Rs. 22,000 per car respectively.

(*f*) There was no opening or closing stock of cars.
Also calculate the total profit for 2009.

[**Ans.** Cost per car Rs. 21,100 (Luxury), Rs. 15,800 (Janta); Profit per car Rs. 8,900 (Luxury), Rs. 6,200 (Janta); Total Profit Rs. 11,60,200]

11. You are the Head of the Costing Department of Explosives Ltd. The Government of a friendly country has invited quotations for explosives for which your Government has granted the necessary permission. Your firm wants to submit the quotation and the Managing Director has instructed you to estimate the cost per tonne by preparing a proper analytical Cost Sheet and suggest a suitable price quotation:

Total Production in 2008	500 Tonnes
	Rs.
Cost of Raw materials	2,00, 000
Carriage inwards	20,000
Direct wages	2,00,000
Indirect wages (Factory)	10,000
Office expenses	1,00,000
Public relations expenses	5,000
Expenses on Testing Lab.	6,000
Selling overhead	1,00,000
Salary of Managing Director	5,000
Payment of Income Tax	30,000

Note:

(*i*) A profit margin of 50 % on cost is provided.

(*ii*) The Government grants a special export subsidy of Rs. 1,000 per tonne.

[**Ans.** Quotation Price Rs. 938]

3

Cost Classification

Cost accounting involves collecting, classifying, recording and appropriate allocation of expenditure for determining the costs of products or services. After costs have been collected, these are properly classified for their identification with cost centres or cost units. Costs have different features or characteristics. Costs are grouped or classified according to their common characteristics. The process of grouping costs according to their common characteristics is known as 'classification of cost'. The various groups into which costs are classified, are known as 'classes'.

Costs may be classified according to different bases or characteristics such as element, nature, variability, controllability, normality, function etc. These bases may be given as follows:

1. Element:

Under this, costs are classified with reference to the factors on which costs are incurred. According to elements, costs may be grouped as:

(*a*) Material Cost,
(*b*) Labour Cost, and
(*c*) Expenses.

Material cost refers to the cost of commodities supplied to an undertaking *e.g.,* in case of textile mill, cost of cotton or cost of yarn, cotton waste for cleaning of machinery, cost of dyes, cost of finishing material etc.

Labour cost refers to the cost of remuneration of the employees in an undertaking and includes salary, wages, commission etc.

Expenses refer to the cost of services provided to an undertaking and includes the notional cost of owned assets e.g., rent of the building, insurance premium of the building, telephone expenses, depreciation of the owned factory building, depreciation of delivery van etc.

2. Nature:

Under this , costs are classified according to their identifiability with cost centres or cost units. According to their nature, costs may be grouped as:

(*a*) Direct Costs, and
(*b*) Indirect Costs.

Direct costs refer to those costs which can be directly and easily traced to or identified with a product, process or department. Materials used and labour employed in manufacturing an article or in a particular process of production are common examples of direct costs.

Indirect costs, on the other hand, refer to those costs which are not traceable to any particular product, process or department, but are common to a number of products, processes or departments *e.g.,* Factory Rent, Factory Insurance, Factory Manager's Salary etc.

3. Variability or Behaviour:

On the basis of their behaviour in relation to changes in the volume of activity, costs (both direct and indirect) may be classified as:

(*a*) Variable Costs,
(*b*) Fixed Costs, and
(*c*) Semi-variable or Semi-fixed Costs.

Variable costs refer to those costs which vary directly in proportion to changes in the volume of output or sales. These costs tend to increase or decrease with the rise and fall in production or sales. Variable costs vary in total but their per unit cost remains constant. Direct material cost, direct wages, direct expenses, consumable stores, commission on sales etc., are the typical examples of variable costs.

Fixed costs refer to those costs which tend to remain unaffected by the changes in the volume of output or sales. In other words, fixed costs remain unchanged with the increase or decrease in output or sales. These costs remain fixed in total but their per unit cost changes with changes in output or sales. These costs depend mainly on effluxion of time and do not vary directly with the changes in the volume of output or sales. Rent, rates, taxes, insurance charges, manager's salary etc., are the typical examples of fixed costs.

It should be remembered that fixed costs are not absolutely fixed for all times. These are fixed only in relation to a certain level of production capacity.

Semi-variable costs refer to costs which tend to vary with changes in the volume of output or sales, but not directly in proportion to such changes. These costs have the characteristics of both fixed and variable costs. A part of semi-variable costs remains constant inspite of changes in the volume of output or sales, while the other part varies in proportion to changes in volume of output or sales. Repairs and maintenance costs of plant, machinery and building, salary of supervisor etc., are the typical examples of semi- variable costs.

4. Controllability:

Under this, costs are classified according to whether or not these are influenced by the action of a given member of an undertaking. The classes of costs are:

(*a*) Controllable Costs, and
(*b*) Uncontrollable Costs.

Controllable costs refer to those costs which can be influenced by the action of a specified member of an undertaking. An undertaking is usually divided into a number of departments or cost centres which are placed under the direct control and supervision of specified persons. The person in charge of a particular department or cost centre can control only those costs which come directly under his control.

Uncontrollable costs, on the other hand, refer to those costs which cannot be influenced by the action of a specified member of an undertaking. Costs which are controllable by a person may be uncontrollable so far as another person is concerned. Thus, the difference between controllable and uncontrollable costs is only in relation to particular individual or level of management.

5. Normality:

Under this, costs are classified according to whether these are costs which are normally incurred at a given level of output in the conditions in which that level of output is normally attained. According to normality, costs may be classified as:

(*a*) Normal or Unavoidable Costs, and
(*b*) Abnormal or Avoidable Costs.

Normal or unavoidable costs refer to those costs which are normally incurred at a given level of output in the conditions in which that level of output is normally attained. Such costs cannot be avoided at all. Cost of normal spoilage of materials and the cost of normal idle time are the typical examples of normal costs.

Abnormal or avoidable costs refer to those costs which are not normally incurred at a given level of output in the conditions in which that level of output is attained. Such costs can be avoided if proper care is taken. Cost of spoilage of material over and above the normal limit is an example of abnormal cost.

6. Function:

From the view point of function performed by the costs, these may be classified as:

(*a*) Production Costs,
(*b*) Administration Costs,
(*c*) Selling Costs, and
(*d*) Distribution Costs.

Production costs refer to those costs which arise in the course of production from the acquisition of raw materials till the finished products have been turned out. Production costs include cost of materials, cost of labour, other factory expenses and cost of primary packing.

Administration costs refer to those costs which are incurred for formulating the business policies, directing the organisation and controlling the operations of an undertaking. These costs should not be related to research, development, production, distribution or selling activities.

Selling costs refer to those costs which are incurred to create and stimulate demand and to secure orders. Thus, these costs are incurred in connection with the marketing of the products.

Distribution costs refer to the costs of the sequence of operations which starts with making the packed product available for despatch and ends with making the reconditioned returned empty packages available for re-use.

7. Time:

From the view point of time, costs can be grouped as:

(*a*) Historical Costs, and
(*b*) Pre-determined Costs.

Historical costs refer to costs ascertained after these have been incurred. Historical costs are determined after goods have been manufactured or services have been rendered. Historical costs simply represent post-mortem of past events and help in ascertaining the profitability but not in exercising cost control.

Pre-determined costs refer to costs which are computed in advance of production on the basis of a specification of all the factors affecting them.

Pre-determined costs can be further divided into:

(*i*) Estimated Costs, and (*ii*) Standard Costs.

Estimated costs refer to costs which, as per studies made, are most likely to be incurred. These are estimated in advance on the basis of the assumption that costs are more or less free to move and that what is made is the best estimate of the cost conditions which will apply when the cost is incurred.

Standard cost refers to a pre-determined cost which is calculated from management's standards of efficient operation and the relevant necessary expenditure. Standard cost is established on the basis of the assumption that costs will not be allowed to move freely but will be controlled as far as possible so that actual cost will be as close to standard cost as possible and any variation of actual from the standard cost will be capable of reasonable explanation.

The basic difference between an estimated cost and a standard cost is that, an estimated cost is a more or less reasonable assessment of what a cost will be when it is incurred. A standard cost, on the other hand, is a specification of what a cost ought to be when it is incurred.

8. Relevance to Decision-Making and Control:

Under this, costs are classified on the basis of their relevance to the decisions to be taken by the management. These costs are as follows:

(*a*) **Marginal Cost:** Marginal cost is defined as "the amount at any given volume of output by which aggregate costs are changed if the volume of output is increased or decreased by one unit." Marginal cost is the increase in total cost resulting from increase in output by one unit. Marginal cost is denoted by variable cost comprising direct material cost, direct labour cost, direct expenses and variable overheads.

(*b*) **Sunk Costs:** Sunk costs refer to those costs which have already been incurred and cannot be altered by any decision in the future. These costs become irrelevant costs for later decisions. For example, if the management decides to replace an existing machine by a new one, the amount of capital invested in the existing machine less scrap value will be irrecoverable and hence it is known as 'Sunk Cost'.

(*c*) **Out of Pocket Costs:** These refer to those costs which signify the present or future cash expenditure regarding a certain decision that will vary depending upon the nature of decision made. Management decisions are directly affected by such costs since they give rise to cash expenditure. For example, a firm has its own vehicles for transporting raw materials and finished goods from one place to another. It seeks to replace these vehicles by employment of public carriers. In making this decision, the depreciation of the vehicles is not to be considered but the management must take into account the present expenditure on fuel, maintenance and salary to drivers. Such costs are treated as out of pocket costs.

(*d*) **Opportunity Costs:** Opportunity cost of a product or service is measured in terms of revenue which could have been earned by employing the resources in some other alternative uses. Opportunity cost can be defined as the cost of the best alternative foregone. Thus, the opportunity cost of yarn produced by a composite spinning and weaving mill and used in the weaving section would be the price that could have been obtained by selling the yarn in the market.

(*e*) **Imputed Costs:** Imputed costs refer to those costs which are not included in costs but are considered for making management decisions. These costs are hypothetical in character. For example, interest on capital, though not actually payable, is often required to be included in order to judge the relative profitability of two products involving unequal outlays of cash.

(*f*) **Differential Costs:** Differential costs refer to the difference in total costs between two alternatives. In case, the choice of an alternative results in an increase in total costs, such increased costs are known as incremental costs. On the other hand, if the choice results in a decrease in total costs, such decreased costs are called decremental costs.

(*g*) **Shut-down Costs:** These are the costs which will still be incurred although a plant is shut down temporarily. Sometimes, it so happens that the normal operations of a business have to be suspended temporarily due to unfavourable market conditions or strike etc. There are some costs which have to be incurred even during suspension of production or other activities. These are treated as 'Shut-down costs'. Examples of such costs are rent of factory premises, salaries of top management etc.

(*h*) **Postponable Costs:** These are the costs which can be postponed or shifted to the future with little or no effect on the efficiency of current operations. These costs are postponable but not avoidable and have to be incurred at a later stage. The concept of postponable cost is very significant in railways and transport undertakings in which cost of repairs and maintenance can be postponed for certain period. In manufacturing concerns also, during depression period, economic crisis can be averted by postponing certain costs.

(*i*) **Replacement Costs:** Replacement cost refers to the cost of replacement of an asset in the current market or at the current price. Thus, the replacement cost of an asset means the cost which would be incurred if the asset was to be purchased at the current market price and not the cost at which it was originally purchased.

(*j*) **Abandonment Costs:** 'Abandonment' refers to complete retirement or withdrawal of a fixed asset from service or utilisation. A fixed asset is abandoned when it is no longer serviceable. Abandonment cost refers to the cost incurred in abandoning a fixed asset *i.e.,* the cost which cannot be recovered or salvaged from the abandoned asset. It is also known as 'Abandonment Loss'.

Other Types of Cost:

(*a*) **Research Cost:** The cost of searching for new or improved products, new applications of materials, or new or improved methods of production, is known as Research Cost.

(*b*) **Development Cost:** The cost of the process, which begins with the implementation of the decision to produce a new or improved product or to employ a new or improved method and ends with the commencement of formal production of that product or by that method, is known as 'Development Cost'.

(*c*) **Pre-production Cost:** It refers to that part of development cost which is incurred in making a trial production run preliminary to formal production.

(*d*) **Conversion Cost:** Conversion costs refer to costs which are incurred for converting raw materials into finished goods and comprise direct labour cost, direct expenses and factory overhead.

OBJECTIVE TYPE QUESTIONS

Multiple Choice Questions

Select the correct answer to the following:

(*a*) Cost incurred to convert raw materials into finished goods is:

(*i*) Direct cost
(*ii*) Controllable cost
(*iii*) Conversion cost
(*iv*) Indirect cost.

(*b*) Interest on capital not actually paid but added to the cost of project for decision making is –

(*i*) Fixed cost
(*ii*) Out of pocket cost
(*iii*) Imputed cost
(*iv*) Uncontrollable cost

(*c*) The estimated cost which is ought to be incurred is –

(*i*) Standard cost
(*ii*) Budgeted cost
(*iii*) Imputed cost
(*iv*) Indirect cost.

(*d*) Revenue or income from an alternative which has been forsaken is –

(*i*) Sunk cost
(*ii*) Variable cost
(*iii*) Imputed cost
(*iv*) Opportunity cost.

(*e*) Sunk costs are –

(*i*) fixed in nature
(*ii*) variable in nature
(*iii*) avoidable
(*iv*) not relevant to present decisions.

[**Ans.** (*a*) (*iii*), (*b*) (*iii*), (*c*) (*i*), (*d*) (*iv*), (*e*) (*i*)]

'True' or 'False' Type questions:

State whether the following statements are true or false:

(*a*) Cost classification is the grouping of costs having common features.

(*b*) On the basis of identifiability, costs are classified into controllable costs and uncontrollable costs.

(*c*) Indirect costs cannot be identified with any particular cost unit.

(*d*) Fixed cost per unit is always fixed.

(*e*) Variable cost per unit is always fixed.

(*f*) Marginal cost is the cost of an additional unit of output.

(*g*) Marginal cost is not relevant to decision making process.

(*h*) Manufacturing costs are incurred to create and stimulate demand.

[**Ans.** (*a*) T, (*b*) F, (*c*) T, (*d*) F, (*e*) T, (*f*) T, (*g*) F, (*h*) F.]

Fill in the blanks:

(*a*) .... costs tend to remain unaffected by changes in output.

(*b*) .... costs tend to change proportionately with changes in level of activity.

(*c*) Grouping of costs on the basis of common .... is known as classification of costs.

(*d*) Costs which have already been incurred are known as .... costs.

(*e*) .... cost is the aggregate of Prime Cost and Variable Overheads.

(*f*) .... costs are hypothetical costs relevant to decision making process.

(*g*) Sunk costs are not relevant to present ....

(*h*) Costs of converting raw materials into finished goods are known as .... costs.

(*i*) Costs of seeking to create and stimulate demand and of securing orders are treated as .... costs.

(*j*) Variable cost per unit is ....

[**Ans.** (*a*) Fixed (*b*) Variable (*c*) characteristics (*d*) historical (*e*) Marginal (*f*) Imputed (*g*) decisions (*h*) conversion (*i*) selling (*j*) fixed.]

SHORT ANSWER TYPE QUESTIONS

1. What is meant by cost classification?
2. How would you classify costs on the basis of variability?
3. Name the various bases of classifying costs.
4. What is meant by fixed cost?
5. What is meant by marginal cost?
6. Explain the meaning of imputed costs.
7. What is out of pocket cost?
8. Give the meaning of development cost.

9. Write notes on:
   (*a*) Pre-production cost;
   (*b*) Conversion cost.
10. How would you classify costs on the basis of controllability?
11. What is meant by functional classification of costs?

LONG ANSWER TYPE OUESTIONS

1. What is classification of costs? How costs are classified?
2. Explain fully the concept of cost. Discuss the various methods of classification of costs. (*H.P. Univ., B.Com., 1995*)
3. Explain fully the concept of 'Cost'. Distinguish between 'Direct Cost' and 'Indirect Cost'. (*B.Com., (Hons.) Delhi*)
4. (*a*) Define Direct Expenditure and Indirect Expenditure and give three example of each cost.
   (*b*) You are required to state how it is important to distinguish between 'fixed' and 'variable' expenses in cost accounting. Give three examples of each type of expenses. (*B.Com., Hons. Calcutta*)
5. Do you agree with the view that cost should be presented in different ways for different purposes? Support your view with suitable illustrations. (*C.A. Inter*)
6. Describe the various costs used in decision-making and explain their characteristics. (*B.Com., Hons., Delhi*)
7. Write notes on:
   (*i*) Conversion Cost
   (*ii*) Sunk Cost
   (*iii*) Opportunity Cost
   (*iv*) Imputed Cost
   (*v*) Differential Cost
   (*vi*) Out-of-pocket Cost.
8. Cost may be classified in a variety of ways according to their nature and the information needs of management. Explain and discuss this statement giving examples of classification required for different purposes. (*H.P.U., B.Com., 2008*)

4

Materials-I

INTRODUCTION

Material is the most important element of cost. In most of the manufacturing concerns 50% to 70% of the total cost of a product is represented by the cost of material. The material cost has been defined by the Institute of Cost and Management Accountants, U.K., as "the cost of commodities supplied to an undertaking." Cost of cotton or cost of cotton yarn in case of a textile mill, cost of cotton cloth in case of a hosiery factory, cost of wood in case of furniture making etc., are the examples of material cost. The term 'material' means and includes raw materials, factory supplies and consumable stores, spare parts, components and packing materials.

Materials may be direct materials or indirect materials. Direct materials comprise:

(*i*) Materials which can be directly related to and identified with cost centres or cost units. In other words, these are the items which form part of the product itself, e.g., cotton used for spinning cotton yarn, cotton yarn used in weaving cotton textiles, wood used in making furniture, leather used in making shoes and bricks and cement used in constructing buildings.

(*ii*) Materials which are purchased specifically for a particular job, work-order or contract.

(*iii*) Finished product of a particular process which forms the raw material of the succeeding process e.g., cost of yarn transferred from spinning process to weaving process.

Indirect materials comprise:

(*i*) Materials which cannot be allocated but can be apportioned to or absorbed by cost centres or cost units e.g., cotton waste for cleaning the machinery, lubricants for oiling the machinery, diesel oil for generating power etc.

(*ii*) Material which are used in such a small quantity that it is not possible to ascertain their per unit cost exactly e.g., cost of thread and nails used in shoe-making.

MATERIAL CONTROL

In an average manufacturing concern, the cost of material constitutes a large proportion of the total product cost and as such there should be a proper system of material control to ensure economy in the cost of production. No system of costing can be said to be complete without proper system of material control. Material control may be defined as safeguarding of company's property in the form of inventory and maintaining it at the optimum level, considering the operating requirements and financial resources of the business. Material control is a system which ensures the provision of the required quantity of materials of the required quality at the required time with the minimum amount of capital investment. The functions of a good system of material control include scheduling the requirements, purchasing, receiving, inspecting, maintaining stock records and stock control. Material control, in practice, is exercised through periodical reports and records relating to purchasing, receiving, inspecting and issuing of direct as well as indirect materials.

OBJECTS OF MATERIAL CONTROL

The main objects of material control may be given as follows:

(*i*) **To Ensure Un-interrupted Production:** The first object of material control is to ensure smooth production by making available all types of required materials in required quantity at the right time. Un-interrupted supply of materials is essential for smooth flow of production which is important for the success of any business.

(*ii*) **To Provide for Required Quality of Materials:** The second object of material control is to ensure the availability of all types of materials of required quality. If the quality of the materials is not proper, it will affect the quality of the product, which in its turn is bound to affect the reputation and sale of the business concern.

(*iii*) **To Minimise Wastages and Losses of Materials:** Material control system also aims at controlling or minimising all types of wastages and losses of materials which may arise due to carelessness in the storing, issuing and handling of materials.

(*iv*) **To Control Investment in Stock of Materials:** Material control system also aims at minimising the capital investment in the stock of materials. Materials are purchased and stored before the actual production commences. A large amount of capital may be locked up in materials which may not be required at that time. Similarly, sometimes there may be under-investment in materials leading to interruptions in production due to non-availability of the required quantity of materials. Efficient material control system helps in ensuring optimum investment of capital in the purchase of materials.

ADVANTAGES OF MATERIAL CONTROL SYSTEM

The main advantages of a good system of material control may be summarised as follows:

1. It helps in preventing production delays due to lack of materials by ensuring regular supply of proper quantities of materials at the right time.
2. It helps in ensuring production of proper quality by ensuring the purchase of materials of proper quality.
3. It helps in eliminating wastage in the use of materials.
4. It reduces the risk of loss from fraud and theft.
5. It reduces the cost involved in the storing and issuing of materials.
6. It minimises the capital investment in the stock of materials.
7. It furnishes quickly and accurately the value of materials used in various departments.
8. It helps in keeping perpetual inventory and other records to facilitate the preparation of accurate material reports.

FUNDAMENTAL PRINCIPLES OR BASIC REQUIREMENTS OF MATERIAL CONTROL

As we already know that the functions of a good system of material control include scheduling of the requirements, purchasing, receiving, inspecting, maintaining stock records etc. To ensure effective and efficient working of the material control system, the following principles should be observed:

(*i*) There should be proper co-ordination among various departments, particularly production department, purchases department, inspection department, stores department, cost department etc.

(*ii*) There should be centralised purchasing set up under the authority of an experienced and competent Purchase Manager.

(*iii*) Standard printed forms should be in use for making requisitions, placing orders, receiving materials, inspection of materials, issue of materials for consumption etc.

(*iv*) There should be a proper system for classification, codification and standardisation of materials.

(*v*) There should be an efficient arrangement for storing of materials in order to avoid the possibility of deterioration of quality, theft, wastage etc.

(*vi*) There should be an effective system of internal check for every aspect so that there is proper control over transactions at every stage. Each transaction in respect of materials must be approved by proper authority.

(*vii*) Different stock levels (*e.g.*, maximum level, re-order level, minimum level etc.) should be fixed for each item of material in the stores.

(*viii*) There should be a proper system for the valuation of materials issued to production since it considerably affects the costing records.

(*ix*) The use of Perpetual Inventory System should be made so that the stock of various items of material is recorded after each transaction.

(*x*) Regular reports on the quantity and value of materials received, issued and balance in hand, should be prepared.

(*xi*) There should be regular reconciliation of the reports on materials with corresponding accounting records.

SCOPE OF MATERIAL CONTROL

Material control comprises the following functions:

1. Purchasing of Materials.
2. Receiving and Inspection of Materials.
3. Storing of Materials.
4. Issue of Materials.
5. Maintenance of Inventory Record.
6. Inventory Control.
7. Accounting for Material Cost. [Discussed under the next chapter – Materials (II)]

PURCHASING OF MATERIALS

Purchasing is a specialised activity of utmost importance in a manufacturing concern. Materials represent a considerable portion of the total cost of production. As such, the Purchase Manager of a business concern is responsible for spending more of its money than any one else. An error on his part can be very expensive. Further, the purchase of sub-standard material would result in low quality of the final product, extra wastage of material and expensive machine break-downs. Hence, it is important to see that the function of purchase of materials is performed effectively, efficiently and economically. According to Alford and Beatty – "Purchasing is the procuring of materials, supplies, machines, tools, and services required for the equipment, maintenance and operation of a manufacturing plant." Purchasing function is performed by a separate Purchase Department set up under an expert 'Buyer' (or Purchase Manager). Purchasing function implies the determination of the following:

(*a*) What to purchase?

(*b*) When to purchase?

(*c*) Where to purchase?

(*d*) How much to purchase?

(*e*) At what price to purchase?

What to Purchase?

Normally some of the spare parts and components which a manufacturing concern requires, may be manufactured in the concern itself rather than being purchased from outside. The various items of stores which the Purchase Department should arrange to procure are:

(*i*) All the items of materials, stores spares and components which the manufacturing concern cannot make.

(*ii*) Other items which it can make but does not want to make.

Decision-making in respect of the items falling under category (*ii*) is an important function of the Purchase Department. The decision in this respect (*i.e.,* whether to buy or make) would depend on various factors like annual requirements of the item, frequency with which it is to be purchased, availability of the spare capacity in the manufacturing concern to produce it, the price advantage arising out of the comparative cost of making and buying, secrecy of the product etc. The decision to give preference to buying is of utmost importance and is taken by the Purchase Department under the guidance of Planning Department and Cost Department.

When to Purchase?

Materials are generally purchased as and when requisitions are received from Stores Department. In case of items available only during particular season, purchases shall be made during the season. In case of items of material restricted by Government control, the time of purchase will be decided with reference to the date of licence, quota or permit, as the case may be.

Where to Purchase?

The Purchase Department generally maintains a list of approved suppliers for various items of materials. Whenever materials are required, purchases are made from these suppliers after inviting quotations from them. In case long-term contracts have to be made for the purchase of materials in bulk, the materials are purchased from some specific supplier/suppliers only. In case of controlled items of materials, purchases are made from the specific supplier/suppliers only.

How Much to Purchase?

The quantity of materials to be purchased is another important decision-making area. The purchase department is guided, in this respect, by the Purchase Requisition received through the Stores Department. However, in case of an organisation using the budgetary control technique, the Purchase Budget prepared and approved in advance, indicates the timings and quantity of purchases. Thus, in such a case, the approved budget is the guiding factor. Some manufacturing concerns adopt control technique of Economic Order Quantity which indicates the quantity and frequency of purchases. Economic

Order Quantity ensures the minimisation of costs involved in purchasing materials and carrying inventory.

At What Price to Purchase?

The 'price' to be paid is one of the main factors affecting the cost of material. In case tenders or quotations have been invited and received, it is the responsibility of the Purchase Department to select the price at which the materials should be purchased. Normally, in this case the tender or quotation offering lowest price is selected. But the terms of delivery, credit period allowed, rate of discount and the reliability and the capacity of the supplier to execute orders, should also be taken into consideration. In case the material is supplied through Controlling Authority, the Purchase Manager has no option but to procure the supply at the price fixed by the concerned authority.

TYPES OF PURCHASING

Purchasing of materials can be done on centralised basis or decentralised basis, keeping in view the nature, size and the requirements of a business concern.

Centralised Purchasing: Under centralised purchasing, the authority to purchase materials for all the departments of an organisation, is placed in one individual or one department (Purchase Department headed by Purchase Manager).

Advantages of Centralised Purchasing: The main advantages of centralised purchasing may be given as follows:

(*i*) A uniform and firm policy can be pursued with regard to conditions of purchasing, *e.g.,* terms of payment.

(*ii*) Purchasing of materials is the sole responsibility of Purchase Department and the operating departmental heads can concentrate on production.

(*iii*) Since the materials are purchased in larger quantities, more advantageous rates can be obtained from suppliers.

(*iv*) A ready standardisation of different items of material can be effected.

(*v*) The buying staff, by concentrating on purchasing alone, develops specialised knowledge and skill leading to expert and economical buying.

(*vi*) Centralised purchasing facilitates the maintenance of one complete set of records for purchase transactions which enables the management to exercise better control over purchases.

(*vii*) Centralised purchasing helps to co-ordinate the entire purchasing activity and by placing authority for purchasing in one person, it avoids duplication and over-lapping.

(*viii*) Centralised purchasing helps in keeping inventories in control and avoiding excessive investment in materials.

Disadvantages of Centralised Purchasing: Centralised purchasing has limitations of its own which may be given as follows:

(*i*) The procedure adopted for the purchase of materials is less flexible which may cause undue delays in obtaining supplies.

(*ii*) Setting up of a separate Purchase Department leads to high administration cost.

Decentralised Purchasing:

Under decentralised purchasing, the authority to purchase materials is decentralised and placed in the hands of more than one individual or department. Under this system, each departmental head makes purchases for his own department. It is also known as 'localised purchasing'.

Decentralised purchasing is beneficial on account of the following reasons:

(*i*) Decentralised purchasing provides for flexibility in the purchase routine which helps in avoiding all types of delays in purchasing materials.

(*ii*) Under decentralised purchasing, the purchasing of materials is made by the departmental heads and no separate buying staff is appointed. Thus, there is saving in administration costs.

(*iii*) Decentralised purchasing is more efficient as the departmental head can assess the requirements and problems of his department well.

But decentralised purchasing has the following disadvantages:

(*i*) Decentralised purchasing is not economic since materials are purchased in smaller lots as a result of which quantity discount and favourable terms and conditions for purchase cannot be obtained.

(*ii*) A uniform policy regarding purchases of materials cannot be possible.

(*iii*) Prices paid for the same materials purchased by different departments may not be uniform.

(*iv*) Expert buying staff cannot be engaged for each department of the organisation.

(*v*) There is no co-ordination among various departments of the organisation in respect of purchases of materials which may lead to duplication and over-lapping of efforts.

(*vi*) The heads of various operating departments, being responsible for purchase of materials, cannot concentrate on their routine duties.

PURCHASE PROCEDURE (OR PURCHASE CYCLE)

Purchase procedure involves the following steps:

(*a*) **Initiating the Purchase:** Purchase of materials is initiated through 'Purchase Requisition' or 'Indent'. A Purchase Requisition or Indent is a form commonly used as a formal request to the Purchase Department for purchasing materials mentioned therein. Purchase Requisition is a document showing quantities, specification and the date when the materials are required, which authorises the Purchase Department to purchase the materials. The Purchase Requisition may be received from:

(*i*) the store-keeper in respect of all items of material in regular use;

(*ii*) the production control department for the special materials required for particular jobs or work-orders;

(*iii*) the plant and maintenance engineer for materials required for capital expenditure or maintenance projects; and

(*iv*) the departmental managers for special items such as filing cabinets, almirah etc.

The Purchase Requisition should specify:

(*i*) Serial number and date of requisition;

(*ii*) Name of the department;

(*iii*) Code Number or Symbol;

(*iv*) Description and quantity of materials required; and

(*v*) The purpose for which the materials are required.

The Purchase Requisition is prepared in triplicate. The original copy is sent to the Purchase Department, second copy is retained by the Stores Department or the department initiating the purchase and the third copy is sent to the costing office for record purposes. The specimen of Purchase Requisition may be given as follows:

ABC Co. Ltd.
Purchase Requisition

No.......................... Date..............................
Name of the Department.......................... Date by which required.........................
Code No. or Symbol...........................
Purpose for which materials are required............................

Serial No.	Particulars	Quantity	Remarks

Approved by........................... Requisitioned by...........................

(*b*) **Determination of the Sources of Supply:** After receiving the Purchase Requisitions, the next step is to select the suppliers with whom the orders are to be placed for the supply of materials. For this purpose, a list of suppliers should be prepared and approved by the Purchase Department each year. These suppliers should be reliable. Tenders or quotations are invited from approved suppliers whenever materials are required. These firms should be required to specify their terms and conditions of supply, delivery time, mode of payment etc., clearly. Out of the various tenders or quotations received, the tender/quotation offering most favourable terms is generally accepted. The specimen of a tender or quotation may be given as follows:

ABC Co. Ltd.
Tender Form/Quotation Form

Tender No............................. Date.............................
Name of Materials.............................

Serial No.	**Name of the Supplier**	**Rate**	**Time of delivery**	**Terms of delivery**	**Remarks**

Purchasing clerk............................. Purchase officer.............................

(c) Placing the Order: After selecting the supplier for obtaining the supplies of material, the Purchase Department prepares and places the purchase order with the supplier. Purchase order is made on a printed form and contains the particulars of materials ordered, quantity, quality, price, time of delivery etc. The specimen of the Purchase Order is given below:

A.B. Co. Ltd.
Purchase Order

Date............................. Purchase Order No.............................
To M/s............................. Department.............................
.... Production Order No.............................
(Vendor) Date by which required.............................

Please supply the following materials as per terms and conditions mentioned below:

Item No.	**Quantity**	**Description**	**Price**	**Amount**	**Remarks**

Signature of Purchase Manager

The number of copies of the purchase order to be prepared depends on the complexity of the organisation and the purchase routine adopted. Generally 4-5 copies are prepared. The original copy of purchase order is sent to the supplier and the copies are sent the Receiving Department, Accounting Department and the department which initiated the purchase requisition. The fifth copy is retained by the Purchase Department for reference purposes.

Receipt and Inspection of Materials

In small and medium sized manufacturing concerns, functions of receipt and inspection of materials are to be performed by the stores department or the store-keeper. But in case of large manufacturing concerns, generally a separate Receiving Department is set up. The Receiving Department has the following functions to perform:

(*i*) To receive, unload and unpack the materials.

(*ii*) To check whether the packages and their contents are intact or not.

(*iii*) To verify and check the quality, quantity and other specifications regarding materials in accordance with the purchase order.

(*iv*) To segregate defective materials from the lot by comparing delivery note sent by the supplier with the copy of the purchase order. Any shortage or breakage of material is intimated alongwith the acknowledgement sent to the supplier for the receipt of material.

(*v*) To pass on the materials from the receiving clerk to the inspector for his thorough inspection of the materials received.

(*vi*) To prepare the 'Goods Received Note' showing the particulars of the materials received.

INSPECTION NOTE

When materials are received by the Receiving Department, they are unpacked and compared with the materials ordered for with the help of the purchase order. If the materials are found to be in order, they are sent to the inspector for the inspection of the quality. If the quality of the materials is found to be fit, the inspector shall prepare an Inspection Note certifying the quality. The specimen of the Inspection Note is given below:

A.B. Co. Ltd.
Inspection Note

Serial No.......................... Date..........................

Identification No.	Description	Quantity Supplied	Rate Rs. P.	Amount Rs. P.	Remarks

The above stores have been thoroughly inspected by us at our/supplier's works/godown and we are of the opinion that they are in accordance with our requirements and are fit for use. We recommend their purchase.

Date..........................

1..........................
2..........................
3..........................

Inspecting Officers

REJECTION NOTE

If the materials received are not found to be in accordance to the purchase order or fit for use, the inspecting staff rejects them for return to the supplier. For this purpose, a document known as Rejection Note is prepared. The specimen of the Rejection Note is given below:

A.B. Co. Ltd. **Rejection Note**				
To be returned to:		Forwarding Note No. Date............		Serial No. Date.............
		Mode of Transport		P.O. No. Date.............
S. No.	**Identification No.**	**Quantity**	**Reasons for Rejection**	**Returned/Kept in Suspense**
Date............				1...................... 2...................... 3...................... Inspecting Officers

MATERIAL RECEIPT BOOK

It is the prime book used for the purpose of store accounting and keeps a date-wise record of the materials received in the stores. The Material Receipt Book provides the following information:

(*a*) Name and address of the supplier.
(*b*) Mode of Transport.
(*c*) Vehicle No.
(*d*) Carrier's Note No. and date and number of packages.
(*e*) Brief description of materials.
(*f*) Daily Receipt Voucher No. (D.R.V. No.) and date.
(*g*) Stock Ledger Folio.

The specimen of Material Receipt Book is given below:

A.B. Co. Ltd. Material Receipt Book										
Date	Consignor's Name and address	Mode of Transport	Vehicle No. (if any)	Carrier's Note No. and Date	No. of Packages and their condition	Brief Description of Goods	D.R.V. No. and Date	Stock Ledger Folio	Receipt Clerk's Initials	Remarks
1	2	3	4	5	6	7	8	9	10	11

MATERIAL RECEIVED NOTE (OR GOODS RECEIVED NOTE)

Some manufacturing concerns prefer to keep a loose card known as Material Received Note. This note is serially numbered and dated and avoids the use of the Material Receipt Book. Material Received Note also replaces the Daily Receipt Voucher. Although the Material Received Note avoids the use of the Material Receipt Book, it is advisable to maintain this book since it is a prime book of store accounting and provides useful information. Normally, five copies of Material Received Note are prepared and are sent to the Purchasing Department, Accounting Department, Stores Department and the department which has initiated the purchase requisition. The last copy is kept by the Receiving Department for future reference. The specimen of a Material Received Note is given below:

A.B. Co. Ltd.
Goods Received Note

G.R. Note No............ — Material Inspection
Purchase Order No............ — Note No..................
Date of Order............ — Delivery Note No.........
Received from............ — Date.......................

S. No.	Description	Symbol	Quantity	Code No.	Remarks

Sd. Received by — Sd. Checked by — Sd. Storekeeper — Sd. Stores Ledger Clerk

DAMAGES/SHORTAGE/EXCESS REPORT

This report is prepared by the receiving section of the stores department on opening the packages and comparing the actual materials received and materials ordered for with the help of the purchase order. Payment to the supplier of materials has to be adjusted according to this document. The proforma of this report is as follows:

A.B. Co. Ltd.
Damage/Shortage/Excess Report

From:
To: Carrier ....
To: Consignor ....
Carrier's Note No....
Date ....
Advice Note No, ...
Date ....

In correspondence, please quote:
Serial No .... Date ....
Purchase Order .... No Date ....

Tick ✓ in the appropriate box:

- ☐ The goods have not yet arrived.
- ☐ The goods have arrived late by .... days.
- ☐ The goods have arrived but the quantities shown below were found damaged on receipt.
- ☐ The goods have arrived but the shortages shown below were found on receipt.
- ☐ The goods have arrived but quantities shown below were found in excess. They are being returned through .... (mode of transport)

Serial No.	Identification No.	Description	Quantity ordered	Discrepancy	Nature of Discrepancy	Remarks
1	2	3	4	5	6	7

Date............ Storekeeper............

Copy to : Purchase Department for information and necessary action

Storage of Materials: After materials purchased have been received and checked, the next step in the process of material control is the storing of materials or store-keeping.

'Store-keeping' refers to the safe custody of all items of raw materials, supplies, finished parts, purchased parts etc., in the store-room for which the store-keeper acts as a trustee. It is said to be the process of receiving and distributing stores or supplies.

According to Alford and Beatty, "Store-keeping is that aspect of material control concerned with the physical storage of goods."

In the words of Wheldon, "Store-keeping is the physical storage of materials carried into the store-room in a scientific and systematic manner with a view to (*i*) saving them from all kinds of damages and losses, and (*ii*) exercising overall control over their movement."

In short, store-keeping refers to the art of preserving raw materials, work-in-progress and finished parts in the stores in the best possible manner. Generally, in small concerns, no importance is given to stores department. But it should be remembered that material pilferage, deterioration of materials and careless handling of materials lead to reduced profits or even losses. As such, it is necessary to maintain a well-equipped stores department to ensure maximum efficiency. Spriegel and Lansburgh have rightly remarked — "Poor control of materials is frequently accompanied by poor store-room administration in a way that may easily throw out of balance any operation programmes which have been adopted."

OBJECTS OF STORE-KEEPING

An efficient system of store-keeping has the following objects:

1. To ensure un-interrupted supply of materials and stores without delay to various production and service departments of the organisation.
2. To prevent over-stocking and under-stocking of materials.
3. To check in all materials as to quality and quantity.
4. To minimise storage cost.
5. To ensure proper and continuous control over materials.
6. To ensure most effective utilisation of available storage space and workers engaged in the process of store-keeping.
7. To protect materials from loss and wastage due to defective storage.
8. To identify and locate materials in the store-rooms without delay.
9. To protect and safeguard material items against pilferage, theft and fire etc.
10. To develop such a system so that fullest information about store items is available in the stores at every time.

FUNCTIONS OF STORE-KEEPING

The principal functions of store-keeping to be performed by the Stores Department in an organisation, are as follows:

1. Issuing purchase requisitions as and when material is required.
2. Receiving purchased stores from the Receiving Department and verifying that every lot of stores is supported by an indent, a purchase order and an inspection note.
3. Preparing 'Goods Received Note' in accordance with the different stores lots received.
4. Ensuring that all the Goods Received Notes are regularly posted to the Bin Card.
5. Placing and arranging stores received at proper and appropriate places

and adhering to the golden principle of store-keeping *i.e.*, 'A place for everything in its place.'

6. Minimising the storage, handling and maintaining costs by preserving and handling the materials in the most economical and efficient manner.
7. Issuing stores to various departments of the business and ensuring that all issues are properly authenticated and accounted for.
8. Ensuring about the adherence to the proper issuing procedure and system followed in the organisation.
9. Taking periodical review of inventory by initiating various inventory control systems viz., perpetual inventory control system and ABC system of inventory control.
10. Disclosing fullest and up-to-date information about the availability of stores whenever required, by maintaining proper stores records with the help of Bin Cards and Stores Ledger.
11. Ensuring proper safety of materials against theft, pilferage and fire, etc.
12. Supervising and co-ordinating the duties of different types of staff working under the headship of the store-keeper.
13. Preventing entry of unauthorised persons in the stores.
14. Maintaining proper stock-levels fixed in respect of every item of stores and replenishing them as and when necessary.

STORE-KEEPER AND HIS DUTIES

As we know that in a manufacturing concern, stores or materials represent an equivalent amount of cash. As such there should be a proper system of store-keeping which will ensure the safe custody of materials, easy location of the various items of stores, economic usage of storage space, regular and efficient flow of materials, maintenance of reliable stores records and an efficient assessment of stock position. For efficient store-keeping, a separate Stores Department under the headship of a 'store-keeper' is set up. The store-keeper is a man of wide experience in stores routine. He is assisted by a number of store-men in the performance of his duties. The store-keeper is responsible for the safe performance of his duties. The main duties and responsibilities of a store-keeper are:

1. To issue requisition on purchase department for purchasing materials at the right time.
2. To accept into stores, materials supplied by suppliers or returned by production departments.
3. To check in all materials as to quality and quantity.
4. To keep all the materials in safe and convenient manner in appropriate bins and containers.
5. To issue materials against proper authorisation.
6. To maintain proper records of receipts, issues and balance of materials.

7. To watch levels of stock and replenish materials when necessary.
8. To prevent the entry of unauthorised persons into the stores.
9. To advise the management on the day-to-day affairs of the stores department.
10. To dispose of scrap or obsolete materials.

LOCATION OF STORES

'Location' means the site for the store. The location of the stores should be carefully planned. An important factor to be considered when establishing a stores set up is the question of locating it in the most appropriate place. The stores must be set up at a convenient and safe place, near to Receiving Department, easily accessible from all parts of the factory and by means of transport and free from the risk of fire, theft, etc. The general principle in determining the location of stores is to minimise the total kg. – km. cost of transportation of materials.

FACTORS DETERMINING THE LOCATION OF STORES

The main factors which determine the location of store in a manufacturing concern may be given as follows:

1. **Minimisation of Material Handling Efforts:** Minimisation of material handling efforts implies location of raw material store near the production shops and location of finished goods store and packing materials store near the assembly shop. The stores should be easily accessible by means of transport.
2. **Nature of the Materials:** The nature of the materials to be stored also affects the location of the store. Material that is not damaged by weather can be stored out of doors in a shed. But materials such as cement, plaster, etc., must not only be protected from weather but must also be stored in a dry place.
3. **Quantity, Weight, etc., of the Materials:** The quantity of each of the goods to be stored must be taken into account for determining the location. When the quantities are known, adequate provision may be made for immediate and future storage needs.
4. **Flow of Materials:** Location of store should be convenient which allows for steady and regular flow of store items without any obstruction.
5. **Free from Risk of Loss:** Store must be set up at a safe place which is free from the risk of loss due to fire, theft, moisture, etc.
6. **Flexibility:** The location of store must be such which provides for its future expansion.

LAYOUT OF STORES

'Layout' of stores refers to the physical arrangement of storage facilities or the internal arrangement or placement of materials inside the stores. Layout of stores aims at effective utilisation of space available for storage of materials, making the receipt and issue of stores convenient, giving better appearance to the store and reducing the chances of damage, wastage, pilferage and accidents. It also aims at reducing the operating cost of storage. The layout of stores should be determined according to the class and quantity of materials to be stored and the general nature of the business. There should be proper and separate arrangement for different items of materials from the view point of economy in space, effective supervision, minimum of wastage and convenience in issue. The materials should be kept in bins, racks, shelves, drawers, drums, packages and containers.

FACTORS TO BE CONSIDERED FOR DETERMINING STORES LAYOUT

1. **Similarity:** Items of similar nature should be stored at one place for the sake of easy identification and convenient issue.
2. **Popularity:** The turnover of each item of stores should be considered so that fast moving items should be stored near the point of issue/usage.
3. **Size of Item:** Items of store which are large or bulky in nature should be stored near the point of use.
4. **Nature of Materials:** Nature of materials to be stored is also important in determining the layout of store. Hazardous, sensitive and perishable goods should be stored separately at safe places.
5. **Physical Movement of Materials:** The principle of 'first-in-first-out' should be strictly adhered to in the matter of physical movement of the materials.
6. **Physical Facilities:** Efficient layout should also consider the various physical facilities such as lighting arrangement, ventilation, wall paints, size of platforms, availability of cranes and handling equipments.

ORGANISATION OF STORES

Stores may be organised as:

(*a*) Centralised Stores,
(*b*) Decentralised Stores, and
(*c*) Centralised Stores with sub-stores.

CENTRALISED STORES

Centralised storing refers to the setting up of a single store-house for the whole organisation. It caters to the needs of all the departments working in the organisation. Such stores are advocated from the point of view of economy and proper control to be exercised over the receipt and issue of materials.

Centralised stores offer the following benefits:

1. Economy in space, storage cost and labour cost can be ensured.
2. Better supervision and effective control over materials and stores can be possible.

3. Capital investment in stock is minimised.
4. Obsolete items in stores are considerably reduced.
5. Appointment of experts can be ensured who can effectively handle intricacies involved in the process of inventory control.
6. Effective forecasting of material requirements can be made.
7. Better layout and effective inventory checks on stores are the other important benefits derived from centralised stores.

However, centralised stores suffer from the following limitations:

1. Increased material handling and transportation costs become unavoidable.
2. Such stores are exposed to greater risk of loss by fire due to concentration of all material items at one central place.
3. Inconvenience and delays are caused in supplying materials to the various departments situated at a distance from the central stores.
4. Accumulation of materials at one place will create problems of storage space and effective control may not be exercised over materials and stores.
5. Break-down in internal transportation system employed for carrying materials from the stores to different departments may cause interruptions in production.

DECENTRALISED STORES

It is the department-wise arrangement of stores whereby store-rooms are located adjacent to the departments they are to serve. The store-keeper of each such department handles the receipt and issue of materials to respective department independently.

Decentralised stores offer the following advantages:

1. Decentralised stores involve lesser internal transportation costs.
2. Undue delays involved in getting the materials issued from centralised stores are avoided.
3. Interruptions in work due to failure of internal transportation system are minimised.

But decentralised stores suffer from the following disadvantages:

1. Lack of specialisation in initiating proper stores control and material handling operations is the most serious drawback of decentralised stores.
2. Setting up of a separate store for each department leads to increased labour cost and occupation of more space for storage purposes.
3. Establishment of decentralised stores usually leads to duplication of clerical work, stores recording and establishment expenses.

CENTRALISED STORES WITH SUB-STORES

In practice a combination of the above two types of store organisation is usually followed which is known as 'Centralised stores with sub-stores'. This system functions on the principle of 'Imprest System'. Under this system, all materials are held in bulk in a centralised store and sub-stores or decentralised stores are set up with each production department. The sub-stores draw their requirements from the centralised or main stores for a specific period (say a month). The sub-store then issues the materials to the department with which it is attached in accordance with the requirements of the department. At the end of the period (say a month), the quantity actually consumed is replenished from the main or centralised stores in order to bring the stock up to the imprest *i.e.*, pre-determined quantity. Thus, the imprest system of stores operates exactly like the imprest system of petty cash.

Centralised stores with sub-stores have the following advantages:

1. They facilitate easy accessibility to the consuming departments or the department for which such stores are established.

2. Interruptions in production are lesser as the items of materials which are immediately required for production are kept in the sub-stores.

3. Specialised control and supervision can be undertaken as limited number of activities are carried out by the store-keeper incharge of the sub-stores.

4. Risks of fire and accidents are diversified.

But these stores suffer from the following disadvantages:

1. Cost of establishment of the centralised store and sub-stores is quite high as there is a need for more storage equipment and additional personnel for controlling such stores.

2. This system lacks uniformity in organising and maintaining the stores.

CLASSIFICATION OF MATERIALS

'Classification' refers to the systematic division, grouping or categorisation of materials or store items with reference to some common characteristic. Classification of materials can be made on different bases namely nature, manufacturing process, value, purpose etc. The important basis of classification of materials may be given as follows:

ON THE BASIS OF NATURE

On the basis of nature, materials may be divided into:

(i) **Direct Materials:** Direct materials are those items of material which can be identified with a product or a group of products in a manufacturing concern and can be easily measured and charged directly to the product. Such materials form the part of the finished product *e.g.*, timber in furniture, cloth in garments, bricks, sand and cement in building, yarn in cloth etc.

(ii) **Indirect Materials:** These are the materials which cannot be traced to a specific product and cannot be charged directly to the various products. These materials do not form part of the product. Examples of indirect materials are—repair and maintenance stores, lubricating oils, cleaning materials, cotton rags etc.

ON THE BASIS OF MANUFACTURING PROCESS

On the basis of the manufacturing process, stores are divided into:

(*i*) **Pre-process Stock:** These are the items of stores which are yet to be taken into the manufacturing process and are obtained prior to the commencement of the manufacturing process or production. These include raw materials, bought-out parts and assemblies, and stock in pipeline of materials in transit.

(*ii*) **Intermediate Stock:** Intermediate stock comprises the parts or assemblies which are manufactured within the factory for use in the final product.

(*iii*) **Finished Goods or Finished Products:** As the name indicates, finished goods are the items which have been duly manufactured in the factory and are ready for shipment or sale to the customers.

ON THE BASIS OF VALUE

On the basis of the value, the stores items may be divided into:

(*i*) **Category 'A':** Category 'A' consists of materials which constitute 5% to 10% of the total items in the stores and represent 70% to 85% of the total stores value.

(*ii*) **Category 'B':** This category consists of materials which constitute 10% to 20% of the total items in the stores and also represent 10% to 20% of the total stores value.

(*iii*) **Category 'C':** This category consists of cheap materials which constitute 70% to 85% of the total items in the stores and represent 5% to 10% of the total stores value.

Category 'A' items constitute costly items calling for greater degree of control for preserving them. A reasonable degree of care may be taken to control category 'B' items while a routine type of care may be applied to control 'C' category or residuary items.

ON THE BASIS OF MOVEMENT OF STORES

On the basis of the movement or rate of consumption, stores items may be divided into:

(*i*) **Fast Moving Stock:** Fast moving stock indicates the items of materials which exhaust at a very fast speed on account of high demand from production departments of a manufacturing concern.

(*ii*) **Slow Moving Stock:** This category indicates the items of stores or materials which are consumed or exhausted at a very slow speed on account of low demand from the production departments of the manufacturing concern.

(iii) **Dormant Stock:** This category covers stores items which do not have any demand at present and may regain demand in future. This category includes seasonal materials which are required during specified seasons.

ADVANTAGES OF CLASSIFICATION

The main advantages of classifying stores items may be given as follows:

1. **Helpful in Grouping of Stores Items:** Classification process helps in the grouping of the different items of materials in the store. Items falling under a particular category can be stored at one place which ensures optimum utilisation of storage space.
2. **Easy Location:** Proper classification of stores items helps in the easy identification of the various items. The store-keeping staff can easily find out the materials whenever these are required in the production departments.
3. **Proper Accounting:** Record-keeping process of properly classified items of stores is simplified. Simplified record-keeping ensures accuracy in posting the receipts and issues in the stores records.
4. **Proper Care:** By classifying the various store items on the basis of value, their relative importance can be ascertained and suitable degree of supervision and control may be exercised over them with reference to such value.
5. **Avoidance of Duplication:** Proper classification of the store items helps in avoiding the possibility of duplication in stocking the same item of material.
6. **Standardisation:** Classification helps in the standardisation of various items in the stores. Standardisation of store items involves the variety reduction through the use of fixed sizes and types. Standardisation aims at having uniform standards for similar items.

CODIFICATION

After having classified or grouped the various items of stores, it is necessary and useful to codify them. Codification is the process of assigning a number or symbol to each store item in addition to its name for making its identification easy and convenient. Codification of store items leads to saving in time and labour on account of substitution of a symbol or number for a longer name. There are different kinds of store codes in use and most of them are specially designed to suit the requirements of a particular organisation. These codes may be based upon the nature of stock items, the purpose for which these items are used or on any other basis which is considered as suitable according to the local circumstances.

METHODS OF CODIFICATION

Some of the common methods of codification of store items may be enumerated as follows:

1. Alphabetical Codification

As the name indicates, this method involves the use of letters of alphabets as codes to facilitate easy and quick identification of the store items. For example:

Symbol	Description
A	Raw Materials
B	Tools and Gauges
C	Spare Parts
D	Capital Stores
E	General Supplies
F	Finished Products

Similarly, alphabets after 'F' *i.e.,* 'G' to 'Z' may be added for the identification of other store items. Alphabetical codification is the most simple method but it lacks flexibility.

2. Mnemonic Codification

It is a modified application of the alphabetical codification and involves the use of the letters of alphabets in such a way as to help memory. This type of codification can be illustrated with the help of the following example:

Code	Item of store
BB	Ball Bearing
CS	Capital Store
SS	Steel Screw
RB	Rubber Belt
SW	Steel Wire
SB	Steel Bolts
WSW	Wind Screen Wiper

Mnemonic method is very simple to operate as it helps in memorising the items of store. But it may create problem if a similar code has been assigned to two different items of store. It also lacks flexibility.

3. Numerical Codification

It is also known as Straight Number Codification. Under this method, numbers are used to represent different items of store. A series of numbers may be allotted to the store items of similar nature. Numerical codification can be illustrated with the help of the following example:

Code No.	Description
0	Raw Materials
1	Bought out items
2	Gauges
3	Tools
4	Scrap
5	Machinery items
6	Finished Product

Series code numbers can be given as follows:

Items of Store	**Code Number**
Steel Screws	1 to 10
Steel Screw $\frac{1}{2}$ cm.	1
Steel Screw $\frac{3}{4}$ cm.	2
Steel Screw 1 cm.	3
Steel Screw $1\frac{1}{4}$ cm.	4
Steel Screw $1\frac{1}{2}$ cm.	5
Steel Nuts	11 to 20
Steel Nuts $\frac{1}{2}$ cm.	11
Steel Nuts $\frac{3}{4}$ cm.	12
Steel Nuts 1 cm.	13
Steel Nuts $1\frac{1}{4}$ cm.	14
Steel Nuts $1\frac{1}{2}$ cm.	15

Numerical codification is simplest and is widely used by manufacturing concerns on account of its flexibility.

4. Decimal Codification

This is also a numerical system with the difference that instead of full numbers, decimals are used under this method. It is generally used in those concerns where mechanised system of accounting is in use. Under this method, whole numbers are used to indicate the main group or the master group and decimals to indicate the sub-groups. For example:

Items	**Code**
Metals	2.00
Aluminium	2.01
Zinc	2.02
Lead	2.03
Nickel	2.04
Copper	2.04
Steel	2.06
Raw Material	3.00
Rubber	3.01
Plastic	3.02
Paints	3.03
Leather	3.04
Paper	3.05

This method has the advantage of flexibility and unlimited expansion. The use of the decimal points make the number easier to read and remember. But the main disadvantage of this method is that it is bit complicated. It also involves the possibility of misplacement or omission of decimals.

5. Alpha-Numeric Codification

It is also known as Alpheno-serial System or Combined Code System. Under this system, the letters of alphabets are used in conjunction with numbers for the purpose of codification of store items. The broader groups of store items are represented by alphabetical symbols while the detailed groups are represented by number. For example:

Description	**Code**
Plywood $\frac{1}{4}$" I Grade	PW 141
Plywood $\frac{1}{4}$" II Grade	PW 142
Plywood $\frac{1}{4}$" III Grade	PW 143
Plywood $\frac{1}{2}$" I Grade	PW 121
Plywood $\frac{1}{2}$" II Grade	PW 122

6. Colour Codification

As the name indicates, under this method, colour markings are used to denote code numbers. This method can be applied for codification of metals, cables, small component parts, drums of oil, and various other items. If the colours are not too complicated, this method affords a ready means of identification on sight. For example – in case of metal, colour code can be used as follows:

Green	for Iron
Blue	for Steel
Red	for Copper
Black	for Aluminium
White	for Zinc

This method is simple but lacks flexibility. With the expansion of store items, it is not possible to expand the number of colours.

PRINCIPLES OF CODIFICATION

The following principles should be kept in mind while assigning code numbers:

1. The code numbers should be easy to understand so that the store-keeping staff may operate them conveniently.

2. There should be no duplication and each code number should relate to only one type of store.
3. The code number should be elastic so that new item of store can be added easily and logically.
4. The code number must identify the material without ambiguity or uncertainty.
5. Code numbers should be brief as large code numbers are subject to errors.
6. Mnemonic codes are both easier to remember and subject to lesser errors.

ADVANTAGES OF CODIFICATION

The main advantages of the process of codification of store items may be given as follows:

1. **Avoidance of Lengthy Description:** Codification helps in avoiding the use of lengthy name and description for store items and thus saves time and energy.
2. **Accurate Identification of Stores:** Codification process assists in the accurate and convenient identification of store items. Easy identification of store items saves time and costs involved in the handling of stores.
3. **Convenience in Issue of Materials:** Codification of store items on scientific lines helps in eliminating the possibility of errors in the issue of materials. It increases the efficiency of the store-keeping staff.
4. **Maintenance of Secrecy:** Every manufacturing concern, necessarily, tries to keep its production activities and processes a secret. Codification of store items helps in maintaining secrecy in production activities.
5. **Simplification of Stores Accounting:** Codification of store items helps in maintaining accurate stores records since scientific codification helps in maintaining stores records mechanically.
6. **Prevention of Duplication:** Codification prevents duplication of items. As all similar items of store are grouped together and when an item is coded once, it is not given an alternative name.
7. **Convenience in Preparation of Material Forms:** Codification of store items makes the preparation of various forms and documents relating to stores easy and convenient *e.g.,* Bill of Material, Purchase Requisition, Material Requisition etc.
8. **Other Advantages:** Codification helps in the standardisation of store items and reduction in their variety. It also helps in reducing storage cost and increasing efficiency.

LOCATION CODE

In case of large manufacturing concerns, use of location code for various items of material in the store is made in order to locate the exact place in the store where a particular item of material is lying. In fact, codification of location is made before codifying the various items of material. The location code may indicate the following details in order to identify the exact location of an item of material:

(*a*) Godown number
(*b*) Column number
(*c*) Rack number
(*d*) Shelf number
(*e*) Bin number.

A location code 1 2 5 9 4 in respect of a particular item of material indicates that it is lying in godown 1, column 2, rack 5, shelf 9 and bin 4.

Thus, location code is helpful in the easy identification of the exact location of the various items of material in the stores.

Determination of Material Levels or Stock Limits:

Proper maintenance of stock items of each type of material is the main function of the stores department. Maintenance of large quantity of stock leads to huge investment in materials, large space coverage, dangers of deterioration in the quality and obsolescence of materials. On the other hand, less stock may result in frequent purchases, higher costs, work stoppages and loss in production etc.

Procurement of proper *quantity* of materials is greatly facilitated by keeping in view certain considerations:

(*a*) Time involved in procurement or placing the order.
(*b*) Availability of floor space.
(*c*) Quantity and type of materials required.
(*d*) Consumption of materials per year in the factory.
(*e*) Price benefit available on account of bulk purchases of material items.
(*f*) Supply of materials, whether it is seasonal or non-seasonal. The fixation of levels of materials will be accordingly affected.
(*g*) The minimum quantity of materials which can be advantageously purchased.

Keeping in view the above mentioned considerations, different types of stock levels are fixed viz., (I) Minimum Level, (II) Re-order Level, (III) Maximum level and (IV) Danger level, which are explained below:

I. Minimum Level

A minimum stock level is that level of an item of material, below which the actual stock should not normally be allowed to fall. In other words, it refers to the minimum quantity of a particular item of material which must be kept in the stores at all times. The fixation of this level acts as a safety measure and hence, it is also known as 'Safety Stock' or 'Buffer Stock'. In case the actual stock falls below this level, there is a danger of stoppage in production and the management has to give top priority to the acquisition of fresh supplies. The main objective of fixing the minimum level of materials is to ensure that the required quantity of each item is available in stores at all times. The main factors which are taken into account in fixing the minimum level are:

(*a*) The average rate of consumption of materials.

(*b*) The time required to obtain fresh supplies under top priority conditions.

(*c*) Re-order level

(*d*) The production requirements as to materials.

(*e*) The minimum quantity of materials which could be procured advantageously.

The minimum stock level can be determined by applying the following formula:

Minimum Stock Level = Re-order Level

– (Normal consumption per day/per week etc. × Normal delivery time).

Following example can be taken to understand the calculation of minimum stock level:

Normal consumption = 300 units per week
Normal delivery time = 7 weeks
Re-order level = 2,400 units.

The minimum stock level will be equal to:

Re-order level – (Normal consumption per day/per week etc. × Normal delivery time).

= 2,400 – (300 × 7) = 2,400 – 2,100 = 300 units

It may be pointed out here that 'Normal delivery time' is taken as the average of maximum and minimum time taken for delivery.

II. Re-order Level or Ordering Level

The re-order or re-ordering level is the stock level fixed between maximum and minimum stock levels, at which an order for the replenishment of stock should be placed. In other words, it is that level of inventory at which purchase order should be placed. The re-order level is generally higher than the minimum level to cover any emergency which may arise as a result of abnormal usage of materials or unexpected delay in obtaining fresh supplies. The factors which are taken into account in fixing the re-order level are:

(*a*) The consumption rate of material.

(*b*) The margin of safety.

(*c*) The time that would elapse between the date of placing the order and the date of the arrival of supplies, or in other words, the normal delivery time or lead time.

(*d*) The minimum level decided to be maintained.

(*e*) Cost of storage and interest on capital employed in materials.

(*f*) Provision for emergencies such as delay in supply and abnormal wastage etc.

The re-ordering stock level is calculated by applying following formula:

Re-order Level = Maximum consumption per day/per week etc.
× Maximum delivery time

Another formula:

Re-order Level = Minimum stock + Average consumption during normal delivery time.

The application of formula depends upon the information supplied in a problem.

The re-order level is revised from time to time by taking into consideration factors which are likely to change supply and demand for goods.

Following example is given to understand the calculation of re-ordering level:

Maximum consumption = 15,000 units per week
Maximum delivery time = 10 weeks
So, Re-order Level = Maximum consumption per day/per week etc. × Maximum delivery time
= 15,000 units × 10 weeks
= 1,50,000 units.

The application of second formula has been illustrated further in solved problem for calculating maximum stock level.

Certain accountants do not make any distinction between 'ordering level' and 'minimum stock level' and regard ordering level as equivalent to minimum stock level, but others make a distinction between the two. The latter is lower, since in its fixation no allowance is made for the margin of safety.

The concepts of 'ordering level and 'minimum stock level' can be illustrated by means of the following diagram:

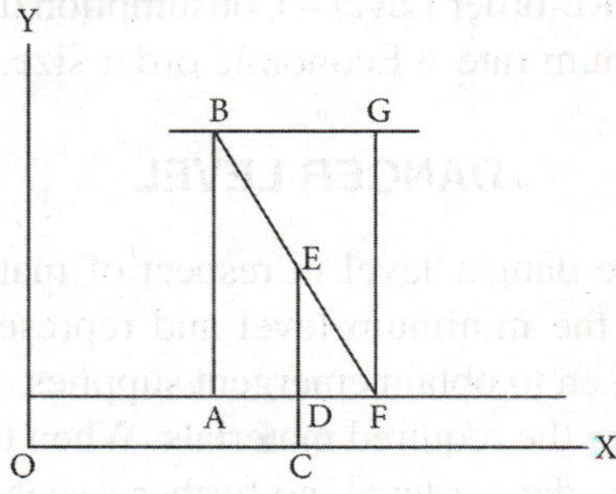

Where:

CD = Minimum Stock or Safety Stock.

E = Re-order Point.

DE = Lead time usage (consumption of materials during the time to obtain fresh supplies).

AB = Economic Order Quantity, which is ordered when stock falls to point E. When stock level falls to point F, next shipment arrives, raising stock to point to G.

III. Maximum Level

Maximum Level is the upper limit of stock above which the stock should not be allowed to exceed under normal circumstances without the prior sanction of the management. The main object for fixing up the maximum stock level is to avoid undue investment of capital leading to loss of interest, obsolescence of materials and additional overheads in the form of higher rents etc. The maximum stock level is determined by taking into account the following factors:

(*a*) Normal consumption rate of material.
(*b*) Time required to obtain new supplies.
(*c*) Amount of working capital available.
(*d*) Availability of storage space.
(*e*) Economic order quantity.
(*f*) Cost of carrying inventory or cost of storage.
(*g*) Risk of deterioration in quality and obsolescence of materials.
(*h*) Seasonal considerations as to price and availability of material.
(*i*) Incidence of insurance costs which may be very important in case of certain types of costly materials.
(*j*) Inherent risks attached with materials and any restrictions imposed by the Government in this regard.

The *maximum stock level* can be determined by applying the following formula:

Maximum Stock level = Re-order Level + Re-order Quantity – (Minimum consumption per day/per week etc. × Minimum time required for delivery.)

It can be represented yet by another formula:

Maximum Level = Re-order Level – Consumption during the time required to get supplies at minimum rate + Economic order size.

DANGER LEVEL

Some firms also use the danger level in respect of materials. Danger level is fixed at a point below the minimum level and represents the limit at which special steps must be taken to obtain emergent supplies of material *i.e.,* sending a man personally to bring the required materials. When the stock of a particular item of materials reaches danger level, no further issues are made by the store-keeper except on the special requisition approved by the works manager. The danger level can be determined by applying the following formula:

Danger Level = Normal Consumption per day/per week/per month etc. × Time required to obtain emergent supplies.

Illustration 1

In a manufacturing concern, material 'X' is used as follows:

Maximum consumption:	9,000 units per week
Minimum consumption:	3,000 units per week
Normal consumption:	6,000 units per week
Re-order quantity:	36,000 units
Time required for delivery: (Lead period)	4 to 6 weeks
Time required for emergent supplies:	1 week

Calculate: (*a*) Re-order level, (*b*) minimum level, (*c*) maximum level, (*d*) danger level and (*e*) average stock level.

Solution:

(*a*) Re-order Level = Maximum consumption per week × Maximum time required to obtain supplies.
= 9,000 units × 6 weeks
= 54,000 units.

(*b*) Minimum Level = Re-order level – (Normal consumption per week × Average time required to obtain supplies).
= 54,000 units – (6,000 units × 5 weeks)
= 24,000 units.

Note: Average time required to obtain supplies has been ascertained as follows:

$$= \frac{\text{Minimum Period} + \text{Maximum Period}}{2}$$

$$= \frac{4 \text{ weeks} + 6 \text{ weeks}}{2}$$

= 5 weeks.

(*c*) Maximum Level = Re-order level + Re-order quantity – (Minimum consumption per week × Minimum time required to obtain supplies.)
= 54,000 units + 36,000 units – (3,000 units × 4 weeks)
= 78,000 units.

(*d*) Danger Level = Normal consumption per week × Time required to obtain emergent supplies.
= 6,000 units × 1 week
= 6,000 units.

(*e*) Average Stock Level = $\frac{1}{2}$ (Minimum Level + Maximum Level)

$= \frac{1}{2}$(24,000 units + 78,000 units)

= 51,000 unit.

Alternatively, it can be calculated as follows:

Average Stock Level = Minimum Stock level + $\frac{1}{2}$(Re-order Quantity)

= 24,000 units + $\frac{1}{2}$(36,000 units)

= 42,000 units

Illustration 2

In a manufacturing concern, two items of materials 'X' and 'Y' are used as follows:

Normal usage:	300 units per week each article.
Minimum usage:	150 units per week each article.
Maximum usage:	450 units per week each article.
Re-order Quantity:	X – 1,800 units
	Y – 2,500 units
Re-order Period:	X – 3 to 5 weeks
	Y – 2 to 4 weeks

Calculate (*a*) Re-order level, (*b*) Maximum level, (*c*) Minimum level, and (*d*) Average level.

Solution

(*a*) Re-order Level:

= Maximum consumption per week × Maximum time required to obtain supplies.

Material 'X'= 450 units × 5 weeks = 2,250 units.

Material 'Y'= 450 units × 4 weeks = 1,800 units.

(*b*) Maximum Level:

= Re-order Level + Re-order Quantity – (Minimum consumption per week × Minimum time required to obtain supplies).

Material 'X'= 2,250 units + 1,800 units – (150 units × 3 weeks)

= 4,050 units – 450 units = 3,600 units.

Material 'Y'= 1,800 units + 2,500 units – (150 units × 2 weeks)

= 4,300 units – 300 units = 4,000 units.

(*c*) Minimum Level:

= Re-order Level – (Normal consumption per week × Average time required to obtain supplies).

Material 'X'= 2,250 units – (300 units × 4 weeks)

= 2,250 units – 1,200 units =1,050 units.

Material 'Y'= 1,800 units – (300 units × 3 weeks)

= 1,800 units – 900 units = 900 units.

(*d*) Average Stock Level:

$$= \frac{1}{2}\text{(Minimum Level + Maximum Level)}$$

$$\text{Material X} = \frac{1}{2}\text{(1,050 units + 3,600 units)}$$

$$= \frac{1}{2}\text{ (4,650 units)}$$

$$= \text{2,325 units.}$$

$$\text{Material Y} = \frac{1}{2}\text{(900 units + 4,000 units)}$$

$$= \frac{1}{2}\text{(4,900 units)}$$

$$= \text{2,450 units.}$$

Illustration 3

ZEE is a product manufactured out of three raw materials 'M', 'N' and 'Q'. Each unit of ZEE requires 10 kgs., 8 kgs., and 6 kgs., of M, N and Q respectively. The re-order levels of 'M' and 'N' are 15,000 kgs. and 10,000 kgs. respectively while the minimum level of 'Q' is 25,000 kgs. The weekly production of ZEE varies from 300 to 500 units, while the weekly average production is 400 units. You are required to compute:

(*i*) The minimum stock level of M.
(*ii*) The maximum stock level of N, and
(*iii*) The re-order level of Q.

The following additional data are given:

	M	N	Q.
Re-order Quantity (in kgs.)	20,000	15,000	20,000
Delivery (in weeks)			
Minimum	2	4	3
Average	3	5	4
Maximum	4	6	5

(*I.C.W.A. Inter 1995*)

Solution

(*i*) Minimum Stock Level of M = Re-order Level – (Normal consumption per week × Average time required to obtain supplies)
= 15,000 kgs. – (400 units × 10 kgs. × 3 weeks)
= 15,000kgs. – 12,000 kgs.
= 3,000 kgs.

(*ii*) Maximum Stock Level of N

= Re-order Level + Re-order Quantity – (Minimum consumption per week × Minimum time required to obtain supplies)

= 10,000 kgs. + 15,000 kgs. – (300 units × 8 kgs. × 4 weeks)

= 25,000 kgs. – 9,600 kgs.

= 15,400 kgs.

(*iii*) Re-order Level of Q:

= Maximum consumption per week × Maximum time required to obtain supplies

= 500 units × 6 kgs. × 5 weeks

= 15,000 kgs.

ECONOMIC ORDER QUANTITY (OR ECONOMIC ORDER SIZE)

This concept relates to the quantity of materials to be purchased by the purchasing department. Economic order quantity is that size of the order which gives maximum economy in purchasing any item of material. In order to determine the economic or optimum order quantity, an analysis of the various costs associated with the ordering quantity is made. These costs may be divided into two parts:

(*a*) Material acquisition costs, and

(*b*) Material carrying costs.

Material acquisition costs arise on account of having to process an order. A part of the wages and operating expenses for departments like production control, purchasing, receiving and stores is incurred for purchasing and possessing the materials. Materials carrying costs include interest charges on investment in materials, insurance costs, storage costs etc. These two types of costs behave quite differently.

The material acquisition costs are related to the number of orders placed during a given period. On the other hand, carrying costs, which are variable or semi-variable in nature, tend to change nearly in direct proportion to the level of stock carried in the manufacturing concern.

Purchasing or buying in large quantities implies low acquisition or purchasing costs (number of purchase orders placed with the suppliers being small) and high carrying costs on account of the amount of stock carried during this period being more. On the other hand, purchasing in small quantities implies high purchasing or acquisition costs and low carrying costs.

The most advantageous or economic quantity will be at a point where the acquisition costs and the costs of carrying stock are equal *i.e.,* where total costs to order and to carry material are minimum.

The other terms used for Economic Order Quantity are 'Economic Lot Quantity' and, 'Economic Buying Quantity.'

Calculation of Economic Order Quantity:

The economic order quantity is ascertained by the following formula:

$$EOQ = \sqrt{\frac{2CO}{I}}$$

Where,

'EOQ' stands for Economic Order Quantity.

'C' stands for annual consumption of material in terms of units.

'O' stands for cost of placing one order including the cost of receiving it.

'I' stands for interest payment per unit per annum (or, carrying cost per unit per annum).

Illustration 4

From the following data calculate economic order quantity:

(*i*) Name of article: A

(*ii*) Rate of material: Rs. 25 per unit.

(*iii*) Consumption of material per annum: 8,000 units

(*iv*) Cost of placing one order: Rs. 100

(*v*) Rate of interest: 10% per annum.

Solution

$$EOQ = \sqrt{\frac{2CO}{I}}$$

$$= \sqrt{\frac{2 \times 8000 \times 100}{25 \times \frac{10}{100}}} = \sqrt{\frac{16,00,000}{2.5}}$$

$$= \sqrt{6,40,000}$$

$$= 800 \text{ units.}$$

Proof:

(*i*) *If the quantity ordered at one point is 800 units:*

Total number of orders to be placed during the year will be $= \frac{8,000}{800} = 10.$

Cost of placing 10 orders (10 × Rs. 100)	= Rs. 1,000
Interest payment for carrying average inventory of 400 units (50% of 800 units) will be (400 units × Rs. 2.50)	= Rs. 1,000
Total Costs	Rs. 2,000

(*ii*) *In case the quantity to be ordered at one point is raised to 1,000 units:*
Total number of orders to be placed during the year will be

$$= \frac{8,000}{1,000} = 8.$$

Cost of placing 8 orders will be (8 × Rs. 100) = Rs. 800
Interest payment for carrying average inventory of 500 units (50% of 1,000 units) will be (500 units × Rs. 2.50) = Rs. 1,250

Total Costs Rs. 2,050

(*iii*) *In case the quantity to be ordered at one point is reduced to 500 units.*

Total number of orders to be placed will be $= \frac{8,000}{500} = 16.$

Cost of placing 16 orders will be (16 × Rs. 100) = Rs. 1,600
Interest payment for carrying average inventory of 250 units (50% of 500 units) will be = Rs. 625
(250 units × Rs. 2.50)

Total Costs Rs. 2,225

The total cost of placing orders and carrying average inventory (50% of the ordering quantity) is the minimum when quantity ordered is 800 units. Hence, 800 units is the economic or optimum order quantity.

Note: It is assumed that the average stock carried in the store is 50% of the order size.

Economic order quantity may also be ascertained by tabular method in the following manner:

TABLE SHOWING THE CALCULATION OF ECONOMIC ORDER QUANTITY

(*a*) Number of orders	(*b*) Quantity per order (units)	(*c*) Average Stock held (units) [(*b*) ÷ 2]	(*d*) Cost of carrying average stock [(*c*) × Rs. 2.50]	(*e*) Ordering Cost [(*a*) × Rs. 100]	(*f*) Total Cost [(*d*) + (*e*)]
			Rs.	Rs.	Rs.
2	4,000	2,000	5,000	200	5,200
5	1,600	800	2,000	500	2,500
8	1,000	500	1,250	800	2,050
10	800	400	1,000	1,000	2,000
16	500	250	625	1,600	2,225
20	400	200	500	2,000	2,500
25	320	160	400	2,500	2,900

The total cost of placing orders and carrying average inventory is the minimum when quantity ordered is 800 units. Hence, 800 units is the economic order quantity.

Illustration 5

Following information relating to a particular type of raw material is available:

Annual demand	2,400 units
Unit price	Rs. 2.40
Ordering cost per order	Rs. 4
Storage cost	2% p.a.
Interest rate	10% p.a.
Lead time	Half month

Calculate Economic Order Quantity and total annual inventory cost in respect of the particular raw material.

(I.C.W.A. Inter 1988)

Solution

$$\text{Economic Order Quantity} = \sqrt{\frac{2CO}{1}}$$

$$= \sqrt{\frac{2 \times 2,400 \times 4}{0.288}}$$

$$= 258 \text{ units (app.)}$$

Calculation of Total Inventory Cost per annum:

Total cost of placing 10 orders p.a.

$$\left(\frac{2,400}{258} = 9.3 \text{ or } 10 \text{ orders}\right)$$

Ordering Cost (10 × Rs. 4)	= 40.00
Cost of Carrying Average Inventory (258 × .288) ÷ 2	= 37.15
Purchase Cost (2,400 units × Rs. 2.40)	= 5,760.00
Total Cost of Inventory	5,837.15

Illustration 6

On inviting tenders, two quotations are received as follows:

(*a*) Rs. 3.60 per unit

(*b*) Rs. 3.30 per unit plus Rs. 9,000 fixed charges to be added irrespective of units ordered. Advise with your arguments with whom orders should be placed and what quantity is to be ordered. The following additional data may be relevant:

	Units
Present stock	1,05,000
Average monthly requirement	30,000
Maximum level	2,40,000
Minimum level	90,000

Sales tax problem may be ignored.

(*C.A. Inter*)

Solution

From the given information it can be found that tender (*a*) is more economical for smaller quantity of purchase. Tender (*b*) becomes economical only when sufficient quantity is ordered to justify the fixed charges of Rs. 9,000.

Price per unit of tender (*a*)	Rs. 3.60
Price per unit of tender (*b*)	Rs. 3.30
Tender (*b*) is cheaper by (per unit)	Rs. 0.30

To justify the fixed charges of Rs. 9,000 the minimum size of the order should be:

$$\frac{\text{Rs.}9{,}000}{\text{Rs.}0.30} = 30{,}000 \text{ units}$$

Therefore, an ordered quantity above 30,000 units becomes economical in case of tender (*b*).

Calculation of Economic Order Size may be given as follows:

Economic Order Size = (Maximum Level – Ordering Level) + Minimum rate of consumption during the time to get fresh supplies.

Present stock	1,05,000 units
Minimum stock level	90,000 units
Excess	15,000 units

This excess quantity of 15,000 units will be consumed within 1/2 month or 15 days since the average monthly consumption is 30,000 units. As such, 15 days should be considered as the time required to obtain fresh supplies.

Ordering Level = Minimum stock + Average rate of consumption × Time required to obtain fresh supplies.

$$= 90{,}000 + \frac{30{,}000}{30} \times 15\text{days}$$

$$= 1{,}05{,}000 \text{ units.}$$

If the rate of consumption of material is considered to be uniform, the minimum rate of consumption shall be the same as the average rate of consumption. Thus, the minimum rate of consumption during the time to get supplies is 15,000 units.

Now applying the formula:

Economic Order Size = (2,40,000 units – 1,05,000) + 15,000
= 1,35,000 + 15,000
= 1,50,000 units

Quantity to be ordered = 1,50,000 units

Thus, tender (*b*) will be more economical since the quantity to be ordered is more than 90,000 units.

ISSUING OF MATERIALS

Whenever certain materials are required in a production department, it has to prepare a Materials Requisition. Materials Requisition or 'Requisition Slip' or 'Materials Requisition Note' can be defined as "*a document which authorises and records the issue of material for use*". In other words, Materials Requisition is a document which is used for drawing materials from the stores and signifies the quantity and quality of materials required and the job No. or work order for which it is required. Materials Requisition is to be signed by the foreman of the department or the works manager to accord it proper authenticity with regard to requirement of materials for a particular job or work order. In other words, it is an authorisation to the store-keeper to issue the quantity and quality of materials specified in the Materials Requisition or Requisition Slip.

After receiving the Materials Requisition, the store-keeper issues the materials to the job and enters the same in the appropriate Bin Card. The signature of the person receiving the materials against the Materials Requisition from the stores must also be obtained by the store-keeper on it.

A specimen of the Materials Requisition is given below:

Materials Requisition
A.B. Co. Ltd.

Department...................... Serial No. ....
Job No. .... Date.......................................

Qty.	Description	Code No.	Bin Card No.	Stores Ledger Folio	Rate	Amount

Authorised by................................. Received by.................................
Store-keeper's Signature.................. Checked by.................................
Materials Abstract prepared by.................................

The rate and amount of the materials are entered in the Materials Requisition by the Costing Office. The Materials Requisition is prepared in duplicate. One copy is sent to the store-keeper and another is retained by the department which initiates it, for future reference.

GATE PASS

Gate pass is a document issued in the name of authority receiving materials from the stores department. It is prepared by the store-keeper. The gate pass issued by the store-keeper authorises the security officer of the stores department to allow the specified person to carry the specified materials out of the store. The specimen of a gate pass is given below:

Gate Pass
A.B. Co. Ltd.

The Security Officer,   Serial No. ....
.... Store,   Date ....
Time..........................

Please allow Shri .... of .... department to carry with him the materials specified below:

S. No.	Description	Quantity	Stock Ledger Folio	Remarks

Signature....................
Designation ....

RETURN AND TRANSFER OF MATERIALS

Return of Materials to Stores. Usually materials obtained for a particular job are not consumed fully or are drawn in excess of requirements. The excess quantity is returned to the stores together with a Material Returned Note. The returned materials should kept by the store-keeper in appropriate Bin and entered in the 'In' or 'Received' column of the Bin Card.

Material Returned Note
A.B. Co. Ltd.

Department......................   Serial No. ....
Job No. ....   Date..........................

Qty.	Code No.	Description	Rate	Amount

Signature of Store-keeper....................   Signature of Foremen....................

The 'Material Returned Note' is prepared in duplicate. One copy is retained by job returning the materials and other is kept by the store-keeper who gets it alongwith materials returned.

It may be pointed out here that there is a considerable similarity between 'Material Returned Note' and 'Material Requisition'. In order to avoid the confusion 'Material Returned Note' may be issued in red ink or printed on paper of different colour.

The Material Returned Note is forwarded to the costing office where the rate and amount are entered and necessary credit for value of materials returned is given to the particular job.

Transfer of Materials

Direct transfer of surplus materials from one job or work-order to another is, as a rule, undesirable and should be discouraged as far as possible. It is, however, justified when an urgent job has to be completed and it is necessary to appropriate the surplus materials in order to avoid the delay which may be caused if the normal routine of returning the materials to stores and, then getting them re-issued is followed. But all such transfers of materials must be accompanied by a Material Transfer Note which is signed by the foremen of the sending and receiving departments and forwarded to the costing office where the necessary adjustments shall be made in the respective job accounts. The specimen of a Material Transfer Note is given below:

Material Transfer Note
A.B. Co. Ltd.

Serial No. .... Date.................

From: To:

Department.............................. Department.............................

Job No. .... Date.......................................

Qty.	Code No.	Description	Rate	Amount

Issued by……………….. Approved by……………….. Received by………………..

MATERIALS ABSTRACT

In order to ascertain the cost of materials used on a particular work-order or job, an analysis of Material Requisitions, Material Returned Notes and Material Transfer Notes is made on sheets specially meant for this purpose which are known as Materials Abstract or Materials Issue Analysis sheet.

Materials Abstract A.B. Co. Ltd. Week ending						
Materials Requisition No.		**Job No.**				
	Amount	**15**	**15**	**17**	**18**	**19**
	Rs. P.	Rs. P.	Rs. P.	Rs. P.	Rs. P.	Rs. P.
Total						

The Materials Abstract is prepared periodically, say, weekly, fortnightly or monthly.

The important benefits of Materials Abstract are:

(*a*) Transactions can be passed in the stores ledger directly from Materials Abstract.

(*b*) Materials cost of each job is calculated without any difficulty.

MAINTENANCE OF INVENTORY RECORDS

Inventory records are maintained to record the quantity, types and values of various items of materials received, issued and held in stock. The inventory records may be of the following types:

(*i*) Bin Card (maintained by the stores department)

(*ii*) Stores Ledger (maintained by the costing office)

(*iii*) Stock Register or Material Control Register.

1. Bin Card (maintained by the Stores Department)

A 'Bin' refers to a rack, container, drawer, shelf or space where materials are kept. The bins are serially arranged in the stores where materials are stored and then issued to different jobs on receiving the material requisitions. Separate Bin Cards are maintained by the store-keeper for each item of material in the store and attached to the respective bin, rack, container, drawer or shelf in which material has been kept. The bin cards show the details of receipts and issues of materials and the balance in hand at any time. Thus, *Bin Card is a document containing a continuous record of receipts, issues and balance of materials*. A bin card has three columns: 'Receipts', 'Issues' and 'Balance'. An entry is made on the Bin Card at the time of each receipt or issue of material and the new balance of stock in hand is calculated. It also depicts maximum, minimum, and ordering levels, ordering quantity, Code No., and Stores Ledger Folio of the respective item of material.

Location code may also be inserted in the Bin Card which is greatly helpful in identifying the placement of material items in the store. The specimen of a Bin Card is given below:

Bin Card
A.B. Co. Ltd.

Description................................	Maximum Level ....
Code No.	Minimum Level ....
Location Code..............................	Ordering Level ....
Stores Ledger Folio......................	Ordering Quantity ....
Unit..	
Bin No.	

Receipts			**Issues**			**Balance**	
Date	**G.R.N. No.**	**Qty.**	**Date**	**Req. No.**	**Qty.**	**Qty.**	**Remarks**

It is notable that a bin card is a quantitative record of receipts, issues and balances of material items in store and does not contain information about the prices of materials.

Illustration 7

The following information regarding receipts and issues of pigments has been obtained from the stores record of a paint manufacturing factory:

April, 2005

1.	Opening Stock of pigments	25,000 kg.
2.	Issued on Requisition No. 1	13,000 kg.
3.	Issued on requisition No. 2	2,000 kg.
4.	Received from a supplier vide Goods Received Note No. 15 of 3-4-05 as per stipulated date of delivery	30,000 kg.
5.	Issued on Requisition No. 3	10,000 kg.
6.	Issued on Requisition No. 4	5,000 kg
7.	Received from a supplier vide Goods Received Note No. 52	10,000 kg.
8.	Issued on Requisition No. 5	4,500 kg.

Examination by stock verifier on the 8th morning revealed a shortage of 500 kg.

Maximum Level was	50,000 kg.
Minimum Level was	8,000 kg.
Ordering Level was	25,000 kg.

You are requested to prepare Bin Card No. 86 for the item 'pigment' for which symbol alloted is x – 40.

Solution

Bin Card
A.B. Co. Ltd.

S. No. : 128 Description: Pigment Material Code No. : x – 40. Location Code : R - 1943 Unit: Kg Bin No. 16	Maximum Level: 50,000 kg. Minimum Level: 8,000 Ordering Level: 25,000 kg. Ordering Quantity: 15,000 kg.

Receipts			Issues			Balance	
Date	**G.R.N. No.**	**Qty.**	**Date**	**Req. No.**	**Qtv.**	**Qty.**	**Remarks**
2005			2005				
April 1						25,000	
			April 2	1	13,000	12,000	
			April 3	2	2,000	10,000	
April 4	15	30,000				40,000	
			April 5	3	10,000	30,000	
			April 6	4	5,000	25,000	
April 7	52	10,000				35,000	
			April 8	Shortage	500	34,500	
			April 8	5	4,500	30,000	

2. Stores Ledger

Stores Ledger is maintained by the costing office. Stores Ledger records the quantity, price and total value of materials received and issued in respective of each item of materials in the store. A balance is recorded after each receipt and issue. The entries in the Stores ledger are parallel to those on the bin cards except that values are shown in the Stores ledger. Stores ledger is generally maintained in the form of loose cards because these can be removed and inserted at convenience.

A specimen of Stores Ledger is being given below.

Stores Ledger Account

Description ....   Folio ....

Code No. ....   Maximum Quantity.........................

Location..............................   Minimum Quantity.........................

Re-order Level..............................

Ordered			Reserved			Receipts					Issues					Balance			
Date	Ref.	Qty.	Date	Ref.	Qty.	Date	G.R.N. No.	Qty.	Rate	Amount	Date	Req. No.	Qty.	Rate	Amount	Qty.	Rate	Amount	Remarks

DIFFERENCE BETWEEN BIN CARD AND STORES LEDGER

The main points of difference between Bin Card and Stores Ledger may be given as follows:

(*i*) Bin card is attached to the 'bin' or 'rack' and is kept in the stores department. Stores Ledger is kept in the costing office.

(*ii*) Bin Card deals with the quantities of materials received, issued and balance in hand. Stores Ledger deals with the quantities and values of materials received, issued and balance in hand.

(*iii*) In Bin Card, receipts and issues of materials are entered on regular basis but these may be entered in Stores Ledger periodically.

(*iv*) Bin Card does not show the inter-departmental transfers of material. But these are recorded in Stores Ledger for cost purposes.

(*v*) Recording of transactions involving receipt and issue of materials is made in Bin Card on the basis of actual quantity of materials received and issued. But in Stores Ledger, the recording of transactions is made with the help of 'Goods Received Note' and 'Material Requisition' etc.

3. Stock Register or Material Control Register

Stock Register contains loose leaves pertaining to each stock item. It is prepared on the same lines as Bin Card. The register is maintained by the store-keeper and gives information regarding stock items lying in the store. It is immensely helpful to the store-keeper in knowing the position of stock items at a glance. It further provides an opportunity of cross checking of material items with the bin cards. The stock register gives information in units (as to quantity of material items).

Inventory Control: In order to exercise effective control over materials, the following systems can be followed:

PERPETUAL INVENTORY SYSTEM

The Institute of Cost and Management Accountants, U.K., has defined the perpetual inventory system as "a system of records maintained by the controlling department, which reflects the physical movement of stocks and their current balance." Perpetual inventory system refers to a system of maintaining such records as will reflect the receipts, issues and balance of all items of materials in the store at all times. The records maintained in a manufacturing concern for material accounting are divided into two parts:

(*a*) Bin Card, and

(*b*) Stores Ledger.

Bin Card is maintained in the Stores Department and shows the quantities of materials received, issued and balance in hand after each receipt and issue. Stores Ledger is maintained by Costing Office and deals with quantities and values of materials received, issued and balance in hand.

In the normal course, the balances of materials in hand as shown by these two records should agree. The difference, if any, between the two may arise due to wrong posting or clerical errors. In case of difference, the balances of these two records should be reconciled and correct balances drawn.

PHYSICAL STOCK VERIFICATION: Having reconciled the balance of Bin Cards and Stores Ledger Accounts, it is necessary to ensure that these book balances agree with the physical balances actually present in the bins or containers in stores. For this purpose, physical stock verification of the various items of materials is necessary. The physical stock verification can be carried on in two ways:

(*i*) Periodic Stock Verification.
(*ii*) Continuous Stock Verification.

Periodic Stock Verification: Under this system, all the items of materials are subject to verification at periodic intervals, generally once a year, at the end of the accounting period. It is done with a view to find out the value of closing stocks for the preparation of final accounts and the Balance Sheet. Sometimes, the physical verification of the stock may be carried on at two or more periodic intervals. For the purpose of periodic verification, the factory work is stopped for the required number of days. On the date fixed for stock verification, the stock verification staff will verify the stock of each item and prepare the relevant stock verification sheets. The stock verification sheets as and when completed, are forwarded to the stores accounting section for carrying out the necessary adjustments in the Stores Ledger. The periodic stock verification system helps the manufacturing concern:

(*a*) in checking automatically the irregularities in store-keeping;
(*b*) in checking the placing of materials in wrong bins; and
(*c*) in checking the correctness of their description in the Bin Card.

But the closing down of the factory for the purpose of carrying out physical stock verification is against its interest and as such this system is not favoured by large manufacturing concerns. Further, the risk of pilferage, loss or theft of materials cannot be minimised due to long interval between two checking periods.

Continuous Stock Verification (or Continuous Stock-taking): Under this system, the stocks are verified throughout the year in a systematic manner. The verification of the stock is carried on by a permanent verification team. The team is entrusted with the work of counting, weighing and listing the actual stock in the store. The team daily verifies the physical stock of different items selected at random. The manufacturing operations go on normally during the checking period. As the verification work is a continuous process, the bulky items of minor value are checked once in a year or two, while items of importance carrying considerable value are verified even twice or thrice a year. The discrepancies, if any, revealed by the physical verification, are thoroughly investigated and corrective entries are made to remove their causes.

Advantages of Perpetual Inventory System:

The main advantages of perpetual inventory system may be given as follows:

(*i*) This system ensures a detailed and reliable checking of the store items in a methodical manner without interfering in any way with the routine work of the factory.

(*ii*) It obviates the necessity of physical stock-taking at the end of the financial year.

(*iii*) It assists in the detection and immediate rectification of clerical errors in the store records.

(*iv*) In case of serious discrepancies, it gives rise to thorough investigation into their causes and prevents the recurrence of similar irregularities.

(*v*) It serves as a moral check upon those who are responsible for the handling of materials.

(*vi*) Any divergence from the pre-determined maximum and minimum stock levels is immediately brought to light.

(*vii*) It ensures more reliability and accuracy in the process of stock verification as it is carried out by expert personnel.

But this system is costly and can be followed only by large manufacturing concerns.

A.B.C. Analysis of Material Control (or Proportional Parts Value Analysis): A.B.C. Analysis is a technique followed for the purpose of exercising control over materials according to their importance or value. Under this system, all the items of material are classified into three categories A, B and C according to their value.

Category 'A' consist of materials which constitute 5% to 10% of the total items in the store and represent 70% to 85% of the total store value ; Category 'B', the items constituting 10% to 20% of the total items in the store and 10% to 20% of the store value and category 'C', the items constituting 70% to 85% of the total items and representing 5% to 10% of the store value. Thus, category 'A' represents items with small quantity but high value, category 'B' represents items with medium quantity and value while category 'C' represents items with high quantity but small value.

The percentages given above are by way of guidelines only and are not fixed. These can be modified as per the choice and requirements of the management.

Under A.B.C. Analysis of materials, items of material falling under category 'A' must be closely controlled at all stages of handling viz., purchasing, receiving, inspecting, storing and issuing. In respect of items falling under category 'C', elaborate control procedures are not necessary. The routine of indenting, purchasing, storing and issuing materials can be simplified for these items. The items under category 'B' receive as much attention as items under category 'A' but the frequency of purchases and issues are so planned as to keep them at the minimum.

A.B.C. Analysis of Materials is also known as 'Always Better Control Method' since it aims at obtaining maximum control over materials and minimum cost of control through equitable distribution of time, attention and cost involved in material control with reference to value.

Advantages of A.B.C. Analysis: The main advantages of A.B.C. Analysis of materials can be given as follows:

(*i*) It ensures closer control over costly items of material in which considerable amount of capital is locked.

(*ii*) It leads to reduction in carrying costs.

(*iii*) It enables to keep enough safety stock for items falling under category 'C'.

(*iv*) It enables to maintain high stock turnover rate.

V.E.D. Analysis: This concept of V.E.D. Analysis is used in connection with the control of spare parts in a manufacturing concern. Under V.E.D. Analysis:

'V' stands for 'Vital',

'E' stands for 'Essential', and

'D' stands for 'Desirable'.

Under this system, spare parts required and used in a manufacturing concern, with reference to their importance, are divided into three categories:

(*i*) Vital Spare Parts *i.e.,* the spares, the stock-out of which even for a very short time will interrupt production for quite some time.

(*ii*) Essential Spare Parts *i.e.,* the spares the absence of which cannot be tolerated for more than a few hours or a day. These spare parts are essential for production otherwise the cost of the production lost is high.

(*iii*) Desirable Spare Parts *i.e.,* the spares which are needed but their non-availability for even a week or so will not lead to interruption in production.

Some spare parts, though carrying very small monetary value, may be vital for ensuring un-interrupted production and require constant attention. Such spare parts may not be given proper attention under A.B.C. Analysis since their value is very small. In such cases, V.E.D. Analysis should be made to ensure the availability of the various types of spare parts at the proper time.

TURNOVER OF MATERIALS

Turnover of materials refers to movement of material into and out of an organisation. It is in the best interest of the organisation to compare the turnover of different types and grades of material as a measure of detecting stock which does not move regularly thereby minimising capital investment in undesirable stock.

Material turnover can be easily calculated by comparing balance of stores with the total issues or withdrawals during a particular period of time. Material turnover ratio can be calculated in this regard as follows:

$$\text{Material Turnover Ratio} = \frac{\text{Value of materials consumed during the period}}{\text{Value of average stock (or, inventory held during the period)}}$$

Average stock can be calculated by adding opening and closing stocks and then dividing by two or it may be put like this:

$$\text{Average stock} = \frac{\text{Opening stock} + \text{Closing stock}}{2}$$

A high material turnover ratio indicates that the material item is fast moving and exhausts easily and investment in that item can be kept minimum. On the other hand, low material turnover ratio in relation to a particular item indicates its slow movement and alarms the organisation to avoid over-stocking of that item in the stores and immediate disposal of such item is in the best interests of the concern.

Materials turnover indicating slow moving items have been classified in the following three categories:

(*a*) *Slow moving materials.* These indicate the items which exhaust at a very slow speed. An attempt should be made to minimise the stock of such items in the store.

(*b*) *Dormant items.* Such material items do not have any demand in present and represent zero turnover ratio. Such stock may regain its demand in future. Store-keeper and other officials of the concern should sit together and decide whether to retain or to dispose of such items in order to save further storing or handling cost.

(*c*) *Obsolete items.* Such material items are no longer in demand and represent zero turnover ratio. Obsolete items should be immediately scrapped or discarded and profit or loss should be transferred to Costing Profit and Loss Account.

Illustration 8

The following figures are taken from the books of M/s Ahuja and Co., Ludhiana for the year ending 31st March, 2008. The valuation of inventory is Re. 1 per kg. or Litre.

Items	Opening stock	Purchases	Closing stock
Material X	700 kg.	11,500 kg.	200 kg.
Material Y	200 Litres	11,000 Litres	1,200 Litres
Material Z	1,000 kg.	1,800 kg.	1,200 kg.

Calculate the material turnover ratio of the above material items and express in number of days the average inventory is held.

Solution

First of all cost of materials consumed pertaining to each item is to be calculated:

Material consumed = Opening stock + Purchases – Closing stock.

Consumption of X material.

= 700 + 11,500 – 200= 12,000 kg.

Consumption of Y material. = 200 + 11,000 – 1200 = 10,000 Litres

Consumption of Z material. = 1,000 + 1,800 – 1,200 = 1,600 kg.

Let us now ascertain the Average Inventory of each material item.

$$\text{Average Inventory} = \frac{\text{Opening stock + Closing stock}}{2}$$

$$\text{Average Inventory of X} = \frac{700 + 200}{2} = 450 \text{ kg.}$$

$$\text{Average Inventory of Y} = \frac{200 + 1200}{2} = 700 \text{ Litres}$$

$$\text{Average Inventory of Z} = \frac{1{,}000 + 1{,}200}{2} = 1{,}100 \text{ kg.}$$

Inventory Turnover Ratio =

$$\frac{\text{Value of Materials consumed during the period}}{\text{Value of Average Inventory held during the period}}$$

Inventory Turnover of:

$$\text{Material X} = \frac{12{,}000}{450} = 26.67 \text{ Times}$$

$$\text{Material Y} = \frac{10{,}000}{700} = 14.29 \text{ times}$$

$$\text{Material Z} = \frac{1{,}600}{1{,}100} = 1.45 \text{ times}$$

The Inventory Turnover as expressed in days can be calculated by applying the following formula:

$$\frac{\text{Value of average inventory} \times \text{Total No. of days during the period}}{\text{Material consumed}}$$

or

$$\frac{\text{Total No. of days during the period}}{\text{Inventory Turnover}}$$

$$\text{Material X} = \frac{450 \times 365}{12{,}000} = \frac{365}{26.67} = 14 \text{ days (approx.)}$$

Material Y $= \dfrac{700 \times 365}{10,000} = \dfrac{365}{14.29} = 26$ days (approx.)

Material Z $= \dfrac{1,100 \times 365}{1,600} = \dfrac{365}{1.46} = 250$ days.

In the above problem inventory turnover ratio is highest is case of material X and lowest in case of material Z. Similarly consumption rate in case of material X is more as compared to Z which is the lowest as indicated by the No. of days calculated. It is suggested that purchase of Z material should be made in limited quantity as and when the need arises, whereas frequent purchases are suggested in case of Material X and moderate purchases in case of Material Y.

MATERIAL LOSSES AND WASTAGES

Material losses take place in one way or the other in the process of material handling, storage and issue to respective departments or jobs. The losses are broadly classified into four categories viz., (*i*) Wastage, (*ii*) Spoilage, (*iii*) Scrap, and (*iv*) Defectives.

These are discussed as follows:

(*i*) **Wastage.** Wastage of materials can be either normal or abnormal. *Normal wastage* is inevitable which occurs due to some of the following reasons:

- (*a*) Evaporation of oil, chemicals and paints etc.
- (*b*) Leakage of certain liquid materials.
- (*c*) Natural decay or deterioration of materials *e.g.,* rusting etc.
- (*d*) Breakage in case of delicate material items.

Normal wastages are not separately recorded in costing books but are covered by *enhancing the production cost by increasing the unit price of materials issued* for recovering the total cost out of a quantity which is actually used.

Abnormal wastages occur when normal limits of wastage are crossed. It is transferred to Costing Profit and Loss account so as to avoid fluctuations in production costs. Following reasons are responsible for such losses, viz.,

- (*a*) Accidents, fire and earth-quake etc.
- (*b*) Defective and careless storage and handling of materials.
- (*c*) Pilferage.
- (*d*) Mischief on account of delibrate destruction and spoilage of materials.
- (*e*) Obsolescence of materials due to improper and irregular issue of materials *i.e.,* issuing fresh supplies earlier than old ones.

With certain care and caution, abnormal wastages can be minimised by controlling certain controllable causes viz., pilferage, defective and careless handling and resorting to proper method of material issues to different jobs or departments etc.

For apprising the authorities with regard to occurrence of wastage and suggesting proper ways and means to control the same, a *Waste Report* is prepared by the foreman or inspector concerned with the inspection of the job. A specimen of *Waste Report* is given as under:

Waste Report
A.B. Co. Ltd.

Department...................... Report No. ....
Cost centre........................ Date..........................

Process or Job No.	Actual Wastage Qty.	Actual Wastage %	Normal Wastage		Abnormal Wastage		Suggested Action	Remarks
			Qty.	%	Qty.	Value Rs.		

Action taken by .... Signature
Report entered by .... of Foreman or Inspector

(*ii*) **Spoilage.** Spoilage refers to the deterioration of goods beyond rectification and are sold out without any further processing. Spoilage is of two types. The first is *normal spoilage* which occurs due to inherent nature of the manufacturing operations. Such a spoilage is uncontrollable. Like normal wastage it is not recorded in the books of cost accounts but its cost is spread over the remaining units.

The second type is *Abnormal spoilage* which takes place due to certain avoidable causes as explained while discussing abnormal wastage. It is debited to Costing Profit and Loss Account.

A specimen of spoilage report is given below:

Spoilage Report
A.B. Co. Ltd

Department...................... Report No. ....
Cost centre........................ Date..........................

Job or Process No.	Actual Spoilage		Standard Spoilage		Cost of spoilage less salvage value Rs.	Cost of Abnormal spoilage Rs.	Reasons and Actions suggested
	Qty.	% age to good units	Qty.	% age to good units			
Total							

Action taken by .... Signature
Report entered by .... Inspector

(*iii*) **Scrap.** Scrap may be defined as "the incidental residue from certain types of manufacture usually of small amount and low value, recoverable without further processing." For example, outlined metal from turnings, borings, saw dust, short lengths from wood work operations and iron dust from machines and foundry works etc.

The difference between scrap and waste is that the former is always available after the completion of a particular production operation while the latter may or not be available in the residue form.

For controlling or minimising scrap, proper standards for scrap should be fixed in advance of actual operations and records in the form of *Scrap Reports* should be prepared and preserved for future references.

A specimen of Scrap Report is given below:

Scrap Report
A.B. Co. Ltd

Department........................ Report No. ....
Cost centre........................ Date........................

Job or Process No.	Scrap Tag No.	Actual Scrap (Qty.)	Actual Scrap% age	Normal Scrap (Qty.)	Normal Scrap % age	Abnormal Scrap		Action Suggested
						Qty.	Amount Rs.	

Action taken by .... Signature
Report entered by .... Inspector

Scrap can be of three types viz.,

(*a*) *Pre-determined* or *Anticipated Scrap* is fixed in advance at the time of anticipation of costs.

(*b*) *Administrative Scrap* occurs due to obsolete design of a product.

(*c*) *Defective Scrap* takes place due to basic defects in raw materials, production processes and other discrepancies leading to unsaleable products.

Accounting Treatment of Scrap. Under the first method, the realisable value of scrap is credited to Costing Profit and Loss Account and termed as abnormal gain. The unit cost of the product includes the value of scrap. This method of recording scrap value is quite simple and can be employed very successfully where the quantum of scrap is negligible. Effective control over scrap lacks under this method as detailed records of scrap values are not prepared and are not identified with different jobs and processes.

Under the second method, the net sale proceeds of scrap (obtained after deducting selling and distribution costs) is deducted from material cost or factory overheads, thereby reducing the overall cost of materials and overheads. This method is most suitable where several production orders are undertaken simultaneously and scrap values are not worked out for each order. Again this method is very suitable in exercising control over scrap arising in different processes and jobs.

Under the third method, which is an improvement over the first two methods, the scrap values realised are credited to each job, process or operation. This is a detailed method and is immensely helpful in identifying scrap values in case of every job, process or operation.

(*iv*) **Defectives.** 'Defectives' signify units or portion of production which can be rectified and turned out as good units by the application of additional materials, labour or other services. Defectives arise due to sub-standard materials, inadequate equipment, inefficient supervision, defective planning, and poor workmanship etc. Usually, it is possible to avoid defects in the units produced but to some extent defectives may be unavoidable. The basic difference between 'defectives' and 'spoilages' is that the former can be sold after rectifying them whereas the latter has got to be rejected or sold as sub-standard or rejected articles.

A "Defective Work Report" is prepared by the inspector specifying information pertaining to defective units, normal defectives, abnormal defectives, cost of rectification, disposal value of defectives and reasons and actions suggested. Following is the specimen of defective work report.

Defective Work Report
A.B. Co. Ltd.

Department........................ Report No. ....
Cost centre........................ Date.......................

Job or Process No.	Defective units	Normal Defectives	Abnormal Defectives	Cost of Rectification	Disposal value of Defectives	Reasons for Defectives and Action Suggested

Action taken by ....
Entered by .... Signature of the Inspector ....

The normal defectives are unavoidable and can be identified with specific jobs and their cost of rectification can be attributed to the job. But if the defective production can not be identified with the specific jobs, the cost of defectives should be added to the factory overheads. In case of defectives arising due to abnormal circumstances, the cost of rectification is treated as an abnormal loss and charged to the Costing Profit and Loss Account.

MISCELLANEOUS ILLUSTRATIONS (SOLVED)

Illustration 9

A factory uses a particular raw material. There are three processes I, II and III. The data relating to inputs, outputs and rejections during the month of April are given below:

	Inputs (in pieces) (Including opening W.I.P)	Rejections (in pieces)	Output (in pieces)
I	18,000	6,000	12,000
II	19,800	1,800	18,000
III	20,400	3,400	17,000

Determine what should be inputs in Process I when the final product transferred from process III is 1,000 pieces.

Calculate the cost of raw materials to produce one piece of the finished product when *(a)* the weight of the finished product is 10 gms. and *(b)* the price of the raw material is Re. 1 per kg.

(*I.C.W.A. Inter 1993*)

Solution

(a)

Process No.	No. of Pcs.		Rejected Pcs.	
	Input	Output	No.	% of output
I	18,000	12,000	6,000	50%
II	19,800	18,000	1,800	10%
III	20,400	17,000	3,400	20%

If 1,000 good pcs. should be the output of Process III, the input should be 1,000 plus 20%, *i.e.,* 1,200 pcs. This input of 1,200 units of Process III should be the output of Process II. The percentage of rejections being 10% in Process II, the input in Process II should be 1,200 plus 10%, i.e., 1,320 pcs. Similarly 1,320 pcs. should be the output of Process I. The rejection being 50%, the input of Process I should be 1,320 plus 50%, i.e., 1,980 pcs. It can be tabulated as follows:

Process	Input	Rejection	%Rejection of output	Output
I	1,980	660	50%	1,320
II	1,320	120	10%	1,200
III	1,200	200	20%	1,000

(*b*) **Given:** Weight of the finished product = 10 gms. per pc.

Assuming that there is no other loss of material, the total material required for 1,980 pcs. of input of Process I shall be:

1,980 pcs. × 10 gms = 19,800 gms.

Rate of material = Re. 1 per kg.

Cost of raw material $= \frac{19{,}800 \times \text{Re.}1}{1{,}000}$ = Rs. 19.80

Cost of raw material per pc. $= \frac{19.80}{1{,}000}$ = Re. 0.0198

Illustration 10

Discuss the considerations that influence the setting of maximum, minimum, and re-order stock levels. Illustrate their computation by using the following information for a component 'ZYP'.

Normal usage .... 50 per week.
Minimum usage .... 25 per week.
Maximum usage .... 75 per week.
Re-order quantity .... 300 units
Re-order period .... 4 to 6 weeks.

(*Bangalore. M.Com. 1976; Punjab, B.Com. Sept. 1983*)

Solution

(**Note:** For considerations influencing the stock levels, read the discussion in the previous pages)

Re-order level = Max. consumption per day/per week etc. × Max. Re-order period
= 75 units × 6 weeks = 450 units

Maximum level = Re-order Level + Re-order Quantity – (Minimum consumption per day/per week etc. × Minimum time required to obtain supplies)
= 450 units + 300 units – (25 units × 4 weeks)
= 750 units –100 units = 650 units

Minimum level = Re-order level – (Normal consumption per day/per week etc. × Average Re-order period)
= 450 units – (50 units × 5 weeks)
= 450 units – 250 units = 200 units

Illustration 11

Two Components, A and B are used as follows:

Normal Usage 50 units per week each
Minimum Usage 25 units per week each
Maximum Usage 75 units per week each

Re-order quantity A : 400 units
B : 600 units
Re-order period A : 4 to 6 weeks
B : 2 to 4 weeks

Calculate for each component

(*i*) Re-order Level
(*ii*) Minimum Level
(*iii*) Maximum Level
(*iv*) Average Stock Level

(*Calicut M.Com.*)

Solution

(*a*) **Re-order Level** = Maximum consumption per day/per week etc. × Maximum Re-order period.
Component A = 75 units × 6 weeks = 450 units
Component B = 75 units × 4 weeks = 300 units

(*b*) **Minimum Level** = Re-order Level – (Normal consumption per day/ per week etc. × Average Re-order period)
Component A = 450 units – (50 units × 5 weeks) = 200 units
Component B = 300 units – (50 units × 3 weeks) = 150 units

(*c*) **Maximum Level** = Re-order Level – Re-order Quantity – (Minimum cosumption per day/per week etc. × Minimum Time required to get supplies)
Component A = 450 units + 400 units – (25 units × 4 weeks)
= 850 units – 100 units = 750 units
Component B = 300 units + 600 units – (25 units × 2 weeks)
= 900 units – 50 units = 850 units

(*d*) **Average Stock Level**= Minimum Level + $\frac{1}{2}$ (Re-order quantity)

Component A 200 units + $\frac{1}{2}$ × 400 units = 400 units

Component B = 150 units + $\frac{1}{2}$ × 600 units = 450 units.

Illustration 12

The following information is available in respect of component D – 20:

Maximum stock level :8,400 units

Budgeted consumption: Maximum 1,500 units per month
Minimum 800 units per month

Estimated delivery period: Maximum 4 months
Minimum 2 months

You are required to calculate:
(*i*) Re-order level;
(*ii*) Re-order quantity. (*I.C.W.A. Inter*)

Solution

(*i*) Re-order Level = Maximum Consumption per day/per week etc. × Maximum Re-order period.
= 1,500 units × 4 months = 6,000 units

(*ii*) Re-order quantity = (Maximum stock level – Re-order level) + Minimum Consumption per day/per week etc. × Minimum delivery period)
= (8,400 units – 6,000 units) + (800 units × 2 months)
= 4,000 units

Illustration 13

Following figures were taken from the records of M/s Dhigra and Co. of Ambala for the year ending 31st March. 2008. The valuation of inventory is Re. 1 per kg:

	Material "X" (kg.)	Material "Y" (kg.)
	Rs.	Rs.
Opening stock	1,700	1,200
Purchases	51,000	32,000
Closing stock	1,200	1,000

Calculate the material turnover ratio and express in number of days the average inventory is held.

(*Punjabi Uni., April 1983*)

Solution

Working notes:

1. Materials consumed

	Material 'X'	Material 'Y'
	(kgs.)	(kgs.)
Opening stock	1,700	1,200
Add: Purchases	51,000	32,000
	52,700	33,200
Less: Closing stock	1,200	1,000
	51,500	32,200

2. Average Inventory

$$\text{Average inventory} = \frac{\text{Opening inventory} + \text{Closing inventory}}{2}$$

$$\text{Material X} = \frac{1{,}700 + 1{,}200}{2} = \frac{2{,}900}{2} = 1{,}450 \text{ kgs.}$$

$$\text{Material Y} = \frac{1{,}200 + 1{,}000}{2} = \frac{2{,}200}{2} = 1{,}100 \text{ kgs.}$$

Material Turnover Ratio

$$= \frac{\text{Material consumed during the period}}{\text{Average inventory}}$$

$$\text{Material 'X'} = \frac{51,500}{1,450} = 35.5 \text{ times (approx.)}$$

$$\text{Material 'Y'} = \frac{32,200}{1,100} = 29.3 \text{ times (approx.)}$$

Number of Days Average Inventory is held

$$= \frac{\text{Total No. of days in the period}}{\text{Material Turnover}}$$

$$\text{Material X'} = \frac{365}{35.5} = 10.3 \text{ days (approx.)}$$

$$\text{Material 'Y'} = \frac{365}{29.3} = 12.5 \text{ days (approx.)}$$

Illustration 14

Do as directed:

Annual consumption: 40,00,000 kgs.
Cost of placing one order: Rs. 100
Cost of carrying one kg. of raw material for one year: 50 Paise
Calculate the Economic Order Quantity.

(G.N.D.U., B.Com., Sept. 1977)

Solution

$$\text{E.O.Q} = \sqrt{\frac{2CO}{I}}$$

$$= \sqrt{\frac{2 \times 40,00,000 \times 100}{0.50}}$$

$$= 40,000 \text{ units.}$$

Illustration 15

Good Luck Company estimates its carrying cost at 15% and its ordering cost at Rs. 9 per order. The estimated annual requirement is 38,000 units at a price of Rs. 4 per unit. What is the most economical number of units to order and how often will an order need to be placed.

(Delhi, M.Com., 1981)
(G.N.D.U., B.Com., 2000, 2002)

Solution

(*a*) Economic Order Quantity $= \sqrt{\frac{2CO}{I}}$

$$= \sqrt{\frac{2 \times 38{,}000 \times 9}{4 \times \frac{15}{100}}}$$

$$= \sqrt{\frac{2 \times 38{,}000 \times 9}{0.6}} = 1{,}067.7 \text{ or } 1{,}068 \text{ units}$$

(*b*) Daily consumption = 38,000 units/365 days = 104.11 units

Period after which order to be placed $= \frac{\text{E.O.Q}}{\text{Daily Consumption}}$

$$= \frac{1{,}068}{104.11} = 10.258 \text{ or } 10 \text{ days}$$

Illustration 16

Find out the Economic Order Quantity and order schedule for raw materials and packing materials with the following data given to you:

1. Cost of ordering:
   Raw materials ... Rs. 1,000 per order
   Packing materials Rs. 5,000 per order
2. Cost of holding inventory
   Raw materials ... 1 Paisa per unit p.m.
   Packing materials ... 5 Paise per unit p.m.
3. Production rate 2,00,000 units per month.

(*C.S. Final*)

Solution

Calculation of E.O.Q $= \sqrt{\frac{2CO}{I}}$

(*a*) Raw materials $= \sqrt{\frac{2 \times 24{,}00{,}000 \times 1{,}000}{0.12}}$

$$= \sqrt{40{,}00{,}00{,}00{,}000} = 2{,}00{,}000 \text{ units.}$$

(*b*) Packing materials $= \sqrt{\frac{2 \times 24{,}00{,}000 \times 5{,}000}{0.60}}$

$$= \sqrt{40{,}00{,}00{,}00{,}000} = 2{,}00{,}000 \text{ units.}$$

Notes: (*i*) Annual Consumption:

Raw materials	= 2,00,000 units × 12 months
	= 24,00,000 units
Packing materials	= 2,00,000 units × 12 months
	= 24,00,000 units

(*ii*) Annual Carrying Cost per unit

= Re. 0.01 × 12
= Re. 0.12

= Re. 0.05 × 12
= Re. 0.60

Illustration 17

The purchase department of your organisation has received an offer of quantity discount on its orders of materials as under:

Price per tonne Rs.	Tonnes
1,400	Less than 500
1,380	500 and less than 1,000
1,360	1,000 and less than 2,000
1,340	2,000 and less than 3,000
1,320	3,000 and above.

The annual requirement of the material is 5,000 tonnes. The delivery cost per order is Rs. 1,200 and the annual stock holding cost is estimated at 20 per cent of the average inventory.

The Purchase Department wants you to consider the following purchase options and advise which among them will be the most economical ordering quantity, presenting the relevant information in a tabular form. The purchase quantity options to be considered are : 400 tonnes, 500 tonnes, 1,000 tonnes, 2,000 tonnes and 3,000 tonnes.

Solution

Statement showing the Calculation of Most Economic Purchase Level

Total Annual Require-ment (Tonnes)	Size of order (Tonnes)	Price per tonne	No. of orders (Anuual requirement ÷ size of order)	Cost of Inventory	Ordering cost	Carrying cost of average inventory	Total Cost
1	2	3	4	5	6	7	8
5,000	400	1,400	12.5	70,00,000	15,000	56,000	70,71,000
	500	1,380	10	69,00,000	12,000	69,000	69,81,000
	1,000	1,360	5	68,00,000	6,000	1,36,000	69,42,000
	2,000	1,340	2.5	67,00,000	3,000	2,68,000	69,71,000
	3,000	1,320	1.67	66,00,000	2,000	3,96,000	69,98,000

From the above table, it is clear that the most economical order size among the given options is 1,000 tonnes since at this order size, the total cost is minimum.

Illustration 18

The annual demand for a product is 6,400 units. The unit cost is Rs. 6 and inventory carrying cost is 25% per annum. If the cost of one procurement is Rs. 75, determine:

(*i*) Economic order quantity
(*ii*) No. of orders per year.
(*iii*) Time between two consecutive orders. (*K.U.K., B.Com., 2006*)

Solution

(*i*)
$$\text{E.O.Q} = \sqrt{\frac{2\text{CO}}{\text{I}}}$$

$$= \sqrt{\frac{2 \times 6400 \times 75}{1.50}}$$

$$= \sqrt{6,40,000} = 800 \text{ units}$$

(*ii*) No. of orders per year
$$= \frac{\text{Annual consumption}}{\text{Size of one order}}$$

$$= \frac{6,400 \text{ Units}}{800 \text{ Units}} = 8 \text{ orders}$$

(*iii*) Time gap between two consecutive orders
$$= \frac{12 \text{ months}}{\text{No. of orders}}$$

$$= \frac{12 \text{ months}}{8 \text{ orders}} = 1.5 \text{ months}$$

Illustration 19

Calculate from the following information:

(*i*) Re-ordering stock level (*ii*) Maximum stock level (*iii*) Minimum stock level (*iv*) Average stock level.

Re-order quantity : 6,000 units

Lead Time:

(*a*) Normal	4 weeks
(*b*) Minimum	2 weeks
(*c*) Maximum	5 weeks
Average consumption	1,400 units
Minimum consumption	1,200 units
Maximum consumption	1,600 units

(*H.P.U., B.Com., 2007*)

Solution

(*i*) Re-ordering Stock Level = Maximum consumption per day/per week etc. × Maximum Lead Time

= 1,600 units × 5 weeks

= 8,000 units

(*ii*) Maximum Stock Level = Re-order Level + Re-order Quantity – (Minimum Consumption per day/per week etc. × Minimum Lead Time)

= 8,000 units + 6,000 units – (1,200 units × 2 weeks)

= 14,000 units – 2,400 units

= 11,600 units

(*iii*) Minimum Stock Level = Re-order level – (Average consumption per day/per week etc. × Normal lead time)

= 8,000 units – (1,400 units × 4 weeks)

= 8,000 units – 5,600 units

= 2,400 units

(*iv*) Average Stock Level $= \frac{\text{Maximum Stock Level} + \text{Minimum Stock Level}}{2}$

$= \frac{11{,}600 \text{ units} + 2{,}400 \text{ units}}{2}$

$= \frac{14{,}000 \text{ units}}{2}$

= 7,000 units

Alternatively:

Average Stock Level= Minimum Stock Level + $\frac{1}{2}$ (Re-order Quantity)

= 2,400 units + $\frac{1}{2}$ (6,000 units)

= 2,400 units + 3,000 units

= 5,400 units

OBJECTIVE TYPE QUESTIONS

A. Multiple choice questions

1. Select the correct answer in each of the following cases:

(*i*) The cost which varies directly in proportion to volume of output is:
(*a*) Fixed cost
(*b*) Variable cost
(*c*) Semi-variable cost.

(*ii*) The most important element of cost is:
(*a*) Material
(*b*) Labour
(*c*) Overheads.

(*iii*) Which of the following records quantity of materials only?
(*a*) Bin Card
(*b*) Stores Ledger
(*c*) Bill of Materials.

(*iv*) Which of the following documents is used for issuing materials to different production departments?
(*a*) Material Requisition
(*b*) Purchase Requisition
(*c*) Purchase Order.

(*v*) Continuous stock-taking is a part of:
(*a*) Annual stock-taking
(*b*) Perpetual Inventory
(*c*) ABC Analysis.

[**Ans.** (*i*) (*b*), (*ii*) (*a*), (*iii*) (*a*), (*iv*) (*a*), (*v*) (*b*)]

B. 'True'/'False' type statements

2. Indicate which of the following statements are true or false:

(*a*) Direct materials include materials which can be directly related to and identified with cost centres or cost units.

(*b*) The terms 'materials' and 'inventory' should not be used synonymously.

(*c*) Bin cards are not the part of accounting records.

(*d*) The re-order or re-ording level is the stock level fixed between the maximum and minimum stock levels.

(*e*) In ABC Analysis, 'A' group of items consists of those materials, the value of which is not high but which are used in large quantities.

(*f*) Perpetual inventory system obviates the necessity of physical stock taking at the end of financial year.

(*g*) Stores Ledger is maintained inside the stores by store-keeper.

(*h*) A high material turnover ratio indicates that the material item is slow moving.

(*i*) Economic order quantity is that size of the order which gives maximum economy in purchasing any item of material.

(*j*) The stock-in-hand should never exceed the maximum stock level.

(*k*) ABC analysis is based on the principle of management by exception.

[**Ans.** True (*a*), (*b*), (*c*), (*d*), (*f*), (*i*) (*k*) False (*e*), (*g*), (*h*), (*j*)]

3. Fill in the blanks

(*a*) Purchase of materials is initiated through ....

(*b*) Goods Received Note is also known as ....

(*c*) The formula for calculating the minimum stock level is ....

(*d*) The formula for calculating the average stock level is ....

(*e*) Material requisition is a document which is used for drawing materials from the ....

(*f*) Bin card is maintained inside the .... by the ....

(g) Stores ledger is kept and maintained in ....

(*h*) Transfer of surplus materials from one job or work order is recorded in ....

(*i*) Allotting code numbers or symbols to different items of materials is known as ....

(*j*) The system of undertaking stock verification after the close of stipulated period is ....

(*k*) Two important opposing factors in fixing the economic order quantity are .... and ....

[**Ans.** (*a*) Purchase Requisition,
(*b*) Material Received Note,
(*c*) Re-order level – (Normal consumption × Normal delivery time),
(*d*) $\frac{1}{2}$(Minimum level + Maximum level)
(*e*) Stores (*f*) Stores, store-keeper,
(*g*) Cost office (*h*) Material Transfer Note
(*i*) Codification
(*j*) Periodic Inventory control system
(*k*) Inventory carrying cost; ordering cost]

SHORT ANSWER TYPE QUESTIONS

4. Answer the following questions in not more than 5 lines each.

(*a*) Define the term 'material control.'

(*b*) Distinguish between Direct Materials and Indirect Materials.

(*c*) What is Economic Order Quantity.

(*d*) What is Inventory Turnover Ratio?

(*e*) Distinguish between Bin Card and Stores Ledger.

(*f*) What is Materials Abstract?

(*g*) What is meant by ABC Analysis?

(*h*) Distinguish between periodical inventory system and perpetual inventory control system.

(*i*) Explain the meaning of Danger Level.

(*j*) Give the meaning and specimen of Material Returned Note.

LONG ANSWER TYPE QUESTIONS

1. What is meant by the term 'Materials'? Give its various types.

Or

Distinguish between Direct and Indirect materials with examples.

2. What is meant by 'Materials Control'? Describe its objectives and importance. State briefly the basic requirements of a materials control system.

(*Punjabi Uni., B.Com., April 1988*)

3. Outline a system of materials control for a large manufacturing concern.

4. Explain briefly the steps involved in purchasing materials from outside by a big production unit.

(*G.N.D.U., B.Com., 2004*)

5. Distinguish between centralised and decentralised purchasing after explaining their respective advantages and disadvantages.

6. (*a*) Enumerate the advantages and disadvantages of a centralised stores system. (*G.N.D.U., B.Com. 1999, 2002*)

(*b*) Define the term 'imprest system of store control'.

7. What is the procedure of organising the stores ? Describe the main duties of a store-keeper.

8. Write short notes on and give specimens of:
   (*i*) Bin card;
   (*ii*) Stores ledger;
   (*iii*) Material Requisition;
   (*iv*) Material Transfer Note.
9. Distinguish between Bin card and Stores ledger. Explain briefly the purposes served by them.
10. What is meant by perpetual inventory control system? Give its advantages and disadvantages. Distinguish it from annual stock-taking.
11. Write short notes on and give specimens of:
   (*i*) Bills of Material;
   (*ii*) Purchase Requisition;
   (*iii*) Materials Abstract;
   (*iv*) Purchase order.
12. What do you understand by maximum level, minimum level and re-ordering level of stores and stocks? What factors are taken into account in fixing these limits?
13. Write a detailed note on ABC Analysis as a technique of material control. (*G.N.D.U., B.Com., 2001, 2002, 2004*)
14. Write short notes on and give specimens of:
   (*i*) Goods Received Note;
   (*ii*) Waste or Scrap Report;
   (*iii*) Spoilage report;
   (*iv*) Defectives Report.
15. "The perpetual inventory system is an integral part of material control". Discuss this statement by bringing out briefly the salient features and advantages of this system. (*G.N.D.U., B.Com., 2000, 2002, 2004*)
16. What do you understand by Inventory Turnover Ratio or Material Turnover Ratio? How is it calculated? Give a practical example to explain the calculation of inventory turnover ratio.
17. How will you treat the scrap, spoilage and defectives in cost accounts?
18. (*a*) What is Economic Order Quantity? How is it determined? (*G.N.D.U., B.Com., 2001, 2003, 2004*)
   (*b*) Write a short note on Danger level. (*G.N.D.U., B.Com., 2004*)
19. What do you understand by normal and abnormal wastages of materials during the process of manufacture?

20. What do you understand by classification and codification of materials? Distinguish between the two.

21. Describe briefly the documents used in an organisation from the time material is received in a factory till it is issued for consumption.

22. What do you mean by material control? Explain the objectives and essentials of effective material control.

(H.P.U., B.Com., 2008)

23. One of the important problems in accounting of materials relates to scrap, spoilage, waste and defectives. Distinguish between these and state how each of them should be accounted for?

(G.N.D.U., B.Com., 2003)

EXERCISES

1. Two components A and B are used as follows:

Minimum usage	150 units per week each
Normal usage	300 units per week each
Maximum usage	450 units per week each
Re-order Quantity	A, 2,400 units; B, 3,600units.
Re-order Period	A, 4 to 6 weeks; B, 2 to 4 weeks.

Calculate for each component:

(*a*) Re-order level,
(*b*) Minimum level,
(*c*) Maximum level,
(*d*) Average stock level.

[**Ans.** (*a*) 2,700 units; 1,800 units (*b*) 1,200 units; 900 units, (*c*) 4,500 units 5,100 units,

(*d*) According to: $\frac{\text{Maximum Level} + \text{Minimum Level}}{2}$

2,850 units; 3,000

or, According to: Minimum stock + $\frac{1}{2}$ (Re-order Qty.) = 2,400

units; 2,700 units.

2. In manufacturing its products, a company uses three raw materials A, B and C in respect of which the following information is available.

Raw Materials	Usage per unit of product (kg.)	Re-order Quantity (kg.)	Price per kg. (Paise)	Delivery Period (weeks)	Order level (kg.)	Minimum level (kg.)
A	10	10,000	10	1 to 3	8,000	
B	4	5,000	30	3 to 5	4,750	
C	6	10,000	15	2 to 4		2,000

Weekly production varies from 175 to 225 units, averaging 200. What would you expect the quantities of the following to be:

(*a*) Minimum Stock of A,
(*b*) Maximum Stock of B,
(*c*) Re-order level of C, and
(*d*) Average Stock level of A. (*C.A. Inter 1989*)

[**Ans.** (*a*) 4,000 kg. (*b*) 7,650 kg. (*c*) 5,400 kg. (*d*) 9,000 kg]

[**Hint:** For (*d*): Minimum Level + $\frac{1}{2}$ (Re-order Qty.)]

3. Calculate the (*i*) minimum stock level, (*ii*) maximum stock level and (*iii*) re-ordering level from the following particulars:

(*a*) Minimum Consumption 100 units per day.
(*b*) Maximum Consumption = 175 units per day.
(*c*) Normal Consumption = 125 units per day.
(*d*) Re-order quantity = 1,500 units.
(*e*) Minimum period for receiving materials = 7 days.
(*f*) Maximum period for receiving materials = 15 days.
(*g*) Normal period for receiving materials = 10 days.

[**Ans.** (*i*) 1,375 units (*ii*) 3,425 units (*iii*) *2,625* units]

4. Two components A and B are used as follows:

Normal usage	50 units per week each.
Minimum usage	25 units per week each.
Maximum usage	75 units per week each.
Re-order Quantity	A: 300 units, B: 500 units.
Re-order period	A: 4 to 6 weeks, B: 2 to 4 weeks.

Calculate for each component (*a*) Re-order level (*b*) Minimum level (*c*) Maximum level and (*d*) Average stock level

(*G.N.D.U., B.Com., April 1995*)

[**Ans.** (*a*) A-450 units, B-300 units
(*c*) 650 units and 750 units
(*d*) 425 units and 450 units
or 350 units and 400 units]

5. Calculate:

(*a*) Maximum stock level.

(*b*) Minimum stock level.

(*c*) Re-order level.

(*d*) Average stock level from the following:

Normal usage	600 units per week.
Maximum usage	900 units per week.
Minimum usage	300 units per week
Re-order quantity	7,200 units
Re-order period	2 to 4 weeks.

(*G.N.D.U., B.Com., April 1996, 1997*)

[**Ans.** (*a*) 10,200 units, (*b*) 1,800 units, (*c*) 3,600 units, (*d*) 6,000 units or 5,400 units]

6. Mr. Sharma buys 1,800 units of a material for which the yearly usage, too, is 1,800 units. The order placing cost is Rs. 500 and the cost of carrying one unit for a year is Rs. 10. Calculate the Economic Order Quantity.

[**Ans.** 424 units]

7. Calculate from the following:

(*i*) Maximum stock level.

(*ii*) Minimum stock level.

(*iii*) Re-order level.

Normal usage	300 units per week.
Minimum usage	150 units per week.
Maximum usage	450 units per week.
Re-order quantity	1,800 units.
Re-order period	2 to 4 weeks.

(*G.N.D.U. B.Com., April, 1997*)

[**Ans.** (*i*) 3,300 units, (*ii*) 900 units, (*iii*) 1,800 units]

8. What do you understand by maximum level, minimum level and re-ordering level?

Calculate the above from the following data:

Re-order quantity	1,500 units.
Re-order period	4 to 6 weeks.
Maximum consumption	400 units per week.
Normal consumption	300 units per week.
Minimum consumption	250 units per week

(*H.P.U., B.Com., 1994*)

[**Ans.** (*i*) 2,900 units, (*ii*) 900 units, (*iii*) 2,400 units]

9. (*a*) Calculate Economic order quantity from the following:

Annual usage = 6,000 units.

Cost of Material per unit = Rs. 20

Cost of placing and receiving one order = Rs. 60

Annual carrying cost of one unit = 10% of inventory value.

(*G.N.D.U., B.Com. April 1996& 1997*)

[**Ans.** 600 units]

(*b*) From the following details, find out economic order quantity:

Estimated requirement for the year: 4,800 units

Cost per unit Rs. 3

Ordering Cost Rs. 60 per order

Carrying Cost 10% of average inventory

(*G.N.D.U., B.Com., April 1998, 2001*)

[**Ans.** 1,386 units]

10. What is Economic Order Quantity? Should the quantity ordered be always equal to EOQ? Calculate the EOQ from the following information:

(*a*) Annual Consumption = 600 units.

(*b*) Ordering Cost = Rs. 12 per order.

(*c*) Carrying Cost = 20%

(*d*) Price per unit = Rs. 20.

[**Ans.** EOQ =60 units]

11. A manufacturer buys casting equipment from outside suppliers @ Rs. 30 per unit. Total annual needs are 80,000 units. The following further data are available:

Annual return on investment 10%

Rent, Insurance, taxes per unit Re. 1 per year.

Cost of placing an order Rs. 100

Determine the Economic Order Quantity. [**Ans.** 2,000 units]

(**Hint:** Total carrying cost per unit = Interest per unit + Rent, Insurance etc., per unit. $\left(\text{Rs.}30\times\frac{10}{100}\right)$ + Re. 1 = 3 + 1 = Rs. 4)

12. The annual demand for raw material 'R' is 4,000 units and the purchase price is expected to be Rs. 90 per unit. The incremental cost of processing an order is Rs. 135 and the cost of storage is estimated to be Rs. 12 per unit.

(*a*) What is the optimal order quantity and the total relevant cost of this order quantity?

(*b*) Suppose that the Rs. 135 estimate of the incremental cost of processing an order is incorrect and should have been 80. Assume that all other estimates are correct. What is the cost of this prediction error assuming that solution to part (*a*) is implemented for one year?

[**Ans.** (*a*) EOQ = 300 units Relevant cost Rs. 3,600. (*b*) Relevant cost = Rs. 3,600 (*b*) Revised EOQ = 231 units – Relevant unit cost = Rs. 2,772]

13. X Company buys its annual requirement of 36,000 units in 6 instalments. Each unit costs Re. 1 and the ordering cost is Rs. 25. The inventory carrying cost is estimated at 20% of unit value. Find out the total annual cost of the existing inventory policy. How much money can be saved by Economic Order Quantity?

[**Ans.** EOQ = 3,000 units; Saving in cost by EOQ Rs. 150]

14. Find out the Economic Order Quantity and Order Schedule for raw materials and packaging materials with the following data:

(*a*) Cost of ordering:
Raw materials Rs. 1,000 per order
Packaging materials Rs. 5,000 per order

(*b*) Cost of holding inventory:
Raw materials 1 paisa per unit p.m.
Packaging materials 5 paise per unit per month

(*c*) Production Rate: 2,00,000 units per month.

[**Ans.** EOQ 2,00,000 units for both; Order schedule – One order per month for both]

15. A company uses a purchased component in an assembly. It follows a policy of economic order quantity for procurement of the component. The purchase price of the component is Rs. 800 each and the cost of carrying one unit is 15% per annum. The cost of placing an order is Rs. 150. The company has estimated the total cost of carrying and order placement at Rs. 36,000. The supplier has offered a discount of 3% on the purchase price if the entire requirement of the component is covered in two purchase orders in a year.

Required:

(*i*) Find the economic order quantity.

(*ii*) Calculate the total cost of the component procurement and storage if the discount offer is accepted. Compare this cost with the total cost of EOQ.

(*iii*) What further discount if any, should be negotiated for minimising the cost.

[*Assume that the inventory carrying cost does not vary according to discount policy.*]

[**Ans.** (*i*) 300 components (*ii*) Rs. 2,90,16,300 (*iii*) 0.625%]

16. N Ltd. manufactures a product and the following particulars are collected for the year ended March, 2002.

Monthly demand (units)	1,000
Cost of placing an order (Rs.)	100
Annual carrying cost (Rs. per unit)	15
Normal Usage (units per week)	50
Minimum usage (units per week)	25
Maximum usage (units per week)	75
Re-order period (weeks)	4 – 6

You are required to calculate

(*i*) Re-order quantity. (*ii*) Re-order level.
(*iii*) Minimum level. (*iv*) Maximum level.
(*v*) Average stock level. (*C.A.Inter*)

[**Ans.** (*i*)186 units (*ii*) 450 units (*iii*) 400 units (*iv*) 536 units (*v*) 368 units]

17. Following information relating to a type of material is available:

Annual Demand	1,200 units.
Unit Price	Rs. 1.20
Ording cost per order	Rs. 400
Storage cost	2% per annum.
Interest rate	10% per annum.
Lead time	Half month

Calculate Economic order quantity and total annual inventory cost in respect of the particular raw material.

[**Ans.** EOQ = 258 units, total inventory cost Rs. 1,477.18]

18. After inviting tenders, two quotations are received as follows:

(*a*) Rs. 1.20 per unit.
(*b*) Rs. 1.10 per unit plus Rs. 3,000 fixed charges to be added irrespective of units ordered.

Advise with your arguments with whom orders should be placed and what quantity is to be ordered?

The following is the additional information:

	Units
Present stock	35,000
Average monthly requirements	10,000
Maximum level	80,000
Minimum level	30,000

Sales Tax problem may be ignored.

[**Ans.** Purchase cost of tender (*a*) Rs. 60,000, and of (*b*) = Rs. 58,000.]

(**Hint:** Tender (*b*), being cheaper for buying 50,000 units, should be preferred to Tender (*a*).)

19. The usage forecast for a particular consumption material is shown below:

Month	Forecast
January	13,300 units
February	13,000 units
March	13,700 units
April	14,800 units
May	16,000 units
June	16,200 units

It normally takes one month from the date of order to seure this material.

Required:

(*a*) The order point to be established during the forecast period.

(*b*) Computation showing the minimum stock to carry.

(*c*) Computation showing the maximum inventory, if the standard order quantity is 15,000 units.

[**Ans.** Order point: 16,200, units, Minimum Level: 1,700 units, Maximum level: 18,200 units]

20. Calculate the material turnover ratio for the year 2008-09 from the following details:

	Material 'A'	Material 'B'
	Rs.	Rs.
Opening Stock	25,000	87,500
Closing Stock	15,000	62,500
Purchases	1,90,000	1,25,000

Determine the fast moving material by expressing in number of days the average inventory is held.

[**Ans.** Material A, 10; Material B, 2; No. of days; A 36.5, No. of days, B 182.5 Material A is fast moving]

21. You are supplied with the following information from the books of a concern:

	Material P	Material Q
	Rs.	Rs.
Opening Stock	28,000	40,000
Purchases	4,60,000	6,72,000
Closing Stock	20,000	48,000

Calculate the materials turnover ratio of the above materials and state which of the two materials is more fast moving.

[**Ans.** 19.5 times and 1.5 times, material P is more fast moving]

(**Hints** 1. Materials Turnover ratio = $\frac{\text{Cost of materials consumed per unit}}{\text{Average Stock}}$

2. To determine the speed of turnover, check the average age of inventory in days, as Average Age = $\frac{365}{\text{Materials Turnover ratio}}$

3. Since the average age of Material P is much less, it is more fast moving)

22. The following information regarding coal is obtained from the stores records of a factory:

Aug. 1 Opening Balance : 200 tons
2 Issued on Requisition No. 273 : 57 tons
4 Issued on Requisition No. *285* : 83 tons
5 Received from supplier by Challan No. 74 of August 5, 2009: 100 tons. The supply was expected on this date.
8 Issued on Requisition No. 341 : 92 tons
12 Issued on Requisition No. 364 : 30 tons
17 Received from supplier by Challan No. 98 of August 17, 2009 100 tons. The supply was expected on this date.
24 Issued on Requisition No. 428 : 69 tons
28 Issued on Requisition No. 447 : 29 tons
30 Received from supplier by Challan No. 171 of August 30, 2009 125 tons. The supply was expected on this date. Received back by credit slip No. 37 : 10 tons.
31 Issued on Requisition No. 483 : 85 tons.

Examination by Stock Verifier on August 25, 2009, revealed a shortage of 5 tons.

The maximum amount of stock of coal permissible at any time is 200 tons, and the minimum 50 tons. The ordering level is 100 tons.

Draw up the Bin Card (No. 23) for Coal with all the necessary details showing the transactions in August, 2009. *(C.A., Final)*

[**Ans.** Balance 105 tons]

23. A timber merchant purchased 1,000 c.ft. of timber logs on first April 2008 @ Rs. 100 per c.ft. and stored them in his timber yard for six months for seasoning. In the timber yard the following items of expenses were incurred during the period of seasoning:

(*i*) Rent Rs. 1,250 p.m.
(*ii*) Salaries of 4 guards @ Rs. 250 p.m.
(*iii*) Incidental expenditure for maintenance, power, lighting etc. Rs. 750 p.m.
(*iv*) Annual share of administration overheads Rs. 10,000.

50% of the floor area of the godown and other connected operations were incurred for stocking the seasoned timber. Loss in volume of the logs due to seasoning should be taken at 10%.

Calculate the selling price of the seasoned timber per c.ft. on 1st October. 2008 assuming that the profit margin on cost was 15%.

(I.C.W.A. Inter, June 1992)

[**Ans.** Rs. 142.47]

24. (*a*) What do you understand by Inventory Turnover? How is it measured?

(*b*) The following figures are taken from the records of a Co. for the year 2001-02. The valuation of inventory is Rs. 2.00 per kg.

	Opening Stock	Purchases	Closing Stock
Material X	1,400 kg.	23,000 kg.	400 kg.
Material Y	2,000 kg.	3,600 kg.	2,400 kg.

Calculate the material turnover ratio of the above two materials and express in number of days the average inventory is held. Also determine which of the two materials is fast moving.

(B.Com., Punjabi 1994)

[**Ans.** (*b*)

	Material X	Material Y
Material Turnover Ratio	26.67	1.45
No. of Days Inventory Held	13.69	251.7

Material X is fast moving].

25. EXE Limited has received an offer of quantity discounts on its order of materials as under:

Price per tonne Rs.	Tonnes Nos.
1,200	Less than 500
1,180	500 and less than 1,000
1,160	1,000 and less than 2,000
1,140	2,000 and less than 3,000
1,120	3,000 and above

The annual requirement for the material is 5,000 tonnes. The ordering cost per order is Rs. 1,200 and the stock holding cost is estimated at 20% of material cost per annum. You are required to compute the most economical purchase level.

(*b*) What will be your answer to the above question if there are no discounts offered and the price per tonne is Rs. 1,500?

(C.A. Inter, Nov. 1990)

[**Ans.** (*a*) Total cost of 5,000 units including ordering and carrying cost is minimum (Rs. 59,22,000) when the order size is of 1,000 tonnes; (*b*) 200 tonnes]

26. Following costs were incurred in producing 800 M.T. of M.S. Rods:

	Rs.
Materials	2,80,000
Labour	1,00,000
Processing Charges	1,00,000
Total Cost	4,80,000

Of the total output, 10% was defective and had to be sold after a discount of 10% of the normal price. The scrap arising out of the production realised a sum of Rs. 8,760. The sale price is calculated to yield 15% profit on sales. You are requested to find out the normal price as well as the discounted price of per M.T. of M.S. Rods.

(*I.C.W.A. Inter, June 1991*)

[**Ans.** Normal Price Rs. 700; Discounted Price Rs. 630]

(**Hint:** Calculation of Equivalent Unit of Sales:

Total Production	800 M.T.
Less : Defective 10%	80 M.T.
Good Production	720 M.T.
Add: Equivalent of Defective Production (90% of 80 M.T.)	72 M.T.
Equivalent Good Production	792 M.T.

Price of Good Production per M.T. = Rs. $\frac{5,54,400}{729}$ = Rs. 700)

5

Materials-II (Valuation of Materials)

One of the main objects of cost accounting is the ascertainment of accurate costs and the accuracy of costs depends upon the ascertainment of the accurate cost of materials consumed and labour used in the production of a particular product. Material is the most important element of cost and it should be valued and charged to cost units in a proper manner. The valuation of materials can be studied under two parts:

(I) Valuation of Materials Purchased (or Received), and
(II) Valuation of Materials Issued.

VALUATION OF MATERIALS PURCHASED

The valuation of the materials received/purchased is made on the basis of actual cost which comprises:

(*i*) The purchase price or invoice price charged by the supplier (less trade discount, if any, allowed by him).

(*ii*) Taxes, duties, packing, freight, carriage & cartage, transit insurance and octroi paid and charged by the supplier or directly paid by the purchaser.

(*iii*) Expenses on purchasing, receiving, inspecting and storing the materials.

The expenses under (*iii*) above are of course incurred in connection with materials purchased but from the view point of convenience and practicability, these are not included in the cost of materials purchased but are treated as part of overhead.

In connection with the calculation of the cost of materials purchased, the following items require a special mention:

1. Discount, and 2. Cost of Containers.

Discount. Discount may be expressed as a concession or reduction in the invoice price of materials bought, allowed by the supplier to the buyer or customer. It may be divided into three parts:

(*a*) **Trade Discount:** It is a reduction off the selling price (or invoice price) allowed by the seller to the buyer on account of a business custom or usage. The amount of trade discount received by the purchaser is deducted from the invoice price of the materials purchased.

(*b*) **Quantity Discount:** It is a type of special concession or reduction off the selling price allowed by seller to buyer on account of bulk purchases. It is allowed to encourage bulk orders and its rate varies according to the quantity ordered and purchased by the buyer. Quantity discount is also deducted from the invoice price of the materials purchased to calculate their cost.

(*c*) **Cash Discount:** Cash discount is a concession or allowance allowed by the creditor (or supplier) to the debtor (or customer) on account of ready cash payment or payment before the expiry of the specified credit period. It represents interest on amount due for the unexpired credit period. As such, cash discount is treated as a financial item not to be deducted from the cost of the materials purchased.

Cost of Containers: The suppliers of materials generally supply the materials in containers. The treatment of the cost of containers may be given as follows:

(*a*) **Non-returnable containers not charged separately by the supplier:** If materials have been supplied in non-returnable containers for which no separate charge has been made in the invoice, no treatment is needed in respect of containers for calculating the cost of materials. If the containers have some realisable value, it should be estimated and deducted either from the cost of materials or from the amount of factory overhead.

(*b*) **Non-returnable containers charged separately by the supplier:** If materials have been supplied in non-returnable containers, which have been charged separately and are neither returnable nor possess any realisable value, their price should be included in the cost of materials.

(*c*) **Returnable containers charged separately by the supplier:** If materials have been supplied in returnable containers which have been charged separately and these can be returned to the supplier or resold, the difference between their cost price and returnable value (or resale value), should be included in the cost of materials.

If the materials are supplied in returnable containers on which the buyer is to get credit for the full price charged (by the supplier) on their return, the cost of containers is not included in the cost of materials on the presumption that these shall be returned to the supplier in due course.

Illustration 1

A manufacturer purchased 5,000 units of material No. X – 51 @ Rs. 15 per unit less trade discount of 2% on invoice price. Freight paid was Rs. 1,000, Carriage and Cartage Rs. 200, Octroi Rs. 750. The expenses of purchasing, receiving and storing for the year amounted to Rs. 5,000. Ascertain the cost of material per unit.

Solution

Statement Showing the Calculation of Cost of Materials

		Rs.	Rs.
Invoice Price (5,000 Units @ Rs. 15 per unit		75,000	
Less Trade Discount @ 2%		1,500	73,500
Add:	Freight		1,000
	Carriage and Cartage		200
	Octroi		750
	Total Cost		75,450

$$\text{Cost per unit} = \frac{\text{Rs. } 75,450}{5,000 \text{ units}} = \text{Rs. } 15.09$$

Note: The expenses of purchasing, receiving and storing are not considered for computing the cost of materials purchased for the purpose of convenience in accounting.

Illustration 2

A consignment consisted of two chemicals A and B. The invoice gave the following data:

	Rs.
Chemical A: 4,000 kgs. @ Rs. 250 per kg.	10,000
Chemical B : 3,200 kgs. Rs. 3.25 per kg.	10,400
Sales Tax	816
Railway Freight	384
	21,600

A shortage of 200 kgs. in A and 128 kgs. in B was noticed due to breakages. What is the stock rate you would adopt for pricing issues, assuming a provision of 5 per cent towards further deterioration?

(*I.C.W.A. Inter*)

Solution

Statement Showing the Issue Rate of Chemicals

	Chemical A	Chemical B
	Kgs.	Kgs.
Quantity Purchased	4,000	3,200
Less Shortage due to breakage	200	128
	3,800	3,072
Less Provision for deterioration @ 5%	190	153.6
Quantity Available for Issue	3,610	2,918.4
	Rs.	Rs.
Purchase Price	10,000	10,400
Sales Tax (apportioned on the basis of purchase value)	400	416
Railway Freight (apportioned in the ratio of weight)	213	171
Total Cost	10,613	10,987
Issue Rate per kg. $\left(\frac{\text{Total Cost}}{\text{Quantity Available for Issue}}\right)$	$= \frac{\text{Rs.}10,613}{3,610\text{ kgs.}}$ = Rs. 2.94	$= \frac{\text{Rs.}10,987}{2,918.4\text{ kgs.}}$ = Rs. 3.76

Note. Shortage of materials due to breakage has been treated as normal loss.

Illustration 3

Dixcy Ltd. received a consignment of two materials viz., A and B. The invoice showed the following:

	Rs.
Material A – 1,600 kgs. @ Rs. 10 per kg.	16,000
Materials B – 1,200 kgs. @ Rs. 7.50 per kg.	9,000
	25,000
Less Quantity Discount	1,000
	24,000
Other Charges:	
Sales Tax, duty and insurance	5,000
Cost of Containers (returnable at 75% of their value)	700
Freight	420
Carriage	280
Total	30,400

Terms: 5% cash discount on payment within a week.

50 kgs. of each material were found short on account of theft in transit. Calculate cost per kg. of each material. The company provides 5% for further deterioration.

Solution

Calculation of Cost of Material per kg

	Material A		Material B	
	Quantity	**Amount**	**Quantity**	**Amount**
	Kgs.	Rs.	Kgs.	Rs.
Purchase Price	1,600	16,000	1,200	9,000
Less Quantity discount (apportioned in the ratio of Invoice Price of 16 : 9)		640		360
		15,360		8,640
Add Expenses:				
Sales Tax, Duty and Insurance (16 : 9)		3,200		1,800
Cost of Containers (apportioned in the ratio of weight 4 : 3)		400		300
Freight (4 : 3)		240		180
Carriage (4 : 3)		160		120
		19,360		11,040
Less Returnable value of containers		300		225
		19,060		10,815
Less Cost of materials lost by theft (Abnormal Loss)	50	595.62	50	450.62
	1,550	18,464.38	1,150	10,364.38
Less Provision for normal loss @ 5%	77.5	–	57.5	–
Cost of Materials	1,472.5	18,464.38	1,092.5	10,364.38

$$\text{Cost per kg} = \frac{18{,}464.38}{1{,}472.50} = \text{Rs. } 12.54 \quad \frac{1{,}0364.38}{1{,}092.5} = \text{Rs. } 9.49.$$

Illustration 4

The following details are available in respect of a consignment of 1,250 kgs. of material 'X'.

(*a*) Invoice Price ~ Rs. 20 per kg
(*b*) Excise Duty ~ 25% on Invoice Price
(*c*) Sales Tax ~ 8% on Invoice Price including excise duty
(*d*) Trade Discount ~ 10% on invoice price
(*e*) Insurance ~ 1% of aggregate net price
(*f*) Delivery charges ~ Rs. 250
(*g*) Cost of containers @ Rs. 60 per container for 50 kgs. of material. Rebate is allowed @ Rs. 40 per container if returned within six weeks, which is a normal feature.
(*h*) One container load of material was rejected on inspection and not accepted.
(*i*) Cost of unloading and handling @ 0.25% of the cost of materials ultimately accepted.

On the basis of the above you are required to find out the landed cost of per kg. of material 'X'. *(I.C.W.A. Inter, 1991)*

Solution

Calculation of Landed Cost of Material 'X'

	Total cost for 1,250 kgs.
	Rs.
Invoice Price (1,250 kgs. @ Rs. 20 per kg.)	25,000.00
Add: Excise Duty (@25% on Rs. 25,000)	6,250.00
Sales Tax (@8% on Rs. 25,000 + Rs. 6,250)	2,500.00
	33,750.00
Less Trade Discount @ 10% on Invoice Price	2,500.00
Net Price	31,250.00
Add: Insurance(@ 10% on Rs. 31,250)	312.50
Delivery Charges	250.00
Cost of Containers	1,500.00
	33,312.50
Less Cost of Materials Returned (One container of 50 kgs.) $\left(\frac{\text{Rs. }33,312.50}{1,250\text{ kgs.}} \times 50\text{ kgs.}\right)$	1,332.50
	31,980.00
Cost of Unloading and Handling (0.25% of Rs. 31,980)	79.95
	32,059.95
Less Credit for Containers Returnable $\left(\frac{1,250\text{ kgs.} - 50\text{ kgs.}}{50\text{ kgs.}} \times \text{Rs.}40\right)$	960.00
Total Landed Cost	31,099.95

$$\text{Landed Cost per kg.} = \frac{\text{Rs.}31,099.95}{1,200\text{ kgs.}} = \text{Rs. }25.92.$$

APPORTIONMENT OF JOINT COST OF MATERIALS

Sometimes a mixture of few qualities/grades of an item of material is purchased in bulk at a single rate. In such a case, it shall be necessary to find out the proper cost of each quality/grade of the material. The cost of the various qualities/grades shall be ascertained with reference to their selling price or market price as explained in the following illustration:

Illustration 5

A truck load of mixed material 'A' was purchased for Rs. 72,000. These were sorted into the following grades, whose market rate is shown against each.

	Units	Selling Rate per unit
Grade 1	10,000	Rs. 6.00
Grade 2	4,000	Rs. 5.00
Grade 3	5,000	Rs. 4.00

Find out the purchase rate per unit of each grade of material assuming that all grades yield the same rate of profit.

(*I.C.W.A. Inter*)

Solution

Calculation of Sales Value of Materials

		Rs.
Grade 1	10,000 units @ Rs. 6 per unit	60,000
Grade 2	4,000 units @ Rs. 5 per unit	20,000
Grade 3	5,000 units @ Rs. 4 per unit	20,000
	19,000 units	1,00,000

Calculation of Rate of Profit on Selling Price

	Rs.
Total Sales value	1,00,000
Less Total Cost	72,000
Profit	28,000

$$\text{Rate of profit on selling price (or sales value)} = \frac{\text{Profit}}{\text{Sales Value}} \times 100$$

$$= \frac{28,000}{1,00,000} \times 100 = 28\%$$

Calculation of Cost Price of Material

Grade	Selling Price per unit	Profit per unit (@ 28% on selling price)	Purchase price per unit
	Rs. P.	Rs. P.	Rs. P.
1	6.00	1.68	4.32
2	5.00	1.40	3.60
3	4.00	1.12	2.88

Illustration 6

Batala Foundry is melting Pig Iron for producing castings. Coke and limestone are used to melt the metal. 150 kgs. of coke and 50 kgs. of limestone are required to melt one tonne of pig iron. The loss in melting is 5% and the rejections amount to 10% of the castings made. Cost of pig iron is Rs. 1,790 per tonne. Cost of coke is Rs. 1,300 per tonne. Cost of limestone is Rs. 200 per tonne. Rejections fetch a rate of Rs. 1.20 per kg. Calculate the cost of raw material per kg. of saleable casting.

(*I.C.W.A. Inter 1993*)

Solution

Calculation of cost of raw material of saleable casting

	Quantity	Amount
		Rs.
Cost of Pig Iron	1,000	1,790
Cost of 150 kgs. of coke @ Rs. 1,300 per tonnne		195
Cost of 50 kgs. of limetstone @ Rs. 200 per tonne		10
		1,995
Less Loss in Melting (5% of weight)	50	—
Castings made	950	1,995
Less Realisation from rejections (10% of 950 kgs.)	95	114
Cost of Material of saleable castings	855	1,881
Cost of raw material of saleable casting per kg.		

$$\frac{\text{Rs.}1{,}881}{855\,\text{kgs.}} = \text{Rs.}\,2.20$$

Illustration 7

Re-Roller Company produced 800 tonnes of M.S. Bars spending Rs. 1,80,000 towards materials and Rs. 60,000 towards rolling charges. 10% of the output was found defective and has to be sold at 10% less than the price for good ones.

If the sales realisations should give the company an overall profit of $12\frac{1}{2}$% on cost, find out the selling price per tonne of both the categories of bars. The scrap arising fetched realisation of Rs. 3,000.

(*I.C.W.A. Inter 1983*)

Solution

Calculation of Selling Price of M.S. Bars

		Rs.
Cost of materials		1,80,000
Rolling charges		60,000
		2,40,000
Less Sale of Scarp		3,000
Total cost		2,37,000
Add Profit @ 12.5% on cost		29,625
Sales value		2,66,625
Effective output		
Quantity of good output (90% of 400 tonnes)		360
Defective output	40 Tonnes	
Less 10% for lower price	4 Tonnes	
Quantity of defective output in terms of good output		36
Total Effective Output		396

$$\text{Selling price per tonne of good output} = \frac{\text{Rs.}\,2{,}66{,}625}{396\ \text{tonnes}} = \text{Rs.}\,673.30$$

$$\text{Selling price per tonne of defective output} = \frac{\text{Rs.}\,673.30 \times 90}{100} = \text{Rs.}\,605.97$$

VALUATION OF MATERIALS ISSUED (OR METHODS OF PRICING OF MATERIALS ISSUED)

Different methods can be used for the purpose of valuing or pricing of materials issued for production in a manufacturing concern. The actual method to be adopted in a manufacturing concern shall depend upon the nature of materials and the nature of the business itself. It is important to note that whichever method of pricing the material issues is followed, the actual issue of materials will always be from the earliest consignment. The important methods applied for pricing material issues are as follows:

1. Cost Price Method.
2. Market Price Method.
3. Average Price Method.
4. Fixed Price Method.
5. Inflated Price Method.
6. Base Stock Method.

1. Cost Price Method:

Under cost price method, materials issued to production, are charged out on the basis of actual cost *i.e.,* the cost at which these have been purchased. As we already know, the actual cost of materials consists of purchase price or invoice price (less trade discount and quantity discount), import duty, sales tax, commission on purchase, freight, carriage, cartage, transit insurance and octroi duty. This method is considered to be the simplest and most scientific as it helps in recovering the actual cost of materials paid, from production. As such, it adheres to the costing principles. Under the actual cost method, the materials issued can be priced out on any of the following basis:

(*a*) First-in-First-out Method (or FIFO Method)

(*b*) Last-in-First-out Method (or LIFO Method)

(*c*) Highest-in-First-out Method (or HIFO Method)

(*d*) Next-in-First-out Method (or NIFO Method)

First-in-First-out Method: Under this method, materials purchased or received first are deemed to be issued first. As such, the price paid for the earliest lot of materials in hand is taken as the basis for charging out the materials issued. Under this method, the various items on the debit side of the Stores Ledger (Receipts Column) are exhausted in chronological order. The stock in hand, under this method, is valued at cost of the current or latest purchases. This method requires the maintenance of the record of quantity and value of every receipt of material.

The operation of this method can be understood by the following example:

Example:

	Materials Received				Materials Issued		
Date	**Qty. (units)**	**Rate**	**Amount**	**Date**	**Qty. (units)**	**Rate**	**Amount**
15.2.05	400	4.00	1,600	18.2.05	300	4.00	1,200
20.3.05	800	3.00	2,400	22.3.05	100	4.00	
30.3.05	900	4.00	3,600		400	3.00	1,600
				2.4. 05	400	3.00	
					200	4.00	2,000

In the above example materials are purchased on three different dates *i.e.,* 15.2.05, 20.3.05 and 30.3.05 at different rates. These materials are issued on different dates *i.e.,* on 18.2.05, 22.3.05 and 2.4.05 by following 'first-in-first-out' principle.

The main advantages of FIFO method may be given as follows:

(*i*) First-in-First-out Method is simple in application.

(*ii*) It adheres to costing principles as the materials are charged to production at actual cost paid for them.

(*iii*) Accounting flow and physical flow of materials is the same.

(*iv*) Under this method, the value of stock in hand would be close to the current market prices.

But this method suffers from the following disadvantages:

(*i*) It involves excessive clerical labour since at the time of each issue of material, the cost clerk is required to find out the price of the lot out of which the issue is being made.

(*ii*) Cost of similar jobs or work orders executed on the same day or during the same week may not be the same simply because the materials have been taken from different lots.

(*iii*) Under the conditions of rising prices, use of FIFO method will mean that costs will not reflect current market conditions.

Illustration 8

Prepare a stores ledger account for material 'X' showing the issue of materials on FIFO method of valuation for August, 2006 from the information given below:

August, 2006	Quantity	Rate per unit
1st Opening balance	500 units	Rs. 20
8th Issues	300 units	
16th Purchases	800 units	Rs. 22
18th Issues	400 units	
25th Issues	300 units	
26th Purchase	400 units	Rs. 25
28th Issues	600 units	

Solution

STORES LEDGER (FIFO Method)

Date	Receipts				Issues				Balance			Remarks
2006	Ref.	Qty. (units)	Rate (Rs.)	Amount (Rs.)	Ref.	Qty. (units)	Rate (Rs.)	Amount (Rs.)	Qty. (units)	Rate (Rs.)	Amount (Rs.)	
Aug. 1									500	20	10,000	
Aug. 8						300	20	6,000	200	20	4,000	
Aug. 16		800	22	17,600					200 800	20 22	4,000 17,600	
Aug. 18						200 200	20 22	4,000 4,400	600	22	13,200	
Aug. 25						300	22	6,600	300	22	6,600	
Aug. 26		400	25	10,000					300 400	22 25	6,600 10,000	
Aug. 28						300 300	22 25	6,600 7,500	100	25	2,500	

Last-in-First-out Method (LIFO)

Under this method, materials received last are deemed to be issued first. As such, the price paid for the latest consignment of materials in hand is used for pricing out the issue of materials. This method also requires the maintenance of the record of quantity and value of every receipt of material. The stock in hand, under this method, is valued at earlier prices paid for. The operation of this method can be explained with the help of the following example:

Materials Received				Materials Issued			
Date	**Qty. (kilos)**	**Rate Rs.**	**Amount Rs.**	**Date**	**Qty. (kilos)**	**Rate Rs.**	**Amount Rs.**
15.2.05	400	2.00	800	18.2.05	300	2.00	600
20.3.05	300	3.00	900	22.3.05	300	3.00	900
					50	2.00	100

The main advantages of this method can be given as follows:

(*i*) This method is also simple in application.

(*ii*) Under this method, material issues are charged out at actual cost and hence it adheres to costing principles.

(*iii*) Under the conditions of rising prices, this method ensures that the issue of materials is charged at the price of the latest consignment or latest purchase. Thus, the cost reflects the current market conditions.

(*iv*) This method helps in preventing over-statement of profits since the current costs are correlated to current selling prices.

But this method has the following disadvantages:

(*i*) It involves too much clerical labour as the cost clerk, at the time of each issue of materials, has to find out the rate of the lots out of which issue is being made.

(*ii*) Cost of similar jobs or work-orders executed on the same day or in the same week may differ on account of the fact that issue of materials has been made out of different lots purchased at different prices.

(*iii*) Valuation of stock in hand (made at the price of earlier consignments) shall not reflect current market conditions. Stock in hand shall either be under-valued or over-valued.

(*iv*) The pricing method does not conform to the physical flow of materials from stores.

Illustration 9

Prepare Stores ledger under LIFO method from the particulars given in Illustration 8.

Solution

STORES LEDGER (LIFO Method)

Date	Receipts				Issues				Balance			Remarks
2006	Ref.	Qty. (units)	Rate (Rs.)	Amount (Rs.)	Ref.	Qty. (units)	Rate (Rs.)	Amount (Rs.)	Qty. (units)	Rate (Rs.)	Amount (Rs.)	
Aug. 1									500	20	10,000	
Aug. 8						300	20	6,000	200	20	4,000	
Aug. 16		800	22	17,600					200	20	4,000	
									800	22	17,600	
Aug.18						400	22	8,800	200	20	4,000	
									400	22	8,800	
Aug. 25						300	22	6,600	200	20	4,000	
									100	22	2,200	
Aug. 26		400	25	10,000					200	20	4,000	
									100	22	2,200	
									400	25	10,000	
Aug.28						400	25	10,000				
						100	22	2,200				
						100	20	2,000	100	20	2,000	

Both FIFO and LIFO methods are based on actual cost and can be conveniently adopted when the transactions of receipts are comparatively few so that it is easy to identify the lot out of which issue is being made. Moreover, it is also essential that price fluctuations are not very wide. If the fluctuations in prices are wide or large, the issue price of materials would also vary to a considerable extent.

Highest-in-First-out Method: Under this method, issues of material are priced out at actual cost on the basis of the principle of 'highest-in-first-out'. Under HIFO method, materials in hand purchased at the highest price are deemed to be issued first. For example, the purchases of material 'X-23' are as follows:

2008: Jan., 1 1,000 units @ Rs. 12
Jan., 2 2,000 units @ Rs. 15
Jan., 15 1,500 units @ Rs. 13

If an issue of 2,300 units is made to production department 'A' on Jan., 20 the issue shall be charged out as follows:

(*i*) 2,000 units @ Rs. 15 = Rs. 30,000
(*ii*) 300 units @ Rs. 13 = Rs. 3,900
Total Cost = Rs. 33,900

Under this method, charging out of issue of materials to production at the highest price leads to an increase in the cost of jobs which ultimately decreases their profit. The main object of this method is to ensure that values of stock in hand are kept at the lowest possible level. Although this method adheres to the costing principles and helps in preventing the over-valuation of stocks, it involves excessive clerical work due to numerous tedious calculations and is not widely adopted.

Next-in-First-out Method: Under this method, issues of material are charged out at the next price *i.e.,* the price at which order for the purchase of materials has been placed but the actual delivery of the materials has not yet been received. In other words, the issues of material are priced out at the latest price at which the manufacturer has placed the order for the next supply, even though the materials have not yet been received in actual. The main object of this method is to price out the issue at a price which is as close as possible to the market price. This method is also not very popular as it involves tedious calculations and excessive clerical labour.

2. Market Price Method

Market Price basis is the second important method of valuation of materials. Under this method, materials are charged to production at the prevailing market price at the time of issuing the material.

Advantages

(*i*) The most important benefit derived from this method is that it reflects current market prices of materials prevailing at the time of manufacturing the products.

(*ii*) This method can be advantageously applied by the contractors and job order manufacturers in calculating the material costs keeping in view the market prices of the materials in their tender statements.

(*iii*) The method is quite simple and does not involve much calculations.

(*iv*) This gives correct financial position of the concern as it provides correct value of materials in stores pertaining to receipts and issues.

Disadvantages

(*i*) The market price is not the real cost of the materials and the total cost of product computed on the basis of this price is not the true cost.

(*ii*) There are usually fluctuations in the market price and sometimes such changes are quite often. These changes also make the issue prices of materials fluctuating. At the same time it becomes very difficult for the store-keeper to keep the proper records of the market prices.

(*iii*) The adoption of market price basis leads to the necessity of making stock adjustments which is certainly complicated and gives rise to errors in the process of valuation of materials.

(*iv*) Adherence to this method poses a serious problem relating to reconciliation of costing and financial books.

3. Average Price Method

This method operates on the basis of the calculation of averages. Under this method all the materials on hand are so inter-mingled that the issues of materials are priced out at the average cost price of materials in hand, a new average being calculated whenever a fresh purchase is made.

Average price method is commendable and can be undertaken with utmost success if the materials are few in number and can be easily mixed together to form one lot. It is better than the former methods as it minimises variances between cost prices and market prices of the materials.

Various methods undertaken for the valuation of materials under Average Price Valuation technique are explained as under:

(A) Simple Average Price.
(B) Weighted Average Price.
(C) Periodic Simple Average Price.
(D) Periodic Weighted Average Price.
(E) Moving Average Price.

(A) Simple Average Price: Simple average price is a price which is calculated by dividing the total of the price of the materials in the stock from which material to be priced could be drawn by the number of prices used in that total. Simply stating, average cost price is calculated by dividing the total of purchase price of materials in hand on the date of issue by the number of prices.

Advantages

(*i*) This method is quite simple in operation and gives reliable results under stable prices.

(*ii*) It minimises the variances in the cost and the market prices.

Disadvantages

(*i*) It does not project accurate total cost because it does not recover actual cost of materials from production.

(*ii*) The method is unscientific in application as it does not take into account the quantity of materials purchased at different prices.

(*iii*) Under-charging and over-charging of material costs give inaccurate profit or loss if this method is resorted to.

(*iv*) Valuation of stock in hand is usually incorrect under this method.

Illustration 10

From the following transactions recorded in respect of material 'x' used in a factory, prepare stores ledger pricing the issues at simple average method.

August, 2006		Quantity	Rate per unit
3rd	Purchases	400 units	Rs. 2.10
15th	Purchases	500 units	Rs. 2.20
20th	Issues	500 units	
26th	Purchases	600 units	Rs. 2.50
28th	Issues	900 units	

Solution

Stores Ledger (Simple Average Method)

Date	Receipts				Issues				Balance			Remarks
2006	Particulars	Qty. (units)	Rate (Rs.)	Amount (Rs.)	Ref.	Qty. (units)	Rate (Rs.)	Amount (Rs.)	Qty. (units)	Rate (Rs.)	Amount (Rs.)	
Aug. 3	G.R.N No.	400	2.10	840					400	2.10	840	
Aug. 15	G.R.N No.	500	2.20	1,100					900	2.15	1,935	
Aug. 20	M.R. No.					500	2.15	1,075	400	2.15	860	
Aug. 26	G.R.N No.	600	2.50	1,500					1,000	2.35	2,350	
Aug. 28	M.R. No.					900	2.35	2,115	100	2.35	235	

Note: Calculation of average price

(*i*) 15th August: $\dfrac{\text{Rs. } 2.10 + \text{Rs. } 2.20}{2} = \text{Rs. } 2.15$

(*ii*) 26th August: $\dfrac{\text{Rs. } 2.20 + \text{Rs. } 2.50}{2} = \text{Rs. } 2.35$

Note: G.R. Note means Goods Received Note and M.R. means Material Requisition.

(B) Weighted Average Price: Weighted average price is one which is calculated by dividing the total cost of materials in the stock from which materials to be priced could be drawn, by the total quantity of materials in that stock. It can be put as:

$$\text{Weighted Average Price} = \frac{\text{Total cost of material in stock}}{\text{Total units in stock}}$$

The average price charged to respective issues remains the same until fresh supply of materials is received which leads to calculation of a new average.

Advantages

(*i*) It is quite simple to understand and easy to operate.

(*ii*) The results shown by this method are more reliable and accurate as compared to simple average price method as it takes into account both the quantities as well as prices of the purchases.

(*iii*) It irons out the fluctuations in the material costs thereby making comparison between different jobs easier.

(*iv*) Total cost of materials is recovered from total production under this method.

Disadvantages

(*i*) The main drawback of this method is that at the time of each purchase of material, a fresh calculation will have to be made to find out the average purchase price. This is indeed tedious.

(*ii*) Closing stock does not represent current market prices.

(*iii*) As the average price is different from the actual price or cost of the material, there may be profit or loss because of over-or under-charging of material costs to jobs.

Illustration 11

Using the information given in illustration 10, how would you present Stores Ledger under Weighted Average Method.

Solution

Stores Ledger

(Method: Weighted Average Method)

Date	Particulars	Receipts			Issues			Balance			Remarks
2006		Qty. (units)	Rate (Rs.)	Amount (Rs.)	Qty. (units)	Rate (Rs.)	Amount (Rs.)	Qty. (units)	Rate	Amount (Rs.)	
Aug. 3	G.R.N No.	400	2.10	840				400	2.10	840	
Aug. 15	G.R.N. No.	500	2.20	1,100				900	2.16	1,940	
Aug. 20	M.R. No.				500	2.16	1,080	400	2.16	860	
Aug. 26	G.R.N. No.	600	2.50	1,500				1,000	2.36	2,360	
Aug. 28	M.R. No.				900	2.36	2,124	100	2.36	236	

Note: Calculation of average price

(*i*) 15th August: $\dfrac{400 \times \text{Rs. } 2.10 + 500 \times \text{Rs. } 2.20}{400 + 500} = \text{Rs. } 2.15$

(*ii*) 26th August: $\dfrac{400 \times \text{Rs. } 2.16 + 600 \times \text{Rs. } 2.50}{400 + 600} = \text{Rs. } 2.36$

(C) Periodic Simple Average Price. Under this method, valuation of material issued is based on the simple average of all prices of materials purchased during a specific period of time, say a month. It can be represented mathematically as:

Periodic Simple Average Price =

$$\frac{\text{Total prices of purchases during the period}}{\text{No. of prices during the period}}$$

It may be pointed out that the price of the opening inventory is not added while calculating the periodic simple average price. In actual routine, the quantities issued are recorded as and when the requisitions are received by the store-keeper, but the pricing is postponed till the end of the month and the periodic simple average issue price or rate is calculated by applying the above formula. This method is also known as the End of Period (EOP) or End of Month (EOM) Average Cost price of pricing materials.

Advantages

(*i*) The method is easier to operate and simple to understand.

(*ii*) It is best suited for large scale industrial undertakings where production is continuously carried over a longer period of time.

(*iii*) The average issue price representing different lots is more representative than the one calculated under simple average price method.

Disadvantages

(*i*) The value of stock in hand does not represent the current market price or actual cost of the product.

(*ii*) Like the simple average method, approximation of figures leads to under- or over-absorption of costs.

(*iii*) Another drawback of this method is that valuation or pricing of material is done at the end of specific period leading to more time lag between recording the issues of materials and calculating periodic average issue price.

(*iv*) On account of delay in calculations, periodic average price work is accumulated leading to heavy clerical work and complications.

Illustration 12

The following receipts and issues pertain to a material item. Calculate the periodic simple average for three months and prepare Stores Ledger.

Date	Receipts Units.	Rs.	Issues Units
1st January, 2005	500	500	–
1st February, 2005	500	400	–
28th February, 2005	–	–	600
1st March, 2005	500	600	–
31st March, 2005	–	–	600

Solution

Stores Ledger

Date		Receipts				Issues				Balance	Remarks	
2005		Ref.	Qty. (units)	Rate (Rs.)	Amount (Rs.)	Ref.	Qty. (units)	Rate (Rs.)	Amount (Rs.)	Qty. (units)	Rate (Rs.)	Amount (Rs.)
Jan.	1		500	1.00	500		–	–	–	500	1.00	500
Feb.	1		500	0.80	400		–	–	–	1,000		900
Feb.	28		–	–	–		600	1.00	600	400		300
March	1		500	1.20	600		–	–	–	900		900
March	31		–	–	–		600	1.00	600	300	1.00	300

Periodic Simple Average Price

$$= \frac{\text{Cost of Materials Received or Purchased during the period}}{\text{Quantity received or purchased}}$$

$$= \frac{\text{Re.}1.00 + \text{Re.}\,0.80 + \text{Rs.}1.20}{3} = \text{Re. } 1$$

(D) Periodic Weighed Average Price. Periodic Weighted Average Price is calculated by dividing the total cost of materials purchased by the total quantity purchased. Like the periodic simple average method, it is also calculated at the end of particular period. In this case weightage is given to the quantities of the material lots purchased.

It can be expressed as:

Periodic Weighted Average Price

$$= \frac{\text{Cost of Materials Received or Purchased during the period}}{\text{Quantity Received or Purchased}}$$

Advantages

(*i*) It is easier to calculate as the only calculation with regard to issue price is to be made at the end of a specific period only.

(*ii*) In industries where there are wide fluctuations in material prices, this method can be successfully employed.

(*iii*) It can be applied with greater success in case of processing industries.

Disadvantages

(*i*) There is every possibility of under-recovery or over-recovery of cost of materials as these are not charged on the basis of actual cost.

(*ii*) Just like the periodic simple average price method, the calculation of periodic weighted average price is delayed till the end of a specific period leading to heavy burden of clerical work. Due to delay, concurrent or simultaneous costing is not possible under this method.

Illustration 13

The following transactions took place in respect of a material item 'A' during the month of May, 2005. Calculate the periodic weighted average price and present the Stores Ledger Account accordingly.

Date 2005	Particulars	Quantity kg.	Rate Per unit Rs.
May 2	Received	2,000	10
May 7	Received	300	12
May 9	Issued	1,200	–
May 11	Received	200	14
May 12	Issued	1,000	–
May 22	Received	300	11
May 31	Issued	200	

Solution

Stores Ledger

Date	Receipts				Issues				Balance			Remarks
2005	Ref.	Qty. (units)	Rate (Rs.)	Amount (Rs.)	Ref.	Qty. (units)	Rate (Rs.)	Amount (Rs.)	Qty. (units)	Rate (Rs.)	Amount (Rs.)	
May 2		2,000	10	20,000			10.6071		2,000			
May 7		300	12	3,600					2,300			
May 9						1,200			1,100			
May 11		200	14	2,800					1,300			
May 12						1,000			300			
May 22		300	11	3,300					600			
May 31						200			400	10.6071	4,243	
		2,800		29,700		2,400		25,487				

Periodic weight average price =

$$= \frac{\text{Cost of Materials Received or Purchased during the period}}{\text{Quantity received or Purchased}}$$

$$= \frac{\text{Rs. } 29{,}700}{2{,}800 \text{ kg}} = \text{Rs. } 10.6071$$

Moving Average Price Method: It is another method to minimise the difficulty arising in case of simple average method. A moving average price is the price obtained by dividing the total of the average price of a number of periods by the number of periods, the last of the periods being that for which material issues are valued. A moving average price may be:

(*a*) Simple Moving Average Price, or (*b*) Weighted Moving Average Price.

To determine the simple moving average price, a number of periods, generally in months *e.g.*, 3 months, 5 months etc., is first decided upon. If it is decided that moving average of last three months is to be considered, we will add the periodic simple average prices of 3 months including and preceding the month for which materials used are valued. The total of the simple average prices divided by three would give us the simple moving average price.

In order to obtain the weighted moving average price, we have to add the weighted average prices of a number of periods including and preceding the month (or period) for which materials used are valued and divide the total by the number of months (or periods).

It should be remembered that if the prices continue to rise over a number of periods, the moving average price tends to be lower than a periodic average price and if the prices continue to fall, the moving average price tends to be higher than the corresponding periodic average. Thus, the prices applied for charging out materials do not reflect the current market price.

(4) Fixed Price Method or Standard Price Method.

Under this method, the material issues are priced out at pre-determined or standard price or fixed price. The standard issue price is fixed for a definite period say a month, quarter or year. As the material issues are made at the same price during a specified period, a record of materials issued can be kept quantity-wise in a single statement.

There are two types of standard prices viz., Basic and Current. Basic standard price is fixed for a longer period of time which is greatly helpful in future planning. Current standard price is fixed for a shorter period which is easily adjusted in accordance with the changed circumstances by keeping in view the future variations in the prices of materials.

The standard price may differ from the actual price of the materials leading to variance. If the actual price paid for the materials is more than the standard price, there is a negative variance representing loss. If the standard price or pre-determined price is more than the actual price there is a positive variance representing profit.

Advantages

(*i*) The method is quite simple in operation and easily understandable.

(*ii*) It considerably reduces the clerical work.

(*iii*) It can be used as an effective tool to initiate effective control over purchases.

Disadvantages

(*i*) Fixation of standard price is a cumbersome process.
(*ii*) As materials are not priced on actual cost basis, there is every possibility of under-recovery or over-recovery of material costs.
(*iii*) The Profit and Loss Account has to be adjusted on account of profit or loss arising due to under-recovery or over-recovery of costs.

(5) Inflated Price Method

This method is applied where the materials are subject to normal wastage which is inevitable or unavoidable. In order to cover the loss arising due to normal wastage, the material issues are priced out at an inflated rate. For example, if 100 units of a certain material item are purchased at Rs. 38 per unit and if it is expected that there shall be a normal wastage of 5 units, 95 units of the material shall be issued at an inflated price of Rs. 40 per unit (Rs. 3,800 ÷ 95 units).

It may be noted here that it is not a separate method of pricing materials. The cost of materials can be inflated in order to recover cost of materials lost.

(6) Base Stock Method

This method works on the assumption that a minimum fixed quantity of materials must be kept in store at all times at original cost. The quantity is known as "Base Stock". The base stock is usually appropriated from the first lot of materials purchased and carried in the books as a fixed asset in the years to come. Any quantity beyond base stock can be valued in accordance with any of the foregoing methods conducive to the organisation.

The materials are charged at the actual cost basis such as LIFO or FIFO under this method which greatly facilitates the calculations. On account of charging at actual cost, under-recovery or over-recovery of material costs resulting in profits or losses is avoided.

The main drawback of this method is that since the stock is not valued at the current market price, the final statements of account do not depict correct working capital position of the concern.

SELECTION OF A PROPER METHOD OF VALUATION

After having discussed the merits and demerits of the various methods of pricing out materials, it should be possible for one to decide as to which method is best suited for application. Selection of the method for pricing out materials is not possible with the help of any particular rules. The selection will be made by taking into account a number of factors which may be given as follows:

(*i*) The nature of production — whether intermittent or continuous.
(*ii*) Volume/frequency of receipts of materials.
(*iii*) Variations and fluctuations in prices and their nature.
(*iv*) Frequency of issue of material.
(*v*) Stock turnover rate.
(*vi*) Effect of pricing method on tax payable.
(*vii*) Clerical labour involved in the method.
(*viii*) Traceability of the issue to the particular lot or consignment.
(*ix*) Nature of the cost accounting system followed.

Pricing of materials returned to vendors

Materials returned to vendors may be recorded at invoice price or in accordance with the method adopted for pricing out material issues. Recording of materials returned at invoice price is not realistic as the price per unit granted by vendor on return of materials cannot be the same as the original invoice cost. Necessary adjustments for discount, freight, carriage inward etc., shall have to be made to arrive at the same. Therefore, returns should be valued according to the method adopted for pricing out material issues and entered in the 'Issued Column' in Stores Ledger.

Pricing of surplus material returned to store

Sometimes all the material requisitioned in a department may not be used in full and the surplus returned to stores. First alternative is to record the materials returned to stores at the price at which they were originally issued and to re-issue them at the same price on the next requisition. Second alternative is to value the return of surplus at the original issue price and to treat the same as an item of new purchase in the 'Received column' of Stores Ledger.

Treatment of Shortage of Materials

If any shortage of materials is noted on making a physical verification of stock of materials, it should be entered in the 'Issued Column' of stores ledger and valued in accordance with the method adopted for pricing out material issues.

Illustration 14

The following is a history of the receipts and issues of materials in a factory during February, 2008:

Feb. 1.	Opening balance	500 Quintals @ Rs. 25
Feb. 3.	Issued	70 Quintals
Feb. 4.	Issued	100 Quintals
Feb. 8.	Issued	80 Quintals
Feb. 13.	Received from vendor	200 Quintals Rs. 24.50
Feb. 14.	Refund of surplus from a work order	15 Quintals @ Rs. 25
Feb. 16.	Issued	180 Quintals
Feb. 20.	Received from vendor	240 Quintals @ Rs. 24.375
Feb. 24.	Issued	304 Quintals
Feb. 25.	Received from vendor	320 Quintals @ Rs. 24.375
Feb. 26.	Issued	112 Quintals
Feb. 27.	Refund of surplus from a work order	12 Quintals @ Rs. 24.50
Feb. 28.	Received from vendor	100 Quintals @ Rs. 25.00

Issues are to be priced on the principle of "First-in-First-out". The stock verifier of the factory noted that on 15th he had found a shortage of 5 quintals and on the 27th another shortage of 8 quintals.

Write out the complete Stores Ledger Account in respect of the above materials.

(C.A.)

Solution

Stores Ledger Account

Date		Receipts			Issues				Balance			Remarks
2008	Ref.	Qty. (Qts.)	Rate (Rs.)	Amount (Rs.)	Ref.	Qty. (Qts.)	Rate (Rs.)	Amount (Rs.)	Qty. (Qts.)	Rate (Rs.)	Amount (Rs.)	
Feb. 1									500	25.00	12,500	
3						70	25.00	1,750	430	25.00	10,750	
4						100	25.00	2,500	330	25.00	8,250	
8						80	25.00	2,000	250	25.00	6,250	
13		200	24.50	4,900					250	25.00	6,250	
									200	24.50	4,900	
14	Refund	15	24.00	360					250	25.00	6,250	
									200	24.00	4,900	
									15	24.00	360	
15					Shortage	5	25.00	125	245	25.00	6,125	
									200	24.00	4,900	
									15	24.00	360	
16						180	25.00	4,500	65	25.00	1,625	
									200	24.00	4,900	
									15	24.00	360	
20		240	24.375	5,850					65	25.00	1,625	
									200	24.00	4,900	
									15	24.00	360	
									240	24.375	5,850	

24						65	25.00	1,625			
						200	24.00	4,900			
						15	24.00	4,900			
						24	24.375	585	216	24.375	5,265
25		320	24.315	7,780.80					216	24.375	5,265
									320	24.315	7,780.80
26						112	24.375	2,730	104	24.375	2,535.00
									320	24.135	7,780.80
27	Refund	12	24.500	294					104	24.375	2,535.00
									320	24.135	7,780.80
									12	24.500	294.00
27					Shortage	8	24.375	195	96	24.375	2,340.00
									320	24.315	7,780.80
									12	24.500	294.00
28		100	25.000	2,500					96	24.375	2,340.00
									320	24.315	7,780.00
									12	24.500	294.00
									100	25.000	2,500.00

Illustration 15

The following receipts and issues were made for a new item of stores:

	Quantity Received (Units)	Cost Rs.	Quantity Issued (Units)
January 1	1,000	1,000	
February 1	1,000	800	
February 28			1,200
March 1	1,000	1,200	
March 31			1,200

Tabulate the values of:

(*i*) issues made 28th February
(*ii*) resulting stock 28th February
(*iii*) issues made 31st March
(*iv*) resulting stock 31st March, when issues are priced on:
  (*a*) LIFO basis
  (*b*) LIFO basis
  (*c*) Average Cost basis.

Solution

Stores Ledger

	Received			Issued			Balance (Stock)		
Date	Units	Rate	Amount	Units	Rate	Amount	Units	Rate	Amount
			Rs.		Rs.	Rs.		Rs.	Rs.
LIFO Basis									
Jan. 1	1,000	1.00	1,000	–	–	–	1,000	1.00	1,000
Feb. 1	1,000	0.80	800	–	–	–	1,000	1.00	1,000
							1,000	0.80	800
Feb. 28	–	–	–	1,000	0.80	800			
				200	1.00	200	800	1.00	800
March 1	1,000	1.20	1,200				800	1.00	800
							1,000	1.20	1,200
March 31	–	–	–	1,000	1.20	1,200			
				200	1.00	200	600	1.00	600
FIFO Basis									
Jan. 1	1,000	1.00	1,000	–	–	–	1,000	1.00	1,000
Feb. 1	1,000	0.80	800	–	–	–	1,000	1.00	1000
							1,000	0.80	800
Feb. 28	–	–	–	1,000	1.00	1,000			
				200	0.80	160	800	0.80	640
March 1	1,000	1.20	1,200				800	0.80	640
							1,000	1.20	1,200
March 31	–	–	–	800	0.80	640			
				400	1.20	480	600	1.20	720
Average Cost Basis									
Jan. 1	1,000	1.00	1,000	–	–	–	1,000	1.00	1,000
Feb. 1	1,000	0.80	800	–	–	–	2,000	0.90	1,800
Feb. 28	–	–	–	1,200	0.90	1,080	800	0.90	720
March 1	1,000	1.20	1,200	–	–	–	1,800	1.00	1,800
March 31	–	–	–	1,200	1.00	1,200	600	1.00	600

[Ans.

	LIFO	FIFO	Average
Issues on 28th Feb.	1,000	1,160	1,080
Stock on 28th Feb.	800	640	720
Issues on 31st March	1,400	1,120	1,200
Stock on 31St March	600	720	600]

Illustration 16

A manufacturing concern purchases from time to time large quantities of a commodity used in the manufacture of one of its products. The following are the details of purchases during the six months ended June 30, 2008.

2008	Units purchased	Cost per 100 units
February 2	10,000	10.00
March 15	25,000	10.50
April 20	20,000	9.50
May 3	15,000	9.00
June 1	12,000	9.00
July 20	3000	8.50

There were 15,000 units in stock on January 1, 2008 which were valued at Rs. 9.50 per 100 units.

Quantities issued from store during the six months were as under:

2008	Units Issued
(*a*) January 25	10,000
(*b*) February 28	8,000
(*c*) March 29	25,000
(*d*) April 30	20,000
(*e*) May 15	18,000
(*f*) June 29	15,000

At what price should the issues be charged and the closing stock valued? Prepare a Store ledger Account, illustrating your views.

Solution

FIFO method is suitable as the prices of purchases show 'downward' trend. FIFO method would enable to recover the higher prices first and the jobs charged at FIFO method would show a well comparative cost. The closing stock should also be valued at FIFO method.

Stores Ledger Account

Material.........................

Maximum Limit.........................
Minimum Limit.........................
Re-order Limit.........................

Date	Received Qty. (units)	Received Rate per 100 (Rs.)	Received Amount (Rs.)	Issued Qty. (Units)	Issued Rate per 100 (Rs.)	Issued Amount (Rs.)	Balance Qty. (Units)	Balance Rate per 100 (Rs.)	Balance Amount (Rs.)
2008									
Jan. 1							15,000	9.50	1,425
Jan. 25				10,000	9.50	950	5,000	9.50	475
Feb. 2	10,000	10.00	1,000				5,000	9.50	475
							10,000	10.00	1,000
Feb. 28				5,000	9.50	475	7,000	10.00	700
				3,000	10.00	300			
March 15	25,000	10.50	2,625				7,000	10.00	700
							25,000	10.50	2,625
March 29				7,000	10.00	700			
				18,000	10.50	1,890	7,000	10.50	735
April 20	20,000	9.50	1,900				7,000	10.50	735
							20,000	9.50	1,900
April 30				7,000	10.50	735			
				13,000	9.50	1,235	7,000	950	665
May 3	15,000	9.00	1,350				7,000	9.50	665
							15,000	9.00	1,350
				7,000	9.50	665			
May 15				11,000	9.00	990	4,000	9.00	360
June 1	12,000	9.00	1,080				4,000	9.00	360
							12,000	9.00	1,080
June 29				4,000	9.00	360			
				11,000	9.00	990	1,000	9.00	90

The closing stock as on 30th June, 2008 is 1,000 units @ Rs. 900 per hundred, for Rs. 90 only.

Illustration 17

Show the Stores Ledger entries as they would appear when using:

(*a*) the weighted average method,

(*b*) the LIFO method,

of pricing issues, in connection with the following transactions:

			Units	Price Rs.
April	1	Balance in hand b/f	300	2.00
April	2	Purchased	200	2.20
April	4	Issued	150	
April	6	Purchased	200	2.30
April	11	Issued	150	
April	19	Issued	200	
April	22	Purchased	200	2.40
April	27	Issued	150	

(*Punjabi, B. Com. April 1984-adapted*)

Solution

(*a*) Weighted Average Method

Stores Ledger Account

Date	Reference	Receipts			Issues			Balance		
		Qty.	Rate	Amount	Qty.	Rate	Amount	Qty.	Rate	Amount
		Units	Rs.	Rs.	Rs.	Rs.	Rs.	Units	Rs.	Rs.
April 1	Balance b/d	–	–	–	–	–	–	300	2.00	600
April 2	G.R. Note No....	200	2.20	440	–	–	–	500	2.08	1,040
Apnl 4	M.R. No. ...	–	–	–	150	2.08	312	350	2.08	728
April 6	G.R. Note No. ...	200	2.30	460	–	–	–	550	2.16	1,188
April 11	M.R. No....	–	–	–	150	2.16	324	400	2.16	864
April 19	M.R. No....	–	–	–	200	2.16	432	200	2.16	432
April 22	G.R. Note....	200	2.40	480	–	–	–	400	2.28	912
April 27	M.R. No....	–	–	–	150	2.28	342	250	2.28	570

Stores Ledger Account

(*b*) Last-in-First-out Method

Date	Reference	Receipts			Issues			Balance		
		Qty.	Rate	Amount	Qty.	Rate	Amount	Qty.	Rate	Amount
		Units	Rs.	Rs.	Rs.	Rs.	Rs.	Units	Rs.	Rs.
April 1	Balance b/d	–	–	–	–	–	–	300	2.00	600
April 2	G.R. Note No...	200	2.20	440	–	–	–	300 200	2.00 2.20	600 440
April 4	M.R. No...	–	–	–	150	2.20	330	300 50	2.00 2.20	600 110
April 6	G.R. Note No...	200	2.30	460	–	–	–	300 50 200	2.00 2.20 2.30	600 110 460
April 11	M.R. No.	–	–	–	150	2.30	345	300 50 50	2.00 2.20 2.30	600 110 115
April 19	M.R. No...	–	–	–	50 50 100	2.30 2.20 2.00	115 110 200	200	2.00	400
April 22	G.R. Note...	200	2.40	480	–	–	–	200 200	2.00 2.40	400 480
April 27	M.R. No...	–	–	–	150	2.40	360	200 50	2.00 2.40	400 120

Illustration 18

Record the following transactions in the Stores Ledger, pricing the materials issued by Weighted Average Price Method. Show the balance of inventory after each transaction.

May 1 Balance, 100 units @ 50 P. per unit, Rs. 50.00.
1 Ordered 400 units, expected May 6, Purchase Order 55.
2 Issued 25 units, Reqn. 101, Dept. A.
4 Ordered 200 units, expected May 8, Purchase Order 65.
6 Received 400 units, Purchase Order 55, @ 60 P. per unit.
7 Issued 150 units, Reqn. 105, Production Order 313.
8 Returned to stock-room 10 units from Dept. A, Reqn. 101.
10 Received150 units, Purchase Order 65, @ 75 P. Per unit.
12 Ordered 100 units, Purchase Order 77, expected May 20.
15 Issued 160 units, Reqn. 125, Production Order 328.
18 Received 50 units balance of Purchase Order 65, @ 75 P. per unit.
21 Issued 60 units Reqn. 130, Dept. B.
23 Returned to vender 20 units from Purchase Order 65, received May 18.
25 Received 100 units, Purchase Order 77, @ 50 P. per unit.
27 Freight on Purchase Order 77, Rs. 25.00.
29 Issued 125 units, Reqn. 140. Production Order 354.

(*Pbi. Univ., B.Com. 2007*)

Solution

Weighted Average Price
Stores Ledger Account

Date	Receipts Qty.	Rate	Amount	Issues Qty.	Rate	Amount	Balance Qty.	Rate	Amount
		Rs.	Rs.			Rs.		Rs.	Rs.
May 1							100	0.50	50.00
,, 2				25	0.50	12.50	75	0.50	37.50
,, 4	400	0.60	240.00				475	0.584	277.50
,, 7				150	0.584	87.63	325	0.584	189.87
,, 8	10	0.50	5.00				335	0.582	194.87
,, 10	150	0.75	112.50				485	0.634	307.37
,, 15				160	0.634	101.44	325	0.634	205.93
,, 18	50	0.75	37.50				375	0.649	243.43
,, 21				60	0.659	38.94	315	0.649	204.49
,, 23				20	0.75	15.00	295	0.642	189.49
				Returned					
,, 25	100	0.75	75.00				395	0.669	264.49
,, 29				125	0.669	83.63	270	0.669	180.86

Closing Stock 270 units @ Re. 0.669 = Rs. 180.86

Illustration 19

A manufacturing company charges out stores to jobs on FIFO basis. Among the stores stocked are 'K-type' screws on which a provision for spoilage by rust (based on experience) is made at 1% of the Stores Account balance at the beginning of each month.

Stock is taken physically at three monthly intervals and the balances of Stores Accounts are appropriately adjusted.

On 1st August, 2008 the stock of K-type screws was 10,000 @ Rs. 9.50 per 100 screws. During the next three months, the transactions were as follows:

	Purchases Quantity	Rate per 100	Issued Quantity
August	40,000	Rs. 10	36,600
September	80,000	Rs. 11	81,367
October	1,00,000	Rs. 12	72,282

At the end of October, stock-taking revealed a shortage of 300 screws.

Prepare Stores Ledger Account for the three months ended 30th October, 2008 and state how would you deal with spoilage by rust and shortage revealed by stock-taking.

Solution

'K-Type Screws Stores Account

Date	Particulars	Qty.	Rate per 100	Amount	Date	Particulars	Qty.	Rate per 100	Amount
2008			Rs.	Rs.	2008			Rs.	Rs.
Aug. 1	To Balance b/d	10,000	9.50	950.00	Aug. 1	By Spoliage by Rust	100	9.50	9.50
Aug. 31	To Purchases	40,000	10.00	4,000.00	31	By Issues	9,900	9.50	940.50
					31	By Issues	26,700	10.00	2,670.00
					31	By Balance c/d	13,300	10.00	1,330.00
		50,000		4,950.00			50,000		4,950.00
Sept. 1	To Balance b/d	13,300	10.00	1,330.00	Sept. 1	By Spoilage by Rust	133	10.00	13.30
Sept. 30	To Purchases	80,000	11.00	8,800.00	30	By Issues	13,167	10.00	1,316.70
					30	By Issues	68,200	11.00	7,502.00
					30	By Balance c/d	11,800	11.00	1,298.00
		93,300		10,130.00			93,300		10,130.00
Oct. 1	To Balance b/d	11,800	11.00	1,298.00	Oct. 1	By Spoilage by Rust	118	11.00	12.98
Oct. 31	To Purchases	1,00,000	12.00	12,000.00	Oct. 31	By Issues	11,682	11.00	1,285.02
					Oct. 31	By Issues	60,600	12.00	7,272.00
					Cot. 31	By Shortage	300	12.00	36.00
					Oct. 31	By Balance c/d	39,100	12.00	4,692.00
		1,11.800		13,298.00			1,11.800		13,298.00

TYPICAL PROBLEMS

1. At the beginning of October 2008 Quality Brush Company had in stock 10,000 brushes valued at Rs. 10 each. Further purchases were made during the month as follows:

7th	October	4,000 Brushes @ Rs. 12.50
14th	October	6,000 Brushes @ Rs. 15.00
24th	October	8,000 Brushes @ Rs. 16.50

Issues to shop floor were as follows:

16th October, 16,000 Brushes
28th October, 10,000 Brushes

You are required:

(*a*) to prepare a stores ledger card for the month of October on the assumption that materials were issued on the First-in-First-out principle, and

(*b*) to state the value of closing stock at the end of October if issues are priced at the weighted average method.

(*C.A. Inter*)

Solution

Stores Ledger Card

Date	Reference	Receipts Qty.	Receipts Rate per unit	Receipts Amount	Issues Qty.	Issues Rate per unit	Issues Amount	Balance Qty.	Balance Rate per unit	Balance Amount
2008		Units	Rs.	Rs.	Units	Rs.	Rs.	Units	Rs.	Rs.
Oct. 1	To Balance	–	–	–	–	–	–	10,000	10	1,00,000
Oct. 7	G.R. Note No.	4,000	12.50	50,000	–	–	–	10,000 4,000	10 12.50	1,00,000 50,000
Oct. 14	G.R. Note No.	6,000	15	90,000	–	–	–	10,000 4,000 6,000	10 12.50 15	1,00,000 50,000 90,000
Oct. 16	Requisition Slip No.	–	–	–	10,000 4,000 2,000	10 12.50 15	1,00,000 50,000 30,000	4,000	15	60,000
Oct. 24	G.R. Note No.	8,000	16.50	1,32,000	–	–	–	4,000 8,000	15 16.50	60,000 1,32,000
Oct. 28	Requisition Slip No.	–	–	–	4,000 6,000	15 16.50	60,000 99,000	2,000	16.50	33,000

(*b*) Value of closing stock on Weighted Average Method.

		Rs.
Opening Stock on Oct. 1:	10,000 brushes @ Rs. 10 each	1,00,000
Receipt on Oct. 7	4,000 brushes Rs. 12.50 each	50,000
Receipt on Oct. 14	6,000 brushes @ Rs. 15.00 each	90,000
	Total value of 20,000 brushes	2,40,000

(Average value per brush = $\frac{2,40,000}{20,000}$ = Rs. 12)

Less:		
Issue on Oct. 16	16,000 brushes @ Rs. 12 each	1,92,000
Balance on Oct. 16	4,000 brushes @ Rs. 12 each	48,000
Receipt on Oct. 24	8,000 brushes @ Rs. 16.50	1,32,000
	Total value of 12,000 brushes	1,80,000

(Average value per brush = $\frac{1,80,000}{12,000}$ = Rs. 15 each)

Less: Issue on Oct. 28:	10,000 brushes @ Rs. 15 each	1,50,000
	Value of closing stock of 2,000 brushes (@Rs. 15 each)	30,000

2. Oil India is a bulk distributor of high octane petrol. A periodic inventory of petrol on hand is taken when the books are closed at the end of each month. The following summary of information is available for the month of June, 2008:

	Rs.
Sales:	9,45,000
General administrative cost	25,000
Opening Stock: 1,00,000 litres @ Rs. 3 per litre	3,00,000
Purchases (including freight in)	
June 1 2,00,000 litres @ Rs. 2.85 per litre	
June 30 1,00,000 litres @ Rs. 3.03 per litre	
Closing Stock, June 30:	1,30,000 litres.

Compute the following data by first-in-and first-out, weighted average and last-in and first-out method of inventory costing:

(*a*) Value of inventory on June 30,

(*b*) Amount of the cost of goods sold for June.

(*c*) Profit or loss for June.

(*C.A. Inter*)

Solution

(A) Stores Ledger Account

Date	Receipts			Issues			Balance		
	Qty.	Price per litre	Amount	Qty.	Price per litre	Amount	Qty.	Price per liter	Amount
	(Litres)	Rs.	Rs.	(Litre)	Rs.	Rs.	(Litres)	Rs.	Rs.
June 1	–	–	–	–	–	–	1,00,000	3.00	3,00,000
June 1	2,00,000	2.85	5,70,000	–	–	–	1,00,000 2,00,000	3.00 2.85	3,00,000 5,70,000
Upto June 30	–	–	–	1,00,000 1,70,000	3.00 2.85	3,00,000 4,84,500	30,000	2.85	85,500
June 30	1,00,000	3.03	3,03,000	–	–	–	30,000 1,00,000	2.85 3.03	85,500 3,03,000

Total Value of Closing Inventory Rs. 3,88,500.

(B) Stores Ledger Account

Date	Receipts			Issues			Balance		
	Qty.	Price per litre	Amount	Qty.	Price per litre	Amount	Qty.	Price per litre	Amount
	(Litres)	Rs.	Rs.	(Litre)	Rs.	Rs.	(Litres)	Rs.	Rs.
June 1	–	–	–	–	–	–	1,00,000	3.00	3,00,000
June 1	2,00,000	2.85	5,70,000	–	–	–	3,00,000	2.90	8,70,000
Upto June 30	–	–	–	2,70,000,	2.90	7,83,000	30,000	2.90	87,000
June 30	1,00,000	3.03	3,03,000	–	–	–	1,30,000	3.00	3,90,000

(C) Stores Ledger Account

Date	Receipts			Issues			Balance		
	Qty.	Price per litre	Amount	Qty.	Price per litre	Amount	Qty.	Price per litre	Amount
	(Litres)	Rs.	Rs.	(Litres)	Rs.	Rs.	(Litres)	Rs.	Rs.
June 1	–	–	–	–	–	–	1,00,000	3.00	3,00,000
June 1	2,00,000	2.85	5,70,000	–	–	–	1,00,000 2,00,000	3.00 2.85	3,00,000 5,70,000
Upto June 30	–	–	–	2,00,000 70,000	2.85 3.00	5,70,000 2,10,000	30,000	3.00	90,000
June 30	1,00,000	3.03	3,03,000	–	–	–	30,000 1,00,000	3.00 3.03	90,000 3,03,000

Total Value of closing inventory = Rs. 3,93,000

Statement of Cost of Goods sold (June 2008)

	FIFO method	Weighted Average method	LIFO method
	Rs.	Rs.	Rs.
Inventory on June 1	3,00,000	3,00,000	3,00,000
Add purchases:			
June 1, 2,00,000 litres @ Rs. 2.85 per litre	5,70,000	5,70,000	5,70,000
June 30, 1,00,000 litres @ Rs. 3.30 per litre	3,03,000	3,03,000	3,03,000
	11,73,000	11,73,000	11,73,000
Less: Inventory on June 30	3,88,500	3,90,000	3,93000
Cost of goods sold for June	7,84,500	7,83,000	7,80,000

Statement of Profit (June 2008)

	FIFO method	Weighted Average method	LIFO method
	Rs.	Rs.	Rs.
Sales	9,45,000	9,45,000	9,45,000
Less: Cost of goods sold	7,84,500	7,83,000	7,80,000
Gross profit	1,60,500	1,62,000	1,65,000
Less: General administrative cost	25,000	25,000	25,000
Profit for June	1,35,500	1,37,000	1,40,000

3. The annual accounts of a trading company are to be made upto October 31 but it was not possible to carry out a stock-taking until November at which date the stock was valued at cost at Rs. 68,567.

The following transactions took place between 1st and 5th November:

	Rs.
Goods received	4,600
Goods returned	200
Sales	10,500
Returns by customer	625

The rate of gross profit is 25% of cost.

Prepare a statement to show the valuation of stock as at October 31.

(*I.C.M.A.-Inter-adapted*)

Solution

Since stock of a previous date (i.e., October 31) has to be calculated, reverse order of movement of goods will have to be adopted.

Statement of Stock Valuation (at Cost)

	Rs.	Rs.
Stock as on November 5		68,567
Add back:		
(*a*) Goods returned to suppliers		200
(*b*) Cost of goods sold:	10,500	
Sale price		
Less: Gross Profit		
(at 25% of cost or 20% of sales)	2,100	8,400
		77,167
Deduct:		
(*a*) Goods received	4,600	
(*b*) Goods returned by customer (at cost)	500	5,100
Stock as on October 31		72,067

4. You are presented with the following information by Om Engineering Company related to the first week of Dec., 2003. The transactions in connection with the materials are as follows:

Days	Receipts		Issues
	Units	Rate per Unit	Units
1st	40	15.00	
2nd	20	16.50	
3rd	–	–	30
4th	50	17.10	–
5th	–	–	20
6th	–	–	40

Calculate the cost of materials issued under (*i*) FIFO method (*ii*) LIFO method, and (*iii*) Weighted Average Method of issue of materials and value of closing stock under the methods aforesaid.

(*H.P.U., B.Com., 2004*)

Solution

(*i*) FIFO Method

Stores Ledger Account

Date	Receipts			Issues			Balance		
	Units	Rate Rs. P.	Amount Rs. P.	Units	Rate Rs. P.	Amount Rs. P.	Units	Rate Rs. P.	Amount Rs. P.
2003									
Dec. 1	40	15.00	600.00				40	15.00	600.00
Dec. 2	20	16.50	330.00				40	15.00	600.00
							20	16.50	330.00
Dec. 3				30	15.00	450.00	10	15.00	150.00
							20	16.50	330.00
Dec. 4	50	17.10	855				10	15.00	150.00
							20	16.50	330.00
							50	17.10	855.00
Dec. 5				10	15.00	150			
				10	16.50	165	10	16.50	165.00
							50	17.10	855.00
Dec. 6				10	16.50	165			
				30	17.10	513	20	17.10	342.00

(Closing Stock 20 units @ Rs. 17.10 per unit at a value of Rs. 342.00)

(*ii*) LIFO Method

Date	Receipts Units	Rate	Amount	Issues Units	Rate	Amount	Balance Units	Rate	Amount
2003									
Dec. 1	40	15.00	600.00				40	15.00	600.00
Dec. 2	20	16.50	330.00				40	15.00	600.00
							20	16.50	330.00
Dec. 3				20	16.50	330.00			
				10	15.00	150.00	30	15.00	450.00
Dec. 4	50	17.10	855.00				30	15.00	450.00
							50	17.10	855.00
Dec. 5				20	17.10	342.00	30	15.00	450.00
							30	17.10	513.00
Dec. 6				30	17.10	513.00			
				10	15.00	150.00	20	15.00	300.00

(Closing Stock 20 units @ Rs. 15 per unit valued at Rs. 300)

(*i*) Weighted Average Method

Stores Ledger Account

Date	Receipts Units	Rate	Amount	Issues Units	Rate	Amount	Balance Units	Rate	Amount
2003									
Dec. 1	40	15.00	600.00				40	15.00	600.00
Dec. 2	20	16.50	330.00				60	15.50	930.00
Dec. 3				30	15.50	465.00	30	15.50	465.00
Dec. 4	50	17.10	855.00				80	16.50	1,320.00
Dec. 5				20	16.50	330.00	60	16.50	990.00
Dec. 6				40	16.50	660.00	20	16.50	330.00

(Closing Stock 20 units @ Rs. 16.50 valued at Rs. 330)

OBJECTIVE TYPE QUESTIONS

A. Multiple Choice Question

Select the correct answer in the following cases:

1. According to which of the following methods of pricing, issues are close to current economic values?
(*a*) Last-in-first-out price
(*b*) First-in-first-out price
(*c*) Highest-in-first-out price
(*d*) Weighted average price.

2. In which of the following methods of pricing, costs lag behind the current economic values?
(*a*) Last-in-first-out price
(*b*) First-in-first-out price
(*c*) Replacement price
(*d*) Weighted average price.

3. In which of the following methods, issues of materials are priced at a pre-determined rate?
(*a*) Inflated price method
(*b*) Standard price method
(*c*) Replacement price method.

4. In which of the following methods, materials are issued at the price prevailing at the time of issue?
(*a*) Inflated price method
(*b*) Standard price method
(*c*) Replacement price method
(*d*) Specific price method.

5. When material prices fluctuate widely, the method of pricing that gives absurd results is:
(*a*) Simple average method
(*b*) Weighted average method
(*c*) Inflated price method.

6. When prices fluctuate widely, the method that will smooth out the effect of fluctuations is:
(*a*) Simple average
(*b*) Weighted average
(*c*) FIFO
(*d*) LIFO.

7. In which of the following methods, the charge to production is not at actual cost?

(*a*) Weighted average
(*b*) Standard price
(*c*) Replacement price
(*d*) All of these.

[**Ans.** 1 (*a*); 2 (*b*); 3 (*b*); 4 (*c*); 5 (*a*); 6 (*b*); 7 (*d*)]

8. Given

Opening stock on 1.1.2006	200 kgs. @ Rs. 4 per kg.
Purchased on 4.1.2006	300 kgs. @ Rs. 5 per kg.
Issued on 8.1.2006	350 kgs.
Market Price on 1.1.2006	Rs. 5 per kg.

On the basis of the above information, select the correct answer in each of the following:

(*i*) At what amount materials issued will be charged if FIFO method is used?
(*a*) Rs. 1,100 (*b*) Rs. 1,550
(*c*) Rs. 1,700 (*d*) Rs. 1,750.

(*ii*) At what amount materials issued will be charged if LIFO method is used?
(*a*) Rs. 1,550 (*b*) Rs. 1,575
(*c*) Rs. 1,700 (*d*) Rs. 1,750.

(*iii*) At what amount materials issued will be charged if weighted average price is used?
(*a*) Rs. 1,550 (*b*) 1,610
(*c*) Rs. 1,625 (*d*) None of these.

(*iv*) At what amount materials issued will be charged if replacement price method is used?
(*a*) Rs. 1,550 (*b*) 1,700
(*c*) Rs. 1,750 (*d*) None of these.

(*v*) What will be the value of closing stock under FIFO method?
(*a*) Rs. 600 (*b*) Rs. 675
(*c*) Rs. 700 (*d*) None of these.

(*vi*) What will be the value of closing stock if weighted average method is applied?
(*a*) Rs. 600 (*b*) 690
(*c*) Rs. 725 (*d*) Rs. 750.

[**Ans.** 8. (*i*) (*b*); (*ii*) (*c*); (*iii*) (*b*); (*iv*) (*c*); (*v*) (*d*); (*vi*) (*b*).]

B. 'True' or 'False' type statements

Indicate whether the following statements are true or false:

1. Weighted average method of pricing issues involves adding all the different prices and dividing by the number of such prices.

2. According to replacement price method of material pricing, issues are at the current economic values.
3. Under Fifo method, materials purchased first are deemed to be issued last.
4. Under the Lifo method, materials purchased last are deemed to be issued first.
5. In Fifo method, closing stock is valued at oldest prices of materials.
6. In Lifo method of pricing, the effect of current market prices is reflected in the cost of production.

[**Ans.** 1. False; 2. True; 3. False; 4. True; 5. False; 6. True.]

C. Filling the blanks

Fill in the blanks:

1. Under the .... method, materials are issued to production at a pre-determined price.
2. .... method of pricing the materials evens out the fluctuations in the purchase prices.
3. Under the .... method, a new issue price is determined after each purchase.
4. .... is a special type of discount allowed for bulk purchases.
5. In .... method of pricing, more than one issue price may have to be adopted for pricing a single requisition.

[**Ans.** 1. Standard price; 2. Weighted Average; 3. Weighted Average; 4. Quantity Discount; 5. LIFO.]

SHORT ANSWER TYPE QUESTIONS

Answer the following questions in not more than four lines each.

1. What is meant by inflated price?
2. What are the advantages of weighted average method of pricing the material issues?
3. Of FIFO and LIFO, which do you think is better?
4. Define replacement price.
5. Give at least four factors which are considered while selecting a method of pricing.

LONG ANSWER TYPE QUESTIONS

1. Explain with suitable examples the following methods of pricing issue of materials: (*a*) FIFO (*b*) LIFO. Which of these methods would you recommend under the conditions of rising prices and why?
2. Discuss the various methods of pricing materials issued for production and point out their respective advantages and disadvantages.

   (*G.N.D.U., B.Com., 2000, 2005, 2008*)
3. "The pricing of materials issued to jobs often becomes a complicated affair where materials have been bought from time to time at different prices." Elucidate this statement and discuss any four important methods of pricing materials issued to jobs.
4. In costing, materials may be charged out to jobs at cost price or at market price. Explain which method, in your opinion, is more appropriate.
5. How would you make the valuation of the materials purchased in a manufacturing concern?
6. Write notes on:

   (*a*) HIFO method (*b*) Base Stock method

   (*c*) Replacement cost price method.

   (*d*) NIFO method
7. State briefly the different methods of pricing material issues and indicate their impact on the ascertainment of profits when there is a general tendency of rising prices.

   (*Pbi. Univ., B.Com., 2008*)

EXERCISES

1. A manufacturer bought 1,000 kgs. of material '*x*' Rs. 10 per kg. less 3% trade discount on invoice price. Freight paid was Rs. 500, carriage and cartage Rs. 100 and octroi @ 5% on the invoice price. The expenses of purchase and storage for the year amount to Rs. 5,000. Ascertain the cost of material per kg.

   [**Ans.** Rs. 10.80]
2. From the following Invoice received from the supplier, calculate the material cost per unit;

Quantity	Particulars	Rate	Amount
			Rs.
500 kgs.	Material 'A'	Rs. 20 per kg.	10,000
1,000 kgs.	Material 'B'	Rs. 15 per kg.	15,000
			25,000
	Less: Trade discount @ 3%		750
	Add:		24,250
	Cost of containers (Nos. 15)		300
	Cartage and Carriage		300
	Octroi duty @ 2% on invoice price		500
	Net Amount		25,350

E. & O.E.

Terms :(*i*) 5% cash discount for payment made within one week.

(*ii*) Return value of containers : Rs. 10 each

Dated: 15.10.2009 Sd. xyz

[**Ans.** Material A Rs. 20.10 per kg.; B Material Rs. 15.15 per kg.]

3. From the following invoice received from the supplier, calculate material cost per unit:

Quantity	Particulars	Rate	Amount
			Rs.
150 kgs.	Material 'X'	Rs. 10 per kg.	1,500
100 kgs.	Material 'Y'	Rs. 12 per kg.	1,200
			2,700
	Less: Trade discount		90
	Add:		2,610
	Cost of containers (Capacity of each 50 kgs.)		60
	Cartage and Carriage		75
	Octroi Duty @ 1%		27
	Total		2,772

Terms: (*i*) 5% cash discount for payment within a week.

(*ii*) Return value of containers: Rs. 9 each.

[**Ans.** X = Rs. 10.126; Y = Rs. 12.08 per kg.]

4. A lorry load of material of mixed grades was purchased for Rs. 9,000. These were sorted into the following grades, whose markets rate is shown against each:

	Units	Selling price per Unit
Grade A	5,000	Rs. 1.20
Grade B	3,000	Rs. 1.00
Grade C	2,000	Rs. 0.50

Find out the purchase rate per unit of each grade of material assuming that all grades yield the same rate of profit. *(I.C.W.A. Inter)*

[**Ans.** (A) Rs. 1.08, (B) Re. 0.90, (C) Re. 0.45]

5. E. Ltd., received a consignment of two chemicals viz., M and N. The invoice showed the following:

	Rs.
Chemical M — 8,000 Kgs. @ Rs. 4 per kg.	32,000
Chemical N — 6,000 Kgs. @ Rs. 3 per kg.	18,000
	50,000
Less Quantity discount	2,000
Other charges:	48,000
Sales tax, duty and insurance	2,500
Containers (returnable at 75% of their value)	350
Carriage etc.	140
Freight	210
Total	51,200

5% cash discount on payment within a week.

500 Kgs. of each material were found short on account of theft in transit. Calculate cost per unit of each chemical. The company provides 5% for further deterioration.

[**Ans.** Cost per kg. M = Rs. 4.29, N = Rs. 3.22]

6. A manufacturer of Surat purchased three chemicals A, B and C from Bombay. The invoice gave the following information:

	Rs.
Chemical A: 3,000 kg. Rs. 4.20 per kg.	12,600
Chemical B: 5,000 kg. @ Rs. 3.80 per kg.	19,000
Chemical C: 2,000 kg. @ Rs. 4.75 per kg.	9,500
Sales Tax	2,055
Railway Freight .	1,000
Total Cost	44,155

A shortage of 200 kg. in Chemical A, of 280 kg. in Chemical B and of 100 kg. in Chemical C was noticed due to breakages. At Surat, the manufacturer paid octroi duty @ Rs. 0.10 per kg. He also paid cartage Rs. 22 for Chemical A, Rs. 63.12 for Chemical B and Rs. 31.80 for

Chemical C. Calculate the stock rate that you would suggest for pricing issue of chemical assuming a provision of 5% towards further deterioration.

(C.A. Inter, Nov. 1991)

[**Ans.** Issue Price per kg. Chemical A = Rs. 5.20 ; Chemical B = Rs. 4.68; Chemical C = Rs. 5.76].

7. A manufacturing organisation has imported four types of materials. The invoice reveals the following data:

	Quantity Kgs.	Rate U.S. $ per kg.
Material A	1,000	1.50
B	2,000	1.25
C	1,500	2.00
D	3,000	1.00
Import duty	....	23% of invoice value
Insurance	....	2% of invoice value.
Freight and Clearing	....	Rs. 30,000
Exchange Rate U.S. $ 1 = Rs. 16.00		

50% of the materials imported are issued to production centres. While determining the value of closing stock 5% allowance is provided to cover up storage loss. Determine the value of closing stock of each type of materials.

(I.C.W.A. Inter, Dec. 1989)

[**Ans.** Value of Closing Stock Material A = Rs. 16,150; Material B = Rs. 27,550; Material C = Rs. 31,350 ; Material D = Rs. 34,200]

[**Hint.** Apportion freight and clearing charges on the basis of quantity of different types of materials.]

8. 2,000 kgs. of wool costing Rs. 72,000 was issued for the manufacture of 40" size pullover. On the completion of manufacture of pullovers, the following information is available:

(*a*) 1,600 good pullovers 40" size of 1 kg. each were manufactured.

(*b*) 50 kgs. of wool is scrapped and realised Rs. 700.

(*c*) 100 kgs. of off-cuts were used in the manufacture of another variety hosiery. The market value of this is Rs. 1,800.

(*d*) 200 pullovers were found defective and were rectified at an additional material cost of Rs. 500.

Your are required to ascertain the cost of material of one pullover.

[**Ans.** Rs. 38.89 per pullover]

9. The following quotation is received from a supplier in respect of material 'Y':

Lot size	Rate per kg.
100 kgs.	Rs. 10
500 kgs.	Rs. 9
1,000 kgs.	Rs. 8

Trade discount is 20% and cash discount 5%, if payment is made within 10 days. One container is required for every 100 kgs. of material and containers are charged @ Rs. 10 each, but credited with Rs. 9 each, if returned within one month. Transportation charges for any order are Rs. 50. Assuming the company makes the payment within the due date, calculate the material cost when the company purchases 500 kgs. of material.

(*B.Com. Banglore 1998*)

[**Ans.** Rs. 7.31 per kg.]

10. The stock of material A as at 1st April, 2004 is 500 units @ Re. 1 per unit. Following purchases and issues of this item were made subsequently. Prepare Stores ledger A/cs under FIFO and LIFO methods.

Purchases			Issues	
Date	**Units**	**Rate**	**Date**	**Units**
2004			**2004**	
April 6	100	1.10	April 9	500
April 20	700	1.20	April 22	500
April 27	400	1.30	April 30	500
May 13	1,000	1.40	May 15	500
May 20	500	1.50	May 22	500
June 17	400	1.60	June 18	500
June 28	600	1.70	June 29	500

[**Ans.** (*i*) Stock in hand 700 units, under FIFO method – 100 units @ Rs. 1.60 and 600 units @ Rs. 1.70

(*ii*) Stock in hand 700 units, under LIFO method –
100 units@ Rs. 1.10
100 unitsRs. 1.20
400 units Rs. 1.40
100 units Rs. 1.70]

11. From the following particulars relating to material A, show how the value of the issues should be arrived at under FIFO method.

1.1. 05	Opening stock 1,000 units at Rs. 5 each.
3.1. 05	Purchased 900 units at Rs. 6 each.
7.1. 05	Issued to Job No. 137, 1,200 units vide M.R. No. 034.
11.1. 05	Purchased 800 units at Rs 6.20 each.
13.1. 05	Purchased 300 units at Rs. 6.40 each
15.1. 05	Issued 400 units to Job No. 141 vide M.R. No. 042.
17.1. 05	Issued 600 units to Job No. 147 vide M.R. No. 048.
19.1. 05	Purchased 200 units at Rs. 6.50 each,
25.1. 05	Issued 600 units to Job No. 150 vide M.R. No. 072.

[**Ans.** Closing stock units 400 Value Rs. 2,580]

12. Prepare the store ledger account for the month of September, 2008 from the following transactions, relating to the receipt and issue of materials on the basis of:

(*a*) Simple Average Price.
(*b*) Weighted Average Price.

Receipts

Date	Quantity	Rate
4.9.2008	200 kg.	Rs. 10 per kg.
18.9.2008	300 kg.	Rs. 12 per kg.
22.9.2008	100 kg	Rs. 16 per kg.
Issues		
6.9.2008	100 kg.	
20.9.2008	200 kg.	
25.9.2008	300 kg.	

[**Ans.** 18th Sept. 22nd Sept.
(*a*) Simple Average Price = Rs. 11.00 Rs. 14.00.
(*b*) Weighted Average Price Rs. 11.50 Rs. 13.00]

13. Following transactions are recorded in respect of a store item:

Date	Receipts kgs.	Rate per unit Rs.	Issues kgs.
3.12.2008	400	1.00	–
11.12.2008	600	1.20	
16.12.2008	–	–	500
19.12.2008	500	1.30	
30.12.2008	–	–	400

Prepare a stores ledger account, pricing the issues at weighted average method.

[**Ans.** Balance Qty. = 600 units
Rate = 1.21 P = Rs. 726]

14. Prepare the Stores Ledger Account by using weighted average method in respect of a material item R during the six months ended on Dec. 31, 2008.

Month	Purchases	Price per Kg.	Issues
	kg.	Rs.	kg.
July	220	2.50	250
August	250	2.40	220
September	240	2.60	200
October	220	2.30	240
November	260	2.50	210
December	200	2.275	210

The opening stock on July 1 was 240 kg. @ Rs. 2.40 per kg.
The closing stock on December, 31 was 300 kg. @ Rs. 2.38 per kg.

[**Ans.** Balance 300 kgs. value = Rs. 716.]

15. Record the following transactions pricing the materials issued according to (*i*) FIFO and (*ii*) LIFO. Show the balance after each transaction and the inventory value on September, 30, 2008.

July	1.	Balance, 1000 units @ Re. 1 per unit.
July	15.	Ordered 500 units, purchase order No. 701. Expected July 20.
July	18.	Issued 250 units, M.R. No. 251 to Department X.
July	21.	Received 300 units, Purchase Order No. 701 @ Re. 1.10 per unit.
July	25	Ordered 500 units, Purchase Order No. 725. Expected August 5.
August	1.	Issued 350 units, M.R. No. 260 to Department Y.
August	10.	Received 400 units, Purchase Order No. 725, @ Re. 1.20 per unit
August	20.	It was discovered that 10 units received on July 21, Purchase Order No. 701, were defective. They were returned to the vendors.
September	1.	Received 200 units, the balance of Purchase order No. 701, @ Rs. 1.10 per unit.
September	15.	Issued 200 units, M.R. No. 275, to Department Z.
September	20.	Department Z returned to stock room for credit, 50 units which were issued on Sept. 15.
September	30.	Issued 250 units M.R. No. 285 to Department X.

[**Ans. 1.** FIFO method Stock in Hand:
290 units@ 1.10, 400 units@1.20, 200 units@ 1.10 = Rs. 1,019.00
2. LIFO method Stock in Hand
700 units@ 1.00, 190 units@ 1.20 = Rs. 928.00]

16. The following information is available in respect of purchase and issue of materials during the month of November, 2008.

Purchases	**Issues**
November 2 .... 200 units Rs. 2.00 per unit,	November 15 .... 250 units
November 10 .... 300 units Rs. 2.40 per unit	November 20 .... 200 units.
November 18 .... 250 units Rs. 2.60 per unit.	

Prepare the Stores Ledger Account showing base stock method of inventory valuation along with LIFO and FIFO methods of pricing materials issued. The normal base quantity is 100 units.

[**Ans.** LIFO:		FIFO:
Qty. in hand	= 300 units	300 units
Value	= Rs. 650	Value Rs. 720]

17. From the following details of stores receipts and issues of material "EXE" in a manufacturing unit, prepare the Stock Ledger using 'Weighted Average' method of valuing the issues:

Nov. 1 Opening stock 2,000 units @ Rs. 5.00 each.
Nov. 3 Issued 1,500 units to Production.
Nov. 4 Received 4,500 units @ Rs. 6.00 each
Nov. 8 Issued 1,600 units to Production
Nov. 9 Returned to stores 100 units by Production Department (from the issues of Nov. 3)
Nov.16 Received 2,400 units @ 6.50 each
Nov. 19 Returned to supplier 200 units out of the quantity received on Nov. 4
Nov. 20 Received 1,000 units Rs. 7.00 each
Nov. 24 Issued to Production 2,100 units
Nov. 27 Received 1,200 units Rs. 7.50 each
Nov. 29 Issued to Production 2,800 units (Use rates upto two decimal places).

(*I.C.W.A. Inter, June 1988*)

[**Ans.** Value of Closing Stock Rs. 19,558]

18. The following information is provided by Sunrise Industries for the fortnight of April, 2008:

Material Exe:

Stock on 1.4.2008 100 units at Rs. 5 per unit.

Purchases

5.4.08	300 units at Rs. 6
8.4.08	500 units at Rs. 7
12.04.08	600 units at Rs. 8

Issues

6.4.08 50 units
10.4.08 400 units
14.4.08 500 units

Required:

(A) Calculate using FIFO and LIFO method of pricing issues

(*a*) the value of materials consumed during the period

(*b*) the value of stock of materials on 15.4.08

(B) Explain why the figures in (*a*) and (*b*) in part (A) of this question are different under the two methods of pricing of material issues used. You need not draw up the Stores Ledger.

(*C.A. Inter, May 1989*)

[**Ans.** (A) (*a*) Value of Materials consumed: Under FIFO Method Rs. 7,800 and Under LIFO Method Rs. 8,300; (*b*) Value of Stock Under FIFO Method Rs. 2,800 and Under LIFO Method Rs. 2,300]

19. The Stock Ledger Account for material 'X' in a manufacturing concern reveals the following data for the quarter ended September 30, 2008:

	Receipts		Issues	
	Quantity Units	**Price per Unit**	**Quantity Units**	**Amount Rs.**
June 1 Balance b/d	1,600	2.00	–	–
June 9	3,000	2.20	–	–
July 13	–	–	1,200	2,556
August 5	–	–	900	917
August 17	3,600	2.40	–	–
August 24	–	–	1,800	4,122
September 11	2,500	2.50	–	–
September 27	–	–	2,100	4,971
September 29	–	–	700	1,656

Physical verification on September 30, 2008 revealed an actual stock of 3,800 units. You are required to:

(*a*) Indicate the method of pricing employed in the above.

(*b*) Complete the above account by making entries you would consider necessary including adjustments, if any, and giving explanations for such adjustments. (*I.C.W.A. Inter, June 1990*)

[**Ans.** (*a*) Weighted Average Method; (*b*) Value of Shortage on September 30, 2008 = Rs. 473 *i.e.*, 200 units @ Rs. 2.37; Value of Closing Stock = Rs. 8,995 *i.e.* 3,800 unit Rs. 2.37 per unit]

6

Labour

INTRODUCTION

Labour cost or wages is the second main element of cost. The Institute of Cost and Management Accountants of U.K., has defined labour cost as "the cost of remuneration of the employees of an undertaking". Labour cost refers to any remuneration paid to the employees in the form of wages, salary, commission, bonus, perquisites, allowances etc. Labour cost may be direct labour cost or indirect labour cost. Direct labour cost is the remuneration of the employees who are directly connected with the manufacturing operations or the conversion of raw materials into finished products. Indirect labour cost is the remuneration of the employees who are not directly connected with manufacturing operations. The important characteristic of direct labour cost (direct wages) is that it can be identified with and allocated to cost centres or cost units. Direct labour cost is incurred for converting raw materials into finished goods. On the other hand, indirect labour cost (indirect wages) cannot be allocated but can be apportioned to or absorbed by cost centres or cost units.

Direct labour cost is also known as 'Productive Wages', 'Process Wages', 'Factory Wages' , 'Manufacturing Wages' or 'Operating Wages'. Direct labour cost is part of 'Prime Cost' while indirect labour cost is treated as part of overhead.

CONTROL OVER LABOUR COST

Control over labour costs requires proper employment and efficient utilisation of labour force. These factors affect the cost and quality of the products of any industrial undertaking and ultimately its profitability. Labour cost control involves employment of efficient workers, proper training of workers, proper time-keeping and time-booking and proper accounting for the wages paid to them.

In a large industrial organisation, control over labour costs is exercised by the following departments:

1. Personnel Department.

2. Engineering and Works Study Department.
3. Time-Keeping Department.
4. Pay-roll Department.
5. Cost Accounting Department.

PERSONNEL DEPARTMENT

Generally, every business has a recruitment policy of its own. However, the general factors governing the recruitment policy of an undertaking are the type of activities undertaken, categories of workers required, volume of operations, seasonal nature of activities, promotions and retirement, rate of labour turnover, legal restrictions arising out of labour legislation etc. For the execution of the recruitment policy of an undertaking, a separate Personnel Department is set up under the headship of a Personnel Manager. The main functions of Personnel Department are recruitment, selection, training, transfers, discharge, promotion and fixation of wages of workmen.

LABOUR PLACEMENT REQUISITION

If in any department, vacancy has been caused within the allowed establishment, the departmental head or manager will send a formal written request to the personnel department in the form of a Labour Placement Requisition. The specimen of a Labour Placement Requisition is shown below:

AB Co. Ltd.

Labour Placement Requisition

Department.......................... Requisition No. ....

Date..

Please arrange workers of the following categories for my department with effect from .... in accordance with the original/revised labour budget.

No. of Workers Requisitioned	Category	Job Specification	Description	Remarks

Requisitioned by........................ Approved by.........................

On receiving the Labour Placement Requisition, the personnel manager arranges for the advertisement in trade journals or newspapers about the requirement of workers or sends a requisition to the employment exchange. Formal applications are received from the candidates and after proper interview, appointments are made. In case of a small organisation, recruitment is made in an informal manner by the departmental head or the factory manager directly.

On the appointment of workers, the personnel department informs the departments concerned about it. When a worker joins the factory, he is allotted a clock number and he is then known by this number. Name of the department, rate of pay, clock number, category etc., of each worker are furnished to pay-roll department.

PERSONNEL RECORD CARD (WORKER'S HISTORY CARD)

For each person employed, the personnel department prepares Personnel Record Card or Worker's History Card which shows the particulars of the employee, name and address of previous employer, cause of leaving the previous employment, previous experience, date of appointment, date of joining and wage rate at commencement.

The details of the following particulars are also recorded in the Personnel Record Card from time to time:

(*i*) Change in the name or address,
(*ii*) Change in the wage rates,
(*iii*) Promotion, transfers,
(*iv*) Sickness and accidents,
(*v*) Date and reasons for leaving the job.

The specimen of personnel record card is given below:

AB Co. Ltd.
Personnel Record Card

Name....................................	Clock No. ....
Father's Name....................................	Date of Appointment....................................
Residential Address:	Date of Joining....................................
Permanent....................................	Date of Birth....................................
Local....................................	Marital Status....................................
References....................................	No. of Children....................................
1.	Height.................... Weight....................
2.	Name of Previous Employer....................................
	Reasons for Leaving
	Previous Employment....................................

Date	Department	Rank	Pay Scale	Present Pay	Allowances

Attendance and Work

Year	Days Absent		Days Sick	Accidents	O.T. Hours	Rewards	Merit rating
	With Pay	Without Pay					

Remarks.................................... Date Left....................................
Reasons for leaving....................................

Engineering and Works Study Department: In order to ensure proper utilisation of labour force in an industrial undertaking, it is necessary to make the use of proper production methods and to provide healthy working conditions to the workers. For this purpose, an Engineering and Works Study Department is set up. This department helps in maintaining control over working conditions, production method, performance on jobs etc., by performing the following functions:

(*a*) Preparing plans and laying down specification for each job scheduled for production.
(*b*) Maintaining safe and efficient working conditions.
(*c*) Initiating and supervising research and experimental work.
(*d*) Undertaking work studies, such as method study, motion study and time study for each operation and job.
(*e*) Undertaking job analysis and job studies.
(*f*) Determining piece work rates.
(*g*) Examining the results of incentive plans introduced in the organisation.

The Engineering and Works Study Department is basically responsible for making work study which comprises the function of studying in detail the technical aspects of production. Work study refers to any method of investigation designed to provide better job of machine performance within a required operation. Work study is made whenever there is a new labour operation or when there is a change in machine, method of operation, types of labour employed or system of wage payment. Work study is carried on to attain the objectives of material conservation, efficient working, time saving, changes in quality, lowest cost etc.

Work Study involves two techniques:

(*i*) Method Study, and (*ii*) Time Study.

Method Study: Method study refers to a systematic procedure for the analysis of work to reduce or eliminate unnecessary work, arrange the remaining work in the best order possible and standardise the usage of proper work methods. Method study involves the systematic recording of the details of the existing methods of work, analytical examination of the existing and proposed methods of doing a work and developing and applying new and improved methods of work for simplifying the existing methods and utilising the available resources in a better way.

Motion Study: Work study also includes the application of motion study. Motion study consists of dividing a work into the most fundamental elements possible, studying these elements separately and in relation to one another and building the method of least waste from the studied elements. Thus, motion study is concerned with the finding out of the most scientific and simple way of performing an operation by eliminating all unnecessary movements and reducing fatigue element. Motion study takes into consideration materials, machines, tools and equipments besides the most important human element.

Time Study: Time study involves the determination of standard time for an operation by direct time measurement. For this purpose, 10 to 12 observations are made for each labour operation and an average time is computed. For the purpose of determining the standard time, due consideration is given to absolutely necessary labour movements, proper tools, proper working conditions and trained, efficient and skilled workers.

Job Analysis: Jobs analysis is also one of the most important functions of Engineering and Works Study Department. It involves the preparation of a description and classification of each job, with a list of qualifications needed by workers to carry on an operation satisfactorily. The job analysis enables the personnel department to assess its labour requirements and assign the best available person to each job.

Thus, work study enables the management to reduce cost through proper planning and controlling output and wages.

TIME-KEEPING DEPARTMENT

For efficient labour organisation, it is necessary that all workers including those who are paid on piece work basis should be punctual. Late arrival or early departure of a worker causes disturbance even as regards the work of others. It is, therefore, necessary to have a good system of recording the time of arrival and departure of workers whether they are paid on the basis of time or piece work. For the purpose of exercising control over arrival and departure of workers, a separate Time-Keeping Department is set up under the headship of a 'Time-Keeper'.

PURPOSE OF TIME-KEEPING

The purpose of time recording or time-keeping is to provide basic data for:

(*i*) Calculation of the wages of time workers.
(*ii*) Ascertainment of labour cost of an operation, product or service.
(*iii*) Maintenance of discipline in attendance.
(*iv*) Distribution of overhead costs if based on wages or labour hours.
(*v*) Attendance records to meet statutory requirements.
(*vi*) Statistical analysis for determining productivity and control of labour cost.

METHODS OF RECORDING TIME

Time recording may be made either manually or mechanically according to the size of the organisation. The principal methods are as follows:

1. **Attendance Register or Muster Roll:** Under this method, each worker is required to sign the Attendance Register upon arrival and departure noting the time in or time out. Instead of the worker signing Attendance Register himself, the time-keeper or foreman or the supervisor may record the time of arrival and departure of workers. This is the oldest method and is suitable where the number of workers is small. There is no possibility of any fraud or mischief unless there is collusion between the worker and the supervisor. But sometimes a worker may dispute the accuracy of the register.
2. **Metal Disc Method:** Under this method, each worker is allotted a number and is supplied with a metal disc or token bearing his number. All the discs or tokens of the workers employed in the factory are hung on a board (kept near the factory gate) on hooks bearing numbers corresponding to those of the discs. On entering the factory, each worker picks up his own disc and drops it into a box which is kept nearby. After the appointed time say 8 a.m., the box is removed and another box is substituted for late corners. This box is removed at the end of the maximum late period allowed. The time of the arrival of each workman is later on noted by the time-keeper in the Attendance Register. This method is useful where the number of workers is not very large. But it suffers from the following drawbacks:
   (*i*) A worker may try to get his friends marked present by dropping their discs in the box.
   (*ii*) If the workers go out for lunch, the process of hanging the discs or taking back on the board will have to be repeated.
   (*iii*) There may be disputes regarding the exact time of arrival of workers, particularly in case of workers coming late.
3. **Time Recording Machines:** In order to avoid the disadvantages of metal disc method, time recording machines are installed. Under this method, each worker is allotted a weekly time card or clock card. All the cards are arranged systematically in the 'Out' tray. On arrival the worker picks up his card from 'Out' tray, inserts it in the clock, gets the exact time of his arrival printed and puts the card in the 'In' tray. The cards remaining in the 'Out' tray will reveal the number of absentees. Similarly, the departure time of workers may be recorded. Late arrival and early departure is printed on the time card in red ink so as to attract the immediate attention of the persons connected with the preparation of wages sheets.

   The main advantage of this method is that exact time of arrival and departure is recorded on the time card and as such there is no possibility of any dispute. But under this method also, a worker may try to get his friends marked present by inserting their cards also in the time recorder. In order to prevent such possibility the time-keeper should be very careful.

Specimen of Time Card or Clock Card

Time Card
A.B. Co. Ltd.

Clock No. ....
Name of Worker................................. Week Ending............................
Department..................................

Day		In	Out	Ordinary	Overtime	Total Hrs.	
						Ordinary	Overtime
Mon.	A.M.						
	P.M.						
Tue.	A.M.						
	P.M.						
Wed.	A.M.						
	P.M.						
Thurs.	A.M.						
	P.M.						
Fri.	A.M.						
	P.M.						
Sat.	A.M.						
	P.M.						

Time Keeper................................. Wages Clerk.................................

4. **Dial Time Recorders:** This type of time recorder has a dial (around the clock), around the edge of which are about 150 holes, each of which bears a number corresponding to the clock number of the worker concerned. In the centre of the dial, there is a radial arm. On entering the factory, the worker has to swing the radial arm and press it into the hole allotted to him. As a result of this operation the time is automatically recorded on a roll of paper inside the machine against the clock number of the worker. Thus the use of a separate time card for each worker is not made under this method.

   But under this method, a worker cannot see the time recorded on the roll of paper inside the machine which may give rise to disputes afterwards.

5. **Key Recorders:** The key recorder is a type of time recorder having a number of keys, each key bearing the clock number of a worker. When a worker enters the factory, he inserts his particular key in the key-hole and gives a turn to it as a result of which the clock number and the clock time are recorded on a sheet of paper kept inside the key recorder. Like dial time recorder, there is no need to keep separate time cards for the workers. But the main problem of this mechanism is that the worker himself is not in a position to see and check his time of arrival and departure as recorded on the sheet of paper inside the recorder.

TIME-BOOKING

Since the main purpose of costing is to find out the true cost of each unit, job or work-order, it is necessary to record the time spent by each worker on each job, work- order or process and the particulars of the work done, in addition to the recording of the attendance of the workers. It is known as 'Time Booking'. In other words, time-booking refers to the analysis of the time of direct workers job-wise. This analysis is also necessary from the point of view of checking the wastage of time and ensuring the proper utilisation of the time paid for. Time-booking is done by means of various cards known as 'Labour Time Records'. The Institute of Cost and Management Accountants, U.K., has defined a 'Labour Time Record' as "a document which records the amount of time spent by an employee, showing the analysis between a number of activities during a payment period. It may record the wages (labour cost) of the time spent."

Time-booking may be made either manually or mechanically according to the size of the organisation. The following are the general methods of booking the time taken on individual jobs:

(*a*) Daily Time Sheet.
(*b*) Weekly Time Sheet.
(*c*) Job Card (for each worker)
(*d*) Job Card for each Job.

(*a*) Daily Time Sheet: Daily Time Sheet is the daily record of the work done by a worker, showing the time spent on different jobs separately. Daily time sheets are generally used in small concerns where the number of workers as well as the number of jobs handled by them are very few. This time sheet is completed by the worker daily and handed over to the foreman who certifies its correctness. The specimen of a Daily Time Sheet is given below:

Daily Time Sheet
A.B. Co. Ltd.

Clock No. .... Week No. ....
Name of the worker........................... Date..
Department...

Work Order No.	**Description of work**	**Qty. of work done**	**Time**		**Total Hours**	**For cost office**			
			On	**Off**		**Rate**		**Amount**	
						Rs.	P.	Rs.	P.

Signature of Worker................ Certified (Foreman)................Calculated by................................
Cost Office Reference..................

(b) Weekly Time Sheet: Weekly Time Sheet is the weekly record of the work done by a worker showing the time spent on different jobs separately. Weekly Time Sheet is completed by the worker at the end of the week as a result of which the number of documents to be prepared is considerably reduced. But as the time sheet is completed at the end of the week, errors in charging time to jobs are likely to occur and the periods of idle time are likely to be forgotten. Hence, this method is not very advantageous but it is extensively used in contract costing *e.g.,* builders, decorators, civil engineers etc. The specimen of Weekly Time Sheet is given below:

Weekly Time Sheet
A.B. Co. Ltd.

Clock No. ....
Name of the worker........................
Department...................................... Week Ending...........................

Day	Job No.	Description of work	Qty. of work done	Time		Total Hours	For cost office	
				On	Off		Rate	Amount
Mon.							Rs. P.	Rs. P.
Tue.								
Wed.								
Thu.								
Fri.								
Sat.								

Signature of Worker................. Certified (Foreman)................Calculated by...............................
Cost Office Reference.................

(c) Job card (For each worker): Under this method, each worker is given a Job Card at the beginning of each week which records the time spent by him on each job during the week. The job numbers are entered on the Job Card either by the foreman or the departmental clerk while the time of starting and completing each job is automatically printed by the time recording machine. At the end of the week, the Job Card is handed over by each worker to the time-keeper who sends it to the wages office and a new card is issued to each worker for the next week. Following is the specimen of a Job Card:

Job Card **A.B. Co. Ltd.**							
Name of the worker.................. Clock No. .... Department......................................				Week Ending............................ Rate..			
Day	**Job No.**	**Brief Description**	**Time**		**Total (Hours)**	**Amount**	
			On	**Off**		Rs.	P.
Mon. Tue. Wed. Thus. Fri. Sat.							
Foreman.................................					Cost Clerk................................. Wages Abstract by....................		

Sometimes the Job Card may be combined with the Time Card. This card recording both, the attendance time and work of a worker is known as 'Combined Time and Job Card' or 'Time and Job Card'.

(*d*) **Job Card for each Job:** This card is issued to record the time spent by different workers on one job so as to show the total labour cost against the individual job. This card travels with the job from worker to worker and is used in those factories where the number of jobs is fairly large and each job passes through different workers. In case a factory uses Job Card for each job, there shall be no need to prepare Wages Abstract in order to ascertain the total labour cost of different jobs. The specimen of such card is given below:

Job Card **A.B. Co. Ltd.**								
Job No. .... Job Description.......................... Started on..................................				Completed on..................................				
Dept.	**Worker No.**	**Time**		**Total Hours**	**Rate**		**Amount**	
		On	**Off**		**Rs.**	**P.**	**Rs.**	**P.**
Total for the Job.................................				Foremen.................................				

PIECE-WORK CARD

In a factory where the workers are paid on the basis of piece work, a Piece-work Card is issued to each worker . On the Piece-work Card, a worker gets recorded the quantity of output done and the time spent upon it in very much the same manner as that in which a worker paid on time basis gets his activities recorded on the Job Card. The worker's output is checked by the Piece-work Inspector who puts his signature on the Piece-work Card if the same is found to be in order.

Piece-Work Card
A.B. Co. Ltd.

Clock No. .... Week Ending....................................
Name of worker.................................... Rate....................................
Department....................................

Day	Time		Total No. of units	No. of units Rejected	No. of units Accepted	Amount	
	On	Off				Rs.	P.
Mon.							
Tue.							
Wed.							
Thu.							
Fri.							
Sat.							

Worker....................................
Inspector.................................... Foreman....................................

PAY-ROLL DEPARTMENT (OR PAY-MASTER'S DEPARTMENT OR WAGES OFFICE)

The pay-roll department is set up for computation and disbursement of wages in a business concern. Pay-roll department is concerned with the computation of gross wages of the workers and making necessary adjustments with a view to ascertain the net amount of wages payable to them. The main functions of pay-roll department are:

(*i*) To maintain a record of the job classification, department and wage rate for each worker.

(*ii*) To verify and summarise the time of each worker as shown by the Daily Time Card.

(*iii*) To calculate the amount of wages earned by each worker.

(*iv*) To prepare the pay-roll or wages sheet for each department showing:

  (*a*) the total amount of wages earned by each worker during a given period.

  (*b*) the various deductions made from the gross wages.

  (*c*) the net amount of wages payable to each worker.

(*v*) To maintain permanent pay-roll records for each worker.

(*vi*) To make the disbursement of wages and salaries to the workers.

Preparation of Wages Sheet or Pay-Rolls

The Wages Sheet is a record of:

(*i*) The gross wages earned by each worker during a particular pay period.

(*ii*) The deductions made therefrom *e.g.,* provident fund contribution, contribution towards Employees' State Insurance (E.S.I.), fines, house rent, co-operative society dues and the recovery of advances, and

(*iii*) The Net Wages payable to him.

When wages are paid on the basis of time, the Wages Sheet is prepared on the basis of Time Cards or Clock Cards. But when the workers are paid on the basis of output, the Wages Sheet is prepared on the basis of Piece-work Cards. Wages Sheets are prepared department-wise, and their preparation is the responsibility of the Wages Office (Pay-Roll Department) which is under the control of Costing Department.

After their completion, the Wages Sheets are passed on to the cashier for the payment of wages to the workers. The specimen of wages sheet is given below:

Cost Centre/Department.............................. Week Ended.............................

Wages Sheet
A.B. Co. Ltd.

Serial No.	Clock No.	Name of Worker	Total Hours Worked	Total units produced	Rate		Wages				Deductions						Net Wages
					Per hour	Per unit	Basic Rs. P.	D.A. Rs. P.	Bonus Rs. P.	Gross Wages Rs. P.	P.F. Rs. P.	E.S.I. Rs. P.	Fines Rs. P.	Advance Rs. P.	Others Rs. P.	Total Rs. P.	Rs. P.
		Total															

Wages Sheet made by..............................
Wages Sheet checked by.........................
Wages Calculated by..............................

Calculations checked by..............................
Paid by...
In the presence of...

Payment of Wages

A proper system of internal check is suggested in order to avoid the possibility of misappropriation of money by including dummy names in the wages sheet. Different persons should be enstrusted to the job of filling different columns and final compilation of the wages sheet. This will considerably reduce the possibility of collusion among the workers. The usual causes of frauds and errors in connection with the preparation of wages sheets and payment of wages are:

(*a*) The inclusion of fictitious names or 'dummy workers' in the wages sheet;
(*b*) Errors or frauds in time and piece-work records;
(*c*) Over-statement of rates of wages; and
(*d*) Under-statement of deductions, etc.

The following guidelines are suggested in order to prevent the possibility of frauds and errors in connection with the payment of wages:

1. There should be a proper and efficient system for maintaining the records of the time spent by workers and actual work performed by them by means of Time Card and Piece-work Card.
2. A proper reconciliation of Job cards and Time cards should be made for knowing accurate time spent by a worker on a job.
3. The wages sheets should include details regarding each worker's number, name, total hours worked, total units produced, rate of wages, amount of wages, allowances, bonus, gross wages, deductions and net amount payable to a worker.
4. The work of compilation of wages sheets must be assigned to a number of clerks. A set of clerks should fill in the clock numbers, names, total time spent, total units produced, rate of wages and deductions to be made. These should then be checked by another set of clerks who should also work out the gross wages and the net amount payable. Another clerk should then check these sheets in respect of rates, calculations and costs.
5. All the persons involved in the preparation of wages sheets should put their initials on the sheets so that responsibility may rest upon them individually, if any error is discovered later on.
6. All the wages sheets should be counter-signed by Works Manager, or a partner or a director of the concern.
7. The wages cheque should be drawn for the exact amount which is shown under the column 'Net Wages.'
8. The wages cheque should be drawn by a person who is not involved in the preparation of wages sheets at any stage.

9. Each worker's wages should be kept in a separate envelope by indicating the name of the worker and the amount contained therein.
10. The foreman of each department should be present at the time of payment, to prevent impersonation for any absent worker.
11. Each worker should be personally present to receive his wages.
12. Wages of the absentees must not be paid to the foreman or a fellow worker in any case.
13. Unclaimed wages should be properly enquired and credited to 'Unpaid Wages' Account. Then, these should be deposited into a separate bank account.
14. The payment of wages to the casual workers should be made in the presence of a responsible official in order to avoid the possibility of any fraud or error in payment.
15. Payment of wages should be made department–wise in the presence of foreman. A pay slip should be given to each employee containing details regarding net wages payable to him.

COST ACCOUNTING DEPARTMENT

Cost accounting department is responsible for the accumulation, classification and analysis of cost data in a business concern following the cost accounting system. Labour cost is one of the important elements of total cost. In a large business concern, representatives of the cost accounting department are located in production department in order to make proper accumulation, classification and analysis of labour costs. These representatives work under the direct supervision and control of the Cost Accountant. They assist the Cost Accountant in computing the labour cost of production by departments, processes, operations, production orders, jobs etc.

PREPARATION OF WAGES ABSTRACT OR WAGES ANALYSIS SHEET

In a factory, a job card is issued to each worker which records the time spent by him on various jobs during the week and the amount of wages payable to him. In order to ascertain the labour cost of all the jobs undertaken during a particular period of time (say, a week), an analysis of Job Cards is made by the Cost Department. Such an analysis is known as Wages Abstract or Wages Analysis Sheet, shown as below:

Wages Abstract A.B. Co. Ltd. Week Ending..................						
Clock No.	**Amount** **Rs. P.**	**Job Nos.**				
		51	**52**	**53**	**54**	**55**
5						
6						
7						
8						
9						
10						
Total						
Prepared by..............................			Cost Ledger posted by.............................. Checked by..............................			

Thus, Wages Abstract shows the analysis of the wages paid during a given period on different jobs, and provides a basis for the allocation of labour cost to different jobs, processes, work-orders, operations etc.

Calculation of Wages Rates for the Purposes of Costing

Amount of wages paid to the workers does not include basic wages only but also a number of other expenses incurred by the employer, for example, contributions towards provident fund, Employees State Insurance (ESI) Corporation premium, holiday pay and production bonus, etc. These payments may be included in indirect expenses or overheads. But it would be appropriate to treat these expenses as direct and add them to direct wages and then divide the figure arrived at by the total effective hours worked. The resulting figure is the labour cost per hour. The total time worked should be multiplied by such a figure in order to calculate labour cost chargeable to different jobs.

Illustration 1

From the following particulars prepare a statement of labour cost, showing the cost per day:

(*i*)	Monthly salary	Rs. 225.
(*ii*)	Leave salary	5% of salary
(*iii*)	Employer's contribution towards provident fund	$8\frac{1}{3}$% of (*i*) and (*ii*)
(*iv*)	Employer's contribution to State Insurance	3% of (*i*) and (*ii*)
(*v*)	Pro-rata expenditure on amenities to labour	Rs. 28 per head per month
(*vi*)	No. of working hours in a month (Assume an 8-hour day).	200

Solution

Labour Cost Statement

	Per Month	Per Day
	Rs.	Rs.
(*i*) Salary	225.00	9.00
(*ii*) Leave salary [5% of(*i*)]	11.25	0.45
(*iii*) Employer's contribution to provident fund $\left[8\frac{1}{3}\% \text{ of } (i) \text{ and } (ii)\right]$	19.69	0.79
(*iv*) Employer's contribution to State Insurance [3% of (*i*) and (*ii*)]	7.09	0.28
(*v*) Pro-rata expenditure on amenities	28.00	1.12
	291.03	11.64
Total Expenses per month = Rs. 291.03. Labour cost per day = Rs. 11.64.		

Idle Time: The question of idle time arises where the direct workers are paid on the basis of time. In case of time workers, there is bound to arise a difference between the time for which they are paid (*i.e.*, the time as shown by Time Card) and the time which they actually spend on production (*i.e.*, the time as shown by Job Card). This difference is known as idle time. The employer has to pay for the idle time but he does not get any benefit from it.

Causes of Idle Time: Idle time may occur owing to:

(*a*) Productive Causes;
(*b*) Administrative causes; and
(*c*) Economic Causes.

(*a*) Productive Causes: The productive causes may be classified as follows:

(*i*) Idle time due to machine break-down.
(*ii*) Power failures.
(*iii*) Waiting for work.
(*iv*) Waiting for tools and/or raw materials.
(*v*) Waiting for instructions.

Idle time caused due to the above mentioned productive factors is controllable internally. A proper preventive maintenance system in the factory can help in minimising the machine break-down. Similarly, any major break-down of machinery can be prevented though a routine check of all the machines at regular intervals. Power failure may occur due to the lack of proper inspection and maintenance of power plant or break-down of the transmission wires. Thus, a proper inspection and maintenance of the power plant and transmission wires can be helpful in reducing idle time. But the management can have no control over power failure from the Main Power Supply.

Waiting for work involves payment of both productive and indirect labour for time lost owing to lack of work. This may occur when there is no proper scheduling of work or proper planning and routing of the job. In a sound organisation, it is expected that all the jobs in hand are properly planned so that machines can always take up the jobs in sequence and the workers have not to wait for them.

A large amount of money is spent as "Idle Time" owing to waiting for materials and/or tools. A proper stores control and tool scheduling system would prevent any such payment for Idle Time. It is expected that materials should be available in time for the jobs loaded on machine. With an effective stores control system this can be ensured.

Instructions and drawings should be clearly laid down for all jobs taken in hand. It is imperative for any production control department to issue clear instructions to the workers as to how to handle the job in sequence, in order to avoid idle time caused by want of instructions.

While all the above items can be controlled by proper planning, it is often found in practice that some amount of Idle Time is bound to occur. It may be due to changing from one job to another. It normally takes some time for setting up the tools for a different job when the previous one is complete. Whatever good planning may there be, this loss of time in tool setting is unavoidable. If, however, a worker handles more than one machine tool changing time may be planned in a way so that when one tool is changed in one changing, the worker can work on the other machine. In some organisations tool changing is done during weekly closed-day.

Idle time owing to all causes should be covered in a report so that action may be taken to control it. Such a report is known as 'Idle Time Report'. The specimen of such report is given below:

A.B. Co. Ltd.
Idle Time Analysis

Works............................ Week No. .... .Week Ended..............................

Production centre	Total Planned Machine Hours	Total lost & Setting Hours	Analysis of Lost & Setting Hours						
			Total Setting Hours	Waiting for Materials	Waiting for Heat Hrs.	Waiting for Tools Hrs.	Waiting for labour Hrs.	Mech. & Elec. Break-down Hrs.	Other Delays Hrs.

(*b*) **Administrative Causes:** Idle Time is sometimes caused by administrative decisions. For instance, when there is a surplus capacity of plant and machinery which the Management decides not to work, there may be some idle time. In times of depression some of the machines have got to work below normal capacity and the regular workers have got to be paid their full amount of wages. As the Managements in such cases are reluctant to get rid of their trained workers temporarily, idle time arising out of this abnormal situation cannot be helped.

(*c*) **Economic Causes:** In many industries, factories work seasonally. In some businesses there is a busy season followed by a slack season. It is not possible to employ a number of workers in the busy season and get rid of them during the slack season. In Coal industries, for example, production cannot be evenly distributed and as such it is normally the case that in slack period the workmen who are not required to do productive jobs, are utilised for doing some other jobs. If such complementary job cannot be found, there will be some unavoidable idle time and this is beyond control.

Types of Idle Time

The idle time may be classified into two different classes:

(*a*) Normal Idle Time

(*b*) Abnormal Idle Time.

(*a*) **Normal Idle Time:** It refers to that loss of time which is natural and unavoidable. For example, time taken in going from the gate of the factory to the department, in going from the department to the factory gate during luncheon break, in changing over from one job to another or from one machine to another and in setting or adjusting the machines etc.

(*b*) **Abnormal Idle Time:** Any loss of time in excess of normal idle time is abnormal idle time. It arises due to certain abnormal causes but can otherwise be avoided. Idle time arising due to break-down of machinery, non-availability of instructions to workmen, irregular supply of materials, delay in the completion of an operation which holds up a subsequent inter-connected operation and other similar conditions is abnormal idle time. Abnormal idle time usually occurs due to the inefficiency on the part of workers and the management.

Treatment of Cost of Normal Idle Time

Cost of normal idle time, since it is inevitable, is to be borne by the output of the factory. It can be treated in any of the following two ways:

(*a*) It may be treated as an item of factory expenses and charged to production as an indirect expense.

(*b*) It may be charged to production as a direct cost by inflating the actual wage rate paid to the workers.

Treatment of Abnormal Idle Time

Since cost of abnormal idle time is the result of abnormal factors viz., floods, strikes and major machinery break-down, it is not allowed to affect the cost of production and hence charged to Costing Profit and Loss Account.

Control Over Idle Time

Control over idle time should be given due consideration by the management. Following steps are suggested for exercising effective control over idle time:

(*i*) Proper planning and control over production is the first important step for controlling idle time. There should be proper planning of jobs to be undertaken and workers to be appointed.

(*ii*) The instructions for doing the work should be issued right in advance of actual performance by the workers. They need not wait unnecessarily for seeking instructions before undertaking a job.

(*iii*) Regular and proper inspection and maintenance of power plant should be undertaken for minimising the power failures.

(*iv*) Idle time card should be prepared regularly in order to know the causes responsible for idle time.

(*v*) Regular and timely supply of materials will also be helpful in checking idle time.

(*vi*) Proper and regular maintenance of plant and machinery will also go a long way in checking idle time.

OVERTIME

Any employment of workers beyond the normal working hours of the factory, is known as overtime. For example, in a factory the workers are required to work for 8 hours a day but if a worker is asked to work 10 hours a day, the time of 2 hours will be treated as overtime. For working beyond the normal hours, the hourly rate of wages is more than the normal rate.

Overtime work is generally required to meet out the increased demand, to complete a job within the specified period as required by the customer, to make up the time lost due to break-down of machinery or power failure and to work as a matter of policy, due to the shortage of labour, machines or factory space.

TREATMENT OF OVERTIME WAGES

As pointed out, overtime is generally paid at a higher rate than the normal time. The overtime wages consist of 'normal wages' and 'overtime premium'. The normal wages form the part of the direct wages, but the overtime premium should be treated in the following manner:

(*i*) Where the overtime work becomes necessary to complete a job within a specified date as required by the customer, the 'overtime premium' or 'overtime cost' should be directly charged to the job concerned by way of direct wages.

(*ii*) Where the overtime work becomes necessary as a result of general pressure of work, the 'overtime premium' should be treated as an item of overheads.

(*iii*) Where the overtime work becomes necessary on account of faulty planning in a department, the overtime premium or cost should be treated as an item of departmental overheads.

(*iv*) Where overtime work is due to abnormal causes *e.g.*, flood, fire etc., the overtime cost should be charged to the Costing Profit and Loss Account.

Illustration 2

Calculate the normal and overtime wages payable to a workman from the following data:

Days	Hours worked
Monday	8 Hours
Tuesday	10 Hours
Wednesday	9 Hours
Thursday	11 Hours
Friday	9 Hours
Saturday	4 Hours

Normal Working Hours: 8 Hours per day.

Normal Rate: Re. 0.50 per hour.

Over Time Rate: Up to 9 hours in a day at single rate and over 9 hours a day at double rate,

Or

Up to 48 hours in a week at single rate and over 48 hours at double rate, whichever is more beneficial to the workman.

Solution

Normal Wages and Overtime Wages according to First Alternative

Day	Hours worked	Normal Hours	Over Time Hours		Normal Wages	Over time Wages	Total Wages
			Single Rate @ 50 Paise per Hour	Double Rate @ 1 per Hour	Rs.	Rs.	Rs.
Monday	8	8	–	–	4.00	–	4.00
Tuesday	10	8	1	1	4.00	1.50	5.50
Wednesday	9	8	1	–	4.00	0.50	4.50
Thursday	11	8	1	2	4.00	2.50	6.50
Friday	9	8	1	–	4.00	0.50	4.50
Saturday	4	4	–	–	2.00	–	2.00
Total	51	44	4	3	22.00	5.00	27.00

Normal Wages and Overtime Wages according to Second Alternative

		Rs.
Normal wages for 44 Hours (Normal) @ 0.50 Paise per hour		22.00
Overtime wages for 7 hours (51 – 44)		
4 Hours @ 0.50 Paise per hour	2.00	
3 Hours @ Re. 1 per hour	3.00	5.00
Total wages		27.00

Night-Shift Allowance

It is quite a common practice to make additional payment for night-shift work which is known as night-shift allowance. It is not fair to charge such allowance directly to the job as the jobs done during the day do not have to bear such cost. The amount of night-shift allowance is treated as an item of departmental overheads.

Holiday Wages

The workers are paid wages for the weekly and other holidays. This payment is treated as an indirect expense and charged to Factory Overheads. An advance estimate with regard to payment of holiday wages is made by the management for the whole year after taking into consideration the normal holidays.

Casual workers

Casual workers are not regular employees in a concern but are generally engaged in case of extra work load in the factory. Casual workers are also usually appointed on temporary basis at the factory gate in case of illness of a regular worker. These workers are paid on daily basis. The remuneration paid to such workers can be treated as factory overheads or direct labour depending upon the nature of work undertaken by such worker.

The task of controlling casual workers and prevention of payment to dummy workers should be entrusted to the foreman. The payment to such workers should be made in the presence of foreman. The foreman should undertake surprise as well as spot checks for proper control over casual workers. It should always be ensured by the foreman that there are no surplus casual workers in the factory. Thus the appointment of casual workers should be made strictly in accordance with the requirements of the factory.

Out-workers

Workers operating outside the factory are known as out-workers. This type of workers are classified into two broad categories:

(*a*) Workers who are given materials to be worked upon in their own houses, and

(*b*) Workers who are sent to sites or customer's premises to perform their work.

In case of the first category of workers doing the work at their houses, proper control must be exercised in the following matters:

(*i*) Issue of materials.

(*ii*) Reconciliation of materials issued with the output.

(*iii*) Inspection of output and rejection of defective work.

(*iv*) Delivery of output within the stipulated time.

The time cards can not be maintained in case of such workers as they perform their work at their houses or work places. The payment to these workers may be more than the workers working inside the factory as such workers use their own premises, furniture, lighting, tools and equipment etc., for doing the job.

In case of the workers of the second category, those who are sent to customer's premises to perform their work, are taken as regular employees of the organization. For example, electricians, plumbers, sanitary workers and gas mechanic etc., are included in this category. For such workers, a strict control over their attendance and work must be exercised and the recording of 'in' and 'out' time is also very essential. The workers may be issued job cards in which actual time spent by them at different places may be recorded. This may prove to be of great help in exercising proper control over their working. For ensuring effective control over such workers 'Out-Work Time Sheet' may be maintained in respect of each such worker. The specimen of 'Out-Work Time Sheet' is shown below:

Out-Work Time Sheet

A.B. Co. Ltd.

Name or the worker...............................

Worker's No. .... Week ending...............................

Day	Description of Work	Time taken	Rate Rs.	Cost Rs.
Monday Tuesday Wednesday Thursday Friday Saturday				
	Total			

Worker............................... Cost Clerk...............................

Foreman...............................

LABOUR TURNOVER

It is a regular feature in every organisation that some workers change or are made to change their employment. The rate at which such a change takes place is known as 'labour turnover'. Labour turnover may be defined as the rate of workers left or discharged during a given period to the average number of workers employed in the organisation during that period.

Causes of Labour Turnover

The main causes of Labour Turnover can be divided into two categories:

(A) Avoidable Causes.
(B) Unavoidable Causes.

(A) Avoidable Causes. These include:

(*a*) Low Wages
(*b*) Dissatisfaction with the job.
(*c*) Unsatisfactory working conditions.
(*d*) Inadequate medical facilities.
(*e*) Lack of recreational facilities.
(*f*) Lack of training facilities.
(g) Dissatisfaction with working hours.
(*h*) Unfair methods of promotion.
(*i*) Unsympathetic attitude of supervisory staff and management.

(B) Unavoidable Causes. These are:

(*a*) Personal betterment.
(*b*) Illness or accident.
(*c*) Retirement or death.
(*d*) Dismissal due to incompetency or inefficiency.
(*e*) Dismissal due to unauthorised long absence.
(*f*) Domestic responsibilities in case of female workers *e.g.*, marriage, pregnancy, etc.

Effects of Labour Turnover

High labour turnover results in increased cost of production due to the following reasons:

(*a*) Interruption in work leading to a decrease in production.
(*b*) Cost of selecting new workers.
(*c*) Increased cost of training.
(*d*) New worker's inefficiency resulting in less economic use of tools and equipment and excessive wastage of materials.
(*e*) Higher accident rate.
(*f*) Overtime wages increase from an excessive number of separations, causing difficulties in adhering to the delivery dates of the contracts.

MEASUREMENT OF LABOUR TURNOVER

There are three principal methods of measurement of labour turnover which may be summarised as follows:

1. **Separation Rate Method:** This method takes into consideration the number of workers left or discharged during the period. Labour turnover is determined by dividing the total number of separations during the

month/year by the average number of workers employed during the month/year and multiplying that by 100.

Thus, Labour Turnover is =

$$\frac{\text{No. of workers separated during the period}}{\text{Average no. of workers during the period}} \times 100$$

Average number of workers employed during the period can be ascertained by means of the following formula:

$$\frac{\begin{array}{c}\text{Number of workers at the} \\ \text{beginning of the period}\end{array} + \begin{array}{c}\text{Number of workers at} \\ \text{the end of the period}\end{array}}{2}$$

2. **Replacement Rate Method:** This method takes into consideration the number of workers replaced during the period irrespective of the number of workers left or discharged. Labour turnover is determined by dividing the number of workers replaced during the month/year by the average number of workers employed during the month/year and multiplying that by 100. Thus labour turnover,

$$= \frac{\text{No. of workers replaced during the period}}{\text{Average number of workers during the period}} \times 100$$

It must be remembered that while calculating the number of replacements, new recruitments made in connection with the expansion programme shall not be considered.

3. **Labour Flux Rate Method:** This method takes into consideration both the number of workers left or discharged and the number of workers replaced during the period. Thus, this method is the combination of the previous two methods. The formula for calculating labour turnover under this method is as follows:

$$\frac{\begin{array}{c}\text{No. of workers separated} \\ \text{during the period}\end{array} + \begin{array}{c}\text{No. of workers replaced} \\ \text{during the period}\end{array}}{\text{Average number of workers during the period}} \times 100$$

Illustration 3

The personnel department of XY Co. Ltd., gives you the following information regarding labour:

No. of workers at the beginning of September, 2007 = 950

No. of workers at the end of September, 2007 = 1050.

During the month 10 workers left while 40 were discharged. 100 workers were recruited during the month of which 45 workers are recruited against the vacancies of those leaving while the rest are recruited in connection with expansion programme. You are required to calculate the labour turnover by using different methods.

Solution

Average number of workers during the month

$$= \frac{\text{Number of workers at the beginning of the month} + \text{Number of workers at the end of the month}}{2}$$

$$= \frac{950 + 1{,}050}{2} = 1{,}000$$

Labour turnover:

(*i*) Separation Rate Method =

$$\frac{\text{No. of workers separated during the month}}{\text{Average no. of workers during the month}} \times 100$$

$$= \frac{50}{1{,}000} \times 100 = 5\%$$

(*ii*) Replacement Rate Method =

$$\frac{\text{No. of workers replaced during the month}}{\text{Average no. of workers during the month}} \times 100$$

$$= \frac{45}{1{,}000} \times 100 = 4.5\%$$

(*iii*) Flux Rate Method =

$$\frac{\text{No. of workers separated} + \text{No. of workers replaced}}{\text{Average no. workers during the month}} \times 100$$

$$= \frac{50 + 45}{1{,}000} \times 100 = 9.5\%$$

Cost of Labour Turnover

The cost of labour turnover can be broadly divided into two parts:

(*a*) Preventive Costs.
(*b*) Replacement Costs.

Preventive costs denote the costs which are incurred to prevent excessive labour turnover by keeping a contented labour force. These include:

(*i*) Cost of personnel administration.
(*ii*) Cost of medical services.
(*iii*) Cost of welfare activities.
(*iv*) Cost of gratuity and pension schemes.
(*v*) A portion of high wages, bonus and perquisites.

Replacement costs refer to the costs of the recruitment, training and absorption of new workers. These include:

(*i*) Cost of recruitment and training of new workers.

(*ii*) Loss of output due to interruption and inefficiency of new workers.

(*iii*) Cost of wastage, scrap and defective work.

(*iv*) Compensation due to frequent accidents.

(*v*) Cost of additional supervision.

Treatment of Cost of Labour Turnover

Cost of labour turnover is treated as an item of overhead and should not be charged directly to a particular job or work-order.

METHODS OF REMUNERATION

The success of an industrial concern depends to a great extent upon the efficiency of labour and the efficiency of labour is considerably affected by the amount of remuneration paid to it. Some persons are of the view that the profits of an industrial concern can be maximised only by reducing the wage rates payable to the workers. But this view is not correct. It should be remembered that low-paid workers are usually inefficient and their inefficiency leads to wastage of materials, less economic use of tools, frequent break-down of machinery and loss of time as a result of which the cost of production goes up. Reasonable and fair wage rates allowed to the workers ultimately lead to more economic use of machines, tools, materials and time. To quote H.J. Wheldon, "Low wages do not necessarily means low costs—in fact, it is now widely recognised that efficiently organised factories may pay the highest wages, and yet have the lowest wages costs".

Therefore, the importance of the method of wage payment must never be under-estimated. Methods of wage payment should be carefully made out and put into action. An ideal system of wage payment must possess the following characteristics:

(*a*) Simplicity: The wage system should be simple to operate and easy to understand. It should avoid complications and should not have any element of uncertainty.

(*b*) Guarantee of Minimum Wages: The system of wage payment should guarantee a minimum wage to every worker irrespective of his efficiency or output so that he can maintain a proper standard of living and enjoy proper health to carry on his duties efficiently.

(*c*) Beneficial to Employer and Employee: The system of wage payment should be such which is gladly acceptable to the employer and the employee. From the view point of employer, the wage system should be economic. At the same time, it should enable the workers to get adequate and proper remuneration for their work.

(*d*) **Flexibility:** The wage system should be flexible enough so that changes may be made according to the requirements of the industrial concerns.

(*e*) **Incentives to Workmen:** The wage system should provide sufficient incentives to workers so that they may put in their best to maximise the output. It would encourage the workers to work hard.

(*f*) **Establishment of Industrial Peace:** The wage system should ensure the establishment of industrial peace. It should help in promoting healthy and cordial relations between the employer and workers.

The principal methods of wage payment may be given as follows:

(1) Time Rate System.
(2) Piece Rate System.
(3) Differential Piece Rate System
(4) Incentive Plans or Bonus Schemes.

TIME RATE SYSTEM

This is the most simple and common method of wage payment. Under this method, the workman is paid an hourly, daily, monthly or yearly rate of wages. The amount of remuneration or total wages payable to the workman thus, depends on the time for which he is employed and the quantity of output given by him is immaterial. The amount of wages payable to a workman under this method, is to be calculated as follows:

Total Wages = Total Time Worked × Rate of Wages per unit of Time

Or

Total Wages = Total Hours Worked × Rate of Wages Per Hour

or Total Wages = T × R

(Where 'T' denotes total time taken and 'R' denotes the rate of wages per unit of time).

The overtime work, under the time rate system, is paid at a higher rate.

ADVANTAGES OF TIME RATE SYSTEM

This method is widely used even at the present time on account of the following advantages:

(*i*) **Simplicity:** This method is simple to operate and easy to understand. The employer as well as the worker can understand this method easily and the amount of wages payable to workmen can be calculated without any tedious calculations.

(*ii*) **Guarantee of Minimum Wages:** This method guarantees minimum basic wages to all workers without any consideration of quantity or quality of output. Interruption in work due to power failure or break-down of machinery is not a cause of worry for the worker. Thus, it creates a sense of security among the workers.

(*iii*) **Quality Production:** Since the amount of wages is not linked with the quantity of output, this method ensures production of better quality due to the careful attention of the workers.

(*iv*) **Unity Among Workers:** Under this method, all workers falling under a particular category, are paid at equal rate without any consideration of their quantity of output. It encourages a feeling of equality among workers on account of which this method is also favoured by workers' trade unions.

(*v*) **Economy:** Under time rate system, there is no need to maintain detailed records regarding the quantity of work done by workers. It leads to reduction in administration overheads. Further, the workers are not in a hurry to maximise their output which leads to most careful and economic use of materials and machines by workers during production. With regular supervision, it proves to be a cheaper form of wage payment resulting in lower cost of production.

But this method has the following disadvantages:

(*i*) **No Incentive to Workers:** This system lacks incentive to efficient workers since all workers are paid equally and no distinction is made between efficient and inefficient workers.

(*ii*) **Encouragement to Go-Slow Policy:** This method encourages 'stretch up' and 'soldiering' leading to poor work performance. The workers, in order to earn higher wages for overtime work, try to make the work last as long as possible which leads to increase in labour cost per unit.

(*iii*) **Discontentment Among Efficient Workers:** The efficient workers are paid wages at the rate equal to that payable to inefficient workers which creates dissatisfaction among efficient workers.

(*iv*) **Payment for Idle Time:** Under this method, idle time of the workers has to be paid for leading to an increase in the cost of production.

(*v*) **Excessive Cost of Supervision:** Since there is no direct link between quantity of output and wages, wastage of time on the part of the workers is more, the avoidance of which requires considerable supervision leading to increase in costs.

(*vi*) **Ascertainment of Labour Cost per Unit Not Possible:** Since there is no link between quantity of output and amount of wages, the exact per unit cost of labour cannot be ascertained.

SUITABILITY OF THE TIME RATE SYSTEM

The time rate system of wage payment is most suitable in the following cases:

(*i*) Where close supervision over workers is possible.

(*ii*) Where quality of production is more important than its quantity.

(*iii*) Where the measurement of work is not simple.

(*iv*) Where production passes through different stages or operations in which delays are unavoidable.

PIECE RATE SYSTEM

Under this system, the workman is paid according to the quantity of the work done and the time spent by him in the factory is immaterial. The wage rate is expressed in terms of per unit of output, per job or per work-order. The amount of wages payable to a worker under this system is:

Total Wages = Total Output × Wage Rate Per Unit of Output

or Total Wages = 0 × R

(Where '0' denotes total output and 'R' denotes the rate of wages per unit of output).

For example, if the rate of wages per unit is Rs. 5 and a worker has made 80 units during a week, the amount of wages payable to him during the week will be Rs. 400 (*i.e.,* 80 units × Rs. 5).

ADVANTAGES OF PIECE RATE SYSTEM

The main advantages of piece rate system can be given as follows:

(*i*) **Simplicity:** Just like time rate system, the piece rate system is simple to operate and easy to understand. It does not involve tedious calculations.

(*ii*) **Incentive to Workers:** This system provides an incentive to the workers to work hard as the wages are paid on the basis of quantity of output and not on the basis of time.

(*iii*) **Ascertainment of Accurate Labour Cost:** Since the wages are paid on the basis of output, the exact cost of labour per unit of output or per job can be ascertained.

(*iv*) **No Payment for Idle Time:** Under the piece rate system, no payment is made to the workers for the idle time as a result of which the cost of supervision is not considerable.

(*v*) **Proper Care and Use of Machine and Tools:** The workers take proper care of their machines and tools since break-down of machine means diminution in output resulting in less remuneration to them.

But this system has the following disadvantages:

(*i*) **Less Attention to Quality:** As the payment of wages is made on the basis of output, the workers, in order to maximise their output, work with a sense of hurry which may affect the quality of the output adversely.

(*ii*) **Uneconomic Use of Machines and Materials:** Since the wages are paid on the basis of quantity of output, an excessive wastage of materials and frequent break-down of machinery may be caused by the workers due to their efforts to obtain maximum output.

(*iii*) **No Guarantee of Minimum Wages:** Since there is direct relationship between quantity of output and wages, the workers suffer if they fail to work efficiently. There is no guarantee of minimum daily wages to workers.

(*iv*) **Dissatisfaction Among Inefficient Workers:** The inefficient workers, who work slowly, become discontended by reason of lower wages as compared to the wages paid to their efficient fellow workers.

(*v*) **Adverse Effect on Workers' Health:** The workers, in a bid to earn more, try to over-work which has an adverse effect on their health and efficiency.

SUITABILITY OF THE PIECE RATE SYSTEM

This system is most suitable in the following cases:

(*i*) Where the work is of a repetitive nature.

(*ii*) Where the measurement of work is simple.

(*iii*) Where the quality and precision of output is not very important.

(*iv*) Where strict supervision is not possible.

DIFFERENTIAL PIECE RATE SYSTEM

Differential piece rate system is a modified form of piece rate system. Under the straight piece rate system, all the output is paid for at the same rate but under differential piece rate system, the output at different levels of efficiency are paid for at different rates, so that at higher levels of production, the worker earns a comparatively higher rate per unit. Differential piece rate system is designed with the object of rewarding efficient workers and encouraging less efficient workers to improve. Payment of wages under the differential piece rate system, can be made according to any of the following methods:

TAYLOR'S DIFFERENTIAL PIECE RATE SYSTEM

This scheme was originated by F.W. Taylor, who is known as the 'father of scientific management'. He was all for maximising output. Under this system, standard output per unit of time is fixed on the basis of time, motion and fatigue studies and two piece rates are fixed – (*a*) a higher rate to workers who attain the standard or go above the standard and (*b*) a lower rate to the workers who fail to attain the standard. Under this system, there is no guaranteed minimum piece rate and the inefficient workers are definitely discouraged. Thus, this system provides encouragement to efficient workers.

Illustration 4

The standard output fixed for the day is 20 units. The rate of payment for workers producing the standard output or more is Rs. 2 per unit and the rate for others is Rs. 1.50 per unit. Calculate the amount of wages payable for the day, if the actual output is (*i*) 25 units; (*ii*) 20 units; (*iii*) 18 units; (*iv*) 12 units.

Solution

Calculation of Wages Payable to Worker

Output (Units)	Rate of Wages per unit	Wages payable for the day
25	2.00	50.00
20	2.00	40.00
18	1.50	27.00
12	1.50	18.00

Taylor's Differential Piece Rate System certainly provides an incentive to workers to maximise production and helps in attracting the most efficient workers. The increase in production reduces the cost of production per unit through decrease in per unit cost of fixed overhead. But this system penalises the inefficient workers by paying them wages at low rates which creates a feeling of discontentment among them. Further, a worker who just fails to reach the standard gets much lower wages than a worker who just reaches the standard. This system does not guarantee a minimum day wage to the worker and as such is opposed by workers' union.

Merrick's Multiple Piece Rate System: Merrick's Multiple Piece Rate System is a modification of the Taylor's Scheme, with the difference that under this system three different piece rate scales are fixed – one for beginners, one for average workers and another for efficient workers. The following rates were suggested by him:

Below 83% of standard task	Basic Piece Rate
From 83% to 100% standard task	110% of Basic Piece Rate
Above 100%	120% of Basic Piece Rate.

This method possesses all the advantages and limitations of Taylor's Differential Piece Rate System.

Emerson's Efficiency Bonus Scheme: Emerson's scheme is yet another modification of the Taylor's scheme. Under this scheme, a minimum time rate is guranteed but the efficiency is certainly rewarded. For determining the level of efficiency of workers, a standard time for a job or a standard output for a unit of time is fixed. If a worker attains the standard, his efficiency is 100% but if he fails to attain the standard, his efficiency is below 100%. For example, if the standard time for a job is 10 hours and the worker does it in 20 hours, his efficiency is 50% and if he does the job in 8 hours, his efficiency is 125%. Bonus becomes payable only when the efficiency level of a worker is $66\frac{2}{3}\%$ or more. For efficiency below $66\frac{2}{3}\%$, the worker becomes entitled only to time wage. Bonus at the efficiency level of $66\frac{2}{3}\%$ is 0.01% of the wages earned but it becomes 20% when efficiency reaches 100%. Beyond the efficiency level of 100%, the rate of bonus is increased by 1% for every increase of 1% in efficiency.

Illustration 5

In a manufacturing concern, a daily wage rate guaranteed for a worker is Rs. 3. The standard output for the month is 1,000 articles representing 100% efficiency. The daily wage rate is paid without bonus to those workers who show upto $66\frac{2}{3}\%$ efficiency. Beyond this, bonus is payable on a graded scale:

Efficiency	Bonus
90%	10%
100%	20%

Further increase of 1% in bonus for every 1% further rise in efficiency.

Calculate the total earnings of A, B, C and D who have worked for 25 days in a month. Workers' output is A-600 articles, B-900 articles, C-1,000 articles and D-1,250 articles.

Solution

Standard output 1,000 units representing 100% efficiency.

Calculation of efficiency and rate of bonus of workers

Name of worker	Actual output (Articles)	Efficiency	% of bonus on wages
A	600	60%	–
B	900	90%	10%
C	1,000	100%	20%
D	1,250	125%	45%

Calculation of Total Earnings

	A	B	C	D
	Rs.	Rs.	Rs.	Rs.
Basic Wages @ Rs. 3 per day for 25 days	75.00	75.00	75.00	75.00
Bonus: A–nil B–10% C–20% D–45%	–	7.50	15.00	33.75
Total Earnings	75.00	82.50	90.00	108.75

Emerson's Efficiency Bonus scheme has the following *advantages:*

(*i*) It guarantees minimum wages to all workers irrespective of the level of efficiency.

(*ii*) It provides an incentive to workers to work hard and increase production.

(*iii*) It makes a proper distinction between beginners, semi-skilled and skilled workers.

But this system suffers from the following *disadvantages:*

(*i*) This system is very complicated and thus difficult to adopt.

(*ii*) The incentive after attaining the standard is very low.

INCENTIVE PLANS

Incentive plans are those plans of remunerating the workers which provide an incentive to them to work harder. The incentive is given to the worker by paying some bonus or premium in addition to their normal wages. Under an incentive plan, normally a standard time is fixed by means of time study of the performance of a specific job and the worker is paid a time rate plus specified proportion of the wages of the time saved by way of bonus. The main object of introducing incentive plans is to reduce the per unit overhead cost by means of an increase in production.

Factors to be considered in formulating and installing incentive plans: There are a number of factors to be taken into account while formulating and introducing an incentive plan for wage payment in an organisation. These may be summarised as follow:

(*a*) The system should be fair to both employer and the employee.

(*b*) The incentive plan should guarantee minimum wages to all the workers irrespective of their level of production.

(*c*) The incentive plans should not fix any upper limit on the possible earnings of an efficient worker.

(*d*) There should be a direct relationship between the amount of incentive and the efficiency of the worker and the amount of incentive should not be influenced by any factor beyond the control of the worker.

(*e*) The standards for production, time allowed etc., fixed under the plan should be such which are attainable by a worker working at the normal efficiency level.

(*f*) The incentive plan should not violate the existing terms and conditions of employment of the workers.

(g) The incentive plan should certainly lead to an increase in the efficiency and productivity of both men and machines.

(*h*) The system should not lead to an increase in the clerical work.

Important Incentive Plans:

The payment of wages may be made according to any of the following incentive plans:

(*a*) **Halsey Premium Plan:** This plan was originated by an American, F.A. Halsey. Under this scheme, an hourly rate is guaranteed to all workers. A standard time is fixed for each unit, job or operation on the basis of time and motion studies and the worker is paid the agreed hourly rate of wages for the actual time taken to complete the unit, job or operation plus a fixed percentage of the wages of the time saved by way of bonus or premium. The amount of bonus or premium payable to the worker is one-half (sometimes one-third) of the wages of the time saved.

The formula for calculating total wages or total earnings of the worker under the Halsey Plan is:

$$\text{Total Wages} = T \times R + \frac{S - T}{2} \times R$$

Where: 'T' stands for actual time taken,
'S' stands for standard time or time allowed, and
'R' stands for rate of wages per hour.

Illustration 6

From the following data, calculate the total wages of a worker under Halsey Premium Plan:

Hourly rate	:	Re. 1.00
Standard Time	:	16 Hours
Time Taken	:	12 Hours.

Solution

Basic wages of the worker will be $= T \times R$
$= 12 \text{ hours} \times \text{Re. } 1$
$= \text{Rs. } 12$

Amount of Bonus will be $= \dfrac{S - T}{2} \times R$

$= \dfrac{16 - 12}{2} \times \text{Re. } 1$

$= \text{Rs. } 2$

Total Earnings $= \text{Rs. } 12 + \text{Rs. } 2$
$= \text{Rs. } 14$

Thus, effective hourly rate of wages $= \dfrac{\text{Total Earnings}}{\text{Total Time taken}}$

$= \dfrac{\text{Rs. } 14}{12 \text{ Hours}}$

$= \text{Rs. } 1.167$

The following *advantages* of the Halsey Plan are worth noting:

(*i*) Every worker is guaranteed minimum wage and even the slow moving worker feels secured.

(*ii*) This plan is easy to follow and relatively simple to operate.

(*iii*) It encourages efficiency among workers by inducing them to finish their job before the standard time.

(*iv*) The benefit from the time saved is shared equally by the employer and the workman.

(*v*) Generally workers do not oppose this method of wage payment as it rewards time saved rather than increased output.

But this method suffers from the following *disadvantages:*

(*i*) Workers are given only 50% of the wages of the time saved and as such the workers may oppose this method.

(*ii*) The workers may be encouraged to rush through work and thus neglect the quality of output to save more time and earn higher bonus.

(*iii*) The standard time fixed for finishing a job may not be scientifically set.

(*b*) **Halsey-Weir Premium Plan:** This plan is just similar to the Halsey Premium Plan but the only difference is in the rate of bonus or premium payable to the worker. Under the Halsey-Weir Premium plan, the rate of bonus payable to the worker is 30% of the wages of time saved.

(*c*) **Rowan Plan:** This plan was originated by David Rowan. This plan also guarantees an hourly rate to all workers. A worker is paid the fixed rate per hour for the actual time spent on the job plus a premium based on the time saved. The amount of bonus or premium is not a fixed percentage of the wages of the time saved but it varies according to the extent of the time saved. The amount of bonus or premium payable under the Rowan Plan is that proportion of the wages of the time taken which the time saved bears to the standard time. The formula for calculating the total earnings under this plan is:

$$\text{Total Wages (Earnings)} = \text{T} \times \text{R} + \frac{\text{S} - \text{T}}{\text{S}} \times \text{T} \times \text{R}$$

Where, 'T' stands for actual time taken,
'R' stands for rate of wages per hour, and
'S' stands for standard time or time allowed.

Illustration 7

Continuing Illustration No. 6, calculate the total earnings of the worker under the Rowan Plan.

Solution

Basic Wages = T × R
= 12 hours × Re. 1
= Rs. 12

$$\text{Amount of Bonus} = \frac{\text{S} - \text{T}}{\text{S}} \times \text{T} \times \text{R}$$

$$= \frac{16-12}{16} \times 12 \times 1$$

= Rs. 3

Total Earnings = Rs. 12 + Rs. 3

= Rs. 15

$$\text{Effective hourly rate} = \frac{\text{Total Earnings}}{\text{Total Time Taken}}$$

$$= \frac{\text{Rs.}15}{12 \text{ hours}}$$

= Rs. 1.25

The *advantages* of the Rowan Plan are:

(*i*) This plan guarantees minimum wage and provides incentives for efficiency.

(*ii*) It does not induce workers to rush through work for increased bonus earning because the bonus increases at a decreasing rate with higher levels of efficiency. Thus, an automatic check for limiting production of inferior quality of goods is ensured.

(*iii*) It is more liberal than the Halsey Plan to provide incentive upto 50% of the time saved.

But this plan suffers from the following *disadvantages:*

(*i*) The ordinary worker finds it very difficult to understand the complicated method of calculation of bonus under this plan.

(*ii*) It does not provide adequate incentives beyond a certain stage *i.e.,* 50% of standard time, as a result of which a worker does not generally exert himself beyond 50% saving in time.

(*iii*) As the worker can earn a more substantial increase over his day wages by moderate exertion than by much harder work, the production is, therefore, kept down. So the system is declining in popularity among employees.

Comparison of Halsey and Rowan Plans: Since under the Halsey Premium Plan 50% of the wages of the time saved is to be paid to the worker as premium or bonus, the two schemes will yield equal wages and bonus if a worker saves exactly half the time allowed to him *(i.e.,* standard time). If a worker saves less than half the standard time, he will be better off under the Rowan Plan. But if he saves more than half the standard time, he will earn more under the Halsey Plan.

(*d*) **Gantt's Task and Bonus Scheme:** This scheme is a combination of time rate, differential piece rate and bonus systems and guarantees a minimum time rate. Under this system, standard output per unit of time is fixed on the basis of time and motion studies. A worker who fails to attain the standard is paid the guaranteed time rate while a worker attaining the standard is paid the time rate plus a bonus at 20% of the time rate. The worker going above the standard is paid a higher piece work rate on his total output. Thus, this system guarantees minimum wages to inefficient workers, encourages the less efficient workers and rewards the efficient workers.

Illustration 8

Calculate the earnings of workers from the following details under Gantt's task and bonus plan:

Standard time	2 hours per unit
Time taken	100 hours
Units produced A –	40 units
B –	50 units
C –	60 units

Rates:

Per hour Rs. 2, per unit Rs. 5.

Solution

Earning of worker A $= T \times R$
$= 100 \times 2$
$=$ Rs. 200

Earning of worker B $= T \times R + T \times R \times 20\%$

$$= 100 \times 2 + 100 \times 2 \times \frac{20}{100}$$

$$= 200 + 200 \times \frac{20}{100}$$

$= 200 + 40$
$=$ Rs. 240

Earning of worker C = Units produced × Rate per unit
$= 60 \times 5$
$=$ Rs. 300

(*e*) Bedaux Point Premium Plan: Under this system, the standard time for a job is determined by time and motion studies. Under this system, every minute of an hour allowed for the work is called a 'point'. Thus, 10 hours' standard time will have 600 points. The worker is paid wages according to his daily or hourly rate plus a bonus equal to 75% of the points saved multiplied by one-sixteeth of the standard rate. The operation of this system can be understood with the help of the following illustration:

Illustration 9

Calculate the amount of earnings of a worker under the Bedaux Point Premium Plan from the following data:

Standard Time : 100 hours.
Actual Time taken : 80 hours.
Rate of wages : Rs. 4 per hour.

Solution

Calculation of Total Earnings

	Rs.
Basic Wages (80 hours × Rs. 4)	320.00
Bonus : (75% of 1,200 points saved × $\frac{1}{60}$ × Rs. 4)	60.00
Total Wages	380.00

(*f*) **Hayne's Bonus System:** A standard time for completing a task is fixed (on the basis of time study) in terms of *Manits*. A manit is a man-minute of work. The value of time saved is distributed among the workers, supervisors and the concern. If the work is not well standardised i.e., up to pre-determined standards, the ratio for dividing the time saved is 5/10th to the operator, 1/10th to the supervisor and 4/10 to the concern. In case of standardised performance, the time saved is distributed between the worker and the supervisor in the ratio of 5 : 1. The bonus is credited to the bonus fund payable to the supervisors. If a product does not pass inspection, no Manits are credited to the workers.

(*g*) **Barth Variable Sharing Scheme:** Although this system is similar to Rowan Plan, it does not guarantee minimum day wages to the workers. Standard time for each job is calculated on the basis of time and motion studies. Under this system, in order to calculate the amount of wages payable, the standard hour is multiplied by the number of hours actually taken to complete the work. Thereafter, the square root of this product is found out and the resulting figure is multiplied by the hourly rate. Thus, wages payable under this system are:

$$= \sqrt{\text{Standard Time} \times \text{Actual Time}} \times \text{Rate of Wages}$$

or $$= \sqrt{ST \times AT} \times R$$

(Where 'ST' denotes Standard Time, 'AT' denotes Actual Time and 'R' denotes Rate of Wages).

Illustration 10

Calculate the amount of wages payable to a worker according to Barth Method:

Standard Time = 20 Hours.
Actual Time Taken = 15 Hours.
Rate of Wages = Rs. 5 per hour.

Solution

$$\text{Wages} = \sqrt{\text{Standard Time} \times \text{Actual Time}} \times \text{Rate of Wages}$$

$$= \sqrt{20 \text{ Hours} \times 15 \text{ Hours}} \times \text{Rs. } 5 = \text{Rs. } 86.60$$

The main problem with the Barth Variable Sharing Scheme is that it involves tedious calculations which a worker cannot understand easily. Further, the amount of wages for lower efficiency is more and it starts falling with the increase in efficiency. As such this scheme is considered good for trainees and unskilled workers.

(*h*) Group Bonus Scheme: Under this system, the bonus is calculated on the collective production of a group of inter-dependent workers and shared among the individual members of the group in agreed proportions. Thus, this system aims at rewarding the joint efforts of the workers but runs counter to the principle of rewarding individual efforts. There is a danger that it may bring performance down to average level. Wages turned to be more constant in such plans since the more industrious worker does not exert more because he does not particularly gain thereby. Such a tendency defeats the basic object of incentive plan. The operation of this scheme can be understood with the help of the following illustration:

Illustration 11

In an engineering concern 30 workers work in a group. If weekly production of the group exceeds 60 units per hour (which is the Standard), each man gets a bonus in addition to his hourly earnings.

Bonus Rule: Each worker's share should be $\frac{1}{2}$ of the percentage in excess of standard production. The bonus shall be payable at this percentage of a wage rate of Rs. 2 per hour. The following particulars relate to working hours during a week in March, 2007:

Day	Hours worked	Output (units)
Monday	300	24,700
Tuesday	320	25,500
Wednesday	290	17,060
Thursday	310	18,050
Friday	340	28,900
Saturday	320	21,150
	1,880	1,35,360

Calculate (*a*) rate and amount of bonus for the week;

(*b*) Total earnings of worker A who worked for 40 hours during the week and his wages are Rs. 1.50 per hour and that of B who worked for 48 hours at Rs. 1.80 per hour basic.

Solution

(*a*) **Calculation of Bonus:**

Actual Output	1,35,360	Units
Standard Output (1,880 × 60)	1,12,800	Units
Excess Output	22,560	Units

Percentage of excess output to standard output:

$$= \frac{\text{Excess Output}}{\text{Standard Output}} \times 100$$

$$= \frac{22,560}{1,12,800} \times 100 = 20\%$$

$$\text{Bonus percentage} = \frac{1}{2} \times 20\% = 10\%$$

$$\text{Bonus Rate per hour} = \text{Rs. } 2 \times \frac{10}{100} \times = \text{Re. } 0.20$$

Amount of Bonus for the week= 1,880 hours @ Re. 0.20
= Rs. 376

(*b*) **Calculation of Earnings of Workers:**

A = 40 hours × Rs. 1.50 + 40 × Re. 0.20
= Rs. 60 + Rs. 8
= Rs. 68

B = 48 hours × Rs. 1.80 + 48 × Re. 0.20
= Rs. 86.40 + Rs. 9.60
= Rs. 96

(*i*) **Profit Sharing Scheme:** It is a scheme whereby the employer allows his workmen a share in the profits over and above their usual wages. This scheme is based on the principle that the workers should be entitled to a share in profits since they contribute to the earnings of the undertaking. The share in the profits to the workers is given in addition to their normal wages. The scheme regarding the calculation of profits for the purpose of bonus is made clear to the workers at the beginning of the year. The benefit of the bonus is given to all workers with reference to the amount of wages and length of service. Normally the amount of bonus is paid in cash but sometimes, it may be paid in the form of bonus shares in the company.

The main advantages of the profit sharing scheme are as follows:

(*i*) It minimises conflicts between workers and employer and thus smoothens the path of co-operation among them.

(*ii*) The workers' interest in the profits economies the use of materials, fuel and power etc., and encourages careful handling of machines and tools.

(*iii*) The workers' interest in the profits reduces the cost of supervision.

(*iv*) The rate of labour turnover is greatly reduced.

But this system has the following limitations:

(*i*) There is no direct link between the personal efforts of a worker and the reward. The payment of bonus is made on group basis and hence the personal or individual efficiency of the worker is not taken into consideration.

(*ii*) Profits of a business concern are not only the results of the efforts of the workers but also depend on a number of other factors *e.g.*, favourable market conditions, monopoly in the market etc. Therefore, the employers may not like to adopt such schemes.

(*iii*) The determination of the share of workers in the profits of the organisation is very difficult since the basis of its calculation is always a matter of dispute between the employer and workers.

(*iv*) There is a time gap between the efforts of the workers and the payment of bonus to them. The payment of the bonus is made at the end of the year when the profits of the business are ascertained. This postponement of the payment of bonus is not liked by the workers.

(*v*) The earning of profits by a business concern involves uncertainty. In case of a loss due to unfavourable circumstances, the workmen will not get any bonus. Similarly, in case of large profits due to favourable conditions, the employers may hesitate to share them with the workers.

(*vi*) The employers may manipulate their accounts to show lower profits with a view to pay smaller amount of bonus to workers.

(*vii*) Employers generally oppose the profit sharing scheme due to the fact that the workers do not have a share in the losses.

MISCELLANEOUS PROBLEMS

Illustration 12

The following particulars relate to the year ending on 31st March, 2007 for 30 workers:

Basic wages	Rs. 50,000	Dearness Allowance	Rs. 25,000
Night Shift Allowance	Rs. 9,600	Overtime Allowance	Rs. 7,000
Bonus	20% on Wages	P.F. deposit for the period	Rs. 12,000
E.S.I. Contribution	Rs. 2,808		

Recovery towards House
Rent Rs. 10,200
Recovery towards Loans Rs. 16,000
Expenses incurred for
amenities to employees Rs. 4,730

P.F. is paid in equal shares by the employer and the employees. The contribution to E.S.I. is in the proportion of 7 : 5 by the employer and the employees respectively. The workers are entitled to 5% of the total days worked as leave on full pay. The number of days worked in the year is 300. Normal idle time is 5%.

Assuming that all items are evenly spread over all the days in the year, ascertain the wages cost per hour, the daily hours worked being eight. Also calculate the amount of cash required to be paid to the workers.

Solution

Statement of Labour Cost for the year ended 31st March, 1997

		Rs.
Basic Wages		50,000
Dearness Allowance		25,000
Night Shift Allowance		9,600
Overtime Allowance		7,000
Bonus (20% of Rs. 50,000)		10,000
Employer's Contribution to P.F.		6,000
Employer's Contribution to E.S.I.		1,638
Expenses on amenities to employees		4,730
Total Labour Cost		1,13,968
Total Hours worked during the Year: (30 workers × 300 days × 8 hours)		72,000
Less:		
(*i*) 5% leave on full pay	3,600 hrs.	
(*ii*) 5% for normal idle time	3,420 hrs.	7,020
Net working hours		64,980
Labour cost per hour: Rs. 1,13,968/64,980 Hrs. = Rs. 1.75 (app.)		

Statement of cash required for payment to direct workers

		Rs.
Basic Wages		50,000
Dearness Allowance		25,000
Night Shift Allowance		9,600
Overtime Allowance		7,000
Bonus (20% of Rs. 50,000)		10,000
		1,01,600
Less Deductions:	Rs.	
Employee's contribution to P.F.	6,000	
Employees' contribution to E.S.I.	1,170	
Recovery of House Rent	10,200	
Recovery of Loan	16,000	
		33,370
Cash required for payment to workers direct		68,230

Illustration 13

Calculate the earnings of workers A and B from the following particulars for a month, and allocate the earnings to each of the jobs X, Y and Z.

	A	B
(*a*) BasicWages	Rs. 100	Rs. 100
(*b*) Dearness Allowance	50%	55%,
(*c*) Provident Fund (on basic wages)	8%	8%
(*d*) Employee's contribution to State Insurance (on basic wages)	2%	2%
(*e*) Overtime	10 hrs.	
(*f*) Idle time and leave	–	16 hrs.

The normal working time for the month is 200 hrs. Overtime is paid at double the normal wages plus Deamess Allowance. Employer's contributions to State Insurance and Provident Fund are at equal rate with the employees' contribution. The month contains 25 working days and one paid holiday. The two workers were employed on jobs X, Y and Z in the following proportions:

Job	X	Y	Z
Worker A	40	30	30
Worker B	50	20	30

Overtime was done on job Y. *(I.C.W.A., Inter)*

Solution

	A	B
	Rs.	Rs.
Basic Wages	100.00	100.00
Deamess Allowance	50.00	55.00
Overtime (basic wages plus D.A.)	15.00	–
Gross Wages earned	165.00	155.00
Less:		
P.F. Contribution (8% on basic wages)	8.00	8.00
E.S.I. Contribution (2% on basic wages)	2.00	2.00
	10.00	10.00
Net Wages due	155.00	145.00
Labour cost chargeable to jobs:		
Gross Wages (excluding overtime)	150.00	155.00
Employer's Contribution to P.F. and E.S.I.	10.00	10.00
	160.00	165.00
Labour cost per hour	0.80	0.825

		Jobs		
	Total	X	Y	Z
	Rs.	Rs.	Rs.	Rs.
A: Ordinary Wages	160	64	48	48
Overtime Wages	15	–	15	–
B: Ordinary Wages	165	83	33	49
	340	147	96	97

Illustration 14

The standard time taken to complete a job is 12 hours at 25 paise per hour.

Time wages are allowed to workers taking more than the time allowed. But workers who complete the job in standard time or less, receive a straight piece-work rate plus 10% bonus *i.e.,* 12 hours at Rs. 0.275.

Calculate the wages earned by A, B, C and D who complete the job in 15, 12, 10 and 8 hours respectively. What will be their effective hourly rate?

If the overhead rate chargeable to production is Re. 0.50 per hour, what will be the "Cost of Conversion" (labour and overhead) per piece produced by each worker?

(*C.A. Final*)

Solution

	A	B	C	D
Time taken in hours	15	12	10	8
Wages due according to the method of remuneration;	Rs.	Rs.	Rs.	Rs.
At Re. 0.25 per hour for 15 hours	3.75	–	–	–
At Re. 0.275 per hour for 12 hours	–	3.30	3.30	3.30
Wages earned by each worker	3.75	3.30	3.30	3.30
Effective rate per hour	0.25	0.275	0.33	0.4125
Cost of labour	3.75	3.30	3.30	3.30
Overhead at Re. 0.50 per hour	7.50	6.00	5.00	4.00
Cost of Conversion	11.25	9.30	8.30	7.30

Illustration 15

Calculate the amount of wages and bonus earned by this worker:

Name of the worker	: Moti Lal
Clock No.	: 88
Job commenced	: Monday, 3rd Jan., 2005, 8 a.m.
Job completed	: Saturday, 8th Jan., 2005, 1 p.m.
Quantity of Pieces of work given out	: 637
Quantity of Pieces of work passed	: 600
Rate of wages	: Re. 1 per hour
Time allowed	: 10 pieces per hour
Bonus	: 40% of time saved

Assume that the employee worked a 9-hour day and no overtime.

Solution

Time allowed for 600 pieces at 10 per hour	60 hours
Time Taken	50 hours
Time saved	10 hours
Bonus @ 40% of time saved	4 hours
Calculation of wages:	Rs. P.
Basic wages @ Re. 1 per hour for 50 hours	50.00
Bonus Re. 1 per hour for 4 hours	4.00
Total Earnings	54.00

Illustration 16

Payment of wage bonus is made in a concern on the following scale on the basis of the percentage of time saved on time allowed:

Time Saved (% of standard)	Bonus (% of time saved)
Upto 25%	10%
Above 25% and upto 35%	(*i*) plus 20% of time saved upto 35%
Above 35%	(*ii*) plus 30% of time saved beyond 35%

Calculate the earnings of a worker (wage rate Rs. 1.20 per hour) who takes 50 hrs. to complete a job, the standard time allowed for which is 100 hours.

(*Punjabi, B.Com, April 1988, G.N.D.U. B.Com. 2008*)

Solution

Time allowed = 100 hours
Time taken = 50 hours
Time saved = 50 hours

%age of time saved on time allowed = $\frac{50}{100} \times 100 = 50\%$

Statement of Earnings

		Rs.	Rs. P.
(*a*) *Time Wages*	(50 hrs. × Rs. 1.20)		60.00
(*b*) Bonus			
(*i*) Time saved upto 25% of time allowed:			
Bonus @ 10%	$\left(\frac{10}{100} \times 25 \text{ hrs.} \times \text{Rs.} 1.20\right)$	3.00	
(*ii*) Time saved above 25%, upto 35% of time allowed:			
Bonus @ 20%	$\left(\frac{20}{100} \times 10 \text{ hrs.} \times \text{Rs.} 1.20\right)$	2.40	
(*iii*) Time saved above 35% of time allowed:			
Bonus @ 30%	$\left(\frac{30}{100} \times 15 \text{ hrs.} \times \text{Rs.} 1.20\right)$	5.40	10.80
	Total Earnings		70.80

Illustration 17

Calculate the earnings of a worker under the *(a)* Halsey Plan, and *(b)* Rowan Plan, from the following particulars:

(1) Hourly rate of wages (guaranteed) : 50 Paise
(2) Standard time for producing 1 dozen articles : 3 hours
(3) Actual Production : 20 dozen articles
(4) Actual time taken : 48 hours.

(*C.A. Inter Nov. 1998*)

Solution

Standard time for 20 dozen articles at 3 hours per dozen: 60 hours

Calculation of Wages

	Halsey Plan Rs. P.	Rowan Plan Rs. P.
Basic wages @ 50 paise per hour for 48 hours	24.00	24.00
Bonus:		
Halsey Plan Rowan Plan		
$\left(\frac{S-T}{2}\times R\right)\left(\frac{S-T}{S}\times T\times R\right)$		
$\left(\frac{60-48}{2}\times 0.50\right)\left(\frac{60-48}{60}\times 48\times 0.50\right)$	3.00	4.80
Total Eamings	27.00	28.80

Where: 'S' stands for standard time
'T' stands for time taken
'R' stands for rate of wages.

Illustration 18

Calculate the total wages earned (including bonus) by a worker for a working day of 8 hours under Halsey and Rowan Plans:

Standard production per hour : 6 units
Total production during the day : 64 units
Rate of wages : Rs. 2 per hour.

(*G.N.D.U. B.Com., April, 1976*)

Solution

Standard time for actual production of 64 units = 10 hrs. 40 minutes

(@6 units per hour) or $10\frac{2}{3}$ Hrs.

Actual time taken : 8 Hours
Rate of wages : Rs. 2 per hour.

Halsey Plan:	**Rs. P.**
Basic wages (Rs. 2 per hour for 8 hours)	16.00
Bonus $\left(\frac{S-T}{2}\times R\right)\left(\frac{10\frac{2}{3}-8}{2}\times 2\right)$	2.67
Total wages	18.67

Rowan Plan:

Basic wages (Rs. 2 per hour for 8 hours)	16.0
Bonus $\left(\frac{S-T}{S} \times T \times R\right) \left(\frac{10\frac{2}{3} - 8}{10\frac{2}{3}} \times 16\right)$	4.00
Total wages	20.00

Note: 'S' stands for Standard Time
'T' for Actual Time Taken
'R' for Rate of wages

Illustration 19

Calculate the earnings of a worker from the following information under

(*a*) Time Rate System, (*b*) Piece Rate System, (*c*) Halsey Plan and (*d*) Rowan Plan.

Standard Time : 100 hours
Time Taken : 80 hours
Rate of Wages : Rs. 2 per hour

Solution

	Rs. P.
(*a*) Under Time Rate System:	
Wages @ Rs. 2 per hour for 80 hours	160.00
Total Earnings	160.00
(*b*) Under Piece Rate System:	Rs. P.
Wages @ Rs. 2 per hour for 100 hrs. (standard time)	200.00
Total Earnings	200.00
(*c*) Under Halsey Plan:	Rs. P.
Wages @ Rs. 2 per hour for 80 hours	160.00
Bonus $\left(\frac{S-T}{2} \times R\right)$ *i.e.*, $\left(\frac{100-80}{2} \times \text{Rs. } 2\right)$	20.00
Total Earnings	180.00
(*d*) Under Rowan Plan:	Rs. P.
Wages @ Rs. 2 per hour for 80 hours	160.00
Bonus $\left(\frac{S-T}{S} \times T \times R\right) \left(\frac{100-80}{100} \times 80 \times \text{Rs. } 2\right)$	32.00
Total Earnings	192.00

Note: Under piece rate system, the worker shall be paid wages for standard time.

Illustration 20

What will be the earnings of a worker at 55 Paise per hour, when he takes 140 hours to do a volume of work for which the standard time allowed is 200 hours? The plan of payment of bonus is on a sliding scale as under:

(*a*) Within the first 10% saving in standard time, the bonus is 40% of the time saved.

(*b*) Within the second 10% saving in standard time, the bonus is 50% of the time saved.

(*c*) Within the third 10% saving in standard time, the bonus is 60% of the time saved.

(*d*) Within the fourth 10% saving in standard time, the bonus is 70% of the time saved.

(*e*) For the rest, the bonus is 75% of the time saved.

(*B.Com. Patna*)

Solution

Standard Time	:	200 Hours
Actual Time taken	:	140 Hours
Time saved	:	60 Hours
10% of the standard time (200 Hours)	:	20 Hours

Calculation of total earnings

	Rs. P.	Rs. P.
Basic wages @ 55 Paise per hour for 140 hours		77.00
Bonus:		
(*a*) For the first 20 hours saved @ 40% of 55 Paise per hour	4.40	
(*b*) For the second 20 hours saved @ 50% of 55 Paise per hour	5.50	
(*c*) For the third 20 hours saved @ 60% of 55 Paise per hour	6.60	16.50
Total Earnings.		93.50

Illustration 21

The following data relate to X, Y and Z in a factory:

Normal labour rate per hour Re. 0.80

Hours worked by the workmen:

X – 40 hrs.

Y – 38 hrs.

Z – 45 hrs.

The merit rating analysis shows the following efficiencies of the workmen:

X – 80%

Y – 110%

Z – 75%

In addition to the wages paid at the adjusted normal rate (*i.e.*, according to the efficiency rates of the workers), a worker is entitled to dearness allowance, as a percentage of his wages at the adjusted rate, based on Cost of Index Number. For every increase of 3 points in Index Number (above 100 points) 1% dearness allowance is to be allowed. Cost of Index Number at present is 124 points. Calculate the wages earned by each worker individually.

Solution

X's Wages:

Adjusted Normal Rate : Re. 0.80 × $\frac{80}{100}$ = Rs. 0.64

Normal Wages	= 40 × 0.64 = Rs. 25.60
Dearness Allowance	= 8% of Rs. 25.60 = Rs. 2.05
Total Wages	= Rs. 25.60 + Rs. 2.05 = Rs. 27.65

Y's Wages:

Adjusted Normal Rate	= Re. 0.80 × $\frac{110}{100}$ = Re. 0.88
Normal Wages	= 38 × Re. 0.88 = Rs. 33.44
Dearness Allowance	= 8% of Rs. 33.44 =Rs. 2.67
Total Wages	= Rs. 33.44 + Rs. 2.67 = Rs. 36.11

Z'sWages:

Adjusted Normal Rate	= Re. 0.80 × $\frac{75}{100}$ = Re. 0.60
Normal Wages	= 45 × Re. 0.60 = Ps. 27.00
Dearness Allowance	= 8% of Rs. 27 = Rs. 2.16
Total Wages	= Rs. 27.00 + Rs. 2.16 = Ps. 29.16

Note: Since the present Index No. is 124 i.e., 24 points' increase over the base period, dearness allowance works out to 8% at the rate of 1% for every 3 points increased.

Illustration 22

The following particulars relate to 3 workers working in a factory

Piece rate = 6 paise per unit.

Production of the workers:

A 125 units per day.

B 80 units per day.

C 150 units per day.

Standard production per day = 120 units.

Calculate the wages of the workers on the basis of Merrick's Differential Piece Rate System, when basic piece rate is guaranteed below standard and the workers get 108% of basic piece rate between 100% and 120%, and 120% of basic piece rate above 120% efficiency.

Solution

Efficiency of the workers:

$$A = \frac{125}{120} \times 100 = 104\%$$

$$B = \frac{80}{120} \times 100 = 67\%$$

$$C = \frac{150}{120} \times 100 = 125\%$$

Piece rate below standard = 6 paise per unit.

Piece rate between 100% to 120% efficiency

$$= 6 \times \frac{108}{100} = 6.48 \text{ paise}$$

Piece rate above 120% efficiency

$$= 6 \times \frac{120}{100} = 7.20 \text{ paise}$$

Earnings of the workers:

A = 125 × 6.48 paise = Rs. 8.10.

B = 80 × 6 paise = Rs. 4.80.

C = 150 × 7.20 paise = Rs. 10.80

Illustration 23

Calculate the earnings of A and B under Straight Piece Basis and Taylor's Differential Piece Rate System, from the following information:

Standard production : 10 units per hour

Factory day : 8 hours.

Normal time rate : 50 paise per hour.

Differential to be applied : 80% of piece rate below standard. 120% of piece rate at or above standard.

Mr. A produces 70 units a day.

Mr. B produces 85 units a day.

Solution

(*i*) Straight Piece Basis

Earnings = No. of units × Rate per unit

Piece Rate = 50 paise ÷ 10 units = 5 paise per unit.

Mr. A's earnings = 70 × 5p = Rs. 3.50.

Mr. B's earnings = 85 × 5p = Rs. 4.25.

(*ii*) Taylor's Differential Piece Rate Basis
Standard production in a Factory day
$= 10 \times 8$ hours
$= 80$ units.

Low piece rate $= 5$ paise $\times \frac{80}{100} = 4$ paise.

High piece rate $= 5$ paise $\times \frac{120}{100} = 6$ paise.

Mr. A's earnings = 70 units × 4 p. = Rs. 2.80
Mr. B's earnings = 85 units × 6 p. = Rs. 5.10.

Illustration 24

A multiple piece rate plan is operated as follows:

(*a*) basic piece rate upto 85% efficiency,
(*b*) 110% basic piece rate between 85% and 100% efficiency,
(*c*) 120% basic piece rate above 100% efficiency.

Guaranteed day rate is equal to 70% efficiency. Assuming that 100% efficiency is 100 pieces per hour, and the piece rate is Re. 0.50 per piece, calculate the labour cost per piece at 5% intervals between 60% and 120% (including 100%) efficiency.

(I.C.W.A. inter)

Solution

Output per hrs. (Units)	Efficiency %	Piece Wages	Guaranteed Time Wages	10% Additional Piece Wages	20% Additional Piece Wages	Total Wages	Wages Per Piece
		Rs.	Rs.	Rs.	Rs.	Rs.	Re.
60	60	30.00	35.00	–	–	35.00	0.583
65	65	32.50	35.00	–	–	35.00	0.538
70	70	35.00	35.00	–	–	35.00	0.500
75	75	37.50	–	–	–	37.50	0.500
80	80	40.00	–	–	–	40.00	0.500
85	85	42.50	–	4.25	–	46.75	0.550
90	90	45.00	–	4.50	–	49.50	0.550
95	95	47.50	–	4.75	–	52.25	0.550
100	100	50.00	–	5.00	–	55.00	0.550
105	105	52.50	–	–	10.50	63.00	0.600
110	110	55.00	–	–	11.00	66.00	0.600
115	115	57.50	–	–	11.50	69.00	0.600
120	120	60.00	–	–	12.00	72.00	0.600

Illustration 25

The following particulars relate to a job:

Normal Time Rate : Rs. 2 per hour.
High Task (Standard) units per week: 36
Piece rate above high task : Rs. 3 per unit. (Bonus standard 20%)
In a 45 hours week, the workers performed as under:

A	30 units,
B	35 units,
C	36 units,
D	40 units,
E	42 units.

Calculate the earnings of the workers under Gantt's Task and Bonus Plan.

Solution

Calculation of Wages in a week of 45 hours under Gantt's Bonus Plan

Actual output		% of Standard Output of 36 units	Piece Rate	Piece Wage Time Wage	Labour Cost per unit
			Rs. P.	Rs. P.	Rs. P.
A	30	83.33%	–	90.00	3.00
B	35	97.22%	–	90.00	2.57
C	36	100%	–	108.00*	3.00
D	40	111.11%	3.00	120.00	3.00
E	42	116.67%	3.00	126.00	3.00

*Time Rate + 20% Bonus

Illustration 26

Ten men work as a group. When the weekly production of the group exceeds the standard (200 pieces per hour), each man in the group is paid a bonus for the excess production in addition to his wages at hourly rates. The bonus is computed as:

The percentage of production in excess of the standard amount is found and one half of this percentage is considered as the men's share. Each man in the group is paid as a bonus, this percentage of a wage rate of Rs. 3.20 per hour. There is no relationship between the individual workman's hourly rate and the bonus rate. The following is the one week's record.

Day	Hours worked	Production units
Monday	90	22,100
Tuesday	88	20,600
Wednesday	90	24,200
Thursday	84	20,100
Friday	88	20,400
Saturday	40	10,200
	480	1,17,600

(*a*) Compute the rate and amount of bonus per week.

(*b*) Compute the total pay of A who worked for $41\frac{1}{2}$ hours and was paid Rs. 2.00 per hour basic and B who worked for $44\frac{1}{2}$ hours and was paid Rs. 2.50 per hour basic.

[*I.C.W.A., UK (adapted)*]

Solution

(*a*) Actual Production for the week — 1,17,600

Standard production (200 × 480) — 96,000

Production in excess of standard — 21,600

Excess production percentage $\frac{21,600}{96,000} \times 100 = 22.5\%$

∴ Bonus percentage for the group $= 22.5 \times \frac{1}{2} = 11.25\%$

∴ Bonus rate = 11.25% of Rs. 3.20

= Re. 0.36.

Amount of bonus = 480 × 0.36 = 172.80

(*b*) Wages Computation for A and B.

A

		Rs.
Basic wages: $41\frac{1}{2}$ hours @ Rs. 2 per hour	=	83.00
Bonus: $41\frac{1}{2}$ hours @ Re. 0.36 per hour	=	14.94
Total Earnings		97.94

B

Basic wages: $44\frac{1}{2}$ hours@ Rs. 2.50 per hour	=	111.25
Bonus: $44\frac{1}{2}$ hours @ Re 0.36 per hour	=	16.02
Total Earnings		127.27

A's Total Earnings — Rs. 97.94

B's total Earnings — Rs. 127.27

Illustration 27

In a factory the hourly rate of pay is Re. 0.50. The standard production per day of 8 hours is 100 units, which is equal to 8 × 60 = 480 'Bs'. Actual production of the day was 120 units. Calculate the bonus and total earnings under Bedaux Point Plan.

Solution

Actual Production $= \frac{480}{100} \times 120 = 576$ 'Bs'

Points Saved $= 576 - 480 = 96$ 'Bs'

Bonus

'Bs' saved, *i.e.*, for $\frac{72}{60}$ 'Bs @ 50 paise = 60 paise.

Wages for one Day = Rs. 4.00 + Re. 0.60 (Bonus)

Total Earnings = Rs. 4.60.

Illustration 28

Jobs are issued to operative X to make 189 units and to operative Y to make 204 units, for which a time allowance of 20 standard minutes and 15 standard minutes per unit respectively, is credited. For every hour saved, bonus is paid at 50% of the base rate, which is Re. 0.665 per hour for both employees. The basic working week is 42 hours. Hours in excess are paid at time plus one third.

X completes his units in 45 hours and Y completes his in 39 hours (but works a full week). Due to defective material, six of X's units and four of Y's units are subsequently scrapped, although all units produced are paid for.

You are required to calculate for each of X and Y:

(*a*) The amount of bonus payable.

(*b*) The total gross wages payable.

(*c*) The wages cost per good unit made.

(*ICWA-Inter, Punjabi, B.Com. Sept. 1989*)

Solution

Operative X

	Time allowance per unit	= 20 minutes
	Time allowed for 189 units (189 × 20)	= 3,780 minutes or 63 hours
	Time actually taken	= 45 hours
	Time saved (63 hours – 45 hours)	= 18 hours
	Rate of bonus per hour (50% of 0.665)	= Re. 0.3325
(*a*)	Bonus for 18 hours (18 × Re. 0.3325)	= Rs. 5.985
(*b*)	Total Gross Wages for 42 hours @ (Re. 0.665 per hour)	= Rs. 27.930

for 3 hours @ (Re. 0.665 + 1/3 of 0.665)	
i.e., @ Re. 0.8 867	= Rs. 2.660
	30.590
Add Bonus (as above)	5.985
Total gross wages payable	36.575

(*c*) Wages Cost per Good Unit:

Saleable units	= Units produced – Defective units
	= 189 units – 6 units
	= 183 units
Wages Cost per unit	= Rs. 36.575 ÷ 183 units
	= Re. 0.1999

Operative Y

Time allowance per unit	= 15 minutes
Time allowance for 204 units (204 × 15)	= 3,060 minutes
	or 51 hours
Time actually taken	= 39 hours
Time saved (51 hours – 39 hours)	= 12 hours
(*a*) Bonus for 12 hours @ Re. 0.3325	= Rs. 3.990
(*b*) Total Gross Wages:	
for 42 hours @ Re. 0.665 per hour	= Rs. 27.930
(Since all the 42 hours are payable)	
Add Bonus as above	= Rs. 3.390
Total gross wages payable	31.920

(*c*) Wages Cost per Good Unit:

Saleable units	= Units produced – Defective units
	= 204 units – 4 units 200 units
Wages Cost per unit	Rs. 31.920 ÷ 200 units
	Re. 0.1596

TYPICAL PROBLEMS

1. Calculate the standard labour hour rate for workmen of Grade III from the following data:

Basic Pay	Rs. 200 P.M.
D.A.	Rs. 150 P.M.
Fringe benefits	Rs. 100 P.M.
Number of working days per year	300 days.

Leave rules:

30 days Privilege leave with full pay

20 days Sick leave with half pay
(Sick leave is usally availed of)

What would be the labour cost per hour if no sick leave is availed of during the year? Assume 8 hourly day.

(I.C.W.A. Inter June, 1977, C.S. Inter 1990 – adapted)
(H.P.U., B.Com. 2008)

Solution

Computation of Standard Labour Rate

	Cost per year
	Rs.
Basic Pay @ Rs. 200 p.m.	2,400
D.A. @ Rs. 150 P.M.	1,800
Fringe benefits @ Rs. 100 p.m.	1,200
Cost without sick leave	5,400
Less : Deduction on account of sick leave:	
Half pay of 20 days. $\left(\frac{200+150+100}{30}\times 20\times\frac{1}{2}\right)$	150
Net labour cost	5,250

Net Working days = Work Days – Days of Leave
= 300 – (30 + 20) = 250 days
Hours per day = 8 (assumed)

Standard Labour Hour Rate $= \frac{\text{Rs. } 5,250}{2,000 \text{ hours}}$

= Rs. 2.63 per hour

In case no sick leave is taken

Standard Labour Hour Rate Rate $= \frac{\text{Rs. } 5,400}{270 \text{ days} \times 8 \text{ hours}} = \frac{\text{Rs. } 5,400}{2,160 \text{ hours}}$

= Rs. 2.50 (per hour)

2. Calculate standard labour time for machining component No. Q – 337 from the following particulars:

Standard batch size	100 pieces
Setting-up time	64 minutes
Operation time (each piece)	
Fixing time for jobs on machine	2 minutes
Cutting time	10 minutes
Removing job from machine	3 minutes.

Allow 10% on total operation time for inspecition during process and allow further 5% on total time for fatigue.

(I.C.W.A. – Inter, adapted)

Solution

Determination of Standard Labour Time (Pieces: 100)

	Minutes	Minutes
Setting-up time		64
Operation time:		
Fixing time for Job @ 2 minutes per piece	200	
Cutting time @ 10 minutes per piece	1,000	
Removing job from machine @ 3 minutes per piece	300	1,500
Machine time		1,564
Add: Inspection time (10% of operation time)		150
Total Time		1,714
Add: Time allowed for fatigue (5% of total time *i.e.,* $\frac{5}{100} \times 1{,}714$)		86
Standard time		1,800

$$\text{Standard time per piece} = \frac{1{,}800 \text{ minutes}}{100 \text{ pieces}}$$

$$= 18 \text{ minutes.}$$

3. Production sections of a factory working on the job order system pay their workers under the Rowan Premium Bonus Scheme. Workers also get a dearness allowance of Rs. 20 per week of 48 hours.

   A worker's basic wage is Rs. 20 per day of 8 hours and his time sheet for a week is summarised below:

Job No.	Time allowed	Time taken
1844	25 hours	20 hours
1926	30 hours	20 hours
Idle time (Waiting)		8 hours.
		48 hours

   Calculate the gross wages he has earned for the week and indicate the accounts to which the wages amount will be debited.

   (*Calcutta, B.Com. modified*)

Solution

Statement of Remuneration of a Worker

	Job No. 1844	Job No. 1926	Total
	Rs.	Rs.	Rs.
Wages	60.00	66.67	126.67
Dearness Allowance	9.09	10.91	20.00
	69.09	77.58	146.67
Idle time (8 hours × Rs. 2.50)			20.00
			166.67

Accounts to be debited:

For, Wages and dearness allowance allowed Job No. 1844 A/c and Job No. 1926 A/c (with respective amounts)

For, idle time cost ...Works Overheads A/c

Working Notes:

Wages rate per hour = Rs. 20 ÷ 8 hours = Rs. 2.50

Wages as per Rowan Plan $= (T \times R) + \dfrac{S - T}{S} \times T \times R$

Wages for the Jobs

Job No. 1844 $= (20 \text{ hrs.} \times \text{Rs. } 2.50) + \dfrac{25 \text{ hrs.} - 20 \text{ hrs.}}{25 \text{ hrs.}} \times 20 \text{ hrs.} \times \text{Rs. } 2.50$

= (20 × Rs. 2.50) + 5/25 × 20 × Rs. 2.50
= Rs. 50 + 10
= Rs. 60

Job No. 1926 $= (20 \text{ hrs.} \times \text{Rs. } 2.50) + \dfrac{30 \text{ hrs.} - 20 \text{ hrs.}}{30 \text{ hrs.}} \times 20 \text{ hrs.} \times \text{Rs. } 2.50$

= (20 × Rs. 2.50) + 10/30 × 20 × Rs. 2.50
= Rs. 50 + 16.67
= Rs. 66.67

Dearness Allowance for the Jobs

Total Allowance = Rs. 20
Time allowed for:
Job No. 1844 = 25 hrs.
Job No. 1926 = 30 hrs.
Deaness Allowance to be divided in the ratio of Time allowed *i.e.,* 25 : 30
Job No. 1844 = Rs. 20 × 25/55 = Rs. 9.09
Job No. 1926 = Rs. 20 × 30/55 = Rs. 10.91

4. The Standard time for a job is 60 hours. The hourly rate of guaranteed wage is Rs. 1.50. Because of the saving in time, a worker gets an hourly wage of Rs. 1.80 under Rowan Premium Bonus system. For the same saving in time, calculate the hourly rate of wages a worker Bansi Lal will get under Halsey- Weir Premium Bonus System (assuring 40% to worker).

(I.C.W.A. Inter)

Solution

Remuneration under Rowan Premium Bonus Plan

$(T \times R) + \frac{S - T}{S} \times T \times R$, where T is actual time taken, S is the standard time and R is rate of wages.

Since actual time taken is not given, let actual time be "T"

Earnings of Bansi Lal= T × Rs. 1.80

$$\text{So, } T \times \text{Rs. } 1.80 = (T \times \text{Rs. } 1.50) + \frac{60 - T}{60} \times T \times \text{Rs. } 1.50$$

$$\text{or } \frac{9}{5}T = \frac{3}{2}T + \frac{60 - T}{60} \times \frac{3}{2}T$$

$$\text{or } \frac{9}{5}T = \frac{3}{2}T + \frac{(60 - T)}{60}$$

Multiplying both sides with 40, we get,

$$72\,T = 60\,T + T\,(60 - T)$$

$$\text{or, } 72\,T - 60\,T = T\,(60 - T)$$

$$\text{or, } 12\,T = T\,(60 - T)$$

Dividing both sides with T, we get,

$$12 = 60 - T$$

$$\text{or } T = 60 - 12 = 48$$

So, time taken = 48 hours.

and, time saved = 60 hours – 48 hours = 12 hours.

Remuneration under Halsey-Weir Plan:

= (T × R) + 40% of Wages of time saved

$$= (48 \times \text{Rs. } 1.50) + \frac{40}{100} \times 12 \times \text{Rs. } 1.50$$

= Rs. 72 + 7.20

= Rs. 79.20

Hourly rate: = Rs. 79.20 ÷ 48 hours

= Rs. 1.65

5. (*i*) From the following informations, compute the wages of workers under (*a*) Time Rate System (*b*) Halsey Plan (*c*) Rowan Plan:

Wage Rate Rs. 3 per hour

Standard Time		80 hours
Actual Time		50 hours

(*ii*)

Standard output =		150 units per day of 8 hours
Piece Rate =		Re. 0.20 per unit
Output of	A	100 units
	B	135 units
	C	180 units

Calculate the earnings of A, B and C under Merrick's differential piece rate system. (*G.N.D.U. B.Com. 1998*)

Solution

(*i*) Calculation of Total Wages

	Time Rate System	Halsey Plan	Rowan Plan
	Rs.	**Rs.**	**Rs.**
Basic wages @ Rs. 3 per hour for 50 hours	150	150	150
Bonus:	Nil		
Halsey Plan: $\frac{S-T}{2} \times R$			
$= \frac{80 \text{ hrs.} - 50 \text{ hrs.}}{2} \times \text{Rs.}\ 3$		45	
Rowan Plan:			
$\frac{S-T}{S} \times T \times R$			
$= \frac{80 \text{ hrs.} - 50 \text{ hrs.}}{80 \text{ hrs.}} \times 50 \text{ hrs.} \times \text{Rs.}\ 3$			56.25
Total Wages	150	195	206.25

S : Standard Time

T : Actual Time taken

R : Rate of Wages

(*ii*) Piece-work Rate payable under Merrick's Differential Piece Rate System:

(*a*) Efficiency below 83% of standard	Basic Rate
(*b*) Efficiency from 83% to 100% of standard	110% of basic rate
(*c*) Efficiency above 100% of standard	120% " " "

Calculation of efficiency level of workers

Worker	Standard Output per day	Actual Output	Level of Efficiency
A	150 units	100 units	$\frac{100}{150}\times100 = 66\frac{2}{3}\%$
B	150 units	135 units	$\frac{135}{150}\times100 = 90\%$
C	150 units	180 units	$\frac{180}{150}\times100 = 120\%$

Calculation of wages:

Worker A (100 units @ Re. 0.20 per unit) = Rs. 20.00
Worker B (135 units @ Re. 0.22 per unit) = Rs. 29.70
Worker C (180 units @ Re. 0.24 per unit) = Rs. 43.20

6. A worker produced 180 units in a week. The guaranteed weekly wage payment for 44 hours is Rs. 77. The expected time to produce one unit is 16 minutes which is further raised by 25% under the incentive scheme. What will be the earnings per hour of the worker under the Halsey and Rowan Schemes. *(H.P.U. B.Com. 2006)*

Solution

(*i*) Hourly Rate of wages = $\frac{\text{Rs. } 77}{44 \text{ hrs.}}$ = Rs. 1.75

(*ii*) Standard Time for actual output:

Actual output = 180 units
Standard time allowed per unit (16 minutes + 25%) = 20 minutes
Standard time for actual output = 180 units × 20 minutes
= 3,600 minutes or 60 hours.
Actual Time Taken = 44 hours.

(iii) Calculation of Wages

	Halsey Plan	Rowan Plan
	Rs. P.	Rs. P.
Basic wages @ Rs. 1.75 per hour for 44 hours	77.00	77.00
Bonus : (a) Halsey Plan : $\frac{S-T}{2}\times R$		
$\left(\frac{60\text{ hrs.}-44\text{ hrs.}}{2}\times 1.75\right)$	14.00	
(b) Rowan Plan: $\frac{S-T}{S}\times T\times R$		
$\left(\frac{60\text{ hrs.}-44\text{ hrs.}}{60\text{ hrs.}}\times 77\right)$		20.53
Total wages	91.00	97.53
(c) Earnings per hour:		
$\left(\frac{\text{Total Wages}}{\text{Actual Time Taken}}\right)$	Rs. 91.00 ÷ 44 hrs	Rs. 97.53 ÷ 44 hrs.
	= Rs. 2.068	= Rs. 2.217

Note: S = Standard Time
T = Actual Time taken
R = Rate of wages

7. Rolex Limited operates in one of its departments a group incentive scheme. A minimum hourly rate is guaranteed to each of the six employees in the group if actual output for the week is less than the standard output. If actual output is greater than the standard output the hourly rate of each employee is increased by 4% for each additional 600 units of output produced. The standard output for the group is 12,000 units for a 40 hour week.

During the week ended 31.12.2001, each employee in the group worked 40 hours; actual output and minimum hourly rates were as under:

	Actual output (in units)	Minimum hourly rate Rs.
A	2,500	0.60
B	2,700	1.00
C	2,400	0.60
D	2,500	0.80
E	2,460	0.60
F	2,440	0.40

You are required to (*i*) Calculate earnings of each employee. (*ii*) Appraise the effectiveness to the company of this group incentive scheme.

(*G.N.D.U. B.Com. 2004*)

Solution

Calculation of Rate of Incentive

Standard weekly output (for the group)	12,000 units
Actual weekly output	15,000 units
Excess of actual output over standard output	3,000 units

Rate of Incentive : 4% of hourly rate for every 600 of additional output

$$\text{Rate of incentive applicable} = \frac{4}{600 \text{ units}} \times 3{,}000 \text{ units} = 20\%$$

Calculation of wages

Name of Worker	Hours Worked	Minimum Hourly Rate	Incentive @ 20%	Effective Rate	Wages at minimum rate	Wages at Effective Rate
		Re.	Re.	Re.	Rs. P.	Rs. P.
A	40	0.60	0.12	0.72	24.00	28.80
B	40	1.00	0.20	1.20	40.00	48.00
C	40	0.60	0.12	0.72	24.00	28.80
D	40	0.80	0.16	0.96	32.00	38.40
E	40	0.60	0.12	0.72	24.00	28.80
F	40	0.40	0.08	0.48	16.00	19.20
					160.00	192.00

Calculation of Effective Wage Rate per unit;

(*i*) At standard minimum output

$$= \frac{\text{Total Wages}}{\text{Standard Output}} = \frac{\text{Rs.}160}{12{,}000 \text{ units}} = \text{Re. } 00.0133 \text{ per unit}$$

(*ii*) $\frac{\text{Total Wages}}{\text{Actual Output}} = \frac{\text{Rs.}192}{15{,}000 \text{ units}} = \text{Re. } 00.0128 \text{ per unit}$

(iii) The adoption of the group incentive scheme has helped the workers in earning wages @ Re. 0.0133 per unit against the minimum of Re. 0.0125 per unit. As such the group incentive plan is effective from the view point of efficiency of workers.

8. Mr. A is working by employing 10 skilled workers. He is considering the introduction of some incentive scheme-either Halsey Scheme (with 50% Bonus) or Rowan Scheme of wage payments for increasing the labour productivity to cope with the increased demand for the product by 25%. He feels that if the proposed incentive scheme could bring about an average 20% increase over the present earnings of the workers, it could act as sufficient incentive for them to produce more and he has accordingly given this assurance to the workers. As a result of this assurance the increase in productivity has been observed as revealed by the following figures for the current month.

Hourly rate of wages (guaranteed) Rs. 2.00

Average time for producing 1 piece by one worker at the previous performance

(This may be taken as time allowed) 2 hours

No. of working days in the month 25

No. of working hours per day for each worker 8

Actual production during the month 1,250 units

Required:

(1) Calculate effective rate of earning per hour under Halsey scheme and Rowan scheme.

(2) Calculate the savings to Mr. A in terms of direct labour cost per piece under the above schemes.

(3) Advise Mr. A about the selection of the scheme to fulfil his assurance.

(*H.P.U., B.Com., 2005*)

Solution

(*i*) Calculation of current piece work rate (previous performance)

Hourly rate of wages (guaranteed) = Rs. 2.00

Average time taken for producing one unit (piece) = 2 hours

Amount of wages per piece = 2 hrs. × Rs. 2

= Rs. 4.

(*ii*) Actual production under incentive plan during the month = 1,250 units

Standard Time Allowed for actual output = 1,250 units × 2 hrs.

= 2,500 hours

Actual Time Taken for actual output

= 25 days × 8 hrs. × 10 workers

= 2,000 hrs.

1. Calculation of Total wages under Incentive Plans

	Halsey Plan	Rowan Plan
	Rs.	Rs.
Basic wages @ Rs. 2 per hour for 2,000 hours	4,000	4,000
Bonus:		
Halsey Plan: $\frac{S-T}{2} \times R$ $\left(\frac{2,500 \text{ hrs.} - 2,000 \text{ hrs.}}{2} \times \text{Rs. } 2\right)$	500	

	Halsey	Rowan
Rowan Plan: $\frac{S-T}{S} \times T \times R$ $\left(\frac{2{,}500 \text{ hrs.} - 2{,}000 \text{ hrs.}}{2{,}500 \text{ hrs.}} \times \text{Rs. } 4{,}000\right)$		800
Total wages	4,500	4,800
Effective Wages Rate $\left(\frac{\text{Total Wages}}{\text{Actual Time Taken}}\right)$	$\frac{\text{Rs. } 4{,}500}{2{,}000 \text{ hrs}}$ = Rs. 2.25 per hour	$\frac{\text{Rs. } 4{,}800}{2{,}000 \text{ hrs}}$ = Rs. 2.40 per hour

2. Calculation of Savings to Mr. A in terms of direct labour cost per piece under Incentive Plans

	Rate of wages per piece	Savings in labour cost per piece
Previous Performance (2 hours per unit @ Rs. 2 per hour)	4.00	–
Halsey Plan $\frac{\text{Rs. } 4{,}500}{1{,}250 \text{ units}}$	3.60	0.40
Rowan Plan $\frac{\text{Rs. } 4{,}800}{1{,}250 \text{ units}}$	3.84	0.16

3. Calculation of Percentage of Increase in earnings

	Current Rate of Wages (Per hour)	Rate of wages under Incentive Plan (Per hour)	Increase over current rate	% of Increase
	Rs. P.	Rs. P.	Rs. P.	
(*i*) Halsey Plan	2.00	2.25	0.25	12.5 $\left(\frac{0.25}{2} \times 100\right)$
(*ii*) Rowan Plan	2.00	2.40	0.40	20.00 $\left(\frac{0.40}{2} \times 100\right)$

In order to fulfil his assurance to the workers that proposed incentive scheme could bring about an average 20% increase in their earnings, Mr. A should follow Rowan Plan as it gives an increase of 20% in effective wage rate over 12.5% under Halsey Plan.

OBJECTIVE TYPE QUESTIONS

A. Multiple Choice Questions

1. Select the correct answer in each of the following cases:

(*i*) Attendance record of the workers is maintained by

(*a*) The Engineering Department,

(*b*) The Time-Keeping Department,

(*c*) The Personnel Department.

(*ii*) Time spent by the worker on each job during a week is recorded on

(*a*) Time Card.

(*b*) Daily Muster Roll,

(*c*) Job Card.

(*iii*) Time, motion and fatigue study is undertaken by

(*a*) The Engineering Department,

(*b*) The Pay Roll department,

(*c*) The Personnel Department.

(*iv*) Labour turnover is measured by

(*a*) Number of worker replaced/average number of workers.

(*b*) Number of workers joining/number in the beginning of the period.

(*c*) Number of workers left/number in the beginning plus number at the end.

(*v*) Cost of idle time arising due to non-availability of raw materials is

(*a*) Charged to Costing Profit and Loss A/c

(*b*) Charged to Factory Overheads

(*c*) Recovered by inflating the wage rate.

(*vi*) The formula for calculating wages under Rowan Plan is

(*a*) $T \times R + \dfrac{S - T}{2} \times R$

(*b*) $T \times R + \% \, (S - T) \times R$

(*c*) $T \times R + \dfrac{S - T}{S} \times T \times R$.

(*vii*) Under Emerson's Efficiency System, no bonus is payable when efficiency is upto

(*a*) 50%

(*b*) $66\frac{2}{3}\%$

(*c*) $83\frac{1}{3}\%$

(*viii*) Wages Sheet is prepared by

(*a*) Time-Keeping Department,

(*b*) Personnel Department,

(*c*) Pay Roll Department.

(*ix*) Under Gantt's Task and Bonus Plan, no bonus is payable to a worker if his efficiency is less than,

(*a*) $66\frac{2}{3}\%$

(*b*) $83\frac{1}{3}\%$

(*c*) 100%

(*x*) Standard time is 8 hours, actual time taken is 6 hours and time rate is Rs. 2 per hour. The total wages under Halsey plan will be:

(*a*) Rs. 16

(*b*) Rs. 18

(*c*) Rs. 14

[**Ans.** (*i*) (*b*), (*ii*) (*c*), (*iii*) (*a*) (*iv*) (*a*) , (*v*) (*a*), (*vi*) (*c*), (*vii*) (*b*), (*viii*) (*c*), (*ix*) (*c*), (*x*) (*c*)]

B. 'True' or 'False' type statements

2. Indicate which of the following statements are 'true' or 'false'

(*a*) Direct labour cost is the remuneration of the employees who are directly connected with the manufacturing operations or the conversion of raw materials into finished products.

(*b*) The Daily Muster Rolls are analysed by the Time-Keeping department in order to calculate wages payable to each worker.

(*c*) Pay Roll department is concerned with disbursing wages and salaries.

(*d*) Overtime wages are paid at double the normal wage rate.

(*e*) The question of idle time arises where the direct workers are paid on time basis.

(*f*) In Rowan Plan, time wages are guaranteed.

(*g*) In Emerson's Efficiency System, bonus is paid only when efficiency is 100%.

(*h*) Taylor's Differential Piece rate system guarantees a minimum day wage.

(*i*) Under Gantt's Task and Bonus Scheme, a worker who fails to attain the standard is paid the guaranteed time rate.

(*j*) Merrick's Differential Piece Rate System is an improvement over Taylor's system.

[**Ans. True** – (*a*), (*c*), (*d*), (*e*), (*f*), (*j*), (*k*) **False** – (*b*), (*g*), (*i*)]

C. Filling the blanks:

3. Fill in the blanks with appropriate words:

(*a*) Wages paid to .... is an example of direct wages.

(*b*) Time and Motion study is conducted by .... department.

(*c*) Wage sheet is prepared by .... department.

(*d*) Cost of normal idle time is charged to ....

(*e*) Under Halsey plan, bonus is paid to the workers equal to .... of the time saved.

(*f*) Formula for calculating wages under Rowan plan is ....

(*g*) .... is concerned with the elimination of useless motions on the job and to find out the best method of job performance.

(*h*) Workers operating outside the factory are known as ....

(*i*) .... are not regular employees in a concern but are generally engaged in case of extra work load in the factory.

(*j*) Time recording clock prints the time on ....

[**Ans.** (*a*) Machinist (*b*) Engineering department (*c*) Pay Roll Department (*d*) Factory Overheads (*e*) 50% (*f*) $T \times R + \frac{S - T}{S} \times T \times R$ (*g*) Motion study (*h*) Out-workers (*i*) Casual workers (*j*) Time Card.]

SHORT ANSWER TYPE QUESTIONS

4. Answer each of the following questions in not more than 5 lines each.

(*a*) Distinguish between direct and indirect labour.

(*b*) What are the main functions of time-keeping department?

(*c*) Name the four incentive payment schemes?

(*d*) Give four examples of normal idle time.

(*e*) What are the causes of labour turnover?

(*f*) What is meant by Profit-sharing?

(*g*) What is Halsey-Weir plan?

(*h*) What is meant by Wages Abstract?

(*i*) What is combined time and job card?

(*j*) What are the main functions of Engineering department?

(*k*) What is Taylor's differential piece rate system?

(*l*) What is Bedeaux Point Premium Plan?

(*m*) What is Group Bonus Scheme of wage payment?

(*n*) What is Merrick's Differential Piece rate system?

(*o*) What is Hayne's Bonus System?

LONG ANSWER TYPE QUESTIONS

1. How is labour cost computed? Distinguish between Direct and Indirect Labour Cost.

2. Briefly explain various methods of time recording. Suggest a suitable method of time recording for a factory employing 1,000 workers.

3. Describe the following methods for recording the daily attendance of workers:

(*a*) Attendance Register
(*b*) Disc Method.
(*c*) Time Recording Card.

4. What is Time-booking ? What are its objects? Explain various methods of Time-booking.

5. (*a*) What do you understand by the term "Labour Turnover"? How is it measured? (*b*) What are its possible effects on production costs of an industrial unit?

6. Briefly discuss the following, giving a specimen of each.

(*i*) Weekly time sheet
(*ii*) Job card
(*iii*) Job Ticket
(*iv*) Time card
(*v*) Combined Time and Job card.

7. Explain briefly the organisation and functioning of the following departments of a manufacturing concern:

(*a*) Personnel Department
(*b*) Engineering Department.
(*c*) Pay Roll Department.

8. How would you ensure that no 'dummy' workers are included in the Pay-roll?

9. Describe briefly the internal checks which you would install to guard against frauds in wage calculations and payments.

10. Give the specimens and explain the procedure of preparing Wages Sheet and Wages Abstract.

11. What is 'idle time'? How is it treated in costing?

Or

(*a*) As a newly appointed Cost Accountant, lay down a procedure for booking idle time for men under various heads in the production shops.

(*b*) While implementing the procedure, a tabulation of the idle time bookings reveals that the maximum time is lost:

(*i*) in waiting for work;
(*ii*) in waiting for material; and
(*iii*) due to frequent power failure. How would you set about finding the causes for these and what remedies would you suggest to reduce idle time under these heads? (*I.C.W.A., Inter*)

12. Explain the following, giving a specimen of each:
(*i*) Daily muster Roll.
(*ii*) Operation Card.
(*iii*) Idle time card.
(*iv*) Employee's History card.

13. Distinguish between 'Normal' and 'Abnormal' idle time. How would you deal with each one of them in cost accounts?

14. What is 'Overtime'? How would you treat the cost of overtime in costing?

15. (*a*) What do you understand by the term 'wages abstract'?
(*b*) In a jobbing factory the productive labour hours are booked to the jobs cost centre-wise. Draw a proforma of a wages abstract for a cost centre.
(*c*) What is the relationship between the hours booked to the jobs and the attendance hours for which wages are paid? (*I.C.W.A. –Inter*)

16. What are the different types of documents that can be used to record labour time and how do they differ from each other? State the advantages and disadvantages of each. (*C.A. Inter Nov. 1973*)

17. How is labour turnover measured? Why is high labour turnover a matter of serious concern to management? (*B.Com., Delhi 1971*)

18. Briefly explain various essentials of a good wage system.

19. What are the advantages and disadvantages of time rate and piece rate systems of wage payment? Explain the circumstances is which each system is effective and useful.

20. Explain and illustrate clearly:

(*a*) Halsey Plan, and (*b*) Rowan Plan. Give a comparative study of the two.

21. What is meant by an 'Incentive plan' of remunerating labour ? Mention any four such plans giving their merits and demerits.

22. "Low wages do not necessarily mean low cost, in fact, it is widely recognised now that efficiently organised factories may pay the highest wages, and yet have the lowest labour costs". Critically examine the statement and give a comparative study of some of the important methods of remunerating labour that are prevalent in the industries these days.

23. Briefly explain Taylor's differential piece rate system and Merrick's multiple piece rate system.

24. Write short notes on:

(*a*) Emerson's efficiency plan.

(*b*) Bedaux system.

(*c*) The Priestman's production bonus plan.

(*d*) Gantt task and Bonus scheme.

25. What is meant by Group Bonus Scheme? Where can it be applied ? What are its advantages over individual bonus?

26. How would you treat the following in cost accounts?

(*a*) Holiday pay.

(*b*) Night shift allowance.

(*c*) Out-workers.

27. What precautionary measures should be adopted in a wage system to prevent payment of wages:

(*a*) To a person who was absent for the whole week or to a fictitious person,

(*b*) To a wrong person, and

(*c*) In excess of hours worked or work done.

28. "With day wages, increased productivity of labour benefits only employers, with piece rate only employees, and with incentive plans both the employers and the employees". Discuss the statement with suitable examples.

29. Explain the profit sharing scheme. Why is it not looked upon with much favour by the workers?

30. What is meant by 'Incentive Scheme' of wage payment? Describe the characteristics and drawbacks of such schemes.(*G.N.D.U. B.Com. 2004*)

EXERCISES

1. From the following data, prepare a statement showing the cost per day of 8 hours engaging a particular type of labour:

(*a*) Monthly salary (Basic plus dearness allowance) ... Rs. 200

(*b*) Leave salary payable to workman 5% of salary

(*c*) Employer's contribution to Provident Fund 8% of salary

[*items* (*a*) *and* (*b*)]

(*d*) Employer's contribution to State Insurance $2\frac{1}{2}\%$ of salary

[*items* (*a*) *and* (*b*)]

(*e*) Pro-rata expenditure on amenities to labour, Rs. 17.95 per head per month.

(*f*) Number of working hours in month ... 200.

[**Ans.** Total labour cost = Rs. 250.00
Labour cost per day = Rs. 10.00]

2. From the following details calculate the normal and overtime wages of a workman in a cotton mill:

Days	No. of hours worked
Monday	7 hours
Tuesday	8 hours
Wednesday	10 hours
Thursday	9 hours
Friday	8 hours
Saturday	5 hours

Normal working hours: 7 hours per day, Normal rate of wages: Re. 1 per hour. Overtime wage rate: upto 8 hours in a day at single rate and over 8 hours in a day at double rate, OR, up to 42 hours in a week at single rate and over 42 hours at double rate, whichever is more beneficial to workman.

[**Ans.** Normal wages = Rs. 42.00
Overtime wages = Rs. 10.00
Total wages Rs. 52.00]

3. From the following information, calculate the net monthly Labour Turnover rate of a company by applying Replacement Rate Method.

Number of employees in the beginning of the month.	1,550
Number of employees at the end of the month	1,850
Number of employees resigned	200
Number of employees discharged	20
Number of employees replaced due to quits and discharges	170
Additional hands employed during the year	350

[**Ans.** 10%]

4. The normal working week in a factory is of 44 hours. A worker is paid 50 paise an hour, overtime is $1\frac{1}{2}$ times the hourly rate and a bonus of 25 paise for every 100 articles produced in excess of 5,000 per week. Calculate his wages for the week from the following particulars taken from his Time and Job Card:

Day	In	Out	In	Out	Output (articles)
Monday	8.00	12.00	1.00	5.30	950
Tuesday	8.00	11.30	–	–	545
Wednesday	8.30	12.00	1.00	8.00	1,106
Thursday	8.00	12.00	1.00	6.00	1,052
Friday	8.00	12.00	1.00	6.30	1,002
Saturday	8.00	12.00	1.00	7.00	1,112

[**Ans.** Total wages = Rs. 29.17]

5. From the following particulars, find the amount of cash required for payment of wages only in a factory for a particular month:

		Rs.
(*i*)	Wages for normal hours worked	20,500
(*ii*)	Wages for Overtime	2,200
(*iii*)	Leave wages	1,700
(*iv*)	Deduction of employee's share to State Insurance contribution	500
(*v*)	Employee's contribution to Provident Fund	1,600
(*vi*)	House rent is to be recovered from 30 employees @ Rs. 10 per month.	

[**Ans.** Cash Required Rs. 22,000]

6. From the following data, calculate total monthly remuneration of 3 workers X, Y and Z:

(*i*) Standard production per month per worker is 1,000 units.

(*ii*) Actual production during the month:
X – 800 units
Y – 700 units
Z – 900 units

(*iii*) Piece-work rate per unit of actual production: 15 Paise.

(*iv*) Dearness Allowance: Rs. 40 per month (fixed)

(*v*) House Rent Allowance: Rs. 20 per month (fixed)

(*vi*) Additional Production Bonus @ Rs. 5 for each percentage of actual production exceeding 75% actual production over standard.

[**Ans.** Total remuneration for the month: X, Rs. 205; Y, Rs. 165; Z, Rs. 270.]

7. Compute the direct labour cost of Job A from the following data:

	Time Employed in Hours	
Day	**Worker X**	**Worker Y**
Monday	10	8
Tuesday	9	10
Wednesday	10	11
Thursday	11	10
Friday	6	5
Saturday	6	4

(*a*) Normal working hours on week days are 8 hours, and on Saturday 4 hours.

(*b*) Overtime is paid for at double the normal rates.

(*c*) Normal Daily wages X, Rs. 3 and Y, Rs. 4.

(*d*) Four hours work on Saturday is paid for full day's wages. Work on Saturdays in excess of 4 hours is treated as over-time and is paid for a $1\frac{1}{2}$ normal wages upto a total of 8 hours work and beyond at double the normal rate.

(*e*) Dearness Allowance is to be added to the total wages including overtime at 50% of wages.

[**Ans.** Total wages of X	= Rs. 36.28
Y	= Rs. 44.25
Direct Labour Cost of Job A	= Rs. 80.53

8. Calculate total earnings and effective wage rate from the following information by using:

(*a*) Time basis,

(*b*) Piece basis.

(*c*) Halsey Plan, and

(*d*) Rowan Plan.

Given: Standard Time = 50 Hours.
Actual Time taken = 40 Hours.
Rate of wages = Re. 1 per hour.
Dearness Allowance = 50 paise per hour worked.

[**Ans.** (*a*) Rs. 60 (*b*) Rs. 70 (*c*) Rs. 65 (*d*) Rs. 68]

9. (*i*) A worker takes 9 hours to complete a job on daily wages and 6 hours on a scheme of payment by results. His day rate is 75 Paise an hour, the material cost is Rs. 4 and the overheads are recovered at 150% of direct wages. Calculate the factory cost of the product under:

(*a*) Piece Work Plan.

(*b*) Rowan Plan.

(*c*) Halsey Plan. [**Ans.** (*a*) Rs. 15.25 (*b*) Rs. 19.00 (*c*) Rs. 18.70]

(*ii*) From the following informations, compute the wages of a worker under, (*a*) Time-Rate System, (*b*) Halsey Plan, (*c*) Rowan Plan:

Wage Rate Rs. 3 per hour
Standard Time 80 hours
Actual Time 50 hours

(*G.N.D.U., B Com., April 1998*)

[**Ans.** (*a*) Rs. 150, (*b*) Rs. 195, (*c*) Rs. 206.25]

10. Calculate the earnings of a workman under the Halsey Premium Plan (50% to worker) and the Rowan Premium Plan for executing a piece of work in 60 hours as against 75 hours allowed. His hourly rate is Re. 1. In addition he gets a dearness allowance of Rs. 2 per day of 8 hours worked.

[**Ans.** Earning under Halsey plan. Rs. 82.50
Rowan plan. Rs. 87.00]

[**Hints:** Bonus under Halsey plan ... $\frac{75-60}{2} \times$ Re. 1

" " Rowan plan ... $\frac{75-60}{75} \times 60 \times$ Re. 1]

11. A Workman normally takes 18 hours to complete a job on daily wages and 12 hours on a scheme of payment by results. His day rate is Re. 1 per hour. The material cost of the job is Rs. 20 and the factory overheads are recovered at 150% of the total direct wages. Calculate the factory cost of the job under (*a*) Time Rate system, (*b*) Piece Rate system, (*c*) Halsey Plan and (*d*) Rowan Plan.

[**Ans.** (*a*) Rs. 65; (*b*) Rs. 50; (*c*) Rs. 57; (*d*) Rs. 60]
(**Hints:** Wages under (*a*) Rs. 18; (*b*) Rs. 18; (*c*) Rs. 15;)

12. A worker under the Halsey method of remuneration has a day rate of Rs. 12 per week of 48 hours, plus a cost of living bonus at 10 Paise per hour worked. He is given an 8 hours task to perform which he accomplishes in 6 hours. He is allowed 30% of the time saved as premium bonus. What would be his total hourly rate of earnings, and what difference would it make if he was paid under Rowan Plan?

[**Ans.** Under Halsey Method, earnings for 6 hours = Rs. 2.25 Under Rowan Plan, earnings for 6 hours = Rs. 2.47]

13. In a concern, 10 men work as a group. When the production of group exceeds the standard output of 200 pieces per hour, each man is paid an incentive for the excess production in addition to his wages at hourly rates. The incentive is at half the percentage the excess production over standard bears to the standard production.

Each man is paid an incentive @ this percentage of a wage rate of Rs. 2 per hour.

There is no relation between individual workman's hourly rate and the bonus rate.

In a week, the hours worked are 500 and the total production is 1,20,000 pieces.

(*a*) Compute the total amount of bonus for the week.

(*b*) Calculate the total earnings of two workers X and Y of the group. X worked for 44 hours and his basic rate per hour was Rs. 2.10, Y worked for 48 hours and his basic rate per hour was Rs. 1.80.

[**Ans.** (*a*) Rs. 100, (*b*) *X* - Rs. 101.20, Y - Rs. 96]

14. The standard time for Job X is 100 hours. The job has been completed by Amar in 60 hours, Akbar in 70 hours and Anthony in 95 hours.

The bonus system applicable to the job is as follows;

Percentage of time saved to time allowed:	Bonus:
Saving upto 10%	10% of time saved
From 11% to 20%	15% of time saved
From 21% to 40%	20% of time saved
From 41% to 100%	25% of time saved

The rate of pay is Re. 1 per hour. Calculate the total earnings of each worker and also the rate of earnings per hour.

(*C.A. Inter, May 1990*)

[Ans.

	Amar	Akbar	Anthony
	Rs.	Rs.	Rs.
Total Earnings	68	76	95.50
Earning per hour	1.133	1.0857	1.005]

15. Calculate the earnings of A and B under Straight Piece Basis and Taylor's Differential Piece Rate System, from the following information:

Standard production: 7 units per hour
Factory day: 8 Hours
Normal time rate : Rs. 2.80 per hour
Differential to be applied : 80% of piece rate below standard, 120% of piece rate at or above standard.
Mr. A produces 50 units a day.
Mr. B produces 60 units a day

(*B.Com., Punjabi, April 1989*)

Ans. [Earnings under Straight Piece Basis: A Rs. 20 B Rs. 24: Earnings under Taylor's Differential Piece Rate System; A Rs. 16; B Rs. 28.80]

16. (*a*) Bonus paid under the Halsey Plan with a bonus at 50% for the time saved equals the bonus paid under the Rowan System. When will this statement hold good?

(Your answer should contain the proof).

(*b*) The time allowed for a job is 8 hours. The hourly rate is Rs. 8. Prepare a statement showing:

(*i*) The bonus earned,
(*ii*) Total earnings of labour, and
(*iii*) Hourly earnings;

under the Halsey System with 50% bonus for time saved and Rowan System for each hour saved progressively.

(*C.A. Inter, May 1991*)

[**Ans.** (*a*) When the time taken is 50% of the time allowed:

(*b*) Time	Bonus Under		Total Earnings		Hourly Earnings	
Taken (Hours)	Halsey System Rs.	Rowan System Rs.	Halsey System Rs.	Rowan System Rs.	Halsey System Rs.	Rowan System Rs.
8	—	—	64	64	8.00	8.00
7	4	7	60	63	8.57	9.00
6	8	12	56	60	9.33	10.00
5	12	15	52	55	10.40	11.00
4	16	16	48	48	12.00	12.00
3	20	15	44	39	14.67	13.00
2	24	12	40	28	20.00	14.00
1	28	7	36	15	36.00	15.00]

17. In a factory Group Bonus System is in use which is calculated on the basis of earnings under time rate.

The following particulars are available for a group of 4 workers P, Q, R and S:

(*i*) Output of the group 16,000 units.

(*ii*) Piece rate per 100 units Rs. 2.50.

(*iii*) Number of hours worked by P 90
Q 72
R 80
S 100

(*iv*) Time rate per hour for P Re. 0.80
Q Re. 1.00
R Rs. 1.20
S Rs. 0.80

Calculate the total of bonus and wages earned by each worker.

(*I.C.W.A. Inter, June 1992*)

[**Ans.** P = Its. 90; Q = Rs. 90; R = Rs. 120; S = Rs. 100]

18. (*i*) What is meant by the term 'Labour Turnover' ? What is the effect of labour turnover on cost of production?

(*ii*) From the following data given by the Personnel Department, calculate the labour turnover rate by applying:

(*a*) Separation Method.

(*b*) Replacement Method.

(*c*) Flux Method.

No. of workers on the payroll	
At the beginning of the month	900
At the end of the month	1,100

During the month 10 workers left, 40 workers were discharged and 150 workers were recruited. Of these 25 workers are recruited in the vacancies of those leaving, while the rest were engaged for an expansion scheme.

(*I.C.W.A. Inter, Dec., 1988*)

[**Ans.** (*ii*) (*a*) 5% : (*b*) 2.5%; (*c*) 7.5%].

19. 'A' an employee of XYZ Co. gets the following emoluments and benefits:

(*a*) Salary	Rs. 250 per month
(*b*) Dearness Allowance	
On lst Rs. 100 of Salary	Rs. 400
On next Rs. 100 of Salary	Rs. 100
On balance every Rs. 100	Rs. 50 or part thereof
(*c*) Employer's Contribution to:	
Provident Fund	8% Salary and D.A.
E.S.I.	4% of Salary and D.A.
(*d*) Bonus	20% of Salary and D.A.
(*e*) Other Allowances	Rs. 2,725 per annum

A works for 2,400 hours per annum, out of which 400 hours are non-productive but treated as normal idle time. A worked for 18 effective hours in Job No. 13, where the cost of direct materials equals A's earning and the overhead applied is 100% of Prime Cost. The Sale Value of the Job is quoted to earn a profit of 10% on such value.

Your are requested to find out:

(*a*) Effective hourly cost of 'A' and

(*b*) The expected sale value of Job. No. 13.

(*I.C.W.A. Inter, June 1991*)

[**Ans.** (*a*) Rs. 7.50; (*b*) Rs. 600]

20. From the following particulars you are required to work out the earnings of a worker for a week under (*a*) Straight piece-rate. (*b*) Differential piece rate, (*c*) Halsey premium scheme (50% sharing) and (*d*) Rowan premium scheme.

Weekly working hours	48
Hourly wage rate	Rs. 7.50
Piece rate per unit	Rs. 3.00
Normal time taken per piece	20 minutes
Normal output per week	120 pieces
Actual output for the week	150 pieces
Differential piece rate	80% of piece rate when output below normal and 120% of piece rate when output above normal.

(*I.C.W.A. Inter, Dec. 1989*)

[**Ans.** (*a*) Rs. 450; (*b*) Rs. 540; (*c*) Rs. 367.50; (*d*) Rs. 374.40]

7
Direct Expenses

Prime Cost consists of direct materials cost, direct wages and direct expenses. Direct materials and direct labour have already been explained in the previous chapters. Direct expenses are those expenses which can be identified with and allocated to cost centres or cost units. These are also known as *chargeable expenses*. Direct expenses include all expenses other than direct materials and direct labour and represent the cost of services rendered to a particular cost unit or cost centre. These services may be external or internal. For example, consultation fees paid to an engineer is the cost of external services while cost incurred for preparing a drawing is the cost of an internal service.

CHARACTERISTICS OF A CHARGEABLE OR DIRECT EXPENSE

For being classified as chargeable expense, an expenditure should have the following characteristics:

(*i*) It is an expenditure other than direct material and direct labour.
(*ii*) It should be an expense necessary for a particular job or product.
(*iii*) It should have been specifically incurred for a particular job or product.
(*iv*) It can be conveniently charged or allocated to that job or product.

ITEMS OF DIRECT EXPENSES

The following items usually come under the heading of direct expenses:

1. Cost of patterns, drawings, or designs specifically prepared for a particular job and which cannot be utilized for other purposes.
2. Hire charges of special machinery, plant or other equipment such as portable cranes, traction engines etc.
3. Cost of any experimental work carried out specially for a particular job.
4. Architects' and surveyors' fees in connection with some particular job or contract.
5. Travelling expenses incurred in connection with a particular contract or job.

6. Carriage and freight charges on materials purchased for particular jobs, if such carriage and freight has not been included in the cost of materials.
7. Royalties paid on the basis of output.

DISTINCTION BETWEEN CHARGEABLE EXPENSES AND OVERHEAD EXPENSES

The main points of difference between chargeable (direct) expenses and overhead expenses may be summarized as follows:

1. Direct expenses are included in prime cost, whereas overhead expenses are not included in it.
2. Direct expenses are incurred for a particular job, contract, product or work-order etc., whereas overheads are incurred for the organisation as a whole or for a number of jobs, products, work-orders or contracts.
3. The direct expenses are variable in nature and as such the amount of direct expenses depends upon the volume of output. On the other hand, overheads include fixed, variable and semi-variable expenses and as such, are not in direct proportion to production.

Whether an expense is a direct expense or overhead expense, depends upon circumstances of each individual case. Some expenses may have to be treated as direct expenses in a particular circumstance while under other circumstances they may have to be treated as overhead expenses. It can be explained with the help of the following illustrations:

(*a*) Hire charges of machinery, tools and equipments like cranes, concrete mixtures, welding machines etc., will be treated as direct expenses if the machinery, tools and equipments are required for a particular job or contract *only*. But if the machinery, tools and equipments are required for general use, the hire charges will be treated as overhead expenses.

(*b*) Consultation fee paid to an engineer or architect will be an item of direct expenses if the consultation is for a particular contract or job. But if the consultation is for a number of contracts or jobs, the consultation fee will be treated as an item of overhead.

(*c*) Cost of preparing patterns or drawings will be treated as direct expenses if the patterns or drawings have been made for a particular job and cannot be used for other jobs. But if the patterns or drawings are of common use for various jobs or products, their cost will be treated as an item of overhead.

QUESTIONS

1. What is meant by direct expenses? Give few examples of direct expenses.
2. Define 'Direct Expenses'. What are their characteristics? How are they treated in cost accounts.
3. How would you make a distinction between direct expenses and overhead expenses? Give three examples of expenses which can be treated both as direct expenses and overhead expenses under different circumstances.

8

Overhead-I

The indirect portion of the total cost constitutes the overhead cost. Overhead cost is defined as *"the aggregate of indirect material costs, indirect wages and indirect expenses.*" The term 'indirect' denotes that which cannot be allocated but which can be apportioned to cost centres or absorbed by cost units. The overhead costs are also sometimes allocated to cost centres. The overhead costs are incurred not for any particular job, work-order, process or unit but for the business as a whole and include all costs other than direct material costs, direct wages and direct expenses. Overhead costs are also denoted by 'supplementary costs' 'non-productive costs', 'indirect costs', 'oncost', 'burden' etc. Of all the terms, 'overhead' is the most common and the Institute of Cost and Management Accountants, London, does not recommend the use of the terms 'oncost' and 'burden'.

CLASSIFICATION OF OVERHEADS

Classification of costs refers to the process of grouping costs according to their common characteristics. Overhead costs may be grouped according to:

1. functions,
2. elements, and
3. behaviour.

1. FUNCTION-WISE CLASSIFICATION

It refers to the classification of overhead costs with reference to the various major activity divisions of a concern. The main groups of overhead on the basis of functions are:

"Overhead costs are the operating cost of a business enterprise which cannot be traced directly to a particular unit of output." *–Blocker and Wheltmer.*

"Overhead may be defined as the cost of indirect materials, indirect labour and such other expenses, including services as cannot conveniently be charged directly to specified cost units. Alternatively, ovreheads are all expenses other than direct expenses."

–Wheldon.

(*a*) Factory Overhead;
(*b*) Office and Administration Overhead;
(*c*) Selling Overhead; and
(*d*) Distribution Overhead.

(*a*) Factory Overhead

Factory overhead refers to all expenses other than direct material costs, direct wages and direct expenses incurred in a factory in connection with manufacturing operations. Examples of factory overhead are: Rent of factory building, municipal taxes and insurance of factory building, depreciation of factory building, depreciation and insurance of factory plant and machinery, repairs and maintenance of factory buildings and machinery, salary of factory manager and other factory staff, factory power and lighting, cost of small tools, consumable stores, lubricating oil, cotton waste, salary of store-keeper, expenses of store-keeping, fuel, gas, water, drawing office salaries, factory stationery, cost of idle time, overtime wages (if not treated as direct cost), telephone charges of factory, cost of training of new workers, labour welfare expenses etc.

(*b*) Administration Overhead

Administration overhead refers to all expenses relating to the direction, control and administration (not connected directly with production, sales or distribution) of an undertaking. Examples of administration overhead are: General management salaries, salaries of general office staff, office rent, depreciation of office building, rates and insurance of office building, office lighting and air-conditioning, depreciation of office furniture and office machinery, repairs and maintenance of office building, office furniture and office machinery, audit fees, legal charges, office stationery, telephone charges of office, bank charges, directors' fees, counting office salaries etc.

(*c*) Selling Overhead

Selling overhead refers to all costs of seeking to create and stimulate demand or of securing orders. Examples of selling overhead are: Sales office expenses, advertisement, salary of sales manager, salaries of other selling staff, commission on sales, travelling expenses, expenses of travelling agents, cost of price lists, catalogues and samples, bad debts, rent of show-room, depreciation of show-room, rates and insurance of show-room, lighting and cleaning of show-room, expenses of branch establishments, expenses of sales and publicity department, cost of training to salesmen, postal expenses relating to sales, legal expenses for recovery of bad debts, cost of entertainment of customers, market research expenses, cost of preparation of tenders etc.

(*d*) Distribution Overhead

Distribution overhead refers to all expenses incurred from the time the product is finished in the factory till its delivery to ultimate customers or consumers.

Examples of distribution overhead are: Rent of warehouse, depreciation of warehouse, insurance, rates and lighting of warehouse, depreciation, running and maintenance of delivery vans, salary of van men, carriage on sales, packing materials and packing charges, cost of after-sales service, salary of warehouse-keeper, and the like.

2. ELEMENT-WISE CLASSIFICATION

It refers to the classification of overhead with reference to the various elements on which costs are incurred. The main groups of overhead on the basis of elements are:

(*a*) Indirect material costs, (*b*) Indirect wages, and
(*c*) Indirect expenses.

(*a*) Indirect Material Costs

Material costs which cannot be allocated but which are to be apportioned to or absorbed by cost centres or cost units, are known as 'Indirect Material Costs'. Examples of indirect material costs are: Consumable stores, cotton waste, small tools, lubricating oil, coal, fuel etc.

(*b*) Indirect Wages

Indirect wages refer to the labour cost or wages which cannot be allocated but which are to be apportioned to or absorbed by cost centres or cost units. Examples of indirect wages are : Salary of foreman, salary of supervisory staff, salary of factory manager, salary of time-keeper, salary of store-keeper, idle time wages, leave pay etc.

(*c*) Indirect Expenses

Indirect expenses refer to expenses (other than indirect material costs and indirect wages) which cannot be allocated but which can be apportioned to or absorbed by cost centres or cost units. Examples of indirect expenses are : Factory rent and rates, depreciation of factory building, insurance of factory building, depreciation of plant and machinery, factory lighting, repairs and maintenance etc.

3. BEHAVIOUR-WISE CLASSIFICATION

By 'behaviour', we mean the reaction of the expenditure for changes in the volume of output. Some overhead costs increase with the increase in the volume of output, some remain constant irrespective of the changes in the level of output, whereas some others do not vary upto a certain volume but vary after that. The main groups on the basis of behaviour or variability are:

(*a*) Fixed Overhead; (*b*) Variable Overhead; and
(*c*) Semi-variable or Semi-fixed Overhead.

(*a*) Fixed Overhead

Fixed overhead refers to expenses which tend to remain constant or unaffected (in aggregate) by changes in the volume of output. For example, if the monthly salary of the Works Manager is Rs. 2,000 and the monthly output is 10,000 units and in a particular month the production falls down to 8,000 units, we cannot make a corresponding cut in the works manager's salary. The monthly expenditure of Rs. 2,000 thus remains constant and is not affected by the fall in output. Similarly, when the output increases, there is no increase in the monthly salary of the works manager. The other examples of fixed overhead are: Rates and taxes on building, insurance of building, factory rent, supervisor's salary, etc. The fixed overhead costs will continue to be incurred even when production completely ceases in a particular period and are, therefore, also known as 'Period Costs', 'Shut-down Costs' or 'Stand-by Costs'.

Fixed overhead costs are not always wholly fixed in nature. This is because over a long period of time, if the concern decides to go in for additional equipments and buildings and appoints some additional staff to cope with the increase in production, these result in a permanent change in the level of production and the fixed charges which were constant within a certain range of plant capacity do also increase now. Thus, the total fixed overhead costs remain constant only within the limits of plant capacity and any appreciable change in the latter affects the fixed overheads.

Another important feature of fixed overhead costs is that since the amount of such costs for an accounting period is constant, the cost per unit decreases with increase in output and increases with decrease in output.

Graphic Presentation of Fixed Costs

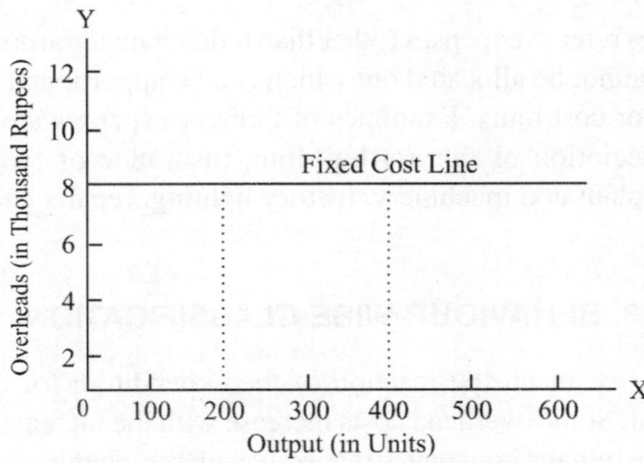

From the above figure, it can be observed that regardless of volume of output, fixed overhead is constant, i.e., Rs. 8,000. Even at zero output, it is the same. Further, as the level of output increases, the fixed overhead per unit of output falls.

(*b*) Variable Overhead

Variable overhead refers to expenses which tend to change (in aggregate) directly with changes in volume of output. Such expenses increase in aggregate as the output goes up and decrease proportionately when the output falls. However, there may not always be a perfect mathematical relation. The examples of variable overhead are: Indirect materials, fuel and power, carriage outward, packing materials, lighting, internal transport, store losses, idle time etc.

Graphic Presentation of Variable Overhead

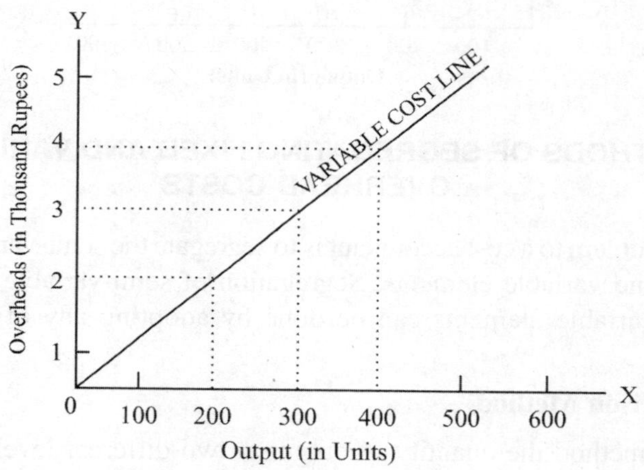

From the above figure, it can be observed that variable overhead costs vary directly with changes in the volume of output. Further, although total amount of variable overhead costs changes with output, the cost per unit of production is constant.

(*c*) Semi-variable Overhead

Semi-variable or semi-fixed overhead costs refer to expenses which are partly fixed and partly variable. These costs are fixed upto a certain volume of output. If, however, the output rises beyond that limit, these costs shall increase in aggregate although the increase in the expenditure will not be proportionate to the increase in output. Examples of semi-variable overhead costs are: Depreciation of plant and machinery, repairs and maintenance, cost of supervision, service department wages, postage and stationery etc.

Graphic Presentation of Semi-variable Overhead

From the figure given below, it can be observed that overhead cost is Rs. 6,000 (a constant amount) upto the output level of 200 units. Beyond 200 units, it increases to Rs. 9,000 but remains constant again for the output between 200 units and 500 units and so on.

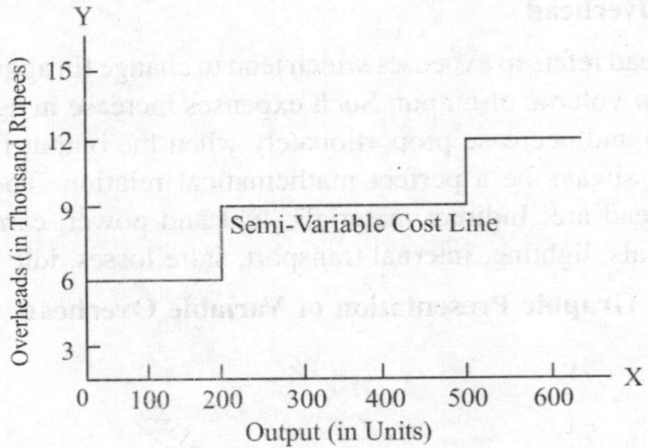

METHODS OF SEGREGATING FIXED AND VARIABLE OVERHEAD COSTS

The main problem to a cost accountant is to segregate the semi-variable overhead into fixed and variable elements. Segregation of semi-variable overhead into fixed and variable elements can be done by adopting any of the following methods.

(*i*) Comparison Method

Under this method the quantity of output at two different levels is compared with corresponding amount of expense. As we know that fixed overhead remains fixed, variable element of overhead is obtained by applying the following formula:

$$\text{Variable cost per unit} = \frac{\text{Change in Amount of Expense}}{\text{Change in Quantity (output)}}$$

Illustration 1

From the following information in respect of a semi-variable expense, obtain the fixed and variable elements:

	Period	Output (Units)	Semi-variable Overhead
Year			Rs.
2008	July	350	3,100
	August	420	3,520
	September	400	3,400
	October	430	3,580
	November	380	3,280
	December	270	2,620

Solution

Month	Production (Units)	Semi-Variable Expense
		Rs.
July, 2008	350	3,100
September, 2008	400	3,400
Change	50	300

Variable cost per unit $= \frac{\text{Change in Amount of Expense}}{\text{Change in Output}} = \frac{\text{Rs. }300}{50 \text{ units}}$

= Rs. 6 per unit

In July, 2008, variable portion of expense = 350 units × Rs. 6 = Rs. 2,100
Hence fixed portion of expense = Rs. 3,100 – Rs. 2,100
= Rs. 1,000

In August, 2008 variable portion = 400 units × Rs. 6
= Rs. 2, 400

Hence fixed portion = Rs. 3,400 – Rs. 2,400
= Rs. 1,000

This method is simple though not scientific and accurate.

(*ii*) High and Low Points Method or Range Method

Under this method, the amount of expense at the highest and lowest levels are compared and related to output attained at those levels. Since fixed overhead remains fixed, the change in the level of overhead must be due to its variable portion. Thus,

$$\text{Variable cost per unit} = \frac{\text{Change in Amount of Expense}}{\text{Change in Output (Units)}}$$

Continuing Illustration (1) and considering highest and lowest points:

Period	Output (Units)	Semi-Variable Overhead
		Rs.
October, 2008	430	3,580
December, 2008	270	2,620
Difference or change	160	960

Variable cost per unit $= \frac{\text{Change in Amount of Expense}}{\text{Change in Output}}$

$= \frac{\text{Rs. }960}{160 \text{ units}}$

= Rs. 6 per unit

For October, 2008: Variable portion of
Overhead = 430 units × Rs. 6
= Rs. 2,580
Fixed portion = Rs. 3,580 – Rs. 2,580
= Rs. 1,000
For December 2008: Variable portion of
Overhead = 270 units × Rs. 6 = Rs. 1,620
Fixed portion = Rs. 2,620 – Rs. 1,620 = Rs. 1,000

(*iii*) Equation Method

Under this method, variable and fixed portions of overhead are ascertained by means of straight line equation. The straight line equation is:

$$Y = mx + C$$

where Y = Total semi-variable cost
C = Fixed costs included in semi-variable costs
m = Variable cost per unit
x = Output or Number of units

Continuing Illustration (1)

Taking the figures of July and August, 2008:

July:	$3{,}100 = 350\,m + C \quad (i)$
August:	$3{,}520 = 420\,m + C \quad (ii)$
Subtracting (*i*) from (*ii*)	$420 \quad = 70\,m$

$$m = \frac{420}{70}$$

= Rs. 6 per unit (Variable cost)

Putting the value of '*m*' in equation (*i*)

$$3{,}100 = 350 \times 6 + C$$
$$3{,}100 = 2{,}100 + C$$

Hence $C = 3{,}100 - 2{,}100$
= Rs. 1,000 (Fixed cost)

(*iv*) Average Method

Under this method segregation of fixed and variable elements is made by first taking the average of two selected groups and then applying the range method or equation method, as the case may be. Continuing Illustration (1) and taking averages of first two and last two months.

	Average Output (units)	Average Semi-variable Overhead (Rs.)
First two months	385	3,310
(July and August, 2008)	$\left(\frac{350+420}{2}\right)$	$\left(\frac{3,100+3,520}{2}\right)$
Last two months	325	2,950
(November and December, 2008)	$\left(\frac{380+270}{2}\right)$	$\left(\frac{3,100+2,620}{2}\right)$
Change	60	360

$$\text{Variable overhead per unit} = \frac{\text{Change in amount}}{\text{Change in output}}$$

$$= \text{Rs. } 360 \div 60 \text{ units} = \text{Rs. } 6 \text{ per unit}$$

Total overhead (Average for July and August)	= Rs. 3,310
Less variable overhead (385 units × Rs. 6)	= Rs. 2,310
Fixed overhead	1,000

(*v*) Graphical Method

Under this method, the portions of variable and fixed overheads are ascertained by plotting the amounts of semi-variable or semi-fixed overheads incurred at various levels of activity on graph paper and drawing the 'line of best fit.' Under the graphical method, volume of output is drawn on horizontal-axis and semi-variable expenses on vertical-axis. Expenses corresponding to each volume are plotted on the graph paper and a straight line, 'the line of best fit' is drawn through the points plotted. This straight line represents the 'total cost line'. The point where the straight line intersects the vertical-axis is taken to be the amount of fixed expenses. A parallel line from the intersection point to the horizontal-axis gives the 'fixed cost line'. Thereafter, the ascertainment of variable cost can be made by means of comparison of fixed cost and total cost.

Illustration 2

From the following information relating to indirect labour cost, obtain the fixed and variable elements by means of Graphical Method:

	Period	Output (Units)	Semi-variable Cost (Rs.)
Year 2008	January	200	2,200
	February	250	2,500
	March	300	2,800
	April	400	3,400

May	350	3,100
June	500	4,000
July	450	3,700
August	600	4,600
September	550	4,300

Solution

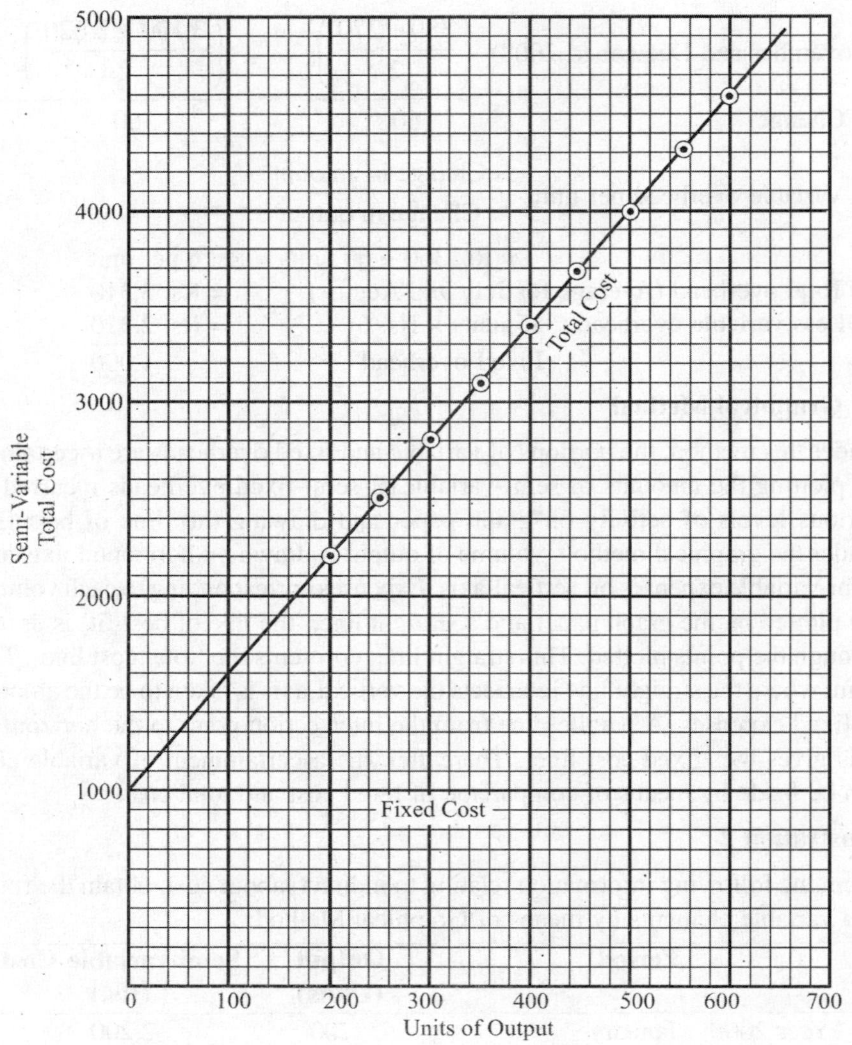

Plotting the points in the graph and drawing the total cost line and fixed element line, it it observed that fixed element is Rs. 1,000. As such:

For the month of April (Total Output 400 units)

		Rs.
Total Semi-variable Cost		3,400
Less Fixed Element		1000
Variable Element		2,400

Variable cost per unit $= \frac{\text{Rs. } 2,400}{400 \text{ units}} = \text{Rs. } 6$

Similarly for any other month say July (Total Output 450 units)

		Rs.
Total Semi-variable Cost		3,700
Less Fixed Element		1,000
Variable Element		2,700

Variable cost per unit $= \frac{\text{Rs. } 2,700}{450 \text{ units}} = \text{Rs. } 6$

Graphical method is also known as Scattergraph Method. This method is fairly good but the results obtained will not be as accurate as under the least squares method.

(*iv*) Least Squares Method

Under this method, segregation of fixed and variable elements of semi-variable overhead is made by finding out a 'line of best fit' for a number of observations with the help of statistical methods.

We know the straight line equation:

$$Y = mx + C$$

By putting the values of various observations, we can have an equation in the following form:

$$y_1 = mx_1 + C$$
$$y_2 = mx_2 + C$$
$$y_3 = mx_3 + C$$
$$\ldots\ldots\ldots\ldots\ldots\ldots$$

$$\text{Adding : } \Sigma y = m\Sigma x + NC \quad \ldots(1)$$

Where
y = Total semi-variable cost
m = Variable cost per unit
x = Output or Number of units
C = Fixed cost included in semi-variable costs
N = Number of observations.

Again, multiplying both sides of the linear equation by x, we get:

$$x_1 y_1 = mx_1^2 + cx_1$$
$$x_2 y_2 = mx_2^2 + cx_2$$
$$x_3 Y_3 = mx_3^2 + cx_3$$

$$\text{Adding: } \Sigma xy = m\,\Sigma x^2 + C\Sigma x \quad \ldots(2)$$

With the help of equations (1) and (2), we can get the values of 'm' (variable cost per unit) and 'C' (fixed cost) and obtain the relationship.

Illustration 3

From the following information relating to an item of semi-variable expense, obtain the fixed and variable elements by the method of least squares:

	Period	Output (Units)	Semi-Variable Expense (Rs.)
Year 2008	Jan.	50	1,250
	Feb.	60	1,400
	March	70	1,550
	April	90	1,850
	May	80	1,700

Solution

Month	Output (x)	Semi-variable (y)	x^2	xy
Jan., 2008	50	1,250	2,500	62,500
Feb., 2008	60	1,400	3,600	84,000
March, 2008	70	1,550	4,900	1,08,500
April, 2008	90	1,850	8,100	1,66,500
May, 2008	80	1,700	6,400	1,36,000
	$\Sigma x = 350$	$\Sigma y = 7{,}750$	$\Sigma x^2 = 25{,}500$	$\Sigma xy = 5{,}57{,}500$

Substituting the value in equations (1) and (2) we get

$$7{,}750 = 350\,m + 5\,\text{C} \quad \ldots(3)$$

$$5{,}57{,}500 = 25{,}500\,m + 350\,\text{C} \quad \ldots(4)$$

Multiplying equation (3) by 70 and by subtracting equation (5) from (4)

$$5{,}57{,}500 = 25{,}500\,m + 350\,\text{C} \quad \ldots(4)$$

$$5{,}42{,}500 = 24{,}500\,m + 350\,\text{C} \quad \ldots(5)$$

$$- \quad - \quad -$$

$$15{,}000 = 1{,}000\,m$$

$$m = \frac{15{,}000}{1{,}000}$$

$$m = 15 \text{ (Variable cost per unit)}$$

Putting this value in equation (3): 7,750 = 5,250 + 5 C

$$\text{C} = \frac{2{,}500}{5} = 500$$

For Jan., 2008: Variable cost = 50 × Rs. 15 = Rs. 750

Fixed cost = Rs. 1,250 – Rs. 750 = Rs. 500.

NECESSITY FOR CLASSIFICATION OF OVERHEAD INTO FIXED AND VARIABLE (OR ADVANTAGES OF CLASSIFYING OVERHEAD INTO FIXED AND VARIABLE)

The necessity for the classification of overhead into fixed and variable elements arises due to the following reasons:

(1) Effective Cost Control

Better control over expenses can be exercised if a proper classification of overhead into fixed and variable elements has been made. Fixed expenses are incurred by management decision and as such can be controlled by the top management while variable expenses can be controlled by lower management.

(2) Helpful in Decision-making

The classification of expenses into fixed and variable elements is of immense help to the management in making a number of business decisions, such as make or buy decision, selection of suitable sales mix, operate or shut-down decision, expansion or contraction of the production of various products etc.

(3) Fixation of Selling Price

This distinction is very helpful in determining the selling price of the products or services. Sometimes, a manufacturer charges different prices for the same article in different markets to meet varying degrees of competition. However, the lowest selling price of any product should atleast cover prime cost plus variable overhead. This classification also helps in determining the price during trade depression or in a special market.

(4) Marginal Costing and Cost-Volume Analysis

The classification of overhead into fixed and variable elements is very essential for the technique of marginal costing and break-even analysis. It helps in ascertaining marginal cost i.e., the total variable cost attributable to one unit of output. Further, it assists in determining the break-even point i.e., the volume of output where there is no profit and no loss.

(5) Helpful in Budgetary Control

This classification is very helpful in the preparation of flexible budgets. A flexible budget is a budget which is designed to change in accordance with the level of activity actually attained. Flexible budget for various levels of activity can be prepared with the help of this classification.

(6) Absorption of Overhead

This classification helps in the proper absorption of the different items of overhead. The method to be adopted for determining the absorption rates depends on the nature of overhead.

But the usefulness of this classification suffers from a number of limitations. Firstly, in classifying the overhead into fixed and variable, factors other than volume such as product specification, product mix, price indices, conditions of efficiency, plant and equipment etc., are ignored. As such, the assumption of the linear behaviour of fixed and variable costs is not always true. Further, the analysis of overhead into fixed and variable elements depends mainly upon historical costs which, in their own turn, suffer from a number of limitations.

COMMENTS ON CERTAIN ITEMS OF OVERHEAD

(A) Depreciation

Depreciation refers to the diminution in the value of an asset due to use and/or the lapse of time. It arises due to physical wear and tear of the asset on account of the usage of asset and passage of time. In cost accounts, the necessity of charging depreciation of an asset arises due to the following reasons:

(*a*) Depreciation represents a charge for the usage of capital resources.

(*b*) The cost of the asset has to be recovered from costs over its life time.

Methods of calculating depreciation

The principal methods of calculating depreciation on assets may be summarised as follows:

(1) **Straight Line Method:** Under this method depreciation is provided by means of periodic charges. The amount of depreciation is a fixed percentage of the original cost of the asset concerned less the residual value, if any. Under this method, the amount of depreciation to be charged remains constant and thus affords better comparative costs.

(2) **Diminishing Balance Method:** Under this method also depreciation is provided by means of periodic charges. The amount of depreciation is a fixed percentage of the balance remaining after deducting from the cost of the asset, aggregate of the amounts of depreciation provided previously. It is argued in favour of this method that a heavier depreciation charge is borne in earlier years when repairs are lighter and that the assumed increasing repair cost is counter balanced in later years, by the reduced annual charge for depreciation.

(3) **Sinking Fund Method:** Under this method a fixed amount is charged for depreciation every year and credited to a sinking fund account and an equivalent amount of money is invested in securities outside the business and allowed to accumulate at compound interest. At the end of the life of the asset, the investments are realised and funds available are used to replace the asset. This is a good method of charging depreciation which ensures the availability of funds at the time of replacement of an asset.

(4) **Annuity Method:** This is the method of providing for depreciation by means of periodic charges, each of which is a constant proportion of the aggregate of the asset depreciated and interest at a given rate per period on the written down value of the asset at the beginning of each period. Under this method, the asset is treated just like an interest bearing investment and the amount of depreciation charged in each period also includes the interest earned on the residual value of the asset at a fixed rate.

(5) **Production Unit Method:** Under this method depreciation is provided by means of a fixed rate per unit of production, obtained by dividing the value of the asset by the estimated number of units to be produced during its life. Thus the amount of depreciation is calculated with reference to actual output and the time factor is ignored.

(6) **Production Hour Method:** Under this method depreciation is provided by means of a fixed rate per hour of production, obtained by dividing the value of the asset by the estimated effective working life of the asset in terms of hours. Thus the amount of depreciation is calculated with reference to the actual number of hours worked by the asset.

(7) **Repairs Reserve Method:** Under this method, depreciation is provided at a combined rate computed to account for depreciation as well as maintenance cost of the asset. The amount of depreciation is a fixed percentage of the original cost of the asset plus the estimated cost of maintenance during its life. Thus the cost of maintenance is uniformly spread throughout the life time of the asset and fluctuations in costs due to heavy repairs in a particular period are avoided.

(8) **Endowment Policy Method:** Under this method, depreciation is provided by means of fixed periodic charges equivalent to the amount of annual premiums paid on an endowment policy taken out for the amount required to meet the cost of the asset on replacement. This method is basically similar to the Sinking Fund Method.

(9) **Revaluation Method:** Under this method, the asset is revalued at the end of each period (generally at the end of each year) and the difference between the value at the beginning of the period and the value re-assessed at the end of the period represents the amount of depreciation chargeable for the period. This method is commonly used for loose tools, patents, livestock etc.

PLANT AND MACHINERY REGISTER

In order to ascertain the annual charge for depreciation relating to each item of plant and machinery employed in a manufacturing concern, generally a separate register known as "Plant and Machinery Register" is maintained. In this register one sheet or page is devoted to each item of plant and machinery. Plant and Machinery Register usually contains the following information:

(1) Description of the machine.
(2) Identification number and location.
(3) Purchase Price.
(4) Date of purchase.
(5) Name and address of suppliers.
(6) Cost of installation.
(7) Estimated life.
(8) Estimated residual value.
(9) Method of depreciation.
(10) Rate of depreciation.
(11) Particulars of repairs carried out.

Plant and Machinery Register

Type of Machine.............	Date of Purchase...............	Estimated Life......................
Identification No.	Makers..................................	Estimated
Location...........................	Suppliers..............................	Scrap Value..........................
Remarks...........................		Method of Depreciation..........................

Ref.	**Description**	**Cost Price**	**Rate of Dep.**	**2005-06**		**2006-07 and so on**		**Date of Sale**	**Sale price**	**Profit or Loss on Sale**
				Depreciation	**Balance**	**Depreciation**	**Balance**			
		Rs.		Rs.	Rs.	Rs.	Rs.		Rs.	Rs.

Illustration 4

New Enterprises Ltd., Calcutta imported a plate bending machine fitted with 10 h.p. motor from the Machine Builders Ltd., Norwich, England, who submitted their invoice MT 101, dated 30.9.2002. The invoice price in Rupees was Rs. 1,26,000, ocean freight Rs. 8,000, insurance Rs. 2,000, customs duty is 30 per cent of C.I.F. value, port trust dues amount to Rs. 1,000, cartage to transport the machine to the works amounted to Rs. 800. Foundation, electric wiring etc., cost Rs. 2,700. It was commissioned on 1st July, 2003 at the north end of the 2nd bay in the shop. Draw a complete Plant Register, charging depreciation @ 10% on the diminishing balance. Ignore development rebate and extra shift allowance.

(*I.C.W.A. Inter-modified*)

Solution

Calculation of cost price

	Rs.
Invoice Price	1,26,000
Freight	8,000
Insurance	2,000
Customs Duty	40,800
Port Trust Dues	1,000
Cartage	300
Installation Cost	2,700
Total Cost	1,80,800

Plant Register

Type of Machine: Plate Bending Machine	Manufacturer:
Identification No. 51	Machine Builder Ltd.,
Location :2nd Bay, North End	Norwich, England
Date of Purchase :30th Sept., 2002	Estimated Life...........
Date of Installation: 1st July 2003	Estimated Scrap Value......
Rate of depreciation : 10 %	Method of Depreciation: Diminishing Balance

Description	Cost Price	Depreciation		Balance	Major repairs or Overhauls
		Year	Amount		
	Rs.		Rs.	Rs.	Rs.
Plate Bending Machine with 10 H.P. Motor		2002-03	18,080	1,62,720	
		2003-04	16,272	1,46,448	
	1,80,800	2004-05	14,645	1,31,803	
		2005-06	13,180	1,18,623	

(B) Obsolescence

Obsolescence is the sudden loss in the value of an asset which arises out of new inventions which can now produce goods better and cheaper. Obsolescence may arise due to change in the method of manufacture, invention of an improved and technically superior model of machine etc. The loss due to obsolescence is an abnormal item as it is difficult to anticipate obsolescence. As such it is advisable to exclude this loss from cost of production and to charge it to Costing Profit and Loss Account.

(C) Interest on Capital

Expert opinion is divided on the inclusion of interest on capital as an item of cost in cost accounts. The main arguments for and against the inclusion of this item in cost accounts may be summarised as follows:

For inclusion in cost accounts

(*i*) Interest is as much an item of cost as wages. Wages are paid to the labour as its reward while interest is the reward of capital.

(*ii*) True profit made in any manufacturing concern cannot be ascertained without taking into consideration the interest on capital employed.

(*iii*) Inclusion of interest on capital in costs facilitates the comparison of costing result of different methods and processes.

(*iv*) Automatic consideration is given to the time element by including interest on capital in costs.

(*v*) Management decisions cannot be made without considering the question of interest on capital involved, e.g., buy or make decision, use of new and improved machinery, replacement of manual operation by machine operation etc.

(*vi*) In case of a manufacturing concern engaged in the manufacture of articles of different values, correct cost of the articles can be worked out only if interest is included in costs.

(*vii*) True cost of maintaining heavy stock of raw materials and finished goods cannot be ascertained without considering the interest on capital involved.

Against inclusion in cost accounts

(*i*) Reward of capital is paid in the form of profits.

(*ii*) Interest on capital is a purely financial matter and cannot be treated as an item of cost, though it is vital to management decisions.

(*iii*) Comparison of cost can be made even without including interest on capital in costs.

(*iv*) Inclusion of interest in cost creates unnecessary complications as the determination of the exact amount of capital employed and the fair rate of interest is very difficult.

(*v*) In case of cost of production per unit being very small and turnover being rapid, it would be inexpedient to include interest in costs.

(*vi*) Inclusion of interest on capital in costs inflates the values of work-in progress and manufactured stock in hand.

The consensus of opinion is against including interest in cost accounts. But the management cannot ignore it at the time of taking a decision which affects the amount of capital employed.

(D) Rent of the Premises

Rent in respect of the premises may be divided into two parts:

(*i*) Rent paid for the rented premises, and

(*ii*) Notional rent of the owned premises.

The amount of rent paid in respect of the rented premises, is an item of fixed overhead costs. The amount of rent paid is to be allocated to manufacturing, administrative, selling or distribution overheads if the amount paid for each premises is known separately. Otherwise it should be apportioned on the basis of floor area of each premises.

In case of owned premises, the amount of notional rent (or fair rental value) of the premises should be included in cost accounts and treated in the same manner as the rent paid. The inclusion of notional rent of the owned premises in cost accounts is more akin to depreciation charges and it puts the cost of use of owned premises on the same footing if the same premises were rented. Further, the notional rent of premises can be computed easily and its inclusion in cost accounts makes costs comparable.

(E) Carriage and Freight Inward

Carriage and freight in respect of materials purchased is usually treated as part of the cost of materials purchased and not as works overhead.

Where carriage charges relate to the faulty or damaged goods returned by customers, their treatment in cost accounts will depend on the cause of the defects. If the goods have been returned due to faulty manufacture, the cost of carriage will be included in works overhead but if they have been returned due to faulty or bad packing , the carriage should be treated as part of selling and distribution overhead.

(F) Cost of Internal Transport

Cost of internal transport facilities for the movement of materials from the stores to the production departments is treated as an item of works overhead.

(G) Carriage and Freight Outward

Where the customer has to pay for the carriage and freight outward, it is a direct charge on individual orders and should be excluded from overhead, otherwise, it is treated as an item of distribution overhead.

(H) Trade Discount and Cash Discount

Trade discount is the concession or reduction allowed by the seller to the customer off the selling price. Trade discount received on the purchase of materials is deducted from the purchase price of materials. On the other hand, trade discount allowed on the sale of finished goods should be included in selling expenses or deducted from selling price

Cash discount is allowed on spot payment for purchases or payment before the expiry of the credit period. Cash discount, by its very nature, represents interest on the employment of liquid funds. As such, the treatment of cash discount in costing shall depend upon the treatment of interest on capital. In practice, however cash discount is considered to be a purely financial item and hence excluded from costs.

(I) Expenditure of Costing Department

The expenditure of costing department includes the salaries of the cost accountant and the clerical staff employed under him, as also the cost of printing, stationery, files, registers etc., used by the department. The expenditure of the costing department is for the benefit of the business as a whole and should be apportioned between factory, administration and selling departments on some equitable basis. But owing to practical difficulties of such apportionment, the total expenditure of the costing department may be included in factory or works overhead.

(J) Packing Charges

Packing charges are divided into two parts: (*a*) cost of packing necessary for preserving or protecting the goods e.g., cost of tubes, bottles, containers, casks, boxes etc., and (*b*) cost of packing necessary for making the manufactured goods ready for sale e.g., cost of wrappers, card board boxes, wooden cases etc.

The packing charges of the first category should be included in the cost of direct materials and thus treated as a part of prime cost. The packing charges of the second category should be treated as an item of distribution overhead.

(K) Advertising

The cost of permanent sign boards, neon signs and electric signs forms part of the capital expenditure which should be apportioned over its effective life and included in selling overhead. The expenditure on the general advertisement of the products (and not for any specific product) is an item of selling overhead to be apportioned to the various products in the ratio of the benefit derived by each product.

(L) Bad Debts

Bad debts represent irrecoverable amount of debts due from customers on account of credit sales. Bad debts may be normal and abnormal. Regular percentage or amount of bad debts is treated as normal and included in selling overhead. Abnormal bad debts represent exceptionally large amount of bad debts. Such bad debts are excluded from cost accounts and charged to Costing Profit and Loss Account.

(M) Royalties

Royalties are expenses in the nature of rent payable in respect of the use of a right (e.g., patent-right, copyright etc.) vested in some other person. Royalties may be paid on the basis of output or sales. If royalties are paid on the basis of output, they should be treated as part of direct expenses. But where royalties are paid on the basis of sales, they should be treated as an item of selling overhead.

(N) Subscription

Subscriptions and donations to welfare schemes and institutions from which benefit is derived by the workers, are treated as part of factory overhead. But where no direct benefit is obtained by the workers from subscriptions and charitable donations, they are excluded from cost accounts.

(O) Defectives

Defectives signify those units or portion of production which can be rectified and turned out as good units by the application of additional material, labour or other services. Defectives arise due to sub-standard materials, inefficient supervision, bad planning, inadequate equipment etc. Usually, it is possible to avoid defects in the units produced but to some extent, defectives may be unavoidable. If the defective production is unavoidable and can be identified with specific jobs, the rectification cost should be charged to the job concerned. But if defective production cannot be identified with specific jobs, the rectification cost should be included in factory overhead. In case of defectives arising due to abnormal circumstances, the rectification cost is treated as an abnormal item and charged to Costing Profit and Loss Account.

(P) Spoilage

'Spoilage' consists of goods damaged, beyond rectification, in the course of manufacturing process and have to be disposed of without further processing. Spoilage arises due to faulty or careless operations or use of defective materials. Generally spoilage is avoidable but to some extent, it is unavoidable. The cost of normal spoilage which is unavoidable is borne by the good units. But the abnormal spoilage, which is otherwise avoidable, should not be allowed to affect the cost of good units. Cost of such spoilage is charged to the Costing Profit and Loss Account.

(Q) Provident Fund

Under the provisions of Employees' Provident Fund Act, a fixed percentage of a workman's wages is deducted every month which is kept as a deposit in his Provident Fund Account together with an equivalent amount paid by the employers as their contribution. While the amount deducted from the worker's wages as his contribution to the Fund remains the part of his gross wages, the employer's contribution to the Fund is treated as an item of overhead cost. The amount is calculated each month and allocated to the departments in which the men are employed.

(R) Head Office Expenses

If a business concern has more than one factory under its control, the expenses incurred in maintaining and running the head office has to be apportioned to the various factories on the basis of services rendered by the head office to each factory. The share of head office expenses charged to each factory is treated as part of administration overhead of the factory concerned. In case of a concern having only one factory, expenses of the head office are treated as part of general administration overhead to be apportioned to the various departments of the factory on some equitable basis.

(S) Dismantling and Installation Cost of Machinery

Installation cost of a newly acquired machinery is added to the cost of the machinery. Sometimes, expenditure is incurred on dismantling and re-installing an old machinery within the same shop or department. The need for such dismantling and re-installation of machinery may arise on account of change in the workshop layout, flow of work or re-arrangement in production processes. Such expenses should be treated as an item of factory overhead since they do not add to the value of the machinery or increase the efficiency of machine.

(T) Taxes

Taxes paid by a concern may be divided into three parts:

(*i*) Municipal taxes or rates;
(*ii*) Sales Tax; and
(*iii*) Income Tax.

Municipal taxes are levied by a local Government or authority on the buildings situated within its jurisdiction. Municipal taxes or rates are allocated or suitably apportioned to the factory, administration, selling and distribution overheads.

Sales tax is paid on the materials and stores purchased by the concern and is added to the cost of materials and stores purchased.

Sales tax realised from the customers on the sale of finished goods is credited to a suspense account as the same is ultimately to be paid to the State Government or the Central Government, as the case may be. Hence, the amount of sales tax realised on the sale of finished goods is not included in cost accounts.

Income tax is levied by the Central Government on the profits of the concern. Income tax paid represents an item of appropriation of profits and is excluded from cost accounts.

(U) Canteen Expenses

Canteens in the factories may be run for the benefit of the workers on no-profit no-loss basis. The expenditure and receipts of the canteen department, in such a case being equal, do not find a place in cost accounts. But in case the expenditure of the canteen department is subsidised, the amount paid is an item of factory overheads and is apportioned to various departments on the basis of number of workers.

(V) Research and Development Costs

It is an important feature of modern industry that manufacturing concerns maintain research departments for developing new products and processes. After the completion of the research and experiments, some further expenditure is incurred for putting the results on a commercial basis. The former type of cost is known as 'Research Cost' and the latter is 'Development Cost'. According to the Costing Terminology of the Institute of Cost and Management Accountants, 'research cost' refers to "the cost of searching for new or improved products, new applications of materials, or new or improved method" and 'development cost' to "the cost of the process which begins with the implementation of the decision to produce a new or improved product or to employ a new or improved method and ends with the commencement of formal production of that product or by that method."

Research embraces all the activities of a concern and depending upon the field covered by a particular research, the research cost is booked to factory, administration, selling and distribution overhead. For example, if research relates to manufacturing methods, the research cost is charged to factory overhead, whereas research cost in respect of management, administration and supervision etc., is an item of office and administration overhead. Similarly, expenses incurred on market research or research on advertising are treated as selling and distribution overhead.

Development cost of new production is treated as an item of deferred revenue expenditure to be spread over a number of periods and booked to factory overhead when production is fully established.

If research is carried on, on general lines not related to the items of regular production of the concern, the expenditure incurred on the same is booked to administration overhead. Sometimes, the research carried on in a manufacturing concern may not be fruitful, the expenditure on such research is excluded from costs and charged to Costing Profit and Loss account.

OBJECTIVE TYPE QUESTIONS

A. Multiple choice questions

Select the correct answer in each of the following

1. Overhead may be classified on the basis of variability as
   (*a*) factory overhead, office overhead and selling overhead
   (*b*) indirect materials, indirect wages and indirect expenses
   (*c*) fixed overhead, variable overhead and semi-variable overhead.

2. Directors' remuneration is treated as
   (*a*) factory overhead (*b*) administration overhead
   (*c*) selling overhead (*d*) distribution overhead

3. Packing cost is an item of
   (*a*) production overhead (*b*) office overhead
   (*c*) selling overhead (*d*) any of the above.

4. Which of the following is a service department
   (*a*) Refining department (*b*) Machining department
   (*c*) Receiving department (*d*) Finishing department

5. Which of the following is not an item of selling overhead ?
   (*a*) Royalty on sales (*b*) Carriage outward
   (*c*) Commission on sales (*d*) General manager's salary.
6. Bad debts are treated as part of
   (*a*) selling overhead (*b*) factory overhead
   (*c*) office overhead.
7. Rent of the warehouse is an item of
   (*a*) factory overhead (*b*) selling overhead
   (*c*) distribution overhead (*d*) office overhead.
8. Variable overheads vary
   (*a*) in aggregate (*b*) per unit
   (*c*) per unit and in aggregate.

[**Ans.** 1. (*c*), 2. (*b*), 3. (*c*), 4. (*c*), 5. (*d*), 6. (*a*), 7. (*c*), 8 (*a*)]

B. 'True'/False' type statements

Indicate whether the following statements are 'true' or false'.

1. Factory overhead includes all production costs other than direct materials and salaries.
2. The term factory overhead is synonymous with general overhead.
3. Variable overheads vary with time.
4. Indirect expenses are also known as chargeable expenses.
5. Rent of the premises is not included in cost accounts when the premises are owned by the manufacturer.
6. Wages paid to the factory manager is a part of the selling overhead.
7. Fixed overheads vary with output and sales.
8. Carriage on direct materials is treated as factory overhead.

[**Ans.** 1. False, 2. False, 3. False, 4. False, 5. False, 6. False, 7. False, 8. False]

C. Filling the blanks

1. Overhead is an aggregate of ...., ...and........... .
2. Salary paid to the foreman of a production department is treated as an item of .... overhead.
3. Overhead cost cannot be........... to cost units or cost centres.
4. Variable overheads vary in aggregate directly in proportion to ....
5. Fixed overheads remain constant at ....

6. Cost of coal used as fuel is an item of ....material.

[**Ans.** (1) indirect material cost, indirect wages and indirect expenses (2) factory (3) allocated (4) output (5) all levels (6) indirect]

SHORT ANSWER TYPE QUESTIONS

Answer each of the following questions in not more than five lines.

1. What is meant by 'overhead'?

2. What is the difference between 'overhead' and 'oncost'?

3. What is the difference between 'overhead' and 'chargeable expenses'?

4. What is a Plant register?

5. How do you treat 'royalties paid' in cost accounts?

6. What is the treatment of interest on capital in cost accounts?

7. How do you treat the hire charges of the plant?

8. How are overhead expenses classified according to functions?

9. How do you classify overhead expenses according to elements?

10. How do you classify overhead expenses according to nature?

LONG ANSWER TYPE QUESTIONS

1. What do you mean by 'overhead'? What are the methods of classifying overheads? *(G.N.D.U., B.Com., 1999, 2001, 2002, 2005)*

2. How would you classify overheads on the basis of functions? Give some examples.

3. Define fixed expenses, variable expenses and semi-variable expenses giving three examples of each. *(I.C.W.A. Inter 1975)*

4. Define 'overhead costs'. Distinguish between fixed, semi-fixed and variable overhead costs giving an example of each. *(I.C.W.A. Inter 1977)*

5. Explain the various methods of segregating fixed and variable overhead costs. *(I.C.W.A. Inter 1975)*

6. What is the advantage of classifying indirect expenses into fixed and variable items? *(I.C.W.A. Inter 1973)*

7. How would you treat the following in cost accounts

(*i*) Carriage	(*ii*) Royalties
(*iii*) Cost office expenses	(*iv*) Cash Discount
(*v*) Bad debts	(*vi*) Trade discount.

8. Classify any eight of the following items of expenses by function and nature:

(*a*) Depreciation on Plant (*b*) Office Telephone Charges
(*c*) Salary paid to Salesman (*d*) Rent of finished goods warehouse
(*e*) Supervisory labour (*f*) General Manager's salary
(*g*) Consumable stores
(*h*) Commission on Sales paid to Salesmen
(*i*) Factory Power (*j*) Delivery Van expenses.

9. How will you treat the following expenses in Cost Accounts?

(*a*) Packaging expenses.
(*b*) Defectives due to bad workmanship and bad material.
(*c*) Expenses of erection of machinery.
(*d*) Expenses of company's lorry which carries raw materials to store house and also delivers finished goods to customers.
(*e*) Cost of patterns and dies.
(*i*) Salaries and wages of trainees and apprentices.
(*g*) Commission to salesmen.
(*h*) Bad Debts. (*C.A. Inter*)

10. How would you account for defectives arising in the course of production?

11. What is depreciation? List the various methods of providing depreciation in accounts.

12. Write notes on the following:

(*a*) Obsolescence (*b*) Straight Line Method
(*c*) Reducing Balance Method (*d*) Residual Value
(*e*) Replacement Cost

13. What is a Plant Register? What details should be shown in such a Register? Give the specimen of a Plant Register.

14. Examine the propriety of including 'Interest on Capital' as an element of cost.

15. What are the arguments for and those against for inclusion of interest on capital in cost accounts?

16. Classification of overhead into 'fixed' and 'variable' is highly helpful to the management for the efficient running of the factory." Discuss. (*G.N.D.U., B.Com., 1981*)

17. What do you understand by 'fixed' and 'variable' overheads? Why it is important to distinguish between two type of expenses for purposes of costing? Give some examples. (*G.N.D.U., B.Com., 1983*)

9

Overhead-II

ALLOCATION, APPORTIONMENT AND ABSORPTION

Steps in Overhead Accounting:

Overhead being indirect expenses cannot be charged directly to cost units or jobs like direct material costs and direct wages. True cost of production can be ascertained only when overhead has been added to the prime cost. Thus, it is necessary to link the indirect expenses to cost units. This linking of indirect costs to cost units involves the following steps:

(1) Classification, Codification and Collection of overhead.

(2) Allocation and Apportionment of overhead.

(3) Re-apportionment of Service Department Costs to Production Departments.

(4) Absorption of overhead.

Classification, Codification and Collection of Overhead

Classification of costs refers to the process of grouping costs according to their common characteristics. As already discussed in the previous chapter, overhead may be classified on the basis of functions, elements and behaviour. In order to make an efficient and effective analysis of expenses in detail, each of the factory, administration, selling and distribution costs, is sub-divided into smaller groups so that items of similar nature can be grouped together under one head. These sub-groups are usually allotted numbers or symbols for quick identification and avoidance of lengthy description. Such a procedure of allotting number or symbol is know as 'Codification'. The code numbers used for covering the items of factory overhead are known as 'Standing Order Numbers', while those covering the administration, selling and distribution overhead items are known as 'Cost Account Numbers'.

A number of plans are used in the manufacturing concerns for the codification of overhead items but the widely used plans are as follows:

(*a*) Numerical System or Straight Number System.

(*b*) Decimal System.

(*c*) Mnemonic System.

(*d*) Combined Code System

Numerical System

Under this system, each type of expenditure is allotted a fixed number or a series of numbers as shown below:

Standing Order Number	Expenditure
1	Lubricating Oil
2	Consumable Stores
3	Spare Parts
15	Factory Manager's Salary
23	Factory Rent
31	Depreciation of Plant and Machinery

A block of numbers may be earmarked to indicate the major heads of expenditure. For example, 1 to 10 for indirect materials, 11 to 20 for indirect labour, 21 to 30 for repairs, 31 to 40 for depreciation, and so on.

Decimal System

This is also numerical system with the difference that instead of full numbers, decimals are used. This method is generally used in those concerns where mechanised system of accounting is in use. Under this method, whole numbers are used to indicate the main group or the master group and decimals to indicate the sub-groups. For example:

Standing Order Number	Item
1	Factory Overhead
1.01	Indirect Materials
1.01.1	Consumable Stores
1,01.2	Lubricating Oil
1.01.3	Cotton Waste
1.01.4	Spare parts
1.02	Indirect Labour
1.02.1	Factory Manager
1.02.2	Time-Keeping
1.02.3	Inspecting and Testing
1.02.3	Foremen and Assistants
1.02.5	Store-keeping
Cost Account Number	**Item**
2	Administration Overhead
2.01	Salaries
2.01.1	Executives and Management
2.01.2	Clerical Staff
2.01.3	Others
3	Selling and Distribution Overhead
3.01	Salaries of Selling Staff
3.01.1	Sales Manager
3.01.2	Salesmen
3.01.3	Travelling Agents
3.01.4	Clerical Staff.
3.02	Advertisement
3.02.1	Display and Exhibition
3.02.2	Newspapers and Magazines
3.02.3	Radio and Television, and so on.

Mnemonic System

This system is also known as Alphabetical System and involves the use of letters of alphabets as codes to facilitate easy and quick identification of the items of overhead. For example:

IM	for Indirect Material
IL	for Indirect Labour
BL	for Building
MA	for Maintenance
RE	for Repairs
AD	for Administration
SA	for Sales, and so on.

Combined Code System

Under this system, the letter of alphabets are used in conjunction with numbers for the purpose of codification of overhead. Under this system, the broader groups are represented by alphabetical symbols whereas the detailed groups are represented by numbers. For example:

Standing Order Number	Item
IM	Indirect Material
IM I	Lubricating Oil
IM 2	Consumable Stores
IM 3	Spare Parts, and so on

Collection of Overhead

The main sources from which overhead expenses are collected are as follows:

(1) Stores Requisition Slips
(2) Wages Analysis Book
(3) Vouchers and Invoices
(4) Petty Cash Book
(5) Subsidiary Records and Statements

1. **Stores Requisition Slips:** Expenditure incurred on indirect materials drawn from the stores are collected from Stores Requisition Slips. Each slip shows the standing order number and name of the department for which indirect materials are drawn.
2. **Wages Analysis Book:** Wages paid to indirect workers against each standing order number and for each department are collected from Wages Analysis Book which is prepared on the basis of the time cards or job cards of indirect workers.
3. **Vouchers and Invoices:** Payments made to outside parties for stores supplied (which are not passed through stores ledger) or services rendered are collected from purchase vouchers or invoices. Such vouchers are generally posted in a Voucher Register which shows the entries relating to overhead in a separate column for 'Expenses.'
4. **Petty Cash Book:** Particulars of the indirect expenses passed through

the Petty Cash Book are collected by making an analysis of the Petty Cash Book.

5. **Subsidiary Records and Statements:** Details of the expenses which do not involve current cash outlay can be collected from subsidiary records and statements which are maintained for this purpose. These items are adjustments in respect of expenses paid in advance, accrued expenses, notional charges for rent, depreciation, share of head office expenses etc.

ALLOCATION AND APPORTIONMENT

Departmentalisation

For ensuring efficient working, effective control and better administration, a factory is divided into a number of sub-divisions known as departments. Each sub-division or department in a factory is engaged in a particular activity. The departments in a factory can be broadly classified as:

(*a*) Production Departments (or Manufacturing Departments),
(*b*) Service Departments (or Auxiliary Departments),
(*c*) Partly-producing Departments.

Production Departments

Production department is one which is engaged in the actual process of production of an article, e.g., conversion of raw materials into finished products, assembling of various parts of a product. The number of production departments in a factory and the names given to each will depend upon the nature of the industry, type of the work performed and the size of factory. For example, a cotton textile mill may have Spinning Department, Weaving Department and Finishing Department and a steel rolling mill may have Hot Mill, Cold Mill, Pickling Shop, Hardening Shop and Polishing and Grinding Shop.

Service Departments

A service department is an auxiliary department not directly engaged in the conversion of raw materials but in rendering a service which contributes in an indirect manner in the manufacture of the product. Examples of service departments are—Purchasing Department, Stores Department, Time-keeping Department, Personnel Department, Power House etc. Each service department renders a particular type of service for the benefit of other departments.

Partly-producing Departments

A partly-producing department is one which according to the nature of work performed by it can be placed in either of the two categories, viz., production and service departments. In some cases, a department which is basically a service department, sometimes does some productive work. For example, a Tool Room, though a service department, may sometimes manufacture special tools for utilisation in the main job order. Similarly, a Carpentry Shop which is basically responsible for the upkeep and repairs of the furniture and fittings, may be required to manufacture wooden boxes for packing purposes. The activity of manufacturing undertaken in Tool Room and Carpentry Shop makes them partly-producing department.

Departmentalisation of Overhead

Departmentalisation of overhead is the process of determining the departments or operations according to which the expenses are to be apportioned. In other words, departmentalisation of overhead refers to the allocation and apportionment of overheads to production and service departments. After overhead costs have been collected under various standing order numbers, the next step is to allocate and apportion them to production and service departments. This process of departmentalisation of overhead is also known as 'Primary Distribution of Overhead'. Departmentalisation of overhead involves two steps namely:

(*a*) Allocation of overhead.
(*b*) Apportionment of overhead.

Allocation of overhead

'Allocation' has been defined by the Institute of Cost and Management Accountants, London, as "the allotment of whole items of cost to cost centres or cost units". Allocation of overhead is the function of identifying overhead items with particular cost centres or production and service departments. Overhead costs arising solely from the existence of a particular department (production as well as service department) can be charged or allocated to that department. Generally the salary of departmental head, foreman's salary and the cost of indirect materials issued to a particular department are allocated to that department.

Apportionment of overhead

'Apportionment' has been defined by the Institute of Cost and Management Accountants as "the allotment of proportions of cost to cost centres or cost units." Apportionment of overhead is the process of distributing those items of overhead which cannot be allocated to a cost centre or department, between cost centres or departments on an equitable basis. Overhead costs such as factory rent, factory insurance, factory lighting, factory power, salary of factory manager etc., incurred for the entire factory require apportionment to different production and service departments on some equitable or reasonable basis.

Overhead Distribution Summary

It refers to a statement or summary prepared on periodical basis, in order to show the allocation and apportionment of overhead costs to production and service departments of the factory. The Overhead Distribution Summary is also known as 'Primary Distribution Summary'.

Principles of Apportionment of Overhead

Selection of a suitable base for the apportionment of overhead to production and service departments is an important aspect of overhead accounting. For this purpose, the following principles may serve as a guide:

1. **Service or Utility:** This is the most important principle of apportionment of overhead and is based on the theory that a department should be burdened with the overhead in proportion to the benefit derived or service utilised by that department on account of overhead. For example, the rent or depreciation of the building may be apportioned on the basis of area occupied by each department in the building. This principle is very consistent and fair but requires the maintenance of detailed records of various facts and figures.
2. **Analysis or Survey:** Sometimes, it may not be possible to ascertain the extent of the benefit derived by various departments on account of overhead. In such a case, an analysis or survey of the expenses with reference to their impact on different departments may be made. For example, the salary of the works manager has to be apportioned on the basis of time devoted by him to different departments.
3. **Ability to Pay:** This principle lays down that the share of overhead apportioned to each department depends upon the ability of the department to bear it. The department making higher profits should be made to bear a higher burden of expenditure. This principle does not take into account the actual cost conditions which render it inequitable.
4. **Efficiency:** This principle is of recent origin. Under this approach, production targets are fixed for each department and overhead costs are apportioned with reference to these targets. If a department fails to achieve the target, its unit cost goes up, indicating its inefficiency. On the other hand, if a department achieves or exceeds the target, it shows its efficiency in the form of reduction in unit cost. Thus, under this approach, a type of incentive is introduced as every departmental head aspires to achieve or exceed the fixed target.

BASES FOR APPORTIONMENT OF OVERHEAD

As regards the basis to be used for apportioning the overhead costs, there is no hard and fast rule. Further, no single basis can be applied to apportion all items of overhead. The basis to be used for apportionment shall be determined with reference to the nature of the particular item of overhead. Some of the common bases for apportionment of overhead may be given as follows:

1. **Floor Area or Floor Space:** Some of the items of overhead are apportioned on the basis of the floor area occupied by various departments. Such expenses include rent, rates and insurance of building, lighting etc.
2. **Direct Wages:** Under this basis, the items of overhead costs are apportioned in proportion to the direct wages of the departments. This base is used for those items which are related to direct wages e.g., contribution to provident fund, contribution to Employees' State Insurance Scheme etc.
3. **Number of Workers:** Under this basis, the overhead costs are apportioned in the ratio of number of workers engaged in each department. This basis is adopted where the expenditure depends on the number of workers in the department e.g., labour welfare expenses, medical expenses, recreational facilities, transport facilities etc.
4. **Direct Labour Hours:** Under this basis, overhead costs are apportioned in proportion to the number of labour hours worked in various departments. Salary of the supervisory staff is apportioned on this basis.
5. **Number of Machine Hours:** This basis is used for the purpose of apportionment of overhead costs to departments where machines are more dominant factor than men.
6. **Value of Assets:** In respect of the expenses relating to capital assets, the values of various assets are used as the basis for apportionment e.g., depreciation, insurance, repairs and maintenance of plant and machinery.
7. **Lighting Points:** The electricity charges of the manufacturing concern are apportioned on the basis of the number of lighting points.
8. **Kilowatt Hours:** This basis is adopted for the apportionment of cost of electric power.
9. **Technical Estimates:** In cases where a conventional basis for apportionment of overhead costs cannot be used, equitable proportion can be estimated by experts on the basis of technical assessment. This basis can be used for steam cost, internal transport etc.

Illustration 1

The following figures are extracted from the records X Y Z Co. Ltd., for the month of April, 2009:

Indirect Materials:		**Rs.**
Production Dept.	X	1,900
Production Dept.	Y	2,400
Production Dept.	Z	400
Maintenance Dept.	A	3,000
Stores Dept.	B	800
Indirect Wages		
Production Dept.	X	2,700
Production Dept.	Y	3,300
Production Dept.	Z	900

Maintenance Dept.	A	2,000
Stores Dept.	B	1,300
Power and Light		15,000
Rent and Rates		5,600
Insurance on assets		3,000
Meal charges		7,500

Depreciation is to be provided @ 12% on capital value of assets, per annum. The following additional information has been given:

	Production Departments			Service Departments	
	X	Y	Z	A	B
Area (sq.ft)	4,000	4,000	3,000	2,000	1,000
Capital value of assets (Rupees)	50,000	60,000	40,000	30,000	20,000
Kilowatt Hours	2,000	2,200	800	750	250
Number of empolyees	90	120	30	40	20

Prepare a summary showing the distribution of overhead.

Solution

Overhead Distribution Summary

Period: April, 2009

Items	Basis of Apportionment	Total	Production Departments			Service Departments	
			X	Y	Z	A	B
		Rs.	Rs.	Rs.	Rs.	Rs.	Rs.
Indirect Materials	Allocation	8,500	1,900	2,400	400	3,000	800
Indirect Wages	Allocation	10,200	2,700	3,300	900	2,000	1,300
Power and Light	Kilowatt hours	15,000	5,000	5,500	2,000	1,875	625
Rent and Rates	Floor Area	5,600	1,600	1,600	1,200	800	400
Insurance on assets	Value of assets	3,000	750	900	600	450	300
Depreciation on assets (for I month)	Value of assets	2,000	500	600	400	300	200
Meal charges	No. of workers	7,500	2,250	3,000	750	1,000	500
Total departmental overhead		51,800	14,700	17,300	6,250	9,425	4,125

Illustration 2

MR Co. Ltd., has three production departments A, B and C and two service departments D and E. The following figures are extracted from the records of the company for the month of March, 2009:

	Rs.
Rent and Rates	10,000
Indirect Wages	3,000
Depreciation of Machinery	20,000
General Lighting	1,200
Power	3,000
Sundries	20,000

The following further details are available

	Total	A	B	C	D	E
Floor space (sq. ft.)	10,000	2,000	2,500	3,000	2,000	500
Light Points	60	10	15	20	10	5
Direct Wages (Rs).	10,000	3,000	2,000	3,000	1,500	500
Horse Power of Machines	150	60	30	50	10	–
Value of Machinery (Rs.)	2,50,000	60,000	80,000	1,00,000	5,000	5,000

Prepare a Primary Overhead Distribution Summary.

Solution

Overhead Distribution Summary

Period: March, 2009

Items	Basis of Apportionment	Total	Production Departments			Service Departments	
			X	Y	Z	A	B
		Rs.	Rs.	Rs.	Rs.	Rs.	Rs.
Direct Wages (of Service Deptts.)	Allocation	2,000	–	–	–	1,500	500
Rent and Rates	Floor Space	10,000	2,000	2,500	3,000	2,000	500
Indirect Wages	Direct Wages	3,000	900	600	900	450	150
Depreciation of Machinery	Value of Machinery	20,000	4,800	6,400	8,000	400	400
General Lighting	Light Points	1,200	200	300	400	200	100
Power	H.P. of Machines	3,000	1,200	600	1,000	200	–
Sundries	Direct Wages	20,000	6,000	4,000	6,000	3,000	1,000
Total departmental overhead		59,200	15,100	14,400	19,300	7,750	2,650

Re-apportionment of Service Department Expenses to Production Departments:

After the apportionment of the overhead costs to production and service departments, the next step is to apportion the total expenses of various service departments to production departments. Since the service departments are not engaged in actual output, it becomes necessary to apportion the costs of the service departments to the production departments. The process of re-apportionment of service department costs to production departments is also known as 'Secondary Distribution.'

Bases of re-apportionment

The service department costs are apportioned to the production departments generally on the basis of the benefits derived by the production departments from the service department. Following is the list of the more conventional bases used for the apportionment of service department costs:

	Service Department	Basis of Apportionment
(*i*)	Time-keeping Department, Wages Office (or Pay Roll Office)	(*a*) Number of workers. (*b*) Labour hours worked. (*c*) Machine hours worked.
(*ii*)	Personnel Department	Number of Employees in each department.
(*iii*)	Purchase Department	(*a*) Number of Purchase Orders placed (*b*) Cost of Materials purchased.
(*iv*)	Stores Department	(*a*) Number of Material Requisitions. (*b*) Value of Materials used.
(*v*)	Maintenance Department	(*a*) Number of Labour Hours worked. (*b*) Machine Hours worked.
(*vi*)	Building Service Department	Floor Space occupied.
(*vii*)	Canteen Department, Welfare Department, Recreation, Ambulance Service.	Number of Employees in each department.
(*viii*)	Internal Transport Department	Weight or Value of Materials handled.

Methods of Re-apportionment:

There are two methods in use for the apportionment of service department costs:

1. Apportionment of service department costs only to production departments.
2. Apportionment of the service department costs to the production as well as other service departments.

Apportionment to Production Departments only:

Under the first method, service department costs are directly apportioned to the production departments and the service rendered to the other service departments is ignored. This method can be explained with the help of the following example:

Illustration 3

RST Co. Ltd., has three Production Departments and two Service Departments. The Departmental expenses as per Primary Distribution Summary for the month of January, 2009 are as follows:

Departments	Rs.
Production Department 'X'	14,700
Production Department 'Y'	17,300
Production Department 'Z'	6,250
Maintenance Department 'A'	9,425
Stores Department 'B'	4,125

The following additional information is available

	Departments		
	X	Y	Z
Direct labour hours	1,800	1,600	1,100
Number of Requisitions	90	60	50

Apportion the service department expenses to production departments, ignoring inter-service department transfer.

Solution

Secondary Distribution Summary

Period: January, 2009

Items	Basis of Apportionment	Total	Production Departments			Service Departments	
			X	Y	Z	A	B
		Rs.	Rs.	Rs.	Rs.	Rs.	Rs.
Total Departmental overhead	——	51,800	14,700	17,300	6,250	9,425	4,125
Expenses of Service Dept. 'A'	Direct labour hours	–	3,770	3,351	2,304	(–)9,425	–
Expenses of Service Dept. 'B'	Number of Requisitions	–	1,856	1,238	1,031	–	(–)4,125
Total Overhead		51,800	20,326	21,889	9,585	–	–

Illustration 4

'XYZ' Company Ltd., has three Production Departments and four Service Departments. The expenses of the departments as per Primary Distribution Summary are as follows:

Production Departments		**Rs.**
X		30,000
Y		20,000
Z		15,000
Service Departments:		Rs.
Purchase Department	(1)	8,000
Time-Keeping and Pay Roll	(2)	6,000
Power House	(3)	4,800
Labour Welfare Department	(4)	1,200

The following information is available:

Departments	1	2	3	4	X	Y	Z
Value of Material Requisitioned (Rs.)	–	–	5,000	–	20,000	20,000	10,000
No. of Employees	6	6	12	6	36	24	12
Horse Power of Machine	–	–	–	–	600	600	400

Prepare a statement showing distribution of overhead costs of Service Departments to Production Departments.

Solution

Secondary Distribution Summary

Items	Basis of Apportionment	Total	Production Departments			Service Departments			
			X	Y	Z	1	2	3	4
		Rs.	Rs.	Rs.	Rs.	Rs.	Rs.	Rs.	Rs.
Departmental Overhead as per Overhead Distribution Summary		85,000	30,000	20,000	15,000	8,000	6,000	4,800	1,200
(*i*) Expenses of Purchase Department	Value of Material Requisitioned	–	3,200	3,200	1,600	(–) 8,000	–	–	–
(*ii*) Expenses of Time-keeping and Pay Roll	No. of Employees	–	3,000	2,000	1,000	–	(–) 6,000	–	–
(*iii*) Expenses of Power House	H.P. of Machines	–	1,800	1,800	1,200	–	–	(–) 4,800	–
(*iv*) Expenses of Labour Welfare Department	No. of Employees	–	600	400	200	–	–	–	(–)1,200
Total Overhead		85,000	38,600	27,400	19,000	–	–	–	–

Illustration 5

A company has three production departments: A, B and C and two service departments X and Y. The following figures relate to the month of July, 2002.

		Production Deptts.			Service Deptts.	
		A	B	C	X	Y
Indirect Materials	Rs.	1,900	2,400	400	3,000	800
Indirect Wages	Rs.	1,800	2,200	600	2,000	1,300
Area (Sq.ft.)		8,000	8,000	6,000	4,000	2,000
Capital value of Assets	Rs.	1,00.000	1,20,000	80,000	60,000	40,000
Kilo-watt hours		4.000	4,400	1,600	1,500	500
No. of Employees		180	240	60	80	40
Service rendered by Service Deptts						
	X	50%	30%	20%		
	Y	30%	40%	30%		

Other expenses were Power and Light Rs. 12,000, Insurance Rs. 2,000, Rent and Rates Rs. 5,600 and Meal expenses Rs. 6,000.

Depreciation is to be provided @ 12% per annum on capital value of assets. Prepare a statement showing the distribution of overheads amongst various departments.

(*M.D.U. Rohtak, B.Com., 2003*)

Solution

Overhead Distribution Summary

Period: July, 2002

Items	Basis of Apportionment	Total	Production Departments			Service Departments	
			X	Y	Z	A	B
		Rs.	Rs.	Rs.	Rs.	Rs.	Rs.
Indirect Materials	Allocation	8,500	1,900	2.400	400	3,000	800
Indirect Wages	Allocation	7,900	1,800	2.200	600	2,000	1,300
Power and Light	Kilowatt Hours	12,000	4,000	4.400	1,600	1,500	500
Insurance (Assets)	Capital Value of assets	2,000	500	600	400	300	200
Rent and Rates	Floor Area	5,600	1,600	1.600	1,200	800	400
Meal Expenses	No. of Employees	6,000	1800	2400	600	800	400
Depreciation on Assets (one month)	Capital Value	4,000	1,000	1.200	800	600	400
Total Departmental Overhead		46,000	12,600	14.800	5.600	9,000	4,000

Secondary Distribution Summary

Period: July, 2002

Items	Basis of Apportionment	Total	Production Departments			Service Departments	
			X	Y	Z	A	B
		Rs.	Rs.	Rs.	Rs.	Rs.	Rs.
Total Departmental overhead (as per- Overhead Distribution Summary)	–	46,000	12,600	14,800	5,600	9,000	4,000
Expenses of Service Deptt.'X'	50 : 30 : 20	–	4,500	2,700	1,800	(–)9,000	–
Expenses of Service Deptt. 'Y'	30 : 40 : 30	–	1,200	1,600	1,200	–	(–)4000
Total Overhead		46,000	18,300	19,100	8,600	–	–

Apportionment to Production Departments and other Service Departments

This method applied for apportioning the service department costs, considers inter-service department distribution on some equitable basis. Inter-service distribution can be done by the following methods:

(*a*) Step Ladder Method.
(*b*) Repeated Distribution Method.
(*c*) Simultaneous Equation Method.
(*d*) Trial and Error Method.

Step Ladder Method:

Under this method, all service departments of a concern are arranged in the order of their utility in terms of their service to the largest number of other departments. Thereafter, the cost of the most serviceable department i.e., the department which serves the largest number of departments, is first apportioned to other service departments and production departments. The service department which serves the next largest number of departments is then taken up and so on in this order till the costs of all the service departments are apportioned. The cost of the last service department will naturally be apportioned only to the production departments. Under this method, the shape of the apportionment chart looks like the steps of a ladder and as such it is known as Step Ladder Method.

Illustration 6

Taking the figures of total department overhead as given in Illustration 4, apportion the service department expenses under the Step Ladder Method.

Solution

For the purpose of solution, first of all, we have to arrange the various service departments in order of their service utility to other departments. The order of

utility may be (*i*) Time-keeping Department, (*ii*) Labour Welfare Department, (*iii*) Purchase Department, and (*iv*) Power House. Thus, the apportionment process shall begin with Time-keeping Department and end with Power House.
Now the solution would be as follows:

Secondary Distribution Summary

Items	Basis of Apportionment	Total	Production Departments			Service Departments			
			X	Y	Z	Time-Keeping	Labour Welfare	Purchase	Power
		Rs.	Rs.	Rs.	Rs.	Rs.	Rs.	Rs.	Rs.
Departmental Overhead as per Distribution Summary		85,000	30,000	20,000	15,000	6,000	1,200	8,000	4,800
(*i*) Expenses of Time-Keeping Department	No. of Employees (36: 24 : 12 : 6 : 6 : 12)	–	2,250	1,500	750	(–) 6,000	375	375	750
(*ii*) Expenses of Labour Welfare Department	No. of Employees (36: 24 : 12 : 6 : 12)	–	630	420	210		(–)1,575	105	210
(*iii*) Expenses of Purchase Department	Value of Material Requisitioned (4: 4 : 2 : 1)	–	3,084	3,084	1,541			(–)8,480	771
(*iv*) Expenses of Power House	Horse Power of Machine (3 : 3 : 2)	–	2,449	2,449	1,633				(–) 6,531
Total Overhead		85,000	38,413	27,453	19,134	–	–	–	–

The Step Ladder method is criticised on account of the fact that it does not take full account of inter-service department costs.

Repeated Distribution Method:

Under this method, the service department costs are repeatedly distributed to other departments (production as well as service) on some equitable basis or on the basis of agreed percentages till the figures of the service departments are exhausted or become negligible.

Illustration 7

A factory has two production departments and two service departments. The overhead departmental distribution summary is as follows:

	Production	Deptt.	Service	Deptt.
	A	B	C	D
Overhead allocated (in Rupees)	6,000	4,000	1,170	1,500

The expenses of the service departments are to be charged out on a percentage basis as follows

	Production	Deptt.	Service	Deptt.
	A	B	C	D
Expenses of Service Deptt. C	40%	50%	–	10%
Expenses of Service Deptt. D	50%	30%	20%	–

Show how the expenses of the two service departments are to be charged to the two Production departments? (*G.N.D.U., B.Com.*)

Solution

Apportionment of service department costs under the Repeated Distribution Method is as follows:

Secondary Distribution Summary

Period.............

Items	Total	Production Departments		Service Departments	
		A	B	C	D
	Rs.	Rs.	Rs.	Rs.	Rs.
Total Departmental Expenses	12,670	6,000	4,000	1,170	1,500
Expenses of Service Dept. 'C'	–	468	585	(–) 1,170	117
Expenses of Service Dept. 'D'	–	809	485	323	(–) 1,617
Expenses of Service Dept. 'C'	–	129	162	(–) 323	32
Expenses of Service Dept. 'D'	–	16	10	6	(–) 32
Expenses of Service Dept. 'C'	–	3	3	(–) 6	–
Total Overhead	12,670	7,425	5,245	–	–

Simultaneous Equation Method:

Under this method, the actual costs of service departments are obtained first by solving simultaneous equations. The costs so obtained are then transferred to production departments on the basis of agreed percentages.

Illustration 8

Continuing Illustration 7 show, the apportionment of service department expenses by Simultaneous Equation Method.

Solution

Let x = Total expenses of Service Dept. 'C' to be apportioned; and
y = Total expenses of Service Dept. 'D' to be apportioned.

$x = 1,170 + \frac{1}{5} y$ (*i*) (since 20% of *y* will be apportioned to Dept. C) and

$y = 1,500 + \frac{1}{10} x$ (*ii*)

So, $5x = 5,850 + y$ (*iii*)
$10y = 15,000 + x$ (*iv*)

Multiplying equation (*iii*) by 10 and adding the two,

$$50x - 10y = 58,500$$
$$-x + 10y = 15,000$$
$$49x = 73,500$$
$$x = 1,500$$
$$y = 1,500 + \frac{1}{10} \times 1,500 = 1,650$$

Secondary Distribution Summary

Period..............

Items	Total	Production Departments		Service Departments	
		A	B	C	D
	Rs.	Rs.	Rs.	Rs.	Rs.
Total Departmental Overhead	12,670	6,000	4,000	1,170	1,500
Expenses of Service Dept. 'C' (Rs. 1,500)	–	600	750	(–)1,500	150
Expenses of Service Dept. 'D' (Rs. 1,650)	–	825	495	330	(–)1,650
Total Overhead	12,670	7,425	5,245	–	–

Trial and Error Method:

Under this method, first of all the cost of the first service department is apportioned to other service departments in the given ratio. Then, the cost of the next service department is apportioned to the first and other service departments. This process goes on till the service department costs are exhausted or become negligible.

Illustration 9

Taking the figures of Illustration 7, apportion the expenses of service departments to production departments on the basis of trial and error method.

Solution

Calculation of Total Expenses of Service Departments

	Service Departments C	D
	Rs. P.	Rs. P.
Departmental Overhead	1,170.00	1,500.00
Share of Expenses of Dept. C (10% to D)		117.00
		1,617.00
Share of Expenses of Dept. D (20% to C)	323.40	
Share of Expenses of Dept. C (10% to D)		32.34
Share of Expenses of Dept. D (20% to C)	6.46	
Share of Expenses of Dept. C (10% to D)		0·65
Total	1,499.86	1,649.99
or (Approximately)	1,500.00	1,650.00

Thus, the total costs of Service Departments 'C' and 'D' are Rs. 1,500 and Rs. 1,650 respectively. Now a Secondary Distribution Summary can be prepared in the same way as was done under the Simultaneous Equation Method.

Illustration 10

The following particulars relate to a manufacturing company which has three production departments A, B and C and two service deptts. X and Y.

Departments

	A	B	C	X	Y
Total Deptt. Overhead as per Primary Distribution (Rs.)	6,300	7,400	2,800	4,500	2,000

The company decided to charge the service departments cost on the basis of the following percentages

Service Deptts.	Production Deptts A	B	C	Service Deptts X	Y
X	40%	30%	20%	–	10%
Y	30%	30%	20%	20%	–

Find the total overheads of production deptts. charging service deptts. cost to production deptts. on Repeated Distribution and Simultaneous Equation Method.

(*Punjabi, B.Com., Sept. 1989*)

Solution

Secondary Distribution Summary
[Method: *Repeated Distribution*]

	Production Departments			Service Departments	
	A	B	C	X	Y
	Rs.	Rs.	Rs.	Rs.	Rs.
Total Departmental overhead as per primary distribution	6,300	7,400	2,800	4,500	2,000
Overhead of Department X apportioned (4 : 3 : 2 :1)	1,800	1,350	900	(–)4,500	450
Overhead of Department Y apportioned (3 : 3 : 2 : 2)	735	735	490	490	(–)2,450
Overhead of Department X apportioned (4 : 3 : 2 : 1)	196	147	98	(–)490	49
Overhead Department Y apportioned (3 : 3 : 2 : 2)	15	15	10	9	(–)49
Overhead of Department X apportioned to production departments (4 : 3 : 2)	4	3	2	(–) 9	
Total Overhead	9,050	9,650	4,300	–	–

(*b*) **Distribution of overhead** [Method: *Simultaneous Equation*] Working note

Let x be the total overhead of service department X, and let y be the total overhead of service department Y.

Thus, $x = \text{Rs. } 4{,}500 + 1/5y$ ... (*i*)

$y = \text{Rs. } 2{,}000 + 1/10x$ ... (*ii*)

or, $5x = \text{Rs. } 22{,}500 + y$ ...(*iii*)

$10y = \text{Rs. } 20{,}000 + x$ ...(*iv*)

Multiplying equation (*iii*) with 10 we get

$50x = \text{Rs. } 2{,}25{,}000 + 10y$ (*v*)

Re-arranging equation (*iv*) and (*v*), and adding the two, we get

$50x - 10y = \text{Rs. } 2{,}25{,}000$

$-x + 10y = \text{Rs. } 20{,}000$

$49x = \text{Rs.} 2{,}45{,}000$

or, $x = \text{Rs.} 2{,}45{,}000 \div 49$

$x = \text{Rs. } 5{,}000$

Putting the value of x in equation (*ii*), we get,

$y = \text{Rs. } 2{,}000 + 1/10x$

$= \text{Rs. } 2{,}500$

Secondary Distribution Summary

	Production Departments			Service Departments	
	A	B	C	X	Y
	Rs.	Rs.	Rs.	Rs.	Rs.
Total Departmental overhead as per primary distribution	6,300	7,400	2,800	4,500	2,000
Overhead of Service Department X (Rs. 5,000 apportioned (4 : 3 : 2 : 1)	2,000	1,500	1,000	(–)5,000	500
Overhead of Service Department Y (Rs. 2,500) apportioned (3 : 3 : 2: 2)	750	750	500	500	(–)2,500
Total Overhead	9,050	9,650	4,300	–	–

Illustration 11

In a factory, there are two service departments P and Q and three production departments A, B and C. In April 2003, the departmental expenses were:

Departments	Rs.
A	6,50,000
B	6,00,000
C	5,00,000
P	1,20,000
Q	1,00,000

The service department expenses are allotted on a percentage basis as follows

Service Department	Production Departments			Service Departments	
	A	B	C	P	Q
P	30	40	15	–	15
Q	40	30	25	5	–

Prepare a statement showing the distribution of the two service departments' expenses to the three production departments. Method of calculation should be shown clearly. *(I.C.W.A. Final)*

Solution

(A) Simultaneous Equation Method

Let x be the total overhead of P Deptt. and y be the total overhead of Q Deptt.

$$x = 1{,}20{,}000 + 5\%\ y$$
$$y = 1{,}00{,}000 + 15\%\ x$$

or $$x = 1{,}20{,}000 + \frac{5}{100}y$$

or $$100x = 1{,}20{,}00{,}000 + 5y \qquad (i)$$

$$y = 1{,}00{,}000 + \frac{15}{100}x \text{ or } 100y = 1{,}00{,}00{,}000 + 15x \qquad (ii)$$

or $$100x - 5y = 1{,}20{,}00{,}000 \ (iii)$$
$$-15x + 100y = 1{,}00{,}00{,}000 \ (iv)$$

By multiplying (*iii*) by (3) and (*iv*) by (20), and adding the two we get

$$= 300x - 15y = 3,60,00,000$$
$$= -300x + 2000y = -20,00,00,000$$
$$1,985y = 23,60,00,000$$
$$y = 1,18,892$$

Substituting the value of *y* in (*iii*) we get

$$100x - 5 \times 1,18,892 = 1,20,00,000$$

or
$$100x = 1,20,00,000 + 5,94,460$$

or
$$x = \frac{1,25,94,460}{100} = 1,25,945$$

Secondary Distribution Summary

Period: April, 2003

Items	Total	Production Departments			Service Departments	
		A	B	C	P	Q
	Rs.	Rs.	Rs.	Rs.	Rs.	Rs.
Departmental Overhead (as perPrimary Distribution Summary)	19,70,000	6,50,000	6,00,000	5,00,000	1,20,000	1,00,000
Expenses of Service Department 'P'	–	37,783	50,378	18,392	(–)1,25,945	18,892
Expenses of Service Department 'Q'	–	47,557	35,667	29,723	5,945	(–)1,18,892
Total Overhead	19,70,000	7,35,340	6,86,045	5,48,515	–	–

(B) Repeated Distribution Method

Secondary Distribution Summary

Period: April, 2003

Items	Total	Production Departments			Service Departments	
		A	B	C	P	Q
	Rs.	Rs.	Rs.	Rs.	Rs.	Rs.
Departmental Overhead	19,70,000	6,50,000	6,00,000	5,00,000	1,20,000	1,00,000
Expenses of Service Dept. 'P'	–	36,000	48,000	18,000	(–)1,20,000	18,000
Expenses of Service Dept. 'Q'	–	47,200	35,400	29,500	5,900	(–)1,18,000
Expenses of Service Dept. 'P	–	1,770	2,360	885	(–)5,900	885
Expenes of Service Dept. 'Q'	–	354	266	221	44	(–)885
Expenses of Service Dept. 'P'	–	13	17	7	(–)44	7
Expenses of Service Dept. 'Q'	–	3	2	2	–	(–)7
Total Overhead	19,70,000	7,35,340	6,86,045	5,48,615	–	–

Illustration 12

Star Co. Ltd., has three production departments and two service departments. The actual expenses of the factory for the month of January, 2003 are as follows:

		Rs.	
Indirect Materials:			
Production Deptt.	'A'	910	
Production Deptt.	B	2,143	
Production Deptt.	C	847	
Service Deptt.	P	300	
Service Deptt.	Q	300	4,500
Indirect Wages:			
Production Deptt.	A	1,200	
Production Deptt.	B	2,000	
Production Deptt.	C	1,000	
Service Deptt.	P	800	
Service Deptt.	Q	1,000	6,000
Rent of the Factory			8,000
Supervision Charges			4,000
Lighting			4,000
Depreciation of Machinery			5,000

The following further details are available:

	Total	A	B	C	P	Q
Area (sq. ft.)	3,000	600	1,200	500	500	200
Light Points	80	16	40	10	8	6
Number of workers	30	6	12	5	5	2
Value of Machinery (Rs.)	50,000	25,000	16,000	2,000	5,000	2,000
Working Hours		1,000	2,500	1,400		

Expenses of Service Departments P and Q are apportioned as follows:

	A	B	C	P	Q
P	30%	40%	20%	–	10%
Q	10%	20%	50%	20%	–

You are required to work out the production hour rate of recovery of overhead in Departments A, B, and C.

(*C.A., Inter*)

Solution

Overhead Distribution Summary

Period: January, 2003

Items	Basis of Apportionment	Total	Production Departments			Service Departments	
			A	B	C	P	Q
		Rs.	Rs.	Rs.	Rs.	Rs.	Rs.
Indirect Materials	Allocation	4,500	910	2,143	847	300	300
Indirect Wages	Allocation	6,000	1,200	2,000	1,000	800	1,000
Rent	Area	8,000	1,600	3,200	1,334	1,333	533
Supervision Charges	Number of Workers	4,000	800	1,600	666	667	267
Lighting	Number of Light Points	4,000	800	2,000	500	400	300
Depreciation on Machinery	Value of Machinery	5,000	2,500	1,600	200	500	200
Total Departmental Overhead		31,500	7,810	12,543	4,547	4,000	2,600

(*a*) Repeated Distribution Method

Secondary Distribution Summary

Period: January, 2003

Items	Total	Production Departments			Service Departments	
		A	B	C	P	Q
	Rs.	Rs.	Rs.	Rs.	Rs.	Rs.
Total Departmental Expenses (as per overhead distribution summary)	31,500	7,810	12,543	4,547	4,000	2,600
Expenses of Service Department 'P'		1,200	1,600	800	(–)4,000	400
Expenses of Service Department 'Q'		300	600	1,500	600	(–)3,000
Expenses of Service Department 'P'		180	240	120	(–)600	60
Expenses of Service Department 'Q'		6	12	30	12	(–)60
Expenses of Service Department 'P'		4	5	3	(–)12	–
Total Overhead	31,500	9,500	15,000	7,000	–	–
Working Hours		1,000	2,500	1,400		
Overhead Rate per hour		Rs. 9.50	Rs. 6.00	Rs. 5.00		

(*b*) Simultaneous Equation Method:

Let x = Total expenses of Service Department 'P' to be apportioned; and

y = Total expenses of Service Deptt. 'Q' to be apportioned.

$$x = 4{,}000 + \frac{1}{5}y \qquad (i)$$

$$y = 2{,}600 + \frac{1}{10}x \qquad (ii)$$

So, $5x = 20{,}000 + y \qquad (iii)$

$10y = 26{,}000 + x \qquad (iv)$

Multiplying equation (*iii*) by 10 and adding the two,

$$\begin{aligned} 50x - 10y &= 2{,}00{,}000 \\ -x + 10y &= 26{,}000 \\ \hline 49x &= 2{,}26{,}600 \\ x &= 4{,}612 \\ y &= 2{,}600 + \frac{1}{10}(4{,}612) = 3{,}061 \end{aligned}$$

Secondary Distribution Summary

Period: January, 2003

Items	Total	Production Departments			Service Departments	
		A	B	C	P	Q
	Rs.	Rs.	Rs.	Rs.	Rs.	Rs.
Total Departmental Overhead	31,500	7,810	12,543	4,547	4,000	2,600
Expenses of Service Dept. P (Rs. 4,612)		1,384	1,845	922	(–)4,612	461
Expenses of Service Dept. Q, (Rs. 3,061)		306	612	1,531	612	(–)3,061
Total Overhead	31,500	9,500	15,000	7,000	–	
Working Hours		1,000	2,500	1,400		
Overhead Rate per hour		Rs. 9.50	Rs. 6.00	Rs. 5.00		

Illustration 13

The New Enterprises Ltd., has three Production Departments A, B, C and two Service Departments D and E. The following figures are extracted from the records of the company:

	Rs.
Rent and rates	5,000
General lighting	600
Indirect wages	1,500
Power	1,500
Depreciation of Machinery	10,000
Sundries	10,000

The following further details are available:

	Total	A	B	C	D	E
Floor Space (sq.ft.)	10,000	2,000	2,500	3,000	2,000	500
Light points	60	10	15	20	10	5
Direct wages (Rs.)	10,000	3,000	2,000	3,000	1,500	500
H.P. of Machines	150	60	30	50	10	–
Value of Machinery (Rs.)	2,50,000	60,000	80,000	1,00,000	5,000	5,000
Working hours	–	6,226	4,028	4,066	–	

The expenses of D and E are allocated as follows:

	A	B	C	D	E
D	20%	30%	40%	–	10%
E	40%	20%	30%	10%	–

What is the total cost of article if its raw material cost is Rs. 50, labour cost Rs. 30 and it passes through Departments A, B and C for 4, 5 and 3 hours respectively? *(I.C.W.A.)*

Solution

Overhead Distribution Summary

Items	Basis of Apportionment	Total	Production Departments			Service Departments	
			A	B	C	D	E
		Rs.	Rs.	Rs.	Rs.	Rs.	Rs.
Direct wages	Actual	2,000	–	–	–	1,500	500
Rent and rates	Re. 0.50 per sq.ft	5,000	1,000	1,250	1,500	1,000	250
General lighting	Rs. 10 per point	600	100	150	200	100	50
Indirect wages	15% of direct wages	1,500	450	300	450	225	75
Power	Rs. 10 per H.P.	1,500	600	300	500	100	–
Depreciation of Machinery	4% of value of machinery	10,000	2,400	3,200	4,000	200	200
Sundries	100% of direct wages	10,000	3,000	2,000	3,000	1,500	500
Total Departmental Overhead		30,600	7,550	7,200	9,650	4,625	1,575

Secondary Distribution Summary

Items	Total	Production Departments			Service Departments	
		A	B	C	D	E
	Rs.	Rs.	Rs.	Rs.	Rs.	Rs.
Total as per Distribution Summary:	30,600	7,550	7,200	9,650	4,625	1,575
Expenses of Dept. D		925	1,387	1,850	(–)4625	463
Expenses of Dept. E		815	408	611	204	(–)2,038
Expenses of Dept. D		41	61	82	(–)204	20
Expenses of Dept. E		8	4	6	2	(–)20
Expenses of Dept. D		–	1	1	(–) 2	–
Total	30,600	9,339	9,061	12,200	–	–
Working hours		6,226	4,028	4,028		
Rate per hour		1.50	2.25	3.03		

Statement of Total Cost of an Article

		Rs.
Direct Material		50
Direct Labour		30
Prime Cost		80
Overheads		
Dept. A 4 hours @ Rs. 1.50 per hour	6.00	
Dept. B 5 hours @ Rs. 2.25 per hour	11.25	
Dept. C 3 hours @ Rs. 3.03 per hour	9.09	26.34
Total Cost		106.34

Absorption of Overhead:

After the overheads have been allocated and apportioned to various production departments, the total overhead cost of a production department shall comprise of:

(*i*) The expenses allocated to the production department e.g., salary of the departmental head, salary of departmental foremen, cost of indirect materials issued to the department etc.

(*ii*) The share of the common expenses apportioned to it e.g., factory rent, salary of works manager, factory power, factory lighting etc.

(*iii*) The share of the expenses of the service departments re-apportioned to it e.g., expenses of personnel department, expenses of the stores department, expenses of time-keeping department etc.

The total amount of overhead accumulated for a production department is ultimately to be charged to the various cost units of that department. The distribution of the accumulated overhead cost of a production department amongst its cost units is known as overhead absorption. Overhead absorption is defined as the allotment of overhead to cost units. Thus, absorption of overhead is the function of apportioning overhead costs to individual units, jobs, production lots, processes, work-orders or such other convenient cost units and is also known as 'recovery' or 'application' of overhead expenses to cost units.

Steps to be taken in the absorption of overheads:

Absorption of overheads involves two steps:

(1) Computation of overhead absorption rate.

(2) Application of the overhead rate to cost units.

Computation of Overhead Absorption Rate

Computation of the overhead absorption rate is made for the purpose of charging the overheads to cost units. For computing overhead absorption rate, a number of methods may be applied. The computation of overhead rate is made by dividing the total overhead costs of a department by the number of units in the 'Base' such as number of units, direct material cost, direct labour cost, prime cost, direct labour hours, machine hours etc. Thus,

$$\text{Overhead Rate} = \frac{\text{Total Overheads of the Department}}{\text{Total Units of Base used}}$$

Application of Overhead Rate to cost units

In order to ascertain the cost of each unit, the overhead rate as calculated above is multiplied to the units of base in the particular cost unit. Thus:

Overhead chargeable to a cost unit = Units of Base in cost unit × Overhead Rate.

For example, if machine hour rate (overhead rate) is Rs. 5 and a particular unit of cost has taken 10 hours of the machine, the amount of overhead to be absorbed by the cost unit will be:

= 10 hours × Rs. 5 = Rs. 50.

METHODS OF FACTORY OVERHEAD ABSORPTION

The common methods applied for absorbing factory overhead are as follows:

(1) Units of Output Method: Under this method, absorption of factory overhead is made on the basis of the number of units manufactured. The overhead rate is obtained by dividing the amount of overhead expenses by the number of units of output. Thus:

$$\text{Overhead Rate} = \frac{\text{Factory Overhead of the Department}}{\text{Number of units of Output}}$$

For example, if the amount of factory overhead for department 'A' for a particular period is Rs. 10,000 and the number of units manufactured by the department during the period is 2,000, the overhead rate per unit will be Rs. 5 (Rs. 10,000 ÷ 2,000 units) and each unit will bear Rs. 5 by way of overhead cost.

This method is a very simple and direct method of overhead absorption and can be applied in single output industries like collieries, brick-making etc., where only one product or a few grades of the same product are manufactured. But this method cannot be applied in multi-product industries where variety of products of different values are manufactured.

(2) Direct Material Cost Method (Percentage on Direct Material Cost): The absorption of overhead, under this method, is made on the basis of direct materials consumed. The overhead rate is expressed as a percentage of the direct material cost and is calculated by dividing the factory overhead for a particular period by the cost of direct materials used during the period and multiplying it by 100. Thus overhead rate is:

$$= \frac{\text{Factoy Overhead}}{\text{Cost of Direct Materials used}} \times 100$$

If the amount of factory overhead for department 'A' for a month is Rs. 10,000 and the cost of direct material consumed is Rs. 25,000, the overhead rate will be 40% on direct material cost $\left(\frac{10,000}{25,000}\times 100\right)$ and if on a job done by department 'A', direct material costing Rs. 200 has been used, the job will absorb Rs. 80 (40% of Rs. 200) by way of overhead.

This method is very simple and equitable where the same type of material is used in all the articles manufactured and the price of such material is not subject to considerable fluctuations. This method is not widely used on account of the following disadvantages:

(1) Cost of materials is often subject to considerable fluctuations which will not be accompanied by similar fluctuations in factory overhead. This basis is, therefore, unstable.

(2) This method ignores time factor involved in production.

(3) The mere fact that a job consumes material of a very expensive nature is no justification for supposing that factory overhead chargeable to it would be proportionately higher.

(4) Factory expenses are affected not only by the materials cost but also by the type of workers employed to do a job. But under this method no distinction is made between the jobs done by skilled workers and those done by unskilled workers.

(3) Direct Labour Cost Method (Percentage on Direct Wages): Under this method, the absorption of overhead is made on the basis of the direct wages. The overhead rate is expressed as a percentage of direct wages and is obtained by dividing the factory overhead for a particular period by the direct wages paid during that period and multiplying it by 100. The overhead rate is obtained by applying the following formula:

$$\frac{\text{Factory Overhead}}{\text{Direct Wages}} \times 100$$

For example, if the factory overhead cost for department 'A' for a particular month is Rs. 10,000 and the total labour cost is Rs. 20,000, the overhead rate will be 50% on direct wages $\left(\frac{10,000}{20,000}\times 100\right)$. And if a job done by department 'A' involves a payment of Rs. 200 by way of direct wages, it will absorb Rs. 100 (50% of Rs. 200) by way of overhead.

This method is very simple and is widely practised on account of the following advantages:

(1) Automatic consideration is given to the time factor as the wages are paid on the basis of time.

(2) Wages rates are more constant than material prices and hence this method provides a stable basis for the absorption of overhead.

(3) Factory expenses, to a great extent, depend on the number of workers employed and hence, this basis is more equitable.

But this method suffers from the following disadvantages:

(1) Variations in the wage rates of skilled and unskilled workers are not taken into account. It is notable that unskilled workers give rise to more factory expenses than skilled workers and hence the jobs done by unskilled workers should bear a higher charge for overhead but the reverse is likely to happen under this method.

(2) No distinction is made between the work of hand workers and that of machine workers. It should be remembered that hand workers give rise to more factory expenses than machine workers.

(3) Time element may be ignored if the workers are paid on the basis of piece-work and not on the basis of time.

(4) Prime Cost Method (Percentage on Prime Cost): Under this method, absorption of overhead is made on the basis of prime cost. This method assumes that both materials and labour give rise to overhead and, therefore, both should be taken into consideration. The overhead rate is expressed as a percentage of the prime cost and can be obtained by the following formula:

$$\frac{\text{Factory Overhead}}{\text{Prime Cost}} \times 100$$

For example, if the factory overhead for department 'A' for a particular month is Rs. 10,000 and the prime cost is Rs. 40,000, the overhead rate will be 25% on prime cost $\left(\frac{10{,}000}{40{,}000} \times 100\right)$ and if the prime cost of a job done by the department is Rs. 300, the job will absorb Rs. 75 (25% of Rs. 300) by way of overhead.

This method is simple to operate and combines the advantages of both direct materials cost and direct labour cost methods. But this method assigns equal weight to materials and labour, though factory overhead is more closely related to labour.

(5) Direct Labour Hour Rate Method: Under this method, absorption of overhead is made on the basis of number of hours for which direct labour is employed. The direct labour hour rate of overhead is obtained by dividing the factory overhead for the department for a given period by the total number of direct labour hours for the period. Thus, overhead rate is:

$$= \frac{\text{Factory Overhead}}{\text{Number of Direct Labour Hours}}$$

For example, if the factory expenses for department 'A' for a particular period amount of Rs. 10,000 and the total number of direct labour hours worked during the period is 5,000, the direct labour hour rate will be Rs. 2 (Rs. 10,000

÷ 5,000 hours). If a particular job done during the period involves 50 hours work of direct labour, it will absorb Rs. 100 (50 hours × Rs. 2) by way of overhead.

Direct labour hour rate is basically a time rate and since most of the items of factory overhead vary with time, this method provides a satisfactory basis for overhead absorption. But this method assumes the pre-dominance of direct labour in production and ignores all other factors of production.

(6) Machine Hour Rate Method: Under this method, overhead absorption is made on the basis of the cost of operating a machinery. This method is applied in highly organised engineering works where most of the work is done by machines. The hourly cost of operating a machine represents the overhead rate and is known as machine hour rate. The machine hour rate is obtained by dividing the factory expenses connected with a machine for a given period by the number of hours worked by the machine during that period.

Thus overhead rate under the machine hour rate method is:

$$= \frac{\text{Factory Overhead (relating to a machine)}}{\text{Number of Machine Hours}}$$

For example, if the factory expenses relating to Machine No. 15 installed in department 'A' for a particular period amount to Rs. 5,000 and the total number of hours worked by the said machine during the period is 1,000, the machine hour rate will be Rs. 5 (Rs. 5,000 ÷ 1,000 hours). If a particular job executed during the period has taken 30 hours of machine No. 15, it will absorb Rs. 150 (30 hours × Rs. 5) by way of factory overhead.

In highly mechanised factories where a considerable portion of the factory overhead is related to the running of the machines, machine hour rate method provides the most scientific basis for the absorption of overhead. But this method is a complicated one as it involves too much mathematical calculations. Moreover, it requires the maintenance of accurate records regarding the life of the machines and the cost of repairs and maintenance.

(7) Dual Hour Rate Method: This is a combination of machine hour rate and direct labour hour rate. It is adopted in those departments where both manual and machine work are equally important. In such cases, overheads are classified into two groups, i.e., overheads which are related to manual work and secondly those related to machine work. The first kind of overheads are absorbed by means of a labour hour rate and the second category of overheads by a machine hour rate.

Illustration 14

The following information relates to a Manufacturing Co., for the year ended 31st March 2005: Materials Used Rs. 60,000; Direct Labour Rs. 30,000; Factory Overhead Rs. 18,000; Direct Labour Hours 12,000; Machine Hours 10,000.

The following information relates to Job No. 75:

Materials used Rs. 1,200; Direct Labour Rs. 650; Direct Labour Hours 265; Machine Hours 255.

Enumerate 4 different methods of absorbing Factory Overheads and prepare a statement showing total cost of Job No. 75 under each of the four methods referred to above.

(G.N.D.U.B. Com. Sept., 1976)

Solution

The main four methods of absorbing factory overhead may be:

(1) A Percentage on Direct Materials.
(2) A Percentage on Direct Labour Cost.
(3) Direct Labour Hour Rate Method.
(4) Machine Hour Rate Method.

First method:

The overhead rate as a percentage on direct materials cost comes to 30%, calculated as follows:

$$\frac{18,000}{60,000} \times 100$$

The factory cost of the Job will be as follows

	Rs.
Materials used	1,200
Direct Labour	650
Prime Cost	1,850
Factory overhead @ 30% of Rs. 1,200	360
Factory Cost	2,210

Second Method:

The overhead rate as a percentage on direct labour cost comes to 60% calculated as follows:

$$\frac{18,000}{30,000} \times 100$$

The factory cost of the Job will be as follows

	Rs.
Materials used	1,200
Direct Labour	650
Prime Cost	1,850
Factory overhead @ 60% of Rs. 650	390
Factory Cost	2,240

Third Method:

The direct labour hour rate of overhead comes to Rs. 1.50, calculated as follows:

$$\frac{\text{Rs.}18{,}000}{12{,}000 \text{ Hrs.}}$$

The factory cost of the job will be as follows:

	Rs.
Materials used	1,200
Direct labour	650
Prime Cost	1,850
Factory overhead @ Rs. 1.50 per labour hour for 265 hours	397.50
Factory Cost	2,247.50

Fourth Method:

The machine hour rate of overhead comes to Rs. 1.80, calculated as follows:

$$\frac{\text{Rs.}18{,}000}{10{,}000 \text{ Hrs.}}$$

The factory cost of the job will be as follows:

	Rs.
Materials consumed	1,200
Direct Labour	650
Prime Cost	1,850
Factory overhead @ Rs. 1.80 per machine hour for 255 hours	459
Factory Cost	2,309

Illustration 15

The following figures have been extracted from the books of a manufacturing company. All jobs pass through the company's two departments:

	Working Deptt.	Finishing Deptt.
Materials used	6,000	500
Direct labour	3,000	1,500
Factory overhead	1,800	1,200
Direct labour hours	12,000	5,000
Machine hours	10,000	2,000

The following information relates to Job No. 17:

	Working Deptt.	Finishing Deptt.
Materials used	120	10
Direct labour	65	25
Direct labour hours	565	70
Machine hours	255	25

You are required:

(*a*) to enumerate four methods of absorbing factory overheads by jobs, showing the rates for each department under the methods quoted, and

(*b*) to prepare a statement showing the different cost results for Job No. 17 under each of four methods referred to.

(*Punjabi Uni., B.Com., 1985*)

Solution

(*i*) Percentage to Direct Material Cost:

$$\frac{\text{Factory Overhead}}{\text{Direct Material Cost}} \times 100$$

$$\text{Working Dept.: } \frac{1{,}800}{6{,}000} \times 100 = 30\%$$

$$\text{Finishing Dept.: } \frac{1{,}200}{500} \times 100 = 240\%$$

(*ii*) Percentage to Direct Labour Cost:

$$\frac{\text{Factory Overhead}}{\text{Direct Wages}} \times 100$$

$$\text{Working Dept.: } \frac{1{,}800}{3{,}000} \times 100 = 60\%$$

$$\text{Finishing Dept.: } \frac{1{,}200}{1{,}500} \times 100 = 80\%$$

(*iii*) Direct Labour hour rate:

$$\frac{\text{Factory Overhead}}{\text{Direct labour hours}}$$

$$\text{Working Dept.: } \frac{1{,}800}{12{,}000} = 15 \text{ p. per hour}$$

$$\text{Finishing Dept.: } \frac{1{,}200}{5{,}000} = 24 \text{ p. per hour}$$

(*iv*) Machine hour rate:

$$\frac{\text{Factory Overheads}}{\text{Machine hours}}$$

$$\text{Working Dept.: } \frac{1{,}800}{10{,}000} = 18 \text{ p. per hour}$$

$$\text{Finishing Dept.: } \frac{1{,}200}{2{,}000} = 60 \text{ p. per hour}$$

Comparative Cost Statement of Job No. 17
For Working Department

Particulars	Material Cost Percentage Rate (*i*)	Direct Labour Cost Percentage Rate (*ii*)	Direct Labour Hour Rate (*iii*)	Machine Hour Rate (*iv*)
	Rs.	**Rs.**	**Rs.**	**Rs.**
Material used	120	120	120	120
Direct Labour	65	65	65	65
Prime Cost	185	185	185	185
Add Factory Overheads				
(*i*) @ 30 % of Material Cost Rs. 120	36			
(*ii*) @ 60 % of Direct Wages Rs. 65		39		
(*iii*) 15 Paise per hr. for 265 hrs.			39.75	
(*iv*) 18 Paise per hr. for 255 hrs.				45.90
Total	221	224	224.75	230.90

Comparative Cost Statement of Job No. 17
For Finishing Department

Particulars	Material Cost Percentage Rate (*i*)	Direct Labour Cost Percentage Rate (*ii*)	Direct Labour Hour Rate (*iii*)	Machine Hour Rate (*iv*)
	Rs.	**Rs.**	**Rs.**	**Rs.**
Direct Material used	10	10	10	10
Labour	25	25	25	25
Prime Cost	35	35	35	35
Add Factory Overheads				
(*i*) @ 240 % of Direct Material Rs. 10.	24			
(*ii*) @ 80 % of Direct Wages Rs. 25		20		
(*iii*) 24 Paise per hr. for 70 hrs.			16.80	
(*iv*) 60 Paise per hr. for 25 hrs.				15
Total	59	55	51.80	50
Total brought from Working Department	221	224	224.75	230.90
Total Cost	280	279	276.55	280.90

Illustration 16

The following expenses were incurred in a leather manufacturing concern during the month of December, 2008:

	Rs.
Factory Rent	1,200
Lighting	200
Supervisory expenses	800
Factory Manager's Salary	1,200
Workers' welfare expenses	600
Organisation expenses	950
Contribution to social security schemes	650

There were 3,000 working hours during the month. Calculate the Direct Labour Hour Rate from the above particulars.

Solution

Calculation of Direct Labour Hour Rate

Direct Labour Hours: 3,000

	Rs.
Factory Rent	1,200
Lighting	200
Supervisory expenses	800
Factory manager's Salary	1,200
Workers' welfare expenses	600
Organisation expenses	950
Contribution to social security scheme	650
Total expenses of the month	5,600

Therefore, Hourly Rate is $\frac{5,600}{3,000}$ = Rs. 1.87

Illustration 17

There are three production departments in a factory namely A, B and C. The total factory expenses were Rs. 79,500 during a month.

The working hours in the different departments were as follows:

Department A

50 skilled workers worked 8 hours per day for 25 days in the month.
20 untrained workers worked 10 hours per day for 25 days in the month.
10 casual workers worked 5 hours per day for 20 days in the month.

Department B

80 skilled workers worked 8 hours per day for 25 days in the month.
30 untrained workers worked 10 hours per day for 22 days in the month.
15 casual workers worked 8 hours per day for 20 days in the month.

Department C

40 skilled workers worked 8 hours per day for 25 days in the month.
15 untrained workers worked 10 hours per day for 24 days in the month.
5 casual workers worked for 5 hours per day for 16 days in the month.

Calculate the 'Man Hour Rate' and distribute the factory overheads in different departments on the basis of the Man Hour Rate.

Solution

Computation of Total Man Hours in the Factory

			Hours.
Department A:			
(*a*) Skilled workers, hours	50 × 8 × 25	10,000	
(*b*) Untrained workers, hours	20 × 10 × 25	5,000	
(*c*) Casual workers, hours	10 x 5 x 20	1,000	16,000
Department B:			
(*a*) Skilled workers, hours	80 × 8 × 25	16,000	
(*b*) Untrained workers, hours	30 × 10 × 22	6,600	
(*c*) Casual workers, hours	15 × 8 × 20	2,400	25,000
Department C:			
(*a*) Skilled workers, hours	40 × 8 × 25	8,000	
(*b*) Untrained workers, hours	15 × 10 × 24	3,600	
(*c*) Casual workers, hours	5 × 5 × 16	400	12,000
	Total working hours		53.000

$$\text{Therefore Man Hour Rate is} = \frac{79,500}{53,000} = \text{Rs. } 1.50$$

Distribution of factory overheads:

		Rs.
Department	A	16,000 × 1.50 = 24,000
Department	B	25,000 × 1.50 = 37,500
Department	C	12,000 × 1.50 = 18,000
		79,500

Computation of Machine Hour Rate

As already discussed, machine hour rate is computed for the recovery or absorption of factory overhead. This basis for recovery of overhead is adopted in those industrial concerns where most of the work is carried on with the help of machines and as such most of the factory expenses are caused by machine operations. Machine hour rate represents the hourly cost of factory overhead for operating a particular machine and is obtained by dividing the factory expenses connected with a machine for a given period by the number of hours worked by the machine during that period. The Institute of Cost and Managements Accountants, London, defines the machine hour rate as "an actual or pre-determined rate of cost apportionment or overhead absorption which is calculated by dividing the cost to be apportioned or absorbed by the number of hours for which a machine or machines are operated or expected to be operated."

For computing the machine hour rate, each machine or a group of similar machines in a production department is considered as a smaller department and the departmental expenses are re-apportioned to the machines or groups of machines in the department. For this purpose the following basic factors are to be considered:

(*i*) Base Period

A *'Base Period'* is to be taken for each machine for computing the machine hour rate. The base period refers to the period of time for which the hourly rate is to be computed and may be a year, a quarter, a month or a week.

(*ii*) Normal Hours of Working

The number of normal or standard working hours of each machine in the base period has to be estimated.

(*iii*) Distribution of Expenses

All the departmental expenses to be considered for computing the machine hour rate are divided into two parts

(*a*) Standing charges (or fixed expenses).

(*b*) Running charges (or variable expenses or machine expenses).

Standing Charges

Standing charges include all those expenses which remain fixed or constant and relate to the department as a whole. These are not affected by the operation of the machines e.g., rent, rates and insurance of factory building, cost of factory supervision, factory lighting, insurance of machine etc.

Running Charges

These include the expenses which are incurred in connection with the operation of the machines e.g., depreciation, repairs and maintenance, power, steam, water etc.

(*iv*) Computation of Hourly Rate of Standing Charges

For computing the machine hour rate all the standing charges relating to the production department will be apportioned to the individual machines on the following bases:

Items	Basis of Apportionment
(*a*) Factory Rent, Rates and Insurance	(*a*) Floor Area occupied by each machine
(*b*) Factory Lighting	(*b*) Number of lighting points Number of workers engaged on each machine or floor area occupied by each machine
(*c*) Factory Supervision	(*c*) Time devoted by supervisory staff to each machine
(*d*) Insurance of machinery	Value of machinery
(*e*) Miscellaneous Expenses e.g., lubricating oil, grease, cotton waste, sundry stores	Actual quantity used (whenever possible) or any other equitable basis.

The standing charges will be taken for the 'base period'. The total of the standing charges apportioned to each machine for the base period will be divided by the total working hours of the machine in the base period to obtain the 'hourly rate of standing charges'.

(*v*) Computation of Hourly Rate of Machine Charges

The hourly rate of various items of 'machine charges' or 'running charges' will be computed separately in the following manner:

(*a*) Depreciation

For the purpose of calculating hourly rate of depreciation of machine, the original cost of the machine, its effective working life in terms of running hours after giving due consideration to the risk of obsolescence and its estimated scrap value (or residual value) at the end of its working life will have to be ascertained. The hourly rate of depreciation of the machine will be calculated by the following formula-

Hourly Rate of Depreciation =

$$\frac{\text{Original Cost of Machine} - \text{Estimated Scrap Value}}{\text{Effective Working Life of Machine in terms of Running Hours}}$$

(*b*) Repairs and Maintenance

Generally, the cost of repairs and maintenance of the machine over its effective working life is estimated on the basis of past experience. The hourly rate of repairs and maintenance cost will be ascertained by applying the following formula-

Hourly Rate of Repairs and Maintenance =

$$\frac{\text{Estimated Cost of Repairs and Maintenance over the life of the machine}}{\text{Effective Working Life of Machine in terms of Running Hours}}$$

(*c*) Power, Steam and Water

The hourly cost of power, steam and water consumed will be ascertained on the basis of-

(*i*) actual hourly consumption, or

(*ii*) estimated hourly consumption ascertained on the basis of past experience.

The hourly rates of standing charges and running charges will be aggregated to obtain the machine hour rate.

Computation of machine hour rate can be explained with the help of the following illustrations:

Illustration 18

From the following information compute a machine hour rate in respect of Machine No. 51 for the month of January, 2008:

Cost of Machine:	Rs. 6,000
Estimated Scrap value:	Rs. 1,000
Effective working life:	5,000 Hours
Hours worked in January, 2008:	100
Estimated cost of repairs and maintenance over the life of machine:	Rs. 1,250
Standing charges allocated to this machine for January, 2008:	Rs. 100

Power consumed by the machine : 10 units per hour at 10 paise per unit.

Solution

Computation of Machine Hour Rate

Machine No. 51

Period : January, 2008
Working hours : 100

	Rs.	Rs.
Standing Charges:		
Allocated to Machine No. 51 for the month	100	
Hourly rate of Standing Charges		1.00
$= \frac{\text{Rs. } 100}{100 \text{ Hours}} = \text{Re. } 1$	100	
Machine Charges:		
(*i*) Depreciation:		
Hourly rate of depreciation:		
$\frac{\text{Original cost} - \text{Scrap value}}{\text{Hours of working life}}$	1.00	
$= \frac{\text{Rs. } 6,000 - 1,000}{5,000 \text{ Hrs.}}$		
(*ii*) Repairs and maintenance:		
Hourly rate		
$= \frac{\text{Estimated cost over working life}}{\text{Hours of working life}}$		
$\frac{\text{Rs. } 1,250}{5,000 \text{ Hrs.}}$	0.25	
(*iii*) Power consumed 10 units per hour at 10 paise per unit	1.00	
Hourly rate of machine charges		2.25
Machine Hour Rate		3.25

Illustration 19

From the following particulars, compute the hourly rate of a machine installed in a department:

Cost of the machine (including installation charges):	Rs. 10,000
Estimated scrap value after the expiry of its life (5 years):	Rs. 1,000
Rent and rates of the department per quarter:	Rs. 400
General lighting of the department per month:	Rs. 60
Salary of supervisor: Rs. 500 per month	
Estimated repairs and maintenance cost of the machine per year:	Rs. 200
Power consumption: 5 units per hour at 20 paise per unit.	
Estimated working hours of the machine per year :	2,000

The machine occupies 1/4 of the total floor area of the department. The supervisor is expected to devote 1/5 of his total time to this machine. General lighting charges are to be apportioned on the basis of floor area.

Solution

Computation of Machine Hour Rate

Machine No. ....

Base-Period: One year
Working Hours : 2,000

			Rs.	Rs.
Standing Charges:				
(*i*) Rent and rates (1/4 of Rs. 1,600)			400	
(*ii*) General Lighting (1/4 of Rs. 720)			180	
(*iii*) Salary of supervisor (1/5 of Rs. 6,000)			1,200	
Total Standing charges			1,780	0·89
Hourly Rate of Standing charges $\frac{\text{Rs. } 1,780}{2,000 \text{ Hrs.}} = 0.89$				
Machine Expenses		Rs.		
(*i*) Depreciation:	Original cost	10,000		
	Estimated scrap value	1,000		
	Amount to be written off during 5 years	9,000	1,800	0.90
Hourly Rate of depreciation = $\frac{\text{Rs. } 1,800}{2,000 \text{ Hrs.}}$				
(*ii*) Repairs and Maintenance			200	0.10
Hourly rate of repairs and maintenance = $\frac{\text{Rs. } 200}{2,000 \text{ Hrs.}}$				
(*iii*) Power consumed : 5 units per hour @ 20 paise per unit				1.00
Machine Hour Rate				2.89

Illustration 20

Prepare a machine hour rate to cover the overhead expenses indicated below:

	Per hour Paise	Per Annum Rs.
Electric Power	75	
Steam	35	
Water	5	
Repairs		1,000
Rent		500
Running hours		2,000

Original Cost: Rs. 15,000
Book Value: Rs. 6,000
Present Replacement Value : Rs. 16,000
Depreciation: 10% per annum on Original Cost.

Solution

Computation of Machine Hour Rate

Machine No. .... Period: ....
Working Hours : 2,000

	Rs.	Rs.
Standing Charges:		
Rent	500	
Total Standing Charges	500	
Hourly Rate of Standing Charges $= \frac{\text{Rs. } 500}{2,000 \text{ Hrs.}}$		0.25
Machine Charges:		
(*i*) Depreciation: 10% on original cost Rs. 15,000 = Rs. 1,500		
Hourly Rate of depreciation $= \frac{\text{Rs. } 1,500}{2,000 \text{ Hrs.}}$	0.75	
(*ii*) Repairs		
Hourly Rate of repairs $= \frac{\text{Rs. } 1,000}{2,000 \text{ Hrs.}}$	0.50	
(*iii*) Electric Power	0.75	
(*iv*) Steam	0.35	
(*v*) Water	0.05	
		2.40
Machine Hour Rate		2.65

Illustration 21

The following annual charges have been incurred in respect of a shop having five identical machines:

		Rs.
(*i*)	Rent and rates	4,800
(*ii*)	Power consumed by the shop @ 5 Paise per unit	3,000
(*iii*)	Repairs and maintenance for the machines	1,000
(*iv*)	Lighting charges for the shop	600
(*v*)	Attendant's salary (there are 2 attendants and each is paid Rs. 100 per month)	
(*vi*)	Supervisor's salary (there is one supervisor for the five machines, his monthly salary Rs. 400)	
(*vii*)	Lubricants and cotton waste for the shop	350
(*viii*)	Depreciation on each machine	600
(*ix*)	Hire-purchase instalment payable for the machines (including Rs. 300 as interest)	2,300
(*x*)	Each machine consumes 10 units of power per hour.	

Compute the machine hour rate for the year.

(*M.D.U. Rohtak, B.Com. 2007*)

Solution

Calculation of the number of working hours is to be made on the basis of the cost of power consumed.

Total cost of power consumed by the shop = Rs. 3,000

Hourly cost of power per machine (10 units × 5 Paise) = 50 Paise

$$\text{Total machines hours worked during the year} = \frac{3{,}000}{0.50} = 6{,}000 \text{ hours}$$

Number of machines in the shop = 5

$$\text{Working hours per machine} = \frac{6{,}000}{5}$$

$$= 1{,}200 \text{ hours per annum.}$$

Computation of Machine Hour Rate

Machine No. .... Period: .... Working Hours : 1,200 per annum

	Per annum Rs.	Per hour Rs.
Standing Charges:		
(*i*) Rent and rates (1/5 of Rs. 4,800)	960	
(*ii*) Lighing charges (1/5 of Rs. 600)	120	
(*iii*) Attendant's Salary (1/5 of Rs. 2,400)	480	
(*iv*) Supervisor's Salary (1/5 of Rs. 4,800)	960	
(*v*) Lubricants and cotton waste (1/5 of Rs.350)	70	
Total standing charges	2,590	
Hourly rate of standing charges $= \frac{\text{Rs. } 2,590}{1,200 \text{ Hrs.}}$		2.16
Machine Charges:		
(*i*) Depreciation: Hourly rate of depreciation $= \frac{\text{Rs. } 600}{1,200 \text{ Hrs.}}$ = Re. 0.50	600	0.50
(*ii*) Repairs and maintenance (1/5 of Rs. 1,000)	200	0.17
Hourly rate $= \frac{\text{Rs. } 200}{1,200 \text{ Hrs.}}$ = Re. 0.17		
(*iii*) Power consumed: 10 units per hour @ 5 Paise per unit		0.50
Machine Hour Rate		3.33

Note: Amount of interest included in hire purchase instalment is a financial item and hence to be ignored while computing the machine hour rate.

Illustration 22

A factory uses three identical big and six identical small machines. The working hours of each of the nine machines are 1,800 hours per annum, while the effective working life is taken as 20,000 hours for each big machine and 12,000 hours for each small machine. The cost of each big machine is Rs. 20,600 and of each small machine Rs. 6,200. Scrap values are estimated at Rs. 600 and Rs. 200 respectively.

Each big machine occupies 1/6 of the workshop and fully employs six workers ; each small machine occupies half the space occupied by a big machine and fully employs four workers.

Each big machine consumes 10 units of power per hour while a small machine consumes 2 units per hour. The cost of power per unit is 10 Paise.

Repairs and maintenance etc., are estimated to cost for each big machine Rs. 5,000 and for each small machine Rs. 1,200 during its effective life. The manager is paid Rs. 1,800 a month and workshop supervision occupies half of his time, which is divided equally among the nine machines.

Other expenses incurred during the month are:

Rent of workshop Rs. 1,200; Lighting (to be apportioned in the ratio of workers engaged) Rs. 252; Insurance: Big machine – Rs. 20; Small machine Rs. 10.

Taking a period of one month as basis, calculate the machine hour rate for a big and a small machine separately.

Solution

Computation of Machine Hour Rate

Working Hours: 150 per month

	Per Month		Per Hour	
	Big Machine	**Small Machine**	**Big Machine**	**Small Machine**
Standing Charges:	**Rs.**	**Rs.**	**Rs.**	**Rs.**
(*i*) Rent of workshop Big Machine 1/6 of Rs. 1,200 Small Machine 1/12 of Rs. 1,200	200	100		
(*ii*) Lighting Big Machine 6/42 of Rs. 252 Small Machine 4/42 of Rs. 252	36	24		
(*iii*) Manager's Salary Big and Small: 1/9 of Rs. 900	100	100		
(*iv*) Insurance	20	10		
Total standing charges	356	234		
Hourly Rate = $\frac{\text{Rs. } 356}{150 \text{ Hrs.}}$ $\frac{\text{Rs. } 234}{150 \text{ Hrs.}}$			2.37	1.56
Machine Charges:				
(*i*) Depreciation: Hourly Rate $= \frac{\text{Cost} - \text{Scrap value}}{\text{Effective working life}}$ Big Machine Small Machine $\frac{\text{Rs. } 20{,}600 - 600}{20{,}000 \text{ Hrs.}}$ $\frac{\text{Rs. } 6{,}200 - 200}{12{,}000 \text{ Hrs.}}$			1.00	0.50
(*ii*) Repairs and Maintenance: Hourly Rate Big Machine Small Machine $\frac{\text{Rs. } 5{,}000}{20{,}000 \text{ Hrs.}}$ $\frac{\text{Rs. } 1{,}200}{12{,}000 \text{ Hrs.}}$			0.25	0.10
(*iii*) Power Consumed Big Machine: (10 units × 10 Paise) Small Machine: (2 units × 10 Paise)			1.00	0.20
Machine Hour Rate			4.62	2.36

Maintenance and Setting-up Time:

Sometimes, a part of the total working hours of a machine is devoted to its maintenance and setting-up. The time required for the maintenance and setting up of the machine (unless it is treated as productive time) should be deducted from the total working hours.

Treatment of the wages of machine operator:

Wages paid to the machine operator form the part of direct wages and hence will be excluded from the overhead to be considered for computing the machine hour rate. But sometimes a manufacturing concern may be interested in calculating a **comprehensive or composite machine hour rate**. The comprehensive machine hour rate also includes the wages of machine operator (direct wages). Thus, in a comprehensive machine hour rate, factory overhead and direct wages are absorbed in a single rate.

Illustration 23

The following particulars refer to a process used in the treatment of material subsequently incorporated in a component forming part of an electric appliance:

(*a*) Original cost of the machine used (purchased in June, 2005 was Rs. 10,000, its estimated life is 10 years, the estimated scrap value at the end of its life is Rs. 1,000 and the estimated working time per year (50 weeks of 44 hours each) is 2,200 hours, of which machine maintenance etc., is estimated to take up 200 hours.
No other loss of working time is expected; setting-up time, estimated at 5% of total productive time, is regarded as productive time. (Bank holidays are to be ignored)

(*b*) Electricity used by machine during production is 16 units per hour at a cost of 9 paise per unit. No current is taken during maintenance or setting-up.

(*c*) The machine requires a chemical solution which is replaced at the end of each week at a cost of Rs. 20 each time.

(*d*) The estimated cost of maintenance per year is Rs. 1,200.

(*e*) Two attendants control the operation of the machine together with five other identical machines. Their combined weekly wages, insurance and the employer's contribution to holiday pay amount to Rs. 120.

(*f*) Departmental and General works overhead allocated to this machine for 2005-06 amount to Rs. 2,000.

You are required to calculate the Machine Hour Rate necessary to provide for recoupment of the costs of operating the machine.

(*M.Com. Agra*)

Solution

Computation of Machine Hour Rate

Machine No. .... Working Hours : 2,000

		Per annum Rs.	Per hour Rs.
Standing Charges:			
(*i*) Departmental and General overheads		2,000	
(*ii*) Attendant's Wages, Insurance and Contribution to Holiday Pay (1/6 of Rs. 6,000)		1,000	
Total Standing charges		3,000	1.50
Hourly Rate of Standing charges = $\frac{\text{Rs. } 3{,}000}{2{,}000 \text{ hrs.}}$			
Machine Charges:			
(*i*) Depreciation: Original cost	10,000		
Less scrap value	1,000		
Amount to be written off over 10 years	9,000	900	0.45
Hourly Rate of Dep. $\frac{\text{Rs. } 900}{2{,}000 \text{ hrs.}}$			
(*ii*) Maintenance		1,200	0.60
(*iii*) Chemical solution (Rs. 20 × 50 weeks)		1,000	0.50
(*iv*) Electricity used $\left[\frac{1{,}900 \text{ hrs} \times 16 \times 9}{2{,}000 \text{ hrs.}}\right]$		2,736	1.37
Machine Hour Rate			4.42

Notes:

(*a*) Calculation of working hours

Total working hours (50 weeks × 44 hrs.)	2,200
Less Maintenance Time	200
Productive Time	2,000

(*b*) Setting-up time has not been deducted as it is also productive time.

Illustration 24

Work out in the appropriate form, the comprehensive machine hour rate of a saw mill with reference to the following items of information extracted from the account books of a wood working shop:

(*i*)	Purchase Price of the Saw Mill	Rs. 90,000
(*ii*)	Railway freight, other incidental charges and installation charges	Rs. 10,000
(*iii*)	Life of the Saw Mill is 10 years @ 2,000 Working hours per year.	
(*iv*)	Repair charges:	50% of depreciation.
(*v*)	Consumption of power:	10 units per hour @ 10 paise per unit
(*vi*)	Lubricating oil	@ Rs. 2 per day of 8 hours
(*vii*)	Consumable stores	@ Rs. 10 per day of 8 hours
(*viii*)	Wages of machine operator	@ Rs. 4 per day of 8 hours.

The residual scrap value of the saw mill is nil.

(*G.N.D.U., B.Com. 2000*)

Solution

Cost of the Saw mill:

	Rs.
Purchase price	90,000
Freight and Installation charges	10,000
Total Cost	1,00,000

Computation of Machine Hour Rate

Machine No. .... Base Period: One day of 8 Hours

	Per Day Rs. P.	Per Hour Rs. P.
Standing Charges:		
(*i*) Lubricating Oil	2.00	
(*ii*) Consumable Stores	10.00	
(*iii*) Wages of Machine Operator	4.00	
Total Standing Charges	16.00	2.00
Hourly rate of standing charges = $\frac{\text{Rs. } 16}{8 \text{ hrs.}}$		
Machine Charges		
(*i*) Depreciation: = $\frac{\text{Cost of Machine} - \text{Scrap Value}}{\text{Effective Working Life}}$		
= $\frac{\text{Rs. } 1,00,000 - \text{Nil}}{20,000 \text{ hrs.}}$		5.00
(*ii*) Repairs (50% of Depreciation)		2.50
(*iii*) Power consumed: 10 units per hour @ 10 Paise per unit		1.00
Machine Hour Rate		10.50

Illustration 25

A department is having 3 machines. The figures indicate the department expenses. Calculate the machine hour rate in respect of these machines from the information given below:

	Rs.
Depreciation of machinery	12,000
Depreciation of building	2,880
Repairs to machinery	4,000
Insurance of machinery	800
Indirect wages	6,000
Power	6,000
Lighting	800
Miscellaneous expenditure	4,200
Total	36,680

	Machine No. 1	Machine No. 2	Machine No. 3
Direct wages	Rs. 1,200	Rs. 2,400	Rs. 2,400
Power units	30,000	10,000	20,000
No. of workers	4	8	8
Light points	8	24	48
Space	400 sq.ft.	800 sq.ft.	800 sq.ft.
Cost of machine	Rs. 3,00,000	Rs. 1,20,000	Rs. 1,80,000
Hours worked	200	300	300

(I.C.W.A. Inter)

Solution

Computation of Machine Hour Rate (Composite)

Items	Basis of Apportionment	Total	Machine No. 1	Machine No. 2	Machine No. 3
		Rs.	Rs.	Rs.	Rs.
Standing Charges:					
Depreciation of Building	Space occupied	2,880	576	1,152	1,152
Indirect wages	No. of workers	6,000	1,200	2,400	2,400
Lighting	Light Points	800	80	240	480
Insurance of Machine	Cost of Machine	800	400	160	240
Miscellaneous Expenditure	Hours worked	4,200	1,050	1,575	1,575
Machine Expenses:					
Depreciation of Machinery	Cost of Machine	12,000	6,000	2,400	3,600
Repairs to Machinery	Cost of Machine	4,000	2,000	800	1,200
Power	Units consumed	6,000	3,000	1,000	2,000
Direct wages	Actual	6,000	1,200	2,400	2,400
Total		42,680	15,506	12,127	15,047
No. of Machine Hours			200	300	300
Machine Hour Rate (Rs.)			77.530	40.423	50.156

Illustration 26

A production department of a manufacturing company has three different machines for each of which it is desired to establish machine hour rate.

The overhead expenses for this Department for the year ending 31 March, 2008 are:

	Rs.	Rs.
Consumable stores:		
Machine No. 1	300	
Machine No. 2	500	
Machine No. 3	600	1,400
Repairs and maintenance:		
Machine No. 1	400	
Machine No. 2	600	
Machine No. 3	800	1,800
Power		720
Heat and Light		400
Rent and Rates		2,400
Insurance of Building		200
Insurance of Machines		480
Depreciation of Machines		7,200
Supervision		4,400
General Charges		1,100
		20,100

Additional operating information is available as follows:

	Effective H.P.	Area occupied (sq.ft.)	Book value of Machinery	Working hrs.
Machine No. 1	5	100	12,000	10,000
Machine No. 2	10	500	20,000	25,000
Machine No. 3	15	400	16,000	20,000

You are required to calculate a Machine Hour Rate for each of the three machines. Show clearly the basis of apportionment that you use.

Solution

Computation of Machine Hour Rate

Items	Basis	Machine No. 1	Machine No. 2	Machine No. 3	Total
		Rs.	Rs.	Rs.	Rs.
Consumable stores	Allocation	300	500	600	1,400
Repairs & Maintenance	Allocation	400	600	800	1,800
Power	Effective H.P	120	240	360	720
Rent & Rates	Area occup.	240	1,200	960	2,400
Heat & light	Area occup.	40	200	160	400
Insurance of Building	Area occup.	20	100	80	200
Insurance of Machine	Book value	120	200	160	480
Dep. of Machine	Machine Hrs.	1,309	3,273	2,618	7,200
Supervision	Area occup.	440	2,200	1,760	4,400
General Charges	Area occup.	110	550	440	1,100
Total		3,099	9,063	7,938	20,100
Machine hours		10,000	25,000	20,000	55,000
Machine hour rate (Re.)		0.31	0.36	0.40	

Illustration 27

In a factory department there are three machines to which the following expenses have been allocated:

A. Rs. 639; B. Rs. 607; C. Rs. 951

In addition, there is an overhead crane to bring material to the machines as necessary. The expenses allocated to this crane is Rs. 570.

During the period of this expenditure, the machines were used as follows

	A Hours	B Hours	C Hours
With use of crane	160	130	480
Without use of crane	428	577	–
	588	707	480

Calculate a machine hour rate for each machine, distinguishing between the hours in which crane is used and those in which it is not.

(*I.C.W.A.*)

Solution

	Machines		
	A	B	C
	Rs.	Rs.	Rs.
(A) Expenses allocated to machines	639	607	951
(B) Hours for which machines used	588	707	480
(C) Rate per hour (without crane (A) ÷ (B))	1.0867	0.8585	1.98
(D) Crane expenses apportioned on the basis of hours used*	118.44	96.23	355.33
(E) Rate per hour (with use of crane)**	1.8267	1.5985	2.72

* The expenses allocated to the crane are Rs. 570. The hours worked by the crane are 160 + 130 + 480 = 770 hrs. So the rate per hour is Rs. 570 ÷ 770 = Rs. 0.74
Crane expenses have been apportioned on the basis of hours used, i.e., 160 hrs., 130 hrs. and 480 hrs. respectively for A, B and C at the rate of Re. 0.74 per hour.

** The rate calculated is as follows:

	A	B	C
Rate without crane	1.0867	0.8585	1.98
Rate for crane expenses	0.74	0.74	0.74
Rate with use of crane	1.8267	1.5985	2.72

Illustration 28

From the following data work out the pre-determined machine hour rates for Departments A and B of a factory:

	Preliminary Estimate of Expenses		
	Total	Dept. A	Dept. B
	Rs.	Rs.	Rs.
Power	15,000		
Spare Parts	8,000	3,000	5,000
Consumable Stores ...	5,000	2,000	3,000
Depreciation of Machinery	30,000	10,000	20,000
Insurance on Machinery ...	3,000		
Indirect Labour	40,000		
Building Maintenance ...	7,000		

The final estimates are to be prepared on the basis of the above figures after taking into consideration the following factors:

(*a*) An increase of 10 per cent in the price of spare parts.

(*b*) An increase of 20 per cent in the consumption of spare parts in Dept. B only.

(*c*) Increase in the straight line rate of depreciation from 10 per cent on the original value of machinery to 12 per cent.

(*d*) 15 per cent general increase in wage rates.

The following further information is available:

	Dept. A	Dept. B
Estimated Direct Labour Hours	80,000	1,20,000
Ratio of KW rating	3	2
Estimated Machine Hours ...	25,000	30,000
Floor Space (sq.ft.)	15,000	20,000

(*I.C.W.A. Inter.*)

Solution

Adjustment of Preliminary Estimates

	Total Rs.	Dept. A Rs.	Dept. B Rs.
1. Spare Parts			
Preliminary estimate	8,000	3,000	5,000
Add for increase in prices (10 % for both depts.)	800	300	500
Total	8,800	3,300	5,500
Add for increase in consumption in spare parts Dept. B only (20%)	1,100	–	1,100
	9,900	3,300	6,600
2. Depreciation			
Depreciation as per preliminary estimate (10% on original value)	30,000	10,000	20,000
Add for increase from 10% to 12%	6,000	2,000	4,000
	36,000	12,000	24,000
3. Indirect Labour			
Preliminary estimate	40,000		
Add for 15% increase in wages	6,000		
	46,000		

Computation of Machine Hour Rate

Items	Basis of apportionment	Total Rs.	Deptt. A Rs.	Deptt. B Rs.
Power	K.W. Rating 3 :2	15,000	9,000	6,000
Spare parts	Final estimates, direct	9,900	3,300	6,600
Consumable stores	Direct	5,000	2,000	3,000
Depreciation of machinery	Final estimates, direct	36,000	12,000	24,000
Insurance on machinery	Value of Machinery (Depreciation Ratio)	3,000	1,000	2,000
Indirect labour	Direct Labour Hours	46,000	18,400	27,600
Building Maintenance	Floor space (3 : 4)	7,000	3,000	4,000
Total		1,21,900	48,700	73,200
Estimated machine hours			25,000	30,000
Pre-determined machine hour rate			1.95	2.44

Choice of Overhead Absorption Method:

At this stage we know that there are a number of methods which can be used for absorbing factory overhead *e.g.*, direct material cost method, direct labour cost method, direct labour hour rate method, machine hour rate method etc. The method selected for absorbing overhead must be most equitable and suitable failing which the costing results may be misleading. The following factors should be taken into account while selecting a method of factory overhead absorption:

(*a*) The type of industry – whether job order or continuous production.

(*b*) Nature of the manufacturing process – whether manual or mechanical.

(*c*) The main constituents of overhead and their nature – whether fixed or variable.

(*d*) The organisational set up of the undertaking into departments, cost centres.

(*e*) Capacity at which the factory is working – full capacity or under-capacity.

(*f*) Policy of the management.

Requisities of a Good Method of Absorption:

A good or satisfactory method of absorption of factory overhead should possess the following characteristics:

1. It should be simple and convenient in its application and should not require the maintenance of unnecessary clerical records.
2. It should be adequate ensuring the recovery of overhead which is more or less equal to the actual amount of overhead.
3. It should give due consideration to the time factor involved in production.
4. It would make proper distinction between the work done by skilled workers and that by unskilled workers.
5. It should also make proper distinction between work done by manual labour and work done on machines.
6. Multiple rates (determined with reference to the difference in the nature of work done in different departments) should be preferred to blanket rate or overall overhead rate of the entire factory.

'Blanket Absorption Rate' and 'Departmental Absorption Rate':

These terms are used in relation to the recovery or absorption of overhead. In case a common absorption rate for overhead is used throughout a factory and for all jobs and units of producton irrespective of the department in which they were produced, it is termed as 'blanket absorption rate'. A common absorption rate is not appropriate in case where there are number of departments in the factory and the jobs or units of production do not spend an equal amount of time in each department or all the jobs or units do not pass through all the departments in the factory. In such cases, departmental overhead rate of respective departments (calculated on the basis of amount of overhead assigned to each department) is applied to the jobs or units of production on the basis of the time spent in each department instead of blanket absorption rate. The overhead absorption rate calculated separately for each department of the factory is termed as 'departmental absorption rate'. It is advisable to establish separate overhead rates for each department in order to ensure that all jobs and units of production are charged with their fair share of overheads in cases where these jobs and units do not spend approximately the same time in each department.

Illustration 29

ABC Ltd., manufacturing engineering components, provides the following budgeted information for the year 2008-09.

Department	Machine hours	Overhead	Machine hours required for Job X
		Rs.	
Fabrication	15,000	1,50,000	40
Machining	12,000	1,80,000	50
Assembly	5,000	1,20,000	30
Finishing	8,000	1,00,000	20

Calculate the blanket and departmental overhead absorption rates and overhead to be charged to Job 'X' under both the methods.

Solution

Calculation of Departmental Overhead Rates

Department (a)	Overhead (b)	Machine hours (c)	Machine hour rate (d) (b) ÷ (c)
	Rs.		Rs.
Fabrication	1,50,000	15,000	10.00
Machining	1,80,000	12,000	15.00
Assembly	1,20,000	5,000	24.00
Finishing	1,00,000	8,000	12.50
	5,50,000	40,000	

Calculation of Blanket Overhead Absorption Rate:

$$\text{Overhead Rate} = \frac{\text{Total Overhead}}{\text{Total Machine Hours}}$$

$$= \frac{\text{Rs. } 5,50,000}{40,000 \text{ machine hours}}$$

$$= \text{Rs. } 13.75$$

Calculation of overhead to be charged to Job 'X' (on the basis of departmental overhead rate)

Department	Machine Hours Required	Departmental Overhead Rate	Overhead to be Absorbed
		Rs.	
Fabrication	40	10.00	400
Machining	50	15.00	750
Assembly	30	24.00	720
Finishing	20	12.50	250
		Total overhead chargeable to Job 'X'	2,120

Calculation of overhead to be charged to Job 'X' (on the basis of blanket overhead rate)

Total machine hours to be used on Job 'X'

= 40 + 50 + 30 + 20 = 140 machine hours

Blanket overhead rate = Rs. 13.75

Overhead to be charged to Job X

= 140 machine hours × Rs. 13.75

= Rs. 1,925

Office and Administration Overhead:

As already discussed, office and administration overhead refers to all expenses relating to the direction, control and administration (not connected directly with production, sales or distribution) of an undertaking. The basic characteristic of office and administration overhead costs is that they are based on time (and as such are known as 'period costs') and are not affected by changes in the volume of output, *e.g.*, office rent, office rates, taxes and insurance, salary of general manager, salary of clerical staff etc. But there are also certain other items of office and administration overhead which are in the nature of semi-variable costs, *e.g.* office lighting, office heating, stationery, postage etc.

The classification, codification and collection of office and administration overhead are done in a manner similar to the one adopted for factory overhead. Office and administration overhead costs are classified according to their type, nature or purpose. Separate Cost Account Numbers are used for the codification of office and administration overhead. For the purpose of control, office and administration overheads are departmentalised. The administrative departments are Main Office or General Office, Accounts Department, Law Department, Executive Department, Personnel Department etc. A periodical Departmental Overhead Summary is prepared for the allocation and apportionment of office and administration overhead.

Treatment of Office and Administration Overhead:

There are three methods of treating office and administration overheads:

(*a*) Apportionment to Manufacturing and Selling and Distribution divisions of a concern;
(*b*) Transfer to Profit Loss Account; and
(*c*) Separate Addition to the Cost of Jobs or Products.

(*a*) **Apportionment to Manufacturing and Selling Divisions:** As the administration is concerned with both production and sales divisions of a manufacturing concern, the office and administration expenses are divided between production and sales divisions on some equitable basis. Share of administrative expenses apportioned to production division is treated as part of factory overhead and the share apportioned to sales division as part of selling and distribution overhead and treated accordingly.

Another method is to treat each of the administrative departments as a separate department having to its debit the share of the administration overhead apportioned to the production division. The overheads charged to each administrative department can be apportioned to production departments on some equitable basis. For example, it may be assumed that in a factory there are five administrative departments. The total administration overhead is Rs. 12,000 out of which an amount of Rs. 8,000 assigned to the manufacturing division is apportioned on a suitable basis to each of these five departments as follows

	Rs.
General Office	3,000
Accounts Department	2,000
Law Department	1,000
Executives Department	1,500
Personnel Department	500
	8,000

In the process of re-apportionment of service department costs to production departments, these five departments will also be treated as service departments and the amount assigned to each will finally be transferred to production departments.

(*b*) **Transfer to Profit and Loss Account:** This method is based on the fact that administration overhead costs are not directly related to production and sales. Further, these are 'period costs' which are fixed in nature remaining unaffected by changes in volume of output. Lastly, there is no equitable basis for the apportionment of administration overhead to production and sales divisions. As such, like other period costs, administration overhead should be transferred to Profit and Loss Account. But if the administration overhead costs are charged to Profit and Loss Account, the cost of production and cost of sales shall be unduly deflated due to the exclusion of administration overhead from overhead costs.

(*c*) **Separate Addition to the Cost of Jobs or Products:** This method is based on the assumption that administration overhead is also an important part of overhead costs like factory and selling overhead and as such should be separately added to the cost of production. The equitable bases that may be selected for absorption of administration overhead are:

(*i*) Factory Cost;
(*ii*) Sales Value;
(*iii*) Selling Cost;
(*iv*) Sales Quantity; and
(*v*) Number of Units manufactured.

The overhead rate is generally pre-determined and is ascertained as follows:

$$\text{Overhead Rate} = \frac{\text{Administration Overhead}}{\text{Quantum or Value of Base}}$$

For example, if the base selected is the Factory Cost, the overhead rate will be:

$$= \frac{\text{Administration Overhead}}{\text{Factory Cost}} \times 100$$

If the administration overhead budgeted for the month of January, 2008 is Rs. 5,000 and the factory cost budgeted for the month is Rs. 50,000, the overhead rate will be:

$$= \frac{5{,}000}{50{,}000} \times 100$$

= 10% on Factory Cost.

If the Factory Cost of a Job 'X' is Rs. 550 comprising of direct materials cost Rs. 200, direct wages Rs. 225, direct expenses Rs. 25 and factory overhead Rs. 100, cost of production will be as follows:

Calculation of Cost of Job 'X'

	Rs.
Direct Materials	200
Direct Wages	225
Direct Expenses	25
Prime Cost	450
Factory Overhead	100
Factory Cost	550
Office overhead (@ 10% on Factory Cost)	55
Cost of Production	605

Selling and Distribution Overhead:

Selling overhead refers to all costs of seeking to create and stimulate demand or of securing orders e.g., sales office expenses, advertisement, salary of sales manager, travelling expenses, rent of show-room etc. Distribution overhead refers to all expenses incurred from the time the product is finished in the factory till its delivery to ultimate customers or consumers e.g., rent of warehouse, lighting of warehouse, running and maintenance of delivery vans, carriage on sales, packing charges etc. For the purpose of distribution, selling and distribution overheads are taken together.

The classification, codification and collection of selling and distribution overheads are done in a manner similar to one adopted for factory overhead. Selling and distribution overhead costs are classified according to their type, nature or purpose. Separate Cost Account Numbers are used for their codification.

Absorption of Selling and Distribution Overheads:

For the purpose of absorption, selling and distribution overheads may be divided into two parts:

(*i*) Expenses which are incurred on the sale of products only and can be directly related to the items sold.

(*ii*) Expenses which are fixed over time and do not depend on sales volume.

Items belonging to category (*i*) can be directly added to the cost of production so as to arrive at the cost of sales. But items under category (*ii*) may be charged to products on the basis of any of the following bases:

(1) An Estimated Rate per Article.

(2) A Percentage on Works Cost.

(3) A Percentage on Selling Price.

(1) An Estimated Rate per Article: Under this method, the total selling and distribution expenses having been ascertained for a product, are divided by the estimated number of units of product to be sold in order to arrive at the rate of selling expenses per unit. The overhead rate, under this method, is computed by applying the following formula:

$$\text{Overhead Rate} = \frac{\text{Estimated Selling and Distribution Expenses}}{\text{Expected Sales in units}}$$

(2) A Percentage on Works Cost: Under this method, the selling and distribution expenses are charged as a percentage on the works cost of articles sold. The overhead rate is computed in advance on the basis of the normal expenses and expected amount of works cost. The overhead rate is computed by applying the following formula:

$$\text{Overhead Rate} = \frac{\text{Selling and Distribution Expenses}}{\text{Works Cost}} \times 100$$

(3) A Percentage on Selling Price: Under this method, the overhead rate is expressed as a percentage of Selling Price and is calculated on the basis on the normal level of such expenses and normal sales volume of the past. The overhead rate is computed by applying the following formula:

$$\text{Overhead Rate} = \frac{\text{Selling and Distribution Expenses}}{\text{Total Sales}} \times 100$$

This method of absorption assumes that selling price would be known and can be adopted successfully where the products are sold at standard prices.

Illustration 30

The factory cost of a certain article was Rs. 200 and the selling price was Rs. 400. The selling and distribution expenses directly incurred were : freight and carriage Rs. 20, insurance Rs. 5, commission Rs. 30, and packing cases Rs. 5. The estimated fixed selling and distribution expenses for the year were Rs. 30,000 and the estimated value of sales for the year was Rs. 1,50,000.

You are required to set out final cost of the article using the method of percentage on sales to recover fixed selling and distribution expenses.

Solution

The percentage of fixed selling and distribution expenses to the estimated value of sales is $\left(\frac{30,000}{1,50,000} \times 100\right) = 20\%$.

Calculation of Total Cost of Article

		Rs.
Factory Cost		200
Selling and Distribution Expenses:		
(*i*) Variable	60	
(Rs. 20 + 5 + 30 + 5)		
(*ii*) Fixed (20% on selling price)	80	140
Total Cost		340

Illustration 31

In a factory the methods mentioned below, are adopted for the allocation of office and selling overheads:

1. Advertising and sales promotion : on factory cost figures
2. Credit and collection expenses : on sales figures
3. Direct selling cost : on sales figures
4. Other items : on factory cost figures

The factory deals with five different types of products viz., A, B, C, D and E. The following information has been collected from books:

	A	B	C	D	E
	Rs.	Rs.	Rs.	Rs.	Rs.
Material	24,000	48,000	66,000	33,000	40,500
Wages	27,000	36,000	57,000	24,000	34,500
Sales	1,12,500	1,65,000	2,62,500	1,09,500	1,60,500

Factory overhead charges are 80% of wages. Office and selling charges are:

	Rs.
1. Direct selling cost	62,100
2. Other items	44,400
3. Credit and collection expenses	9,000
4. Advertisement and sales promotion	75,840

Calculate the profit earned on each type of product.

Solution

Statement showing Allocation of Expenses

	A	B	C	D	E
	Rs.	Rs.	Rs.	Rs.	Rs.
Materials	24,000	48,000	66,000	33,000	40,500
Wages	27,000	36,000	57,000	24,000	34,500
Prime Cost	51,000	84,000	1,23,000	57,000	75,000
Factory overhead @ 80% on wages	21,600	28,800	45,600	19,200	27,600
Factory Cost	72,600	1,12,800	1,68,600	76,200	1,02,600
Direct Selling cost (in Sales Ratio)	6,468.75	9,487.75	15,093.75	6,296.25	9,228.75
Advertisement and sales promotion (in Factory Cost Ratio)	7,713.75	11,985.00	17,913.75	8,096.25	10,901.25
Credit and Collection Expenses (in Sales Ratio)	937.50	1,374.75	2,187.75	912.75	1,337.25
Other Items (in Factory Cost Ratio)	4,537.50	7,050.00	10,537.50	4,762.50	6,412.50
Cost of Sales	92,257.50	1,42,697.25	2,14,332.75	96,267.75	1,30,479.75
Sales	1,12,500.00	1,65,000.00	2,62,500.00	1,09,500.00	1,60,500.00
Profit	20,242.50	22,302.75	48,167.25	13,232.25	30,020.25

Notes: (*i*) Sales Ratio 75 : 110 : 175 : 73 : 107

(*ii*) Factory Cost Ratio 121 : 188 : 281 : 127 : 171

Illustration 32

Prosperous India sells its goods directly through salesmen in the zones A, B and C. The company keeps accounts under three sales service departments at the head-quarter besides the three zones.

Details regarding other expenses are as follows:

	Rs.	Basis of Distribution
Subscription and other expenses	200	Allocate to general and advertising deptt.
Advertising	5,000	Net sales
Rent, rates on building	400	Floor space
Fire insurance on building	100	Floor space
Dep. of sales equipment	500	Value of equipment
Light and water	200	Floor space

Selling costs of general and advertising department as well as credit and collection departments are to be apportioned over various zones on the basis of net sales. The shipping and warehouse expenses are to be charged in the ratio of 4 : 2 : 4 to Zones A, B and C respectively.

The following information is supplied to you for the month of March, 2002.

Items		Zones			Departments			Total
		A	B	C	General and Advertising	Shipping and Warehouse	Credit and Collection	
Net sales	Rs.	50,000	30,000	20,000	–	–	–	1,00,000
Sales Equipment	Rs.	14,400	7,600	5,800	8,400	4,200	9,600	50,000
Supplies	Rs.	6	24	92	41	28	9	200
Salesmen's Salaries	Rs.	3,750	2,900	2,450	–	–	–	9,100
Office Salaries	Rs.	–	–	–	1,800	1,100	500	3,400
Travelling Expenses	Rs.	–	–	–	490	120	290	900
Floor space (sq. ft.)		–	–	–	1,100	600	300	2,000

From the information you are required to determine a selling and distribution overhead rate based on sales for each of the territories.

Solution

Overhead Distribution Summary

Items	Amount	Basis of Apportionment	Department			Zones		
			General & Advertising	Shipping & Warehouse	Credit & Collection	A	B	C
	Rs.		Rs.	Rs.	Rs.	Rs.	Rs.	Rs.
Salesmen Salaries	9,100	Allocation				3,750	2,900	2,450
Office Salaries	3,400	”	1,800	1,100	500			
Subscription and Others	200	”	200	–	–	–	–	–
Advertising	5,000	Net Sales	–	–	–	2,500	1,500	1,000
Travelling Exp.	900	Allocation	490	120	290	–	–	–
Rent, Rates on Building	400	”	220	120	60	–	–	–
Fire Insurance on Building	100	”	55	30	15	–	–	–
Depreciation on Sale Equipment	500	Value of Equipment	84	42	96	144	76	58
Light & water	200	Floor space	110	60	30	–	–	–
Supplies	200	Space allocation	41	28	9	6	24	92
Total	20,000		3,000	1,500	1,000	6,400	4,500	3,600
Cost of General Advertising department		Net Sales	(–)3,000	–	–	1,500	900	600
Cost of credit and collection		”			(–)1,000	500	300	200
Cost of shipping and warehouse deptt.		4 : 2 : 4		(–)1,500		600	300	600
Total Selling and Distribution Cost for zones	20,000		–	–	–	9,000	6,000	5,000

Computation of Selling Distribution Overhead Rate

Items	Total	Zones		
		A	B	C
Selling and distribution costs	Rs.20,000	Rs. 9,000	Rs. 6,000	Rs. 5,000
Net sales	Rs.1,00,000	Rs. 50,000	Rs. 30,000	Rs. 20,000
Selling and distribution overhead rate (as a percentage of sales)	20%	18%	20%	25%

Illustration 33

The XYZ company operates a standard cost system in connection with its manufacturing operations. It produces products A, B and C whose standard manufacturing costs per unit are as follows.

	A	B	C
	Rs.	Rs.	Rs.
Fixed	1.00	0.50	2.00
Variable	1.00	2.50	1.00
Total	2.00	3.00	3.00

The company's selling and distribution costs are high and the company's profits have been declining.

Selling and distribution costs for the period just ended are summed below:

	Rs.
Advertising	4,000
Direct selling	12,000
General office expenses (related to sales)	3,480
Ordering and billing	2,450
Packing	3,600
Storage	5,060

Additional data concerning the company's operations are:

	A	B	C
Advertising space	30%	40%	30%
Average time in storage	10 days	20 days	12 days
No. of Invoices	80	40	160
Sales values	24,000	18,000	18,000
Space occupied per unit of product	I cu. ft.	2 cu. ft.	1/2 cu.ft.
Salesmen's time	40%	30%	30%
Time required for packing		3/4 A	1/4 A
Units sold	4,000	2,000	2,000

You are required to:

(*a*) Prepare an analysis of selling and distribution costs by products A, B and C;

(*b*) Prepare an income statement for each product based on standard manufacturing costs and the analysis just completed.

(*I.C.W.A. Inter, June 1983*)

Solution

(*a*) Statement Showing the Analysis of Selling and Distribution Costs

Sr. No.	Nature of selling expenses	Basis of apportionment	Total amount	A	B	C
			Rs.	Rs.	Rs.	Rs.
1.	Advertising	Advertising space (3:4:3)	4,000	1,200	1,600	1,200
2.	Direct selling	Salesmen's time (4:3:3)	12,000	4,800	3,600	3,600
3.	Central Office Expenses	Sales volume (4:3:3)	3,480	1,392	1,044	1,044
4.	Ordering and billing	No. of invoices (2:1:4)	2,450	700	350	1,400
5.	Packing	Packing time * (4:3:1)	3,600	1,800	1,350	450
6.	Storage	# (10:20:3)	5,060	1,533	3,067	460
	Total selling and distribution cost		30,590	11,425	11,011	8,154

(*b*) Statement Showing the Income Statement of Three Products

	Total	A	B	C
	Rs.	Rs.	Rs.	Rs.
Sales	60,000	24,000	18,000	18,000
Less: Variable Mfg. Cost	11,000	4,000	5,000	2,000
Contribution	49,000	20,000	13,000	16,000
Less: Fixed Mfg. Cost	9,000	4,000	1,000	4,000
Gross margin	40,000	16,000	12,000	12,000
Less: Selling and Distribution Cost	30,590	11,425	11,011	8,154
Profit	9,410	4,575	989	3,846

* It is given in the additional information that time required for packing products B and C is 3/4 and 1/4 of A respectively. In other words, if product A requires 1 hour of packing time, product B requires 3/4 hour and product C requires 1/4 hour. The proportion of packing time, thus is 4 : 3 :1 for products A, B and C respectively.

	A	B	C
# [Storage time × Space occupied × Units sold]	10 × 1 × 4,000	20 × 2 × 2,000	12 × 1/2 × 2,000
	or	or	or
	40,000	80,000	12,000
	or	or	or
	10	20	3

Illustration 34

XYZ Ltd. a manufacturing company, having an extensive marketing network throughout the country, sells its products through four zonal sales offices, viz., A, B, C and D. The budgeted expenditure for the year is given below:

			Rs.
Sales Manager's salary			1,20,000
Expenses relating to Sales Manager's office			80,000
Travelling Salesmen's Salaries			3,20,000
Travelling Expenses			36,000
Advertisement			30,000
Godown Rent: Zone	'A'	15,000	
	'B'	25,200	
	'C'	9,800	
	'D'	18,000	
			68,000
Insurance on inventories			20,000
Commission on sales @ 5% on sales			6,00,000

The following further particulars are also available:

Zone	Sales in Rs. Lakhs	No. of Salesmen	Total Mileage Covered	Allocation of advertisement	Average stock Rs. Lakhs
A	36	5	6,000	30%	6
B	48	6	14,000	30%	8
C	16	2	4,500	20%	4
D	20	3	5,500	20%	2

Based on the above details, compute zone-wise selling overheads as percentage to sales.

(*I.C.W.A Inter*)

Solution

Statement Showing Distribution of Selling Overhead

S.No.	Items	Basis of Distribution	Total	Zones			
				A	B	C	D
			Rs.	Rs.	Rs.	Rs.	Rs.
1.	Sales Manager's Salary	Sales	1,20,000	36,000	48,000	16,000	20,000
2.	S.M. Office Expenses	Sales	80,000	24,000	32,000	10,667	13,333
3.	Salesmen's Salaries	No. of Salesmen	3,20,000	1,00,000	1,20,000	40,000	60,000
4.	Travelling Expenses	Mileage Covered	36,000	7,200	16,800	5,400	6,600
5.	Advertisement	Allocation Ratio	30,000	9,000	9,000	6,000	6,000
6.	Godown Rent	Actuals	68,000	15,000	25,200	9,800	18,000
7.	Insurance	Average Stock Holding	20,000	6,000	8,000	4,000	2,000
8.	Commission on Sales	Sales	6,00,000	1,80,000	2,40,000	80,000	1,00,000
9.	Total		12,74,000	3,77,200	4,99,000	1,71,867	2,25,933
10.	Value of Sales		1,20,00,000	36,00,000	48,00,000	16,00,000	20,00,000
11.	Selling Overhead as % of Sales		10.62%	10.48%	10.40%	10.74%	11.30%

Illustration 35

A firm is producing three types of products A, B, and C. The sales territory of the company is divided into three areas X, Y and Z. The estimated sales for the year are as under:

Territory		X	Y	Z
Product	A	Rs. 40,000	Rs.16,000	–
	B	Rs. 24,000	–	Rs. 64,000
	C	–	Rs. 56,000	Rs. 32,000

Budgeted cost for advertisement is as under:

Territory	Total	X	Y	Z
Local cost	Rs. 9,520	Rs. 2,560	Rs. 3,600	Rs. 3,360
General	Rs. 4,640	–	–	–

Calculate the advertisement cost percent sales for each product and territory showing how will you present the statement to the management.

(*I.C.W.A., Inter*)

Solution

At the first stage, advertisement costs are to be apportioned to the products on the basis of estimated sales.

Territory	X	Y	Z
	Rs.	**Rs.**	**Rs.**
	(10:6)	(2 :7)	(2 :1)
Product A	1,600	800	–
Product B	960	–	2,240
Product C	–	2,800	1,120
	2,560	3,600	3,360

The next step is to apportion the general advertisement expenses to various products and territories. Since no information is given, these may be apportioned on the basis of sales.

Total General Expenses		Rs. 4,640
Total Sales:		Rs.
	X	64,000
	Y	72,000
	Z	96,000
		2,32,000

$$\text{Percentage of General Expenses on Total Sales} = \frac{4,640}{2,32,000} \times 100 = 2\%$$

Hence, general expenses would be apportioned as follows:

Territory		X	Y	Z
		Rs.	**Rs.**	**Rs.**
Products	A	800	320	–
	B	480	–	1,280
	C	–	1,120	640
		1,280	1,440	1,920

Estimated Advertisement Cost Analysis

Product	Territory	Sales	Advertisement Cost					
			Local	%	General	%	Total	%
		Rs.	Rs.		Rs.		Rs.	
A	X	40,000	1,600	4	800	2	2,400	6
	Y	16,000	800	5	320	2	1,120	7
B	X	24,000	960	4	480	2	1,440	6
	Z	64,000	2,240	3.5	1,280	2	3,520	5.5
C	Y	56,000	2,800	5	1,120	2	3,920	7
	Z	32,000	1,120	3.5	640	2	1,760	5.5

Illustration 36

A company is supplying its products to the ultimate consumer through the wholesaler to retailers. The Managing Director thinks that if they sell through the retailers or to the consumers direct, they can increase their sales, earn better prices and make more profit. As a Cost Accountant of the company, you are required to advise the Managing Director in selecting the channels of distribution from the following information:

	I	II	III
Channels of distribution	To consumers direct	To retailers direct	To wholesaler
Sales price per unit (Rs.)	4.75	4.25	3.75
Estimated sales per year (nos.)	12,00,000	11,40,000	10,80,000
Selling and distribution cost per unit (Rs.)	1.50	0.80	0.45
Cost of Production			
Variable cost @ Rs. 2 per unit			
Fixed cost Rs. 10,00,000			

In selecting the channels of distribution what factors besides cost would you consider? (*I.C.W.A., Inter*)

Solution

Statement of Profit Per Unit

	I To Consumer	II To Retailer	III To Wholesaler
	Rs.	Rs.	Rs.
Variable cost	2.00	2.00	2.00
Fixed cost	0.83	0.88	0.93
Cost of production	2.83	2.88	2.93
Selling and distribution cost	1.50	0.80	0.45
Cost of sales	4.33	3.68	3.38
Selling price	4.75	4.25	3.75
Profit	0.42	0.57	0.37

Channel II is the most profitable as it provides maximum amount of profit per unit. Other factors to be considered in selecting the channel may be:

(*i*) By eliminating wholesalers, we may lose the advantage of credit facilities, effective advertisement and efficient sales organisation.

(*ii*) Selling goods direct to retailers or consumers, would mean more capital requirement, more credit selling, more collection expenses and more bad debts.

(*iii*) The name of the product, the nature of its demand and market conditions should be properly assessed.

(*iv*) The possibilities of future expansion should be considered.

(*v*) The possibilites of competitors of the company taking the field to oblige the wholesalers must be considered.

Actual Overhead Rate and Pre-determined Overhead Rate:

Overhead rates set up for the absorption of overhead may be divided into two parts:

(*a*) Actual Rate.

(*b*) Pre-determined Rate.

Actual overhead rate is that which is based on the actual amount of overhead to be absorbed and the actual quantum or value of the base selected such as direct wages, materials cost, machine hours, direct labour hours etc. Actual overhead rate enables the recovery of actual amount of overhead but its main drawback is that it is historical in nature which can be ascertained only after the overhead costs have been incurred and measured. As such the actual overhead rate is useless from the point of view of cost control.

Pre-determined rate is based on anticipated amount of overhead and the anticipated quantum or value of the base. It is worked out by dividing the estimated amount of overhead by the estimated value of the base before actual production commences and is applied for absorption of overhead during the period for which it has been computed.

Under-absorption and Over-absorption of Overhead:

Where the absorption of overhead is made by a rate based on actual data, the overhead absorbed must be equal to the actual overhead incurred. But where a pre-determined rate is employed, there is generally a difference between the overhead absorbed and the overhead incurred. If the absorbed amount is less than the actual overhead, there is said to be under-absorption of overhead. For example, if during the month of March, 2007, overheads absorbed are Rs. 9,500 and the actual overheads are Rs. 10,000, there is an under-absorption of overheads to the extent of Rs. 500. In case of under-absorption, the cost of production is deflated to the extent of amount under-absorbed. On the other hand, if the absorbed amount is in excess of the actual overhead, there is said to be over-absorption of overhead. For the example, if during April, 2007, overheads absorbed are Rs. 10,800 and the actual overheads are Rs. 10,000, there is an over-absorption of overhead to the extent of Rs. 800. In case of over-absorption, the cost of production is inflated to the extent of over-absorption.

Causes of Under-absorption or Over-absorption of Overhead

The main causes responsible for under-absorption and over-absorption of overhead are:

(*i*) Under-utilisation of the production capacity.
(*ii*) Seasonal fluctuations in production in case of seasonal factories.
(*iii*) Errors in anticipating the overhead costs or the quantum or value of the base.
(*iv*) Major change in the method of production.
(*v*) Change in the working capacity.

Treatment of under- or over-absorbed overhead:

The under- or over-absorbed overhead costs may be disposed of in any of the following manners:

(1) Use of Supplementary Rate: Under this method, under-or over-absorbed overhead is apportioned to work-in-progress inventory, finished goods inventory and cost of sales by means of supplementary overhead rate. The amount of under-absorbed overhead is adjusted by adding it back to the cost of production by applying a positive supplementary rate while over-absorbed overhead is deducted through a negative supplementary rate. The supplementary rate is obtained by applying the following formula:

$$\left.\begin{array}{r}\text{Supplementary}\\ \text{Overhead Rate}\end{array}\right\} = \frac{\text{Overhead Incurred} - \text{Overhead Absorbed}}{\text{Quantum of Base}}$$

This method has the ultimate effect of charging actual overhead to the cost of production and thus the distinction between the recovery at pre-determined rates and at actual rates no longer exist. The use of this method is generally recommended in the following cases :

(*i*) When there is a serious error in anticipating or estimating the overhead cost or quantum or value of base and the extent of under-absorption or over-absorption is considerable.
(*ii*) When there is a major change in the method of production leading to a significant difference between the overhead incurred and the overhead absorbed.
(*iii*) When there is a change in the working capacity of the manufacturing concern disturbing the estimates of overhead and quantum of base.
(*iv*) When contracts or work-orders are undertaken on cost plus basis.

(2) Carry Forward to the Next Year's Accounts: Under this method, the amount of overhead remaining under-or over-absorbed at the end of the year is transferred to an Overhead Reserve or Suspense Account to be carried forward to the next year's accounts for absorption. This method can be applied when the normal business cycle extends over more than one year and overhead rates are pre-determined on a long term basis. This method is not commonly used.

(3) **Transfer to Costing Profit and Loss Account:** Under this method, which is applied in case of unusual circumstances causing abnormal increase or decrease in actual overhead costs, the amount of overhead under- or over-absorbed is transferred to the Costing Profit and Loss Account. If the pre-determined overhead rate is applicable for a year, there will be no problem in transferring the difference between overhead absorbed and overhead incurred to Costing Profit and Loss Account but if the same is applicable to shorter periods, the work of comparison between actual and estimated overhead will have to be done at frequent intervals. The other main disadvantage of this method is that the stocks of work-in-progress and finished goods remain under- or over-valued and are carried forward at the same values to the next period.

Illustration 37

The total overhead expenses of a factory are Rs. 4,50,608. Taking into account the normal working of the factory, overhead was recovered in production at Rs. 1.25 per hour. The actual hours worked were 2,93,104. How would you proceed to close the account of works assuming that besides 7,800 units produced of which 7,000 were sold, there were 200 equivalent units in work-in-progress. On investigation, it was found that 50 per cent of the unabsorbed overhead was on account of increase in the cost of indirect material and indirect labour and the other 50 per cent was due to factory inefficiency. *(I.C.W.A., Inter)*

Solution

	Rs.
Amount of overhead recovered in production:	
2,93,104 hrs. × Rs. 1.25	3,66,380
Actual overhead incurred	4,50,608
Overhead under-recovered	84,228

50% of unabsorbed overheads is due to increase in cost of indirect material and indirect labour. So 50% of Rs. 84,228 *i.e.*, Rs. 42,114 be recovered by a supplementary rate.

Total Number of units produced or in work-in-progress

= 7,800 + 200 = 8,000 units

$$\text{Supplementary rate} = \frac{42,114}{8,000} = \text{Rs. } 5.26425 \text{ per unit}$$

So this amount of Rs. 42,114 be apportioned as follows:

		Rs.
Cost of Sales	7,000 units × Rs. 5.26425	36,849.75
Finished Goods	800 units × Rs. 5.26425	4,211.40
Work-in-progress	200 units × Rs. 5.26425	1,052.85
	Total	Rs. 42,114.00

The balance 50% difference caused due to factory inefficiency should be transferred to Costing Profit and Loss Account as it is an abnormal loss.

Illustration 38

The Cost Accountant of Novo Chemicals Ltd., determined the overhead recovery rate for the year 2006-07 based on direct labour hours, with the following estimates:

	Rs.
Indirect labour	1,15,000
Inspection	70,000
Factory supervision	50,000
Depreciation and maintenance	1,25,000
Total factory overheads	3,60,000
Direct Labour hours (Estimates)	75,000
Hourly Wage Rate (Estimates)	Rs 15

The actual results for the year are as follows:

	Rs.
Indirect labour	99,000
Inspection	73,000
Factory Supervision	51,000
Depreciation and maintenance	1,15,000
Total actual factory overheads	3,38,000
Direct actual labour hours	67,600
Actual hourly wage rate	Rs. 16

Calculate the pre-determined overhead recovery rate and find out the amount of over/under absorption, it any. How would you treat the over/under-absorbed amount in cost accounts? (*Delhi Univ. B.Com. Hons*)

Solution

Calculation of pre-determined overhead recovery rate:

$$\left.\begin{array}{l}\text{Estimated overhead recovery rate}\\ \text{(per direct labour hour)}\end{array}\right\} = \frac{\text{Estimated factory overheads}}{\text{Estimated direct labour hours}}$$

$$= \frac{\text{Rs. } 3{,}60{,}000}{75{,}000 \text{ labour hours}}$$

= Rs. 4.80 per labour hour

Amount of factory overhead recovered in production

= Actual labour hours worked × Overhead recovery rate
= 67,600 labour hours × Rs. 4.80
= Rs. 3,24,480

Calculation of factory overhead over/under-absorbed:

	Rs.
Factory overhead recovered	3,24,480
Actual factory overhead incurred	3,38,000
Factory overhead under-absorbed	13,520

The under-absorbed amount of factory overhead may be disposed of in any of the following manners:

(*i*) Apportionment to work-in-progress inventory, finished goods inventory and cost of sales by means of a positive supplementary overhead rate.

(*ii*) Carrying forward to the next year's accounts.

(*iii*) Transferring to Costing Profit and Loss Account.

Illustration 39

The factory overhead costs of four production departments of a company engaged in executing job orders, for an accounting year, are as follows:

A	19,300
B	4,200
C	4,000
D	2,000

Overhead has been applied as under:

Deptt. A Rs. 1.50 Per Machine Hour for 14,000 hours.
Deptt. B Rs. 1.30 per Direct Labour Hour for 3,000 hours.
Deptt. C Rs. 80% of Direct Labour Cost of Rs. 6,000
Deptt. D Rs. 2 per piece, for 950 pieces.

Find out the amount of department-wise under-or over-absorbed factory overheads. (*I.C.W.A. Inter*)

Solution

Statement of Under/Over-absorption of Factory Overheads

	Departments			
	A	**B**	**C**	**D**
	Rs.	**Rs.**	**Rs.**	**Rs.**
Factory Overheads incurred	19,300	4,200	4,000	2,000
Factory Overheads absorbed				
A : 14,000 hrs. × Rs. 1.50	21,000			
B : 3,000 hrs. × Rs. 1.30		3,900		
C : 80% of Rs. 6,000			4,800	
D : 950 pieces × Rs. 2				1,900
Under-recovery (–)		(–) 300		(–) 100
Over -recovery (+)	(+) 1,700		(+) 800	

MISCELLANEOUS PROBLEMS

1. 'A' Ltd. an engineering company having 25 different types of automatic machines, furnishes the following data for 2008-09 in respect of machine 'B'.

1. Cost of the Machine Life 10 years. Rs. 50,000
2. Overhead Expenses are:

	Rs.
Factory Rent	50,000 p.a.
Heating and Lighting	40,000 p.a.
Supervision	1,50,000 p.a.
Reserve Equipment for Machine B 5,000 p.a.	
Area of the Factory	80,000 Sq.ft.
Area occupied by machine "B"	3,000 Sq.ft.
Power cost 50 paise per hour while in operation	

3. Wages of operator is Rs. 24 per day of 8 hours including all fringe benefits. He attends to one machine when it is under set up and two machines while under operation
4. Estimated production hours 3,600 per annum
   Estimated set up time 400 hours per annum

   Prepare a schedule of comprehensive machine hour rate and find the cost of the following Jobs:

	Job 1102	Job 1308
Set up time (Hours)	80	40
Operation time (Hours)	130	160

(*C.A. Inter*)

Solution

Computation of Comprehensive Machine Hour Rate of Machine B.

		Details Rs.	Amount Rs.
Standing Charges (for the year 2008-09)			
1. Factory Rent	$\frac{50{,}000}{80{,}000}\times 3{,}000$	1,875	
2. Heating and Lighting	$\frac{40{,}000}{80{,}000}\times 3{,}000$	1,500	
3. Supervision	$\frac{1{,}50{,}000}{25}$	6,000	
4. Reserve Equipment		5,000	
5. Depreciation	$\frac{50{,}000}{10}$	5,000	
Standing Charges per hour =	$\frac{19{,}375}{4{,}000 \text{ hr.}}$ = Rs. 4.844		19,375

	Set-up cost per hour	Operation cost per hour
	Rs.	Rs.
Machine Charges.		
Power per hour	–	0.500
Add: Standing charges per hour 4.844	4.844	4.844
Add: Wages of Operator: $\frac{24}{8} \times \frac{1}{2}$	3.000	1.500
Comprehensive Machine Hour Rate	7.844	6.844

Statement of Cost

	Job. 1102		Job. 1308	
	Hours	Amount Rs.	Hours	Amount Rs.
Set up cost @ Rs. 7.844 per hour	80	627.52	40	313.76
Operation cost @ Rs. 6.844 per hour	130	889.72	160	1,095.04
Total:		1,517.24		1,408.80

2. With the following figures, compute a composite machine hour for machine 'Angel' for a four week period. The machine is expected to be working for 108 hours:

	Rs.
Rent and Rates	150
Lighting	20
Depreciation	100
Indirect Wages	100
Power	60
Sundries	150
Canteen Expenses	10
Repair etc.	40
	630

Machines	Angel	Beta	Cherry
Space Occupied (Sq. Feet)	100	200	300
Light Points	1	3	6
Cost of Machine (Rs.)	2,500	1,500	1,000
Workers	1	2	2
Power (Actual consumption)	25	15	20
Direct Wages (Rs.)	200	300	500

(*I.C.W.A., 1967; Punjabi, B.Com., April, 1989*)

Solution

Computation of Machine Hour Rate

Items of Expenses	Basis of Apportionment	Machines		
		Angel	**Beta**	**Cherry**
Sending Chages:		**Rs.**	**Rs.**	**Rs.**
Rent and Rates	Space Occupied	25	50	75
Lighting	Light Points	2	6	12
Indirect Wages	Direct Wages	20	30	50
Sundries	Equal	50	50	50
Canteen Expenses	No. of Workers	2	4	4
		99	140	191
Machine Expenses:				
Depreciation	Cost of Machine	50	30	20
Power	Actual Consumption	25	15	20
Repairs etc.	Cost of Machine	20	12	8
Total Expenses		194	197	239
Ordinary Machine Hour Rate		Rs.194 / 108 hrs	Rs.197 / 108 hrs.	Rs.239 / 108 hrs.
	Rs.	1.796	1.824	2.213
Hourly Rate of Direct Wages	Rs.200/108 | Rs.300/108 | Rs.500/108	1.851	2.777	4.629
Composite Machine Hour Rate (Rs.)		3.647	4.601	6.842

3. From the following information, calculate Machine Hour Rate of 'A' Machine.

	Rs.
Consumable Stores	
Machine 'A'	600
Machine 'B'	1,000
Repairs:	
Machine 'A'	800
Machine 'B'	1,200
Heat and Light	360
Rent	1,200
Insurance of Building	4,800
Insurance of Machines	800
Depreciation of Machines	700
Room Service	60
General charges	90

Additional Information:

	Working Hours	Area (in sq.feet)	Book Value Rs.
'A' Machine	10,000	100	12,000
'B' Machine	25,000	500	20,000

(*M.D.U. Rohtak B.Com. 2002*)

Solution

Computation of Machine Hour Rate

Machine No. 'A' **Working Hours : 10,000**

	Total Rs.
Standing Charges:	
Consumable stores	600
Heat and light (apportioned on the basis of area) (1/6 of Rs. 360)	60
Rent (apportioned on the basis of area occupied) (1/6 of Rs. 1,200)	200
Insurance of Building (apportioned on the basis of area occupied) (1/6 of Rs. 4,800)	800
Insurance of machines (apportioned on the basis of book value $\frac{12,000}{32,000} \times 800$)	300
Room service (apportioned on the basis of area 1/6 of Rs. 60)	10
General charges (apportioned on the basis of area 1/6 of Rs. 90)	15
Machine Expenses	
(*i*) Depreciation $\left(700 \times \frac{12,000}{32,000}\right)$	262.50
(*ii*) Repairs	800
Total overhead	3,047.50

$$\text{Machine Hour Rate} = \frac{\text{Rs. } 3,047.50}{10,000 \text{ Hours}} = \text{Re. } 0.30475$$

4. The following data was obtained from the books of M/s. Manmohan Singh Chidambram Co., for the year ending 30th June, 2007.

Items	P_1	P_2	P_3	Office	Stores	Work-shop	Total
	(Rs.)	(Rs.)	(Rs.)	(Rs.)	(Rs.)	(Rs.)	(Rs.)
Direct Wages	20,000	25,000	30,000	–	–	–	75,000
Direct Material	30,000	35,000	45,000	–	–	–	1,10,000
Indirect Material	2,000	3,000	3,000	1,000	2,000	2,000	13,000
Indirect Wages	3,000	3,000	4,000	10,000	10,000	5,000	35,000
Area Sq. Metre	200	250	300	150	100	250	1,250
Value of Machinery	30.000	35,000	25,000	–	–	15,000	1,05,000
H.P. of Machine	15	20	25	–	–	5	65
Machine Hours Worked	10,000	20,000	15,000	–	–	5,000	50,000

General Expenses: Rent Rs. 12,500, Insurance Rs. 1,050, Depreciation 15% of Value of Machine, Power Rs. 3,800, Light Rs. 1,250.

You are required to prepare an Overhead Analysis Sheet for the department showing clearly the basis of Apportionment and Re-apportionment of Overheads.

(P.U. B.Com 2008)

Solution

Primary Overhead Distribution Summary

Period: Year ending 30.6.07

Items	Basis of apportionment	Total	Production Departments			Service Departments		
			P1	p2	p3	Office	Stores	Work shops
		Rs.	Rs.	Rs.	Rs.	Rs.	Rs.	Rs.
Indirect Material	Allocation	13,000	2,000	3,000	3,000	1,000	2,000	2,000
Indirect Wages	Allocation	35,000	3,000	3,000	4,000	10,000	10,000	5,000
Rent	Area occup.	12,500	2,000	2,500	3,000	1,500	1,000	2,500
Insurance	Value of Mach.	1,050	300	350	250	–	–	150
Depreciation	Value of mach.	15,750	4,500	5,250	3,750	–	–	2,250
Power	H.P. × Machine Hours	3,800	600	1,600	1,500	–	–	100
Light	Area occup.	1,250	200	250	300	150	100	250
Departmental Overhead		82,350	12,600	15,950	15,800	12,650	13,100	12,250

Secondary Distribution Summary

Period: Year ending 30.6.07

Items	Basis of apportionment	Total	Production Departments			Service Departments		
			P1	p2	p3	Office	Stores	Work shops
		Rs.	Rs.	Rs.	Rs.	Rs.	Rs.	Rs.
Departmental overhead	–	82,350	12,600	15,950	15,800	12,650	13,100	12,250
Expenses of Office	Direct Wages	–	3,373	4,217	5,060	(–)12,650		
Expenses of Stores	Direct Materials	–	3,573	4,168	5,359		(–)13,100	–
Expenses of Workshop	Machine Hours Worked	–	2,722	5,445	4,083	–	–	(–) 12,250
Total Overhead		82,350	22,268	29,780	30,302	–	–	–

5. Calculate the machine hour rate from the following Particulars:

	Rs.
Cost of Machine	1,00,000
Installation charges	10,000
Scrap value	5,000
Life of Machine	10 years
Estimated Working Hours per year	2,200 hours
Rent, Rates for the shop per month	250
Supervisor's salary per month	700
General lighting for the shop per month	300
Rate of power per 100 units	50
Power consumption per hour	10 units.

Machine occupies 1/4th area of shop.

The supervisor is spending 1/5th of his time on this machine.

(H.P.U. B.Com. 2008)

Solution

Computation of Machine Hour Rate

Machine No. .... **Period: One Year**

No. of Working Hours : 2,200

Particulars	Per Annum	Per Hour
	Rs.	Rs. P.
Standing Charges		
(*i*) Rent & Rates of shop (1/4th of Rs. 3,000)	750	
(*ii*) Supervisor's Salary (1/5th of Rs. 8,400)	1,680	
(*iii*) General Lighting (1/4th of Rs. 3,600)	900	
Total Standing charges	3,330	
Hourly Rate of standing charges = Rs. 3,330/2,200 hrs.		1.51
Machine Charges:		
(*i*) Depreciation		
Hourly Rate $\left(\dfrac{\text{Rs. } 1,10,000 - 5,000}{2,200 \text{ hrs.} \times 10 \text{ yrs.}}\right)$		4.77
(*ii*) Power consumed 10 units per hour (@) Re. 0.50 per unit		5.00
Machine Hour Rate		11.28

6. The T Manufacturing Company has been accused of discriminating against its small order customers (25 to 30 cases) in Territory 1 as compared with the same class of customers in Territories 2, 3 and 4. The company has broken down its selling and distribution costs by territories, and now desires to pro-rate the territorial costs between classes of customers within each territory. The following is a tabulation of the average selling and distribution costs per year in Territory 1:

Expenses	Amount
Advertising:	Rs.
Direct to customer catalogues	7,200
Radio and newspapers	18,000
Salesmen's salaries	72,000
Salesmen's commissions	96,000
Delivery expenses	57,600
Travelling costs of salesmen	21,600
	2,72,400

The cost department has tabulated the following information to assist in pro-rating costs in Territory between small-order, medium-order and large-order customers:

	Small order	Medium order	Large order
Net sales (Rs.)	1,50,000	2,20,000	3,50,000
No. of sales orders taken	2,500	2,000	1,500
No. of cases of product sold	1,00,000	1,50,000	2,50,000
Relative shipping cost (per order) (Rs.)	1	2	3
Number of customers	1,500	1,500	2,000
Relative no. of miles travelled per day	4	10	16
No. of salesmen	13	6	5

All salesmen are paid the same salary, each salesman works within a single class of customer.

Prepare a statement showing the pro-ratio of the selling and distribution costs of Territory I to the classes of customers. Indicate the base or bases on which you make each pro-ratio.

Solution

Statement Showing the Pro-ratio of Selling and Distribution Cost

Particulars	Base of apportionment	Total	Small order	Medium order	Large order
		Rs.	Rs.	Rs.	Rs.
Advertising:					
Direct to customer catalogues	No. of orders (5:4:3)	7,200	3,000	2,400	1,800
Radio and newspapers	No. of cases (2:3:5)	18,000	3,600	5,400	9,000
Salesmen's commission	Net sales (15:22:35)	96,000	20,000	29,333	46,667
Salesmen's salaries	No of salesmen (13:6:5)	72,000	39,000	18,000	15,000
Delivery expenses	Shipping cost × No. of orders taken (5:8:9)	57,600	13,091	20,945	23,564
Travelling cost of salesmen	Km. run per day (2:5:8)	21,600	2,880	7,200	11,520
		2,72,400	81,571	83,278	1,07,551

7. Progressive Company Ltd., manufactures three products A, B and C and sells them direct through own sales force in three zones X, Y and Z. The overall control of distribution and sales is taken care of at the Headquarters, responsible also for sales promotion.

You are presented with the following data for the year ended 31st March, 2007:

		Sales	Direct selling and distribution expenses
		Rs.	Rs.
Zone X : Product	A	1,50,000	10,200
	B	1,00,000	10,500
	C	50,000	5,300
		3,00,000	26,000
Zone Y : Product	A	2,00,000	14,200
	B	2,00,000	18,800
	C	1,00,000	10,500
		5,00,000	43,500
Zone Z : Product	A	50,000	4,200
	B	40,000	3,400
	C	1,10,000	14,400
		2,00,000	22,000

Selling and sales promotion expenses at the Headquarters are as follows:

Selling expenses	Rs. 18,000
Advertisement expenses	Rs. 20,000
Other expenses	Rs. 24,000

While advertisement expenses are allocated to zones and products on the basis of sales, the other two types of expenses are allocated equally to zones and products.

Cost of the sales should be taken as following percentage of sales:

Product	A	80%
	B	75%
	C	70%

You are required to tabulate the above information to present comparative profit and loss statements for each zone and for each product.

(I.C.W.A., Inter June 1992)

Solution

Comparative Zone-wise Profit/(Loss) Statement for the year ended 31st March 2007

Particulars	Zone 'X'	Zone 'Y'	Zone 'Z'	Total
	Rs.	Rs.	Rs.	Rs.
1. Sales	3,00,000	5,00,000	2,00,000	10,00,000
2. Cost of sales				
Product A (80% of sales)	1,20,000	1,60,000	40,000	3,20,000
B (75% of sales)	75,000	1,50,000	30,000	2,55,000
C (70% of sales)	35,000	70,000	77,000	1,82,000
Total	2,30,000	3,80,000	1,47,000	7,57,000
3. Margin (1-2)	70,000	1,20,000	53,000	2,43,000
4. Direct selling expenses	26,000	43,500	22,000	91,500
5. Selling cost allocated (Indirect at headquarters)				
Selling expenses	6,000	6,000	6,000	18,000
Advertisement expenses	6,000	10,000	4,000	20,000
Other expenses	8,000	8,000	8,000	24,000
Total Selling cost (4-5)	46,000	67,500	40,000	1,53,500
Profit	24,000	52,500	13,000	89,500

Comparative Product-wise Profit/Loss Statement for the year ended 31st March, 2007

Particulars	Product A	Product B	Product C	Total
	Rs.	Rs.	Rs.	Rs.
1. Sales				
Zone X	1,50,000	1,00,000	50,000	3,00,000
Zone Y	2,00,000	2,00,000	1,00,000	5,00,000
Zone Z	50,000	40,000	1,10,000	2,00,000
	4,00,000	3,40,000	2,60,000	10,00,000
2. Cost of sales	3,20,000	2,55,000	1,82,000	7,57,000
3. Margin (1-2)	80.000	85,000	78,000	2,43,000
4. Direct selling expenses	28,600	32,700	30,200	91,500
5. Indirect selling expenses (At headquarters)				
Selling expenses	6,000	6,000	6,000	18,000
Advertisement expenses	8,000	6,800	5,200	20,000
Other expenses	8,000	8,000	8,000	24,000
Total Selling expenses	Rs. 50,600	53,500	49,400	1,53,500
Profit	Rs. 29,400	31,500	38,600	89,500

8. A cost centre in a factory furnishes the following conditions:

Normal working week	40 hours
Number of machines	15
Number of weekly loss of hours on maintenance etc.	4 hours per machine
Estimated annual overheads	Rs. 1,55,520
Estimated direct wages rate	Rs. 3 per hour
Number of weeks worked per year	48
Actual results in respect of a 4-week period are	
Overheads incurred	Rs. 15,000
Wages incurred	Rs. 7,000
Machine hours produced	Rs. 2,200

You are required to (*a*) calculate the overhead rate per machine hour, and (*b*) calculate the amount of under- or over-absorption of both wages and overheads.

(*CA-Inter, May 1978; Delhi, B.Com. Hons. 1982*)

Solution

Estimated annual overheads:	= Rs. 1,55,520
Normal annual working hours:	
No. of weeks worked	= 48
No. of machines	= 15
No. of hours per week (Less loss of hours)	= 40 – 4
	= 36
No. of working hours per annum	= 48 × 15 × 36
	= 25,920
(*a*) Overhead rate per machine hour	= Rs. 1,55,520 ÷ 25,920
	= Rs. 6
(*b*) Machine hours produced	= 2,200
Overhead rate per machine hour	= Rs. 6
Overheads absorbed (i.e., 2,200 × 6)	= Rs. 13,200
Overheads incurred	= Rs. 15,000
Under-absorption of overheads:	= Rs. 15,000 – Rs. 13,200
	= Rs. 1,800
Wages absorbed @ Rs. 3 per hour for a 4 week period	= (15 × 40) × 4 × Rs. 3
	= Rs. 7,200
Wages incurred	= Rs. 7,000
Over-absorption of wages	= Rs. 7,200 – Rs. 7,000
	= Rs. 200

9. In a manufacturing unit, overhead was recovered at pre-determined rate of Rs. 25 per man-day. The total factory overhead expenses incurred and the man-days actually worked were Rs. 41.50 lakhs and 1.5 lakh days respectively.

Out of the 40,000 units produced during a period, 30,000 were sold.

On analysing the reasons it was found that 60% of the unabsorbed overheads were due to defective planning and the rest were attributable to increase in overhead costs.

How would unabsorbed overheads be treated in cost accounts?

(Delhi, B.Com. Hons.)

Solution

Overhead rate	= Rs. 25 per man-day
Actual man-days	= 1.50 lakh man-days
So, overhead recovered	= Actual man-days × Overhead rate
	= 1.50 lakh man-days × Rs. 25
	= Rs. 37.50 lakhs
Actual overheads	= Rs. 41.50 lakhs
Overhead under- recovered	= Rs. 41.50 lakhs – Rs. 37.50 lakhs
	= Rs. 4 lakhs.
Reasons for under-recovey overhead:	
(*i*) Defective planning	= 60% Rs. 4 lakhs = Rs. 2.40 lakbs
(*ii*) Increase in overheads costs.	= 40% of Rs. 4 lakhs
	= Rs. 1.60 lakhs

Treatment of under-recovery of overhead in cost accounts

(*i*) Defective planning is an abnormal phenomenon and hence Rs. 2.40 lakhs be treated as an abnormal loss. It should be transferred to the debit of Costing Profit and Loss A/c.

(*ii*) Increase in overhead costs should be passed on to the cost of the finished goods. Since 30,000 units have been sold and 10,000 units are lying unsold, Rs. 1.60 lakhs should be debited to Finished Goods Stock A/c and Cost of Sales A/c in the ratio of 1 : 3.

OBJECTIVE TYPE QUESTIONS

A. Multiple Choice Questions

Select the correct answer in each of the following:

1. Which of the following is a production department?

(*a*) Stores department (*b*) Receiving department
(*c*) Personnel department (*d*) Refining department

2. Which of the following is a service department?
(*a*) Weaving department (*b*) Spinning department
(*c*) Finishing department (*d*) Purchase department

3. The allotment of whole items of cost to cost centres or cost units is known as
(*a*) allocation (*b*) apportionment (*c*) absorption.

4. The allotment of proportions of cost to cost centres or cost units is known as
(*a*) allocation (*b*) absorption (*c*) apportionment

5. The code numbers used for covering the items of factory overhead are known as
(*a*) standing order numbers (*b*) cost account numbers
(*c*) code numbers.

6. Allocation means.
(*a*) allotment of whole items of cost to cost centres or cost units.
(*b*) allotment of proportions of cost to cost centres or cost units.

7. Absorption means
(*a*) charging of overhead to cost centres
(*b*) charging of overhead to cost units
(*c*) charging of overhead to cost centres or cost units.

8. Which method of absorption of factory overhead would you recommend in a concern which produces only one uniform item of product?
(*a*) Direct labour cost (*b*) Machine hour rate
(*c*) Direct labour hour rate (*d*) A rate per unit of output
(*e*) Any of the above.

9. When the amount of overhead absorbed is less than the amount of overhead incurred, it is known as
(*a*) under-absorption of overhead
(*b*) over-absorption of overhead
(*c*) proper absorption of overhead.

10. When the amount of overhead incurred is less than the amount of overhead absorbed, it is known as
(*a*) under-absorption (*b*) over-absorption (*c*) proper absorption.

[**Ans.** 1. (*d*) 2. (*d*) 3. (*a*) 4. (*c*) 5. (*a*) 6. (*a*) 7. (*b*) 8. (*d*) 9. (*a*) 10. (*b*)]

B.'True'/'False' Type Questions

1. When actual overheads are more than absorbed overheads, it is known as over-absorption.

2. Cash discount allowed is generally included in cost accounts

3. Cost of indirect materials is apportioned to various departments.
4. Pre-determined overhead rates are used only in standard costing.
5. Under-absorption of overheads means that the absorbed overheads are more than actual overheads.
6. The pre-determined rate of overhead is based on past cost data.
7. The application of pre-determined overhead rate is one of the reasons for the difference in costing and financial profit or loss.
8. The terms 'allocation', 'apportionment' and 'absorption' carry the same meaning.
9. The use of actual overhead absorption rates leads to delays in ascertainment of cost of production.
10. Machine hour rate is applied for the recovery of office overhead.
11. Machine hour rate is calculated for each machine separately.
12. Calculation of machine hour rate takes into account the machine expenses only.
13. Office overhead may be recovered by means of a percentage on direct labour cost.
14. Machine hour rate for the recovery of overhead is applied in those factories where most of the work is done by machines.
15. Over-absorption of overhead leads to over-statement of cost.
16. Allotment of the whole items of cost to cost centres or cost units is known as apportionment.

[**Ans.** 1. False, 2. False, 3. False, 4. False, 5. False, 6. True, 7. True, 8. False, 9. True, 10. False, 11. True, 12. False, 13. False, 14. True, 15. True, 16. False]

C. Filling the Blanks

Fill in the blanks with appropriate words

1. Machine hour rate method of absorption is appropriate when production is carried out on ....
2. The charging of overheads to cost units is technically known as ....
3. The problem of under- or over-absorption of overheads arises only when overheads are absorbed by .... rate.
4. .... denotes the allotment of whole items of cost to cost centres or cost units.
5. .... is the allotment of proportions of items of cost to cost centres or cost units.

6. The .... rate is computed by dividing the factory overhead by the total number of direct labour hours.
7. Two of the main reasons of under- or over-absorption of overhead are .... and ....
8. Expenses of personnel department are apportioned to various departments on the basis of ....

[**Ans.** 1. machines, 2. absorption, 3. pre-determined, 4. allocation, 5. apportionment, 6. labour hour, 7. under-utilisation of production capacity and seasonal fluctuations in production, 8. number of workers employed]

SHORT ANSWER TYPE QUESTIONS

Answer the following questions in not more than five lines.

1. What is meant by allocation of overhead?
2. What is meant by apportionment of overhead?
3. What is meant by absorption of overhead?
4. Name four service departments in a manufacturing concern.
5. What is the difference between allocation and apportionment.
6. Why should we use pre-determined overhead rates?
7. What is meant by under- and over-absorption of overhead?
8. What is meant by standing order numbers?
9. What is primary overhead distribution summary?
10. What is secondary overhead distribution summary?
11. What is meant by departmentalisation of overhead?

LONG ANSWER TYPE QUESTIONS

1. State the main sources from which overhead expenses are collected in the cost accounts.
2. What are the steps involved in the accounting and control of overhead expenses?
3. What are standing order numbers? What is their necessity? What are the ways of alloting standing order numbers?
4. Distinguish between:
   (*i*) Cost classification and cost allocation.

(ii) Cost allocation and cost apportionment

(iii) Cost apportionment and cost absorption.

5. What are the principal bases or methods for apportionment of overhead expenses among departments? Name the overheads for which each basis or method will be suitable.

6. Explain atleast six bases of apportionment of overheads to departments with illustrations as to the item of expenses.

7. What is the difference between apportionment of overheads and absorption of overheads? Explain the different methods of absorption of factory overheads.

(G.N.D.U., B.Com. 2001, 2008)

(H.P.U. B.Com, 2008, K.U.B.Com., 1984)

8. Discuss the various methods of allocating works overhead charges. Give the merits and demerits of each system.

(K.U., B.Com. April, 1984)

(G.N.D.U., B.Com., 1983, 1981)

9. Discuss the principles on which apportionment of overhead expenses can be based.

10. What are the various methods of distribution of service department expenses to production departments? *(G.N.D.U., B.Com. 2008)*

11. What is Machine Hour Rate? How it is computed?

12. What is meant by absorption of overhead? Discuss briefly the different methods for the absorption of factory overheads.

13. Define 'Selling Overhead' and `Distribution Overhead'. Explain how selling and distribution overheads are allocated to products.

(K.U., B.Com. 1882)

14. What are the methods of absorption of Administration and Selling and Distribution overheads to different products?

15. What are the requisites of a good method of absorption of factory overheads?

16. What factors would you consider before formulating overhead rates ?

17. What do you mean by 'Overhead Rates'? Distinguish between actual rate and pre-determined rate of overheads.

18. What is the difference between apportionment of overheads and absorption of overheads? What are the common bases used for the absorption of overheads in products? *(G.N.D.U., B.Com., 1985)*

19. What is meant by under-absorption and over-absorption of overhead? How would you treat in accounts any under- or over-absorbed overhead charges? *(G.N.D.U., B.Com., 1984, 1980)*

20. What information is necessary to calculate a machine hour rate for overhead absorption? State with reasons, the conditions under which this method is most effective.

21. What is meant by 'Actual Overheads' and 'Recovered Overheads'? Under what circumstances do overheads stand under-absorbed or over-absorbed? How will you account for these under/over-absorption of overhead?

22. What do you know of 'Machine Hour Rate' and 'Direct Labour Hour Rate'? Describe briefly the methods of their compilation.

23. What is the difference between Apportionment of overheads and Absorption of overheads? State with the help of imaginary figures how you would make the apportionment of overheads in the production departments and auxiliary services. *(K.U., B.Com., 1976)*

24. "The treatment of under- and over-absorbed overheads depends upon the extent of under- or over-absorption and the circumstances leading to it." Explain. *(G.N.D.U., B.Com. Sept. 1979)*

25. Discuss fully the accounting of overheads under cost accounting. *(G.N.D.U., B.Com., 2003)*

26. Write an explanatory note on accounting of overheads. *(G.N.D.U., B.Com. 2004, H.P.U., B.Com., 2005)*

27. Explain the term 'oncost'. Discuss briefly the various methods of charging oncost to different jobs. Explain the merits of each method. *(G.N.D.U., B.Com., April 1979)*

EXERCISES

1. The Modern Co., is having four departments. A, B and C are the producing departments and D is a servicing department. The actual costs for a period are as follows:

Rent	Rs. 2,000	Insurance on stock	Rs. 1,000
Repair	Rs. 1,200	Employer's Liability	
Depreciation	Rs. 900	for Insurance	Rs. 300
Light	Rs. 200	Power	Rs.1,800
Supervision	Rs.3,000		

The following data are also available in respect of four departments:

	Dept. A	Dept. B	Dept. C	Dept. D
Area sq.ft.	150	110	90	50
Number of workers	24	16	12	8
Total wages	Rs. 8,000	Rs. 6,000	Rs. 4,000	Rs. 2,000
Value of plant	Rs. 24,000	Rs. 18,000	Rs. 12,000	Rs. 6,000
Value of stock	Rs. 15,000	Rs. 9,000	Rs. 6,000	–

Apportion the costs to the various departments on the most equitable method.

[**Ans.** Dept. **A**, Rs. 4,205; **B**, Rs. 2,265; **C**, Rs. 2,135, **D**, Rs. 3, 095 including wages]

2. The "Prabhat Ltd." is divided into two production cost centres, A and B and two service cost centres X and Y. The following is the summary of overhead costs for a particular period:

	Rs.
Works Manager's salary	4,000
Power	21,000
Contribution to Provident Fund	9,000
Plant maintenance	4,000
Depreciation of plant and machinery	20,000
Canteen Expenses	12,000
Rent	6,000

Following information is made available for the various departments:

	Dept. A	Dept. B	Dept. X	Dept. Y
No. of employees	16	8	4	4
Area occupied (in sq.ft.)	2,000	3,000	500	500
Value of Plant (Rs.)	75,000	1,00,000	25,000	–
Wages (Rs.)	40,000	20,000	10,000	5,000
Horse power ratio	3	3	1	–

Apportion the costs to the various departments on most suitable bases.

[**Ans. A**-Rs. 32,800, **B**-Rs. 30,400, **X**-Rs. 19,700, **Y**-Rs. 8,100]

3. The following expenses were incurred during the month of June, 2008 in various departments.

		Rs.
Production Department:	X	10,000
	Y	15,000
	Z	25,000
Service Department:	L	6,000
	M	8,000
	N	2,000

Distribute the expenses of service departments in the following order.

	X	Y	Z	M	N
Expenses of L Deptt.	20%	25%	30%	10%	15%
Expenses of M Deptt.	15%	30%	30%	–	25%
Expenses of N Deptt.	25%	25%	50%	–	–

[**Ans.** **X**- Rs. 13,752.50 **Y**-Rs. 20,342.50 **Z**- Rs. 31,905.00]

4. A manufacturing concern has three production departments and two service departments. In July, 2008 the departmental expenses were as follows:

Production departments:

	Rs.
A	8,000
B	6,500
C	7,000
	21,500

Service departments:

E	2,000
F	3,000
	5,000

The service department expenses are charged out on a percentage basis viz:

	A	B	C	E	F
Expenses of Dept. E	20%	25%	35%	–	20%
Expenses of Dept. F	25%	25%	40%	10%	–

Prepare a statement showing the apportionment of service department expenses to production departments on the basis of:

(*a*) Repeated Distribution Method, and

(*b*) Simultaneous Equation Method.

[**Ans.** **A**- Rs, 9,337, **B**- Rs. 7,954, **C**-Rs. 9,209]

5. A company has three production depts. and two service depts. and for a period the departmental distribution summary has the following totals:

		Rs.
Production Depts.	A	800
	B	700
	C	500
Service Depts.	1	234
	2	300
		2,534

The expense of the service departments is charged out on a percentage basis as follows:

Depts.	A	B	C	1	2
1	20%	40%	30%	–	10%
2	40%	20%	20%	20%	–

You are required to show the apportiomnent of overhead by (*i*) Repeated Distribution Method and (*ii*) Simultaneous Equation Method.

[**Ans.** Dept. A Rs. 992, Dept. B Rs. 887, Dept. C Rs. 655]

6. X and Y are two service departments with respective total of Rs. 3,000 and 2,000 of overhead which are to be apportioned on inter service departmental basis on the basis of percentage given in the chart below. Find out the total overhead of production departments A, B and C assuming the totals of A, B and C being Rs 4,000, 5,000 and 3,500 respectively before distribution:

	A	B	C	X	Y
X	30	40	20	–	10
Y	30	30	20	20	–

Re-distribute the expenses of service departments to production departments by (a) Repeated Distribution, and (b) Simultaneous Equation Method. *(H. P. University, B.Com., 1994)*

[**Ans.** Dept. A Rs. 5,745, Dept. B Rs. 7,092, Dept. C Rs. 4,663]

7. ABC Ltd. is a manufacturing company having three production departments A, B and C and two service departments X and Y. The following is the budget for Oct., 2002:

	Total Rs.	A Rs.	B Rs.	C Rs.	X Rs.	Y Rs.
Direct Material	10,000	1,000	2,000	4,000	2,000	1,000
Direct Wages	18,000	5,000	2,000	8,000	1,000	2,000
Factory Rent	4,000					
Power	2,500					
Depreciation	1,000					
Other Overheads	9,000					
Additional Information:						
Area (Sq. ft.)		500	250	500	250	500
Capital Value of Assets (Rs. lacs)		20	40	20	10	10
Machine Hours		1,000	2,000	4,000	1,000	1,000
Horse Power of Machines		50	40	20	15	25

A technical assessment for the apportionment of expenses of service departments is as under:

	A %	B %	C %	X %	Y %
Service Department X	45	15	30	–	10
Service Department Y	60	35	–	5	–

You are required to prepare:

(*a*) A statement showing distribution of overheads to various departments.

(*b*) A statement of re-distribution of service departments expenses to production departments.

(*H.P. University B.Com. 1995*)

[**Ans.** (*a*) Dept. A Rs. 4,200, Dept. B Rs., 2,700, Dept. C Rs. 6,000, Dept. X Rs. 4,250, Dept. Y Rs. 5,350
(*b*) Dept. A Rs. 9,726, Dept. B Rs. 5,412, Dept. C Rs. 7,362]

8. List of indirect expenses:

	Rs.
Factory Rent	2,000
Factory Insurance	200
Organisational Expenses	1,500
Works Manager's Salary	2,500
Lighting	800
Contribution of Social Security Scheme	800
Welfare Expenses	2,200
Total Labour Hours	5,000 hours.

Calculate the Labour Hour Rate from the above figures. [**Ans.** Rs. 2]

9. There are three production departments A, B, C and one service department S. The following figures are available for one month of 25 working days of 8 hours each day. All departments work all these days with full attendance:

Expenses	**Total**	**Service Dept. S**	**Prod. Dept. A**	**Prod. Dept. B**	**Prod. Dept. C**
	Rs.	**Rs.**	**Rs.**	**Rs.**	**Rs.**
Power and Lighting	1,100	240	200	300	360
Supervisor's salary	2,000	–	–	–	–
Rent	500	–	–	–	–
Welfare	600	–	–	–	–
Others	1,200	200	200	400	400
	5,400				
Supervisor's salary		20%	30%	30%	20%
Number of workers		10	30	40	20
Floor Area in Sq.ft		500	600	800	600
Service rendered by Service Dept. to Production Depts.		–	50%	30%	20%

Calculate Labour Hour Rate for each of the Departments, A, B and C.

[**Ans.** A 30 Paise, B 25 Paise, C 40 Paise]

10. The Production Department of a Factory furnishes the following information for the month of October:

Materials used (Rs.)	54,000
Direct sages (Rs.)	45,000
Labour Hours worked	36,000
Hours of Machine operation	30,000
Overhead chargeable to the dept. (Rs.)	36,000

For an order executed by the department during the period, the relevant information was as under:

	Rs.
Materials used	6,000
Direct wages	3,200
Labour hours worked	3,200
Hours of machine operation	2,400

Calculate the overhead charges chargeable to the job by the following methods:

(1) Direct materials cost percentage rate,
(2) Labour hour rate, and
(3) Machine hour rate.

[**Ans.** Overhead rate (1) 66 2/3% (2) Rs. 1.00 (3) Rs. 1.20
Overhead Charges (1) Rs. 4,000 (2) 3,200 (3) 2,880]

11. Four types of commodities were produced in a factory during the month of December, 2008 with following expenditure:

	A (Rs.)	**B** (Rs.)	**C** (Rs.)	**D** (Rs.)
Material consumed	10,000	12,000	8,000	10,000
Wages	12,000	15,000	9,000	14,000
Works overhead (combined) Rs.	20,000			

Calculate the works cost for the each type of article apportioning the works overhead on the following basis:

(*i*) In the ratio of material consumed.
(*ii*) In the ratio of direct labour.
(*iii*) In the ratio of prime cost

[**Ans.** (*i*) 27,000, 33,000, 21,000, 29,000.
(*ii*) 26,800, 33,000, 20,600, 29,600.
(*iii*) 26,889, 33,000, 20,778, 29,333]

12. The following data were obtained from the books of Light Engineering Company for the half-year ended 30th September, 2009. Calculate the departmental overhead rates for each of the production departments assuming that the overheads are recovered as a percentage of direct wages.

		Production Departments			Service Departments	
		A	B	C	X	Y
Direct Wages	Rs.	7,000	6,000	5,000	1,000	1,000
Direct Materials	Rs.	3,000	2,500	2,000	1,500	1,000
Employees	Nos.	200	150	150	50	50
Electricity	Kwh.	8,000	6,000	6,000	2,000	3,000
Light points	Nos.	10	15	15	5	5
Assets values	Rs.	50,000	30,000	20,000	10,000	10,000
Area occupied	sq.yds.	800	600	600	200	200

The expenses for six months were:

	Rs.		Rs.
Stores overhead	400	Depreciation	6,000
Motive Power	1,500	Repairs and Maintenance	1,200
Electric Lighting	200	General overheads	10,000
Labour welfare	3,000	Rent and Taxes	600

Apportion the expenses of Department X in the ratio of 4 : 3 : 3 and that of Department Y in proportion to direct wages, to Departments A, B and C respectively.

(*C.A: Inter*)

[**Ans.** A- Rs. 11,396, B- Rs. 8,663, C- 7,341]

13. Calculate the Machine Hour Rate for Machine A from the following data:

Cost of machine	Rs. 16,000
Estimated scrap value	Rs. 1,000
Effective working life	10,000 hours
Running time per four weekly period	160 hours
Average cost of repairs and maintenance charges per four weekly period	Rs. 120
Standing charges allocated to machine per four weekly period	Rs. 40
Power used by machine	4 units per hour at a cost of 5 paise an hour.

(*B.Com. Delhi*)

[**Ans.** Rs. 2.55]

14. Calculate the Machine Hour Rate for Machine No. 10 installed in a factory from the following particulars:

	Per Annum (Rs.)	Per Hour
Supervisor's Salary	4,500	
Repairs and Maintenance	90	
Rent of Factory	2,400	
Insurance Premium	I50	
Running Hours	1,500 hours	
Electric Power consumed		15 units
Water		Re. 0.10
Steam		Re. 0.015

1/10th time was devoted by the supervisory staff for this machine. Machine No. 10 occupied ¼ th floor area of the factory, rate of electricity Re. 0.10 per unit.

Original cost of machine	Rs. 15,000
Book Value	Rs. 5,000
Present Replacement Cost	Rs. 20,000

Depreciation @10% per annum on original cost. [**Ans.** Rs. 3.61]

15. The following figures are extracted from the records of a cycle manufacturing concern regarding a machine used for production during a month:

	Rs.
Repairs and maintenance	250
Rent	150
Organisational expenses	180
Supervisory expenses	160
Attendants' remuneration	90
Insurance	30
Indirect material	10
Depreciation per annum	360
Power consumed	240

Machine consumed 8 units per hour and the rate of electricity was 15 paise per unit. Calculate the machine hour rate from the above details.

[**Ans.** Rs. 5.70]

16. A manufacturing company uses two indentical large and four indentical small machines. Each large machine occupies one quarter of the workshop and fully employs three workers, each small machine occupies half the space of a large machine and fully employs two workers. The workers are paid by piece work.

Each of the six machines is estimated to work 1,440 hours per year, while the effective working life is taken as 12,000 working hours for each large machine and 9,000 working hours for each small machine.

Large machines cost Rs. 20,000 each and small machines Rs. 4,000 each. Scrap values are Rs. 4,000 and Rs. 100 respectively.

Repairs, maintenance and oil are estimated to cost for each large machine Rs. 6,000 and each small machine Rs. 1,800 during its effective life.

Power consumption costs 5 paise per unit and amounts for a large machine to 20 units per hour and for a small machine to 2 units per hour.

The manager is paid Rs. 4,800 a year and workshop supervision occupies half of his time, which is divided equally among the six machines. Details of other expenses are:

Rent and rates of workshop: Rs. 3,200 a year.

Lighting (total apportioned in the ratio of workers employed) : Rs. 1,820 a year.

Taking a period of three months as a basis, calculate the machine-hour rate for a large machine and a small machine.

[**Ans.** Big, Rs. 3.93 small, Rs. 1.47]

17. From the following particulars, compute a machine hour rate in respect of Machine No. 65 for the month of April, 2003:

Original cost of the machine	Rs. 31,000
Estimated scrap value	Rs. 1,000
Effective working life of the machine	40,000 hours
Standing charges allocated to the machine for the month	Rs. 120
Working hours during the month	240 hours
Estimated repairs and maintenance over the life of the machine	Rs. 8,000

Power used by machine: 10 units per hour at 5 paise per unit.

[**Ans.** Rs. 1.95]

18. Work out in the appropriate form the Machine Hour Rate of a Saw Mill with reference to the following items of information extracted from the account books of wood working shop:

(*i*) Purchase price of the Saw Mill Rs. 70,000

(*ii*) Railway freight, other incidental charges and installation charges Rs.10,000

(*iii*) Life of the Saw Mill is 8 years @ 2,000 working hours per year.

(*iv*) Repair charges : 50% of depreciation.

(*v*) Consumption of electric power: 10 units per hour @ 7 p. per unit.

(*vi*) Lubricating oil @ Rs. 2 per day of 8 hours

(*vii*) Consumable stores @ Rs. 10 per day of 8 hours

(*viii*) Wages of Machine Operator @ Rs. 4 per day of 8 hours.

[**Ans.** Rs. 9.70]

19. From the data given below, calculate the machine hour rate:

	Per annum
	Rs.
Rent of the department (space occupied by this machine 1/5 of the dept.)	780
Lighting (number of men in the dept. 12, two men engaged on this machine)	288
Insurance for the machine	36
Cotton waste, oil etc. for the machine	60
Salary of foreman (one-fourth of the foreman's time is occupied by this machine and the remainder equally by the other two machines)	6,000

The cost of the machine is Rs. 9,200 and it has an estimated scrap value of Rs. 200.

It is ascertained from past experience:

(*i*) that the machine will work for 1,800 hours per annum;

(*ii*) that it will incur expenditure of Rs. 1,125 in respect of repairs and maintenance;

(*iii*) that it consumes 5 units of power at the cost of 6 paise per unit; and

(*iv*) that the working life of the machine will be 18,000 hours.

[**Ans.** Rs. 1.86]

20. In allocating overheads to production, what do you understand by the term 'machine hour rate'? The following figures relate to a department having three machines. A, B and C. Compute the machine hour rate of machine A from the data given below:

	Rs.
The machine A is expected to work for 200 hours	
Power	1,500
Lighting	200
Depreciation of machinery	3,000
Insurance on machinery	200
Indirect wages	1,500
First Aid post	50
Civil Maintenance	720
Repair to Machinery	1,000
Miscellaneous Expenditure	1,000
	Rs. 9,170

	A	**B**	**C**
Space occupied	100 sq.ft.	200 sq.ft.	200 sq.ft.
Light points	2	6	12
Cost of machine	Rs.75,000	Rs. 30,000	Rs. 45,000
Number of workers	1	2	2
Power units recorded	7,500	2,500	5,000
Direct wages	Rs. 300	Rs. 600	Rs. 600

[**Ans.** Rs.19.12]

21. The machine costs Rs. 90,000 and is deemed to have a scrap value of 5% at the end of its effective life (19 years). Ordinarily the machine is expected to run for 2,400 hrs. per annum but it is estimated that 150 hours will be lost for normal repairs and maintenance and further 750 hours will be lost due to staggering. The other details in respect of the machine shop are:

		Rs.	
(*a*)	Wages, bonus and provident fund contribution of each of the two operators (each operator is incharge of two machines)	6,000	per year
(*b*)	Rent and rates of the shop	3,000	per year
(*c*)	General lighting of the shop	250	per month
(*d*)	Insurance premium for the machine	200	per quarter
(*e*)	Cost of repairs and maintenance for machine	250	per month
(*f*)	Shop supervisor's salary	500	per month
(*g*)	Power consumption of the machine per hour-20 units, rate of power 100 units	10	
(*h*)	Other factory overheads attributable to the shop	4,000	per year

There are four identical machines in the shop. The supervisor is expected to devote one-fifth of his time for supervising the machine. Compute a comprehensive machine hour rate from the above details.

(*Punjabi, B.Com., April 1988*)

[**Ans.** Rs. 12]

[**Hints:** 1. Running hours = 2,400 – 150 – 750 – 1,500

2. Operator's wages = Rs. 3,000 ÷ 1,500

= Rs. 2 per hour]

22. With the following figures compute a machine hour rate for machines A, B and C for a four-week period. The machines are expected to be working 108 hours.

	Rs.
Rent and Rates	150
Lighting	20
Depreciation	100
Indirect Wages	100
Power	60
Sundries	150
Canteen Expenses	10
Repairs, etc.	40
	630

	A	B	C
Space occupied	100 sq.ft.	200 sq.ft	300 sq.ft
Light points	1	3	6
Cost of machine	Rs.2,500	Rs.1,500	Rs.1,000
No. of Workers	1	2	2
Power (actual)	Rs. 25	Rs. 15	Rs. 20
Direct wages	Rs. 200	Rs. 300	Rs. 500

(*I.C.W.A., Inter*)

[**Ans.** Machine Hour Rate: A-Rs. 1.796. B -Rs. 1.824, C Rs. 2.213 Composite Rate: A Rs. 3.647. B Rs. 4.601, C Rs. 6.842)

23. Alpha Ltd. has three manufacturing depts. A, B and C and one service dept. S.

The following figures are available for one month of 25 working days of 8 hours each day. All depts. worked all days with full attendance.

(*I*) Expenses	**Total Rs.**	**Dept. S Rs.**	**Dept. A Rs.**	**Dept. B Rs.**	**Dept. C Rs.**
Power and Lighting	2,200	480	400	600	720
Supervision	2,000				
Rent	1,000				
Welfare	1,200				
Others	2,400	400	400	800	800
	8,800				

(*II*) Other information	**S**	**A**	**B**	**C**
Supervisor's salary	30%	30%	20%	20%
No. of Workers	10	30	40	20
Floor area (sq.ft.)	500	600	800	600
Service to Production Departments		50%	30%	20%

Calculate labour hour rate of each dept.

[**Ans.** Dept. A-Rs. 0.4833, Dept. B-Rs. 0.3925. Dept. C-Rs. 0.69]

24. Four machines namely A, B, C and D were used in a factory for the production during a certain period with and without use of crane. You are given the following list of expenses regarding these machines:

	A	B	C	D
	Rs.	**Rs.**	**Rs.**	**Rs.**
Depreciation	15	12	18	10
Repairs and maintenance	8	7	9	6
Power	86	78	92	80
Oil and the other indirect materials	10	6	12	8
Supervisor's salary	120	110	150	115
Insurance	15	8	20	10
Foreman's Salary	125	110	160	120
Rent	45	30	50	40
Other Sundry expenses	18	10	20	15
	442	371	531	404

The expenses regarding crane are following:

	Rs.
Depreciation	125
Repairs and Maintenance	45
Oil and Sundry Materials	15
Sundry expenses	25
Power consumed	10
Salary of Crane driver	110
	330

The machines were used for production for the following number of hours.

	A	B	C	D
Without use of crane	325	250	420	310
With use of crane	75	50	80	90
Total no. of hours	400	300	500	400

Compute the Machine Hour Rate regarding each machine.
(*a*) Without use of crane and (*b*) with use of crane.

[**Ans.** (*a*) Rs. 1.11; Rs. 1.24; Rs. 1.06; Rs. 1.01
(*b*) Rs. 2.23; Rs. 2.36; Rs. 2.10; Rs. 2.13]

25. The works cost of a certain article is Rs. 400 and its selling price is Rs. 800. The following direct selling and distribution expenses were incurred:

Freight	40
Insurance	10
Commission	60
Packing	10

The estimated fixed selling and distributive expenses for the year were Rs. 30,000 and the estimated value of sales for the year was Rs. 1,50,000.

You are required to set out the final cost of the article using the method of percentage on sales volume to recover fixed selling and distributive expenses.

(*C.A. Final*)

[**Ans.** Total cost Rs. 680]

26. Reliance Works Ltd., is producing a single product in three sizes A, B and C. Prepare a statement showing the selling and distribution expenses apportioned over three sizes applying the appropriate basis for such apportionment in each case from the particulars indicated.

Express the total of the costs apportioned to each size as:

(*i*) Cost per unit sold (nearest paise)

(*ii*) A percentage of sales turnover (nearest two places of decimal.)

The expenses are:

Item	Amount	Basis of apportionment (Rs.)
Sales salaries	10,000	Direct Charge
Sales commission	6,000	Sales turnover
Sales office exp.	2,096	No. of orders
Advertising – General	5,000	Sales turnover
Advertising – Specific	22,000	Direct charge
Packing exp.	3,000	Volume in cubic ft. of product sold
Delivery exp.	4,000	Volume in cubic ft. of product sold
Warehouse exp.	1,000	Volume in cubic ft. of product sold
Credit collection expenses	1,296	No. of orders
Total	54,392	

Data available relating to three sizes

	Total	Size A	Size B	Size C
1. No. of Salesmen (all paid same salary)	10	4	5	1
2. Units sold	10,400	3,400	4,000	3,000
3. No. of orders	1,600	700	800	100
4. % of specific advertising	100%	30%	40%	30%
5. Sales turnover Rs.	2,00,000	58,000	80,000	62,000
6. Volume in cubic ft. Per unit of finished product	–	5	8	17

(*I.C.W.A. Inter*)

[**Ans.** (*i*) A-Rs. 4.89, B-Rs. 5.61. C-Rs. 5.10

(*ii*) A = 28.6%, 13 = 28.07, C = 24.68%]

27. The Madras Chemicals has five salesmen working in its Goa Branch. The following information is available in the Branch office records for the month of March. In assessing the performance of each salesman, the branch office costs of Rs. 60,000 are apportioned as a percentage of cost of goods sold. The results of the salesmen B and E are considered unsatisfactory and their discharge is recommended. Do you consider the method of apportionment equitable and support the recommendation? Prepare a Salesmen's Comparative Profit and Loss statement showing contribution margin and net profit:

Sales men	Net sales	Cost of goods sold	Travelling Expenses and Contingencies
	Rs.	Rs.	Rs.
A	80,000	60,000	2,800
B	160,000	1,48,000	2,400
C	40,000	24,000	1,600
D	1,20,000	96,000	2,000
E	80,000	72,000	2,400

(*I.C.W.A. Final*)

[**Ans.** Contribution Rs. 68,800 and Net profit 8,800]

(**Hint.** Apportion selling expenses on the basis of sales. B and E should not be discharged.)

28. A company is making a study of the relative profitability of the two products A and B. In addition to direct costs, indirect selling and distribution costs to be allocated between the two products are as under:

	Rs.
Insurance charges for inventory (finished)	78,000
Storage Cost	1,40,000
Packing and forwarding charges	7,20,000
Salesman salaries	8,50,000
Invoicing cost	4,50,000

Other details are:

	Product A	Product A
Selling price per unit (Rs.)	500	1,000
Cost per unit (exclusive of indirect costs) (Rs.)	300	600
Annual sales in units	10,000	8,000
Average Inventory (Units)	1,000	800
Number of Invoices	2,500	2,000

One unit of product A requires storage space twice as much as main product B. The cost to pack and forward one unit is same for both the products. Salesman are paid salary plus commission @ 5% on sales and equal amount of efforts are put forth on the sales of each of the products.

Required:

(*i*) Set up a schedule showing the apportionment of the indirect selling and distribution cost between the two products.

(*ii*) Prepare a statement showing the relative profitability of the two products.

(*C.A., Inter, May 1996*)

[**Ans.** (*i*) Product A-Rs. 14,55,000, Product B-Rs. 14,33,000
(*ii*) Product A-Rs. 5,45,000, Product B-17,67,000]

29. A company is producing three types of products A, B and C. The sales territory of the company is divided into three areas X, Y and Z.

Products	**Territories**		
	X	**Y**	**Z**
	Rs.	**Rs.**	**Rs.**
A	25,000	10,000	–
B	15,000	–	40,000
C	–	35,000	20,000

Advertising Cost:

	Territories			**Total**
	X	**Y**	**Z**	
	Rs.	**Rs.**	**Rs.**	**Rs.**
Local direct cost	3,200	4,500	4,200	11,900
Common cost	–	–	–	5,800
				17,700

You are required to prepare a statement showing territory-wise advertising cost expressed as a percentage of sales. The allocation of advertising cost should be based on sales as given above.

(*I.C.W.A., Inter*)

[**Ans.** Overhead Rate X-12%, Y-14%, Z -11%]

30. Dixy Creation Ltd. has been supplying its products to the ultimate consumer through the wholesaler to retailers. The Managing Director thinks that if they sell through the retailers or to the consumers direct, they can increase their sales, earn better prices and make more profit. As a Cost Accountant of the company, you are required to advise the Managing Director in selecting the channels of distribution from the following information:

	I	II	III
Channels of distribution	To consumers direct	To retailers direct	To wholesalers
Sale price per unit (Rs.)	14.25	12.75	11.25
Estimated sales per annum (Nos.)	18,00,000	17,10,000	16,20,000
Selling and distribution cost per unit (Rs.)	4.50	2.40	1.35

Cost of production:

Variable cost @ Rs. 6 per unit. Fixed cost Rs. 20,00,000

[**Ans.** Profit : Channel I II III
Rs. 2.64 3.18 2.67
Channel II is most profitable]

31. J.B. Mangaram produces three types of special biscuits called A_1, A_2 and A_3. Their estimates for sales for the year 2007:

Area		**X_1**		**X_2**		**X_3**	
Salesmen		**K_1**	**K_2**	**J_1**	**J_2**	**L_1**	**L_2**
		Rs.	**Rs.**	**Rs.**	**Rs.**	**Rs.**	**Rs.**
Product	A_1	15,000	30,000	30,000	39,000	–	–
	A_2	48,000	33,000	–	–	42,000	51,000
	A_3	–	–	45,000	33,000	30,000	24,000

Salesmen are given a commission of 5%, 3% and 4% on the sales of A_1, A_2 and A_3 respectively. They also receive yearly remuneration which is as follows:

K_1 Rs. 630	J_1 Rs. 750	L_1 Rs. 720
K_2 Rs. 630	J_2 Rs. 720	L_2 Rs. 750

Other selling expenses are budgeted to be Rs. 63,000.

Production cost of A_1, A_2 and A_3 are expected to be 60%, 60%, and 70%, of sales respectively.

You are required to calculate the profit or loss on each product and on each salesman. (*I.C.W.A., Inter*)

[**Ans.** Product A_1: Rs. 2,850; Rs. 5,700; Rs. 5,700, Rs. 7,410,
A_2: Rs. 10,080; Rs. 6,930; Rs 8,820; Rs. 10,710,
A_3: Rs. 4,500; Rs. 3,300; Rs. 3,000: Rs. 2,300]

32. A company manufactures two models of a machine and distributes them in three sales areas. The budgeted profit and loss account for a year is:

Sales

Area	Large	Small	Total
	Rs.	Rs.	Rs.
A	12,500	25,000	37,500
B	25,000	37,500	62,500
C	37,500	62,500	1,00,000
	75,000	1,25,000	2,00,000

Production cost of sales:		
Large (60% of sales)	45,000	
Small (70% of sales)	87,500	1,32,500
Gross Profit		Rs. 67,500

Direct selling and distribution costs:

Area	A	B	C	Total
Salesmen's salaries	3,625	4,000	1,875	9,500
Salesmen's expenses	1,125	750	625	2,500
Sales office costs	1,150	1,550	1,800	4,500
Advertising	350	850	400	1,600
Carriage	675	600	725	2,000

Indirect selling and distribution costs:

Advertising	Rs. 6,000	
Carriage	Rs. 1,100	
Warehousing	Rs. 3,850	
Credit control	Rs. 2,200	
General Administration	Rs. 4,000	Rs. 17,150
Budgeted Net Profit		Rs. 30,250

The budgeted analysis of sales is:

	Large		Small	
Sales area	Sales Volume (machines)	No. of orders	Sales Volume (machines)	No. of orders
A	2,000	300	2,000	400
B	4,000	500	3,000	500
C	6,000	200	5,000	300

The cost manual of the company states that:

(*i*) Indirect selling and distribution costs are to be apportioned to sales areas as follows:
Advertisement and general administration: On the basis of sales value
Carriage and warehousing : Sales volume
Credit Control : No. of Orders

(*ii*) Selling and distribution costs of sales areas are to be apportioned to models on the basis of sales value.

You are required to:

(*a*) Prepare a comparative statement showing an analysis of budgeted selling and distribution costs by sales areas;

(*b*) Prepare a comparative budgeted profit and loss statement for each model by sales areas;

(*c*) Show the budgeted average net profit per unit for each model in each sales area. (*I.C.M.A.*)

Ans

Net Profit:	A	B	C
	Rs.	Rs.	Rs.
Large Model	1,334	4,620	10,200
Small Model	166	3,180	10,750

33. In a manufacturing unit overhead was recovered at a pre-determined rate of Rs. 20 per labour hour. The total factory overhead incurred and the labour hours actually worked were Rs. 45,00,000 and 2,00,000 labour hours respectively. During this period 30,000 units were sold. At the end of the period 5,000 units were held in stock while there was no opening stock of finished goods. Similarly, though there was no stock of incompleted units at the beginning of the period, at the end of the period, there were 10,000 incompleted units which may he reckoned at 50% complete. On analysing the reasons, it was found that 60% of the unabsorbed overheads were due to defective planning and rest were attributable to increasing overhead costs. How would unabsorbed overheads be treated in Cost Accounts.

(*C.A., Inter, Nov., 1995*)

[**Ans** : Under-absorption Rs. 5,00,000]

34. Separate departmental overhead application rates based on direct labour hours are being used by a manufacturing company. At the end of the year, the following information is supplied to you:

	Deptt. I	Deptt. II	Deptt. III
	Rs.	Rs.	Rs.
Overhead Absorption Rates used	4.00	3.00	7.00
Actual overhead incurred	81,900	1,20,960	79,360
Overhead Absorbed	72,800	1,00,800	86,800

Direct Labour Hours recorded against:

Work in Progress	2,900	4,930	820
Finished Goods Stock	5,400	3,700	1,210

(*a*) Calculate the revised overhead application rate in rupees per direct labour hour (to the nearest paisa) in the light of the actual figures for the year supplied to you.

(*b*) Calculate also the total amounts by which the work-in-progress and finished goods stock in each department will have to be increased or decreased in the light of the revision of the overhead application rate. (*I.C.W.A., Inter*)

[**Ans.** Revised Rates I Rs. 4.50, II Rs. 3.60. III Rs. 6.40]

35. A machine was purchased on January 1, 2003, for 5 lakhs. The total cost of all machinery inclusive of the new machinery was Rs. 75 lakhs. The following further particulars are available.

Expected life of the machine	10 years
Scrap value at the end of ten years	Rs. 5,000

Repairs and maintenance for the machine during the year Rs. 2,000.
Expected number of working hours of the machine per year 4,000 hours.
Insurance premium annually for all the machines Rs. 4,500.
Electricity consumption for the machine per hour (@ 75 paise per unit) 25 units.
Area occupied by the machine 100 sq.ft.
Area occupied by other machines 1,500 sq.ft.
Rent per month of the department Rs. 800
Lighting charges for 20 points for the whole department out of which three points are for the machine Rs. 12 per month.
Compute the machine hour rate for the new machine on the basis of the data given above.

(*C.A., Inter, May 1990*)

[**Ans.** Rs. 31.904]

36. (*a*) What do you mean by the term 'under/over-absorption of production overheads'? How does it arise? How is it treated in cost accounts?

(*b*) In a factory, overhead of a particular department are recovered on the basis of Rs. 5 per machine hour. The total expenses incurred and the actual machine hours for the department for the month of August were Rs. 80,000 and 10,000 hours respectively. Of the amount of Rs. 80,000, Rs. 15,000 became payable due to an award of the labour court and Re. 5,000 was in respect of expenses of the previous year booked in the current month (August). Actual production was 40,000 units of which 30,000 units were sold. On analysing the reasons, it was found that 60% of the under-absorbed overhead was due to defective planning and the rest was attributed to normal cost increase. How would you treat the under-absorbed overhead in cost accounts?

(*C.A., Inter, Nov. 1989*)

[**Ans.** Rs. 6,000 (60%) due to defective planning should be debited to Costing Profit and Loss Account. Balance Rs. 4,000 (40%) should be distributed over Finished Goods and Cost of Sales by supplementary rate.]

37. Deccan Manufacturing Ltd., have three departments which are regarded as production departments. Service departments' costs are disributed to these production departments using the *Step Ladder Method* of distribution. Estimates of factory overhead costs to be incurred by each department in the forthcoming year are as follows. Data required for distribution is also shown against each department:

Department	Factory Overhead Rs.	Direct-Labour Hours	No. of Employees	Area in sq.ft.
Production:				
X	1,93,000	4,000	100	3,000
Y	64,000	3,000	125	1,500
Z	83,000	4,000	85	1,500
Service:				
P	45,000	1,000	10	500
Q	75,000	5,000	50	1,500
R	1,05,000	6,000	40	1,000
S	30,000	3,000	50	1,000

The overhead costs of the four service departments are distributed in the same order, viz. P, Q, R and S respectively on the following basis.

Department	-	Basis
P	-	Number of employees
Q	-	Direct Labour Hours
R	-	Area in Square metres
S	-	Direct Labour Hours

You are required to:

(*a*) Prepare a schedule showing the distribution of overhead costs of the four service departments to the three production departments, and

(*b*) Calculate the overhead recovery rate per direct labour hour for each of the three production departments. (*C.A., Inter*)

Ans.

	[X	Y	Z
(*a*)	Rs. 3,00,000	Rs. 1,35,000	Rs. 1,60,000
(*b*)	Rs. 75	Rs. 45	Rs. 40]

38. A Machine shop has 8 identical Drilling Machines manned by 6 operators. The machines cannot be worked without an operator wholly engaged on them. The original cost of all these 8 machines works out to Rs. 8 lakhs. These particulars are furnished for a 6 months period:

Normal available hours per month	208
Absenteeism (without pay) hours	18
Leave (with pay) hours	20
Normal idle time (unavoidable) hours per month	10
Average rate of wages per day of 8 hours	Rs. 20
Production Bonus estimated	15% on wages
Value of power consumed	Rs. 8,050
Supervision and Indirect labour	Rs. 3,300
Lighting and Electricity	Rs. 1,200

These particulars are for a year:

Repairs and maintenance including consumables 3% on value of machine.

Insurance Rs. 40,000

Depreciation 10% on original cost

Other sundry works expenses Rs. 12,000

General Management Expenses allocated Rs. 54,530

You are required to work out a comprehensive machine hour rate for the machine shop. (*C.A., Inter, Nov., 1986; I.C.W.A., Inter, 1990*)

[**Ans.** Rs. 23.87]

[**Notes:**

1. Calculation of wages:
   Hours paid for = Normal Hours – Absenteeism Hours without Pay
   = 208 – 18 = 190 Hours per month
   Hourly Wage Rate = Rs. 20 ÷ 8 hrs. = Rs. 2.50
   Total wages for six months = 190 hrs. × 6 operators × 6 months × Rs. 2.50 = Rs. 17,100
2. Calculation of Machine Hours Worked:
   Normal Hours – (Absenteeism + Leave + Idle Hours)
   = 208 – (18 + 20 + 10) = 160 Hours per month.
   Total Hours for six months for six operators = 160 × 6 × 6 = 5,760 hrs.
   Since the machines could not work without an operator, total hours for all machines worked were also 5,760 hours.]

10

Single (or Output) Costing-I

This method of costing is applied to ascertain the total and per unit cost of a standard product turned out in a manufacturing concern. Output costing method (which is also known as Single Costing*) is generally applied to industries where the following features are present:

(*a*) The output of production is continuous.

(*b*) The units of output are identical.

(*c*) The units of output are natural.

(*d*) It is desirable to ascertain the cost per unit of output *e.g.*, per metre, per kilogram, per ton etc.

The above mentioned features are present in industries like, collieries, brick works, flour mills, quarries, cement mills, paper mills, iron and steel mills, sugar mills etc., which are engaged in producing only one type of product or a few grades of same product.

Objects of Output Costing

The main objects of Output and Single Costing method are:

(*i*) to ascertain the total cost and per unit cost of production during a specified period;

(*ii*) to make comparative study of the cost of production; and

(*iii*) to ascertain or to determine the selling price per unit of goods manufactured.

Costing Procedure

Unit costing method is adopted with a view to ascertain the total cost and also the per unit cost by making a detailed analysis of different elements of cost (*i.e.*, direct material cost, direct labour cost, direct expenses and overhead) under various heads *e.g.*, Prime Cost, Works Cost, Office Cost and Total Cost. This method does not require a detailed apportionment of overheads since all

* "Single or Output Cost System is used in businesses where a standard product is turned out and it is desired to find out the cost of a basic unit of production."

– *J.R. Batliboi*

overheads are incurred on identical units but the production of few grades or various sizes of the same commodity shall require a careful apportionment of overhead to these grades and sizes.

The analysis of cost may be presented periodically in the form of a statement (known as Cost Sheet or Statement of Cost) or an account (known as Production Account).

COST SHEET

Cost Sheet is a statement, prepared at given intervals of time, which provides information regarding elements of cost incurred in production. It discloses the total cost as well as the cost per unit of the product manufactured during the given period. If it is desired to compare the costing results of a particular period with any of the preceding periods, comparative columns can be provided in the Cost Sheet.

Cost Sheet Vs. Statement of Cost

Some people make a distinction between 'Cost Sheet' and 'Statement of Cost', the former denoting a statement presenting cost analysis on unit basis* and the latter (Statement of Cost) denoting a statement showing the total cost figures. However, both terms may be used inter-changeably.

Features of Cost Sheet

The basic features of Cost Sheet are as follows:

(*i*) This statement is usually prepared under the output costing method, where the object is to ascertain the per unit cost of production.

(*ii*) A cost sheet is prepared for a specified period of time, generally for a month, quarter, half year or year.

(*iii*) The cost sheet generally contains the following information:

- (*a*) Period,
- (*b*) Total Output,
- (*c*) Cost of raw materials consumed,
- (*d*) Cost of direct labour,
- (*e*) Details of chargeable expenses
- (*f*) Details of overheads namely factory, office and administration and selling and distribution, and
- (*g*) Aggregate of elements of cost at various stages *e.g.*, Prime Cost, Works Cost, Office Cost and Total Cost.

---

* "The expenditure which has been incurred upon production for a period is extracted from the financial books and the store records set out in a memorandum statement. If this statement is confined to the disclosure of the cost of units produced during the period, it is termed as Cost Sheet."

– *W.W. Bigg.*

Advantages of Cost Sheet

The main advantages of Cost Sheet available to a manufacturing concern are as follows

1. **Disclosure of Cost:** Cost Sheet enables the manufacturer to ascertain exact cost per unit in a scientific manner. Further, it also discloses the extent to which each element of the expenditure contributes to the total cost.
2. **Determination of Selling Price:** By disclosing the actual cost of production, the cost sheet provides the manufacturer with a reliable basis for fixing competitive selling price of his product. Thus, it saves the manufacturer from losses which arise due to injudicious fixation of prices without looking to the cost of production.
3. **Cost Control:** A cost sheet, by providing a comparative study of various elements of current costs with the cost of the previous period enables the manufacturer to find out the causes of variations in cost and to eliminate the adverse factors and conditions which go to increase the total cost.
4. **Determination of Tender Price:** Cost sheet provides a reliable basis for preparing tenders or quotations at which the manufacturer offers to supply goods to a prospective customer at some future date.

Specimen of Cost Sheet

The Cost Sheet of a manufacturing concern can be prepared in the forms given below:

SPECIMEN NO. 1

Cost Sheet

Period .... **Output ....**

Particulars	Total Cost	Cost per Unit
	Rs. P.	**Rs. P.**
Direct Materials	× × ×	× × ×
Direct Wages	× × ×	× × ×
Direct Expenses	× × ×	× × ×
Prime Cost	× × ×	× × ×
Works Overhead	× × ×	× × ×
Works Cost	× × ×	× × ×
Office and Administration Overhead	× × ×	× × ×
Cost of Production	× × ×	× × ×
Selling and Distribution Overhead	× × ×	× × ×
Total Cost	× × ×	× × ×
Profit	× × ×	× × ×
Sales	× × ×	× × ×

SPECIMEN NO. 2

Cost Sheet

Previous Year's Figures		Particulars	Current Year's Figures	
Output .... Units			Output .... Units	
Total Cost	Cost per Unit		Total Cost	Cost per Unit
Rs. P.	Rs. P.		Rs. P.	Rs. P.
		Direct Materials Direct Wages Direct Expenses		
		Prime Cost Works Overhead		
		Works Cost Office Overhead		
		Cost of Production		

Cost Sheet Vs. Cost Account

It is desirable to understand the difference between a cost sheet and a cost account. A cost sheet is a statement, prepared at given intervals of time, which provides information regarding elements of cost incurred in production. It discloses the total cost as well as the cost per unit of output and provides for the comparison of costing results of a particular period with any of the preceding periods through comparative columns. In short, it is a statement prepared on memorandum basis and does not form part of the double entry system in cost accounts.

A cost account, on the other hand, is an account forming part and parcel of the double entry system of cost accounting which discloses the details of expenditure actually incurred upon a particular job, contract or a process. Unlike a cost sheet, a cost account deals with the result of a one operation or job and does not disclose the result of the whole operation for a given period of time.

The main distinction between the Cost Sheet and Cost Account may be summarised as follows:

Cost Sheet	Cost Account
1. It is a statement showing cost of production per unit or total output.	Cost account is a ledger account maintained in the Cost Ledger on the principles of double entry.
2. It is an independent and isolated summary of costs relating to a job or a certain volume of output.	Every cost account is a part of integrated cost accounting system of the entire organisation.
3. It is prepared for a short period, say for three or six months while production continuous.	Cost accounts are kept for accounting period as a whole and are prepared when the production is completed.

4. It shows the costing data in an analytical manner to suit the purpose for which it is prepared.	Cost accounts make a presentation of total amount of costs without analysis.
5. It presents costing data on unit basis.	Cost account does not depict unit cost.
6. It is prepared for the purpose of cost determination, cost comparison, pricing, cost control and cost estimation.	Cost accounts make a record of actual costs incurred for the purpose of preparing Costing Profit and Loss Account.

Illustration 1

From the following details, prepare a cost sheet for three months ended 31st March, 2006:

	Rs.
Direct Material Consumed	75,000
Direct Wages	1,20,000
Direct Expenses	20,000
Factory Overhead	50,000
Office Overhead	30,000
Selling and Distribution Overhead	60,000

Total Output : 2,000 units.

Solution

Cost Sheet

Period: Three months ending 31st March, 2006 — Output: 2,000 units

Particulars	Total	Per Unit
	Rs.	Rs.
Direct Material Consumed	75,000	37.50
Direct Wages	1,20,000	60.00
Direct Expenses	20,000	10.00
Prime Cost	2,15,000	107.50
Factory Overhead	50,000	25.00
Factory Cost	2,65,000	132.50
Office Overhead	30,000	15.00
Cost of Production	2,95,000	147.50
Selling and Distribution Overhead	60,000	30.00
Total Cost	3,55,000	177.50

Illustration 2

The accounts of Poonam Manufacturing Co., for the year ended 31st March, 2006, show the following information:

	Rs.
Production Wages	2,50,000
Direct Material used	3,10,000
Chargeable Expenses	30,000
Sales	8,00,000
Drawing Office Salaries	10,000

Counting Office Salaries	18,800
Carriage on Direct Materials	8,200
Cash Discount allowed	3,000
Carriage outward	5,400
Bad Debts written off	8,500
Rent, Rates and Taxes	
(*i*) Office	4,000
(*ii*) Works	15,400
Travelling Expenses	3,600
Travellers' Salaries and Commission	8,500
Depreciation on Plant and Machinery	6,500
Depreciation on Office Furniture	1,000
Directors' Fee	12,000
Gas and Water (3/4 Factory, 1/4 Office)	2,800
Manager's Salary (3/4 Factory, 1/4 Office)	24,000
General Expenses	4,000
Haulage Hire	5,000

Prepare a statement showing (*i*) Prime Cost (*ii*) Factory Overhead and its percentage on Wages (*iii*) Factory Cost (*iv*) General overhead and its percentage on factory cost (*v*) Total Cost and (*vi*) Net Profit.

Solution

Statement of Cost

Period: Year ended 31st March, 2006

Particulars		**Rs.**
Direct Material used		3,10,000
Production Wages		2,50,000
Carriage on Direct Materials		8,200
Chargeable Expenses		30,000
Prime Cost		5,98,200
Factory Overhead:		
Drawing Office Salaries	10,000	
Rent, Rates and Taxes (Works)	15,400	
Depreciation on Plant and Machinery	6,500	
Gas and Water (3/4)	2,100	
Manager's Salary (3/4)	18,000	
Haulage Hire	5,000	57,000
Factory Cost		6,55,200
General Overhead:		
Counting Office Salaries	18,800	
Carriage Outward	5,400	
Bad Debts written off	8,500	
Rent, Rates and Taxes (Office)	4,000	
Travelling Expenses	3,600	
Travellers' Salaries and Commission	8,500	
Depreciation on Office Furniture	1,000	
Directors' Fees	12,000	
Gas and Water (1/4)	700	
Manager's Salary (1/4)	6,000	
General Expenses	4,000	72,500
Total Cost		7,27,700
Net Profit		72,300
Sales		8,00,000

Calculations:

(*i*) Percentage of Factory Overhead on Wages $= \frac{\text{Factory Overhead}}{\text{Wages}} \times 100$

$= \frac{57,000}{2,50,000} \times 100 = 22.8\%$

(*ii*) Percentage of General Overhead on Factory Cost $= \frac{\text{General Overhead}}{\text{Factory Cost}} \times 100$

$= \frac{72,500}{6,55,200} \times 100$

$= 11.065\%$

Note: Cash discount is a financial item and hence excluded from costs.

Illustration 3

The accounts of Zenith Manufacturing Co., for the year ended 31st March, 2007, show the following:

	Rs.
Drawing Office Salaries	6,500
Counting Office Salaries	12,600
Cash Discount allowed	2,900
Carriage on direct materials	7,150
Carriage outwards	4,300
Bad Debts written off	6,500
Repairs to Plant and Machinery	4,450
Rent, Rates, Taxes and Insurance	
(i) Factory	8,500
(ii) Office	2,000
Sales	4,61,100
Direct Material Used	2,00,000
Travelling Expenses	2,100
Travellers' Salaries and Commission	7,700
Productive Wages	1,26,000
Depreciation on Plant and Machinery	6,500
Depreciation on Office Furniture	300
Directors' Fee	6,000
Gas and Water (3/4 Factory, 1/4 Office)	1,600
Manager's Salary (3/4 Factory, 1/4 Office)	12,000
General Expenses	3,400

Prepare a statement showing (*i*) Prime Cost (*ii*) Factory Overhead and its percentage on Wages (*iii*) Factory Cost (*iv*) General Overhead and its percentage on Factory Cost (*v*) Total Cost and (*vi*) Net Profit.

Statement of Cost

Period: Year ended 31st March, 2007

Particulars		**Amount**
		Rs.
Direct Material Used		2,00,000
Productive Wages		1,26,000
Carriage on Direct Materials		7,150
Prime Cost		3,33,150
Factory Overhead:	Rs.	
Drawing Office Salaries	6,500	
Repairs to Plant and Machinery	4,450	
Rent, Rates and Taxes etc. (Factory)	8,500	
Depreciation on Plant and Machinery	6,500	
Gas and Water (3/4)	1,200	
Manager's Salary (3/4)	9,000	36,150
Factory Cost		3,69,300
General Overhead:	Rs.	
Counting Office Salaries	12,600	
Carriage outward	4,300	
Bad Debts written off	6,500	
Rent, Rates, Taxes etc. (Office)	2,000	
Travelling Expenses	2,100	
Travellers' Salaries etc.	7,700	
Depreciation of Office Furniture	300	
Directors' Fees	6,000	
Gas and Water (1/4)	400	
Manager's Salary (1/4)	3,000	
General Expenses	3,400	48,300
Total Cost		4,17,600
Profit		43,500
Sales		4,61,100

(1) Calculation of Percentage of Overheads:

(*i*) Percentage of Factory Overhead on Direct Wages $= \frac{\text{Factory Overhead}}{\text{Direct Wages}} \times 100$

$$= \frac{36{,}150}{1{,}26{,}000} \times 100$$

$$= 28.7\%$$

(*ii*) Percentage of General Overhead on Factory Cost $= \frac{\text{General Overhead}}{\text{Factory Cost}} \times 100$

$$= \frac{48{,}300}{3{,}69{,}300} \times 100$$

$$= 13.07\%$$

(2) Cash discount allowed (Rs. 2,900) is a financial item and hence excluded from cost accounts.

Illustration 4

From the following particulars, prepare a Cost Sheet showing the comparative cost per tonne for each of the two periods:

Six Months Ended

	30.09.2006	31.3.2007
	Rs.	Rs.
Factory Wages	48,000	75,000
Raw Material	1,08,000	1,80,000
Administration Expenses	18,000	18,000
Factory Taxes and Insurance	1,000	1,000
Light and Water	2,000	3,000
Direct Expenses	18,000	27,000
Depreciation on Machinery	5,000	5,000
Factory Rent	3,000	3,000
Indirect Wages	45,000	60,000
Factory Power	3,000	4,500
	2,51,000	3,76,500
Output	10,000 Tonnes	12,000 Tonnes

Solution

Cost Sheet

Six Months ended 30-09-06 Output: 10,000 Tonnes		Particulars	Six Months ended 31-03-07 Output: 12,000 Tonnes	
Total	Cost per Tonne		Total	Cost per Tonne
Rs.	Rs.		Rs.	Rs.
1,08,000	10.80	Raw Material	1,80,000	15.00
48,000	4.80	Factory Wages	75,000	6.25
18,000	1.80	Direct Expenses	27,000	2.25
1,74,000	17.40	Prime Cost	2,82,000	23.50
		Works Overhead		
1,000	0.10	Factory Taxes and Insurance	1,000	0.08
2,000	0.20	Light and Water	3,000	0.25
5,000	0.50	Depreciation on Machinery	5,000	0.42
3,000	0.30	Factory Rent	3,000	0.25
45,000	4.50	Indirect Wages	60,000	5.00
3,000	0.30	Factory Power	4,500	0.38
2,33,000	23.30	Factory Cost	3,58,500	29.88
		Administration		
18,000	1.80	Expenses	18,000	1.50
2,51,000	25.10	Cost of Production	3,76,500	31.38

Treatment of Stocks

(i) Stock of Raw Materials:

While preparing a cost sheet, it is necessary to ascertain the cost of raw materials consumed. In order to arrive at the cost of raw materials consumed, the value of the opening stock of raw materials is added to the cost of raw materials purchased and the value of the closing stock of raw materials is deducted from the same. Calculation of cost of raw materials can be shown as follows:

	Rs.			
Opening Stock of Raw Materials	x	x	x	x
Add Purchases of Raw Materials	x	x	x	x
Add Carriage on Purchases of Raw Materials, if any	x	x	x	x
	x	x	x	x
Less Closing Stock of Raw Materials	x	x	x	x
Cost of Raw Materials Consumed	x	x	x	x

Material Scrap or Wastage

These are materials which are useless for their original purpose. If the scrap materials are in a raw condition, the cost of materials used should be reduced by the amount realised from the sale of scrap. If the scrap materials are derived or obtained in the course of manufacturing process, the amount realised from the sale of such scrap, if any, should be deducted from works overhead or from the works cost.

Illustration 5

From the following information calculate the cost of raw materials consumed during January, 2008:

	Rs.
Stock of Raw Materials (1-1-2008)	15,000
Purchases of Raw Materials	1,50,000
Stock of Raw Materials (31-1-2008)	18,000
Amount realised from Scrap of Materials	2,000

Solution

Calculation of Cost of Raw Materials Consumed:

	Rs.
Opening Stock of Raw Materials	15,000
Add Purchases of Raw Materials	1,50,000
	1,65,000
Less Closing Stock of Raw Materials	18,000
	1,47,000
Less Sale of Scrap of Materials	2,000
Cost of Raw Materials Consumed	1,45,000

Illustration 6

From the following particulars, calculate the Works Cost of output made during January, 2008:

	Rs.
Direct Materials used	60,000
Direct Wages	80,000
Direct Expenses	10,000
Works Overhead	30,000
Sale of Factory Scrap	1,000

Solution

Calculation of Works Cost:

			Rs.
Direct Materials used			60,000
Direct Wages			80,000
Direct Expenses			10,000
	Prime Cost		1,50,000
Works Overhead		30,000	
Less Sale of Factory Scrap		1,000	29,000
	Works Cost		1,79,000

(*ii*) *Stock of Work-in-progress:*

Work-in-progress refers to partly finished goods or the goods which are yet in the manufacturing process. The stock of work-in-progress may be valued at Prime Cost or at Works Cost. In case work-in-progress is valued at prime cost, the cost of work-in-progress shall consist of cost of direct materials consumed, direct wages paid and other direct expenses incurred for the work-in-progress.

The adjustment for work-in-progress *valued at prime cost* should be made at the stage of ascertaining the Prime Cost.

Illustration 7

Show the treatment of the following items in the Statement of Cost:

	Rs.
Raw Materials used	30,000
Direct Wages	40,000
Direct Expenses	10,000
Opening stock of work-in-progress (Valued at Prime Cost)	5,000
Closing stock of work-in-progress (Valued at Prime Cost)	3,000
Factory Overhead	15,000

Solution

Statement of Cost

		Rs.
Raw Materials used		30,000
Direct Wages		40,000
Direct Expenses		10,000
		80,000
Add Opening Stock of Work-in-progress (at Prime Cost)		5,000
		85,000
Less Closing Stock of Work-in-progress (at Prime Cost)		3,000
	Prime Cost	82,000
Factory Overhead		15,000
	Factory Cost	97,000

But where the work-in-progress is valued at works cost, the cost of work-in-progress shall consist of cost of direct materials consumed, direct wages paid and direct expenses incurred for the work-in-progress and a proportionate part of the total works overhead. Generally, the valuation of the stock of work-in-progress is made on the basis of works cost. In case, the basis for the valuation of work-in-progress has not been given, it should be assumed that the same has been made on the basis of works cost. The adjustment for the stock of work-in-progress valued at works cost should be made at the time of calculating the Works Cost.

Illustration 8

Show the treatment of the following items in the Statement of Cost:

	Rs.
Raw Materials used	80,000
Direct Wages	60,000
Direct Expenses	25,000
Factory Overhead	45,000
Opening Stock of Work-in-progress (at Works Cost)	8,000
Closing Stock of Work-in-progress (at Works Cost)	6,000

Solution

Statement of Cost

		Rs.
Raw Materials used		80,000
Direct Wages		60,000
Direct Expenses		25,000
	Prime Cost	1,65,000
Factory Overhead		45,000
		2,10,000
Add Opening Stock of Work-in-progress		8,000
		2,18,000
Less Closing Stock of Work-in-progress		6,000
	Works Cost	2,12,000

(*iii*) *Stock of Finished Goods:*

The stock of finished goods or completed units is valued on the basis of Office Cost (or Cost of Production) and hence the adjustment for the stock of finished goods is made after ascertaining the Office Cost or Cost of Production. The cost of opening stock of finished goods is added to the cost of production, while the cost of closing stock of finished goods is deducted from the cost of production and the adjusted figure so arrived at shall be the 'Cost of Goods Sold'. The treatment of stock of finished goods in cost sheet can be given as follows:

	Rs.
Works Cost	x x x x
Office and Administration Overhead	x x x x
Cost of Production	x x x x
Add Opening Stock of Finished Goods	x x x x
	x x x x
Less Closing Stock of Finished Goods	x x x x
Cost of Goods Sold	x x x x

Illustration 9

From the following particulars, prepare a statement of cost of production for the year ended 31st March, 2008 and show what percentage each individual item of cost bears to the total cost. Calculate factory overheads @ 20% on prime cost and office overheads @ 80% on factory overheads.

	Rs.
Opening Stock of Raw Materials	1,44,000
Purchase of Raw Materials	8,64,000
Closing Stock of Raw Materials	2,16,000
Direct Wages	3,60,000

(Agra, B.Com.)

Solution

Statement of Cost

		Total Cost Rs.	% on Total Cost
Raw Materials Consumed			
Opening Stock of Raw Materials	1,44,000		
Add Purchases of Raw Materials	8,64,000		
	10,08,000		
Less Closing Stock of Raw Materials	2,16,000	7,92,000	50.55
Direct Wages		3,60,000	22.98
Prime Cost		11,52,000	
Factory Overheads @ 20% on Prime Cost $\left(\frac{11,52,000 \times 20}{100}\right)$		2,30,400	14.71
Factory Cost		13,82,400	
Office Overheads @ 80% on Factory Overheads $\left(\frac{2,30,400 \times 80}{100}\right)$		1,84,320	11.76
Cost of Production		15,66,720	100.00

Illustration 10

The following particulars have been extracted from the books of M. Manufacturing Co., for the year ended 31st March, 2007:

	Rs.		Rs.
Stock of Raw Materials on 1.4.2006	47,000	Cash discount allowed	3,400
Stock of Raw Materials on 31.3.2007	50,000	Bad Debts written off	4,700
Materials purchased	2,08,000	Repairs to Plant	10,600
Drawing Office Salaries	9,600	Rent, Rates, Taxes and Insurance (Factory)	3,000
Counting office salaries	14,000	Office Rent, Rates and Taxes	1,000
Carriage Inward	8,200	Travelling Expenses	3,100
Carriage Outward	5,100	Directors' Fees	6,000
Travellers' Salaries and Commission	8,400	Gas and Water charges (Factory)	1,500
Production Wages	1,40,000	Gas and Water charges (Office)	300
Depreciation on machinery, plant and tools	7,100	Manager's Salary	12,000
		General Charges	5,000
Depreciation on Furniture	600		

Out of 48 hours in a week, the time devoted by the manager to the factory and office was on an average 40 hours and 8 hours respectively throughout the accounting year. Prepare a statement giving the following information:

(*a*) Prime Cost (*b*) Factory oncost and the percentage of factory oncost on production wages (*c*) Factory Cost (*d*) General oncost and the percentage on factory cost and (*e*) Total Cost.

Solution

STATEMENT OF COST

Period: Year ending 31st March, 2007

	Rs.	Rs.
Raw Materials Consumed:		
Opening Stock of Raw Materials	47,000	
Add Purchases	2,08,000	
Carriage Inward	8,200	
	2,63,200	
Less Closing Stock of Raw Materials	50,000	2,13,200
Production Wages		1,40,000
Prime Cost		3,53,200
Factory Oncost:		
Drawing Office Salaries	9,600	
Repairs to plant	10,600	
Rent, Rates, Taxes and Insurance (Factory)	3,000	
Depreciation on Machinery, Plant and Tools	7,100	
Gas and Water charges (Factory)	1,500	
Manager's Salary (12,000 × 40/48)	10,000	41,800
Factory Cost		3,95,000
General Oncost:		
Counting House Salaries	14,000	
Carriage Outward	5,100	
Bad Debts written off	4,700	
Rent, Rates and Taxes (Office)	1,000	
Travelling Expenses	3,100	
Travellers' Salaries and Commission	8,400	
Depreciation on Furniture	600	
Directors' Fees	6,000	
Gas and Water charges (Office)	300	
General Charges	5,000	
Manager's Salary (12,000 × 8/48)	2,000	50,200
Total Cost		4,45,200

Note: Cash discount allowed is a financial item and as such has been excluded from cost accounts.

Percentage of Factory Oncost to Production Wages:

$$= \frac{\text{Factory Oncost}}{\text{Production Wages}} \times 100$$

$$= \frac{41,800}{1,40,000} \times 100 = 29.85\%$$

Percentage of General Oncost to Factory Cost:

$$= \frac{\text{General Oncost}}{\text{Factory Cost}} \times 100$$

$$= \frac{50{,}200}{3{,}95{,}000} \times 100$$

$$= 12.7\%$$

Illustration 11

A factory produces a standard product. The following information is given to you from which you are required to prepare "Cost Sheet" for the period ended on 31st March, 2007:

	Rs.		
Consumable Materials:		Office Overheads 10% of Works Cost	
Opening Stock	10,000	Selling and Distribution	
Purchases	85,000	Expenses Rs. 2 per unit sold	
Closing Stock	4,000		
Direct Wages	20,000	Units of Finished Products:	
Other Direct Expenses	10,000	In hand at the beginning	
		of the period	1,000 (value Rs. 16,000)
Factory Overheads 100% of Direct Labour		Produced during the Period	10,000
		In hand at the end of the Period	2,000

Also, find out the selling price per unit on the basis that profit make-up is uniformly made to yield a profit of 20% of the selling price. There was no work-in-progress either at the beginning or at the end of the period.

(Bombay, B.Com.)

Solution

Cost Sheet

Period: Ended 31.3.2007 — Output: 10,000 units

Particulars		Total Rs.	Per Unit Rs. P.
Materials Consumed			
Opening Stock	10,000		
Add Purchases	85,000		
	95,000		
Less Closing Stock	4,000	91,000	9.10
Direct Wages		20,000	2.00
Direct Expenses		10,000	1.00
Prime Cost		1,21,000	12.10
Factory Overhead @ 100% of Direct Wages		20,000	2.00
Works Cost		1,41,000	14.10
Office Overhead @ 10% of Works Cost		14,100	1.41
Cost of Production		1,55,100	15.51

Note: The statement showing the calculation of selling price can be prepared separately in the following manner:

Statement of Selling Price

Particulars	Units	Amount Rs. P.
Opening Stock of Finished Products	1,000	16,000
Add Cost of Goods Produced during the period	10,000	1,55,100
	11,000	1,71,100
Less Closing Stock of Finished Products @ Rs. 15.51 per unit	2,000	31,020
Cost of Goods Sold	9,000	1,40,080
Selling and Distribution Expenses @ Rs. 2 per unit sold		18,000
Cost of Sales		1,58,080
Profit @ 20% on Selling Price $\left[\text{Rs.}1{,}58{,}080 \times \frac{20}{80}\right]$		39,520
Selling Price	9,000	1,97,600

$$\text{Selling Price per unit} = \frac{\text{Total Sales}}{\text{Total No. of units sold}}$$

$$= \frac{1{,}97{,}600}{9{,}000} = \text{Rs. } 21.96$$

Illustration 12

The following data relate to the manufacturer of a standard product during the month of March, 2007:

	Rs.
Raw Materials Consumed	80,000
Direct Wages	48,000
Machine Hours Worked	8,000
Machine Hours Rate: Rs. 4	
Office Oncost: 10% of Works Cost	
Selling Oncost: Rs 1.50 per unit sold.	
Units Produced: 4,000	
Units Sold: 3,600 @ Rs. 50 each.	

You are required to prepare a Cost Sheet in respect of the above showing:

(*i*) Cost per Unit

(*ii*) Profit for the Period.

Solution

Cost Sheet

Period: March, 2007 Output: 4,000 Units

Particulars	Total Rs.	Cost Per Unit Rs. P.
Raw Materials Consumed	80,000	20.00
Direct Wages	48,000	12.00
Prime Cost	1,28,000	32.00
Works Overheads @ Rs. 4 per machine hour for 8,000 hours	32,000	8.00
Works Cost	1,60,000	40.00
Office Overheads @ 10% on Works Cost	16,000	4.00
Cost of Production (4,000 Units)	1,76,000	44.00
Less Closing Stock of Finished Goods (400 units @ Rs. 44 each)	17,600	–
Cost of Goods Sold (3,600 Units)	1,58,400	–
Selling Overheads @ Rs. 1.50 per unit sold	5,400	1.50
Cost of Sales	1,63,800	45.50
Profit	16,200	4.50
Sales (3,600 units @ Rs. 50 each)	1,80,000	50.00

Illustration 13

The directors of a manufacturing business require a statement showing the production results of the business for the month of March, 2004. The cost accounts reveal the following information:

	Rs.
Stock on hand 1st March, 2004:	
Raw Material	25,000
Finished Goods	17,360
Stock on Hand, 31st March, 2004	
Raw Material	26,250
Finished Goods	15,750
Purchases of Raw Materials	21,900
Work-in-progress, 1st March 2004	8,220
Work-in-progress, 31st March 2004	9,100
Sale of Finished Goods	72,310
Direct Wages	17,150
Non-productive Wages	830
Works Expenses	8,340
Office and Administrative Expenses	3,160
Selling and Distributive Expenses	4,210

You are required to construct the statement so as to show (*a*) the value of materials consumed; (*b*) the total cost of production; (*c*) the cost of goods sold; (*d*) the profit on goods sold and (*e*) the net profit for the month.

(*H.P. Uni., B.Com. 1994*)

Solution

Statement of Cost

Period: March, 2004

		Rs.	Rs.
Opening Stock of Raw Materials		25,000	
(+) Purchases of Raw Materials		21,900	
		46,900	
(–) Closing Stock of Raw Materials		26,250	
(*a*) Materials Consumed			20,650
Direct Wages			17,150
	Prime Cost		37,800
Non-productive Wages		830	
Works Expenses		8,340	9,170
			46,970
(+) Work-in-progress (1.3.04)			8,220
			55,190
(–) Work-in-progress (31.3.04)			9,100
	Works Cost		46,090
Office and Administrative Expenses			3,160
(*b*) Total Cost of Production			49,250
(+) Stock of Finished Goods (1.3.04)			17,360
			66,610
(–) Stock of Finished Goods (31.3.04)			15,750
(*c*) Cost of Goods Sold			50,860
(*d*) Gross Profit on Goods sold			21,450
	Sales		72,310

Net Profit:

		Rs.
Cost of Goods Sold		50,860
Selling and Distribution Expenses		4,210
Cost of Sales		55,070
Net profit for the month		17,240
	Sales	72,310

Illustration 14

The following extracts of costing information relate to commodity Y for the half year ended 30.9.2006

	Rs.
Purchases of Raw Materials	1,32,000
Direct Wages	1,10,000
Rent, Rates, Insurance and Works Overhead	44,000
Carriage Inward	1,584
Stock – 1st April, 2006	
Raw Material	22,000
Finished Product – 1,600 tons	17,600
Stock – 30th Sept., 2006	
Raw Material	24,464
Finished Product – 3,200 tons	35,200
Work-in-progress, 1st April, 2006	5,280
Work-in-progress, 30th Sept., 2006	17,600
Cost of Factory Supervision	8,800
Sales – Finished Product	3,30,000

Advertising, Discounts allowed and Selling Costs amounted to 75 Paise per ton sold. 25,600 tons of commodity were produced during the period.

You are required to ascertain (*a*) the value of Raw Materials used; (*b*) the cost of the output for the period; (*c*) the cost of the turnover for the period; (*d*) the net profit for the period and (*e*) the net profit per ton of the commodity sold.

(*Agra, M.Com., Adapted*)

Solution

Statement of Cost

Period: Six months ended 30th Sept., 2006 — Output: 25,600 Tons

	Rs.	Rs.
Raw Materials Consumed:		
Opening Stock of Raw Materials	22,000	
Add Purchases of Raw Materials	1,32,000	
Add Carriage Inward	1,584	
	1,55,584	
Less Closing Stock of Raw Materials	24,464	
		1,31,120
Direct Wages		1,10,000
Prime Cost		2,41,120
Factory Overhead:		
Rent, Rates, Insurance and Works Overhead	44,000	
Cost of Factory Supervision	8,800	
		52,800
		2,93,920
Add Opening Stock of Work-in-progress		5,280
		2,99,200
Less Closing Stock of Work-in-progress		17,600
Works Cost (Cost of Output)		2,81,600

$$\text{Cost of output per ton} = \frac{\text{Cost of Output}}{\text{Total Output}} = \frac{\text{Rs. } 2,81,600}{25,600 \text{ Tons}} = \text{Rs. 11 per ton.}$$

Statement of Profit can be shown separately in the following manner:

Statement of Profit

	Tons	Rs.
Stock of Finished Products (as on 1.4. 2006)	1,600	17,600
Add Cost of Output during six months	25,600	2,81,600
	27,200	2,99,200
Less Stock of Finished Product (as on 30.9. 2006).	3,200	35,200
Cost of Goods Sold	24,000	2,64,000
Advertising Discounts and Selling Costs (@ 75 Paise per ton sold for 24,000 tons)		18,000
Cost of Sales		2,82,000
Net Profit		48,000
Sales		3,30,000

(*a*) Value of Raw Materials used = Rs. 1,31,120
(*b*) Cost of Output = Rs. 2,81,600
(*c*) Cost of Goods Sold = Rs. 2,64,000
(*d*) Net Profit for the period = Rs. 48,000
(*e*) Profit per ton = Rs. 48,000/24,000 Tons = Rs 2.00

Illustration 15

A.C. Ltd., are manufacturing room heaters and the following details are given in respect to its factory operations for the year ended 31st March, 2005:

	Rs.	Rs.
Work-in-process, 1st April, 2004		
At Prime Cost	25,500	
Manufacturing Expenses	7,500	
		33,000
Work-in-process, 31st March, 2005		
At Prime Cost	22,500	
Manufacturing Expenses	4,500	
		27,000
Stock of Raw Materials, 1st April, 2004		1,12,500
Purchases of Raw Materials		2,38,500
Direct Wages		85,500
Manufacturing Expenses		42,000
Stock of Raw Materials 31st March, 2005		1,02,000

On the basis of above data, prepare a statement showing the cost of production. Also indicate separately the amount of manufacturing expenses which enter into cost of production.

Solution

(Showing the valuation of Work-in-progress at Prime Cost)

Statement of Cost

	Rs.	Rs.
Raw Material Consumed:		
Opening Stock of Raw Materials	1,12,500	
Add Purchases of Raw Materials	2,38,500	
	3,51,000	
Less Closing Stock of Raw Materials	1,02,000	
		2,49,000
Direct Wages		85,500
		3,34,500
Add Work-in-progress (1.4.2004) (at Prime Cost)		25,500
		3,60,000
Less Work-in-progress (31.3.2005) (at Prime Cost)		22,500
Prime Cost		3,37,500
Manufacturing Expenses	42,000	
Add Manufacturing Expenses included in opening Work-in-progress	7,500	
	49,500	
Less Manufacturing Expenses included in closing Work-in-progress	4,500	45,000
Works Cost		3,82,500

Illustration 16

A Factory Produces 100 units of each of the commodities A and B. The costs of production are:

	A	B
	Rs.	Rs.
Direct Materials	12,000	10,000
Direct Wages	8,000	5,000
Chargeable Expenses	1,000	1,000

The overhead expenses are (*i*) Factory, Rs. 6,500 and (*ii*) Office, Rs. 3,480. If a profit of 25% on sales is to be realised, what should be the selling price of each article?

Solution

Cost Sheet

Particulars	A (100 units)		B (100 units)	
	Total	Cost Per unit	Total	Cost Per unit
	Rs.	Rs.	Rs.	Rs.
Direct Materials	12,000	120	10,000	100
Direct Wages	8,000	80	5,000	50
Chargeable Expenses	1,000	10	1,000	10
Prime Cost	21,000	210	16,000	160
Factory Overheads (apportioned on the basis of Direct Wages in 8 : 5 ratio)	4,000	40	2,500	25
Factory Cost	25,000	250	18,500	185
Office Overheads (apportioned on the basis of Factory Cost in 250 : 185 ratio)	2,000	20	1,480	14.80
Cost of production	27,000	270	19,980	199.80
Profit @ 25% on Sales $\left(\frac{\text{Cost} \times 25}{100-25}\right)$	9,000	90	6,660	66.60
Selling Price	36,000	360	26,640	266.40

Illustration 17

M/s A.B. Shoes Co. manufactures two types of shoes A and B. Production costs for the year ended 31st March, 2005 were:

Direct Material	Rs. 15,00,000
Direct Wages	8,40,000
Production Overhead	3,60,000
	27,00,000

There was no work-in-progress at the beginning or at the end of the year. It is ascertained that (*a*) Direct materials in type A shoes consist twice as much as that in type B shoes. (*b*) The direct wages for type B were 60% of those of type A shoes. (*c*) Production Overhead was the same per pair of A and B type. (*d*) Administrative Overhead for each type was 150% of direct wages. (*e*) Selling Cost was Rs. 1.50 per pair. (*f*) Production during the year were : Type A 40,000 pairs of which 36,000 were sold; Type B 1,20,000 pairs of which 1,00,000 were sold. (*g*) Selling Price was Rs. 44 for type A and Rs. 28 for type B per pair. Prepare a statement showing cost and profit.

Solution

Statement of Cost and Profit

For the year ending 31st March, 2005

Particulars	**Type A**		**Type B**	
	Total	**Per Pair**	**Total**	**Per Pair**
	Rs.	**Rs.**	**Rs.**	**Rs.**
Direct Material	6,00,000	15.00	9,00,000	7.50
Direct Wages	3,00,000	7.50	5,40,000	4.50
Prime Cost	9,00,000	22.50	14,40,000	1200
Production Overhead	90,000	2.25	2,70,000	2.25
Production Cost	9,90,000	24.75	17,10,000	14.25
Administrative Expenses	4,50,000	11.25	8,10,000	6.75
Cost of Production	14,40,000	36.00	25,20,000	21.00
Less Closing Stock	1,44,000		4,20,000	
Cost of Goods Sold	12,96,000	36.00	21,00,000	21.00
Selling Expenses	54,000	1.50	1,50,000	1.50
Cost of Sales	13,50,000	37.50	22,50,000	22.50
Profit	2,34,000	6.50	5,50,000	5.50
Sales	15,84,000	44.00	28,00,000	28.00

Notes: (1) Material Cost has been allocated as follows:

Suppose type B material cost is $= x$

Then, type A material cost $= 2x$

$1,20,000\,x + 80,000\,x$ = Rs. 15,00,000

$2,00,000\,x$ = Rs.15,00,000

x = Rs. 7.50

∴ Type B Material Cost = Rs. 7.50 per pair

Type A Material Cost = Rs. 15.00 per pair

(2) Wages have been allocated as follows:

Suppose labour charges for type A $= x$

Labour charges for type B $= \frac{60x}{100}$

∴ $40,000\,x + 1,20,000 \times \frac{60x}{100}$ = Rs. 8,40,000

Rs. 40,000 x + 72,000 x = Rs. 8,40,000

x = Rs. 7.50 per pair

∴ Labour charges for type A = Rs. 7.50 per pair

Labour charges for type B $= 7.50 \times \frac{60}{100}$

= Rs. 4.50 per pair

(3) Production Overhead has been distributed in the ratio of production as charge for each pair is the same.

Illustration 18

Trading and Profit and Loss Account of Electric Engineering Limited

For the year ending on 31st March, 2005

		Rs.			Rs.
To Cost of Material:			By Sales:		
A	10,000		A	31,000	
B	8,000		B	25,000	
C	6,000	24,000	C	24,000	80,000
To Wages					
A	12,000				
B	7,000				
C	11,000	30,000			
To Manufacturing Expenses		6,000			
To Gross Profit c/d		20,000			
		80,000			80,000
To General Expenses		1,200	By Gross Profit b/d		20,000
To Staff Salaries		2,300			
To Director's Fees		2,500			
To Office Expenses		3,300			
To Selling Expenses		2,700			
To Net Profit		8,000			
		20,000			20,000

Prepare the statement showing the cost and profit of different articles A, B and C separately, if:

(*i*) units manufactured and sold of A, B and C articles were 1,600, 800 and 600 respectively.

(*ii*) Manufacturing expenses are to be apportioned in the ratio of direct wages.

(*iii*) General expenses, staff salaries, director's fees and office expenses should be distributed in the ratio of works cost of different articles.

(*iv*) Selling expenses incurred equally on per unit sold.

Solution

Statement Showing Cost and Profit of Articles A, B and C
(Produced and sold during the year ended 31st March, 2005)

Particulars		Article A		Article B		Article C	
		Cost of 1,600 units	Cost per unit	Cost of 800 units	Cost per units	Cost of 600 units	Cost per unit
		Rs.	Rs.	Rs.	Rs.	Rs.	Rs.
Direct Material		10,000	6.25	8,000	10.00	6,000	10.00
Direct Labour		12,000	7.50	7,000	8.75	11,000	18.33
Prime Cost		22,000	13.75	15,000	18.75	17,000	28.33
Manufacturing Expenses (12 : 7 : 11)		2,400	1.50	1,400	1.75	2,200	3.67
Works Cost		24,400	15.25	16,400	20.50	19,200	32.00
Administrative expenses (61 : 41 : 48)							
General Expenses	1,200						
Staff Salaries	2,300						
Director's Fees	2,500						
Office Expenses	3,300						
	9,300	3,782	2.36	2,542	3.18	2,976	4.96
Cost of Production		28,182	17.61	18,942	23.68	22,176	36.96
Selling Expenses (8 : 4 : 3)		1,440	0.90	720	0.90	540	0.90
Cost of Sales		29,622	18.51	19,662	24.58	22,716	37.86
Profit		1,378	0.86	5,338	6.67	1,284	2.14
Sales		31,000	19.37	25,000	31.25	24,000	40.00

Illustration 19

Prepare a Cost Sheet from the following information:

(*i*) Direct Materials $\frac{1}{3}$ of cost of sales.

(*ii*) Direct Labour $\frac{1}{4}$ of cost of sales.

(*iii*) Direct Expenses $\frac{1}{12}$ of cost of sales.

(*iv*) Works overheads 20% of Prime Cost.

(*v*) Office Overheads, Selling Expenses and Distribution Expenses are in the ratio of $\frac{3}{9}:\frac{4}{9}:\frac{2}{9}$ respectively.

(*vi*) Profit is $\frac{1}{10}$ of sales.

(*vii*) Sales less direct cost is Rs. 8,00,000.

(*viii*) There is no work-in-progress or stock of finished goods.

Solution

Let us suppose that sales = x

$$\text{Profit } (\frac{1}{10} \text{ of sales}) = 0.10x$$

$$\text{Cost of sales} = \text{Sales} - \text{Profit}$$
$$= x - 0.10x$$
$$= 0.9x$$

Direct Cost = Direct materials + Direct wages + Direct expenses = $\frac{1}{3}+\frac{1}{4}+\frac{1}{12}=\frac{2}{3}$ of cost of sales.

$$\text{Cost of sales} = 0.9x$$

$$\text{Hence Direct cost} = \frac{0.9x}{\frac{2}{3}} = 0.6x$$

Given: Sales – Direct cost = Rs. 8,00,000

Hence $x - 0.6x$ = Rs. 8,00,000

or $0.4x$ = Rs. 8,00,000

$$x = \frac{8,00,000}{0.4}$$

Hence Sales = Rs. 20,00,000

Profit = Rs. 2,00,000

Cost of sales = Rs. 20,00,000 – Rs. 2,00,000 = 18,00,000

Indirect cost = Cost of sales – Direct cost
= Rs. 18,00,000 – Rs. 12,00,000
= Rs. 6,00,000

Cost Sheet

	Amount Rs.
Direct Materials (1/3rd of cost of sales)	6,00,000
Direct labour (¼ of cost of sales)	4,50,000
Direct expenses (1/12 of cost of sales)	1,50,000
Prime cost	12,00,000
Works overhead @20% on Prime Cost	2,40,000
Works cost	14,40,000
Office overheads (Rs.6,00,000 – 2,40,000 = 3,60,000 × $\frac{3}{9}$)	1,20,000
Cost of Production	15,60,000
Selling and distribution overheads	
(*i*) Selling overheads (3,60,000 × $\frac{4}{9}$)	1,60,000
(*ii*) Distribution Overheads 3,60,000 × $\frac{2}{9}$	80,000
Total cost or Cost of sales	18,00,000
Profit	2,00,000
Sales	20,00,000

Illustration 20

From the under-mentioned particulars, prepare Cost Sheet of a brick works showing cost and profit per 1,000 bricks

Wages (clay-getting, machining, drying, setting, burning, drawing, sorting etc.) Rs. 1,50,000

Coal : 5,000 tons @ Rs. 15 per ton.

Royalties : Rs. 1.50 per 1,000 bricks made. Depreciation on plant and machinery at 10% (Capital outlay, Rs. 3,00,000)

Removal of overburden at Re. 1 per 1,000 bricks.

Works Overhead: 10% of Wages and Coal.

Office Overhead: 2½% of Wages and Coal.

Bricks Made : 1,01,52,284 (allow for waste 1½% of output)

Bricks Sold : 80,00,000 at Rs. 40 per 1,000.

Stock of Bricks on 1st January, 1994 : 20,00,000 @ Rs. 30 per 1,000.

Stock of Bricks on 31st January 1994 : 40,00,000 @ Rs. 30 per 1,000.

(Agra, M.Com.)

Solution

Cost Sheet

Bricks Made 1,01,52,284 less 1½% for wastage **Effective Output 1,00,00,000 Bricks**	**Total**	**Cost per 1,000 Bricks**
	Rs.	**Rs. P.**
Wages (clay getting, machining, drying, setting, burning, drawing)	1,50,000	15.00
Coal (5,000 Tons at Rs. 15 per Ton)	75,000	7.50
Royalties (at Rs. 1.50 per 1,000 bricks on 1,00,00,000 Bricks)	15,000	1.50
Prime Cost	2,40,000	24.00
Works Expenses:		
Removal of Overburden (at Re. 1 per 1,000 bricks)	10,000	1.00
Depreciation on plant and machinery (10% on Rs. 3,00,000)	30,000	3.00
Works Overheads (@ 10% on Wages and Coal, Rs. 2,25,000)	22,500	2.25
Works Cost	3,02,500	30.25
Office Overheads (@ 2.5% on Wages and Coal Rs. 2,25,000)	5,625	0.56
Cost of Production	3,08,125	30.81

Statement of Profit

Particulars	**No. of Bricks**	**Amount**
		Rs.
Opening Stock @ Rs. 30 per 1,000 Bricks	20,00,000	60,000
Add Cost of Production during the year	1,00,00,000	3,08,125
	1,20,00,000	3,68,125
Less Closing Stock @ Rs. 30 per 1,000 Bricks	40,00,000	1,20,000
Cost of Bricks sold during the year	80,00,000	2,48,125
Profit		71,875
Sales : (80,00,000 Bricks @ Rs. 40 per 1,000 Bricks)	80,00,000	3,20,000

Profit per 1,000 Bricks = $\frac{71,875}{80,00,000} \times 1,000 =$ Rs. 8.98

Illustration 21

From the following particulars of a colliery for the month of February, 2006 prepare a Cost Sheet:

	Rs.
Wages:	
Underground	15,000
Surface	2,500
Working Expenses:	
Repairs & Renewals	600
Timber	350
Royalties and Wayleaves	500
Stable Expenses	150
Stores	200
Rent, Rates & Taxes	175
Depreciation	300
Administrative Expenses:	
General, Administrative, Selling and Distribution Charges	700
Saleable tons raised : 5,000 tons	

Solution

Cost Sheet

Period: February, 2006 — Output: 5,000 Tons

Particulars	Rs.	Total Rs.	Per Unit Rs.
Wages:			
Under Ground	15,000		
Surface	2,500	17,500	3.50
Works Expenses:			
Repairs & Renewals		600	0.12
Timber		350	0.07
Royalties and Wayleaves		500	0.10
Stable Expenses		150	0.03
Stores		200	0.04
Rent, Rates and Taxes		175	0.035
Depreciation		300	0.060
	Works Cost	19,775	3.955
Administration, Selling & Distribution Expenses		700	0.140
	Total Cost	20,475	4.095

Illustration 22

From the following particulars of Mohan Meakins Ltd., for the three months ending 31st March, 2007, prepare the Cost Sheet of Beer, showing:

(*a*) Prime Cost per barrel.
(*b*) Works Cost per barrel.
(*c*) Cost of Production per barrel.
(*d*) Profit per barrel.

Wages Rs. 12,000; Coal and Oil Rs. 11,200; Cooperage, Corks and Shives Rs. 4,000; Malt Rs. 40,000; Hops Rs. 10,800; Beer Duty Rs. 2,80,000; Water

Rs. 1,000; Factory Rent and Rates Rs. 6,000; Sale of Bye-products Rs. 3,600; Sugar Rs. 14,000; Preservatives Rs. 1,600; Other materials Rs. 1,200; Repairs Rs. 1,800; Depreciation Rs. 1,200; Office and Establishment Expenses Rs. 24,000; Selling and Distribution Expenses Rs. 30,000.

Opening Stock of Beer (300 Barrels) Rs. 40,500;
Closing Stock of Beer (500 Barrels) Rs. 67,500;
Beer brewed during the period; 3,000 Barrels;
Beer Sales (2,800 Barrels) Rs. 4,98,000.

(*Punjab, B.Com., 1970*)

Solution

Cost Sheet

Period ....   Output: 3,000 Barrels

Particulars	Total Rs.	Per Barrel Rs. P.
Material Consumed:		
Malt	40,000	13.33
Hops	10,800	3.60
Sugar	14,000	4.67
Preservatives	1,600	0.53
Other Materials	1,200	0.40
Water	1,000	0.33
	68,600	22.86
Less Sale of By-products	3,600	1.20
	65,000	21.66
Wages	12,000	4.00
Beer Duty	2,80,000	93.33
Prime Cost	3,57,000	118.99
Factory Overheads:		
Coal & Oil	11,200	3.73
Cooperage, Corks and Shives	4,000	1.33
Factory Rent and Rates	6,000	2.00
Repairs	1,800	0.60
Depreciation	1,200	0.40
Factory Cost	3,81,200	127.05
Office and Establishment Expenses	24,000	8.00
Cost of Production	4,05,200	135.05

Statement of Profit

Particulars	Barrels	Amount Rs.
Opening Stock of Beer	300	40,500
Cost of Beer brewed during the Period	3,000	4,05,200
	3,300	4,45,700
Less Closing Stock of Beer	500	67,500
Cost of Beer Sold	2,800	3,78,200
Add Selling and Distribution Expenses	–	30,000
Cost of Sales	2,800	4,08,200
Profit for the Period		89,800
Sales	2,800	4,98,000

Calculation of Profit per barrel:

$$= \frac{\text{Total Profit}}{\text{No. of barrels sold}}$$

$$= \frac{\text{Rs. } 89,800}{2,800 \text{ Barrels}} = \text{Rs. } 32.07$$

Illustration 23

In a Brass Foundry three types of building accessories, namely A, B and C are manufactured involving complicated designs. Each type is manufactured from the same mixture of molten brass but requires skilled labour and care in moulding of each type. Draw up a Cost Sheet in the appropriate form showing the cost of production per cwt. for each type of products A, B and C with reference to following data:

Direct Material:

(1) Brass Ingots : 200 cwt. @ Rs. 500 per cwt.
(2) Coke : 50 cwt. @ Rs. 20 per cwt.
(3) Cupola labour : 20 men @ Rs. 5 each per day for one day.
(4) Depreciation on Melting Furnace Equipment @ 50 Paise per cwt. of ingot melt.

Molten brass taken out of the cupola is distributed as 50% for A, 30% for B and 20% for C.

Direct Labour:

Moulding labour:

Article A – 200 men @ Rs. 5 per day for one day
Article B – 150 men @ Rs. 6 per day for one day
Article C – 100 men @ Rs. 7 per day for one day.

Foundry Overheads:

Article A – 100 p.c. of direct labour.
Article B – 200 p.c. of direct labour.
Article C – 300 p.c. of direct labour.

General Overhead:

10% on Works Cost

Assume no loss in melting and no rejection in moulding.

(*C.A. Final*)

Solution

Cost Sheet

Particulars	Rs.	Article 'A' Rs.	Article 'B' Rs.	Article 'C' Rs.
Direct Materials:				
Brass Ingots (200 cwt.)	1,00,000			
Coke (50 cwt.)	1,000			
Cupola labour (20 Men × Rs. 5)	100			
Depreciation on Melting Furnace Equipment (200 cwt. × 0.50)	100			
(To be divided in the ratio of 50 : 30 : 20)	1,01,200	50,600	30,360	20,240
Direct Labour (Moulding) A – 200 Men @ Rs. 5 per day for one day B – 150 Men @ Rs. 6 per day for one day C – 100 Men @ Rs. 7 per day for one day		1,000	900	700
Prime Cost		51,600	31,260	20,940
Foundry Overheads : A – 100% of direct labour B – 200% of direct labour C – 300% of direct labour		1,000	1,800	2,100
Works Cost		52,600	33,060	23,040
General Overhead (10% on Works Cost)		5,260	3,306	2,304
Total Cost		57,860	36,366	25,344
Output in cwt. (200 cwt. in 50 : 30 : 20 ratio)		100	60	40
Cost per cwt.		578.60	606.10	633.60

Illustration 24

The following particulars are obtained from the records of a factory:

Materials issued – Rs. 64,000.

Wages paid – Rs. 56,000.

Factory overhead – 60% of Wages.

Out of the materials issued. Rs. 800 worth of goods have been returned to the stores and Rs. 400 transferred to other jobs.

10 per cent of the production has been scrapped as bad and a further 20 per cent has been brought up to the specification by increasing the factory overheads to 80 per cent of the wages.

If the scrapped production fetches only Rs. 470, find out the production cost per unit of the finished product (including the quantity scrapped) be 100 units.

(*H.P. University, B.Com, 1994*)
(*G.N.D.U., B.Com., 2000*)

Solution

Statement of Cost

Particulars			Units	Cost per Unit	Total Cost
				Rs.	Rs.
Material used:					
Material issued		Rs. 64,000	100		
(–) Returned to Store	800			628	62,800
Transferred	400	1,200			
Wages				560	56,000
		Prime Cost		1,188	1,18,800
Factory Overhead, 60% of Wages				336	33,600
				1,524	1,52,400
(–) Scrapped as bad			10		470
			90		1,51,930
Additional Factory Overhead for 20 units @ 20% i.e., (80% – 60%) on wages *i.e.*, Rs. 112 × 20 units					2,240
		Cost of Production	90	1,713	1,54,170

Illustration 25

Work out in the Cost Sheet form the unit cost of production per metre of Khaki Drill Cloth in a Textile Factory from the following data obtained for the month of May, 2007:

Khaki cotton thread:

4,000 kgs. @ Rs. 3.50 per kg.

Direct labour:

200 men @ Rs. 4.50 per day for 20 days.

Stores overhead at the rate of 10 % on Direct material.

Shop overhead:

Variable 50%
Fixed 100% } on Direct labour.

Credit on account of sale of cotton waste, 400 kgs. @ Re. 1 per kg. recovered from Khaki drill cloth weaving shop of factory.

Administration overhead 10% on factory cost.

Total output for the month: 33,000 mts.

There is no work-in-progress at the beginning of the month or at the end of the month.

(C.A. Final., Raj., B.Com. III)

Solution

Textile Factory Cost Sheet

(Month: May, 2007) (Output: 33,000 mts.)

Particulars		Cost per metre	Amount
		Rs.	Rs.
Materials		0.424	14,000
Direct labour		0.545	18,000
	Prime Cost	0.969	32,000
Stores overhead		0.042	1,400
Shop overhead			
Variable		0.273	9,000
Fixed		0.546	18,000
		1.830	60,400
Less Sale of cotton waste		.012	400
	Factory Cost	1.818	60,000
Administration overhead		.182	6,000
	Total Cost	2.000	66,000

Illustration 26

Two branches of an Engineering Works A and B, machine and shape identical types and size of steel frames out of steel forgings in automatic lathes in the month of Jan., 2008. But the method of remuneration of labour in A is piece work rate whereas that in B is a premium bonus system, namely, time rate plus 50% of the time saved out of standard time fixed.

Work out the unit rate and total cost of each steel frame turned out by each of these two branches A and B with reference to the following data:

Direct Material

Steel forgings (each forging weighing 5 lbs. @ Rs. 2 per lb.)

Branch A : 2,000 Nos.

Branch B : 3,000 Nos.

Direct Labour:

Piece rate : Re. 1 each

Time rate : Rs. 2 per day of 8 hours.

Standard time fixed: 12,000 hours.

Time taken in Completion : 8,000 hours.

Factory Overhead:

Variable 50%, Fixed 150% } on Direct labour.

Sale value of Steel Scraps (realised at Rs. 20 per cwt.)

Branch A : 50 cwt.

Branch B : 75 cwt.

Administration, selling and distribution overheads, 50% on the factory cost.

There was no work-in-progress either in the beginning or at the end of the month. There was also no rejection and no defective work in course of machining and shaping. } in either of two branches

(*C.A.*)

Solution

Cost Sheet of Steel Frames

(For the month of January, 2008)

Particulars	2,000 Frames Branch A Total Cost	2,000 Frames Branch A Cost per Frame	3,000 Frames Branch B Total Cost	3,000 Frames Branch B Cost per Frame
	Rs.	Rs.	Rs.	Rs.
Direct Material – Steel forgings	20,000	10.00	30,000	10.00
Direct Labour	2,000	1.00	2,500*	0.83
Prime Cost	22,000	11.00	32,500	10.83
Factory Overheads				
Variable, 50% on Direct Labour	1,000	0.50	1,250	0.42
Fixed, 150% on Direct Labour	3,000	1.50	3,750	1.25
	26,000	13.00	37,500	12.50
Less Sale proceeds of steel scraps	1,000	0.50	1,500	.50
Factory Cost	25,000	12.50	36,000	12.00
Administration, Selling and Distribution overhead (50% on Factory Cost)	12,500	6.25	18,000	6.00
Total Cost	37,500	18.75	54,000	18.00

Premium on Time saved:

Standard Time	= 12,000 hrs.
Time taken	= 8,000 hrs.
Time Saved	= 4,000 hrs.
Premium for Time Saved	= 4,000 × ½ × Rs. 0.25
Total Wages	= Basic Wages + Premium
	= Rs. 2,000 + Rs. 500
	= Rs. 2,500

* This has been calculated as follows:
Time taken = 8,000 hours or 1,000 days
Wages @ Rs. 2 per day = Rs. 2,000

Illustration 27

Find out the appropriate Cost Sheet form the selling rate per ton of special paper manufactured by a Paper Mill for the Government in January, 2005, under the following divisions of cost:

(*a*) Prime Cost,

(*b*) Works Cost,

(*c*) Total Cost and

(*d*) Selling Price.

The Cost Sheet is to be prepared with reference to data given below:

Direct Materials:

Paper Pulp – 500 tons @ Rs. 50 per ton.

Other miscellaneous materials – 100 tons @ Rs. 30 per ton

80 Skilled men @ Rs. 3 per day for 25 days.

40 Unskilled men @ Rs. 2 per day for 25 days

Special equipments – Rs. 3,000.

Special dyes – Rs. 1,000.

Works overhead:

Variable @ 100% } on direct wages
Fixed @ 60% }

Administration overhead @ 10% } on Works Cost
Selling and distribution overhead @ 15% }

Profit 10% on Total Cost.

Finished paper manufactured – 400 tons.

Credit on account of sale of wastage – Rs. 800.

There was no work-in-progress at the beginning or at the end of the month.

The scrap value of the special equipment after utilisation in manufacture is nil.

Solution

Cost Sheet of Special Paper

(Output : 400 tons)

Particulars		Total	Cost per Unit
	Rs.	Rs.	Rs.
Direct Materials:			
Paper pulp (500 tons @ Rs. 50 per ton)	25,000		
Other Materials 100 tons @ Rs. 30 per ton)	3,000	28,000	70
Direct Labour:			
80 Skilled men			
@ Rs. 3 per day for 25 days	6,000		
40 Unskilled men			
@ Rs. 2 per day for 25 days	2,000		
		8,000	20
Direct Expenses:			
Special equipments	3,000		
Special dyes	1,000	4,000	10
Prime Cost		40,000	100
Works Overhead:			
Variable at 100% on Direct Wages	8,000		
Fixed at 60% on Direct Wages	4,800	12,800	32
		52,800	132
Less Sale of waste		800	2
Works Cost		52,000	130
General Overhead:			
Administration at 10% on Works Cost	5,200		
Selling and distribution at 15% on Works Cost	7,800	13,000	32.50
Total Cost		65,000	162.50
Profit @ 10% on Cost		6,500	16.25
Selling Price		71,500	178.75

Note: The output is 400 tons. Therefore, the selling rate per ton of the special paper manufactured is Rs. 178.75.

Illustration 28

The following figures are collected from the books of the Iron Foundry after the close of the year:

	Rs.
Raw materials:	
Stock in the beginning of the year	7,000
Purchases during the year	50,000
Stock at the end of the year	5,000
Direct Wages	10,000

Works Overhead 50% of Direct wages

Stores Overhead on Materials 10% on the cost of materials.

10% of the castings were rejected being not upto the specification and a sum of Rs. 400 was realised on sale as scrap.

10% of the finished castings were found to be defective in manufacture and were rectified by expenditure of additional works overhead charges to the extent of 20% on the proportionate direct wages.

The total gross output of castings during the year was 1,000 tons. Find out the manufacturing cost of the saleable casting per ton.

(*M.D. University B.Com. 1976*)

Solution

Cost Sheet Showing the Manufacturing Cost Per Ton

Particulars		Qty. Tons	Amount
Total gross output of castings during the year		1,000	Rs.
Raw Materials Consumed			
Opening Stock	7,000		
Purchases during the year	50,000		
	57,000		
Less Closing Stook	5,000		52,000
Direct Wages			10,000
Works Overhead			5,000
Stores Overhead on materials			5,200
Total Cost of gross output		1,000	72,200
Less Sale of rejected castings		100	400
Cost of Good Finished castings		900	71,800
Additional Works Overhead charges on 90 tons of casting at 20% of the proportionate direct wages			180
Manufacturing Cost of Saleable Castings		900	71,980

Manufacturing cost of the saleable castings per ton is = $\frac{\text{Rs. } 71{,}980}{900 \text{ Tons}}$

= Rs. 79.98

Illustration 29

A foundry produces castings having the following contents:

50% Material A, costing 2,000 per ton

20% Material B, costing 800 per ton

10% Material C costing 1,200 per ton

20% scrap of identical mixture, charged at the average price of metal content.

5% of metal charged is lost in melting, 30% of melted metal is returned to scrap. There is a proposal to use the market price (Rs. 1,000 per ton) for valuing foundry's own scrap. Present a report to management on the subject giving consideration to the positions which arise when

(*a*) All scrap cannot be used in future melting processes,

(*b*) The scrap returned to store after pouring is (*i*) lower than, (*ii*) equal to, and (*iii*) higher than, the input of scrap.

(*I.C.W.A. Inter*)

Solution

Cost per 100 Tons of Castings

Particulars	At average weight tons	Rate	Amount	At market weight tons	Rate	Amount
		Rs.	Rs.		Rs.	Rs.
Raw Material	50	2,000	1,00,000			
A						
B	20	800	16,000			
C	10	1,200	12,000			
	80		1,28,000	80		1,28,000
Scrap	20	1,600	32,000	20	1,000	20,000
	100		1,60,000	100		1,48,000
Melt loss 5%	5		–	5		–
Net weight poured	95		1,60,000	95		1,48,000
Less: 30% scrap	28.5	1,600	45,600	28.5	1,000	28,500
Weight of castings	66.5		1,14,400	66.5		1,19,500
Cost per ton			1,720			1,800

It is clear from the above analysis that the use of market value for scrap would increase the product cost but reduce the value of scrap inventory.

When all scrap cannot be used in future melting process the surplus has to be sold at the prevailing market rate. From this point of view charging scrap at average cost would result in inflated value of inventory and resultant loss on realisation. Moreover, when a part of the scrap is used and balance is sold, the issue price should not be different for different purposes. A common price at market rate would ensure consistency in scrap accounting.

Moreover, when market price of Rs. 1,000 is used for scrap, a change in the ratio of used scrap to returned scrap would have corresponding effects on product cost and inventory as follows:

(*a*) When returned scrap is less than input scrap, product cost will be less by Rs. 600 for each ton returned less.

(*b*) When returned scrap is equals to scrap, product cost remains unaltered.

(*c*) When returned scrap is more than input scrap, product cost will be more than Rs. 600 per ton returned more.

Illustration 30

The standard production for a particular work order is 20 units per day and piece-rate wages is 60 paise per unit if daily production is 20 units or more. The rate is 50 paise per unit if production is less than 20 units. Cost of material is 30 paise per unit. It is proposed to charge factory overheads under one of the following methods:

(*i*) 100% on labour cost (*ii*) 80% on prime cost.

Tabulate the above data in the form of a suitable statement and indicate the factory cost per unit, under each of the above methods, if the daily production is (*a*) 15 units, (*b*) 20 units, (*c*) 25 units. (*I.C.W.A., Inter, June 1986*)

Solution

(*i*) Statement Showing Factory Cost per unit by charging Overheads at 100% on Labour Cost

Production per day (units)	**15**	**20**	**25**
Material cost @ 30 paise per unit	Rs. 4.50	Rs. 6.00	Rs. 7.50
Labour cost @ 50 paise for 15 units and @ 60 paise for 20 and 25 units	7.50	12.00	15.00
Prime cost	12.00	18.00	22.50
Factory overheads @ 100 % on labour cost	7.50	12.00	15.00
Total Factory Cost	19.50	30.00	37.50
Factory cost per unit (Factory Cost ÷ Production)	1.30	1.50	1.50

(*ii*) Statement Showing Factory Cost per unit by charging Overheads at 80% of Prime Cost

Production per day (units)	**15**	**20**	**25**
Prime Cost as at (*i*) above	Rs. 12.00	Rs. 18.00	Rs. 22.50
Factory Overhead @ 80% of prime cost	9.60	14.40	18.00
Total Factory Cost	21.60	32.40	40.50
Factory Cost per unit	1.44	1.62	1.62

PRODUCTION ACCOUNT

The analysis of cost presented in the form of an account is known as 'Production Account' or 'Manufacturing Account'. Production Account, prepared for a given period, shows the output made, the total cost and per unit cost incurred and their components, as also the profit or loss made for that period. The form of Production Account differs from industry to industry but the common forms of Production Account can be given as follows:

Production Account

Period........... Output...........

Particulars	Per unit Rs.	Total Rs.	Particulars	Per unit Rs.	Total Rs.
To Raw Materials Consumed			By Cost of Production		
To Direct Wages					
To Direct Expenses					
Prime Cost					
To Factory Overhead					
Factory Cost					
To Office and Administration Overhead					

"The term 'Production Account' is used to denote a particular form of manufacturing account prepared in conjunction with the functional accounts in order to show the actual cost of producing the goods manufactured during the period under review."

– *G.R. Grover & R.G. Williams*

Production Account

Period........... Output...........

Particulars	Amount Rs.	Particulars	Amount Rs.
To Raw Materials Consumed		By Prime Cost c/d	
To Direct Wages			
To Direct Expenses			
To Prime Cost b/d		By Factory Cost c/d	
To Factory Overhead			
To Factory Cost b/d		By Cost of Production	
To Office and Administration Overhead			

Production Account

Period........... Output...........

Particulars	Amount Rs.	Particulars	Amount Rs.
To Raw Materials Consumed		By Cost of Production c/d	
To Direct Wages			
To Direct Expenses			
Prime Cost			
To Works Overhead			
Works Cost			
To Office and Administration Overhead			
To Opening Stock of Finished Goods			
To Cost of Production b/d		By Sales	
Less Closing Stock of Finished Goods			
Cost of Goods Sold			
To Selling and Distribution Overhead			
Cost of Sales			
To Net Profit			

Illustration 31

From the following information, prepare Pig Iron Production Account showing cost per ton of each class of expenditure and of the pig iron produced:

	Coal Rs.	Coke Rs.	Limestone Rs.	Iron Rs.	Sundries Rs.
Opening Stock 1.4.2004	4,720	3,580	1,450	3,930	2,700
Purchases during the year	21,880	29,470	5,080	18,690	7,810
Closing Stock 31.3.2005	3,600	2,050	1,530	3,620	3,010

Total output of Pig Iron	32,000 Tons
Sale of Slag:	Rs 10,500
Wages:	Rs. 17,000
General Works Charges:	Rs. 4,500

Solution

Pig Iron Production Account

Period : Year ended 31.3.2005 (Output 32,000 Tons)

Particulars		Cost per Ton	Total	Particulars	Cost per Ton	Total
		Rs. P.	Rs.		Rs. P.	Rs. P.
To Coal consumed:						
Opening Stock	4,720			By Sale of		
Add Purchases	21,880			Slag	0.33	10,500
	26,600					
Less Closing Stock	3,600	0.72	23,000	By Cost of Production	3.01	96,500
To Coke Consumed						
Opening Stock	3,580					
Add Purchases	29,470					
	33,050					
Less Closing Stock	2,050	0.97	31,000			
To Limestone Consumed:						
Opening Stock	1,450					
Add Purchases	5,080					
	6,530					
Less Closing Stock	1,530	0.16	5,000			
To Iron Ore Consumed:						
Opening Stock	3,930					
Add Purchases	18,690					
	22,620					
Less Closing Stock	3,620	0.59	19,000			
To Sundries Consumed:						
Opening Stock	2,700					
Add Purchases	7,810					
	10,510					
Less Closing Stock	3,010	0.23	7,500			
To Wages		0.53	17,000			
To Works Charges		0.14	4,500			
		3.34	1,07,000		3.34	1,07,000

Illustration 32

From the following particulars, you are required to prepare a Production Account for the three months ending 31st March, 2004 assuming stock of finished goods at the end of the period to be valued at cost, showing:

(*a*) Value of materials consumed;
(*b*) Works Cost;
(*c*) Cost of Production;
(*d*) Cost of goods sold;
(*e*) Gross profit; and
(*f*) Net profit.

	(1st Jan., 2004)	(31st March, 2004)
Stocks:	Rs.	Rs.
Raw materials	20,000	24,700
Finished Good	14,300	8,400
Work-in-progress	6,200	6,900
Purchases of raw material	17,600	
Direct Wages	14,000	
Indirect Wages	500	
Works Expenses	7,400	
Office Expenses	2,600	
Selling Expenses	3,000	
Sales	56,800	

Solution

Production Account
for three months ending 31st March, 2004

Particulars	Amount	Particulars	Amount
To Opening stock of	Rs.		Rs.
Raw Materials	20,000		
To Purchase of Raw		By Cost of	
Materials	17,600	Production c/d	36,700
	37,600		
Less Closing Stock of			
Raw Materials	24,700		
Cost of Raw Materials			
Consumed	12,900		
To Direct Wages	14,000		
Prime Cost	26,900		
To Works Overheads			
Indirect Wages	500		
Works Expenses	7,400		
To Opening Stock of			
Work-in-progress	6,200		
	41,000		
Less Closing Stock of			
Work-in-progress	6,900		
Works Cost	34,100		
To Office Expenses	2,600		
	36,700		36,700
To Opening Stock of			
Finished Goods	14,300	By Sales	56,800
To Cost of Production b/d	36,700		
	51,000		
Less Closing Stock of			
Finished Goods	8,400		
Cost of Goods Sold	42,600		
To Gross Profit c/d	14,200		
	56,800		56,800
To Selling Expenses	3,000	By Gross Profit b/d	14,200
To Net Profit	11,200		
	14,200		14,200

Illustration 33

The following Impersonal Ledger balances appeared in the books of X Y Z Co. Ltd., on 31 March 2007:

	Rs.
Wages paid	6,04,000
Timber used	58,000
Sundry Stores and Maintenance of Mines	97,000
Rent, Taxes and General Charges (One-third applicable to Talcum Powder)	72,000
Wages paid and stores used for the manufacture of Talcum Powder	71,000
Royalties paid on Mica produced	72,000
Ropes used	12,000
Salaries paid (1/4 applicable to Talcum Powder)	28,000
Mica sold 1,94,000 tons	7,02,000
Talcum Powder sold 72,000 tons	4,50,000

The total production of the company was 3,04,000 tons of Mica and 72,000 tons of Talcum Powder, 1,10,000 tons of Mica were used for making Talcum Powder.

You are required to prepare Mica Production Account and Talcum Powder Production Account showing the profit resulting from the sale of Mica and Talcum Powder respectively and showing the cost per ton of Mica and the cost per ton of Talcum Powder, taking Mica used for Talcum Powder at cost price.

Solution

Mica Production Account

(Output: 3,04,000 tons)

	Rs.		Rs.
To Timber used	58,000	By Cost of Production	
To Wages paid	6,04,000	@ Rs. 3 per ton	9,12,000
To Stores and Maintenance of Mines	97,000		
To Ropes used	12,000		
To Royalties paid	72,000		
To Salaries (3/4) paid	21,000		
To Rent, Taxes and General Charges (2/3)	48,000		
	9,12,000		9,12,000
To Cost of Production	9,12,000	By Sales – 1,94,000 tons	7,02,000
To Profit & Loss A/c	1,20,000	By Talcum Powder Production	
		A/c (1,10,000 tons @ Rs. 3 per ton)	3,30,000
	10,32,000		10,32,000

Talcum Powder Production A/c

(Output: 72,000 tons)

	Rs.		Rs.
To Mica Production A/c	3,30,000	By Cost of Production	
To Wages paid and Stores used	71,000	@ Rs. 6 per ton	4,32,000
To Rents, Taxes and General (1/3)	24,000		
To Salaries (1/4)	7,000		
	4,32,000		4,32,000
To Cost of Production	4,32,000	By Sales – 72,000 tons	4,50,000
To Profit & Loss A/c	18,000		
	4,50,000		4,50,000

Illustration 34

The following are the balances of the Impersonal Ledger of a colliery, relating to the month of March, 2007:

	Rs.
Wages paid for coal production deptt.	5,556
Stores used for coal production deptt.	270
Repairs and renewal for coal production deptt.	869
Stable expenses for coal production deptt.	293
Timber used for coal production deptt.	467
Rent, rates and taxes for coal production deptt.	281
Royalties for coal production deptt.	735
Depreciation for coal production deptt.	381
Administration expenses for coal production deptt.	885
General sales of coal 12,100 tons	10,285
Of the stock of coal on 1st March, 2007, 6,900 tons were sold to the Coke production deptt. at Rs. 10 per ton	
Other raw materials used in coke production	315
Wages paid for coke production	850
Repairs and Renewals – Coke production deptt.	790
Salaries and general charges – Coke production deptt.	417
Sales of Coke 4,800 tons	8,400
Sales of by – products	1,372

The stock of coal at 1st March was 7,000 tons valued at Rs. 10 per ton and at 31st March 3,000 tons valued at Rs. 12 per ton. The stock of coke at 1st March was 2,000 tons valued at Rs. 25 per ton and at 31st March, 1,900 tons valued at Rs. 28 per ton. The total production at the colliery was 15,000 tons of coal and 4,700 tons of coke.

Prepare separate Production Accounts for the coal and coke, showing the cost of each item of expenses per ton of coal and coke respectively.

Solution

Coal Production A/c

Period: March, 2007 (Output: 15,000 Tons)

Particulars	Cost per Ton	Amount	Particulars	Cost per Ton	Amount
	Rs. P.	Rs.		Rs. P.	Rs. P.
To Wages	0.3704	5,556	By Cost of Production c/d (15,000 tons)	0.6490	9,737
To Stores	0.0180	270			
To Repairs and Renewals	0.0579	869			
To Stable Expenses	0.0195	293			
To Timber used	0.0311	467			
To Rent, Rates and Taxes	0·0187	281			
To Royalties paid	0.0490	735			
To Depreciation	0.0254	381			
To Administration expenses	0.0590	885			
	0.6490	9,737		.6490	9,737

	Tons	Rs.		Tons	Rs.
To Opening Stock @ Rs. 10 per ton	7,000	70,000	By Sales	12,100	10,285
			By Coke Production A/c @ Rs. 10 per ton	6,900	69,000
To Cost of Production b/d @ Re.0.6490 per ton	15,000	9,737	By Closing Stock @ Rs. 12 per ton	3,000	36,000
To Profit and Loss A/c.		35,548			
	22,000	1,15,285		22,000	1,15,285

Cokc Production A/c

(Output: 4,700 tons)

Particulars	Cost per Ton	Amount	Particulars	Cost per Ton	Amount
	Rs. P.	Rs.		Rs. P.	Rs. P.
To Coal Production A/c 6,900 tons @ Rs. 10 per ton	14.68	69,000	By Sales of By-products	0.29	1,372
			By Cost of Production c/d	14.90	70,000
To Raw Material	0.07	315			
To Wages	0.18	850			
To Repairs Renewals	0.17	790			
To Salaries and General Charges	0.09	417			
	15.19	71,372		15.19	71,372
	Tons	Rs.		Tons	Rs.
To Opening Stock @ Rs. 25 per ton	2,000	50,000	By Sales	4,800	8,400
			By Closing Stock @ Rs. 28 per ton	1,900	53,200
To Cost of production b/d @ Rs. 14.90 per ton	4,700	70,000	By P & L A/c (Loss)		58,400
	6,700	1,20,000		6,700	1,20,000

Illustration 35

From the following information in respect of a factory manufacturing plastic material goods of two varieties, prepare the accounts of plastic goods and find out the profit and loss per unit of each variety.

	I Variety	II Variety
Weight of finished product	1,216 lbs.	684 lbs.
Wages	Rs. 2,540	Rs. 1,840
Sales	Rs. 14,880	Rs. 10,208
No. of units of finished product	2,480	1,276

Factory overhead is 60% of wages and office overhead is 25% of factory cost. The cost of plastic materials is Rs. 3 per lb. and the wastage in the process of manufacture is 5%. There is no opening or closing balance of raw plastic materials or work-in-progress.

N. B.: Each work order is to be debited with the cost of the gross weight of materials issued for it.

Solution

Plastic Goods Account – I Variety

(2,480 units)

Particulars	Weight lbs.	Amount	Particulars	Weight lbs.	Amount
		Rs.	By Loss in Weight	64	Rs. –
To Raw Materials	1,280	3,840			
To Wages		2,560	By Cost of Production @ Rs. 4 per unit	1,216	9,920
To Factory Overhead @ 60% of Wages		1,536	(Rs. 9,920/2,480 units = Rs. 4.00)		
Factory Cost		7,936			
To Office Overhead @ 25% of Factory Cost		1,984			
	1,280	9,920		1,280	9,920
To Cost of Production		9,920	By Sales		14,880
To Profit and Loss A/c		4,960			
		14,880			14,880

Plastic Goods Account – II Variety

(1,276 units)

Particulars	Weight lbs.	Amount	Particulars	Weight lbs.	Amount
To Raw Materials	720	2,160	By Loss in Weight	36	–
To Wages		1,840	By Cost of Production (@ Rs. 5 per unit)	684	6,380
To Factory overhead (@ 60% of Wages)		1,104	(Rs. 4,380/1,276 units = Rs. 5.00)		
Factory Cost		5,104			
To Office overhead @ 25% of Factory Cost		1,276			
	720	6,380		720	6,380
To Cost of Production		6,380	By Sales		10,208
To Profit and Loss Account		3,828			
		10,208			10,208

Note: The weight of gross raw materials has been arrived by multiplying the net weight by 100/95.

A = 1,216 × 100/95 = 1,280; B = 684 × 100/95 = 720.

Illustration 36

A firm manufactures a standard article in three qualities of which they produced during 2005-06:

500 articles of Quality X
1,000 articles of Quality Y
1,200 articles of Quality Z

The stocks of finished goods at 1st April, 2005 were: Quality X – 60 articles Quality Y – 40 articles; Quality Z – 76 articles. Sales during the year 2005-06 were:

Quality X – 510 articles at Rs. 60.
Quality Y – 960 articles at Rs. 67.50.
Quality Z – 1,248 articles at Rs. 75.

All the following figures, in respect of the year 2005-06 were extracted from books of account:

	Rs.
Work-in-progress (1st April, 2005)	15,000
Work-in-progress (31st March, 2006)	18,000
Cost of raw materials used in manufacture	43,500
Cost of stores used in manufacture	6,000
Manufacturing Wages	78,000
Depreciation (works)	9,000
Works overhead	16,500

From the above particulars, prepare Manufacturing and Trading Account for the year, showing the amount of gross profit carried to Profit and Loss Account. Assume that the rate per cent of gross profit is the same for all the three kinds of articles.

(*Ranchi B.Com.*) (*M.D.U., B.Com, 2004*)

Solution

Manufacturing and Trading Account for the year ending 31st March, 2006

Particulars	Rs.	Rs.	Particulars	Rs.	Rs.
To Opening Stock of Work-in-progress		15,000	By Closing Stock of Work-in-progress		18,000
To Raw Materials used		43,500	By Cost of Manufacture		
To Stores used		6,000	X – 500 articles @ Rs. 48 each	24,000	
To Manufacturing Wages		78,000	Y – 1,000 articles @ Rs. 54 each	54,000	
To Depreciation (works)		9,000			
To Works Overhead		16,500	Z – 1,200 articles @ Rs. 60 each	72,000	1,50,000
		1,68,000			1,68,000
To Opening Stock of Finished Goods:			By Sales:		
X – 60 articles @ Rs. 48 each	2,880		X – 510 articles @ Rs. 60 each	30,600	
Y – 40 articles @ Rs. 54 each	2,160		Y – 960 articles @ Rs. 67.50 each	64,800	
Z – 76 articles @ Rs. 60 each	4,560	9,600	Z – 1,248 articles @ Rs. 75 each	93,600	1,89,000
To Cost of Goods Manufactured:			By Closing Stock of Finished Goods:		
X – 500 articles @ Rs. 48 each	24,000		X – 50 articles @ Rs. 48 each	2,400	
Y – 1,000 articles @ Rs. 54 each	54,000		Y – 80 articles @ Rs. 54 each	4,320	
Z – 1,200 articles @ Rs. 60 each	72,000	1,50,000	Z – 28 articles @ Rs. 60 each	1,680	8,400
To Gross Profit (20% on Sales)		37,800			
		1,97,400			1,97,400

Notes: (*i*) The cost per unit of articles X, Y and Z has been calculated as follows:

Total Cost of manufacture as per Manufacturing Account:

$$\left.\begin{array}{l}X-500\text{ articles}\\Y-1{,}000\text{ articles}\\Z-1{,}200\text{ articles}\end{array}\right\}\text{Rs.}1{,}50{,}000$$

Sales Value of Goods manufactured:

X – 500 articles	@ Rs. 60 each	30,000
Y – 1,000 articles	@ Rs. 67.50 each	67,500
Z – 1,200 articles	@ Rs. 75.00 each	90,000
	Total sales value	1,87,500

Total Gross Profit on goods manufactured
= Rs. 1,87,500 – Rs. 1,50,000
= Rs. 37,500

Rate of Gross Profit on Sales

$$\text{(same for X, Y and Z)} = \frac{37{,}500}{1{,}87{,}500} \times 100$$

$$= 20\%$$

	Selling Price Per article	Gross Profit (20%) on Selling Price	Cost of Manufacture per article
	Rs.	Rs.	Rs.
X	60.00	12.00	43.00
Y	67.50	13.50	54.00
Z	75.00	15.00	60.00

(*ii*) It has been assumed that the cost of opening stock of finished goods is the same at which goods have been manufactured during 2005-06.

(*iii*) Calculation of the no. of articles of closing stock:

Opening stock	Manufactured during the year (+)	Sold during the year (–)	Closing stock (=)
X – 60 articles	500 articles	510 articles	50 articles
Y – 40 articles	1,000 articles	960 articles	80 articles
Z – 76 articles	1,200 articles	1,248 articles	28 articles

Illustration 37

From the following particulars of Swadeshi Cotton Mills Ltd., for the half year ended 31st March, 2006, prepare two separate Production Accounts showing: (*a*) Gross Profit, (*b*) Total Quantity produced, (*c*) Total Cost of production, and (*d*) Cost of production per lb.

	Rs.		Ns.
Opening stock of yarn at cost		Cotton purchased	
(60,000 Lbs.)	30,000	(10,40,000 Lbs.)	2,60,000
Opening stock of cloth at cost		Wages-weaving	60,000
(1,20,000 Lbs.)	90,000		
Wages-spinning	30,000	Stores-weaving	40,000
Stores-spinning	20,000		
Fuel-spinning	10,000	Fuel-weaving	10,000
Yarn sales (2,00,000 Lbs.)	40,000	Sale of waste of yarn	
Stock at end at cost:		(2,11,000 Lbs.)	29,000
Yarn (2,00,000 Lbs.)	41,000	Cloth sales	
Cloth (2,05,000 Lbs.)	1,50,000	(4,20,000 Lbs.)	3,00,000

Stores consumed increase the weight of production by 4,000 Lbs. for the spinning stores and 1,20,000 Lbs. for the weaving stores.

Solution

Yarn Production Account

Particulars	Weight in Lbs.	Amount	Particulars	Weight in Lbs.	Amount
		Rs.			Rs.
To Cotton	10,40,000	2,60,000			
To Stores	4,000	20,000	By Sale of Waste	2,11,000	29,000
To Wages		30,000	By Cost of Production c/d	8,33,000	2,91,000
To Fuel		10,000	(@ Re. 0.349 per lb.)		
	10,44,000	3,20,000		10,44,000	3,20,000
To Opening Stock	60,000	30,000	By Sales	2,00,000	40,000
To Cost of Production b/d	8,33,000	2,91,000	By Cloth Production A/c (Transfer)	4,93,000	1,77,215
			By Closing Stock	2,00,000	41,000
			By Profit and Loss A/c (Loss)		62,785
	8,93,000	3,21,000		8,93,000	3,21,000

Calculation of Yarn transferred to Cloth Production A/c:

Opening stock of Yarn	60,000 lbs.
Add Yarn produced	8,33,000 lbs.
	8,93,000 lbs.
Less Yarn sold and in hand at close	4,00,000 lbs.
Transferred to Cloth Production A/c	4,93,000 lbs.

Cost of Yarn transferred to Cloth Production A/c

$$\frac{\text{Rs. } 3,21,000}{8,93,000 \text{ lbs.}} \times 4,93,000 \text{ lbs.} = \text{Rs. } 1,77,215$$

Cloth Production Account

Particulars	Weight in lbs.	Amount Rs.	Particulars	Weight in lbs.	Amount Rs.
To Yarn Production A/c	4,93,000	1,77,215			
To Stores	1,20,000	40,000			
To Wages		60,000	By Loss in Weight	1,08,000	–
To Fuel		10,000	By Cost of Production c/d	5,05,000	2,87,215
	6,13,000	2,87,215		6,13,000	2,87,215
To Opening Stock	1,20,000	90,000	By Sales	4,20,000	3,00,000
To Cost of Production b/d	5,05,000	2,87,215	By Closing Stock	2,05,000	1,50,000
To Gross Profit c/d		72,785			
	6,25,000	4,50,000		6,25,000	4,50,000

Calculation of Loss in weight in weaving

Weight of cloth sold and stock in hand at close	6,25,000 lbs.
Less opening stock of cloth	1,20,000 lbs.
Weight of Production during the period	5,05,000 1bs.
Total weight put in (4,93,000 + 1,20,000)	6,13,000 lbs.
Weight of production during the year	5,05,000 lbs.
Loss in weight	1,08,000 lbs.

Illustration 38

(Cost Sheet in the form of Account)

From the following particulars, make out a monthly Cost Sheet and Production Account of the Coke and By-products Company:

	January, 2007
Coal used 5,000 tons	@ Rs. 25 per ton
Coke produced 3,500 tons	@ Rs. 50 per ton
Tar produced 210 tons	@ Rs. 100 per ton
Sulphate of Ammonia produced 49 tons	@ Rs. 300 per ton
Benzol produced 48 tons	@ Rs. 130 per ton
Raw Materials used to the value of	Rs. 17,500
Wages paid	Rs. 7,170
Repairs & Renewals	Rs. 5,630
Salaries and General Charges	Rs. 8,100

Show the percentage of each product to the weight of coal used.

Solution

Cost Sheet (in the form of Account for January, 2007)

Particulars	Percentage of coal used	Quantity (tons)	Price per ton	Total	Particulars	Percentage to coal	Quantity (in tons)	Price per ton	Total
			Rs.	Rs.				Rs.	Rs.
To Coal used	100	5,000	25.00	1,25,000	By Coke produced	70.00	3,500	50.00	1,75,000
To Raw Materials				17,500	By Tar produced	4.20	210	100.00	21,000
To Wages paid				7,170	By Sulphate of Ammonia	0.98	49	300.00	14,700
To Repairs and Renewals				5,630	By Benzol	0.96	48	130.00	6,240
To General Charges				8,100	By Loss in Weight	23.86	1,193	—	—
Total Cost				1,63,400					
To Profit and Loss A/c (Profit)				53,540					
	100%	5,000		2,16,940		100%	5,000		2,16,940

OBJECTIVE TYPE QUESTIONS

A. Multiple Choice Questions

1. Select the correct answer in each of the following:

1. Unit costing system is applicable to

(*a*) Chemical works (*b*) Transport undertakings
(*c*) Printing press (*d*) Steel mills
(*e*) None of these.

2. An under-statement of closing work-in-progress inventory will

(*a*) Under-state cost of goods sold
(*b*) Over-state cost of goods sold
(*c*) Over-state gross profit
(*d*) Over-state current assets.

3. An over-statement of opening inventory of work-in-progress will

(*a*) Under-state cost of goods sold
(*b*) Over-state cost of goods sold
(*c*) Over-state net profit
(*d*) Over-state gross profit.

4. Aggregate of direct materials cost, direct labour cost and direct expenses is known as

(*a*) Factory Cost (*b*) Office Cost
(*c*) Selling Cost (*d*) Prime Cost.

5. A Cost Sheet should have

(*a*) one column (*b*) two columns
(*c*) three columns
(*d*) as many columns as may be required.

[**Ans.** 1. (*d*) 2. (*b*) 3. (*b*) 4. (*d*) 5. (*b*)]

B. 'True'/'False' type Statements

2. Indicate whether the following statements are 'true' or 'false'.

1. Direct expenses form the part of factory overhead.
2. Cost sheet is prepared to show the total cost and the per unit cost.
3. Aggregate of prime cost and factory overheads is known as the office cost.
4. A cost sheet is used to collect, classify and summarise costs.
5. Unit costing is also known as operating costing.
6. While preparing a cost sheet, after adjusting, opening and closing the stocks of finished goods in cost of production, we arrive at cost of sales.

[**Ans.** 1. False, 2. True, 3. False, 4. False 5. False 6. False]

C. Filling the Blanks

3. Fill in the blanks with appropriate words:

1. Under unit costing system, cost accounts may take the form of a .... or .... account.
2. Aggregate of direct material cost, direct labour and direct expenses is known as ....
3. Aggregate of prime cost and factory overhead is known as ....
4. Office cost is also known as ....
5. Cost of sales is calculated by adding .... to cost of goods sold.
6. Amount realised from the sale of factory scrap may be deducted from .... or ....

[**Ans.** 1. cost sheet or production, 2. prime cost, 3. factory cost, 4. cost of production, 5. selling and distribution expenses, 6. factory overhead or factory cost]

SHORT ANSWER TYPE QUESTIONS

Answer each of the following questions in not more than five lines:

1. What is unit costing?
2. To which industries is unit costing system applicable?
3. What is cost sheet?
4. What is meant by production account?
5. What is the difference between a cost sheet and a statement of cost?
6. What is the basic difference between unit costing and contract costing?

LONG ANSWER TYPE QUESTIONS

1. What is meant by Output Costing? What are its main features? Name the undertakings to which it is most suited.
2. What is meant by 'Cost Sheet'? How it is prepared? How does it differ from a Production Account?
3. What is Cost Sheet? What are its advantages? How does it differ from Cost Account?
4. Distinguish between a Cost Sheet and a Production Account?
5. How does a Cost Sheet help in knowing the tender price? Elucidate with example.
6. What is a Cost Sheet? Prepare Cost sheet of a manufacturing concern with imaginery figures.
7. What is unit costing? In which industries this method is applied? Why is this method considered significant from Cost Accounting point of view? (*Pbi. Univ. B.Com., 2008*)

EXERCISES

1. Calculate the cost of raw materials consumed from the following information:

	Rs.
Opening Stock of Raw Materials	25,000
Closing Stock of Raw Materials	32,000
Raw Materials purchased	1,90,000
Carriage on purchases of Raw Materials	2,000

[**Ans.** Rs. 1,85,000]

2. From the data given below, calculate the Cost of Raw Materials consumed during the year 2005-06:

	Rs.
Stock of Raw Materials	
on 1.4.2005	35,000
on 31.3.2006	42,000
Purchases of Raw Materials during the year	2,35,000
Return of Materials to suppliers	8,000
Carriage on purchases	6,000
Sale of scrap of Raw Materials	3,000

[**Ans.** Rs. 2,23,000]

3. From the following details of Kishore Enterprises, calculate the Prime Cost for the month of October, 2006:

	Rs.
Direct Materials	
(*i*) Opening stock	10,000
(*ii*) Closing stock	8,000
(*iii*) Purchases during the month	92,000
Carriage on direct materials	3,000
Royalties on output	5,000
Excise Duty	4,000
Direct Wages	60,000
Indirect Wages	15,000

[**Ans.** Rs. 1,66,000]

4. Swami Enterprises supply you the following data for the month of April, 2006 for product 'X'

	Rs.
Prime Cost	1,50,000
Factory Overhead	40,000
Office Overhead	15,000

Stock of Work-in-progress:	
(*i*) 1.4.2006	6,000
(*ii*) 30.4.2006	9,000
Sale of Factory scrap	1,000

Calculate Factory Cost.

[**Ans.** Rs.1,86,000]

5. From the following data, ascertain the Prime Cost:

	Rs.
Factory Cost	2,15,000
Factory overhead	42,000
Opening Stock of Work-in-Progress	12,000
Closing stock of Work-in-Progress	15,000
Sale of Factory scrap	2,000

[**Ans**. 1,78,000]

6. Calculate the amount of cost of production and cost of goods sold from the following:

Factory cost	2,20,000
Factory overhead	40,000
Office overhead	20,000
Opening Stock of Finished Goods	22,000
Closing Stock of Finished Goods	30,000

[**Ans.** Cost of Production Rs. 2,40,000 Cost of Goods Sold Rs. 2,32,000]

7. From the data given below, ascertain the cost of the sales:

	Rs.
Factory cost	2,15,000
Office overhead	25,000
Factory overhead	45,000
Opening Stock of Finished Goods	18,000
Closing Stock of Finished Goods	25,000
Selling and Distribution Overhead	36,000

[**Ans.** Rs. 269,000]

8. The following expenses are related to the production of 1,000 units during the month of August, 2007:

	Rs.
Direct Materials	12,000
Wages	10,000
Factory Rent & Rates	1,000

Depreciation on machinery	500
Supervisor's Salary	1,500
Indirect Material	200
Indirect Labour	300
Office Expenses	1,500
Other Factory Expenses	500
Office Salaries	1,800
Printing and Stationery	200
Administrative Expenses	2,500

Prepare a Statement of Cost showing:

(*a*) Prime Cost (*b*) Works Cost, (*c*) Total Cost of Production (*d*) Cost of one unit, (*e*) Percentage of various expenses on Total Cost.

[**Ans.** (*a*) Rs. 22,000 (*b*) Rs. 26,000 (*c*) 32,000 (*d*) Rs. 32.]

9. The Accounts of Swadeshi Manufacturers Ltd., for the year ended 31st March 2007, show the following:

	Rs.
Stock of Materials, 1.4.2006	67,200
Materials purchased	2,59,000
Counting House Salaries	17,640
Bad Debts Written off	9,100
Travellers' Salaries and Commission	10,780
Depreciation written off (office furniture)	420
Drawing Office Salaries	9,100
Rent, Rates, Taxes and Insurance (Factory)	11,900
Productive Wages	1,76,400
Director's Fees	8,400
General Expenses	4,760
Gas and Water (Factory)	1,680
Travelling Expenses	2,940
Sales	6,45,540
Manager's Salary ($\frac{2}{3}$ Factory, $\frac{1}{3}$ Office)	15,000
Depreciation Written off Plant, Machinery & Tools	9,100
Cash discounts allowed	4,060
Repairs of Plant, Machinery & Tools	6,230
Carriage & Cartage Outwards	6,020
Direct expenses	10,010
Rent, Rates, Taxes and Insurance (Office)	2,800
Gas and Water (Office)	560
Stock of materials 31st March 2007	87,920

Prepare a Statement giving the following information:
(*a*) Materials consumed
(*b*) Prime Cost
(*c*) Factory Oncost and its percentage on Wages
(*d*) Factory Cost
(*e*) General Oncost, and its percentage on Factory Cost
(*f*) Total Cost; and
(*g*) Net Profit.

[**Ans.** (*a*) Rs. 2,38,280 (*b*) Rs. 4,24,690 (*c*) Rs. 48,010 (27.22%) (*d*) Rs. 4,72,700 (*e*) 68,420 (14.47%) (*f*) Rs. 5,41,120 (*g*) Rs. 1,04,420.

10. From the following particulars, prepare a cost sheet showing the comparative cost per ton for each of two periods.

	Three months ended	
	31-3-07	30-6-07
	Rs.	Rs.
Productive Wages	72,000	98,000
Administration	12,000	12,000
Raw materials	36,000	49,000
Taxes and Insurance (Factory)	750	750
Light and Water	1,000	1,000
Direct Expenses	9,000	12,500
Depreciation	2,000	2,000
Factory Rent	1,500	1,500
Unproductive Labour	30,000	41,000
Factory Repairs	3,000	4,500
	1,67,250	2,22,250
Output	6,000 Tons	8,000 Tons

[**Ans.** Cost per ton Period I – Rs. 27.875 Period II – Rs. 27.781]

11. The following information has been taken from Profit & Loss Account of a manufacturer for the past two years:

	Year ended 31st March	
	2006	2007
	Rs.	Rs.
Finished Products on hand		
Beginning of the year	50,000	1,00,000
End of the year	1,00,000	1,72,000
Materials used	1,00,000	1,60,000
Direct Labour	60,000	96,000
Indirect Labour	7,500	9,000
Fuel & Power	11,000	17,500

Depreciation of Machinery & Equipment	5,000	6,000
Repairs & Maintenance	3,500	6,500
Sundry Manufacturing Expenses	3,000	5,000
Sales	2,00,000	3,00,000

Prepare a comparative statement of cost.

[**Ans.** Cost of Production (*i*) Rs. 1,90,000 (*ii*) Rs. 3,00,000]

12. The following data are extracted from the books of a television manufacturing company related to the year ended 31.3.2007.

	Rs.
Purchases of Material	3,50,000
Direct Labour Employed	4,20,000
Direct Expenses	80,000
Factory Rent	25,000
Foreman's Salary	35,000
Production Manager's Salary	84,000
Other Factory Expenses	16,000
Factory Lighting	7,000
Supervisory Expenses	23,000
Stock on 1st April, 2006:	
Raw Material	1,50,000
Work-in-Progress	90,000
Stock on 31st March, 2007:	
Raw Material	1,00,000
Work-in-Progress	120,000
Directors' Fees	50,000
Legal Expenses	12,000
Office Rent	23,000
Office Expenses	10,000
Printing & Stationery	5,000

Number of televisions produced during the year 500 units.

Find out the cost per television by preparing a cost sheet.

[**Ans.** Rs. 2,320 per T.V.]

13. You are given the following details of expenses incurred in a factory during the six monthly period ending on 31st March, 2007:

	Rs.		Rs.
Opening Stock of Raw Material	23,200	Repairs and Maintenance	150
Purchases of Raw Material	31,700	Factory cleaning	100
Carriage thereon	1,300	Factory Rent & Rates	1,800
Productive wages	32,000	Factory Lighting and Heating	250
Royalty paid	6,000	Power consumed	3,100
Non-productive wages	1,200	Foreman's salary	1,900
Indirect Material	1,300	Depreciation on Machinery	400
Haulage	500	Estimating Expenses	440
Drawing Office Salary	800	Salesman Salary	1,300
Director's Fees (Director devoted 1/3 of his time for factory)	3,600	Travelling Expenses	700
Interest on capital	2,000	Advertising Expenses	600
Supervisor's Salary	1,200	Carriage outward	200
Loose Tools written off	300	Cash discount allowed	1,500
Bank Charges	150	Warehouse rent	300
Legal Expenses	350	Delivery Van's Depreciation	150
Printing and Stationery (Office)	500	Upkeep of Delivery Vans	50
Printing and Stationery (Factory)	100	Sales Manager's Salary	1,500
Postage	150	Commission on Sales	270
Bad debts	830	Opening Work-in-Progress	9,900
Water Supply	260	Opening Stock of Finished Goods	28,200
Office Rent	1,200		
Depreciation on Office Furniture	190	Closing Stock of Raw Material	13,100
Chargeable Expenses	2,900	Closing Work-in-Progress	8,900
Office Superintendent's Salary	1,000	Closing Stock of Finished Goods	32,100
Miscellaneous Office Expenses	2,060	Units produced during the period	2,000 units
		Sales	Rs. 1,30,000

Find out the following from the above details:

(*a*) Cost of material consumed, (*b*) Prime cost, (*c*) Factory cost (*d*) Cost of production (*e*) Total cost and (*f*) Net Profit.

[**Ans.** (*a*) Rs. 43,100, (*b*) Rs. 84,000, (*c*) Rs. 1,00,000, (*d*) Rs. 1,08,000, (*e*) Rs. 1,10,000, (*f*) Rs. 20,000

14. The following Trading & Profit & Loss Account has been prepared for a factory for the year ended 31st December, 2002.

Particulars	Rs.	Particulars	Rs.
To Opening Stock of Raw Materials	10,000	By Sales	4,44,000
To Purchase of Raw Materials	1,50,000	By Closing Stock of Raw Materials	12,000
To Wages	1,24,000		
To Power	36,000		
To Gross Profit	1,36,000		
	4,56,000		4,56,000
To Establishment (Office)	15,000	By Gross Profit	1,36,000
To Establishment (Factory)	8,000		
To Rent (Office)	3,000	By Investment Income	1,200
To Rent (Factory)	2,000		
To Advertisements & samples	6,000		
To Travellers' Commission	4,000		
To Maintenance of Delivery Vans	5,000		
To Rent and Maintenance of Warehouse	2,500		
To Telephone (Office)	500		
To Telephone (Factory)	300		
To Electric Charges (Office)	400		
To Electric Charges (Factory)	200		
To Dep. of Furniture (Office)	700		
To Depreciation of Plant and Machinery	3,000		
To Misc. Expenses (Office)	9,000		
To Interest on Capital	1,000		
To Misc. Expenses (Factory)	2,000		
To Net Profit	74,600		
	1,37,200		1,37,200

The following information is supplied:

(*a*) Office establishment consists of 40% for sales establishment, 10% for distribution section and 50% for administration section.

(*b*) The sales rooms & adjuncts occupy 60% of the entire office areas.

(*c*) 40% of the telephone charges are for the sales section, 10% for the warehouse and rest for the office.

(*d*) 70% of the electric charges are for the sales section, 5% for the warehouse and the balance for the office.

(*e*) 65% of the furniture is in the sales section, 15% in the warehouse and 20% in the office.

(*f*) Miscellaneous office expenses are allocated as follows: 25% to sales section, 10% to the warehouse and 65% to the office.

Prepare a Cost Sheet making suitable assumptions.

[**Ans.** Profit Rs. 74,400]

(**Hint:** Interest on capital is considered as financial loss and hence excluded from cost accounts)

15. The following extract of costing information relates to Commodity A for the year ending 31.3.2007:

	Rs.
Purchases – raw materials	60,000
Direct wages	50,000
Rent, rates, insurance and works overheads	20,000
Carriage inwards	1,000
Stocks-1st April, 2006	
Raw materials	10,000
Finished products – 2,000 tonnes	8,000
Stock-31st March, 2007	
Raw materials	11,000
Finished products – 4,000 tonnes	
Work-in-Progress – 1st April, 2006	2,400
Work-in-Progress – 31st March, 2007	8,000
Cost of factory supervision	4,000
Sales–finished products	1,50,000

Advertising, discount allowed and selling costs Re. 0.40 per tonne sold. 32,000 tonnes of the commodity were produced during the period.

Ascertain:

(*a*) the cost of the output for the period and the cost per tonne of production:

(*b*) the net profit per tonne of the commodity.

(*Delhi*, *B.Com*)

[**Ans.** (*a*) Rs. 1,28,400, Rs. 4.01, (*b*) Re. 0.588 per tonne)

(**Hint:** Closing Stock of Finished goods 4,000 tonnes has been valued at actual cost *i.e.*, Rs. 1,28,400 ÷ 32,000 × 4,000 = Rs. 16,050)

16. From the following figures prepare the Cost Sheet to show the cost of production of one unit of the goods manufactured. Also, prepare a statement to show the profit earned.

	Rs.		Rs.
Depreciation of Plant and Machinary	1,300	Carriage on Raw Materials	391
Stock on 30th June, 2006		Office Salaries	940
Manufactured Goods (350 units)	974	Carriage on Sales	233
Raw Materials (500 units)	300	General Expenses	217
Cash Discount on Sales	374	Factory Rent and Rates	2,271
Printing and Stationery	93	Manufacturing Wages	10,000
Purchases:		Manufacturing Salaries	1,029
Raw Materials (10,000 units)	8,726	Travelling Expenses	279
Manufactured Goods (510 units)	1,274	Sales	29,942
Repairs to Machinery	250	Stock on 31st July, 2006	
Office Rent and Rates	650	Manufactured goods (1,070 units)	2,794
Coal	579	Raw Materials (300 units)	200

There was no wastage during the production.

(**Hint:** Since there is no wastage, output will be equal to the units of materials used.)

[**Ans.** Cost of production per unit Rs. 2,602, Profit Rs. 3,430)

17. From the following particulars you are required to prepare a Statement showing:

(*i*) The cost of materials consumed
(*ii*) Prime Cost
(*iii*) Works Cost
(*iv*) Total Cost
(*v*) Percentage of works oncost to wages.

	Rs.
On April 1, 2006	
Stock of Raw Materials	33,280
Stock of Finished goods	72,800
On March 31, 2007	
Stock of Raw Materials	35,360
Stock of Finished Goods	78,000
Purchases of Raw Materials	7,59,200
Sale of Finished Goods	15,39,200
Productive Wages	5,16,880
Works Overhead Charges	1,29,220
Office and General Charges	70,000

(*B.Com., Mysore*)

[**Ans.** Cost of Goods sold Rs.14,68,020]

18. The Modern Manufacturing Co., submits the following information on 31st March, 2006.

Sales for the Year	Rs. 2,75,000
Inventories at the beginning of the year –	
	Rs.
Finished Goods	7,000
Work-in-progress	4,000
Purchases of Material for the year	1,10,000
Materials Inventory –	
at the beginning of the year	Rs. 3,000
at the end of the year	Rs. 4,000
Direct Labour	Rs. 65,000

Factory overhead was 60% of the direct labour cost. Inventories at the end of the year–

Work-in-progress	Rs. 6,000
Finished Goods	Rs. 8,000

Other expenses for the year were –

Selling expenses 10% of Sales

Administrative expenses 5% of the sales

Prepare Statement of Cost.

(*C.A. Inter, 1977 May*)

[**Ans.** Cost of Sales Rs. 2,51,250]

19. From the following figures ascertain (*a*) The cost of materials used; (*b*) Value of output of manufactured goods; and (*c*) Percentage of Gross Profit on sales.

Trading Account

		Rs.			Rs.
To Stock			By Sales		8,40,000
Finished Goods	80,000		By Closing Stock		
Raw Materials	24,000	1,04,000	Finished Goods	70,000	
			Raw Materials	28,000	98,000
To Purchases		2,40,000			
To Wages		4,00,000			
To Carriage		20,000			
to Gross Profit		1,74,000			
		9,38,000			9,38,00C

(*Shivaji, B.Com.*

[**Ans.** (*a*) Rs. 2,56,000; (*b*) Rs. 6,56,000 and (*c*) $\frac{290}{14}$% *i.e.* 20.715% approx.

(**Hint:** Carriage is to be treated as a part of material cost)

20. A factory produces 100 units of a commodity. The cost of production is –

Direct Materials	10,000
Direct Wages	5,000
Direct Expenses	1,000
Factory Overheads	6,500
Administration overheads	3,480

If profit of 25% is to be realised. what would be the selling price of each unit of the commodity.

(*B.Com., Delhi*) [**Ans.** Rs.340.40]

21. The following data relate to the manufacture of a standard product during the 4 weeks to 28th February, 2007:

Raw materials consumed	Rs. 20,000
Direct Wages	Rs. 12,000
Machine hours worked	500
Machine hour rate	Rs. 4
Office Overhead	15% of Works Cost
Selling Overhead	37 paise per unit
Units Sold	18,000 at Rs. 2.50 each

You are required to prepare a cost sheet in respect of the above, showing (*a*) the cost per unit, (*b*) the profit for the 4 weekly period.

(*Bombay, B.Com.*)

[**Ans.** (*a*) Cost per unit: Rs. 2.542 approx., (*b*) Loss: Rs. 7601

22. Jai Electricals manufactures two types of fans–major and minor models, From the following information, prepare a statement showing cost and profit per fan sold. There were no stocks.

	Major	**Minor**
	Rs.	**Rs.**
Labour	15,600	62,920
Materials	27,300	1,08,680

Factory overheads are recovered at 80% on labour and office overheads at 15% on factory cost. The selling price of each fan of both models is Rs. 1,000. 78 Major and 286 Minor fans were sold.

(G.N.*D.U., B.Com. April 1998*)

23. A manufacturer makes two kinds of spray pumps, *viz.*, 'Super' and 'Delux'. The following information relates to these pumps:

	Super	**Delux**
	Rs.	**Rs.**
Direct Materials	7,000	6,000
Direct Wages	5,000	4,000
Chargeable Expenses	500	–
	12,500	10,000

Other costs:

Factory Overhead	Rs. 3,600
Packing and Forwarding charges	Rs. 600
Administration and Selling Overhead	Rs. 2,610

Pumps Produced during the year: 'Super' 30 and 'Delux' 20.

The common costs are to be allocated on the following basis:

(*a*) Factory cost to be charged on the basis of the Prime Cost.

(*b*) Administration and selling expenses to be divided in the ratio of works cost.

(*c*) Packing and Forwarding charges to be apportioned in proportion to the units manufactured.

Prepare the Cost Sheet.

[**Ans.** Cost Per unit: Super Rs. 543.67; Delux Rs. 650]

24. Shri Jain Metal Works manufactures two types of articles X and Y. The production during January, 2007 was: X = 500 and Y = 750 and expenses incurred during the month were:

	Rs.
Material	2,00,000
Wages	40,000
Stores Overhead	10,000
Depreciation	20,000
Machine operating expenses	30,000
Labour Welfare Expenses	2,800
General Works Expenses	36,000
Adm. and Selling Overheads	84,700

The releveant data furnished to you are:	X		Y
Material Cost Ratio per unit	3	:	2
Labour Cost Ratio per unit	1	:	2
Machine Utilisation Ratio per unit	1	:	1

Calculate cost of each article. Make assumptions supported by proper reason wherever necessary.

[**Ans.** Cost per unit X – Rs. 361.75, Y – 323.50]

(**Hint:** Selling and Administration expenses have been apportioned in the ratio of Factory Cost.)

25. Five different varieties of a product are manufactured in factory and the following information is collected:

Variety	Materials Rs.	Wages Rs.	Sales Rs.
A	34,000	30,000	1,44,000
B	19,000	20,000	90,000
C	15,200	16,000	72,000
D	33,800	24,000	1,26,000
E	48,600	28,000	1,62,000

Factory overhead charges are 80% of wages. The total administrative overhead charges amount to Rs. 1,08,900 and total selling overhead charges (including distribution charges) amount to Rs. 61,776.

All the commodities produced in the factory have been sold. On the basis of the data given, what in your opinion should be the best method for allocation of administration and selling overhead charges over the different varieties of the product? Also calculate the profit earned by each production section.

[**Ans**

1. Production section	**Profit earned**	**2. Basis of allocation**	
A	14,624	(*a*) Administrative oncost	In the ratio of works cost.
B	9,140	(*b*) Selling and Distribution oncost	In the ratio of sales.]
C	7,312		
D	12,796		
E	16,452		

26. The Pen Manufacturing company is producing two types of pen – 'Delux' and 'Popular', The manufacturing costs for the year ended 31st March, 2008 were:

	Rs.
Direct Material	2,00,000
Direct Wages	1,12,000
Production Overhead	48,000
	3,60,000

It is ascertained that:

(*a*) Direct materials in 'Delux' type cost twice as much that of Popular type.

(*b*) Direct Wages of 'Popular' type were 60% of those for 'Delux' type.

(*c*) Production overhead was 30 paise per pen for both types.

(*d*) Administrative overhead for each type was 200% of direct labour.

(*e*) Selling cost was 25 paise per pen for both the types.

(*f*) Production during the year was:

Delux Type	40,000 pens of which 36,000 were sold
Popular Type	1,20,000 pens of which 1,00,000 were sold

(*g*) Selling price were Rs. 7 per pen of 'Delux' type and Rs. 5 per pen of 'Popular' type.

Prepare a statement showing the total cost per pen of each type and the profit made on each type of pen.

(*M.D. University. B.Com. 1993*)

[**Ans.** Total Cost per fan – Delux-Rs. 5.76, Popular-Rs. 3.48
Profit per fan – Delux-Rs. 1.24, Popular-Rs. 1.52]

27. A Company is manufacturing building bricks and fire bricks. Two processes-Brick Forming and Heat Treating – are required for completion of the products.

Time required (in hours)

	Building Bricks	Fire Bricks
Brick Forming, per 100 bricks	3	2
Heat Treating per 100 bricks	2	5

Total cost of the two processing departments in a particular month were:

Bricks Forming : Rs. 21,200
Heat Treating : Rs. 48,800

Production during that month was :

Building Bricks : 1,30,000 pieces
Fire Bricks : 70,000

Prepare a statement of manufacturing costs for the two varieties of bricks.

(*I.C.W.A. Inter,, Dec. 1991*)

[**Ans.** Manufacturing Cost Per brick: Building Brick Rs. 0.28, Fire Brick Re. 0.84]

28. A factory produces a standard product, The following information is given to you from which you are required to prepare 'Cost Sheet' for the period ended 31st March, 2008:

	Rs.
Consumable Materials:	
Opening Stock	10,000
Purchases	85,000
Closing stock	4,000
Direct Wages	20,000
Other Direct Expenses	10,000
Factory Overhead of direct labour	100%
Office Overhead	10% of Works Cost
Selling and Distribution Expenses	Rs. 2 per unit sold
Units of Finished product:	
In hand at the beginning of the period (value Rs. 16,000)	1,000
Produced during the year	10,000
In hand at the end of the period	2,000

Also find out the selling price per unit on the basis that profit make-up is uniformly made to yield a profit of 20% of the selling price. There was no work-in-progress at the beginning or at the end of the period.

(*H.P. University, B.Com., September 1995*)

[**Ans.** Cost of production – Rs. 1,55,100, Cost of sales – Rs. 1,78,080, Selling Price per unit – Rs. 11.72]

29. The following particulars of a work-order are obtained from the cost records of a manufacturer:

	Rs.
Raw Materials	1,28,000
Direct Wages	1,12,000
Factory Overhead	60% of Wages
Materials returned to store	1,600
Materials transferred to other jobs	800

10% of the production has been scrapped as bad and further 20% has been brought upto specification by increasing factory overheads to 80% of wages. If the scrapped production fetches only Rs. 940, find the production cost per unit of the finished goods if the total production (including scrapped) be 200 units.

(*G.N.D.U., B.Com., 2000*) [**Ans.** Rs.1,713]

30. From the under-mentioned particulars appearing in the books of the Bombay Bricks Works, you are required to prepare monthly Cost sheet of bricks made in January, 2007, showing cost and profit per 1,000 bricks:

	Rs.	**Oncost**
Materials:		
Coal	31,500	Works 25% on Prime Cost
Royalty	5,550	Office 10% on Works Cost
Stores	15,000	
Labour:		
Brick-making	50,000	
Indirect	15,000	
Production per month		74,00,000 Bricks
Sales per Month		70,00,000 Bricks
@ Rs. 27.50 per 1,000		
Stock 1st January, 2007		2,00,000 Bricks
Stock 31st January, 2007		6,00,000 Bricks

You have to assume that opening stock was valued at the same rate per thousand bricks as the production for January, 2007.

Calculations may be made to the nearest paisa.

[**Ans.** Cost per 1.000 bricks Rs. 21.193 – Profit Rs. 6.307]

31. The following particulars have been extracted from the books of the Bharat Slate Co. Ltd., for the year ended 31st March, 2008:

Slate quarried : 6,500 tons, all of which was used, wages (quarrying, splitting and dressing) Rs. 50 per 1,000 slates made.

Internal transport costs: Rs. 32,500

Royalties: Rs. 1.50 per ton of slate quarried.

Works Overhead 20% of Wages and Office Overhead is 60% of Works Overhead.

Stock of Slates on 1st April, 2007 : 30,00,000
Valued at Rs. 60 per 1,000.
Stock of Slates on 31st March, 2008 : 25,00,000 to be valued at cost during the year.
Slates sold during the year : 70,00,000 at Rs. 90 per 1,000.
Prepare statements showing (*a*) the total cost of each 1,000 slates made during the year and (*b*) the profit made for the year ended 31st March, 2008.

[**Ans.** Cost per 1,000 slates Rs. 72.50, Profit Rs. 1,60,000)

32. From the following information prepare Pig Iron Production Account showing Cost per ton of each class of expenditure and of the Pig Iron produced:

	Coal	Coke	Lime Stone	Iron Ore	Sundries
	Rs.	Rs.	Rs.	Rs.	Rs.
Stock on 1st April, 2005	7,080	5,370	2,175	5,895	4,050
Purchases during the year	32,820	44,205	17,620	28,035	11,715
Stock on 31st March, 2006	5,400	3,075	2,295	5,430	4,515

The total production of Pig Iron to amounted to 40,000 tons : Sale of Slag Rs. 10,500 : General Working charges Rs. 6,750 : Wages Rs. 25,500.

[**Ans.** Cost per ton Rs. 4]

33. From the following particulars you are required to prepare a Profit and Loss Account in such a form as you consider would be most useful to the Costing Department:

	Rs.		Rs.
Opening Stock:		Rent, Rates and Taxes (*a*)	3,360
Raw Materials	24,500	Fuel, Gas etc. (*a*)	960
Finished Goods	5,450	Repairs to Plant and Machinery	650
Closing Stock:			
Raw Materials	21,450	Depreciation on Machinery	1,050
Finished Goods	3,900		
Wages:		Repairs to Premises (*a*)	800
Productive	17,350	Office Expenses	1,970
Non-productive	3,250	Purchases of Materials	73,650
Salaries	3,460		
Carriage on purchases	550	Sales	1,24,700
Carriage on Sales	950		

One-sixteenth of items marked (*a*) to be taken as in respect of the office as distinct from the works. (*C.A., Inter*)

[**Ans.** (*a*) Works Cost Rs. 1,04,350 (*b*) Cost of Production Rs. 1,10,100 (*c*) Net Profit Rs. 12,100]

34. A manufacturing concern requires a statement, showing the results of its production for the month of September, 2007. The cost records give the following information:

Stock on 1st September, 2007	
(*a*) Raw Materials	1,00,000
(*b*) Finished Goods	71,500
Stock on 30th September, 2007	
(*a*) Raw Materials	1,23,500
(*b*) Finished Goods	42,000
Purchases of Raw Materials	88,000
Work-in-progress on 1st September, 2007	31,000
Work-in-progress on 30th September, 2007	34,500
Sales	2,84,000
Direct Wages	70,000
Indirect Wages	2,500
Works Charges	37,000
Administration expenses	13,000
Selling and Distribution Expenses	15,000

You are required to prepare a concise account which will show: (*a*) the value of materials consumed : (*b*) the cost of production : (*c*) the cost of stock sold : (*d*) the net profit for the month.

[**Ans.** (*a*) Rs. 64,500, (*b*) Rs. 1,83,500, (*c*) 2,13,000, (*d*) Rs, 56,000]

35. Prepare the Production Account from the following information for the period ended on 31st March, 2008:

	Rs.
Opening Balances:	
Raw Material	17,000
Work-in-progress	8,200
Purchases of Raw Material	22,000
Carriage	1,000
Productive Wages	32,000
Non-Productive Wages	5,000
Factory Expenses	3,000
Direct Expenses	8,000
Factory Rent and Rates	1,500
Office Expenses	2,500
Manager's Salary	1,800
Advertisement	2,250
Bad Debts	1,125
Salesman's Salary	450
Staff Salaries	1,500

[**Ans.** Cost of Production Rs. 1,03,500]

36. Given below is the Cloth and Yarn Manufacturing Account of Arvind Mills for the year ended 31st March, 2006:

Particulars		Rs.	Particulars		Rs.
To Opening stock	Rs.		By Sales of 2,24,000 lbs. of waste being that portion of 11, 53,600 lbs. of cotton as per contra which could not be utilised in yarn manufacture		28,000
Yarn 44,800 lbs.	33,600		" Yarn Sales 1,68,000 lbs.		1,89,000
Cloth 88,200 lbs.	88,200	1,21,800	" Cloth Sales 7,56,000 lbs.		8,97,750
To Cotton Consumed 11,53,600 lbs.		9,01,250	" By Closing Stock:		
" Spinning Wages		57,050	Yarn lbs 1,40,000	Rs. 1,48,750	
" Weaving Wages		91,700	Cloth 1,90,400 lbs.	Rs. 2,14,200	3,62,950
" Stores Consumed in spinning which increased Yarn 5,600 lbs in weight		41,300			
" Store and sizing materials consumed in weaving which increased cloth by 1,86,200 lbs. in weight		1,48,400			
" Spinning Fuel		36,050			
" Weaving Fuel		22,400			
" Gross Profit		57,750			
		14,77,700			14,77,700

In the above Manufacturing Account (where the closing stock of yarn and cloth is taken at actual cost) it is contended by the Income Tax Authorities that the closing stock is valued below the cost price in order to suppress the gross profit actually made.

For the satisfaction of authorities you are required to prepare from the above Manufacturing Account, a separate Yarn Production Account and separate Cloth Production Account showing the following details:

(*a*) Gross profit of the departments.

(*b*) Total quantity produced (including the opening balance).

(*c*) Total cost of production (including the value of Opening Stock which was at Cost).

(*d*) Cost of production per pound (including the quantity of the opening stock in total quantity and the cost of opening stock in total cost).

In manufacturing cloth 6,72,000 lbs. of Yarn was consumed which is to be adjusted at the actual cost arrived at in the manner stated above.

[Ans.	**Gross Profit Rs.**	**Total Quantity Produced Lbs.**	**Total Cost of Production Rs.**	**Cost of Production per pound**
Yarn A/c	10,500	9,80,000	10,41,250	1.0625
Cloth A/c	47,250	9,46,400	10,64,700	1.125]

37. Given below is the Manufacturing Account of Star Spinning and Weaving Mills Ltd., for the year ended 31st March, 2008:

Particulars	Rs.	Particulars	Rs.
To Opening Stock:		By Sales of 3,20,000 lbs. of waste being that portion of 16,48,000 lbs. of Cotton as per Contra which could not be used in manufacture	40,000
Yarn 64,000 lbs.	48,000		
Cloth 1,26,000 lbs.	1,26,000		
To Cotton consumed: 16,48,000 lbs.	12,87,500		
To Spinning Wages	81,500		
To Weaving Wages	1,31,000	By Yarn sales (2,40,000 lbs.)	2,70,000
To Stores used in spinning which increased yarn by 8,000 lbs. in weight	59,000	By Cloth sales (10,80,000 lbs.)	12,82,500
To Stores and sizing material used in weaving which increased Cloth by 2,66,000 lbs. in weight	2,12,000	By Closing Stock:	
		Yarn 2,00,000 lbs.	2,12,500
		Cloth 2,72,000 lbs.	3,06,000
To Spinning Fuel	51,500		
To Weaving Fuel	32,000		
To Gross Profit	82,500		
	21,11,000		21,11,000

In the above Manufacturing Account (where the Closing Stock of Yarn and Cloth is taken at actual cost) it is contended by the Income-Tax Officer that the closing stock is valued below cost price in order to suppress the gross profit actually made. For his satisfaction you are required to prepare from the above account a separate Yarn Production Account and a separate Cloth Production Account, showing the following details:

(*a*) Gross Profit
(*b*) Total Quantity produced (including opening balance)
(*c*) Total Cost of Production (including the opening stock which was valued at Cost) and
(*d*) Cost of production per lb. (including the quantity of the opening stock in total quantity and the cost of opening stock in the total cost).

In manufacturing Cloth 9,60,000 lbs. of Yarn was consumed which is to be adjusted at actual cost arrived at in the manner stated above.

Ans.	Gross Profit	Total Quantity Produced	Total Cost	Cost of Production per pound
Yarn A/c	Rs. 15,000	14,00,000	Rs. 14,87,500	Rs. 1.0625
Cloth A/c	Rs. 67,500	13,52,000	Rs. 15,21,000	Rs. 1.1249

38. The following are the balances of the Impersonal Ledger of a colliery relating to revenue at the at the end of the year:

	Rs.
Wages paid for coal production	5,80,000
Coal for colliery consumption	45,000
Timber used in coal production	64,000
Ropes used in coal production	12,000
Stores used in coal production	76,000
Royalties paid	42,000
General charges (for coal production)	70,000
Salaries	36,000
Coal sold (including colliery) 1,12,000 tonnes	8,84,000
Wages paid for coke making	50,000
Stores used for coke making	37,000
Salaries for coke making	8,000
Coke sold (43,500 tonnes)	5,40,000

The stock of coal at the beginning of the year amounted to 7,000 tonnes valued at Rs. 5 per tonne and at the end of the year 15,000 tonnes valued at the same rate. The stock of coke at the beginning of the year amounted to 2,000 tonnes valued at Rs. 10 per tonne and at end of the year 500 tonnes valued at the same rate.

The total production of the colliery was 1,85,000 tonnes of coal and 42,000 tonnes of coke, 65,000 tonnes of coal being used for coke making. Prepare separate Production Accounts for coal and coke, showing the cost of each item of expense per tonne of coal and coke respectively, taking coal used for coke making at cost price.

(B.Com. Delhi, M.Com. Agra)

[**Ans.** Coal per ton Rs. 5, Coke per ton Rs. 10)

39. The Empire Industries Ltd., manufacture a standard article in three qualities of which they produced during the year ending 31st March,2008 the following:

4,200 articles of quality X
4,800 articles of quality Y
6,500 articles of quality Z

The stocks of Finished Goods on 1st April 2007 were:
Quality X 200 articles, Quality Y 300 articles, Quality Z 100 articles.
Sales during the year were:
Quality X 4,000 articles at Rs. 12 each
Quality Y 5,000 articles at Rs. 8 each
Quality Z 6,000 articles at Rs. 4 each

and the following further figures were extracted from the company's books in respect of the year

	Rs.
Work-in-Progress on lst April, 2007	4,700
Work-in-Progress on 31st March, 2008	1,600
Cost of Raw Materials used in manufacture	26,000
Cost of stores used in manufacture	3,600
Manufacturing Wages	41,400
Depreciation (Works)	2,000
Works Oncost	10,000

Assuming the rate per cent of Gross Profit to be the same in the case of all three qualities, prepare accounts showing the Gross Profit on trading to be carried to the company's Profit and Loss Account for the year.

[**Ans.** Cost per unit
X – Rs. 9
Y – Rs. 6
Z – Rs. 3 Gross Profit = Rs. 28,000]

11

Single (or Output) Costing-II

(Calculation of Estimates, Tender Price and Quotation Price)

Very often a manufacturer is required to quote prices and submit tenders to a prospective customer. The receipt of orders depends on the acceptance of the quotation or tender submitted by the manufacturer. Tender or quotation price must be competitive. For calculating a competitive tender price, the manufacturer makes a careful analysis of the expenditure incurred during the period preceding the date of the submission of the tender. For this purpose each and every item of cost of production is considered separately and a proper analysis of indirect expenses into fixed, variable and semi-variable elements is made. Tender price or quotation price comprises the following:

(*a*) Cost of direct material required;
(*b*) Cost of direct labour and direct expenses to be paid;
(*c*) Amount of works overhead to be incurred;
(*d*) Amount of office overhead to be incurred;
(*e*) Amount of selling overhead to be incurred; and
(*f*) Estimated amount of profit to be made.

Calculation of direct material cost, direct wages and direct expenses for tender or quotation:

The direct material cost, direct labour cost and direct expenses per unit shall be the same as in the previous production period (as shown in the cost sheet for the previous period) since these items of cost, in the absence of any other information, are treated as variable. If any increase or decrease in the previous level of cost of these items is anticipated, the same shall be added to or deducted from the previous cost level.

Calculation of Factory Overhead for tender

(*i*) Fixed Factory Overhead:

Fixed amount of factory overhead shall be the same in aggregate as given in the previous period's cost sheet.

***(ii)* Variable Factory Overhead:**

(*a*) shall bear the same percentage on direct wages as in the previous period's cost sheet;

OR

(*b*) shall be the same amount per unit as in the previous period's cost sheet (+) or (–) expected increase or decrease.

Calculation of Office Overhead for Tender:

***(i)* Fixed Overhead:**

Fixed amount of office overhead shall be the same amount in aggregate as given in the previous period's cost sheet.

***(ii)* Variable Overhead:**

Variable overhead shall bear the same percentage on factory cost as in the previous period's cost sheet or shall be the same amount per unit as in the previous period's cost sheet

(+) or (–) expected increase or decrease.

Calculation of Selling and Distribution Overhead for Tender:

***(i)* Fixed Overhead:**

Fixed amount of selling and distribution overhead shall be the same amount in aggregate as given in the previous period's cost sheet.

***(ii)* Variable Overhead:**

Variable overhead shall bear the same percentage on factory cost (or any other given item) as in the previous period's cost sheet or shall be the same amount per unit as in the previous period's cost sheet

(+) or (–) expected increase or decrease.

Calculation of Profit for Tender:

In order to ascertain the tender price, a certain amount of profit, by way of a percentage (specifically given or calculated on the basis of previous period's cost sheet) on total cost or on selling price, is added to the total cost of the tender. The amount of profit to be added to the cost of the tender can be calculated as follows:

(*a*) If the amount of profit is a certain percentage on total cost:

$$\text{Profit} = \text{Total Cost} \times \frac{\text{Rate of Profit}}{100}$$

(*b*) If the amount of profit is a certain percentage of selling price or tender price:

$$\text{Profit} = \text{Total Cost} \times \frac{\text{Rate of Profit}}{100 - \text{Rate of Profit}}$$

Calculation of Percentage of different items of Overhead:

The following are the formulae to be applied to find out the percentage which the various items of overhead bear to a given item or basis:

(*i*) For percentage of Factory Overhead to Direct Wages –

$$\frac{\text{Factory Overhead}}{\text{Direct Wages}} \times 100$$

(*ii*) For percentage of Factory Overhead to Direct Materials Cost –

$$\frac{\text{Factory Overhead}}{\text{Direct Material Cost}} \times 100$$

(*iii*) For percentage of Factory Overhead to Prime Cost –

$$\frac{\text{Factory Overhead}}{\text{Prime Cost}} \times 100$$

(*iv*) For percentage of Office Overhead to Works Cost –

$$\frac{\text{Office Overhead}}{\text{Works Cost}} \times 100$$

(*v*) For percentage of Selling Overhead to Works Cost –

$$\frac{\text{Selling Overhead}}{\text{Works Cost}} \times 100$$

Type I. *When no instructions are given about tender:*

Illustration 1

The following figures relate to the costing of a manufacturer of electric fans of uniform size and quality for a period of three months ending 31st March, 2007:

	Rs.
Completed stock on 1.1.2007	Nil
Completed stock on 31.3.2007	20,000
Stock of Raw Materials (1.1.2007)	15,000
Stock of Raw Materials (31.3.2007)	5,000
Materials Purchased	65,000
Factory Wages	1,50,000
Indirect Expenses	35,000
Sales	3,00,000

The number of fans manufactured during three months was 5,000. Prepare a statement showing the cost per fan and the price to be quoted for 1,250 fans to realise the same percentage of profit as was realised during the three months referred to above, assuming identical costs.

Solution

Cost Sheet

Period: Three Months ending 31st March, 2007 — Output: 5,000 Fans

Particulars		Total Rs. P.	Per Fan Rs. P.
Raw Materials Consumed:			
Opening Stock of Raw Materials	15,000		
Add Purchases of Raw Materials	65,000		
	80,000		
Less: Closing Stock of Raw Materials	5,000	75,000	15.00
Factory Wages		1,50,000	30.00
Prime Cost		2,25,000	45.00
Indirect Expenses		35,000	7.00
Cost of Production		2,60,000	52.00
Less: Completed Stock on 31st March, 2007		20,000	
Cost of Goods sold		2,40,000	
Profit		60,000	
Sales		3,00,000	

Calculation of percentage of profit on cost:

$$= \frac{\text{Profit}}{\text{Cost of Goods Sold}} \times 100 = \frac{60,000}{2,40,000} \times 100 = 25\%$$

Statement Showing the Calculation of Tender Price for 1,250 Fans

	Amount Rs.
Raw Materials $\left(\frac{75,000}{5,000} \times 1,250\right)$	18,750
Factory Wages $\left(\frac{1,50,000}{5,000} \times 1,250\right)$	37,500
Prime Cost	56,250
Indirect Expenses $\left(\frac{35,000}{5,000} \times 1,250\right)$	8,750
Total Cost	65,000
Profit @ 25% on cost $\left(65,000 \times \frac{25}{100}\right)$	16,250
Tender Price	81,250

Alternatively, if indirect expenses to be charged to tender are based on direct wages:
Percentage of Indirect Expenses on Direct Wages:

$$= \frac{\text{Indirect Expenses}}{\text{Direct Wages}} \times 100$$

$$= \frac{35,000}{1,50,000} \times 100 = 23.333\%$$

Statement Showing the Calculation of Tender Price for 1,250 Fans

Particulars		Amount Rs.
Raw Materials $\left(\frac{75,000}{5,000}\times1,250\right)$		18,750
Factory Wages $\left(\frac{1,50,000}{5,000}\times1,250\right)$		37,500
	Prime Cost	56,250
Indirect Expenses @ 23.333 % on Direct Wages $\left(\frac{35,000\times23.333}{100}\right)$		8,750
	Total Cost	65,000
Profit @ 25% on cost $\left(65,000\times\frac{25}{100}\right)$		16,250
	Tender Price	81,250

Type II. *When there is a change in prices of materials and/or labour:*

Illustration 2

On 30th April, 2004, an Electric Meter Manufacturer desired to quote for a contract for the supply of 5,000 meters. From the following data prepare a statement showing the price to be quoted to give the same percentage of net profit on turnover as was realised during the six months to 31st March 2004:

	Rs.
Stock of Raw Materials (1st Oct., 2003)	50,000
Stock of Raw Materials (31st March, 2004)	7,000
Purchases of Raw Materials during the six months	75,000
Factory Wages for six months	1,50,000
Indirect Charges for six months	25,000
Sales for six months	2,70,000
Completed Stock (1st Oct., 2003)	Nil
Completed stock (31st March, 2004)	50,000

The number of meters manufactured during the six months was 6,000 including those in stock at the close of the period. The meters to be quoted for are of uniform size and quality and are similar to those manufactured during the six months to 31st March, 2004. As from 1st April, 2004, the cost of factory labour has increased by 10%.

(*G.N.D.U., B.Com., 1983 Modified*)

Solution

Cost Sheet

Period: Six months ended 31st March, 2004 — Output: 6,000 meters

Particulars		Total Rs. P.	Per Unit Rs. P.
Raw Materials consumed:			
Opening Stock of Raw Materials	50,000		
Add Purchases of Raw Materials	75,000		
	1,25,000		
Less Closing Stock of Raw Materials	7,000	1,18,000	19.67
Factory Wages		1,50,000	25.00
Prime Cost		2,68,000	44.67
Indirect Charges		25,000	4.17
Cost of Production		2,93,000	48.84
Less Completed Stock on 31st March, 2004		50,000	
Cost of Goods sold		2,43,000	
Profit		27,000	
Sales		2,70,000	

(*i*) Calculation of percentage of profit on Sales:

$$= \frac{\text{Profit}}{\text{Sales}} \times 100 = \frac{27{,}000}{2{,}70{,}000} \times 100 = 10\%$$

(*ii*) Calculation of percentage of indirect charges on factory wages:

$$= \frac{\text{Indirect Charges}}{\text{Factory Wages}} \times 100 = \frac{25{,}000}{1{,}50{,}000} \times 100 = 16.667\%$$

Statement showing the Calculation of Quotation Price for 5,000 Meters

Particulars		Rs.
Raw Materials $\left(\frac{1{,}18{,}000}{6{,}000} \times 5{,}000\right)$		98,333
Factory Wages $\left(\frac{1{,}50{,}000}{6{,}000} \times 5{,}000\right)$	= 1,25,000	
Add Increase @ 10%	= 12,500	1,37,500
Prime Cost		2,35,833
Indirect Charges @ 16.667% on Wages $\left(1{,}37{,}500 \times \frac{16.667}{100}\right)$		22,917
Cost of Production		2,58,750
Profit @ 10% on Sales $\left(2{,}58{,}750 \times \frac{10}{90}\right)$		28,750
Tender Price		2,87,500

Illustration 3

On 4th April, 2006 a manufacturer of bicycles was required to quote for a contract to supply 500 bicycles. From the following details, prepare a statement showing the price to be quoted to give the same percentage of profit on sales as was realised during the six months to 31st March, 2006:

	Rs.
Stock of Raw Materials on 1st Oct., 2005	1,00,000
Stock of Raw Materials on 31st March, 2006	14,000
Purchases of Materials during the six months	1,50,000
Factory Wages for six months	3,00,000
Indirect charges for six months	50,000
Stock of Finished Goods on 1st Oct., 2005	Nil
Stock of Finished Goods on 31st March, 2006	1,00,000
Sales	5,40,000

The number of bicycles manufactured during the six months was 2,000 including those in stock at the end of the period. The bicycles to be quoted are of uniform size and quality and similar to those manufactured during the six months to 31st March, 2006. As from 1st April, 2006, the cost of factory labour has increased by 10% and that of materials by 15%.

Solution

Cost Sheet

Period: Six months ended 31st March, 2006 Output: 2,000 Bicycles

Particulars		Total Rs. P.	Per Bicycle Rs. P.
Raw Materials Consumed:			
Opening Stock of Raw Materials	1,00,000		
Add Purchases of Raw Materials	1,50,000		
	2,50,000		
Less Closing Stock of Raw Materials	14,000	2,36,000	118.00
Factory Wages		3,00,000	150.00
Prime Cost		5,36,000	268.00
Indirect Charges		50,000	25.00
Cost of Production		5,86,000	293.00
Less Closing Stock of Finished Goods		1,00,000	
Cost of Goods Sold		4,86,000	
Profit		54,000	
Sales		5,40,000	

(*i*) Calculation of percentage of Profit on Sales

$$= \frac{\text{Profit}}{\text{Sales}} \times 100 = \frac{54,000}{5,40,000} \times 100 = 10\%$$

(*ii*) Calculation of percentage of Indirect Charges on Factory Wages:

$$= \frac{\text{Indirect Charges}}{\text{Factory Wages}} \times 100 = \frac{50,000}{3,00,000} \times 100 = 16.667\%$$

Statement Showing Quotation Price for 500 Bicycles

Particulars		Amount Rs.
Raw Materials $\left(\frac{2,36,000}{2,000}\times 500\right)$	59,000	
Add Increase @ 15%	8,850	67,850
Direct Wages $\left(\frac{3,00,000}{2,000}\times 500\right)$	75,000	
Add Increase @ 10%	7,500	82,500
Prime Cost		1,50,350
Indirect Charges @ 16.667% on Wages $\left(\frac{82,500\times 16.667}{100}\right)$		13,750
Cost of Production		1,64,100
Profit @ 10% on Selling Price $\left(1,64,100\times\frac{10}{90}\right)$		18,233
Quotation Price		1,82,333

Type III. *When number of units manufactured during the preceding period is not given but the amount of material and labour required for the tender is given without specifying the basis for calculating the amount of overhead for tender.*

In this case, for ascertaining tender price, factory overhead should be based on direct wages and office overhead on works cost.

Illustration 4

From the following information find out (*a*) the cost of raw materials consumed, (*b*) prime cost, (*c*) works cost and (*d*) total cost:

		Rs.
Stock of Raw Materials	(1st April, 2004)	30,000
Purchases of Raw Materials		7,50,000
Stock of Raw Materials	(31st March, 2005)	32,000
Productive Wages		6,00,000
Sales of Finished Goods		17,30,000
Works Overheads		1,20,000
Office Overheads		1,46,800

The company has to give a tender for the manufacture of a machine in 2005. The costing department estimates that the material required would cost Rs. 40,000 and direct wages would cost Rs. 50,000. The tender is to be made at a profit of 20% on the selling price. Show the calculation of the tender price.

Solution

Statement of Cost

Period: Six months ended 31st March, 2005

Particulars	Amount Rs.	Amount Rs.
Raw Materials Consumed:		
Opening Stock of Raw Materials	30,000	
Add Purchases of Raw Materials	7,50,000	
	7,80,000	
Less Closing Stock of Raw Materials	32,000	7,48,000
Direct Wages		6,00,000
Prime Cost		13,48,000
Works Overhead		1,20,000
Works Cost		14,68,000
Office Overhead		1,46,800
Cost of Production		16,14,800
Profit		1,15,200
Sales		17,30,000

(*i*) Calculation of Percentage of Works Overhead to Direct Wages:

$$= \frac{\text{Works Overhead}}{\text{Direct Wages}} \times 100 = \frac{1,20,000}{6,00,000} \times 100 = 20\%$$

(*ii*) Calculation of Percentage of Office Overhead to Works Cost:

$$= \frac{\text{Office Overhead}}{\text{Works Cost}} \times 100 = \frac{1,46,800}{14,68,000} \times 100 = 10\%$$

Statement Showing the Calculation of Tender Price of Machine

Particulars	Amount Rs.
Materials	40,000
Direct Wages	50,000
Prime Cost	90,000
Works Oncost @ 20% on Direct Wages $\left(50,000 \times \frac{20}{100}\right)$	10,000
Works Cost	1,00,000
Office Oncost @ 10% on Works Cost $\left(1,00,000 \times \frac{10}{100}\right)$	10,000
Total Cost	1,10,000
Profit @ 20% on Selling Price $\left(1,10,000 \times \frac{20}{100-20}\right)$	27,500
Tender Price	1,37,500

Type IV. *When the amount of material and labour required for the tender and basis for recovery of overheads are given.*

Illustration 5

From the following particulars, you are required to prepare the statement showing:

(*a*) The Cost of Materials Consumed, (*b*) Prime Cost, (*c*) Works Cost, (*d*) Total Cost, (*e*) The Percentage of Works Oncost to Productive Wages and (*f*) The Percentage of General Oncost to Works Cost:

	Rs.
Stock of Finished Goods – 1.4.2005	72,800
Stock of Raw Materials – 1.4.2005	33,280
Purchases of Raw Materials	7,59,200
Productive Wages	5,16,880
Sales of Finished Goods	15,39,200
Stock of Finished Goods – 31.3.2006	78,000
Stock of Raw Materials – 31.3.2006	35,360
Works Overhead Charges	1,29,220
Office & General Expenses	70,161

The company is about to send tender for a large plant. The costing department estimates that the materials required would cost Rs. 52,000 and the wages to workmen for making the plant would cost Rs. 31,200. The tender is to be made at a profit of 20% on selling price. Show what the amount of the tender would be if based on the above percentages.

Solution

Statement of Cost

Particulars	Amount Rs.
Raw Materials (Opening Stock on 1.4.2005)	33,280
Add Raw Materials Purchased	7,59,200
	7,92,480
Less Raw Materials (Closing Stock on 31.3.2006)	35,360
(*a*) Cost of Materials Consumed	7,57,120
Productive Wages	5,16,880
(*b*) Prime Cost	12,74,000
Works Overhead Charges	1,29,220
(*c*) Works Cost	14,03,220
Office & General Expenses	70,161
(*d*) Total Cost	14,73,381

(*e*) Percentage of Works Oncost to Productive Wages

$$= \frac{\text{Works Oncost}}{\text{Productive Wages}} \times 100$$

$$= \frac{1,29,220}{5,16,880} \times 100 = 25\%$$

(*f*) Percentage of General Oncost to Works Cost

$$= \frac{\text{General Oncost}}{\text{Works Cost}} \times 100$$

$$= \frac{70{,}161}{14{,}03{,}220} \times 100 = 5\%$$

Tender for Large Plant

	Rs.
Raw Materials	52,000
Wages	31,200
Prime Cost	83,200
Works Oncost (25% on Wages)	7,800
Works Cost	91,000
General Oncost (5 % of Works Cost)	4,550
Total Cost	95,550
Profit @ 20% on Selling Price $\left(95{,}550 \times \frac{20}{80}\right)$	23,888
Tender Price	1,19,438

Illustration 6

In respect of a factory the following figures have been obtained for the year ended 31st March, 2006:

	Rs.
Cost of Materials	6,00,000
Wages for Labour	5,00,000
Factory Overhead	3,00,000
Administrative Charges	3,36,000
Selling Charges	2,24,000
Distribution Charges	1,40,000
Profit	4,20,000

A work order has been executed in 2006-07 and the following expenses have been incurred:

	Rs.
Materials	8,000
Wages of Labour	5,000

Assuming that during 2006-07 the rate of Factory Overhead has gone up by 20%, Distribution Charges have gone down by 10% and Selling and Administration Charges have each gone up by 12½%, at what price should the product be sold so as to earn the same rate of profit on the Selling Price as in 2005-06.

Factory Overhead is based upon Direct Labour and Administration, Selling and Distribution Overhead on Factory Cost.

(*G.N.D.U., B.Com. 1978, 1983*)

Solution

Statement of Cost for the year Ended 31st March, 2006

Particulars		Amount
		Rs.
Materials Consumed		6,00,000
Direct Labour		5,00,000
	Prime Cost	11,00,000
Factory Overhead		3,00,000
	Factory Cost	14,00,000
Administration Charges		3,36,000
	Office Cost	17,36,000
Selling Charges		2,24,000
Distribution Charges		1,40,000
	Total Cost	21,00,000
	Profit	4,20,000
	Sales	25,20,000

(*a*) Percentage of Factory Overhead on Direct Labour

$$= \frac{3,00,000}{5,00,000} \times 100 = 60\%$$

(*b*) Percentage of Administration Charges on Factory Cost

$$= \frac{3,36,000}{14,00,000} \times 100 = 24\%$$

(*c*) Percentage of Selling Charges on Factory Cost

$$= \frac{2,24,000}{14,00,000} \times 100 = 16\%$$

(*d*) Percentage of Distribution Charges on Factory Cost

$$= \frac{1,40,000}{14,00,000} \times 100 = 10\%$$

(*e*) Percentage of Profit on Selling Price

$$= \frac{4,20,000}{25,20,000} \times 100 = 16.67\%$$

Estimate for the Work Order

	Rs.	Rs.
Materials		8,000
Wages		5,000
Prime Cost		13,000
	Rs.	
Factory Overhead (60% on Wages)	3,000	
Add 20% Increase	600	
		3,600
Factory Cost		16,600
Administration Charges (24% on Factory Cost)	3,984	
Add 12½% increase	498	4,482
Office Cost		21,082
Selling Charges (16% on Factory Cost)	2,656	
Add 12½%, increase	332	2,988
Distribution Charges (10% on Factory Cost)	1,660	
Less 10% decrease	166	1,494
Total Cost		25,564
Add Profit @ 16.67% on the Selling Price $\left\{25{,}564\times\frac{16.67}{(100-16.67)}\right\}$ or $\left(25{,}564\times\frac{16.67}{83.33}\right)$		5,114
Selling Price		30,678

Type V. *When*

(*i*) *The number of units manufactured during the preceding year,*

(*ii*) *The number of units to be manufactured, and*

(*iii*) *The nature and various classes of overhead, are given.*

Illustration 7

The Bharat Cooling Manufacturers Ltd., manufactured and sold 1,000 coolers during the year ending 31st March, 2006. The summarised Trading and Profit and Loss Account is set out below:

Trading and Profit and Loss Account
for the year ending 31st March, 2006

	Rs.		Rs.
To Cost of Materials	80,000	By Sales	4,00,000
To Direct Wages	1,20,000		
To Manufacturing Costs	50,000		
To Gross Profit c/d	1,50,000		
	4,00,000		4,00,000
		By Gross Profit b/d	1,50,000
To Management and Staff Salaries	60,000		
To Rent, Rates and Insurance	10,000		
To Selling Expenses	30,000		
To General Expenses	20,000		
To Net Profit	30,000		
	1,50,000		1,50,000

For the year ending 31st March, 2007, it is estimated that:

(*a*) Output and Sales will be 1,200 coolers;

(*b*) Price of materials will rise by 20% on the previous year's level;

(*c*) Wages will rise by 5%;

(*d*) Manufacturing cost will rise in proportion to the combined cost of Materials and Wages;

(*e*) Selling costs per unit will remain unchanged;

(*f*) Other expenses will remain unaffected by the rise in output.

Prepare a cost statement, showing the price at which the coolers will be marketed so as to show a profit of 10% on the selling price.

(Agra, M.Com., I.A.S., Punjab. B.Com.)
(G.N.D.U., B.Com., 1978, 2006)

Solution

Cost Sheet

Period: Year Ending 31st March, 2006 — Output: 1,000 Coolers

Particulars	Total Rs. P.	Per Unit Rs. P.
Material	80,000	80
Direct Wages	1,20,000	120
Prime Cost	2,00,000	200
Manufacturing Costs	50,000	50
Works Cost	2,50,000	250
Office Overheads:		
Management and Staff Salaries	60,000	60
Rent, Rates and Insurance	10,000	10
General Expenses	20,000	20
Cost of Production	3,40,000	340
Selling Expenses	30,000	30
Total Cost	3,70,000	370
Profit	30,000	30
Sales	4,00,000	400

Calculation of percentage of Manufacturing Costs on Materials and Wages

(*i.e.*, on Prime Cost) = $\frac{50,000}{2,00,000} \times 100 = 25\%$

Statement Showing the Estimated Selling Price of 1,200 Coolers

Particulars		Total Rs. P.	Per Unit Rs. P.
Materials $\left(\frac{80,000}{1,000} \times 1,200\right)$	96,000		
Add Increase @ 20%	19,200	1,15,200	96.00
Direct Wages: $\left(\frac{1,20,000}{1,000} \times 1,200\right)$	1,44,000		
Add Increase @ 5%	7,200	1,51,200	126.00
Prime Cost		2,66,400	222.00
Manufacturing Costs @ 25% on Prime Cost		66,600	55.50
Works Cost		3,33,000	277.50
Office Overheads:			
Management and Staff Salaries		60,000	50.00
Rent, Rates and Insurance		10,000	8.33
General Expenses		20,000	16.67
Cost of Production		4,23,000	352.50
Selling Overheads (Variable)		36,000	30.00
Total Cost		4,59,000	382.50
Profit @ 10% on Selling Price $\left(\frac{4,59,000 \times 10}{100-10}\right)$		51,000	42.50
Selling Price		5,10,000	425.00

Type VI. *Miscellaneous Problems*:

Illustration 8

Following are the particulars for the production of 2,000 sewing machines of Datta Engineering Co. Ltd., for the year ended 31.3.2006.

Cost of Materials Rs. 1,60,000; Wages Rs. 2,40,000; Manufacturing Expenses Rs. 1,00,000; Salaries Rs, 1,20,000; Rent, Rates and Insurance Rs. 20,000; Selling expenses Rs. 60,000; General expenses Rs. 40,000; Sales Rs. 8,00,000.

The company plans to manufacture 3,000 sewing machines during 2006-07. You are required to submit a statement showing the price at which machines would be sold so as to show a profit of 10% of the selling price. The following additional information is supplied to you:

(*a*) Price of materials will rise by 20% over the previous year's level.
(*b*) Wages rates are expected to show an increase of 5%.
(*c*) Manufacturing expenses will rise in proportion to the combined cost of materials and wages.
(*d*) Selling expenses per unit will remain the same.
(*e*) Other expenses will remain unaffected by the rise in the output.

(*M.D. University, B.Com. 1993*)

Solution

Cost Sheet

Period: 2005-06 (Output: 2,000 units)

Particulars		Total Rs.	Per Unit Rs.
Direct Materials		1,60,000	80
Direct Wages		2,40,000	120
Prime Cost		4,00,000	200
Manufacturing Expenses		1,00,000	50
Factory Cost		5,00,000	250
Office Expenses:			
Salaries	1,20,000		
Rent, Rates & Insurance	20,000		
General Expenses	40,000	1,80,000	90
Cost of Production		6,80,000	340
Selling Expenses		60,000	30
Total Cost		7,40,000	370
Profit		60,000	30
Sales		8,00,000	400

(*i*) Percentage of Manufacturing Expenses to cost of Materials and Direct Wages = 25%.

(*ii*) Selling expenses per unit = Rs. 30.

Statement Showing the Estimated Cost of 3,000 Machines

Particulars		Total Rs.	Per Unit Rs.
Direct Materials:			
(3,000 × Rs. 80)	2,40,000		
Add increase @ 20%	48,000		
		2,88,000	96.00
Direct Wages:			
(3,000 × Rs. 120)	3,60,000		
Add increase @ 5%	18,000		
		3,78,000	126.00
Prime Cost		6,66,000	222.00
Manufacturing Expenses @ 25% of Prime Cost (25% of Rs. 6,66,000)		1,66,500	55.50
Factory Cost		8,32,500	277.50
Office Expenses:			
Salaries	1,20,000		
Rent, Rates etc.	20,000		
General Expenses	40,000		
		1,80,000	60.00
Cost of Production		10,12,500	337.50
Selling Expenses		90,000	30.00
Total Cost		11,02,500	367.50
Profit @ 10% on Selling Price		1,22,500	40.83
Selling Price		12,25,000	408.33

Illustration 9

A manufacturer finds that an advance in the cost of production has taken place and that, whereas formerly his goods cost Raw Materials 30%, Wages 20%, Rent, Rates etc. 5%, Fuel 10%, General Expenses 15%, now there has been an increase of 50% in fuel, 30% in materials, 25% in wages and 20% in Rent and Rates etc.

He consults you as to what percentage he must add to the selling price in order to obtain the same profit. What would be the results of your calculations and how would you prove to him that they were correct?

(*M.D.U. B.Com., 2001*)

(*Agra. B.Com., Ranchi, B.Com.*)

Solution

Assuming the selling price of the commodity to be Rs. 100, the cost of production and profit (before increase in the cost of production) has been as follows:

	Rs.
Raw Materials	30
Wages	20
Fuel	10
Rent and Rates	5
General Expenses	15
Total Cost	80
Profit @ 25% on Cost	20
Selling Price	100

Since an advance in the cost of production has taken place, the position will be as follows:

Particulars		Amount
		Rs.
Raw Materials	30	
Add increase @ 30%	9	39
Wages	20	
Add increase @ 25%	5	25
Fuel	10	
Add increase @ 50%	5	15
Rent and Rates	5	
Add increase @ 20%	1	6
General Expenses		15
Total Cost		100
Add Profit @ 25% on Cost		25
Selling Price		125

It is clear that selling price must be increased by 25% in order to obtain the same percentage of profit as was earned before the increase in the cost of production.

Illustration 10

The cost of manufacturing 5,000 units of a commodity comprises:

Materials Rs. 20,000, Wages Rs. 25,000, Chargeable Expenses Rs. 400, Fixed Overhead Rs. 16,000, Variable Overhead Rs. 4,000.

For manufacturing every 1,000 extra units of the commodity, the cost of production increases as follows:

Materials : Proportionately.
Wages : 10% less than proportionately.
Chargeable Expenses : No extra cost.
Fixed Overheads : Rs. 200 extra.
Variable Overheads : 25% less than proportionately.

Calculate the estimated cost of production of 8,000 units of the commodity and show by how much it would differ if a flat rate of factory overhead based on wages were charged. (*Agra, M.Com. 1989*)

Solution

Statement of Cost

Particulars	5,000 Units	3,000 units	8,000 units
	Rs.	**Rs.**	**Rs.**
Materials	20,000	12,000	32,000
Wages	25,000	13,500	38,500
Chargeable Expenses	400	–	400
Prime Cost	45,400	25,500	70,900
Factory Overheads:			
Fixed	16,000	600	16,600
Variable	4,000	1,800	5,800
Cost of Production	65,400	27,900	93,300

Calculation of Flat Rate of factory overheads on direct wages:

$$= \frac{20{,}000 \text{ (Total Factory Overheads)}}{25{,}000 \text{ (Direct Wages)}} \times 100$$

= 80% on Wages

Cost of production of 8,000 units if factory expenses are charged at flat rate:

	Rs.
Materials	32,000
Wages	38,500
Chargeable Expenses	400
Prime Cost	70,900
Factory Overheads @ 80% on Wages	30,800
Cost of Production	1,01,700

Cost of production would differ by Rs. 8,400 (Rs. 1,01,700 – Rs. 93,300) if factory overheads are charged at a flat rate based on wages.

Illustration 11

Janta Fans Ltd., produces a pedestal fan that sells for Rs. 650 per piece. The only figures available are that:

(*a*) Material costs so far have been 50% of cost of sales;

(*b*) Labour costs have been 40% of cost of sales; and

(*c*) Overhead costs have been 10% of cost of sales.

An increase of 15% in cost of materials, of 10% in cost of labour and of 5% in overhead costs is anticipated next year which would cause a 40% reduction in the amount of present gross profit if the present selling price is maintained.

Prepare a Cost Sheet showing the new as well as old cost per unit and also calculate next year's Selling Price if the management wants the same percentage of gross profit as before. *(G.N.D.U., B.Com., 1976)*

Solution

Selling Price = Rs. 650

Let us assume that the Cost of Sales = x

Then:

Particulars	Present Conditions	Anticipated Conditions
Material	$.5\ x$	$.575\ x$
Labour	$.4\ x$	$.440\ x$
Overhead	$.1\ x$	$.105\ x$
Total cost	x	$1.12\ x$
Profit (Sales – Total Cost):	$(650 - x)$	$(650 - 1.12\ x)$

It should be remembered that if there is no change in the selling price per unit, any increase in total cost would cause a corresponding decrease in the amount of profit.

In the problem, it is given that if the present selling price is maintained, the anticipated increase in cost would lead to a reduction of 40% in the amount of present profit.

Hence:

Anticipated increase in cost = 40% of present profit

or $(650 - x) - (650 - 1.12\ x) = 40\%$ of $(650 - x)$

or
$$-x + 1.12\ x = 260 - .4\ x$$
$$-x + 1.12\ x + .4\ x = 260$$
$$.52\ x = 260$$
$$x = 500$$

Hence present cost per unit = Rs. 500

Cost Sheet

Particulars		Present Conditions	Anticipated Selling Price Unchanged	Conditions Selling Price Increased
		Rs. P.	Rs. P.	Rs. P.
Materials		250.00	287.50	287.50
Labour Cost		200.00	220.00	220.00
	Prime Cost	450.00	507.50	507.50
Overhead		50.00	52.50	52.50
	Total Cost	500.00	560.00	560.00
	Profit	150.00	90.00	168.00 (30% on Cost)
	Selling Price	650.00	650.00	728.00

Illustration 12

The managing director of a small manufacturing concern consults you as to the minimum price at which he can sell the output of one of the departments of the company which is intended for mass production in future. The company's records show the following particulars for this deparment for the last year:

Production and Sales	100 Units
	Rs.
Materials	13,000
Direct Labour	7,000
Direct Charges	1,000
Works Oncost	7,000
Office Oncost	2,800
Selling Oncost	3,200
Profit	5,000
	39,000

You ascertain that 40% of the works oncost fluctuates directly with production and 70% of the selling oncost fluctuates with sales. It is anticipated that the department would produce 500 units per annum and that direct labour charges per unit will be reduced by 20%, while fixed works oncost charges will increase by Rs. 3,000. Office oncost and fixed selling oncost charges are expected to show an increase of 25% but otherwise no changes are anticipated.

Prepare a statement for submission to your client.

(Agra, M.Com., G.N.D.U., April 1980, Sept. 1980)
(K.U.K., B.Com. 2007)

Solution

Statement of Cost of 100 Units

Particulars	Total Rs.	Per Unit Rs. P.
Materials	13,000	130.00
Direct Labour	7,000	70.00
Direct Charges	1,000	10.00
Prime Cost	21,000	210.00
Works Oncost:		
Variable (40%)	2,800	28.00
Fixed (60%)	4,200	42.00
Works Cost	28,000	280.00
Office Oncost:	2,800	28.00
Office Cost	30,800	308.00
Selling Oncost:		
Variable (70%)	2,240	22.40
Fixed (30%)	960	9.60
Total Cost	34,000	340.00
Profit	5,000	50.00
Selling Price	39,000	390.00

$$\text{Calculation of Percentage of Profit on Total Cost} = \frac{\text{Profit}}{\text{Total Cost}} \times 100$$

$$= \frac{5,000}{34,000} \times 100 = 14.706\%$$

Statement Showing the Estimated Selling Price of 500 Units

Particulars	Rs.	Total Rs.	Per Unit Rs. P.
Materials (500 units × Rs. 130)		65,000	130.00
Direct Labour (500 units × Rs. 70)	35,000		
Less Decrease @ 20%	7,000	28,000	56.00
Direct Charges		5,000	10.00
Prime Cost		98,000	196.00
Works Oncost:			
Variable (500 units × Rs.28)		14,000	28.00
Fixed	4,200		
Add Increase	3,000	7,200	14.40
Works Cost		1,19,200	238.40
Office Oncost:	2,800		
Add Increase @ 25%	700	3,500	7.00
Office Cost		1,22,700	245.40
Selling Oncost:			
Variable (500 units × Rs. 22.40)		11,200	22.40
Fixed	960		
Add Increase @ 25%	240	1,200	2.40
Total Cost		1,35,100	270.20
Profit @ 14.706% on Cost		19,860	39.72
Selling Price		1,54,960	309.92

Illustration 13

A factory's normal capacity is 1,20,000 units per annum. The estimated costs of production are as under:

Direct Material	Rs. 3.00 per unit
Direct Labour	Rs. 2.00 per unit (Subject to a minimum of Rs. 12,000 per month)
Indirect Expenses:	
Fixed	Rs. 1,60,000 per annum
Variable	Rs. 2.00 per unit
Semi-variable	Rs. 60,000 per annum upto 50% capacity and extra Rs. 20,000 for every 20% increase in capacity or a part thereof.

Each unit of raw material yields scrap which is sold at 20 paise. In 2005-06, the factory worked at 50% capacity for first three months, but it was expected to work at 80% capacity for the remaining 9 months. During the first three months, the selling price per unit was Rs. 12. What should be the selling price per unit in the remaining 9 months to earn a total profit of Rs. 2,18,000?

(G.N.D.U., B.Com., 1981 Modified)

Solution

Statement of Cost and Selling Price

(Normal Capacity: 1,20,000 units per annum or 10,000 units per month)

Particulars	First 3 months (50% capacity 15,000 units)	Last 9 months (80% capacity 72,000 units)	Total (87,000 units)
	Rs.	Rs.	Rs.
Direct Materials @ Rs. 3 per unit	45,000	2,16,000	2,61,000
Less Sale of Scrap @ 20 Paise per unit	3,000	14,400	17,400
	42,000	2,01,600	2,43,600
Direct Labour @ Rs. 2 per unit (Subject to a minimum of Rs. 12,000 p.m.)	36,000	1,44,000	1,80,000
Prime Cost	78,000	3,45,600	4,23,600
Indirect Expenses:			
(*i*) Fixed: Rs. 1,60,000 p.a.	40,000	1,20,000	1,60,000
(*ii*) Variable: @ Rs. 2 per unit	30,000	1,44,000	1,74,000
(*iii*) Semi-Variable	15,000	75,000	90,000
(*a*) First 3 months @ Rs. 60,000 p.a. or Rs. 5,000 p.m. upto 50% capacity			
(*b*) Last 9 months: (Rs. 60,000 + Rs. 20,000 + Rs. 20,000 × $\frac{9}{12}$)			
Cost of Production	1,63,000	6,84,600	8,47,600
Profit	17,000	2,01,000	2,18,000
Selling Price	1,80,000 @ Rs. 12 per unit	8,85,600 @ Rs. 12.30 (approx.)	10,65,600

Notes: (*i*) For the purpose of sale of scrap, it has been assumed that quantity of raw material is equal to the quantity of the output.

(*ii*) Output for the first three months has already been sold @ Rs. 12 per unit giving a profit of Rs. 17,000.

(*iii*) Profit to be made during the remaining 9 months of the year is Rs. 2,01,000 (Rs. 2,18,000 – Rs. 17,000 already made).

(*iv*) Calculation of Selling Price per unit for the remaining 9 months of the year has been made as follows:

Cost of 72,000 units = Rs. 6,84,600
Add Profit required = Rs. 2,01,000
Total Sales Required = Rs. 8,85,600

$$\text{Selling Price per unit} = \frac{\text{Rs. } 8,85,600}{72,000 \text{ units}} = \text{Rs. } 12.30.$$

Illustration 14

Following is the schedule of expenses incurred during three months ending on 31st March, 2006 in Modern Chemical Co.

		Rs.
Direct Materials		18,900
Labour Cost		19,000
Direct Expenses		5,100
Overheads:		
Fixed	6,200	
Variable @ Rs. 4 per unit	4,800	11,000
Units produced:	1,200 Units	
Sales (@ Rs. 50 per unit)	Rs. 60,000	

Find out (*i*) Total cost of production (*ii*) % of Profit on Sale (*iii*) Estimated price of commodity if 2,000 units were produced during the next quarter ending on 30th June, 2006.

Solution

Statement of Cost and Profit

For the quarter ending on 31st March, 2006

Particulars		Cost of 1,200 units	Cost of one unit
		Rs.	Rs.
Direct Materials		18,900	15.75
Labour Cost		19,000	15.83
Direct Expenses		5,100	4.25
Prime Cost		43,000	35.83
Overheads:			
Fixed	6,200		
Variable	4,800		
		11,000	9.17
Cost of Production		54,000	45.00
Profit (@ 10% on Sales)		6,000	5.00
Sales		60,000	50.00

Statement Showing the Estimated Cost of 2,000 Units

Particulars		Cost of 2,000 units	Cost of one unit
		Rs.	Rs.
Direct Material		31,500	15.75
Labour		31,660	15.83
Direct Expenses		8,500	4.25
Prime Cost		71,660	35.83
Overheads			
Fixed	6,200		
Variable	8,000	14,200	7.10
Cost of Production		85,860	42.93
Profit @10% on Sales		9,540	4.77
Sales		95,400	47.70

Illustration 15

'A' Commodity is manufactured in a factory. The factory has a capacity of producing 2,500 units per week. From the following information related to 4 weeks, state as to what will be the selling price per unit if 2,000 units are produced in one week. The company charges profit @ 12.5% on selling price.

	Per week Production units	Direct Materials	Direct Labour	Works Oncost	Office Oncost
	Rs.		Rs.	Rs.	Rs.
I Week	800	2,400	4,000	6,400	3,840
II Week	1,000	3,000	5,000	7,000	4,500
III Week	1,500	4,500	7,500	8,500	6,150
IV Week	1,800	5,400	9,000	9,400	7,140

Solution

If we make a careful analysis of the information given above, the following facts shall be revealed:

(*a*) The material cost has shown a proportionate increase *i.e.*, Rs. 3 per unit.

(*b*) Labour cost varies proportionately *i.e.*, Rs. 5 per unit.

(*c*) Works oncost includes fixed as well as variable elements. Generally, works oncost is dependent on labour cost. Fixed works oncost will remain fixed while variable will vary according to production.

Works oncost at 800 units is Rs. 6,400, whereas, at 1,000 units it is Rs. 7,000. Thus there is an increase of Rs. 600 for an increase of 200 units. Similarly works oncost at 1,500 units is Rs. 8,500 and at 1,800 units Rs. 9,400, thereby showing an increase of Rs. 1,500 as against an increase of 500 units and further an increase of Rs. 900 against the increase in output of 300 units. It is clear that every unit of commodity shows an increase of Rs. 3. Thus, variable works oncost is Rs. 2,400; 3,000; 4,500 and 5,400 in all the 4 weeks. As such fixed works oncost is Rs. 6,400 – 2,400 = 4,000; Rs. 7,000 – 3,000 = 4,000; Rs. 8,500 – 4,500 = 4,000; Rs. 9,400 – 5,400 = 4,000.

Thus, fixed works oncost = Rs. 4,000 and variable oncost = Rs. 3 per unit or 60% of labour.

(*d*) Office oncost will be based on Works Cost.

	Works Cost	Office Oncost	Percentage of Office Oncost on works cost
	Rs.	Rs.	
I Week	12,800	3,840	30%
II Week	15,000	4,500	30%
III Week	20,500	6,150	30%
IV Week	23,800	7,140	30%

Thus, office oncost is 30% of Works Cost.

Statement of Cost

Output: 2,000 units

Particulars		Per unit Rs. P.	Total Rs. P.
Direct Material		3.00	6,000
Direct Labour		5.00	10,000
Prime Cost		8.00	16,000
Works Oncost:			
Fixed	4,000		
Variable (@ Rs. 3 per unit)	6,000		
		5.00	10,000
Works Cost		13.00	26,000
Office Oncost @ 30% of Works Cost		3.90	7,800
Cost of Production		16.90	33,800
Profit @ 12.5% on Sales $\left(\frac{\text{Cost} \times \text{Rate}}{100 - \text{Rate}}\right)$		2.41	4,829
Selling Price		19.31	38,629

EXERCISES

1. The following figures relate to the costing of the manufacturers of electric fans (of one uniform quality) for the period of three months:

	Rs.
Completed stock on 1st Jan., 2006	Nil
Completed stock on 31st March, 2006	20,250
Stock of Raw Material – 31st March, 2006	3,500
Stock of Raw Material – 1st Jan., 2006	5,000
Factory Wages	75,000
Indirect Charges	12,500
Material Purchased	32,500
Sales	1,12,590

The number of fans manufactured during the three months was 3,000. Prepare a statement showing the cost per fan and the price to be quoted for 750 fans to realise the same percentage of profit as was realised during the three months referred to above, assuming identical costs.

(B.Com., Punjab 1966 – Year changed)

[**Ans.** Cost per fan Rs. 40.60, Quotation price of 750 fans, Rs. 33,777]

2. The following figures relate to the costing of a tarpaulin in respect of a certain type of sheet for a period of three months.

	Rs.
Stock of Raw Materials – 1st January	5,500
Stock of Raw Materials – 31st March	3,500
Factory Wages	83,000
Material Purchased	61,500
Sales	1,41,000
Indirect Expenses	13,000
Completed stock – 1st January	Nil
Completed stock – 31st March	29,000

The number of sheets manufactured during the three months was 2,200 and the price was to be quoted for 648 sheets in order to realise the percentage of profit as for the period under review assuming no alteration in the rates of wages and cost of materials.

Prepare the statement of cost for the manufacture of 2,200 sheets and quotation for 648 sheets.

(Punjab, B.Com., Agra, B.Com)

[**Ans.** Cost of 2,200 Sheets Rs. 1,19,500
Price of 648 Sheets Rs. 50,760
Rate of Profit on cost 8.046%]

3. On 30th April, 2007 a manufacturer was required to quote for a contract to supply 1,000 Electric Stoves. From the following data, prepare the statement showing the price to be quoted to give the same percentage of net profit on turnover as was realised during the six months to 31st March, 2007:

	Rs.
Stock of Materials, 1st October, 2006	35,000
Stock of Materials, 31st March, 2007	4,900
Purchases of Materials, six months to 31st March, 2007	52,500
Factory Wages	95,000
Factory Expenses	17,500
Establishment Expenses	10,000
Completed Stock in hand, 1st October, 2006	Nil
Completed Stock in hand, 31st March, 2007	35,000
Sales	1,89,000

The number of stoves manufactured during the six months was 4,000 including those sold and those in stock at the close of the period. The stoves to be quoted are of uniform quality and make and similar to those manufactured during the six months to 31st March, 2007. As from 1st April, 2007, the cost of factory labour has increased by 10% and material cost by 15%.

(Punjab Univ., B.Com., 2007)
(Agra, M.Com. 1963, H.P. University, B.Com., 1996)

[**Ans.** Cost of 4,000 Stoves Rs. 2,05,100. Tender Price Rs. 63,874.78 by charging Factory Expenses on the basis of Direct Wages and Establishment expenses on the basis of Factory Cost)

4. The following informations are extracted firm the books of a Blanket manufacturer who intends to quote for the supply of 5,000 Blankets. Prepare a statement showing what price he should quote so that he may get the same percentage of net profit on turnover which he got during the last year for which the particulars are given.

	Rs.
Stock of Materials on 1st April, 2006	1,00,000
Materials purchased during the year	1,50,000
Factory Wages	3,00,000
Indirect Expenses	50,000
Sales	5,40,000
Stock of Materials, 31st March, 2007	14,000
Completed Stock in hand on 1st April, 2006	Nil
Completed Stock in hand on 31st March, 2007 (2,047 Nos. of Blankets)	1,00,000
Output during the year (Blankets)	12,000

Provision has to be made in the estimate for the expected increase of 10% in the Cost of Factory Labour and 5% in the Material Cost.

[**Ans.** Cost of 12,000 blankets Rs. 5,86,000, Tender Price Rs. 2,92,963 by charging Indirect Expenses @ 16.667% on Wages)

5. The accounts of 'T' Products Ltd., who are engaged in the manufacture of electric pumps, show for 2005-06:

Materials used	Rs. 1,00,000
Direct Wages	Rs. 2,00,000
Works Overhead Expenses	Rs. 50,000
Office Overhead Expenses	Rs. 35,000

Show the Prime Cost, the Works Cost and the Total Cost of manufacture, the percentage that the works overhead expenses bear to the direct wages and the percentage that office overhead expenses bear to the works cost.

What price should the company quote to manufacture an electric pump which, it is estimated will require material worth Rs. 800 and Rs. 1,000 for wages, so that it will yield a profit of 10 percent on the selling price?

(*Meerut, B.Com. B.H.U., B.Com., Agra, B.Com., G.N.D.U., B.Com., 1991*)

[**Ans.** Prime Cost Rs. 3,00,000, Works Cost Rs. 3,50,000, Total Cost Rs. 3,85,000; Percentages – 25% and 10% respectively)

6. The accounts of a machine manufacturing company disclose the following information for the six months ending 31st March, 2006:

	Rs.
Material used	1,50,000
Productive Wages	1,20,000
Factory Overhead Expenses	24,000
Administrative Expenses	17,640

Prepare the cost sheet of the machines and calculate the price which the company should quote for the manufacture of a machine requiring the materials valued at Rs. 1,250 and expenditure in productive wages of Rs. 750 so that the price may yield a profit of 20% of the selling price.

(*B.Com., Delhi*) [**Ans.** Rs. 2,848.75]

7. You are given the following details of expenses incurred during three months ending on 31st March, 2007 in the Standard Plastic Manufacturing & Co.

		Rs.
Raw Material		5,000
Direct Wages		6,000
Direct Expenses		1,000
Overheads:		
Fixed	2,000	
Variable @ Rs. 3 per unit	3,000	5,000
Units Produced		1,000 units
Sales		Rs. 20,000

Find out (*i*) total cost of production, (*ii*) percentage of profit on sales and (*iii*) estimated cost of a commodity if 500 units were produced during the next three months ending on 30th June, 2007.

(*G.N.D.U., B.Com. 1992*)

[**Ans.** (*i*) Rs.17,000 (*ii*) 15% (*iii*) Rs. 9,500]

8. A manufacturer of scooters finds that in 2005-06, it cost him Rs. 6,16,000 to manufacture 200 scooters which he sold at Rs. 4,000 each. Cost was made up of:

Materials	Rs. 2,00,000
Direct Wages	Rs. 3,00,000
Factory Overhead Expenses	Rs. 60,000
Office Overhead Expenses	Rs. 56,000
	Rs. 6,16,000

For 2006-07 season, he estimates,

(*a*) That each scooter will require materials to the value of Rs. 1,000 and wages of Rs. 1,500.

(*b*) That the factory overhead expenses will bear the same relation to direct wages as in the previous year.

(*c*) The percentage of office overhead expenses on factory cost will be the same as in the previous year.

Prepare the statement showing the profit he should make per unit if he enhances the price of the scooter by Rs. 50.

(B.Com., B.H.U., B.Com., Raj.)

[**Ans.** Prime Cost Rs. 2,500; Factory Cost Rs. 2,800; Total Cost Rs. 3,080, Profit Rs. 1,000; Amount of estimate Rs. 4,050).

9. The accounts of the Progressive Co. Ltd. for 2005-06 show:

	Rs.
Materials used	7,00,000
Direct Manual and Machine Labour Wages	5,40,000
Works Overhead Expenditure	1,62,000
Establishment and General Expenses	1,12,160

Show the works cost and the total cost of manufacture, the percentage that the Works Overhead Cost bears to the Manual and Machine Labour Wages and the percentage Establishment and General Expenses bear to the Works Cost.

What price should the company quote to manufacture a refrigerator, which, it is estimated, will require an expenditure of Rs. 720 in material and Rs. 600 in wages so that it will yield a profit of 15% on the total cost?

(G.N.D.U., B.Com., 1984, Punjab, B.Com)

[**Ans.** Rs. 14,02,000; Rs. 15,14,160; 30%, 8%, Rs. 1,863]

10. The accounts of a machine manufacturing company disclose the following information for the six months ending March, 2001:

Matrials used	1,50,000
Production wages	1,20,000
Factory overhead expenses	24,000
Office and General expenses	17,640

Prepare in proper form a cost sheet for the machines, and calculate the price which the company should quote for the manufacture of machine requiring materials valued at Rs. 12,500 and productive wages of Rs. 7,500 so that the price may yield a profit to 20 per cent on the selling price.

(B.Com. Punjab)

[Ans. Quotation price Rs. 28,487.50]

11. The following particulars have been extracted from the accounts of Hindustan Motors Ltd., a manufacturer of 14 H.P. motor cars, for the year ended 31st March, 2005:

	Rs.
Opening Stock of Raw Material	50,000
Purchases of Raw Material	12,00,000
Carriage on Raw Material	60,000
Wages to manual labour and also that working on Machine	7,00,000
Works Overhead	1,96,000
Establishment and General Charges	1,49,170
Closing Stock of Raw Material	75,000

Find out the Works Cost and Total Cost of motor car, the percentage that Works Overhead bears to the wages and percentage that establishment charges bear to Works Cost. Work out what price the company should quote for a motor car, which it is estimated will require an expenditure of Rs. 5,500 in raw material and Rs. 4,000 in wages, so that it would yield a profit of 25% on total cost and 20% on the selling price.

(H.P. University, B.Com., 1995)

[Ans. Quatation Price Rs. 14,204.25]

12. Pleasant Co. Ltd., manufactured and sold 2,000 Refrigerators during the year ending 31st March, 2006. The summarised Trading and P & L A/c is set out below:

Particulars	**Rs.**	**Particulars**	**Rs.**
To Cost of Materials	1,60,000	By Sales	8,00,000
To Direct Wages	2,40,000		
To Manufacturing Costs	1,00,000		
To Gross Profit c/d	3,00,000		
	8,00,000		8,00,000
To Management and Staff Salaries	1,20,000		
To Rent, Rates and Insurance	20,000	By Gross Profit b/d	3,00,000
To Selling Expenses	60,000		
To General Expenses	40,000		
To Net Profit	60,000		
	3,00,000		3,00,000

For the year ending 31st March, 2007, it is estimated that:

(*i*) Output and sales will be 2,400 Refrigerators.

(*ii*) Price of Materials will rise by 20% on the previous level.

(*iii*) Wages rates will rise by 5%.

(*iv*) Manufacturing costs will rise in proportion to the combined costs of materials and wages.

(*v*) Selling costs per unit will remain unchanged.

(*vi*) Other expenses will remain unaffected by rise in output.

You are required to submit a statement for the Board of Directors showing the price at which the refrigerators should be marketed so as to show a profit of 10% on selling price.

(*Karnataka, M.Com. 1966*)

[**Ans.** Estimated price of 2,400 Refrigerators Rs. 10,20,000; Per unit Rs. 425]

13. The All-India Water Proof Manufacturers Ltd., manufactured and sold 850 waterproofs during the year ending 31st March, 2006. The summarised Trading and Profit & Loss Account is given below:

	Rs.		**Rs.**
To Cost of Materials	64,000	By Sales	3,20,000
To Direct Wages	96,000		
To Manufacturing Expenses	40,000		
To Gross Profit c/d	1,20,000		
	3,20,000		3,20,000
To Office Salaries	48,000	By Gross Profit b/d	1,20,000
To Rent, Rates and Taxes	8,000		
To Selling Expenses	16,000		
To General Expenses	24,000		
To Net Profit	24,000		
	1,20,000		1,20,000

For the year ending 31st March, 2007, it has been estimated that:

(*a*) Output and Sales will be 1,000 waterproofs.

(*b*) Price of materials will rise by 25% on the previous year's level.

(*c*) Wages will rise by 12½%.

(*d*) Manufacturing expenses will rise in proportion to the combined cost of materials and wages.

(*e*) Selling cost per unit will remain unchanged.

(*f*) Other expenses will remain unaffected by the rise in output.

Prepare the Cost Statement, showing the price at which the waterproofs would be marketed so as to show a profit at 12% on the selling price.

[**Ans.** Estimated Price Rs. 4,26,472, Price per unit Rs. 426.47]

14. The undermentioned figures have been collected from the books of a company:
Cost of materials Rs. 4,00,000; Cost of Labour Rs. 3,00,000; Factory Charges Rs. 1,50,000; Administration Charges Rs. 1,70,000; Selling Charges Rs. 42,500; Distribution Charges Rs. 42,500.
On the basis of the above figures a work-order has been executed and the following expenses have been incurred thereon:
Materials Rs. 10,000, Labour Rs. 6,000.
Factory Overhead is based on direct wages. Administration, Selling and Distribution charges are based on Factory Cost. Assuming that the factory overhead has gone up by 10% and other overheads maintaining the same percentage and profit charged is 20% on the total cost, find out the total price of the work order.

(*M.D. University, B.Com., 1994*)

[**Ans.** Price of work-order Rs. 30,108]

15. In respect of a factory, the following figures have been obtained for the year ended 31st March, 2005:
Cost of Materials Rs. 90,000; Direct Wages Rs. 75,000; Factory Overhead Rs. 45,000; Administration Charges Rs. 50,400; Selling Charges Rs. 33,600; Distribution Charges Rs. 21,000; Sales Rs. 3,78,000.
On the basis of the above figures, a work-order has been executed in 2005-06 and the following expenses have been incurred:

	Rs.
Materials	4,000
Wages	2,500

Assuming that in 2005-06, the rate of factory overhead has gone up by 20%, distribution charges have gone down by 10% and selling and administration charges each have gone up by 12½%, at what price should the product be sold so as to earn the same percentage of profit on selling price as in 2004-05.
Factory overhead is based on direct labour and administration, selling and distribution overhead on factory cost.

[**Ans.** Total Cost for 2004-05 – Rs. 3,15,000,
Price of Work-order Rs. 15,338)

16. The Managing Director of a small manufacturing concern consults you as to the minimum price at which he can sell the output of one of the departments of the company which is intended for mass production in future. The company's records show the following particulars for this department for the past year:

Production and Sales:	100 units
	Rs.
Materials	3,900
Direct Labour	2,100
Direct Charges	300
Works Oncost	2,100
Office Oncost	840
Selling Oncost	960
Profit	1,500
Sales	11,700

It is ascertained from the records that 40% of the works oncost fluctuates directly with production and 70% of the selling oncost fluctuates with sales. It is anticipated that the department would produce 1,000 units per annum and the direct labour charges per unit will be reduced by 20%, while the fixed works oncost charges will increase by Rs. 900. Office oncost and fixed selling oncost charges are expected to show an increase of 25%. Besides the above, no other changes are anticipated.

Prepare a statement for submission to your client.

(*Nagpur, M.Com.*)

[**Ans.** Estimated Selling Price: Rs. 88,886]

17. The Metal Product Company produces a sewing machine that sells for Rs. 300. An increase of 15% in cost of materials and of 10% in cost of labour is anticipated.

If the only figures available are given below, what must be the selling price to give the same percentage of Gross Profit as before?

(*a*) Material costs have been 45% of cost of sales.

(*b*) Labour costs have been 40% of cost of sales.

(*c*) Overhead costs have been 15% of cost of sales.

(*d*) The anticipated increased costs in relation to the present sales price would cause a 35% decrease in the amount of the present Gross Profit.

(*Delhi, B.Com., 1971*)

[**Ans.** Rs. 332.25]

18. The cost structure of an article, the selling price of which is Rs. 500, is as follows:

Direct Materials	:	50% of the total cost
Direct Labour	:	30% of the total cost
Overhead	:	Balance

Due to anticipated increase in existing material price by 20%, and in the existing labour rate by 10%, the existing profit would come down by 30% if the selling price remains unchanged.

Prepare the comparative statement showing the cost, profit and sale price under the present conditions and with the increase expected for the future assuming the same percentage of profit on cost as under present conditions (calculations may he made to the nearest rupee) had to be earned.

(I.C.W.A., Final)

[**Ans.** Present Cost Rs. 350, Anticipated Cost Rs. 395, Anticipated Selling Price Rs. 565 to earn a profit of 30% on Sales Price.]

19. The following information is available from the account books of Mysore Industries Ltd., for the year ended 31st March, 2006. Prepare a cost sheet:

	Rs.
Opening Stock:	
Raw Materials	1,40,000
Finished Goods	20,000
Purchases of Raw Materials	2,10,000
Factory Wages	3,80,000
Factory Overhead	70,000
Administrative Overhead	40,000
Closing Stock:	
Raw Materials	19,600
Finished Goods	1,60,000
Sales	7,56,000

The number of products manufactured was 4,000 including those sold and those in the stock at the end.

The company wishes to supply 1,000 units of the product in the coming period on the basis of the above figures. It is likely that the cost of material and labour will increase by 15% and 10% respectively. Calculate the price to be quoted.

(Mysore, B.Com, 1976)

[**Ans.** Present Gross Profit is Rs. 75,600; Price to be quoted for the coming period is Rs. 255.51 per unit]

20. The cost structure of an article, the selling price of which is Rs. 45,000 is as follows:

Direct materials	50%
Direct wages	20%
Overheads	30%

An increase of 15% in the cost of materials and 25% in the cost of labour is anticipated. These increased costs in relation to the present selling price would cause a 25% decrease in the amount of present profit per article. You are required:

(*i*) To prepare a statement of profit per article at present and

(*ii*) The revised selling price to give the same percentage of profit on sales as before. [**Ans.** Selling price Rs. 50,625]

21. The following is the cost of manufacturing 4,000 units:

Materials	Rs. 15,000
Wages	Rs. 2,000
Direct Expenses	Rs. 300
Fixed Overheads	Rs. 14,000
Variable Overheads	Rs. 3,000

It is estimated that for manufacturing every 1,000 units (over and above 4,000 units) the manufacturing cost will increase by following rate:

(*a*) Materials will increase proportionately.

(*b*) Wages will be 10% less than the proportionate amount.

(*c*) Direct expenses will not increase.

(*d*) Fixed overheads will increase by Rs. 2,000.

(*e*) Variable overheads will be 20% less than the proportionate amount.

Calculate the cost to produce 7,000 units and show by how much amount this cost would differ if all the factory overheads were charged at 10% of direct wages.

(*Shivaji, B.Com.*) [**Ans.** Total Cost Rs. 54,700]

22. In 2008 when selling price was Rs.10 per article, total sales were Rs. 1,00,000. In 2009 selling price was increased by 10%. Total sales realised Rs.1,26,500.

In 2008 materials cost 40% of sales value. In 2009, price of raw materials rose by 10%. In 2008, wages were Rs. 30,000. In 2009, the cost was Rs. 33,000. In 2008, other expenses were 10% of sales value. These expenses rose in 2009 by the sum of Rs. 1,500.

Prepare cost statements for the years 2008 and 2009 and find out net profit for 2008 and 2009.

[**Ans.** Profit: 2008 Rs. 20,000, 2009 Rs. 31,400]

23. The management of a manufacturing concern has approached the Costing Dept. to find out the cost of 3,000 units. The cost analysis of 2,000 units gives the following results:

Materials Rs. 45,000; Labour Rs. 25,000; Direct Expenses Rs. 500; Factory Overheads Rs. 1,000; Administration Overheads Rs. 800 and Selling and Distribution overheads Rs. 400.

The further details in this connection are as follows:

(*a*) An increase of 10% is expected in the cost of raw materials and 5% in the cost of the labour.

(*b*) 70% of the factory overheads are fixed and 30% variable.

(*c*) The ratio of fixed and variable expenses in administration overheads is 60:40.

(*d*) Half of the selling and distribution overheads are fixed.

The management desires to charge 25% profit on the sale price. Ascertain selling price. [**Ans.** Profit Rs. 38,995; S.P. Rs. 1,55,980]

24. The following is a summary of the trading results of a company selling an electrical appliance for the year ended 31st March, 2000 during which 80,000 units were sold:

	Rs. (lakhs)	**Rs. (Lakhs)**
Sales		96
Costs:		
Direct Materials	36	
Direct Labour	15	
Indirect Labour	06	
Other Costs	18	75
Profit		21

Taking into consideration the following matters, prepare a summary of the expected results for the following year:

(*a*) The selling price is to be reduced by Rs. 7.50.

(*b*) Sales volume is expected to increase by 40%.

(*c*) Suppliers have agreed to give a discount of 5% on all purchases of materials.

(*d*) Direct workmen are to be paid incentive bonus of 2.5% in order to stimulate production. Indirect labour is not expected to increase during the following year.

[**Ans.** Profit Rs. 25,39,500]

25. Analysis of the total cost per unit at the maximum capacity of 10,000 units is given below:

	Rs.
Materials	25
Direct Wages	15
Factory Overhead:	
Fixed	10
Variable	20
	70
Administration Expenses (Fixed)	10
Selling and Distribution Expenses:	
Fixed	9
Variable	6
	95
Profit	25
Selling Price	120

However, it is expected that there would be alround rise in all variable expenditure by 5% in future, although fixed expenses may remain the same.

In view of increased demand, the management has decided to increase plant capacity to 15,000 units. The implications of this policy are summarised below:

(*a*) The additional capacity will require additional finance of Rs. 5,00,000 on which interest would amount to 6% p.a.

(*b*) There will be an increase of 20% in all fixed overheads.

(*c*) There is no need for changing the price for the purpose of boosting sales.

Prepare a comparative statement of cost showing anticipated profit for the present output and the proposed output in the future for the managerial decision.

[**Ans.** Total Cost Rs. 14,17,500 (15,000 units), Cost per unit: 94.50]

26. The following cost data relate to a light engineering concern producing standardised article. The information is accumulated on the weekly basis.

Output per week (Units)	Direct Material Rs.	Direct Wages Rs.	Factory Overhead Rs.
1,000	3,000	4,000	2,400
1,200	3,600	4,800	2,600
1,500	4,500	6,000	2,900

You are required to analyse behaviour of costs in relation to the output and determine selling price for a weekly output of 2,000 units. The factory has sufficient idle capacity to permit the increase in the volume. Further, the management expects a return of 20% on the selling price.

[**Hint:** Material Cost per unit, Rs. 3; Labour Cost per unit, Rs. 4; Variable overheads per unit, Re. 1 and Fixed Overheads, Rs. 1,400]

27. The following particulars relate to a manufacturing company:

	2003-04	2004-05	2005-06
Materials	Rs. 75,000	50,000	1,00,000
Labour	Rs. 50,000	40,000	60,000
Works Overheads	Rs. 35,000	30,000	40,000
Administrative Overheads	Rs. 20,000	20,000	20,000
Selling Overheads	Rs. 10,000	9,000	8,000
Output in units	15,000	10,000	20,000

Prepare an estimate for 40,000 units, a profit of 25% on Works Cost will be sufficient.

[**Hint:** Selling expenses for 2006-07 to be assumed as Rs. 7,000]

[**Ans.** Selling Price: Rs. 4,77,000]

28. The Inner Co. Ltd. has received an enquiry for supply of 10,000 steel folding chairs. The costs are estimated as under:

Raw Materials – 1,00,000 kgs. at Re. 1 per kg.

Direct Wages – 10,000 hours at Rs. 4 per hour.

Variable Overheads: Factory, Rs. 2.40 per labour hour, Selling and Distribution, Rs. 16,000.

Fixed Overheads: Factory, Rs. 6,000, Selling and Distribution, Rs. 14,000.

Prepare statement showing the price to be fixed which will result in a profit of 20% on selling price.

(*C.A., Inter*)

[**Ans.** Selling Price Rs. 25 per unit]

29. A factory can produce 60,000 units per annum at the optimum (100%) capacity. The estimated costs of production are as under:

Direct Material	Rs. 3 per unit
Direct Labour	Rs. 2 per unit
Indirect Expenses:	
Fixed	Rs. 1,50,000 per annum
Variable	Rs. 5 per unit

Semi-variable: Rs. 50,000 per annum upto 50% capacity and an extra expense of Rs. 10,000 for every 25% increase in capacity or part thereof.

The factory produces only against orders and not for own stock. If the production programme of factory is as indicated below and the management desires to earn a profit of Rs. 1,00,000 for the year, work out the average selling price at which each unit should be quoted:

First 3 months of the year	50% of capacity
Remaining 9 months	80% of the capacity.

Ignore Selling, Distribution and Administration overheads.

(*C.A. Final, Bombay, M.Com.*)

[**Ans.** Average Selling Price Rs. 17.24 per unit]

30. The following information has been obtained from the costing records of a factory for 2005-06:

	Rs.
Rates of Factory	1,400
Lighting of Factory	2,600
Depreciation of Plant	3,500
Clerical Salaries	12,000
Management Expenses	6,000
Power	4,500
Factory Indirect Wages	12,250
Plant Repairs and Maintenance	10,000

Rectification of Defective Work	2,800
Consumable Stores	7,500
Selling Expenses	7,330
General Expenses	4,600
Receipts from the sale of scrap	1,200
Profit from canteen	500

Production has been 1,00,000 units, the prime cost of which has been materials 90 paise and wages 60 paise per unit and selling price was Rs. 2.35 per unit, all units being sold.

In 2006-07 selling price is reduced to Rs. 2.25 per unit and production increased by 50% without extra shift.

Prepare Statement showing–

(1) Various elements of cost during 2005-06.

(2) The estimated cost and profit during 2006-07 assuming that 1,50,000 units will be produced and sold.

(Mysore, B.Com.)

[**Ans.** Estimated total cost and profits for 1,50,000 units Rs. 3,00,345, Rs, 37,155 (Profit from canteen has been excluded from cost sheet]

[**Hints:**

(*i*) All factory expenses have been treated as fixed as the increased production does not require overtime or extra-shift.

(*ii*) Cost of rectification, receipt from sale of scrap and profit from canteen have been excluded.

(*iii*) Selling expenses have been treated as variable in relation to number of units sold.]

12

Job Costing and Batch Costing

Job costing is the method of costing which is applied to ascertain the costs of specific jobs or work-orders which are treated as contracts of small size. These jobs are generally dissimilar, of non-repetitive nature and may not be comparable with each other. This method is also known as 'Job Lot Costing' or 'Lot Costing'.

SPECIAL FEATURES OF JOB COSTING

The special features of job costing may be summarised as follows:

(*i*) Under job costing, production is carried on by a manufacturer against customer's order and not for stock.

(*ii*) Each job or work-order is of a separate nature.

(*iii*) The jobs or work-orders are generally executed in factories, work-shops and repair-shops. But sometimes the job work is also done outside the factory or work-shop *e.g.*, plumbering job, sewerage work etc.

(*iv*) The unit of costing, under this method, is a job or specific work-order.

(*v*) Under this method, the production and its requirements are determined first and then the expenses are ascertained in relation to it.

SUITABILITY OF JOB COSTING

Job costing method is most suitable to such activities as printing press, painting and decorating, automobile garages, repair shops, electrical fittings, ship building, engineering works, plumbering works etc., where work is done according to the customer's specifications.

PROCEDURE OF JOB ACCOUNTING

The various steps in the job accounting may be summarised as follows:

(*a*) Job Number

Production in any job industry is dependent upon the receipt of an order from the customer. When an order for a job is received and is accepted by the manufacturer, the order as well as the job are given specific number by which they are known or identified. Such number is known as 'Job Number'.

(*b*) Production Order

After the acceptance of the order, the Production Planning Department prepares a document known as 'Production Order'. The Production Order contains the following particulars:

(*i*) Production Order No.
(*ii*) Date of the Order
(*iii*) Name of the Customer
(*iv*) Quantity
(*v*) Description of the Job
(*vi*) Drawings and Designs
(*vii*) Bill of Materials No.
(*viii*) Particulars of Operations to be Carried Out
(*ix*) Departments and Machines Allotted for the Job
(*x*) Date of Commencement of Job
(*xi*) Date of Completion
(*xii*) Special Instructions, if any.

The Production Order is in the form of instructions issued to the foreman to proceed with the job. Thus, it serves as an authority to the foreman for starting the work. The specimen of a Production Order is as follows:

A B Co. Ltd.,
Production Order

Name of customer..................................	Job No. ....
Date of commencement..........................	Date..
Date of completion................................	Bill of Materials No. ....
Special Instructions...............................	Drawing Attached: Yes/No.

Quantity	Description	Machines to be used	Tools required

Production Authorised
....
(Signature)
Head of Production Control Department

(*c*) Bill of Materials

A Bill of Materials is a list of all materials and parts required for a specific job. This document contains details of stores required and serves as an advance intimation to the storekeeper who may issue materials for the execution of the job on the basis of the Bill rather than on separate material requisitions. The responsibility for the preparation of Bill of Materials lies with the Production Planning Department. The foreman receives a copy of Bill of Materials along with the Production Order. The Bill of Materials authorises the foreman to call for and receive the specified materials from the stores. If certain special tools are required for the Job, a separate list thereof, known as Tool List, is also prepared.

(*d*) Recording of Costs

For recording all direct and indirect costs incurred in respect of each job, a Job Cost Card or Job Cost Sheet is prepared by the costing department. The Job Cost Sheet shows the direct material costs, direct wages and overheads applicable to respective Jobs. A Job Cost Card or Job Cost Sheet has to be designed to suit the needs of the organisation. The specimen of a Job Cost Sheet is given below:

A B Co. Ltd.,
Job Cost Sheet

Job/Production Order No. .... Customer..................................
Particulars of Job.. Quantity..................................
Date of Commencement..............................
Special Instructions...................................... Date of Completion...............

Material Cost				Labour Cost					Overhead (absorbed)				
Date	Department	Material Requisition No.	Amount (Rs.)	Date	Department	Hours	Rate	Amount (Rs.)	Date	Department	Hours	Rate	Amount (Rs.)
Total (Rs.)													

Profit/Loss		**Cost Summary**			
			Estimated Cost	Actual Cost	Difference
	Rs.	Materials	Rs.	Rs.	Rs.
Price Quoted	x x x	Wages			
Less Cost	x x x	Overhead			
Profit or Loss	x x x	Total			

Material Costs

Materials to job are issued from stores on the basis of Bill of Materials or Material Requisitions. Material costs of a job can be ascertained from Bill of Materials or from the Materials Abstract prepared by the costing department on the basis of Material Requisitions. If any special material is purchased for a job, it is directly charged to the job concerned on the basis of Invoice. In case any surplus material is returned from the job to the stores, the Job Account is given due credit for the value of the same.

Labour Costs

The labour cost of a job is ascertained on the basis of Job Cards. A circulating Job Card is issued with each job to record the labour hours spent on different operations and the total labour cost is calculated on the completion of the job.

Overhead Costs

Overhead costs are accumulated on departmental basis and then apportioned to the various jobs executed by each department on some equitable basis *e.g.*, direct labour hours, machine hours spent on each job. But in order to avoid delays in distributing overheads on actual cost basis, overheads are generally charged at the pre-determined rates worked out on the basis of previous period's figures. Progress Reports are received from departments to assess the extent of work completed from time to time so as to ensure that the job is completed within the stipulated time.

(*e*) Completion of Job

On completion of a job, a Job Completion Report is sent to the costing department. The total cost of a job is ascertained by posting all costs related to that job to the Job Cost Sheet. If a job consists of a number of units of production, the total cost of the job is divided by the number of units in order to arrive at the cost per unit.

(*f*) Profit or Loss on Job

The amount of profit or loss on a job is computed by comparing the total cost of the job with sales price.

CALCULATION OF WORK-IN-PROGRESS

In order to ascertain the cost of incomplete jobs or work-in-progress, a 'Composite Work-in-Progress Account' may be opened for the entire factory. This account is debited with all costs incurred on various jobs during a period and credited with the cost of completed jobs. The debit balance on the Composite Work-in-Progress Account shall represent the cost of work-in-progress. Alternatively, in order to ascertain the cost of work-in-progress department-wise, a Composite Work-in-Progress Account may be opened for each department separately. Costs incurred on various jobs in a department shall be debited to this account and cost of finished jobs credited to the same, leaving a debit balance on the account representing the cost of work-in-progress.

ADVANTAGES OF JOB COSTING

The main advantages of job costing can be summarised as follows:

(*i*) Job costing enables the manufacturer to know the profitability of each job separately.

(*ii*) It provides for the collection and analysis of costs by elements, functions, departments and jobs which enables the management to know the trend of costs and to control the efficiency of various operations, materials and machines by suitable comparisons.

(*iii*) By providing for collection and analysis of costs by elements, functions, departments and jobs, job costing method provides a suitable basis for future planning and preparing quotations and estimates.

(*iv*) Job costing facilitates cost control through the comparison of actual costs with estimated costs.

(*v*) The recovery of overheads under job costing is generally made on the basis of pre-determined rates. This use of pre-determined rates necessitates the adoption of budgetary control of overhead. Thus, the manufacturing concern enjoys the advantages of budgetary control.

(*vi*) Spoilage and defective work can be easily identified with a specific job or work-order and the responsibility for the same can be fixed on departments and individuals.

LIMITATIONS OF JOB COSTING

Job costing method suffers from the following limitations:

(*i*) It involves too much clerical work which increases the chances of errors.

(*ii*) This method is historical in nature and thus fails to provide prompt remedial action in case of inefficiency.

(*iii*) Due to the recovery of overhead at pre-determined rates, job costing involves the problem of over/under-recovery of overheads.

(*iv*) The scheme of budgetary control may not be complete since it may not be extended to material and labour costs.

Illustration 1

The following direct costs were incurred on Job No. 105 of ABC Engineering Works:

Materials		Rs. 3,415
Wages	:	
Department 'A'	:	80 hours @ Rs. 2.50 per hour
Department 'B'	:	60 hours @ Rs. 4.00 per hour

Overhead expenses were estimated as follows:

(*i*) Variable Overhead:

Department A	:	Rs. 5,000 for 4,000 direct labour hours.
Department B	:	Rs. 6,000 for 3,000 direct labour hours.

(*ii*) Fixed Overhead:

Estimated at Rs. 7,500 for 10,000 hours normal working time of the factory.

You are required to calculate the cost of Job No. 105 and estimate the percentage of profit earned if the price quoted was Rs. 4,750.

Solution

Cost Sheet

Job No. 105

Particulars		Amount
		Rs.
Direct Materials		3,415
Direct Wages		
(*i*) Dept. A:		
80 hours @ Rs. 2.50 per hour	200	
(*ii*) Dept. B:		
60 hours @ Rs. 4.00 per hour	240	440
Prime Cost		3,855
Overheads:		
(*i*) Variable:		
Dept. A:		
80 hours @ Rs. 1.25 per hour	100	
Dept. B:		
60 hours @ Rs. 2.00 per hour	120	220
(*ii*) Fixed:		
140 hours @ Rs. 0.75 per hour		105
Total Cost		4,180
Profit @ 13.6% on cost		570
Selling Price		4,750

Working Notes:

(1) Overhead rates have been computed as follows:

Variable overhead rates:

$$(i)\text{ Department A} = \frac{\text{Rs. } 5{,}000}{4{,}000\text{ hrs.}}$$

$$= \text{Rs. } 1.25 \text{ per direct labour hour}$$

$$(ii)\text{ Department B} = \frac{\text{Rs. } 6{,}000}{3{,}000\text{ hrs.}}$$

$$= \text{Rs. } 2.00 \text{ per direct labour hour.}$$

Fixed overhead rate:

$$= \frac{\text{Rs. } 7{,}500}{10{,}000\text{ hrs.}} = \text{Rs. } 0.75 \text{ per direct labour hour.}$$

(2) Percentage of profit on cost has been calculated as follows:

$$= \frac{\text{Profit}}{\text{Total Cost}} \times 100$$

$$= \frac{570}{4{,}180} \times 100$$

$$= 13.6\% \text{ on cost.}$$

Illustration 2

A Job No. 58 passes through three departments namely X, Y and Z. The following information is given to you regarding this job:

	Departments X	Y	Z
Materials Issued to Job	Rs. 8,000	Rs. 1,000	Rs. 500
Direct Labour hours for Job	1,000	2,000	5,000
Rate of Direct Labour per hour	Re. 1.00	Rs. 1.50	Rs. 2.00
Sale of Scrap of Materials Arising from Job	Rs. 1,000	Rs. 150	Rs. 100
Total Overheads for the Departments	Rs.10,000	Rs.15,000	Rs.25,000
Total Labour hours for the Departments	10,000	30,000	40,000

Calculate the cost of Job No. 58 from the above figures.

Solution

Job Cost Sheet

Job No. 58

Particulars		Rs.
Materials (less scrap)	Rs.	
Dept. X	7,000	
Dept. Y	850	
Dept. Z	400	8,250
Direct Wages		
Deptt. X : 1,000 hours @ Re. 1 per hour	1,000	
Deptt. Y : 2,000 hours @ Rs. 1.50 per hour	3,000	
Deptt. Z : 5,000 hours @ Rs. 2 per hour	10,000	14,000
	Prime Cost	22,250
Overheads:	Rs.	
Department X	1,000	
Department Y	1,000	
Department Z	3,125	5,125
	Total Cost	27,375

Note: Calculation of overheads chargeable to Job No. 58 has been made as follows:

Department X:

$$\frac{\text{Total Overheads in the Department}}{\text{Total Labour hours in the Department}} \times \text{Labour hours in the Department for Job No. 58}$$

$$= \frac{10,000}{10,000} \times 1,000 = \text{Rs. } 1,000$$

Department Y:

$$= \frac{15,000}{30,000} \times 2,000 = \text{Rs.} 1,000$$

Department Z:

$$= \frac{25,000}{40,000} \times 5,000 = \text{Rs. } 3,125.$$

Illustration 3

The following expenses were incurred for a job during the year ended on 31st March, 2008:

	Rs.
Direct Materials	30,000
Direct Wages	40,000
Chargeable Expenses	10,000
Factory Overheads	20,000
Selling & Distribution Overheads	20,000
Administrative Overheads	30,000

Selling price for the above job was Rs. 1,80,000. You are required to prepare a Statement showing the profit earned during the year ended 31.3.2008 from the job and an estimated price of a job which is to be executed in the year 2008-09, charging the same percentage of profit on sales as it was during the year 2007-08. Materials, wages and chargeable expenses will be required of Rs. 50,000, Rs. 70,000 and Rs. 20,000 respectively for the job. The various overheads should be recovered on the following basis while calculating the estimated price:

(*a*) Factory overheads as a percentage of direct wages.

(*b*) Administrative and selling and distribution overheads as a percentage of factory cost. (*H.P. University, B.Com., 1995*)

Solution

Job Cost Sheet

(For the Year ending on 31st March, 2008

Particulars	Amount
	Rs.
Direct Materials	30,000
Direct Wages	40,000
Chargeable Expenses	10,000
Prime Cost	80,000
Factory Overheads	20,000
Factory Cost	1,00,000
Administrative Overheads	30,000
Total Cost	1,30,000
Selling & Distribution Overheads	20,000
Selling Cost	1,50,000
Profit	30,000
Selling Price	1,80,000

Notes: Calculation of various overheads rates, and percentage of profit on sales:

$$(a)\ \text{Factory Overheads Rate} = \frac{\text{Factory Overheads}}{\text{Direct Wages}} \times 100 = \frac{20{,}000}{40{,}000} \times 100$$

$$= 50\%$$

(*b*) Administrative Overheads Rate $= \dfrac{\text{Administrative Overheads}}{\text{Factory Cost}} \times 100$

$= \dfrac{30,000}{1,00,000} \times 100 = 30\%$

(*c*) Selling & Distribution Overheads Rate =

$\dfrac{\text{Selling \& Distribution Overheads}}{\text{Factory Cost}} \times 100$

$= \dfrac{20,000}{1,00,000} \times 100 = 20\%$

(*d*) Percentage of profit on sales $= \dfrac{\text{Profit}}{\text{Selling Price}} \times 100$

$= \dfrac{30,000}{1,80,000} \times 100 = 16\frac{2}{3}\%$

Statement Showing the Estimated Price for Job to be Executed in 2008-09

Particulars	Amount Rs.
Materials	50,000
Wages	70,000
Chargeable Expenses	20,000
Prime Cost	1,40,000
Factory Overheads (50% on wages)	35,000
Factory Cost	1,75,000
Administrative Overheads (30% on Factory Cost)	52,500
Cost of Production	2,27,500
Selling & Distribution Overheads (20% on Factory Cost)	35,000
Total Cost	2,62,500
Profit ($16\frac{2}{3}\%$ on Sales)	52,500
Estimated Sales Price	3,15,000

Illustration 4

A factory engaged in making non-standard products to customer's specifications processes all production through 3 departments. The cost figures of the factory for the month of September, 2004 are furnished below:

Nature of Expenses	Total Expenses	Departments		
		A	B	C
	Rs.	Rs.	Rs.	Rs.
Direct Materials	18,600	7,500	6,400	4,700
Labour	15,000	6,000	5,000	4,000
Total Overhead Expenses	7,500	3,000	2,500	2,000
	41,100	16,500	13,900	10,700

Prepare a simple cost sheet for products X and Y on the basis of data furnished below:

Product	Cost Elements	Expenses Incurred in		
		Dept. A	Dept. B	Dept. C
X	Direct Material	100	200	300
X	Direct Labour	50	60	70
Y	Direct Material	50	90	140
Y	Direct Labour	70	60	80

(*C.A. Final*)

Solution

Cost Sheet

Particulars	Product X		Product Y	
	Rs.	Rs.	Rs.	Rs.
Direct Material:				
Dept. A	100		50	
Dept. B	200		90	
Dept. C	300	600	140	280
Direct Labour:				
Dept. A	50		70	
Dept. B	60		60	
Dept. C	70	180	80	210
Overheads: (as percentage to direct wages)				
Dept. A : $\frac{3,000}{6,000}\times 100 = 50\%$	25		35	
Dept. B : $\frac{2,500}{5,000}\times 100 = 50\%$	30	90	30	105
Dept. C : $\frac{2,000}{4,000}\times 100 = 50\%$	35		40	
Total Cost		870		595

Illustration 5

A shop-floor supervisor of small factory presented the following costs for Job No. 421 to determine the selling price:

	Per Unit Rs.
Material	70
Direct Wages (18 hrs. @ Rs. 2.50)	45
(Dept. X –8 hrs. Dept. Y–6 hrs. Dept. Z –4 hrs.)	
Chargeable Expenses (Special Stores Items)	5
	120
Add $33\frac{1}{3}\%$ for expenses	40
Cost	160

Analysis of the Profit and Loss Account for the previous year 2007 shows the following:

Particulars		Rs.	Particulars	Rs.
Material used		1,50,000		
Direct Wages:			Sales Less Returns	2,50,000
Dept. X	10,000			
Dept. Y	12,000			
Dept. Z	8,000	30,000		
Special Stores Items		4,000		
Overheads:				
Dept. X	5,000			
Dept. Y	9,000			
Dept. Z	2,000	16,000		
		2,00,000		
Gross Profit c/d		50,000		
		2,50,000		2,50,000
Selling Expenses		20,000	Gross Profit b/d	50,000
Net Profit		30,000		
		50,000		50,000

It is also noted that average hourly wages for the three departments X, Y and Z are similar. You are required to:

(*i*) Draw up a Job Cost Sheet.

(*ii*) Calculate and enter revised cost using 2007 actual figures as basis.

(*iii*) Add 20% to total cost to determine selling price. (*I.C.W. A. Inter*)

Solution

Job Cost Sheet

Job No. 421

	Rs. P.
Materials	70.00
Direct Wages:	
Dept. X (8 hrs. @ Rs. 2.50 per hour)	20.00
Dept. Y (6 hrs. @ Rs. 2.50 per hour)	15.00
Dept. Z (4 hrs. @ Rs. 2.50 per hour)	10.00
Chargeable Expenses	5.00
Prime Cost	120.00
Overhead:	
Dept. X (8 hrs. @ Rs. 1.25 per hour)	10.00
Dept. Y (6 hrs. @ Rs. 1.875 per hour)	11.25
Dept. Z (4 hrs. @ Rs. 0.625 per hour)	2.50
Total Cost	143.75
Profit @ 20% on total cost	28.75
Selling price	172.50

Working Notes:

Calculation of Overhead Absorption Rates:

(*i*) Dept. X $= \dfrac{5{,}000 \times 2.50}{10{,}000} =$ Rs. 1.25

(*ii*) Dept. Y $= \frac{9{,}000 \times 2.50}{12{,}000}$ = Rs. 1.875

(*iii*) Dept. Z $= \frac{1{,}000 \times 2.50}{8{,}000}$ = Re. 0.625

Illustration 6

M/s. Perfect Printers Ltd., operate a printing press. During November 2008, the plant was operating at full capacity. The material and labour costs of Job 101, and all other jobs worked on, in November, are shown below:

	Job 101	All other Jobs	Total
	Rs.	Rs.	Rs.
Materials	10,000	70,000	80,000
Direct labour	12,000	28,000	40,000
Overtime premium	4,000	–	4,000

In addition to the foregoing costs, factory overhead incurred in November amounted to Rs. 44,000. Overhead is allocated to production on the basis of direct labour costs. You are required to:

(*i*) Show what the factory Profit or Loss on Job 101 would be, using two different methods of accounting for overtime premium. Assume that the contract price for this Job is Rs. 40,000.

(*ii*) Indicate under what circumstances each method should be used.

(*iii*) State whether the profit or loss of the company during November would be affected by the choice of one method or another.

(*I.C.W.A. Inter*)

Solution

$$\text{Factory Overhead Recovery Rate} = \frac{\text{Factory Overhead}}{\text{Direct Labour Cost}} \times 100$$

$$= \frac{44{,}000}{44{,}000} \times 100$$

$$= 100\%$$

(*i*) (*a*): If overtime premium is fully charged to Job No. 101:

Job Cost Sheet

Job No. 101 — Period.............

	Rs.
Materials	10,000
Direct Wages (including overtime premium)	16,000
Prime Cost	26,000
Factory Overhead @ 100% on Direct Wages	16,000
Total Cost	42,000
Loss	(–) 2,000
Contract Price	40,000

(*i*) (*b*): If overtime premium is charged pro-rata to all Jobs:

Job Cost Sheet

Job No. 101 Period..............

	Rs.
Materials	10,000
Direct Wages (including overtime premium)	13,200
Prime Cost	23,200
Factory Overhead @ 100% on Direct Wages	13,200
Total Cost	36,400
Profit	3,600
Contract Price	40,000

(*ii*) Overtime premium should be charged fully to Job 101 if it was a rush Job and it was done at the request of the customer. But if the overtime work was due to limited production capacity and it was accidental that Job 101 was done during overtime then the premium should be charged *pro-rata* to all Jobs.

(*iii*) Profit and Loss of the company during November will be affected by the choice of any of the methods if all the jobs performed during the month are not completed by the end of the month. If overtime premium is fully charged to Job 101 but it is not completed by 30th November then the loss on this Job will not be taken in the account of November 2008. Similarly, if overtime premium is charged *pro rata* to all the Jobs and profit or loss on any Job remaining incomplete will be carried over to the next month.

Illustration 7

As a Cost Accountant, you find that the selling price of a product has been calculated as follows:

	Rs.
Materials	24.00
Direct Wages	
20 hrs. @ Re. l per hour	20.00
(Dept. 1 – 10 hrs.	
Dept. 2 – 6 hrs.	
Dept. 3 – 4 hrs)	
Prime cost	44.00
Plus 50% on the cost	22.00
Selling price	66.00

An analysis of the previous year's profit and loss account shows the following:

	Rs.		Rs.
Materials	35,000	Factory Overheads	
Direct Wages:		Dept. 1	5,000
Dept. 1	5,000	Dept. 2	3,000
Dept. 2	6,000	Dept. 3	3,000
Dept. 3	4,000	Selling and Distribution Overheads	12,200

You are required to (*a*) draw up a Job Cost Sheet (*b*) calculate and enter the revised cost using the previous year's figures as a basis and (*c*) add to the total job cost 10% for profit and give the final selling price.

Solution

In order to draw up the Job Cost Sheet, the analysis of the percentages of the overhead for the previous year shall be made as follows:

(A) Factory Overhead Rates

		Dept. 1	Dept. 2	Dept. 3
(*i*)	Factory overheads Rs.	5,000	3,000	3,000
(*ii*)	No. of direct labour hours (Direct wages ÷ 1)	5,000	6,000	4,000
(*iii*)	Rate per hour	$\frac{\text{Rs. } 5{,}000}{5{,}000 \text{ hrs.}}$ = Re. 1.00	$\frac{\text{Rs. } 3{,}000}{6{,}000 \text{ hrs.}}$ = Re. 0.50	$\frac{\text{Rs. } 3{,}000}{4{,}000 \text{ hrs.}}$ = Re. 0.75

(B) Percentage of Selling and Distribution Overhead on Works Cost

$$= \frac{\text{Selling Overheads}}{\text{Works Cost}} \times 100 = \frac{12,200}{61,000} \times 100 = 20\%$$

Cost Sheet

Job No. ....

		Rs.
Materials		24.00
Direct Wages		
Dept. 1	10.00	
Dept. 2	6.00	
Dept. 3	4.00	20.00
Prime Cost		44.00
Factory Overhead		
Dept. 1	10 hrs. × Re. 1 = 10.00	
Dept. 2	6 hrs. × Re. 0.50 = 3.00	
Dept. 3	4 hrs. × Re. 0.75 = 3.00	16.00
Works Cost		60.00
Selling Overhead @ 20% on Works Cost		12.00
Cost of sales		72.00
Profit @ 10% on Cost		7.20
Selling Price		79.20

Illustration 8

The following information for the year ended 31st March, 2007 is obtained from the books and records of a factory:

	Completed Jobs	Work-in-progress
	Rs.	Rs.
Raw Materials Supplied from Stores	90,000	30,000
Wages	1,00,000	4,000
Chargeable Expenses	10,000	4,000
Materials Transferred To Work-in-Progress	2,000	2,000
Materials Returned to Stores	1,000	–

Factory overhead is 80% of wages and office overhead is 25% of factory cost.

The value of executed jobs during the year ended 31st March, 2007 was Rs. 4,10,000.

Prepare (*i*) Consolidated Completed Jobs Account showing the profit made or loss incurred thereon, and (*ii*) Consolidated Work-in-Progress Account.

(*H.P. University, B.Com., 2008*)

Solution

Consolidated Completed Jobs Account

Particulars		Amount Rs.	Particulars	Amount Rs.
To Raw Materials Consumed:			By Contractee's A/c (Value of Completed Jobs)	4,10,000
Supplied from Stores		90,000		
Less: Transferred to Work-in Progress	2,000			
Returned to Stores	1,000	3,000		
		87,000		
To Wages		1,00,000		
To Chargeable Expenses		10,000		
Prime Cost		1,97,000		
To Factory Overhead (80% of wages)		80,000		
Factory Cost		2,77,000		
To Office Overhead (25% of Factory Cost)		69,250		
Cost of Production		3,46,250		
To Profit Transferred to Profit and Loss A/c		63,750		
		4,10,000		4,10,000

Consolidated Work-in-Progress Account

Particulars		Amount Rs.	Particulars	Amount Rs.
To Raw Materials Consumed:			By Balance c/d	1,35,000
Supplied from Stores	30,000			
Transferred from completed Jobs	2,000	32,000		
To Wages		40,000		
To Chargeable Expenses		4,000		
Prime Cost		76,000		
To Factory Overhead (80% of wages)		32,000		
Factory Cost		1,08,000		
To Office Overhead (25% on Factory Cost)		27,000		
		1,35,000		1,35,000

Illustration 9

The following particulars are drawn from the costing books of a contractor for the month of December, 2004:

	Rs.	Rs.
(*i*) Stores Abstract:		
Balance on 30th November:		52,865
Purchases		10,900
Received from Job No. 201		855
		64,620
Issued to Job No. 202		5,280
Balance on 31st December, 2004		59,340
(*ii*) Wages Abstract:		
Job No. 201	575	
Job No. 202	7,190	7,765
Establishment		640
		8,405

The respective Job Accounts showed the following balances in Contract Ledger on 30th November, 2004:

Job No. 201	Rs. 3,21,580
Job No. 202	Rs. 1,41,865

A certificate of completion was obtained for Job No. 201; of the balance of this account standing on 30th Nov., 2004, Rs. 61,500 was in respect of plant and machinery, the remainder consisting of wages and materials. A machine costing Rs. 5,500 specially brought for this contract, was sold during December, 2004 for Rs. 2,000. Of the remainder of the balance on plant and machinery Rs. 40,000 worth had been utilised on the Job for eight months and the rest for six months. Of the former, half was transferred to Job No. 202 and the whole of the remaining plant was returned to stores. The contract price for Job No. 201 was fixed at Rs. 3,75,000.

Prepare Contract Accounts for the two Jobs and state the profit made on the job certified as completed, allowing depreciation on machinery at 15 per cent per annum. Assume 10 per cent for establishment charges on cost of wages and materials consumed.

(*Raj. M.Com.*)

Solution

Job No. 201 Account

Particulars	Rs.	Particulars	Rs.
To Balance b/d	3,21,580	By Stores Returned	855
To Wages	575	By Plant Sold (Cost Rs. 5,500)	2,000
To Establishment Charges (10% on Rs. 2,59,800)*	25,980	By Profit and Loss Account (Loss on Sale of Plant)	3,500
To Profit and Loss A/c	84,020	By Plant Transferred to Job No. 202	18,000
		By Plant Returned to Stores	18,000
		By Plant Returned to Stores	14,800
		By Contractee's A/c (Contract Price)	3,75,000
	4,32,155		4,32,155

Working Notes:

1. Establishment charges in respect of Job No. 201 A/c have been calculated as follows:

	Rs.
Opening Balance	3,21,580
Less Cost of Plant	61,500
	2,60,080
Add Wages	575
	2,60,655
Less Stores Returned	855
Cost of Materials & Wages	2,59,800

2. Depreciation on plant and value of plant returned to stores have been calculated as follows:

	Rs.
Original Cost of Plant	61,500
Less Cost of Plant Sold	5,500
	56,000

Plant Costing Rs. 40,000 has been used for 8 months and plant costing Rs. 16,000 for 6 months.

	Cost of Plant	Period of Use	Depreciation @ 15% p.a.	Depreciated Value
	Rs.		Rs.	Rs.
(i)	40,000	8 months	4,000	36,000
(ii)	16,000	6 months	1,200	14,800

Half of the plant having the total depreciated value of Rs. 36,000 has been transferred to Job No. 202.

Job No. 202 Account

	Rs.		Rs.
To Balance b/d	1,41,865	By Work-in-Progress	1,72,335
To Wages	7,190		
To Stores	5,280		
To Plant Transferred from Job No. 201	18,000		
	1,72,335		1,72,335

BATCH COSTING

Batch Costing is a varied form of Job Costing. While Job Costing is concerned with the ascertainment of the cost of executing jobs by a jobber according to the specifications given by the customers, Batch Costing is concerned with the ascertainment of the cost of a group of identical products manufactured for own stock. Batch Costing is generally applied in the manufacture of medicines, component parts of complex products (such as motor cars, scooters, computers, watches, televisions etc.), biscuits, food products, readymade garments etc. The products manufactured in a batch are to be used for a particular purpose (e.g., spare parts of complex or composite products are to be used in a particular model only) or to be consumed within a specified period (e.g., medicines, biscuits and food products are to be consumed within a given period otherwise they become harmful).

Costing Procedure:

For the purpose of costing, each batch or group of identical products is allotted a serial number (known as Batch Number) just like a job number. The presentation of the various items of cost is made in the form of a statement known as 'Batch Cost Sheet.'

The Batch Cost Sheet includes the Cost of Direct Material, Cost of Direct Labour and Direct Expenses which can be directly identified with a particular batch. The share of overhead chargeable to the batch (calculated on some equitable basis) is also included in the statement. The total cost of a batch as shown by the Batch Cost Sheet divided by the total number of products in the batch will give us the cost per product in the batch.

Illustration 10

You are required to prepare a Batch Cost Sheet of an engineering works showing the cost of Batch No. 8801 of 1,000 units from the following information. You are given that the batch passes through three departments, X, Y and Z. Costs incurred for the batch are:

Direct Materials Issued	
Dept. X	5,400 kgs. @ Rs. 10 per kg.
Dept. Y	600 kgs @ Rs. 8 per kg.
Dept. Z	500 kgs. @ Rs. 20 per kg.
Direct Wages:	
Dept. X	1,000 hours @ Rs. 2 per hour.
Dept. Y	200 hours @ Rs. 2.50 per hour.
Dept. Z	1,000 hours @ Rs. 1.50 per hour.
Factory Overhead:	
Dept. X	150% on Direct Wages.
Dept. Y	@ Rs. 10 per Labour hour.
Dept. Z	$66\frac{2}{3}\%$ on Direct Wages.

After the batch is complete, 600 kgs. of raw materials issued to Dept. X are found to be surplus and returned to stores.

Solution

Batch Cost Sheet

Period .... Batch No. 8801

		Rs.
Direct Materials Consumed:		
Dept. X : 5,400 kgs. @ Rs. 10 per kg.	Rs. 54,000	
Less Material Returned 600 kgs. @ Rs. 10 per kg.	Rs. 6,000	48,000
Dept. Y : 600 kgs. @ 8 per kg.		4,800
Dept. Z : 500 kgs. @ Rs. 20 per kg.		10,000
		62,800

Direct Wages:		
Dept. X : 1,000 hrs. @ Rs. 2 per hour	2,000	
Dept. Y : 200 hrs. @ Rs. 2.50 per hour	500	
Dept. Z : 1,000 hrs. @ Rs. 1.50 per hour	1,500	4,000
Prime Cost		66,800
Factory Overhead:		
Dept. Z : 150% of Direct Wages	3,000	
Dept. Y : Rs. 10 per Labour hour	2,000	
Dept. Z : $66\frac{2}{3}\%$ of Direct Wages	1,000	6,000
Total Cost		72,800

$$\text{Cost per unit} = \frac{\text{Rs. } 72,800}{1,000 \text{ units}} = \text{Rs. } 72.80$$

OBJECTIVE TYPE QUESTIONS

A. Multiple Choice Questions

1. Select the correct answer in each of the following:

1. In a job cost system, costs are accumulated
(*a*) by specific job (*b*) by kind of material used
(*c*) by department or process (*d*) on a monthly basis.

2. The most suitable cost system where the products differ in type of materials and work performed is
(*a*) Job costing (*b*) Process costing
(*c*) Operating costing (*d*) none of these

3. Job costing is used in
(*a*) repair shops (*b*) printing presses
(*c*) furniture making (*d*) automobile garages
(*e*) all of these

[**Ans.** 1. (*a*), 2. (*a*), 3. (*e*)]

B. 'True'/ 'False' Type Statements.

2. Indicate whether the following statements are 'true' or 'false'

1. Job order costing is most suitable for a large steel mill.

2. Job cost sheet may be used for estimating profit on the job.

3. Job costing cannot be used in industries using standard costing.

4. Job costing can be more suitably used in concerns producing any specific uniform product.

5. Job costing can be applied only in small concerns.

6. In job costing method, a cost sheet is prepared for each job.

[**Ans.** 1. False, 2. True, 3. True, 4. False, 5. False, 6. True]

C. Fill the Blanks

3. Fill in the blanks

1. Costs are accumulated by jobs under .... system, and by process or department under .... system.

2. Under job order cost system, each job is assigned one identifying job........

3. In job costing, each .... is cost unit to which material, labour and overhead costs may be assigned.

[**Ans.** 1. job costing, process costing, 2. number, 3. job]

SHORT ANSWER TYPE QUESTIONS

Answer each of the following questions in not more than five lines each.

1. What is the basic difference between job costing and process costing?

2. What is the difference between job costing and contract costing?

3. Name three such industries where batch costing may be used.

LONG ANSWER TYPE QUESTIONS

1. What is Job Costing? Mention the type of industries in which this system would be suitable.

2. What are the main features of Job Order Costing? Give a proforma Cost Sheet under such a system. (*G.N.D.U., B.Com., 2008*)

3. Discuss the procedure of recording or collecting costs under Job Costing system.

4. What is Job Order Number? Explain how costs are booked against Job Numbers.

5. Write notes on:
(*i*) Job Cost Sheet
(*ii*) Production Order
(*iii*) Calculation of profit or loss on jobs.

6. What is Job Costing? How does it differ from contract costing? Explain. (*M.D.U., B.Com., 1993*)

EXERCISES

1. A Job No. 19 passed through three departments *i.e.*, A, B and C. The following informations are supplied to you regarding this job for the month of June, 2004:

Materials consumed by the Job	Rs. 20,000	Rs. 6,000	Rs. 4,000
Direct Labour Hours for the Hob	5,000	12,000	15,000
Sale of Scrap of Materials from Job	Rs. 2,000	Rs. 400	Rs. 100
Rate of Direct Labour per Hour	Re. 0.80	Re. 1.00	Re. 0.60
Total Overheads for the Departments	Rs. 8,000	Rs. 10,000	Rs. 20,000
Total Labour Hours for the Departments	40,000	25,000	50,000

Calculate the cost of Job No. 19 from the above figures.

[**Ans.** Rs. 64,300]

2. The following information relates to job No. 112:

Materials – Rs. 6,900;

Wages: Depts.	Casting	120 hours at Rs. 3 per hour
	Machining	40 hours at Rs. 4 per hour
	Finishing	30 hours at Rs. 2 per hour

Fixed Overheads were Rs. 10,000 for 5,000 working hours.

Variable Overheads:

Depts.	Casting	Rs. 4,000 for 2,000 labour hours
	Machining	Rs. 6,000 for 1,500 labour hours
	Finishing	Rs. 2,000 for 500 labour hours

What should be the price to be quoted, if profit expected is 20% on the selling price? [**Ans.** Price Rs. 10,975]

3. The Modern Foundry prepares metal castings for specific orders using job order cost system. During the month of January, Job 203 calling for 10,000 machine parts was started and completed. Information for this order is summarised as follows:

(*a*) Material requisitioned: 22,000 pounds @ 54 p. per pound.

(*b*) Labour hours expended: 2,000 @ 1.75 per hour.

(*c*) Manufacturing expenses charged to production @ 90 p. per direct labour hour.

(*d*) Material returned to stores: 800 pounds @ 54 p. per pound.

(*e*) Castings completed: 9,800

Required: the unit cost of production on accuracy to 2 decimal places.

[**Ans.** Cost per unit: Rs. 1.71; Loss of 200 units is treated as normal loss]

4. The following particulars are extracted from the books and other relevant sources in respect of M/s A and Co.:

(*i*) Estimated Material Cost of job is Rs. 50,000 and the direct labour cost is likely to be Rs. 10,000.

(*ii*) In machine shop it will require machining by German machine for 20 hours and Japanese machine for 6 hours.

(*iii*) The Machine Hour rates for German and Japanese machines are Rs. 100 and Rs. 150 respectively.

(*iv*) The direct wages in all other shops last year amounted to Rs. 8,00,000 as against Rs. 4,80,000 factory overheads.

(*v*) Last year factory cost of all jobs amounted to Rs. 25,00,000 as against Rs. 3,75,000 office expenses.

Make out a quotation with 20% profit on selling price.

(*Bombay, M.Com.*) [**Ans.** Selling Price Rs. 99,043.75]

5. A factory uses job costing. The following data are obtained from its books for the year ended 31st March, 2007:

	Rs.
Direct Materials	90,000
Direct Wages	75,000
Factory Overheads	45,000
Administration Overheads	42,000
Selling and Distribution Overheads	52,500
Profit	60,900

(*a*) Prepare a Job Cost Sheet indicating the Prime Cost, Works Cost, Production Cost, Cost of Sales and the Sales Value.

(*b*) In 2007-08 the factory receives an order for a number of jobs. It is estimated that direct materials required will be Rs. 1,20,000 and direct labour will cost Rs. 75,000. What should be the price for these jobs if factory intends to earn the same rate of profit on sales assuming that the selling and distribution overheads have gone up by 15%? The factory recovers factory overheads as a percentage of direct wages and administration and selling and distribution overheads as a percentage of works cost, based on cost rates prevailing during the previous year.

(*C.A., Inter.*)

[**Ans.** Selling Price for 2007-08 : Rs. 4,28,400]

6. GR Co. Ltd. has absorbed overhead by means of a blanket rate based on direct labour hours. As from 1st January, 2004, it decides to adopt separate rates for the three main activities – store-keeping and material handling, machining and assembly. The estimates of costs and absorption rates for selling and distribution cost remain unchanged.

Overhead absorption rates are,

Prior to lst January, 2004:

Production overhead – Re. 0.50 per direct labour hour. Selling and distribution overhead 25% of production cost.

From 1st January, 2004:

Production overhead : Store-keeping and material handling –10% of direct material cost; Machining – Re. 0.75 per machine hour; Assembly – Re. 0.30 per labour hour. Selling and distribution overhead 25% of production cost.

Direct costs of Job No. 101 have been : Direct material cost Rs. 90; Direct wages: Machining, 20 hours @ Re. 0.60: Assembly: 100 hours @ Re. 0.40.

Contract price of the job is Rs. 525 and it requires 180 machine hours to complete.

Show the Job Cost Sheet for Job No. 101:

(*a*) as it would appear if the job had been completed prior to 1st January, 2004.

(*b*) as it would appear if the job were completed in January, 2004.

[**Ans.** (*a*) Profit Rs. 25 (*b*) Loss Rs. 5]

7. The following information for the year ending 31st March, 2007 is obtained from the books and records of a factory:

	Completed Jobs Rs.	Work-in-Progress Rs.
Raw Materials Supplied from Stores	18,000	6,000
Wages	20,000	8,000
Direct Expenses	2,000	800
Materials Transferred to Work-in-Progress	400	400
Materials Returned to Stores	200	-

Factory overhead is 80% of wages and office overhead is 25% of factory cost. The price of the executed jobs during 2006-07 was Rs. 82,000. Prepare:

(*a*) Consolidated Completed Jobs Account, showing the profit or loss thereon.

(*b*) Consolidated Work-in-Progress Account.

[**Ans.** Profit Rs. 12,750 completed Jobs]

(*K.U., B.Com., 1984*)

8. The estimated material cost of a job is Rs. 5,000 and direct labour cost is likely to be Rs. 1,000. In machine shop it will require machining by Machine No. 8 for 20 hours, and by Machine No. 11 for 6 hours. Machine hour rates for Machine No. 8 and Machine No. 11 are respectively Rs. 10 and 15. Considering only machine shop cost, the direct wages in all other shops last year amounted to Rs. 80,000 as against Rs. 48,000 factory overhead. Last year factory cost of all jobs amounted to Rs. 2,50,000 as against Rs. 37,500 office expenses.

Prepare a quotation which guarantees 20% profit on selling price.

[**Ans.** Quotation price Rs. 9,905 – by charging factory oncost @ 60% on wages and office expenses @ 15% on factory cost.]

9. During March, 2005 'The New Machine Manufacturing Company' worked on four orders numbered consecutively 101 to 104. Jobs 101 and 104 were completed during the month, Jobs 102 and 103 were in process at the end of the month, order 104 was sold in March to Mr. Amit on credit for cost plus 50 per cent.

The records disclose the following data for March:

(1) Material purchases (all on credit) aggregated Rs. 4,500.

(2) Materials requisitions were:

	Rs.	Rs.
Direct – For Job Order		
101	440	
102	480	
103	560	
104	520	2,000
Indirect – For Factory Overhead		
Maintenance	300	
Repairs	250	550
		2,550

(3) Labour time sheets summary:

Direct – For Job Order	Hours	Amount Rs.
101	1,400	410
102	1,340	335
103	1,900	475
104	1,360	345
	6,000	1,565

Indirect – For Factory Overhead	Rs.	
Supervision	450	
Repairs	180	
Maintenance	220	850
		2,415

(4) Other factory overhead items for the month were as follows:

	Rs.
Payroll Tax (accrued)	75
Repairs, Materials and Supplies (on credit)	425
Depreciation	800
Rent (paid in cash)	650
Insurance (accrued)	250
	2,200

Factory overhead was applied on the normal direct labour hour method, normal factory overhead per month is Rs. 4,000, and normal direct labour hours are 8,000.

(*a*) Prepare a schedule showing the cost of each job for the month.

(*b*) Present a revenue statement for the month and a trial balance as at the end of March.

[**Ans.** Cost of Job No. 101 Rs. 1,550; Job No. 102 Rs. 1,485; Job No. 103 Rs. 1,985; Job No. 104 Rs. 1,545]

10. In a factory following the Job Costing Method, an abstract from the work-in-progress as at 30th September was prepared as under:

Job No.	Materials	Direct Labour		Factory Overheads (80% on Direct Labour Cost)
	Rs	Hrs.	Rs.	Rs.
115	1,325	400	800	640
118	810	250	500	400
120	765	300	475	380
	2,900		1,775	1,420

Materials used in October were as follows:

Materials Requisition No.	Job No.	Cost Rs.
54	118	300
55	118	425
56	118	515
57	120	665
58	121	910
59	124	720
		3,535

A summary of labour hours deployed during October is as under:

Job No.	Number of Hours Shop A	Number of Hours Shop B
115	25	25
118	90	30
120	75	10
121	65	–
124	20	10
	275	75
Indirect Labour		
Waiting for Material	20	10
Machine Breakdown	10	5
Idle Time	5	6
Over Time Premium	6	5
	316	101

A shop credit slip was issued in October, that material issued under Requisition No. 54 was returned to stores as being not suitable. A material transfer note issued in October indicated that material issued under Requisition No.55 for Job 118 was directed to Job 124.

The hourly rate in Shop A for labour is Rs. 3 per hour while at Shop B it is Rs. 2 per hour. The factory overhead is applied at the same rate as in September. Jobs 115, 118 and 120 were completed in October.

You are asked to compute the factory cost of the completed jobs. It is the practice of the management to put a 10% on the factory cost to cover administration and selling overheads and invoice the job to the customer on the total cost plus 20% basis. What would be the invoice price of these 3 jobs.

(*C.A., Inter, Nov., 1985*)

[**Ans.** Job No.	115	118	120
Invoice Price	Rs. 3,946.80	Rs. 3,721.08	3,598.32]

11. A manufacturing unit has pre-determined the overhead recovery rates as 400% on direct wages, 20% on works cost and 25% on cost of production for works expenses, management expenses and commerical expenses respectively.

At the end of the year, it has been found that the works overheads stand under-absorbed to the extent of 30% of the total productive wages, management overheads show under-recovery of one-eighth of the absorbed amount, and the recovery of commerical expenses result in an over-absorption of one-third of the total amount absorbed.

If the prime costs of three jobs are as under, find the profit/loss on the respective selling prices (both on the basis of standard cost and on the basis of full absorption of overheads):

	Job A	**Job B**	**Job C**
	Rs	**Rs.**	**Rs.**
Direct Materials	45.50	32.60	26.80
Direct Wages	15.20	8.60	7.20
Prime Cost	60.70	41.20	34.00
Selling Price	200.00	130.00	90.00

(*I.C.W.A., Inter, 1995*)

	Job A	**B**	**C**
[**Ans.** Profit/loss (1) At Standard Cost	Rs. 17.75	Rs. 16.60	(–) Rs. 4.20
(2) At Actual Cost	Rs. 22.30	Rs. 19.69	(–) Rs. 1.65]

12. Two fitters, a labourer and a boy undertake a job on piece rate basis for Rs.1,290. The time spent by each of them is 220 ordinary working hours. The rates of pay on time basis, are Rs. 1.50 per hour for each of the two fitters, Re. 1 per hour for the labourer and Re. 0.50 per hour for the boy. Calculate:

(*a*) The amount of piece-work premium and the share of each worker, when the piece-work premium is divided proportionately to the wages paid.

(*b*) The selling price of the above job on the basis of the following additional data: Cost of Direct Material Rs. 2,010, Works overhead @ 20% of Prime Cost, Selling Overhead at 10% of Works Cost and Profit at 25% of Cost of Sales. (*I.C.W. A., June, 1998*)

[**Ans.** (*a*) Rs. 300, (*b*) Rs. 5,445]

13. Mayur Engineering Co. engaged in job work has completed all the jobs in hand on 30th December, 2008 except Job No. 447. The cost sheet on 30th December showed direct material and direct labour cost of Rs.40,000 and Rs. 30,000 respectively as having been incurred on Job No. 447. The costs incurred by the business on 31st December, 2008 the last date of the accounting year, were as follows:

	Rs.
Direct Material	2,000
Direct Labour	8,000
Indirect Labour	2,000
Misc. Factory Overheads	3,000

The company follows the practice to make the job absorbed factory overheads on the basis of 120% of direct labour cost. Prepare a composite Job Cost Sheet for Job 447 showing analytical computations, if any, of the value of WIP on Job No. 447.

[**Ans.** Total Cost Rs. 1,25,600]

14. You are appointed as Cost Accountant in a factory and you find that the selling price of Job No. 134 has been calculated on the following basis:

	Rs.
Material	12.08
Direct Wages - 22 hours @25 Paise per hour	5.50
Dept. A 10 hours	
Dept. B 4 hours	
Dept. C 8 hours	17.58
Plus $33\frac{1}{3}\%$ on Prime Cost	5.86
Selling Price	23.44

An analysis of the previous year's profit and loss account shows the following:

	Rs.		Rs.
Materials Used	77,500	Factory Overheads:	
Direct Wages:		Dept. A	2,500
Dept. A	5,000	Dept. B	4,000
Dept. B	6,000	Dept. C	1,000
Dept. C	4,000	Selling Overhead	30,000

You are required to (*a*) draw up a Job Cost Sheet; (*b*) calculate and enter the revised costs using the previous year's figures as a basis; (*c*) add to the total job cost 10% for profit and give the final selling price.

(**Ans.** Rs. 28.42)

15. XY Manufacturing Company uses job cost system. Following data refer to the month of December, 2002:

	Job No. 410 Rs.	Job No. 411	Total Rs.
Opening Balances of Job in hand on 1st Dec. 2002:			
Direct Material	80	420	500
Direct Labour:	150	450	600
Factory overheads absorbed	200	400	600
	430	1,270	1,700

(*b*) Direct material requisition during the month of December 2002:

	Rs.
Job No. 410	120
Job No. 411	280
Job No. 412	225
Job No. 413	300
	925

(*c*) Direct labour distribution:

	Hours	Rs.
Job No. 410	400	600
Job No. 411	200	450
Job No. 412	300	675
Jon No. 413	100	225
	1000	1,950

(*d*) Factory overheads are applied to jobs on production according to direct labour rate which is Rs. 2.

(*e*) Factory overhead incurred in December 2002: Rs. 2,100.

(*f*) Job No. 411 and 412 were completed during the month. They were billed to customer at a price which included 15% of the price of job for selling and administration expenses and another 10% of job price for the profit. Prepare:

(*i*) Job Cost Sheet for Job Nos. 411 and 412.

(*ii*) Determine the billing price for the job.

(*iii*) Calculate the value of WIP inventory.

(*iv*) Prepare an income statement showing gross profit for the month of December, 2002.

[**Ans.** Billing Price Job No. 411, Rs. 3,200 Job No. 412 Rs. 2,000; Work-in-Progress Total Rs. 2,675; Gross Profit Rs. 1,200)

16. One of your clients, a Jobbing Engineer, has hitherto based his quotations on cost of materials and labour plus a percentage to cover overheads and profit. He has now accepted your advice to relate costs to departments (*viz*., X, Y and Z) through which the work passes and in pursuance of this policy to charge overhead to jobs on the basis of department direct labour hours.

He has compiled the following cost data from records for the year ending 31st March, 2004:

Expenses

	Rs.	Suggested base for apportionment to departments
Consumable Stores	500	Direct labour hours
Rent, Rates and Insurance	3,000	Floor area
Depreciation	2,500	Plant value
Indirect Labour	4,000	Direct labour hours
Repairs and Renewals	1,000	Technical estimate, *i.e.*, 3 : 3 : 4 respectively
Labour Amenities	1,500	No. of employees
E.S. Insurance	400	– do –
Works Manager's Salary	3,600	Equally
General Administration	6,000	Ratio of quotations in previous year, *i.e.*, 5 : 4 : 3
Sundry Expenses	400	12 : 7 : 1

Departments	**X**	**Y**	**Z**
Direct Labour Hours	5,000	3,000	2,000
Wages Rate per Hour (Re.)	0.60	0.50	0.40
No. of Employees	20	20	10
Floor Area (in sq.ft.)	3,000	2,000	1,000
Value of Plant (Rs.)	15,000	9,000	6,000

You are required to:

(*a*) calculate the hourly overhead rates to be charged for work in each department;

(*b*) prepare a quotation for a job to which the following data relates:

Material	Rs. 300
Direct Labour:	
X	20 hours
Y	15 hours
Z	10 hours

Profit = 20% of Selling Price.

[**Ans.** Labour Hour Rate: Dept. X Rs. 2.00 Dept. Y Rs. 2.50 Dept. Z Rs. 2.70 Selling Price of Job Rs. 535]

17. Job No. 2198 was commenced on 10th October, 2006 and completed on 1st November, 2006. Material used were Rs. 600 and labour charged directly to the job was Rs. 400. Other information was as follows:

Machine No. 215 used for 40 hours @ Rs. 3.50 per hour.

Machine No. 160 used for 30 hours @ Rs. 4.00 per hour.

6 welders worked on the job for 5 days of 8 hours each; the direct labour rate for welders is 20 paise. Other expenditure of the concern not apportioned for calculating the machine hour or the direct labour hour rates amounted to Rs. 20,000, total direct wages for the period being Rs. 20,000. Ascertain the cost of Job No. 2198.

(G.N.D.U., B.Com., April, 1998)

[**Ans.** Rs. 1,756 charging other expenses @ 100% of direct wages including that of welders]

18. Indian Products Ltd. have received an enquiry for the supply of 2,00,000 numbers of a special type of machine screw. Capacity exists for manufacture of the screws in the company's Unit No. 3 but a fixed investment of Rs. 60,000 and working capital to the extent of 25% of the sale value will be required if the job is undertaken. The costs are estimated as follows:

Raw material –20,000 lbs. at Rs. 2.30 per lb.

Labour hours-direct 18,000 of which 2,000 would be overtime hours payable at double the labour rate.

Labour rate-Re. 1 per hour.

Factory overhead-Re. 1 per direct labour hour.

Selling and distribution cost-Rs. 23,000.

Material recovered as scrap at the end of the operations is estimated at Rs. 2,000.

The company expects a net return of 25% on the capital employed.

Prepare a cost and price statement indicating the price which should be quoted to the customer.

[**Ans.** Quotation Price Rs. 1,28,000]

19. (*a*) What do you understand by Batch Costing? In what industries is it applied?

(*b*) Leo Ltd. undertakes to supply 1,000 units of a component per month for the months of January, February and March, 2007. Every month a batch order is opened against which material and labour cost are booked at actuals and overhead are levied at a rate per labour hour. The selling price is contracted at Rs. 15 per unit.

From the following data, present the cost and profit per unit of each batch order for 3,000 units:

Months	Batch Output (No.)	Material Cost (Rs.)	Labour Cost Rs.	Overheads Rs.	Total Labour Hours
Jan. 2007	1,250	6,250	2,500	12,000	4,000
Feb. 2007	1,500	9,000	3,000	9,000	4,500
Mar. 2007	1,000	5,000	2,000	15,000	5,000

(*C.A. Inter, May, 1987*)

[Ans.

	Jan.	Feb.	March
Cost per unit (Rs.)	10	10	10
Profit per unit (Rs.)	5	5	5

Overall position for 3,000 units – Profit Rs. 15,000]

13 Contract Costing

Contract costing is the method of costing which is applied in a business where separate contracts of non-repetitive nature are undertaken. According to Sharle, "Contract or terminal cost accounts are applicable to a concern which makes specific contracts and requires to know the cost of each." A contract is a job of large size which may extend even beyond one accounting period. The person executing the contract is known as Contractor and the person for whom it is executed is known as Contractee.

Features of Contract Costing

The main features of Contract Costing may be summarised as follows:

(*a*) Contracts are executed at contract site away from executor's or contractor's premises.

(*b*) Contracts are jobs of large size and may continue over more than one accounting period.

(*c*) Each contract is treated as a separate unit of cost for the purpose of cost ascertainment.

(*d*) The contracts are executed as per the specifications given by the contractee.

(*e*) Since the work is executed at the contract site, most of the items of cost to be incurred are direct in nature.

(*f*) The contract is executed by the contractor for some agreed amount of consideration known as Contract Price.

(*g*) The payments by the contractee are made to the contractor in instalments on the basis of the extent of the work already completed by him and certified as complete by contractee's engineer or architect.

Contract costing is most suitable to ship-building, road construction, building construction, civil engineering works etc.

CONTRACT COSTING, JOB COSTING AND TERMINAL COSTING

Contract Costing, Job Costing and Terminal Costing do not differ from each other so far as the nature of the work involved is concerned. But contract costing differs from job costing in as much as a contract is executed at the site outside the factory premises of the contractor, whereas a job is executed by the contractor inside his factory premises. Moreover, the ascertainment of the cost of a contract is very simple as compared to the ascertainment of the cost of a job. A contract is executed at the site of the contract outside the factory premises and as such most of the expenses incurred by the contractor in its execution are direct in nature. A job is performed inside the factory premises where a number of different jobs are completed simultaneously and a number of items of indirect expenses have to be apportioned to these jobs on some equitable basis.

Contract costing and job costing differ slightly from terminal costing as in case of terminal costing a deadline is fixed by the contractee within which a job or contract must be completed failing which the contractor shall pay damages to the contractee on account of loss suffered by him due to the delay in the completion of the job or contract.

Objects of Contract Costing

The main objects of Contract Costing are:

(*i*) to ascertain the total cost of a contract, and

(*ii*) to ascertain the profit or loss on the contract.

Costing Procedure

A contractor maintains a Contract Ledger in which a separate account is opened for each contract undertaken by him. The Contract Ledger should be ruled out as to give maximum information. A specimen ruling of the Contract Ledger is given below:

Contract Ledger

Contract No. .... Contract Price...................
Site.................................. Terms of Payment.................
Started on .... Retention Money..................
Completed on..................... Work Certified......................
Remarks........................... Date .... Rs. ....
Date .... Rs. ....

Date	Particulars	Materials	Wages	Direct Charges	Indirect Charges	Total
		Rs.	Rs.	Rs.	Rs.	Rs.
	Total					

When a contract has been accepted by the contractor, a separate account is opened for each contract in order to bring together all costs relating to a particular contract, and a serial number is given to each contract. All expenses incurred on account of a contract *i.e.*, materials, wages, direct expenses, cost of sub-contracts, cost of special plant, indirect expenses etc., are debited to Contract Account. Similarly, expenses accrued or outstanding on the contract at the end of the accounting period are also debited to Contract Account. Materials returned to supplier, materials and plant returned to store, transferred to other contracts, stolen, destroyed, sold and in hand at the end of the accounting period will appear on the credit side of the Contract Account. Materials and plant stolen or destroyed are abnormal losses and should be charged to Profit and Loss Account. Similarly, profit or loss arising from the sale of the plant or materials should also be transferred to Profit and Loss Account by way of abnormal items. The other items to be shown on the credit side of the Contract Account are Contract Price (in case of completed contracts) and the work-in-progress consisting of value of certified work and cost of uncertified work (in case of incomplete contracts). A specimen of Contract Account may be given as follows:

Contract No. 4 .... Account

Particulars	Amount	Particulars	Amount
	Rs.		Rs.
To Materials:		By Materials:	
(*i*) Direct Purchases		(*i*) Returned to Suppliers	
(*ii*) Issued from Stores		(*ii*) Returned to Stores	
(*iii*) Transferred from other Contracts		(*iii*) Transferred to other Contracts	
To Wages		(*iv*) Sold	
To Plant		(*v*) In Hand	
(*i*) Cost of Special Plant		By Plant	
(*ii*) Depreciation of General Plant		(*i*) Returned to Stores	
To Direct Expenses		(*ii*) Transferred to other Contracts	
To Cost of Sub-contracts		(*iii*) Sold	
To Cost of Extra Work		(*iv*) In Hand	
To Indirect Expenses		By Profit and Loss A/c	
To Expenses Accrued		(*i*) Materials Lost, Stolen or Destroyed	
		(*ii*) Plant Lost, Stolen or Destroyed	
		By Contractee's A/c	
		(Contract Price in case of a completed contract)	
		OR	
		By Work-in-Progress A/c	
		(*i*) Value of Certified Work	
		(*ii*) Cost of Uncertified Work	
		(In case of an incomplete contract)	

The treatment of the various items included in the Contract A/c has been discussed hereunder:

(A) Materials:

The cost of materials purchased directly or issued from the stores will appear on the debit side of Contract A/c. Materials returned to suppliers and stores will appear on the credit side. Amount received from the sale of surplus materials will be credited to Contract A/c, any profit or loss arising therefrom to be transferred to Profit and Loss Account by way of abnormal item. Materials lost, stolen or destroyed by accident, fire etc., will be charged to Profit and Loss A/c by way of abnormal loss. Values of material in hand at the end of the accounting period will appear on the credit side of Contract A/c. Sometimes, materials are transferred from one contract to another contract. In such a case, the contract receiving the materials is debited and the contract sending the materials is credited. The treatment of the various items of material in Contract Account can be explained with the help of the following example.

Example

B undertook a Contract No. 5 for the construction of a cinema building. He purchased material for the contract at a cost of Rs. 80,000. Issues from stores were Rs. 45,000. Materials valued Rs. 3,000 were returned to stores while materials costing Rs. 2,000 were stolen and those costing Rs. 500 were destroyed by fire. Materials costing Rs. 5,000 were sold for Rs. 4,800. Materials worth Rs. 25,000 were received from Contract No. 3 which was completed. Materials worth Rs. 1,000 were transferred to Contract No. 15. Materials in hand at the end of accounting period were valued at Rs. 10,000. Show the treatment of the materials in Contract Account No. 5.

Solution

Contract Account No. 5

	Rs.			Rs.
To Materials				
(*i*) Purchased Directly	80,000	By Materials		
(*ii*) Issued from Stores	45,000	Returned to Stores		3,000
(*iii*) Transferred from Contract No. 3	25,000			
		By Profit and Loss A/c:		2,500
		Materials Stolen	2,000	
		Materials Destroyed	500	
		By Materials Sold (Cost Rs. 5,000)		4,800
		By Profit and Loss A/c (Loss on Sale of Materials)		200
		Cost 5,000		
		Sold for 4,800		
		By Materials Transferred to Contract No. 15		1,000
		By Materials in Hand		10,000

(B) Labour Cost:

All the workers engaged at the site of a particular contract, irrespective of the nature of the work performed by them, are treated as direct workers and the amount of wages paid to them as direct wages. Such wages are to be charged to the particular contract directly. In case a worker (generally the supervisory staff) is engaged at two or more contracts, his total wages may be apportioned to different contracts on the basis of time devoted to each contract or on some other equitable basis. Wages accrued or outstanding at the end of the accounting period should appear on the debit side of the Contract Account.

Example

The following data are available for the year ending 31st March, 2007 relating to Contract No. 2, commenced on 1st April, 2006.

Direct Wages paid Rs. 85,000

Wages Accrued on 31st March, 2007 Rs. 12,000

Show the treatment of these items in Contract No. 2 Account.

Contract No. 2 Account

	Rs.		Rs.
To Direct Wages	8,5000		
To Wages Accrued	12,000		

(C) Plant:

The plant purchased by the contractor for executing the contract may be divided into two parts–Special Plant and General Plant.

Special plant refers to the plant which is specially purchased for a particular contract and is expected to the used for that contract over a long period. The value of special plant at the commencement of the use period (*i.e.*, the original cost including installation charges or written down value) is debited to the Contract Account. At the end of the accounting period, value of the plant after providing appropriate amount of depreciation *i.e.*, depreciated value, shall be credited to Contract Account. In this way the amount of depreciation on plant is automatically charged to the contract account. While calculating the value of plant in hand, the value of plant returned to store, plant sold, and plant destroyed, etc., should also be taken into account.

Example

A plant costing Rs. 80,000 was purchased for Contract No. 5 on 1.4.2004. Plant worth Rs. 4,000 was returned to store and plant costing Rs. 4,000 was sold for Rs. 6,000. Plant worth Rs. 2,000 was stolen and worth Rs. 8,000 destroyed by fire. Value of plant in hand at the end of the year 31.3.2005 was Rs. 40,000. Show how the plant would be treated in Contract Account No. 5.

Solution

Contract No. 5 Account

2004		Rs.	2004			Rs.
April 1	To Special Plant Purchased	80,000		By Plant Returned to Stores		4,000
	To Profit and Loss A/c (Profit on Sale of Plant)	2,000		By Plant Sold		6,000
				By Profit and Loss A/c:		10,000
				Plant Stolen	2,000	
				Plant Destroyed	8,000	
			2005 March 31	By Plant in Hand		40,000

Example

B purchased a plant for Contract No. 5 on 1st July, 2004 at a cost of Rs. 40,000. Show the treatment of plant in contract account by depreciating it by (*i*) 10 per cent and (*ii*) 10 per cent per annum, assuming that accounts are closed on 31st March, each year.

Solution

(*i*) **Contract No. 5 Account**

2004		Rs.	2005		Rs.
July 1	To Plant Purchased	40,000	March 31	By Plant in Hand Cost 40,000 Less Dep. @ 10% 4,000	36,000

(*ii*) **Contract No. 5 Account**

2004		Rs.	2005			Rs.
July 1	To Plant Purchased	40,000	March 31	By Plant in Hand Cost Rs. 40,000 Less Dep. @ 10% p.a.	3,000	37,000

Example

A contractor purchased a plant on 1.4.2004 for Contract No. 3 at a cost of Rs. 1,00,000. Plant costing Rs. 20,000 was returned to stores on 31.12.2004. Plant costing Rs. 5,000 was lost in an accident on 30.9.2004. Plant costing Rs. 10,000 was found unsuitable and sold immediately at Rs. 11,500. Show the treatment of the plant by providing depreciation at 20% per annum. The books are closed on 31st March, each year.

Solution

Contract No. 3 Account

2004		Rs.	2004			Rs.
April 1	To Plant Purchased	1,00,000	April 1	By Plant Sold		11,500
	To Profit and Loss A/c (Profit on Sale of Plant) (Rs. 11,500 – Rs. 10,000)	1,500	Sept. 30	By Profit and Loss A/c (Plant lost)		4,500
				Cost Rs.	5,000	
				Less Dep. @ 20% for 6 months	500	
			Dec. 31	By Plant Returned to Stores		
				Cost	Rs. 20,000	
				Less Dep. @ 20% for 9 months	3,000	17,000
			2005 March 31	By Plant in Hand		
				Cost Rs.	65,000	
				Less Dep. @ 20%	13,000	52,000

Calculation of cost of plant in hand on 31.3.2005:

	Rs.	Rs.
Cost of Plant		1,00,000
Less:		
(*i*) Cost of Plant Sold	10,000	
(*ii*) Cost of Plant Lost	5,000	
(*iii*) Cost of Plant Returned	20,000	
		35,000
Cost of Plant in Hand		65,000

General Plant

General Plant refers to the plant which is purchased for use at two or more contracts. In case of general plant, an hourly, daily, weekly or monthly rate of depreciation may be ascertained and the amount of depreciation can be charged to each contract according to the actual use of the plant at the site of the contract. The treatment of depreciation on general plant can be explained with the help of the following example:

Example

A plant was purchased for Rs. 52,000 on 1st April, 2004. It was expected that the life of the plant is 5 years and at the end of the 5th year its scrap value will be Rs. 2,000. The plant was used for 73 days on Contract No. 31. Show the treatment of plant in Contract No. 31 Account.

Solution

	Rs.
Cost Price of the Plant	52,000
Less Scrap Value	2,000
Depreciation to be provided over 5 years or 1,825 days (365 days × 5)	50,000

Amount of Depreciation to be Charged

$$\text{to Contract No. 31} = \frac{\text{Rs. } 50{,}000}{1{,}825 \text{ days}} \times 73 \text{ days} = \text{Rs. } 2{,}000$$

Contract No. 31 Account

	Rs.		Rs.
To Depreciation on Plant	2,000		

(D) Direct Expenses:

All expenses (other than material cost and direct wages) which have been incurred specifically for a particular contract are direct expenses and shall be debited to contract account. Examples of direct expenses are: hire charges of special plant (not owned), carriage on materials purchased, travelling expenses relating to contract etc.

(E) Indirect Expenses:

There are certain expenses which cannot be directly charged to a particular contract e.g., salary of general manager, salary of architect engaged at a number of contracts simultaneously, salary of store-keeper, expenses of store and office expenses. Since these expenses are incurred for the business as a whole, they are to be apportioned to the different contracts on some equitable basis.

(F) Cost of Sub-contracts:

Generally, the work of a specialised character e.g., road construction in a building, installation of lifts, electrical fittings, is passed on to some other contractor by the main contractor. In such cases, the work performed by the sub-contractor forms a direct charge to the contract concerned and the sub-contract price paid shall be debited to Contract Account.

(G) Cost of Extra Work:

Sometimes, in case of a contract, some additional work or variations of the work originally contracted for, may be required by the contractee. Since the additional work required will not be covered by the terms and conditions of original contract, it will be the subject of a separate charge. If the additional work required by the contractee is quite substantial, it should be treated as a separate contract and dealt with in a separate account to be opened for it. But in case the additional work is not substantial, the expenses incurred on extra work should be debited to contract account as Cost of Extra Work and the extra amount which the contractee has agreed to pay to the contractor should be added to the original contract price.

(H) Contract Price:

The contract price is the agreed price at which the contractor undertakes to execute the contract. The contract account is credited with the contract price if it has been completed. In such a case, the amount of contract price is debited to the Contractee's Personal Account and credited to the Contract Account. No entry is passed in respect of the contract price in case of incomplete contracts.

(I) Work-in-Progress:

The amount of work-in-progress to be included on the credit side of the contract account in respect of an incomplete contract comprises:

(*i*) Work Certified, and
(*ii*) Work done but not certified.

(*i*) Work Certified

In case of large contracts, it is usual for the contractor to receive sums on account from the contractee from time to time. These sums will be paid against certificates issued by the contractee's architect, surveyor or engineer as to the value of the work so far completed by the contractor. The work completed by the contractor and certified to be complete by the contractee's architect or engineer is known as Work certified or Work completed and certified.

(*ii*) Work done but not Certified

Work relating to an incomplete contract which has been done but has not yet been certified by contractee's engineer or architect is known as Uncertified Work or Work done but not Certified. It comprises the work done since the date of the last certification and should be valued on the basis of actual cost.

The amount of work-in-progress (work certified and work done but not certified) in case of incomplete contracts at the end of accounting period is debited to Work-in-Progress Account and credited to Contract Account. At the beginning of the next accounting period, such amount is debited to Contract Account and credited to Work-in-Progress Account.

Retention Money

Generally, the terms of the contract provide that the whole of the amount shown by the architect's certificate shall not be paid to the contractor but a specified percentage or portion (say 10% or 20%) thereof shall be retained by the contractee till the completion of the contract. The money so retained is known as Retention Money. Suppose, the total value of work certified is Rs. 1,00,000 and it is agreed that 20% of the work certified shall be retained till the completion of the contract, the contractee shall pay Rs. 80,000 to the contractor immediately and keep Rs. 20,000 (20% of Rs. 1,00,000) as Retention Money till the completion of contract.

COST PLUS CONTRACTS

Sometimes contractors may accept contracts on the condition that the contractee would bear all costs incurred in executing a contract plus a fixed rate or percentage of profit calculated with reference to total cost. Such contracts are known as Cost Plus contracts and are generally adopted in cases where the probable cost of contract cannot be ascertained in advance with a reasonable degree of accuracy. Cost-plus-contracts are given frequently by Government for production of special articles not usually manufactured, e.g., production of newly designed aircraft component, or in case of urgent repair of ships, vehicles, power house etc., or in case of constructions during war period. From the contractor's point of view, this method protects him from the risks of fluctuations in market prices of material, labour, and other services. In case of these contracts, the contractor knows in advance, the profit he can expect on contract when executed. From the contractor's point of view, this method ensures that the price will depend on cost rather than on arbitrary commitment to a specific price.

ESCALATION CLAUSE

In order to reduce the element of risk by market fluctuations, an 'escalator clause' or 'escalation clause' may be included in the contract. According to this clause, one of the conditions of the contract would be, that in case of a change in the prices of materials, labour and other services during the course of the execution of the contract, the contract price shall be adjusted accordingly. In case these are the rise in the prices of materials, labour and other services beyond a particular level, the contractee would bear such additional costs. Similarly, if there is a fall in the price of material and/or labour beyond the specified level, the contractor shall allow a rebate in his bill to the contractee.

CALCULATION OF PROFIT/LOSS ON CONTRACTS

The procedure for the determination of profit or loss on contracts under different circumstances may be given as follows:

1. Profit on Completed Contracts:

In case of contracts completed during the accounting year, the full contract price, whether payable in lump sum on the completion of contract or payable by instalments, shall be debited to the Contractee's Personal Account and credited to the Contract Account. The difference between the total of the two sides of Contract Account shall be transferred to Profit and Loss Account of the contractor by way of profit or loss. Sometimes, under the terms of the agreement, the contractor undertakes to rectify the defects, if any, in the contract work which may arise during a specified period (known as Maintenance Period) after the date of the completion of the contract. The amount of profit or loss on contracts in such a case should be ascertained only after making a sufficient provision for cost of maintenance expected to be incurred during the maintenance period.

2. Profit on Incomplete Contracts:

As a general rule, profits on incomplete contracts should not be taken credit for. A number of arguments are given against the calculation of profits on incomplete contracts. Firstly, the anticipation of profits is against the general accounting principles. Secondly, the true profit on a contract cannot be ascertained until a contract is finished since a contract which appears to be profitable in its early stages may finally result into a loss on account of unexpected losses. Lastly, income tax will be paid on profits at an earlier date than would otherwise be necessary.

But, it is counter-argued that by including profit on incomplete contracts in the Profit and Loss Account, undue fluctuations in the profits and dividends paid can be avoided. Secondly, some contracts may take several years to complete and if profits are calculated on such contracts on completion, it shall appear that the entire amount of profit has been earned in one year, which is not correct. Therefore, profits on incomplete contracts should be calculated very cautiously and only a portion of it may be credited to Profit and Loss Account.

The computation of profit on incomplete contracts has two aspects:

(*a*) Computation of Notional Profit at the End of the Accounting Period on Incomplete Contract.

For this purpose, the value of Certified Work and cost of Uncertified Work at the end of the accounting period are credited to the Contract Account. The amount of notional profit shall be:

Value of Work Certified	x x x x x x
Add Cost of Work not yet Certified	x x x x x x
	x x x x x x
Less Total Cost of Contract to Date	x x x x x
Notional Profit	x x x x x x

(*b*) Computation of the Proportion of the Notional Profit to be Transferred to Profit and Loss Account.

The entire amount of notional profit at the end of the accounting period is not transferred to Profit and Loss Account. In view of the future uncertainties involved in contract work, only a portion of the notional profit is transferred to Profit and Loss Account and the remaining portion is kept by way of a provision to cover future contingencies. The following principles are generally followed for the purpose of ascertaining the proportion of notional profit to be transferred to Profit and Loss Account.

(*i*) Incomplete Contracts with Little Progress:

These are the contracts which have just commenced or where only a small portion of the contract (as a general rule, less than $\frac{1}{4}$) has been finished. In case of such contracts, it is not prudent to take credit for any profit made thereon, since it is impossible to see the future position of such contracts clearly. The entire amount of notional profit on such contracts is kept by way of provision for contingencies and is transferred to the credit of Work-in-Progress Account so as to bring it down to its actual cost.

(*ii*) Incomplete Contracts with Appreciable Progress:

A contract is generally said to have made appreciable progress if at least $\frac{1}{4}$ of the contract has been completed. The proportion of the notional profit to be transferred to Profit and Loss Account in respect of such contracts is computed as follows:

(*a*) When work certified is $\frac{1}{4}$ or more than $\frac{1}{4}$ but less than $\frac{1}{2}$ of the contract price, the amount of profit to be transferred to Profit and Loss account should be:

$$= \text{Notional Profit} \times \frac{1}{3} \times \frac{\text{Cash Received}}{\text{Work Certified}}$$

(*b*) When work certified is $\frac{1}{2}$ or more than $\frac{1}{2}$ of the contract price, but the contract is not nearing completion, the profit to be transferred to Profit and Loss Account should be:

$$= \text{Notional Profit} \times \frac{2}{3} \times \frac{\text{Cash Received}}{\text{Work Certified}}$$

(*iii*) Incomplete Contracts Nearing Completion:

These are the contracts which are nearing completion and the future costs to be incurred on their completion can reasonably be estimated. The amount of profit to be transferred to Profit and Loss Account, in this case, shall be ascertained on the basis of estimated profit. Estimated Profit, in case of contract nearing completion is the difference between contract price and the total estimated cost of contract on completion and can be ascertained as follows :

Total Contract Price	x x x x x
Less Estimated Cost of Contract on Completion	x x x x x
Estimated Profit on Completion	x x x x x

The calculation of the Estimated Cost of Contract on Completion shall be calculated as follows:

Net Expenditure Incurred on Contract to Date	x x x x x
Add: Estimated Expenditure yet to be Incurred to Complete the Contract	x x x x x
Estimated Cost of Contract on Completion	x x x x x

Moreover, only a proportion of the estimated profit is to be transferred to Profit and Loss Account, leaving the balance to guard against future contingencies. The proportion of estimated profit to be transferred to Profit and Loss Account can be calculated by any of the following formulae:

(*a*) $\text{Estimated Profit on Completion} \times \dfrac{\text{Value of Work Certified}}{\text{Contract Price}}$

(*b*) $\text{Estimated Profit on Completion} \times \dfrac{\text{Value of Work Certified}}{\text{Contract Price}} \times \dfrac{\text{Cash Received}}{\text{Value of Work Certified}}$

(*c*) $\text{Estimated Profit on Completion} \times \dfrac{\text{Cost to Date}}{\text{Total Estimated Cost}}$

Loss on Incomplete Contracts:

When an incomplete contract reveals a loss, the whole of the amount of such loss must be charged to the Profit and Loss Account of the accounting year.

Problems of Various Types:

(*A*) *Contracts commenced and completed during the same financial year.*

Illustration 1

The Contract Ledger of a company showed the following particulars in respect of Contract No. 50 which was commenced on 1st April, 2006:

	Rs.
Materials Issued	76,000
Direct Wages	80,000
Cost of Special Plant	20,000
Chargeable Expenses	7,000
Establishment Charges	5,000

The contract was completed by 31st March, 2007 and the contract price was Rs. 2,00,000. The value of materials and plant returned to store on 31st March, 2007 was 6,000 and Rs. 12,000 respectively. Contract price was received in full on 31st March.

Prepare Contract Account and Contractee's Personal Account.

Solution

Contract No. 50 Account

	Rs.		Rs.
To Materials Issued	76,000	By Materials to Store	6,000
To Direct Wages	80,000	By Value of Plant Returned to Store	12,000
To Cost of Special Plant	20,000		
To Chargeable Expenses	7,000	By Contractee's A/c (Contract Price)	2,00,000
To Establishment Charges	5,000		
To Profit and Loss A/c (Profit)	30,000		
	2,18,000		2,18,000

Contractee's Account

2007		Rs.	2007		Rs.
March 31	To Contract No. 50 A/c (Contract Price)	2,00,000	March 31	By Bank A/c	2,00,000
		20,00,000			2,00,000

Illustration 2

The following is the summarised record as on 31st March, 2007, relating to Contract No. 414 completed during the year:

	Rs.
Materials Purchased Directly	1,270
Materials Supplied from Stores	520
Wages	2,144
Expenses Directly Chargeable	294
Materials Returned to Stores	240
Contract Price	5,000
Works Oncost-25% on Direct Wages	
Office Oncost-10% on Prime Cost	

Prepare the Contract Account from the above particulars.

Solution

Contract No. 414 Account

		Rs.		Rs.
To Materials Consumed:				
(*i*) Materials Purchased	1,270			
(*ii*) Issued from Stores	520			
	1,790			
Less Materials Returned to Stores	240	1,550.00		
To Wages		2,144.00		
To Direct Expenses		294.00		
Prime Cost		3,988.00	By Contractee's Account (Contract Price)	5,000.00
To Works Oncost @ 25% on Direct Wages $\left(\frac{2,144 \times 25}{100}\right)$		536.00		
Works Cost		4,524.00		
To Office Oncost @ 10% on Prime Cost $\left(\frac{3,988 \times 10}{100}\right)$		398.80		
Total Cost		4,922.80		
To Profit and Loss A/c (Profit)		77.20		
		5,000.00		5,000.00

Illustration 3

From the following particulars, write up Contract No. 5 Account and find out the value of the tender (contracted) price

Materials used	30,000
Productive wages	25,000
Direct Expenses	500

Provide 60% on productive wages for works overheads and $12\frac{1}{2}$% on works cost for office overhead. Profit to be realised 15% on tender price.

(G.N.D.U., B.Com., 2000)

Solution

Contract No. 5 Account

	Rs.		Rs.
To Materials Used	30,000		
To Productive Wages	25,000		
To Direct Expenses	500	By Contract Price	93,308.82
	55,500	(Tender Price)	
To Works Overhead $\left(\frac{25{,}000 \times 60}{100}\right)$	15,000		
Works Cost	70,500		
To Office Overhead $\left(\frac{70{,}500 \times 12.5}{100}\right)$	8,812.50		
Total Cost	79,312.50		
To Profit @ 15% on Tender Price $\left(\frac{79{,}312.50 \times 15}{100 - 15}\right)$	13,996.32		
	93,308.82		93,308.82

Illustration 4

Xavier undertook a contract for constructing a building from Yakub on 1st January, 2008, the contract price being Rs. 75,000. He incurred the following expenses:

	Rs.
Materials Consumed	25,000
Materials in Hand at End	1,000
Wages	35,000
Direct Expenses	20,000
Plant Purchased	10,000

The contract was completed on 30th June, 2008 and the contract price was duly received. Provide depreciation @ 10% on plant and charge indirect expenses @ 20% on wages. Prepare Contract Account in the books of Xavier.

Solution

Contract Account

	Rs.		Rs.
To Materials Purchased	26,000	By Materials in hand	1,000
To Wages	35,000	By Plant at site	9,000
To Direct Expenses	20,000	(Cost Rs. 10,000 less Depreciation @ 10% Rs. 1,000)	
To Plant Purchased	10,000	By Yakub (Contract Price)	75,000
To Indirect Expenses @ 20% on Wages $\left(\frac{35,000 \times 20}{100}\right)$	7,000	By Profit and Loss Account (Loss)	13,000
	98,000		98,000

Note: Calculation of materials purchased has been made as follows:

	Rs.
Materials Consumed	25,000
Add: Materials in Hand at the End	1,000
Materials Purchased	26,000

Illustration 5

A contractor undertook a contract on 1st April, 2004 and incurred the following expenses:

	Rs.
Materials Purchased	70,000
Wages Paid	25,000
Cost of Special Plant	20,000
Direct Expenses	10,000
Indirect Expenses	4,000
	1,29,000

Other particulars are:

Contract Price	1,50,000
Value of Plant at the End	15,000
Materials Returned to Stores	4,000

The contract was actually finished on 30th November, 2004 but the contract could not be considered as completed until the maintenance period of 6 months had expired on 31st May, 2005. The cost of maintenance is estimated to be Rs. 6,000. Prepare contract account.

Solution

Contract Account

	Rs.		Rs.
To Materials Purchased	70,000	By Plant at End	15,000
To Wages	25,000	By Materials Returned to Stores	4,000
To Special Plant	20,000		
To Direct Expenses	10,000	By Contractee's A/c (Contract Price)	1,50,000
To Indirect Expenses	4,000		
To Provision for Maintenance	6,000		
To Profit and Loss A/c (Profit)	34,000		
	1,69,000		1,69,000

(*B*) Incomplete Contracts

When work certified is less than $\frac{1}{4}$ of the contract.

Illustration 6

On 1st April, 2006 Contractors Ltd. commenced to build a cinema hall, the contract price being Rs. 6,00,000. During the year ended 31st March 2007, they incurred the following expenses:

	Rs.
Materials Purchased Directly	50,000
Materials Issued from Stores	10,000
Direct Wages	42,000
Plant	10,000
Overhead Charges	3,000

Work to the value of Rs 1,20,000 had been certified on 31st March, 2007 of which 75% had been received in cash. Cost of work completed but not certified was Rs. 10,500. Materials valued at Rs. 5,000 were on hand at site.

After allowing depreciation @ 20% p.a. on plant, prepare an account showing the profit earned to date and the amount of profit for which company may take credit in its accounts on 31st March, 2007. Also prepare Work-in-Progress Account.

Solution

Contract Account

	Rs.			Rs.
To Materials Purchased	50,000	By Materials at Site		5,000
To Materials Issued from Stores	10,000	By Plant at Site		8,000
To Direct Wages	42,000	By Work-in-Progress A/c		
To Plant (cost)	10,000	Value of Certified Work	1,20,000	
To Overhead Charges	3,000	Cost of Uncertified Work	10,500	1,30,500
To Work-in-Progress A/c (Profit Reserved)	28,500			
	1,43,500			1,43,500

Work-in-Progress Account

		Rs.		Rs.
To Contract A/c:		1,30,500	By Contract A/c (Profit reserved)	28,500
Value of Certified Work	1,20,000			
			By Balance c/d	1,02,000
Cost of Uncertified Work	10,500			
		1,30,500		1,30,500

Note: Since the value of Work Certified (Rs. 1,20,000) has been less than $\frac{1}{4}$th of the total contract price, the entire notional profit of Rs. 28,500 has been kept as reserve for contingencies.

Incomplete Contracts–*When work certified is* $\frac{1}{4}$ *or more than* $\frac{1}{4}$ *of the contract price but less than* $\frac{1}{2}$ *of the contract price:*

Illustration 7

A building contractor took a contract for the construction of a certain building on 1st April, 2004. The contract price was agreed at Rs. 4,00,000. The contractor had made the following expenditure during the year ended 31st March, 2005:

	Rs.
Direct Materials Purchased	40,000
Materials Issued from Stores	15,000
Direct Labour	25,000
Special Plant	40,000
Indirect Expenses	10,000
	1,30,000

From the following further information, prepare Contract Account for the year and show the amount of the Work-in-Progress which will be shown in the Balance Sheet of the contractor:

	Rs.
Value of Plant on 31st March, 2005	30,000
Stock of Materials on 31st March, 2005	5,000
Materials Returned to Stores	1,000
Value of Certified Work	1,20,000
Cash Received from Contractee	90,000
Cost of Uncertified Work	4,000

Solution

Contract Account

	Rs.			Rs.
To Materials Purchased	40,000	By Materials Returned to Stores		1,000
To Materials Issued from Stores	15,000	By Value of Materials in Hand		5,000
To Direct Labour	25,000	By Plant at Site		30,000
To Special Plant	40,000	By Work-in-Progress A/c		1,24,000
To Indirect Expenses	10,000	(*i*) Value of Certified Work	1,20,000	
To Balance c/d (Notional Profit)	30,000	(*ii*) Cost of Uncertified Work	4,000	
	1,60,000			1,60,000
To Profit and Loss A/c $\left(30{,}000 \times \frac{1}{3} \times \frac{90{,}000}{1{,}20{,}000}\right)$	7,500	By Balance b/d		30,000
To Work-in-Progress A/c (Profit not taken)	22,500			
	30,000			30,000

Work-in-Progress Account

		Rs.		Rs.
To Contract A/c		1,24,000	By Contract A/c (Profit not taken)	22,500
Value of Certified Work	1,20,000		By Balance c/d	1,01,500
Cost of Uncertified Work	4,000			
		1,24,000		1,24,000

Notes:

(*i*) Since less than $\frac{1}{2}$ of the contract has been certified, $\frac{1}{3}$ of the realised profit has been taken to Profit and Loss A/c.

(*ii*) Work-in-progress will appear in Balance Sheet at Rs. 1,01,500.

Incomplete Contracts–*When the work certified is $\frac{1}{2}$ or more than $\frac{1}{2}$ of contract price but the contract is not nearing completion:*

Illustration 8

The Punjab Engineering Co. Ltd., undertakes large contracts. On 31st March, 2007 when the annual accounts were prepared, the position of a bridge contract which commenced on 1st July, 2006 was as follows:

Materials purchased Rs. 60,000; Wages paid Rs. 70,000; Sundry expenses Rs. 3,000; Plant despatched to site at cost Rs. 10,000; Wages accrued Rs. 1,000; Materials on hand Rs. 2,400.

The value of certified work was Rs. 1,44,000 of which Rs. 1,08,000 had been received. The work finished but uncertified was valued at Rs. 4,000. The plant on the site on 3lst March, 2007 was valued at Rs. 8,000. The contract price was 2,40,000.

You are required to prepare Contract Account, showing the profit which should reasonably be transferred to Profit and Loss A/c and to calculate Work-in-Progress as at 31st March, 2007.

(B.Com. G.N.D.U. Sept. 1983 Modified)

Solution

Bridge Contract Account

		Rs.			Rs.
To Materials		60,000	By Materials at site		2,400
To Wages Paid	70,000		By Plant at site		8,000
Add Accrued Wages	1,000	71,000	By Work-in-Progress A/c:		
To Plant		10,000	Value of certified work	1,44,000	1,48,000
To Sundry Expenses		3,000	Cost of uncertified work	4,000	
To Balance c/d (Notional Profit)		14,400			
		1,58,400			1,58,400
To Profit and Loss A/c $\left(14,400 \times \frac{2}{3} \times \frac{1,08,000}{1,44,000}\right)$		7,200	By Balance b/d (Notional Profit)		14,400
To Work-in-Progress A/c (Profit not taken)		7,200			
		14,400			14,400

Work-in-Progress Account

		Rs.		Rs.
To Contract A/c:		1,48,000	By Contract A/c:	7,200
Value of Certified Work	1,44,000		(Profit not taken)	
Cost of Uncertified Work	4,000		By Balance c/d	1,40,800
		1,48,000		1,48,000

Illustration 9

The following particulars relate to a contract undertaken by a firm of contractors:

	Rs.
Materials Sent to Site	85,349
Labour Engaged on Site	74,375
Plant Installed at Site	15,000
Direct Expenditure	3,167
Establishment Charges	4,126
Materials Returned to Store	549
Work Certified by Architects	1,95,000
Cost of Work not yet Certified	4,500
Materials on hand, 31st March	1,883
Wages Accrued on 31st March	2,400
Direct Expenses Accrued on 31st March	240
Value of Plant on 31st March	11,000

The contract price has been agreed at Rs. 2,50,000. Cash received from contractee was Rs. 1,80,000. You are required to prepare Contract A/c, Contractee's Account, and to show suitable items in the Balance Sheet of the contractors as on 31st March .

(*Agra, M.Com., 1964, 1970, G.N.D.U., B.Com., 1978, 1984 Pbi. Uni. B.Com., 1996*)

Solution

Contract Account

	Rs.			Rs.
To Materials to Site	85,349	By Materials Returned to Store		549
To Labour Engaged	74,375	By Materials at Site		1,883
To Plant Installed	15,000	By Value of Plant as Site		11,000
To Direct Expenditure	3,167			
To Establishment Charges	4,126	By Work-in-Progress A/c		
To Wages Accrued	2,400	Value of Certified Work	1,95,000	
To Direct Expenses Accrued	240	Cost of Uncertified Work	4,500	
To Balance c/d (Notional Profit)	28,275			1,99,500
	2,12,932			2,12,932
To Profit and Loss A/c $\left(28,275\times\frac{2}{3}\times\frac{1,80,000}{1,95,000}\right)$	17,400	By Balance b/d (Notional Profit)		28,275
To Work-in-Progress A/c (Profit not taken)	10,875			
	28,275			28,275

Work-in-Progress Account

		Rs.		Rs.
To Contract A/c:				
Value of Certified Work	1,95,000	1,99,500	By Contract A/c	10,875
Cost of Uncertified Work	4,500		(Profit not taken)	
			By Balance c/d	1,88,625
		1,99,500		1,99,500

Contractee's Account

	Rs.		Rs.
To Balance c/d	1,80,000	By Bank A/c	1,80,000
	1,80,000		1,80,000

Balance Sheet as on 31st March

Liabilities	Rs.	Assets		Rs.
		Work-in-Progress	1,88,625	
Wages Accrued	2,400	Less Cash		
Direct Expenses Accrued	240	Received from Contractee	1,80,000	8,625
		Materials in Store		549
		Materials at Site		1,883
		Plant at Site		11,000

Illustration 10

Bharat Construction Co. Ltd. has undertaken the construction of multi-storey building for a contract price of Rs. 25 lacs. The retention money agreed is 20% and the contractee is to make payment for 80% of the work certified by the engineer. The following are the details as shown in the books on 31st March, 2004.

	Rs.
Materials sent Direct to Site	8,40,000
Materials Issued from Stores	2,12,400
Labour on Site	8,10,000
Hire and use of Plant	24,200
Materials Destroyed at Site (cost)	10,000
Direct Expenses	46,000
General Expenses Allocated to Contract	74,200
Materials Sold at Site at a Profit of 20% on Selling Price Costing	40,000
Materials in Hand on March 31, 2004	12,600
Wages Accrued on March 31, 2004	15,600
Direct Expenses Accrued on March 31, 2004	3,200
Work not yet Certified at Cost	33,000
Work Certified by the Engineer	22,00,000
Cash Received from the Contractee	17,60,000

You are required to prepare:

(*a*) Contract Account,

(*b*) Contractee's Account, and

(*c*) To show the items as they would appear in the balance sheet of the contractor.

(*G.N.D.U., B.Com.1975*)

Solution

Contract Account

	Rs.		Rs.
To Materials Sent Direct to Site	8,40,000	By Profit and Loss A/c	10,000
To Materials Issued from Store	2,12,400	(Materials destroyed)	
To Labour on Site	8,10,000	By Sale of Materials	
To Hire and use of Plant	24,200	(Selling Price)	50,000
To Direct Expenses	46,000	By Materials in Hand	12,600
To General Expenses		74,200 By Work-in-Progress A/c:	
To Wages Accrued	15,600	Value of Work Certified 22,00,000	
To Direct Expenses Accrued	3,200	Cost of Uncertified Work 33,000	22,33,000
To Profit and Loss A/c	10,000		
(Profit on Sale of Materials)			
To Balance c/d (Notional Profit)	2,70,000		
	23,05,600		23,05,600
To Profit and Loss A/c	1,44,000	By Balance b/d	2,70,000
$\left(2,70,000 \times \frac{2}{3} \times \frac{80}{100}\right)$			
To Work-in-Progress A/c			
(Profit not taken)	1,26,000		
	2,70,000		2,70,000

Work-in-Progress Account

	Rs.		Rs.
To Contract Account:		By Contract A/c	1,26,000
Value of Work Certified 22,00,00	22,33,000	(Profit not taken)	
Cost of Work Uncertified 33,000		By Balance c/d	21,07,000
	22,33,000		22,33,000

Contractee's Account

	Rs.		Rs.
To Balance c/d	17,60,000	By Bank A/c	17,60,000
	17,60,000		17,60,000

(D) Incomplete Contracts – *When Cost of Uncertified Work has to be ascertained:*

Illustration 11

M/s Promising Company undertook a contract for erecting a sewerage treatment plant for Prosperous Municipality for a total value of Rs. 24 lakhs. It was estimated that the job would be completed by 31st January, 2006. You are asked to prepare the Contract Account for the year ending 31st January, 2005 from the following particulars:

(*i*)	Materials	Rs. 3,00,000
(*ii*)	Wages	Rs. 6,00,000
(*iii*)	Overhead Charges	Rs. 1,20,000

(*iv*) Special Plant Rs. 2,00,000

(*v*) Work certified was for Rs. 16,00,000 and 80% of the same was received in cash.

(*vi*) Materials lying on site as on 31.1.2005 was Rs. 40,000.

(*vii*) Depreciate Plant by 10%.

(*viii*) 5% of the value of material issued and 6% of wages may be taken to have been incurred for the portion of the work completed but not yet certified. Overheads are charged as a percentage of direct wages.

(*ix*) Ignore depreciation of Plant for use on uncertified portion of the work.

(*x*) Ascertain the amount to be transferred to Profit and Loss Account on basis of realised profit.

(*G.N.D.U, B.Com., 1972, Punjabi, B.Com., April, 1988*)

Solution

Contract Account

	Rs.			Rs.
To Materials	3,00,000	By Materials on Site		40,000
To Wages	6,00,000	By Value of Plant at Site		
To Overhead Charges	1,20,000	Cost	Rs. 2,00,000	
To Special Plant	2,00,000	Depreciation 10%	20,000	1,80,000
		By Work-in-Progress A/c:		
		Value of Certified Work	16,00,000	
To Balance c/d (Notional Profit)	6,58,200	Cost of Uncertified Work	58,200	16,58,200
	18,78,200			18,78,200
To Profit and Loss A/c $\left(6,58,200 \times \frac{2}{3} \times \frac{80}{100}\right)$	3,51,040	By Balance b/d (Notional Profit)		6,58,200
To Work-in-Progress A/c (Profit not taken)	3,07,160			
	6,58,200			6,57,200

Working Notes:

(*i*) Calculation of percentage of overhead charges on direct wages:

$$\frac{\text{Overhead Charges}}{\text{Direct Wages}} \times 100 = \frac{1,20,000}{6,00,000} \times 100$$

$$= 20\% \text{ on direct wages}$$

(*ii*) Calculation of the cost of uncertified work:

	Rs.
Materials : 5% of Rs. 3,00,000 (Materials issued):	15,000
Wages : 6% of Rs. 6,00,000	36,000
Overhead Charges : 20% on Direct Wages (Rs. 36,000)	7,200
	58,200

Illustration 12

Given below is a summary of entries in a Contract Ledger as at 31st March, 2005 in respect of Contract No. 223.

	Rs.
Materials	26,500
Wages	24,420
Direct Expenses	6,710
Establishment Charges	8,000
Plant	34,200
Sale of Scrap	1,820

You are required to prepare an account for Contract No. 223 after taking into account the following information and to indicate what profit should be taken to the Profit and Loss Account for the year ending 31st March, 2005.

(*a*) Accruals on 31st March, 2005 are: Wages Rs. 800, Establishment charges Rs. 1,120.
(*b*) Depreciation of the plant up to 31st March, 2005 was Rs. 8,550.
(*c*) Included in the summary of entries are: Wages Rs. 1,000, Other expenses Rs. 1,500, Materials used Rs. 2,080 since certification of work done.
(*d*) Materials on site at 31st March, 2005 cost Rs. 10,000.
(*e*) Rs. 62,500 has been the total work certified up to 20th March, 2005 when three-eights of the contract remained incompleted.
(*f*) The total contract price was Rs. 1,00,000.
(*g*) Ignore depreciation of plant in respect of work uncertified.
(*h*) Cash received has been 75% of work certified.

Solution

Contract No. 223 Account

	Rs.			Rs.
To Materials	26,500	By Sale of Scrap		1,820
To Wages	24,420	By Value of Plant		
To Direct Expenses	6,710	Cost Rs.	34,200	
To Establishment Charges	8,000	Less Depreciation	8,550	25,650
To Plant	34,200			
To Accrued Wages	800			
To Accrued Establishment Charges	1,120	By Materials on Site		10,000
		By Work-in-Progress A/c:		
		Value of Certified Work	62,500	
To Balance c/d (Notional Profit)	2,800	Cost of Uncertified Work	4,580	67,080
	1,04,550			1,04,550
To Profit and Loss A/c: $\left(2{,}800 \times \frac{2}{3} \times \frac{75}{100}\right)$	1,400	By Balance b/d		2,800
To Work-in-Progress A/c (Profit not taken)	1,400			
	2,800			2,800

Working Notes:

(*i*) Calculation of Cost of work done but not certified has been made as follows:
Expenses incurred since the date of certification of work done:

	Rs.
Materials used	2,080
Wages Paid	1,000
Other Expenses	1,500
Cost of Uncertified Work	4,580

(*ii*) Depreciation on plant in respect of uncertified work has been ignored.

(*iii*) Since more than 1/2 of the contract has been completed and certified, 2/3 of the realised amount of notional profit has been transferred to Profit and Loss A/c.

Illustration 13

Prepare Contract Account and Contractee's Account from the following particulars:

	Rs.
Materials Sent to Site	24,000
Direct Wages	23,000
Chargeable Expenses	20,000
Plant Installed	40,000
Indirect Expenses	15,000
Wages Accrued	12,000
Materials Returned to Store	4,000
Plant at Site at the End	30,000
Materials at Site at the End	4,000
Cash Received (being 75% of work certified)	75,000
Work Completed	3/5
Contract Price	2,50,000

Solution

Contract Account

	Rs.		Rs.
To Materials Sent to Site	24,000	By Materials Returned to Store	4,000
To Direct Wages	23,000	By Materials at Site	4,000
To Chargeable Expenses	20,000	By Plant at Site	30,000
To Plant Installed	40,000		
To Indirect Expenses	15,000	By Work-in-Progress A/c	
To Wages Accrued	12,000	Value of Work Certified 1,00,000	
To Balance c/d (Notional Profit)	36,000	Cost of Work Uncertified 32,000	
			1,32,000
	1,70,000		1,70,000
To Profit and Loss A/c $\left(36,000 \times \frac{1}{3} \times \frac{75}{100}\right)$	9,000	By Balance b/d	36,000
To Work-in-Progress A/c (Profit reserved)	27,000		
	36,000		36,000

Contractee's Account

	Rs.		Rs.
To Balance c/d	75,000	By Bank A/c	75,000
	75,000		75,000

Note: Calculation of cost of work uncertified has been made as follows:

Cost of Work Uncertified:

Total expenditure for 3/5th contract:

		Rs.
Materials		24,000
Wages		23,000
Chargeable Expenses		20,000
Plant Installed		40,000
Indirect Expenses		15,000
Wages Accrued		12,000
		1,34,000
Less:	Rs.	
Materials Returned to Stores	4,000	
Materials at Site	4,000	
Plant at Site	30,000	38,000
		96,000

Total Estimated Cost for the whole Contract:

$$96{,}000 \times \frac{5}{3} = \text{Rs. } 1{,}60{,}000$$

Estimated Cost for the Work Certified:

$$\text{Total Estimated Cost} \times \frac{\text{Value of Work Certified}}{\text{Contract Price}}$$

$$1{,}60{,}000 \times \frac{1{,}00{,}000}{2{,}50{,}000} = \text{Rs. } 64{,}000$$

Therefore, Cost of Work Uncertified:

Total Expenses Incurred for 3/5th Contract – Estimated Cost for Work Certified

= 96,000 – 64,000
= Rs. 32,000

Illustration 14

The following figures are extracted from the books of a contractor for the year ending 31st March, 2005:

	Rs.	Rs.
Work-in-Progress on 31st March, 2004	8,50,000	
Less Advances	5,50,000	
		3,00,000
Materials Supplied to Contracts Direct		60,000
Materials Issued from Stores		1,05,000

Wages	85,000
Working Expenses	15,000
Administration Expenses (of which Rs. 2,500 is chargeable to General Profit and Loss A/c)	12,500
Plant Issued	25,000
Materials Returned from Contracts Direct to Suppliers	4,500
Materials Returned to Stores	5,500
Contracts Finished	2,25,000
Works Certified	1,50,000
Profit Taken from Contracts	1,15,000
Advances from Contractees	4,00,000

Prepare the Contract Ledger account (as in General Ledger) and the Total Contractees' account. Show also how the Work-in-Progress would appear in the Balance Sheet as on 31st March, 2005.

(*G.N.D.U., B.Com., Sept., 1981*)

Solution

Contract Ledger Account

	Rs.			Rs.
To Work-in-Progress b/d	8,50,000	By Materials Returned to Suppliers		4,500
To Materials		By Materials Returned to Stores		5,500
(*i*) Supplied to Contracts Direct	60,000	By Total Contractees' A/c (Contracts finished)		2,25,000
(*ii*) Issued from Stores	1,05,000	By Work-in-Progress A/c		
To Wages	85,000	Work Certified	1,50,000	
To Working Expenses	15,000	Work Uncertified	8,80,000*	10,30,000*
To Administration Expenses	10,000			
To Plant Issued	25,000			
To Profit and Loss A/c (Profit taken)	1,15,000			
	12,65,000			12,65,000

(*Balancing figure)

Working notes:

(*i*) Since the amount of profit on contracts taken to Profit and Loss A/c has been given, the balancing figure on the credit side of Contract A/c (Rs. 10,30,000) shall represent Work-in-Progress.

(*ii*) The cost of uncertified work has been calculated as follows:

	Rs.
Total Amount of Work-in-Progress	10,30,000
Less Value of Certified Work (given)	1,50,000
Cost of Uncertified Work	8,80,000

Total Contractees' Account

		Rs.			Rs.
2005			2004		
March, 31	To Contract Ledger A/c (Contracts Finished)	2,25,000	April 1	By Balance b/d	5,50,000
			2005		
March 31	To Balance c/d	7,25,000	March 31	Bank A/c	4,00,000
		9,50,000			9,50,000

Balance Sheet
as on 31st March 1995
(Assets Side)

		Rs.
Work-in-Progress	10,30,000	
Less Advance from Contractees	7,25, 000	3,05,000

Illustration 15

A contractor prepares his accounts for the year ending 31st December each year. He commenced a contract on 1st April, 2008. The following information relates to the contract as on 31st Dec., 2008.

	Rs.
Materials Issued	2,51,000
Labour Charges	5,65,600
Salary to Foreman	81,300

A machine costing Rs. 2,60,000 has been on the site for 146 days, its working life is estimated at 7 years and final scrap value at Rs. 15,000. A supervisor, who is paid Rs. 8,000 per month, has devoted one-half of his time to this contract. All other expenses and administration charges amount to Rs. 1,36,500. Materials in hand at site cost Rs. 35,400 on 31st Dec., 2008. The contract price is Rs. 20 lakhs. On 31st Dec., 2008, two-third of the contract was completed. The architect issued certificates covering 50% of the contract price, and the contractor has been paid Rs. 7,50,000 on account. Prepare Contract A/c and show how much profit or loss should be included in financial accounts to 31st Dec., 2008.

(B.Com., H.P. Univ., 1996)

Solution

Contract Account

	Rs.		Rs.
To Materials Issued	2,51,000	By Value of Materials at Site	35,400
To Labour Charges	5,65,600		
To Salary to Foreman	81,300	By Work-in-Progress A/c	12,62,250
To Depreciation on Machine	14,000	(*i*) Value of Certified Work	
To Salary of Supervisor	36,000	= 10,00,000	
$\left(8{,}000 \times 9\text{ms} \times \frac{1}{2}\right)$		(*ii*) Cost of Uncertified Work	
		= 2,62,250	
To Other Expenses	1,36,500		
To Balance c/d (Notional Profit)	2,13,250		
	12,97,650		12,97,650
To Profit and Loss A/c	1,06,625	By Balance b/d. (Notional Profit)	2,13,250
To Work-in-Progress A/c (Profit not taken)	1,06,625		
	2,13,250		2,13,250

Note: (*i*) Calculation of Depreciation on Machine

$$\frac{2,60,000 - \text{Rs.}15,000}{7 \text{ years}} \times \frac{146}{365}$$

$$= \text{Rs. } 14,000$$

(*ii*) Calculation of Cost of Uncertified Work:

Work Completed = 2/3rd of contract

Cost of Work Completed

= (Rs. 2,51,000 + 5,65,600 + 81,300 + 14,000 + 36,000 + 1,36,500 – 35,400) = 10,49,000

$$\text{Total estimated cost of contract on completion} = 10,49,000 \times \frac{3}{2}$$

= Rs.15,73,500

Estimated cost of work certified;

$$= \text{Total Estimated Cost} \times \frac{\text{Value of Certified Work}}{\text{Contract Price}}$$

$$= 15,73,500 \times \frac{10,00,000}{20,00,000}$$

= Rs. 7,86,750

Cost of Uncertified Work =

Total Expenses Incurred – Estimated Cost of Certified Work

= Rs. 10,49,000 – 7,86,750

= Rs. 2,62,250

(*iii*) Amount of Profit transferred to Profit and Loss A/c (Since 1/2 of the contract has been certified)

$$= \text{Notional Profit} \times \frac{2}{3} \times \frac{\text{Cash Received}}{\text{Value of Certified Work}}$$

$$= 2,13,250 \times \frac{2}{3} \times \frac{7,50,000}{10,00,000}$$

= 1,06,625.

(E) Incomplete Contracts Showing Loss

Illustration 16

The following is a summary of expenditure on Contract No. 31 to March 31, 2004.

	Rs.
Direct Wages	6,900
Direct Materials	34,000
Stores Issued	3,800
Stores Returned	550
Sub-Contract Costs	6,300
Plant	12,000

You obtain the following informations:

(*i*) The contract was begun in April, 2003 and the total contract price is Rs. 60,000.

(*ii*) The architects and certified that four-fifths of the contract had been completed on 15th March, 2004.

(*iii*) Depreciation of plant upto 15th March, 2004 is Rs. 4,800.

(*iv*) The summary set out above includes items relating to the period since March 15th, as follows:

	Rs.
Wages	700
Materials used	1,620

(*v*) Materials on site on 31st March, 2004 had cost Rs. 5,000 and stores on site had cost Rs. 400.

(*vi*) Establishment charges are 40% on direct wages.

(*vii*) A fine of Rs. 1,000 is likely to be imposed for late completion. Prepare Contract No. 31 Account.

Solution

Contract No. 31 Account

	Rs.			Rs.
To Direct Materials	34,000	By Stores Returned		550
To Direct Wages	6,900			
To Cost of Plant	12,000	By Value of Plant in Hand		
To Stores Issued	3,800	Cost	12,000	
To Sub-contract Costs	6,300	Depreciation	4,800	7,200
To Establishment Charges (40% of Rs. 6,900)	2,760			
		By Materials at Site		5,000
		By Stores at Site		400
		By Work-in-Progress A/c:		
		Value of Certified Work (60,000 × 4/5)	48,000	
		Cost of Uncertified Work	2,600	50,600
		By Profit and Loss A/c (Loss)		2,010
	65,760			65,760

Working Notes:

(*i*) Fine of Rs. 1,000 likely to be imposed for late completion of contract is an abnormal item of loss and is to be debited to Profit and Loss A/c by creating a provision.

(*ii*) The following expenses incurred since March, 2004 (date of certification of work) constitute uncertified work:

	Rs.
Materials	1,620
Wages	700
Establishment charges (40% of wages)	280
	2,600

(*iii*) Depreciation on plant in respect of use for uncertified work has been ignored.

(F) Incomplete Contracts Nearing Completion

Illustration 17

Bharat Construction Ltd., undertake contracts. They secured a contract to supply and erect machinery for Rs. 7,50,000. They started work on 1st April, 2005 and incurred the following expenditure during the year ended 31st March, 2006:

	Rs.
Plant and Tools	70,000
Machinery and Stores	2,00,000
Wages	1,50,000
Sundry Expenses	30,000
Establishment Expenses	40,000
	4,90,000

A part of the machinery costing Rs. 20,000 was unsuited to the contract and was immediately sold at a profit of Rs. 5,000. The value of plant and tools on 31st March, 2006 was Rs. 40,000 and the value of machinery and stores then on hand was Rs. 30,000. By 31st March, 2006 they had received payments on account amounting to Rs. 4,38,750, being 90% of the certified value of work done up to 31st March, 2006.

In order to calculate the profit made on the contract to 31st March, 2006, the contractors estimated further expenditure that would be incurred in completing the contract and decided to take to the credit of the Profit and Loss Account of the year that proportion of the estimated net profit to be realised on the contract which the value of work certified bore to the contract price.

Their estimates were as follows:

(1) That the contract would be completed by 30th Sept., 2006.

(2) That the plant and tools would have a residual value of Rs. 10,000 upon completion.

(3) That the cost of machinery and stores required in addition to those in stock on 31st March, 2006, would be Rs. 1,00,000 and that further sundry expenses of Rs. 20,000 would be incurred.
(4) That the wages on the contract for the six months to 30th Sept., 2006 would amount to Rs. 80,000;
(5) That the establishment expenses would cost the same sum per month as in the previous year; and
(6) That 2½% of the total cost of the contract (excluding this percentage) should be provided for contingencies.

Prepare the Contract Account for the year ended 31st March, 2006 and show your calculation of the profit to be credited to the Profit and Loss Account for that year.

Solution

Contract Account

for the year ending 31st March, 2006

	Rs.		Rs.
To Machinery and Stores	2,00,000	By Sale of Machinery	25,000
To Plant and Tools	70,000	By Machinery and Stores on Hand	30,000
To Wages	1,50,000		
To Sundry Expenses	30,000	By Value of Plant and Tools	40,000
To Establishment Expenses	40,000	By Work-in-Progress A/c	4,87,500
To Profit and Loss A/c (Profit on Sale of Machinery)	5,000	(Value of Certified Work $4,38,750 \times \frac{100}{90}$)	
To Balance c/d (Notional Profit)	87,500		
	5,28,500		5,82,500
To Profit and Loss A/c	34,450	By Balance b/d (Notional Profit)	87,500
To Work-in-Progress A/c (Profit not taken)	53,050		
	87,500		87,500

Calculation of Profit to be transferred to Profit and Loss A/c:

Ist Step: Calculation of Estimated Cost of Contract on Completion:

Gross Expenditure incurred to date:

		Rs.
Machinery and Stores		2,00,000
Plant and Tools		70,000
Wages		1,50,000
Sundry Expenses		30,000
Establishment Expenses		40,000
		4,90,000
Less:		
Part of Machinery Sold (at cost)	20,000	
Machinery and Stores on Hand	30,000	
Value of Plant and Tools	40,000	90,000
Net Expenditure Incurred (upto 31.3.2006)		4,00,000

		Rs.	Rs.
Add:	Additional cost to be incurred to complete the contract:		
	Machinery and Stores (Rs. 1, 00,000 + Rs. 30,000)	1,30,000	
	Plant and Tools		
Less:	Residual Value (Rs. 40,000 – Rs. 10,000)	30,000	
	Wages	80,000	
	Sundry Expenses	20,000	
	Establishment Expenses $\left(40{,}000 \times \frac{6}{12}\right)$	20,000	2,80,000
			6,80,000
Add:	Provision for Contingencies (2½% of 6,80,000)		17,000
	Estimated Total Cost		6,97,000

2nd Step: Calculation of Estimated Profit on Completion of Contract

	Rs.
Contract Price	7,50,000
Less Estimated Total Cost of Contract	6,97,000
Estimated Profit on Completion	53,000

3rd Step: Calculation of amount of profit to be transferred to Profit and Loss A/c on incomplete contract:

Profit to be transferred to Profit and Loss A/c:

$$= \text{Estimated Profit on Completion} \times \frac{\text{Work Certified}}{\text{Contract Price}}$$

$$= 53{,}000 \times \frac{4{,}87{,}500}{7{,}50{,}000}$$

= Rs. 34,450.

Illustration 18

Compute a conservative estimate of profit on a contract (which has been 80% complete) from the following particulars. Illustrate four methods of computing the profit:

	Rs.
Total Expenditure to Date	1,70,000
Estimated Further Expenditure to Complete the Contract (including contingencies)	34,000
Contract price	3,06,000
Work Certified	2,00,000
Work not Certified	17,000
Cash Received	1,63,200

(C.A. Inter, May, 1998)

Solution

1. ***Computation of Estimated Profit:***

		Rs.
Contract Price		3,06,000
Less: Estimated Expenditure to Date	1,70,000	
Estimated Further Expenditure to Complete the Contract	34,000	2,04,000
Estimated Profit		1,02,000

2. ***Computation of Notional Profit:***

Value of Work Certified + Work Uncertified (2,00,000 + 17,000)	2,17,000
Less: Total Expenditure to Date	1,70,000
Notional profit	47,000

Four methods of computing the conservative estimate of profit to be transferred to P & L Account.

(*i*) $\text{Estimated Profit} \times \dfrac{\text{Work Certified}}{\text{Contract Price}}$

$$= \text{Rs. } 1{,}02{,}000 \times \frac{\text{Rs. } 2{,}00{,}000}{\text{Rs. } 3{,}06{,}000}$$

$$= \text{Rs. } 66{,}666.67$$

(*ii*) $\text{Estimated Profit} \times \dfrac{\text{Work Certified}}{\text{Contract Price}} \times \dfrac{\text{Cash Received}}{\text{Work Certified}}$

$$= \text{Rs. } 1{,}02{,}000 \times \frac{\text{Rs. } 2{,}00{,}000}{\text{Rs. } 3{,}06{,}000} \times \frac{\text{Rs. } 1{,}63{,}200}{\text{Rs. } 2{,}00{,}000}$$

$$= \text{Rs. } 54{,}400$$

(*iii*) $\text{Notional Profit} \times \dfrac{2}{3} = \text{Rs. } 47{,}000 \times \dfrac{2}{3}$

$$= \text{Rs. } 31{,}333.33$$

(*iv*) $\text{Notional Profit} \times \dfrac{2}{3} \times \dfrac{\text{Cash Received}}{\text{Work Certified}}$

$$= \text{Rs. } 47{,}000 \times \frac{2}{3} \times \frac{\text{Rs. } 1{,}63{,}200}{\text{Rs. } 2{,}00{,}000}$$

$$= \text{Rs. } 25{,}568$$

MISCELLANEOUS PROBLEMS

Illustration 19

The following information is available in respect of three contracts undertaken by a contractor in 2008:

	Contract No.100	Contract No.101	Contract No.102
Materials Issued	25,000	2,80,000	2,50,000
Wages Paid	22,000	2,60,000	3,00,000
General Charges	9,000	35,000	40,000
Plant Installed at Site	–	1,00,000	2,00,000
Hire and use of Plant Upkeep Account	22,000	–	–
Materials in Hand at Close	13,000	10,000	40,000
Wages Accrued	5,000	30,000	25,000
Work Certified	80,000	5,00,000	6,00,000
Work Completed but not Certified	10,000	25,000	40,000
Cash Received	50,000	4,00,000	4,50,000
Materials Transferred to other Contracts	10,000	–	5,000
Materials Received from other Contracts	–	15,000	–
Depreciation on Plant per Annum	–	10%	20%
Contract Price	5,00,000	8,00,000	10,00,000
Date of Commencement of Contracts	1st January, 2008	1st April, 2008	1st July, 2008

Prepare the Contract Accounts in tabular form.

Solution

Contract Accounts

Particulars	Contract No.100 (Rs.)	Contract No.101 (Rs.)	Contract No.102 (Rs.)	Particulars	Contract No.100 (Rs.)	Contract N0.101 (Rs.)	Contract No.102 (Rs.)
To Materials Issued	25,000	2,80,000	2,50,000	By Materials in Hand	13,000	10,000	40,000
To Materials Received from other Contracts	–	15,000	–	By Materials Transferred to other Contracts	10,000	–	5,000
To Wages paid	22,000	2,60,000	3,00,000	By Plant at the end	–	92,500	1,80,000
To General Charges	9,000	35,000	40,000	By Work-in-Progress A/c: Value of Work Certified	80,000	5,00,000	6,00,000
To Plant Installed	–	1,00,000	2,00,000				
To Plant Upkeep	22,000	–	–	Cost of Work Uncertified	10,000	25,000	40,000
To Wages Accrued	5,000	30,000	25,000	By Profit & Loss A/c (Loss on Contract)	–	92,500	–
To Work-in-Progress A/c (Profit not taken)	30,000	–	–				
To Balance c/d	–	–	50,000				
	1,13,000	7,20,000	8,65,000		1,13,000	7,20,000	8,65,000
To Profit & Loss A/c $\left(50,000 \times \frac{2}{3} \times \frac{4,50,000}{6,00,000}\right)$	–	–	25,000	By Balance b/d	–	–	50,000
To Work-in-Progress A/c (Profit not taken)	–	–	25,000				
	–	–	50,000		–	–	50,000

Notes:

1. Work completed on Contract No. 100 is less than $\frac{1}{4}$ of the total contract, therefore no amount of profit is transferred to profit and loss account on this contract.
2. Contract No. 101 shows a loss of Rs. 92,500. The full amount of loss has been transferred to profit and loss account.
3. Valuation of plant at site at the end of the period has been made as follows regarding various contracts.

$$\text{Contract No. 101} = \left[1{,}00{,}000 - \left(1{,}00{,}000 \times \frac{10}{100} \times \frac{9}{12}\right)\right]$$
$$= [1{,}00{,}000 - 7{,}500]$$
$$= \text{Rs. } 92{,}500$$

$$\text{Contract No. 102} = \left[2{,}00{,}000 - \left(2{,}00{,}000 \times \frac{20}{100} \times \frac{6}{12}\right)\right]$$
$$= [2{,}00{,}000 - 20{,}000]$$
$$= \text{Rs. } 1{,}80{,}000$$

Illustration 20

Building Contractors Ltd., undertook a contract for Rs. 15,00,000 on an arrangement that 80% of the value of the work done, as certified by architect of the contractee, shall be paid immediately and the remaining 20% be retained until the completion of the contract.

In 2001, the amounts expended were: Materials Rs. 1,80,000; Wages Rs. 1,70,000; Carriage Rs. 6,000; Cartage Rs. 1,000; Sundry Expenses Rs. 3,000. The work was certified for Rs. 3,75,000 and 80% of this was paid as agreed.

In 2002, the amounts expended were: Materials Rs. 2,20,000; Wages Rs. 2,30,000; Carriage Rs. 23,000; Cartage Rs. 2,000; Sundry Expenses Rs. 4,000. Three-fourths of the contract were certified as done by 31st December and 80% of this was received. The value of unused stock and work-in-progress uncertified was ascertained at Rs. 20,000.

In 2003, the amounts expended were: Materials Rs. 1,26,000; Wages Rs. 1,70,000; Cartage Rs. 6,000; Sundry Expenses Rs. 3,000 and on 30th June the whole contract was completed.

Show how the Contract Account as also the contractee's account would appear for each of these years in the books of the contractor, assuming that the balance due to them was received on completion of the work. Show also what amount of profit will have to be carried to P & L account for each of these years, and how the amount of work-in-progress will appear in the Balance Sheet until the work is finished.

Solution

Contract Account

Date	Particulars	Rs.	Date	Particulars	Rs.
2001		**Rs.**	2001		**Rs.**
Dec. 31	To Materials	1,80,000	Dec. 31		
	To Carriage	6,000		By Work-in-Progress	
	To Cartage	1,000		A/c (Work Certified)	3,75,000
	To Wages	1,70,000			
	To Sundry Expenses	3,000			
	To Balance c/d				
	(Notional Profit)	15,000			
		3,75,000			3,75,000
Dec. 31	To Profit & Loss A/c	4,000	Dec. 31	By Balance b/d	15,000
				(Notional Profit)	
	$\left(15,000\times\frac{1}{3}\times\frac{80}{100}\right)$				
	To Work-in-Progress A/c	11,000			
	(Profit not taken)				
		15,000			15,000
2002			2002		
Jan. 1	To Work-in-Progress b/d	3,64,000	Dec. 31	By Work-in-Progress A/c	11,45,000
	(3,75,000 – 11,000)				
Dec. 31	To Materials	2,20,000		Work	
	To Carriage	23,000		Certified 11,25,000	
	To Cartage	2,000		Work	
	To Wages	2,30,000		Uncertified 20,000	
	To Sundry Expenses	4,000			
	To Balance c/d	3,02,000			
	(Notional Profit)				
		11,45,000			11,45,000
2002		**Rs.**	2002		**Rs.**
Dec. 31	To Profit and Loss A/c	1,61,066	Dec. 31	By Balance b/d	3,02,000
	$\left(3,02,000\times\frac{2}{3}\times\frac{80}{100}\right)$				
	To Work-in-Progress A/c	1,40,934			
	(Profit not taken)				
		3,02,000			3,02,000
2003			2003		
Jan. 1	To Work-in-Progress b/d		June 30	By Contractee's A/c	15,00,000
	(Rs. 11,45,000 – 1,40,934)	10,04,066		(Contract Price)	
June 30	To Materials	1,26,000			
	To Cartage	6,000			
	To Wages	1,70,000			
	To Sundry Expenses	3,000			
	To Profit and Loss				
	A/c (Profit)	1,90,934			
		15,00,000			15,00,000

Contractee's Account

		Rs.			Rs.
2001			2001		
Dec. 31	To Balance c/d	3,00,000		By Bank A/c (80% of Rs. 3,75,000)	3,00,000
		3,00,000			3,00,000
2002			2002		
Dec. 31	To Balance c/d	9,00,000	Jan. 1	By Balance b/d	3,00,000
				By Bank A/c (80% of Rs, 7,50,000 additional work certified)	6,00,000
		9,00,000			9,00,000
2003			2003		
June 30	To Contract A/c (Contract Price)	15,00,000	Jan. 1	By Balance b/d	9,00,000
			June 30	By Bank A/c	6,00,000
		15,00,000			15,00,000

Work-in-Progress Account

		Rs.			Rs.
2001			2001		
Dec. 31	To Contract A/c	3,75,000	Dec. 31	By Contract A/c (Profit not taken)	11,000
				By Balance c/d	3,64,000
		3,75,000			3,75,000
2002			2002		
Jan. 1	To Balance b/d	3,64,000	Jan. 1	By Contract A/c (Transfer)	3,64,000
Dec. 31	To Contract A/c: Work Certified 11,25,000 Work Uncertified 2 0,000	11,45,000	Dec.31	By Contract A/c (Profit not taken)	1,40,934
				By Balance c/d	10,04,066
		15,09,000			15,09,000
2003			2003		
Jan. 1	To Balance b/d	10,04,066	Jan. 1	By Contract A/c (Transfer)	10,04,066
		10,04,066			10,04,066

Balance Sheet
as on 31.3.01
(Assets Side)

		Rs.
Work-in-Progress	3,64,000	
Less Cash received from Contractee	3,00,000	64,000

Balance Sheet
as on 31.3.2002
(Assets Side)

		Rs.
Work-in-Progress	10,04,066	
Less: Cash Received from Contractee	9,00,000	1,04,066

Illustration 21

M/s Deep Ltd., undertook a contract for Rs. 3,00,000 on 1st April, 2002 and completed the same on 30th June, 2002. You are given the following information for the contract:

2000-01 : Materials issued Rs. 40,000; Wages Rs. 20,000; Other Direct Charges Rs. 10,000; Cost of Special Plant Rs. 80,000. On 31st March, 2001 Materials on site Rs. 4,000; Work certified Rs. 70,000.

2001-02 : Materials issued Rs. 70,000; Wages Rs. 50,000; Other Direct Charges Rs. 5,000.
On 31st March, 2002 Materials on site Rs. 10,500; Work certified this year Rs. 1,55,000; Work completed but uncertified Rs. 25,000.

2002-03 : Materials issued Rs. 5,000, Wages Rs. 12,500 and Direct Charges Rs. 1,200.
On 30th June, 2002 Materials returned to store Rs. 1,000. Plant was returned to store at a value ascertained after charging 10% depreciation annually on the original cost. 80% of the value of certified work was received in cash every year.

Prepare Contract Account, Contractee's Account and Work-in-Progress Account for each year.

Solution

Contract Account (2000-01)

	Rs.		Rs.
To Materials Issued	40,000	By Materials on Site	4,000
To Wages	20,000	By Value of Plant	
To Direct Charges	10,000	Cost Rs. 80,000	
To Cost of Special Plant	80,000	Less Dep. 8,000	72,000
		By Work-in-Progress A/c (Work Certified)	70,000
		By Profit and Loss A/c (Loss Transferred to Profit and Loss A/c)	4,000
	1,50,000		1,50,000

Work-in-Progress Account

		Rs.			Rs.
2001			2001		
March 31	To Contract A/c	70,000	March 31	By Balance c/d	70,000
		70,000			70,000

Contractee's Account

		Rs.			Rs.
2001			2000-01		
March 31	To Balance c/d	56,000		By Bank A/c (80% of Rs. 70,000)	56,000
		56,000			56,000

Contract Account (2001-02)

	Rs.		Rs.
1.4.01		31.3.02	
To Work-in-Progress A/c	70,000	By Materials on Site	10,500
To Materials on Site	4,000	By Plant on Site	64,000
To Value of Plant	72,000	(Rs.72,000 – Rs.8,000 10% on 80,000)	
31.3.02			
To Materials Issued	70,000	By Work-in-Progress A/c:	
To Wages	50,000	Work Certified 2,25,000 (70,000 + 1,55,000)	
To Direct Charges	5,000	Work Uncertified 25,000	
To Balance c/d (Notional Profit)	53,500		2,50,000
	3,24,500		3,24,500
To Profit and Loss A/c $\left(53,500\times\frac{2}{3}\times\frac{80}{100}\right)$	28,534	By Balance b/d (Notional Profit)	53,500
To Work-in-Progress A/c (Profit not taken)	24,966		
	53,500		53,000

Work-in-Progress Account

			Rs.			Rs.
2001 April, 1	To Balance b/d		70,000	2001 April, 1	By Contract A/c (Transfer)	70,000
2002 March, 31	To Contract A/c			2002 March, 31	By Contract A/c (Profit not taken)	24,966
	Work Certified	2,25,000				
	Work Uncertified	25,000	2,50,000			
				March, 31	By Balance c/d	2,25,034
			3,20,000			3,20,000

Contractee's Account

		Rs.			Rs.
2002 March 31	To Balance c/d	1,80,000	2001 April, 1	By Balance b/d	56,000
			2002 March 31	By Bank A/c (80% of 1,55,000)	1,24,000
		1, 80,000			1, 80,000

Contract Account (2002-03)

	Rs.		Rs.
1.4.02		31.6.02	
To Work-in-Progress	2,25,034	By Materials Returned to Store	1,000
To Materials on Site	10,500		
To Plant on Site	64,000	By Plant Returned to Store (Rs. 64,000 – Rs. 2,000 10% on 80,000 for 3 months)	62,000
30.6.02			
To Materials Issued	5,000		
To Wages	12,500	By Contractee's A/c (Contract Price)	3,00,000
To Direct Charges	1,200		
To Profit and Loss A/c (Profit)	44,766		
	3,63,000		3,63,000

Work-in-Progress Account

		Rs.			Rs.
2002 April, 1	To Balance b/d	2,25,034	2002 April, 1	By Contract A/c (Transfer)	2,25,034
		2,25,034			2,25,034

Contractee's Account

		Rs.			Rs.
2002 June, 30	To Contract A/c (Contract Price)	3,00,000	2002 April, 1	By Balance b/d	1,80,000
			June, 30	By Bank A/c (Balance of Contract Price)	1,20,000
		3,00,000			3,00,000

Illustration 22

Work out the financial result in respect of contract for construction of buildings undertaken by a firm. Your answer should be based on the following figures extracted from the financial books of the firm, for the year ended 31.3.2006.

The term of the contract is Rs. 10 per sq. foot of the covered floor area as accepted and certified by the engineer of the contractee.

(*a*) **Materials:** Building materials in stock at the commencement of work Rs. 10,000; purchases during the currency of the contract: Cement 7,500 bags @ Rs. 6 per bag, bricks 1,25,000 @ Rs. 40 per thousand, Sand 10,000 c.ft. @ Rs. 10 per 100 c.ft., Wood work 900 c.ft. @ Rs. 10 per c.ft., Value of materials in hand after completion of work, Rs. 10,000.

(*b*) **Labour:** 100 masons at Rs. 4 per day for 25 days, 400 mazdoors at Rs. 2 per day for 25 days.

(*c*) **Tools and Plants:** Two new concrete mixtures were purchased at Rs. 10,000 each at the commencement of the contract. Residual value as assessed after completion of the contract is Rs. 3,500 for each mixture.

(*d*) **Supervision:** 50 per cent of two engineers' pay at Rs. 1,000 per month for each engineer for two months, 50 per cent of ten overseers' pay at Rs. 200 per month for each overseer for 4 months.

(*e*) **Administration Overhead:** 20% of Head office expenses for the period of contract, the total Head office expenses for this period are Rs. 5,000.

(*f*) **Quantity of work done:** Work accepted and certified by the engineer: 12,000 sq.ft. of covered floor area.

Solution

Building Contract A/c

	Rs.		Rs.
To Materials in Stock (opening)	10,000	By Materials in hand	10,000
To Materials Purchased:		By Tools & Plants as site : 2 × Rs. 3,500	7,000
Cement: 7,500 bags @Rs. 6 each	45,000	By Contractee's A/c:	
Bricks: 1,25,000 @ Rs. 40 per 1,000	5,000	12,000 sq.ft. @ Rs. 10 per sq.ft.	1,20,000
Sand: 10,000 c.ft. @Rs. 10 per 100 c.ft.	1,000		
Wood Work: 900 c.ft. @ Rs. 10 per c.ft.	9,000		
To Labour:			
100 masons @ Rs. 4 per day for 25 days	10,000		
400 mazdoors @ Rs. 2 per day for 25 days	20,000		
To Tools & Plant: 2 Concrete Mixtures @ Rs. 10,000 each	20,000		
To Supervision Charges:			
2 Engineers × Rs. 1,000 p.m. × 2 months × 50%	2,000		
10 Overseers × Rs. 200 p.m. × 4 months × 50%	4,000		
To Administration Overheads: (20% of Rs.5,000)	1,000		
To P & L A/c (Profit)	10,000		
	1,37,000		1,37,000

Illustration 23

The following figures relate to two jobs of a road contractor:

	Contract A	Contract B
	Rs.	Rs.
Total Expenditure to 31st March, 2005	1,94,460	86,035
Wages Paid (2005-06)	51,180	10,548
Materials & haulage hire	78,915	3,572
Indirect Expenses Charged (2005-06)	2,625	287
Plant Transferred at Valuation to Other Contracts on 28th Feb., 2006 (Originally Charged at Cost to these Contracts)	1,375	95
Total Contract Price	3,47,262	68,945

In each case the work was actually finished on 28th Feb., 2006 but the contracts could not be considered as completed until the maintenance period of six months had expired on 31st August, 2006.

Write up the two Contract Accounts and state what profit or loss (if any) should be brought into the Profit & Loss Account for the year ended 31st March 2006.

Solution

Contract Accounts

Particulars	A	B	Particulars	A	B
	Rs.	Rs.		Rs.	Rs.
To Work in Progress b/d	1,94,460	86,035	By Plant Transferred to other Contracts	1,375	95
To Wages	51,180	10,548			
To Materials and Haulage Hire	78,915	3,572	By Contractees' Account (Contract Price)	3,47,262	68,945
To Indirect Expenses	2,625	287	By Balance (being loss)	–	31,402
To Balance (being Profit)	21,457	–			
	3,48,637	1,00,442		3,48,637	100,442

Note: As these two contracts cannot be considered as completed until the expiry of the maintenance period of six months ending on 31st Aug., 2006, amount of the maintenance cost must be estimated before any profit or loss is brought into the Profit and Loss Account of 2005-06.

In case of contract 'A', the total profit earned Rs. 21,457 less than adequate provision for maintenance may be credited to Profit and Loss Account of 2005-06 while in case of contract 'B', the whole amount of loss (Rs. 31,402) plus the estimated cost of maintenance to be provided should be charged to Profit and Loss Account of 2005-06.

Illustration 24

The following particulars relate to two houses which a firm of builders had in course of construction under contract:

	House A Rs.	House B Rs.
Work-in-Progress on 1st April, 2005 (Excluding Rs. 800 Estimated Profit which was taken to Profit and Loss A/c in 2004-05)	14,000	
Materials Purchased	23,000	16,600
Wages	20,000	14,000
Electrical Fittings	1,400	300
Road Making Charges	8,000	–
Contract Price (including Road Making)	60,000	40,000
Percentage of Cash Received to Work Certified	100%	$66\frac{2}{3}$%
Cash Received to 31st March, 2006	60,000	24,000
Value of Materials in Hand on 31st March, 2006	400	540
Completed Work not Certified	–	2,500
Value of Plant used on Sites	12,000	6,000
Periods for which Plant Remained on Sites During the year	10 months	8 months

The total establishment expenses incurred during the year 2005-06 amounted to Rs. 12,240 and are to be charged to two contracts in proportion to wages. Depreciation on plant is to be provided at 10% p.a.

Prepare the two Contract Accounts in columnar form for the year ending 31st March, 2006.

(P.U., B.Com., G.N.D.U., B.Com.)

Solution

Contract Accounts

Particulars	House A	House B	Particulars	House A	House B
	Rs.	Rs.		Rs.	Rs.
To Work-in-Progress (including Profit taken to P & L A/c)	14,800	–	By Materials on Hand	400	540
			By Value of Plant (after Depreciation)	11,000	5,600
To Materials	23,000	16,600			
To Wages	20,000	14,000	By Work-in-Progress A/c:		
To Electrical Fittings	1,400	300	Value of Certified Work 36,000		
To Road Making Charges	8,000	–	Cost of Uncertified Work 2,500	–	38,500
To Plant	12,000	6,000	By Contractee's Account (Contract Price)	60,000	–
To Establishment Expenses (in 20:14 Ratio)	7,200	5,040			
To Balance c/d	–	2,700	By Profit and Loss A/c (Loss)	15,000	–
	86,400	44,640		86,400	44,640

Particulars	House A	House B	Particulars	House A	House B
	Rs.	Rs.		Rs.	Rs.
To Profit and Loss A/c $\left(2{,}700\times\frac{2}{3}\times\frac{66\frac{2}{3}}{100}\right)$	–	1,200	By Balanced b/d	–	2,700
To Work-in-Progress A/c (Profit not taken)	–	1,500			
	–	2,700		–	2,700

Illustration 25

The Thekedar Contractors Ltd., having an authorised capital of Rs. 1,00,000 divided into 10,000 equity shares of Rs. 10 each, commenced operations on 1st January, 2006 and during the year ended 31st March, 2006 were engaged on one contract of which the contract price was Rs. 4,00,000. The trial balance extracted from their books on 31st March, 2006 stood as under:

	Rs.	Rs.
Share Capital:		
Equity Shares of Rs. 10 each, Rs. 8 paid		80,000
Sundry Creditors		8,000
Land and Buildings (Cost)	34,000	
Cash at Bank	9,000	
Contract No. 1 Account:		
Materials	75,000	
Plant	20,000	
Wages	1,05,000	
Expenses	5,000	
Cash Received, being 80% of Work Certified		1,60,000
	2,48,000	2,48,000

Of the plant and materials charged to the Contract, plant costing Rs. 3,000 and materials costing Rs. 2,400 were destroyed in an accident. On 31st March, 2006 plant which cost Rs. 4,000 was returned to store. The value of materials on site was Rs. 3,000 and the cost of work done but not certified was Rs. 2,000.

Charge 10% depreciation off plant, carry to Profit and Loss A/c two-third of profits received and compile Contract No. 1 Account for the year ended 31st March, 2006 and the Balance sheet as on 31st March, 2006.

Solution

Contract No. 1 Account

Particulars	Rs.	Particulars	Rs.	Rs.
To Materials	75,000	By Profit and Loss A/c:		
To Wages	1,05,000	Materials Lost	2,400	
To Plant	20,000	Plant Lost	3,000	5,400
To Expenses	5,000	By Materials on Site		3,000
To Balance c/d	20,700	By Plant Returned to Store (Cost less depreciation) (Rs. 4,000 – Rs. 400)		3,600
		By Plant at Site		11,700
		By Work-in-Progress A/c:		
		Value of Certified Work	2,00,000	
		$\left(1,60,000\times\frac{100}{80}\right)$		
		Cost of Uncertified Work	2,000	2,02,000
	2,25,700			2,25,700
To Profit and Loss A/c $\left(20,700\times\frac{2}{3}\times\frac{80}{100}\right)$	11,040	By Balance b/d		20,700
To Work-in-Progress A/c (Profit not taken)	9,660			
	20,700			20,700

Profit and Loss Account

Particulars		Rs.	Particulars	Rs.
To Contract No. 1 A/c			By Contract No. 1 A/c	11,040
Materials Lost	2,400	5,400		
Plant Lost	3,000			
To Net Profit		5,640		
		11,040		11,040

Work-in-Progress Account

Date	Particulars		Rs.	Date	Particulars	Rs.
2006 March 31	To Contract No. 1 A/c			2006 March 31	By Contract No. 1 A/c (Profit not taken)	9,660
	Value of Certified Work	2,00,000		March 31	By Balance c/d	1,92,340
	Cost of Uncertified Work	2,000	2,02,000			
			2,02,000			2,02,000

Balance Sheet of Thekedar Contractors Ltd.
as at 31st March, 2006

Liabilities	Amount	Assets		Amount
Share Capital:	**Rs.**	Fixed Assets:		**Rs.**
Authorised	1,00,000	Land and Buildings		34,000
Issued and Subscribed:		Plant (Cost less Depreciation)		
		at site	11,700	
10,000 Equity shares of Rs. 10 each, Rs. 8 per share called up	80,000	in store	3,600	15,300
		Current Assets:		
Reserves & Surplus:		Work-in-Progress	1,92,340	
Profit & Loss A/c	5,640			
		Less Cash received from Contractee	1,60,000	
Current Liabilities:				
Sundry Creditors	8,000			32,340
		Materials at site		3,000
		Cash at Bank		9,000
	93,640			93,640

Illustration 26

The following is the trial balance of Premier Construction Co., engaged in the execution of Contract No. 747 as on 31st March, 2008:

	Dr. Rs.	Cr. Rs.
Contractee's Account (Amount Received)		3,00,000
Buildings	1,60,000	
Creditors		72,000
Bank Balance	35,000	
Share Capital		5,00,000
Materials	2,00,000	
Wages	1,80,000	
Expenses	47,000	
Plant	2,50,000	
	8,72,000	8,72,000

The work on Contract No. 747 was commenced on 1st April, 2007. Materials costing Rs. 1,70,000 were sent to the site of the contract but those of Rs. 6,000 were destroyed in an accident. Wages of Rs. 1,80,000 were paid during the year. Plant costing Rs. 50,000 was used on the contract all through the year. Plant which cost Rs. 2,00,000 was used from 1st April to 31st December and was then returned to the stores. Materials of the cost of Rs. 4,000 were at site on 31st March, 2008.

The contract was for Rs. 6,00,000 and the contractee pays 75% of the work certified. Work certified was 80% of the total contract price as on 31st March, 2008. Uncertified work was estimated at Rs. 15,000 on 31st March, 2008. Expenses are charged to contract at 25% of wages and plant is to be depreciated at 10% for the entire year.

Prepare Contract No. 747 Account for the year ended 31st March, 2008 and make out the Balance Sheet as on 31st March, 2008 in the books of Premier Construction Co. *(Delhi, B.Com. Hons., 1979)*

Solution

Contract No. 747 Account

	Rs.			Rs.
To Materials Issued	1,70,000			
To Wages	1,80,000	By Profit and Loss A/c		
To Expenses	45,000	(Materials Destroyed)		6,000
(25% on Wages)				
To Plant	2,50,000	By Plant Returned to Stores		
		Cost	2,00,000	
		Less Depreciation		
		@ 10% for 9 months	15,000	1,85,000
		By Plant at Site		
		Cost	50,000	
		Less Depreciation @10%	5,000	45,000
		By Materials at Site		4,000
		By Work-in-Progress A/c		
To Balance c/d	90,000	Value of Work Certified	4,80,000	
(Notional Profit)		$\left(6,00,000\times\frac{80}{100}\right)$		
		Uncertified Work	15,000	4,95,000
	7,35,000			7,35,000
To Profit and Loss A/c	37,500	By Balance b/d		90,000
$\left(90,000\times\frac{2}{3}\times\frac{3,00,000}{4,80,000}\right)$		(Notional Profit)		
To Work-in-Progress A/c	52,500			
(Profit not taken)				
	90,000			90,000

Profit and Loss Account
for the year ending 31st March, 2008

Particulars	Rs.	Particulars	Rs.
To Contract A/c	6,000	By Contract A/c	37,500
(Materials Destroyed)		(Profit taken)	
To Depreciation on Plant	5,000		
(10% on Rs. 2,00,000 for 3 months)			
To Expenses	2,000		
(47,000 – 45,000)			
To Net Profit	24,500		
	37,500		37,500

Note: Depreciation on Plant is to be charged @ 10% for the whole year. Plant costing Rs. 2,00,000 has been used at the site of the contract for 9 months only. As such depreciation on this plant for 9 months has been charged to Contract No. 747 A/c and for remaining 3 months to Profit & Loss A/c.

Work-in-Progress Account

			Rs.			Rs.
2008 March 31	To Contract A/c			2008 March 31	By Contract A/c (Profit not taken)	52,500
	Work Certified	4,80,000		2008 March 31	Balance c/d	4,42,500
	Work Uncertified	15,000	4,95,000			
			4,95,000			4,95,000

Balance Sheet as on 31st March, 2008

Liabilities	Amount	Assets		Amount
	Rs.			Rs.
		Buildings		1,60,000
Share Capital	5,00,000			
Profit and Loss A/c	24,500	Plant (cost less Dep.)		
		(*i*) In Store		1,80,000
Sundry Creditors	72,000	(*ii*) At Site		45,000
		Materials		
		(*i*) In Store		30,000
		(*ii*) At Site		4,000
		Work-in-Progress	4,42,500	
		Less Cash Received from Contractee	3,00,000	1,42,500
		Bank Balance		35,000
	5,96,500			5,96,500

Illustration 27

A builder and contractor makes up his accounts to March, 31 in each year. Contract No. 534 was commenced on July, 1, 2007. The cost records yield the following information on March 31, 2008:

	Rs.
Material Charged out to Site	2,150
Labour	5,011
Foreman's Salary	631

A machine costing Rs. 1,500 has been on site for 73 days. Its working life is estimated at 5 years, its final scarp value is at Rs. 100.

A supervisor, who is paid Rs. 1,200 per annum, has spent approximately one half of his time on this contract.

All other expenses and administration amounted to Rs. 1,261. Materials in store at site at year end cost Rs. 248.

The contract price is Rs. 20,000. On 31st March, 2008 two thirds of the contract was completed. Architect's certificate has been issued covering Rs. 10,000; Rs. 8,000 has so far been paid on account, cost of work not yet certified Rs. 2,328.

Prepare a contract account and state how much profit or loss should be included in respect of Contract No. 534 in the financial accounts to 31st March, 2008.

Solution

Contract No. 534 Account

	Rs.			Rs.
To Materials Charged out to Site	2,150	By Materials at the Site		248
To Labour	5,011	By Work-in-Progress A/c		
To Foreman's Salary	631	Work Certified	10,000	
To Depreciation on Machine	56	Work Uncertified	2,328	12,328
To Supervisor's Salary	450			
To Other Expenses	1,261			
To Balance c/d (Notional Profit)	3,017			
	12,576			12,576
To Profit and Loss A/c $\left(3{,}017\times\frac{2}{3}\times\frac{8{,}000}{10{,}000}\right)$	1,609	By Balance b/d		3,017
To Work-in-Progress A/c (Profit not taken)	1,408			
	3,017			3,017

Working Notes:

(*i*) Depreciation on machine, chargeable to Contract No. 534 A/c. has been calculated as follows:

Cost of Machine	Rs. 1,500
Less Scrap Value	Rs. 100
Amount to be Written off over 5 years	1,400

$$\text{Annual Depreciation} = \frac{\text{Rs. } 1{,}400}{5 \text{ yrs}} = \text{Rs. } 280$$

$$\text{Depreciation for 73 days} = \text{Rs. } 280\times\frac{73 \text{ days}}{365 \text{ days}} = \text{Rs. } 56$$

(*ii*) Since $\frac{1}{2}$ of the contract has been completed and certified, the profit transferred to Profit and Loss A/c has been ascertained as follows:

$$\text{Notional profit} \times\frac{2}{3}\times\frac{\text{Cash received}}{\text{Work certified}}$$

(*iii*) Portion of the Supervisor's salary from 1st July, 2007 to 31 March, 2008 chargeable to Contract No. 534 has been calculated as follows:

$$= \text{Rs. } 1{,}200 \times \frac{9}{12}\times\frac{1}{2} = \text{Rs. } 450$$

Illustration 28

Hindustan Builders Ltd., have undertaken the construction of a building for a contract price of Rs. 50 lakhs. The retention money agreed is 15% and the contractee is to make payment for 85% of the work certified by the engineer. The following are the details as shown in the books of the contractor:

Opening Balances:

2006		**Rs.**
April 1.	Work-in-Progress Account (excluding Rs. 80,000 profit transferred to Profit and Loss Account upto 31st March, 2006)	16,00,000
April 1.	Plant at Site	80,000
April 1.	Materials at Site	25,000
April 1.	Outstanding Wages	12,000
April 1.	Cash Received from the Contractee	13,80,000

Transactions during the Year:

Materials Sent to Site Direct	6,90,000
Materials Issued from Stores	3,99,800
Wages Paid	9,32,000
Additional Plant Purchased	1,30,000
Material Destroyed at Site (cost)	10,000
Direct Expenses Paid	92,000
General Expenses Allocated	1,48,400
Materials Sold at Site at a Profit of 20% on the Selling Price	80,000
Cash Received from the Contractee during the Year	21,40,000

Closing Balances:

2007		**Rs.**
March 31	Materials on Hand at Site	25,200
March 31	Wages Accrued but not Paid	37,600
March 31	Value of Plant at Site	1,61,600
March 31	Work Certified	44,00,000
March 31	Work done but not Certified (at cost)	66,000

You are required to prepare:

(*a*) The Contract Account in Contractor's Books.

(*b*) The Work-in-Progress Account.

(*c*) The Balance Sheet to show the relevant items.

(*G.N.D.U., B.Com.*)

Solution

Contract Account

	Rs.		Rs.
2006		2006	
April 1		April 1	
To Work-in-Progress b/d (including Rs. 80,000 being Profit taken to Profit & Loss A/c)	16,80,000	By Outstanding Wages (Opening)	12,000
" To Plant at Site	80,000	2007	
" To Materials at Site	25,000	March 31	
		By Profit and Loss A/c (Materials Destroyed)	10,000
		By Bank A/c (Sale of Materials)	80,000
2007			
March 31			
To Materials Sent to Site (direct)	6,90,000	By Value of Materials at Site	25,200
		By Plant at Site	1,61,600
To Materials Issued from Stores	3,99,800	By Work-in-Progress A/c:	
To Wages Paid	9,32,000	Value of Certified Work 44,00,000	
To Cost of Additional Plant	1,30,000	Cost of Uncertified Work 66,000	44,66,000
To Direct Expenses	92,000		
To General Expenses	1,48,400		
To Profit and Loss A/c (Profit on sale of Materials)	16,000		
To Wages Outstanding (closing)	37,600		
To Balance c/d (Notional Profit)	5,24,000		
	47,54,800		47,54,800
To Profit and Loss A/c (5,24,000 × 2/3 × 35,20,000/44,00,000)	2,79,467	By Balance b/d (Notional profit)	5,24,000
To Work-in-Progress A/c (Profit not taken to Profit and Loss A/c)	2,44,533		
	5,24,000		5,24,000

Work-in-Progress Account

		Rs.		Rs.
2007			2007	
March 31			March 31	
To Contract A/c			By Contract A/c (Profit not taken to Profit and Loss A/c)	2,44,533
Value of Certified Work	44,00,000			
Cost of Uncertified Work	66,000	44,66,000	By Balance c/d	42,21,467
		44,66,000		44,66,000

Balance Sheet as on 31st March, 2007

Liabilities	Amount	Assets		Amount
	Rs.			Rs.
Outstanding Wages	37,600	Work-in-Progress	42,21,467	
		Less: Cash Received from Contractee	35,20,000	7,01,476
		Materials at Site		25,200
		Plant at Site		1,61,600

Illustration 29

Write up Contract No. 200 from the following particulars:

	Rs.
Direct Materials	39,000
Wages	26,400
Special Plant	17,600
Stores Issued	7,040
Loose Tools	3,300
Costs of Tractor:	
Running Materials	2,200
Wages of Drivers, etc.	3,520
Other Direct Charges	2,640

The contract was completed in 13 weeks, at the end of which period plant was returned subject to depreciation of 15% on the original cost. The value of loose tools and stores returned were Rs. 2,200 and Rs. 890 respectively. The value of the tractor was Rs. 20,000 and depreciation was to be charged to this contract at the rate of 15% per annum. You are required to provide for administrative expenses at the rate of 10% on total works cost.

(*Bombay, B.Com.*)

Solution

Contract No. 200 Account

		Rs.			Rs.
To Direct Materials		39,600	By Plant	17,600	
To Wages		26,400	Less 15% Dep. on the Original Cost	2,640	
To Special Plant		17,600			14,960
To Stores Issued		7,040	By Loose Tools Returned		2,200
To Loose Tools		3,300	By Stores Returned		890
To Costs of Tractor:			By Balance being Works Cost c/d		85,000
(*i*) 15% p.a. Depreciation for 13 weeks $\left(\text{Rs. } 20{,}000 \times \frac{15}{100} \times \frac{13}{52}\right) = 750$					
(*ii*) Running Materials	2,200				
(*iii*) Driver's Wages	3,520	6,470			
To Other Direct Charges		2,640			
		1,03,050			1,03,050
To Balance being Works Cost b/d		85,000	By Total Cost		93,500
To Administrative Expenses (10% of Works Cost)		8,500			
		93,500			93,500

Illustration 30

Modern Constructions (Private) Ltd., Civil Engineering Contractors proposing to tender for the construction of a "Community Hall" in a new township, estimate their direct costs as Rs. 1,50,000:

	Rs.
Direct Materials	60,000
Direct Labour (21,000 man-days of various categories)	63,000
Cost of transport of men and materials to work site	17,000
Other Direct Expenses	10,000

Existing commitments of Modern Constructions for the year necessitate an overhead expenses of Rs. 8,50,500 against execution of works the direct labour costs of which amounts to Rs. 5,67,000.

Assuming that whole of the overhead expenses is variable (for the sake of simplicity and tendering), calculate the estimated value of tendering duly providing for (*a*) necessary overheads, (*b*) interest at 5% on the average of capital, and (*c*) 10% margin. (*C.A. Final*)

Solution

Modern Construction (Private) Ltd.

Statement of Estimated Value of Tender

		Rs.
Direct Materials		60,000
Direct Labour (Various Categories)		63,000
Cost of Transport of Men and Materials to Work Site		17,000
Other Direct Expenses		10,000
		1,50,000
Add: Overhead Expenses (150% of Direct Labour Cost)		94,500
	Capital Outlay	2,44,500
Add: Interest on Capital Outlay (5% on the average)		6,113
	Total Estimated Cost	2,50,613
Add: Margin of Profit (10%)		25,061
	Tender Value	2,75,674

Notes:

(*i*) Percentage of Overhead Expenses on Direct Labour:

$$\frac{\text{Rs. } 8,50,500}{5,67,000} \times 100 = 150\%$$

(*ii*) Interest on Capital Outlay

		Rs.
	Total Capital Outlay	= 2,44,500
Average Capital Outlay		$= \frac{2,44,500}{2}$
		= 1,22,250

Illustration 31

Kapur Engineering Company undertakes long term contract which involves the fabrication of pre-stressed concrete blocs and the erection of the same on consumer's site.

The following information is supplied regarding the contract which is incomplete on 31st March, 2008.

Cost incurred:		
Fabrication cost to date:		
Direct Materials		2,80,000
Direct Labour		90,000
Overheads		75,000
		4,45,000
Erection Cost to Date		15,000
Total:		4,60,000
Contract Price		8,19,000
Cash Received on Account		6,00,000
Technical Estimate of Work Completed to Date:		
Fabrication:		
Direct Materials	80%	
Direct Labour and Overhead	75%	
Erection	25%	

You are required to prepare a statement for submission to the management indicating:

(*a*) the estimated profit on the completion of the contract.
(*b*) the estimated profit to date on the contract.

(*I.C.W.A. Inter; C.A. Inter Adapted*)

Solution

Statement of Cost

Items of Cost	Cost to Date % age	Cost to Date Amt. Rs.	Estimated Additional Costs % age	Estimated Additional Costs Amt. Rs.	Total (100%) Rs.
A. Fabrication Costs:					
Direct Materials	80%	2,80,000	20%	70,000	3,50,000
Direct Labour	75%	90,000	25%	30,000	1,20,000
Overheads	75%	75,000	25%	25,000	1,00,000
		4,45,000		1,25,000	5,70,000
B. Erection Costs	25%	15,000	75%	45,000	60,000
Total Estimated Cost (A + B)		4,60,000		1,70,000	6,30,000

Statement of Profit

Total Estimated Profit = Contract Price – Total Estimated Cost
= Rs.8,19,000 – Rs.6,30,000
= Rs. 1,89,000

Profit to be taken to Profit and Loss A/c (as per formula)

$$= \text{Total Estimated Profit} \times \frac{\text{Cost to Date}}{\text{Total Estimated Cost}}$$

$$= \text{Rs. } 1{,}89{,}000 \times \frac{4{,}60{,}000}{6{,}30{,}000}$$

= Rs.1,38,000

OR

$$= \text{Total Estimated Profit} \times \frac{\text{Cash Received}}{\text{Contract Price}}$$

$$= \text{Rs. } 1{,}89{,}000 \times \frac{6{,}00{,}000}{8{,}19{,}000}$$

= Rs.1,38,462

Illustration 32

The following particulars relating to a contract have been taken from the books of Kulkarni Contractors (P) Ltd. for the year ended 31st March, 2008:

(*a*) Work-in-Progress as on March 31, 2007:

	Rs.
Value of Work Certified	2,00,000
Cost of Work Uncertified	10,000
	2,10,000
Less Profit in Reserve	10,000
	2,00,000

(*b*) Contractee's Personal account as on March 31, 2007 showed a credit balance of Rs. 1,60,000.

(*c*) Transactions relating to the contract during the year ended March 31, 2008:

Materials Purchased for the Contract	Rs. 1,25,000
Materials Issued from Stores	Rs. 11,00,000
Wages (including Rs. 10,000 accrued)	Rs. 2,50,000
Materials Costing Rs. 10,000 sold at a Profit of 20% on Selling Price	

Machine Hiring charges for 200 hours at Rs. 30 per hour.

A second hand plant acquired for Rs. 50,000 and commissioned at the contract on Oct. 1, 2007, after getting it re-conditioned at a cost of Rs. 10,000 (Half of this plant was transferred to another contract on January 1, 2008).

A supervisor at a salary of Rs. 24,000 p.a. devoted 1/4th of his time on the contract. Power and fuel for the plant paid, Rs. 2,000.

(*d*) You are further told that:

(*i*) Work certified as per contractor's certification on March 10, 2008, Rs. 15,00,000 (excluding the previous certification).

(*ii*) Included in the cost items above, expenses incurred since certification were:

Materials Rs. 5,000 and wages Rs. 2,000.

(*iii*) Overhead are to be allocated at 25% of wages.

(*iv*) Depreciation on plant at 20% p.a. on diminishing value method.

(*v*) Contractors paid 80% of the work certified.

(*vi*) Materials at site :

as on March 31, 2007 Rs. 15,000

as on March 31, 2008 Rs. 25,000

Prepare Contract Account and Contractee's Personal Account.

Solution

Contract Account

Particulars		Amount Rs.	Particulars		Amount Rs.
To Work-in-Progress b/d:			By Sale of Materials (10,000 + 2,500)		12,500
Value of Work Certified	2,00,000		By Plant Transferred:	30,000	
Cost of Work Uncertified	10,000		*Less:* Dep.	1,500	28,500
	2,10,000				
Less Profit in Reserve	10,000	2,00,000			
To Materials at Site (Opening)		15,000	By Plant a Site	30,000	
			Less: Depreciation	3,000	27,000
To Material Purchased		1,25,000	By Material at Site (closing)		25,000
To Materials Issued from Stores		11,00,000	By Work-in-Progress:		
To Wages Paid	2,40,000		Value of Work Cert.	17,00,000	
Add: Accrued Wages	10,000	2,50,000	Uncertified Work	7,500	17,07,500
To Profit & Loss A/c (Profit on Material Sold)		2,500	By Profit & Loss A/c – Loss		28,500
To Hire of Machine (200 hrs. × Rs. 30)		6,000			
To Plant (50,000 + 10,000)		60,000			
To Supervisor's Salary (24,000 ÷ 4)		6,000			
To Power and Fuel		2,000			
To Overhead (25% of Wages)		62,500			
		18,29,000			18,29,000

Contractee's Personal Account

	Rs.		Rs.
To Balance c/d	13,60,000	By Balance b/d	1,60,000
		By Bank A/c	12,00,000
	13,60,000		13,60,000

Working Note:

Cost of Uncertified Work:

	Rs.
Materials	5,000
Wages	2,000
Overhead $\left(2{,}000\times\frac{25}{100}\right)$	500
	7,500

Illustration 33

Rex Limited commenced a contract on 1.10.2007. The total contract price was Rs. 5,00,000 but Rex Limited accepted the same for Rs. 4,50,000. It was decided to estimate the total profit and to take to the credit of Profit & Loss Account that proportion of estimated profit on cash basis which the work completed bore to the total contract. Actual expenditure till 31.3.08 and estimated expenditure in 2008-09 are given below:

Expenses	Actuals Till 31.3.08	Estimated For 2008-09
	Rs.	Rs.
Materials	75,000	1,30,000
Labour	55,000	60,000
Plant Purchased (Original Cost)	40,000	–
Misc. Expenses	20,000	35,500
Plant Returned to Stores on 31.3.08 at Original Cost	10,000	25,000 as at 31.12.08
Materials at Site	5,000	Nil
Work Certified	2,00,000	Full
Work Uncertified	7,500	Nil
Cash Received	1,80,000	Full

The plant is subject to annual depreciation @ 20% of original cost. The contract is likely to be completed on 31.12.2008.

You are required to prepare the contract account for the year ended 31.3.08. Workings should be clearly given.

It is the policy of the company to charge depreciation on time basis

(*C.A. Inter. Nov., 1990*)

Solution

Contract Account

(For the period ended 31 March, 2008)

	Rs.		Rs.
To Materials	75,000	By Plant Returned	
To Wages	55,000	to Stores	9,000
To Cost of Plant	40,000	(Rs. 10,000 – Rs. 1,000 Dep.)	
To Miscellaneous Expenses	20,000	By Plant at Site	27,000
To Balance c/d		(Rs. 30,000 – Rs. 3,000 Dep.)	
(Notional Profit)	58,500	By Materials at site	5,000
		By Work-in-Progress A/c	
		(*i*) Value of certified Work 2,00,000	
		(*ii*) Cost of uncertified Work 7,500	2,07,500
	2,48,500		2,48,500
To Profit and Loss A/c (Profit taken)	24,900	By Balance b/d	58,500
To Work-in-Progress A/c (Profit Reserved)	33,600		
	58,500		58,500

Estimated Contract Account

(From 1.10.07 to 31.12.08)

	Rs.		Rs.
To Materials (Rs. 75,000 + 1,30,000)	2,05,000	By Plant Returned to stores	27,750
To Wages (Rs. 55,000 + 60,000)	1,15,000	(*i*) 10,000 – 1,000 Dep. = 9,000	
		(*ii*) 25,000 – 6,250 Dep.	
To Cost of Plant	40,000	for 15 months = 18,750	
To Miscellaneous Expenses (Rs. 20,000 + 35,500)	55,500	By Contractee (Contract Price)	4,50,000
To Estimated Profit on Completion	62,250		
	4,77,750		4,77,750

Notes:

(*i*) Calculation of Profit to be transferred to Profit and Loss A/c:

$$= \text{Estimated Profit on Completion} \times \frac{\text{Cash Received}}{\text{Work Certified}} \times \frac{\text{Work Certified}}{\text{Total Contract Price}}$$

$$= \text{Rs. } 62{,}250 \times \frac{1{,}80{,}000}{2{,}00{,}000} \times \frac{2{,}00{,}000}{4{,}50{,}000}$$

= Rs. 24,900

(*ii*) It has been assumed that plant costing Rs. 5,000 would be exhausted at the site of the contract during the course of the second year. Hence, it is to be treated as a normal loss.

Illustration 34

During the year 2004-05, British Contractors Ltd. undertook three contracts, one on 1st April, second on 1st October and third on 1st January. On 31st March, 2005, when their accounts were made up, the position was as follows:

	Contract No. 1	Contract No. 2	Contract No. 3
	Rs.	Rs.	Rs.
Contract Price	2,00,000	1,35,000	1,50,000
Expenditure:			
Materials	39,400	29,000	10,000
Wages	63,250	56,200	7,000
General Expenses	2,000	1,400	500
Plant Installed	10,000	8,000	6,000
Materials on Hand	2,000	2,000	1,000
Wages Accrued	1,700	1,800	800
General Expenses Accrued	300	200	100
Work Certified	1,20,000	80,000	18,000
Cash Received on Work Certified	90,000	60,000	13,500
Work Finished but not yet Certified	3,000	4,000	1,050

Contract No. 1 has been negotiated in 2002-03 with an escalation clause providing that should material prices and wage rates increase by more than 2½%, the contractee would increase the contract price by 20% of the rise in the cost of materials and 40% of the rise in the wage rates beyond 2½% in each case. It is agreed that since the signing of the agreement, the material prices had gone up by 10% and wage rates by 15%. The value of work certified does not take into account the effect of the escalation clause.

The plant was installed on the dates of the contracts and depreciation is taken at 10% per annum. Prepare the respective accounts in Contract Ledger. Columnar form may be used and the dates may be omitted.

(Adapted C.A. Final)

Solution

Contract Accounts

Particulars	Contract No. 1	Contract No. 2	Contract No. 3	Particulars	Contract No. 1	Contract No. 2	Contract No. 3
	Rs.	Rs.	Rs.		Rs.	Rs.	Rs.
To Materials	39,400	29,000	10,000	By Materials at Hand	2,000	2,000	1,000
To Wages Paid & Accrued	64,950	58,000	7,800	By Work-in-Progress A/c (Value of Certified Work plus Cost of Uncertified Work)	1,26,334 (including escalation)	84,000	19,050
To General Expenses Paid & Accrued	2,300	1,600	600				
To Depreciation on Plant	1,000	400	150				
To Balance c/d (Notional Profit)	20,684	–	1,500	By Profit and Loss A/c (Loss)	–	3,000	–
	1,28,334	89,000	20,050		1,28,334	89,000	20,050
To Profit and Loss A/c (Profit taken)	10,342	–	–	By Balance b/d (Notional Profit)	20,684	–	1,500
To Work-in-Progress A/c (Profit Reserved)	10,342	–	1,500				
	20,684	–	1,500		20,684	–	1,500

Notes:

(*i*) Effect of escalation on Contract No. 1 has been calculated as follows:

	Total Increase	Increase @ 2½	Balance
	Rs.	Rs.	Rs.
(*a*) *Materials:* Effect of Increase in Price			
$37{,}400 \times \frac{10}{110}$	= 3,400	850	2,550
(*b*) *Wages:* Effect of Increase in Wage Rates			
$64{,}950 \times \frac{15}{115}$	= 8,472	1,412	7,060

Increase in Contract Price

20% of Rs. 2,550	= 510
40% of Rs. 7,060	= 2,824
	3,334

(*ii*) Contract No. 2 shows a loss which is to be transferred to Profit and Loss A/c.

(*iii*) Since very small portion of work has been completed and certified (less than 1/4 th of the total contract price) on Contract No. 3, the entire amount of notional profit has been transferred to Work-in-Progress A/c by way of profit reserved.

(*iv*) In case of Contract No. 1 more than ½ of the total contract has been completed and certified. As such the amount of profit to be transferred to Profit and Loss A/c has been calculated as follows:

$$\text{Notional Profit} \times \frac{2}{3} \times \frac{\text{Cash Received}}{\text{Value of Work Certified}}$$

$$= 20{,}684 \times \frac{2}{3} \times \frac{90{,}000}{1{,}20{,}000} = \text{Rs. } 10{,}342$$

Illustration 35

New Century Builders have entered into a contract to build an office building complex for Rs. 480 lakhs. The work started in April, 2007 and it is estimated that the contract will take 15 months to be completed. Work has progressed as per schedule and the actual costs charged till March, 2008 are as follows:

	Rs. (in lakhs)
Materials	112.20
Labour	162.00
Hire Charges for Equipment and other Expenses	36.00

Establishment Charges	32.40
	342.60

The following informations are available;

	Rs. (in lakhs)
Materials in Hand (March 31, 2008)	6.60
Work Certified (of which Rs. 324 lakhs have been paid) at March 31, 2008	400.00
Work not yet Certified at March 31, 2008, at cost	7.50

As per management estimates, the following further expenditure will be incurred to complete the work:

	Rs. (in lakhs)
Materials	10.50
Labour	16.00
Sub-contractors	20.00
Equipment Hire and other Charges	3.00
Establishment Charges	6.90

You are required to compute the value of work-in-progress as on March 31, 2008 after considering a reasonable margin of profit and show the appropriate accounts. Make a provision for contingencies amounting to 5% of total costs.

(*I.C.W.A. Inter, Dec., 1998*)

Solution

Contract Account

	Rs. lakhs			**Rs. lakhs**
To Materials	112.20	By Materials in hand		6.60
To Labour	162.00	By Work-in-Progress A/c		
To Hire of Equipment	36.00	(*i*) Value of Certified Work	400.00	
To Establishment Charges	32.40	(*ii*) Cost of Uncertified Work	7.50	407.50
Total	342.60			
To Balance c/d (Notional Profit)	71.50			
	414.10			414.10
To Profit and Loss A/c (Profit taken)	50.00	By Balance b/d		71.50
To Work-in-Progress A/c (Profit Reserved)	21.50			
	71.50			71.50

Note: Total Estimated Profit on completed contract

Expenditure upto 31-3-2008 (342.60 – 6.60)	336.00
Estimated further Expenditure:	
Materials (10.50 + 6.60)	17.10
Labour	16.00
Sub-contractors	20.00
Hire of Equipment	3.00
Establishment Charges	6.90
	63.00
Total Cost (336.00 + 63.00)	399.00

Add: Provision for Contingency (399 × 5/95)	21.00
Total Estimated Cost	420.00
Total Estimated Profit	60.00
Contract price	480.00

Proportionate profit to be considered for the year ending 31-3-08

$$= \frac{\text{Work Certified}}{\text{Contract Price}} \times \text{Total Estimated Profit} = \frac{400}{480} \times 60 = \text{Rs. 50 lakhs.}$$

Work-in-Progress A/c

	Rs. (lakhs)		Rs. (lakhs)
To Contract A/c	407.50	By Contract A/c (Profit Reserved)	21.50
		By Balance c/d	386.00
	407.50		407.50

Illustration 36

A construction company undertaking a number of contracts, furnished the following data relating to its incompleted contracts as on 31st March, 2006:

Contract Numbers	Rs. (lakhs) 723	726	729	731
Total Contract Price	23.20	14.40	10.08	28.80
Estimated Costs on Completion of Contract	20.50	11.52	12.60	21.60
Expenses for the year ended 31.3.06				
Direct Materials	5.22	1.80	1.98	0.80
Direct Wages	2.32	4.32	3.90	2.16
Overheads (Excluding Depreciation)	1.06	2.60	2.62	1.05
Profit Reserve as on 1.4.05	1.50	–	–	–
Plant Issued at Cost	5.00	3.50	2.75	3.00
Materials at Site on 1.4.05	0.75	–	–	–
Materials at Site on 31.3.06	0.45	0.20	0.08	0.05
Work Certified Till 31.3.05	4.65	–	–	–
Work Certifed during the year 2005-06	12.76	13.26	7.56	4.32
Work Uncertified as on 31.3.06	0.84	0.24	0.14	0.18
Progress Payments Received during the year	9.57	9.00	5.75	3.60

Depreciation @ 20% per annum is to be charged on plant issued. While the Contract No. 723 was carried over from last year, the remaining contracts were started in the 1st week of April, 2005.

Required:

(*i*) Determine the profit/loss in respect of each contract for the year ended 31st March, 2006.

(*ii*) State the profit/loss to be carried to Profit & Loss A/c for the year ended 31st March, 2006.

(*C.A. Inter*)

Solution

Contract Accounts for the year ending 31-3-2006 (fig. in Rs. Lakhs)

Contract No.	723	726	729	731	Contract No.	723	726	729	731
To WIP Certified					By WIP A/c				
	4.65				Certified Work	17.41	13.26	7.56	4.32
Mat. at Site Work	0.75				Uncertified Work	0.84	0.24	0.14	0.18
	5.40				By Mat.				
Less: Reserve	1.50				at site	0.45	0.20	0.08	0.05
	3.90								
To D. Materials	5.22	1.80	1.98	0.80					
To D. Wages	2.32	4.32	3.90	2.16	Loss. Tr. To	–	–	1.27	0.06
To Overheads	1.06	2.60	2.62	1.05	P&L A/c				
To Depreciation	1.00	0.70	0.55	0.60					
To Notional Profit	5.20	4.28	–	–					
	18.70	13.70	9.05	4.61		18.70	13.70	9.05	4.61
* To P&L A/c	2.60	1.80	–	–	By Notional				
To W1P A/c	2.60	2.48	–	–	Profit	5.20	4.28	–	–
	5.20	4.28	–	–		5.20	4.28	–	–

*Working Notes

(*i*) Contract No. 723

$$\textbf{Transfer to P\&L A/c} = \text{Notional Profit} \times \frac{2}{3} \times \frac{\text{Cash Received}}{\text{Work Certified}}$$

$$= 5.20 \times \frac{2}{3} \times \frac{9.57}{12.76} = \text{Rs. } 2.60$$

(*ii*) **Contract No. 726:** This contract is 92% (*i.e.*, 13.26 ÷ 14.40) complete
Transfer to P&L : A/c =

$$\text{Estimated Profit on Completion} \times \frac{\text{Work Certified}}{\text{Contract Price}} \times \frac{\text{Cash Received}}{\text{Work Certified}}$$

$$= (14.40 - 11.52) \times \frac{13.26}{14.40} \times \frac{9.00}{13.26} = \text{Rs. } 1.80$$

OBJECTIVE TYPE QUESTIONS

A. Multiple Choice Questions

1. *Select the correct answer in each of the following.*

1. Most of the expenses are direct in
(*a*) job costing (*b*) batch costing
(*c*) contract costing.

2. When a contract is not completed at the end of the accounting year, profit on incomplete contract is
(*a*) transferred to Profit and Loss Account
(*b*) transferred to reserve
(*c*) transferred partly to Profit and Loss Account and partly to reserve.

3. When a contract is not completed at the end of the year, loss on incomplete contract is
(*a*) transferred to Profit and Loss Account
(*b*) transferred to work-in-progress
(*c*) transferred partly to Profit and Loss Account and partly to work-in-progress.

4. When $\frac{1}{2}$ of the contract is complete, the amount of profit to be taken credit for is usually
(*a*) the amount of profit estimated
(*b*) 50% of the estimated profit
(*c*) two-thirds of the estimated profit multiplied by cash ratio.

5. In contract costing, work-in-progress account represents
(*a*) Cost of certified work
(*b*) Cost of certified and uncertified work
(*c*) Cost of certified work, cost of uncertified work and amount of profit transferred to Profit and Loss Account.

6. Cost-plus contract is usually entered into those cases where
(*a*) cost can be easily estimated
(*b*) it is not possible to compute cost in advance with a reasonable degree of accuracy
(*c*) contractor wants to earn a fixed amount of profit.

7. Contract price is not fixed in case of
(*a*) cost-plus contracts (*b*) escalation clause
(*c*) de-escalation clause (*d*) all of the above.

8. In contract costing, contract account is prepared by the
(*a*) contractor (*b*) contractee
(*c*) both by contractor and contractee.

9. In a building contract of Rs. 2,40,000, at the end of the year work certified is Rs. 1,60,000 and the estimated profit is Rs. 30,000. What is the amount of profit to be credited to Profit and Loss Account assuming cash ratio is 80%

(*a*) Rs. 20,000 (*b*) Rs.16,000 (*c*) Rs. 25,000

[**Ans.** 1. (*c*), 2. (*c*), 3. (*a*), 4. (*c*), 5. (*c*), 6. (*b*), 7. (*a*), 8. (*a*), 9. (*b*)]

B. 'True'/ 'False' type statements

2. *Indicate whether the following statements are 'true' or 'false'*

1. Contract costing is a variant of job costing.

2. Most of the items of cost are direct in nature in contract costing.

3. In cost-plus contracts, the contractor runs a risk of incurring a loss.

4. In case of cost-plus contracts, the final contract price is not certain.

5. Escalation clause in a contract provides that contract price is fixed.

6. In contract costing, credit is taken for full amount of estimated profit on incomplete contracts.

7. In contract costing , the unit of cost is a job.

8. In contract costing, profit on contracts is calculated when they are completed.

[**Ans.** 1. True, 2. True, 3. False, 4. True, 5. False, 6. False, 7. False, 8. False]

C. Filling the blanks.

3. *Fill in the blanks.*

1. In contract costing, the cost unit is ....

2. .... in a contract provides that in the event of a specified contingency, the contract price would be suitably enhanced.

3. When there is a loss on incomplete contract, it is treated as .... and transferred to ....

4. When 75% of the contract price is certified as complete, the profit to be transferred to Profit and Loss Account will be equal to ....

5. .... contracts provide for payment of actual cost plus an agreed percentage of profit.

6. For a contract which is almost complete, the amount of profit to be transferred to Profit and Loss Account should be equal to ....

7. When a contract account is debited with the original cost of the plant, at the end of the year, it should be credited with ....

[**Ans.** 1. Per contract, 2. Escalation clause, 3. Loss, Profit and Loss A/c, 4. Two-thirds of the estimated profit multiplied by cash ratio, 5. Cost-plus, 6. Estimated Profit on completion $\times \frac{\text{Value of certified work}}{\text{Contract Price}}$, 7. Depreciated value]

SHORT ANSWER TYPE QUESTIONS

Answer each of the following in not more than 5 lines:

1. What is contract costing?
2. To what type of industries is contract costing applicable?
3. What is certified work?
4. What is uncertified work?
5. What is meant by cost-plus contracts?
6. What is escalation clause in contract costing?
7. What is meant by notional profit?
8. What is the difference between special plant and general plant?
9. What is a sub-contract?
10. What is meant by contract price?

LONG ANSWER TYPE QUESTIONS

1. What do you understand by Contract Costing? How does it differ from Job Costing and Terminal Costing? To what undertakings is this method of costing is considered to be the most suitable?
2. Theoretically, it may be incorrect to bring into account any profit or loss on incomplete contracts, but in practice strict adherence to this principle may have important consequences. Discuss the pros and cons of the question.
3. What are the different methods of calculating profit on incomplete contracts? Illustrate your answer. (*G.N.D.U., B.Com., 2008*)
4. Write notes on
   (*a*) Work Certified
   (*b*) Work done but not Certified
   (*c*) Cost-plus Contracts
   (*d*) Retention Money.

5. What do you understand by cost-plus method of placing contracts? In what cases is this method usually employed? Discuss its advantages and disadvantages.

6. What is a Contract Account? How is it prepared? Discuss the various items which are included in a Contract Account.

7. Discuss the method of ascertaining the profit on the following contracts:
   (*i*) When the contract is completed;
   (*ii*) When the contract is not completed; and
   (*iii*) When the contract is nearing completion.

8. What items are included in the valuation of work-in-progress relating to contracts? How are they shown in the Balance Sheet?

9. How would you calculate profit on contracts which are nearing completion?

(*G.N.D.U., B.Com., 2008*)

EXERCISES

1. The details regarding Contract No. 88 which was completed by 31st March, 2005 are as follows:

	Rs.
Contract Price	5,00,000
Net expenditure incurred on contract till completion	4,15,000
Maintenance Period in respect of contract after completion	6 Months
Estimated cost of maintenance during maintenance period	12,000

Calculate the amount of profit to be transferred to Profit and Loss Account in respect of the contract.

[**Ans.** Rs. 73,000]

2. (*a*) The following figures are available at the end of a financial year relating to a contract:

	Rs.
Total cost of work done to date	= 1,65,525
Cost of work uncertified	= 12,450
Contract price	= 8,70,000
Value of work certified	= 2,10,420

Determine the amount of profit to be taken to Profit and Loss Account.

(*G.N.D.U., B.Com. April 1996*)

[**Ans.** Notional profit Rs. 57,345 Profit to be transferred to Profit and Loss A/c = Nil since the value of work certified is less than $\frac{1}{4}$ th of total contract.]

(*b*) From the following data, calculate the profit to be transferred to Profit and Loss Account:

Cost of contract	Rs. 8,85,200
Work not certified	Rs. 30,000

Cash received being 80% of work certified Rs. 7,20,000.

(*G.N.D.U., B.Com., April 1997*)

[**Ans.** Notional Profit Rs. 44,800, transferred to Profit and Loss A/c Rs. 23,893 assuming that more than 1/2 of the contract has been certified.]

3. From the following particulars relating to Contract No. 374 for the year ending 31st March, 2006, calculate the amount of profit to be transferred to Profit and Loss A/c:

	Rs.
Total Contract Price	6,00,000
Total Expenditure incurred on contract to date	1,41,000
Value of work certified	1,80,000
Cash received from contractee	1,35,000
Cost of work not yet certified	6,000

[Ans. Notional Profit Rs. 45,000 Profit transferred to Profit and Loss A/c ($\frac{1}{3}$rd of realised portion of notional profit) Rs. 11,250]

4. Following particulars relate to Contract No. 18 at the end of the financial year 2005-06:

	Rs.
Total contract price	12,50,000
Value of work certified	11,00,000
Cost of work not yet certified	16,500
Total cost of contract	9,81,500

Cash received on account Rs. 8,80,000. Calculate the amount of profit to be transferred to Profit and Loss A/c

[**Ans.** Notional profit Rs. 1,35,000 Profit transferred to Profit and Loss A/c Rs.72,000]

5. From the following particulars relating to Contract No. 181, for the year ended 31st March, 2005, calculate the cost of uncertified work and the amount of profit to be transferred to Profit and Loss A/c:

	Rs.
Contract price	5,00,000
Work completed	3/5
Cash received (being 75% of work certified)	1,50,000
Net Expenditure incurred on contract to date	1,92,000

[**Ans.** (*i*) Estimated cost of contract on completion = 1,92,000 × 5/3 = 3,20,000

(*ii*) Estimated cost of work certified = $3{,}20{,}000 \times \dfrac{2{,}00{,}000}{5{,}00{,}000} = 1{,}28{,}000$

(*iii*) Cost of uncertified work = Rs. 1,92,000 – 1,28,000 = Rs. 64,000

(*iv*) Notional Profit = Rs. 72,000

(*v*) Transfer to Profit & Loss A/c: Rs. 18,000]

6. The details regarding Contract No. 35 undertaken by Jainco Builders for the year ended 31st March, 2006 are as follows:

	Rs.
Contract price	7,50,000
Net expenditure incurred to date	3,80,000
Cash received on contract (90% of work certified)	4,38,750
Estimated expenditure yet to be incurred for completing the contract	3,10,000
Provision for contingencies	10,000

Calculate the amount of profit to be taken to Profit and Loss A/c on the contract which is nearing completion.

[**Ans.** (*i*) Estimated cost of contract on completion Rs. 7,00,000

(*ii*) Estimated Profit on completion Rs. 50,000

(*iii*) Profit to be transferred to Profit and Loss A/c: = $50{,}000 \times \dfrac{4{,}38{,}750}{7{,}50{,}000}$]

7. A contractor undertook a contract of Rs. 50,000 on 1st January, 1987 to be completed over a period of two years. His accounting year ends on 31st Dec. State with reasons at what value the work-in-progress on 1st January, 1988 will appear in the contract account in each of the following cases:

(*a*) Work-in-progress on 1st January, 1988 Rs. 14,000 (including Rs. 800 estimated profit which was taken to profit and loss account in 1987).

(*b*) Work-in-progress Rs. 14,000 on 1st January, 1988 (including Rs. 800 estimated profit which was not taken to P&L Account in 1987).

(*c*) Work-in-progress on 1st January, 1988 Rs. 14,000 (excluding Rs. 800 estimated profit which was not taken to P&L Account in 1987).

(*d*) Work-in-progress on 1st January, 1988 Rs. 14,000 (excluding Rs. 800 estimated profit which was taken to profit and loss account in 1987).

[**Ans.** (*a*) Rs. 14,000, (*b*) Rs. 13,200, (*c*) Rs. 14,000, (*d*) Rs. 14,800]

8. Calculate the amount to be transferred to Profit and Loss A/c

Total Contract Price	8,00,000
Total Cost Incurred	3,00,000
Cash received upon contract	2,00,000
Amount of work certified	5,00,000
Uncertified work	10,000

(*B.Com. Pbi. Univ., 1998*)

[**Ans.** 56,000]

9. Prepare the Contract Account on 31.10.04 and state the amount of profit to be credited to Profit and Loss Account from the following figures:

	Rs.
Materials purchased	75,000
Materials on hand	3,000
Wages paid	87,500
Wages outstanding	1,250
Indirect expenses	3,750
Cost of plant	12,500

The value of work certified was Rs.1,80,000 of which Rs. 1,35,000 had been received, work completed but uncertified was valued at Rs. 5,000. The contract price was Rs. 3,00,000. The plant on site was valued at Rs. 10,000 on 31.10.04.

(*G.N.D.U., B.Com. III, 1995*)

[**Ans.** Notional Profit Rs. 18,000 Transferred to Profit and Loss A/c Rs. 9,000. Material on hand taken as Closing Stock]

10. A firm of building contractors started its business on 1st April, 2003. Following was the expenditure on contract for Rs. 3,00,000.

Materials issued to contract	51,000
Plant issued for contract	15,000
Wages incurred	81,000
Other expenses incurred	5,000

Cash received on account upto 31-3-04 amounted to Rs.1,28,000 being 80% of the work certified. Of the plant and materials charged to the contract, plant which cost Rs. 3,000 and materials which cost Rs. 2,500 were lost. On 31.3.04 plant which cost Rs. 2,000 was returned to stores. The cost of work done but uncertified was Rs. 1,000 and materials costing Rs. 2,300 were in hand on site.

Charge 15% depreciation on plant and show what profit or loss would be taken into account for the year ended on 31.3.04.

[**Ans.** Notional Profit Rs. 27,000, Transferred to Profit and Loss A/c Rs. 14,400]

(*G.N.D.U. B.Com. III, April, 1996, H.P. Univ., B.Com. 111, April, 1996*)

11. Given below is the summarised record as on 31st March, 2008, of all transactions relating to Contract No. 75 which was duly completed:

	Rs.
Materials purchased directly	6,450
Materials supplied from Stores	2,600
Direct Wages	10,720
Direct Expenses	1,470
Materials returned to stores	1,200
Contract Price	25,000
Work overhead	25% on Direct Wages
Office overhead	10% on Prime Cost

You are required to prepare Contract No. 75 Account showing the profit made.

[**Ans.** Prime Cost Rs. 20,040, Profit Rs. 276]

12. Ganpathi & Co., undertook a contract which was started on 1st April, 2007. During the year, the following expenses were incurred:

	Rs.
Materials purchased	5,000
Materials issued from stores	10,000
Materials transferred from other contracts	8,000
Wages paid	15,000
Direct Expenses	500
Establishment Expenses	500
Cost of Special Plant	20,000

The contract price was Rs. 50,000. On 31st March, 2008, the work was completed and the contract price duly received. On this date, the position of the contract revealed the following:

Materials returned to stores	1,500
Materials in hand on 31st March	500
Value of Plant on 31st March	19,000

You are required to prepare Contract Account and Contractee's Personal Account.

[**Ans.** Profit: Rs. 12,000]

13. A contractor undertook a contract of Rs. 5,00,000 on 1st January, 2008. The work was completed on 30th June, 2008. Following are the details of this contract:

	Rs.
Materials sent to site from stores	30,200
Materials purchased directly from vendor	45,500
Materials received from other contracts	20,300
Labour engaged	1,35,000
Direct charges	42,000

Plant installed at site	40,000
General expenses	32,000
Establishment charges	18,000
Wages accrued	12,000
Direct charges accrued	3,000
General charges accrued	5,000
Materials returned to stores	15,000
Materials at site	13,000
Materials transferred to other contracts	11,000
Materials sold (costing Rs. 8,000)	9,000
Plant sold (costing Rs. 15,000)	10,000
Materials destroyed by fire	8,000

Prepare a contract account charging depreciation on plant @ 10% per annum from the above particulars.

[**Ans.** Profit to Profit & Loss A/c Rs. 2,10,750]

(**Hint:** It is assumed that plant has been sold in the beginning)

14. A building contractor took a contract for the construction of a certain building on 1st April, 2002. The contract price was agreed at Rs. 4,00,000. The contractor has made the following expenditure during the year ended 31st March, 2003:

	Rs.
Direct materials purchased	20,000
Materials issued from stores	5,000
Direct labour	15,000
Plant	40,000
Indirect expenses	10,000
Total	90,000

From the following further information prepare a contract account for the year ended 31st March, 2003. Also show the amount of work-in-progress which will be shown in the Balance Sheet of contractor.

	Rs.
Value of plant on 31st March, 2003	30,000
Stock of materials on 31st March, 2003	5,000
Materials returned to stores	1,000
Work certified by architects	75,000
Cash received from contractee	70,000
Cost of work not yet certified	4,000

[**Ans.** Notional profit Rs. 25,000]

(**Hint:** No amount of profit is transferred to P&L A/c as the value of work certified is less than $\frac{1}{4}$ of contract price.)

15. Bharat Constructions Ltd., obtained a contract for the construction of Arts Faculty of a university at 10% less of the estimated cost amounting to Rs. 20,00,000.

The work was taken up on 1st April, 2007. On 31st March, 2008, the expenses on the contract were as follows:

		Rs.
Materials issued to the contract	...	3,60,000
Material at site at the end	...	15,000
Wages	...	4,93,200
Plant and machinery specially bought for contract (subject to depreciation at 10% for the whole year for costing purposes)	...	60,000
Direct expenses incurred	...	25,800
General overhead (share of the contract)	...	15,200
Cost of completed work not certified as on 31st March, 2008	...	30,000

Upto the close of the year, a total sum of Rs. 7,20,000 was received by the contractors, being 80% of the amount payable (on the basis of net value of contract) on Architect's certificate.

Prepare the contract account showing the profit earned on the contract.

(*Meerut, B.Com. Agra, M.Com.*)

[**Ans.** Notional Profit Rs. 44,800, Profit to P&L A/c Rs. 23,893]

16. The following is a summary of the expenditure on Contract No. 375 to 31st March, 2006:

	Rs.
Direct Wages	13,800
Direct Material	68,000
Stores issued	7,600
Stores returned	1,100
Sub-contract costs	12,600
Plant	24,000

You obtain the following information:

(*i*) The contract was begun in 2005-06 and the contract price was Rs. 1,20,000 (*ii*) The architects had certified that 4/5 of the contract had been completed on 15th March, 2006 (*iii*) Depreciation of plant to 15th March, 2006, is Rs. 9,600 (*iv*) The summary set out above includes items relating to the period since certification (15-03-06) as follows: Wages Rs. 1,400 and Materials used Rs. 3,240 (*v*) Materials on site on 31st March, 2006 had cost Rs. 10,000 and stores on site had cost Rs. 800. (*vi*) Establishment charges are 40% on direct wages. (*vii*) A fine of Rs. 5,000 is likely to be imposed for the late completion of the contract.

You are required (*a*) to prepare Contract No. 375 Account, (*b*) to show clearly and separately what profit or loss has arisen on the work certified and (*c*) to suggest what amount should be taken to the Profit and Loss Account for the year ending 31st March, 2006.

(*B.Com. Agra*)

[**Ans.** Loss transferred to P&L A/c Rs. 4,020]

17. The Hindustan Construction Co. Ltd. have undertaken the construction of a bridge over the River Yamuna for a Municipal Corporation. The value of the contract is Rs. 12,50,000 subject to a retention of 20% until one year after the certified completion of the contract, and final approval of the Corporation's engineer. The following are the details as shown in the books on 30th June, 2007:

	Rs.
Labour on site	4,05,000
Material direct to site less returns	4,20,000
Material from stores	81,200
Hire and use of plant–plant upkeep account	12,100
Direct expenses	23,000
General Overhead allocated to the contract	37,100
Materials on hand June 30,2007	6,300
Wages accrued on June 30, 2007	7,800
Direct expenses accrued on June 30, 2007	1,600
Work not yet certified – at cost	16,500
Amount certified by the Corporation's engineer	11,00,000
Cash received on account	8,80,000

Prepare (*a*) Contract account, (*b*) Contractee's account and (*c*) show how work-in-progress would appear in the Balance Sheet.

[**Ans.** Notional Profit Rs. 1,35,000 Profit to P&L A/c. Rs. 72,000.]

18. A building contractor, having undertaken construction work at a contract price of Rs. 5,00,000 began execution of the work on 1st April, 2008. The following are the particulars of the contract upto 31st March, 2009.

	Rs.
Machinery installed at site	30,000
Materials sent to site	1,70,750
Labour at site	1,48,698
Direct expenses	6,334
Overhead charges allocated	8,251
Materials returned from site	1,098
Work certified by architect	3,90,000
Cash received	3,60,000
Cost of work not yet certified	9,000

Materials on hand on 31.03.09	3,765
Wages accrued on 31.03.09	5,380
Value of machinery as at 31.03.09	22,000

It was decided that the profit made on the contract in the year should be arrived at by deducting the cost of work certified from the total value of architect's certificates, that one-third of the profit so arrived at should be regarded as a provision against contingencies and that such provision should be increased by taking to the credit of Profit and Loss Account, such portion of the two-third profit as the cash received bore to the work certified.

Prepare the Contract Account for the year and show the amount taken to the credit of the Profit and Loss Account.

(Punjab B.Com.)

[**Ans.** Notional Profit Rs. 56,450, Profit to P&L A/c Rs. 34,738]

19. A contract account in the books of Contractors Ltd. appears as follows:

2007		**Rs.**
June 30	Materials issued to site	5,000
	Plant issued to site	12,500
	Direct Labour	4,600
	Indirect Labour	640
	Overhead expenses	1,950

You are informed that it is the practice of the firm to take credit for two-thirds of the profit earned on the contracts in progress after taking into account the value of the work certified for payment by architects. You are required to:

(*a*) Compile the contract account to June 30.

(*b*) Show the amount which you would transfer to Profit and Loss Account along with necessary calculations.

(*c*) Show relevant entries in the Balance Sheet as on 30th June.

For this purpose you are supplied with the following further information as at that date:

	Rs.
Value of work certified for payment	10,000
Cost of work carried out, but not certified	3,800
Stock of materials not used	950
Value of plant on site after depreciation	11,875

(Delhi B. Com. Hons.)

[**Ans.** Notional Profit Rs. 1,935; Profit to P and L A/c
1,935 × 2/3 = 1,290]

20. Ashoka Building Construction Ltd., undertook a contract for Rs. 1,00,000. The following expenses were incurred regarding this contract during the year 2003-04:

	Rs.
Materials sent to site	31,000
Direct wages paid	28,000
Chargeable expenses	6,000
Plant installed	10,000
General expenses	9,000
Establishment charges	7,000

The architects of contractee certified the work of Rs. 60,000 at the end of the year. The cost of work uncertified was Rs. 5,000 on that date. The materials and plant were at site of Rs. 3,000 and Rs. 6,000 respectively at the end of the year.

Prepare (*i*) Contract Account (*ii*) and also show how these transactions will appear in the Balance Sheet of the contractor at the end of the year.

[**Ans.** Loss to P&L A/c Rs. 17,000]

21. Prepare the contract accounts in tabular form from the following particulars for the year ending on 31st March, 2003:

	Contract A	**Contract B**	**Contract C**
	Rs.	**Rs.**	**Rs.**
Materials sent to site	28,000	22,000	40,000
Labour engaged	16,000	25,000	38,000
Plant installed	30,000	–	80,000
Plant hired–plant upkeep account	–	8,000	–
Materials returned to store	1,000	3,000	5,000
Materials sold (costing Rs. 6,000)	7,000	–	–
Materials destroyed	–	–	2,000
Materials transferred to other contracts	–	3,000	1,000
Materials received from other contracts	4,000	–	–
Depreciation on plant (per annum)	10%	–	15%
Wages accrued	6,000	–	–
Value of work certified	35,000	60,000	1,00,000
Cost of work uncertified	8,000	10,000	16,000
Cash received	30,000	50,000	80,000
Contract price	1,50,000	3,00,000	2,50,000
Date of commencement	1st July, 2002	1st April, 2002	1st Sept., 2002

Also show how the above transactions would appear in the balance sheet as on 31st March, 2003.

[**Ans.** Contract A –Loss to P and L A/c Rs. 6,250 : Contract B –Balance of Contract A/c Rs. 21,000;Contract C–Profit to P and. L A./c Rs. 10,400]

22. The following figures relate to two jobs of a contractor. You are required to prepare Contract Accounts for both the contracts and state what profit or loss (if any) should be brought to the Profit and Loss Account for the year ended 31st March, 2002.

	Contract A	Contract B
	Rs.	Rs.
Total expenditure upto 31-3-2001	9,00,000	6,75,000
Wages (2001-02)	1,05,000	21,500
Materials and Haulage Hire (2001-02)	1,57,500	7,500
Indirect expenses	5,250	600

Plants which were originally charged at cost were valued at the close of the year at Rs. 2,50,000 and Rs. 3,75,300 respectively for Contracts A and B. The Contract Price for A was Rs. 12,00,000 and for B Rs. 3,00,000. The work in each case was actually finished on 28th Feb., 2002 but the contracts could not be considered as complete until the maintenance period of six months as stipulated in Contract has expired on 31st August, 2002. The cost of maintenance is estimated at Rs. 5,000 for Contract A and Rs. 3,500 for Contract B.

[**Ans.** Contract A –Profit 2,77,250; B –Loss, Rs. 32,800]

23. The following Trial Balance was extracted on 31st March, 2003 from the books of Singhania Co. Ltd., Contractors:

	Rs.	Rs.
Share Capital		
Shares of Rs. 10 each		3,51,800
Profit and Loss A/c on 1st April, 2002		25,000
Provision for Depreciation on Plant and Tools		63,000
Cash received on account: Contract No.777		12,80,000
Creditors		81,200
Land & Buildings (cost)	74,000	
Plant and Tools (cost)	52,000	
Bank	45,000	
Contract No. 777:		
Materials issued	6,00,000	
Direct Labour	8,30,000	
Expenses	40,000	
Plant and Tools on site at cost	1,60,000	
	18,01,000	18,01,000

Contract No. 777 was begun on 1st April, 2002. The contract price is Rs. 27,00,000 and the customer has so far paid Rs. 12,80,000, being 80% of the work certified. The cost of work done since certification is estimated at Rs. 16,000.

On 31st March 2003, after the above trial balance was extracted, Plant costing Rs. 32,000 was returned to stores and materials then on site were valued at Rs. 27,000. Provision is to be made for direct labour accrued Rs. 6,000 and for for depreciation of all plant and tools at 12½% on cost.

You are required to (*a*) write up the Contract Account and (*b*) submit the Balance Sheet as on 31st March, 2003.

[**Ans.** Notional profit Rs. 1,47,000. Profit to P&L A/c Rs. 78,400. Total of Balance Sheet: Rs. 6,05,400]

24. Bharat Construction Engineers undertook a contract of Rs. 20,00,000 which was completed in three years commencing from 1st April, 2005. Following are the details of expenditure of this contract for various years.

In 2005-06: Direct materials Rs. 1,20,000, Direct Wages Rs. 1,00,000. Depreciation on plant Rs. 30,000 and other expenses Rs. 20,000. The engineers certified a work of Rs. 3,00,000 upto 31st March, 2006 of which 80% was received in cash. The cost of work uncertified was Rs. 10,000.

In 2006-07: Direct Materials Rs. 3,80,000, Wages Rs. 2,80,000, Depreciation on plant Rs. 80,000 and other expenses Rs. 50,000. The value of work certified was Rs. 10,00,000 (80% received in cash) and the cost of work done but not certified upto 31st March, 2007 was Rs. 20,000.

In 2007-08: Direct Materials Rs. 1,40,000, Wages Rs. 1,60,000, Depreciation on plant Rs. 50,000 and other expenses Rs. 20,000. The contract was completed at the end of the year and full amount has been received from contractees.

Prepare the contract account for three years and show how it would appear in the Balance Sheet for the various years.

[**Ans.** 2005-06 –Balance of Contract A/c Rs. 40,000 (as no profit transferred to P & L A/c since work certified is less than 1/4th total contract),
2005-07 –Loss to P&L A/c Rs. 40,000,
2008-09 –Profit to P&L A/c Rs. 6,10,000]

25. Pleasant Co. Ltd. undertook a contract on 1st April, 2000 which was completed on 30th June, 2002. Following particulars are given to you in respect of the contract:

2000-01: Materials issued Rs. 40,000 Wages, Rs. 20,000, Other Direct expenses Rs. 2,000 Materials on site on 31st March, 2001 Rs. 4,000, Value of Certified work Rs. 75,000.

2001-02: Materials issued Rs. 10,000 Wages, Rs. 50,000, Other Indirect expenses Rs. 5,000, Special Plant Rs. 80,000, Materials on site on 31st March, 2002 Rs.10,500, Value of work certified during the year Rs.1,50,000, Work completed but uncertified Rs. 25,000.

2002-03: Materials issued Rs. 5,000; Wages Rs. 12,500 and direct expenses Rs. 1,200. Materials returned to stores on 30th June, 2002 Rs. 1,000.

Plant returned to stores after charging depreciation @ 10% p.a. Cash received on work certified each year: 80%. Total Contract Price Rs. 3,00,000. Prepare Contract Account, Contractee's Account and Work-in-Progress Account and show how Work-in-Progress Account will appear in Balance Sheet each year.

(M.D.U., B.Com. III, 1996)

[**Ans.** Year 2000-01 Notional Profit- Rs. 17,000; 2001-02 Notional Profit- Rs. 1,20,967; 2002-03 Net Profit-Rs. 76,451]

26. Prepare a Contract Account and Contractee's account from the following particulars:

	Rs.
Materials sent to site	58,000
Direct wages	65,000
Chargeable expenses	35,000
Plant installed	40,000
Indirect expenses	25,000
Wages accrued	30,000
Materials returned to store	8,000
Plant at site at the end	25,000
Materials at site at the end	10,000
Cash received (being 80% of work certified)	2,00,000
Work completed	¾
Contract price	4,00,000

[**Ans.** Profit to P & L A/c Rs. 40,000; Cost of work uncertified Rs. 35,000]

27. A contractor, who prepares his accounts on 31st December each year, commenced a contract on 1st April, 2005. The costing records concerning the said contract reveal the following information on 31st December, 2005:

	Rs.
Materials charged to site	2,58,100
Labour engaged	5,60,500
Foreman's salary	79,300

Plants costing Rs. 2,60,000 have been on site for 146 days. Their working life is estimated at 7 years and their final scrap value at Rs. 15,000. A supervisor, who is paid Rs. 4,000 p.m., has devoted approximately three-fourths of his time to this contract. The administrative and other expenses amount to Rs. 1,40,000. Materials in hand at site on 31st December,

2005 cost Rs. 25,400. Some of the material costing Rs. 4,500 was found unsuitable and was sold for Rs. 4,000 and a part of the plant costing Rs. 5,500 (on 31.12.05) unsuited to the contract was sold at a profit of Rs. 1,000.

The contract price was Rs. 22,00,000 but it was accepted by the contractor for Rs. 20,00,000. On 31st December, 2005, two-thirds of the cost of the contract work was completed. Architect's certificate has been issued covering 50% of cost of contract and Rs. 7,50,000 had so far been paid on account. Prepare contract account and state how much profit or loss should be included in the financial accounts to 31st December, 2005. Workings should be clearly given. Depreciation is charged on time basis.

Also prepare the Contractee's account and show how these accounts would appear in the Balance Sheet on 31st December; 2005.

(Adapted C.A. Inter, Nov, 1991)

[**Ans.** Notional profit Rs. 2, 13,350; profit transferred to P/L A/c Rs. 1,06,675; WIP Rs. 11,55,675; Cost of uncertified work Rs. 2,62,250 (*i.e.*, cost of work done 10,49,000 –Rs. 7,86,750 *i.e.*, 50% of cost of contract].

28. A B Ltd. has obtained a contract for construction of a building. The value of contract is Rs. 12 lakhs and work commenced on 1st Oct., 2004. The following details are shown in their books for the year ended 30th Sept., 2005:

Plant purchased Rs. 60,000, Wages paid Rs. 3,40,000; Materials issued to site Rs. 3,36,000, Direct expenses Rs. 8,000, General overhead apportioned Rs. 32,000, Wages accrued as on 30.9.05 Rs. 2,800, Material at site on 30.9.05 Rs. 4,000, Direct expenses accrued as on 30.9.05 Rs. 1,200. Work not yet certified at cost Rs. 1,400. Cash received being 80% of the work certified Rs. 6,00,000. Life of plant purchased is 5 years and scrap value is nil. You are required to (*i*) prepare the Contract Account for the year ended 30th Sept., 2005 and (*ii*) Show the amount of profit which you consider might be fairly taken on the contract and how you have calculated it.

(H.P.U. B.Com. 1997)

[**Ans.** Notional Profit Rs 23,400]

29. Alcon Construction Company Ltd., commenced its business of construction on 1-1-2008. On 31.12.2008, their books showed the following balances:

	Dr. (Rs)	Cr. (Rs.)
Paid-up Share Capital		1,00,000
Cash received on account of contract (80% of work certified)		1,20,000
Land and Buildings	30,000	
Machinery at cost (75% at site)	40,000	
Bank	4,000	
Materials at site	40,000	
Direct labour	55,000	
Expenses at site	2,000	
Lorries and Vehicles	30,000	
Furniture	1,000	
Office equipment	10,000	
Postage and Telegrams	500	
Office expenses	2,000	
Rates and Taxes	3,000	
Fuel and Power	2,500	
	2,20,000	2,20,000

The contract price is Rs. 3,00,000 and work certified is Rs. 1,50,000. The work completed since certification is estimated at Rs. 1,000 (at cost). Machinery costing Rs. 2,000 was returned to stores at the end of the year. Stock of material at site on 31-12-2008 was of the value of Rs. 5,000, Wages outstanding were Rs. 200. Depreciation on machinery at 10%. You are required to prepare Contract Account and show how the work-in-progress will appear in balance sheet as on 31-12-2008.

(*B.Com. Hons. Delhi 1990*)

[**Ans.** *Profit Rs. 47,800 B/S total Rs. 1,24,693*]

30. P. Ltd. undertook a contract for the construction of building at contract price of Rs. 15,00,000. During the first year, the following amounts were spent against which a sum of Rs. 5,62,500 (representing 90% of the work certified) was received by the contractor:

	Rs.
Materials used	2,62,500
Wages paid to the workers	1,50,000
Overhead expenses	37,500

During the second year, the contractor spent the following amounts:

	Rs.
Materials used	3,75,000
Wages paid to the workers	3,00,000
Overhead expenses	75,000

In the second year, the contract was completed and a sum of Rs. 8,75,000 was received by the contractor. You are required to prepare the Contract Accounts and the contractee's accounts for both the years and determine the profit.

Note: Only 40% of the notional profit is to be taken to the credit of Profit and Loss Account in the first year as the work done was less than 50% of the contract.

[**Ans.** Profit Rs. 2,30,000]
(*I.C.W.A. Inter Dec., 1992*)

31. Modern contruction company with a paid up share captal of Rs. 50 lakhs undertook a contract to construct LIG houses. The contract work commenced on 1.1.2004 and the contract price was Rs. 50 lakhs. Cash received on account of contract on 31.12.2004 was Rs. 18 lakhs (90% of the work certified). Work completed but not certified was estimated at Rs. 1,00,000. As on 31.12.04, material at site was estimated at Rs. 30,000 and machinery at site costing Rs. 2,00,000 was returned to stores. Plant and machinery at site is to be depreciated at 5%. Wages outstanding on 31.12. 04 were Rs. 5,000.

The following were ledger balances (Dr.) as per Trial Balance as on 31.12.04.

	Rs.
Land and buildings	15,00,000
Plant and machinery at cost (60% at site)	25,00,000
Lorries and other vehicles	8,00,000
Furniture	50,000
Office equipment	10,000
Materials sent to site	14,00,000
Fuel & Power	1,25,000
Site expenses	5,000
Office Expenses	4,000
Rates & Taxes	8,000
Postage & Telegrams	15,000
Cash at bank	1,33,000
Wages	2,50,000

Prepare the Contract Account to ascertain the profit from the contract and show the WIP in the Balance Sheet.

[**Ans.** Notional Profit 2,43,000; Total of Balance Sheet Rs. 50,77,900]
(*I.C.W.A. Inter, Dec. 1995*)

32. The following figures are disclosed by the books of a Contractor for the year ending 31st March, 2009:

	Rs.	**Rs.**
Work-in-Progress as on 31st March, 2008		
Less Advances	1,70,000	
from Contractees as on 31st March, 2008	1,10,000	60,000
Transactions during the year 2008-09:		
Materials supplied to Contracts directly by merchants		12,000
Materials issued from stores		21,000
Wages		17,000
Working expenses		3,000
Administrative expenses (of which Rs. 500 are chargeable to Profit & Loss A/c)		2,500
Plant issued		5,000
Material returned from contracts directly to merchants		900
Materials returned to stores		1,100
Contracts finished		45,000
Works certified		30,000
Profit taken upon contracts		23,000
Advances from contractees		80,000

Prepare Contract Ledger Account (as in General Ledger) and the Total Contractees' Account and show the Work-in-Progress which would appear in Balance Sheet as on 31st March, 2009.

(*Bombay, B.Com.; Agra, B.Com.*)

[**Ans.** Cost of work uncertified Rs. 1,76,000]

33. A and B, Contractors obtained a contract to build houses, the Contract Price being Rs. 4,00,000.

Work commenced on 1st April, 2003 and upon it the following expenditure was incurred during the year: Plant and Tools Rs. 20,000; Stores and Materials Rs. 72,000; Wages Rs. 65,000; Sundry expenses Rs. 5,300; and Establishment charges Rs.11,700.

Some of the materials costing Rs. 12,000 were were unsuited to the contract and were sold for Rs. 14,500. A portion of the plant was scrapped and sold for Rs. 2,300.

The value of plant and tools on site on 31st March, 2004 was Rs. 6,200 and the value of stores and materials on hand Rs. 3,400. Cash received on account was Rs. 1,40,000 representing 80% of the work certified. The cost of work done but not certified was Rs. 21,900; this was certified later for Rs. 25,000.

A and B decided to estimate what further expenditure would be incurred in completing the contract, to compute from this estimate and the expenditure already incurred the total profit that would be made on the contract and to take credit to Profit and Loss Account for the year 2003-04 that proportion of the total which corresponded to the work certified by 31st March.

The estimate was as follows:

(*a*) That the contract would be completed by 31st Dec., 2004.

(*b*) That the wages on the contract in 2004-05 would amount to Rs. 71,500.

(*c*) That the cost of stores and materials required in addition to those in stock on 31st March, 2004 would be Rs. 68,600 and that the further sundry expenses would amount to Rs. 6,000.

(*d*) That a further Rs. 25,000 would have to be laid out on plant and tools and that the residual value of the plant and tools on 31st December, 2004 would be Rs 3,000.

(*e*) That the establishment charges would cost the same per month as in 2003-04.

(*f*) That 2½% of the total cost of the contract would be due to defects, temporary maintenance and contingencies.

Prepare Contract Account for the year ended 31st March, 2004 and show your calculation of the amount credited to Profit and Loss Account for that year.

[**Ans.** Notional Profit on Incomplete Contract, Rs. 46,800. Estimated Profit on completion Rs. 54,795. Profit to P & L A/c

$$= \text{Rs. } 54{,}795 \times \frac{1{,}75{,}000}{4{,}00{,}000} = \text{Rs. } 23{,}973]$$

34. Prepare Contract Account and Contractee's Account assumiug that the amount due from the contractee was duly received.

		Rs.
Direct Material		20,250
Direct Wages		15,500
Stores Issued		10,500
Loose Tools		2,400
Tractor expenses:		
Fuel, oil etc.	2,300	
Wages of Drivers	3,000	5,300
Other Direct Charges		2,650

The contract price was Rs. 90,000 and the contract took 13 weeks in its completion. The value of Loose Tools and Stores returned at the end of the period were Rs. 200 and Rs. 3,000 respectively. The plant was also returned at a value of Rs. 16,000 after charging depreciation at 20 %. The value of tractor was Rs. 20,000 and the depreciation was to be charged to the contract @ 15 % per annum. The administrative and office expenses are to be provided at 10% on works cost.

[**Ans.** Profit to P & L A/c Rs. 26,035]

(*Rajasthan, B.Com., G.N.D.U. B.Com.*)

35. A contractor makes up his accounts on 31st March each year. Contract No. 41 was commenced on 1st July, 2004. The costing records yield the following information on 31st March, 2005:

	Rs.
Materials charged out to site	43,000
Labour	1,00,220
Foreman's Salary	12,620

A machine costing Rs. 30,000 has been on the site for 73 days. Its working life is estimated at five years and its scrap value at Rs. 2,000.

A supervisor, who is paid Rs. 2,000 per month has spent approximately one half of his time on the contract. All other expenses and administration amounted to Rs. 25,220. Materials in stores at site on 31st March, 2005 cost Rs. 4,960.

The contract price is Rs. 4,00,000 and on 31st March, 2005, 2/3 of the contract was completed, architect's certificate had been issued covering 50% of contract price, Rs. 1,60,000 has so far been paid on contract.

Prepare a Contract Account and state how much profit or loss should be included in the Financial Accounts to 31st March, 2005.

(G.N.D.U., B.Com., 1981)

[**Ans.** Notional profit Rs. 60,335 profit to Profit & Loss A/c Rs. 32,179]

[**Hint:** Calculation of cost of uncertified work: Cost of 2/3 work completed Rs. 1,86,220

Cost of full contract $= 1{,}86{,}220 \times \frac{3}{2}$

= Rs. 2,79,330

Cost of certified work = Rs. 1,39,665
(½ of contract)

Cost of uncertified work = Rs. 1,86,220 – Rs. 1,39,665

= Rs. 46,555]

36. A commenced business as a building contractor and invested Rs. 5,00,000 in capital equipment. He undertook a contract for Rs. 1,00,00,000 to be completed in four years. He was to be paid 90% of the value of work completed as certified by the architects immediately, the balance to be paid on the completion of the contract.

A's records showed the following position:

Year	Wages	Materials	Carriage	Miscellaneous Expenses	Stock and uncompleted works at the end
	Rs.	Rs.	Rs.	Rs.	Rs.
1	5,00,000	4,70,000	20,000	20,000	1,00,000
2	10,00,000	8,00,000	40,000	10,000	3,00,000
3	20,00,000	25,00,000	1,50,000	18,000	4,00,000
4	8,00,000	5,00,000	15,000	8,000	50,000

Architect's certificates were for Rs. 10,00,000 during the first year, for Rs. 20,00,000 during second year and Rs. 50,00,000 and Rs. 20,00,000 for the third and fourth year, respectively.
A was duly paid in accordance with the terms of the contract. His capital equipment at the end was valued at Rs. 4,00,000.
Show the Contract A/c and Contractee's A/c in A's Books.

[Ans.	**Total work certified**	**Notional Profit Rs.**	**Profit to P & L A/c**
1st year	10,00,000	65,000	Nil
2nd year	30,00,000	3,90,000	1,17,000
3rd year	80,00,000	6,80,000	4,08,000
4th year	1,00,00,000		5,74,000)

37. Modern Construction Ltd., commenced a contract on 1st April, 2002. The total contract was for Rs. 10,00,000 (estimated by the contractor) and was accepted by Modern Construction Ltd. at 10% less. It was decided to estimate the total profit and to take to the credit of Profit and Loss Account, that proportion of estimated profit on cash basis which the work completed bore to the total contract. Actual expenditure in 2002-03 and estimated expenditure in 2003-04 are given below:

	2002-03 (Actual)	**2003-04**
	Rs.	**Rs.**
Materials	1,50,000	2,60,000
Labour (*i*) Paid	1,00,000	1,20,000
(*ii*) Accrued	10,000	–
Plant purchased	80,000	–
Plant returned to store on 31st March (cost)	20,000	50,000 (On 31st Dec., 2003)
Expenses	40,000	71,000
Materials at site	10,000	–
Work certified	4,00,000	Full
Work uncertified	15,000	–
Cash received	3,00,000	Full

The plant is subject to annual depreciation @ 20% on cost. The contract is likely to be completed on 31st Dec., 2003. Prepare Contract Account.

(*M.D.U., B.Com. III 1993-dates changed*)

[**Ans.** Estimated Profit Rs. 1,27,500; Amount credited to Profit and Loss A/c Rs. 42,500]

38. Rahul Engineers undertake long term contracts which involve the fabrication of pre-stressed concrete blocs and the erection of the same on consumer's site. The following information is supplied regarding Contract No. 88 which is incomplete on 31st March, 2004:

Costs incurred:

	Rs.
Fabrication cost to date:	
Direct materials	56,000
Direct wages	18,000
Overhead	15,000
Erection cost to date	3,000
Total	92,000
Contract price	1,63,800
Cash received on account	1,20,000

Technical estimate of work completed to date:

Fabrication:	
Direct Materials	80%
Direct wages and overhead	75%
Erection	25%

You are required to prepare a statement for submission to management indicating:

(*i*) the estimated profit on completion of the contract,
(*ii*) the estimated profit to date on the contract.

[**Ans.** (*i*) Rs. 37,800 (*ii*) 27,692 or Rs. 27,600]

39. The following information is supplied regarding a contract in progress:

	Rs.	Stage of completion
Erection cost to date:	7,500	25%
Fabrication Cost to date:		
Material	60,000	60%
Wages	40,000	50%
Overhead	7,500	50%
	1,15,000	

Contract price Rs. 2,00,000

Calculate (*i*) the estimated profit or loss at the completion of the contract, and (*ii*) the estimated profit or loss to date.

[**Ans.** (*i*) Rs. 25,000 (Loss) (*ii*) Rs. 12,778 (Loss)]

40. Deluxe Limited undertook a contract for Rs. 5,00,000 on 1st July, 2006. On 30th June, 2007 when the accounts were closed, the following details about the contract were gathered:

	Rs.
Material Purchased	1,00,000
Wages Paid	45,000
General Expenses	10,000
Plant Purchased	50,000
Material on Hand 30-6-07	25,000
Wages Accrued 30-6-07	5,000
Work Certified	2,00,000
Cash Received	1,50,000
Work Uncertified	15,000
Depreciation of Plant	5,000

The above contract contained an escalation clause which read as follows: "In the event of prices of materials and rates of wages increase by more than 5%, the contract price would be increased accordingly by 25% of the rise in the cost of materials and wages beyond 5% in each case."

It was found that since the date of signing the agreement the prices of materials and wage rates increased by 25%. The value of the work does not take into account the effect of the above clause.

Prepare the contract account. Working should from part of the answer.

(*C.A. Inter, Nov. 1987; I.C.W.A. Inter, Dec. 1991*)

[**Ans.** Profit transferred to P/L Account Rs. 20,000]

14

Process Costing-I

The method of process costing is applied to ascertain the cost of production in those industries, where a product passes through different processes or stages of production before its completion. Under process costing, there is a finished product at each stage which becomes the raw material of the subsequent stage or next process till the final stage of completion.

Process costing method is generally employed in industries like chemicals, distilled products, canned products, food products, oil refineries, edible oils, soap, paper, textiles etc.

Main Features of Process Costing

The main features of process costing may be given as follows:

(*i*) The production is divided into various stages (known as processes) and each process is carried out by separate cost centre or department.

(*ii*) The production is continuous and the final product or end product is the result of a sequence of processes or operations.

(*iii*) The finished product of each process is treated as the raw material of the subsequent process.

(*iv*) The units of the commodity produced are homogeneous and identical in nature.

(*v*) The cost of production per unit is the average cost which is obtained by dividing the total process cost by the total number of units manufactured.

(*vi*) The sequence of processes and operations employed is pre-determined.

(*vii*) There is indispensable loss in the process of production. It is known as normal loss. It may be due to inherent nature of the material used for production *i.e.*, loss may occur due to chemical action, loss in weight and evaporation etc. The normal loss is absorbed by the cost of good units.

(*viii*) The processing of raw material may lead to joint products and by-products.

(*ix*) There may occur abnormal loss and abnormal gain. These are treated separately under process costing.

(*x*) Inter-process profits are also kept in mind while transferring the output at market price to another process. It will depict the market price and will be helpful in checking the inefficiency and losses taking place in a process.

(*xi*) The concept of equivalent production is also considered under process costing. It means that when some units are in semi-finished stage, these are to be expressed in terms of equivalent completed units or effective units.

(*xii*) Costing profit and loss is calculated after taking into account the opening balance of finished stock and the closing balance of the finished stock. The process accounts are helpful in the proper valuation of the raw material, work-in-progress (semi-finished goods) and finished goods. These stocks are shown in the Balance Sheet.

To sum up these principles, W.W. Big. has nicely remarked, "The fundamental principle involved in process cost accounts is simple. A separate account is opened for each process or distinct operation to which all expenditure incurred thereon is charged.

When the process or operation has been completed, the partially worked out product is passed into a process stock account from which it will be requisitioned as and when required by the next process or it may become automatically the raw material of the next process and be charged to the Process Account immediately."

DISTINCTION BETWEEN PROCESS COSTING AND JOB COSTING

A comparative study of process and job costing will help in understanding the process costing system in a better way.

Process Costing	Job Costing
1. Costs are calculated process-wise and per unit cost is the average cost ascertained by dividing the total cost of the process by the number of units produced.	1. Costs are separately calculated for each job, which is a cost unit.
2. Production of standardised and identical products is undertaken.	2. Production of non-standardised and unidentical items is undertaken in accordance with the instructions and specifications of the customers.
3. Costs are calculated at the end of a particular period.	3. Costs are ascertained on the completion of a job.
4. As there are series of processes employed, the cost of one process is transferred to the other process.	4. As the job as a whole is considered as a single unit, there is no transfer of one part of job to another.

5. The nature of production is continuous, there is usually work-in-progress in the beginning as well as at the end.	5. The work-in-progress may or may not occur in the beginning and at the end of the accounting period.
6. On account of continuous and uninterrupted production, cost control is comparatively easier.	6. Cost control becomes difficult due to intermittent nature of production.
7. Production is taken to stores.	7. Production is undertaken against orders from the customers.

COSTING PROCEDURE

Under process costing, the manufacture of a product is divided into well-defined processes. A separate account is opened for each process to which all costs incurred thereon, are charged. The total number of units produced during a given period is calculated and by dividing the total cost of a process by the total number of units produced, the cost per unit shall be obtained. The finished material of one process constitutes the raw material of the next or subsequent process and therefore, the finished material as also the cost of each process is transferred to the next process till it is transferred to the Finished Stock Account. The process costing procedure can be explained by means of the following illustration:

Illustration 1

A product passes through three processes, Process A, Process B and Process C, to completion. The production of the commodity was 1,000 tonnes. The costs were as follows:

	Process A	Process B	Process C
	Rs.	Rs.	Rs.
Material	3,000	1,500	1,500
Labour	1,500	3,000	5,250
Manufacturing Expenses	1,500	4,500	5,250

Assume that there was no work-in-progress either at the beginning or at the end. Show the process costs for each process and the total cost of the finished product.

Solution

Process A Account

Particulars	Cost per Tonne	Total Cost	Particulars	Cost per Tonne	Total Cost
	Rs. P.	Rs. P.		Rs. P.	Rs. P.
To Materials	3.00	3,000	By Process B A/c	6.00	6,000
To Labour	1.50	1,500	(Output transferred)		
To Manufacturing Expenses	1.50	1,500			
	6.00	6,000		6.00	6,000

$$\text{Cost per unit} = \frac{\text{Cost of input}}{\text{Output}} = \frac{\text{Rs. } 6{,}000}{1{,}000 \text{ tonnes}} = \text{Rs. 6 per tonne.}$$

Process B Account

Particulars	Cost per Tonne	Total Cost	Particulars	Cost per Tonne	Total Cost
	Rs. P.	Rs. P.		Rs. P.	Rs. P.
To Process A A/c	6.00	6,000	By Process C A/c	15.00	15,000
To Materials	1.50	1,500	(Output transferred)		
To Labour	3.00	3,000			
To Manufacturing Expenses	4.50	4,500			
	15.00	15,000		15.00	15,000

$$\text{Cost per unit} = \frac{\text{Rs. } 15{,}000}{1{,}000 \text{ tonnes}} = \text{Rs. 15 per tonne.}$$

Process C Account

Particulars	Cost per Tonne	Total Cost	Particulars	Cost per Tonne	Total Cost
	Rs. P.	Rs. P.		Rs. P.	Rs. P.
To Process B A/c	15.00	15,000	By Finished Stock A/c	27.00	27,000
To Materials	1.50	1,500	(Output transferred)		
To Labour	5.25	5,250			
To Manufacturing Expenses	5.25	5,250			
	27.00	27,000		27.00	27,000

$$\text{Cost per unit} = \frac{\text{Rs. } 27{,}000}{1{,}000 \text{ tonnes}} = \text{Rs. 27 per tonne.}$$

Finished Stock Account

Particulars	Cost per Tonne	Total Cost	Particulars	Cost per Tonne	Total Cost
	Rs. P.	Rs. P.		Rs. P.	Rs. P.
To Process C A/c	27.00	27,000	By Balance c/d	27.00	27,000
	27.00	27,000		27.00	27,000

Illustration 2

A product passes through three distinct processes to completion. These processes are numbered respectively 1, 2 and 3. During the week ended 31 January, 1,000 units are produced. The following information is obtained:

	Process 1	Process 2	Process 3
Materials	6,000	3,000	2,000
Labour	5,000	4,000	5,000
Direct Expenses	1,000	200	1,000

The indirect expenses for the period were Rs. 2,800 apportioned to the processes on the basis of wages.

Prepare Process Accounts.

Solution

Process 1 Account

Output = 1,000 units — Week ended 31st Jan.

Particulars	Cost per unit	Total Cost	Particulars	Cost per unit	Total Cost
	Rs. P.	Rs. P.		Rs. P.	Rs. P.
To Materials	6.00	6,000.00	By Process 2 A/c	13.00	13,000
To Labour	5.00	5,000.00	(Output transferred)		
To Direct Expenses	1.00	1,000.00			
To Indirect Expenses	1.00	1,000.00			
	13.00	13,000.00		13.00	13,000

Process 2 Account

Output = 1,000 units — Week ended 31st Jan.

Particulars	Cost per unit	Total Cost	Particulars	Cost per unit	Total Cost
	Rs. P.	Rs. P.		Rs. P.	Rs. P.
To Process 1 A/c	13.00	13,000.00	By Process 3 A/c	21.00	21,000.00
To Materials	3.00	3,000.00	(Output transferred)		
To Labour	4.00	4,000.00			
To Direct Expenses	0.20	200.00			
To Indirect Expenses	0.80	800.00			
	21.00	21,000.00		21.00	21,000.00

Process 3 Account

Output = 1,000 units — Week ended 31st Jan.

Particulars	Cost per unit	Total Cost	Particulars	Cost per unit	Total Cost
	Rs. P.	Rs. P.		Rs. P.	Rs. P.
To Process 2 A/c	21.00	21,000.00	By Finished Stock A/c	30.00	30,000.00
To Materials	2.00	2,000.00	(Output transferred)		
To Labour	5.00	5,000.00			
To Direct Expenses	1.00	1,000.00			
To Indirect Expenses	1.00	1,000.00			
	30.00	30,000.00		30.00	30,000.00

Finished Stock Account

Output = 1,000 units — Week ended 31st Jan.

Particulars	Cost per unit	Total Cost	Particulars	Cost per unit	Total Cost
	Rs. P.	**Rs. P.**		**Rs. P.**	**Rs. P.**
To Process 3 A/c	30.00	30,000	By Balance c/d	30.00	30,000
	30.00	30,000		30.00	30,000

Note: Indirect Expenses have been allocated on the basis of labour *i.e.*, in the ratio of 5 : 4 : 5.

Illustration 3

A manufacturing company produces two types of articles P and Q in which materials used are identical in all respects. Each type of article undergoes two processes *i.e.*, (*i*) Factory and (*ii*) Finishing. The direct labour cost is recorded separately. The material is allocated in the ratio of output and the general expenses are treated similarly. Factory and Finishing overhead charges are apportioned on the basis of direct labour ratio of each process. Prepare process accounts from the following particulars showing total cost and cost per unit of each product. Also show percentage of profit assuming that selling prices of the articles are per unit P Rs. 400 and Q Rs. 450.

Output: Product P = 2,000 units and Product Q = 1,000 units.

	Rs.
Opening Stocks:	
Factory Materials	10,600
Finishing Materials	5,000
Purchases:	
Factory	3,17,400
Finishing	1,35,000
Closing Stocks:	
Factory Materials	82,000
Finishing Materials	44,000
Factory Wages (Direct) P	1,60,000
Factory Wages (Direct) Q	1,20,000
Finishing Wages (Direct) P	90,000
Finishing Wages (Direct) Q	30,000
Factory Overheads	63,000
Finishing Overheads	24,000
General Expenses	1,44,000

Solution

Factory Process Account

Particulars		Product P		Product Q		Particulars	Product P		Product Q	
		Total Cost	Cost Per Unit	Total Cost	Cost Per Unit		Total Cost	Cost Per Unit	Total Cost	Cost Per Unit
		Rs.	Rs.	Rs.	Rs.		Rs.	Rs.	Rs.	Rs.
To Materials Consumed:										
Opening Stock	10,600					By Transfer to Finishing Process A/c	3,60,000	180	2,29,000	229
Add Purchases	3,17,400									
	3,28,000									
Less Closing Stock	82,000									
(Divided in the ratio of 2: 1)	2,46,000	1,64,000	82	82,000	82					
To Direct Wages		1,60,000	80	1,20,000	120					
To Factory Overheads (4 :3)		36,000	18	27,000	27					
		3,60,000	180	2,29,000	229		3,60,000	180	2,29,000	229

Finishing Process Account

Particulars		Product P Total Cost	Product P Cost Per Unit	Product Q Total Cost	Product Q Cost Per Unit	Particulars	Product P Total Cost	Product P Cost Per Unit	Product Q Total Cost	Product Q Cost Per Unit
		Rs.	Rs.	Rs.	Rs.		Rs.	Rs.	Rs.	Rs.
To Transfer from Factory Process		3,60,000	180	2,29,000	229	By Transfer to Finished Stock A/c	5,32,000	266	2,97,000	297
To Materials Consumed:										
Opening Stock	5,000									
Add Purchases	1,35,000									
	1,40,000									
Less Closing Stock	44,000									
Divided in the ratio of 2 : 1	96,000	64,000	32	32,000	32					
To Direct Wages		90,000	45	30,000	30					
To Finishing Overheads (3 : 1)		18,000	9	6,000	6					
		5,32,000	266	2,97,000	297		5,32,000	266	2,97,000	297

Statement Showing Total Cost and Profit

Particulars	Product P 2,000 units		Product Q 1,000 units	
	Total	Per Unit	Total	Per Unit
	Rs.	Rs.	Rs.	Rs.
Cost of Factory and Finishing Processes	5,32,000	266	2,97,000	297
General Expenses (Rs.1,44,000 divided in the ratio of 2 : 1)	96,000	48	48,000	48
	6,28,000	314	3,45,000	345
Profit	1,72,000	86	1,05,000	105
Selling Price	8,00,000	400	4,50,000	450
Percentage of Profit to Cost	27.4%		30%	

Note: In the absence of any specific information, General Expenses have not been apportioned to Factory and Finishing Processes.

PROCESS LOSS OR WASTAGE

In processing industries, some loss or wastage of materials is inevitable and attempts are made to avoid it or to minimise it. The process loss or wastage may be divided into two parts:

(*i*) Normal Wastage, and (*ii*) Abnormal Wastage.

Normal Wastage: It is the quantity of wastage which is unavoidable and is bound to take place. It cannot be avoided though efforts can be made to minimise it. Normal Wastage generally arises on account of the nature of materials used or the nature of the manufacturing process involved. The extent of normal wastage can be ascertained on the basis of past experience.

Treatment of Normal Wastage in Process Accounts: The cost of normal wastage or loss in the process is borne by the goods units produced in the process. The quantity of normal wastage or loss is shown in the 'units column' on the credit side of the Process Account. If the normal loss or wastage has some realisable value, the Process Account is credited with such realisable value. Thus, the total process cost less any realisable value (scrap value) of normal wastage divided by the number of good units produced in the process, shall give us the cost per unit.

Normal Effectives: In relation to normal wastage or normal loss, it is necessary to know the meaning of Normal Effectives. Normal Effectives are the good units produced when the wastage is normal. Normal Effectives are also known as 'Normal Output' and may be expressed in the form of an equation as follows:

Normal Effectives (units) = Total Input (units) – Normal Wastage (units)

If, in a particular process, the number of units put in is 1,000 and 2% of the input is normal wastage or normal loss, normal effectives will be:

= 1,000 units – 20 units (*i.e.*, 2% of 1,000 units)

= 980 units.

Treatment of normal wastage in process costing can be explained with the help of the following illustration:

Illustration 4

10,000 units have been issued to Process 'X' at a cost of Rs. 20,000. The other expenses are as follows:

	Rs.
Materials	12,000
Direct Wages	16,000
Factory Expenses	5,000

From past experience it is ascertained that wastage incurred in the process is 2% of input and it realises Rs. 50 per 100 units. The actual output of process is 9,800 units.

Prepare Process 'X' Account and Normal Wastage Account.

Solution

Process X Account

	Units	Rs.		Units	Rs.
To Units Introduced	10,000	20,000	By Normal Wastage A/c (2% of 10,000 units)	200	100
To Materials		12,000			
To Direct Wages		16,000			
To Factory Expenses		5,000	By Next Process A/c (Output transferred) (Cost per unit = Rs. 52,900/9,800 = Rs. 5.40 (app.))	9,800	52,900
	10,000	53,000		10,000	53,000

Normal Wastage Account

	Units	Rs.		Units	Rs.
To Process X A/c (2% of 10,000 units)	200	100	By Cash A/c (Sale of wastage)	200	100
	200	100		200	100

Abnormal Wastage: Any wastage or loss arising over and above the normal wastage or normal loss is treated as abnormal wastage or abnormal loss. Such a wastage or loss is otherwise avoidable and arises due to unexpected or abnormal reasons such as sub-standard materials, defective machinery, negligence, carelessness, slackness, accidents etc.

Treatment of Abnormal Wastage: The cost of abnormal wastage is not allowed to affect the cost of good units produced. Abnormal wastage of a process is valued at actual cost (*i.e.*, the cost of material, labour and appropriate overhead incurred by the wastage) by applying the following formula:

Cost of Abnormal Wastage =

$$\frac{\text{Cost of Normal Effectivcs}}{\text{Normal Effectives (units)}} \times \text{Abnormal Wastage (units)}$$

or

$$= \frac{\text{Total Process Cost} - \text{Realisable Value of Normal Wastage}}{\text{Input (units)} - \text{Normal Wastage (units)}} \times \text{Abnormal Wastage (units)}$$

The cost of abnormal wastage is debited to Abnormal Wastage Account and credited to the concerned Process Account. Abnormal Wastage Account is, then, credited with the realisable value or scrap value, if any, of such abnormal wastage and the balance of the account is transferred to Costing Profit and Loss Account by way of abnormal loss.

The treatment of abnormal loss in process account can be explained with the help of the following example:

Illustration 5

10,000 units have been issued to Process 'A' at a cost of Rs. 20,000. The other expenses are as follows:

Materials	Rs. 15,000
Direct Wages	Rs. 25,000
Factory Overhead	Rs. 10,000

From past experience, it is ascertained that 2% of input is wastage which realises Re. 1 per unit. The actual output of process is 9,700 units. Prepare Process Account, Normal Wastage A/c and Abnormal Wastage A/c.

Solution

Process 'A' Account

	Units	Rs.		Units	Rs.
To Units Introduced	10,000	20,000	By Normal Wastage A/c (2% of 10,000 units)	200	200
To Materials		15,000			
To Direct Wages		25,000	By Abnormal Wastage A/c	100	712
To Factory Overhead		10,000			
			By Next Process A/c (Transfer) (Cost per unit Rs. 69,088/9,700 units = Rs. 7.12)	9,700	69,088
	10,000	70,000		10,000	70,000

Normal Wastage Account

	Units	Rs.		Units	Rs.
To Process 'A' A/c	200	200	By Cash A/c (Sale)	200	200
	200	200		200	200

Abnormal Wastage Account

	Units	Rs.		Units	Rs.
To Process 'A' A/c	100	712	By Cash A/c (Sale)	100	100
			By Costing Profit and Loss A/c (Loss)	–	612
	100	712		100	712

Note: Calculation of Cost of Abnormal Wastage:

Total Input = 10,000 units

Normal Wastage (2% of Input) = 200 units

Normal Effectives = Input – Normal Wastage
= 10,000 units – 200 units
= 9,800 units

Cost of Normal Effectives = Total Process Cost – Realisable Value of Normal Wastage
= Rs. 70,000 – Rs. 200
= Rs. 69,800

$$\text{Cost per unit} = \frac{\text{Rs. } 69{,}800}{9{,}800 \text{ units}} = \text{Rs. } 7.12$$

Actual Output = 9,700 units

Abnormal Wastage = Normal Effectives – Actual Output
= 9,800 units – 9,700 units
= 100 units

Cost of Abnormal Wastage @ Rs. 7.12 per unit = Rs. 712

Illustration 6

A product passes through three processes namely. A, B and C. 10,000 units at a cost of Rs. 1.10 per unit were issued to Process A. Other expenses were as follows:

	Process A	Process B	Process C
	Rs.	Rs.	Rs.
Sundry Materials	1,500	1,500	1,500
Direct Labour	4,500	8,000	6,500
Direct Expenses	1,000	1,000	1,503

The scrap of Process A was 5% and in Process B 4% of input. The scrap of Process A was sold @ Re. 0.25 per unit, that of Process B at Re. 0.50 per unit and that of Process C at Re. 1.00 per unit. Overhead charges were 160% of direct labour. The final product was sold at Rs. 10 per unit, fetching a profit of 20% on sales.

Prepare three processes accounts and find out the number of units of scrap in Process C. *(G.N.D.U., B.Com. 2004)*

Solution

Process A Account

Particulars	Units	Amt. Rs.	Particulars	Units	Amt. Rs.
To Units Introduced	10,000	11,000	By Sale of Scrap (5% of 10,000 units)	500	125
To Sundry Materials		1,500			
To Direct Labour		4,500	By Process B A/c (Output transferred)	9,500	25,075
To Direct Expenses		1,000			
To Overhead Charges (160% of Rs. 4,500)		7,200	(Cost per unit $\frac{\text{Rs. } 25,075}{9,500 \text{ units}}$ = Rs. 2.64)		
	10,000	25,200		10,000	25,200

Process B Account

Particulars	Units	Amt. Rs.	Particulars	Units	Amt. Rs.
To Process A A/c	9,500	25,075	By Sale of Scrap (4% of 9,500 units)	380	190
To Sundry Materials		1,500			
To Direct Labour		8,000	By Process C A/c (Output transferred)	9,120	48,185
To Direct Expenses		1,000			
To Overhead Charges (160% of Rs. 8,000)		12,800	(Cost per unit $\frac{\text{Rs. } 48,185}{9,120 \text{ units}}$ = Rs. 5.28)		
	9,500	48,375		9,500	48,375

Process C Account

Particulars	Units	Amt. Rs.	Particulars	Units	Amt. Rs.
To Process B A/c	9,120	48,185	By Sale of Scrap	696	696
To Sundry Materials		1,500			
To Direct Labour		6,500			
To Direct Expenses		1,503	By Finished		
To Overhead Charges (160% of Rs. 6,500)		10,400	Stock A/c (Output transferred @ Rs. 8 per unit) (cost)	8,424	67,392
	9,120	68,088		9,120	68,088

Notes: (i) Calculation of cost per unit of output of Process C:

Selling Price = Rs. 10 per unit

Less Profit @ 20% = Rs. 2 per unit

Cost per unit = Rs. 8

(*ii*) Calculation of units scrapped in Process C:

Total Cost of Process C = Scrap Value of Process C + Total Cost of Finished Product.

Let us suppose that No. of units scrapped = X

$$\text{Rs. } 68{,}088 = 1(X) + 8\,(9{,}120 - X)$$
$$68{,}088 = X + 72{,}960 - 8\,X$$
$$68{,}088 = 72{,}960 - 7\,X$$
$$7\,X = 72{,}960 - 68{,}088$$
$$X = \frac{4{,}872}{7} = 696$$

Abnormal Effectives (or Abnormal Saving or Abnormal Gain):

Sometimes, the actual wastage or loss in a process may be less than the normal wastage or normal loss. In such a case, the good units produced in excess of normal effectives (or normal output), are treated as abnormal effectives or abnormal gain. Abnormal effectives or abnormal gain may arise due to exceptionally good quality of materials, exceptionally high degree of efficiency on the part of workers and supervisory staff etc. Such conditions are not normally expected.

In the form of equation, abnormal effectives or abnormal gain may be expressed as follows:

Abnormal Effectives (units) = Actual Output (units) – Normal Effectives (units)
or = Normal Wastage (units) – Actual Wastage (units)

Suppose, in a process, 5,000 units of basic raw material are introduced. It is ascertained on the basis of past experience that 5% of the input is normal wastage. If the actual output is 4,800 units, there is an abnormal gain of 50 units calculated as follows:

Normal Effectives = Input – Normal Wastage
= 5,000 units – 250 units = 4,750 units.

Actual Output = 4,800 units

Abnormal Effectives = Actual Output – Normal Effectives
= 4,800 units – 4,750 units = 50 units.

Alternatively: Normal Wastage = 250 units (5% of 5,000 units)

Actual Wastage = Input – Output
= 5,000 units – 4,800 units = 200 units.

Abnormal Effectives = Normal Wastage – Actual Wastage
= 250 units – 200 units = 50 units.

Accounting Treatment of Abnormal Effectives:

Abnormal effectives or abnormal gain, arising due to abnormal conditions, are not allowed to reduce the cost of good units. In case of abnormal effectives, the Normal Wastage Account is debited and the concerned Process Account is credited with the quantity (in units column) and realisable value, if any (in

Amount Column), of normal wastage (which is notional). Thereafter, the value of abnormal effectives is ascertained at the rate at which good units would have been valued, had there been normal wastage only. The value of abnormal effectives is calculated by applying the following formula:

Value of abnormal effectives =

$$\frac{\text{Cost of Normal Effectives}}{\text{Normal Effectives (units)}} \times \text{Abnormal Effectives (units)}$$

$$\text{or} = \frac{\text{Total Process Cost} - \text{Realisable value of Normal Wastage}}{\text{Input (units)} - \text{Normal Wastage (units)}} \times \text{Abnormal Effectives (units)}$$

The value of abnormal effectives thus determined will be debited to Process Account concerned and credited to Abnormal Effectives Account (or Abnormal Gain Account). The realisable value of actual wastage (which is less than the notional quantity of normal wastage) is credited to the Normal Wastage Account. The debit balance of Normal Wastage Account, denoting the excess of quantity and value of notional normal wastage over the quantity and value of actual wastage, is transferred to the Abnormal Effectives Account. Thereafter, the credit balance of Abnormal Effectives Account is closed by transfer to Costing Profit and Loss Account by way of abnormal gain or profit.

The treatment of abnormal effectives can be explained with the help of the following example:

Illustration 7

10,000 units have been issued to Process 'A' at a cost of Rs. 20,000. The other expenses are as follows:

Materials Rs. 15,000; Direct Wages Rs. 25,000; Factory overhead Rs. 10,000.

From past experience it is known that 2% of the input is wastage and realises Re. 1 per unit. The actual output of the process is 9,900 units. Prepare Process A/c, Normal Wastage A/c and Abnormal Effectives A/c showing the calculation of value of abnormal effectives.

Solution

Process 'A' Account

	Units	Rs.		Units	Rs.
To Units Introduced	10,000	20,000	By Normal Wastage A/c (2% of 10,000 units)	200	200
To Materials		15,000			
To Direct Wages		25,000			
To Factory Overhead		10,000			
To Abnormal Effectives A/c	100	712	By Next Process A/c (Transfer) (Cost per unit Rs. 70,512/9,900 units = Rs. 7.12)	9,900	70,512
	10,100	70,712		10,100	70,712

Normal Wastage Account

	Units	Rs.		Units	Rs.
To Process 'A' A/c	200	200	By Cash A/c (Sale of actual wastage)	100	100
			By Abnormal Effectives A/c (Transfer)	100	100
	200	200		200	200

Abnormal Effectives Account

	Units	Rs.		Units	Rs.
To Normal Wastage A/c	100	100	By Process 'A' A/c	100	712
To Costing Profit and Loss A/c	–	612			
	100	712		100	712

Note: Calculation of Cost of Abnormal Effectives:

Total Input = 10,000 units

Normal Wastage (2% of Input) = 200 units

Normal Effectives = Input – Normal Wastage
= 10,000 units – 200 units = 9,800 units

Cost of Normal Effectives = Total Process Cost – Realisable Value of Normal Wastage
= Rs.70,000 – Rs.200
= Rs. 69,800

Cost per unit $= \dfrac{\text{Rs. } 69{,}800}{9{,}800 \text{ units}} = \text{Rs. } 7.12$

Actual Output = 9,900 units

Abnormal Effectives = Actual Output – Normal Effectives
= 9,900 units – 9,800 units
= 100 units

Cost of Abnormal Effectives @ Rs. 7.12 per unit = Rs. 712

Cost of Actual Output $= \dfrac{\text{Rs. } 69{,}800}{9{,}800 \text{ units}} \times 9{,}900 \text{ units} = \text{Rs. } 70{,}512$

Illustration 8

1,500 units were introduced into a process at a cost of Rs. 15,000. The additional cost incurred for the process was Rs. 3,750. A normal loss equal to one-sixth of the input is expected which has a scrap value of Rs. 2 per unit. The actual output for the period was 1,300 units. Prepare Process Account and show how abnormal effectiveness/gain will be treated in accounts.

Solution

Process Account

	Units	Rs.		Units	Rs.
To Units Introduced	1,500	15,000	By Normal Wastage A/c	250	500
To Sundry Expenses		3,750	By Next Process A/c	1,300	18,980
To Abnormal Effectives A/c	50	730	(Cost per unit Rs. 18,980/1,300 units = Rs. 14.60)		
	1,550	19,480		1,550	19,480

Normal Wastage Account

	Units	Rs.		Units	Rs.
To Process ... A/c	250	500	By Cash A/c (Sale of actual wastage)	200	400
			By Abnormal Effectives A/c	50	100
	250	500		250	500

Abnormal Effectives Account

	Units	Rs.		Units	Rs.
To Normal Wastage A/c	50	100	By Process ... A/c	50	730
To Costing Profit and Loss A/c (Profit)	–	630			
	50	730		50	730

Illustration 9

The product of a manufacturing concern passes through two processes A and B and then to Finished Stock. It is ascertained on the basis of past experience that in each process 2% of the total weight put in is lost and 10% is scrap which from process A and B realises Rs. 100 per kg. and Rs. 150 per kg. respectively. The process figures are as follows:

	Process A	Process B
Materials Consumed in Kgs.	1,000	70
Cost of Material per kg.	Rs. 120	Rs. 200
Wages	Rs.17,500	Rs.10,000
Manufacturing Expenses	Rs. 5,380	Rs. 5,342

Prepare Process Accounts, showing the cost of the output of each process and the cost per kg.

Solution

Process A Account

	Kgs.	Rs.		Kgs.	Rs.
To Materials	1,000	1,20,000	By Loss in weight (2% of 1,000 kgs.)	20	–
To Wages		17,500	By Sale of Scrap (10% of 1,000 kgs.)	100	10,000
To Manufacturing Expenses		5,380	By Process B A/c (Output Transferred) (Cost per kg. Rs. 1,32,880/880 kgs. = Rs. 151)	880	1,32,880
	1,000	1,42,880		1,000	1,42,880

Process B Account

	Kgs.	Rs.		Kgs.	Rs.
To Process A A/c (Transfer)	880	1,32,880	By Loss in weight (2% of 950 kgs.)	19	–
To Materials Consumed	70	14,000	By Sale of Scrap (10% of 950 kgs.)	95	14,250
To Wages		10,000			
To Manufacturing Expenses		5,342	By Finished Stock A/c (Output Transferred) (Cost per kg. = Rs. 1,47,972/836 kgs. = Rs. 177)	836	1,47,972
	950	1,62,222		950	1,62,222

Finished Stock Account

	Kgs.	Rs.		Kgs.	Rs.
To Process B A/c (Output Transferred)	836	1,47,972	By Balance c/d	836	1,47,972
	836	1,47,972		836	1,47,972

Illustration 10

A manufacturer's product passes through two distinct processes A and B and then to Finished Stock. It is known from the past experience that wastage occurs in the process as under:

In process A, 5% of the units entering the process and in Process B, 10% of units entering the process. The scrap value of the wastage in process A is Rs. 8 per 100 units and in process B is Rs. 10 per 100 units.

The process figures are:

	Process A	Process B
Materials Consumed	Rs. 3,000	Rs. 1,500
Wages	Rs. 3,500	Rs. 2,000
Manufacturing Expenses	Rs. 1,000	Rs. 1,000
5,000 units were brought into Process A costing Rs. 2,500		
The outputs were	4,700 units	4,150 units

Prepare Process Cost Accounts showing the cost of the output.

(P.U., B.Com.)

Solution

Process A Account

	Units	Rs.		Units	Rs.
To Units Introduced	5,000	2,500	By Normal Wastage A/c (5% of 5,000 units.)	250	20
To Materials		3,000			
To Labour		3,500	By Abnormal Wastage A/c	50	105
To Manufacturing Expenses		1,000	By Process B A/c (Transfer) (Cost per unit Rs. 9,875/4,700 units = Rs. 2.10)	4,700	9,875
	5,000	10,000		5,000	10,000

Calculation of the cost of Abnormal Wastage:

Input = 5,000 units
Normal Wastage = 250 units
Normal Effectives = Input – Normal Wastage
= 5,000 units – 250 units
= 4,750 units

Cost of Normal Effectives = Total Process Cost – Realisable Value of Normal Wastage
= Rs. 10,000 – Rs. 20
= Rs. 9,980

Actual Output = 4,700 units
Abnormal Wastage = 4,750 units – 4,700 units
= 50 units

Cost of Abnormal Wastage

$$= \frac{\text{Cost of Normal Effectives}}{\text{Normal Effectives}} \times \text{Abnormal Wastage}$$

$$= \frac{\text{Rs. } 9,980}{4,750 \text{ units}} \times 50 \text{ units} = \text{Rs. } 105 \text{ (app.)}$$

Process B Account

	Units	Rs.		Units	Rs.
To Process A A/c	4,700	9,875	By Normal Wastage A/c (10% of 4,700 units)	470	47
To Materials		1,500			
To Wages		2,000	By Abnormal Wastage A/c	80	271
To Manufacturing Expenses		1,000	By Finished Stock A/c (Cost per unit Rs. 14,057/4,150 units = Rs.. 3.39)	4,150	14,057
	4,700	14,375		4,700	14,375

Calculation of Cost of Abnormal Wastage:

Input = 4,700 units
Normal Wastage = 470 units
Normal Effectives = Input – Normal Wastage
= 4,700 units – 470 units
= 4,230 units

Cost of Normal Effectives = Total Process Cost – Realisable Value of Normal Wastage
= Rs. 14,375 – Rs. 47
= Rs. 14,328

Actual output = 4,150 units

Abnormal Wastage = 4,230 units – 4,150 units

= 80 units

Cost of Abnormal Wastage

$$= \frac{\text{Cost of Normal Effectives}}{\text{Normal Effectives}} \times \text{Abnormal Wastage}$$

$$= \frac{\text{Rs. }14,328}{4,230 \text{ units}} \times 80 = \text{Rs. } 271$$

Illustration 11

Samantar Ltd. manufactures a product which passes through two consecutive processes viz., Purvardha and Uttarardha. The company furnishes you with the following information for the year ended 31st March, 2002.

	Purvardha	**Uttarardha**
Basic Material	5,000 Units	–
Rate per unit	Rs. 2.20	–
	Rs.	Rs.
Process Material	4,000	3,000
Wages	3,000	4,000
Factory Overheads	2,000	2,650
Process Loss as Percentage of Input	10%	10%
Scrap value of Process Loss (per 100 units)	40	60

Prepare Process Accounts and other relevant accounts under the following two alternative circumstances assuming that the entire process loss is

Circumstance 1 – Normal Loss and

Circumstance 2 – Abnormal Loss.

The entire output of Uttarardha Process was sold for Rs. 30,000. Show the consequent reflection of the final results in Profit and Loss Account under both the circumstances. (*Mumbai Univ. B.Com. 1996*)

Solution

Case 1

Purvardha Process Account

	Units	Amt.		Units	Amt.
		Rs.			Rs.
To Units Introduced	5,000	11,000	By Normal Loss A/c (10% of 5,000 units)	500	200
To Process Materials		4,000	By Uttarardha Process A/c	4,500	19,800
To Wages		3,000	(Output Transferred)		
To Factory Overheads		2,000	(cost per unit $\frac{\text{Rs.}19,800}{4,500}$ = Rs. 4.40)		
	5,000	20,000		5,000	20,000

Uttarardha Process Account

	Units	Amt.		Units	Amt.
		Rs.			Rs.
To Purvardha Process A/c	4,500	19,800	By Normal Loss A/c (10% of 4,500 units)	450	270
To Process Materials		3,000	By Finished Stock A/c	4,050	29,180
To Wages		4,000	(Output Transferred)		
To Factory Overhead		2,650	(Cost per unit $\frac{\text{Rs. } 29{,}180}{4{,}050 \text{ units}}$ = Rs. 7.20)		
	4,500	29,450		4,500	29,450

Finished Stock A/c

	Units	Amt.		Units	Amt.
		Rs.			Rs.
To Uttarardha Process A/c	4,050	29,180	By Sales	4,050	30,000
To Profit Loss A/c (Profit)	–	820			
	4,050	30,000		4,050	30,000

Normal Loss Account

	Units	Amt.		Units	Amt.
		Rs.			Rs.
To Purvardha Process A/c	500	200	By Cash A/c (Sale of scrap of P. Process)	500	200
To Uttarardha Process A/c	450	270	By Cash A/c (Sale of scrap of U. Process)	450	270
	950	470		950	470

Case 2

Purvardha Process Account

	Units	Amt.		Units	Amt.
		Rs.			Rs.
To Units Introduced	5,000	11,000	By Abnormal Loss A/c	500	2,000
To Process Materials		4,000	$\left(\frac{\text{Rs. } 20{,}000}{5{,}000 \text{ units}} \times 500\right)$ (at cost)		
To Wages		3,000			
To Factory Overheads		2,000			
			By Uttarardha Process A/c (Output Transferred) (Cost per unit $\frac{\text{Rs. } 18{,}000}{4{,}500 \text{ units}}$ = Rs. 4	4,500	18,000
	5,000	20,000		5,000	20,000

Uttarardha Process Account

	Units	Amt. Rs.		Units	Amt. Rs.
To Purvardha Process A/c	4,500	18,000	By Abnormal Loss A/c (at cost)	450	2,765
To Process Material		3,000	$\left(\frac{\text{Rs. }27{,}650}{4{,}500\text{ units}} \times 450\text{ units}\right)$		
To Wages		4,000			
To Factory Overheads		2,650			
			By Finished Stock A/c (Output Transferred)	4,050	24,885
			(Cost per unit $\frac{\text{Rs. }24{,}885}{4{,}050\text{ units}} = \text{Rs. }6.144$)		
	4,500	27,650		4,500	27,650

Finished Stock Account

	Units	Amt. Rs.		Units	Amt. Rs.
To Uttarardha Process A/c	4,050	24,885	By Sales	4,050	30,000
To Profit and Loss A/c		5,115			
	4,050	30,000		4,050	30,000

Abnormal Loss Account

	Units	Amt. Rs.		Units	Amt. Rs.
To Purvardha Process A/c	500	2,000	By Cash A/c (Sale of scrap of P process)	500	200
To Uttarardha Process A/c	450	2,765	By Cash A/c (Sale of scrap of 'U' process)	450	270
			By Profit and Loss A/c (loss)	–	4,295
	950	4,765		950	4,765

Profit and Loss Account

	Rs.		Rs.
To Abnormal Loss A/c	4,295	By Finished Stock A/c	5,115
To Net Profit	820		
	5,115		5,115

Illustration 12

The finished product of a factory has to pass through three processes (A, B and C). The normal wastage of each process is 2% in A, 5% in B and 10% in C. The percentage of waste is computed on the number of units entering each process. The scrap value of the wastage of process A, B and C is Rs. 10, Rs. 40 and Rs. 20 per 100 units respectively.

The output of each process is transferred to the next process and the finished products are transferred from process C into stock. The following further information is obtained:

	Process A	Process B	Process C
	Rs.	Rs.	Rs.
Materials Consumed	12,000	4,000	4,000
Direct Labour	8,000	6,000	6,000
Manufacturing Expenses	2,000	4,000	2,000

20,000 units were put into process A at a cost of Rs. 16,000. The output of each process has been: A 19,600 units; B 18,400 units; and C 16,700 units.

There was no stock of work-in-progress in any process. Prepare Process Accounts, Normal Wastage A/c, Abnormal Wastage A/c and Abnormal Effectives A/c.

(*Pb. U., B.Com.,1968*) (*G.N.D.U., B.Com., 2002*)

Solution

Process A Account

	Units	Rs.		Units	Rs.
To Units Issued	20,000	16,000	By Normal Wastage A/c (2% of 20,000 units)	400	40
To Materials		12,000			
To Direct Labour		8,000			
To Manufacturing Expenses		2,000	By Process B A/c (Transfer) (Cost per unit Rs. 37,960/19,600 units = Rs. 1.94)	19,600	37,960
	20,000	38,000		20,000	38,000

Process B Account

	Units	Rs.		Units	Rs.
To Process A A/c	19,600	37,960	By Normal Wastage A/c	980	392
To Materials		4,000	(5% of 19,600 units)		
			By Abnormal Wastage A/c	220	609
To Direct Labour		6,000			
			By Process C A/c	18,400	50,959
To Manufacturing Expenses		4,000	(Transfer) (Cost per unit Rs. 50,959/18,400 units = Rs. 2.77)		
	1 9,600	51,960		19,600	51,960

Calculation of Cost of Abnormal Wastage:

Input = 19,600 units

Normal Wastage = 980 units

Normal Effectives = Input – Normal Wastage
= 18,620 units (i.e., 19,600 units – 980 units)

Cost of Normal Effectives = Total Process Cost – Realisable Value of Normal Wastage
= Rs. 51,960 – Rs. 392
= Rs. 51,568

Actual output = 18,400 units

Abnormal Wastage = 18,620 units – 18,400 units = 220 units

Cost of Abnormal Wastage

$$= \frac{\text{Cost of Normal Effectives}}{\text{Normal Effectives}} \times \text{Abnormal Wastage}$$

$$= \frac{\text{Rs. } 51{,}568}{18{,}620 \text{ units}} \times 220 \text{ units} = \text{Rs. } 609.$$

Process C Account

	Units	Rs.		Units	Rs.
To Process B A/c	18,400	50,959	By Normal Wastage A/c (10% of 18,400 units)	1,840	368
To Materials		4,000			
To Direct Labour		6,000			
To Manufacturing Expenses		2,000	By Finished Stock A/c (Transfer)	16,700	63,120
To Abnormal Effectives A/c	140	529	(Cost per unit Rs. 63,120/16,700 units = Rs. 3.78)		
	18,540	63,488		18,540	63,488

Calculation of Cost of Abnormal Effectives:

Input = 18,400 units

Normal Wastage = 1,840 units

Normal Effectives = Input – Normal Wastage
= 18,400 – 1,840
= 16,560 units

Cost of Normal Effectives = Total Process Cost – Realisable Value of Normal Wastage
= Rs. 62,959 – Rs. 368
= Rs. 62,591

Actual Output = 16,700 units

Abnormal Effectives = 16,700 units – 16,560 units
= 140 units

Cost of Abnormal Effectives

$$= \frac{\text{Cost of Normal Effectives}}{\text{Normal Effectives}} \times \text{Abnormal Effectives}$$

$$= \frac{\text{Rs. } 62{,}591}{16{,}560 \text{ units}} \times 140 \text{ units} = \text{Rs. } 529.$$

Abnormal Wastage Account

	Units	Rs.		Units	Rs.
To Process B A/c	220	609	By Cash A/c (Sale @ Rs. 40 per 100 units)	220	88
			By Costing Profit and Loss A/c	–	521
	220	609		220	609

Abnormal Effectives Account

	Units	Rs.		Units	Rs.
To Normal Wastage A/c	140	28	By Process C A/c	140	529
To Costing Profit and Loss A/c (Profit)	–	501			
	140	529		140	529

Normal Wastage Account

	Units	Rs.		Units	Rs.
To Process A A/c	400	40	By Cash A/c (Sale of Wastage of Process A)	400	40
To Process B A/c	980	392	By Cash A/c (Sale of Wastage of Process B)	980	392
To Process C A/c	1,840	368	By Cash A/c (Sale of Actual Wastage of Process C)	1,700	340
			By Abnormal Effectives A/c (Transfer)	140	28
	3,220	800		3,220	800

Illustration 13

A product passes through three processes, A, B and C. The normal wastage of each process is as follows:

Process A	3 per cent
Process B	5 per cent
Process C	8 per cent

Loss of process A was sold at 25 paise per unit, that of process B at 50 paise per unit and that of process C at Re. 1 per unit. 10,000 units were issued to process A in the beginning of January at a cost of Re. 1 per unit. The other expenses were as follows:

Process	A	B	C
	Rs.	Rs.	Rs.
Sundry Material	1,000	1,500	500
Labour	5,000	8,000	6,500
Direct Expenses	1,050	1,188	2,009
Actual Output in Units	9,500	9,100	8,100

Prepare the Process Cost accounts, assuming there was no opening or closing stock.

(*B.Com. Punjab*)
(*G.N.D.U., B.Com., 2000*)

Solution

Process A Account

	Units	Rs.		Units	Rs.
To Units Introduced	10,000	10,000	By Normal Loss A/c (3% of 10,000 units)	300	75
To Sundry Materials		1,000	By Abnormal Loss A/c	200	350
To Labour		5,000	By Process B A/c	9,500	16,625
To Direct Expenses		1,050	(Output Transferred)		
	10,000	17,050		10,000	17,050

$$\text{Cost of Abnormal Loss} = \frac{\text{Cost of Normal Output}}{\text{Normal Output (units)}} \times \text{Abnormal Loss (units)}$$

$$= \frac{\text{Rs. } 17{,}050 - 75}{9{,}700 \text{ units}} \times 200 \text{ units}$$

$$= \text{Rs. } 350.$$

Process B Account

	Units	Rs.		Units	Rs.
To Process A A/c	9,500	16,625	By Normal Loss A/c (5% of 9,500 units)	475	238
To Sundry Materials		1,500	By Process C A/c	9,100	27,300
To Labour		8,000	(Output Transferred)		
To Direct Expenses		1,188			
To Abnormal Effectives A/c	75	225			
	9,575	27,538		9,575	27,538

$$\text{Cost of Abnormal Effectives} = \frac{\text{Cost of Normal Output}}{\text{Normal Output}} \times \text{Abnormal Effectives}$$

$$= \frac{\text{Rs. } 27{,}313 - 238}{9{,}025 \text{ units}} \times 75 \text{ units} = \text{Rs. } 225.$$

Process C Account

	Units	Rs.		Units	Rs.
To Process B A/c	9,100	27,300	By Normal loss A/c (8% of 9,100 units)	728	728
To Sundry Material		500	By Abnormal Loss A/c	272	1,156
To Labour		6,500	By Finished Stock A/c	8,100	34,425
To Direct Expenses		2,009	(Output Transferred)		
	9,100	36,309		9,100	36,309

$$\text{Cost of Abnormal Loss} = \frac{\text{Cost of Normal Output}}{\text{Normal Output}} \times \text{Abnormal Loss}$$

$$= \frac{\text{Rs. } 36{,}309 - 728}{8{,}372 \text{ units}} \times 272 \text{ units} = \text{Rs. } 1{,}156.$$

Illustration 14

Product Z is obtained after it passes through three distinct processes. The following information is obtained from the accounts for the month ending 31.12.2004.

Items	Total	Processes I	II	III
	Rs.	Rs.	Rs.	Rs.
Direct Material	7,542	2,600	1,980	2,962
Direct Wages	9,000	2,000	3,000	4,000
Production Overhead	9,000			

1,000 units of Rs. 3 each were introduced in Process I. There was no stock of materials or work-in-progress at the beginning or at the end of the period. The output of each process passes direct to the next process and finally to finished stock. Production overhead are recovered at 100 percent of direct wages. The following additional data are obtained:

Process	Output during the month	% of Normal Loss to Input	Value of Scrap per unit
I	950	5%	Rs. 2
11	840	10%	Rs. 4
111	750	15%	Rs. 5

Prepare Process Accounts and Normal Loss Account.

(G.N.D.U, B.Com. April, 1996, 1997, 2001)
(Delhi, B.Com. (Hons) 1979) (H.P.U., B.Com., 2006)

Solution

Process I Account

	Units	Rs.		Units	Rs.
To Units Introduced	1,000	3,000	By Normal Wastage A/c	50	100
To Direct Materials		2,600	(5% of 1,000 units)		
To Direct Wages		2,000	By Process II A/c	950	9,500
To Production Overhead		2,000	(Output Transferred)		
(100% of direct wages)			(Cost per unit Rs.		
			9,500/950 units = Rs. 10)		
	1,000	9,600		1,000	9,600

Process II Account

	Units	Rs.		Units	Rs.
To Process I A/c	950	9,500	By Normal Wastage A/c	95	380
To Direct Materials		1,980	(10% of 950 units)		
To Direct Wages		3,000	By Abnormal Wastage A/c	15	300
To Production Overhead		3,000			
(100% of direct wages)			By Process III A/c		
			(Output Transferred)	840	16,800
			(Cost per unit Rs.		
			16,800/840 = Rs. 20)		
	950	17,480		950	17,480

$$\text{Cost of Abnormal Loss} = \frac{\text{Rs.}17{,}480 - 380}{950 \text{ units} - 95 \text{ units}} \times 15 \text{ units}$$

$$= \frac{\text{Rs. }17{,}100}{855 \text{ units}} \times 15 \text{ units}$$

$$= \text{Rs. } 300.$$

Process III Account

	Units	Rs.		Units	Rs.
To Process II A/c	840	16,800	By Normal Wastage A/c	126	630
To Direct Materials		2,962	(15% of 840 units)		
To Direct Wages		4,000			
To Production Overhead		4,000	By Finished Stock A/c	750	28,500
(100% of direct wages)			(Output Transferred)		
To Abnormal Effectives A/c	36	1,368	(Cost per unit		
			Rs. 28,500/750 = Rs. 38)		
	876	29,130		876	29,130

$$\text{Cost of Abnormal Effectives} = \frac{\text{Rs. }27{,}762 - 630}{840 \text{ units} - 126 \text{ units}} \times 36 \text{ units}$$

$$= \text{Rs. } 1{,}368$$

Abnormal Wastage Account

	Units	Rs.		Units	Rs.
To Process II A/c	15	300	By Cash A/c	15	60
			(Sale @ Rs. 4 per unit)		
			By Costing Profit and Loss A/c	–	240
	15	300		15	300

Abnormal Effectives Account

	Units	Rs.		Units	Rs.
To Normal Wastage A/c	36	180	By Process III A/c	36	1,368
To Costing Profit and Loss A/c (Profit)	–	1,188			
	36	1,368		36	1,368

Normal Wastage Account

	Units	Rs.		Units	Rs.
To Process I A/c	50	100	By Cash A/c	50	100
			(Sale of wastage of Process I)		
To Process II A/c	95	380			
To Process III A/c	126	630	By Cash A/c	95	380
			(Sale of Wastage of Process II)		
			By Cash A/c	90	450
			(Sale of Actual Wastage of Process III)		
			By Abnormal Effectives A/c	36	180
	271	1,110		271	1,110

TRANSFER OF A PART OF OUTPUT TO WAREHOUSE FOR SALE

In process costing, at the time of the completion of each process, there is a finished product. It may be sold directly in the market (without further processing) or transferred to the next process as its raw material. Sometimes, a manufacturer may transfer a part of production of a process to next process for further processing while the remaining part may be transferred to warehouse for sale. In such a case, both the cost of output transferred to next process and the cost of output transferred to warehouse for sale are shown on the credit side of the concerned Process Account. The treatment can be shown by means of the following illustration:

Illustration 15

The product of a manufacturing concern passes through three processes. Details of costs and production during March, 2007 were as follows:

	Process A	Process B	Process C
Raw Materials used (Tons)	200	71	164
Cost per ton	Rs.100	Rs.300	Rs.50
Direct Wages	Rs. 8,000	Rs. 3,490	Rs. 2,850
Overheads	Rs. 2,520	Rs.2,400	Rs.3,820
Sale of scrap per ton	Rs. 80	Rs. 60	Rs. 120

The product of the three processes is dealt with as follows:

Sent to warehouse for sale	25%	50%	100%
Sent to next Process	75%	50%	–

In each process 6% of total weight is lost and 8% is scrap. You are required to prepare Process Account showing the cost per ton of each process.

Solution

Process A Account

	Tons	Rs.		Tons	Rs.
To Raw Materials used	200	20,000	By Loss of weight (6% of 200 Tons)	12	–
To Direct Wages		8,000	By Sale of scrap (8% of 200 tons)	16	1,280
To Overheads		2,520	By Transfer to Warehouse	43	7,310
			By Transfer to Process B A/c (Cost per ton 21,930/129 = Rs. 170)	129	21,930
	200	30,520		200	30,520

Process B Account

	Tons	Rs.		Tons	Rs.
To Transfer from Process A	129	21,930	By Loss of Weight (6% of 200 Tons)	12	–
To Raw Materials used	71	21,300	By Sale of Scrap (8% of 200 Tons)	16	960
To Direct Wages		3,490	By Transfer to Warehouse	86	24,080
To Overheads		2,400	By Transfer to Process C (Cost per ton 24,080/86 = Rs. 280)	86	24,080
	200	49,120		200	49,120

Process C Account

	Tons	Rs.		Tons	Rs.
To Transfer from Process B	86	24,080	By Loss of Weight (6% of 250 Tons)	15	–
To Raw Materials used	164	8,200	By Sale of Scrap (8% of 250 Tons)	20	2,400
To Direct Wages		2,850			
To Overheads		3,820	By Transfer to Warehouse (Cost per ton 36,550/215 = Rs. 170)	215	36,550
	250	38,950		250	38,950

Illustration 16

Bharat Chemicals Ltd., manufacture and sell their chemicals produced by the consecutive processes. The products of these processes are dealt with as under:

	Process I	Process II	Process III
Transferred to Next Process	$66\frac{2}{3}\%$	60%	–
Transferred to Warehouse for Sale	$33\frac{1}{3}\%$	40%	100%

In each process 4% of the weight put in is lost and 6% is scrap which from Process I realised at Rs. 3 per tonne, from Process II Rs. 5 per tonne and from Process III Rs. 6 per tonne.

The following particulars relate to January 2008.

	Process I	Process II	Process III
Raw materials used in tonnes	1,400	160	1,260
Rate per tonne	Rs. 10.00	Rs. 16.00	Rs. 7.00
Wages and other Expenses	Rs. 5,152	Rs. 3,140	Rs 2,898

Prepare Process Accounts showing cost per tonne of each product.

(*Punjab Univ. B.Com. 1998*)

Solution

Process No. I Account

	Tonnes	Rs.		Tonnes	Rs.
To Raw Materials @ Rs. 10 per tonne	1,400	14,000	By Loss in weight (4% of 1,400 tonnes)	56	–
To Wages and other Expenses		5,152	By Sale of scrap (6% of 1,400 tonnes @ Rs. 3)	84	252
			By Transfer to warehouse ($33\frac{1}{3}\%$ of output 1,260 tonnes costing Rs. 18,900 @ Rs. 15 per tonne)	420	6,300
			By Process II A/c ($66\frac{2}{3}\%$ of output transferred @ Rs. 15 per tonne)	840	12,600
	1,400	19,152		1,400	19,152

Process No. II Account

	Tonnes	Rs.		Tonnes	Rs.
To Process I A/c	840	12,600	By Loss in Weight (4% of 1,000 Tonnes)	40	–
To Raw Materials	160	2,560	By Sale of Scrap (6% of 1,000 Tonnes) (60 Tonnes @ Rs.5 per Tonne)	60	300
To Wages and other Expenses		3,140	By Transfer to Warehouse (40% of 900 Tonnes)	360	7,200
			By Process III A/c (Cost per tonne Rs. 10,800/540 = Rs.20)	540	10,800
	1,000	18,300		1,000	18,300

Process No. III Account

	Tonnes	Rs.		Tonnes	Rs.
To Process II A/c	540	10,800	By Loss in Weight (4% of 1,800 Tonnes)	72	–
To Raw Materials	1,260	8,820	By Sale of Scrap (6% of 1,800 Tonnes)	108	648
To Wages and other Expenses		2,898	By Transfer to Warehouse (Cost per tonne Rs. 21,870/1,620 Tonnes = Rs. 13.50)	1,620	21,870
	1,800	22,518		1,800	22,518

Illustration 17

A product passes through three processes i.e., A, B and C. The details of expenses incurred on these during 2003 were as under:

Process	A	B	C
Units Issued	1,000	–	–
Cost per unit	50	–	–
Sundry Materials	1,000	1,500	500
Labour	2,600	8,000	6,392
Direct Expenses	600	1,815	2,720
Sale price of output (per unit)	70	100	200

Actual output of the three processes was 930 units of A, 540 units of B and 210 units of C.

Two-thirds of output of process A and one-half of the output of process B was passed on to the next process and the balance was sold. Entire output of C was also sold.

Normal loss of the three processes, calculated on the input of every process was:

Process A- 5%; Process B- 15%; Process C- 20%. Process loss of A was sold at Re. 1 per unit, that of process B at Rs. 3 per unit, and that of process C at Rs. 6 per unit. Selling expenses Rs. 9,000 (chargeable to income statement not allocable to the processes). Prepare three process accounts and the income statement.

(G.N.D.U., B.Com. 2003)

Solution

Process A Account

Particulars	Units	Amount Rs.	Particulars	Units	Amount Rs.
To Units Issued	1,000	50,000	By Normal Loss A/c	50	50
To Sundry Materials		1,000	By Abnormal Loss A/c	20	1,140
To Labour		2,600	By Process B A/c (2/3rd output)	620	35,340
To Direct Expenses		600	By Transfer to Warehouse for sale (1/3rd output) (Cost per unit Rs. 57)	310	17,670
	1,000	54,200		1,000	54,200

Process B Account

Particulars	Units	Amount Rs.	Particulars	Units	Amount Rs.
To Process A A/c	620	35,340	By Normal Loss A/c	93	279
To Sundry Materials		1,500	By Process C A/c (1/2 output)	270	23,760
To Labour		8,000			
To Direct Expenses		1,815	By Transfer to Warehouse for sale (1/2 output) (Cost per unit Rs. 88)	270	23,760
To Abnormal Gain A/c	13	1,144			
	633	47,799		633	47,799

Process C Account

Particulars	Units	Amount Rs.	Particulars	Units	Amount Rs.
To Process B A/c	270	23,760	By Normal Loss A/c	54	324
To Sundry Materials		500	By Abnormal Loss A/c	6	918
To Labour		6,392	By Transfer to Warehouse for sale (Cost per unit Rs.153)	210	32,130
To Direct Expenses		2,720			
	270	33,372		270	33,372

Profit and Loss Account

	Rs.		Rs.
To Cost of goods sold:		By Sales:	
Process A	17,670	Process A (310 units × Rs. 70)	21,700
Process B	23,760	Process B (270 units × Rs. 100)	27,000
Process C	32,130	Process C (210 units × Rs. 200)	42,000
To Abnormal loss:			
Process A (Rs. 1,140 – Rs. 20)	1,120		
Process C (Rs. 918 – Rs. 36)	882	By Abnormal Gain: Process B (Rs. 1,144 – Rs. 39)	1,105
To Selling Expenses	9,000		
To Net Profit	7,243		
	91,805		91,805

PROCESS STOCKS

Sometimes there may arise the question of stocks in the various processes of a manufacturing concern. These stocks may be of:

(*i*) Raw Materials,

(*ii*) Finished Goods, or of

(*iii*) Semi-Finished Goods or Work-in-progress (dealt with in detail in the chapter of Process Costing –III – Equivalent Production).

STOCK OF RAW MATERIALS

Stock of raw materials represents the stock of unused materials in various processes. Stock of raw material in the first process of a product in a manufacturing concern, if any, shall represent the basic raw material of that concern to be returned to the Stores Department. But the stock of raw material in the subsequent processes (opening as well as closing) shall be treated as the finished product of the preceding process to be valued at the rate at which it was transferred from the preceding process to the concerned process. The opening stock is shown on the debit side of the account prepared for the process concerned while the closing stock is shown on its credit side.

Treatment of stocks of raw material in the process accounts can be explained with the help of the following example:

Illustration 18

From the following figures, show the cost of the three processes of manufacture. The production of each process is passed on to the next process immediately on completion:

	Process X	Process Y	Process Z
	Rs.	Rs.	Rs.
Wages and Materials	3,040	1,200	2,925
Works Overhead	560	525	600
Production (in units)	3,600	3,750	4,800
Stock (Units from Preceding Process) on 1st January, 2006	–	400	1,650
Stock (Units from Preceding Process) on 31st January, 2006	–	100	550

Solution

Process X Account

	Units	Rs.		Units	Rs.
To Wages and Materials	3,600	3,040	By Process Y A/c	3,600	3,600
To Works Overhead		560	(Output Transferred) (Cost per unit Rs. 3,600/3,600 units = Re. 1)		
	3,600	3,600		3,600	3,600

Process Y Account

	Units	Rs.		Units	Rs.
To Balance b/d (Opening Stock @ Re. 1 per unit)	400	400	By Normal Wastage (Balance Fig.)	150	–
To Process X A/c	3,600	3,600	By Process Z A/c (Output Transferred) (Cost per unit Rs. 5,625/3,750 units = Rs. 1.50)	3,750	5,625
To Wages and Materials		1,200			
To Factory Overhead		525			
			By Balance c/d (Closing stock @ Re. 1 per unit)	100	100
	4,000	5,725		4,000	5,725

Process Z Account

	Units	Rs.		Units	Rs.
To Balance b/d (Opening Stock @ Rs. 1.50 per unit)	1,650	2,475	By Normal Wastage	50	–
To Process Y A/c	3,750	5,625	By Finished Stock A/c (Cost per unit Rs. 10,800/4,800 units = Rs. 2.25)	4,800	10,800
To Wages and Materials		2,925			
To Works Overhead		600	By Balance c/d (Closing stock @ Rs. 1.50 per unit)	550	825
	5,400	11,625		5,400	11,625

Notes: (*i*) It has been assumed that wastage in each process is normal wastage, the cost of which is to be borne by good units.

(*ii*) In Process X, input has been assumed to be equal to output as the quantity of input is not given.

Illustration 19

The information given below is extracted from books of a factory producing a commodity in the manufacture of which three processes are involved. Prepare Process Cost Accounts showing the cost of output and the cost per unit at each stage of manufacture assuming that:

(*i*) The operations in each process are completed daily.

(*ii*) The value at which the units are to be charged to processes two and three, is the cost per unit of processes one and one plus two respectively.

	Process No. 1	2	3
	Rs.	Rs.	Rs.
Direct Wages	7,500	15,000	19,500
Machine Expenses	4,200	3,600	3,600
Factory Oncost	3,300	4,650	2,700
Raw Material Consumed	24,000	–	–
	Units	Units	Units
Production (Gross)	2,750	–	
Wastage	150	210	200
Stock, 1st April, 2006	–	250	500
Stock, 31st March, 2007	–	440	100

Solution

Process No. 1 Account

	Units	Rs.		Units	Rs.
To Raw Material Consumed	2,750	24,000	By Wastage	150	–
To Direct Wages		7,500	By Process No. 2 Account	2,600	39,000
To Machine Expenses		4,200	(Output Transferred)		
To Factory Oncost		3,300	(Cost per unit Rs. 39,000/2,600 Units = Rs. 15)		
	2,750	39,000		2,750	39,000

Process No. 2 Account

	Units	Rs.		Units	Rs.
To Balance b/d	250	3,750	By Wastage	210	–
(@ Rs. 15 per unit)			By Process No. 3 A/c	2,200	59,400
To Process No. 1 A/c	2,600	39,000	(Output Transferred)		
To Direct Wages		15,000	(Cost per unit Rs. 59,400/2,200 units = Rs. 27)		
To Machine Expenses		3,600			
To Factory Oncost		4,650	By Balance c/d	440	6,600
			(@ Rs. 15 per unit)		
	2,850	66,000		2,850	66,000

Process No. 3 Account

	Units	Rs.		Units	Rs.
To Balance b/d	500	13,500	By Wastage	200	–
(@ Rs. 27 per unit)					
To Process No. 2 A/c	2,200	59,400	By Finished Stock A/c	2,400	96,000
To Direct Wages		19,500	(Output Transferred)		
To Machine Expenses		3,600	(Cost per unit Rs.		
To Factory Oncost		2,700	96,000/2,400 units = Rs.40)		
			By Balance c/d (@ Rs. 27 per unit)	100	2,700
	2,700	98,700		2,700	98,700

Notes: (*i*) Production (Gross) in Process No. 1 represents input. (*ii*) Wastage in each process has been assumed to be normal wastage.

Stock of Finished Goods: In some cases, the entire output of a process may not be transferred to the subsequent process and a part of it may be held in the processing department in its finished form. Such stock of finished goods (opening as well as closing) is valued on the basis of the cost per unit as shown by the concerned process account (in which stock is held) for the relevant periods. For the purpose of dealing with the stocks of finished goods, a separate Process Stock Account is prepared with each process. The output of each process is first transferred to its Process Stock Account and from there to the next process account.

Illustration 20

The product of a company passes through two processes, namely A and B respectively. From past experience the percentage of loss, which is computed on the number of units entering the process concerned, is ascertained as under:

Process A : 2%   Process B : 5%

The loss of each process has a scrap value. The wastage of Process A is sold at Rs. 10 per 100 units and that of Process B at Rs. 20 per 100 units. The following information is available for the year ended 31st March, 2006:

	Process A	Process B
	Rs.	Rs.
Materials Consumed	8,000	2,800
Direct Wages	12,200	14,000
Manufacturing Expenses	3,080	1,000
	Units	Units
Finished Products	39,000	38,500
Stocks:		
1st April, 2005	4,000	6,000
31st March, 2006	3,000	8,000

40,000 units of crude materials were introduced in Process A at a cost of Rs. 16,000. Stock valuation on April 1 (per unit) Process A: Re. 0.90

Process B: Rs. 1.47

Stocks at 31st March are to be valued at the cost as shown by the year's process accounts.

Prepare the necessary accounts. *(G.ND.U, B. Com. 1979, 1985)*

(Pbi. Univ. B.Com., 2007)

Solution

Process A Account

	Units	Rs.		Units	Rs.
To Units Introduced	40,000	16,000	By Normal Wastage	800	80
To Materials		8,000	By Abnormal Wastage	200	200
To Direct Wages		12,200			
To Manufacturing Expenses		3,080	By Process A Stock A/c	39,000	39,000
			(Cost per unit:		
			Rs. 39,000/39,000 units		
			= Re. 1.00)		
	40,000	39,280		40,000	39.280

Process A Stock Account

	Units	Rs.		Units	Rs.
April 1, 2005					
To Balance b/d	4,000	3,600	By Process B A/c	40,000	39,600
(@ Re. 0.90 per unit)			(Units transferred)		
To Process A A/c	39,000	39,000	March 31, 2006		
			By Balance c/d	3,000	3,000
			@ Rs. 1 per unit)		
	43,000	42,600		43,000	42,600

Process B Account

	Units	Rs.		Units	Rs.
To Process A Stock A/c	40,000	39,600	By Normal Wastage	2,000	400
To Materials		2,800			
To Direct Wages		14,000			
To Manufacturing Expenses		1,000	By Process B Stock A/c	38,500	57,750
To Abnormal Effectives	500	750	(Cost per unit Rs. 57,750/ 38,500 units = Rs. 1.50)		
	40,500	58,150		40,500	58,150

Process B Stock Account

	Units	Rs.		Units	Rs.
April 1, 2005					
To Balance b/d (@ Rs. 1.47 per unit)	6,000	8,820	By Finished Stock A/c	36,500	54,570
To Process B A/c	38,500	57,750	March 31, 2006		
			By Balance c/d (@ Rs. 1.50 per unit)	8,000	12,000
	44,500	66,570		44,500	66,570

Calculation of Cost of Abnormal Wastage and Abnormal Effectives

Process A:

$$\text{Abnormal Wastage} = \text{Rs. } 39,200 \times \frac{200}{39,200} = \text{Rs. } 200$$

Process B:

$$\text{Abnormal Effectives} = \text{Rs. } 57,000 \times \frac{500}{38,000} = \text{Rs. } 750.$$

INTER-PROCESS PROFITS

In process costing, the usual practice is to transfer the output of each process to the next process and from the last process to the Finished Stock Account at actual cost price. But in some of the manufacturing concerns, the transfer of output from one process to another and from last process to Finished Stock Account, is made at cost plus a certain percentage of profit, which is known as 'Transfer Price' or 'Inflated Price'. In this way, each process shows a profit which is credited to Profit and Loss Account.

The practice of transferring the output at cost plus profit or at inflated price, has some advantages. Inflated price or transfer price is generally equal to the market value of the output. As such, the level of efficiency or inefficiency at each stage will be immediately known through the comparison of the cost of the process with the market value of the output at that stage of completion. Secondly, this practice also helps in making a decision as to whether to buy a partly processed material from outside supplier or to process it in the factory itself.

But the above practice creates a number of accounting problems. As regards units sold, there is no problem because the Profit and Loss Account absorbs the difference between the cost and sales value of these units. But the problem arises in respect of stock unsold. The inflation of inter-process transfer prices has the effect that process stocks appear in accounting records at an amount in excess of cost. Further, the inflated values of stock cannot be directly included in the Balance Sheet of the business since these values, if included in balance sheet, will not show the correct position of the business.

Therefore, the inter-process profit included in the stocks should be eliminated, as this profit is not yet realised. The calculation of the actual cost and the element of profit included in the process stocks is made by providing additional columns for 'Cost' and 'Profit' on memorandum basis along with 'Total' or 'Amount' Column on both sides of each Process Account and Finished Stock Account. The cost of stock in each process and finished stock account shall be calculated by applying the following formula:

$$\text{Cost of Stock} = \frac{\text{Total of Cost Column}}{\text{Total of Total Column}} \times \text{Value of Stock}$$

The element of unrealised profit included in the value of stock shall be ascertained as follows:

Amount of Unrealised Profit = Value of Stock – Cost of Stock.

The amount of unrealised profit included in the stocks of each process and of the finished stock account, calculated in the manner given above, shall be debited to Profit and Loss Account and credited to 'Reserve for Unrealised Profit' in order to ascertain the actual process profits. Thus, the actual amount of profit can be calculated as follows:

Actual Profit = Apparent Profit from Process – Unrealised Profit included in closing stock.

These calculations can be explained with the help of the following illustrations:

Illustration 21

A product passes through two processes A and B. Output of Process A is transferred to Process B at cost plus 25% profit and the output of Process B is similarly transferred to Finished Stock Account at cost plus 25% profit. There was no Work-in-Progress in either process on 31st March, 2006. On this date, the following further information was available:

	Process A	**Process B**
	Rs.	**Rs.**
Materials Consumed	8,000	24,000
Wages	12,000	16,000
Closing Stock (Valued at Prime Cost)	4,000	12,000

Out of the finished stock, a portion remained at hand valued at Rs. 18,000 and the balance sold for Rs. 58,000. Prepare the Process and Finished Stock Accounts. Question of oncost should be ignored. Also calculate the amount of reserve that should be made in respect of unrealised profit.

(*G.N.D.U., B.Com., 1995*)

Solution

Process A Account

	Total	Cost	Profit		Total	Cost	Profit
	Rs.	Rs.	Rs.		Rs.	Rs.	Rs.
To Material	8,000	8,000	–				
To Wages	12,000	12,000	–				
Total	20,000	20,000					
Less Closing Stock	4,000	4,000	–				
Prime Cost	16,000	16,000		By Process B A/c (Transfer)	20,000	16,000	4,000
To Profit (25% on Rs. 16,000)	4,000	–	4,000				
	20,000	16,000	4,000		20,000	16,000	4,000

Process B Account

	Total	Cost	Profit		Total	Cost	Profit
	Rs.	Rs.	Rs.		Rs.	Rs.	Rs.
To Process A A/c	20,000	16,000	4,000				
To Materials	24,000	24,000	–				
To Wages	16,000	16,000	–				
Total	60,000	56,000	4,000				
Less Closing Stock	12,000	11,200	800	By Finished Stock A/c (Transfer)	60,000	44,800	15,200
Prime Cost	48,000	44,800	3,200				
To Profit (25% on Rs. 48,000)	12,000	–	12,000				
	60,000	44,800	15,200		60,000	44,800	15,200

Finished Stock Account

	Total	Cost	Profit		Total	Cost	Profit
	Rs.	Rs.	Rs.		Rs.	Rs.	Rs.
To Process B A/c	60,000	44,800	15,200				
Less Closing Stock	18,000	13,440	4,560	By Sales	58,000	31,360	26,640
	42,000	31,360	10,640				
To Profit	16,000	–	16,000				
	58,000	31,360	26,640		58,000	31,360	26,640

Note: Calculation of Profit on Closing Stock:

Cost of the closing stock can be ascertained by applying the following formula:

$$\text{Cost of Closing Stock} = \frac{\text{Total of Cost Column}}{\text{Total of Total Column}} \times \text{Value of Stock}$$

Process A: Closing stock has been valued at prime cost and hence it includes no profit.

Process B: $\frac{\text{Total of Cost Column}}{\text{Total of Total Column}} \times \text{Value of Stock}$

$$= \frac{56{,}000}{60{,}000} \times 12{,}000 = \text{Rs. } 11{,}200$$

Profit = Rs. 12,000 – Rs. 11,200 = Rs. 800

Finished Stock: $\frac{\text{Total of Cost Column}}{\text{Total of Total Column}} \times \text{Value of Stock}$

$$= \frac{44{,}800}{60{,}000} \times 18{,}000 = \text{Rs. } 13{,}440$$

Profit = Rs. 18,000 – 13,440 = Rs. 4,560

Calculation of Actual Profit:

	Apparent Profit from Process	Unrealised Profit in Closing Stock	Actual Profit
	Rs.	Rs.	Rs.
Process A	4,000	–	4,000
Process B	12,000	800	11,200
Finished Stock	16,000	4,560	11,440
	32,000	5,360	26,640

Illustration 22

The product of a manufacturing concern passes through three processes A, B and C. The output of process A and B is charged to the next process to give a profit of 25% on cost, while the output of process C is charged to Finished Stock Account which gives process C, a profit of 25% on cost.

From the following particulars prepare the Process Accounts and Finished Stock Account and calculate the amount of unrealised profit included in the closing stock and the amount of actual profit made by the concern. There was no opening stock and closing stock in each process has been valued at prime cost.

	Processes		
	A	B	C
	Rs.	Rs.	Rs.
Materials Used	14,000	21,000	7,000
Labour	21,000	14,000	28,000
Closing Stock	7,000	14,000	21,000
Sales:	Rs. 1,26,000		

Closing Stock of Finished Goods amounted to Rs. 14,000.

(*Punjab Univ. B.Com., 2007*)

Solution

Process A Account

	Total	Cost	Profit		Total	Cost	Profit
	Rs.	Rs.	Rs.		Rs.	Rs.	Rs.
To Materials	14,000	14,000	–				
To Labour	21,000	21,000	–				
	35,000	35,000	–				
Less Closing Stock	7,000	7,000	–				
Prime Cost	28,000	28,000	–	By Process B A/c	35,000	28,000	7,000
To Profit (25% on Cost Rs. 28,000)	7,000	–	7,000				
	35,000	28,000	7,000		35,000	28,000	7,000

Note: Closing Stock of Process A has been valued at Prime Cost. Hence it includes no Profit.

Process B Account

	Total	Cost	Profit		Total	Cost	Profit
	Rs.	Rs.	Rs.		Rs.	Rs.	Rs.
To Process A A/c	35,000	28,000	7,000				
To Materials	21,000	21,000	–				
To Labour	14,000	14,000	–				
	70,000	63,000	7,000				
Less Closing Stock	14,000	12,600	1,400				
Prime Cost	56,000	50,400	5,600				
To Profit (25% on Rs. 56,000)	14,000	–	14,000	By Process C A/c	70,000	50,400	19,600
	70,000	50,400	19,600		70,000	50,400	19,600

$$\text{Cost of Closing Stock of Process B} = \frac{\text{Total of Cost Column}}{\text{Total of Total Column}} \times \text{Value of Stock}$$

$$= \frac{63,000}{70,000} \times 14,000 = \text{Rs. } 12,600$$

Process C Account

	Total	Cost	Profit		Total	Cost	Profit
	Rs.	Rs.	Rs.		Rs.	Rs.	Rs.
To Process B A/c	70,000	50,400	19,600				
To Materials	7,000	7,000	–				
To Labour	28,000	28,000	–				
	1,05,000	85,400	19,600				
Less Closing Stock	21,000	17,080	3,920				
Prime Cost	84,000	68,320	15,680	By Finished Stock A/c	1,05,000	68,320	36,680
To Profit (25% on Rs. 84,000)	21,000	–	21,000				
	1,05,000	68,320	36,680		1,05,000	68,320	36,680

$$\text{Cost of Closing Stock of Process C} = \frac{\text{Total of Cost Column}}{\text{Total of Total Column}} \times \text{Value of Stock}$$

$$= \frac{85,400}{1,05,000} \times 21,000 = \text{Rs. } 17,080$$

Finished Stock Account

	Total	Cost	Profit		Total	Cost	Profit
	Rs.	Rs.	Rs.		Rs.	Rs.	Rs.
To Process B A/c	1,05,000	68,320	36,680				
Less Clossing Stock	14,000	9,110	4,890				
	91,000	59,210	31,790	By Sales	1,26,000	59,210	66,790
To Profit	35,000	–	35,000				
	1,26,000	59,210	66,790		1,26,000	59,210	66,790

$$\text{Cost of Finished Stock Unsold} = \frac{\text{Total of Cost Column}}{\text{Total of Total Column}} \times \text{Value of Stock}$$

$$= \frac{68{,}320}{1{,}05{,}000} \times 14{,}000 = \text{Rs. } 9{,}110$$

Calculation of Actual Profit:

	Apparent Profit from Process	Unrealised Profit in closing stock	Actual Profit
	Rs.	Rs.	Rs.
Process A	7,000	–	7,000
Process B	14,000	1,400	12,600
Process C	21,000	3,920	17,080
Finished Stock	35,000	4,890	30,110
	77,000	10,210	66,790

Illustration 23

A certain product passes through three processes before it is transferred to finished stock. These processes are known as A, B and C. The following information is obtained for the month of January, 2007:

	Process A	Process B	Process C	Finished Stock
	Rs.	Rs.	Rs.	Rs.
Opening Stock (at Prime Cost)	1,000	1,200	800	3,000
Direct Materials	2,000	2,100	3,000	–
Wages	1,500	1,500	1,600	–
Overheads	1,400	600	4,000	–
Closing Stock (at Prime Cost)	500	600	400	1,500
Inter-Process Profits for Opening Stock	–	200	200	1,100
Profit (% on transfer price to next process)	25%	20%	20%	–

Sales of finished stock during January, 2007 amounted to Rs. 35,000. You are required to:

(*a*) Prepare Process Cost Accounts; and

(*b*) Calculate Actual Realised Profit.

Solution

Process A Account

	Total	Cost	Profit		Total	Cost	Profit
	Rs.	Rs.	Rs.		Rs.	Rs.	Rs.
To Opening Stock	1,000	1,000	–				
To Materials	2,000	2,000	–				
To Wages	1,500	1,500	–				
	4,500	4,500	–	By Process B A/c			
Less Closing Stock	500	500	–	(Transfer)	7,200	5,400	1,800
Prime Cost	4,000	4,000	–				
To Overheads	1,400	1,400	–				
	5,400	5,400	–				
To Profit (25% on Tranfer Price)	1,800	–	1,800				
	7,200	5,400	1,800		7,200	5,400	1,800

Process B Account

	Total	Cost	Profit		Total	Cost	Profit
	Rs.	Rs.	Rs.		Rs.	Rs.	Rs.
To Opening Stock	1,200	1,000	200				
To Process A A/c	7,200	5,400	1,800				
To Materials	2,100	2,100	–				
To Wages	1,500	1,500	–				
	12,000	10,000	2,000				
Less Closing Stock	600	500	100				
Prime Cost	11,400	9,500	1,900	By Process C A/c	15,000	10,100	4,900
To Overheads	600	600	–				
	12,000	10,100	1,900				
To Profit (20% on Transfer Price)	3,000	–	3,000				
	15,000	10,100	4,900		15,000	10,100	4,900

Process C Account

	Total	Cost	Profit		Total	Cost	Profit
	Rs.	Rs.	Rs.		Rs.	Rs.	Rs.
To Opening Stock	800	600	200				
To Process B A/c	15,000	10,100	4,900				
To Materials	3,000	3,000	–				
To Wages	1,600	1,600	–				
	20,400	15,300	5,100				
Less Closing Stock	400	300	100				
Prime Cost	20,000	15,000	5,000	By Finished Stock A/c (Transfer)	30,000	19,000	11,000
To Overheads	4,000	4,000	–				
	24,000	19,000	5,000				
To Profit (20% on Transfer Price)	6,000	–	6,000				
	30,000	19,000	11,000		30,000	19,000	11,000

Finished Stock Account

	Total	Cost	Profit		Total	Cost	Profit
	Rs.	Rs.	Rs.		Rs.	Rs.	Rs.
To Opening Stock	3,000	1,900	1,100				
To Process C A/c	30,000	19,000	11,000				
	33,000	20,900	12,100	By Sales	35,000	19,950	15,050
Less Closing Stock	1,500	950	550				
	31,500	19,950	11,550				
To Profit	3,500	–	3,500				
	35,000	19,950	15,050		35,000	19,950	15,050

Note: Amount of profit by way of % on transfer price, which is to be charged on the transfer of the output of each process to next process has been calculated by the following formula:

$$\frac{\text{Cost} \times \% \text{ of Profit}}{100 - \% \text{ of Profit}}$$

Calculation of Cost of Process Stocks at the close of the period:

Process A: Closing Stock of Process A has been valued at Prime Cost and hence it does not include any profit.

Process B: $\frac{\text{Total of Cost Column}}{\text{Total of Total Column}} \times \text{Value of Stock} = \frac{10{,}000}{12{,}000} \times 600 = \text{Rs. } 500$

Process C: $\frac{\text{Total of Cost Column}}{\text{Total of Total Column}} \times \text{Value of Stock} = \frac{15{,}300}{20{,}400} \times 400 = \text{Rs. } 300$

Finished Stock: $\frac{\text{Total of Cost Column}}{\text{Total of Total Column}} \times \text{Value of Stock} = \frac{20{,}900}{33{,}000} \times 1{,}500 = \text{Rs. } 950$

Unrealised Profit:

Process A: Nil
Process B: Rs. 600 – Rs. 500 = Rs. 100
Process C: Rs. 400 – Rs. 300 = Rs. 100
Finished Stock: Rs. 1,500 – Rs. 950 = Rs. 550
Total Unrealised Profit = Rs. 750

Calculation of Actual Profit

	Apparent Profit from Process	Unrealised Profit Opening Stock (+)	Unrealised Profit Closing Stock (–)	Actual Profit
	Rs.	Rs.	Rs.	Rs.
Process A	1,800	–	–	1,800
Process B	3,000	200	100	3,100
Process C	6,000	200	100	6,100
Finished Stock	3,500	1,100	550	4,050
	14,300	(+) 1,500	(–) 750	15,050

Illustration 24

A chemical product passes through three consecutive processes. In the first process the raw material are broken down and blended. Heat treatment and further blending are carried out in second process, and the final or warehouse-operation consists of packing into cartons for sale.

There are no quantity losses in process. The output of process 1 is charged to process 2 at a figure which shows a profit of 10 per cent on the transfer price, and that of process 2 to process 3 at a figure which shows a profit of 25 per cent on such price.

The stocks carried by process 2 are valued at the cost of the year's production.

The following particulars are supplied for the year to 31st March, 2002:

			Kgs.	Rs.
Process 1				
Raw materials used			15,680	78,400
Wages: Crushing and Mixing				1,37,200
Overhead: Management Salary				40,000
Process 2				
Transfer from Process 1				
Raw Materials used			3,920	9,000
Coal and Coke				10,000
Wages: Furnace and Mixing				1,47,000
Overhead: Management Salary				40,000
Process stock	Kgs.	Rs.		
April 1, 2001	1,500	32,500		
(Subject to stock provision Rs. 2,500)				
March 31, 2002	1,100			
Process 3				
Transfer from Process 2				
Including all Opening Stock			20,000	
Cartons				12,500
Wages				67,500
Overhead: Management Salary				60,000
Sales			18,000	9,00,000
Selling Expenses				1,22,100

In respect of the year to March 31, 2002, it is required:

(*a*) to write the process accounts in detail, and

(*b*) to give up the Profit and Loss Account, introducing such provisions as may be necessary to reduce stocks to cost.

Solution

Process 1 Account

Particulars	Kgs.	Total	Cost	Profit	Particulars	Kgs.	Total	Cost	Profit
		Rs.	Rs.	Rs.			Rs.	Rs.	Rs.
To Raw Materials used	15,680	78,400	78,400	–					
To Wages	–	1,37,200	1,37,200	–	By Process	15,680	2,84,000	2,55,600	28,400
To Overhead	–	40,000	40,000	–	2 Account				
		2,55,600	2,55,600	–	(Output Transferred)				
To Profit and Loss A/c		28,400	–	28,400					
(Profit@ 10% on transfer price)									
	15,680	2,84,000	2,55,600	28,400		15,680	2,84,000	2,55,600	28,400

Process 2 Account

Particulars	Kgs.	Total	Cost	Profit	Particulars	Kgs.	Total	Cost	Profit
		Rs.	Rs.	Rs.			Rs.	Rs.	Rs.
To Process 1 A/c	15,680	2,84,000	2,55,600	28,400					
To Raw Materials used	3,920	9,000	9,000	–	By Process 3 A/c	20,000	6,60,000	4,65,694	1,94,306
To Coal & Coke	–	10,000	10,000	–					
To Wages	–	1,47,000	1,47,000	–					
To Overhead	–	40,000	40,000	–					
	19,600	4,90,000	4,61,600	28,400					
Add Opening Stock	1,500	32,500	30,000	2,500					
	21,100	5,22,500	4,91,600	30,900					
Less Closing Stock	1,100	27,500	25,906	1,594					
	20,000	4,95,000	4,65,694	29,306					
To Profit & Loss A/c (25% on Transfer price)	–	1,65,000	–	1,65,000					
	20,000	6,60,000	4,65,694	1,94,306		20,000	6,60,000	4,65,694	1,94,306

Process 3 Account

Particulars	Kgs.	Total	Cost	Profit	Particulars	Kgs.	Total	Cost	Profit
		Rs.	Rs.	Rs.			Rs.	Rs.	Rs.
To Process 2 A/c	20,000	6,60,000	4,65,694	1,94,306					
To Cost of Cartons	–	12,500	12,500	–	By Sales	18,000	9,00,000	6,67,225	2,32,775
To Wages	–	67,500	67,500	–					
To Overhead	–	60,000	60,000	–					
	20,000	8,00,000	6,05,694	1,94,306					
Less									
Closing Stock	2,000	80,000	60,569	19,431					
Cost of Goods Sold	18,000	7,20,000	5,45,125	1,74,875					
To Selling Expenses	–	1,22,100	1,22,100	–					
Cost of Sales	18,000	8,42,100	6,67,225	1,74,875					
To Profit & Loss A/c	–	57,900	–	57,900					
	18,000	9,00,000	6,67,225	2,32,775		18,000	9,00,000	6,67,225	2,32,775

Profit and Loss Account

	Rs.		Rs.
To Stock Reserve A/c	21,025	By Process 1 A/c	28,400
Process 2 A/c: 1,594		By Process 2 A/c	1,65,000
Process 3 A/c: 19,431		By Process 3 A/c	57,900
To Net Profit	2,32,775	By Stock Reserve A/c (Opening - Process 2A/c)	2,500
	2,53,800		2,53,800

Notes: (*i*) Calculation of the Cost of Closing Stock in Process 2:

$$\text{Cost of Stock} = \frac{\text{Total of Cost Column}}{\text{Total of Total Column}} \times \text{Value of Stock}$$

$$= \frac{\text{Rs. 4,91,600}}{\text{Rs. 5,22,500}} \times \text{Rs.27,500} = \text{Rs. 25,906.}$$

(*ii*) Calculation of the Cost of Closing Stock of Process 3:

$$\text{Cost of Stock} = \frac{\text{Total of Cost Column}}{\text{Total of Total Column}} \times \text{Value of Stock}$$

$$= \frac{\text{Rs. 6,05,694}}{\text{Rs. 8,00,000}} \times \text{Rs.80,000} = \text{Rs. 60,569.}$$

MISCELLANEOUS PROBLEMS

Illustration 25

A manufacturer produced three products in consecutive processes A, B and C. It is known from the past experience that wastage occurs in the process as under:

Process A: 5%; Process B: 5%; Process C: 10% of the total weight put in the process.

The scrap value of wastages in Process A is Rs. 10 per kg., in Process B is Rs. 15 per kg. and in Process C Rs. 20 per kg.

The product of three processes is dealt with as follows:

Processes	A	B	C
Output passed to the next process	60%	80%	–
Output sent to warehouse for sale	40%	20%	100%
The figures relating to the processes are:			
Raw Materials Consumed	2,000 kg.	1,000 kg.	500 kg.
Rate of raw Materials (per kg.)	Rs. 20	Rs. 50	Rs. 100
Sundry Materials and Direct Wages	Rs. 32,000	Rs. 35,000	Rs. 48,000
Manufacturing Expenses	Rs. 24,000	Rs. 20,640	Rs. 23,900
Output	1,800 kg.	2,000 kg.	1,800 kg.

Prepare the process accounts, showing cost per kg. of each product.

Solution

Process A Account

(Output: 1,800 kg.)

	Weight Kgs.	Rs.		Weight Kgs.	Rs.
To Raw Materials Consumed	2,000	40,000	By Normal Wastage (5% of 2,000 kgs.)	100	1,000
To Sundry Materials and Direct Wages		32,000	By Abnormal Wastage	100	5,000
To Manfacturing Exp.		24,000	By Transfer to Warehouse (40% of 1,800 kgs.,)	720	36,000
			By Process B A/c (60% of 1,800 kgs.)	1,080	54,000
	2,000	96,000		2,000	96,000

Process B Account

(Output: 2,000 kg.)

	Weight Kgs.	Rs.		Weight Kgs.	Rs.
To Process A A/c	1,080	54,000	By Normal Wastage (5% of 2,080 Kgs.)	104	1,560
To Raw Materials Consumed	1,000	50,000	By Transfer to Warehouse (20% 2,000 Kgs.)	400	32,000
To Sundry Materials and Direct Wages		35,000	By Process C A/c (80% of 2,000 Kgs.)	1,600	1,28,000
To Manufacturing Exp.		20,640			
To Abnormal Effectives	24	1,920			
	2,104	1,61,560		2,104	1,61,560

Process C Account

(Output: 1,800 kg.)

	Weight Kgs.	Rs.		Weight Kgs.	Rs.
To Process B A/c	1,600	1,28,000	By Normal Wastage (10% of 2,100 Kgs.)	210	4,200
To Raw Materials	500	50,000			
To Sundry Materials and Direct Wages		48,000	By Abnormal Wastage	90	11,700
To Manufacturing Exp.		23,900	By Transfer to Warehouse	1,800	2,34,000
	2,100	2,49,900		2,100	2,49,900

Illustration 26

The finished product of a manufacturing company passes through three processes, viz., I, II and III. The normal wastage in each process is 5%, 7% and 10% for the processes I, 1 and III respectively (calculated with reference to the number of units fed into each process). The scrap generated out of wastage has a sale value of 70 paise per unit, 80 paise per unit and Rupee 1 per unit in process I, II and III respectively. The output of each process is transferred to the next process and the finished output emerges from the process III and transferred to stock. There was no stock of work-in-progress in any process in a particular month. The details of cost data for the month are given below:

	Process I	Process II	Process III
Materials used (Rs.)	1,20,000	40,000	40,000
Direct Labour Cost (Rs.)	80,000	60,000	60,000
Production Expenses (Rs.)	40,000	40,000	28,000
Output in Units (actual)	38,000	34,600	32,000

Process I was fed with 40,000 units of raw input at a cost of Rs. 3,20,000. Prepare the process accounts.

(*I.C.W. A. Inter, June 1996*)

Solution

Process I Account

	Units	Amount Rs.		Units	Amount Rs.
To Units Introduced	40,000	3,20,000	By Normal loss (5%) @ 70p. per unit	2,000	1,400
To Materials	–	1,20,000			
To Direct Labour Cost	–	80,000	By Transfer to Process II @ Rs. 14.70 *per unit.	38,000	5,58,600
To Production Expenses	–	40,000			
	40,000	5,60,000		40,000	5,60,000

$$\text{*Cost per unit} = \frac{\text{Rs. } 5{,}60{,}000 - 1{,}400}{40{,}000 - 2{,}000 \text{ units}} = \frac{\text{Rs. } 5{,}58{,}600}{38{,}000 \text{ units}} = \text{Rs. } 14.70$$

Process II Account

	Units	Amount Rs.		Units	Amount Rs,
To Transfer from Process I A/c	38,000	5,58,600	By Normal Loss (7%) @ 80 paise per unit	2,660	2,128
To Materials	–	40,000	By Abnormal Loss @ Rs. 19.7078 *per unit.	740	14,584
To Direct Labour	–	60,000			
To Production Expenses		40,000	By Transfer to Process III *@ 19.7078	34,600	6,81,888
	38,000	6,98,600		38,000	6,98,600

$$\text{*Cost per unit} = \frac{\text{Rs. } 6{,}98{,}600 - 2{,}128}{38{,}000 - 2{,}660 \text{ units}} = \frac{\text{Rs. } 6{,}96{,}472}{35{,}340 \text{ units}} = \text{Rs. } 19.7078$$

Process III Account

	Units	Amount Rs.		Units	Amount Rs.
To Tr. from Process II A/c	34,600	6,81,888	By Normal Loss	3,460	3,460
To Materials		40,000	By Transfer to Stock @ * Rs. 25.897 per unit	32,000	8,28,700
To Direct Labour		60,000			
To Production Expenses		28,000			
To Abnormal Gain @ Rs. 25.897	860	22,272			
	35,460	8,32,160		35,460	8,32,160

$$\text{*Cost per unit} = \frac{\text{Rs. } 8{,}09{,}888 - 3{,}460}{34{,}600 - 3{,}460 \text{ units}} = \frac{\text{Rs. } 8{,}06{,}428}{31{,}140 \text{ units}} = \text{Rs. } 25.897$$

Illustration 27

The following details are available for the year 2003:

	Process I Rs.	Process II Rs.	Process III Rs.
Raw Materials Used - 1,000 Tons			
Cost per ton	200	–	–
Manufacturing Wages and Expenses	72,500	40,800	10,710
Weight Lost	5%	10%	20%
Scrap (sold at Rs. 50 per ton)	50 tons	30 tons	51 tons
Sale price per ton	350	500	800

Management expenses were Rs. 17,500; Selling expenses Rs. 10,000; and Interest on borrowed capital Rs. 4,000.

2/3 output of Process I and 1/2 output of Process II are passed on to the next process and the balance are sold.

You are required to prepare a cost statement in a suitable form.

(G.N.D.U., B.Com., 2000)

Solution

Statement of Cost

	Tons	Rs.
Proceess I:		
Raw Materials at Rs. 200 per ton	1,000	2,00,000
Manufacturing Wages and Expenses		72,500
		2,72,500
Less Loss in weight @ 5%	50	–
	950	2,72,500
Less Scrap at Rs. 50 per ton	50	2,500
Cost of Production (Rs. 300 per ton)	900	2,70,000
2/3 Output Transferred to Procees II at Cost	600	1,80,000
1/3 Output Sold at Cost	300	90,000
Selling Price of 1/3 Output (at Rs. 350 per ton)	300	1,05,000
Cost Price of 1/3 Output (at Rs. 300 per ton)	300	90,000
Profit on Sales	–	15,000
Process II:		
Output from Process I:	600	1,80,000
Manufacturing Wages and Expenses		40,800
		2,20,800
Less Loss in weight @ 10%	60	–
	540	2,20,800
Less Scrap at Rs. 50 per ton	30	1,500
Cost of Production (at Rs. 430 per ton)	510	2,19,300
1/2 of the Output Transferred to Process III at Cost	255	1,09,650
1/2 of the Output Sold at Cost	255	1,09,650
Selling Price of 1/2 Output (at Rs. 500 per ton)	255	1,27,500
Cost price of 1/2 Output (at Rs. 430 per ton)	255	1,09,650
Profit on Sales	–	17,850

Process III:

Output from Process II at Rs. 430 per ton	255	1,09,650
Manufacturing Wages and Expenses		10,710
	255	1,20,360
Less: Loss in Weight @ 20%	51	–
	204	1,20,360
Less: Scrap sold at Rs. 50 per ton	51	2,550
Cost of Production (at Rs. 770 ton)	153	1,17,810
Selling Price of 153 tons at Rs. 800 per ton	153	1,22,400
Cost of Production at Rs. 770 per ton	153	1,17,810
Profit on Sales	–	4,590

Statement of Profit

		Rs.
Profit:		
Process I : Rs. 15,000		
Process II : Rs. 17,850		
Process III: Rs. 4,590		37,440
Less:		
Management Expenses	Rs. 17,500	
Selling Expenses	Rs. 10,000	
		27,500
	Net Profit	9,940

Note: Interest on borrowed capital (Rs. 4,000) has been excluded as it is a financial item.

Illustration 28

An article passes through five hand operations as follows:

Operation No.	Time per Article	Grade of Worker	Wage Rate per Hour
1.	15 minutes	M	Re. 0.65
2.	25 minutes	N	Re. 0.50
3.	10 minutes	O	Re. 0.40
4.	30 minutes	P	Re. 0.35
5.	20 minutes	Q	Re. 0.30

The factory works at 40 hours per week and the production target is 7,200 articles per week. Prepare a statement showing for each operation and in total the number of operators required, the labour cost per doz. and the total labour cost per week to produce the total target output.

(*Madras, B. Com. May 1982-Adapted*)

Solution

Production target = 7,200 articles per week.

Time required for 7,200 articles (Operation-wise):

Operation 1 $7{,}200 \times \frac{15}{60} = 1{,}800$ hours.

Operation 2 $7{,}200 \times \frac{25}{60} = 3{,}000$ hours.

Operation 3 $7{,}200 \times \frac{10}{60} = 1{,}200$ hours.

Operation 4 $7{,}200 \times \frac{30}{60} = 3{,}600$ hours.

Operation 5 $7{,}200 \times \frac{20}{60} = 2{,}400$ hours.

Working of the factory is 40 hours a week. So, the number of operators required can be calculated by dividing the total hours of an operation by 40, as given in column No. 3 in the statement below:

Statement of Labour Cost

1	2	3	4	5	6
Operation No.	**No. of Hours**	**Operators Required** (Col. 2) ÷ 40	**Wage Rate per Hour**	**Labour Cost per Week** (Col. 2) × Rate	**Labour Cost per doz. of Articles** (Col. 5) × $\frac{12}{7,200}$
			Rs.	Rs.	Rs.
1.	1,800	45	0.65	1,170	$1{,}170 \times \frac{12}{7{,}200} = 1.95$
2.	3,000	75	0.50	1,500	$1{,}500 \times \frac{12}{7{,}200} = 2.50$
3.	1,200	30	0.40	480	$480 \times \frac{12}{7{,}200} = 0.80$
4.	3,600	90	0.35	1,260	$1{,}260 \times \frac{12}{7{,}200} = 2.10$
5.	2,400	60	0.30	720	$720 \times \frac{12}{7{,}200} = 1.20$
				5,130	8.55

Illustration 29

A product passes through three processes – P, Q and R.

The details of expenses incurred on the three processes during the year 2001 were as follows:

	P	Q	R
Units issued	10,000		
	Rs.	Rs.	Rs.
Cost per Unit	100		
Sundry Materials	10,000	15,000	5,000
Labour	30,000	80,000	65,000
Direct Expenses	6,000	18,150	27,200
Sale price of Output (per unit)	120	165	250

Management expenses during the year were Rs. 80,000 and selling expenses were Rs. 50,000. These are not allocable to the processes.

Actual output of the three processes was : Process P- 9,300 units; Process Q- 5,400 units; Process R- 2,100 units.

Two-thirds of the output of Process P and one-half of the output of Process Q was passed on to the next process and the balance was sold. The entire output of Process R was sold.

The normal wastage of the three processes, calculated on the input of every process, was: Process P – 5% : Process Q – 15% and Process R – 20%.

The wastage of Process P was sold at Rs. 2 per unit, that of Process Q at Rs. 5 per unit and yet that of Process R at Rs. 10 per unit.

Prepare the three process accounts and a statement of income

(*Delhi, B.Com. Hons. 1982; C.A. Inter May, 1993*)

Solution

Process P Account

Particulars	Units	Amount	Particulars	Units	Amount
		Rs.			Rs.
To Units Issued	10,000	10,00,000	By Normal Loss	500	1,000
To Sundry Materials		10,000	By Abnormal Loss @ Rs. 110 each	200	22,000
To Labour		30,000	By Process Q A/c - @ Rs. 110 each	6,200	6,82,000
To Direct Expenses		6,000	By Statement of Income - @ Rs. 110 each	3,100	3,41,000
	10,000	10,46,000		10,000	10,46,000

Process Q Account

Particulars	Units	Amount	Particulars	Units	Amount
		Rs.			Rs.
To Process P A/c	6,200	6,82,000	By Normal Loss	930	4,650
To Sundry Materials		15,000	By Process R A/c - @ Rs. 150 each	2,700	4,05,000
To Labour		80,000	By Statement of Income		
To Direct Expenses		18,150	- @ Rs. 150 each	2,700	4,05,000
To Abnormal Gain @ Rs. 150 each	130	19,500			
	6,330	8,14,650		6,330	8,14,650

Process R Account

Particulars	Units	Amount	Particulars	Units	Amount
		Rs.			Rs.
To Process Q A/c	2,700	4,05,000	By Normal Loss	540	5,400
To Sundry Materials		5,000	By Abnormal Loss		
To Labour		65,000	(Rs. 230 each)	60	13,800
To Direct Expenses		27,200	By Statement of Income - @ Rs. 230 each	2,100	4,83,000
	2,700	5,02,200		2,700	5,02,200

Statement of Income

Particulars	Units	Amount Rs.	Particulars	Units	Amount Rs.
To Process P A/c			By Sale of Units		
- @ Rs. 110 each	3,100	3,41,000	Process P @ Rs. 120 each	3,100	3,72,000
To Process Q A/c - @: Rs. 150 each	2,700	4,05,000	Process Q @ Rs. 165 each	2,700	4,45,500
To Process R A/c - @ Rs. 230 each	2,100	4,83,000	Process R @ Rs. 250 each	2,100	5,25,000
To Management Expenses		80,000	By Abnormal Loss		18,850
To Selling Expenses		50,000	By Net Loss		32,450
To Abnormal Loss		34,800			
	7,900	13,93,800		7,900	13,93,800

Working Notes:

Abnormal Loss

$$\text{Process P} = \frac{\text{Rs. }10,46,000 - \text{Rs. }1,000}{10,000 \text{ units} - 500 \text{ units}} \times 200 \text{ units} = \text{Rs. } 22,000$$

$$\text{Process R} = \frac{\text{Rs. }5,02,200 - \text{Rs. }5,400}{2,700 \text{ units} - 540 \text{ units}} \times 60 \text{ units} = \text{Rs. } 13,800$$

Abnormal Gain

$$\text{Process Q} = \frac{\text{Rs. }7,95,150 - \text{Rs. }4,650}{6,200 \text{ units} - 930 \text{ units}} \times 130 \text{ units} = \text{Rs. } 19,500$$

Illustration 30

The input to a purifying process was 16,000 kgs. of basic material purchased @ 1.20 per kg. Process wages amounted to Rs. 720 and overhead was applied @ 240% of the labour cost. Indirect materials of negligible weight were introduced into the process at a cost of Rs. 336. The actual output from the process weighed 15,000 kgs. The normal yield of the process is 92%. Any difference in weight between the input of basic and output of purified material (product) is sold @ 0.50 per kg.

The process is operated under a licence which provides for the payment of royalty @ Re. 0.15 per kg. of the purified material produced.

Prepare:

(*i*) Purifying Process Account
(*ii*) Normal Wastage Account
(*iii*) Abnormal Wastage/Yield Account
(*iv*) Royalty Payable Account.

(*C.A. Inter*)

Solution

Purifying Process Account

Particulars	Kgs.	Amount	Particulars	Kgs.	Amount
		Rs.			Rs.
To Units Introduced	16,000	19,200	By Normal Wastage A/c	1,280	640
To Wages		720	By Output	15,000	24,000
To Overhead		1,728			
To Indirect Materials		336			
To Royalty Payable		2,208			
To Abnormal Yield A/c	280	448			
	16,280	24,640		16,280	24,640

$$\text{*Cost per kg.} = \frac{\text{Rs. } 24,192 - 640}{16,000 - 1,280 \text{ kgs.}} = \text{Rs.}1.60$$

Normal Wastage Account

Particulars	Kgs.	Amount	Particulars	Kgs.	Amount
		Rs.			Rs.
To Purifying Process A/c	1,280	640	By Cash (Sale)	1,000	500
			By Abnormal Yield A/c	280	140
	1,280	640		1,280	640

Abnormal Yield Account

Particulars	Kgs.	Amount	Particulars	Kgs.	Amount
		Rs.			Rs.
To Normal Wastage A/c	280	140	By Purifying Process A/c	280	448
To Costing P&L A/c		266			
To Royalty Payable (on 280 kgs.)		42			
	280	448		280	448

Royalty Payable Account

Particulars	Kgs.	Amount	Particulars	Kgs.	Amount
		Rs.			Rs.
To Lessor	15,000	2,250	By Purifying Process A/c	14,720	2,208
			By Abnormal Yield A/c	280	42
	15,000	2,250		15,000	2,250

OBJECTIVE TYPE QUESTIONS

A. Multiple Choice Questions

Select the correct answer in each of the following cases:

(*a*) Normal loss in a process
  (*i*) is unavoidable
  (*ii*) is avoidable
  (*iii*) arises due to defective machinery
  (*iv*) arises due to inefficient supervision.

(*b*) The process loss not allowed to affect the cost of good units is:
  (*i*) Normal Loss
  (*ii*) Standard Loss
  (*iii*) Abnormal Loss
  (*iv*) Material Loss.

(*c*) The cost of normal wastage less scrap value, if any, is borne by:
  (*i*) Process A/c
  (*ii*) Abnormal Wastage
  (*iii*) Normal Effectives
  (*iv*) None of these.

(*d*) Accounting entry for writing off Abnormal Loss in process costing is;
  (*i*) Abnormal Loss A/c Dr. To Process A/c
  (*ii*) Costing Profit and Loss A/c Dr. To Abnormal Loss A/c
  (*iii*) Abnormal Loss A/c Dr. To Costing Profit and Loss A/c
  (*iv*) Process A/c Dr. To Costing Profit and Loss A/c.

(*e*) In Process A 1,000 units are introduced. The normal loss is 5%. If the actual output is 940 units, there is;
  (*i*) an abnormal loss
  (*ii*) an abnormal gain
  (*iii*) a normal loss only
  (*iv*) neither abnormal loss nor abnormal gain.

(*f*) In Process 'A' 2,000 units are introduced. The normal loss is 10%. If the actual output is 1,850 units, there is:
  (*i*) an abnormal loss
  (*ii*) an abnormal gain
  (*iii*) a normal loss only
  (*iv*) neither normal loss nor abnormal loss.

[**Ans.** (*a*) (*i*), (*b*) (*iii*), (*c*) (*iii*), (*d*) (*ii*), (*e*) (*i*), (*f*) (*ii*)]

B. True/False Type Statements

Indicate whether the following statements are true or false;

(*i*) Process Costing is generally applied in case of large contracts.

(*ii*) Process Costing is similar to contract costing.

(*iii*) Cost of normal process loss is borne by normal output.

(*iv*) Cost of abnormal process loss is borne by good units.

(*v*) The value of abnormal effectives reduces the cost of normal output.

(*vi*) In case of inter-process transfers at a profit, the cost of closing stock is calculated as follows:

$$\frac{\text{Total of Cost Column}}{\text{Total of Total Column}} \times \text{Value of Closing Stock}$$

(*vii*) Output of preceding process cannot be transferred to succeeding process at market price.

[**Ans.** (*i*) False (*ii*) False (*iii*) True (*iv*) False (*v*) False (*vi*) True (*vii*) False]

C. Filling the Blanks

Fill in the blanks:

(*i*) Average unit cost of each process is calculated by dividing the total process cost by ....

(*ii*) Abnormal Process loss is transferred to ....

(*iii*) Cost of normal loss is borne by ....

(*iv*) Cost of .... loss is not borne by good units.

(*v*) If the actual loss in a process is less than the normal loss, the difference is known as ....

(*vi*) For accounting purpose, stock must be valued at .... or .... whichever is less.

[**Ans.** (*i*) Units of output (*ii*) Costing Profit and Loss A/c (*iii*) Normal output (*iv*) abnormal (*v*) abnormal gain (*vi*) cost price, market price

SHORT ANSWER TYPE QUESTIONS

1. What is Process Costing?
2. What is the costing procedure in process costing?
3. How would you treat 'Normal Loss' in process account?
4. Discuss the treatment of 'Abnormal Loss' in process costing.
5. How would you treat abnormal gain in process accounts.

LONG ANSWER TYPE QUESTIONS

1. What is meant by Process Costing? In what type of industries is process costing generally applied?
2. What is Process Costing? What are the basic differences between Job Costing and Process Costing?
3. What are the basic differences between Job order and Process cost systems? (B. *Com, Madras*)
4. Define normal and abnormal process losses explaning the possible causes. How are these dealt with in cost accounts? (*Punjab Univ., B.Com.*)
5. Describe briefly the main features of process costing. Also compare Process Costing with Job Costing.
6. What do you understand by the term 'inter-process profits'? Give advantages and disadvantages of its adoption in process costing.
7. Explain 'Normal Wastage,' 'Abnormal Wastage' and 'Abnormal Gain' and discuss their treatment in process accounts. (*Pbi. Univ. B.Com., 2008*)
8. Define Process Costing. Discuss the special characteristics of process costing. Also distinguish between job costing and process costing. (*H.P.U. B.Com., 2008*)

EXERCISES

1. An article passes through three processes of manufacture. From the following figures, show the cost of each of the three processes during the month of January, 2004.

	Process No 1	**Process No. 2**	**Process No. 3**
Material used	15,000	5,000	2,000
Labour	8,000	20,000	6,000
Direct Expenses	2,600	7,200	2,500

The indirect expenses amounting to Rs. 8,500 may be apportioned on the basis of wages. No account need be taken of stocks in hand and Work-in-Progress at the beginning and close of the month. The number of articles produced during the month was 240.

(*Agra, B.Com., G.N.D.U., B.Com., 1995*)

[**Ans.** Cost per article Process A – Rs. 115, B – Rs. 270, C – Rs. 320]

2. A product passes through three processes of production. The output of preceding process is transferred to the next process.
The output for the month is 100 tons and the following expenses were incurred:

	A – Process	**B – Process**	**C – Process**
	Rs.	Rs.	Rs.
Material	10,000	2,000	1,000
Wages	5,000	8,000	7,000
Direct Expenses	3,000	1,000	2,000

Total indirect expenses during the month of July, 2003 were Rs. 2,000. Prepare Process Accounts.

[**Ans.** Cost per ton A-Rs. 185, B-Rs. 303, C-Rs. 410]

3. Two types of articles A and B are produced in a factory in which the materials used are identical and in which each undergoes two processes-factory and finishing. The wages are separately recorded ; materials used and general expenses are divided in output ratio ; factory and finishing charges are apportioned in the labour ratio of each process.

You are required to prepare a Statement of Process Cost per hundred articles from the following particulars and to show the percentage of profit if the selling price of article A is Re. 0.25 and of article B Re. 0.30.

Output A-3,18,600; B-1,27,440.

	Rs.
Factory Materials	
Opening Stock	9,600
Purchases	27,200
Closing Stock	7,400
Finishing Materials	
Opening Stock	3,800
Purchases	9,200
Closing Stock	3,200
Factory Wages	
A	15,600
B	11,400
Finishing Wages	
A	6,400
B	2,400
Factory Charges	5,400
Finishing Charges	2,200
General Expenses	12,600

4. A factory makes two types of articles A and B which are subjected to two processes - factory and finishing and in respect of which labour is recorded separately. Similar materials are used in each article, the raw material cost being the same. Prepare statements showing the process cost for each type of articles and percentage of profit thereon from the following information:

		Article A	Article B
		Rs.	Rs.
Output		3,220	1,380
Selling Price		125	155
Materials:			
Purchased	- Factory	1,35,000	
	- Finishing	43,000	
Opening stock	- Factory	50,000	
	- Finishing	12,000	
Closing stock	- Factory	37,000	
	- Finishing	12,000	
Labour	Factory -A	90,000	
	- Factory -B	60,000	
	- Finishing -A	37,500	
	- Finishing -B	12,500	
General charges:	Factory	50,000	
	- Finishing	27,200	

Apportion general charges in the ratio of labour for each process.

[**Ans.** Cost per unit : A B
Factory process Rs. 69.44 Rs. 90.14
Finishing process Rs. 96.77 Rs. 113.48]

5. In Process A, 4,000 units of crude material are introduced at a cost of Rs. 16,000. Normal loss in the process is 5% of units entering the process and has a scrap value of Rs. 1.50 per unit. The other expenses in the process are:

	Rs.
Direct Materials	5,000
Direct Wages	8,000
Overhead	3,000

Actual output in the process is 3,800 units. Prepare Process A Account and Normal Loss Account. [**Ans.** Cost per unit Rs. 8.34]

6. In Process I, 1,000 kgs. of crude material are introduced at a cost of Rs. 60 per kg. On the basis of past experience it is known that 3% of the weight put in is lost and another 8% is scrapped which realises Rs. 10 per kg. The other expenses in the process are:

	Rs.
Direct Materials	15,000
Direct Wages	12,000
Factory Overhead	8,000

Prepare Process I Account.

[**Ans.** Cost per kg. Rs. 105.84]

7. In Process A, 5,000 units of crude material are introduced at a cost of Rs. 25,000. Normal wastage in the process is 5% of input having a realisable value of Rs. 2 per unit. The other expenses of the process are:

	Rs.
Direct Materials	10,000
Direct Wages	12,000
Production Overhead	6,000

Actual output in the process is 4,600 units. Prepare Process A Account, Normal Wastage Account and Abnormal Wastage Account.

[**Ans.** Abnormal Wastage 150 units, Cost per unit Rs. 11.05]

8. In Process I, 5,000 units of crude material are introduced at a cost of Rs. 20,000. Normal Wastage in the process is 5% of input having a realisable value of Re. 1 per unit. The other expenses of the process are:

	Rs.
Direct Materials	12,000
Direct Wages	10,000
Production Overhead	5,000

Actual output in the process is 4,800 units. Prepare Process I Account, Normal Wastage Account and Abnormal Effectives Account.

[**Ans.** Abnormal Effectives 50 units Cost per unit Rs. 9.84]

9. The product of a manufacturing company passes through two processes A and B and then to finished stock. It is ascertained that in each process 5% of the total weight put in is lost and 10% is scrap which from Processes A and B realises Rs. 80 per ton and Rs. 200 per ton respectively.

	Process A	**Process B**
Materials consumed in tons	1,000	70
Cost of Materials per ton in Rupees	125	200
Wages in Rupees	18,000	12,000
Manufacturing Expenses in Rupees	6,000	5,000

Prepare Process Cost Accounts showing the cost of the output of each process and the cost per ton.

[**Ans.** Cost per ton A - Rs. 165.88, B - 196.42]

10. A product passes through two processes to completion, namely Process A and Process B. The weight lost is 4% in Process A and 3% in Process B. Wastage has no realisable value.

During the year ending 31st March, 2003 : 8,000 units of materials costing Rs. 8 per unit were introduced in Process A. The other information as per cost records is as under:

	Process A	Process B
	Rs.	Rs.
Other Materials	–	8,125
Labour	16,000	12,000
Overheads	4,480	6,500
Output (Units)	7,500	7,300

The output of the Process B is transferred to Finished Stock Account. Out of the output transferred to Finished Stock Account 6,500 units were sold at Rs. 20 per unit and the selling and distribution expenses incurred were Rs. 3 per unit sold.

Prepare Process Accounts and Finished Stock Account.

[**Ans.** Process A Abnormal loss 180 units Rs. 1980
Process B Abnormal Gain 25 units Rs. 375]

11. In a factory the product passes through two processes A and B. A loss of 5% is allowed in process A and 2% in process B, nothing could be realised by disposal of wastage.

During April, 2002, 10,000 units of materials costing Rs. 6 per unit were introduced in process A. The other costs are as follows:

	Process A	Process B
	Rs.	Rs.
Materials	–	6,140
Labour	10,000	6,000
Overheads	6,000	4,600

The output was 9,300 units from process A. 9,200 units were produced by process B, which were transferred to the warehouse. 8,000 units of the finished product were sold @Rs.15 per unit, the selling and distribution expense were Rs. 2 per unit.

Prepare process accounts and statement of profit.

[**Ans.**

Process A :	**Process B :**	**Profit**
Abnormal Loss 200 Units Rs. 1,600	Abnormal Gain 86 units Rs. 860	Rs. 24,000
Cost of Output Rs. 74,400	Cost of output Rs. 92,000	Net profit Rs. 23,260)

12. The following information is available in respect of three processes P, Q and R:

	Process P	Process Q	Process R
Wastage	2%	4%	10%
(To be calculated on input in process)			
Scrap value (per unit)	Rs. 250	Rs. 250	Rs. 500
Materials	3,00,000	2,00,000	1,00,000
Wages	4,00,000	3,00,000	1,50,000

Machine Expenses	50,000	50,000	75,000
Other Expenses	87,500	95,000	1,05,000

50,000 units had been put in Process P at a cost of Rs. 5,00,000. The output of each process is as follows:

Process P 48,750 Units, Process Q 47,000 Units, Process R 42,000 Units.

There was no opening or closing stock of work-in-progress in any of the processes. Prepare the Process Accounts, Abnormal Gain Account and Abnormal Wastage Account. (*B.U. April 1990*)

[**Ans.**

Process —P- Cost per unit Rs. 27.25 Ab. Wastage - 250 units.

Q - Rs. 42.06 & Ab. Gain - 200 units.

R - Rs. 56.34 & Ab. Loss - 300 units.]

13. Bajpai Manufacturing Company's product passes through two distinct processes A and B and then to finished stock. It is known from past experience that wastage occurs in the process as under:

In Process A 5% of the units entering the process and in Process B 10% of the units entering the process.

The scrap value of wastage in Process A is Rs. 16 per 100 units and in Process B is Rs. 20 per 100 units.

The process figures are:

	Process A	Process B
	Rs.	Rs.
Materials Consumed	6,000	3,000
Wages	7,000	4,000
Manufacturing Expenses	2,000	2,000

5,000 units were brought into Process A, costing Rs 5,000. The outputs were:

Process A	4,700 units
Process B	4,150 units

Prepare Process Cost Accounts showing the cost of the output.

[**Ans.** Process A- A.W. 50 units Rs. 210, B - A.W. 80 units Rs. 542]

14. Product 'P' passes through three processes to completion. Following are the relevant details:

(*a*) Elements of Cost

Particulars	Total	No. I	No. 2	No. 3
	Rs.	Rs.	Rs.	Rs.
Direct Material	8,482	2,000	3,020	3,462
Direct Labour	12,000	3,000	4,000	5,000
Direct Expenses	726	500	226	–
Production Overhead	6,000	–	–	–

(*b*) 1,000 units at Rs. 5 each were issued to Process No. 1.

(*c*) Output of each process was:

Process No. 1	920 units
Process No. 2	870 units
Process No. 3	800 units

(*d*) Normal Loss per process was estimated as:

Process No. 1	10% of units introduced
Process No. 2	5% of units introduced
Process No. 3	10 % of units introduced

(*e*) The Loss in each process represented scrap which could be sold to a merchant at value as follows:

Process No. 1	Rs. 3 per unit
Process No. 2	Rs. 5 per unit
Process No. 3	Rs. 6 per unit

(*f*) There was no stock of material or work-in-progress in any department at the beginning or end of the period. The output of each process passes direct to the next process and finally to finished stock. Production overhead is allocated to each process on the basis of 50% of the cost of Direct Labour. Show process accounts.

(*B.U. April, 1983*)

[**Ans.** Process 1 - Cost per unit Rs. 13, Ab. Gain: 20 units.
Process 2 - Cost per unit Rs. 24, Ab. wastage: 4 units
Process 3 - Cost per unit Rs. 40, Ab. Gain: 17 units.]

15. Product P is obtained finally after it passes through Process A, Process B and Process C. 4,000 units @ Rs. 10 per unit were introduced in the Process A. Other details pertaining to each process were as under:

	Process A	**Process B**	**Process C**
	Rs.	**Rs.**	**Rs.**
Sundry Materials	8,000	5,000	10,000
Direct Wages	10,000	15,000	12,000
Direct Expenses	7,000	9,000	8,000

Production overheads were charged to each process at 100% of direct wages. The actual output was:

Process	A	3,800 Units
	B	3,400 Units
	C	2,900 Units

Percentage of normal loss in each process was:

Process	A	5%
	B	10%
	C	15%

Scrap value per unit in each process was:

Process	A	Rs. 3
	B	Rs. 5
	C	Rs. 10

You are required to prepare all the three process accounts and abnormal loss and abnormal gain accounts.

[**Ans.** Process A Rs. 19.58 : B Rs. 34.06 : C Rs. 52.84]

(*B.U. March 1993*)

16. A product passes through three processes I, II and III before being finally transferred to Finished Stock Account.

10,000 units were introduced in process I at the cost of Rs. 5 per unit. The other direct expenses were:

	Process I	**Process II**	**Process III**
	Rs.	**Rs.**	**Rs.**
Sundry Materials	5,000	8,000	6,000
Direct Labour	10,000	12,000	15,000
Direct Expenses	4,000	5,000	7,000
Output (Units)	9,000	5,700	1,824
Normal Wastage	10%	5%	4%
Value of Scrap per unit	5	6	5

Production overheads are charged at 60% of direct labour to each process. The semi-finished product of each process being saleable, 1/3 output of process I and 2/3 output of process II was sold in the market at profit of 20% and 25% on cost to each process respectively. The remaining output was transferred to the next process.

Prepare three process accounts.

[**Ans.** Process I Rs 7.73 : II Rs. 13.52: III Rs. 34.16]

17. In a factory three processes are employed. The output of Process A is transferred to B and B to C. It has been the experience that wastage in Process A is 2%, Process B 5%, and Process C 10%.

The scrap value of wastage in Process A and B is Rs. 20 per 100 units and in process C Rs. 50 per 100 units.

The expenses were as follows:

	Process A	**Process B**	**Process C**
	Rs.	**Rs.**	**Rs.**
Material	10,000	8,000	6,000
Wages	5,000	4,000	3,000
Manufacturing Expenses	3,000	3,000	1,000
Oncost	2,000	2,000	500

In Process A, 5,000 units were purchased at Rs. 10,000.

The outputs were as follows:

Process	A	4,500 units
Process	B	4,400 units
Process	C	3,500 units

Prepare Process Accounts.

[**Ans.** Process A-A.W. 400 units Rs. 2,447, B-A.E. 125 units Rs. 1,301, C-A.W. 460 units Rs. 6,513]

18. A product passes through three processes A, B and C. The normal loss of each process is as follows:

Process A-3%, Process B-5% and Process C-8%

Loss of Process A was sold at 25 paise per unit, that of B at 50 paise per unit and that of C at Re. 1.00 per unit. 10,000 units were introduced to Process A at Re. 1.00 per unit. The other expenses were as follows

	Process		
	A	**B**	**C**
	Rs.	**Rs.**	**Rs.**
Materials	1,000	1,500	500
Labour	5,000	8,000	6,500
Direct Expenses	1,050	1,188	2,009
Actual Output (in units)	9,500	9,100	8,100

Prepare the Process Accounts, assuming that there were no opening or closing stocks.

(*B.Com. Delhi*)

[**Ans.** Process A - Abnormal Loss 200 units at Rs. 350; Process B - Abnormal Gain 75 units at Rs. 225; Process C - Abnormal Loss 272 units at Rs. 1,156]

19. A Product is finally obtained after it passes through three distinct processes. The following information is available from the cost records.

	Process I	**Process II**	**Process III**	**Total**
	Rs.	**Rs.**	**Rs.**	**Rs.**
Material	2,600	2,000	1,025	5,625
Direct Wages	2,250	3,680	1,400	7,330
Production overhead	–	–	–	7,330

500 units @ Rs. 4 per unit were introduced in Process I. Production overheads are absorbed as a percentage of direct wages.

The actual output and normal loss of the respective processes are given below:

	Output (units)	**Normal Loss as a Percentage of Input**	**Value of Scrap per Unit**
Process I	450	10%	Rs. 2
Process II	340	20%	Rs. 4
Process III	270	25%	Rs. 5

Prepare the process accounts and the abnormal gain/loss accounts.

(*I.C.W.A. Inter, June 1991*)

[**Ans.** Process I : Cost per unit Rs. 20 ; Process II : Abnormal Loss 20 units at Rs. 1,000; Process III : Abnormal Gain 15 units at Rs. 1,200]

20. The product of a company passes through three distinct processes to completion. From the past experience, it is ascertained that wastage is incurred in each process as under: Process A 2%; Process B 5%; Process C 10%.

The Wastage of Processes A and B is sold at Rs. 10 per 100 units and that of Process C at Rs. 80 per 100 units.

Following is the information regarding the production of March, 2007:

	Process A	Process B	Process C
	Rs.	Rs.	Rs.
Materials	12,000	8,000	4,000
Direct Labour	16,000	12,000	6,000
Machine Expenses	2,000	2,000	3,000
Other Factory expenses	3,500	3,800	4,200

20,000 units have been issued to Process A at a cost of Rs. 20,000. The output of each process has been as under:

Process	A	19,500 units
Process	B	18,800 units
Process	C	16,000 units

There was no Stock or Work-in-Progress in any process in the beginning and at the end of March.

Prepare Process Cost Accounts.

[**Ans.** Process A-A.W. 100 units Rs. 273, B-A.E. 275 units Rs. 1,171, C-A.W. 920 units Rs. 5,207]

21. A product passes through two processes A and B. The normal wastage in Process A is 3 p.c. and in Process B is 5 p.c. Wastage of Process A is sold at 25 Paise per unit and that of Process B at 50 paise per unit. 10,000 units were introduced into Process A in the beginning of March, 2005 at a cost of Re. 1 per unit. The other expenses were as follows:

	Process A	Process B
	Rs.	Rs.
Materials	1,000	1,500
Labour	5,000	8,000
Direct Expenses	1,050	1,188

Actual output was Process A 9,500 and B 9,100 units. Prepare the two Process Accounts and Abnormal Wastage and/or Abnormal Effectives Accounts, if any, assuming that there were no opening or closing work-in-progress.

(B.*Com.*, *G.N.D.U.*)

[**Ans.** Process A-Abnormal Wastage 200 units at Rs. 350, Process B-Abnormal Effectives 75 units at Rs. 225]

22. A product passes through two processes A and B. The output of process A is transferred to Process B and that of Process B to Finished Stock Account at cost. The normal wastage in Process A is 3% and in Process B is 5% of the units introduced. 25,000 units were introduced in Process A in the beginning of January, 2007 at cost of Rs. 2 per unit. Wastage of Process A is sold at 50 paise per unit and that of Process B at Re. 1 per unit. Other expenses during the month were:

	Process A Rs.	Process B Rs.
Sundry Raw Materials	5,000	7,500
Direct Labour	25,000	40,000
Production Overhead	5,250	6,500
Actual Output	24,000 units	23,000 units

Assuming that there was no opening or closing stock of either raw materials or work-in-progress, prepare Process Accounts, the Abnormal Wastage and Abnormal Effectives Accounts for January, 2007.

(B.*Com. G.N.D.U., April 1977*)

[**Ans.** Process A-Abnormal Wastage 250 units at Rs. 875, Process B-Abnormal effectives 200 units at Rs. 1,200]

23. A material passes through three processes to manufacture a finished product. The information relating to the year 2005 is as follows:

	Process I	Process II	Process III
Raw Materials used (Tons)	1,000		
Cost per Ton (Rs.)	200		
Manufacturing Wages (Rs.)	87,500	39,500	10,710
Weight Lost (Percentage of input of the Process)	4%	10%	20%
Scrap (sale Price Rs. 50 per ton) (Tons)	50	30	51
Sale Price per ton (Rs.)	360	500	800
Factory Overhead (Rs.)	31,300	11,167	15,837

Prepare Process Cost Accounts assuming that 2/3rd output of Process I and 1/2 output of Process II are passed on to the next process and the balance are sold.

[Ans. Process I-Profit Rs. 3,763; Process II- Loss Rs. 1,075; Process III- Loss Rs. 30,072]

24. In a factory a product passes through three processes: A, B and C. In each process 5% of the total weight put in is lost and 10% is scrap which realises Rs. 10 per ton from process A, Rs. 15 per ton from Process B and Rs. 20 per ton from Process C.

The following further details are available:

	Processes		
	A	**B**	**C**
Materials used in Tons	3,300	2,000	1,000
	Rs.	Rs.	Rs.
Cost of Materials per ton	30	40	50
Labour	8,000	5,000	2,000
Oncost	7,000	2,000	1,000

The Products are dealt with as follows:

	A	B	C
Sent to Warehouse	25%	50%	100%
Sent to Next Process	75%	50%	–

Prepare Process Accounts.

[**Ans.** Cost per unit-Process A Rs. 39.465; Process B Rs. 46.98; Process C Rs. 55.497]

25. The product of a company passes through three distinct processes to completion. From the past experience it is ascertained that wastage occurred in each process is as under: Process A 2%; Process B 5%; Process C 10%.

The wastage of process A and B is sold at Rs. 5 per 100 units and that of process C at Rs. 20 per 100 units. Following is the information regarding the production of March, 2006:

	Process A	**Process B**	**Process C**
Materials	4,000	2,000	1,000
Direct Wages	6,000	4,000	3,000
Works Overhead	1,000	1,000	1,500

20,000 units have been issued to process A at a cost of Rs. 8,000. The output of each process has been as under:

Process A	19,500 units
Process B	18,800 units
Process C	16,000 units

There is no stock or work-in-progress in any process. Prepare Process Cost Accounts.

(H.P.U. B.Com., 2007)

[**Ans.** Process A Abnormal Wastage 100 units Rs. 97; Process B Abnormal Effectives 275 units Rs. 384; Process C Abnormal Wastage 920 units Rs. 1,704]

26. A product is obtained after passing it through three processes. The following information is collected for April, 2007:

	Processes		
	I	II	III
Direct Materials	Rs. 5,200	Rs. 3,960	Rs. 5,924
Direct Wages	Rs. 4,000	Rs. 6,000	Rs. 8,000
Output in units during the month	950	840	750
Normal Loss	5%	10%	15%
Value of Scrap per unit	Rs. 4	Rs. 8	Rs. 10

ADDITIONAL INFORMATION:

1,000 units at Rs. 6 each were introduced in Process 1. There was no stock of materials or work-in-progress at the beginning or at the end of that month. The production overhead was Rs. 18,000 for that month. Prepare the Process Accounts indicating Normal Loss, Abnormal Loss and Abnormal Gain.

(C.A. Inter)

[**Ans.** Process I - Cost Rs. 20 per unit : Process II - Cost Rs. 40 per unit; Abnormal Loss 15 units - Rs. 600; Process III - Cost Rs. 76 per unit; Abnormal Gain 36 units - Rs. 2,736]

27. The output from Process A totalled 3,500 units. It was considered that 100 units were an abnormal loss. Normal loss allowed was 10%. The other information is given below:

Material	@ Rs. 5 per unit
Labour	Rs. 4,000
Overheads	Rs. 3,350
Wastage Realised	Rs. 2.50 per unit
Direct Expenses	Rs. 650

The output from Process B is normally 95% of input into the process. The actual output, however, was of 3,350 units. The costs incurred in Process B were:

Labour — Rs. 5,250

Overheads — 10% of the cost of units transferred from Process A plus Labour cost but after deducting the overheads.

Direct Expenses — Rs. 2,736

The units scrapped are sold @ Rs. 3 per unit. From Process B, the finished output is obtained. Prepare Process A, Process B, Abnormal Gain and Abnormal Loss Accounts. Also show the working.

[**Ans.** Input of A Process 4,000 units, Abnormal Loss in A Process 100 units Rs. 750, Abnormal Gain in Process B 25 units Rs. 275]

28. From the following figures, show the three processes of manufacture. The production of each process is passed on to the next process immediately on completion.

	A	B	C
	Rs.	Rs.	Rs.
Wages and Materials	30,400	12,000	29,250
Works Oncost	5,600	5,250	6,000
Production in Units	36,000	37,500	48,000
Stock (units from preceeding Process 1st July, 2009)	–	4,000	16,500
Stock (units from preceeding Process) 31st July, 2009	–	1,000	5,500

[**Ans.** Cost per unit A – Re. 1.00, B – Rs. 1.50, C – Rs. 2.25]

29. From the following particulars of X Chemical Corporation Private Ltd., prepare process cost accounts showing the cost of the output and unit at each stage of manufacture. The value at which units are charged to processes two and three is the cost per unit of processes I and I plus II respectively.

	Process I	Process II	Process III
	Rs.	Rs.	Rs.
Raw Materials	10,000	–	–
Factory Wages	3,500	6,000	8,500
Machine Expenses	3,000	2,500	3,500
Sundry Factory Expenses	4,000	3,800	3,710
Sundry Materials	–	7,380	–

The gross production in Process I was 515 gallons. The wastage in different processes were Process I, 15 gallons, Process II, 20 gallons, and Process III, 10 gallons. There were opening stocks of 20 and 40 gallons in Process II and III respectively. At the end of the period there were stocks of 100 gallons in Process II and of 20 gallons in Process III.

[**Ans.** Cost per gallon - I - Rs. 41, II - Rs. 92.25, III - Rs. 132.82]

30. The information given below is extracted from the books of a Factory producing a commodity in the manufacture of which three processes are involved. Prepare Process Cost Accounts showing the cost of output and the cost per unit at each stage of manufacture.

(1) The operations in each process are completed daily.

(2) The value at which units are to be charged to Processes two and three is the cost per unit of Processes one and one plus two respectively.

	Process No.		
	1	**2**	**3**
	Rs.	**Rs.**	**Rs.**
Direct Wages	2,500	5,000	6,500
Machine Expenses	1,400	1,200	1,200
Factroy Oncost	1,100	1,550	900
Raw Material consumed	8,000	–	–
	Units	Units	Units
Production (gross)	2,750	–	–
Wastage	150	210	200
Stock, 1st Jan. 2004	–	250	500
Stock, 31st Jan. 2004	–	440	100

[**Ans.** Cost per unit Process 1 - Rs. 5.00, Process 2 - Rs. 9.00, Process 3 - Rs. 13.33]

31. The product of a company passes through two processes X and Y. It is ascertained from past experience that the loss incurred in two processes has been 2% and 5% respectively on the units entering the process concerned. The loss of process X and Y has a scrap value of Rs. 2 per unit.

For the month of April, 2007 the following information has been given:
Units Introduced in Process X : 4,000 units at a cost of Rs. 8 per unit.

Other Expenses were:

	Process X	**Process Y**
	Rs.	**Rs.**
Materials Used	16,000	6,000
Direct Wages	24,000	16,000
Factory Overhead	4,000	2,000
	Units	Units
Output	3,900	3,850
Stock : April 1	400	600
April 30	300	800
Stock Valuation on April 1, per unit	19	27

Stocks on 30th April are to be valued at cost as shown by month's process accounts. Prepare Process Accounts and Process Stock Accounts.

[**Ans.** Process X : Abnormal Loss 20 units at Rs. 387; Process cost per unit Rs. 19.35; Process Y : Abnormal gain 50 units @ Rs. 1,327; Process Cost per unit Rs. 26.54]

32. The product of company passes through three different processes P, Q and R. It is ascertained from the past experience that loss in each process is incurred as under:

Process	P	2%
	Q	5%
	R	10%

The percentage of loss in each process is computed on the basis of number of units entering the process concerned. The loss of each process has a scrap value. The loss of processes P and Q is sold at Rs. 3 per unit and that of process R at Rs. 12 per unit. The company gives the following information for the month of March 2002:

2,000 units of crude materials were introduced in process P at a cost of Rs. 24 per unit:

	P	**Q**	**R**
	Rs.	**Rs.**	**Rs.**
Material Consumed	24,000	9,000	6,000
Direct Labour	36,000	24,000	18,000
Works Expenses	6,000	3,000	9,000
	Units	Units	Units
Output	1,950	1,925	1,590
Stock (March 1st)	200	300	500
Stock (March 31st)	150	400	–
Stock Valuation on March 1st (per unit)	57	81	109.5

Stock on 31st March, 2002 is to be valued at cost as shown by month's production accounts. Prepare the Process Accounts.

[**Ans.** P Rs. 58.10; Q Rs. 79.83; R Rs. 107.70]

(*B.U. October 1992*)

33. The product of a company passes through three different processes A, B, and C. It is ascertained from past experience that loss in each process is incurred as under:

Process A : 2%, Process B : 5%, Process C : 10%.

The percentage of loss in each case is computed on the basis of number of units entering the process concerned.

The loss of each process has a scrap value. The loss of processes A and B is sold at Re. 1 per unit and that of process C at Rs. 4 per unit.

The company gives you the following information for the month of July, 2003:

2,000 units of crude material were introduced in process A at a cost of Rs. 8 per unit. Besides this, the following were other expenses:

	Process A	Process B	Process C
Materials consumed	8,000	3,000	2,000
Direct Labour	12,000	8,000	6,000
Works expenses	2,000	1,000	3,000
	Units	Units	Units
Output	1,950	1,925	1,590
Stock: July 1	200	300	500
July 31	150	400	–
Stock: Valuation	Rs.	Rs.	Rs.
On July 1, per unit	19	27	36.5

Stocks on 31st July, 2003 are to be valued at cost as shown by month's production accounts. Prepare the Process Accounts.

[**Ans.** Process A – Abnormal Loss (10 units) Rs. 194, Process cost per unit Rs. 19.368; Process B – Abnormal Gain (25 units) Rs. 665; Process Cost per unit Rs. 26.611 Process C – Abnormal Loss (52 units) Rs. 1,867. Process Cost per unit Rs. 35.90].

34. A product passes through two processes – A and B. Output of Process A is passed to Process B at cost plus 25% profit and finished output is similarly transferred to Finished Stock Account at cost plus 25% profit. There was no partly finished work in either process on 31st March, 2007, on which date the following further information was available:

	Process A	Process B
	Rs.	Rs.
Materials Consumed	6,000	18,000
Labour	9,000	12,000
Closing Stock (at prime Cost)	3,000	9,000

Out of the output of the finished stocks, a portion remained at hand valued at Rs. 13,500 and the balance was sold for Rs. 43,500.

Prepare the necessary accounts and calculate the unrealised profit included in closing stock and actual profit made.

[**Ans.** Profit A Rs. 3,000; B Rs. 9,000; Finished Stock 12,000; Unrealised Profit Rs. 4,020; Actual Profit Rs. 19,980]

35. The following are the details in respect of two processes, X and Y, of a process industry:

	Process X	Process Y
	Rs.	Rs.
Material	10,000	–
Labour	12,000	20,000
Overheads	6,000	10,000
Closing stock (valued at total cost)	4,000	8,000

The output of process X is transferred to Process Y at a price calculated to give a profit of 20% on the transfer price and the output of Process Y is charged to Finished Stock on a similar basis.

Of the output transferred to Finished Stock, stock costing Rs. 10,000 remained unsold at the end of accounting period and the balance realised Rs. 1,00,000. There was no opening or closing work-in-progress. Show Process Accounts, Finished Stock A/c and prepare a statement of total profits.

(*B.U. May 1982*)

[**Ans.** Profit: X Rs. 6,000, Y – Rs. 13,000, Finished Goods Rs. 45,000 and Total Rs. 64,000]

36. A product passes through three processes to completion-A, B and C. The output of each process is charged to the next process at a price calculated to give a profit of 25% on cost. The output of Process C is charged to Finished Stock Account on a similar basis. There was no work-in-progress in any process at 31st March, 2005, on which date the following information was obtained:

	Process A	Process B	Process C
	Rs.	Rs.	Rs.
Materials Used	4,000	6,000	2,000
Labour	6,000	4,000	8,000
Stock (at Prime Cost) 31st March, 2005	2,000	4,000	6,000

There was no stock in hand on 1st April, 2004 and the question of overheads has been ignored. Of the goods passed into Finished Stock, Rs. 4,000 remained in hand on 31st March, 2005 and the balance was sold for Rs. 36.000.

Prepare Process Accounts and calculate the amount of unrealised profit and actual profit made.

[**Ans.** Profit A Rs. 2,000, B Rs. 4,000, C Rs. 6,000; Finished Stock Rs. 10,000; Unrealised Profit Rs. 2,917; Actual Profit Rs. 19,083]

37. Product A passes through three processes before it is completed. The output of each process is charged to the next process at a price calculated to give a profit of 20% on transfer price (*i.e.*, 25% on cost price). The output of Process III is charged to finished stock account on a similar basis. There was no work-in-progress at the beginning of the year and overheads have been ignored. Stocks in each process have been valued at prime cost of the process. The following data are obtained at the end of March, 2004.

Details	Process I	Process II	Process III	Finished Stock.
	Rs.	Rs.	Rs.	Rs.
Direct Materials	20,000	5,000	4,000	–
Direct Wages	15,000	10,000	20,000	–
Stock on 31st March	5,000	6,500	9,500	5,000
Sales during the year	–	–	–	1,10,000

From the above information prepare:

(*a*) Process cost accounts showing the profit element at each stage;

(*b*) Actual realised profit, and

(*c*) Stock valuation as would appear in the Balance Sheet.

[**Ans.** (*a*) Profit: Process I – Rs. 7,500, Process II – Rs. 11,500, Process III – Rs. 18,000 and Finished Stock Rs. 25,000 (*b*) Rs. 57,078, (*c*) Rs. 21,078]

38. Product B passes through three processes before it is transferred to finished stock. The following information is obtained for the month of December:

Details	Process I	Process II	Process III	Finished Stock
	Rs.	Rs.	Rs.	Rs.
Opening Stock	5,000	8,000	10,000	20,000
Direct Materials	40,000	12,000	15,000	–
Direct Wages	35,000	40,000	35,000	–
Production Overheads	20,000	24,000	20,000	–
Closing Stock	10,000	4,000	15,000	30,000
Profit % on Transfer price (to next process)	25%	20%	10%	–
Inter-process Profit for Opening Stock	–	1,395	2,690	6,534

Stocks in processes are valued at prime cost and finished stock has been valued at the price at which it is received from Process III. Sales during the period were Rs. 4,00,000.

Prepare and compute:

(*a*) Process cost accounts showing profit element at each stage:

(*b*) Actual realised profit, and

(*c*) Stock valuation for Balance Sheet purpose.

(*G.N.D.U., B.Com., April 1998*)

[**Ans.** (*a*) Process I – Rs. 30,000, Process II – Rs. 50,000, Process III – Rs. 35,000 and Finished Stock – Rs. 60,000, (*b*) Rs. 1,71,084, (*c*) Rs. 44,465]

15

Process Costing-II
(Joint Products and By-Products)

In many industries, the manufacture of some products is accompanied by the manufacture of some other commodities. The manufacture of these other commodities is unavoidable and these may be treated as Joint Products or By-Products.

Joint products refer to a group of individual products of significant relative sales value simultaneously produced from the same raw material. The basic essential features of joint products are:

(*i*) These products cannot be produced separately.

(*ii*) These products are obtained or produced simultaneously from the common process and common raw material.

(*iii*) These products carry almost equal economic importance or sales value.

Oil refining is the typical example of joint products. In the process of refining oil, joint products such as motor spirit, kerosene, fuel oil, lubricating oil, wax, tar and asphalt are obtained from crude petroleum. Other examples are tobacco manufacturing, canned-product industry, meat-packing industry etc.

By-products refer to any saleable or usable value incidentally produced in addition to the main product. The basic essential features of by-products are as follows:

(*i*) These products cannot be produced separately.

(*ii*) By-products emerge in the process of manufacturing the main product.

(*iii*) These products have a sale value (or economic importance) which is comparatively lower than that of the main product.

For example, in case of sugar industry, the production of sugar is accompanied by bagasse and molasses. Bagasse and molasses cannot be produced separately and their sale value is lower than that of sugar which is treated as the main product.

Thus, the industries producing joint products and those producing by-products basically have the difference in degree and not in kind. If a manufacturing concern is engaged in producing two or more commodities from the same raw material and equal economic importance is attached to these commodities, the manufacturing concern can be said to be producing joint products. But where one or more of these commodities are considered relatively less important than the others, the manufacturing concern is said to be manufacturing by-products.

Co-products and Joint products: Generally speaking, no distinction is made between co-products and joint products and both are treated as the same thing. But it should be remembered that co-products do not always arise from the same manufacturing operation or the same raw material and the manufacturer carries the necessary control over the quantity of co-products. In a bakery, bread, cake, pastry, cake-rusk and biscuits of various types produced in different quantities as per its requirements, are the examples of co-products. On the other hand, in case of a meat packing concern, the quantity of various joint products remains unchanged and these are obtained in the common process from the same raw material.

OBJECTIVES OF ACCOUNTING FOR JOINT PRODUCTS AND BY-PRODUCTS

The principal objectives of analysis of costs and accounting of joint products and by-products are:

(*i*) To determine the unit cost of joint products and by-products.
(*ii*) To determine the profit or loss on each line of product.
(*iii*) To assist in the proper inventory valuation.
(*iv*) To determine the pattern of production and the most profitable sales-mix.
(*v*) To study the effect on costs and profits due to change in the production of joint and by-products for the ultimate aim of price fixation.

ACCOUNTING FOR JOINT PRODUCTS

The various joint products of an industry cannot be identified as different individual products until a certain stage of production known as 'split-off point' or `separation point'. It is the stage or the point at which joint products are separated from each other. All costs incurred prior to the split-off point are known as 'pre-split-off point costs' or 'Joint product costs' while the costs incurred after the split-off point are known as 'Post-split-off point costs' or 'separate costs' or 'subsequent costs'. The separate costs can be identified with and charged to the various joint products directly and conveniently since these costs are incurred for specific joint products. But the basic problem in joint product costing is the apportionment of the joint product costs to different products. The apportionment of the joint costs is generally made on an arbitrary base which may not be very logical. As such it becomes very difficult to determine the true or the accurate cost of joint products. The principal methods of apportioning joint product costs to various products are:

(*i*) Average Unit Cost Method
(*ii*) Physical Units Method
(*iii*) Market Value Method
(*iv*) Points Value Method or Survey Method
(*v*) Contribution Margin Method
(*vi*) Reverse Cost Method or Net Value at Separation Point Method.

(*i*) Average Unit Cost Method

Under this method, the joint costs of manufacture incurred prior to the split-off point, are divided by the total quantity of joint products produced, to get an average cost per unit. This method assumes that since all the units of joint products are obtained in the same process, these should be made to bear the joint costs equally. The basic advantage of this method is its simplicity but it can be adopted only if all the products, obtained from the common process, can be expressed in terms of the same unit. Under this method, the joint cost per unit of each joint product shall be the same. The application of this method can be explained with the help of the following example:

Illustration 1

AB Co. produces three products X, Y and Z which originate from a common process. The joint costs of manufacture amount to Rs. 77,500. The output of X, Y and Z is 3,000, 5,000 and 7,500 units respectively. Apportion the joint costs of manufacture to various products on the basis of Average Unit Cost Method.

Solution

$$\text{Average cost per unit} = \frac{\text{Total Joint Costs}}{\text{Total Output}}$$

$$= \frac{\text{Rs. } 77{,}500}{15{,}500 \text{ units}}$$

= Rs. 5 per unit.

As such the joint costs of manufacture will be apportioned @ Rs. 5 per unit.

Statement showing the Apportionment of Joint Costs

Product	No. of Units	Cost per unit	Share in Joint Costs
X	3,000	5.00	15,000
Y	5,000	5.00	25,000
Z	7,500	5.00	37,500
	15,500		77,500

(*ii*) Physical Unit Method

Under this method, joint costs are apportioned to the various joint products on the basis of some physical co-efficient, e.g., unit or weight of products, percentage of raw material content, calories etc. For example, if the content of raw material in joint product 'A' is 40% and in joint product 'B' 60%, the joint cost of Rs. 1,500 will be apportioned to products A and B in the ratio of 40 : 60.

The loss, if any, arising in the process, shall also be apportioned to the various joint products in the ratio of their physical units. This method can be applied where the joint products are measurable in terms of common physical unit.

Illustration 2

The following data have been extracted from the books of North Coke Co.:

Items	Yield in kgs. per ton of coal
Coke	648
Coal Tar	45
Benzol	18
Sulphate of Ammonia	9
Gas	180
Waste	100
	1,000 kgs.

The price of coal is Rs. 150 per ton. Direct labour and overhead costs to point of split-off are Rs. 250 and Rs. 400 respectively per ton of coal.

Calculate material, labour, overhead and total cost of each product on the basis of weight.

Solution

Statement of Cost

Products	Yield per ton of coal (in Kgs.)	% of total yield	Apportioned Cost			Total Cost
			Material	Labour	Overhead	
			Rs. P.	Rs. P.	Rs. P.	Rs.
Coke	648	72	108.00	180.00	288.00	576
Coal Tar	45	5	7.50	12.50	20.00	40
Benzol	18	2	3.00	5.00	8.00	16
Sulphate of Ammonia	9	1	1.50	2.50	4.00	8
Gas	180	20	30.00	50.00	80.00	160
Total	900	100	150.00	250.00	400.00	800

Note: Waste having no value has been ignored. Alternatively, the weight of waste may be distributed among various products on the basis of weight and joint costs apportioned accordingly. The result will, however, be the same.

(iii) Market Value Method

Market value for the purpose of apportioning joint product costs may be of two types:

(*a*) Market Value at Separation Point, and
(*b*) Market Value after further processing.

Market Value at Separation Point

Under this method, joint product costs are apportioned to different products on the basis of the selling prices or sales values at the separation point. Thus, this method takes into account a product's ability to absorb the costs. But so far as the use of selling prices in apportioning joint costs is concerned, the results shall be completely invalid and as such the use of sales values is made to apportion joint costs equitably. Sales value refers to the weighted sales value i.e., quantity produced × selling price per unit of joint product.

Market Value after Further Processing

Under this method, joint product-costs are apportioned to different products on the basis of the selling prices or sales value obtained after further processing. This method is generally applied where the market value of the products at the point of separation cannot be ascertained and the cost of further processing is proportionate to the sales prices or sales values.

Illustration 3

The joint cost of manufacturing 1,000 units of A, 2,000 units of B and 3,000 units of C is Rs. 24,000. The selling prices of products A, B and C are Rs. 5, Rs. 4 and Rs. 3 respectively. The products do not require any further processing costs after split-off point.

Your are required to apportion the joint costs

(*a*) on sales price basis; and

(*b*) on sales value basis.

Solution

(*a*) Statement Showing the Apportionment of Joint Cost on Sales Price basis

Products	Production (units)	Selling Price (Per unit)	Apportioned Joint Cost (5:4:3)	Joint Cost per unit
		Rs.	Rs.	Rs.
A	1,000	5.00	10,000	10.00
B	2,000	4.00	8,000	4.00
C	3,000	3.00	6,000	2.00
	6,000		24,000	

(b) Statement Showing the Apportionment of Joint Cost on Sales Value basis

Products	Production (units)	Selling Price (Per unit)	Total Sales Value	Apportioned Joint Cost (5:8:9)	Joint Cost per unit
		Rs.	Rs.	Rs.	Rs. P.
A	1,000	5	5,000	5,455	5.455
B	2,000	4	8,000	8,727	4.364
C	3,000	3	9,000	9,818	3.273
	6,000		22,000	24,000	

Illustration 4

The cost of 100 litres of crude oil and processing it into different products is Rs. 120 in XYZ Oil Refinery Ltd. The standard yield per 100 litres of crude oil and its market value per litre are indicated below. Compute the unit cost of each product:

	Standard yield per 100 litres of crude	Market value per litre Rs.
Petrol	32.0	1.20
Lubricating Oil	5.0	2.00
Fuel Oil	50.0	0.50
Kerosene	8.0	0.75
Gas Oil	3.0	0.30
Loss	2.0	0.00
	100.0	

(*I.C.W.A. Final*)

Solution

Products	Production (Litres)	Market Value per litre Rs. P.	Total Market Value Rs. P.	Apportioned Joint Cost Rs. P.	Cost per litre Rs. P.
Petrol	32.0	1.20	38.40	57.40	1.80
Lubricating Oil	5.0	2.00	10.00	15.00	3.00
Fuel Oil	50.0	0.50	25.00	37.30	0.74
Kerosene	8.0	0.75	6.00	9.00	1.12
Gas Oil	3.0	0.30	0.90	1.30	0.43
	98.0		80.30	120.00	

Note: Loss having no value has been ignored. Alternatively, the weight of loss may be distributed among various products on the basis of weight and joint costs apportioned accordingly. The result will, however, be the same.

(*iv*) Points Value Method or Survey Method

Under this method, joint costs are apportioned on the basis of point values or percentages assigned to individual products to denote their relative importance. These point values are determined after considering all the important factors involved in the production and sale of joint products through extensive survey.

Illustration 5

The joint costs of manufacturing 500 units of A, 3,000 units of B and 2,000 units of C are as follows:

	Rs.
Materials	15,000
Wages	9,000
Overhead	6,000
Total	30,000

You are required to apportion the joint costs to the products if the values assigned for A, B, and C on the basis of technical estimates are 4, 3 and 2 per unit respectively.

Solution

Statement Showing the Apportionment of Joint Costs

Products	Production (units)	Point Value Assigned per unit	Total Value	Apportioned Joint Cost (2:9:4 ratio)	Joint Cost per unit
				Rs.	Rs.
A	500	4	2,000	4,000	8
B	3,000	3	9,000	18,000	6
C	2,000	2	4,000	8,000	4
	5,500		15,000	30,000	

(v) Contribution Margin Method

This method involves the use of marginal costing technique for the apportionment of joint costs. Under this method, the variable cost or marginal cost of the joint process is apportioned on the basis of the weight or quantity of joint products and the fixed cost on the basis of marginal contribution provided by each of them. This method provides useful information to the management for determining the most profitable product-mix or sales-mix.

Illustration 6

From the following information relating to joint products A, B, and C, apportion the marginal cost and fixed cost on suitable basis and ascertain the profit or loss for each of the joint products:

Sales: Product A : 250 kgs. @ Rs. 60 per kg.
Product B : 300 kgs. @ Rs. 30 per kg.
Product C : 200 kgs. @ Rs. 50 per kg.

Joint Costs:

Variable Cost	Rs. 15,000
Fixed Cost	Rs. 11,400
	26,400

Solution

Statement of Cost and Profit

Products	Sales Value	Pro-rated Variable Cost (25:30:20 ratio)	Marginal Contribution	Pro-rated Fixed Cost (10:3:6 ratio)	Profit
	Rs.	Rs.	Rs.	Rs.	Rs.
A	15,000	5,000	10,000	6,000	4,000
B	9,000	6,000	3,000	1,800	1,200
C	10,000	4,000	6,000	3,600	2,400
		15,000	19,000	11,400	7,600

(*vi*) Reverse Cost Method or Net Value Method

Under this method, the joint product costs are apportioned to different products on the basis of the estimated cost at the separation point. The estimated cost at the separation point is ascertained by deducting from the sales value of each joint product, the estimated net profit, selling and distribution expenses, if any, and the subsequent processing costs after separation point.

Illustration 7

A factory produces three products A, B and C which originate from a joint process. The actual joint costs are:

	Rs.
Materials	10,200
Labour	11,500
Overhead	7,500
	29,200

Subsequent expenses are as follows:

	A	B	C
Material	2,500	1,200	1,400
Labour	1,900	1,600	2,000
Overhead	1,500	900	1,050
	5,900	3,700	4,450
Selling Prices	30,000	20,000	15,000
Estimated Profit on Sales	40%	30%	25%

Prepare a statement showing the apportionment of joint costs over different products.

Solution

Statement Showing the Apportionment of Joint Costs

	A	B	C	Total
	Rs.	Rs.	Rs.	Rs.
Selling Price	30,000	20,000	15,000	65,000
Less: Estimated Profit	12,000	6,000	3,750	21,750
Total Cost	18,000	14,000	11,250	43,250
Less: Subsequent Expenses	5,900	3,700	4,450	14,050
Basis of Apportionment of Joint Costs	12,100	10,300	6,800	29,200

Joint product costs shall be apportioned in the ratio of 121:103:68. Hence, A's share in joint costs will be: Rs.

$$29{,}200 \times \frac{12{,}100}{29{,}200} = 12{,}100$$

B's share in joint costs will be:

$$29{,}200 \times \frac{10{,}300}{29{,}200} = \quad 10{,}300$$

C's share in joint costs will be:

$$29{,}200 \times \frac{6{,}800}{29{,}200} = \quad 6{,}800$$

Total 29,200

Illustration 8

A factory produces three products, A, B, and C, which originate from a joint process. The joint costs of manufacture are:

	Rs.
Materials	1,00,000
Wages	18,000
Overheads	8,000
	1,26,000

Subsequent costs of processing are:

	Product A	**Product B**	**Product C**
Materials	7,000	6,500	2,900
Wages	2,100	2,000	1,900
Overheads	900	500	1,200
Total	10,000	9,000	6,000
Total Sales Values	1,00,000	70,000	60,000
Estimated Profit on Sales Value	20%	30%	40%

Prepare a statement showing the apportionment of joint costs and prepare necessary accounts showing total cost of joint products.

Solution

Statement Showing Apportionment of Joint Costs

	Product A	**Product B**	**Product C**	**Total**
	Rs.	**Rs.**	**Rs.**	**Rs.**
Sales Value	1,00,000	70,000	60,000	2,30,000
Less: Estimated Profit	20,000	21,000	24,000	65,000
Total Cost	80,000	49,000	36,000	1,65,000
Less: Selling and Distribution Expenses Apportioned in the Ratio of Sales Value	6,087	4,261	3,652	14,000
Cost of Production	73,913	44,739	32,348	1,51,000
Less: Subsequent Costs	10,000	9,000	6,000	25,000
Share in Joint Cost of Manufacture	63,913	35,739	26,348	1,26,000

(*i*) Joint costs of manufacture are to the apportioned in the ratio of 63, 913 : 35, 739 : 26, 348.

(*ii*) Calculation of selling and distribution expenses has been made as follows:

Total Cost of Products A, B and C	1,65,000
Less: Subsequent Process Costs (Total)	25,000
Total Joint Cost	1,40,000
Total Joint Cost of Manufacture	1,26,000
Balance taken as Selling and Distribution Expenses	14,000

Product A Account

	Rs.		Rs.
To Share in Joint Cost of Manufacture	63,913	By Total Cost	80,000
To Materials (Separate)	7,000		
To Wages (Separate)	2,100		
To Overheads (Separate)	900		
Cost of Production	73,913		
To Selling and Distribution Expenses	6,087		
	80,000		80,000

Product B Account

	Rs.		Rs.
To Share in Joint Cost of Manufacture	35,739	By Total Cost	49,000
To Materials (Separate)	6,500		
To Wages (Separate)	2,000		
To Overheads (Separate)	500		
Cost of Production	44,739		
To Selling and Distribution Expenses	4,261		
	49,000		49,000

Product C Account

	Rs.		Rs.
To Share in Joint Cost of Manufacture	26,348	By Total Cost	36,000
To Materials (Separate)	2,900		
To Wages (Separate)	1,900		
To Overheads (Separate)	1,200		
Cost of Production	32,348		
To Selling and Distribution Expenses	3,652		
	36,000		36,000

ACCOUNTING FOR BY-PRODUCTS

The various methods of accounting for by-products may be grouped as follows:

(1) Non-cost Methods, and (2) Cost Methods.

Non-cost methods are also known as sales value methods. Under these methods, costs are not assigned to by-products but income or revenue arising from the sale of by-products is credited to Profit and Loss Account or to the Main-Product Account.

Under the cost methods, an attempt is made to apportion a part of the joint costs to the by-products in the most equitable manner with a view to ascertain the cost of by-products separately.

Non-cost Methods: The principal of non-cost methods of accounting for by-products may be given as follows:

(*i*) Crediting the Sale Value of By-products to Other Income: This method is generally adopted in cases where the value of the by-product is very small or negligible. Under this method, the sale value of by-product is credited to Profit and Loss Account as other income. If the by-product is not sold and is kept in stock, its value for Balance Sheet purposes shall be taken as nil. Thus, if there is a time gap between production and sale of by-products, this method is going to give inaccurate results.

(*ii*) By-product Sales Added to Main-product Sales: Under this method, the sales value of by-product is added to the sales of the main-product and profit or loss is computed by deducting the total cost from the combined sales figures of main-product and by-product. This method is based on the assumption that by-products are sold in the form in which they emerge in the manufacturing process. Stock of by-products in hand, has no value for balance sheet purposes.

Illustration 9

In manufacturing 1,000 units of a product 'A', 50 units of by-product 'B' emerge. The process costs are:

Material	28,000
Wages	12,000
Overhead	5,000
	45,000

Sales value:

(*i*) Main-product 'A'	Rs. 62 per unit
(*ii*) By-product 'B'	Rs. 10 per unit

Ascertain the profit or loss by adding the sales of by-product to the sales value of main product 'A'.

Solution

Statement of Profit

		Rs.
Sales of Main-Product 'A' (1,000 units @ Rs. 62 per unit)		62,000
Sale of By-product 'B' (50 units @ Rs. 10 per unit)		500
Total Sales		62,500
Less Process Costs:	Rs.	
Materials	28,000	
Wages	12,000	
Overhead	5,000	45,000
Profit		17,500

(*iii*) By-product Value Deducted from Total Cost:

Under this method, the sales value of by-product is deducted from the total cost of the main-product. The sales value of the by-product may be deducted either from the cost of production or cost of sales of the main-product. Thus, the cost of the main-product is reduced by the sales value of the by-product. Stock of by-product in hand for balance sheet purposes is shown at its selling price:

Illustration 10

The cost of processing and selling product 'X' is as follows:

Direct Materials	5,000
Direct Wages	2,500
Factory Overhead	1,500
Administration and Selling Overhead	1,400

A by-product 'N' emerges in the processing which is sold for Rs. 500. Calculate the total cost of the main-product 'X' by deducting the by-product value from cost of production of 'X'.

Solution

Statement of Cost of Product 'X'

		Rs.
Direct Materials		5,000
Direct Wages		2,500
Factory Overhead		1,500
		9,000
Less: Sale of By-product 'N'		500
	Factory Cost	8,500
Administration and Selling Overhead		1,400
Total Cost		9,900

Illustration 11

A particular brand of phenyle passes through three important processes. During the week ending 31st March, 2007, 300 gross bottles were produced. The cost books show the following data:

	Process A	Process B	Process C
Materials	4,200	2,400	1,500
Wages	3,000	2,700	2,400
Direct Expenses	600	400	450
Cost of Bottles	–	1,500	–
Cost of Corks	–	–	150

The indirect expenses for the week were Rs. 1,350. The by-products of process B were sold for Rs. 300. The residue of Process C was sold for Rs. 50.

Prepare the Process Accounts.

Solution

Process A Account

(Output : 300 Gross Bottles)

	Rs.		Rs.
To Materials	4,200		
To Wages	3,000		
To Direct Expenses	600	By Process B A/c (Cost per gross Bottles = Rs. 27.67)	8,300
To Indirect Expenses	500		
	8,300		8,300

Process B Account

(Output : 300 Gross Bottles)

	Rs.		Rs.
To Process A A/c	8,300	By Sale of By-products	300
To Materials	2,400		
To Wages	2,700		
To Direct Expenses	400	By Process C A/c	15,450
To Cost of Bottles	1,500	(Cost per gross Bottles = Rs. 51.50)	
To Indirect Expenses	450		
	15,750		15,750

Process C Account

(Output : 300 Gross Bottles)

	Rs.		Rs.
To Process B A/c	15,450	By Sale of Residue	50
To Materials	1,500		
To Wages	2,400		
To Direct Expenses	450	By Finished Stock A/c	20,300
To Cost of Corks	150	(Cost per gross Bottles = Rs. 67.67)	
To Indirect Expenses	400		
	20,350		20,350

Note: Indirect expenses amounting to Rs. 1,350 have been apportioned to three processes in the ratio of wages.

Illustration 12

The following details are extracted from the costing records of Amrit Oil Mills for the year ended 31st March, 2006:

Purchase of Copra : 5,400 Tons at a cost of Rs. 2,20,000.

	Crushing Rs.	Refining Rs.	Finishing Rs.
Cost of Labour	2,750	1,100	1,650
Electric Power	660	396	264
Sundry Materials	110	2,200	–
Repairs to Machinery	308	363	154
Steam	660	495	495
Factory Expenses	1,452	726	242
Cost of Casks	–	–	8,250

3,200 Tons of crude oil were produced. 2,600 tons of oil were produced by the Refining Process. 2,550 Tons of Refined oil were finished for delivery.

Copra sacks sold	Rs. 440
1,925 Tons of Copra Residue Sold	Rs. 12,100
Loss: in weight in crushing	275 Tons
500 Tons of by-product obtained from Refining Process sold for	Rs. 7,425

Prepare (*i*) Copra Crushing Process A/c (*ii*) Refining Process A/c and (*iii*) Finishing Process including Casking A/c.

Solution

Copra Crushing Process Account

Particulars	Tons	Rs.	Particulars	Tons	Rs.
To Copra used	5,400	2,20,000	By Sale of Copra Residue	1,925	12,100
To Cost of Labour		2,750	By Sale of Copra Sacks	–	440
To Electric Power		660	By Loss in weight in Crushing	275	–
To Sundry Materials		110			
To Repairs of Machinery		308	By Refining Process A/c (Transfer) (Cost per ton Rs. 2,13,400/3,200 Tons = Rs. 66.69)	3,200	2,13,400
To Steam		660			
To Factory Expenses		1,452			
	5,400	2,25,940		5,400	2,25,940

Refining Process Account

Particulars	Tons	Rs.	Particulars	Tons	Rs.
To Crushing Process A/c	3,200	2,13,400	By Sale of By-Products	500	7,425
To Cost of Labour		1,100			
To Electric Power		396	By Loss in weight in Refining	100	–
To Sundry Materials		2,200			
To Repairs to Machinery		363	By Finishing Process A/c (Transfer) (Cost per ton Rs. 2,11,255/2,600 Tons = Rs. 81.25)	2,600	2,11,255
To Steam		495			
To Factory Expenses		726			
	3,200	2,18,680		3,200	2,18,680

Finishing Process (Including Casking A/c)

Particulars	Tons	Rs.	Particulars	Tons	Rs.
To Refining Process A/c	2,600	2,11,255	By Loss in weight in Finishing	50	–
To Cost of Labour		1,650			
To Electric Power		264	By Finished Stock A/c (Cost per ton Rs. 2,22,310/2,550 Tons Rs. 87.18)	2,550	2,22,310
To Repairs to Machinery		154			
To Steam		495			
To Factory Expenses		242			
To Cost of Casks		8,250			
	2,600	2,22,310		2,600	2,22,310

(iv) Crediting Sales Value Less Selling and Distribution Expenses of By-product to the Main-product:

Under this method, selling and distribution expenses incurred for selling the by-product are deducted from the sales value of the by-product and the net sales value is deducted from the total cost of the main-product.

Illustration 13

Continuing Illustration 10, if the selling and distribution expenses of the by-product amount to Rs. 100 and the total sales of the main-product amount to Rs. 12,500, calculate the profit on main-product 'X'.

Solution

Statement of Cost and Profit

		Rs.
Direct Materials		5,000
Direct Wages		2,500
Factory Overhead		1,500
		9,000
Less: Sale of By-product 'N'	500	
Less: Selling and Distribution Expenses	100	400
Factory Cost		8,600
Administration and Selling Overhead	(Product X)	1,400
Total Cost		10,000
Profit		2,500
Sales		12,500

(v) Crediting Sales Value Less Selling and Distribution Costs and other Costs Incurred on By-product after Split-off Point:

This method is used when the by-product is subjected to further processing after the split-off point. Under this method, the subsequent costs and the selling and distribution cost of the by-product are deducted from its sales value and the net amount so arrived is deducted from the total cost of the main-product. Closing stock of by-product for balance sheet purposes, is valued at selling price less an estimated amount for selling and distribution costs and further processing costs after split-off point.

Illustration 14

In manufacturing 500 units of the main-product 'A', 100 units of a certain by-product are obtained. The costs of the process are:

	Rs.
Materials	15,000
Wages	9,000
Overhead	6,000
	30,000

The market value of the by-product is Rs. 15 per unit. The by-product requires further processing at a cost of Rs. 300. Selling and distribution expenses of the by-product are Rs. 100. Calculate the cost of main-product.

Solution

Statement of Cost of Main-product 'A'

Processing Costs:			
Materials			15,000
Wages			9,000
Overhead			6,000
			30,000
Sales Value of 100 Units of By-product		Rs. 1,500	
Less: Further Processing Cost	300		
Selling and Distribution Expenses	100	400	1,100
Cost of Main-product			28,900

$$\text{Cost per unit} = \frac{\text{Rs. } 28{,}900}{500 \text{ units}} = \text{Rs. } 57.80$$

(*vi*) Crediting to the main product, the sales value of by-product less selling and distribution expenses, costs incurred after split-off point and the estimated profit on by-product (i.e., Reverse Cost Method):

Under this method, the net estimated cost of the by-product is calculated by deducting from its sales value, the following:

(*a*) estimated profit on by-product,
(*b*) selling and distribution expenses of by-product, and
(*c*) costs incurred for further processing of by-product after the split-off point.

The net estimated cost of the by-product is credited to the main-product account to find out its cost.

Illustration 15

A by-product 'Beta' is derived in the course of manufacturing a product 'Alpha'. The by-product is further processed for sale. From the following data available from the cost records, prepare an account showing the cost per kg. of the product 'Alpha' and the by-product 'Beta':

	Joint Expenses	Separate Expenses	
		'Alpha'	'Beta'
	Rs.	Rs.	Rs.
Materials	10,000	6,000	500
Labour	7,000	5,000	2,000
Overheads	2,500	1,500	600

The quantities produced during the period under consideration were: Alpha 100 kg. and Beta 50 kg. The selling price of Beta was Rs. 120 per kg. on which the profit earned was estimated at 30 per cent.

(*B.Com., Punjab, B.Com. G.N.D.U., 1973, 2001*)

Solution

Calculation of Beta's Share in Joint Expenses		Rs.
Selling Price of Beta 50 kgs. @ Rs. 120 per kg.		6,000
Less: Estimated Profit @ 30%		1,800
Total Cost		4,200
Less: Separate Expenses:		
Materials	500	
Labour	2,000	
Overheads	600	3,100
Share in Joint Expenses		1,100

Alpha (Main-product) Account

		Rs.		Rs.
To Materials:				
Joint	10,000		By Beta (By-Product) A/c (Share in Joint Expenses)	1,100
Separate	6,000	16,000		
To Labour:				
Joint	7,000			
Separate	5,000	12,000		
To Overheads:			By Cost of Production (Alpha 100 kgs. @ Rs. 309 per kg.)	30,900
Joint	2,500			
Separate	1,500	4,000		
		32,000		32,000

Beta (By-product) Account

	Rs.		Rs.
To Alpha (Main) Product) A/c (Share in Joint Expenses)	1,100		
To Materials (separate)	500	By Cost of Production (50 kgs. @ Rs. 84 per kg.)	4,200
To Labour (separate)	2,000		
To Overheads (separate)	600		
	4,200		4,200

Illustration 16

A company manufactures product X, which yields by-products Y and Z. The actual joint expenses of manufacturing for a period were Rs. 80,000. It was estimated that the profit on each product as a percentage of sales would be 30%, 25% and 15% respectively. Subsequent costs are as under:

	X	Y	Z
	Rs.	Rs.	Rs.
Materials	1,000	750	250
Direct Wages	2,000	1,250	500
Overheads	1,500	1,250	750
	Rs. 4,500	Rs. 3,250	Rs. 1,500
Sales	Rs. 60,000	Rs. 40,000	Rs. 25,000

Prepare a statement showing the apportionment of the joint expenses of manufacture over the different products and prepare the necessary accounts.

(B.Com., G.N.D.U.)

Solution

Statement Showing the Apportionment of Joint Costs

	Main-product X	By-product Y	By-product Z	Total
	Rs.	Rs.	Rs.	
Sales	60,000	40,000	25,000	1,25,000
Less: Profit	18,000	10,000	3,750	31,750
Total Cost	42,000	30,000	21,250	93,250
Less: Selling and Distribution Expenses	1,920	1,280	800	4,000
Cost of Production	40,080	28,720	20,450	89,250
Less: Subsequent Costs	4,500	3,250	1,500	9,250
Share in Joint Costs	35,580	25,470	18,950	80,000

Calculation of Selling and Distribution Expenses

	Rs.
Total Cost (of Products X, Y and Z)	93,250
Less Subsequent Costs (Rs. 4,500 + 3,250 + 1,500)	9,250
Total Joint Costs	84,000
Joint Cost of Manufacture	80,000
Difference to be taken as Selling and Distribution Expenses (to be apportioned in sales ratio)	4,000

Main-product X Account

	Rs.		Rs.
To Sundry Joint Costs	80,000	By By-product Y A/c (Share in Joint Costs)	25,470
To Materials (Separate)	1,000		
To Wages (Separate)	2,000	By By-product Z A/c (Share in Joint Costs)	18,950
To Overhead (Separate)	1,500		
To Selling and Distribution Expenses	1,920	By Total Cost	42,000
	86,420		86,420

By-product Y Account

	Rs.		Rs.
To Main-product X A/c (Share in Joint Costs)	25,470	By Total Cost	30,000
To Materials (Separate)	750		
To Wages (Separate)	1,250		
To Overheads (Separate)	1,250		
To Selling and Distribution Expenses	1,280		
	30,000		30,000

By-product Z Account

	Rs.		Rs.
To Main-product X A/c (Share in Joint Costs)	18,950	By Total Cost	21,250
To Materials (Separate)	250		
To Wages (Separate)	500		
To Overheads (Separate)	750		
To Selling and Distribution Expenses	800		
	21,250		21,250

Cost Methods: The main cost methods of accounting for by-products may be given as follows:

(*i*) Replacement Cost Method or Opportunity Cost Method:

Under this method, the by-products are valued on the basis of their replacement cost or opportunity cost i.e., the price at which the by-products would have been purchased from outside suppliers, had they not been produced in the factory. For example, the production of 800 kgs. of a product 'A' yields 100 kgs. of a by-product 'X'. The by-product X is available in the market at a price of Rs. 16 per kg. The opportunity cost of 100 kgs. of by-product X is Rs. 1,600, which should be credited to the main-product 'A' A/c. The replacement cost method is adopted in those cases in which the by-products obtained are used in the factory itself as raw material for some other process.

Illustration 17

A factory manufactures a commodity which passes through three processes A, B, and C. The finished product of process A becomes the raw material of process B and the finished product of process B forms the raw material of process C which delivers the end product. The by-products of process A and B are sold direct from the factory.

	A	B Rs.	C Rs.
Materials	1,000 tons @ Rs. 12 per ton	700	600
Wages	Rs.10,000	20,000	36,000
Factory Overheads (Percentage of Wages)	75%	60%	50%
Wastage (of no sales value)	2 Tons	3 Tons	2 Tons
Sales Proceeds of By-products	8 tons @ Rs. 30 per ton	5 tons @ Rs. 24 per ton	–

Draw up Process Accounts and By-products Recoveries Account, assuming that the by-products are valued at estimated market price of Rs. 25 per ton for process A and Rs. 20 per ton for process B at the point of above separation.

(C.A. Inter)

Solution

Process A Account

Particulars	Tons	Rs.	Particulars	Tons	Rs.
To Materials	1,000	12,000	By Wastage	2	–
To Wages		10,000	By By-products Recoveries A/c @ Rs. 25 per ton	8	200
To Factory Overheads (75% of Wages)		7,500	By Process B A/c (Output Transferred) (Cost per ton = $\frac{\text{Rs. } 29,300}{990 \text{ Tons}}$ = Rs. 29.60)	990	29,300
	1,000	29,500		1,000	29,500

Process B Account

Particulars	Tons	Rs.	Particulars	Tons	Rs.
To Process A A/c	990	29,300	By Wastage	3	–
To Materials		700	By By-products Recoveries A/c @ Rs. 20 per ton	5	100
To Wages		20,000			
To Factory Overheads (60% of Wages)		12,000	By Process C A/c (Output Transferred) (Cost per ton = $\frac{\text{Rs. } 61,900}{982 \text{ Tons}}$ = Rs. 63.03)	982	61,900
	990	62,000		990	62,000

Process C Account

Particulars	Tons	Rs.	Particulars	Tons	Rs.
To Process B A/c	982	61,900	By Wastage	2	–
To Materials		600	By Finished Stock A/c	980	1,16,500
To Wages		36,000	(Output Transferred) (Cost		
To Factory Overheads (50% of Wages)		18,000	per ton $\frac{\text{Rs. }1,16,500}{980\text{ Tons}}$ = Rs. 118.88)		
	982	1,16,500		982	1,16,500

By-products Recoveries Account

Particulars	Tons	Rs.	Particulars	Tons	Rs.
To Process A A/c	8	200	By Cash A/c (Sale of by-products of Process A)	8	240
To Process B A/c	5	100			
To Profit and Loss A/c	–	60	By Cash A/c (Sale of by-products of Process B)	5	120
	13	360		13	360

(*ii*) Standard Cost Method:

Under this method, a standard cost is fixed for each by-product on the basis of past experience and the by-products are valued on the basis of the standard cost. A credit equal to the standard cost of the by-product is given to the main-product while ascertaining the cost of the main-product. The standard cost of a by-product is not fixed for ever. It is subject to changes according to change in the conditions of the production of the main-product.

In case the value of the by-products is considerable, the by-products may be given the status of joint-products and joint costs may be apportioned to them on any equitable basis. Thus, the basis to be adopted for the valuation of by-products becomes arbitrary in nature, and may involve a number of complicated calculations. The method of valuing the by-products by an equitable method is generally followed in cases where these are further processed in the factory with a view to utilise the idle plant capacity.

Illustration 18

The following details are available from the costing records of a factory in which two processes are employed:

	Process A	Process B
Materials	1,000 Tons @ Rs. 50 per ton	–
Direct Wages	Rs. 25,000	Rs. 20,000
Factory Overhead	80% of Direct Wages	60% of Direct Wages
Wastage	50 Tons	40 Tons
Sale of By-products	150 Tons at cost plus 20%	60 Tons at cost plus 25%

Prepare Process Accounts and By-product Accounts.

Solution

Process A Account

Particulars	Tons	Rs.	Particulars	Tons	Rs.
To Materials @ Rs. 50 per ton	1,000	50,000	By Wastage	50	–
To Direct Wages		25,000	By Process A By-Product A/c $\left(95{,}000 \times \frac{150}{950}\right)$	150	15,000
To Factory Overhead (80% of Wages)		20,000	By Process B A/c	800	80,000
	1,000	95,000		1,000	95,000

Process A By-product A/c

Particulars	Tons	Rs.	Particulars	Tons	Rs.
To Process A A/c	150	15,000	By Sale of By-products (Cost plus 20%)	150	18,000
To Profit and Loss A/c (Profit on Sale of By-products)		3,000			
	150	18,000		150	18,000

Process B Account

Particulars	Tons	Rs.	Particulars	Tons	Rs.
To Process A A/c	800	80,000	By Wastage	40	–
To Direct Wages		20,000	By process B By-Product A/c $\left(1{,}12{,}000 \times \frac{60}{760}\right)$	60	8,842
To Factory Overhead (60% of Wages)		12,000	By Finished Stock A/c	700	1,03,158
	800	1,12,000		800	1,12,000

Process B By-product A/c

Particulars	Tons	Rs.	Particulars	Tons	Rs.
To Process B A/c	60	8,842	By Sale of By-products (Cost plus 25%)	60	11,052.50
To Profit and Loss A/c (Profit)		2,210.50			
	60	11,052.50		60	11,052.50

Illustration 19

The yield of a certain process is 80% as to the main-product, 15% as to the by-product and 5% as to the process loss. The material put in process (5,000 units) cost Rs. 23.75 per unit and all other charges are Rs. 14,250, of which power cost accounted for $33\frac{1}{3}$%. It is ascertained that power is chargeable as to the main-product and by-product in the ratio of 10:9.

Draw up a statement showing the cost of the by-product. *(C.A. Inter)*

Solution

Yield per 5,000 units of Input

	Percentage of Yield	Yield in Units
Main-product	80%	4,000
By-product	15%	750
Process Loss	5%	250
	100%	5,000

Statement Showing the Cost of By-product

	Rs.
Material Cost (5,000 units × 23.75) × $\frac{750}{4,750}$	18,750
Other Charges (Except Power) $\left(14,250 \times 66\frac{2}{3}\%\right) \times \frac{750}{4,750}$	1,500
Power $\left(14,250 \times 33\frac{1}{3}\% \times \frac{9}{19}\right)$	2,250
Total Cost	22,500

Illustration 20

In manufacturing the main product A, a company processes the resulting waste materials into two by-products B and C. Using the method of working back from sales value to an estimated cost, prepare a comparative profit and loss statement of the three products from the following data:

(*i*) Total Cost upto separation point was : Rs. 34,000

		A	B	C
(*ii*)	Sales (all Production)	Rs. 82,000	Rs. 8,000	Rs. 12,000
(*iii*)	Costs after Separation		Rs. 2,400	Rs. 3,600
(*iv*)	Estimated Net Profit as percentage of Sales Value	–	20%	30%
(*v*)	Estimated Selling Expenses as percentage of Sales Value	20%	20%	20%

Solution

Statement Showing the Apportionment of Joint Costs

	Product B	Product C
	Rs.	Rs.
Sales	8,000	12,000
Less: Estimated Net Profit	1,600	3,600
Cost of Sales	6,400	8,400
Less: Selling Expenses	1,600	2,400
Cost of Production	4,800	6,000
Less: Cost after Separation	2,400	3,600
Share in Joint Costs	2,400	2,400

Total Cost upto Separation Point : Rs. 34,000

Less: Share of By-products in Joint Costs:

By-product B : Rs. 2,400

By-product C : Rs. 2,400

Rs. 4,800

Share of main-product A in Joint Costs Rs. 29,200

Comparative Statement of Profit and Loss

Particulars	A	B	C
	Rs.	Rs.	Rs.
Share in Joint Costs	29,200	2,400	2,400
Costs after Separation	–	2,400	3,600
Cost of Production	29,200	4,800	6,000
Selling Expenses @ 20% on Selling Price	16,400	1,600	2,400
Cost of Sales	45,600	6,400	8,400
Profit	36,400	1,600	3,600
Selling Price	82,000	8,000	12,000

Illustration 21

The following particulars are extracted from the records of a refinery:

	Oil No. 1	Oil No. 2
	Rs.	Rs.
Production of Crude Oil:		
Materials	10,000	8,000
Wages	200	150
Steam for Heating	60	60
Sale of By-products	160	120
Refining:		
Materials	400	300
Wages	250	200
Steam for Heating	140	130
Sale of By-products	600	300
Blending:		
Wages	Rs. 100	
Steaming and Heating	Rs. 30	

Rent, rates and taxes amounted to Rs. 900. These are apportioned equally to each process and in production of crude and refining Oil No. 1 and Oil No. 2 are to be charged in the proportion of 7/12 and 5/12 respectively.

From the above particulars you are required to prepare accounts showing separately the cost of each process and the total cost of the finished product which is a blend of Oils No. 1 and 2.

Solution

Crushing (Crude Oil) Process Account

Particulars	Oil No. 1	Oil No. 2	Particulars	Oil No. 1	Oil No. 2
	Rs.	Rs.		Rs.	Rs.
To Materials	10,000	8,000	By Sale of By-products	160	120
To Wages	200	150			
To Steam for Heating	60	60			
To Rent, Rates and Taxes (1/3 of Rs. 900 apportioned in 7:5 Ratio)	175	125	By Refining Process A/c (Transfer)	10,275	8,215
	10,435	8,335		10,435	8,335

Refining Process Account

Particulars	Oil No. 1	Oil No. 2	Particulars	Oil No. 1	Oil No. 2
	Rs.	Rs.		Rs.	Rs.
To Crushing (Crude Oil) Process A/c	10,275	8,215			
To Materials	400	300	By Sale of By-products	600	300
To Wages	250	200			
To Steam for Heating	140	130			
To Rent, Rates and Taxes (1/3 of Rs. 900 Apportioned in 7:5 Ratio)	175	125	By Blending Process A/c (Transfer)	10,640	8,670
	11,240	8,970		11,240	8,970

Blending Process Account

	Rs.		Rs.
To Refining Process A/c (Cost of Refined Oil)			
Oil No. 1	10,640		
Oil No. 2	8,670	By Finished Stock A/c	19,740
To Wages	100		
To Steam for Heating	30		
To Rent, Rates and Taxes (1/3 of Rs. 900)	300		
	19,740		19,740

Illustration 22

A chemical process yields 60% of the material introduced as Main-product A, 15% by-product B, 20% by-product C, and 5% being the wastage.

The ratio of absorption of Raw materials and Labour in the processing of products is as follows:

1. One unit of Product C requires half the raw material required for one unit of B, one unit of product A requires $1\frac{1}{2}$ times the raw material required for product B.

2. Product A requires double the time needed for the production of one unit of B and one unit of C.
3. Product C requires half the time required for the production of one unit of product B.
4. Overheads are to be absorbed in the ratio of 6 : 1 : 1.
5. Cost Data: Input 1,000 units Cost Rs. 4,600
   Direct Labour Rs.4,100
   Overheads Rs.6,000.

Solution

The total number of units introduced		= 1,000 units
A Main Product	60% of 1,000 units	= 600 units
B By-product	15% of 1,000 units	= 150 units
C By-product	20% of 1,000 units	= 200 units
Wastage	5% of 1,000 units	= 50 units
	Total	= 1,000 units

Apportionment of Joint Cost

Particulars	Ratio	Total Cost	Main-product A		By-product B		By-product B	
			Amount	Cost per Unit	Amount	Cost per Unit	Amount	Cost per Unit
		Rs.	Rs.	Rs.	Rs.	Rs.	Rs.	Rs.
Material	18 : 3 : 2	4,600	3,600	6.00	600	4.00	400	2.00
Labour	36 : 3: 2	4,100	3,600	6.00	300	2.00	200	1.00
Overhead	6: 1 : 1	6,000	4,500	7.50	750	5.00	750	3.75
		14,700	11,700	19.50	1,650	11.00	1,350	6.75

Notes: 1. Material ratio between A, B and C is 3 : 2 : 1 on the basis of consumption. Hence ratio will be 600 × 3 : 150 × 2 : 200 × 1 or 18 : 3 : 2.

2. Labour ratio between A, B and C will be as follows:
A takes double the time of B + C or A = 2 (2 + 1) = 6 units of time.
The ratio is therefore 6 : 2 : 1.
Multiplying time into units, the ratio will be 600 × 6 : 150 × 2 : 200 × 1 or 36 : 3 : 2.

Illustration 23

The Premier Processing Factory carries out 10 batches of production in a year, with 1,000 kgs. of raw material M per batch of production and after processes recovers five joint products – Products A, B, C and D and a gas G. The following details are available:

	Rs.
Plant and Machinery (Net)	80,000
Land and Buildings	40,000
Other Assets	30,000
Cash, Stock and Debtors	70,000
Current Liabilities	20,000

Product	Production (per 1, 000 kgs. of M)	Unit Selling Prices
	Kg.	Rs.
A	50	30
B	200	25
C	100	40
D	300	15
G	2,500 litres	2

Processing cost (conversion cost) is estimated at Rs. 6,410 per batch, material handling charges at Rs. 680 per 1,000 kgs. of M and selling and distribution expenses at 10% of sales. The factory works on a 10% return on investments.

One per cent of the raw material is retrieved at the end of the process at original cost (without handling charges) and is used for the next batch of production. The balance of raw material unaccounted for its invisible waste.

Work out the purchase price per kg. of M in order to achieve the above result and compute the unit cost of sales of each of the joint products based on their sales value.

Solution

	Rs.
Plant and Machinery (Net)	80,000
Land and Buildings	40,000
Other Assets	30,000
Cash, Stocks and Debtors	70,000
Total Assets	2,20,000
Less: Current Liabilities	20,000
Net Investment	2,00,000

Return on Investment 10% of 2,00,000 = Rs. 20,000.

Return on Investment per Batch = 20,000 ÷ 10 = Rs. 2,000.

Product	Output	Sales Price	Sales	Cost of Sales	Cost per unit
		Rs.	Rs.	Rs.	Rs. P.
A	50 kgs.	30	1,500	1,350	27.00
B	200 kgs.	25	5,000	4,500	22.50
C	100 kgs.	40	4,000	3,600	36.00
D	300 kgs.	15	4,500	4,050	13.50
G	2,500 litres	2	5,000	4,500	1.80
			20,000	18,000	

Cost of Sales per Batch (20,000 –2,000)			18,000
Less: Selling cost 10% of 20,000		2,000	
Conversion Cost		6,410	
Handling Cost		680	9,090
Cost of Material M			8,910
Material M Input	1,000 kgs.		
Less: Material Retrieved 1%	10 kgs.		
	990 kgs.		

Price of Material M = $\frac{8,910}{990}$ = Rs. 9 per kg.

Illustration 24

In a concern engaged in process industry four products emerge from a particular process of operation. The total cost of input for the period ended 30th September, 2002 is Rs. 2,53,500. The details of output, additional cost after "split-off point" and sales value of the products are appended below.

Products	Output Kgs.	Additional process cost after split-off point	Sales value
A	8,000	Rs. 60,000	Rs. 1,68,000
B	5,000	10,000	1,10,000
C	3,000	–	60,000
D	4,000	20,000	90,000

If the products are sold at "split-off point" without further processing, the sales value would have been:

A	Rs. 1,15,000
B	90,000
C	55,000
D	80,000

You are required to prepare a statement of profitability based on the products being sold (*i*) after further processing, and (*ii*) at the split-off point.

Solution

(*i*) Statement Showing Profitability After Further Processing

Products	Sales Value	Additional Processing Cost	Equivalent Sales value at split-off-point	Joint Cost	Profit
	Rs.	Rs.	Rs.	Rs.	Rs.
A	1,68,000	60,000	1,08,000	81,000	27,000
B	1,10,000	10,000	1,00,000	75,000	25,000
C	60,000	–	60,000	45,000	15,000
D	90,000	20,000	70,000	52,500	17,500
	4,28,000	90,000	3.38,000	2,53,500	84,500

Note: Joint cost has been apportioned on the basis of equivalent sales value at the split-off point.

(*ii*) Statement of Profitability if Sold at Split-off Point

Products	Sales Value	Joint Cost	Profit
	Rs.	Rs.	Rs.
A	1,15,000	85,743	29,257
B	90,000	67,103	22,897
C	55,000	41,007	13,993
D	80,000	59,647	20,353
	3,40,000	2,53,500	86,500

Note: Joint cost has been apportioned on the basis of sales value.

Illustration 25

Bright Chemicals Ltd., electrolyses common salt to obtain three joint products – caustic soda, chlorine and hydrogen. During a costing period, the expenditure relating to the inputs for the common process amounted to Rs. 3,50,000. After separation, expenses amounting to Rs. 1,60,000, Rs. 75,000, and Rs. 10,000 were incurred for caustic soda, chlorine and hydrogen respectively. The entire production was sold and Rs. 3,75,000, Rs. 2,50,000 and Rs. 60,000 were realised for caustic soda, chlorine and hydrogen respectively. The selling expenses were estimated at 5% of realisations from sale. The management expected profits @ 15%, 10% and 5% of realisations from sale of caustic soda, chlorine and hydrogen respectively.

Draw a columnar statement showing the apportionment of joint costs and the profitability of each product. (*I.C.W.A. Inter, Dec., 1991*).

Solution

Statement Showing the Apportionment of Joint Costs

	Caustic Soda	Chlorine	Hydro-gen	Total
	Rs.	Rs.	Rs.	Rs.
Sales	3,75,000	2,50,000	60,000	6,85,000
Less: Profit	56,250 (15% on sales)	25,000 (10% on sales)	3,000 (5% on sales)	84,250
Total Cost (Estimated)	3,18,750	2,25,000	57,000	6,00,750
Less: Selling Expenses (5% on Sales)	18,750	12,500	3,000	34,250
Cost of Production (Estimated)	3,00,000	2,12,500	54,000	5,66,500
Less: After Separation Costs	1,60,000	75,000	10,000	2,45,000
Share in Joint Costs (Estimated)	1,40,000	1,37,500	44,000	3,21,500
Estimated Percentage of Share of Joint Costs in Total Joint Cost	43.5%	42.8%	13.7%	100%

Statement of Profitability

	Caustic Soda	Chlorine	Hydrogen	Total
	Rs.	Rs.	Rs.	Rs.
Actual Share of Joint Costs (43.5 : 42.8 : 13.7)	1,52,250	1,49,800	47,950	3,50,000
After Separation Costs	1,60,000	75,000	10,000	2,45,000
Cost of Production (Actual)	3,12,250	2,24,800	57,950	5,95,000
Selling Expenses (5% on Sales)	18,750	12,500	3,000	34,250
Total Cost (Actual)	3,31,000	2,37,300	60,950	6,29,250
Profit/Loss	44,000	12,700	(–) 950	55,750
Sales	3,75,000	2,50,000	60,000	6,85,000

Illustration 26

XY Company buys crude vegetable oil. The refining of this oil results in four products A, B, C and D. The cost of oil refined in 2001 was Rs. 2,72,000 and the refining department had total processing costs of Rs. 7,00,000. The output and sales for the four products in 2001 were as follows:

Products	Output	Sales	Additional Process cost after Split-off
		Rs.	Rs.
A	5,00,000 gallons	11,50,000	3,00,000
B	10,000 gallons	1,00,000	60,000
C	5,000 gallons	40,000	–
D	9,000 gallons	3,00,000	10,000

Required:

(*i*) Assume that the net realizable value at split-off is used for allocating joint costs. What is the net income for products A, B, C and D? Joint costs total Rs. 9,76,000.

(*ii*) The company had been tempted to sell out at split-off directly to other processors. If that alternative had been selected, sales per gallon would have been A – Rs. 1.50; B – Rs. 5.00; C – Rs. 8.00 and D – Rs. 30. What would the net income have been for each product under this alternative?

(*iii*) The company expects to operate at the same level of production and sales in the forthcoming year. Could the company increase net income by altering its processing decisions? If so what would be the expected overall net income? Which products should be processed further and which should be sold at split-off. Assume that all costs incurred after split-off are variable.

(I.C.W.A. Inter Adapted)

Solution

(*i*) Allocation of Joint Cost on the basis of Net Realisable Value

Products	Sales (Rs. '000)	Cost after Split-off (Rs. '000)	Net Realisable Value (Rs. '000)	Joint Cost Apportioned (Rs. '000)
A	1,150	300	850	680
B	100	60	40	32
C	40	–	40	32
D	300	10	290	232
	1,590	370	1,220	976

The net income for the products are:

Product A	850 – 680 =	170 thousand rupees
Product B	40 – 32 =	8 thousand rupees
Product C	40 – 32 =	8 thousand rupees
Product D	290 – 232 =	58 thousand rupees
Total		244 thousand rupees

(*ii*) If the products are sold out at the point of split-off

Products	Output ('000 gallons)	Price Rs.	Sales (Rs. '000)	Joint Cost Apportioned (Rs. '000)	Net Income (Rs. '000)
A	500	1.50	750	680	70
B	10	5.00	50	32	18
C	5	8.00	40	32	8
D	9	30.00	270	232	38
Total			1,110	976	134

It appears that if all the products are sold at split-off then total net income will drop from 244 to 134 thousand rupees which is not advisable. Rather products B and C (the latter does not require further processing) can be sold at split-off to increase the total net income.

(*iii*) If the above suggestion is accepted then the net income position will be as under

Products	Sales (Rs. '000)	Cost after Split-off (Rs. '000)	Joint Cost (Rs. '000)	Net Income (Rs. '000)
A	1,150	300	680	170
B	50	–	32	18
C	40	–	32	8
D	300	10	232	58
	1,540	310	976	254

Thus the total net income will increase by 10 thousand rupees if the suggestion is accepted as the additional processing cost of product after split-off can be saved (Rs. 60,000) and the fall in revenue being Rs. 50,000 the net gain is Rs. 10,000.

Illustration 27

Three products X, Y and Z alongwith a by-product B are obtained again in a crude state which require further processing at a cost of Rs. 5 for X; Rs. 4 for Y; and Rs. 2.50 for Z per unit before sale. The by-product is however saleable as such to a nearby factory. The selling prices for the three main products and by-product, assuming they should yield a net margin of 25 per cent on cost, are fixed at Rs. 13.75, Rs. 8.75, Rs. 7.50 and Re. 1.00 respectively – all per unit quantity sold.

During a period, the joint input cost including the material cost was Rs. 90,800 and the respective outputs were:

X	8,000 units
Y	6,000 units
Z	4,000 units, and
B	1,000 units

By-product should be credited to the joint cost and only the net joint costs are to be allocated to the main products. Calculate the joint cost per unit of each product and the margin available as a percentage on cost.

(C.A. Final, May 1992)

Solution

Working Notes:

1. Computation of allocation ratio of joint costs

	Products X	Products Y	Products Z
	Rs.	Rs.	Rs.
Selling Price	13.75	8.75	7.50
Less: Anticipated margin @ 25% on Cost or 20% on Sales	2.75	1.75	1.50
Cost of sales	11.00	7.00	6.00
Less: Post split-off Cost	5.00	4.00	2.50
Pre-split-off Net Joint Cost per unit	6.00	3.00	3.50
Output (units)	8,000	6,000	4,000
Total Output Cost	48,000	18,000	14,000
Allocation Ratio for Joint Costs	24	: 9	: 7

2. Computation of Net Allocable Joint Costs:

	Rs.	*Rs.*
Joint Output Cost Including Material Cost		90,800
Less: Credit for Realisation from By-product B		
Sales Revenue (1,000 units x Re. 1)	1,000	
Less: Profit 25% on Cost or 20% on Sales	200	800
Net Joint Costs to be Allocated		90,000

(Allocation of net joint costs of Rs. 90,000 in the ratio of 24 : 9 : 7 to products X, Y and Z).

Determination of joint cost per unit of each product:

Products	Net Joint Costs Allocation	Output (units)	Joint Cost per Unit
	Rs.		Rs.
X	54,000	8,000	6.75
Y	20,250	6,000	3.38
Z	15,750	4,000	3.94
	90,000		

Profit margin available on each product as a percentage on cost:

Products	Joint Cost	Post Split-off Cost	Total Cost	Selling Price	Margin	Margin % on Cost
X	6.75	5.00	11.75	13.75	2.00	17.0
Y	3.38	4.00	7.38	8.75	1.37	18.6
Z	3.94	2.50	6.44	7.50	1.06	16.5

Illustration 28

Two products P and Q are obtained in a crude form and require further processing at a cost of Rs. 5 for P and Rs. 4 for Q per unit before sales. Assuming a net margin of 25 per cent on cost, their sale prices are fixed at Rs. 13.75 and Rs. 8.75 per unit respectively. During the period, the joint cost was Rs. 88,000 and the outputs were:

P 8,000 units
Q 6,000 units

Ascertain the joint cost per unit. *(C.A. Inter, May, 1998)*

Solution

Statement of Apportionment of Joint Cost

	Products	
	P	Q
Output (units)	8,000	6,000
	Rs.	Rs.
Selling Price per Unit	13.75	8.75
Less : Profit (25% on Cost or 20% on Sales)	2.75	1.75
Cost of Sales	11.00	7.00
Less : After Split-off Cost	5.00	4.00
Share in Joint Cost per Unit	6.00	3.00

Total Cost 8,000 units × Rs. 6 = Rs.48,000   6,000 units × Rs. 3 = Rs.18,000

Ratio between P and Q is 48,000 : 18,000 or 8 : 3.

Total joint cost of Rs. 88,000 is apportioned to P and Q in the ratio of 8 : 3 i.e., Rs. 64,000 for P and Rs. 24,000 for Q.

Illustration 29

A company processes a raw material in its Department 1 to produce three products, viz., A, B and X at the same split-off stage. During a period 1,80,000 kgs. of raw material were processed in Department 1 at a total cost of Rs. 12,88,000 and the resultant output of A, B and X were 18,000 kgs., 10,000 kgs. and 54,000 kgs. respectively. A and B were further processed in Department 2 at a cost of Rs. 1,80,000 and Rs. 1,50,000 respectively. X was further processed in Department 3 at a cost of Rs. 1,08,000. There is no waste in further processing.

The details of sales effected during the period were as under:

		A	B	X
Quantity Sold	(kgs.)	17,000	5,000	44,000
Sales Value	(Rs.)	12,24,000	2,50,000	7,92,000

There were no opening stocks. If these products were sold at split-off stage, the selling prices of A, B and X would have been Rs. 50, Rs. 40 and Rs. 10 per kg. respectively.

Required:

(*i*) Prepare a statement showing the apportionment of joint costs to A, B and X.

(*ii*) Present a statement showing the cost per kg. of each product indicating joint cost, further processing cost and total cost separately.

(*iii*) Prepare a statement showing the product-wise and total profit for the period.

(*iv*) State with supporting calculations as to whether any or all the products should be further processed or not.

(*C.A. Inter, Nov., 1996*)

Solution

(i) Statement of Apportionment of Joint Cost

Products	Output kg. (a)	S.P. at Split-off Point (b)	Sales Value (a × b)	Share in Joint Cost in Ratio of Sales Value
		Rs.	Rs.	Rs.
A	18,000	50	9,00,000	6,30,000
B	10,000	40	4,00,000	2,80,000
X	54,000	10	5,40,000	3,78,000
				12,88,000

(ii) Statement of Cost per kg.

	Products		
	A	B	X
(A) Share in Joint Cost (Rs.)	6,30,000	2,80,000	3,78,000
(B) Output in kg.	18,000	10,000	54,000
(C) Cost per kg. (A ÷ B) (Rs.)	35	28	7
(D) Further Processing Cost per kg. (Rs.) (Further Processing Cost ÷ Output)	10	15	2
(E) Total Cost per kg. (C + D)	45	43	9

(iii) Statement of Profit

	Products			Total
	A	B	X	
Output (kg.)	18,000	10,000	54,000	
Sales (kg.)	17,000	5,000	44,000	
Closing Stock (kg.)	1,000	5,000	10,000	
	Rs.	Rs.	Rs.	Rs.
Sales	12,24,000	2,50,000	7,92,000	22,66,000
Add: Closing Stock (at cost)	45,000	2,15,000	90,000	3,50,000
(A) Value of Production	12,69,000	4,65,000	8,82,000	26,16,000
Share in Joint Cost	6,30,000	2,80,000	3,78,000	
Further Processing Cost	1,80,000	1,50,000	1,08,000	
(B) Total cost	8,10,000	4,30,000	4,86,000	17,26,000
Profit (A-B)	4,59,000	35,000	3,96,000	8,90,000

(iv) Statement of Incremental Profit/Loss

By Further Processing

	Products		
	A	B	X
	Rs.	Rs.	Rs.
Selling Price after Further Processing per kg.	72	50	18
Less: Selling Price at Split-off Point	50	40	10
Incremental Selling Price	22	10	8
Less: Incremental Cost (further processing cost)	10	15	2
Incremental Profit/Loss (–)	12	(-) 5	6

***Conclusion*:** Product A and X should be processed further because these give incremental profits. Product B should be sold at split-off point because by further processing, it results into a loss.

OBJECTIVE TYPE QUESTIONS

A. Multiple Choice Question

Select the correct answer in each of the following.

(*a*) The typical example of joint product manufacturing is:
- (*i*) Oil refinery
- (*ii*) Colliery
- (*iii*) Automobile industry
- (*iv*) Engineering industry.

(*b*) Two or more products of considerable sales value obtained simultaneously from the same raw material are termed as:
- (*i*) Common products
- (*ii*) By-products
- (*iii*) Main-products
- (*iv*) Joint products.

(*c*) Any saleable or usable value incidentally obtained in addition to the main-product, is termed as:
- (*i*) Co-product
- (*ii*) By-product
- (*iii*) Joint product
- (*iv*) None of these.

(*d*) Costs incurred prior to the split-off point of various products are termed as:
- (*i*) Separate costs
- (*ii*) Direct costs
- (*iii*) Joint costs
- (*iv*) Processing costs.

(*e*) Trimmings in timber industry should be treated as:
- (*i*) Joint product
- (*ii*) By-product
- (*iii*) Defectives
- (*iv*) Scrap.

(*f*) Which of the following methods of by-product accounting should be used when the by-product is to be used in the undertaking itself as raw material for some other process:
- (*i*) Other Incomes Method
- (*ii*) Opportunity Cost Method
- (*iii*) Reverse Cost Method
- (*iv*) Sales Value Method.

[**Ans.** (*a*) (*i*), (*b*) (*iv*), (*c*) (*ii*), (*d*) (*iii*), (*e*) (*iv*), (*f*) (*ii*).]

B. True/False Type Statements.

Indicate whether the following statements are true or false:

(*a*) Costs incurred prior to the split-off point are known as 'Joint Costs.'

(*b*) Costs incurred for the further processing of the joint costs are known as 'Joint Costs'.

(*c*) By-products are never subjected to further processing.

(*d*) No distinction can be made between 'Co-products' and 'Joint products'.

(*e*) There is no need to apportion joint costs to joint products.

(*f*) Separate costs should be apportioned to various joint products on some equitable basis.

[**Ans:** (*a*) True (*b*) False (*c*) False (*d*) False (*e*) False (*f*) False.]

C. Filling the blanks.

Fill in the blanks.

(*a*) The stage of production at which separate products are identified is known as ....

(*b*) The .... product generally has a greater sale value than by-products.

(*c*) The costs incurred upto the split-off point are known as ....

(*d*) .... costs are incurred after the split-off point.

(*e*) Under the 'other income method' of accounting of by-products, the sales value of the by-products is credited to ....

[**Ans:** (*a*) split-off point (*b*) main (*c*) joint costs (*d*) Subsequent (*e*) Profit and Loss A/c]

SHORT ANSWER TYPE QUESTIONS

1. What is meant by 'Joint Products' and By-products?

2. Distinguish between 'Joint Products' and 'By-products'.

3. What is meant be pre-split-off point costs.?

4. What are subsequent costs?

5. List out four bases of apportionment of Joint costs.

6. What is the difference between co-products and joint products?

7. Write notes on

(*i*) Joint products

(*ii*) By-products

(*iii*) Joint costs.

LONG ANSWER TYPE QUESTIONS

1. Define Joint products and By-products and cite an example of each. Explain the various methods of apportionment of joint costs to joint products. *(C.A., Inter)*

2. Distinguish between Joint products and By-products. Explain the various methods of apportionment of joint expenses with illustrations. *(I.C.W.A., Inter)*

3. "The distinction between joint products and by-products is a matter of judgement only." Comment.

4. Define each of the term given below:

(*a*) (*i*) Normal Loss (*ii*) Abnormal Loss

(*b*) (*i*) By-products (*ii*) Joint Products

Describe how would you evaluate and deal in the process accounts with each of these items. *(Punjab, B.Com., 1983)*

5. Define 'By-products'. Discuss the methods of accounting for by-products. *(C.A., Inter)*

EXERCISES

1. S.K. Corporation produces four products in a manufacturing process. The output of four products has been as follows:

Product A 7,500 units
Product B 6,000 units
Product C 4,000 units
Product D 7,500 units.

The joint costs of the four products are Rs. 3,00,000. Using the average unit cost method (*a*) calculate the unit cost and (*b*) show the apportionment of joint costs to joint products.

[**Ans.** Average unit cost Rs. 12, Cost apportioned : A Rs. 90,000, B Rs. 72,000, C Rs. 48,000, D Rs. 90,000]

2. The following data have been extracted from the books of M/s. East India Coke Co. Ltd.,

Joint Products	**Yield in lb. of Recovered Products per ton Coal**
Coke	1,420
Coal Tar	120
Benzol	22
Sulphate of Ammonia	26
Gas	412
	2,000

The price of coal is Rs. 80 per ton. Direct labour and overhead costs to point of split-off are Rs. 40 and Rs. 60 respectively per ton of coal. Calculate material, labour and overhead and total cost of each product on the basis of weight. (*I.C.W.A. Final*)

[**Ans.** Total cost per ton : Coke Rs. 127.80, Coal Tar Rs. 10.80, Benzol Rs. 1.98, Sulphate Rs. 2.34 and Gas Rs. 37.08].

3. The following particulars have been obtained about three joint products manufactured from the same raw material:

	A	B	C
	Rs.	**Rs.**	**Rs.**
Market Price (sale)	50	40	50
Cost of Manufacture after the Stage at which the Products are Separated	30	15	20

The joint cost of manufacture before the products are separated is Rs. 60. Allocate the cost of the joint products. (*I.C.W.A., Inter*)

[**Ans.** A Rs. 16; B Rs. 20: C Rs. 24]

4. The Joint Cost of manufacturing 500 units of A, 3,000 units of B and 2,000 units of C are as follows:

Materials	15,000
Labour	9,000
Overheads	6,000
Total	30,000

You are required to apportion the Joint Costs to the products if the technical estimates assign 4, 3 and 2 points to A, B and C respectively.

[**Ans.** Cost per unit A Rs. 8, B Rs. 6 and C Rs. 4)

5. From a common process two joint products A and B come out. Expenses after separation for A and B are Rs. 10 and Rs. 16 respectively per unit. Total expenses in the common process amount to Rs. 3,22,000. Selling price of A and B are Rs. 40 and Rs. 55 respectively per unit. Output of A and B are 7,000 units and 6,000 units respectively. Find out the cost of A and B after completion, if profit on sales is 20%.

[**Ans.** Cost per unit A, Rs. 32 and B, Rs. 44]

6. In a manufacturing company 10,000 kilolitres of 'A' is processed to produce 6,000 kilolitres of 'B' and 4,000 kilolitres of 'C'. The joint cost before separation point came to an amount of Rs. 24,000. From the following particulars, calculate the apportionment of joint cost and the profit of each product under (*a*) physical measurement, (*b*) market value at separation point, and (*c*) market value after further processing.

	B	C
	Rs.	Rs.
Unit Selling Price at Separation Point	5.00	3.75
Unit Selling Price after Further Processing	7.00	7.50
Further Processing Costs after Separation	5,000	7,500

(*I.C.W.A., Inter June, 1992*)

[**Ans.**	**B**	**C**
	Rs.	**Rs.**
(*a*)	15,600	5,400
(*b*)	14,000	7,000
(*c*)	23,000	12,500]

7. In a process industry, the input of materials gives an output of three joint products. The relative market value method is used in allocating the joint costs among the products. Calculate the cost per unit of each product from the following data:

Input	**Quantity**	**Cost per unit**
		Rs.
Material A	100 lbs.	0.12
Material B	50 gallons	0.15
Direct Labour	3 hrs.	2.00
Mfg. Overhead	3 hrs.	3.50
Output Product	**Quantity**	**Rs.**
I	30 lbs.	0.60
II	60 lbs.	0.40
III	20 gallons	0.30

(*I.C.W.A.*)

[**Ans.** Product 1 Re. 0.45; II Re. 0.30; III Re. 0.225]

8. A manufacturing company produced three joint products at a joint cost of Rs. 1,00,000. Two of these products were processed further. Production and sales were:

	Weight	**Sales**	**Additional Processing Costs**
		Rs.	**Rs.**
A	3,00,000 lbs.	2,45,000	2,00,000
B	1,00,000 lbs.	30,000	–
C	1,00,000 lbs.	1,75,000	1,00,000

Calculate if:

(*i*) **The approximated relative value of allocating joint costs is used. What is the net income for products A, B and C?**

(*ii*) **The company had been tempted to sell at split-off directly to other processors. If that alternative had been selected, sales would have been:**

A – Rs. 50,000; B – Rs. 30,000; and C – Rs. 60,000. What would the net income have been for each product under this alternative?

(*iii*) The company expects to operate at the same level of production and sales in the forthcoming year. Could the company increase net income by altering its processing decisions? If so, what would be the expected overall net income?

Which products should be processed further and which should be sold at split-off? Assume that all costs incurred after split-off are variable.

[**Ans.** (*i*) Net Income A Rs. 15, 000; B Rs. 10,000; C Rs. 25,000,
(*ii*) A Rs. 14,287; B Rs. 8,571; C Rs. 17,143 ,
(*iii*) Net Income A Rs. 15,000; B Rs. 10,000; C Rs. 25,000]

9. Three joint products X, Y and Z are produced from a common process. The joint expenses of manufacture are:

Material	Rs. 57,000
Labour	Rs. 30,000
Overhead	Rs. 2,100
Total	Rs. 89,100

Subsequent expenses are as follows:

	X	Y	Z
	Rs.	Rs.	Rs.
Materials	24,000	12,000	6,000
Labour	12,000	9,000	3,000
Overheads	1,800	1,500	1,500
Total	37,800	22,500	10,500
Sales	1,53,000	63,000	30,000
Estimated profit on Sales	40%	30%	20%

Show the manner in which you want to apportion the joint expenses of production.

[**Ans.** Joint expenses will be apportioned in the ratio of 20 : 8 : 5,
Total Cost A-Rs. 91,800, B-Rs. 44,100 and C-Rs. 24,000]

10. A certain chemical process yields 75% of material introduced as main product 20% as a by product and 5% being lost. The percentage of material consumed by main-product and by-product is 80:20. Time taken to produce one unit of by-product is half the time taken to produce one unit of the main-product. Overheads have been allocated @ 200% of wages of each product.

Cost data:

	Rs.	Units
Raw Material	10,000	2,000
Labour	8,500	
Overheads	17,000	
Total	35,500	

Ascertain the cost of two products.

[**Ans.** Total Cost of Main product- Rs. 30,500 and By-product Rs. 5,000]

[**Hint:** Ratio of Labour Expenses = Proportionate Time × Units Produced.

Main Product	:	By-product
2 × 1,500	:	1 × 400
3,000	:	400
15	:	2]

11. The following details are available from the costing records of factory in which two processes are employed:

	Process A	**Process B**
Materials	1,000 tons @ Rs. 50 per ton	–
Direct Wages	Rs. 25,000	Rs. 20,000
Factory Overhead	80% of Direct Wages	60% of Direct Wages
Wastage	50 tons	40 tons
Sale of By-product	150 tons at Cost Plus 20%	60 tons at Cost Plus 25%

Prepare process accounts and by-product accounts.

[**Ans.** Process A-Output 800 tons @ Rs. 100 per ton, by-product A 150 tons and profit on sale of by-product A-Rs. 3,000; Process B-Output 700 tons @ 147.37 per ton, by product B-60 tons and profit on sale of by-product-B Rs. 2,210.50]

12. A factory producing article P also produces a by-product Q, which is further processed into finished product. The joint cost of manufacture is given below:

	Rs.
Material	5,000
Labour	3,000
Overheads	2,000
Total	10,000

Subsequent costs are given below:

	P	Q
	Rs.	Rs.
Materials	3,000	1,500
Labour	1,400	1,000
Overheads	600	500
Total	5,000	3,000

Selling prices of P and Q are Rs. 16,000 and Rs. 8,000 respectively. Estimated profits on selling prices are 25% for P and 20% for Q. Assume that selling and distribution expenses are in proportion of sales price. Show how would you apportion joint costs of manufacture and prepare a statement showing cost of production of P and Q.

(*C.A. Inter*)

[**Ans.** Cost of production, P-Rs. 11,733 and Q-Rs. 6,267, Total Selling Expenses-Rs. 400]

13. A factory producing article A also yields B and C as by-products. The joint cost of manufacture is:

	Rs.
Material	10,000
Labour	2,000
Overheads	8,000
	20,000

Subsequent costs are as under:

	A	B	C
	Rs.	Rs.	Rs.
Material	1,500	1,300	1,000
Labour	200	150	100
Overheads	800	550	400
	2,500	2,000	1,500
Selling Prices	30,000	24,000	20,000
Estimated Profits on Selling Price	30%	25%	20%

Show how you would propose to apportion the joint costs of manufacture and prepare the necessary statement in respect of A, B and C.

[**Ans.** Share in joint cost of manufacture; A Rs.6,743; B Rs. 6,595; C Rs. 6,662)

14. Calculate the estimated cost of production of by-products X and Y at the point of separation from the main product.

	By-product X	By-product Y
Selling Price per unit	Rs. 12	Rs. 24
Cost after Separation per unit	Rs. 3	Rs. 5
Units Produced	500	200

Selling expenses amount to 25% of total works cost i.e., including both pre-separation and post-separation works cost.

Selling prices are arrived at by adding 20% of total cost i.e., the sum of works cost and selling expenses. (C.A. *Final*)

[**Ans.** Cost at Point of Separation, By-product X-Rs. 5 and By-product Y-Rs. 11]

15. A factory is engaged in the production of a chemical BOMEX and in the course of its manufacture, a by product BRUCIL is produced, which after further processing has a commercial value. For the month of April, 2008, the following are the summarised cost data:

	Joint Expenses	Separate Expenses BOMEX	Separate Expenses BRUCIL
	Rs.	Rs.	Rs.
Materials	1,00,000	6,000	4,000
Labour	50,000	20,000	18,000
Overhead	30,000	10,000	6,000
Selling Price per unit		98	34
Estimated Profit per unit on Sale of BRUCIL			4
		Units	Units
No. of Units Produced		2,000	2,000

The factory uses reverse cost method of accounting for by-products whereby the sales value of by-products after deduction of the estimated profit, post separation costs and selling and distribution expenses relating to the by-products is credited to the joint process cost account.

You are required to prepare statement showing:

(*i*) the joint cost allocable to BOMEX.

(*ii*) The product-wise and overall profitability of the factory for April, 2008. (*C.A. Inter May, 1990*)

[**Ans.** (*i*) Rs. 1,48,000; (*ii*) Bomex Rs. 12,000. Brucil Rs. 8,000 Total Profit Rs. 20,000]

16. A medical product passes through three distinct processes to completion. These processes are numbered respectively 1, 2 and 3. During the week ended 15th January, 2004, 500 gross of bottles are produced. The cost books show the following information:

	Process 1	Process 2	Process 3
Materials	3,000	1,500	1,000
Labour	2,500	2,000	2,500
Direct Expenses	50	100	500
Cost of Bottles	–	2,060	–
Cost of Corks	–	–	405

The indirect expenses for the period were Rs. 1,400. The by-products were sold for Rs. 145.75 (Process 2).

Residue sold Rs. 166.75 (Process 3).

Prepare the account in each of the process showing its cost of production of the finished product per gross of bottles.

[**Ans.** Cost per gross Process 1 = Rs. 12.10, 2 = Rs. 23.93, 3 = Rs. 33.405]

17. The following details are extracted from the costing records of an oil company for the year ended 31st March, 2003: Purchase of 500 tons Copra Rs. 2,00,000.

	Crushing	**Refining**	**Finishing**
	Rs.	**Rs.**	**Rs.**
Cost of Labour	2,500	1,000	1,500
Electric Power	600	360	240
Sundry Materials	100	2,000	–
Steam	600	450	450
Repairs of Machinery	280	330	140
Factory Expenses	1,320	660	220
Cost of Casks			7,500

300 Tons of crude oil were produced.
250 Tons of oil were produced by the refining process. 248 Tons of refined oil were finished for delivery. Copra sacks sold for Rs. 400.
175 Tons of copra residue sold for Rs. 11,000.
Loss in weight in crushing 25 tons, 45 tons of by-products obtained from Refining Process Rs. 6,750.
You are required to show the accounts in respect of each of the following stages of manufacture for the purpose of arriving at the cost per ton of each process and the total cost per ton of the finished oil : (*a*) Copra Crushing Process (*b*) Refining Process, (*c*) Finishing Process including Casking.

[**Ans.** Cost per ton-Crushing Process : Rs. 646.67
Refining Process : Rs. 768.20 Finishing Process : Rs. 814.92]

18. Swastik Oil Factory Limited is a manufacturing concern. Their main product passes through three processes namely Crushing, Refining and Finishing. The following particulars were extracted from the books for the month ending 31st March, 2003:

	Kernels consumed 1,000 tons Rs. 4,50,000		
	Crushing	**Refining**	**Finishing**
	Rs.	**Rs.**	**Rs.**
Wages	16,000	11,800	11,750
Power and Stores	2,400	2,000	3,000
Repairs and Stores	800	–	–
Rent and Taxes	1,800	1,500	1,200
Sundry Works Expenses	400	500	700
Office and Establishment Charges	6,900		
Sundry Materials for Refining		3,800	
Barrels for Storing Finished Oil		–	42,050

Cake sales 400 tons for Rs. 30,000, Crude Oil obtained 550 tons, Sundry bags sold Rs. 1,800, Refined oil 500 tons. Finished oil stored in barrels 480 tons and 20 tons Sundry sales realised Rs. 2,200. Establishment charges are to be apportioned as Rs. 2,800, Rs. 2,600 and Rs. 1,500 respectively, to three processes.

You are required to prepare a Crushing Process A/c, Refining Process A/c and Finishing Process A/c.

[**Ans.** Cost per ton : Crude oil Rs. 804.36, Refined oil Rs. 929.20, Finished Oil Rs. 1,088.75]

19. The following particulars are taken from the books of an oil mill for the month of September, 2008:

Purchase of 100 tonnes of oil seeds at Rs. 10,000 per tonne.

	Crushing	**Refining**	**Finishing**
	Rs.	**Rs.**	**Rs.**
Wages	10,000	7,000	9,000
Stores used	2,000	6,000	1,000
Power	4,000	3,500	2,000
Steam	3,000	2,500	2,000
Factory Overheads	5,000	4,000	3,000
Containers			23,500

60 tonnes of crude oil were produced.

51 tonnes of oil were produced in the refining process. 50 tonnes of refined oil were finished for delivery. Empty bags of oil seeds are sold for Rs. 1,000.

35 tonnes of oil cake was sold at Rs. 600 per tonne. Loss in weight in crushing was 5 tonnes.

8.5 tonnes of by-products from the finished process were valued at Rs. 25,500.

Prepare accounts in respect of each process and calculate the cost of the product per tonne at the end of each process.

[**Ans.** Cost per tonne: Crushing Rs. 16,700; Refining Rs. 19,598; Finishing Rs. 20,800]

20. In manufacturing the main-product A, a company processes the resulting waste material into by-products M_1 and M_2. Using the method of working back from sales value to estimated cost, you are required to prepare comparative profit and loss statement of three products from the following data:

(*i*) Total Cost upto Separation Point was Rs. 1,36,000.

	A	**M_1**	**M_2**
(*ii*) Sales (all production)	Rs. 3,28,000	Rs. 32,000	Rs. 48,000
(*iii*) Cost after Separation	–	Rs. 9,600	Rs. 14,400
(*iv*) Estimated net Profit as Percentage of Sales Value	–	20%	30%

(v) Estimated Selling Expenses as Percentage of Sales Value	20%	20%	20%

(*I.C.W.A. Inter*)

[**Ans.** Profit: A-Rs. 1,45,600, M_1-Rs. 6,400, and M_2-Rs. 14,400; Share in joint Cost-M_1-Rs. 9,600 and M_2-Rs. 9,600]

21. A factory manufactures a commodity which passes through three processes A, B and C. The finished product of process A becomes the raw material of process B and the finished product of process B forms the raw material of process C which delivers the end product. The by-products of process A and B are sold direct from the factory.

	A	B	C
		Rs.	Rs.
Materials	1,000 tons @ Rs. 22 per ton	700	600
Wages	Rs. 20,000	30,000	36,000
Factory Overheads (Percentage on Wages)	75%	60%	50%
Wastage (of no sale value)	2 tons	3 tons	2 tons
Sales Proceeds of by-products	8 tons @ Rs. 40 per ton	5 tons @ Rs. 34 per ton	–

Draw up process accounts and by-products recoveries accounts, assuming that the by-products are valued at estimated market price of Rs. 25 per ton for process A and Rs. 20 per ton for process B at the point of the above separation. (*C.A. Inter*)

[**Ans.** Cost of production. Process A-Rs. 57.37, Process B-Rs. 107.33 and Process C-Rs. 163.27, By-product recoveries profit Rs. 190]

22. A factory is engaged in the production of a chemical X, and in the course of its manufacture a by-product Y is produced, which after a separate process has a commercial value. For the month of August, 2008, the following are the summarised costing data:

	Joint Expenses	Separate X	Expenses Y
	Rs.	Rs.	Rs.
Materials	19,200	7,360	780
Labour	11,700	7,680	2,642
Oncost	3,450	1,500	544

The output for the month was 142 tonnes of X and 49 tonnes of Y and the selling price of Y averaged Rs. 280 per tonne.

Assuming that the profit on Y is estimated at 50% of the selling price, prepare an account showing the cost of X per tonne.

[**Ans.** Product X Rs. 338 per tonne ; Product Y Rs. 140 per tonne.]

23. From the following information, find the profit made by each product apportioning joint costs on sales-value basis:

		Rs.
Joint Costs		
Direct materials		1,26,000
Power		25,000
Petrol, Oil, Lubricants		5,000
Labour		7,500
Other charges		4,100
	Product X	**Product Y**
	Rs.	**Rs.**
Selling costs	40,990	59,050
Sales	1,52,000	1,68,000

(*I.C.W.A.*)

[**Ans.** Profit X Rs. 31,400; Y Rs. 20,960]

24. In the course of the manufacture of the main-product 'P', by-products 'A' and 'B' also emerge. The joint expenses of manufacture amount to Rs. 1,19,550. All the three products are processed further after separation and sold as per details given below:

	Main Product	**By-Products**	
	'P'	**A**	**B**
Sales	Rs. 90,000	Rs. 60,000	Rs. 40,000
Cost Incurred after Separation	Rs. 6,000	Rs. 5,000	Rs. 4,000
Profit as %Age on Sale	25%	20%	15%

The fixed selling expenses are 10% of total cost of sales which are apportioned to the three products in the ratio of 20 : 40 : 40.

(*i*) Prepare a statement showing the apportionment of joint costs to the main-product and the two by-products.

(*ii*) If the by-product A is not subjected to further processing and is sold at the point of separation, for which there is a market at Rs. 58,500 without incurring any selling expenses, would you advise its disposal at this stage? Show the working.

(*C.A. Inter*)

[**Ans.** (*a*) P - Rs. 58,510; A - Rs. 37,020; B - Rs. 24,020
(*b*) Advisable to sell before further processing.]

25. From the following particulars make out a weekly cost sheet showing profit on main-product of mini petroleum company:

Crude oil used	5,00,000 Litres @ Re. 0.50
Petrol produced (Main product)	1,50,000 Litres @ Rs. 2.50

By-products:

(1) Lubricating oil produced 50,000 Litres @ Rs. 2.00

(2) Fuel oil produced 2,50,000 Litres @ Re. 1.00

(3) Kerosene oil produced 30,000 Litres @ Re 0.80

Raw Materials consumed Rs. 48,000; Wages paid Rs. 1,20,000; Repairs and Renewals Rs. 86,000; Salaries and General charges Rs. 50,000.

Show the percentage of each product to the weight of crude oil used.

(*C.A., Inter*)

[**Ans.** Cost of petrol Rs. 1 ,80,000; Profit Rs. 1,95,000, Percentage of each product to the weight of crude oil used: Petrol 30%; Lubricating oil 10%; Fuel oil 50%; Kerosene 6% and Wastage 4%)

26. From a single raw material, a chemical company produces three products A, B and C. Product A is considered to be a by-product and products B and C are treated as major joint products.

In process I, by-product A is obtained and the remaining output passes to process II, where products B and C are obtained.

During April, 2007 the cost of materials consumed was Rs. 3,600 and operating costs were:

Process I Rs. 6,000 and Process II Rs. 7,500.

Work-in-progress was negligible both at the beginning and end of the month.

Production and Sales data for the month are given below:

Product	Production	Sales
A	6,000 Litres	3,000 litres at 5 paise per litre
B	9,000 kgs.	7,500 kgs. @ Rs. 2 per kg.
C	2,500 kgs.	1,500 kgs. @ Rs. 4.80 per kg.

Stock on 1 April, 2007 were:

A 600 Litres at 5 paise per litre

B 750 kgs. at Rs. 1.50 per kg.

C 50 kgs. at Rs. 3.75 per kg.

You are required to prepare statements showing (*a*) the value of stock of each product as on 30th April, 2007, employing market price for A and apportioning the remaining costs between B and C according to the sales value of the output and (*b*) gross profit for April, 2007.

[**Ans.** (*a*) A-Rs. 180 B-Rs.2,520 C-2,822.40
(*b*) A-Nil B-Rs. 6,315 C-3,114.90
Share of B and C in joint cost Rs. 10,080 and Rs. 6,720 respectively]

27. A Chemical Processing company produces four different products A, B, C and D from a single raw material. All the four products are produced simultaneously at a single split-off point. Product C does not require further processing. The other three products require further processing before being sold. The company adopts the suitable sale value method of allocating joint costs to products.

The cost of the material used for the year just ended was Rs. 18,000 and the initial processing cost amounted to a further Rs. 30,000. The output, sales and additional processing cost for the relevant year were as follows:

Product	Output (units)	Sales Rs.	Additional Processing Costs Rs.
A	4,000	36,000	5,000
B	3,500	14,000	1,750
C	2,500	20,000	–
D	1,200	12,000	3,250

(*a*) Prepare a comparative Profit and Loss Statement showing the profit or loss made on each product separately.

(*b*) A proposal has been made by the management to sell of split-off directly to other processors. If that alternative has been selected, sales price per unit would have been:
A-Rs. 7.00, B-Rs. 3.50, C-Rs. 8.00 and D-Rs. 9.00. What would be the overall net profit of the company under this alternative?

(*c*) Give your recomendations as to the future course of action to be followed by management in regards to its processing of products from the view point of profit improvement.

[**Ans.** (*a*) Profit A - Rs. 10,333, B - Rs. 4,083, C - Rs. 6,667, D - Rs. 2,917 (*b*) Rs. 23,050 (*c*) A should be processed further and D should be sold at split-off point]

28. Three joint products are produced by passing chemicals through two consecutive processes. Output from process 1 is transferred to process 2 from which the three joint products are produced and immediately sold. The data regarding the processes for April, 2009 is given below:

	Process I	Process 2
Direct Material 2,500 kilos at Rs. 4 per kilo	Rs. 10,000	
Direct Labour	Rs. 6,250	Rs. 6,900
Overheads	Rs. 4,500	Rs.6,900
Normal Loss	10% of input	Nil
Scrap Value of Loss	Rs. 2 per kilo	–
Output	2,300 kilos	Joint products A - 900 Kilos B - 800 Kilos C - 600 Kilos

There were no opening or closing stocks in either process and the selling prices of the output from process 2 were:

Joint product A	Rs. 24 per kilo
Joint product B	Rs. 18 per kilo
Joint product C	Rs. 12 per kilo

Required:

(*a*) Prepare an account for process 1 together with any Loss or Gain Accounts you consider necessary to record the month's activities.

(*b*) Calculate the profit attributable to each of the joint products by apportioning the total costs from process 2:

(*i*) According to weight of output;

(*ii*) By the market value of production.

(*C.A. Inter, May 1991*)

[**Ans.** (*a*) Process 1: Transfer to process 2 (2,300 kgs.) Rs. 20,700; Abnormal Gain (50 kg.) Rs. 450;

(*b*)	(*i*)	(*ii*)
A	8,100	4,350
B	2,400	2,900
C(1,800)	Loss	1,450]

16

Process Costing-III
(Equivalent Production)

The problem of work-in-progress in process industries is very important. In continuous processes, there must be some work-in-progress at the beginning and at the end of a period and the degree of completion of closing work-in-progress may be quite different from the degree of completion of opening work-in-progress. Work-in-Progress can be valued on the basis of actual cost, *i.e.*, an attempt may be made to find out how much materials have been used on the incomplete units and how much amount of labour and expenses have been spent on them.

But the problem of valuation of work-in-progress can also be solved by calculating what is known as 'Equivalent Production' or 'Effective Production'. Equivalent or effective production represents the production of a process expressed in terms of completed units. The formula for calculating equivalent production is:

Equivalent Production = Actual Number of units in process of manufacture × Percentage of work completed.

Thus, closing stock of 200 units in a process, 60% complete in respect of material, wages and overhead, is equivalent to 120 units (*i.e.*, 200 × 60%) which are 100% complete.

COMPUTATION OF EQUIVALENT PRODUCTION

The computation of the units of equivalent production shall be made with the help of the following steps:

(*i*) At the first place, the equivalent production of opening work-in-progress will be ascertained by taking into account the degree of work to be done on it during the current period. For example, if the opening work-in-progress is 500 units, 40% complete in all respects, then the degree of work required to be performed on it during the current period is 60%. As such, the equivalent production for opening work-in-progress during the current period will be 300 units (*i.e* 500 × 60%).

(*ii*) At the second place, the number of units introduced and completed during the current period will be computed. It can be done by deducting the closing work-in-progress from the units introduced in the process during the current period.

(*iii*) At the third place, the equivalent production for closing work-in-progress will be ascertained by taking into account the number of units of closing work-in-progress and the degree of work completed on them. If the closing work-in-progress is 800 units, 70% complete in all respects, the equivalent production of closing work-in-progress will be 560 units (*i.e.*, 800 × 70%).

(*iv*) At the end, the equivalent production calculated under the above-mentioned three steps, will be aggregated tc ascertain total output in terms of equivalent units or equivalent production.

Computation of equivalent production can be understood with the help of the following illustrations:

Illustration 1

In Process 'A' 2,000 units were introduced during April, 2007. 600 units, 30% complete in all respects remained as work-in-progress at the end of the month.

Compute the Equivalent Production for April, 2007.

Solution

Statement of Equivalent Production

Input		Output		Equivalent Production	
Items	**Units**	**Items**	**Units**	**Units**	**% of Completion**
Units Introduced during the month	2,000	(*i*) Units Introduced and completed during the month	1,400	1,400	100%
		(*ii*) Closing Work-in-Progress	600	180	30%
	2,000		2,000	1,580	

Illustration 2

In Process 'A' opening work-in-progress in May, 2007 was 500 units 40% complete. 3,000 units were introduced during the month. 3,200 completed units were transferred to next process and 300 units remained as closing work-in-progress 60% complete.

Compute Equivalent Production for the month of May, 2007.

Solution

Statement of Equivalent Production

Input		Output		Equivalent Production	
Items	**Units**	**Items**	**Units**	**Units**	**% of Completion**
Opening Work-in-Progress	500	(*i*)Completion of Opening W.I.P.	500	300	60%
Units Introduced during the month	3,000	(*ii*)Units Introduced and completed during the month	2,700	2,700	100%
		Transfer to next Process	3,200		
		(*iii*)Closing Work-in-Progress	300	180	60%
	3,500		3,500	3,180	

Illustration 3

The following data are available in respect of Process 'A' for the month of April, 2007:

Opening Work-in-Progress:	900 units
Degree of completion:	Material 80%, Labour and overhead 60%
Input of materials during the month:	6,000 units
Closing work-in-progress:	700 units
Degree of completion:	Material 70%, Labour and overhead 60%
Units transferred to next process:	6,200 units.

Compute Equivalent Production for the month of April, 2007.

Solution

Statement of Equivalent Production

Input		Output		Equivalent Production			
Items	**Units**	**Items**	**Units**	**Materials**		**Labour and Overhead**	
				Units	**% of Completion**	**Units**	**% of Completion**
Opening Work-in-progress	900	(*i*) Completion of Opening W.I.P.	900	180	20%	360	40%
Units Introduced during the month	6,000	(*ii*) Units introduced and completed during the month	5,300	5,300	100%	5,300	100%
		Transfer to next process	6,200				
		(*iii*) Closing work-in-progress	700	490	70%	420	60%
	6,900		6,900	5,970		6,080	

EVALUATION OF EQUIVALENT PRODUCTION

The evaluation of equivalent production is usually made by preparing the following three statements

(*i*) **Statement of Equivalent Production:** This statement shows the number of equivalent completed units.

(*ii*) **Statement of cost per Equivalent unit:** This statement is prepared to compute the element-wise cost per equivalent unit. For this purpose, the cost of each element (*i.e.*, material, labour and overhead) is divided by the equivalent units of production of that element.

(*iii*) **Statement Showing the Apportionment of Costs or Statement of Evaluation:** This statement shows the apportionment of the total process cost to the finished output and work-in-progress of the process.

I Case – When there is closing work-in-progress without any process loss:

Illustration 4

In Process 'A' 10,000 units were introduced during April, 2007. 2,000 units 80% complete in respect of materials and 60% complete in respect of labour and overhead remained as work-in-progress at the end of the month. The process costs during the month were:

	Rs.
Materials	48,000
Labour	27,600
Overhead	18,400

There is no loss in the process.

Prepare (*i*) Statement of Equivalent Production.

(*ii*) Statement of cost per unit of Equivalent Production.

(*iii*) Statement showing the apportionment of process costs.

Solution

Statement of Equivalent Production

Input		Output		Equivalent Production			
				Materials		Labour and Overhead	
Items	Units	Items	Units	Units	% of Completion	Units	% of Completion
Units Introduced during the month	10,000	(*i*) Units Introduced and completed during the month	8,000	8,000	100%	8,000	100%
		(*ii*) Closing work-in-progress	2,000	1,600	80%	1,200	60%
	10,000		10,000	9,600		9,200	

Statement of cost per unit of Equivalent Production

Elements	Cost	Equivalent Production	Cost per unit
	Rs.	Units	Rs.
Materials	48,000	9,600	5.00
Wages	27,600	9,200	3.00
Overhead	18,400	9,200	2.00
Total Cost	94,000		10.00

Statement Showing the Apportionment of Costs

	Equivalent Production Units	Cost per unit Rs.	Cost Rs.	Total Rs.
(*i*) Units Introduced and completed				
Materials	8,000	5.00	40,000	
Wages	8,000	3.00	24,000	
Overhead	8,000	2.00	16,000	80,000
(*ii*) Closing Work-in-Progress				
Materials	1,600	5.00	8,000	
Wages	1,200	3.00	3,600	14,000
Overhead	1,200	2.00	2,400	
Total Costs				94,000

II Case: When there is closing work-in-progress accompanied by process loss:

Process operations are subject to loss which may be normal loss or abnormal loss. Normal loss is borne by normal output. As such, in case of normal loss, nothing is added as equivalent production while preparing the 'Statement of Equivalent Production'. If the normal loss (units scrapped) has some realisable value, the same should be deducted from the cost of materials while preparing 'Statement of cost per unit of Equivalent Production'. Abnormal loss is not allowed to affect the cost of other units. It is added to equivalent production and is valued at the cost applicable to the good units.

In case the actual loss is less than the normal loss, the saving is treated as 'abnormal gain' or 'abnormal effectives'. The units of abnormal gain are deducted in the 'Statement of Equivalent Production' while computing equivalent production.

Illustration 5

4,000 units of basic material were introduced in Process 'A' at a cost of Rs. 11,600 in April, 2007. The normal loss is estimated at 5% of input and has a realisable value of Re. 1 per unit.

At the end of the month, 2,800 units were completed and transferred to next process, 920 units were incomplete and 280 units had been scrapped. The degree of completion of closing work-in-progress was as follows:

Materials	75%
Labour	50%
Overhead	50%

Process costs were as under:

Direct Materials	Rs. 2,880
Direct Wages	Rs. 6,680
Overhead	Rs. 3,340

Units scrapped passed through the process and were 100% completed as regards material, labour and overhead. Find out (*a*) Equivalent Production, (*b*) Cost per unit, and make the apportionment of process costs. Also prepare Process A Account.

Solution

Statement of Equivalent Production

Input		Output		Equivalent Production			
Items	Units	Items	Units	Materials		Labour and Overhead	
				Units	% of Completion	Units	% of Completion
Units Introduced during the month	4,000	(*i*) Units Introduced and completed during the month	2,800	2,800	100%	2,800	100%
		(*ii*) Normal Loss	200	–	–	–	–
		(*iii*) Abnormal Loss	80	80	100%	80	100%
		(*iv*) Closing work-in-progress	920	690	75%	460	50%
	4,000		4,000	3,570		3,340	

Statement of Cost per unit of Equivalent Production

Elements	Cost	Equivalent Production (Units)	Cost per unit
	Rs.		Rs.
Materials:			
Cost of Units Introduced	11,600		
Direct Materials	2,880		
	14,480		
Less Scrap value of Normal loss (200 units × Re. 1)	200		
	14,280	3,570	4.00
Direct Wages	6,680	3,340	2.00
Overhead	3,340	3,340	1.00
Total Cost	24,300		7.00

Statement Showing the Apportionment of Process Costs

	Equivalent Production Units	Cost per unit Rs.	Cost Rs.	Total Cost Rs.
(*i*) Units Introduced and completed:				
Materials	2,800	4.00	11,200	
Wages	2,800	2.00	5,600	
Overhead	2,800	1.00	2,800	19,600
(*ii*) Abnormal Loss:				
Materials	80	4.00	320	
Wages	80	2.00	160	
Overhead	80	1.00	80	560
(*iii*) Closing Work-in-Progress				
Materials	690	4.00	2,760	
Wages	460	2.00	920	4,140
Overhead	460	1.00	460	
Total Costs				24,300

Process A Account

Particulars	Units	Amount Rs.	Particulars	Units	Amount Rs.
To Units Introduced	4,000	11,600	By Normal Loss	200	200
To Direct Materials		2,880	By Abnormal Loss	80	560
To Direct Wages		6,680			
To Overhead		3,340	By Process B A/c (Output Transferred)	2,800	19,600
			By Balance c/d (Closing work-in-progress)	920	4,140
	4,000	24,500		4,000	24,500

Abnormal Loss Account

Particulars	Units	Amount Rs.	Particulars	Units	Amount Rs.
To Process A A/c	80	560	By Cash A/c (Sale @ Re. 1 per unit)	80	80
			By Costing Profit and Loss A/c	–	480
	80	560		80	560

III Case: When there is opening as well as closing work-in-progress without process loss:

In case both the opening work-in-progress and closing work-in-progress are given, the valuation of completed units and work-in-progress can be made on the basis of First-in-First-Out Method, Last-in-First-Out Method or Average Method.

(*a*) First-in-First-Out Method

Under the first-in-first-out (FIFO) method the basic assumption is that materials in the process move on first-in-first-out basis which means that the units entering the process first are to be completed first. Thus the opening work-in-progress shall first be completely processed and then the units introduced during the current period are taken up. Accordingly, under this method the cost put in during the current period is pro-rated to the production necessary to complete the opening work-in-progress, to complete the units introduced and completed during the period and to partially completed units of closing work-in-progress.

(*b*) Last- in- First- Out Method:

Last- in- First- Out (Lifo) Method is based on the assumption that materials in the process move on last-in-first-out basis which means that the units entering the process last are to be completed first. As such, the units of material introduced during the current period shall be deemed to have been completed first and these units will be shown at their current cost. The closing stock of work-in-progress may comprise the units out of the current period's input which could not be completed and the units of opening work-in-progress.

(*c*) Average Method:

Average method of valuation is employed where the degree of completion of opening stock of work-in-progress is not given. Under this method the cost of opening work-in-progress is added to the cost put into the process during the current period to ascertain the 'total process cost'. The total process cost is then divided by the equivalent production obtained by adding the number of units completed and transferred and the effective units of closing work-in-progress.

Illustration 6

From the following details, prepare Statement of Equivalent Production, Statement of Cost and Statement showing apportionment of cost by following First-in-First-Out Method:

Opening Work-in-Progress: 2,000 units

	Rs.
Materials (100% Complete)	5,000
Labour (60% Complete)	3,000
Overhead (60% Complete)	1,500
	9,500

Units introduced into the process during the current period: 8,000.

There are 2,000 units in progress at the end of the period and the stage of completion is estimated to be:

Materials	100%
Labour	50%
Overhead	50%.

8,000 units are transferred to next process. There is no process loss and the process costs for the period are:

	Rs.
Material	88,000
Labour	62,400
Overhead	31,200
	1,81,600

Solution

Statement of Equivalent Production

Input		Output		Equivalent Production			
				Materials		Labour & Overhead	
Items	Units	Items	Units	Units	% of Completion	Units	% of Completion
Opening Stock of Work-in-Progress	2,000	(*i*) Completion of opening work-in-progress	2,000	–	–	800	40%
Units Introduced during the period	8,000	(*ii*)Units Introduced and Completed during the period	6,000	6,000	100%	6,000	100%
		Transfer to Next Process	8,000				
		(*iii*)Closing work-in-progress	2,000	2,000	100%	1,000	50%
	10,000		10,000	8,000		7,800	

Statement of per unit Cost of Equivalent Production

Element	Cost	Equivalent Production (Units)	Cost per unit
	Rs.		Rs.
Material	88,000	8,000	11.00
Wages	62,400	7,800	8.00
Overhead	31,200	7,800	4.00
Total Cost	1,81,600		23.00

Statement Showing the Apportionment of Costs

	Equivalent Production (Units)	Cost per unit	Cost	Total Cost
		Rs.	Rs.	Rs.
(*i*) Completion of Opening Work-in-progress				
Materials	–	–	–	
Wages	800	8.00	6,400	
Overhead	800	4.00	3,200	9,600
(*ii*) Units Introduced and Completed:				
Materials	6,000	11.00	66,000	
Wages	6,000	8.00	48,000	
Overhead	6,000	4.00	24,000	1,38,000
(*iii*) Closing Work-in-progress:				
Materials	2,000	11.00	22,000	
Wages	1,000	8.00	8,000	
Overhead	1,000	4.00	4,000	34,000
Total Cost				1,81,600

Illustration 7

From the following particulars relating to Process A for the month of April, 2003, calculate the equivalent production units and the value of finished production and work-in-progress using the Lifo method

Opening work-in-progress on 1st April, 2003: 5.000 units (50% complete)

	Cost (Rs.)	
Material	12,000	
Labour	16,000	
Overhead	16,000	
		44,000

Units introduced into the process during the month: 10,000

	Cost (Rs.)	
Material	60,000	
Labour	1,05,000	
Overhead	1,40,000	
		3,05,000

During the period, 7,500 units were completed and transferred to next process. Closing work-in-progress on 30th April: 7,500 units (50 % complete).

Solution

Statement of Equivalent Production

Input		Output		Equivalent Production			
Items	Units	Items	Units	Materials		Labour & Overhead	
				Units	% of Completion	Units	% of Completion
Opening Work-in -progress	5,000	Units Introduced - completed and transferred to next process during the month	7,500	7,500	100%	7,500	100%
Units introduced during the month	10,000	Closing work-in-progress					
		(*i*) Out of the units introduced during the month	2,500	1,250	50%	1,250	50%
		(*ii*) Out of opening work-in-progress	5,000	–	–	–	–
	15,000		15,000	8,750		8,750	

Since the units in the opening work in progress were already 50% complete, no additional work has been performed on these units during the current period.

$$\text{Cost per unit of Equivalent Production} = \frac{\text{Total Process Cost}}{\text{Equivalent Production}}$$

$$= \frac{\text{Rs.}3{,}05{,}000}{8{,}750 \text{ units}}$$

$$= \text{Rs.}34.857 \text{ or Rs. } 34.86$$

Valuation of Finished Production and Work-in-Progress:

(*i*) Finished Production: 7,500 Units × Rs. 34.86 = Rs. 2,61,450

(*ii*) Closing work-in-progress: Rs. 44,000 + (1,250 × Rs. 34.86) = Rs. 87,575

Illustration 8

From the following information for January, 2009, prepare process cost accounts for Process A by average method:

Opening Stock	:	10,000 units
Materials	:	Rs. 40,000
Wages	:	Rs. 38,000
Overhead	:	Rs. 32,000
Units Introduced	:	40,000 units
Materials	:	Rs. 2,10,000
Labour	:	Rs. 1,50,000
Overhead	:	Rs. 1,00,000

During the period 35,000 units were completed and transferred to Process B.

Closing Stock	:	15,000 units
Degree of completion :		
Materials	:	100%
Labour	:	80%
Overhead	:	60%

Solution

Statement of Equivalent Production (Average Method)

Input		Output		Equivalent Production					
Items	Units	Items	Units	Materials		Labour		Overhead	
				Units	% of comp.	Units	% of compl.	Units	% of compl.
Opening work-in-progress	10,000	(*i*) Opening work-in-progress (Costs also added)	10,000	10,000	100%	10,000	100%	10,000	100%
Units Introduced	40,000	(*ii*) Units Introduced and completed	25,000	25,000	100%	25,000	100%	25,000	100%
		Transfer to Process B	35,000						
		(*iii*) Closing work-in-progress	15,000	15,000	100%	12,000	80%	9,000	60%
	50,000		50,000	50,000		47,000		44,000	

Statement of Average Cost of Each Element

Element	Opening Cost	Cost in Process A	Total Cost	Equiv. Production	Cost per unit
	Rs.	Rs.	Rs.	Units	Rs.
Materials	40,000	2,10,000	2,50,000	50,000	5.00
Labour	38,000	1,50,000	1,88,000	47,000	4.00
Overhead	32,000	1,00,000	1,32,000	44,000	3.00
Total	1,10,000	4,60,000	5,70,000		12.00

Statement Showing the Apportionment of Costs

	Equivalent Production Units	Cost per unit Rs.	Cost Rs.	Total Cost Rs.
(*i*) Units completed and Transferred:				
Materials	35,000	5.00	1,75,000	
Labour	35,000	4.00	1,40,000	
Overhead	35,000	3.00	1,05,000	4,20,000
(*ii*) Closing work-in-progress:				
Materials	15,000	5.00	75,000	
Labour	12,000	4.00	48,000	
Overhead	9,000	3.00	27,000	1,50,000
Total Costs				5,70,000

Process A Account

Particulars	Units	Amount Rs.	Particulars	Units	Amount Rs.
To Balance b/d (Opening work-in-progress)	10,000	1,10,000	By Process B A/c (Units completed and transferrd)	35,000	4,20,000
To Units of Materials Introduced	40,000	2,10,000	By Balance c/d (Closing work-in-progress)	15,000	1,50,000
To Labour		1,50,000			
To Overhead		1,00,000			
	50,000	5,70,000		50,000	5,70,000

IV Case: When there is opening as well as closing work-in-progress accompanied by process loss:

Illustration 9

The following data are available in respect of Process A for June, 2007:

Opening Work-in-Progress	:	450 units at Rs. 2,250.
Degree of completion	:	Material 100%, Labour and overhead 60%
Input of materials	:	4,550 units at Rs. 13,650.
Direct wages	:	Rs. 4,100
Overhead	:	Rs. 8,200
Units scrapped	:	600 units
Degree of completion	:	Material 100%, Labour and overhead 70%
Closing Work-in-Progress	:	500 units
Degree of completion	:	Material 100%, Labour and overhead 80%
Units transferred to next process	:	3,900 units
Normal Loss	:	10% of total input (opening stock plus units put in) scrap value Rs. 3 per unit.

Compute Equivalent Production and show the apportionment of costs to production and work-in-progress and prepare Process A Account.

Solution

Statement of Equivalent Production

Input		Output		Equivalent Production			
				Materials		Labour & overhead	
Items	Units	Items	Units	Units	% of completion	Units	% of completion
Opening Work-in-Progress	450	(i) Completion of Opening Work-in-Progress	450	–	–	180	40%
Units Introduced	4,550	(ii) Units introduced and completed during the period	3,450	3,450	100%	3,450	100%
		Transfer to next process	3,900				
		(iii) Normal Loss (10% of 5,000)	500	–	–	–	–
		(iv) Abnormal loss (600-500)	100	100	100%	70	70%
		(v) Closing Work-in-Progress	500	500	100%	400	80%
	5,000		5,000	4,050		4,100	

Statement of Cost per Equivalent unit

		Cost	Equivalent Production	Cost per unit
	Rs.	Rs.	Units	Rs.
Materials Introduced	13,650			
Less Sale of Scrap	1,500	12,150	4,050	3.00
Direct wages		4,100	4,100	1.00
Overhead		8,200	4,100	2.00
Total Cost		24,450		

Statement showing the Apportionment of Costs

	Equiv. Produc. (units)	Cost per unit	Cost	Total Cost
		Rs.	Rs.	Rs.
(i) Completion of opening work-in-progress				
Materials	–	–	–	–
Wages	180	1	180	
Overhead	180	2	360	540
(ii) Units introduced and completed				
Materials	3,450	3	10,350	
Wages	3,450	1	3,450	
Overhead	3,450	2	6,900	20,700
(iii) Abnormal Loss				
Materials	100	3	300	
Wages	70	1	70	
Overhead	70	2	140	510
(iv) Closing Work-in-progress				
Material	500	3	1,500	
Wages	400	1	400	
Overhead	400	2	800	2,700
Total Costs				24,450

Process A Account

Particulars	Units	Rs.	Particulars	Units	Rs.
To Balance b/d	450	2,250	By Normal Loss	500	1,500
To Materials Introduced	4,550	13,650	By Abnormal Loss	100	510
To Direct Wages		4,100	By Next Process A/c (Transfer)	3,900	23,490
To Overhead		8,200	By Balance c/d	500	2,700
	5,000	28,200		5,000	28,200

Illustration 10

The following data are available in respect of Process 1 for the month of April, 2003:

(*i*) Opening stock of work-in-progress: 400 units at a total cost of Rs. 8,000.

(*ii*) Degree of completion of opening work-in-progress:

Material	100%
Labour	60%
Overhead	60%

(*iii*) Input of materials during April, 2003: 4,600 units at a cost of Rs. 70,400.

(*iv*) Direct wages Rs. 33,480.

(*v*) Production overhead Rs. 16,740.

(*vi*) Units scrapped: 600 units

Degree of completion

Material	100%
Labour	80%
Overhead	80%

(*vii*) Closing work-in-progress: 450 units

Degree of completion

Material	100%
Labour	70%
Overhead	70%

(*viii*) 3,950 units were completed and transferred to the next process.

(*ix*) Normal loss : 8% of total input (opening stock + units put in)

(*x*) Scrap value : Rs. 8 per unit.

You are required to

(*a*) Compute equivalent production.

(*b*) Calculate cost per unit for each element.

(*c*) Calculate the cost of abnormal loss.

(*d*) Calculate the cost of units transferred to next process and closing work-in-progress by using Last-in-First-out Method.

(*e*) Prepare the Process 1 Account for April, 2003.

Solution

Statement of Equivalent Production

Input		Output		Equivalent Production			
				Materials		Labour & Overhead	
Items	Units	Items	Units	Units	% of Completion	Units	% of Completion
Opening Work- in progress	400	(*a*) Units Introduced completed and transferred to Process II (out of current input)	3,950	3,950	100%	3,950	100%
Units introduced during the month	4,600	(*b*) Normal Loss	400	–	–	–	–
		(*c*) Abnormal Loss	200	200	100%	160	80%
		(*d*) Closing work-in-progress					
		(*i*) Out of current input	50	50	100%	35	70%
		(*ii*) Out of opening work-in-progress	400	–		40	10%
	5,000		5,000	4,200		4,185	

Statement of Cost per Unit of Equivalent Production

Elements	Cost	Equivalent Production (Units)	Cost per Unit
	Rs.		Rs.
Material	70,400		
Less Realisabale value of normal loss	3,200		
	67,200	4,200	16.00
Labour	33,480	4,185	8.00
Overhead	16,740	4,185	4.00
	1,17,420		28.00

Statement of Evaluation

	Equivalent Production	Cost per Unit	Cost	Total Cost
	Units	Rs.	Rs.	Rs.
(*a*) Units introduced and completed during the month				
Material	3,950	16	63,200	
Labour	3,950	8	31,600	
Overhead	3,950	4	15,800	1,10,600
(*b*) Abnormal Loss:				
Material	200	16	3,200	
Labour	160	8	1,280	
Overhead	160	4	640	5,120
(*c*) Closing work- in- progress				
(*i*) Out of current input				
Material	50	16	800	
Labour	35	8	280	
Overhead	35	4	140	1,220
(*ii*) Out of opening work- in -progress				
Material	–	–	–	
Labour	40	8	320	
Overhead	40	4	160	480
Total cost				1,17,420

Process I Account

Particulars	Units	Amount Rs.	Particulars	Units	Amount Rs.
			By Normal Loss A/c	400	3,200
To Opening Work-in-progress	400	8,000	By Abnormal Loss A/c	200	5,120
To Units Introduced	4,600	70,400	By Process II A/c	3,950	1,10,600
To Wages		33,480	By Closing work-in progress	450	9,700
To Overhead		16,740			
	5,000	1,28,620		5,000	1,28,620

Illustration 11

From the following information for April, 2007 prepare process cost accounts for Process 'B':

Opening stock of Work-in-progress in

Process 'B'	:	600 units at Rs. 2,100
Transfer from Process 'A'	:	11,000 units at Rs. 11,000
Direct materials added in process 'B'	:	Rs. 9,640
Direct wages	:	Rs. 14,310
Production overhead	:	Rs. 19,080
Transferred to process 'C'	:	8,800 units
Units scrapped during the month	:	1,200 units
Closing stock of Work-in-Progress	:	1,600 units

Degree of completion:

	Opening stock	Closing stock	Scrap
Material	80%	70%	100%
Labour	60%	60%	70%
Overhead	60%	60%	70%

There was a normal loss of 10% of production and units scrapped were sold at Re. 1 per unit.

Solution

Statement of Equivalent Production

Input		Output		Equivalent Production							
Items	Units	Items	Units	Material A		Material B		Wages		Overhead	
				Units	% of Comp	Units	% of Comp.	Units	% of Comp.	Units	% of Comp
Opening Stock of Work-in-Progress	600	(*i*) Completion of opening Work-in-Progress	600	–	–	120	20%	240	40%	240	40%
Transfer from Process A	11,000	(*ii*) Units Introduced and Completed	8,200	8,200	100%	8,200	100%	8,200	100%	8,200	100%
		Transfer to Process C	8,800								
		(*iii*) Normal Loss	1,000	–	–	–	–	–	–	–	–
		(*iv*) Abnormal Loss	200	200	100%	200	100%	140	70%	140	70%
		(*v*) Closing Work-in-Progcsss	1,600	1,600	100%	1,120	70%	960	60%	960	60%
	11,600		11,600	10,000		9,640		9,540		9,540	

Notes: (*i*) Material 'A' refers to the finished product of Process 'A' which shall always be 100% completed. Material 'B' refers to matcrial added to Process 'B'.

(*ii*) Production of Process 'B' has been calculated as follows:

Opening stock + Units introduced – Closing stock
= 600 units + 11,000 units – 1,600 units
= 10,000 units.

(*iii*) Normal Process Loss = 10% of 10,000 units
= 1,000 units.

(*iv*) Abnormal Process Loss = Actual Loss – Normal Loss
= 1,200 units – 1,000 units
= 200 units.

Statement of Cost for Each Element

		Cost Rs.	Equivalent Production Units	Cost per unit Rs.
Material 'A'				
(Materials from Process A)	Rs. 11,000			
Less Sale of Scrap 1,000 units	Rs. 1,000			
@ Re. 1 per unit (Normal Loss)		10,000	10,000	1.00
Material 'B' (added in Process B)		9,640	9,640	1.00
Direct Wages		14,310	9,540	1.50
Production Overhead		19,080	9,540	2.00
Total Cost		53,030		

Statement showing the Apportionment of Costs

	Equiv. Prod. Units	Cost per unit Rs.	Cost Rs.	Total Cost Rs.
(*i*) Completion of Opening Work-in-Progress:				
Material A	–	–	–	–
Material B	120	1.00	120	
Wages	240	1.50	360	
Overhead	240	2.00	480	960
(*ii*) Units Introduced and Completed:				
Material A	8,200	1.00	8,200	
Material B	8,200	1.00	8,200	
Wages	8,200	1.50	12,300	
Overhead	8,200	2.00	16,400	45,100
(*iii*) Abnormal Loss:				
Material A	200	1.00	200	
Material B	200	1.00	200	
Wages	140	1.50	210	
Overhead	140	2.00	280	890
(*iv*) Closing Work-in-Progress:				
Material A	1,600	1.00	1,600	
Material B	1,120	1.00	1,120	
Wages	960	1.50	1,440	
Overhead	960	2.00	1,920	6,080
Total Costs				53,030

Process B Account

Particulars	Units	Rs.	Particulars	Units	Rs.
To Balance b/d	600	2,100			
To Process A A/c	11,000	11,000	By Normal Loss	1,000	1,000
			By Abnormal Loss	200	890
To Materials		9,640	By Process C A/c	8,800	48,160
To Wages		14,310			
To Overhead		19,080	By Balance c/d	1,600	6,080
	11,600	56,130		11,600	56,130

Illustration 12

From the following information for January, 2007, prepare process cost accounts for Process B:

Opening stock of work-in-progress	:	3,200 units at Rs. 28,000
Degree of completion		Material 70%, Labour 60%, Overhead 60%
Transfer from Process A	:	20,400 units at Rs. 96,000
Transfer to Process C	:	18,200 units
Direct materials added in Process B	:	Rs. 53,760
Direct Labour	:	Rs. 35,040
Overhead	:	Rs. 17,520
Units scrapped	:	1,800 units
Degree of completion	:	Material 100%, Labour 70%, Overhead 70%.
Closing stock of work-in-progress	:	3,600 units.
Degree of completion	:	Material 60%, Labour 40%, Overhead 40%

Normal Loss in the process was 10% of *production and scrap was sold at Rs. 2 per unit.*

Solution

Statement of Equivalent Production

Input		Output		Equivalent Production							
				Material A		Material B		Wages		Overhead	
Items	Units	Items	Units	Units	% of Comp.	Units	% of Comp.	Units	% of Comp.	Units	% of Comp.
Opening Stock of Work-in-Progress	3,200	(*i*) Completion of opening Work-in-Progress	3,200	–	–	960	30%	1,280	40%	1,280	40%
Transfer from Process A	20,400	(*ii*) Units introduced and completed	15,000	15,000	100%	15,000	100%	15,000	100%	15,000	100%
		Transfer to Process C	18,200								
		(*iii*) Normal Loss	2,000	–	–	–	–	–	–	–	–
		(*iv*) Closing Work-in-Progesss	3,600	3,600	100%	2,160	60%	1,440	40%	1,440	40%
			23,800	18,600		18,120		17,720		17,720	
		(*v*) Less Abnormal Gain	200	200	100%	200	100%	200	100%	200	100%
	23,600		23,600	18,400		17,920		17,520		17,520	

Notes: (*i*) Material 'A' refers to the finished product of Process A which shall always be 100% completed.

(*ii*) Production of Process B has been calculated as follows:

Production = Opening stock + Units introduced – Closing stock
= 3,200 + 20,400 – 3,600
= 20,000 units.

(*iii*) Normal Process Loss = 10% of 20,000 units
= 2,000

(*iv*) Abnormal Gain = Normal Loss – Actual Loss
= 2,000 units – 1,800 units
= 200 units.

Statement of Cost for each Element

		Cost Rs.	Equivalent Production Units	Cost per unit Rs.
Material 'A'				
(Materials from process A)	Rs. 96,000			
Less Sale of scrap of normal loss (2,000 units at 2 per unit)	Rs. 4,000	92,000	18,400	5.00
Material 'B' (added in Process B)		53,760	17,920	3.00
Labour		35,040	17,520	2.00
Overhead		17,520	17,520	1.00
Total cost		1,98,320		

Statement Showing the Apportionment of Costs

	Equiv. Prod. Units	Cost per unit Rs.	Cost Rs.	Total Cost Rs.
Completion of Opening W.I.P.:				
Material A	–	–	–	–
Material B	960	3.00	2,880	
Labour	1,280	2.00	2,560	
Overhead	1,280	1.00	1,280	6,720
Units Introduced and Completed:				
Material A	15,000	5.00	75,000	
Material B	15,000	3.00	45,000	
Labour	15,000	2.00	30,000	
Overhead	15,000	1.00	15,000	1,65,000
Closing Work-in-progress:				
Material A	3,600	5.00	18,000	
Material B	2,160	3.00	6,480	
Labour	1,440	2.00	2,880	
Overhead	1,440	1.00	1,440	28,800
				2,00,520
Less Abnormal gain:				
Material A	200	5.00	1,000	
Material B	200	3.00	600	
Labour	200	2.00	400	
Overhead	200	1.00	200	2,200
				1,98,320

Process B Account

Particulars	Units	Rs.	Particulars	Units	Rs.
To Balance b/d	3,200	28,000	By Normal Loss	2,000	4,000
To Process A A/c	20,400	96,000			
To Materials		53,760	By Process C A/c (Output transferred)	18,200	1,99,720
To Labour		35,040			
To Overhead		17,520			
To Abnormal Gain A/c	200	2,200	By Balance c/d	3,600	28,800
	23,800	2,32,520		23,800	2,32,520

Illustration 13

1. The following data pertains to Process A for March, 2003 of Alpha Textiles Ltd.

   Opening Work-in-progress 1,500 units for Rs. 15,000
   Degree of completion:

   Materials 100%, Labour and Overheads $33\frac{1}{3}\%$

   Input of Materials 18,500 units at Rs. 52,000
   Direct Labour Rs. 14,000
   Overheads Rs. 28,000
   Closing Work-in-progress 5,000 units
   Degree of completion:
   Materials 90%, Labour and Overheads 30%
   Normal process loss is 10% of total input
   (Opening Work-in-progress units + Units put in)
   Scrap value Rs. 2.00 per unit.
   Units transferred to the next process 15,000 units.
   You are required to:
   (*a*) Compute equivalent units of production.
   (*b*) Compute cost per equivalent unit for each cost element i.e., materials, labour and overheads.
   (*c*) Compute the cost of finished output and closing work-in-progress.
   (*d*) Prepare the process and other accounts.
   Assume:
   (*i*) FIFO method is used by the company.
   (*ii*) The cost of opening work-in-progress is fully transferred to next process.

(G.N.D.U., B.Com., 2000, C.A. Inter 1990)

Solution

Statement of Equivalent Production

Input		Output		Equivalent Production			
				Materials		Labour & Overhead	
Items	Units	Items	Units	Units	% of Completion	Units	% of Completion
Opening Work-in-progress	1,500	(*i*) Completion of opening work-in-progress	1,500	–	–	1,000	$66\frac{2}{3}$%
Units Introduced during the month	18,500	(*ii*) Units Introduced & completed during the month	13,500	13,500	100%	13,500	100%
		Output transferred to Next Process	15,000				
		(*iii*) Normal Loss (10% of 20,000 units)	2,000	–	–	–	–
		(*iv*) Closing Work-in-progress	5,000	4,500	90%	1,500	30%
			22,000	18,000		16,000	
		(*v*) Less Abnormal Gain	2,000	2,000	100%	2,000	100%
	20,000		20,000	16,000		14,000	

Statement of per unit Cost of Each Element

Elements	Cost Rs.	Equivalent Production (Units)	Cost per unit Rs.
Materials	52,000		
Less Sale of scrap	4,000		
	48,000	16,000	3.00
Wages	14,000	14,000	1.00
Overheads	28,000	14,000	2.00
	90,000		6.00

Statement Showing the Apportionment of Costs

	Equivalent Production (Units)	Cost per unit Rs.	Cost Rs.	Total Cost Rs.
(*i*) Completion of Opening Work-in-progress:				
Materials	–	–	–	
Wages	1,000	1.00	1,000	
Overhead	1,000	2.00	2,000	3,000
(*ii*) Units Introduced and Completed during the month				
Materials	13,500	3.00	40,500	
Wages	13,500	1.00	13,500	
Overhead	13,500	2.00	27,000	81,000
(*iii*)Closing Work-in-progress				
Materials	4,500	3.00	13,500	
Wages	1,500	1.00	1,500	
Overhead	1,500	2.00	3,000	18,000
				1,02,000
(*iv*)Less Abnormal Gain:				
Materials	2,000	3.00	6,000	
Wages	2,000	1.00	2,000	
Overhead	2,000	2.00	4,000	12,000
	Total Cost			90,000

Process A Account

Particulars	Units	Amount Rs.	Particulars	Units	Amount Rs.
To Opening W.I.P	1,500	15,000	By Normal Loss A/c	2,000	4,000
To Units Introduced	18,500	52,000	By Process B A/c	15,000	99,000
To Wages		14,000	By Closing Work-in-Progress	5,000	18,000
To Overhead		28,000			
To Abnormal Gain A/c	2,000	12,000			
	22,000	1,21,000		22,000	1,21,000

Abnormal Gain Account

Particulars	Units	Amount Rs.	Particulars	Units	Amount Rs.
To Normal Loss A/c	2,000	4,000	By Process A A/c	2,000	12,000
To Costing Profit and Loss A/c	–	8,000			
	2,000	12,000		2,000	12,000

Normal Loss Account

Particulars	Units	Amount Rs.	Particulars	Units	Amount Rs.
To Process A A/c	2,000	4,000	By Abnormal Gain A/c	2,000	4,000
	2,000	4,000		2,000	4,000

Illustration 14

A Chemical Company carries on production operations in two processes. Materials first pass through Process I, where a compound is produced. A loss in weight takes place at the start of processing. The following data, which can be assumed to be representative, relates to the month just ended:

	kgs.
Quantities:	
Material Input	2,00,000
Opening Work-in-process (half processed)	40,000
Work Completed	1,60,000
Closing Work-in-process (two-thirds completed)	30,000
Costs:	Rs.
Material Input	75,000
Processing Costs	1,02,000
Opening Work-in-process:	
Materials	20,000
Processing Costs	12,000

Normal process loss in quantity may be assumed to be 20% of material input.

Any quantity of the compound can be sold for Rs. 1.60 per kg. Alternatively, it can be transferred to Process II for further processing and packing to be sold as Supercomp, for Rs. 2.00 per kg. Further materials are added in Process II which yield two kgs of Supercom for every kg. of the Process I compound used.

Of the 1,60,000 kgs. per month of work completed in Process 1,40,000 kgs. are sold as compound and 1,20,000 kgs. are passed through Process II for sale as Supercomp. Process II has facilities to handle upto 1,60,000 kgs. of compound per month, if required. The monthly costs incurred in Process II (other than the cost of the compound) are:

	1,20,000 kgs. of Compound Inputs	**1,60,000 kgs. of Compound Inputs**
	Rs.	**Rs.**
Materials	1,20,000	1,60,000
Processing Costs	1,20,000	1,40,000

Required

(*a*) Determine, using the average cost method, the cost per kg. of the compound in Process I and the value of both completed and closing work-in-process for the month just ended.

(*b*) Is it worthwhile processing, 1,20,000 kgs. of compound further?

(*c*) Calculate the minimum acceptable selling price per kg. if a potential buyer could be found for the additional output of Supercomp that could be produced with the remaining compound.

(*CA. Final Nov. 1990*)

Solution

Process - I

Statement of Equivalent Production (Average Method)

Input		Output		Equivalent Production			
				Materials		Processing Costs	
Items	Units	Items	Units	Units	% of Compl.	Units	% of Compl.
Opening work-in-progress	40,000	(*i*) Completion of opening work-in-progress	40,000	40,000	100%	40,000	100%
Units Introduced	2,00,000	(Costs also added up) (*ii*) Units Introduced & Completed	1,20,000	1,20,000	100%	1,20,000	100%
		Total units completed	1,60,000				
		(*iii*) Normal Loss (20% of 2,00,000 kgs.)	40,000	–	–	–	–
		(*iv*) Abnormal Loss (Balancing Figure)	10,000	10,000	100%	10,000	100%
		(*v*) Closing Work-in-progress	30,000	20,000	$66\frac{2}{3}$% or 2/3 rds	20,000	$66\frac{2}{3}$% or 2/3 rds
	2,40,000		2,40,000	1,90,000		1,90,000	

Statement of cost per unit of Equivalent Production

Elements	Opening cost	Cost in Process I	Total cost	Equivalent Production	Cost per unit
	Rs.	Rs.	Rs.	(units)	Rs.
Materials	20,000	75,000	95,000	1,90,000	0.50
Processing costs	12,000	1,02,000	1,14,000	1,90,000	0.60
	32,000	1,77,000	2,09,000		1.10

Statement of Evaluation

Items	Equivalent Production (Units)	Cost per unit Rs.	Cost Rs.	Total Cost Rs.
Units Completed:				
Materials	1,60,000	0.50	80,000	
Processing costs	1,60,000	0.60	96,000	1,76,000
Abnormal Loss:				
Materials	10,000	0.50	5,000	
Processing Costs	10,000	0.60	6,000	11,000
Closing work-in-progress:				
Materials	20,000	0.50	10,000	
Processing costs	20,000	0.60	12,000	22,000
Total Process costs				2,09,000

(b) Evaluation of Further Processing of 1,20,000 kgs. of compound

	Rs.
Cost in Process I (Opportunity cost) (1,20,000 × Rs. 1.60)	1,92,000
Material cost	1,20,000
Processing Costs	1,20,000
Total Cost of Processing 2,40,000 kgs. of supercom	4,32,000
Sales value (2,40,000 kgs × Rs. 2.00)	4,80,000
Profit	48,000

Therefore, it is profitable to further process 1,20,000 kgs. of compound.

(c) Calculation of Minimum Selling Price per kg.

Cost of Processing 40,000 kgs. further:	Rs.
Cost in Process I (Opportunity cost) (40,000 kgs × Rs. 1.60)	64,000
Materials (Rs. 1,60,000 – Rs. 1,20,000)	40,000
Processing Costs (Rs. 1,40,000 – Rs. 1,20,000)	20,000
Total cost	1,24,000
Quantity of Supercom Produced	= 80,000 kgs.
Minimum Selling Price per kg. of Supercom (atleast equal to cost)	$= \frac{\text{Rs. } 1,24,000}{80,000 \text{ kgs.}}$ = Rs. 1.55

Illustration 15

From the information given below relating to Process X for a certain period, you are required to prepare:

(*a*) A statement of equivalent whole units of production.

(*b*) An account of the process showing the total and unit costs with other relevant information.

Work-in-progress at beginning of period: Units 500:.

		Rs.
Transfer from previous process and Material A		6,250
Material B		1,500
Material C		300
Labour and Overhead		2,700
		10,750
		Rs.
Costs incurred during the period:		
Transfer from previous process 3,600 units		32,750
Material A	9,000	
Material B	16,500	
Material C	6,300	31,800
Labour and Overhead		28,710
Units completed during the period		2,950
Units scrapped during the period		100
Abnormal loss		50

The units scrapped were:

100% complete for materials and 80% complete for labour and overheads.

Work-in-progress at end of period:

		Units 1,000	% completed
Materials		A	100
		B	60
		C	30
Labour and Overhead			50

(*I.C.M.A. Adapted*)

Solution

Statement of Equivalent Production

(Average Method)

Input		Output		Equivalent Production							
Items	Units	Items	Units	Mat. A		Mat. B		Mat. C		Labour & Overhead	
				Units	% of Compl.	Units	% of Compl.	Units	% of Compl.	Units	% of Compl.
Opening Work-in-Progress	500	(*i*) Completion of opening work-in-progress (Costs Added)	500	500	100%	500	100%	500	100%	500	100%
Units Transferred from Previous Process	3,600	(*ii*) Units Introduced and completed during the period	2,450	2,450	100%	2,450	100%	2,450	100%	2,450	100%
		Units Completed	2,950								
		(*iii*) Normal Loss	100	–	–	–	–	–	–	–	–
		(*iv*) Abnormal Loss	50	50	100%	50	100%	50	100%	40	80%
		(*v*) Closing work-in-progress	1,000	1,000	100%	600	60%	300	30%	500	50%
	4,100		4,100	4,000		3,600		3,300		3,490	

Statement of Average Cost per unit of Equivalent Production

Elements	Opening Cost	Cost in Process X	Total Cost	Equivalent Production	Cost per unit
	Rs.	Rs.	Rs.	(Units)	Rs.
Material A	6,250	41,750 (32,750 + 9,000)	48,000	4,000	12.00
Material B	1,500	16,500	18,000	3,600	5.00
Material C	300	6,300	6,600	3,300	2.00
Labour & Overhead	2,700	28,710	31,410	3,490	9.00
	10,750	93,260	1,04,010		28.00

Statement of Evaluation

	Equivalent Production (Units)	Cost per unit Rs.	Cost Rs.	Total cost Rs.
(*i*) Units completed during the period:				
Transfer from Previous Process and Mat. 'A'	2,950	12.00	35,400	
Material 'B'	2,950	5.00	14,750	
Material 'C'	2,950	2.00	5,900	
Labour & Overhead	2,950	9.00	26,550	82,600
(*ii*) Abnormal Loss:				
Mat. A	50	12.00	600	
Mat. B	50	5.00	250	
Mat. C	50	2.00	100	
Labour & Overhead	40	9.00	360	1,310
(*iii*) Closing Work-in-Progress				
Mat. A	1,000	12.00	12,000	
Mat. B	600	5.00	3,000	
Mat. C	300	2.00	600	
Labour & Overhead	500	9.00	4,500	20,100
Total cost				1,04,010

Process X Account

Particulars	Units	Amount Rs.	Particulars	Units	Amount Rs.
To Opening Work-in-Progress	500	10,750	By Normal Loss	100	–
To Transfer from Previous Process and Material A (Rs. 32,750 + 9,000)	3,600	41,750	By Abnormal Loss	50	1,310
			By Finished Output @ Rs. 28 per unit	2,950	82,600
To Material B		16,500			
To Material C		6,300	By Closing Work-in-Progress	1,000	20,100
To Labour & Overhead		28,710			
	4,100	1,04,010		4,100	1,04,010

Illustration 16

A food preserver has four processing centres for a brand of baby food. With the following particulars draw a process cost sheet showing for each centre the total cost by elements, cost per unit of work-in-progress, the cost per unit transferred and the cost per unit of final output.

	Grinding	Cooking	De-hydrating	Packing
(*i*) Elements of Cost	Rs.	Rs.	Rs.	Rs.
Materials	85,000	1,500	–	7,800
Wages	30,000	5,400	2,400	3,800
Fixed charges (Total Rs. 35,000)	40%	30%	17.5%	12.5%
Service charges	15,000	4,500	3,600	1,200
(*ii*) Quantities	lbs.	lbs.	lbs.	lbs.
Input	1,40,000	1,10,000	90,000	55,000
Output	1,20,000	1,00,000	60,000	53,000
Work-in-progress	10,000	10,000	6,000	1,000

Work-in-Progress is assessed to be equivalent to 50% finished in grinding centre; 80% in cooking centre; 90% in de-hydrating centre and at the input stage at the packing centre.

Prepare a Profit and Loss Account with a sale of 90% of the final output at Rs. 3.50 per lb.

Solution

Grinding Process Account

Particulars	Lbs.	Amount Rs.	Particulars	Lbs.	Amount Rs.
To Materials	1,40,000	85,000	By Normal Loss	10,000	–
To Wages		30,000	By Cooking Process A/c (Output Transferred)	1,10,000	1,26,720
To Fixed Charges (40% of Rs. 35,000)		14,000			
To Service Charges		15,000	By Grinding Process Stock A/c	10,000	11,520
			By Work-in-Progress A/c (Equivalent to 50% of Finished Product of Grinding Process)	10,000	5,760
	1,40,000	1,44,000		1,40,000	1,44,000

Notes:

(*i*) Calculation of Loss in Grinding Process:

Input	1,40,000 Lbs.
Output	1,20,000 Lbs.
	20,000
Work-in-Progress	10,000 Lbs.
Difference being normal loss	10,000 Lbs.

(*ii*) Since out of the total output of 1,20,000 Lbs. of Grinding Process, only 1,10,000 Lbs. (input of Cooking Process) have been transferred to Cooking Process, the balance of 10,000 Lbs. is to be taken as the stock of Grinding Process.

(*iii*) Calculation of cost per Lbs. of output in Grinding Process:

Total Process Cost Rs. 1,44,000

Total Output = 1,20,000 + 5,000 (*i.e.*, 50% of 10,000 Lbs. of finished product)

= 1,25,000 Lbs.

$$\text{Cost per Lb.} = \frac{\text{Rs. } 1{,}44{,}000}{1{,}25{,}000 \text{ Lbs.}} = \text{Rs. } 1.152$$

Cooking Process Account

Particulars	Lbs.	Amount Rs.	Particulars	Lbs.	Amount Rs.
To Grinding Process A/c	1,10,000	1,26,720	By De-hydrating Process A/c (Output Transferred)	90,000	1,21,930
To Materials		1,500			
To Wages		5,400	By Cooking Process Stock A/c	10,000	13,548
To Fixed Charges (30% of Rs. 35,000)		10,500			
To Service Charges		4,500	By Work-in Progress A/c (Equivalent to 80% of Finished product)	10,000	13,142
	1,10,000	1,48,620		1,10,000	1,48,620

Notes:

(*i*) Total Equivalent Output = 1,00,000 Lbs. + 8,000 Lbs. (i.e., 80% of 10,000 Lbs.)

= 1,08,000 Lbs.

(*ii*) Calculation of cost of work-in-progress (10,000 Lbs.)

	Rs.
Cost upto Grinding Process (100% complete) (10,000 units × Rs. 1.152)	11,520
Cost Incurred in Cooking Process (80%) $\left(\frac{\text{Rs. } 21{,}900}{1{,}08{,}000 \text{ Lbs.}} \times 8{,}000\right)$	1,622
	13,142

(*iii*) Cost of Output transferred to De-hydrating Process:

$$\frac{\text{Rs. } 1{,}48{,}620 - 13{,}142}{1{,}00{,}000 \text{ Lbs.}} \times 90{,}000 \text{ Lbs.} = \text{Rs. } 1{,}21{,}930$$

De-hydrating Process A/c

Particulars	Lbs.	Amount Rs.	Particulars	Lbs.	Amount Rs.
To Cooking Process A/c	90,000	1,21,930	By Normal Loss	24,000	–
To Wages		2,400	By Packing Process A/c (Output Transferred)	55,000	1,14,515
To Fixed Charges (17.5% of Rs. 35,000)		6,125			
To Service Charges		3,600	By De-hydrating Process Stock A/c	5,000	10,410
			By Work-in-Progress A/c	6,000	9,130
	90,000	1,34,055		90,000	1,34,055

Notes:

(*i*) Equivalent output in De-hydrating Process:
= 60,000 Lbs. + 5,400 Lbs. (90% 6,000 Lbs.)
= 65,400 Lbs.

(*ii*) Calculation of Cost of Work-in-progress:

	Rs.
Cost upto Cooking Process (100% complete) $\left(6{,}000 \text{ Lbs.} \times \frac{\text{Rs. } 1{,}21{,}930}{90{,}000 \text{ Lbs.}}\right)$	8,129
Cost incurred in De-hydrating Process $\left(\frac{\text{Rs. } 12{,}125}{65{,}400 \text{ Lbs.}} \times 5{,}400 \text{ Lbs.}\right)$	1,001
	9,130

(*iii*) Cost of output transferred to Packing Process:

$$= \frac{\text{Rs. } 1{,}34{,}055 - 9{,}130}{60{,}000 \text{ Lbs.}} \times 55{,}000 \text{ Lbs.} = \text{Rs. } 1{,}14{,}515$$

(*iv*) Since the nature of loss in the de-hydrating process has not been specified, it has been taken as normal loss.

Packing Process Account

Particulars	Lbs.	Amount Rs.	Particulars	Lbs.	Amount Rs.
To De-hydrating Process A/c	55,000	1,14,515	By Normal Loss	1,000	–
To Materials		7,800	By Finished stock A/c (Output transferred)	53,000	1,29,608
To Wages		3,800			
To Fixed Charges (12.5% of Rs. 35,000)		4,375	By Work-in-Progress A/c	1,000	2,082
To Service Charges		1,200			
	55,000	1,31,690		55,000	1,31,690

Note:

(*i*) Calculation of cost of work-in-progress (on the basis of the cost at the input stage of packing process) = $\frac{1,14,515}{55,000 \text{ Lbs}} \times 1,000$ Lbs. = Rs.2,082

(*ii*) Cost of output transferred to Finished Stock A/c Rs. 1,31,690 – 2,082 = Rs. 1,29,608

Profit and Loss Account

		Rs.			Rs.
To Costs Incurred:			By Sales (90% of final output i.e., 90% of 53,000 Lbs.) (= 47,700 Lbs. @ Rs. 3.50 per Lb.)		1,66,950
Materials	94,300				
Wages	41,600				
Fixed Charges	35,000				
Service Charges	24,300	1,95,200	By Process Stocks:		
Less Cost of Work-in-Progress					
Grinding	5,760		Grinding	11,520	
Cooking	13,142		Cooking	13,548	
De-hydrating	9,130		De-hydrating	10,410	35,478
Packing	2,082	30,114			
Cost of Production		1,65,086	By Finished Stock (10% of 53,000 Lbs.) $\left(\frac{\text{Rs. } 1,29,608}{53,000 \text{ Lbs.}} \times 5,300 \text{ Lbs.}\right)$		12,961
To Gross Profit		50,303			
		2,15,389			2,15,389

OBJECTIVE TYPE QUESTIONS

A. Multiple Choice Questions

Select the correct answer:

(*a*) Equivalent production of 1,000 units, 60% complete in all respects, is:

(*i*) 1,000 units (*iii*) 600 units

(*ii*) 1,600 units (*iv*) 1,060 units.

(*b*) Equivalent production of 1,500 units of opening work-in-progress 40% complete in all respects completed during the current period and transferred to next process, is:

(*i*) 900 units (*iii*) 600 units

(*ii*) 1,500 units (*iv*) 2,100 units.

(*c*) In a process opening work-in-progress (60% complete), units introduced during current period and closing work-in-progress (70% complete) were 1,000 units, 8,000 units and 2,000 units respectively. Assuming FIFO method, equivalent production during the period was:

(*i*) 11,000 units (*iii*) 7,700 units

(*ii*) 7,800 units (*iv*) 6,600 units.

(*d*) In a process 8,000 units are introduced during a period. 5% of input is normal loss. Closing work-in-progress 60% complete is 1,000 units. 6,600 completed units are transferred to next process. Equivalent production for the period is:

(*i*) 9,000 units (*iii*) 7,440 units
(*ii*) 5,400 units (*iv*) 7,200 units

[**Ans:** (*a*) (*iii*); (*b*) (*i*); (*c*) (*ii*); (*d*) (*iv*)]

True/False Type Questions

Indicate whether the following statements are True or False:

(*a*) Equivalent production of 1,500 units 40% complete in all respects is 600 units.

(*b*) The cost of opening work-in-progress is added to the process cost for the current period under FIFO method.

(*c*) FIFO method is followed for evaluation of equivalent production when prices are fluctuating.

(*d*) Average Price Method is adopted for evaluation of equivalent production when prices are fluctuating.

(*e*) Work-in-progress is the inherent feature of processing industries.

[**Ans:** (*a*) True; (*b*) False; (*c*) False; (*d*) True; (*e*) True]

Filling the Blanks

Fill in the blanks:

(*a*) Equivalent production represents the production of a process in terms of .... units.

(*b*) Two principal methods of evaluation of equivalent production are .... and ....

(*c*) Statement of cost per unit of Equivalent production shows the per unit cost ....

(*d*) ....units of closing work-in-progress 70% complete are equivalent to 1,400 units.

[**Ans:** (*a*) Completed; (*b*) FIFO Method, Average method; (*c*) Element-wise (*d*) 2,000]

SHORT ANSWER TYPE QUESTIONS

1. What is meant by work-in-progress?

2. What is Equivalent Production?

3. What is Statement of Equivalent Production?
4. List out the various statements which are prepared for computing and valuing equivalent production.
5. What is the basic assumption of FIFO method of evaluation of equivalent production?

LONG ANSWER TYPE QUESTIONS

1. What is meant by Equivalent Production ? How is it computed ? Illustrate your answer.
2. Discuss the FIFO and Average price methods of evaluating equivalent production with suitable example.
3. What is meant by 'equivalent production'?

EXERCISES

1. In Process X, 5,000 units were introduced during January, 2006. 1,000 units, 40% complete in all respects remained as work-in-progress at the end of the month. Compute the Equivalent production for January, 2006.
   [Ans. 4,400 units]
2. In process I, opening work-in-progress in January, 2007 was 2,000 units 40% complete. 10,000 units were introduced during the month. 3,000 units remained as closing work-in-Progress 70% complete. 9,000 units were transferred to next process. Compute Equivalent production for January, 2007. **[Ans.** 10,300 units]
3. The following data are available in respect of Process I for the month of April, 2006:

Opening work-in-progress	:	450 Units
Degree of completion	:	Material 80%, Labour and overhead 60%
Input of Materials during the month	:	3,000 units
Closing Work-in-progress	:	350 units
Degree of completion	:	Material 70%, Labour and overhead 60%
Units transferred to next process	:	3,100 units.

   Compute Equivalent Production for the month of April, 2006.
   [Ans. Equivalent Production Materials : 2,985 units
   Labour and overhead : 3,040 units.]
4. In Process A 4,000 units were introduced during January, 2007. 1,000 units 40% complete in all respects remained as closing work-in-progress

at the end of the month. Total process costs during the month were Rs. 10,200. Compute the Equivalent production and ascertain the cost of work-in-progress.

[**Ans.** Equivalent production : 3,400 units
Cost of work-in-progress : Rs. 1,200]

5. In Process A, 6,000 units of materials were introduced at a cost of Rs. 20,475. The wages and overheads for the process were Rs. 11,520 and Rs. 14,100 respectively. 5,400 units were completed and transferred to process B. The closing work-in-progress was 600 units on which the work completed was as follows:

Material	75%
Labour	60%
Overheads	40%

Calculate the cost of one completed unit. [**Ans.** Cost per unit, Rs. 8]

6. In a process 10,000 units of materials are introduced at a cost of Rs. 2 per unit. The amount spent on wages and overheads are Rs. 26,400 and Rs. 14,700 respectively. 10% of the units put into process are normally lost which have a realisable value of 65 P. each. The actual output during the period is 7,500 units. The work-in-progress at the end of the period is 1,000 units. The degree of completion of work-in-progress is Material 60%, Labour 80% and Overheads 40%.

You are required to prepare:

(*a*) Statement of Equivalent production
(*b*) Statement of Cost
(*c*) Statement of Evaluation
(*d*) Process account.

[**Ans.** Equivalent Production: Material, 8,600 units
Labour 8,800 units and Overheads 8,400 units
Abnormal loss, 500 units at Rs. 3,500 Cost per unit, Rs. 7]

7. AB Ltd. is engaged in the process engineering industry. During the month of April 2003, 2,000 units were introduced in Process 'X'. The normal loss is estimated at 5% of Input. At the end of the month 1,400 units had been produced and transferred to process 'Y', 460 were incomplete units and 140 units had to be scrapped at the end of the process. The incomplete units reached the following degree of completion:

Materials	:	75%
Labour	:	50%
Overheads	:	50%

Following are the further details regarding process 'X':

Cost of 2,000 units introduced	Rs. 58,000
Additional materials consumed	Rs. 14,400
Direct labour	Rs. 33,400

Allocated overheads Rs. 16,700

Note: The scrapped units fetched Rs. 10 each.

Required:

(*i*) Statement of equivalent production

(*ii*) Statement of cost;

(*iii*) Statement of evaluation;

(*iv*) Process 'X' Account. (*I.C.W.A. InterJune 1999*)

[**Ans.** Equivalent Production : Material 1,785 units; Labour & overhead 1,670 units; Cost per unit Rs. 70; Abnormal Loss 40 units at Rs. 2,800]

8. From the following data, find out the equivalent units of production to determine the per unit processing cost, which was incurred evenly during the month of March, 2009:

Opening Work-in-Progress	5,000 units (20% completed)
Fresh units started	16,000 units
Finished goods	12,000 units
Closing work-in-progress	8,000 units (60% completed)

No loss was permissible in the process.

Entire stock of opening work-in-progress was completed during the month of March, 2009 without any loss/rejection.

(*B.Com. Hons., Delhi 1991*) [**Ans.** 16,800]

9. X Ltd., a manufacturer of a specialised product, is having a process costing system. The stock of work-in-progress at the end of each month is valued on FIFO basis. At the beginning of a month, the stock of work-in-progress was 400 units (40 per cent complete) which was valued as follows:

Materials	Rs. 3,600
Labour	Rs. 3,400
Overheads	Rs. 1,000
	Rs. 8,000

During the month, actual issue of materials for production purpose was Rs. 68,500. Wages and overheads in the month amounted to Rs. 79,800 and Rs. 21,280 respectively. Finished production taken into the stock in the month was 2,500 units. There was no loss in the process. At the end of the month, the stock of work-in-progress was 500 units (60 percent complete as to labour and overheads and 80 percent complete as to materials). Prepare a Process Cost Sheet showing total and unit costs.

(*I.C.W.A. Inter, June 1992*).

[**Ans.** Effective units: Materials 2,740: Labour and overhead 2,640 each: Cost per equivalent unit. Material Rs. 25, Labour Rs. 30.227, Overhead Rs. 8.061; Cost of Production (2,500 units) Rs. 1,56,094: Closing W.I.P. Rs. 21,486].

10. The accountant of a chemical company provides you the following data:

	Units	Amount (Rs.)
Work-in-Progress, beginning of period	2,000	
Direct materials		4,200
Direct labour and manufacturing overhead		1,950
Addition to work-in-process in April	4,000	
Direct materials		9,000
Direct labour and manufacturing Overhead		7,500
Total		22,650
Work-in-Process, end of period	1,500	

Further, work-in-process at the beginning of the period is complete to the extent: materials 100% and labour and manufacturing overhead 75%. Work-in-process at the end of the period is complete to the extent : materials 100% and direct labour and manufacturing overhead only 50%. You are required to:

(*i*) Calculate the number of units of product transferred to finished goods stock during the period. Assume no units are lost in process.

(*ii*) Calculate the number of equivalent whole units of work completed during the period.

(*iii*) Calculate the unit cost for materials during the month of April using a first-in-first-out method of inventory issue.

(*B.Com. Hons.. Delhi 1992*)

[**Ans.** (*i*) 4,500 units, (*ii*) Effective units – Material 4,000; Labour and Overhead Rs. 3,750, (*iii*) Rs. 2.25].

11. From the following data of Pratap Industries Ltd., calculate (*a*) Equivalent Production, (*b*) Cost per unit of Equivalent Production, and (*c*) Cost of units completed and awaiting completion.

	Rs.
Number of units introduced in the process	4,000
Number of units completed and transferred to next process	3,500
Number of units in process at the end of the period	400
Stage of Completion:	
Materials	80%
Labour	50%
Overheads	50%

Normal process loss at the end of the process 100 units.

	Rs.
Value of scrap	Re. 1 per unit
Value of raw materials	7,740
Wages	11,100

Overhead	7,400

[**Ans.** Equivalent Production : Materials 3,820; Labour and overhead 3,700; Cost per unit Materials Rs. 2; Labour Rs. 3; Overhead Rs. 2 Value of Finished Goods Rs. 24,500 Work-in-progress Rs. 1,640].

12. Find out the equivalent production from the following data under the FIFO method:

Opening work-in-progress	2,000 units	
Degree of completion:	Materials	80%
	Labour	60%
	Overheads	60%
Units introduced	8,000	
Closing work-in-progress		3,000 units
Degree of completion:		
Materials		80%
Labour		60%
Overheads		60%

Assume there are no process losses.

(*B.Com. Hons., Delhi 1993*)

[**Ans.** Effective units; Material 7,800; Labour and overhead 7,600 units each].

13. During January, 2005, 6,000 units were introduced into Process No. I. The Process costs for the month were:

Direct Material	Rs. 55,200
Direct labour	Rs. 30,600
Production overheads	Rs. 14,400

The normal loss was estimated to be 10% of the input. At the end of the month 4,000 units had been processed and transferred to Process No. 2 A/c, 500 units had been scrapped, and 1,500 units were incomplete. The stage of completion of 1,500 units was estimated thus:

Material	100%
Labour	80%
Overheads	60%

The units scrapped had been completely processed and it was estimated that these had a realisable value of Rs. 2 per unit. Compute (*a*) Equivalent production (*b*) Cost per unit of Equivalent production (*c*) Evaluation and (*d*) prepare the necessary accounts.

[**Ans.** Equivalent production Material 5,400 units,
Labour 5,100 units and Overheads 4,800 units
Cost per unit Rs. 19
Abnormal Gain 100 units, Rs. 1,900
Cost of Finished units Rs. 76,000
Work-in-progress 24,900]

14. Dixcy Ltd. furnishes you the following information relating to process 'B' for the month of April, 2007:

(*i*) Opening work-in-progress Nil

(*ii*) Units introduced 10,000 units @ Rs. 3 per unit

(*iii*) Expenses debited to the process:

	Rs.
Direct materials	14,650
Labour	21,148
Overheads	42,000

(*iv*) Normal loss in process - one per cent of input

(*v*) Closing work-in-progress 350 units

Degree of completion:

Material	100%
Labour and overheads	50%

(*vi*) Finished output 9,500 units

(*vii*) Degree of completion of abnormal loss

Material	100%
Labour and overheads	80%

(*viii*) Units scrapped as normal loss were sold at Re. 1 per unit.

(*ix*) All the units of abnormal loss were sold at Rs. 2.50 per unit.

Prepare:

(*a*) Statement of equivalent production

(*b*) Statement of cost

(*c*) Process 'B' account, and

(*d*) Abnormal loss account.

[**Ans.** Equivalent Production: Material 9,900, Labour and overhead 9,715. Cost per unit : Materials Rs. 4.50; Labour and Overhead Rs. 6.50; Value of closing stock of Rs. 2,713; Abnormal loss Rs. 485, Finished goods Rs. 1,04, 500].

15. From the following details prepare statement of equivalent production, statement of cost and find the value of:

(*a*) Output transferred, and

(*b*) Closing work-in-progress by following average cost method.

Opening work-in-progress, 2,000 units.

Material	(100% complete)	Rs. 7,500
Labour	(60% complete)	Rs. 3,000
Overhead	(60% complete)	Rs. 1,500

8,000 units were introduced into process.

There are 2,000 units in process and the stage of completion is estimated to be:

Material	100%
Labour	50%
Overheads	50%

8,000 units were completed and transferred to next process. The process costs for the period are:

Material	Rs. 1,00,000
Labour	Rs. 78,000
Overhead	Rs. 39,000

(*C.A. Inter*)

[**Ans.** No. of Equivalent units for Materials, 10,000 units, Labour 9,000 units and Overheads 9,000 units, Cost per unit Materials Rs. 10.75, Labour Rs. 9 and Overheads Rs. 4.50, Value of output transferred Rs. 1,94,000, Cost of closing work-in-progress Rs. 35,000]

16. The product manufactured by a light engineering factory undergoes two operations: Machining and Finishing. The following data are available relating to expenses incurred on production during November 2001:

	Machining	**Finishing**
Units as input	90,000	60,000
Expenses incurred in process:	Rs.	Rs.
Direct Material	2,70,000	Nil
Direct Labour	1,28,000	45,000
Overheads	64,000	1,35,000

At the end of the month there were 30,000 units lying incomplete in machining operation. While the full quantity of materials had been consumed for the total production, the expenditure on labour and overheads was estimated to be $66\frac{2}{3}\%$ in respect of the incomplete products.

You are required to prepare a detailed cost statement showing the final cost per unit assuming:

(*i*) Completed units of machining operation are transferred to the finishing operation.

(*ii*) Finishing operation has completed all the units received from the earlier operation during November, 2001, leaving no work-in-process at the end of the month.

(*I.C.W.A., Inter Dec., 1991*)

[**Ans.** Cost per unit: Machining Rs. 5.40 Finishing Rs. 8.40]

17. The following information is submitted for Process I of R.S. Ltd. The average method of pricing work-in-process is used.

Work-in-Process on April 1:

	Rs.
Materials on 1,000 units	1,800
Labour on 1,000 units	2,000
Factory overheads on 1,000 units	800
	4,600

Production Cost for April:

Material	15,600
Labour	18,300
Factory Overheads	12,250
	46,150

Production completed during April:
1,000 units from April 1 Work-in-process.
4,000 units from products received during April.
5,000 Total units completed.
Work-in-Process on April 30:
800 units – 25% completed as to material, labour and overheads.
Write up the Process I Account for April.

[**Ans.** Equivalent Production : Materials, Labour and Overheads 5,200 each; Cost per unit: Materials Rs. 3.3462; Labour Rs. 3.9038 and overhead Rs. 2.5096. Valuation of finished goods Rs. 48,798 and Work-in-progress Rs. 1,952].

18. The following details relate to an intermediary process in a factory:

	% Degree Completion	No. of Units	Cost Rs.
Opening Work-in-progress:		300	12,300
(*a*) Material	50%		
(*b*) Labour	80%		
(*c*) Overheads	80%		
Transfer from previous process	100%	3,800	1,36,800
Process material added			7,900
Direct Wages			37,400
Overheads			14,960
Transfer to next process (Finished)	100%	3,500	
Closing Work-in-progress:			
(*a*) Material	100%		
(*b*) Labour	80%		
(*c*) Overheads	80%		

Prepare:
(*a*) Process cost accounts for the intermediary process,
(*b*) Statement of equivalent units (on FIFO) basis,
(*c*) Statement of distribution of cost on the basis of equivalent units.

[**Ans.** Equivalent Production : Materials (*i*) 3,800 units, Materials (*ii*) 3,950 units Labour and overheads, 3,740 units each. Cost per unit-Materials (*i*) Rs. 36, Materials (*ii*) Rs. 2, Labour – Rs. 10, Overheads Rs. 4, Total cost Rs. 52 ; Value of closing work-in-progress Rs. 29,520, Transfer price to next process 3,500 units at Rs. 1,79,840].

19. The finished product of a factory pass through two processes. From the following production and cost data relating to the first process, work out the value of the closing inventory and the value of the material transferred to the second process:

Process I

	Rs.
Opening Inventory	10,000
Material	27,500
Labour	50,000
Manufacturing overheads	40,000
	Kgs.
Opening Inventory (25% complete)	4,000
Put into process	12,000
Transferred to II process	10,000
Closing Inventory (20% complete)	5,000
Spoilage during process	1,000

Use FIFO Method. *(I.C.W.A. Final)*

[**Ans.** Equivalent production Material, labour and overheads 10,000 each. Cost per unit Material Rs. 2.75. Labour Rs. 5.00 and Overheads Rs. 4.00 Apportionment of current cost:

Opening W.I.P	Rs. 35,250
Finished units	Rs. 70,500
Closing W.I.P	Rs. 11,750

Value of goods transferred Rs. 1,15,750]

20. A company manufactures a product which involves two consecutive processes viz., Pressing and Polishing. For the month of Oct., 2008, the following information is available:

	Pressing Rs.	Polishing Rs.
Opening Stock	–	–
Input of units in Process	1,200	1,000
Units Completed	1,000	500
Units under process	200	500
Materials Cost (Rs.)	96,000	8,000
Conversion Cost (Rs.)	3,36,000	54,000

For incomplete units in process, charge materials cost at 100 per cent and conversion cost at 60 per cent in the Pressing Process and 50 percent in Polishing Process. Prepare a statement of cost and calculate the selling price per unit which will result in 25 percent profit on sale price.

(C.A. Inter, Nov. 1991)

[Ans.	Pressing	Polishing
Effective units		
Material	1,200	1,000
Conversion Cost	1,120	750
Cost per equivalent unit		
Material	Rs. 80.00	Rs. 388.00
Conversion	Rs. 300.00	72.00
work-in-progress	Rs. 52,000	Rs. 2,12,000

Selling price per unit Rs. 613.33].

21. The following data are available in respect of Process I for February, 2009:

(*i*) Opening stock of work in progress: 800 units at total cost of Rs. 4,000.

(*ii*) Degree of completion of opening work in progress:

Material	100%
Labour	60%
Overheads	60%

(*iii*) Input of materials at a total cost of Rs. 36,800 for 9,200 units.

(*iv*) Direct wages incurred Rs. 16,740.

(*v*) Production overhead Rs. 8,370.

(*vi*) Units scrapped 1,200 units. The stage of completion of these units was:

Material	100%
Labour	80%
Overheads	80%

(*vii*) Closing work-in-progress 900 units. The stage of completion of these units was:

Material	100%
Labour	70%
Overheads	70%

(*viii*) 7,900 units were completed and transferred to the next process.

(*ix*) Normal loss is 8% of the total input (opening stock plus units put in).

(*x*) Scrap value is Rs. 4 per unit.

You are required to:

(*a*) Compute equivalent production.

(*b*) Calculate the cost per equivalent unit for each element.

(*c*) Calculate the cost of abnormal loss (or gain) closing work-in-progress and the units transferred to the next process using the FIFO method.

(*d*) Show the Process Account for February, 2009.

(*C.A. Inter, May 1990*)

[**Ans.** (*a*) Materials: 8,400 units; labour and overhead: 8,370 units.

(*b*)	Material cost per unit	Rs. 4
	Labour cost per unit	Rs. 2
	Overhead cost per unit	Rs. 1
		7
(*c*)	Abnormal loss (400 units)	Rs. 2,560
	Closing W.I.P (900 units)	Rs. 5,490
	Finished Goods (7,900 units)	Rs. 54,660
		[4,960 + 49,700]

22. Product 'N' passes through three processes. In April 2007, the following information is obtained in respect of Process II.

Opening Stock : 2,800 units valued at Rs. 1,200 made up of Rs. 700 for materials, Rs. 150 for labour and Rs. 350 for overhead.

Degree of Completion: Material 60%, Labour 40%, Overhead 40%.

Transfer from Process I : 14,000 units @ Re. 0.20 each.

Transfer to Process III : 12,000 units

	Rs.
Direct Materials added in process II	1.560
Direct labour amounted to	2,000
Production overheads incurred	4,400

Units scrapped: 2,000 on completion of Process II.

Closing stock: 2,800 units

Degree of completion: Materials 80%, Labour 60%, Overhead 60%.

Note: 10% loss during production considered normal loss. Units scrapped realised Re. 0.40 each.

Prepare a statement of cost of Process II and show the unit cost of units transferred to Process III using FIFO method.

[**Ans.** Equivalent Production: Materials I – 12,600, Materials, Labour and Overhead each 13,160. Cost per unit: Material I Re. 0.1777, Material II Re. 0.1185, Labour Re. 0.1519, Overhead Re. 0.3343, Value of Opening Stock Rs. 950; Abnormal Loss Rs. 470, Finished Goods Rs. 7,198 Closing work-in-progress Rs. 1,582].

23. The following data relate to Process Q:

(*i*) Opening work-in-process: 4,000 units

Degree of completion:

Materials	100%	Rs. 24,000
Labour	60%	Rs. 14,400
Overheads	60%	Rs. 7,200

(*ii*) Received during the month of April, 2003 from Process P:

40,000 units Rs.1,71,000

(*iii*) Expenses incurred in Process Q during the month:

Materials	Rs. 79,000
Labour	Rs. 1,38,230

Overheads Rs. 69,120

(*iv*) Closing work-in-process 3,000 units

Degree of completion: Materials 100%; Labour & Overheads 50%.

(*v*) Units scrapped 4,000 units

Degree of completion: Materials 100%; Labour & Overheads 80%.

(*vi*) Normal loss: 5% of current input.

(*vii*) Spoiled goods realised Rs. 1.50 each on sale.

(*viii*) Completed units are transferred to warehouse.

Required:

Prepare: (*i*) Equivalent units statement (*ii*) Statement of cost per equivalent unit and total costs (*iii*) Process Q Account (*iv*) Any other account necessary. (*C.A. Inter, May. 1998*)

[**Ans.** Equivalent Production: Material P & Material Q 38,000 units Labour & Overhead 37,700 units; Cost per unit Rs. 12; Abnormal Loss 2,000 units]

24. Roy & Johnson (P) Ltd. gives the following particulars relating to Process A in its plant for the month of December, 2002:

		Cost	Rs.
Work-in-Progress			
(Opening balance) on 1.12.2002 – 500 units:		Material	4,800
		Labour	3,200
		Overheads	6,400
			14,400
Units Introduced during the month – 19,500			
Processing costs incurred during the month:			
Materials		Rs. 1,86,200	
Labour		72,000	
Overheads		1,06,400	Rs.3,64,600
Output:	Units transferred to process B		18,200
	Units scrapped (completely processed)		1,400
	Work-in-progress (Closing balance)		400

[Degree of completion: Materials –100% Labour and overhead – 50%]

Normal loss in processing is 5% of total input and normal scrapped units fetch Re 1 each. Prepare the following statements for Process A for December, 2002:

(*a*) Statement of equivalent production;

(*b*) Statement of cost;

(*c*) Statement of evaluation;

(*d*) Process 'A' Account. (*I.C.W.A. Inter, June 1998*)

[**Ans.** Equivalent Production: Material 19,000 units; Labour & Overhead 18,800 units; Cost per unit Rs. 20 by Average Method]

25. From the following information relating to Process A for the month of April, 2003, calculate the equivalent production units and the value of finished production and work-in-progress, using the Lifo method. Also prepare Process A Account.

Opening work-in-progress: 5,000 units 50% complete in respect of material, labour and overhead.

	Cost (Rs.)
Material	6,000
Labour	8,000
Overhead	8,000
	22,000

10,000 units introduced into the process during the month of April, 2003:

	Cost (Rs.)
Material	30,000
Labour	52,500
Overhead	70,000
	1,52,500

Normal loss: 5% of units introduced during the current period.
No. of units scrapped: 700 units
Realisable value of scrap: Re. 1 per unit
Units completed and transferred to Process B = 8,000 units
Closing work-in-progress: 6,300 units
Degree of completion of closing work-in-progress

Material	80%
Labour	70%
Overhead	70%

[**Ans.** Equivalent Production Material 10,740 units, Labour and Overhead 10,110 units; Cost per unit Rs. 14.863; Closing W.I.P. 1,300 units at Rs. 13,883 and 5,000 units at Rs. 38,239]

17

Operating Costing

Operating costing is the method of costing employed to ascertain the cost of providing or operating a service. This method of costing is employed in those undertakings which are engaged in providing or operating services rather than in manufacturing tangible products. This method is applicable to road transport undertakings, railways, tramways, airways, shipping companies, electricity companies, gas companies, hospitals, cinemas, hotels, canteens, water works etc.

CHARACTERISTICS

The undertakings where operating costing is applied, generally possess the following characteristics:

(*i*) These undertakings are engaged in rendering services of unique nature to their customers.

(*ii*) These undertakings are required to invest a large proportion of their total capital in fixed assets *e.g.*, trucks, buses, ships, aircrafts, railway engines, wagons, railway lines, etc.

(*iii*) The amount of working capital required to meet out the day-to-day expenses, is comparatively less.

(*iv*) In the case of these undertakings, a proper distinction between fixed and variable cost is of utmost importance since the economies and scale of operations considerably affect the cost per unit of service rendered. For example, in case of a transport company if the buses run capacity packed, the fixed cost per passenger shall be lower.

UNIT OF COST

The main problem in operating costing is the selection of a unit of cost. In case of some of the operating undertakings, the unit of cost is simple and obvious. For instance,

Types of undertakings	*Unit of cost*
(*i*) Electricity companies	Per unit or kilowatt
(*ii*) Water works	Per 1000 litres
(*iii*) Gas companies	Per cylinder

(*iv*) Hospitals — Per bed

(*v*) Canteen — Per cup of tea

But in case of other undertakings, a composite unit of cost is used. For example, in case of transport undertakings, it will be per passenger kilometre or per ton kilometre. The calculation of the composite unit of cost in case of a transport undertaking can be illustrated with the help of the following example:

Suppose:

(*i*)	Total number of buses in the undertaking:	4
(*ii*)	Number of days operated in the month:	25
(*iii*)	Trips made by each bus daily:	2
(*iv*)	Distance of route:	100 kms. (one side)
(*v*)	Capacity of one bus:	50 Passengers
(*vi*)	Normal passengers travelling:	80% of capacity

Total kilometres and total passenger kilometres are to be ascertained. Total kilometres (in a month) shall be = Number of buses × Number of days operated in the month × Number of trips made by each bus × Distance of route (both ways)

$$= 4 \times 25 \times 2 \times 200 \text{ kms.} = 40{,}000 \text{ kms.}$$

Total Passenger kilometres shall be = Total kilometres × Seating Capacity (Number of passengers) × % of capacity operated

$$= 40{,}000 \times 50 \times \frac{80}{100} = 16{,}00{,}000 \text{ Passenger kilometres.}$$

PROCEDURE OF COSTING

The method of ascertainment of costs under operating costing is on lines similar to output or unit costing. All costs incurred in operating a service are accumulated under suitable headings in the form of a Cost Sheet and the costs are expressed in terms of the unit of service rendered. The only difference lies in the method of collecting cost data and its allocation to cost units.

Transport Costing: In transport undertakings, most of the cost data required for the purpose of ascertainment of cost are available from *Daily Log Report* which is maintained for each vehicle separately by the driver of the vehicle. In order to prepare the cost sheet for a transport undertaking, the costs are sub-divided into three parts:

(*i*) **Fixed Costs or Standing Costs:** These are constant costs and are incurred whether the vehicle operates or not. These are more or less fixed in nature in a transport undertaking. These include insurance, depreciation, road tax, licence fee, garage rent, administration, general supervision, interest on capital etc.

(*ii*) **Operating and Running Costs:** These costs are incurred on the actual running of the vehicles. These are variable in nature and include cost of petrol and fuel, oil, grease, wages of drivers and conductors (though these wages are not wholly variable).

(iii) **Maintenance Costs:** These costs are incurred on the repairs and maintenance of vehicles so as to keep them in proper gear. These are considered to be semi-variable in nature and include tyres and tubes, repairs, overhauling of vehicles, painting etc.

Amount of depreciation on vehicle needs a special mention in relation to the above classification of costs. Opinions differ as to whether depreciation is to be regarded as a fixed cost or variable cost. It is thus sometimes regarded as a variable or running cost and sometimes as a fixed cost. If the life of the vehicle has been given in terms of mileage or kilometreage, depreciation may be treated as part of running costs.

The total operating, maintenance and fixed costs divided by the total number of units shall give us the cost per unit. The specimen of a Cost Sheet prepared in transport undertakings is given below:

Cost Sheet

Vehicle No...................   Period..........................
No. of cost units...........

Items	Amount Rs.
(i) **Fixed Costs:**	
Garage Rent	
Insurance	
Depreciation	
Road Tax	
Licence Fee	
Administration	
Interest on Capital	
Total	
(ii) **Operating Costs:**	
Petrol	
Lubricating Oil	
Grease	
Wages of Operating Staff.	
Total	
(iii) **Maintenance Costs:**	
Tyres and Tubes	
Repairs	
Overhauling	
Total	
Grand Total *(i)* + *(ii)* + *(iii)*	
Total units	
Cost per unit	

Illustration 1

The following data relate to a vehicle of a transport company. The vehicle in question runs, on an average, 20 kms. per hour. After charging interest on cost of vehicle @ 5 % p.a., compute cost per km. run by the vehicle:

Estimated life	2,00,000 kms.
Annual kilometreage	60,000 kms.
	Rs.
Cost of vehicle	50,000
Driver's wages per hour	6
Petrol per gallon	5
Repairs per km.	0.25
Tyre allocation per km.	0.10
Annual Expenses:	
Licence	1,000
Insurance	1,100
Garage Rent	800
Supervision and salaries	1,500

The vehicle runs 20 kms. per gallon.

Solution

Cost Sheet

Vehicle No.................. Period................................

No. of cost units: 60,000 kms.

		Rs.
(i)	**Fixed Costs (per annum)**	
	Licence	1,000
	Insurance	1,100
	Garage Rent	800
	Supervision and Salaries	1,500
	Interest on Capital (5% on Rs. 50,000)	2,500
		6,900
	Fixed costs per km. (Rs. 6,900/60,000 kms.)	0.115
(ii)	**Running Costs (per km.)**	
	Driver's Wages (Rs. 6 per 20 kms.)	0.30
	Petrol (Rs. 5 per 20 kms.)	0.25
	Depreciation (Variable) (Rs. 50,000/2,00,000 kms.)	0.25
	Running Costs per km.	0.80
(iii)	**Maintenance Costs (per km.)**	
	Repairs	0.25
	Tyre Allocation	0.10
	Maintenance Costs per km.	0.35
	Total Cost per Running km. *(i)* + *(ii)* + *(iii)*	1.265

Illustration 2

Mr. Subramanyam runs a tempo service in the city and has two vehicles. He furnishes the following particulars and wants you to compute the cost per running-km:

	Vehicle A	Vehicle B
	Rs.	Rs.
Cost of Vehicle	25,000	15,000
Road Licence Fees per year	750	750
Supervision and Salaries (yearly)	1,800	1,200
Driver's wages per hour	4	4
Cost of fuel per litre	1.50	1.50
Repairs and maintenance per km.	1.50	2.00
Tyre cost per km.	1.00	0.80
Garage Rent per year	1,600	550
Insurance Premium (Yearly)	850	500
Kms. run per litre	6	5
Kilometreage run during the year	15,000	6,000
Estimated life of Vehicle	kms. 1,00,000	kms. 75,000

Charge interest at 10 per cent per annum on cost of vehicle.

The vehicles run 20 kms. per hour on an average.

Solution

Cost Sheet

Vehicle No. A and B — Period..........................

Cost units A : 15,000 Kms. B : 6,000 Kms.

	Particulars	Vehicle A	Vehicle B
(i)	**Fixed Costs:**	**Rs. P.**	**Rs. P.**
	Road Licence Fees	750	750
	Insurance Premium	850	500
	Garage Rent	1,600	550
	Supervision and Salaries	1,800	1,200
	Interest @ 10% on Cost of Vehicle	2,500	1,500
	Total Fixed Cost	7,500	4,500
	Fixed Cost per kms.		
	A : Rs. 7,500/15,000 km.	0.50	
	B : Rs. 4,500/6,000 kms.		0.75
(ii)	**Running Costs (per km.)**		
	Driver's Wages (at Rs. 4 per 20 kms.)	0.20	0.20
	Cost of Fuel	0.25	0.30
	Depreciation (variable)	0.25	0.20
	Vehicle A: $\frac{\text{Rs. } 25{,}000}{1{,}00{,}000 \text{ kms.}}$ Vehicle B: $\frac{\text{Rs. } 15{,}000}{75{,}000 \text{ kms.}}$		
	Running Cost per km.	0.70	0.70
(iii)	**Maintenance Costs (per km.)**		
	Repairs and Maintenance	1.50	2.00
	Tyre Cost	1.00	0.80
	Maintenance Cost per km.	2.50	2.80
	Total Cost per km. *(i)* + *(ii)* + *(iii)*	3.70	4.25

Illustration 3

A transport service company is running four buses between two towns which are 100 kms. apart. The seating capacity of each bus is 40 passengers. The following particulars were obtained from its books for October, 2006:

	Rs.
Wages of Drivers, Conductors and Cleaners	4,800
Salaries of Office Staff and Inspectors	2,000
Diesel Oil and Lubricants	8,000
Repairs and Maintenance	1,600
Road Tax and Insurance	3,200
Depreciation	5,200
Interest and other Charges	4,000
Total	28,800

Actual passengers carried were 75% of the seating capacity. All the buses ran for 30 days. Each bus made one round trip per day.

Find out the cost per passenger kilometre. *(Delhi. B.Com.)*

Solution

Calculation of total passenger kilometres = Number of buses × Number of days in month × Distance of route (both ways) × Number of passengers per bus × %age of seating capacity used

$$= 4 \times 30 \times 200 \times 40 \times \frac{75}{100}$$

= 7,20,000 passenger kilometres

Cost Sheet

Period: Oct. 2006
Total Passenger kms.: 7,20,000

		Rs.
(i)	**Fixed Costs:**	
	Salaries of Office Staff and Inspectors	2,000
	Road Tax and Insurance	3,200
	Depreciation (Fixed)	5,200
	Interest and other Charges	4,000
	Total Fixed Costs	14,400
(ii)	**Operating Costs:**	
	Wages of Drivers, Conductors and Cleaners	4,800
	Diesel and Lubricants	8,000
	Total Operating Costs	12,800
(iii)	**Maintenance Costs:**	
	Repairs and Maintenance	1,600
	Total Maintenance Costs	1,600
	Total Costs *(i)* + *(ii)* + *(iii)*	28,800
	Total Passenger kms.	7,20,000
	Cost per Passenger km. (Rs. 28,800/7,20,000)	0.04

Illustration 4

Prepare a Statement of Operating Cost per passenger km. for bus No. 27 for the month of August, 2006 from the following particulars:

Cost of Bus	Rs. 40,000
Estimated Life of the bus	80,000 kms.
kms. during the month of August	2,000
Average number of passengers per km.	50
Salaries of drivers, conductors and cleaners etc.	1,000
Insurance	50
Road Tax	30
Licence fee	80
Staff Salaries	500
Garage Rent	200
Petrol	600
Depreciation on tyres	100
Repairs and maintenance expenses	200
Terminal office expenses	500
Bus fare per passenger km.	0.06

Solution

Statement of Operating Cost

Bus No. 27 — Period: August, 2006

		Rs.
(i)	**Fixed Costs:**	
	Depreciation of vehicle	1,000
	Insurance	50
	Road Tax	30
	Licence Fee	80
	Staff Salaries	500
	Garage Rent	200
	Terminal Office Expenses	500
	Total Fixed Costs	2,360
(ii)	**Running Costs:**	
	Salaries of Drivers and Conductors etc.	1,000
	Petrol	600
	Depreciation on Tyres (assumed to be variable)	100
	Total Running Costs	1,700
(iii)	**Maintenance Costs:**	
	Repairs and Maintenance Expenses	200
	Total Maintenance Costs	200
	Total Costs *(i)* + *(ii)* = *(iii)*	4,260
	Total units (50 × 2,000 = 1,00,000 passenger kms.)	1,00,000 Passenger kms.
	Operating Cost per unit	Re. 0.426
	Total Fare during the Month (Re. 0.06 × 1,00,000)	Rs. 6,000
	Profit Earned during the Month (Rs. 6,000 – Rs. 4,260)	Rs. 1,740

Illustration 5

Work out in appropriate Cost Sheet form the unit cost per passenger km. for the year 2003-04 for a fleet of passenger buses run by a Transport Company from the following figures extracted from its books:

5 passenger buses costing Rs. 50,000, Rs. 1,20,000, Rs. 45,000, Rs. 55,000 and Rs. 80,000 respectively. Yearly depreciation of vehicles –20% of the cost. Annual repairs, maintenance and spare parts –80% of depreciation.

Wages of 10 drivers	@ Rs. 100 each per month
Wages of 20 cleaners	@ Rs. 50 each per month
Yearly rate of interest	@ 4% on capital
Rent of six garages	@ Rs. 50 each per month
Director's fees	@ Rs. 400 per month
Office establishment	@ Rs. 1,000 per month
Licence and taxes	@ 1,000 every six months
Realisation by sale of old tyres and tubes	@ Rs. 3,200 every six months

900 passengers were carried over 1,600 kms. during the year

(*I.C.W.A. Final*)

Solution

Total passenger kms. =1,600 × 900 = 14,40,000

Operating Cost Statement

Passenger kms. =14,40,000

		Rs.
(*i*)	**Fixed Costs (Annual)**	
	Interest on Capital (4% on Rs. 3,50,000)	14,000
	Rent for six Garages Rs. 50 p.m.	3,600
	Director's Fees	4,800
	Office Establishment	12,000
	Licence and Taxes	2,000
	Wages of Drivers (10 × 12 × 100)	12,000
	Wages of Cleaners (20 × 12 × 50)	12,000
	Depreciation (Fixed) (20 % on Rs. 3, 50, 000)	70,000
	Total Fixed Costs	**1,30,400**
(*ii*)	**Maintenance Costs (Annual)**	
	Repairs and Maintenance Charges (80 % of depreciation)	56,000
	Total Maintenance Costs	**56,000**
	Total costs (*i*) + (*ii*)	1,86,400
	Less: Recovery from Sale of Tyres and Tubes	6,400
		1,80,000
	Total Passenger kms.	14,40,000
	Cost per Passenger km. Rs. 1,80,000 ÷ 14,40,000 Pass. kms.	Re. 0.125

Note: Wages of drivers and cleaners have been taken as fixed costs as these have been given in terms of per month.

Illustration 6

Mr. R. Mathur owns a bus which runs between Delhi to Chandigarh and back, for 10 days in the month. The distance from Delhi to Chandigarh is 150 kms. The bus completes the trip from Delhi to Chandigarh and back in the same day. The bus goes another 10 days in a month towards Agra. The distance from Delhi to Agra is 120 kms. The trip is also completed in the same day. For the rest 4 days of its operation in a month it runs in the local city. Daily distance covered in local city is 40 kms. Calculate the rate Mr. R. Mathur should charge from passengers when he wants to earn the profit of $33\frac{1}{3}\%$ on his takings. The other informations are given below:

	Rs.
Cost of the bus	60,000
Depreciation (20% p.a.)	
Salary of driver	350 per month
Salary of conductor	350 per month
Salary of part-time accountant	160 per month
Insurance	1,680 per annum
Diesel consumption 4 kms. per litre costing	1 per litre
Token tax	600 per annum
Lubricant Oil	10 per 100 kms.
Repairs and maintenance	500 per month
Permit fee	284 per month
Normal capacity	50 persons

The bus is generally occupied 90% of the capacity when it goes to Chandigarh and 80% when it goes to Agra. It is always full when it runs within the city. Passenger tax is 20% of his net takings.

Solution

Operating Cost Sheet

Period: One month

		Per month
(i)	**Fixed Costs:**	Rs.
	Salary of Driver	350
	Salary of Conductor	350
	Salary of Part-time Accountant	160
	Insurance (Rs. 1,680/12)	140
	Token Tax (Rs. 600/12)	50
	Permit Fee	284
	Depreciation $\left(\frac{(60,000 \times 20)}{100 \times 12}\right)$	1,000
	Total Fixed Cost	2,334
(ii)	**Operating Costs:**	
	Diesel Consumption	1,390
	Lubricant Oil	556
	Total Operating Cost	1,946

(iii) **Maintenance Costs:**		
Repairs and Maintenance		500
Total Maintenance Cost		500
Total Cost *(i)*, *(ii)*, *(iii)*		4,780
Total Cost for the month	4,780	
Add: Profit @ $33\frac{1}{3}\%$ on takings	2,390	
	7,170	
Add: Passenger Tax @ 20% on takings	1,434	
	8,604	

Total passenger kms. 2,39,000

$$\text{Rate per passenger km.} = \frac{\text{Rs. } 8{,}604}{2{,}39{,}000} = \text{Re.}0.036$$

Charges per passenger

(i) for Chandigarh = 150 × 0.036 = Rs. 5.40

(ii) for Agra = 120 × 0.036 = Rs. 4.32

Notes:

(i) Calculation of Total Passenger kms. (effective)

(a) Chandigarh

$$1 \text{ round trip} \times 150 \text{ kms.} \times 2 \times 10 \text{ days} \times 50 \text{ persons} \times \frac{90}{100} \text{ Capacity} = 1{,}35{,}000$$

$$(b) \text{ Agra} \quad 1 \times 120 \times 2 \times 10 \times 50 \times \frac{80}{100} = 96{,}000$$

$$(c) \text{ Local} \quad 4 \times 40 \times 50 = 8{,}000$$

Total = 2,39,000

(ii) Cost of Diesel and Lubricant Oil:

Total kms. covered

Chandigarh (150 × 2 × 10)	3,000
Agra (120 × 2 × 10)	2,400
Local (40 × 4)	160
	5,560

$$\text{Cost of Diesel} = \frac{5{,}560}{4} \times \text{Re. } 1 = \text{Rs. } 1{,}390$$

$$\text{Cost of Lubricant Oil} = \frac{5{,}560}{100} \times \frac{10}{1} = \text{Rs. } 556$$

Illustration 7

The Union Transport Company has been given a twenty kilometre long route to ply a bus. The bus costs the company Rs. 1,00,000. It has been insured at 3% per annum. The annual road tax amounts to Rs. 2,000. Garage rent is Rs. 400

per month. Annual repair is estimated to cost Rs. 2,360 and the bus is likely to last for five years.

The salary of the driver and the conductor is Rs. 600 and Rs. 200 per month respectively in addition to 10% of takings as commission to be shared equally by them. The manager's salary is Rs. 1,400 per month and stationery will cost Rs. 100 per month. Petrol and oil will cost Rs. 50 per 100 kilometres. The bus will make three round trips per day carrying on an average 40 passengers in each trip. Assuming 15% profit on takings and that the bus will ply on an average 25 days in a month, prepare operating cost statement on a full year basis and also calculate the bus fare to be charged from each passenger per kilometre.

(*C.A. Inter, May 1992*)

Solution

Operating Cost Sheet

		Rs.
(A)	**Fixed Costs:**	
	Manager's Salary	16,800
	Driver's Salary	7,200
	Conductor's Salary	2,400
	Road Tax	2,000
	Insurance (3% of Rs. 1,00,000)	3,000
	Garage Rent	4,800
	Stationery	1,200
	Depreciation (Rs. 1,00,000/5 years)	20,000
	Total Fixed Costs	**57,400**
(B)	**Running Costs:**	
	Petrol and Oil $\left(36{,}000 \text{ kms.} \times \frac{\text{Rs.}50}{100 \text{ kms.}}\right)$	18,000
	Total Running Costs	18,000
(C)	**Maintenance Costs:**	
	Repairs	2,360
	Total Maintenance Costs	**2,360**
	Total Costs (A) + (B) + (C)	77,760
	Add: 10% of takings for Commission of Driver and Conductor and 15% for Desired Profits *i.e.*,	
	25% on takings $\left(77{,}760 \times \frac{25}{100-25}\right)$	25,920
		1,03,680
	Rate to the Charged per km.:	**Rs. 1,03,680 ÷** 14,40,000 kms. = 7.2 Paise

Notes: (*i*) Calculation of Distance Covered
= (20 kms. × 2 × 3 × 25 × 12) : 36,000 kms. per annum

(*ii*) Effective passenger kms. = (2 × 20 kms. × 3 trips × 40 passengers × 25 days × 12 months) = 14,40,000 kms.

Illustration 8

The following were the expenses incurred by a company in operating two lorries (for the conveyance of raw material) and a bus (for the conveyance of staff) during a selected month.

	Monthly Cost		
	Lorry A	**Lorry B**	**Bus**
	Rs.	**Rs.**	**Rs.**
Driver's salaries	110	115	120
Cleaner's wages	120	120	60
Petrol	170	240	110
Oil	18	25	20
Repairs	150	150	100
Depreciation	330	220	350
Supervision	70	70	70
Garage overhead	130	110	75
Road and other tax	45	45	309
Other overhead expenses	35	40	20

The above vehicles carried the following raw materials and passengers during the month:

Lorry A	100 tons of raw material
Lorry B	120 tons of raw material
Bus	25 passengers daily for 25 days

At the same time their respective kilometreage during the same period were:

Lorry A	3,000
Lorry B	4,500
Bus	2,000

From the above statistics prepare an Operating Cost Sheet in summary form for the three vehicles. Also explain the unit of costing selected.

(*I.C.W.A., Final*)

Solution

Operating Cost Sheet

	Lorry A	Lorry B	Bus
	Rs.	Rs.	Rs.
(A) Fixed Costs:			
Depreciation	330	220	350
Road and Other Taxes	45	45	30
Other Overhead Expenses	35	40	20
Supervision	70	70	70
Total (A)	480	375	470
(B) Maintenance Costs:			
Repairs	150	150	100
Garage Overhead	130	110	75
Total (B)	280	260	175

(C) Running Costs:			
Petrol	170	240	110
Oil	18	25	20
Driver's Salaries	110	115	120
Cleaner's Wages	120	120	60
Total (C)	418	500	310
(D) Total Operating Costs (A)+(B)+(C)	1,178	1,135	955
(E) Ton-kms.			
A	10,000		
B		18,000	
Passenger-kms. Bus			50,000
(F) Cost per Ton-km. of Lorry A and Lorry B	Re. 0.1178	Re.0.06305	Re. 0.0191 per passenger km.

Notes:

The unit cost for lorry carrying raw materials is per ton-km..and that of bus carrying passengers is per passenger-km., calculated as:Total Tons × kms. and total Passengers × kms. respectively.

So units of cost as above are:

$$\text{Lorry A} = \frac{100 \text{ tons} \times 3{,}000 \text{ kms.}}{30 \text{ days}} = 10{,}000 \text{ ton-kms.}$$

$$\text{Lorry B} = \frac{120 \text{ tons} \times 4{,}500 \text{ kms.}}{30 \text{ days}} = 18{,}000 \text{ ton-kms.}$$

Bus = 25 passengers × 2,000 kms. = 50,000 passenger-kms.

Illustration 9

A Transport Ltd. operates a fleet of lorries. The records for a lorry reveal the following information for the month of Nov., 2002.

Days available	26
Days operated	22
Total kms. covered	880
Total trips made	33
Total tonnage carried	330

Following information has also been supplied:

Estimated days operated in the year 2002, 275 days, Operating Cost (November) petrol, oil and grease Rs. 300.

Wages: driver Rs. 200 p.m.: cleaner Rs. 100 per month.

Maintenance cost (estimated for 2002):

Tyres, Repairs, Overheads Rs. 2,720, Mechanic wages Rs. 100 p.m.

Fixed cost (Estimated for 2002):

Insurance Rs. 96

Road tax Rs. 550, Sundries Rs. 400.

Capital cost Rs. 21,600, residual value estimated Rs. 1,600.

Effective life 5 years.

Administrative and other overheads are estimated Rs. 5,500 for the year 2002.

Prepare a cost sheet for the month showing inter-alia cost per commercial tonne-km., per absolute tonne-km., cost per day operated, cost per km. operated, cost per trip operated.

Solution

Operating Cost Sheet

Period: Nov., 2002

	Rs.
(*i*) Fixed Costs:	
Insurance $\left(960\times\frac{22}{275}\right)$	76.80
Road Tax $\left(550\times\frac{22}{275}\right)$	44.00
Sundries $\left(400\times\frac{22}{275}\right)$	32.00
Capital Cost $\left(4{,}000\times\frac{22}{275}\right)$	320.00
Administrative Cost $\left(5{,}500\times\frac{22}{275}\right)$	440.00
Total Fixed Cost	912.80
(*ii*) Maintenance Costs:	
Tyres, Repairs and Overhead $\left(2{,}720\times\frac{22}{275}\right)$	217.60
Mechanic's Salary	100.00
Total Maintenance Costs	317.60
(*iii*) Operating Costs:	
Petrol, Oil and Grease	300.00
Driver's Wages	200.00
Cleaner's Wages	100.00
Total Operating Cost.	600.00
Total Cost for the month	1,830.40

$$\text{Cost per Absolute tonne-km.} = \frac{\text{Rs. } 1{,}830.40}{8{,}800} = \text{Paise } 20.8$$

$$\text{Cost per Commercial tonne-km.} = \frac{\text{Rs. } 1{,}830.40}{4{,}400} = \text{Paise } 41.6$$

$$\text{Cost per day operated} = \frac{\text{Rs. } 1{,}830.40}{22} = \text{Rs. } 83.20$$

$$\text{Cost per km. operated} = \frac{\text{Rs. } 1{,}830.40}{880} = \text{Rs. } 2.08$$

$$\text{Cost per trip operated} = \frac{\text{Rs. } 1{,}830.40}{33} = \text{Rs. } 55.46$$

Working Notes:

Calculation of Absolute tonne-km.

Average kms. per day operated = $\frac{880}{22}$ = 40 kms. per day

Average kms. per trip = $\frac{880}{33} = \frac{80}{3}$

Average tonnes per trip $\frac{330}{33}$ = 10 tonnes

$\therefore$ Absolute tonne-kms. per trip = $\frac{80}{3} \times 10 = \frac{800}{3}$

Absolute tonne-kms. for the month = $\frac{800}{3} \times \frac{33}{1}$ = 8,800 tonne-kms.

Commercial tonne-km.

Per trip = $\frac{80}{3} \times 10 \times \frac{1}{2} = \frac{400}{3}$

Per month = $\frac{400}{3} \times \frac{33}{1}$ = 4,400 tonne-kms.

Illustration 10

An entrepreneur, who looks after the marketing function personally travels on an average 30,000 kms. per annum in his new car costing Rs. 45,000, the life of which he estimates as 3 years. A driver is engaged to drive the car and he is paid on an hourly basis on the assumption that he would be able to do on average 25 kms. per hour. Based on these facts, the costs per km. of running the car works out to 332 paise as under:

	Cost per km. (Paise)
Licence	3
Petrol and repairs	165
Insurance	2
Garage rent	2
Driver's wages	14
Tyre wear (usage)	80
Depreciation	50
Establishment	4
Interest	12
	332

(*i*) What would be the cost per km. if the businessman requires to cover only 20,000 kms. per annum?

(*ii*) In his average run of 30,000 kms. per annum he also includes about 5,000 kms. which is needed by his family to attend to the domestic charges like shopping etc. For this purpose, he proposes to buy an exactly similar car at the same price with similar facilities for his family's usage and between the two car a run of 30,000 kms. per annum to be made. In this way, the businessman thinks, that the total cost per km. may not go up and only he has to find Rs. 45,000 for the second car. Do you agree? If not, what would be the total cost per km. if the second car is bought?

(*iii*) Sometimes, when he travels for business to a nearby town at a distance of 100 kms. he gives a lift to another businessman who is his neighbour who wants to go to the same place on the understanding that between them they will share the costs half and half. The businessman is charging his neighbour, a sum of Rs. 161.00 per trip on such thinking, taking it as very fair. Do you agree? If not, what is the fair amount that should be charged?

Solution

(*i*) Operating Cost Sheet

	Per km.	Total
(*a*) Operating Costs:		Rs. P.
Petrol and Repairs	1.65	49,500
Driver's Wages	0.14	4,200
Tyre Wear	0.80	24,000
Total Operating Costs	2.59	77,700
(*b*) Fixed Costs:		
Licence	0.03	900
Insurance	0.02	600
Garage Rent	0.02	600
Depreciation	0.50	15,000
Interest	0.12	3,600
Establishment	0.04	1,200
Total Fixed Cost	0.73	21,900
Total Cost (*a* + *b*) (30,000 kms.)	3.32	99,600

If the businessman covers only 20,000 kms. per annum the operating costs will be reduced but fixed costs will remain unaltered. Thus,

Operating costs for 20,000 kms. @ 2.59	51,800
Fixed cost	21,900
Total cost	73,700

Cost per km. = Rs. 73,700 ÷ 20,000 = Rs. 3.685

(*ii*) If the businessman buys another car for use of his family for domestic purpose then his fixed costs will be double the original costs although operating costs may remain the same.

	Ist car	2nd car*	Total
Operating cost @ 2.59 p.m.	64,750	12,950	77,700
Fixed Cost	21,900	21,900	43,800
	86,650	34,850	1,21,500

Cost per km. 1,21,500 ÷ 30,000 = Rs. 4.05

(*iii*) Since the businessman's total cost per km. (when his average annual run is 30,000 kms.) is 332 paise, the total cost per trip of 100 kms. will be Rs. 332. If 50 % of this amount is to be charged to the neighbour, the amount to be charged is Rs. 166. To that extent the charge of Rs. 166 per trip of 100 kms. is reasonable. But if fixed costs are considered as sunk costs which are to be incurred even if the trips are not made, the fair amount to be charged to the neighbour should be variable cost. In that case the charge to be made shall be:

50% of 100 × 2.59 = Rs. 129.50

Working Notes:

25,000 × 2.59 = Rs. 64,750

5,000 × 2.59 = Rs. 12,950

POWER-HOUSE COSTING

It is concerned with the ascertainment of cost per unit of steam or electricity produced. The costs of producing steam used in power house for the generation of electricity is also included in the power house costs. The specimen of cost sheet prepared by power-house may be given as follows:

Specimen No. 1

Cost Sheet

Period: Output...............

Particulars	Total Rs. P.	Per kwt. Rs. P.
(A) Fixed Expenses:		
Plant Supervision		
Administration Overheads		
Depreciation		
(B) Variable Expenses:		
Operating Labour		
Repairs and Maintenance		
Coal Consumed		
Lubricants, Spares and Stores		

Specimen No. 2

(*Power-house using steam for generating electricity*)

Cost Sheet

Period.............
Steam produced.............. Units of Electricity
Steam used for Generation.............. Generated...........

Particulars	Total	Per Therm
(A) Steam Production Costs:		
Coal		
Water		
Water Softener		
Wages:		
(*i*) Coal Handling		
(*ii*) Stoking		
(*iii*) Ash Disposal		
Repairs and Maintenance		
Stores Depreciation		
Supervision		
Therms (units)		
Total Production for the Period		
Less: used in Heating		
Steam used for Generation		
(B) Electricity Generation Costs:		
Cost of Steam used		
Operator's Wages		
Stores		
Repairs and Maintenance		
Depreciation		
Supervision		
Total Cost of Electricity Generated		

Illustration 11

From the following data pertaining to the year 2002-03, prepare a Cost Sheet showing the cost of electricity generated per unit of kwh. by Chambal Thermal Power Station:

Total units generated 20,00,000 kwh.

	Rs.
Operating Labour	50,000
Repairs and Maintenance	50,000
Lubricants, Spares and Stores	40,000
Plant supervision	30,000
Administrative Overheads	20,000

Coal consumed per kwh. for the year is 2.5 kgs. @ Re. 0.02 per kg.

Depreciation charge @ 5% on capital cost of Rs. 2,00,000

(*C.A. Inter. Adapted*)

Solution

Cost Sheet

Period: Year 2002-03 Output: 20,00,000 Kwh.

Particulars	Total Rs. P.	Per kwh. Rs. P.
Fixed Expenses:		
Plant Supervision	30,000	
Administrative Overheads	20,000	
Depreciation (5% on Rs. 2,00,000)	10,000	
	60,000	0.030
Variable Expenses:		
Coal Consumed	1,00,000	0.050
Operating Labour	50,000	0.025
Repairs and Maintenance	50,000	0.025
Lubricants, Spares and Stores.	40,000	0.020
	3,00,000	0.150

Note: Cost of coal consumed has been calculated as follows:
= 20,00,000 kwh. × 2.5 kgs × Re.0.02 = Rs. 1,00,000

Illustration 12

From the following data find out, in an appropriate cost sheet form, the generating cost of electricity per unit in an Iron and Steel Works during the month of April, 2003.

1. **Fuel:** Coal at the beginning of the month 500 tons
   Supply during the month 1,100 tons
   Balance at the end of the month 400 tons
   Annual contract for supply of coal F.O.R. colliery at Rs. 10 per ton. Add 10% to cover freight and handling charges.
2. Oil: 10 tons at Rs. 250 per ton.
3. Water: 50,000 gallons, pumping charges at 25 paise per 100 gallons.
4. Depreciation of Steam Boiler: Capital value Rs. 24,000 and the rate of depreciation 12 % per annum.
5. Salaries and wages of the Boiler House:
   10 men at Rs. 100 per month each.
   40 coolies at Rs. 20 per month each.
6. Recovery on account of sale of ashes: 100 tons at Re. 1 per ton.
7. Salaries and wages of the generating station:
   50 men at Rs. 100 per month each;
   20 coolies at Rs. 20 per month each.
8. Repairs and maintenance of the generating equipment: Rs. 2, 600.
9. Depreciation on Generating Equipment: Capital value Rs. 1,20,000 and the rate of depreciation 12½% p.a
10. Share of administration charges: Rs. 1,750.
11. Number of units generated: 1,46,000.
12. Loss in the process: 2,000 units generated. (*Karnataka, M.Com. Adapted*)

Solution

Cost Sheet

Month: April, 2003 — Net output 1,44,000 units

Particulars	Rs.	Rs.
(A) Steam Production Cost:		
1. Fuel: Coal: Opening stock: 500 tons @ Rs. 11	5,500	
Supply during the month: 1,100 tons @ Rs. 11	12,100	
	17,600	
Less: Closing stock: 400 tons @ Rs. 11	4,400	
		13,200
2. Oil consumed: 10 tons Rs. 250 per ton		2,500
3. Water 50,000 gallons @ 25 Paise per 100 gallons		125
4. Depreciation of Steam Boiler: $\frac{12}{100} \times 24,000 \times \frac{1}{12}$		240
5. Salaries and Wages of the Boiler House:		
10 men @ Rs. 100 per month	1,000	
40 coolies @ Rs. 20 per month	800	1,800
		17,865
6. *Less*: Recovery from sale of ashes		100
Cost of Producing Steam c/d		17,765
Cost of Producing Steam b/d		17,765
(B) Electricity Generation Costs:		
7. Salaries and wages : 50 men @ Rs. 100 p.m.	5,000	
20 coolies @ Rs. 20 p.m.	400	
		5,400
8. Repairs and maintenance of equipment		2,600
9. Depreciation on equipment		
$\frac{1,20,000}{100} \times \frac{25}{2} \times \frac{1}{12}$		1,250
Cost of Generating Electricity		27,015
10. Administrative charges		1,750
Total Cost		28,765
Cost Per Unit =Rs. 28,765 ÷ 1,44,000 units		Re. 0.20 approx.

Note: Rate of Coal = Price Rs. 10 + Handling Charges Re. 1 = Rs. 11 per ton.

CINEMA HOUSE COSTING

The object of Cinema house costing is to ascertain the cost of operating a cinema theatre. In case of a cinema house the unit of cost is "a man-show".

Illustration 13

A cinema hall has seating capacity of 800. It runs daily 4 shows on all 30 days of a month. It is generally full to the extent of 80% of its capacity. Find out the number of man-shows during the month.

Solution

Total man-shows = Number of shows per day × Number of days during the month × Number of Persons per show

$$= 4 \text{ shows} \times 30 \text{ days} \times 800 \times \frac{80}{100}$$

= 76,800 man-shows.

Illustration 14

The following data relate to Lal Rattan Cinema for the year ending 31st March, 2003:

Salaries	**Rs.**
1 Manager	800 p.m.
10 gate-keepers	200 p.m. each
2 Operators	400 p.m. each
4 Clerks	250 p.m. each
Other Expenses:	Rs.
Electricity	11,655
Carbon	7,235
Miscellaneous expenditure	5,425
Advertisement	34,710
Administrative expenses	18,000
Hire for Print	1,40,700

The premises are valued at Rs. 6,00,000 and its estimated life is 15 years. Projector and other equipment cost Rs. 3,20,000 on which 10% depreciation is to be charged. Daily 3 shows are run throughout the year. Total capacity is 625 seats which are divided into three classes as follows:

'B' Circle:	250 seats
'A' Circle:	250 seats
Balcony:	125 seats

Ascertain cost per man-show, assuming that

(*a*) 20% of the total seats remain vacant, and

(*b*) Weightage to be given to the three classes in the ratio of 1 : 2 : 3.

Determine the rates for each class if the management expects 30% return on gross proceeds. Ignore entertainment taxes.

Solution

Statement of Cost

Period: Year ending 31st March, 2003

	Rs.	Rs.
(A) Fixed Costs		
Manager's Salary (Rs. 800 × 12)	9,600	
Gate-keepers' Salaries (10 × 200 × 12)	24,000	
Operators' Salaries (2 × 400 × 12)	9,600	
Clerks' Salaries (4 × 250 × 12)	12,000	
Administrative Expenses	18,000	
Depreciation on Machinery (10% on Rs. 3,20,000)	32,000	
Depreciation on Premises $\left(\frac{\text{Rs.}6,00,000}{15}\right)$	40,000	
		1,45,200
(B) Variable Costs		
Electricity	11,655	
Carbon	7,235	
Hire for Print	1,40,700	
Advertisement	34,710	
Miscellaneous Expenditure	5,425	
		1,99,725
Total Cost		3,44,925

(*i*) Capacity used

'B' Circle = 250 × 80%
= 200 Seats

'A' Circle = 250 × 80%
= 200 Seats

Balcony = 125 × 80%
= 100 Seats

(*ii*) Total number of shows during the year
= 365 days × 3 shows per day
= 1,095 shows

(*iii*) Calculation of man-shows:

	No. of Seats	×	No. of Shows	×	Weight-age	=	Man-shows
'B' Bircle	200	×	1,095	×	1	=	2,19,000
'A' Circle	200	×	1,095	×	2	=	4,38,000
Balcony	100	×	1,095	×	3	=	3,28,500
					Total man-shows	=	9,85,500

(*iv*) Cost per man-show $= \text{Rs. } \frac{3,44,925}{9,85,500}$

= Re. 0.35

Add Profit @ 30% on gross proceeds = Re. 0.15

$\left(\text{Re.}0.35 \times \frac{30}{70}\right)$

Rate to be charged per man-show = Re. 0.50

(*v*) Rates (with due weightage) to be charged for different classes

	Rs.
'B' Circle	Re. 0.50 × 1 = 0.50
'A' Circle	Re. 0.50 × 2 = 1.00
Balcony	Re. 0.50 × 3 = 1.50

HOTEL COSTING

A hotel is engaged in providing food, accommodation and other comforts to its customers. Costs incurred by a hotel may be fixed or variable. Fixed costs may include salaries of staff, depreciation of fixed assets etc., while variable costs may comprise lighting and power charges, wages of room attendants etc. The object of hotel costing is to ascertain the cost per room or cost per man.

Illustration 15

Following is the information given by the owner of hotel. You are required to advise him what rent should be charged from customers per day so that he is able to earn 25 profit on cost other than interest.

(1) Staff salaries Rs. 80,000 per annum.

(2) Room Attendant's salary Rs. 2 per day. The salary is paid on daily basis and services of room attendant are needed only when the room is occupied. There is one attendant for one room.

(3) Lighting, Heating and power : The normal lighting expenses for a room if it is occupied for the whole month is Rs. 50 per room. Power is used only in winter and normal charge per month, if occupied, for a room is Rs. 20.

(4) Repairs to Buildings Rs. 10,000 per annum.

(5) Linen etc. Rs. 4,800 per annum.

(6) Sundries Rs. 6,600 per annum.

(7) Interior decoration and furnishing Rs. 10,000 per annum.

(8) Cost of Building Rs. 4,00,000 rate of depreciation is 5%

(9) Other Equipment Rs. 1,00,000, Rate of depreciation is 10%

(10) Interest @ 5% may be charged on its investments of Rs. 5,00,000 in the buildings and equipments.

(11) There are 100 rooms in the hotel and 80% of the room are normally occupied in summer and 30% of the rooms are occupied in winter.

You may assume that period of summer and winter is six months each. Normal days in a month may be assumed to be 30.

Solution

Statement of Cost

Period: One year — Room-days: 19,800

Particulars		Amount Rs.
(1) Staff Salaries		80,000
(2) Room Attendants' Salaries		39,600
(3) Lighting, Heating and Power		36,600
(4) Repairs to Buildings		10,000
(5) Linen etc.		4,800
(6) Sundries		6,600
(7) Interior Decoration and Furnishings		10,000
(8) Depreciation:		
Building @ 5%	20,000	
Other Equipment @ 10%	10,000	30,000
(9) Interest on Investments @ 5% on Rs. 5,00,000		25,000
Total Cost		2,42,600
Add: Profit @ 25% on cost other than interest (25% on Rs. 2,17,600)		54,400
Total Room rent for the year		2,97,000
Total Number of Room-days		19,800
Rent per room per day $\left(\frac{\text{Rs. } 2{,}97{,}000}{19{,}800 \text{ days}}\right)$		15.00

Working Notes:

(*i*) Calculation of Total number of room-days

(*a*) Summer: (100 Rooms × 6 months × 30 days × 80 %) = 14,400

(*b*) Winter (100 Rooms × 6 months × 30 days × 30 %) = 5,400

19,800

(*ii*) Calculation of Room Attendants' Salaries:

Rs.

(*a*) Summer (100 Rooms × 6 months × 30 days × 80% × Rs. 2) = 28,800

(*b*) Winter (100 Rooms × 6 months × 30 days × 30% × Rs. 2) = 10,800

39,600

(*iii*) Calculation of Cost of Lighting and Power:

(*a*) Lighting: Rs.

Summer (100 Rooms × 6 months × 80% × Rs. 50) = 24,000

Winter (100 Rooms × 6 months × 30% × Rs. 50) = 9,000

33,000

(*b*) Power: (100 Rooms × 6 months × 30% × Rs. 20) = 3,600

Total Cost of Lighting and Power 36,600

Illustration 16

A hotel has three types of suites viz., single room suite, double room suite, and three room suite. You are requested to suggest what rent should be charged for each type of suite on the basis of the following information:

(1) The rent of double room suite is to be fixed as 1½ times the single suite and that of three room suite as 2 times the single room suite.

(2) *Total accommodation*

Single room suites	100
Double room suites	30
Three room suites	20

(3) *Room occupancy ratio*

	Summer	**Winter**
Single room	90%	50%
Double room	80%	20%
Three room	60%	20%

(4) *Annual expenses are as follows*:

Staff salaries Rs. 2,20,000

Room attendant's salary *(daily)*

	Summer	**Winter**
	Rs.	**Rs.**
Single room occupied	2	3.00
Double room occupied	3	4.50
Three room occupied	4	6.00

Lighting, heating and power:

Lighting: Rs. 40 for single room suite per month if occupied for full month for both summer and winter.

Rs. 60 for double room suite per month and Rs. 80 for three room suite per month if occupied for full month for both summer and winter.

	Rs.
Repairs and Renovations	42,000
Linen etc.	45,000
Interior Decoration	50,000
Sundries	31,550

Depreciation: Building @ 5% on Rs. 14,00,000

Furniture and Fittings @ 10% on Rs. 1,00,000

Air Conditioners @ 10% on Rs. 2,00,000

(5) Summer 7 months, Winter 5 months } in a year

Normal working days in a month may be taken as 30.

(6) Profit on cost 25%, so that interest on investment may also be covered in such profits.

Solution

Cost Sheet

			Rs.
Staff Salaries			2,20,000
Room Attendant's Salary			
	Summer	63,000	
	Winter	30,150	93,150
Linen etc.			45,000
Depreciation	Building Rs. 14,00,000, 5%		70,000
	Furniture and Fittings Rs. 1,00,000, 10%		10,000
	Air Conditioners Rs. 2,00,000, 10%		20,000
Power:			
	Single room set	17,600	
	Double room set	5,940	
	Three room set	4,160	27,700
Lighting and Heating			
	Single room set	35,200	
	Double room set	11,880	
	Three room set	8,320	55,400
Repairs and Renovation			42,000
Interior Decoration			50,000
Sundries			31,550
	Total Cost		6,64,800
	Profit 25% on Cost		1,66,200
			8,31,000
		Room Days	41,550

Rent for one day $\dfrac{8,31,000}{41,550}$ = Rs. 20 per day

∴ Rent for single room suite Rs. 20 per day

Rent for double room suite = $\dfrac{20 \times 3}{2}$ = Rs. 30 per day

Rent for three room suite = 20 × 2 = Rs. 40 per day

Working Notes:

1. Calculation of Room Days:

(*a*) Single Room Suite

Summer: No. of rooms × Percentage occupied × Days in month × No. of months

$= 100 \times \dfrac{90}{100} \times 30 \times 7 = 18{,}900$ room days

Winter $= \dfrac{100 \times 50}{100} \times 30 \times 5 = 7{,}500$ room days

Total single room days = 26,400

(*b*) Double Room Suite

Summer: $30 \times \frac{80}{100} \times 30 \times 7 = 5{,}040$ room days

Winter: $30 \times \frac{20}{100} \times 30 \times 5 = 900$ room days

Total room days for double room suite = 5,940

(*c*) Three Room Suite

Summer: $20 \times \frac{60}{100} \times 30 \times 7 = 2{,}520$

Winter: $20 \times \frac{20}{100} \times 30 \times 5 = 600$

Total room days for three room suite = 3,120

Total Single Room Days

The rent of double room suite should be 1½ times and that of three-room suite twice of single room. Therefore room days of double room suite and three room suite may be converted to room days of single room by multiplying those with 1½ and 2 respectively.

	Single room days
Single room suite	= 26,400
Double room suite $\frac{5{,}940}{2} \times 3$	= 8,910
Three room suite 3,120 × 2	= 6,240
	= 41,550

(2) Room Attendant's Salary = Room days × Daily rate of pay

Summer:

			Rs.
Single room suite	18,900 × 2	=	37,800
Double room suite	5,040 × 3	=	15,120
Three room suite	2,520 × 4	=	10,080
	Total for Summer		63,000

Winter:

			Rs.
Single room suite	7,500 × 3	=	22,500
Double room suite	900 × 4.50	=	4,050
Three room suite	600 × 6	=	3,600
	Total for Winter		30,150

(3) Lighting = Room days × $\dfrac{\text{Monthly charge}}{\text{No. of days in a month}}$

Summer and Winter

			Rs.
Single room suite	= $\dfrac{26{,}400 \times 40}{30}$	=	35,200
Double room suite	= $\dfrac{5{,}940 \times 60}{30}$	=	11,880
Three room suite	= $\dfrac{3{,}120 \times 80}{30}$	=	8,320
	Total		55,400

Power:

Summer and Winter

			Rs.
Single room suite	$\dfrac{26{,}400 \times 20}{30}$	=	17,600
Double room suite	$\dfrac{5{,}940 \times 30}{30}$	=	5,940
Three room suite	$\dfrac{3{,}120 \times 40}{30}$	=	4,160
	Total		27,700

CANTEEN COSTING

The object of canteen costing is to ascertain the cost per meal, cost per cup of tea etc. In a canteen, the expenses are generally classified as follows:

1. Wages and salaries of staff e.g., cooks, helpers, waiters and supervisors.
2. Provisions like meat, fish, fruits, flour, oil, milk, sugar, cream, tea, coffee, and soft drinks.
3. Services like steam, gas, electricity, power, water etc.
4. Consumable stores like cutlery, crockery, glassware, table linen, mops and washing up clothes, drying up clothes, cleaning materials, dust pans and brushes.
5. Miscellaneous overheads like rent, rates, depreciation and insurance.

A monthly operating cost statement is usually prepared to ascertain the total cost and cost per meal. As most factory canteens are subsidised by the employer to some extent, the amount of subsidy is deducted from the total cost.

Illustration 17

Progressive Enterprises Ltd., runs a canteen for the benefit of its workmen and provides subsidy of Rs. 15,000 per month to the canteen. During the month of May, 2007, the following purchases were made:

	Quantity (kgs.)	**Rate per kg.**
Tea	4	100.00
Sugar	50	30.00
Milk	60	20.00
Flour	230	20.00
Vegetable ghee	30	110.00
Besan	12	40.00
Dal	30	35.00
Potato	90	20.00
Green vegetable	20	15.00
Spices	2	240.00

Opening stock was: Tea 2 kgs.; Sugar 10 kgs.; Flour 30 kgs.

Closing stock was: Tea 1 kg.; Sugar 5 kgs.; Flour 20 kgs.

Other expenses for the month were:

(*a*) Rickshaw fare Rs. 200 (*b*) Salary to cook (1) Rs. 2,500 p.m. (*c*) Wages to waiters (2) Rs. 1,500 per month each (*d*) Supervisor's salary Rs. 3,000 p.m. (*e*) Fuel, gas, coal etc., Rs. 4,000 (*f*) Crockery and glassware Rs. 1,000 (*g*) Depreciation of utensils and furniture Rs. 1,500. Sale of coupons: 8,000 @ Rs. 1.50 per coupon. Prepare a cost statement of the canteen and ascertain the profit or loss of the canteen.

Solution

Canteen Cost Statement

Period: May, 2007

Particulars	Rs.	Rs.
Wages and Salaries Rs.	Rs.	
Cook 2,500		
Waiters 3,000		
Supervisor 3,000		8,500
Provisions Consumed:		
Opening Stock: Tea (2 kgs. × Rs. 100)	200	
Sugar (10 kgs. × Rs. 30)	300	
Flour (30 kgs. × Rs. 20)	600	
Add Purchases:		
Tea (4 kgs. × Rs. 100)	400	
Sugar (50 kgs. × Rs. 30)	1,500	
Milk (60 kgs. × Rs. 20)	1,200	
Flour 230 kgs. × Rs. 20)	4,600	
Vegetable ghee (30 kgs. × Rs. 110)	3,300	
Besan (12 kgs. Rs. 40)	480	
Dal (30 kgs. × Rs. 35)	1,050	
Potato (90 kgs. × Rs. 20)	1,800	
Vegetables (20 kgs. × Rs. 15)	300	
Spices (2 kgs. × Rs. 240)	480	
	16,210	
Rickshaw fare	200	
	16,410	
Less: Closing Stock:		
Tea (1 kg. × Rs. 100) 100		
Sugar (5 kgs. × Rs. 30) 150		
Flour (20 kgs. × Rs. 20) 400	650	15,760
Miscellaneous Expenses:		
Fuel, gas, coal etc. 4,000		
Crockery and Glassware 1,000		
Depreciation 1,500		6,500
Total cost		30,760
Less subsidy		15,000
		15,760
Loss		(–) 3,760
Sale of Coupons (8,000 @ Re. 1.50)		12,000

HOSPITAL COSTING

A hospital is engaged in providing various medical services to the patients and hospital costing is applied to determine the cost of these services. A hospital may have the following departments on the basis of functions performed by them:

(*i*) Outdoor Patient Department (O.P.D.)
(*ii*) Indoor Patient Department (Medical Wards)
(*iii*) Medical Service Departments e.g., X-Ray Department, Scanning Centre, Pathology Laboratory etc.
(*iv*) General Service Departments e.g., Boiler House, Power House, Catering Department, Laundry Room, Administrative Office, Works Maintenance Department etc.
(*v*) Miscellaneous Service Departments i.e., the departments engaged in providing services to the above four departments such as transport department, dispensary, general porting etc.

The operating costs of Outdoor Patient Department, Indoor Patient Department, Medical Service Departments and General Service Departments are determined with reference to the suitable unit of cost and in doing so the costs of miscellaneous service departments are apportioned to them on some suitable basis.

The common units of cost of various departments in a hospital are follows:

(*a*) Outdoor Patient Department	Per Out-patient attended.
(*b*) Indoor Patient Department	Per Room-day.
(*c*) X-Ray Department	Per 100 units.
(*d*) Scanning Centre	Per Case
(*e*) Pathology Laboratory	Per 100 Requests
(*f*) Laundry Department	Per 100 items laundered
(*g*) Catering Department	Per Patient Per Week.

The costs of a hospital are divided into fixed and variable costs. Fixed costs may comprise salaries of administrative staff, depreciation of building, rent of building, depreciation of surgical and medical equipments etc., while variable costs may comprise light and power, water, laundry charges, food supplied to patients etc. The preparation of cost sheet can be explained with the help of the following illustrations:

Illustration 18

Dr. Sanjeev Sharma and Dr. (Mrs.) Sharma hire a building to run a nursing home. The building has 8,000 square feet of area consisting of 40 rooms of 150 square feet each. The rest is general area. The monthly rent has been agreed at Rs. 10 per square feet. Lighting and heating expenses come to Rs. 10,000 per month. The staff would consist of the following:

5 doctors @ Rs. 20,000 p.m.

10 nurses @ Rs. 8,000 p.m.

6 general helpers @ Rs. 2,500 p.m.

It is expected that 90% of the rooms will always remain occupied. If a margin of 25% on total takings is desired, ascertain the rent to be charged per day assuming a month of 30 days.

Solution

Cost Sheet

(Period: One month)

Staff salaries:		Rs.
(*i*) 5 Doctors @ Rs. 20,000 per month each	= Rs.1,00,000	
(*ii*) 10 Nurses @ Rs. 8,000 per month	= Rs. 80,000	
(*iii*) 6 General helpers @ Rs. 2,500 p.m.	= Rs. 15,000	1,95,000
Rent of Building @ Rs. 10 per square feet for 8,000 sq.ft.		80,000
Lighting and heating expenses		10,000
Total Cost		2,85,000
Add Margin (Profit) @ 25% on total takings	$\left(\frac{2,85,000 \times 25}{100 - 25}\right)$	95,000
Total Takings (or Rent chargeable)		3,80,000

Calculation of Room-days:

$$\text{Room days} = \text{No. of rooms} \times \text{Percentage occupied} \times \text{No. of days in a month.}$$
$$= 40 \text{ Rooms} \times 90\% \times 30 \text{ days} = 1,080 \text{ Room-days}$$

$$\text{Rent to be charged per day} = \frac{\text{Total Takings}}{\text{Total Room-days}} = \frac{\text{Rs. } 3,80,000}{1,080} = \text{Rs.}351.85$$

Illustration 19

Appollo Hospital runs an Intensive Care Unit in a hired building at a rent of Rs. 7,500 p.m. The hospital has undertaken to bear the cost of repairs and maintenance.

The Intensive Care Unit consists of 35 beds and 5 more beds can be conveniently accommodated whenever required. The permanent staff attached to the unit are as follows:

2 Supervisors, each at a salary of Rs. 2,500 per month.

4 Nurses, each at salary of Rs. 2,000 per month.

4 Ward boys, each at a salary of Rs. 500 per month.

Though the unit was open for the patients all the 365 days in a year but it was found that only 150 days in a year, the unit had the full capacity of 35 patients per day and for another 80 days it had on an average 25 beds only occupied per day. But there were occasions when the beds were full, extra beds were hired from outside at a charge of Rs. 10 per bed per day. This did not come to more than 5 beds extra above the normal capacity any one day. The total hire charges for the extra beds incurred for the whole year amounted to Rs. 7,500.

The unit engaged expert doctors from outside to attend on the patients and fees were paid on the basis of the number of patients attended and time spent by them on an average worked out to Rs. 25,000 per month in the year 2003. The other expenses for the year were as under:

	Rs.
Repairs and Maintenance (Fixed)	8,100
Food supplied to patients (Variable)	88,000
Janitor and other services for patients (Variable)	30,000
Laundry charges for their bed linen (Variable)	60,000
Medicines supplied (Variable)	75,000
Cost of Oxygen, X-ray, etc., other than directly borne for treatment of patients (Fixed)	1,08,000
General Administration charges allocated to the unit (Fixed)	1,00,000

(*i*) Calculate the profit per patient day made by the unit in the year 2003 if the unit recovered on overall amount of Rs. 200 per day on an average from each patient.

(*ii*) The unit wants to work on a budget for the year 2004, but the number of patients requiring intensive care is a very uncertain factor. Assuming that same revenue and expenses prevail in 2004 in the first instance, work out the number of patient days required by the unit to break-even.

Solution

Calculation of No. of Patient-days

(*i*)	35 beds × 150 days =	5,250
(*ii*)	25 beds × 80 days =	2,000
(*iii*)	Extra bed days = $\left(\frac{\text{Rs. } 7{,}500}{10}\right)$	750
		8,000

Statement of Profit

	Per Annum: Rs.	Rs.
1. Income Received (Rs. 200 × 8,000 patient-days)		16,00,000
2. Variable Costs (Marginal Costs)		
Food	88,000	
Janitor and other Services	30,000	
Laundry Charges	60,000	
Medicines Supplied	75,000	
Doctors' Fees (Rs. 25,000 × 12)	3,00,000	
Hire Charges for Extra-beds	7,500	5,60,500
Contribution		10,39,500
3. Fixed Costs		
Salaries:		
Supervisors (2 × 2,500 × 12)	60,000	
Nurses (4 × 2,000 × 12)	96,000	
Ward Boys (4 × 500 × 12)	24,000	
Rent (7,500 × 12)	90,000	
Repairs & Maintenance	8,100	
Cost of Oxygen etc.	1,08,000	
General Administration	1,00,000	4,86,100
Profit		5,53,400

$$\text{Profit per Patient-day} = \frac{\text{Rs. } 5{,}53{,}400}{8{,}000 \text{ Patient-days}} = \text{Rs. } 69.175$$

$$\text{Break-even Point} = \left(\frac{\text{Fixed Cost}}{\text{Contribution}} \times \text{Income}\right)$$

$$\left(\frac{\text{Rs. } 4{,}86{,}100}{\text{Rs.} 10{,}39{,}500} \times 16{,}00{,}000\right)$$

= Rs. 7,48,206

Break-even Point for Patient-days =

$$\frac{\text{Rs. } 7{,}48{,}206}{\text{Rs. } 200} = 3{,}741 \text{ Patient-days}$$

OBJECTIVE TYPE QUESTIONS

A. Multiple Choice Questions.

Select the correct answer in each of the following:

1. Classification and accumulation of costs by fixed and variable elements is of special importance in:

(*a*) process costing (*b*) unit costing
(*c*) operating costing (*d*) none of these.

2. Operating costing is applicable to:

(*a*) transport undertakings (*b*) electricity undertakings
(*c*) hospitals (*d*) cinemas
(*e*) all of these

3. Cost of service under operating costing is ascertained by preparing:
   (*a*) cost sheet (*b*) production account
   (*c*) process account (*d*) job cost sheet.

[**Ans.**1. (*c*), 2. (*e*), 3. (*a*)]

B. 'True'/'False' type statements.

Indicate whether the following statements are 'true' or 'false':

1. Operating costing is applied to ascertain the cost of products.
2. Operating costing is also known as operation costing.
3. Under operating costing, the main problem relates to the calculation of normal and abnormal loss.
4. The problem of equivalent production arises in case of operating costing.
5. The unit of cost in case of transport undertakings is per ton km. or per passenger km.
6. Cost of operating the services is ascertained by preparing Job Account.

[**Ans.** 1. false, 2. false, 3. false, 4. false, 5. True, 6. false]

C. Filling the blanks.

Fill in the blanks:

1. The method of costing used in undertakings like gas companies, cinema houses, hospitals etc., is known as ....
2. In motor transport costing, two examples of fixed cost are .... and ....
3. In transport undertakings, a .... is maintained for each vehicle to record details of trips made by vehicles during a specified period of time.
4. In hospitals, the cost unit is ....
5. In electricity companies, the cost unit is ....

[**Ans.** 1. Operating Costing, 2. Insurance and depreciation, 3. Daily Log Report, 4. per bed, 5. Per unit or kilowatt]

SHORT ANSWER TYPE QUESTIONS

Answer each of the following questions in not more than four lines.

1. What is operating costing?
2. To what type of undertaking is operating costing applicable?
3. What is Daily Log Report in case of transport undertakings?
4. Where do service undertakings invest a large proportion of their total capital?

LONG ANSWER TYPE QUESTIONS

1. What do you understand by 'Operating Costing'? What are its main features? Give examples of situations where operating costs are computed.

2. Explain units of cost used in transport undertakings. How are they computed?

EXERCISES

1. Following are the particulars in respect of a bus owned by Prestige Transporters for the month of April, 2006.

No. of days operated in the month : 25

Trips made by the bus daily : 4

Distance of route 80 kms. (one side)

Capacity of the bus : 52 passengers

Normal passengers travelling : 80 % of capacity

Calculate Total kms. and total passenger-kms. covered by the bus during the month.

[**Ans.** (*i*) Total kms. 1 × 25 × 4 × 80 kms. = 8,000

(*ii*) Total passenger-kms. $(8{,}000 \times 52 \times \frac{80}{100} = 3{,}32{,}800)$]

2. A transport service company is running two buses between two towns which are 150 kms. apart. The seating capacity of each bus is 40 passengers. Actual passengers carried were 75% of the seating capacity. All the buses ran for 30 days during the month. Each bus made one round trip per day. Calculate the total number of passenger kms. of the fleet for the month.

[**Ans.** 2 × 30 days × 300 kms. × 40 passengers × $\frac{75}{100}$ = 5,40,000 passenger-kms.]

3. D.G. Transport Company supplies the following details in respect of a truck of 10 ton capacity:

Month : October, 2006 No. of days of operation : 25

The truck carries goods to and from the city covering a distance of 200 kms. each way. On outward trip, freight is available to the extent of full capacity and on return 50% of capacity. Calculate the number of ton-kms. of the truck for the month.

[**Ans.** 1 × 25 × 200 kms. × 10 tons = 50,000

1 × 25 × 200 kms × 10 tons × $^{50}/_{100}$ = 25,000

No. of ton-kms. = 75,000]

4. From the following data, calculate the cost per km. of a vehicle:

	Rs.
Cost of vehicle	30,000
Road licence fee per year	1,000
Insurance charges per year	200
Garage rent per year	1,200
Driver's wages per month	400
Cost of petrol per litre	4.80
Kms. per litre : 8	
Proportionate charges for tyre and maintenance per km.	0.40
Estimated life: 1,50,000 kms.	
Annual kilometreage (estimated) 6,000 kms.	

[**Ans.** Cost per km. Rs. 2.40]

5. A transport company is running 4 buses between two towns which are 50 kms. apart. Seating capacity of each bus is 40 passengers. The following particulars were obtained from their books for the month of April, 2007:

	Rs.
Wages of drivers, conductors etc.	2,400
Salaries of office and supervisory staff	1,000
Diesel oil and other oils	4,000
Repairs and maintenance	800
Tax, Insurance etc.	1,600
Depreciation	2,600
Interest and other charges	2,000
	14,400

Actual passengers carried were 75% of the seating capacity. All the four buses run on all the days for the month. Each bus made one round trip per day. Find out cost per passenger km.

(*C.A. Inter, I.C.W.A. June, 1992*)

[**Ans.** Cost per passenger-km. Re. 0.04]

6. Union Transport Company supplies the following details in respect of a truck of 5 ton capacity:

Cost of truck	Rs. 90,000
Estimated life	10 years
Diesel, oil, grease	Rs. 15 per trip each way
Repairs and maintenance	Rs. 500 per month
Driver's wages	Rs. 500 per month
Cleaner's wages	Rs. 250 per month
Insurance	Rs. 4,800 per year
Tax	Rs. 2,400 per year
General Supervision Charges	Rs. 4,800 per year

The truck carries goods to and from the city covering a distance of 50 kms. each way. On outward trip, freight is available to the extent of full capacity and on return 20% of capacity.

Assuming that the truck runs on an average 25 days a month, work out

(*a*) Operating cost per ton-km.

(*b*) Rate per ton per trip that the company should charge if a profit of 50% on freightage is to be earned. (*C.A. Inter*)

(**Hint:** Assumed that truck makes only one trip a day)

[**Ans.** Cost per ton km. : Re. 0.50 Freightage per ton per trip Rs. 50]

7. From the following data relating to two different vehicles A and B, compute the cost per running km.

	Vehicle A	**Vehicle B**
Kilometres Run (Annual)	15,000	6,000
	Rs.	**Rs.**
Cost of Vehicle	25,000	15,000
Road Licence (Annual)	750	750
Insurance (Annual)	700	400
Garage Rent (Annual)	600	500
Supervision and Salaries (Annual)	1,200	1,200
Driver's wages per hour	3	3
Cost of petrol per gallon	3	3
Repairs and maintenance per km.	1.65	2
Tyre allocation per km.	0.80	0.60
Kilometres run per gallon	20 kms.	15 kms.
Estimated life of Vehicles	1,00,000 kms.	75,000 kms.

You are to charge interest on cost of vehicles at 5% per annum. The vehicles run 20 kms. per hour on an average.

(*I.C.W.A. Inter; C.A. Inter May*)

[**Ans.** A : Rs. 3.30, B : Rs. 1.75]

8. Kapoor Transport Co., which keeps a fleet of lorries, supply the following information:

Kilometres run for April, 2005	30,000
Expenses for April, 2005	**Rs.**
Operating Wages	2,000
Petrol	4,000
Original cost of vehicles	80,000
Depreciation @ 25% p.a. on the original cost	
Repairs	6,000
Garage Rent	2,000
Insurance Premium for the year	3,000

Prepare a Cost Sheet for April, 2005 showing the cost per running kilometre. [**Ans.** Total cost per km. Re. 0.53]

9. Prakash Automobiles distributes its goods to a regional dealer using a single lorry. The dealer's premises are 40 kilometres away by road. The lorry has a capacity of 10 tonnes and makes the journey twice a day fully loaded on the outward journeys and empty on return journeys. The following information is available for a four weekly period during the year 2008:

Petrol consumption	8 kilometres per litre
Petrol cost	Rs. 13 per litre
Oil	Rs. 100 per week
Driver's wages	Rs. 400 per week
Repairs	Rs. 100 per week
Garage rent	Rs. 150 per week
Cost of lorry (excluding tyres)	Rs. 4,50,000
Life of lorry	80,000 kilometres
Insurance	Rs. 6,500 per annum
Cost of tyres	Rs. 6,250
Life of tyres	25,000 kilometres
Estimated sale value of lorry at end of its life	Rs. 50,000
Vehicle licence cost	Rs. 1,300 per annum
Other overhead cost	Rs. 41,600 per annum

The lorry operates on a five day week.

Required:

(*a*) A statement to show the total cost of operating the vehicle for the four weekly period analysed into running costs and fixed costs.

(*b*) Calculate the vehicle cost per kilometre and per tonne-kilometre.

(*C.A. Inter, May, 1991*)

[**Ans.** (*a*) Rs. 28,800; (*b*) Rs. 9 and Rs. 1.80]

10. National Roadways has a fleet of 20 trucks. Each truck covers a distance of 300 kms. per day and the carrying capacity of the trucks is ten tons. On an average, loading available for the trucks is only 90%. Effective working days in a month are 25, excluding the days of lay-off on account of repairs which are estimated to be 5%. Information about the costs is as follows:

1. Cost of trucks – Rs. 1,60,000
2. Estimated useful life – 5 years.
3. Resale value after 5 years – Rs. 60,000.
4. Salary to drivers and cleaners – Rs.1,000 per truck per month.
5. Taxes and insurance – Rs. 2,500 per truck per year.
6. Total expenditure on maintenance and repairs through owned workshop for all trucks – Rs. 24,000 per year.
7. Tyre and tubes and other accessories – Rs. 7,200 per truck per year.

8. Diesel, oil etc. – Rs. 40 per 100 kms.

Calculate the cost of operating the truck per ton-km.

[**Ans.** Re. 0.10 per ton-km. approximately. Total ton-kms. per month 64,125]

11. A chemical factory runs its boiler on furnace oil obtained from Indian Oil and Bharat Petroleum, whose depots are situated at a distance of 12 and 8 kms. from the factory site. Transportation of furnace oil is made by the company's own tank lorries of 5 tons capacity each. Onward trips are made only on full load and the lorries return empty. The filling-in time takes an average 40 minutes for Indian Oil and 30 minutes for Bharat Petroleum. But the emptying time in the factory is only 40 minutes for all. From the records available, it is seen that the average speed of the company's lorries works out to 24 kms. per hour. The varying operating charges average 60 paise per km. covered and fixed charges give an incidence of Rs. 7.50 per hour of operation.

Calculate the cost per ton-km. for each source. (*C.A. Inter*)

[**Ans.** Indian Oil 53 paise; Bharat Petroleum 58 paise]

12. Shankar has been promised a contract to run a tourist car on a 20 kms. long route for the Chief Executive of a multi-national firm. He buys a car costing Rs. 1,50,000. The annual cost of insurance and taxes are Rs. 4,500 and Rs. 900 respectively. He has to pay Rs. 500 per month for a garage where he keeps the car when it is not in use. The annual repair costs are estimated at Rs. 4,000. The car is estimated to have a life of 10 years at the end of which the scrap value is likely to be Rs. 50,000. He hires a driver who is to be paid Rs. 300 per month plus 10% of the takings as commission. Other incidental expenses are estimated at Rs. 200 per month.

Petrol and oil will cost Rs. 100 per 100 kms. The car will make 4 round trips each day. Assuming a profit of 15% on takings is desired and that the car will be on the road for 25 days on an average per month, what should he charge per round-trip? (*C.A. Inter*)

[**Ans.** Rs. 88.22 per round trip]

13. Mr. X owns a bus which runs according to the following schedule:

(*i*) Delhi to Chandigarh and back, the same day
Distance covered: 150 kms. one way
Number of days run each month: 8
Seating capacity occupied: 90%

(*ii*) Delhi to Agra and back, the same day
Distance covered: 120 kms. one way
Number of days run each month: 10
Seating capacity occupied: 85%.

(*iii*) Delhi to Jaipur and back, the same day
Distance covered: 270 kms. one way
Number of days run each month: 6
Seating capacity occupied 100%

(*iv*) Following are the other details:

Cost of the bus	Rs. 6,00,000
Salary of the driver	Rs. 2,800 p.m.
Salary of the Conductor	Rs. 2,200 p.m.
Salary of the part-time Accountant	Rs. 200 p.m.
Insurance of the bus	Rs. 4,800 per annum.
Diesel consumption 4 kms. per litre at	Rs. 6 per litre
Road tax	Rs. 1,500 p.a.
Lubricant oil	Rs. 10 per 100 kms.
Permit fee	Rs. 315 p.m.
Repairs and maintenance	Rs. 1,000 p.m.
Depreciation of the bus	@ 20 % p.a.
Seating capacity of the bus	50 persons.

Passenger tax is 20% of the total takings. Calculate the bus fare to be charged from each passenger to earn a profit of 30% on total takings. The fares are to be indicated per passenger for the journeys:

(*i*) Delhi to Chandigarh (*C.A. Inter, 1994*)
(*ii*) Delhi to Agra
(*iii*) Delhi to Jaipur.

[**Ans**. (*i*) Rs. 24; (*ii*) Rs. 19.20; (*iii*) 43.20]

14. An Iron and Steel Works which generates its own power for the purpose of using the same for running the factory gives the following information:

(*a*) Coal-consumed 1,000 quintals @ Rs. 12 per quintal.
Oil-15 quintals @ Rs.1,000 per quintal.
Water 2,00,000 litres @ Re. 1.00 per 100 Lts.
Cost of steam boiler Rs. 60,000, which has a residual value of Rs. 12,000, and a life of 10 years.

(*b*) Salaries and wages for generating plant:
10 skilled workers @ Rs. 300 p.m.
15 unskilled workers @ Rs. 100 p.m.

(*c*) Generating plant cost Rs. 1,50,000, depreciation @ 10%

(*d*) Share of administrative charges Rs 2,050 per month.

(*e*) Salaries and wages for the Boiler House
20 men @ Rs. 150 p.m.
40 women @ Rs. 60 p.m.

(*f*) Repairs and maintenance of steam boiler and generating plant Rs. 1,000 p.m.

(*g*) No. of units generated 2,00,000.

(*h*) Sale of ash Rs. 1,300.

(*i*) 1/10 of units generated were used by Generating Department itself.

Calculate cost per unit of electricity generated.

[**Ans.** 25 paise]

15. The following cost data pertaining to the year 2005-06 are collected from the books of Amritsar Power Supply Co. Ltd. Prepare a cost sheet showing the cost of generation of power per unit of kwh.

Total units generated 15,00,000 kwhs.

	Rs.
Operation Labour	16,500
Plant Supervision	5,250
Lubricants and Supplies	10,500
Repairs and Maintenance	21,000
Administration Overhead	9,000
Capital Cost	1,50,000

Coal consumed per kwh. for the year is 1.5 lbs. and the cost of coal delivered to the Power Station is Rs. 33.06 per metric tonne. Depreciation rate chargeable is 4% p.a. and interest on capital is to be taken at 1% higher than the Reserve Bank rate of 6% p.a.

[**Ans.** Total Cost Rs. 1,12,485 Per kwh. Re. 0.075]

[**Hint:** for calculating cost of coal consumed:

One metric tonne = 2,205 lbs.

Cost of one metric tonne = Rs. 33.06

Coal consumed = 15,00,000 kwhs. × 1.5 lbs.

= 22,50,000 Lbs.

Cost of Coal $= 22{,}50{,}000 \text{ Lbs.} \times \dfrac{33.06}{2{,}205}$

= Rs. 33,735 (approximately)]

16. From the following particulars, prepare a Cost Sheet in proper form showing the total cost and cost per unit of electricity generated:

	Rs.
Coal used	10,000
Water	100
Wages for coal handling	600
Wages for stoking	900
Repairs and maintenance of Boiler House	300
Lubricating oil	50
Depreciation of Boiler House	800
Supervisory Labour	250
Total Steam produced	20,000 lbs.
Steam used for generation of power	15,000 lbs.

The other expenses incurred in the power house are as follows:

	Rs.
Wages for operators	900
Depreciation of Generator and other equipments	700
Repairs	500
Supervision Charges	400
Electricity generated :	10,000 units.

[**Ans.** Total Cost of generation Rs. 12,250; Cost per unit Rs. 1.225]

17. From the following information, calculate the cost of generating electricity per unit:

1. Coal used 1,200 Tonnes @ Rs. 10 per tonne.
2. Freight and handling charges : 10% of the value of coal used.
3. Oil : 10 tonnes @ Rs. 350 per tonne.
4. Water : 50,000 litres @ Re.0.25 per 100 litres.
5. Depreciation of steam boiler, Rs. 250.
6. Salaries and wages of Boiler House:
   10 men @ Rs. 100 each
   40 coolies @ Rs. 50 each
7. Recovery on account of sale of ashes:
   100 tonnes @ Re. 1 per tonne.
8. Salaries and wages of generating station:
   40 men @ Rs. 150 each
   30 coolies @ Rs. 50 each
9. Repairs and maintenance of generating equipment, Rs. 500.
10. Depreciation of generating equipment, Rs. 5,000
11. Share of Administrative Expenses, Rs. 2,000
12. Total Number of units generated, 2,02,000
13. Normal Loss in the process, 2,000 units generated.

[**Ans.** Re. 0.174 per unit]

18. A lodging home is being run in a small hill station with 50 single rooms. The home offers concessional rates during six off-season months in a year. During this period, half of the full-room rent is charged. The management's profit margin is targeted at 20% of the room rent. The following are the cost estimates and other details for the year ending 31st March, 2003 (assume a month to be of 30 days):

(*a*) Occupancy during the season is 80%, while in the off season is 40% only

(*b*) Expenses:

	Rs.
(*i*) Staff Salary (excluding room attendants)	2,75,000
(*ii*) Repairs to buildings	1,30,500
(*iii*) Laundry & linen	40,000

(*iv*) Interior and tapestry 87,000

(*v*) Sundry expenses 95,400

(*c*) Annual depreciation is to be provided, for buildings at 5% and on furniture and equipments at 15%, on straight line basis.

(*d*) Room attendants are paid Rs. 5 per room-day on the basis of occupancy of the rooms in a month.

(*e*) Monthly lighting charges are Rs. 120 per room, except in four months of winter when it is Rs. 30 per room and this cost is on the basis of full occupancy for a month.

(*f*) Total investment in the home is Rs. 100 lakhs of which Rs. 80 lakhs relate to buildings and balance for furniture and equipments.

You are required to work out the room rent chargeable per day both during the season and off-season months, on the basis of the foregoing information.

[**Ans.** Room Rent (*i*) Rs. 197 (*ii*) Rs. 98.50]

19. The Holiday Hotel has 40 bed rooms with a maximum occupancy of 490 sleeper nights per week. Average occupancy is 60% throughout the year. Meals provided to guests have been costed and the average food cost per person per day is as follows:

	Rs.
Breakfast	3.60
Lunch	11.00
Dinner	13.40
Total	28.00

Direct wages and staff meals per week are as under:

House-keeping	1,952
Restaurant and kitchen	3,430
General	1,760

Direct expenses per annum are Rs. 45,760 for house-keeping and Rs. 52,000 for the restaurant.

Indirect expenses amounting to Rs. 3,41,120 which should be apportioned on the basis of floor areas are:

Bed rooms	3,600 Sq. metres
Restaurant	1,200 Sq. metres
Service area	600 Sq. metres

A net profit of 10% each must be made on the restaurant takings and accommodation takings.

You are required to calculate what inclusive terms per person should be charged per day. Show the split between meals and accommodation charges.

[**Ans.** For Food Rs. 60.36; For Accommodation Rs. 29.64; Inclusive Rs. 90]

20. Dr. Rajesh Sodhi and Dr. Monika Sodhi hire a building to run a Nursing Home. The building has 40 rooms and the monthly rent is Rs. 1,20,000. The lighting, power and heating charges come to Rs. 15,000 per month. The following staff members are engaged

(*i*) 8 Doctors @ Rs. 25,000 p.m. each.
(*ii*) 16 Nurses @ Rs. 5,000 p.m. each.
(*iii*) 10 General Helpers @ Rs. 2,000 p.m. each.

The room occupancy is expected to be 80%. If a margin of 20% on total takings is desired, ascertain the amount of rent to be charged per room day taking a month to be of 30 days.

[**Ans.** Rs. 566.41]

21. Mumbai Health Centre runs an Intensive Care Unit. For this purpose it has hired a building at a rent of Rs. 5,000 p.m. with the understanding that it would bear the repairs and maintenance charges also.

The unit consists of 25 beds and 5 more beds can be comfortably accommodated when the occasion demands. The permanent staff attached to the unit are as follows:

2 Supervisors, each at a salary of Rs. 500 per month.
4 Nurses, each at a salary of Rs. 300 per month.
2 Wards Boys, each at a salary of Rs. 150 per month.

Though the unit was open for the patients all the 365 days in a year, scrutiny of accounts of 2002 revealed that only for 120 days in a year, the unit had the full capacity of 25 patients per day and for another 80 days it had on an average 20 beds only occupied per day, but there were occasions when the beds were full, extra beds were hired from outside at a charge of Rs. 5 per bed day. The total hire charges for the extra beds incurred for the whole year amounted to Rs. 2,000.

The unit engaged expert doctors from outside to attend on the patients and the fees were paid on the basis of number of patients attended and time spent by them on an average worked out to Rs. 10,000 per month in 2002. The other expenses for the year were as under:

	Rs.
Repairs and maintenance (Fixed)	3,600
Food supplied to patients (Variable)	44,000
Janitor and other services for them (Variable)	12,500
Laundry charges for their bed linen (Variable)	28,000
Medicines supplied (Variable)	25,000
Cost of Oxygen, X-ray etc. other than directly borne for treatment of patients (Fixed)	54,000
General Administration charges allocated to the unit (Fixed)	49,550

(*i*) If the unit recovered an overall amount of Rs. 100 per day on an average from each patient, what is the profit per patient-day made by the unit in the year 2002.

(*ii*) The unit wants to work on a budget for the year 2003, but the number of patients requiring intensive care is a very uncertain factor. Assuming that same revenue and expenses prevail in 2003 in the first instance, work out the number of patient days required by the unit to break even.

[Ans. (*i*) Rs. 12 27, (*ii*) 3,813 patient days]

22. The management of New Hotel has prepared the budget, which shows the following room occupancy:

	Average %
January – March	45
April – June	60
July – September	90
October – December	55

Revenue for the year is estimated to be Rs. 30,00,000 and arises from three profit centres:

Accommodation	45%
Restaurant	35%
Bar	20%
Total	100%

The accommodation revenue is earned from several different categories of guest, each of which pays a different rate per room.

The three profit centres have the following percentage gross margins:

	Accommodation		**Restaurant**		**Bar**	
		%		**%**		**%**
Revenue		100		100		100
Wages	20		30		15	
Cost of sales	–		40		50	
Direct costs	10	30	10	80	5	70
		70		20		30

Fixed costs for the year are estimated to be Rs. 5,65,000.

Capital employed is Rs. 70,00,000.

As a means of improving the Return of Capital Employed (ROCE) two suggestions have been made;

(*i*) to offer special two-night holidays at a reduced price of Rs. 25 per night. It is expected that those accepting the offer would spend an amount equal to 40% of the accommodation charge in the restaurant, and 20% in the bar. The gross margin percentages for the three profit centers would remain same as above.

(*ii*) to increase prices, management is confident that there will be no drop in volume of sales if restaurant prices are increased by 10% and bar prices by 5%. Accommodation prices would also need to be increased.

You are required:

(*a*) to calculate the budgeted return on capital employed before tax; and

(*b*) to calculate:

(*i*) how many two-night holidays would need to be sold each week in the three off-peak quarters to improve the return on capital employed by a further 4% above the percentage calculated in (*a*) above.

(*ii*) by what percentage the prices of accommodation would need to be increased to achieve the desired increase in ROCE shown in (*b*) (*i*) above.

(*I.C.W.A., Final June, 1992*)

[**Ans.** (*a*) 11%, (*b*) (*i*) 171 (*ii*) 11%]

18

Reconciliation of Cost and Financial Accounts

In a business concern, cost accounts and financial accounts can be maintained on the basis of non-integral system or integral system of accounting. Under non-integral system of accounting, cost accounts and financial accounts are maintained separately. Cost accounts are maintained by Cost Accountant as per the principles of cost accounting to ascertain the total and per unit cost of products and jobs at different stages of production or execution. Financial accounts are maintained by financial accountant as per the principles of financial accounting to record the day-to-day transactions of a business with a view to find out their net effect on the profitability and financial position of the business. Thus, the aims, objects, principles and the methods of maintaining cost accounts and financial accounts are not the same. As such, the profit shown by cost accounts may not agree with the profit shown by financial accounts. The conflicting information provided by these two sets of accounts may not be helpful in taking correct policy decisions.

Thus, the system of costing should be capable of reconciliation with financial accounts. Since the cost accounts, largely dependent upon estimates, comprise a detailed analysis of financial expenditure and unless such analysis is reconciled with financial accounts, cost accounts cannot be relied upon. In this connection, H.J. Wheldon is of the opinion that "no system is complete unless it is linked up with financial accounts so that the results shown by both cost and financial accounts may be reconciled."

MEANING OF RECONCILIATION

Reconciliation may be expressed as the process of tallying the working results or profits as shown by cost accounts with that of financial accounts. According to Eric L. Kohler — "Reconciliation is the determination of the items necessary to bring the balances of two or more related accounts or statements into agreement. Efforts are also made to judge the arithmetical accuracy of the profits revealed by two different sets of books." Thus, reconciliation of cost accounts and financial accounts involves the process of identifying and accounting for the items which have led to the difference in working results as shown by cost accounts and financial accounts. The reconciliation is made in an analytical form presented in the shape of a statement (known as Reconciliation Statement) or a memorandum account (known as Memorandum Reconciliation Account).

NEED FOR RECONCILIATION

The necessity for reconciliation of cost accounts and financial accounts arises due to the following reasons:

(*i*) Reconciliation assists in ascertaining the accuracy and reliability of the various sets of books of account maintained in a business concern.

(*ii*) It facilitates internal control since it discloses the reasons for the variation in profit or loss in an analytical manner.

(*iii*) It assists in effecting co-operation and co-ordination between costing office and accounting office.

(*iv*) It helps in formulating proper policies regarding overhead absorption, depreciation and stock valuation.

CAUSES OF DISAGREEMENT OF RESULTS SHOWN BY COST ACCOUNTS AND FINANCIAL ACCOUNTS

Under the non-integral system of accounting, when cost accounts and financial accounts are maintained separately, the documents used for ascertaining the amount of expenditure to be charged in respect of some of the items, are the same (e.g., cost of materials used and the cost of labour paid are to be ascertained with the help of Material Requisitions and Wages Sheets respectively), yet there may arise a difference in the profit (or loss) as shown by the two sets of accounts, due to one or more of the following reasons:

1. **Under/Over-Absorption of Overhead:** The financial accounts comprise the actual expenditure in respect of the factory, office, administration, and selling and distribution overheads whereas the cost accounts comprise an approximate charge in respect of these items on the basis of past records or pre-determined absorption rate. As such, overheads are generally under/over-absorbed in cost accounts.
2. **Items of Receipts/Income shown in Financial Accounts Only:** The following items of receipts and income are shown or included in financial accounts but excluded from cost accounts:
   (*a*) Interest and discount received.
   (*b*) Rent received.
   (*c*) Dividend received.
   (*d*) Commission received.
   (*e*) Transfer fees received.
   (*f*) Profit from the sale of fixed assets and investments.

3. **Items of Expenses/Losses Shown in Financial Accounts Only:** The following items of expenses and losses are charged in financial accounts but are not shown in cost accounts:
   (*a*) Interest allowed on loan.
   (*b*) Interest on capital.
   (*c*) Cash discount allowed.
   (*d*) Interest paid on debentures.
   (*e*) Expenses and losses on issue of shares and debentures.
   (*f*) Loss on sale of fixed assets and investments.
   (*g*) Items of appropriation of profit i.e., income tax paid or provision for income tax, transfer to reserves, dividends paid on shares etc.
   (*h*) Preliminary expenses written off.
   (*i*) Goodwill written off.
   (*j*) Donations and charity paid.
4. **Items of Abnormal Profit/Loss Included in Financial Accounts Only:** There are various items of abnormal profit/loss which are included in financial accounts but are excluded from cost accounts. These items are:
   (*a*) Cost of abnormal loss of materials.
   (*b*) Cost of abnormal idle time of workers.
   (*c*) Cost of abnormal saving of materials.
   (*d*) Exceptional bad debts.
   (*e*) Penalties and fines paid for violation of Government rules and regulations.
5. **Items of Expenses Included in Cost Accounts Only:** The following items of expenses are recorded in cost accounts only and are not considered in financial accounts:
   (*a*) Notional rent for owned premises.
   (*b*) Depreciation on assets which do not carry any book value in financial accounts.
6. **Difference in the Basis for Charging Depreciation on Assets:** The methods for calculating depreciation on fixed assets in cost accounts and financial accounts may differ leading to a difference in working results. In financial accounts, depreciation is generally provided on the basis of diminishing balance (written-down value) method or original cost method. But in cost accounts, machine hour rate or production unit method of depreciation may be followed.
7. **Difference in Bases for Valuation of Stock:** The stock of raw material in financial accounts is valued at cost price or market price, whichever is less, while in cost accounts, it is valued by adopting any of the methods like FIFO, LIFO, AVERAGE price methods etc. The stock of work-in-progress for the purpose of cost accounts may be valued on the basis of prime cost or factory cost while in financial accounts, it is valued by taking into account, a part of office and administration expenses. The

stock of finished goods in financial accounts is valued on the basis of cost price or market price, whichever is less, while in cost accounts, it is valued on the basis of actual cost.

RECONCILIATION OF COSTING AND FINANCIAL RESULTS

Where there is a difference between the results of working as disclosed by cost accounts and as disclosed by financial accounts, the following steps should be taken to locate the reasons for such difference :

1. The extent of the difference between actual indirect expenses as recorded in financial accounts and the charges made in cost accounts should be ascertained.
2. A schedule of all expenses and losses which have been included in the Trading and Profit and Loss Account but not in cost accounts should be prepared.
3. A schedule of all income and profit which have been credited to Profit and Loss Account but excluded from cost accounts should be prepared.
4. A schedule of all items which have been included in cost accounts but excluded from financial accounts should be prepared.
5. The basis on which stocks of raw materials, work-in-progress and finished goods have been valued for balance sheet purposes must be ascertained and compared with the valuations appearing in cost accounts and their difference must be ascertained.
6. Lastly, all items which have been included in cost accounts as well as financial accounts but differ in value should be ascertained.

After the discrepancies have been located, a Reconciliation Statement should be prepared by starting with profit as disclosed by cost accounts. The following items should then be added to the profit as per cost accounts :

(*i*) Indirect expenses (factory, office and administration and selling and distribution) over-absorbed or over-recovered in cost accounts or under-absorbed in financial accounts.

(*ii*) Items of receipts shown in the financial books but not in cost accounts.

(*iii*) Over-valuation of opening stock (of raw material, work-in-progress or finished goods) in cost accounts.

(*iv*) Under-valuation of closing stock (of raw material, work-in-progress or finished goods) in cost accounts.

(*v*) Items of abnormal efficiency (abnormal saving) shown in financial books but not in cost accounts.

The following items should be deducted from profit as per cost accounts:

(*i*) Under-absorption of indirect expenses in cost accounts or over-absorption in financial accounts.

(*ii*) Items of expenses shown in the financial accounts but not in cost accounts.

(*iii*) Under-valuation of opening stock (of raw material, work-in-progress or finished goods) in cost accounts.

(*iv*) Over-valuation of closing stock in cost accounts.

After making the above adjustments, the profit as per cost accounts will agree with the profit as per financial accounts.

Specimen of Reconciliation Statement

	Rs.	Rs.
Profit as per Cost Accounts		?
Add:		
(*i*) Over-recovery of Overheads in Cost Accounts	?	
(*ii*) Items of Income /Receipts Credited in Financial Accounts only.	?	
(*iii*) Over-valuation of Opening Stock of Raw Materials, Work-in-Progress or Finished Goods in Cost Accounts	?	
(*iv*) Under-valuation of Closing Stock of Raw Materials, Work-in-Progress or Finished Goods in Cost Accounts		?
Less:		
(*i*) Under-recovery of Overheads in Cost Accounts	?	
(*ii*) Items of expenses/losses debited in Financial Accounts only.	?	
(*iii*) Under-valuation of Opening Stock of Raw Materials, Work-in-Progress or Finished Goods in Cost Accounts	?	
(*iv*) Over-valuation of Closing Stock of Raw Materials, Work-in-Progress or Finished Goods in Cost Accounts.	?	?
Profit as per Financial Accounts		?

MEMORANDUM RECONCILIATION ACCOUNT

Reconciliation of Cost Accounts and Financial Accounts may also be presented in the form of an account prepared on memorandum basis. Such an account is known as "Memorandum Reconciliation Account". The amount of profit as per cost accounts is shown on the credit side of this account. The various items to be added to the profit as per cost accounts, are credited to the Memorandum Reconciliation Account and the items to be deducted from profit as per cost accounts, are debited to it. The difference between the two sides of the account will reveal the amount of profit or loss as per financial accounts. The specimen of a Memorandum Reconciliation Account may be given as follows:

Memorandum Reconciliation Account

Particulars	Amount	Particulars	Amount
	Rs.		Rs.
To Under-Recovery of Overheads in Cost Accounts	?	By Profit as per Cost Accounts	?
To Items of Expenses and Losses not included in Cost Accounts	?	By Over-Recovery of Overheads in Cost Accounts	?
To Under-Valuation of Opening Stock in Cost Accounts	?	By Items of Incomes and Receipts not included in Cost Accounts	?
To Over-Valuation of Closing Stock in Cost Accounts	?	By Over-Valuation of Opening Stock in Cost Accounts	?
To Profit as per Financial Accounts	?	By Under-Valuation of Closing Stock in Cost Accounts	?

Illustration 1

Profit disclosed by a company's cost accounts for the year was Rs. 50,000 whereas the net profit as disclosed by the financial accounts was Rs. 46,000. Following information is available:

(*a*) Overheads as per cost accounts were estimated at Rs. 55,555. The charge for the year shown by the financial accounts was Rs. 50,000

(*b*) Director's fees shown in financial accounts only Rs. 1,000

(*c*) The company allocated Rs. 2,000 as provision for doubtful debts.

(*d*) In financial accounts, depreciation was charged more in comparison with cost accounts by Rs. 3,000

(*e*) Share-transfer fees received during the year Rs. 445

(*f*) Provision for Income tax was Rs. 4,000

From the above, prepare a statement reconciling the figures shown by the cost and financial accounts.

Solution

Reconciliation Statement

	Rs.	Rs.
Profit as per Cost Accounts		50,000
Add:		
(*i*) Over-recovery of Overheads in Cost Accounts (Rs. 55,555 – Rs. 50,000)	5,555	
(*ii*) Share Transfer Fees Received not included in Cost Accounts	445	6,000
		56,000
Less:		
(*i*) Director's Fees not shown in Cost Accounts	1,000	
(*ii*) Provision for Doubtful Debts not made in Cost Accounts	2,000	
(*iii*) Excess Amount of Depreciation charged in Financial Accounts	3,000	
(*iv*) Provision for Income Tax not made in Cost Accounts	4,000	10,000
Profit as per Financial Accounts		46,000

Illustration 2

The net profits of a manufacturing company appeared at Rs. 64,500 as per financial records for the year ended 31st March, 2007. The cost books, however, showed a net profit of Rs. 86,460 for the same period. A careful scrutiny of the figures from both the sets of accounts revealed the following facts:

		Rs.
(*i*)	Income tax provided in financial books	20,000
(*ii*)	Bank interest credited in financial books	250
(*iii*)	Works overhead under-recovered in cost books	1,550
(*iv*)	Depreciation charged in financial books	5,600
(*v*)	Depreciation recovered in costing books	6,000
(*vi*)	Administrative overheads over-recovered	850
(*vii*)	Loss due to obsolescence charged in financial accounts	2,800
(*viii*)	Interest on investments not included in cost accounts	4,000

(*ix*) Stores adjustments (Credited in financial books) 240

(*x*) Loss due to depreciation in stock values charged in Financial Books 3,350

Prepare (*a*) the Reconciliation Statement

(*b*) a Memorandum Reconciliation Account.

Solution

Reconciliation Statement

	Rs.	Rs.
Profit as per Cost Accounts		86,460
Add:		
(*i*) Bank Interest credited in financial books	250	
(*ii*) Excess depreciation recovered in cost accounts	400	
(*iii*) Administrative overheads over-recovered in Cost Accounts	850	
(*iv*) Interest on Investments not included in Cost Accounts	4,000	
(*v*) Stores adjustments credited in Financial Books	240	5,740
		92,200
Less:		
(*i*) Income tax provided in Financial Books	20,000	
(*ii*) Works Overhead Under-recovered in Cost Books	1,550	
(*iii*) Loss due to obsolescence charged in Financial Accounts	2,800	
(*iv*) Loss due to depreciation in stock values charged in Financial Books	3,350	27,700
Profit as per Financial Accounts		64,500

Memorandum Reconciliation Account

	Rs.		Rs.
To Income tax provided in Financial Books	20,000	By Profit as per Cost Accounts	86,460
To Works Overhead Under-recovered in Cost Accounts	1,550	By Bank Interest Credited in Financial Books	250
To Loss due to obsolescence charged in Financial Books	2,800	By Excess Depreciation recovered in Cost Accounts	400
To Loss due to Depreciation in Stock Values charged in Financial Books	3,350	By Administrative Overheads Over-recovered in Cost Accounts	850
To Profit as per Financial Accounts	64,500	By Interest on Investments not included in Cost Accounts	4,000
		By Stores Adjustments credited in Financial Books	240
	92,200		92,200

Illustration 3

From the following figures prepare a Reconciliation Statement:

	Rs.
Net Loss as per Financial Records	2,08,045
Net Loss as per Costing Records	1,72,400
Works Overhead under-recovered in Costing	3,120
Administrative Overhead recovered in Excess	1,700
Depreciation charged in Financial Records	11,200
Depreciation recovered in Costing	12,500
Interest Received not included in Costing	8,000
Obsolescence Loss Charged in Financial Books	5,700
Income-tax provided in Financial Books	40,300
Bank Interest Credited in Financial Books	750
Stores Adjustments (Credited in Financial Books)	475
Value of Opening Stock in Cost Accounts	52,600
In Financial Accounts	54,000
Value of Closing Stock in Cost Accounts	52,000
In Financial Accounts	49,600
Interest Charged in Cost Accounts but not in Financial Accounts	6,000
Preliminary Expenses Written off in Financial Accounts	800
Provision for Doubtful Debts in Financial Accounts	150

(*C.S. Inter, 1997*)

Solution

Reconciliation Statement

	Rs.	Rs.
Net Loss as per Cost Accounts		(–) 1,72,400
Add:		
(*i*) Over-recovery of Administrative overheads in Cost Accounts	1,700	
(*ii*) Depreciation over-recovered in Cost Accounts	1,300	
(*iii*) Interest Received not included in Cost Accounts	8,000	
(*iv*) Bank Interest Credited in Financial Accounts	750	
(*v*) Stores Adjustments Credited in Financial Accounts	475	
(*vi*) Interest Charged in Cost Accounts but not in Financial Accounts	6,000	
		(+) 18,225
Less:		(–) 1,54,175
(*i*) Works Overhead under-recovered in Cost Accounts	3,120	
(*ii*) Obsolescence Loss Charged in Financial Accounts	5,700	
(*iii*) Income tax provided in Financial Books	40,300	
(*iv*) Under-valuation of Opening Stock in Cost Accounts	1,400	
(*v*) Over-valuation of Closing Stock in Cost Accounts	2,400	
(*vi*) Preliminary Expenses Written off in Financial Accounts	800	
(*vii*) Provision for Doubtful Debts made in Financial Accounts	150	
		(–) 53,870
Net Loss as per Financial Accounts		(–) 2,08,045

Illustration 4

From the following profit and loss account, draw up a Memorandum Reconciliation Account, showing the profit as per cost accounts.

Profit and Loss Account
for the year ended 31.03.2007

	Rs.		Rs.
To Office Salaries	11,282	By Gross Profit	54,648
To Office Expenses	6,514	By Dividend received	400
To Salesmen's Salaries	4,922	By Interest on bank deposits	150
To Sales Expenses	9,304		
To Distribution Expenses	2,990		
To Loss on Sale of Machinery	1,950		
To Fines	200		
To Discount on Debentures	100		
To Net Profit	17,936		
	55,198		55,198
To Income Tax	8,000	By Net Profit	17,936
To Reserve	1,000		
To Dividend	4,000		
To Balance c/d	4,936		
	17,936		17,936

The cost accountant of the company has ascertained a profit Rs. 19,636 as per his books.

Solution

Memorandum Reconciliation Account

Dr.	Rs.		Cr. Rs.
To Incomes excluded from Cost Accounts:		By Profit as per Profit and Loss A/c	4,936
Dividend Received	400	By Items not Charged in Cost Accounts:	
Interest on Bank Deposits	150	Loss on Sale of Machinery	1,950
		Fines	200
		Discount on Debentures	100
		Income Tax	8,000
To Profit as per Cost Accounts	19,636	Reserve	1,000
		Dividend	4,000
	20,186		20,186

Illustration 5

X is the manufacturer of a standard product. His Trading and Profit and Loss Account for the year ended 31st March, 2007 appears as under:

Trading and Profit and Loss Account for the year ended 31st March, 2007

	Rs.		Rs.
To Material Consumed	3,84,310	By Sales	7,20,000
To Carriage Inward	3,860		
To Direct Wages	2,12,640		
To Works Expenses	81,420		
To Gross Profit c/d	37,770		
	7,20,000		7,20,000
To Office and Administrative Expenses	21,930	By Gross Profit b/d	37,770
To Selling and Distribution Expenses	3,270		
To Net Profit	12,570		
	37,770		37,770

In his Cost Accounts, X has charged works and office and administrative expenses to production during the year of Rs. 82,350 and Rs. 21,260 respectively while selling overhead has been ignored. His Cost Accounts reveal a profit of Rs. 15,580 for the year. Prepare a statement reconciling the results shown by the two sets of accounts.

Solution

Reconciliation Statement

	Rs.	Rs.
Profit as Per Cost Accounts		15,580
Add:		
Over-absorption of works expenses in Cost Accounts (Rs. 82,350 – Rs. 81,420)	930	930
		16,510
Less:		
(*i*) Under-absorption of office and administrative expenses in Cost Accounts (Rs. 21,930 – 21,260)	670	
(*ii*) Selling and Distribution expenses not shown in Cost Accounts	3,270	
		3,940
Profit as per Financial Accounts		12,570

Illustration 6

A radio manufacturing company, which commenced business in 1st April, 2005, supplies you with the following information and asks you to prepare a statement showing the profit per radio set sold. Wages and materials are to be charged at actual cost, works oncost at 75% on wages and office oncost at 30% on works cost. You are also required to prepare a statement reconciling the profit as shown by the Cost Accounts with the profit as shown by Profit and Loss Account for the year ending 31st March, 2006.

There were no radio sets in stock, or in course of manufacture on 31st March, 2006, and the number of radio sets sold during the year was 540. The particulars given are as follows:

Material per set	Rs. 240
Wages per set	Rs. 80
Selling price per set	Rs. 600

Prepare the necessary statement showing the actual profit for the year, if works expenses were Rs. 32,160 and the office expenses Rs. 61,800

(*P.U. B.Com., 1968*)

Solution

Profit and Loss Account
for the year ended 31st March, 2006

	Rs.		Rs.
To Material Consumed (Rs. 240 × 540 sets)	1,29,600	By Sales (Rs. 600 × 540 sets)	3,24,000
To Wages (Rs. 80 × 540 sets)	43,200		
To Works Expenses	32,160		
To Office Expenses	61,800		
To Net Profit	57,240		
	3,24,000		3,24,000

Cost Sheet

Output: 540 Radio sets

		Per Set	Total
		Rs.	Rs.
Direct Materials		240	1,29,600
Direct Wages		80	43,200
	Prime Cost	320	1,72,800
Works Overheads @ 75% on Wages		60	32,400
	Works Cost	380	2,05,200
Office Overheads @ 30% on Works Cost		114	61,560
	Cost of Production	494	2,66,760
	Profit	106	57,240
	Sales	600	3,24,000

Reconciliation Statement

	Rs.
Profit as per Cost Accounts	57,240
Add: Over-recovery of Works Expenses in Cost Accounts (Rs. 32,400 – Rs. 32,160)	240
	57,480
Less: Under-recovery of Office Expenses in Cost Accounts (Rs. 61,800 – Rs. 61,560)	240
Profits as per Financial Accounts	57,240

Illustration 7

The net profits shown by financial accounts of a company amounted to Rs. 28,550 whilst the profits disclosed by company's cost accounts for that period were Rs. 38,660. On reconciliation, the following differences were discovered:

1. The following items are not included in cost accounts:

	Rs.
Directors' fee (Dr.)	650
Bank Interest (Cr.)	30
Income Tax (Dr.)	8,300

2. A provision for Bad and Doubtful Debts made in financial books did not occur in cost accounts, Rs. 570.
3. Overheads absorbed in cost accounts were Rs. 8,500 while the actuals as shown by financial accounts were Rs. 8,320.
4. The expenditure on a work started during the year on a new factory was Rs. 16,000. Depreciation @ 5% was provided in financial books.

Prepare a statement reconciling the figures of profit as shown by the two sets of books.

Solution

Reconciliation Statement

		Rs.	Rs.
Profit as shown by Cost Accounts			38,660
Add:			
(*i*) Overheads overcharged in cost accounts:			
Cost Accounts	Rs. 8,500		
Financial Accounts	Rs. 8,320		
		180	
(*ii*) Bank interest credited in financial books but not included in cost books		30	
			210
			38,870
Less:			
(*i*) Expenses not charged in Cost Accounts:			
Income Tax		8,300	
Directors' fees		650	
Reserve for Bad and Doubtful debts		570	
Depreciation @ 5% on Rs. 16,000		800	10,320
Profit as per Financial Books			28,550

Illustration 8

From the following particulars prepare (*a*) Statement of cost of manufacture, charging factory overheads @ 25% on Prime Cost and office overheads @ 75% of factory oncost (*b*) A statement of profit as per Cost Accounts (*c*) Profit and Loss Account in the financial books (*d*) A statement reconciling the Profit and Loss Account. The selling price is fixed at cost plus 25%.

	Rs.
Stock on 1st April, 2006	
Raw Materials	4,000
Finished Goods	8,000
Stock on 31st March, 2007:	
Raw Materials	6,000
Finished Goods	2,000
Purchases of Raw Materials	24,000

Direct Wages	10,000
Sales	65,000
Works overhead	7,750
Office overhead	6,100

Solution

Statement of Cost

Period: Year ended 31st March, 2007

		Rs.
Raw Materials Consumed		
Opening Stock of R.M.	4,000	
Add: Purchases of R.M.	24,000	
	28,000	
Less: Closing Stock of R.M.	6,000	22,000
Direct Wages		10,000
Prime Cost		32,000
Factory Overhead @ 25% on Prime Cost		8,000
Factory Cost		40,000
Office Overhead @ 75% on Factory Oncost $\left(8{,}000\times\frac{75}{100}\right)$		6,000
Cost of Production		46,000

Statement of Profit

	Rs.
Opening Stock of Finished Goods	8,000
Add: Cost of Production	46,000
	54,000
Less: Closing Stock of Finished Goods	2,000
Cost of Goods Sold	52,000
Profit @ 25% on Cost	13,000
Sales	65,000

Profit and Loss Account for the Year Ending 31st March, 2007

	Rs.		Rs.
To Opening Stock		By Sales	65,000
(*i*) Raw Materials	4,000		
(*ii*) Finished Goods	8,000	By Closing Stock	
To Purchases of Raw Materials	24,000	(*i*) Raw Materials	6,000
To Wages	10,000	(*ii*) Finished Goods	2,000
To Works Expenses	7,750		
To Office Expenses	6,100		
To Net Profit	13,150		
	73,000		73,000

Reconciliation Statement

	Rs.
Profit as per Cost Accounts	13,000
Add: Over-recovery of Factory Overhead in Cost Accounts (Rs. 8,000 – Rs. 7,750)	250
	13,250
Less: Under-recovery of Office Overhead in Cost Accounts (Rs. 6,100 – Rs. 6,000)	100
Profit as per Financial Accounts	13,150

Illustration 9

A factory turns out two products A and B. The cost of materials and labour is as follows:

	A	B
	Rs.	Rs.
Materials (per unit)	12.50	7.50
Wages Direct (per unit)	10.00	6.00

Works overhead is charged at 100% of wages and office overhead at 25% of works cost. 200 units of A and 500 units of B were produced and sold at Rs. 50 and Rs. 30 per unit respectively, there being no opening and closing stocks.

If actually the works expenses amounted to Rs. 4,800 and office expenses to Rs. 4,200, reconcile the results shown by Cost Accounts and Financial Accounts.

Solution

Statement of Cost and Profit

(as per cost accounts)

	Product A		Product B	
	Cost per unit	**Cost of 200 units**	**Cost per unit**	**Cost of 500 units**
	Rs.	**Rs.**	**Rs.**	**Rs.**
Materials	12.50	2,500	7.50	3,750.00
Wages	10.00	2,000	6.00	3,000.00
Prime Cost	22.50	4,500	13.50	6,750.00
Works Overhead @ 100% on Wages	10.00	2,000	6.00	3,000.00
Works Cost	32.50	6,500	19.50	9,750.00
Office Overhead @ 25% of Works Cost	8.125	1,625	4.875	2,437.50
Total Cost	40.625	8,125	24.375	12,187.50
Profit	9.375	1,875	5.625	2,812.50
Sale Price	50.00	10,000	30.00	15,000.00

Total Profit as per Cost Accounts

	Per unit	Total
	Rs.	Rs.
A	9.375	1,875.00
B	5.625	2,812.50
		Rs. 4,687.50

Profit and Loss Account (Financial Books)

		Rs.		Rs.
To Materials	A 2,500		By Sales	
	B 3,750	6,250	A 200 × Rs. 50 = 10,000	
To Wages	A 2,000		B 500 × Rs. 30 = 15,000	25,000
	B 3,000	5,000		
To Works Expenses		4,800		
To Office Expenses		4,200		
To Net Profit		4,750		
		25,000		25,000

Reconciliation Statement

			Rs.
Profit as per Cost Books			4,687.50
Add:	Works overhead charged in excess in cost accounts:		
	Cost Books (2,000 + 3,000)	5,000	
	Financial Books	4,800	200.00
			4,887.50
Less:	Office overhead under-charged in cost accounts:		
	Financial Books	4,200.00	
	Cost Books (1,625 + 2,437.50)	4,062.50	137.50
Profit as per Financial Books			4,750.00

Illustration 10

A.K. Singh commenced business on 1st April, 2006 as a manufacturer of fountain pens, making three standard types of fountain pens which he designated as A, B and C. His Trading and Profit & Loss Account for the year ended 31st March, 2007 is as follows:

Trading and Profit and Loss Account of A.K. Singh
for the year ended 31st March, 2007

	Rs.			Rs.
To Materials	24,500	By Sales		66,000
To Direct Labour	15,000	By Stock of Finished Goods		6,900
To Works Expenses	14,600	By Work-in-progress		
To Gross Profit c/d	20,800	Materials	1,000	
		Labour	500	
		Works Overhead	500	2,000
	74,900			74,900
To Office Expenses	13,800	By Gross Profit b/d		20,800
To Net Profit	7,000			
	20,800			20,800

He has charged out materials and labour at actual cost, works overhead at 100% on labour and office overhead at 25% on works cost. Finished fountain pens in stock and work-in-progress are valued at 'works cost'.

The following figures are taken from his Cost Accounts:

	A	B	C
	Rs.	Rs.	Rs.
Average cost of materials per finished fountain pen	2.00	2.50	3.00
Average cost of labour per finished fountain pen	1.00	1.50	2.00
Sale Price per fountain pen	6.00	8.00	10.00
Number of finished fountain pens manufactured	2,000	3,000	4,000
Fountain pens sold	1,800	2,400	3,600

From the above particulars, you are requested to prepare:

(*a*) Statement showing profit per fountain pen sold and the total profit per Cost Accounts, and

(*b*) Reconciliation of Profit per Cost Accounts with profit per Financial Accounts explaining the difference, if any.

Solution

(A) Statement Showing Profit Per Fountain Pen Sold as Per Cost Accounts

	A	B	C
	Rs.	Rs.	Rs.
Direct Materials	2.00	2.50	3.00
Direct Labour	1.00	1.50	2.00
Prime Cost	3.00	4.00	5.00
Works Overhead (100% on Labour)	1.00	1.50	2.00
Works Cost	4.00	5.50	7.00
Office Overhead (25% on Works Cost)	1.00	1.375	1.75
Total Cost	5.00	6.875	8.75
Profit	1.00	1.125	1.25
Selling Price	6.00	8.00	10.00

Statement Showing Total Profit as Per Cost Accounts

	Rs.
A – 1,800 fountain pens sold at a profit of Rs. 1.00 each	1,800.00
B – 2,400 fountain pens sold at a profit of Rs. 1.125 each	2,700.00
C – 3,600 fountain pens sold at a profit of Rs. 1.25 each	4,500.00
	9,000.00

(B) Reconciliation Statement

		Rs.	Rs.	Rs.
Profit as per Cost Accounts				9,000
Add: Works Overhead Over-charged in Cost A/cs				
Works Overhead:	A – 2,000 × 1.00	2,000		
	B – 3,000 × 1.50	4,500		
	C – 4,000 × 2.00	8,000	14,500	
Works Expenses as per Profit and Loss Account (Rs. 14,600 – 500 Closing work-in-progress)			14,100	400
				9,400
Less: Office Overhead under-charged on Cost A/cs				
Office Overhead:	A – 2,000 × 1.00	2,000		
	B – 3,000 × 1.375	4,125		
	C – 4,000 × 1.75	7,000		
		13,125		
Office Expenses as per Profit and Loss Account			13,800	
Office Overhead as per Cost Accounts			13,125	675
				8,725
Less: Office Overhead not included in the valuation of unsold stock of fountain pens for the purpose of Financial A/cs:				
A – 200 (unsold)	× 1.00	200		
B – 600	× 1.375	825		
C – 400	× 1.75	700		1,725
Profit as per Profit & Loss Account (Financial Books)				7,000

Illustration 11

A Company's Trading and Profit & Loss Account was as follows:

Dr.	Rs.		Cr. Rs.
To Purchases	25,210	By Sales: 50,000 units	
Less: Closing Stock	4,080	@ Rs. 1.50 each	75,000
	21,130		
To Direct Wages	10,500	By Discount Received	260
To Works Expenses	12,130	By Profit on Sale of Land	2,340
To Selling Expenses	7,100		
To Administration Expenses	5,340		
To Distribution Expenses	1,100		
To Net Profit	20,300		
	77,600		77,600

The profit as per Cost Accounts was only Rs. 19,770.

Reconcile the financial and cost profits using the following information:

(*a*) Cost accounts valued closing stock at Rs. 4,280.

(*b*) The works expenses in cost accounts were taken as 100% of direct wages.

(*c*) Selling and administration expenses were charged in the Cost Accounts at 10% of sales and Re. 0.10 per unit respectively.

(*d*) Depreciation in Cost Accounts was Rs. 800.

(*C.A. Inter*)

Solution

Reconciliation Statement

		Rs.	Rs.
Profit as per Cost Accounts			19,770
Add:			
(*i*) Over-absorption of selling expenses in Cost Accounts		400	
(*ii*) Sundry incomes not included in Cost Accounts:			
Discount	Rs. 260		
Profit on Sale of Land	Rs. 2,340	2,600	
(*iii*) Depreciation Charged in Cost Accounts		800	3,800
			23,570
Less:			
(*i*) Over-valuation of closing stock in cost accounts		200	
(*ii*) Under-absorption of works expenses in Cost Accounts		1,630	
(*iii*) Under-absorption of administration expenses in Cost Accounts		340	
(*iv*) Distribution expenses not charged to cost accounts		1,100	3,270
Profit as per Financial Accounts			20,300

Illustration 12

The following is the Trading and Profit & Loss Account of Time and Tide Limited for the year ended 31st March, 2002:

	Rs.			Rs.
To Materials Consumed	27,40,000	By Sales (60,000 units)		60,00,000
To Direct Wages	15,10,000	By Finished Stock		1,60,000
To Factory Expenses	8,30,000	(2,000 units)		
To Administration Expenses	3,82,400	By Work-in-progress:		
To Selling and Distribution		Materials	64,000	
Expenses	4,50,000	Wages	36,000	
To Preliminary Expenses	60,000	Factory Expenses	20,000	1,20,000
To Net Profit	3,25,600	By Dividends		18,000
	62,98,000			62,98,000

Manufacturing a standard unit, the companys' cost records show that:

(*i*) Factory Expenses have been allocated to production at 20% on prime cost.

(*ii*) Administrative Expenses have been recovered at Rs. 6 per finished unit.

(*iii*) Selling and Distribution Expenses have been recovered at Rs. 8 per unit sold. Prepare Costing Profit and Loss Account and reconcile the same with financial profit.

(*B.Com., Delhi, G.N.D.U. B.Com. 2003*)

Solution

Costing Profit and Loss Account

	Rs.		Rs.
To Material Consumed	27,40,000	By Cost of Production (62,000	
To Direct Wages	15,10,000	units) (Cost per unit Rs.	53,52,000
Prime Cost	42,50,000	53,52,000/62,000 units =	
		Rs. 86.32)	
To Factory Expenses @ 20% on Prime Cost	8,50,000		
	51,00,000		
Less: Work-in-progress (Closing)	1,20,000		
Works Cost	49,80,000		
To Administration Expenses @ Rs. 6 per finished unit for 62,000 units	3,72,000		
	53,52,000		53,52,000
To Cost of Production b/d (62,000 units)	53,52,000	By Sales (60,000 units)	60,00,000
Less: Closing Stock (2,000 units @ Rs. 86.32 per unit)	1,72,645		
Cost of Goods Sold	51,79,355		
To Selling and Distribution Expenses @ Rs. 8 per unit for 60,000 units	4,80,000		
Cost of Sales	56,59,355		
To Net Profit	3,40,645		
	60,00,000		60,00,000

Reconciliation Statement

	Rs.	Rs.
Profit as per Cost Accounts		3,40,645
Add:		
(*i*) Over-recovery of Works Expenses in Cost Accounts	20,000	
(*ii*) Over-recovery of Selling and Distribution Expenses in Cost Accounts	30,000	
(*iii*) Dividends received not recorded in Cost Accounts	18,000	68,000
		4,08,645
Less:		
(*i*) Under-recovery of Administration Expenses in Cost Accounts	10,400	
(*ii*) Over-valuation of closing stock in Cost Accounts	12,645	
(*iii*) Preliminary Expenses not charged to Cost Accounts	60,000	83,045
Profit as per Financial Accounts		3,25,600

Notes:

(*i*) Value of work-in-progress in cost accounts has been calculated as follows:

	Rs.
Materials	64,000
Wages	36,000
Prime Cost	1,00,000
Factory Expenses @ 20% on Prime Cost	20,000
	1,20,000

Thus, the value of work-in-progress is the same in Cost and Financial Accounts.

(*ii*) The Closing Stock of finished goods in Cost Accounts has been valued on the basis of actual cost i.e., Rs. 86.32 per unit.

Illustration 13

Following are the figures extracted from the Cost Ledger of a manufacturing unit:

Stores: (*a*) Opening Balance Rs. 15,000; (*b*) Purchases Rs. 80,000; (*c*) Transfer from Work-in-progress Rs. 40,000; (*d*) Issues to Work-in-progress Rs. 80,000; (*e*) Issue to repairs and maintenance Rs. 10,000; (*f*) Sold some quantity as a special case at cost Rs. 5,000; (*g*) Shortage in the year Rs. 3,000.

Work-in-Progress: (*a*) Opening Balance Rs. 30,000; (*b*) Direct Labour Cost charged Rs. 30,000; Overhead cost charged Rs. 1,20,000; (*d*) Closing Balance Rs. 20,000.

Finished Products: Entire output is sold at 10% profit on actual cost from work-in-progress.

Others: Wages for the period Rs. 35,000
Overhead Expenses Rs. 1,25,000

You have to find out profit and loss as per Financial Accounts and Cost Accounts and reconcile them.

Solution

Profit and Loss Account (Financial)

		Rs.			Rs.
To Stock (Opening):			By Sales (made at cost)		5,000
Stores	15,000		By Sales (Finished Goods)		2,20,000
Work-in-progress	30,000	45,000	By Stock (Closing)		
To Purchases (stores)		80,000	Stores	37,000	
To Wages		35,000	Work-in-progress	20,000	57,000
To Overhead Expenses		1,25,000	By Net Loss		3,000
		2,85,000			2,85,000

Costing Profit and Loss Account

		Rs.		Rs.
To Direct Materials	80,000			
Less: Transferred	40,000	40,000	By Sales	2,20,000
To Direct Wages		30,000		
To Overhead Charged		1,20,000		
To Work-in-Progress				
Opening	30,000			
Less: Closing	20,000	10,000		
		2,00,000		
To Net Profit		20,000		
		2,20,000		2,20,000

Reconciliation Statement

	Plus Items	Minus Items
	Rs.	Rs.
Net Profit as per cost books	20,000	
1. Wages under-charged in cost books (Rs. 35,000 – 30,000)		5,000
2. Stores issued for repairs and maintenance not recorded in cost books		10,000
3. Shortage of stores not taken into account in cost books		3,000
4. Overheads under-recovered in cost books (Rs. 1,25,000 – 1,20,000)		5,000
	20,000	23,000

Total of Minus Items:	Rs. 23,000
Total of Plus Items	Rs. 20,000
Net loss as per financial books	Rs. 3,000

Working Notes:

1. Closing balance of stores Rs. 37,000 has been ascertained by preparing a Stores Account.

Stores Account

	Rs.		Rs.
To Balance b/d	15,000	By Issue to Work-in-progress	80,000
To Purchases	80,000	By Issue to repairs etc.	10,000
To Transferred from Work-in-progress	40,000	By Sale (at Cost)	5,000
		By Shortage of Stores	3,000
		By Balance c/d	37,000
	1,35,000		1,35,000

2. In financial books, the net charge of stores is as follows:

	Rs.
Opening Balance of Stores	15,000
Purchases of Stores	80,000
	95,000
Less: Sale at Cost	5,000
	90,000
Less: Closing Balance	37,000
	53,000

3. The break-up of Rs. 53,000 is as follows:

	Rs.
Stores consumed in jobs (Rs. 80,000 – 40,000)	40,000
Stores for repairs and maintenance	10,000
Stores Lost (in shortage)	3,000
	53,000

4. Since the charge of stores in cost books is Rs. 40,000 (*i.e.* Rs. 80,000 – 40,000), it implies that stores for repairs Rs. 10,000 and shortage of Rs. 3,000 have not been charged in cost books.

Illustration 14

The profit as per cost accounts is Rs. 1,65,300. The following details are ascertained on comparison of the cost and financial accounts

	Cost Accounts	**Financial Accounts**
	Rs.	**Rs.**
(*i*) Opening Stocks:		
Materials	32,600	33,000
Work-in-progress	20,000	21,000
(*ii*) Closing Stocks:		
Materials	36,000	34,400
Work-in-progress	16,000	15,200
Finished Goods	8,000	9,000

(*iii*) Directors' fees paid Rs 1,000, Interest paid Rs. 800, Reserve for bad debts Rs. 500, Transfer fees collected Rs. 300 and dividends received Rs. 200 are exclusively taken in Financial Accounts, but ignored in cost accounts.

(*iv*) Rent charged in costing, but not in Financial Accounts Rs. 6,000

(*v*) Preliminary expenses written off Rs. 13,000 but not charged in costing.

(*vi*) Overheads charged in financial accounts Rs. 1,21,200 but recovered in cost Rs. 1,26,200.

Find out profit as per Financial Accounts and draw up a Reconciliation Statement.

(*G.N.D.U., B.Com., 1995*)

Solution

Reconciliation Statement

	Rs.	Rs.
Profit as per Cost Accounts		1,65,300
Add: (*i*) Under-valuation of closing stock of finished goods in Cost Accounts	1,000	
(*ii*) Transfer fees collected and Dividends received not included in Cost Accounts (Rs. 300 + Rs. 200)	500	
(*iii*) Rent charged in Cost Accounts but not in Financial Accounts	6,000	
(*iv*) Over-recovery of overheads in Cost Accounts	5,000	12,500
		1,77,800
Less: (*i*) Under-valuation of opening stock in Cost Accounts:		
Materials	400	
Work-in-Progress	1,000	
(*ii*) Over-valuation of closing stock in Cost Accounts:		
Materials	1,600	
Work-in-Progress	800	
(*iii*) Items debited in Financial Accounts but not in Cost Accounts		
Directors' Fees	1,000	
Interest Paid	800	
Reserve for Bad Debts.	500	
Preliminary Expenses	13,000	19,100
Profit as per Financial Accounts		1,58,700

Illustration 15

From the following information (*i*) determine the profit as it would be shown by cost accounts; and (*ii*) prepare a statement reconciling it with profit shown by financial accounts:

Trading and Profit & Loss Account
For the year ended 31st March, 2007

	Rs.		Rs.
Materials Consumed	1,00,000	Sales (1,00,000 units)	2,00,000
Direct Wages	50,000		
Indirect Expenses	30,000		
Office Expenses	9,000		
Selling and Distribution Expenses	6,000		
Net Profit	5,000		
	2,00,000		2,00,000

The normal output of the factory is 1,50,000 units. Works expenses of a fixed nature are Rs. 18,000. Office Expenses are for all practical purposes constant. Selling and Distribution expenses are constant to the extent of Rs. 3,000 and the balance varies directly with sales.

(*G.N.D.U., B.Com., Prof. 2008*)

Solution

Statement of Cost and Profit

		Rs.
Materials Consumed		1,00,000
Direct Wages		50,000
Prime Cost		1,50,000
Works Expenses		
2/3 of fixed overheads*	12,000	
Variable overheads (Rs. 30,000 – Rs.18,000)	12,000	24,000
Works Cost		1,74,000
Office Expenses		
2/3 of fixed expenses*		6,000
Cost of Production		1,80,000
Selling and Distribution expenses		
2/3 of fixed expenses*	2,000	
Variable overheads (Rs. 6,000 – Rs. 3,000)	3,000	5,000
Cost of Sales		1,85,000
Profit		15,000
Sales		2,00,000

*Out of total factory overheads Rs. 18,000 are fixed. The fixed factory overhead rate in financial accounts must have been determined on the basis of normal output *i.e.*, 1,50,000 units. Therefore fixed factory overheads recovered in cost accounts must be Rs. 12,000 (*i.e.*, 2/3 of Rs. 18,000). Similarly, the fixed office overheads and fixed selling overheads recovered in cost accounts must be Rs. 6,000 (*i.e.*, 2/3 of Rs. 9,000) and Rs. 2,000 (*i.e.* 2/3 of Rs. 3,000) respectively.

Reconciliation Statement

		Rs.
Profit as per Cost Accounts		15,000
Less: Under-recovery of Works Expenses	6,000	
Under-recovery of Office Expenses	3,000	
Under-recovery of Selling & Distribution Expenses	1,000	10,000
Profit as per Financial Accounts		5,000

QUESTIONS

1. What is the necessity of preparing Reconciliation Statement? Explain various causes responsible for disagreement of profits shown by financial and by costing books.
2. "It has has been stated that an efficient costing system will not necessarily produce accounts which in their result will agree with the financial accounts". Comment upon this statement.
3. List out ten items, either debit or credit, which appear in the financial accounts but do not appear in the cost accounts?

4. "It is impossible to form a completely accurate agreement between cost accounts and financial accounts for the same concern." Discuss the statement, showing the points of difference between the two systems and give your opinion as to the possibility of reconciliation and the degree of accuracy attainable.

5. At the end of an accounting period, it is found that the profit as shown by the financial accounts falls considerably short of the profits according to the cost accounts. Indicate how the discrepancy may have arisen.

6. What is the purpose of reconciling cost and financial accounts? Indicate the possible sources of difference between them. How will you prepare reconciliation statement to reconcile cost and financial accounts?

(*G.N.D.U., B.Com., 2001*)

7. Why a reconciliation between cost and financial accounts is needed? How such reconciliation is done? (*G.N.D.U., B.Com., 2002*)

8. Discuss the reasons of differences between cost accounting profit and financial accounting profit. (*G.N.D.U., B.Com., 2008*)

EXERCISES

1. The net profit of a manufacturing concern for the year ended 31st December was Rs. 2,57,510 as shown by the financial books. The cost accounts for same period disclosed a profit of Rs. 3,44,800. On an examination of both sets of accounts, the following facts were discovered:

		Rs.
(*i*)	Works overhead under-recovered in cost accounts	6,240
(*ii*)	Office overhead over-recovered in cost books	3,400
(*iii*)	Depreciation charged in financial books	22,400
(*iv*)	Depreciation recovered in cost books	25,000
(*v*)	Interest on investments not included in cost accounts	16,000
(*vi*)	Obsolescence loss charged in financial accounts	11,400
(*vii*)	Income Tax provided for financial accounts	80,600
(*viii*)	Bank interest and dividends received (in financial books)	2,450
(*ix*)	Loss due to depreciation in stock values charged in financial accounts	13,500

Prepare a statement showing the reconciliation between the figure of net profit as per Cost Accounts and the figure of net profit shown in the financial books.

2. Prepare a Reconciliation statement from the following information:

	Rs.
Net Loss as per Cost Accounts	3,44,800
Net Loss as per Financial Accounts	4,32,090
Works overhead under-recovered in Cost Accounts	6,240
Depreciation over-charged in Cost Accounts	2,600
Administration overhead recovered in excess	3,400
Interest on Investments	17,500
Goodwill written off in financial books	11,400
Income tax paid	80,600
Stores adjustments (credited in financial books)	950
Depreciation in stock values charged in financial books	13,500

3. The profit as per Cost Accounts is Rs. 86,250. The following points are found out on comparison between Cost Accounts and Financial Accounts:

	Cost Accounts Rs.	**Financial Accounts Rs.**
(1) Opening Stock:		
Materials	10,300	10,500
Work-in-progress	8,000	8,500
(2) Closing Stock:		
Materials	15,000	14,200
Work-in-Progress	6,000	5,600

(3) Dividend and interest received Rs. 600

(4) Loss on the sale of investments Rs. 1,000

(5) Rs. 1,500 interest charged by bank but not considered in financial accounts.

(6) Goodwill Rs. 2,500 and Preliminary expenses Rs. 3,000 have been written off during the year.

(7) Overheads incurred Rs. 40,600 but overheads recovered amounted to Rs. 38,500.

Find out the profit as per financial accounts by drawing a Memorandum Reconciliation Account.

(*P.U., B.Com.*)

[**Ans.** Profit as per Financial Books Rs. 76,350]

(**Hint.** *Note:* Item no. 5 needs no reconciliation as interest charged by bank is not recorded in costing books)

4. The following figures are available from financial accounts for the year ended 31st March, 2008:

	Rs.
Direct Material consumption	2,50,000
Direct Wages	1,00,000

Factory overheads	3,80,000
Administration overheads	2,50,000
Selling and distribution overheads	4,80,000
Bad debts	20,000
Preliminary Expenses (written off)	10,000
Legal charges	5,000
Dividend received	50,000
Interest on Deposit Received	10,000
Sales (1,20,000 units)	7,00,000
Closing stock:	
Finished Stock (40,000 units)	1,20,000
Work-in-progress	80,000

The Cost Accounts revealed:

Direct Material Consumption	Rs. 2,80,000

Factory overhead recovered at 20% on Prime Cost.
Administration overhead at Rs. 3 per unit of production.
Selling and Distribution overhead at Rs. 4 per unit sold.

Prepare:

(*a*) Costing Profit and Loss Account
(*b*) Financial Profit and Loss Account
(*c*) Statement reconciling the profits disclosed by the Costing Profit and Loss Account and Financial Profit and Loss Account.

(*G.N.D.U., B.Com., April, 1985*)

[**Ans.** (*i*) Net Loss Rs. 4,22,000 as per cost accounts
(*ii*) Net Loss Rs. 5,35,000 as per financial accounts.]

5. From the following particulars prepare:

(*a*) Statement of profit as per cost accounts,
(*b*) Profit and Loss Account, and
(*c*) A Reconciliation Statement.

	Rs.
Raw Materials Consumed	14,600
Wages	23,200
Factory Expenses	22,840
Office Expenses	12,420
Sale Price	88,400

Works overhead is 100% on labour and office overhead is 20% of works cost.

[**Ans.** Profit as per Cost Accounts, Rs. 15,200;
Profit as per Financial Accounts Rs. 15,340]

6. From the following particulars prepare (*a*) Statement of Cost of Manufacture and percentage of each item of cost to total cost, calculating factory oncost at 25% on Prime Cost, and office oncost at 75% on factory oncost (*b*) A statement of Profit as per Cost Accounts (*c*) Profit and Loss Account in the financial books (*d*) A statement reconciling the Profit and Loss Account. The selling price is fixed at cost plus 25%.

	Rs.
Stock, 1st April 2004:	
Raw Materials	8,000
Finished Product	16,000
Stock 31st March. 2005:	
Raw Materials	12,000
Finished Product	4,000
Purchases of Raw Materials	48,000
Wages	20,000
Sales	1,30,000
Works Expenses	15,500
Office Expenses	12,200

[**Ans.** (*a*) Cost of manufacture, Rs. 92,000
(*b*) Profit as per cost accounts, Rs. 26,000
(*c*) Profit as per profit and loss account, Rs. 26,300]

7. A company manufacturing bicycles, which commenced business on 1st April, 2004, supplies you the following information. You are required to prepare a statement showing the profit per bicycle sold. Wages and materials are to be charged at actual cost, works oncost at 80% on wages, and office oncost at 20% on works cost. You are also required to prepare a statement reconciling the profit as shown by the cost accounts with the profit as shown by profit and loss account for the year ended 31st March, 2005.

Two types of bicycles are manufactured, viz., Model A and Model B. There were no bicycles in stock or in the course of manufacture on 31st March, 2005 and the number of bicycles sold during the year were Model A, 120 and Model B, 84.

The particulars given are as under:

	Model A	**Model B**
	Rs.	**Rs.**
Materials per bicycle	40	50
Wages per bicycle	20	30
Selling price per bicycle	100	150

Prepare the necessary statements, showing the actual profit for the year, if the works expenses were Rs. 4,000 and the office expenses Rs. 3,500

[**Ans.** Costing Profit = Rs. 3,172.80 Financial Profit = Rs. 3,180.00]

8. V.G. Jog who commences business on 1st April, 2004 as a violin manufacturer places before you the following information and asks you to prepare a statement showing the profit per violin sold charging labour and material at actual cost, works oncost at 100% on labour and office oncost at 25% on works cost, and a statement showing a reconciliation between profit as shown by Cost Accounts and the profit shown by the Profit and Loss Account for the year ended 31st March, 2005.

Two grades of violins manufactured are known as No. 1 and No. 2. There are no violins in stock or in course of manufacture on 31st March, 2005. The other details are given as under:

	No. 1	**No. 2**
	Rs.	**Rs.**
Average cost of material per violin	100	80
Average cost of labour per violin	190	140
Sale price per violin	750	550

The works expenses were Rs. 52,400 and the office expenses Rs. 31,660. 118 violins of No. 1 grade and 205 violins of No. 2 grade were sold during the year. You are required to prepare necessary statements, showing the actual profit for the year.

[**Ans.** (*a*) Costing profit = Rs. 38,200. (*b*) Financial profit= Rs. 37,870.]

9. Paliwal Engineering Co. Ltd., manufactures two sizes of machine components, size A and size B. The following details refer to the year ended 31st March, 2007:

	Size A	**Size B**
Production	125 units	400 units
Sales	120 units	360 units
Wages cost per unit	Rs. 40	Rs. 30
Material cost per unit	Rs. 15	Rs. 12
Sale price per unit	Rs. 125	Rs. 90

All expenses other than wages and materials are analysed as under "works overheads" which during the year amounted to Rs. 9,000 and "office overheads" which amounted to Rs. 10,000.

In fixing the selling price, it was estimated that the works overhead expenses should be taken at 50% on wages and office overhead expenses at $33\frac{1}{3}\%$ on works cost.

You are required to compute the following:

(*a*) The total cost of each unit on the basis of above overhead percentages.

(*b*) The net profit for the year as shown by the financial accounts, valuing unsold stocks at actual materials and wages cost plus works overheads at 50% on wages.

(*c*) The reconciliation of net profit in (*b*) above with the estimated total net profit based on the cost figures.

[**Ans.** (*a*) Costing Profits, Rs. 8,040 (*b*) Financial Profit, Rs. 7,380.]

10. During the year a company's profits have been estimated from the costing system to be Rs. 23,063, whereas the final accounts prepared by the auditors disclose a profit of Rs. 16,624. Given the following information, you are required to prepare a Reconciliation Statement showing clearly the reasons for the difference.

Profit and Loss Account
for the year ended 31st March, 2005

		Rs.		**Rs.**
To Opening Stock	2,47,179		By Sales	3,46,500
Add Purchases	82,154			
	3,29,333			
Less: Closing Stock	75,121	2,54,212		
To Direct Wages		23,133		
To Factory Overheads		20,826		
To Gross Profit c/d		48,329		
		3,46,500		3,46,500
To Administrative Expenses		9,845	By Gross Profit b/d	48,329
To Selling Expenses		22,176	By Sundry Income	316
To Net Profit		16,624		
		48,645		48,645

The Costing records show:

(*a*) a stock ledger closing balance of Rs. 78,197;

(*b*) a direct wages absorption account with a closing credit balance of Rs. 24,867;

(*c*) a factory overhead absorption account with a closing credit balance of Rs. 19,714;

(*d*) administration expenses calculated @ 3% on the selling price;

(*e*) Selling price include 5% for selling expenses;

(*f*) no mention of sundry income.

11. Prepare a reconciliation statement with the help of the following information:

Following is the Trading and Profit and Loss account of a manufacturer, specialising in a product:

Trading and Profit & Loss Account

	Rs.			Rs.
To Materials	2,91,500	By Sales		7,50,000
To Wages	1,86,100	By Stock of Finished Goods		18,125
To Factory Expenses	1,40,550	By Work-in-progress:		
To Gross Profit c/d	2,05,275	Materials	28,000	
		Wages	15,600	
		Factory Expenses	11,700	55,300
	8,23,425			8,23,425
To Administrative Expenses	1,36,500	By Gross Profit b/d		2,05,275
To Net Profit	68,775			
	2,05,275			2,05,275

1,550 patented articles were produced and 1,500 were sold during the year. The costing records showed that the factory expenses worked out at Rs. 82.50 and administrative expenses at Rs. 90.625 per article produced. The cost accounts showed profit of Rs. 70,312.50 for the year. Prepare the necessary accounts, showing the under and over-recovery of various overheads and reconciliation statement.

12. For the year ended 31st December, 2008, the Financial A/cs showed Rs. 60,000 as profit after taxation. The following items have been included in the accounts:

	Rs.		Rs.
Interest Received	3,000	Interest Paid	4,000
Fines	60	Loss on Sale of Plant	1,500
Audit Fees	2,000	Dividends Received	3,400
Income Tax	40,000		

The costing profit and loss account showed a profit of Rs. 1,06,560 after including notional rent of Rs. 3,000. The stocks were valued as follows:

	Financial Accounts		Cost Accounts	
	Opening Rs.	Closing Rs.	Opening Rs.	Closing Rs.
Raw Materials	2,55,000	2,84,200	2,81,600	2,98,000
Work-in-progress	1,04,000	1,10,000	1,10,000	1,23,800
Finished Goods	1,49,000	1,42,800	1,57,200	1,64,400

Prepare a statement reconciling the profit shown by financial accounts with that of cost accounts.

13. The financial Profit and Loss Account of Seema Manufacturing Company for the year ended 30th June, 2008, is given below:

	Rs.		Rs.
Opening Stock:		Sales:	9,20,000
Raw Materials	60,000		
Finished Stock	80,000	Closing Stock:	
Work-in-Progress	35,000	Raw Material	60,000
Purchases	2,40,000	Finished Stock	30,000
Factory Wages	60,000	Work-in-Progress	41,000
Factory Electric Power	66,000		
Factory Overhead	90,000		
Gross Profit b/d	4,20,000		
	10,51,000		10,51,000
Administration Expenses	25,000	Gross Profit b/d	4,20,000
Selling & Distribution Exps.	1,15,000	Misc. Income	20,000
Bad Debts	30,000		
Net Profit	2,70,000		
	4,40,000		4,40,000

The cost accounts of the Company showed a profit of Rs. 2,81,750. It is observed that the Costing Profit and Loss Account is prepared on the basis of figures furnished below:

	Rs.
Opening Stock:	
Raw Materials	80,000
Finished Stock	60,000
Work-in-progress	40,000
Closing Stock:	
Raw Materials	70,000
Finished Stock	20,000
Work-in-progress	44,000
Selling and Distribution Expenses	1,27,000
Administrative Expenses	18,000

A plant is purchased on 1st July, 2005 for Rs. 80,000. Rate of Depreciation is 25% p.a.

Financial accounts charge depreciation according to straight line method and it is included in factory overhead of Rs. 90,000 whereas cost accounts charge depreciation according to written down value method.

Prepare a statement reconciling the difference in the Profit and Loss Accounts.

(*B.U. April, 1995*)

[**Ans.** Costing; Profit Rs. 17,032]

14. A Company's Trading and Profit and Loss Account was as follows:

	Rs.		Rs.
Purchases:	25,210	Sales: 50,000 Units at Rs. 1.50 each	75,000
Less: Closing Stock	4,080	Discount Received	260
	21,130	Profit of Sale of Land	2,340
Direct Wages	10,500		
Works Expenses	12,000		
Selling Expenses	7,100		
Adm. Expenses	5,470		
Depreciation	1,100		
Net Profit	20,300		
	77,600		77,600

The Profit as per Cost Accounts was only Rs. 19,770. Reconcile the Financial and Cost Profits using the following information:

(*a*) Cost Accounts value of closing stock Rs. 4,280.

(*b*) The works expenses in Cost Accounts were taken as 100% of direct wages.

(*c*) Selling and Administration Expenses were charged in the Cost Accounts at 10% of sales and Re. 0.10 per unit respectively.

(*d*) Depreciation in the Cost Accounts was Rs. 800.

[**Ans.** Costing profit Rs. 19,770]

15. A commenced business on 1st April, 2006, as a perambulator manufacturer making three types A, B and C. The following is his Trading and Profit & Loss Account for the year ended 31st March, 2007.

Particulars	Amount	Particulars	Amount
	Rs. P.		Rs. P.
To Materials	27,269.05	By Sales	71,940.00
To Direct Labour	16,535.00	By Stock of Finished Goods	2,790.65
To Works Expenses	15,720.00	By Work-in-Progress:	
To Gross Profit c/d	19,906.60	Materials	3,100.00
		Labour	800.00
		Works Oncost	800.00
	79,430.65		79,430.65
To Office Expenses	11,150.00	By Gross Profit b/d	19,906.60
To Net Profit	8,756.60		
	19,906.60		19,906.60

He has kept costing records in respect of each type, charging out materials and labour at actual cost, works oncost at 100% on labour cost and office oncost at 20% on works cost. From the following information and the above particulars, you are required to prepare:
(*a*) Statement showing profit per perambulator sold and total profit as per Cost Accounts and, (*b*) Reconciliation of Profit as per Cost Accounts and Profit and Loss Account, explaining the difference, if any.

	A	B	C
	Rs. P.	**Rs. P.**	**Rs. P.**
Average cost of materials per finished perambulator	15.37	16.75	11.41
Average cost of labour per finished perambulator	9.50	11.00	8.75
Sale price per perambulator	47.00	52.00	40.00
Number of finished perambulators	845	470	290
Perambulators sold	820	450	250

[**Ans.** Profit as per costing records Rs. 8,521.92]

16. Profit disclosed by a company's cost accounts for the year was Rs. 70,000, whereas the net profit as disclosed by the financial accounts was Rs. 49,750. Following information is available:

(*a*) Overheads as per cost accounts were estimated at Rs. 8,500. The charge for the year shown by the financial accounts was Rs. 7,000.
(*b*) Directors' fee shown in the financial accounts only Rs. 2,000.
(*c*) The company allowed Rs. 5,000 as provision for doubtful debts.
(*d*) Work was commenced during the year on a new factory and expenditure of Rs. 30,000 was made. Depreciation at 5% p.a. was provided for in the financial accounts for six months.
(*e*) Share transfer fees received during the year were Rs. 1,000.
(*f*) Provision for Income Tax was Rs. 15,000.

From the above, prepare a statement reconciling the figures shown by the cost and financial accounts.

(*H.P.U., B.Com., 1994*)

17. The following are the Trading and Profit & Loss Accounts of a factory manufacturing a single product:

Trading and Profit and Loss Account
for the year ended 31st March, 2005

	Rs.		Rs.
To Materials consumed	3,00,000	By Sales (50,000 units)	7,50,000
To Direct wages	2,00,000		
To Works expenses	1,20,000		
To Office expenses	42,000		
To Selling and Ditribution expenses	80,000		
To Net Profit	8,000		
	7,50,000		7,50,000

The normal output of the factory is 60,000 units. Factory expenses are constant upto Rs. 60,000 and office expenses are fixed for all practical purposes. However, selling and distribution expenses vary with sales to the extent of Rs. 50,000 and the rest are fixed. Prepare a cost sheet and also a reconciliation statement.

(H.P.U., B.Com., 1995)

18. From the following information, prepare a cost statement and a statement to reconcile the profit shown as per Cost Accounts with the profit shown as per Financial Accounts.

Profit and Loss Account
for the Year Ending 31.03.2009

	Rs.		Rs.
To Materials Consumed	2,50,000	By Sales (1,50,000 Units)	6,00,000
To Wages (Direct)	1,00,000		
To Factory Overheads	75,000		
To Office Expenses	30,000		
To Selling Expenses	20,000		
To Net Profit	1,25,000		
	6,00,000		6,00,000

Normal production of the factory is 2,25,000 units. Factory expenses of a fixed nature are Rs. 45,000. Office expenses are all of a fixed nature. Selling expenses are fixed to the extent of Rs. 6,000 and the balance varies with the sales.

19. The following is the Trading and Profit and Loss Account of Time and Tide Limited for the year ended 31st December, 2008:

	Rs.			Rs.
To Materials Consumed	7,08,000	By Sales – 30,000 Units		15,00,000
To Direct Wages	3,71,000	By Finished Stock (1,000 Units)		40,000
To Works Overheads	2,13,000	By Work-in-progress:		
To Administration Overheads	95,500	Materials	17,000	
To Selling and Distribution		Wages	8,000	
Overheads	1,13,500	Works Overheads	5,000	30,000
To Net Profit for the year	69,000			
	15,70,000			15,70,000

Manufacturing a standard unit the Company's cost records show that:

(*a*) Works overheads have been charged to work-in-progress at 20% on Prime Cost.

(*b*) Administration overheads have been recovered at Rs. 3 per finished unit.

(*c*) Selling and Distribution overheads have been recovered at Rs. 4 per unit sold.

(*d*) The under-absorbed or over-absorbed overheads have not been adjusted into Costing Profit and Loss A/c.

Prepare:

(*i*) Costing Profit and Loss Account indicating net profit.

(*ii*) A Statement reconciling the profit as disclosed by cost accounts and that shown in financial accounts.

(*Bombay, B.Com,1990., I.C.W.A., Inter June 1992*)

[**Ans.** Costing profit Rs. 66,000]

20. The net profit of a company amounted to Rs. 60,412 for the year ended 31st March, 2006 as per its financial records. The cost records, however, revealed a different figure. A scrutiny of the two sets of accounts disclosed the following facts:

(*a*) Works overhead recovered in Cost Accounts during the period amounted to Rs. 28,450 while the actual amount of these expenses was Rs. 21,390 only.

(*b*) Actual office expenses for the period were Rs. 19,850 whereas the office overhead recovered in Cost Accounts amounted to Rs. 14,500.

(*c*) The annual rental value of premises owned by the company, amounting to Rs. 40,800 was charged in Cost Accounts but not in Financial Accounts.

(*d*) Selling and Distribution Expenses for the period amounting Rs. 16,490 were excluded from costing records.

(*e*) Excess depreciation charged in Cost Accounts Rs. 2,400.

(*f*) Expenses not included in Cost Accounts and shown in Financial Accounts:

	Rs.
Interest on Bank Loan	1,600
Bank Charges	160
Director's Fees	750
Penalty due to late completion of contract	2,500

(*g*) Gains during the year not included in Cost Accounts:

	Rs.
Transfer Fees	45
Profit on Sale of Investment	4,250

(*h*) The following appropriations had been made before arriving at the profit figure at Rs. 60,412 shown above:

	Rs.
Transfer to Dividend Equalisation Fund	10,500
Transfer to Income Tax Reserve	6,400
Transfer to Debenture Redemption Fund	9,000

(*i*) A sum of Rs. 10,000 given as donation to the Prime Minister's Relief Fund had been charged to Profit and Loss Account as business expense.

Prepare a reconciliation statement and find out the amount of net profit/loss as per costing records.

[**Ans.** Costing profit Rs. 68,607]

21. Following are the figures extracted from the Cost Ledger of a Manufacturing Unit:

Stores : (*a*) Opening Balance Rs. 30,000; (*b*) Purchases Rs. 1,60,000 (*c*) Transfer from Work-in-progress Rs. 80,000; (*d*) Issue to Work-in-progress Rs. 1,60,000; (*e*) Issue to Repairs and Maintenance Rs. 20,000; (*f*) Sold some quantity as a special case at cost Rs. 10,000; (*g*) Shortage in the year Rs. 6,000.

Work-in-progress : (*a*) Opening Inventory Rs. 60,000; (*b*) Direct Labour Cost charged Rs. 60,000; (*c*) Overhead Cost charged Rs. 2,40,000; (*d*) Closing Balance Rs. 40,000.

Finished products : Entire output is sold at 10% profit on actual cost from Work-in-progress

Others : Wages for period : Rs. 70,000; Overhead Exps. : 2,50,000

You have to find out profit or loss as per Financial Accounts and Cost Accounts and reconcile them.

19

Budgeting and Budgetary Control

The three main functions of management are planning, operating and control. Planning relates to the future, operating to the present and control to the past. For assisting the management in the functions of planning and control, two techniques are applied viz., budgetary control and standard costing systems. Budgetary control system is usually operated with a system of standard costing since both the systems are inter-related but it should be remembered that these two systems are not inter-dependent.

In the context of Budgetary Control System, we should now discuss the three common terms viz., Budget, Budgeting and Budgetary control.

BUDGET

The term 'Budget' has been derived from the French word 'Bougette' which means a leather bag from which the Minister of the Government would take out his proposals regarding the expenditure and revenue of the Government during the coming financial period. Now-a-days, the budget is not restricted to Government affairs only. It covers domestic, business and institutional affairs as well.

In business, a budget may be defined as a formal expression of the expected income and expenditure for a definite future period. According to J. Fred Meston– "A budget is the expression of a firm's plan in financial form for a period of time in future." According to J.L. Brown and L.R. Howard– "A budget is a pre-determined statement of management policy during a given period which provides a standard for comparison with the result actually achieved." George R. Terry has defined "Budget" as "an estimate of future needs arranged according to an orderly basis, covering some or all the activities of an enterprise for definite period of time." The Institute of Cost and Management Accountants has defined a budget as "a financial and/or quantitative statement, prepared prior to a defined period of time, of the policy to be pursued during that period for the purpose of attaining a given objective."

A careful study of the above definitions brings out the following features of a budget:

(*i*) **A Budget is a plan:** A budget is an expression of the plan of the operations of an enterprise. The operations of an enterprise are affected by a number of factors–both external (such as general business conditions, government policy and size and composition of population) and internal (such as manufacturing processes, promotional programmes). The budget covers both external and internal factors and expresses partly what the management expects to happen and partly what the management intends to happen.

(*ii*) **It is comprehensive:** A budget is comprehensive which means that it covers the activities and operations of all the segments or divisions of an organisation. Budgets are prepared for each segment or division of an organisation and all these are integrated into a Master Budget.

(*iii*) **It provides for a co-ordinated plan:** The budgets are prepared for the various segments or divisions of an organisation after considering the conditions and problems of each segment. The budgets for all the components are prepared in harmony with one another.

(*iv*) **It is prepared in advance:** A budget is prepared in advance and denotes the future course of action. Thus, a budget is forward-looking in approach.

(*v*) **It relates to a specified future period:** A budget always relates to a specified future period. A budget becomes meaningless if it is not related to a time horizon. Thus, budgeted output, sales, profit etc., are planned to be achieved in a pre-determined time framework.

(*vi*) **It is a plan for Operations and Resources:** A budget is a mechanism to plan for the operations and resources of an organisation. The operations are expressed in terms of revenues and expenses.

The plan also covers the planning of the resources of the organisation. Resources refer to the various assets and the sources of capital available to finance these operations.

(*vii*) **It is expressed in Financial and/or Quantitative Terms:** A budget is always expressed in financial or monetary terms. It is due to the fact that monetary unit is a common denominator. The various activities and operations of a business concern may be expressed in different units e.g., Material Budget is expressed in terms of weight, Labour Budget in terms of labour hours, Sales budget in terms of sales territories. But for the purpose of integration into a plan, all these budgets have to be expressed in terms of some comparable unit of measurement. This comparable unit is provided by monetary unit.

(*viii*) **It provides a yardstick for the comparison of actual performance:** A budget provides for the comparison of actual achievements with the specified goals. This comparison is of utmost importance for exercising effective control over business operations since it helps in fixing the responsibility for variances between actual performance and budgeted performance.

BUDGETING

Budgeting refers to the mechanism of preparing budgets. According to J.Batty—"The entire process of preparing the budgets is known as budgeting." Preparation or formulation of business budgets involves a careful study of the conditions of the business, the objectives of the management and the capacity of the business concern for attaining those objectives. Thus, it can be said that budgeting involves the entire process of making busines plans. Budgeting process involves the following steps:

(*i*) To forecast sales indicating what quantity and quality of goods should be made available.

(*ii*) To determine management policy regarding range of products, stock levels, channels of distribution, investments etc.

(*iii*) To prepare a Production Budget in accordance with the forecast and policies and to plan the needs for materials, labour and services alongwith the costs involved.

(*iv*) To prepare financial estimates as regards cash requirements for planned operations and investments.

(*v*) To prepare a 'Master Budget' combining and co-ordinating the individual budgets.

BUDGETARY CONTROL

Budgetary control is a system whereby the budgets are used as a means of planning and controlling costs. Budgeting lays down as to what is to be attained and how it is to be attained while control ensures that the objectives are realised and actual results do not deviate from the planned course more than necessary. According to J.L. Brown and L.R. Howard–"Budgetary control system is a system of controlling costs which includes the preparation of budgets, co-ordinating the departments and establishing responsibilities, comparing actual performance with the budgeted and acting upon results to achieve maximum profitability." According to J. Batty–"Budgetary Control is a system which uses budgets as a means of planning and controlling all aspects of producing and/or selling commodities or services." The Institute of Cost and Management Accountants has defined budgetary control as "the establishment of budgets relating to the responsibilities of executives to the requirements of a policy and the continuous comparison of actual with budgeted results, either to secure by individual action the objective of that policy or to provide a basis for its revision." From these definitions, it is clear that budgetary control operates through different budgets. It aims at laying down a policy, co-ordinating the different activities of the business and exercising necessary control so that the individual targets set by different budgets can be achieved. The targets set up under the system are such that they can be directly compared with the actual performances, and the difference, if any, can be traced to an individual who is responsible for the same. This building up of a sense of responsibility in accounting is the main feature of budgetary control.

EXERCISE OF BUDGETARY CONTROL

The exercise of the system of budgetary control involves the following main steps:

(*a*) The establishment of budgets for each section or department of the organisation;

(*b*) The measurement of actual performances;

(*c*) The continuous comparison of actual performances with budgeted performances so as to determine the deviations or variances; and

(*d*) The ascertainment of reasons for such variances and taking suitable actions to remedy the defects in order to achieve the objective under the original policy or to provide a basis for its revision.

OBJECTIVES OF BUDGETARY CONTROL

The general objectives of budgetary control can be summarised as follows:

(*i*) To plan the policy of a business for the coming period for achievement of the firm's objectives and its translation into monetary and quantitative terms.

(*ii*) To determine the responsibility of each department and executive so that they are made accountable for definite and precise results.

(*iii*) To co-ordinate the activities of a business so that each is a part of an integral total.

(*iv*) To provide for continuous comparison of actual and budgeted performance in terms of results achieved and costs incurred so that cause for any inefficiency is immediately detected and removed.

(*v*) To control and direct each function so that best possible results may be obtained.

(*vi*) To provide for the revision of budgets for future in the light of experience gained.

Essentials of effective Budgeting and Budgetary Control: The main essentials for an effective and successful system of budgetary control can be given as follows:

1. **Support of Top Management:** In order to make the budgeting system successful, it is necessary that it must have the whole hearted support of every person involved in the organisational set up. In this regard, the initiative must come from the top management. The budgetary control system can be effective if the persons at the various levels of management feel that the top management considers the system as valuable. For this

purpose, it is necessary that the top management must show its commitment to the ideas, principles and philosophy of budgeting and budgetary control.

2. **Definite and Reasonable Targets or Goals:** For the successful operations of the budgetary control system, the targets fixed in the budgets should be definite, realistic and attainable. This feeling should come from the various executives who have been assigned the responsibility of various budget centres.
3. **Well-defined Organisation:** In order to ensure maximum benefits from budgeting system, well defined budget centres should be created within the organisation so that the responsibility of each executive in the organisation may be clearly laid down.
4. **Well Defined Policy:** The budgets are prepared to establish the responsibilities of executives to the requirements of a particular policy. As such the policy of the business to be followed during budget period should be clearly defined.
5. **Active Participation by Executives:** The various executives who are made responsible for different budget centres, should be actively involved in the preparation of the budget. It will ensure the proper implementation of the business policy as laid down in the budget.
6. **Efficient Budget Education:** The various executives responsible for putting into effect the budgetary proposals, should take active interest in the operation of the budgeting system. It is possible only if these executives are constantly educated about the objectives, potentials and techniques of budgeting. It can be done through regular meetings of executives where all matters regarding preparation of budgets and actual results achieved can be discussed.
7. **Adequate Accounting System:** Budgeting is closely related to accounting since compilation of budget is done on the basis of historical data provided by the Accounting Department. These data form the basis for making estimates. As such the accounting system should be designed to the requirements of responsibility accounting.
8. **Cost of the Budgeting System:** The cost of operation of the budgeting system should be within the financial capability of the business and should not exceed, in any case the total benefits accruing from it to the organisation.
9. **Efficient Reporting:** It is necessary that prompt reports on the comparison of actual performance with the budgeted figures should be made available to the management for ensuring timely action on the points of inefficiency.
10. **Flexibility:** The budget programme of the business concern should not be too rigid. It should be flexible and should provide for possible contingencies.

11. **Integration with Standard Costing System:** If the business concern decides to introduce standard costing system, it should be completely integrated with budgetary control system in respect of compilation of budgets and analysis of variances.

ADVANTAGES OF BUDGETARY CONTROL SYSTEM

The main advantages of budgetary control system may be given as follows:

1. **Helps in Planning:** Continuous use of the budgetary control system enhances the ability and power of the management to foresee or think ahead. It enables them to forecast future operational problems and difficulties and to arrange for suitable or corrective actions well in advance. It certainly brings an improvement in planning process and it becomes more clear, precise and effective. To quote Charles T. Horngren, budgetary control "helps managers to focus on operating and financial problems early enough for effective planning and action."
2. **Encourages Cost Consciousness:** Under budgetary control system, the establishment of budgets, fixation of responsibility and communication of the targets to be achieved by various executives, make every executive and worker cost conscious. The cost consciousness leads to the elimination of the causes of inefficiency and reduction in cost.
3. **Leads to Economy in Operations:** Budgetary control system brings economy in the overall working of the business concern. Budgets aim at regulating and controlling expenditure by exposing all types of wastages and inefficiencies and thus help in the efficient operation of the business.
4. **Promotes Co-operation and Co-ordination:** Budgetary control system promotes co-operation and co-ordination among the various functionaries and departments of the business concern. All persons and departments engaged in production, sales, personnel, finance, service etc., work as a team in harmony and co-ordination in the realisation of a common objective. Every person in the organisation thinks as a group and not as an individual.
5. **Encourages Safe Delegation of Responsibility:** Where budgets have been prepared, top executives may delegate responsibility safely and may control the departmental executives by their actions through budget reports.
6. **Helps in Effective Cost Control:** Budgets are treated as yardsticks against which actual performance and actual costs can be compared and deviations ascertained. Analysis of deviations helps in ascertaining their reasons and the points of inefficiency and provides for corrective action to avoid their recurrence.
7. **Gives Motivation to Workers:** The budgets provide incentive and motivation to work with greater vigour and vigilance for attaining the budget targets. It increases the overall efficiency and productivity.

8. **Serves as a Media of Communication:** Budgets translate the goals and targets of a business concern in quantitative and monetary terms. The departmental targets and overall goals are communicated to all the concerned persons. Further, the actual performance and variance reports prepared under budgetory control system are also sent to various executives at different levels of management. These reports serve as a media of communication between different executives.
9. **Encourages Management by Exception:** Variance analysis and reporting are based on the principles of management by exception. The top management is interested only in variances so that corrective measures may be taken in time. By highlighting the minority of items which are not proceeding as planned, the time of the management is saved as close attention need not be given to the majority of the items which have proceeded smoothly.

Limitations of Budgetary Control System: Budgetary Control system is not a foolproof tool and has its own limitations. The main limitations may be given as follows:

1. **Use of Estimated Figures:** Budgeting relates to future and involves forecasting and estimation which may not be accurate to the full extent. If the estimates are not correct, the budget targets may become useless.
2. **Expensive System:** The installation and operation of budgetary control system is very costly since it requires the engagement of a large force of technical and qualified staff. As such, budgetary control system is not suitable for smaller undertakings having limited financial resources.
3. **Extensive Decentralisation:** The system of budgetary control involves an extensive decentralisation of authority and powers and if a proper co-ordination of different business activities is not achieved, the attainment of the objectives of budgetary control system shall become doubtful.
4. **Opposition by Staff:** Budgets provide yardsticks against which the performance of the executives and workers is to be measured. The inefficiency on the part of any person involved in the organisation is immediately known which calls for corrective action. As such inefficient executives and workers generally create difficulties in the way of operating this system.
5. **It is Simply a Tool of Management:** The system of budgeting cannot eliminate the necessity of superior executive ability in every business decision. As such budgeting is simply a tool of management and cannot take the place of management.
6. **Lack of Flexibility:** Budgets are prepared after a lot of ground work done by different departments. The business executives treat the budgets figures as the final figures and stick to them.

ORGANISATION FOR BUDGETARY CONTROL

For the purpose of effective cost control, the system of budgetary control should take into account the following preliminaries:

1. **Creation of Budget Centres:** An organisation is broken down into a number of budget centres to facilitate the control of planned activities. A budget centre refers to a department or other location to which income or expenses may be attached and of which the responsibility is borne by an individual. The Institute of Cost and Management Accountants defines a budget centre as "a section of the organisation of an undertaking defined for the purposes of budgetary control." For each budget centre, a separate budget is prepared.
2. **Introduction of Suitable Accounting Records:** The preparation of various budgets for the purpose of budgetary control, requires the provision of adequate accounting records. As such, it is necessary that accounting system should be able to provide the required information in an analytical form. For this purpose, a chart of accounts corresponding with the budget centres should be maintained
3. **Preparation of Organisation Chart:** There should be a well-defined organisation chart for budgetary control. This organisation chart shows the functional responsibilities of each executive and assists him in ascertaining his position in the organisation and his relationship with other executives. The design of the organisation chart shall depend upon the nature and size of the organisation but a simple organisation chart may be given as follows:

Organisation Chart for Budgetary Control

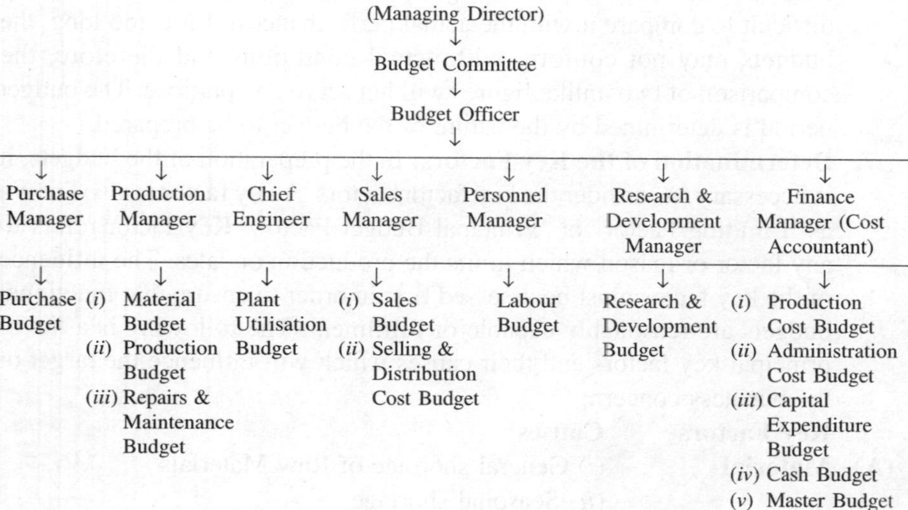

4. **Setting up of a Budget Committee:** In small concerns, the preparation of the budget is usually the responsibility of Accountant or Cost Accountant. In large concerns, the preparation of the budget is entrusted to a Budget Committee which is headed by the Chief Executive of the organisation. The budget committee is composed of the representatives of various departments e.g., Sales, Production, Purchases and Works Engineering etc. The responsibility for operating the system of budgetary control is undertaken by the Budget Officer who is a senior member of the Accounting Department. The main functions of a Budget Committee are:
   (*a*) To receive and scrutinise different budget estimates;
   (*b*) To decide detailed policy to be followed;
   (*c*) To suggest revision of functional budgets, where necessary;
   (*d*) To approve budgets; and
   (*e*) To receive and to deal with budget and comparison statement and to recommend action to be taken under the circumstances.
5. **Preparation of a Budget Manual:** In large undertakings, generally, a Budget Manual is prepared which guides the Budget Officer and various departmental heads. Budget manual is a document which contains:
   (*a*) Standard instructions for compilation of budgets.
   (*b*) Specific responsibilities and limits of each executive concerned with the budget.
   (*c*) Method of compilation of the various schedules and co-ordinating with related figures of some other schedule.
6. **Fixation of the Budget Period:** Budget period is defined as the period for which a budget is prepared and employed. There is no specific rule governing the selection of the budget period but it should neither be too long nor too short. In case budget period is too short, it will be very difficult to compare it with the actual performances. If it is too long, the budgets may not conform with actual conditions and therefore, the comparison of two unlike figures will not serve any purpose. The budget period is determined by the nature of the budget to be prepared.
7. **Determination of the Key Factors:** In the preparation of the budgets, it is necessary to consider the key factor/factors. A key factor is also known as 'Limiting Factor' or 'Principal Budget Factor.' Key factor refers to any factor or reason which limits the production or sales. The influence of the key factor must be assessed first in order to ensure that functional budgets are reasonably capable of fulfilment. The following is a list of principal key factors and their causes which will influence the target of the business concern:

	Key Factors	**Causes**
(A)	**Material**	(*i*) General shortage of Raw Materials
		(*ii*) Seasonal shortage

	(*iii*) Restrictions on imports
	(*iv*) Restriction of quota or licence.
(B) Labour	(*i*) Overall shortage of workers
	(*ii*) Shortage of particular type of skilled workers
(C) Plant	(*i*) Shortage of plant and machinery
	(*ii*) Shortage of capital/funds
	(*iii*) Shortage of space/accommodation for plant
	(*iv*) Bottlenecks in different processes.
(D) Sales	(*i*) Consumer Resistance
	(*ii*) Inadequate Advertising
	(*iii*) Shortage of sales force
	(*iv*) Dumping by a foreign country
(E) Management	(*i*) Lack of capital
	(*ii*) Lack of technical knowledge
	(*iii*) Shortage of experienced managers.

In most of the business concerns, sales is the most important key factor. If a limiting factor cannot be avoided by any means, then all the functional budgets will have to be built around that factor.

8. **Determination of Level of Activity:** For the purpose of planning production and controlling costs, it is necessary to establish the normal level of activity of the business concern. Normal level of activity is the level of activity at which the business concern is expected to operate under the present conditions. The budget estimates should also provide for necessary allowance to the made in the budget figures and suggest what the figure should have been with the level of activity actually attained.

9. **Budget Officer or Budget Controller:** A 'Budget Officer' or 'Budget Controller' is appointed to link up the various operations to bring them together and to co-ordinate their efforts in the matter of the preparation of budgets. Budget Officer is more or less the Secretary to the Budget Committee. But it should be remembered that Budget Controller does not control the preparation of budgets. He is an advisor and he does not issue instructions. His principal duties are:

   (*i*) To render assistance in the preparation of various budgets and their co-ordination and compilation into the Master Budget.

   (*ii*) To compile information about actual performance on a continuous basis,comparing it against the budgeted figures, ascertaining cause of variances and preparing reports based thereon and sending them to appropriate executive.

   (*iii*) To bring to the notice of the management the need for revision of budgets.

   (*iv*) To compile information of all types for the purpose of efficient preparation of budgets.

CLASSIFICATION OF BUDGETS

Budgets may be classified on the basis of:

(A) Functions involved;

(B) Conditions (on which these are based);

(C) Periods; and

(D) Activity levels.

(A) Classification on the basis of functions

On the basis of functions budgets may be divided into:

(*i*) Functional Budgets and (*ii*) Master Budget.

A functional budget refers to a budget which relates to any of the functions of an undertaking, e.g., sales, production, finance, purchases, administration etc.

Functional Budgets:

In a manufacturing concern, generally the following detailed functional budgets are prepared:

(1) Sales Budget

Under the system of budgetary control, the starting point is the preparation of Sales Budget. Sales budget is the forecast of sales during a given period, both in quantity and value. Sales budget is said to be the most difficult budget to prepare since it is not easy to estimate consumer's demand, especially in case a new product is being introduced in the market. The responsibility for the preparation of the sales budget lies with the Sales Manager. This budget is classified under a number of headings, namely–product or product group, territories, areas and countries, type of customer, e.g., National Government, State Governments, export, country customers, salesman and period etc. The specimen of a Sales Budget has been given below:

Sales Budget

Period: 2007-08

Zone	Products	Budget for 2007-08			Budget for 2006-07 (Current Year)			Actual sales for Current Year 2006-07		
		Quantity (Units)	Price Rs.	Value Rs.	Quantity (Units)	Price Rs.	Value Rs.	Quantity (Units)	Price Rs.	Value Rs.
North:	A									
	B									
	Total									
West:	A									
	B									
	Total									
South:	A									
	B									
	Total									
East:	A									
	B									
	Total									
	Grand Total									

Illustration 1

C. Bros, sells two products which are manufactured in one plant. During the year 2007-08 it plans to sell the following quantities of each product:

Sales Budget (units)

	First quarter	Second quarter	Third quarter	Fourth quarter	Total
Product 1	90,000	2,30,000	3,00,000	80,000	7,00,000
Product 2	85,000	75,000	55,000	85,000	3,00,000

Each of these two products is sold on a seasonal basis. Product 1 tends to sell better in summer months, while product 2 sells better during the winter. C. Bros. plan to sell product 1 throughout the year at a price of Rs. 10 a unit and product 2 at a price of Rs. 20 a unit.

A study of the past experiences reveals that C. Bros. has lost about 3% of its billed revenue each year because of returns (constituting 2% of loss of revenue), allowances and bad debts (1% loss).

Prepare a budget incorporating the given information.

Solution

Sales Budget

Period: Year 2007-08

	I Quarter	II Quarter	III Quarter	IV Quarter	Total
Product No. 1, Sale Price Rs. 10	9,00,000	23,00,000	30,00,000	8,00,000	70,00,000
Product No. 2, Sale Price Rs. 20	17,00,000	15,00,000	11,00,000	17,00,000	60,00,000
1. Total Sales	26,00,000	38,00,000	41,00,000	25,00,000	1,30,00,000
Loss for Returns @ 2% of total sales	52,000	76,000	82,000	50,000	2,60,000
Loss for Bad Debts and allowances @ 1% of total sales	26,000	38,000	41,000	25,000	1,30,000
2. Total Deductions	78,000	1,14,000	1,23,000	75,000	3,90,000
3. Net Sales 1–2	25,22,000	36,86,000	39,77,000	24,25,000	1,26,10,000

(2) Selling and Distribution Cost Budget

This budget shows the cost of selling and distribution for the quantities shown in the sales budget. The main factors which affect the selling and distribution cost budget are the channels through which sales are to effected, the sales promotion plan to be pursued, the sales territories to be covered and the mode of despatch of products to the customers. Selling and distribution cost budget is drawn up by the Sales Manager and in the compilation, he is assisted by Distribution Manager, Advertising Manager, Sales Office Manager and the Accountant. For compiling this budget, the expenses are grouped according to elements *e.g.*, direct selling expenses, sales office expenses, distribution expenses and advertising expenses.

Illustration 2

The following table shows the selling and distribution expenses of X Ltd., incurred during the year ended on 31st March, 2007:

Items of Expenditure	Sales Divisions			Head Office	Total
	West	East	North		
	Rs.	Rs.	Rs.	Rs.	Rs.
Salesmen's Salaries	30,000	32,000	15,000	–	77,000
Commission	18,000	20,000	9,000	–	47,000
Travelling Expenses	9,000	13,000	6,000	–	28,000
Sales Depots & Showrooms	16,000	20,000	8,000	–	44,000
Discounts & Rebates	3,000	5,000	2,000	–	10,000
Credit Collection Exp.	2,000	4,000	3,000	–	9,000
Rent of Warehouse	15,000	25,000	14,000	–	54,000
Packing Expenses	4,000	10,000	8,000	–	22,000
Advertisement	22,000	25,000	10,000	14,000	71,000
Sales Managers' Salaries	15,000	20,000	12,000	20,000	67,000
Misc. Expenses	16,000	26,000	13,000	16,000	71,000
Total	1,50,000	2,00,000	1,00,000	50,000	5,00,000

The following additional informations are also given to you for next year:

1. Management decided to participate in 'The International Trade Fair' to be held in February, 2008 and it was estimated that an expenditure of Rs. 40,000 will be incurred in this connection which will be met by head office.
2. It was estimated that to increase the sales in North Division 4 additional salesmen will be appointed next year. They will be paid Rs. 300 per month each.
3. Management also decided to promote the sales in South through an independent sales division (South). This will increase the expenditure as follows:
   Salesmen Salaries Rs. 5,000, Travelling Expenses Rs. 2,000, Sales Depot and Showrooms Expenses Rs. 5,000, Advertisement Rs. 10,000, Misc. Expenses Rs. 7,000, Sales Manager's Salaries Rs. 9,000.
4. Extensive advertisement programmes will be adopted for which Rs. 20,000 will be spent by head office.
5. Commission will be given @ 5% on sales.
6. There will be an expenditure for credit collection @ 1% on sales.
7. Customers will be allowed discount and rebate @ 10% on sales.
8. Other Expenses will remain unchanged.
9. Estimated Sales for the next year will be as follows:
   West: Rs. 5,00,000; East: Rs. 8,00,000;
   North: Rs. 6,00,000; and South: Rs. 3,00,000.
   Prepare the Selling and Distribution Cost Budget for the year ending on 31st March, 2008 from the above details.

Solution

X Ltd.
Selling & Distribution Cost Budget
(For the year ended on 31st March, 2008)

Items of Expenditure	Sales Divisions				Head Office	Total
	West	East	North	South		
	Rs.	Rs.	Rs.	Rs.	Rs.	
Salesmen's Salaries	30,000	32,000	29,400	5,000	–	96,400
Commission	25,000	40,000	30,000	15,000	–	1,10,000
Travelling Expenses	9,000	13,000	6,000	2,000	–	30,000
Sales Depots & Show-rooms	16,000	20,000	8,000	6,000	–	50,000
Discounts & Rebates	50,000	80,000	60,000	30,000	–	2,20,000
Credit Collection charges	5,000	8,000	6,000	3,000	–	22,000
Rent of Warehouse	15,000	25,000	14,000	3,000	–	57,000
Packing Expenses	4,000	10,000	8,000	5,000	–	27,000
Advertisement	22,000	25,000	10,000	10,000	34,000	1,01,000
Sales Managers' Salaries	15,000	20,000	12,000	9,000	20,000	76,000
Trade Fair Expenses	–	–	–	–	40,000	40,000
Misc. Expenses	16,000	26,000	13,000	7,000	16,000	78,000
Total	2,07,000	2,99,000	1,96,400	95,000	1,10,000	9,07,400

(3) Production Budget

A Production Budget is defined as an estimate of quantity of goods that must be produced during the budget period. This budget is prepared by the Production Manager keeping in view the following factors:

(*a*) Estimated sales.

(*b*) Expected opening stock and desired closing stock of each article.

(*c*) Available physical resources of plant, power, factory space, materials and machines.

(*d*) The policy of the management regarding manufacture or purchase of components.

The Production Budget may be classified under following heads:

(*i*) Products

(*ii*) Manufacturing Departments

(*iii*) Months, Quarters etc.

Illustration 3

Prepare 'Production Budget' from the following particulars for the year ended 31st March, 2008:

	Products			
	A Units	B Units	C Units	D Units
Estimated Sales	80,000	60,000	50,000	20,000
Estimated Opening Balances	30,000	25,000	10,000	5,000
Desired Closing Balances	35,000	20,000	20,000	10,000

Solution

Production Budget

Period.............

	Products			
	A	B	C	D
	Units	Units	Units	Units
Estimated Sales	80,000	60,000	50,000	20,000
+ Desired Stock at the end	35,000	20,000	20,000	10,000
Total	1,15,000	80,000	70,000	30,000
– Estimated Stock in the beginning	30,000	25,000	10,000	5,000
Budgeted Production	85,000	55,000	60,000	25,000

(4) Production Cost Budget

This budget is also known as Factory Cost Budget and it shows the estimated cost of carrying out the production plan given in the Production Budget. The production cost includes direct materials cost, direct labour cost, direct expenses and factory overheads. Production Cost Budget is generally classified under the following headings:

(*i*) Products
(*ii*) Manufacturing Departments
(*iii*) Months, Quarters etc.
(*iv*) Elements of Costs.

Illustration 4

Your company manufactures two products A and B. A forecast of the number of the units to be sold in the first seven months of the year is given below:

	Product A	Product B
January	1,000	2,800
February	1,200	2,800
March	1,600	2,400
April	2,000	2,000
May	2,400	1,600
June	2;400	1,600
July	2,000	1,800

It is anticipated that (*i*) there will be no work-in-progress at the end of any month, (*ii*) finished units equal to half the sales for the next month will be in stock at the end of each month (including the previous December).

Budgeted production and production costs for the whole year are as follows:

	Product A	Product B
Production (Units)	22,000	24,000
Per unit	Rs.	Rs.
Direct Material	12.50	19.00
Direct Labour	4.50	7.00
Total Factory Overhead, apportioned	66,000	96,000

Prepare for the six months period ending 30th June, a production budget for each month and a summarised production cost budget.

(*I.C.W.A., Final*)

Solution

(a) **Production Budget**

(For six months ending 30th June)

	Jan. (Units)	Feb. (Units)	March (Units)	April (Units)	May (Units)	June (Units)	Total (Units)
Product A							
Sales	1,000	1,200	1,600	2,000	2,400	2,400	
(+) Closing Stock	600	800	1,000	1,200	1,200	1,000	
	1,600	2,000	2,600	3,200	3,600	3,400	
(–) Opening Stock	500	600	800	1,000	1,200	1,200	
Production Budget	1,100	1,400	1,800	2,200	2,400	2,200 =	11,100
Product B							
Sales	2,800	2,800	2,400	2,000	1,600	1,600	
(+) Closing Stock	1,400	1,200	1,000	800	800	900	
	4,200	4,000	3,400	2,800	2,400	2,500	
(–) Opening Stock	1,400	1,400	1,200	1,000	800	800	
Production Budget	2,800	2,600	2,200	1,800	1,600	1,700 =	12,700

(b) **Summarised Production Cost Budget**

	Product A		Product B		Total
	Rate	Amount	Rate	Amount	
	Rs.	Rs.	Rs.	Rs.	
Direct Material	12.50	1,38,750	19.00	2,41,300	3,80,050
Direct Labour	4.50	49,950	7.00	88,900	1,38,850
Factory Overhead	3.00	33,300	4.00	50,800	84,100
Total	20.00	2,22,000	30.00	3,81,000	6,03,000

(5) Purchases Budget

The purchases budget represents the total purchases to be made during the budget period. These purchases represent the requirements of direct and indirect materials, fixed assets, services and finished goods for resale but the most important item is that of raw materials. The requirements of the items to be purchased are expressed in terms of quantities as well as money. This budget is prepared on the basis of Sales, Production Cost, Capital Expenditure, Research and Development Cost Budgets. Purchases budget facilitates the management of finances by defining the cash requirements in respect of the purchases to be made during the budget period and enables the Purchases Department to plan its purchases in time so that long-term forward contracts may be made when advantageous.

Illustration 5

The Sales Director of a manufacturing company reports that next year he expects to sell 54,000 units of a certain product.

The production manager consults the storekeeper and casts his figures as follows:

Two kinds of raw materials, A and B are required for manufacturing the product. Each unit of the product requires 2 units of A and 3 units of B. The estimated opening balances at the commencement of the next year are:

Finished product – 10,000 units.

A – 12,000 units.

B – 15,000 units.

The desirable closing balances at the end of the next year are:

Finished Product – 14,000 units

A – 13,000 units B – 16,000 units.

Draw up a quantitative chart showing the Material Purchase Budget for the next year.

(Calcutta University, M.Com.)

Solution

Production Budget
(For Finished Product)

	Units
Expected sales during next year	54,000
Add: Closing Balance desired (at the end of next year)	14,000
	68,000
Less: Opening Balance (at the beginning of next year)	10,000
Estimated Production for the next year	58,000

Raw Material Purchase Budget
(in Quantity)

	Raw Material	
	A (Units)	B (Units)
Raw Material required for 58,000 units of finished product	1,16,000	1,74,000
Add Desired Closing Stock of Raw Material (at the end of next year)	13,000	16,000
	1,29,000	1,90,000
Less Opening Stock of Raw Material (at the beginning of next year)	12,000	15,000
Raw Materials to be purchased next year	1,17,000	1,75,000

(6) Labour Cost Budget

The Labour Cost Budget represents in terms of money, number and grades of personnel, number of working hours or other appropriate units, the direct and indirect labour required to carry out the programme laid down in the Sales, Production, Capital Expenditure and Research and Development Expenditure Budgets. Thus, this budget is a forecast of planned outlay on direct and indirect labour of a concern during the budget period.

(7) Plant Utilisation Budget

Plant Utilisation Budget forecasts the plant and machinery requirements to meet the Production Budget. This budget is expressed in terms of working hours or other convenient units and it indicates the machine load on each manufacturing department, machine or group of machines and the extent of over-loading or under-loading so that the management may take corrective action.

(8) Administration Cost Budget

This budget is a forecast of general administration costs of the undertaking during the budget period. General administration cost includes the cost of formulating the policy, directing the organisation and controlling the operations of an undertaking. Most of the items of administration cost are fixed in nature but a clear distinction shall have to be made between 'fixed' and 'variable' items.

(9) Capital Expenditure Budget

This budget expresses in detail the anticipated expenditure to be incurred on fixed assets during the budget period e.g., plant and machinery, land, buildings, patents etc. Capital Expenditure Budget is normally a long-term budget providing for the acquisition of the assets necessitated by the replacement of existing assets, additions to the existing assets, or by the installation of an improved type of machinery to take the advantage of new production techniques.

(10) Research and Development Cost Budget

This budget is a planned outlay on research and development activities of an undertaking and expresses in terms of money, the permissible limits within which the research and development activities are to be pursued and the directions for the same.

(11) Cash Budget

The cash budget is a forecast of the cash position for a period and represents the cash receipts and payments and the estimated cash balance each month of the budget period. This budget is practically the nerve centre of the whole budgetary control system since the most carefully prepared budgets are incapable of fulfilment if adequate cash is not available at proper time. The main functions of this budget may be summarised as follows:

(*i*) It ensures that sufficient cash is available to meet the requirements of the organisation.

(*ii*) It reveals any expected shortage of cash so as to enable the management to arrange for cash in time by means of bank overdraft or loan etc.

(*iii*) It reveals any expected surplus of cash available for investment outside the business.

This budget is prepared after all the functional budgets have been drawn up.

Cash Budget of a business concern can be prepared by Receipts and Payments Method, Adjusted Profit and Loss Method and Balance Sheet Method. But the Receipts and Payments Method is the most popular method and is commonly used by business concerns. Under this method, cash budget is prepared just like a summarised cash book. For the purpose of preparing cash budget, all types of 'Cash Receipts' or 'Cash Inflows' (including opening balance of cash/bank) are to be estimated in a logical manner period-wise, keeping in view the past figures, existing trends and expected changes in future. Similarly, all types of 'Cash payments' or 'cash outflows' are also estimated period-wise. Thereafter, a comparison of total estimated cash receipts and total estimated cash payments is made to ascertain the amount of excess or shortage of cash. In case of expected shortage or shortfall, arrangements shall be planned to raise funds by means of short-term loans or bank overdraft etc.

Illustration 6

Estimate the cash requirement of Meerut Fruit Co. Ltd. for June, 2008 on the basis of data given:

(*i*) Sales

February, 2008 Rs. 25,000
March, 2008 Rs.20,000
April to June, 2008 Rs. 30,000 per month

Half the sales are for cash. 90% of credit sales are collected in the month following the month of sale and the balance one month later.

(*ii*) Fruits are always bought of cash to avail a cash discount of 5%. The purchase budget for the second quarter (April to June) was 15,000 baskets per month at Re. 1 per basket.

(*iii*) Wages and salaries for the second quarter were budgeted at Rs. 5,000 per month.

(*iv*) Manufacturing and other expenses for the quarter were:

Cash expenses Rs. 4,500
Depreciation Rs. 7,500
Selling expenses Rs. 3,000
Administrative expenses Rs. 2,000 (equally in April and May only)

Solution

Cash Budget (For three months ending 30th June, 2008)

Particulars	April Rs.	May Rs.	June Rs.
Opening Cash Balance	–	2,500	9,250
Add: Cash Inflows:			
(*i*) Cash Sales (1/2 of sales)	15,000	15,000	15,000
(*ii*) Cash Collected from Debtors	10,250	14,500	15,000
(A) Total Cash Available	25,250	32,000	39,250
Cash Outflows:			
(*i*) Cash Purchases (Less Trade discount)	14,250	14,250	14,250
(*ii*) Wages and Salaries	5,000	5,000	5,000
(*iii*) Cash Expenses	1,500	1,500	1,500
(*iv*) Selling Expenses	1,000	1,000	1,000
(*v*) Administrative Expenses	1,000	1,000	–
(B) Total Payments	22,750	22,750	21,750
(C) Closing Cash Balance (A) – (B)	2,500	9,250	17,500

Working Notes:

(*i*) As the opening cash balance for the month of April has not been given in the question, it has been assumed to be nil.

(*ii*) Closing cash balance of a month becomes the opening balance of the next month.

(*iii*) Cash collections from debtors have been calculated as follows:

	Feb.	March	April	May	June
	Rs.	Rs.	Rs.	Rs.	Rs.
Credit Sales (being 1/2 of Sales)	12,500	10,000	15,000	15,000	15,000
Cash collected form debtors:					
(*a*) 90% of previous month's credit sales			9,000	13,500	13,500
(*b*) 10% of credit sales of two months earlier			1,250	1,000	1,500
			10,250	14,500	15,000

Illustration 7

A company making for stock in the first quarter of the year is assisted by its bankers with overdraft accommodation. The following are the relevant budget figures:

	Sales	Purchases	Wages
	Rs.	Rs.	Rs.
November	60,000	41,500	4,900
December	64,000	48,000	5,000
January	36,000	81,000	4,000
February	58,000	82,000	3,800
March	42,000	89,500	5,200

Budgeted cash at the bank on 1st January is Rs. 8,600. Credit terms of sales are payment by the end of the month following the month of supply. On an average, one half of the sales are paid on the due date, while the other half are paid during the next month. Creditors are paid during the month following the month of supply.

You are required to prepare a Cash Budget for the quarter from 1st January to 31st March, showing budgeted amount of bank facilities required at each month-end.

Solution

Cash Budget (For the quarter ending 31st March)

Particulars	January Rs.	February Rs.	March Rs.
Opening Bank Balance	8,600	18,600	(–) 16,200
Add: Cash Inflows:			
Collection from debtors	62,000	50,000	47,000
(A) Total Cash Available	70,600	68,600	30,800
Cash Outflows:			
(*i*) Payments to creditors for purchases	48,000	81,000	82,000
(*ii*) Payment of wages	4,000	3,800	5,200
(B) Total Payments	52,000	84,800	87,200
(C) Closing Bank Balance (A) – (B)	18,600	(–) 16,200	(–) 56,400

Working Notes:

(*i*) Collections from debtors have been calculated as follows:

	Nov. Rs.	Dec. Rs.	Jan. Rs.	Feb. Rs.	March Rs.
Credit Sales	60,000	64,000	36,000	58,000	42,000
Amount Collected					
(*i*) For Sales during preceding month (1/2 of sales)			32,000	18,000	29,000
(*ii*) For sales during the month preceding the previous month (1/2 sales)			30,000	32,000	18,000
Total Collections			62,000	50,000	47,000

(*ii*) Since the lag in payment of wages has not been given, these shall be treated to be payable in the same month.

(*iii*) The company has to arrange for the bank overdraft facility for Rs. 16,200 at February-end and for Rs. 56,200 at March-end.

Illustration 8

From the following forecasts of income and expenditure, prepare a Cash Budget for the half-year ended on 30th June, 2009:

Months	Sales (Credit)	Purchases (Credit)	Wages	Manufacturing Expenses	Administration Expenses	Selling Expenses
2008	Rs.	Rs.	Rs.	Rs.	Rs.	Rs.
November	25,000	10,000	2,500	1,100	1,000	600
December	30,000	15,000	2,800	1,200	975	650
2009						
January	20,000	10,000	2,000	1,250	1,060	550
February	25,000	15,000	2,200	1,150	1,040	650
March	30,000	17,500	2,400	1,300	1,105	750
April	30,000	20,000	2,600	1,350	1,120	800
May	40,000	22,500	2,800	1,450	1,180	825
June	45,000	25,000	3,000	1,500	1,185	875

(1) A sales commission of 5% on sales and due two months after sales is payable in addition to the above selling expenses. (2) Capital Expenditure-Plant purchased, 1st January for Rs. 10,000, its payment being immediately due. Building purchased in January for Rs. 80,000, payable in two half-yearly instalments, the first payable in February. (3) A dividend of Rs. 5,000 (net) is payable in April. (4) Period of credit allowed by creditors and to customers is 2 months. (5) Lag in the payment of wages-1/8th month, (6) Lag in the payment of other expenses-1 month, (7) Cash Balance on January 1, 2009, was expected to be Rs. 37,500.

(M.Com. Agra)

Solution

Cash Budget

(For the half year ended on 30th June, 2009)

Particulars	Jan. Rs.	Feb. Rs.	March Rs.	April Rs.	May Rs.	June Rs.	Total Rs.
Opening balance of Cash	37,500	36,325	4,790	8,575	6,595	11,550	
Receipts: Received from Customers	25,000	30,000	20,000	25,000	30,000	30,000	1,60,000
Total:	62,500	66,325	24,790	33,575	36,595	41,550	
Less: Payments	26,175	61,535	16,215	26,980	25,045	27,930	
Closing balance of Cash	36,325	4,790	8,575	6,595	11,550	13,620	
Payments:							
Paid to Creditors	10,000	15,000	10,000	15,000	17,500	20,000	87,500
Wages*	2,100	2,175	2,375	2.575	2,775	2,975	14,975
Manufacturing Expenses	1,200	1,250	1,150	1,300	1,350	1,450	7,700
Administration Expenses	975	1,060	1,040	1,105	1,120	1,180	6,480
Selling & Distribution Expenses	650	550	650	750	800	825	4,225
Sales Commission	1,250	1,500	1,000	1,250	1,500	1,500	8,000
Purchase of Plant	10,000	–	–	–	–	–	10,000
Instalment payment of Building	–	40,000	–	–	–	–	40,000
Dividend	–	–	–	5,000		–	5,000
Total Payments	26,175	61,535	16,215	26,980	25,045	27,930	1,83,880

*Amount of Wages which is being paid actually in various months is calculated as per table given below:

Months	Wages for the month	Lag in payment of 1/8 month	Amount actually paid in the month		
			for the month 7/8	Lag payment	Total
	Rs.	Rs.	Rs.	Rs.	Rs.
December, 2008	2,800	350	–	–	–
January, 2009	2,000	250	1,750	350	2,100
February, 2009	2,200	275	1,925	250	2,175
March, 2009	2,400	300	2,100	275	2,375
April, 2009	2,600	325	2,275	300	2,575
May, 2009	2,800	350	2,450	325	2,775
June, 2009	3,000	375	2,625	350	2,975

Note: It is assumed that wages have been incurred equally throughout the month.

Master Budget: A Master Budget is a summary of all the functional budgets. It is defined as the Summary Budget, incorporating its components functional budgets, which is finally approved, adopted and employed. When the Master Budget is complete, its details shall be considered by the Budget Committee and if approved, it will be submitted to the Board of Directors. However, once it is finally approved, it becomes the target for the organisation during the budget period.

The master budget is usually prepared in the form of a Budgeted Profit and Loss Statement. It begins with the sales budget figures, from which Production Cost Budget figures and overheads are deducted in order to arrive at the figure of budgeted profit.

Illustration 9

Glass manufacturing company requires you to calculate and present the budget for the next year from the following information:

Sales:	Toughened glass	Rs. 3,00,000
	Bent Toughened glass	Rs. 5,00,000
	Direct Material cost	60% of sales
	Direct wages	20 workers @ Rs. 150 p.m.
	Factory Overheads	
	Indirect Labour:	
	Works Manager	Rs. 500 p.m.
	Foreman	Rs. 400 p.m.
	Stores and spares	$2\frac{1}{2}\%$ on sales
	Depreciation on Machines	Rs. 12,600
	Light and Power	Rs. 5,000
	Repairs etc.	Rs. 8,000
	Other Sundries	10% of direct wages

Administration, Selling and Distribution expenses Rs. 14,000 per year

(*C.A. Inter*)

Solution

Master Budget

Period ....

Sales:	Rs.	Rs.
(*i*) Toughened glass	3,00,000	
(*ii*) Bent Toughened glass	5,00,000	8,00,000
Less: **Cost of Production**		
Direct Material (60% of sales)	4,80,000	
Direct wages (20 × 150 × 12)	36,000	
Factory Overheads:		
Works manager's salary	6,000	
Foreman's salary	4,800	
Stores and Spare parts	20,000	
Depreciation on Machines	12,600	
Light and Power	5,000	
Repairs etc.	8,000	
Sundries	3,600	5,76,000
Gross Profit		2,24,000
Less Operating Expenses:		
Administration, Selling and Distribution		14,000
Net Profit before Tax		2,10,000

(B) Classification on the basis of conditions

On the basis of conditions on which they are based, budgets may be divided into:

(*i*) Basic Budgets, and (*ii*) Current Budgets.

Basic budget is a budget which is established for use unaltered over a long period of time while a current budget is one which is established for use over a short period of time and is related to current conditions.

(C) Classification on the basis of period

On the basis of period for which they are prepared, budgets may be divided into:

(*i*) Short Term Budgets and (*ii*) Long Term Budgets.

A short term budget is one which is prepared for a period of one year or less than one year. Such budgets cover those expenses or activities, the trend in which is difficult to be foreseen over longer periods. Cash Budget and Materials Budget are the examples of short term budgets.

A long term budget is that which is prepared for a period longer than a year. Long term budgets normally help in business forecasting and future planning. Capital Expenditure Budget and Research and Development Expenditure Budget are the examples of long term budgets.

(D) Classification on the basis of Activity Levels

On the basis of activity levels or capacity, the budgets may be classified as:

(*i*) Fixed Budgets and (*ii*) Flexible Budgets.

The Institute of Cost and Management Accountants has defined fixed budget as "a budget which is designed to remain unchanged irrespective of the level of activity actually attained." The fixed budget shows an inflexible or rigid plan. There is one set of conditions, one volume of output, and a simple collection of costs and the management expects all conditions etc., to operate without any variation. On the other hand, flexible budget is a budget which is designed to change in accordance with the level of activity actually attained. The figures used in this type of budget are made adaptable to any given set of operating conditions. The compilation of flexible budgets requires the classification of all costs or expenses into fixed, variable and semi-variable. Fixed costs remain fixed or constant at all levels of activity, semi-variable costs vary with different levels of activity while variable costs vary directly in proportion to changes in the volume of output or sales.

Illustration 10

The expenses budgeted for production of 10,000 units in a factory are furnished below:

	Per Unit Rs.
Materials	70
Labour	25
Variable Overheads	20
Fixed Overheads (Rs. 1,00,000)	10
Variable Expenses (Direct)	5
Selling Expenses (10% Fixed)	13
Distribution Expenses (20% Fixed)	7
Administration Expenses (Rs. 50,000)	5
Total Cost of Sale Per unit	155

Prepare a budget for production of–

(*a*) 6,000 units, and

(*b*) 8,000 units.

Assume that administration expenses are rigid at all levels of production.

Solution

Alternative 1 – Traditional Approach
ABC Co. Ltd.
Flexible Budget

Period ....   Budgeted Output:

Particulars	6,000 units	8,000 units	10,000 units
	Rs.	Rs.	Rs.
Materials	4,20,000	5,60,000	7,00,000
Labour	1,50,000	2,00,000	2,50,000
Direct Expenses	30,000	40,000	50,000
Prime Cost	6,00,000	8,00,000	10,00,000
Factory overheads:			
(*i*) Fixed	1,00,000	1,00,000	1,00,000
(*ii*) Variable	1,20,000	1,60,000	2,00,000
Factory cost	8,20,000	10,60,000	13,00,000
Administration overhead (Fixed)	50,000	50,000	50,000
Cost of Production	8,70,000	11,10,000	13,50,000
Selling overhead:			
(*i*) Fixed	13,000	13,000	13,000
(*ii*) Variable	70,200	93,600	1,17,000
Distribution overhead			
(*i*) Fixed	14,000	14,000	14,000
(*ii*) Variable	33,600	44,800	56,000
Total Cost	10,00,800	12,75,400	15,50,000
Cost per unit $\left(\dfrac{\text{Total Cost}}{\text{Budgeted output}}\right)$	166.80	159.425	155.000

Alternative 2 – Marginal Costing Approach
ABC Co. Ltd.
Flexible Budget

Period ....   Budgeted Output:

Particulars	6,000 units	8,000 units	10,000 units
	Rs.	Rs.	Rs.
(A) Variable Costs:			
Materials	4,20,000	5,60,000	7,00,000
Labour	1,50,000	2,00,000	2,50,000
Direct Expenses	30,000	40,000	50,000
Factory overhead	1,20,000	1,60,000	2,00,000
Selling overhead	70,200	93,600	1,17,000
Distribution overhead	33,600	44,800	56,000
Total Variable Costs	8,23,800	10,98,400	13,73,000
(B) Fixed Costs:			
Factory overhead	1,00,000	1,00,000	1,00,000
Administration overhead	50,000	50,000	50,000
Selling overhead	13,000	13,000	13,000
Distribution overhead	14,000	14,000	14,000
Total Fixed Costs	1,77,000	1,77,000	1,77,000
Total Cost (A) + (B)	10,00,800	12,75,400	15,50,000
Cost per unit $\left(\dfrac{\text{Total Cost}}{\text{Budgeted output}}\right)$	166.80	159.425	155.00

Illustration 11

The cost of an article 'X' at a capacity level of 5,000 units is given under 'A' below. For a variation of 25% in capacity above or below this level, the individual expenses vary as under 'B' below:

	A	B
	Rs.	
Material cost	25,000	100% varying
Labour cost	15,000	100% varying
Power	1,250	80% varying
Repairs and Maintenance	2,000	75% varying
Stores	1,000	100% varying
Inspection	500	20% varying
Depreciation	10,000	100% varying
Administration overheads	5,000	25% varying
Selling overheads	3,000	50% varying
Total	62,750	

Find out the cost of the product at production levels of 4,000 units and 6,000 units.

(G.N.D.U., B.Com. Hons., 1998)

Solution

Flexible Budget

Period ....

Particulars	Budgeted Production: 5,000 units	4,000 units	6,000 units
	Rs.	Rs.	Rs.
Materials	25,000	20,000	30,000
Labour	15,000	12,000	18,000
Prime Cost	40,000	32,000	48,000
Factory Overhead:			
Power:			
Fixed	250	250	250
Variable	1,000	800	1,200
Repairs and maintenance:			
Fixed	500	500	500
Variable	1,500	1,200	1,800
Stores (Variable)	1,000	800	1,200
Inspection:			
Fixed	400	400	400
Variable	100	80	120
Depreciation (Variable)	10,000	8,000	12,000
Factory Cost	54,750	44,030	65,470
Administrative Overheads			
Fixed	3,750	3,750	3,750
Variable	1,250	1,000	1,500
Cost of Production	59,750	48,780	70,720
Selling Overheads:			
Fixed	1,500	1,500	1,500
Variable	1,500	1,200	1,800
Total Cost	62,750	51,480	74,020
Cost per unit	12.55	12.87	12.34

Illustration 12

Monu Products Ltd., produce a standard product. The estimated costs per unit are given below:

	Rs.
Raw Material	10
Direct Wages	8
Direct Expenses	2
Variable Overheads	3
	23

Semi-variable overheads at 100% activity level (10,000 units) are expected to be Rs. 40,000 and these overheads vary in steps of Rs. 2,000 for each change in output of 1,000 units. Fixed overheads are estimated at Rs. 50,000. Selling price per unit is expected to be Rs. 40.

Prepare a flexible budget at 50%, 70% and 90% level of activity.

Solution

Flexible Budget

Period ....

Normal Activity Level
100% (10,000 units)
Budgeted Production

Capacity Units	100% 10,000	50% 5,000	70% 7,000	90% 9,000
	Rs.	Rs.	Rs.	Rs.
Direct Materials	1,00,000	50,000	70,000	90,000
Direct Wages	80,000	40,000	56,000	72,000
Direct Expenses	20,000	10,000	14,000	18,000
Prime Cost	2,00,000	1,00,000	1,40,000	1,80,000
Overheads:				
Fixed	50,000	50,000	50,000	50,000
Variable	30,000	15,000	21,000	27,000
Semi-Variable	40,000	30,000	34,000	38,000
Total Cost	3,20,000	1,95,000	2,45,000	2,95,000
Profit	80,000	5,000	35,000	65,000
Sales	4,00,000	2,00,000	2,80,000	3,60,000
Cost per unit	32.00	39.00	35.00	32.78
Profit per unit	8.00	1.00	5.00	7.22

Illustration 13

The following data are available in a manufacturing concern for the year 2007-08:

Fixed Expenses:	Rs. (in Lakhs)
Wages and Salaries	8.4
Rent Rates and Taxes	5.6
Depreciation	7.0
Sundry Administrative Expenses	8.9
	29.9

Semi-variable Expenses:	
(at 50% Capacity)	
Maintenance and Repairs	2.5
Indirect Labour	9.9
Salaries of Sales Dept.	2.9
Sundry Administrative Expenses	2.6
	17.9
Variable Expenses:	
(at 50% Capacity)	
Materials	24.0
Labour	25.6
Other Expenses	3.8
	53.4

Assume that fixed expenses remain constant for all levels of production, semi-variable expenses remain constant between 45% and 65% of capacity, increasing by 10% between 65% and 80% capacity and by 20% between 80% and 100% capacity.

Sales at various levels are:

	Rs. (in Lakhs)
60%	100.00
75%	120.00
90%	150.00
100%	170.00

Prepare a flexible budget for the year and forecast the profits at 60%, 75%, 90% and 100% of capacity.

Solution

Flexible Budget

Period .... Capacity Level

Particulars	50% Rs. (Lakhs)	60% Rs. (Lakhs)	75% Rs. (Lakhs)	90% Rs. (Lakhs)	100% Rs. (Lakhs)
Fixed Expenses:					
Wages and Salaries	8.4	8.4	8.4	8.4	8.4
Rent, Rates & Taxes	5.6	5.6	5.6	5.6	5.6
Depreciation	7.0	7.0	7.0	7.0	7.0
Sundry Administrative Expenses	8.9	8.9	8.9	8.9	8.9
	29.9	29.9	29.9	29.9	29.9
Variable Expenses:					
Materials	24.0	28.8	36.0	43.2	48.0
Labour	25.6	30.72	38.4	46.08	51.2
Other Expenses	3.8	4.56	5.7	6.84	7.6
	53.4	64.08	80.1	96.12	106.8
Semi-variable Expenses:					
Maintenance and Repairs	2.5	2.5	2.75	3.0	3.0
Indirect Labour	9.9	9.9	10.89	11.88	11.88
Salaries of Sales Department	2.9	2.9	3.19	3.48	3.48
Sundry Administrative Expenses	2.6	2.6	2.86	3.12	3.12
	17.9	17.9	19.69	21.48	21.48
Total Cost	101.2	111.88	129.69	147.50	158.18
Sales Forecast	–	100.00	120.00	150.0	170.00
Profit/Loss	–	11.88 (Loss)	9.69 (Loss)	2.5 (Profit)	11.82 (Profit)

Illustration 14

A company produces a standard product. The estimated costs per unit are as follows:

Raw Materials Rs. 4; Direct labour Rs. 2; Variable overheads Rs. 5.

The semi-variable costs are: Indirect Materials Rs. 235; Indirect Labour Rs. 156; Maintenance and Repairs Rs. 570. The variable costs per unit included in semi-variables are: Indirect Materials Re. 0.05; Indirect Labour Re. 0.08; Maintenance and Repairs Re. 0.10.

The fixed costs are:

Factory Rs. 2,000; Administration Rs. 3,000;
Selling and Distribution Rs. 2,500.

The above costs are for 70% of normal capacity producing 700 units. The selling price is Rs. 30 per unit. Prepare Flexible Budget for 60%, 80% and 100% normal capacities with the help of above.

(G.N.D.U., B.Com., 1982)

Solution

Analysis of Semi-Variable Costs at 70% Capacity

	Indirect Materials	Indirect Labour	Maintenance & Repairs
	Rs.	Rs.	Rs.
Total Cost	235.00	156.00	570.00
Less: Variable portion	35.00 (700 × 0.05)	56.00 (700 × 0.08)	70.00 (700 × 0.10)
Fixed portion	200.00	100.00	500.00

ABC Co. Ltd.
Flexible Budget

Period .... **Capacity:**

Particulars	60%	70%	80%	100%
	600 units	700 units	800 units	1,000 units
	Rs.	Rs.	Rs.	Rs.
Variable Costs:				
Raw Materials	2,400	2,800	3,200	4,000
Direct Wages	1,200	1,400	1,600	2,000
Variable Overheads	3,000	3,500	4,000	5,000
Indirect Materials @ Re. 0.05 per unit	30	35	40	50
Indirect Labour @ Re. 0.08 per unit	48	56	64	80
Maintenance and Repairs @ Re. 0.10 per unit	60	70	80	100
(A) Total Variable Cost	6,738	7,861	8,984	11,230
Fixed Costs:				
Factory Expenses	2,000	2,000	2,000	2,000
Administration Expenses	3,000	3,000	3,000	3,000
Selling and Distribution Expenses	2,500	2,500	2,500	2,500
Indirect Materials	200	200	200	200
Indirect Labour	100	100	100	100
Maintenance and Repairs	500	500	500	500
(B) Total Fixed Costs	8,300	8,300	8,300	8,300
Total Cost (A) + (B)	15,038	16,161	17,284	19,530
Profit	2,962	4,839	6,716	10,470
Sales @ Rs. 30 per unit	18,000	21,000	24,000	30,000

Illustration 15

The operating results of GOE Ltd., for the year ending 31st March, 2009 are summarised below:

	Rs. in lakhs
Sales – 40,000 units	48.00
Less: Trade discount	2.40
Net sales:	45.60
Cost of sales:	
Direct materials	14.40
Direct labour	12.60
Factory overheads	6.30
Administration overheads	3.60
Selling and distribution overheads	4.50

The following changes are to be incorporated in the budget for the year 2009-10:

(*a*) Sales (units) to be increased by 25%;
(*b*) Material price to increase by 15%;
(*c*) Direct wages to go up by 12%;
(*d*) Overheads – Factory overheads will increase by 15%. In addition, a new facility will be added to the factory laboratory at a recurring cost of Rs. 12,500 per year. Administrative and selling and distribution overheads are estimated to increase by 10% and 14% respectively;
(*e*) Inventory – no change;
(*f*) Profit target for the year has been fixed at Rs. 6 lakhs; and
(*g*) No change in the rate of trade discount.

Calculate the unit selling price and present the budget for 2009-10 in a meaningful format.

(*I.C.W.A. Inter, Dec. 1995*)

Solution

Budget for the year 2009-10

	(Fig in Rs. lakhs) Year 2009-10 (50,000 units)	Year 2008-09 (40,000 units)
Sales	64.00	48.00
Less: Trade discount	3.20	2.40
(A) Net Sales	60.80	45.60
Cost of sales:		
Direct materials	20.70	14.40
Direct labour	17.64	12.60
Factory overhead	7.37	6.30
Adm. overhead	3.96	3.60
Selling and dist. overhead	5.13	4.50
(B) Total Cost	54.80	41.40
Profit (A – B)	6.00	4.20

$$\text{Unit Selling Price} = \frac{\text{Rs. } 64{,}00{,}000}{50{,}000 \text{ units}} = \text{Rs. } 128$$

Working Notes:

For the year 2009-10, figures are calculated as follows:

1. Sales units = 40,000 × 125% = 50,000 units
2. Material cost = 14.40 × 1.15 × 125% = Rs. 20.70
3. Labour cost = 12.60 × 1.12 × 125% = Rs. 17.64
4. Factory overhead = (6.30 × 1. 15) + 0.125 = Rs..7.37
5. Adm. overhead 3.60 × 110% = Rs. 3.96
6. Selling and Distribution overhead 4.50 × 114% = Rs. 5.13

Illustration 16

Viveka Elementary School has a total of 150 students consisting of 5 sections with 30 students per section. The school plans for a picnic around the city during the week-end to places such as the zoo, the amusement park, the planetarium etc. A private transport operator has come forward to lease out the buses for taking the students. Each bus will have a maximum capacity of 50 (excluding 2 seats reserved for the teachers accompanying the students). The school will employ two teachers for each bus, paying them an allowance of Rs. 50 per teacher. It will also lease out the required number of buses. The following are the other cost estimates:

	Cost per student Rs.
Breakfast	5
Lunch	10
Tea	3
Entrance fee at zoo	2

Rent Rs. 650 per bus.

Special Permit Fee Rs. 50 per bus.

Block Entrance Fee at the Planetarium Rs. 250.

Prizes to students for games Rs. 250

No costs are incurred in respect of the accompanying teachers (except the allowance of Rs. 50 per teacher).

You are required to prepare:

(*a*) A flexible budget estimating the total cost for the levels of 30, 60, 90 120 and 150 students. Each item of cost is to be indicated separately.

(*b*) Compare the average cost per student at these levels.

(*c*) What will be your conclusions regarding the break-even level of students if the school proposes to collect Rs. 45 per student?

Solution

Flexible Budget to Estimate Total Cost

No. of students	30	60	90	120	150
	Rs.	Rs.	Rs.	Rs.	Rs.
Variable Costs:					
Breakfast	150	300	450	600	750
Lunch	300	600	900	1,200	1,500
Tea	90	180	270	360	450
Entrance fee at zoo	60	120	180	240	300
	600	1,200	1,800	2,400	3,000
Semi-fixed Costs:					
Rent of bus	650	1,300	1,300	1,950	1,950
Permit fee	50	100	100	150	150
Allowance to teachers	100	200	200	300	300
	800	1,600	1,600	2,400	2,400
Fixed Costs:					
Block Entrance fee at Pl.	250	250	250	250	250
Prizes to students for games	250	250	250	250	250
	500	500	500	500	500
Total Cost	1,900	3,300	3,900	5,300	5,900
(*b*) Average Cost per Student	Rs. 1,900 / 30 = Rs.63.33	Rs. 3,300 / 60 = Rs.55	Rs. 3,900 / 90 = Rs.43.33	Rs. 5,300 / 120 = Rs.44.17	Rs. 5,900 / 150 = Rs.39.33

(*c*) Break-even Level

	Rs.
Collection per student	45
Variable cost per student	20
Contribution per student.	25

Since the semi-fixed cost changes for every 50 students, fixed costs + semi-fixed costs for three level of students to be covered are:

Level	Upto 50	51 to 100	101 to 150
	Rs.	Rs.	Rs.
Fixed costs (including semi-fixed costs)	1,300	2,100	2,900
Contribution per student	25	25	25
Break-even point (No. of students to recover fixed costs including semi-fixed costs)	$\frac{\text{Rs.}1,300}{25}$ = 52	$\frac{\text{Rs. }2,100}{25}$ = 84	$\frac{2,900}{25}$ = 116

The number of students required to recover fixed costs at levels upto 50, 51 to 100 and 101 to 150 are 52, 84 and 116 respectively. The figure of 52 students lies outside the first level i.e., upto 50, but the remaining figures 84 and 116 are within their prescribed levels. Therefore, 84 and 116 students represent two break-even points.

Illustration 17

Draw up a flexible budget for overhead expenses on the basis of the following data and determine the overhead rates at 70%, 80% and 90% plant capacity.

	At 70% Capacity Rs.	At 80% Capacity Rs.	At 90% Capacity Rs.
Variable overheads:			
Indirect Labour	–	12,000	–
Stores including spares	–	4,000	–
Semi-variable overheads:			
Power (30% fixed, 70% variable)	–	20,000	–
Repairs and maintenance (60% fixed, 40% variable)	–	2,000	–
Fixed overheads:			
Depreciation	–	11,000	–
Insurance	–	3,000	–
Salaries	–	10,000	–
Total overheads	–	62,000	–
Estimated direct labour hours	–	1,24,000 Hours	–

(*I.C.W.A. Inter*)

Solution

Flexible Budget

Period ....

Capacity	70%	80%	90%
Variable Overheads:	Rs.	Rs.	Rs.
Indirect Labour	10,500	12,000	13,500
Stores including Spares	3,500	4,000	4,500
Semi-variable Overheads:			
Power:			
Fixed	6,000	6,000	6,000
Variable	12,250	14,000	15,750
Repairs and Maintenance:			
Fixed	1,200	1,200	1,200
Variable	700	800	900
Fixed Overheads:			
Depreciation	11,000	11,000	11,000
Insurance	3,000	3,000	3,000
Salaries	10,000	10,000	10,000
Total overheads	58,150	62,000	65,850
Estimated direct labour hours	1,08,500 Hrs.	1,24,000 Hrs.	1,39,500 Hrs.
Direct Labour Hour Rate $\left(\frac{\text{Total Overheads}}{\text{Direct Labour Hours}}\right)$	$\frac{58,150}{1,08,500}$ = Rs. 0.536	$\frac{62,000}{1,24,000}$ = Rs. 0.50	$\frac{65,850}{1,39,500}$ = Rs. 0.472

Illustration 18

Assuming the following overhead expenses in a factory when operating at 50% of normal capacity, draw up a flexible budget of the factory for operating at 75%, 100% and 125% of normal capacity.

Indicate the basis upon which you have estimated each item of expense for the different operating levels.

	Rs.
Foreman's Salary	1,200
Assistant Foreman's Salary	800
Inspector's Salary	1,300
Shop Labourers' Wages	800
Machinery Repairs	2,000
Defective work	500
Consumable Stores	400
Machine Depreciation	2,200
	9,200

Solution

Items	Capacity				Basis of Revision, if any
	50%	75%	100%	125%	
	Rs.	Rs.	Rs.	Rs.	
Foreman's Salary	1,200	1,200	1,200	1,200	It will remain fixed at all capacity levels.
Assistant Foreman's Salary	800	1,200	1,200	1,600	Additional supervision will be necessary with rising levels of activity (Semi-variable).
Inspector's Salary	1,300	1,800	2,400	2,800	Inspection cost will rise with activity levels (Semi-variable).
Shop Labourers' Wages	800	1,200	1,600	2,000	It will increase directly with production (Variable).
Machine Repairs	2,000	3,000	4,000	5,500	Machine repairs cost will rise with capacity levels (and more than proportionately if 100% capacity is exceeded) (Semi-variable).
Defective Work	500	800	1,200	1,600	Defective work shall increase more than proportionately on account of fatigue.
Consumable Stores	400	600	800	1,000	It is an item of variable cost.
Machine Depreciation	2,200	2,800	3,100	4,000	Depreciation is an item of semi-variable cost but excess provision shall have to be made over 100% capacity on account of excessive wear and tear.
Total Cost	9,200	12,600	15,500	19,700	

CONTROL RATIOS

Under the system of budgetary control, the actual performances are compared with budgeted performances so as to determine the deviations or variances. The deviations or variances may be favourable or unfavourable and may be expressed in terms of absolute figures or in terms of ratios. The ratios in terms of which the deviations or variances are expressed, are known as Control Ratios. These Control Ratios are:

(*i*) Capacity Ratio (*ii*) Activity Ratio (*iii*) Efficiency Ratio.

Capacity Ratio: It is also known as Actual Usage of Budgeted Capacity Ratio. It denotes the relationship between the actual number of working hours and the budgeted number of working hours. This ratio indicates the extent to which the available facilities were actually utilised during the budget period. Capacity Ratio may be expressed or calculated as follows:

$$\text{Capacity Ratio} = \frac{\text{Actual Hours}}{\text{Budgeted Hours}} \times 100$$

Activity Ratio: Activity Ratio is the number of standard hours equivalent to the work produced, expressed as a percentage of the budgeted standard hours. This ratio measures the level of activity at which a business concern is operating and may be expressed as follows:

$$\text{Activity Ratio} = \frac{\text{Actual Production in terms of Standard Hours}}{\text{Budgeted Production in terms of Standard Hours}} \times 100$$

Efficiency Ratio: Efficiency Ratio is the number of standard hours equivalent to the work produced, expressed as a percentage of the actual hours spent in producing that work. This ratio measures the efficiency of the operation of the firm and may be expressed as follows:

$$\text{Efficiency Ratio} = \frac{\text{Actual Production in terms of Standard Hours}}{\text{Actual Hours worked}} \times 100$$

Interpretation of the Results of Control Ratios: The results of control ratios may be interpreted as follows:

	Result	**Interpretation**
(*i*)	100%	No deviation
(*ii*)	Above 100%	Favourable deviation
(*iii*)	Below 100%	Unfavourable deviation

Illustration 19

Product X takes 5 hours to make and Y requires 10 hours. In a month of 25 effective days of 8 hours a day, 1,000 units of X and 600 units of Y were produced. The company employs 50 workers in the production department. The budgeted hours are 1,02,000 for the year. Calculate Capacity Ratio, Activity Ratio and Efficiency Ratio.

(*Punjabi University, B.Com.*)

Solution

Given: Budgeted hours for the year = 1,02,000 hrs.

Budgeted hours for the month $= \frac{1{,}02\ 000}{12} = 8{,}500$ hours.

Actual hours worked = 10,000 hrs
(50 workers × 25 days × 8 hours per day)

Standard hours for Actual output

(*i*) Hours allowed for 1,000 units of Product 'X' (1,000 units × 5 hrs) = 5,000

(*ii*) Hours allowed for 600 units of Product Y (600 units × 10 hrs) = 6,000

11,000

(*a*) $\text{Capacity Ratio} = \frac{\text{Actual Hours}}{\text{Budgeted Hours}} \times 100$

$= \frac{10{,}000 \text{ hrs.}}{8{,}500 \text{ hrs.}} \times 100$

$= 117.65\%$

(*b*) $\text{Activity Ratio} = \frac{\text{Actual Production in terms of standard hours}}{\text{Budgeted Production in terms of standard hours}} \times 100$

$= \frac{11{,}000}{8{,}500} \times 100 = 129.41\%$

(*c*) $\text{Efficiency Ratio} = \frac{\text{Actual Production in terms of standard hours}}{\text{Actual Hours worked}} \times 100$

$= \frac{11{,}000}{10{,}000} \times 100 = 110\%$

Illustration 20

A factory produces two products 'X' and 'Y'. Standard time to manufacture product 'X' is 2 hours and product 'Y' 10 hours. The budgeted and actual production in December, 2009 were as follows:

	Budgeted Production	Actual Production
Product 'X'	250 units	200 units
Product 'Y'	60 units	48 units

Total actual hours worked were 1,320. Compute the Capacity Ratio, Efficiency Ratio and Activity Ratio.

Solution

(*i*) Standard hours produced (or actual production in terms of standard hours)–

Product X : 200 units × 2 Hrs. = 400 Hrs.

Product Y : 48 units × 10 Hrs. = 480 Hrs.

880 Hrs.

(*ii*) Standard Hours budgeted (or budgeted production in terms of standard hours)–

Product X : 250 units × 2 Hrs = 500 Hrs.

Product Y : 60 units × 10 Hrs. = 600 Hrs.

1,100 Hrs.

(*iii*) Actual Hours worked: 1,320 Hrs.

$$\text{Capacity Ratio} = \frac{\text{Actual Hours}}{\text{Budgeted Hours}} \times 100$$

$$= \frac{1{,}320}{1{,}100} \times 100 = 120\%$$

$$\text{Efficiency Ratio} = \frac{\text{Actual Production in terms of Standard Hours}}{\text{Actual Hours worked}} \times 100$$

$$= \frac{880}{1{,}320} \times 100 = 66.67\%$$

$$\text{Activity Ratio} = \frac{\text{Actual Production in terms of standard hours}}{\text{Budgeted Production in terms of standard hours}} \times 100$$

$$= \frac{880}{1{,}100} \times 100 = 80\%$$

Alternatively:

Capacity Ratio × Efficiency Ratio = Activity Ratio

120% × 66.67% = 80%

ZERO-BASE BUDGETING (Z.B.B.)

Under traditional budgeting, functional budgets are prepared on the basis of previous year's budgets. For the purpose of budgeting, previous year's figures are taken as 'Base', to which necessary adjustments are made for impact of inflation, proposed increase in the level of activity, expected increase in the resources and past experience. As such budget figures are generally obtained by adding some percentage to the expenditure of the previous year. The Budget Committee and top management also accept and approve the budget figures obtained by the above method and practically no enquiry is made into the justification of the base figures. In Government Departments and public enterprises particularly, there is a feeling that the actual expenditure should be in line with budgeted figures. In case the actual expenditure is less than the budgeted figures, the budget allocation for the next year shall be reduced by higher authorities. In order to ensure that the future allocation is atleast at the previous year's level, the person incharge of the expenditure, spends the whole amount without going into its desirability and justification. Thus, traditional budgeting is considered to be of no value if the management wants to review and re-evaluate every task with a view to ensure better performance and efficient utilisation of scarce resources. In such a case, Zero-base Budgeting may provide a solution.

Concept of Zero-base Budgeting

The concept of zero-base budgeting is of recent origin and was originally developed by Peter A. Pyhrr in Texas Instruments of U.S.A. and later on introduced by Ex-President Jimmy Carter of U.S.A., then Governor of the State of Georgia, as a means of controlling state expenditure. Peter A. Pyhrr has defined zero-base budgeting as "an operating planning and budgeting process, which requires each manager to justify his entire budget request in detail from scratch (hence zero base) and shifts the burden of proof to each manager to justify why he should spend any money at all." The 'zero-base' refers to a `nil budget' as the starting point. As an activity is budgeted, costs are objectively budgeted. It starts with the premise that the budget for the next period is `zero' so long as the demand for a function, process, project or activity is not justified. The assumption is that without such justification no spending will be allowed. Each manager is responsible to justify why the money should be spent at all and to explain in detail as to what would happen if the proposed activity is not carried out and no money is spent. Thus, each manager or functional head in the organisation, is required to make cost-benefit-analysis of each of the activities or projects under his control and for which he is responsible. Hence, 'Zero-base Budgeting' is a resource planning and re-deployment process rather than a cost reduction control. The process of zero-base budgeting:

(*i*) deals with all aspects of budget requests of managers;

(*ii*) reviews both existing and newly proposed activities critically;

(*iii*) sets priorities in respect of different activities and re-deploys the resources accordingly.

Areas where zero-base budgeting is applicable

Zero-base Budgeting is more suitably applicable to discretionary cost areas. These costs may have no relation to volume or activity and generally arise as a result of management policies. Where standards are determinable, those costs associated with the inputs should be controlled through the use of standard costing. On the other hand, if output as a function of input cannot be specified, Zero-base Budgeting may be more suitably applied. Thus, service or support-type activities are more suitable for Z.B.B.

PROCESS OF ZERO-BASE BUDGETING OR STEPS INVOLVED IN ZERO-BASE BUDGETING

The process of Zero-Base Budgeting involves the following steps:

(*i*) Identification of 'Decision units.'

(*ii*) Preparation and development of decision packages.

(*iii*) Ranking of priority.

(*iv*) Approval and Funding.

Identification of Decision Unit: A decision unit refers to a tangible activity or group of activities for which a single manager has the responsibility for successful performance. Thus, decision unit is a programme or a project or a segment of the organisation for which separate budgets are to be prepared.

Preparation of Decision Packages: Preparation of decision packages is a set of documents which identify and describe activities of the unit in such a way that the management can evaluate and rank them against others competing for resources (limited) and decide whether to approve or disapprove.

Ranking of Priority: The third step involved in Z.B.B. is the ranking of proposed alternatives included in decision packages for various decision units or of various decision packages for the same decision unit.

Funding: Funding involves the allocation of available resources of the organisation to various decision units keeping in mind the alternative which has been selected and approved through ranking process.

Advantages of Zero-Base Budgeting: The main advantages of zero-base budgeting are as follows:

(*i*) Z.B.B. ensures more careful planning before the preparation of the budget itself.

(*ii*) The involvement of lower and middle level management in the budgeting process is increased.

(*iii*) It ensures the optimum utilisation of financial resources since allocation is made on the basis of ranking with reference to cost-benefit-analysis.

(*iv*) It provides for eliminating all types of wastages and inefficiency leading to reduction in cost.

(*v*) It provides the management with significant data base and may be helpful to operational audit. Thus it ensures higher organisational efficiency and effectiveness.

OBJECTIVE TYPE QUESTIONS

A. Multiple Choice Questions.

Select the correct answer.

(*a*) A budget is expressed in
   (*i*) financial terms only
   (*ii*) quantitative terms only
   (*iii*) both financial and quantitative terms
   (*iv*) financial and/or quantitative terms.

(*b*) Which of the following budgets is usually prepared for a long period of time:
   (*i*) Production Budget
   (*ii*) Materials Purchase Budget
   (*iii*) Cash Budget
   (*iv*) Capital Expenditure Budget

(*c*) A flexible budget takes into account:
   (*i*) fixed costs only
   (*ii*) variable costs only
   (*iii*) semi-variable costs only
   (*iv*) fixed, variable and semi-variable costs.

(*d*) Master Budget denotes the summary of:
   (*i*) Cash Budget
   (*ii*) Sales Budget
   (*iii*) Sales and Production Budgets
   (*iv*) all functional budgets.

(*e*) A budget is prepared for:
   (*i*) one year
   (*ii*) five years
   (*iii*) a specified period
   (*iv*) one month.

[**Ans.** (*a*) (*iv*), (*b*) (*iv*), (*c*) (*iv*), (*d*) (*iv*), (*e*) (*iii*)]

B. True/False Type Questions.

State whether the following statements are 'True' or 'False'.

(*a*) A budget manual is a summary of all functional budgets.

(*b*) A budget is presented in financial and/or quantitative terms.

(*c*) The Master Budget is prepared first and all other budgets are sub-ordinate to it.

(*d*) The key factors should not be taken into account while preparing budgets.

(e) A system of budgetary control can be used even when standard costing is not in use in a manufacturing concern.

[**Ans.** (*a*) False (*b*) True (*c*) False (*d*) False (*e*) True]

C. Filling the blanks.

Fill in the blanks.

(*a*) The budget for .... is prepared first and all other budgets are sub-ordinate to it.

(*b*) .... is the summary of all the functional budgets.

(*c*) .... shows the expected sources and utilisation of cash.

(*d*) For preparing flexible budget, all costs are classified into ....

(*e*) A .... budget is prepared for more than one levels of activity.

[**Ans.** (*a*) Principal key Factor (*b*) Master Budget (*c*) Cash Budget (*d*) Fixed, variable and semi-variable (*e*) Flexible]

SHORT ANSWER TYPE QUESTIONS

1. What is a budget?

2. Explain Sales Budget. (*G.N.D.U., B.Com, 1996, 1997*)

3. Define Materials Budget. (*G. N.D.U., B.Com, 1995*)

4. Define Overheads Budget. (*G.N.D.U., B.Com., 1995*)

5. What is Budget Period?

6. What is Budget Factor'?

7. What is a Master Budget?

8. What is meant by Budget Manual?

9. What is a flexible budget?

10. What is Budgetary Control?

11. Define 'Budgeting'.

12. Discuss the meaning of Cash Budget.

13. What is meant by Control Ratios?

14. What is meant by Budget Committee?

LONG ANSWER TYPE QUESTIONS

1. Explain the various types of budgets. (*G.N.D.U., B.Com., 1996, 1997*)

2. What is Budgetary Control? Discuss its main objectives.
(*C.A. Inter, G.N.D.U., B.Com., 1990*)

3. Write an essay on Budgetary Control System. (*Punjab, B.Com., 1977*)
4. Define 'budget' & 'budgetary control'. State the advantages of budgetary control in an organisation.
5. Discuss briefly the objectives and limitations of budgetary control.
6. Describe briefly the fundamental functions of business budgets.
7. Define budgetary control and discuss the objectives of introducing a budgetary control in an organisation. (*G.N.D.U., B.Com., 1995*)
8. Define budgetary control. State its objectives. Explain the process by which the various budgets are prepared.
9. What do you think are the essentials of an effective budgetary control system.
10. What do you understand by budgetary control? Discuss briefly some of the problems encountered in operating any scheme of budgetary control.
11. A budget has been defined as "a financial or quantitative interpretation prior to a defined period of time, of policy to be pursued for that period to attain a given objective." Bring out, from the above definition, the essentials of budget.
12. What do you understand by budgetary control? State its advantages in a large manufacturing concern.
13. Define and explain briefly what do you understand by the following: (*a*) Sales budget (*b*) Materials budget (*c*) Labour budget (*d*) Overhead budget.
14. Distinguish between:
    (*i*) Budgeting and Budgetary control (*ii*) Budgets and forecasts
    (*iii*) Fixed and Flexible budgets.
15. Describe briefly objectives and limitations of 'Budgetary Control'.
16. What is 'Budgetary control' and how is it exercised? Discuss various advantages and essentials for the success of budgetary control.
17. What do you mean and understand by flexible budget? How is it prepared?
18. Define and explain the term 'Flexible budget'. How is flexible budget constructed and what difficulties would you expect in its compilation? Explain the usefulness of a flexible budget to management.
19. What are functional budgets? Which are the fundamental budgets most commonly used by management?
20. Write notes on
    (*a*) Budget period (*c*) Budget Manual
    (*b*) Key factor (*d*) Zero-base budgeting
21. Give advantages of Budgetary control. (*G.N.D.U. B.Com., 2008*)

EXERCISES

1. Prepare a Production Budget of the Dixcy Enterprises Ltd., from the following particulars:

Product	Budgeted Sales (units)	Estimated stocks (units) Jan. 1	Dec. 31
A-1	50,000	3,000	3,500
A-2	30,000	1,500	1,200
A-3	8,000	80	70

[**Ans.** 50,500 units ; 29,700 units ; 7,990 units]

2. M/s Manubhai & Sons make their products by using single raw materials. Each unit of product consumes 2 kgs. of the raw materials. The price of the raw material is Rs. 12.50 per kg. The following additional information is also given:

Production Schedule:

April, 2009	... 20,000 units.
May, 2009	... 20,500 units
June, 2009	... 22,000 units

Closing inventory of raw materials required:

On March 31, 2009	... 5,000 kgs.
On April, 30, 2009	... 6,000 kgs.
On May 31, 2009	... 7,000 kgs.
On June 30, 2009	... 8,000 kgs.

Prepare Materials Purchase Budget for the quarter ended June 30, 2009. Give physical quantity as well as monetary outlays.

[**Ans.** Quantity, 41,000 kgs; 42,000 kgs; 45,000 kgs.
Amount Rs. 5,12,500; Rs. 5,25,000; Rs. 5,62,500]

[**Hint:** Quantity to be purchased
= Quantity required + Closing inventory – Opening inventory]

3. Shangrila Food Products Limited has prepared the following Sales Budget for the first five months of 2002:

	Sales Budget (in units)
January	10,800
February	15,600
March	12,200
April	10,400
May	9,800

The inventory of finished products at the end of every month is to be equal to 25 per cent of the sales estimate for the next month. On 1 January 2002, there were 2,700 units of product on hand. There is no work-in-progress at the end of any month.

Every unit of product requires two types of materials in the following quantities:

Material A	–	4 kg.
Material B	–	5 kg.

Materials equal to one-half of the next month's production are to be in hand at the end of every month. This requirement was met on 1 January 2002.

Budgeted prices for the purchase of materials are:

Material A – Rs. 3 per kg. Material B – Rs. 2 per kg.

Prepare a Materials Budget for the first quarter of 2002 in a logical form showing the quantities of each type of material to be purchased every month. Also prepare a Purchase Budget.

(I.C.W.A. Inter, B.Com. Hons. Delhi, 1999, Adapted)

[**Ans.**

	Material Budget		**Purchases Budget**	
	A	**B**	**A**	**B**
Jan	53,500 Kgs.	66,875 Kgs.	Rs. 1,60,500	Rs. 1,33,750
Feb	53,000 Kgs.	66,250 Kgs.	Rs. 1,59,000	Rs. 1,32,500
March	44,000 Kgs.	55,000 Kgs.	Rs. 1,32,000	Rs. 1,10,000]

4. The following are the estimated sales of a company for eight months ending 30.11.2002:

Months	**Estimated Sales (units)**
April, 2002	12,000
May, 2002	13,000
June, 2002	9,000
July, 2002	8,000
August, 2002	10,000
September, 2002	12,000
October, 2002	14,000
November, 2002	12,000

As a matter of policy, the company maintains the closing balance of finished goods and raw materials as follows:

Stock item	**Closing balance of a month**
Finished goods	50% of the estimated sales for the next month.
Raw materials	Estimated consumption for the next month.

Every unit of production requires 2 kgs. of raw material costing Rs. 5 per kg. Prepare Production Budget (in units) and Raw Material Purchase Budget (in units and cost) of the company for the half year ending 30th September, 2002. *(I.C.W.A. Inter., June, 1999)*

[**Ans.**

	April	**May**	**June**	**July**	**Aug.**	**Sep.**
Production Budget (Units)	12,500	11,000	8,500	9,000	11,000	13,000
Purchase Budget (Rs.)	1,10,000	85,000	90,000	1,10,000	1,30,000	1,30,000]

5. P. Ltd. manufactures two products using one type of material and one grade of labour. Shown below is an extract from the company's working papers for the next period's budget:

	Product A	**Product B**
Budgeted sales (units)	3,600	4,800
Budgeted material consumption, per product (kg.)	5	5
Budgeted material cost Rs. 12 per kg.		
Standard hours allowed per product	5	4
Budgeted wage rate Rs. 8 per hour		

Overtime premium is 50% and is payable if a worker works for more than 40 hours a week. There are 90 direct workers.

The target productivity ratio (or efficiency ratio) for the productive hours worked by the direct workers in actually manufacturing the products is 80%; in addition, the non-productive downtime is budgeted at 20% of the productive hours worked.

There are twelve 5 day weeks in the budget period and it is anticipated that sales and production will occur evenly throughout the whole period.

It is anticipated that stock at the beginning of the period will be: Product A 1,020 units; Product B 2,400 units; Raw material 4,300 kgs.

The target closing stock, expressed in terms of anticipated activity during the budget period are: Product A 15 days sales; Product B 20 days sales; Raw material 10 days consumption.

Required: Calculate the Material Purchases Budget and the Wages Budget for the direct workers, showing the quantities and values, for the next period. (*C.A. Inter, Nov. 1995*)

[**Ans.** Purchases Budget Rs. 3,60,000; Wages Budget Rs. 4,28,400]

6. Study the following data for Subramanium Carpet Company Ltd., Madras:

(*a*) **Sales Budget (in units):**	**Product X**	**Product Y**
Area 'K'	2,500	2,000
Area 'L'	4,000	4,800
Area 'M'	10,000	5,000
Total Sales (Units)	16,500	11,800

(*b*) Stock as on Sept. 30, 2008:

Product X, 1,000 units; Product Y, 1,500 units.

(*c*) Stock as on Sept. 30, 2009:

Estimated to be 10% in excess of opening stock.

You are asked to prepare a Production Budget for the year ended Sept. 30, 2009, in case:

(*i*) There is no loss in production:

(*ii*) There is a normal loss in production of 5% each in Product X and Y.

[**Ans.** (*i*) Product X, 16,600 units, Product Y, 11,950 units.
(*ii*) Product X, 17,474 units, Product Y, 12,579 units]

[**Hints:** For (*i*): Production figure = Units of sales budget + Closing stock - Opening stock.

For (*ii*): Since there is normal loss of 5%, the net production is 95% of the input. So, production should be so increased to have the output as per (*i*). So, the production will be arranged for 16,600 × $\frac{100}{95}$ *i.e.* 17,474 units of X and 11,950 × $\frac{100}{95}$ *i.e.* 12,579 units of Y].

7. A firm expects to have Rs. 30,000 in bank on 1st May, 2008 and requires you to prepare an estimate of the cash position during the three months from May to July, 2008. The following information is supplied to you:

Month	Sales	Purchases	Wages	Factory expenses	Office expenses	Selling expenses
	Rs.	Rs.	Rs.	Rs.	Rs.	Rs.
March	40,000	24,000	6,000	3,000	4,000	3,000
April	46,000	28,000	6,500	3,500	4,000	3,500
May	50,000	32,000	6,500	4,000	4,000	3,500
June	72,000	36,000	7,000	4,400	4,000	4,000
July	84,000	40,000	7,250	4,250	4,000	4,000

Other information:

(*i*) 25 per cent of the sale is for cash, remaining amount is collected in the month following that of sale.

(*ii*) Suppliers supply goods at two months' credit.

(*iii*) Delay in payment of wages and all other expenses, one month.

(*iv*) Income tax of Rs. 10,000 is due to be paid in July.

(*v*) Preference share dividend of 10 per cent on Rs. 1,00,000 is to be paid in May.

(*Punjab, B.Com., Sept., 1982*)

[**Ans.** Bank balances at the end of: May, Rs 25,500; June, Rs. 35,000; July, Rs. 48,600]

8. Summarised below are the income and expenditure forecasts for the months of March to August, 2009:

Months	Sales (all credit)	Purchases (all credit)	Wages	Manufacturing Expenses	Office Expenses	Selling Expenses
	Rs.	Rs.	Rs.	Rs.	Rs.	Rs.
March	60,000	36,000	9,000	4,000	2,000	4,000
April	62,000	38,000	8,000	3,000	1,500	5,000
May	64,000	33,000	10,000	4,500	2,500	4,500
June	58,000	35,000	8,500	3,500	2,000	3,500
July	56,000	39,000	9,500	4,000	1,000	4,500
August	60,000	34,000	8,000	3,000	1,500	4,500

You are given the following further informations:

(*a*) Plant costing Rs. 16,000 is due for delivery in July payable 10% on delivery and the balance after three months.

(*b*) Advance Tax of Rs. 8,000 is payable in March and June each.

(*c*) Period of credit allowed (*i*) by suppliers 2 months and (*ii*) to customers 1 month.

(*d*) Lag in payment of manufacturing expenses $\frac{1}{2}$ month.

(*e*) Lag in payment of all other expenses 1 month.

You are required to prepare a Cash Budget for three months starting on 1st May, 2009 when there was a cash balance of Rs. 8,000.

(*C.A. Final; Bhopal, M. Com.*)

9. The cost per unit of article 'A' is Rs. 15 at a capacity level of 5,000 units. The details are given under 'X' below. For a variation up to 25% in capacity above or below this level, the individual expenses vary as indicated under 'Y' below:

	X	Y
	Rs.	**Rs.**
Material cost	35,000	100% varying
Labour cost	15,000	100% varying
Power	2,000	80% varying
Repair & Maintenance	3,000	75% varying
Stores	1,000	100% varying
Inspection	600	20% varying
Depreciation	10,000	100% fixed
Admn. Overheads	5,400	20% varying
Selling Overheads	3,000	50% varying
	Rs. 75,000	

Calculate the cost per unit of product, showing individual expenses at production levels of 4,000 units & 6,000 units. (*I.C.W.A – Inter*)

[**Ans.** Total Cost: Rs. 63,490 and 86,510. Per unit : Rs. 15.87, 14.42]

10. With the following data for 60% activity, prepare a budget for production at 80% and 100% capacity:

Production at 60% capacity: 600 units

Materials Rs. 100 per unit

Labour Rs. 40 per unit

Direct Expenses Rs. 10 per unit

Factory overheads Rs. 40,000 (40% fixed)

Administration Expenses Rs. 30,000 (60% fixed)

(*Punjabi, B.Com., 1985, M.D.U., B.Com., 1984*)

[**Ans.** At 80% capacity: Total cost Rs. 2,02,000; Cost per unit Rs. 252.50
At 100% capacity: Total cost Rs. 2,44,000; Cost per unit Rs. 244]

11. Prepare a flexible budget for production at 80% and 100% of activity:

Production at 50% capacity	5,000 units
Raw Materials	Rs. 80 per unit
Direct Labour	Rs. 50 per unit
Variable Expenses (Direct)	Rs. 10 per unit
Factory Overheads	Rs. 50,000 (50% fixed) at 50% capacity operation.
Office Overheads	Rs. 60,000 (40% fixed) at 50% capacity operation.

(*G.N.D.U., B.Com. 1996, 2000, 2001*)

[**Ans.** 80% Capacity: Total cost Rs. 12,66,600, Per unit cost Rs. 158.325, 100% Capacity: Total cost Rs. 15,71,000, Per unit cost Rs.157.10]

12. For the production of 10,000 electrical automatic irons the following are the budgeted expenses:

	Per unit Rs.
Direct Material	60
Direct Labour	30
Variable Overheads	25
Fixed Overheads (Rs. 1,50,000)	15
Variable expenses (direct)	5
Selling expenses (10% fixed)	15
Administration expenses (Rs 50,000 rigid for all levels of production)	5
Distribution expenses (20% fixed)	5
Total cost of sale per unit	160

Prepare a budget for production of 6,000; 7,000; 8,000 irons.

(*C.A. Inter; Punjab B.Com., April 1980, April 1988*)

[**Ans.** Total Cost 6,000 units Rs. 10,50,000 7,000 units Rs. 11,87,500; 8,000 units Rs. 13,25,000]

13. Prepare a Flexible Budget from the following data:

Capacity	40%	
Volume	12,000 units	
Selling Price per unit	Rs. 300	
Material	Rs. 150	
Labour	Rs. 45	
Factory Overhead	Rs. 45	(Rs. 18 Fixed)
Office Overhead	Rs. 30	(Rs. 15 Fixed)

At 70% working, material cost per unit decreases by 2% and selling price per unit falls by 2%. At 90% working, selling price per unit falls by

5% and material cost per unit decreases by 5%. Estimate the profit at 70% and 90% working. (*G.N.D.U., B.Com. 2000*)

[**Ans.** Budgeted Profit 70% Rs. 8,64,000; 90% Rs. 11,02,500]

14. The following data relate to a manufacturing company for the year 2007-08:

	Rs.
(Fixed Expenses)	
Wages and Salaries	16,00,000
Depreciation	6,60,000
Sundry Administrative Expenses	7,40,000
(Semi-variable Expenses) (at 50% capacity)	
Maintenance & Repairs	6,30,000
Indirect Labour	7,90,000
Sales Department Salaries	3,80,000
(Variable Expenses) (at 50% capacity)	
Materials	21,70,000
Wages	20,40,000
Other Expenses	7,90,000

Semi-variable Expenses remain constant between 45% & 65% of capacity, increasing by 10% between 65% and 80% capacity & by 20% between 80% and 100% capacity. If sales at 50% capacity level were Rs. 1,00,00,000, prepare a flexible budget for the year 2008-09 and forecast the profits at 75% and 90% capacity utilisation level. (*Pbi. Univ. B. Com. 1996*)

[**Ans.** Budgeted Profit 75% Rs. 25,20,000; 90% Rs. 38,40,000]

15. Excellent Manufacturers can produce 4,000 units of a certain product at 100% capacity. The following information is obtained from the books of account:

	Aug. 2002	Sept. 2002
Units produced	2,800	3,600
	Rs.	Rs.
Repairs and maintenance	500	560
Power	1,800	2,000
Shop labour	700	900
Consumable stores	1,400	1,800
Salaries	1,000	1,000
Inspection	200	240
Depreciation	1,400	1,400

Rate of production per hour is 10 units. Direct material cost per unit is Re. 1 and direct wages per hour is Rs. 4.

You are required to:

(*i*) Compute the cost of production at 100%, 80% and 60% capacity showing the variable, fixed and semi-variable items under the flexible budget.

(*ii*) Find out the overhead absorption rate per unit at 80% capacity.

(*C.S. Inter, Dec. 1995*)

[**Ans.** (*i*) Rs. 13,950; Rs. 11,930; Rs. 9,910; (*ii*) Rs. 2.33]

16. From the information given below prepare flexible budget at 60 and 80 per cent capacities and fix the total overhead rates as a per cent on direct wages at these capacities:

	At 60% Capacity Rs.	At 75% Capacity Rs.	At 80% Capacity Rs.
Variable overheads:			
Indirect materials		7,500	
Indirect labour		22,500	
Semi-variable overheads:			
Electricity (40% fixed, 60% variable)		37,500	
Repairs and maintenance (80% fixed, 20% variable)		3,750	
Fixed overheads:			
Salaries		1,00,000	
Insurance		5,000	
Depreciation		25,000	

Estimated direct wages, Rs. 40,250 at 75% capacity

(*I.C.W.A. Inter*)

[**Ans.** At 60% = 592%, at 75% = 500%; at 80% = 477%]

17. Prepare a flexible budget from the following information and show the forecast of profit or loss at 60, 70, 90 and 100 per cent capacity working:

	Capacity Worked 50% Rs.	Rs.
Fixed Expenses:		
Salaries	50,000	
Rent & Taxes	40,000	
Depreciation	60,000	
Administration Exp.	70,000	2,20,000
Variable Expenses:		
Materials	2,00,000	
Labour	2,50,000	
Others	40,000	4,90,000
Semi-variable Expenses:		
Repairs	1,00,000	
Indirect Labour	1,50,000	
Others	90,000	3,40,000

It is estimated that the fixed expenses remain constant for all levels of capacity worked, semi-variable expenses do not move when capacity worked ranges between 45% and 60% of capacity, rise by 10% when production goes beyond 60% but is not more than 75% of capacity and further rise by another 5% as soon as the production crosses the 75% capacity figure and thereafter there is no change upto 100% of capacity. Possible sales at various levels of working are:

Capacity worked per cent	Sales (Rs.)
60	11,00,000
70	13,00,000
90	15,00,000
100	17,00,000

(*M.Com. Agra, 1970*)

[**Ans.** 60% Loss Rs. 48,000; 70% Profit Rs. 20,000; 90% Profit Rs. 7,000; 100% Profit Rs. 1,09,000]

18. From the following data prepare a flexible budget for 70%, 80% and 100% activity level when sales are Rs. 450 lakhs, Rs. 500 lakhs & Rs. 600 lakhs respectively. Fixed expenses remain constant upto 100% level, while semi-variable expenses vary by 10% in amount between 75% & 90% activity and by 20% between 90% and 100%. The expenses and sales at 60% activity are as under:

	Rs/lakhs
A. Variable	
1. Materials	80
2. Labour	60
3. Other expenses	10
4. Total	150
B. Semi-variable	
1. Repairs & Maintenance	10
2. Indirect Labour	30
3. Sales Dept. Expenses	15
4. Others	10
5. Total	65
C. Fixed Expenses	
1. Wages & Salaries	40
2. Rent, Rates & Office Expenses	10
3. Depreciation	15
4. Sundry expenses	35
5. Total	100
D. Sales	400

Calculate at each level of activity, the cost of sales, profit and percentage of profit to sales.

(*I.C.W.A., Final*)

[**Ans.** Cost of Sales (Rs. Lakhs): 340, 371.5 and 428, Profit (Rs. Lakhs): 110, 128.5, 172]

19. The annual flexible budget of a company is as follows:

Cost (Rs. Thousands)	Capacity 60%	80%	100%
Direct Material	180	240	300
Direct Wages	240	320	400
Factory Overheads	126	138	150
Administrative overheads	62	66	70
Selling and Distribution overheads	68	74	80
Total	676	838	1,000

On account of severe competition in the market, the company is presently working at 50% capacity, the sales value of production at current prices charged by the company being Rs. 6.00 lakhs. It is anticipated that a 10% discount in the selling price will enable the company to improve its competitive position thereby enabling the company to operate at 75% capacity. Present a suitable statement to the management analysing the implications giving your recommendations.

[**Ans.** A discount of 10% in selling price will increase profit by Rs. 7,500 : Profit at 50% capacity Rs. 5,000]

20. The following particulars are available from the records of a manufacturing company for two periods:

Output	**Period I**	**Period II**
	60,000 units	80,000 units
Cost:	Rs.	Rs.
Direct Materials	1,20,000	1,60,000
Direct Wages	3,00,000	4,00,000
Direct Expenses	60,000	80,000
Prime Cost	4,80,000	6,40,000
Overheads:		
Consumable Stores	15,000	20,000
Shop Labour	6,000	8,000
Maintenance and Repairs	8,000	10,000
Inspection	1,600	1,800
Depreciation	10,000	10,000
Insurance	5,000	5,000
Salaries	6,000	6,000
Total Overheads	51,600	60,800
Total Factory Cost	5,31,600	7,00,800

Total production at 100% capacity is 1,00,000 units. Prepare a flexible budget for 70% and 90% capacity.

[**Ans.** 70% Capacity, Total cost Rs. 6,16,200, Per unit cost Rs. 8.80, 90% Capacity, Total cost Rs. 7,85,400, Per unit cost Rs. 8.726]

21. Budget manager of Jupiter Electricals Limited is preparing flexible budget for the accounting year starting from 1st July, 2008.

The company produces, one product-DETX II. Direct material costs Rs. 7 per unit. Direct labour averages Rs. 2.50 per hour and requires 1.6 hours to produce one unit of DETX II. Salesmen are paid a commission of Re. 1 per unit sold. Fixed selling and administration expenses amount to Rs. 85,000 per year.

Manufacturing overhead is estimated in the following amounts under specified conditions of volume:

Volume of production (in units)	1,20,000	1,50,000
Expenses:		
	Rs.	Rs.
Indirect Materials	2,64,000	3,30,000
Indirect labour	1,50,000	1,87,500
Inspection	90,000	1,12,500
Maintenance	84,000	1,02,000
Supervision	1,98,000	2,34,000
Depreciation-Plant & Equipment	90,000	90,000
Engineering Services	94,000	94,000
	9,70,000	11,50,000

Normal capacity is 1,25,000 units.

Prepare a budget of total cost at 1,40,000 units of production.

[*B.Com. Hons. Delhi*]

[**Ans.** Total Cost Rs. 28,56,200 ; Cost per unit Rs. 20.40]

22. From the following data, calculate Activity Ratio, Capacity Ratio and Efficiency Ratio:

A factory manufactures two products 'A' and 'B'. Standard time to manufacture 'A' is 2 hours and product 'B' is 10 hours. The budgeted and actual production in Dec., 2009 were as follows:

	Budgeted Production	**Actual Production**
Product A	125 Units	100 units
Product B	30 units	24 units

Total actual hours worked were 660. [**Ans.** 80%; 120%; $66\frac{2}{3}$ %]

23. Two articles A and B are produced in a factory. Their specifications show that 4 A's or 2B's can be produced in one hour. Budgeted production for Jan. 2009 is 800 A's and 200 B's. The actual production at the end of month is 900 A's and 180B's. Actual labour hours spent were 350. Find out capacity, activity, and efficiency ratio for January, 2009.

[**Ans.** Capacity ratio 116.67%, Activity ratio 105% and Efficiency ratio 90%]

20

Standard Costing

Standard Costing is the second technique of cost control (the first being the Budgetary Control) and is one of the most recently developed refinements of cost accounting. The standard costing technique has been introduced in many industries on account of the limitations of Historical Costing. Historical costing, which refers to the ascertainment of costs after they have been incurred, provides the management with a record of what has happened. Thus, it is simply a post-mortem of a case and has its own limitations. The main limitations of historical costing are:

1. **Expensive Nature:** Historical costing is very expensive since it requires the maintenance of large volume of accounting records.
2. **Delay in Availability of Data:** Historical cost records are available too late as a result of which the management fails to take corrective action in time in respect of mistakes, deviations and inefficiencies.
3. **No Suitable Yardsticks for Comparison:** Historical costing does not provide any yardstick to measure actual performances so as to assist the management in the evaluation of performances. It simply indicates what the actual cost is and not what the cost should be.
4. **No Assistance in Ascertaining the Reasons for Cost Deviations**: Historical costing fails to bring to light the reasons for cost deviations, such as excessive wastage of materials, defective materials, excessive idle time, defective machines and tools etc. As such, the responsibility for inefficiency cannot be fixed.
5. **No Assistance in Planning:** Historical costing records are not helpful in production planning and control. The periods to which historical costs relate may have peculiar conditions which are not relevant to the future.
6. **Doubtful Accuracy of Cost Data:** The total cost determined under historical costing is the aggregate of direct material cost, direct labour cost and overheads apportioned. The determination of the cost of these elements generally involves estimation. As such, the accurate cost of products and services may not be ascertainable.

MEANING OF STANDARD COSTING

The technique of standard costing is applied in order to overcome the various limitations of historical costing. Standard costing technique involves the preparation and use of standard costs, their comparison with actual costs and the analysis of the deviations to their causes so as to provide for corrective action. According to W.B. Lawrence – "A standard cost system is a method of cost accounting in which standard costs are used in recording certain transactions and the actual costs are compared with the standard costs to learn the amount and reason for any variations from the standard."

According to Brown & Howard, "Standard Costing is a technique of cost accounting which compares the standard cost of each product or service with actual cost to determine the efficiency of the operation, so that any remedial action may be taken immediately."

According to the Institute of Cost and Management Accountants - "Standard Costing is the preparation and use of standard costs, their comparison with actual costs and the analysis of variances to show their causes and points of incidence."

The definition of standard costing as given by W.W. Bigg is more clear and comprehensive. He is of the opinion that – "Standard Costing discloses the cost of deviations from standard and classifies these as to their causes, so that management is immediately informed of the sphere of operations in which remedial action is necessary."

After discussing these definitions, it can be said that standard costing is basically a technique of cost control under which cost data for each activity are pre-determined on the basis of normal levels of operation. The efficiency and costs incurred at actual performance are compared with pre-determined standards and deviation or variance, if any, is ascertained. Thereafter, an analysis of variances is made with reference to their causes with a view to fix the responsibility of the particular executive. A report on such analysis is submitted to the management to enable it to take corrective measures to ensure that actual costs are consistent with standard costs in future. The main features of standard costing, drawn on the basis of the above definitions, may be given as follows :

(*i*) Standard costing is primarily a technique of cost accounting concerned with cost control.

(*ii*) It determines standards for each element of total costs (i.e., material, labour and overhead) for each product or service.

(*iii*) These standards are determined well in advance and are treated as 'Standard Costs'.

(*iv*) It also determines and records the actual costs when these are incurred.

(*v*) It makes a comparison of actual costs with standard costs to find out the variances or deviations of actuals from standards. These variances reveal the level of efficiency or otherwise of the business operations.

(*vi*) A systematic analysis of the variances is made to ascertain the reasons responsible for them.

(*vii*) Variances are reported to the management for the purpose of taking remedial actions.

MEANING OF STANDARD COST

The various definitions of standard costing lay emphasis on the determination and use of standard cost and hence it is desirable to understand the meaning of 'Standard Cost'. Actually speaking, standard costs are those costs which are determined in advance for a normal level of efficiency of operation and which are used periodically as a basis for comparison with actual costs. These may be termed as 'commonsense costs' reflecting the best judgement of management as to what costs ought to be if the business operations are conducted with high degree of efficiency. According to Brown & Howard – "The Standard Cost is a pre-determined cost which determines what each product or service should cost under given circumstances." Blocker has defined 'Standard Cost' as "a pre-determined cost based upon engineering specifications and representing highly efficient production for quality standard with a fixed amount expressed in terms of `Dollars' for materials, labour and overhead for any estimated quantity of production." The Institute of Cost and Management Accountants has defined `Standard Cost' as "a pre-determined cost which is calculated from management's standards of efficient operation and the relevant necessary expenditure. It may be used as a basis for price fixation and for cost control through variance analysis."

In the above definition, the term 'management's standards of efficient operation, is important since standard cost will be ascertained on this basis. The standard of efficient operation may be determined on the basis of past experience, study or experiments. The standard is generally that which is attainable though only after a good effort. Standard cost serves as a measure against which actual cost is compared. If actual cost does not exceed standard cost, the performance will be treated as fully efficient. Thus, standard cost is of great importance in judging the performance of people. Through an analysis of the difference between the actual and standard costs, the management is in a position to know the factors leading to such difference in costs. Standard costs also assist the management in deciding the long term pricing matters.

The main features of standard cost may be given as follows:

(*i*) Standard cost is a pre-determined cost.

(*ii*) It is based on past experience and is termed as 'common sense cost' reflecting the best judgement of the management.

(*iii*) It relates to a product, service, process or an operation.

(*iv*) Standard cost is determined for a normal level of efficiency of operation.

(*v*) Standard cost is used for measuring the efficiency of future production or future operations and thus provides a basis for cost control.

(*vi*) Standard cost may be expressed in terms of money or quantity.

APPLICABILITY OF STANDARD COSTING

The technique of standard costing can be applicable under certain conditions which can be given as follows:

(*i*) There should be output or production of sufficient volume of some standard product.

(*ii*) The methods, operations and processes of production should be capable of standardisation.

(*iii*) The costs should be capable of being controlled.

Standard costing technique can be applied successfully in all those industries which are engaged in producing standardised products and following process costing method. Examples of such industries are : sugar, fertilisers, cement, footwear, breweries and distilleries etc. Public utility concerns like transport undertakings, electricity supply undertakings, water works etc., can also apply this technique for controlling costs and increasing efficiency. In jobbing industries and industries producing non-standardised products, this technique cannot be applied with advantage.

DISTINCTION BETWEEN STANDARD COST AND ESTIMATED COST

Both, standard cost and estimated cost are pre-determined costs and are considered to carry the same meaning. But it is not so. The objectives of both these costs are different. The main points of difference between standard cost and estimated cost are as follows:

1. Estimated cost is a reasonable assessment of what a cost 'will be', whereas standard cost is a specification of what a cost 'should be'.

2. Estimated cost is ascertained on the basis of expected actuals. Standard cost is said to be a planned cost ascertained on scientific basis.

3. Estimated cost is an expression of likely cost in future and cannot be used to measure efficiency or otherwise. Standard cost is used as a barometer of efficiency. Standard cost is compared with actual cost with a view to ascertain operational efficiency.

4. The use of estimated cost is made in a business concern where historical costing is in operation whereas standard cost is used in a concern making the use of standard costing system.

5. Estimated cost does not serve any control purpose but standard cost serves as a tool of exercising control over costs.

DIFFERENCE BETWEEN STANDARD COSTING AND BUDGETARY CONTROL

Both the systems aim at controlling the business operations by means of predetermined standards with the objects of having better efficiency and of reducing costs. But these systems differ in following respects:

(I) Budgetary control deals with the operation of a department or business as a whole while standard costing mainly applies to manufacturing of a product or providing a service. As such budgetary control system is more extensive as it relates to the operations of the business as a whole and covers capital, sales and financial expenses in addition to production. But standard costing is more intensive and is concerned with controlling amount involved in various elements of cost.

(II) Standard costing can be adopted in a business without any particular policy. Its sole object is to maximise efficiency in operation by determining standard costs before hand. But in case of budgetary control it is necessary to lay down the objective or the policy of the firm for the period for which budgets are being laid down.

(III) Budgetary control is exercised by statistically putting the budgets and actuals side by side. Variances are not revealed through the accounts. But under the Standard Costing system, actuals are recorded in accounts and thus the variances are revealed through different accounts.

(IV) Budgetary control system can be employed in parts such as budget for cash, selling and distribution expenses, research and development expenses, but the question of the partial application of standard costing system does not arise at all.

(V) In budgetary control system, the variances are revealed in total but their analysis in detail according to originating causes is not possible. But in standard costing, the different variances are analysed in detail according to their originating causes.

(VI) Budgetary control is the projection of financial accounts, whereas standard costing is the projection of cost accounts.

Preliminaries To Be Considered Before Establishment Of Standard Costing System:

While introducing the technique of standard costing in a business concern, certain preliminaries have to be taken into consideration. These preliminaries are:

1. Establishment of Cost Centres.
2. Classification and Codification of Accounts.
3. Types of Standards.
4. Setting the Standards.

Establishment of Cost Centres

A cost centre is a location, person, or item of equipment (or a group of these) for which costs may be ascertained and used for the purpose of cost control. Cost centres may be personal cost centres or impersonal cost centres. Personal cost centre is related to a person while impersonal cost centre is related to a location or item of equipment. Establishment of cost centres is necessary for determination of responsibilities and defining lines of authority.

Classification and Codification of Accounts

Classification or grouping of accounts is most essential for standard costing. Accounts should be classified in such a way that cost elements of every cost centre are clearly and precisely reflected. Codes and symbols are assigned to different accounts to make the collection and analysis of costs more quick and convenient.

Types of Standards

A standard is pre-determined measure relating to material, labour or overhead and is reflection of what under stated conditions, is expected of plant and personnel. A standard is basically an expression of quantity and a standard cost is its monetary expression *i.e.*, quantity multiplied by price. It shows what the cost should be. In setting standards, the cardinal question is to decide the type of standard which is to be used in fixing the cost. Basically there are two types of standards *viz*.,

(*a*) Basic Standard, and
(*b*) Current Standard.

Basic Standard

The Institute of Cost and Management Accountants has defined 'Basic Standard' as "a standard which is established for use unaltered over a long period of time." The principle in fixing the basic standard is similar to that of index numbers. Basic standard is set up for some base year and is not revised with changed conditions. It remains in force for a long period of time. Basic standard permits the calculation of variance which reflects trends and thus is of no practical importance for cost control.

Current Standard

'Current Standard' has been defined by the Institute of Cost and Management Accountants as "a standard which is established for use over a short period of time, and is related to current conditions." A current standard is meant to incorporate into the basic standard, temporary conditions which are likely to prevail in the current period. Current standards are more consistent, useful and capable of attainment. Current standards may be based upon :

(*i*) Ideal Standard, or
(*ii*) Expected Standard.

The Institute of Cost and Management Accountants has defined 'Ideal Standard' as "the standard which can be attained under the most favourable conditions possible." Ideal standard is a theoretical standard and is based on perfect performance which is rather impossible to attain with the result that when actual costs are compared with such standard costs, large variances are shown which do not represent a true and fair position.

'Expected Standard' has been defined by the Institute as "the standard which may be anticipated to be attained during a future specified budget period." This is a practical standard and represents an attainable level of good performance. Reasonable allowance is made for unavoidable waste and inefficiency before setting expected standards. As such expected standards are regarded as more realistic and are best suited from the point of view of cost control.

There is one more type of standard which is known as 'Normal Standard.' Normal Standard is an average standard which it is anticipated can be attained over a future period of time preferably long enough to cover one trade cycle. Normal standard does not require frequent adjustments but it is not useful for the purpose of cost control.

Setting the Standards or Establishment of Standard Cost

Establishment of standard cost for each element viz., material, labour and overhead, is a complex task and requires the collaboration of a number of executives. For this purpose a Standards Committee is set up. The Standards Committee generally consists of:

(*i*) Production Manager,
(*ii*) Purchase Manager,
(*iii*) Personnel Manager,
(*iv*) Production Engineer,
(*v*) Sales Manager, and
(*vi*) the Cost Accountant.

The Budget Committee and the Standards Committee can also be combined into one committee. The Standards Committee is responsible for fixing standards. It also assists in the effective application of the standards and to make changes therein that may be necessary as the new circumstances render previous standards obsolete. Before fixing standards, a detailed study of the functions involved in the manufacture of the product will be necessary. While fixing standard costs, the fundamental principle to be observed is that the set standards are attainable so that these are taken as yardsticks for measuring the efficiency of actual performances. The setting up of standard costs requires the consideration of quantities, price or rates and qualities or grades for each element of cost entering into a product *i.e.*, material, labour and overhead. The standard costs should be fixed as follows:

DIRECT MATERIAL

The establishment of standard cost of direct material for each product will involve determination of:

(*i*) Standard quantity of materials, and

(*ii*) Standard price of materials.

The object of the determination of standard quantity of material is to achieve maximum economies in material usage. The planning of the standard specification of materials as to qualities and grades must precede the determination of quantities of materials. In fixing standard quantities, yield and loss factors should be taken into consideration. Reasonable provision must be made for unavoidable waste. The Cost Accountant will be helped by the Production Engineer in fixing the standard quantity for each type of material.

For translating the standard quantity of material into standard cost, the standard price is fixed. The object of fixing the standard price is to increase efficiency in purchasing and store-keeping and thus to keep down the material prices. The setting up of the standard price of materials will be done by Cost Accountant in collaboration with Purchase Manager.

DIRECT LABOUR COST

The setting up of the standard costs for direct labour will involve the determination of:

(*i*) Standard time, and

(*ii*) Standard rate.

The standard time indicates the precise time that labour of a particular grade should take to perform a given operation. The main object of fixing standard time for labour is to achieve maximum efficiency. The establishment of standard time requires the standardisation of working conditions as well as grade of workers. Standard time may be fixed either on the basis of past performance or by means of test runs with time and motion studies, but due allowance must be made for unavoidable losses.

The standard labour rate indicates the wage rate which should be paid to workman of a particular grade. The object of fixing the standard rate is to foretell, as far as possible, the actual wage rate which should be paid to the labour. The standard wage rate shall be determined by the Cost Accountant in collaboration with Personnel Manager by keeping in view the guaranteed minimum wage, future trend of wages and collective agreement between labour and management.

Variable Overhead

Variable Overhead indicates the overhead cost which tends to vary directly with variation in volume of output. Therefore, it is necessary to calculate standard variable overhead per unit or per hour.

Fixed Overhead

Fixed Overhead refers to the overhead cost which tends to be unaffected by variation of volume of output. Setting up the standard fixed overhead cost will involve the determination of budgeted fixed overhead for a period and the corresponding budgeted output in units or standard hours. Budgeted overheads are apportioned to production and service departments and service department expenses are ultimately apportioned to production departments on some equitable basis. Standard rate of fixed overhead is ascertained by dividing the total fixed overheads for each department by a suitable base *e.g.*, labour hours, machines hours, direct wages, prime cost etc.

Standard Cost Card

When standard costs have been fixed for materials, labour and overhead, they are properly recorded on a card known as "Standard Cost Card". One such card is normally prepared for each major component of product made which shows the quantity and price of each type of material required, the time and rate of each grade of labour, the overhead rate, and the total of each element of cost for the product. The maintenance of Standard Cost Card is an important part of the standard costing system. The information contained in the standard cost card is used by the management in formulating the price and cost policies. The form of Standard Cost Card is given below:

Standard Cost Card

No.......................
Product .... For the Period ....
Description ....

Items	Cost Per Unit	Remarks
1. Direct Materials	Rs. P.	
Material A 5 kgs. @ Rs. 2 per kg.	10.00	
Material B 3 kgs. @ Rs. 5 per kg.	15.00	
2. Direct Wages		
5 hours @ Rs. 2 per hour	10.00	
3. Variable Overhead		
5 hours @ Rs. 0.50 per hour	2.50	
4. Fixed Overhead		
5 hours @ Re. 0.75 per hour	3.75	
Total Standard Cost	41.25	
Standard Profit Margin	6.75	
Sale Price	48.00	

Advantages of Standard Costing

Standard costing is said to be a tool of control in the hands of management which helps the management in a number of ways in controlling and reducing costs through the elimination of wastages and inefficiencies of all types. The main advantages of standard costing may be given as follows:

1. **Valuable Aid to Management:** The technique of standard costing enables the management to perform the functions of planning, organising, co-ordinating, motivating and controlling effectively. Determination of standard costs involves a careful analysis of different activities of the business concern. Thus, it helps the management to plan effectively. Further, it helps in determining the responsibility of the various executives of a business concern through the preparation of organisation chart. Standard costing is also helpful in achieving co-ordination in the working of the business concern. While determining standard costs, the various activities of busines concern are to be considered in cohesion. Lastly, the standard costing technique involves the comparison of actual costs with standard costs which is an essence of control function. This comparison helps the management in evaluating performance and determining efficiency or inefficiency of various operations and taking corrective action, where and when necessary.
2. **Formulation of Production and Price Policies:** Standard costing system facilitates the ascertainment of estimated costs promptly and thus helps the management in formulating production policies. The estimation of total cost in advance helps in fixing the selling price in advance.
3. **Facilitates Delegation of Authority:** Standards Costing system enables the top management to delegate authority through the establishment of cost and profit centres and to control the departmental executives by their actions through costing reports.
4. **Assists in Detecting and Preventing Inefficiency:** The measurement and analysis of variances assist the management in detecting inefficiencies which in their own turn enable the management to investigate into their originating causes and take corrective action.
5. **Promotes Cost Consciousness:** Standard costing system stimulates cost consciousness of all executives as the variance analysis indicates the responsibility of various executives for favourable or unfavourable performances.
6. **Encourages Management by Exception:** Under standard costing system, the principle of 'management by exception' can be applied. The management need not spend time and efforts in respect of activities which proceed according to plans and can concentrate on other important matters.
7. **Quick Reporting:** Standard costing makes possible the quick communication of operating data. The preparation of cost reports does not obstruct the routine activities of the business. The quick and immediate reporting helps the management in taking suitable and timely measures.
8. **Economy:** Standard costing system is economical too. Standard costing system does not require the maintenance of detailed cost records. Standard

Cost Cards are prepared for each product or job and on that basis, material cost, labour cost and other expenses are arranged. Material Requisition Slips, Time Records and other job records are not frequently used under the standard costing system. Thus, it saves both, time and money.

9. **Assistance in Budgetary Planning:** Standards set up in respect of materials, labour and overheads under the standard costing technique, are of great help in preparing the various budgets. A proper knowledge of variations between actual and standard increases the capacity to anticipate about the changing conditions in the future. Thus, a more accurate and effective budget can be prepared for the future.

Limitations of Standard Costing

The technique of standard costing suffers from the following limitations:

1. Introduction of standard costing system is very expensive. Establishment of standard costs not only requires high degree of skill but is also very costly. As such, small business concerns find it difficult to adopt standard costing system due to their financial limitations.
2. Under standard costing system, executives are held responsible for unfavourable variances caused due to the factors within their control. As such it is necessary to make a distinction between controllable and uncontrollable factors, which is a tedious task.
3. The standards to be fixed under standard costing system should be realistic, accurate and close to the actuals. If the standards are not properly fixed, these are not going to help the management.
4. Any change in the original factors or circumstances under which standards were fixed, requires the revision of standards. If it is not done, the standards become rigid and incapable of being used effectively. But the revision of the standards is also a very tedious and difficult task.
5. Standard costing is not suitable for all types of business concerns. If a business concern deals with non-standardised products and jobs, the system of standard costing shall be found to be unsuitable.
6. Implementation of standard costing system requires a lot of interest on the part of the management and co-operation from employees. High standards may have adverse psychological effects on workers. It may discourage the workers.

VARIANCES

When the actual costs are recorded and compared with the standard costs, some deviations or variations are observed. These deviations or variations are commonly known as 'variances'. A variance may be defined as the difference between a standard cost and comparable actual cost incurred during a period. If the standard cost specified is Rs. 10,000 and the actual cost incurred is

Rs. 11,200, the difference of Rs. 1,200 is to be treated as 'variance'. Variances may be divided into:

(*i*) Controllable Variances and Uncontrollable Variances.

(*ii*) Favourable Variances and Unfavourable Variances.

Controllable variance is that cost variance which can be identified as the primary responsibility of a specified person. For example, excess usage of material by a production department is controllable being the responsibility of the foreman of the department. On the other hand, if a cost variance is due to some abnormal or extra-ordinary cause beyond the control of any individual *e.g.*, increase in the wage rates of the workers under the national wage policy, it is known as uncontrollable variance.

When the actual cost is less than the standard cost, the difference or the variance is known as 'favourable'. On the other hand, when actual cost exceeds the standard cost, the variance is treated as 'unfavourable' or 'adverse'. A favourable variance is a reflection of efficiency while an unfavourable variance indicates inefficiency. These variances can be justified only if standard costs have been correctly fixed otherwise the variances become meaningless.

VARIANCE ANALYSIS

The calculation and the analysis of variances is one of the most important features of standard costing. Variance analysis is a process of analysing variances by sub-dividing the total cost variance in such a way that the management can assign the responsibility for off production performance. Variances are calculated and analysed in respect of the three major elements of cost (*viz*., direct material, direct labour and overhead) and sales. Thus, the main Cost Variances are:

(1) Direct Material Cost Variance,

(2) Direct Labour Cost Variance, and

(3) Overhead Variance.

MATERIAL VARIANCES

Material Cost Variance: Material Cost Variance is the difference between the standard cost of direct materials specified for the output achieved and the actual cost of direct materials used. It may be calculated as follows:

Material Cost Variance = Standard Cost – Actual Cost

OR

Material Cost Variance = (Standard Quantity × Standard Price) – (Actual Quantity × Actual Price)

or MCV = (SQ × SP) – (AQ × AP)

Note: While calculating material cost variance, the standard quantity must relate to actual production.

Material Cost Variance may be divided into:

(*a*) Material Price Variance (*b*) Material Usage Variance.

Material Price Variance: Direct Material Price Variance is that portion of Direct Material Cost Variance which is due to the difference between the standard price specified and the actual price paid. It is calculated as follows:

Material Price Variance = (Standard Price – Actual Price) × Actual Quantity

or MPV = (SP – AP) × AQ

Reasons for Material Price Variance: The main reasons for material price variance may be:

(*i*) Change in the basic prices of materials.

(*ii*) Failure to purchase standard quality, leading to the payment of a different price.

(*iii*) Change in the quantity of materials purchased leading to different rates of quantity discount.

(*iv*) Defective purchasing.

(*v*) Change of delivery costs.

(*vi*) Rush purchases.

(*vii*) Change in the rates of excise duty, purchase tax etc., on materials.

Material Usage Variance: It is also known as 'Material Quantity Variance' and represents that portion of the direct material cost variance which is due to the difference between the standard quantity specified and the actual quantity used. It may be calculated as follows:

Material Usage Variance = (Standard Quantity – Actual Quantity) × Standard Price

or MUV = (SQ – AQ) × SP

Reasons for Material Usage Variance: The main reasons responsible for material usage variance may be:

(*i*) Use of sub-standard or defective materials

(*ii*) Negligence or carelessness in the handling and use of materials.

(*iii*) Pilferage of materials.

(*iv*) Defects in machinery and equipments.

(*v*) Changes in the quality of materials.

(*vi*) Use of substitute materials.

(*vii*) Use of non-standard material mixture.

(*viii*) Changes in the yield from materials.

Note: The total of the material price variance and material usage variance should be equal to material cost variance.

Thus:

Material Cost Variance = Material Price Variance + Material Usage Variance

or MCV = MPV + MUV

Now, calculation of material variances can be explained with the help of the following illustrations:

Illustration 1

From the following particulars, calculate Material Cost Variance, Material Price Variance and Material usage variance:

Name of the product: X

	Standard	Actual
Quantity of Material	500 kgs.	450 kgs.
Price of Material	Rs. 6 per kg.	Rs. 8 per kg.

Solution

Material Cost Variance = (Standard Quantity × Standard Price) – (Actual Quantity × Actual Price)
= (500 kgs. × Rs. 6) – (450 kgs. – Rs.8)
= Rs. 3,000 – Rs. 3,600
= Rs. 600 (Adverse).

(*a*) Material Price Variance = (Standard Price – Actual Price) × Actual Quantity
= (Rs. 6 – Rs. 8) × 450 kgs.
= Rs. 900 (Adverse).

(*b*) Material Usage Variance = (Standard Usage – Actual Usage) × Standard Price
= (500 kgs. – 450 kgs.) × Rs. 6
= Rs. 300 (Favourable)

Proof: MCV = MP V + MUV
Rs. 600 (A) = Rs. 900 (A) + Rs. 300 (F)

Illustration 2

A furniture company uses Sunmica tops for tables. It provides the following data:

Standard quantity of sunmica per table 4 sq.ft.
Standard price per sq.ft. of sunmica = Rs. 5
Actual production of tables = 10,000
Sunmica actually used = 43,000 sq.ft.
Actual price of sunmica per sq.ft. Rs. 5.50
Calculate Material Variances.

(*P.U., B.Com., 1974, 1984*)

Solution

Material Cost Variance = (Standard Quantity × Standard Price) – (Actual Quantity × Actual Price)
= (40,000 sq.ft. × Rs. 5) – (43,000 sq.ft. × Rs. 5.50)
= Rs. 2,00,000 – Rs. 2,36,500
= Rs. 36,500 (Adverse)

(*a*) Material Price Variance = (Standard Price – Actual Price) × Actual Quantity
= (Rs. 5 – Rs. 5.50) × 43,000 sq.ft.
= Rs. 21,500 (Adverse)

(*b*) Material Usage Variance = (Standard Quantity – Actual Quantity) × Standard Price
= (40,000 sq.ft. – 43,000 sq.ft.) × Rs. 5
= Rs. 15,000 (Adverse)

Proof: MCV = MPV + MUV
Rs. 36,500 (A) = Rs 21,500 (A) + Rs. 15,000 (A)

Illustration 3

From the following particulars find out the (*i*) Material Cost Variance, (*ii*) Material Usage Variance, (*iii*) Material Price Variance:

Quantity of material purchased	= 3,000 units
Value of material purchased	= Rs. 9,000
Standard quantity of materials required per tonne of the finished product	= 25 units
Standard rate of material	= Rs. 2 per unit
Opening stock of material	= Nil
Closing stock of material	= 500 units
Finished production during the period	= 80 tonnes

(*G.N.D.U., B.Com. 1992*)

Solution

Standard Quantity of Material Required for actual production
= 80 tonnes × 25 units = 2,000 units

Actual Quantity of materials used = Quantity Purchased + Quantity of Opening Stock – Quantity of Closing Stock
= 3,000 units + Nil – 500 units
= 2,500 units

Standard Price of Material = Rs. 2 per unit

Actual Price of Material $= \dfrac{\text{Rs. } 9{,}000}{3{,}000 \text{ units}} =$ Rs. 3 per unit

(*i*) Material Cost Variance = (Standard Quantity × Standard Price) – (Actual Quantity × Actual Price)
= (2,000 units × Rs. 2) – (2,500 units × Rs. 3)
= Rs. 4,000 – Rs. 7,500
= Rs. 3,500 (Adverse)

(*ii*) Material Usage Variance = (Standard Quantity – Actual Quantity) × Standard Price
= (2,000 units – 2,500 units) × Rs. 2
= Rs. 1,000 (adverse)

(*iii*) Material Price Variance = (Standard Price – Actual Price) × Actual Quantity
= (Rs. 2 – Rs. 3) × 2,500 units = Rs. 2,500 (Adverse)

MCV = MUV + MPV
Rs. 3,500 (A) = Rs. 1,000 (A) + Rs. 2,500 (A)

Material Sub-Variances: Material Usage Variance is further divided into two parts:

(*a*) **Material Mix Variance** (*b*) **Material Yield Variance.**

Material Mix Variance: Material Mix Variance arises in those industries where two or more items of material are physically mixed in some standard ratio in the manufacturing process. Material mix variance is that portion of direct materials usage variance which arises due to the difference between the standard and actual composition of a mixture. Material Mix Variance is calculated as follows:

(*i*) **When the total weight (or total volume) of actual mix and the total weight (or total volume) of standard mix do not differ:**

Material Mix Variance = (Standard Quantity – Actual Quantity) × Standard price per unit

or, Alternatively,

Material Mix Variance = Standard Cost of Standard Mix – Standard Cost of Actual Mix

Here, standard cost of standard mix is calculated by aggregating the standard cost of the standard quantity of each material while standard cost of actual mix is calculated by aggregating the standard cost of actual quantity of each material.

Illustration 4

From the following data, calculate the Material Mix Variance:

	Standard Mix	Actual Mix
Material A	160 kgs. @ Rs. 3 per kg.	150 kgs. @ Rs. 4 per kg.
Material B	40 kgs. @ Rs. 5 per kg.	50 kgs. @ Rs. 6 per kg.
	200 kgs.	200 kgs.

Solution

Material Mix Variance = (Standard Quantity – Actual Quantity) × Standard Price per unit

Material A = (160 kgs. – 150 kgs.) × Rs. 3 = Rs. 30 (F)

Material B = (40 kgs. – 50 kgs.) × Rs. 5 = Rs. 50 (A)

Rs. 20 (A)

Alternatively:

	Standard Cost of Standard Mix	Standard Cost of Actual Mix
	Rs.	Rs.
Material A	160 kgs. × Rs. 3 = 480	150 kgs. × Rs. 3 = 450
Material B	40 kgs. × Rs. 5 = 200	50 kgs. × Rs. 5 = 250
	680	700

Material Mix Variance = Standard Cost of Standard Mix – Standard Cost of Actual Mix

= Rs. 680 – Rs. 700 = Rs. 20 (Adverse)

In the above case, if we calculate the Material Usage Variance, it shall be equal to Material Mix Variance as shown below:

Material Usage Variance = (Standard Quantity – Actual Quantity) × Standard Price

Material A = (160 kgs. – 150 kgs.) × Rs. 3 = Rs. 30 (F)
Material B = (40 kgs. – 50 kgs.) × Rs. 5 = Rs. 50 (A)
= Rs. 20 (A)

Such a situation arises when:

(1) Total weight of standard and actual mix is the same, and
(2) The materials are not subjected to normal loss.

Revision of Standard Mix

In some cases, standard quantity of materials is changed due to the shortage of the one type of materials. In such cases, the Material Mix Variance is calculated by using the 'Revised Standard Quantity' in the following manner :

Material Mix Variance = (Revised Standard Quantity – Actual Quantity) × Standard Price per unit

Illustration 5

From the following information, calculate the Material Mix Variance:

	Standard	Actual
Material A	200 kgs. @ Rs. 12 per kg.	160 kgs. @ Rs. 14 per kg.
Material B	100 kgs. @ Rs. 10 per kg.	140 kgs. @ Rs. 10 per kg.
	300 kgs.	300 kgs.

Due to shortage of material 'A', standard mix of material A and B was changed from 2 : 1 to 1 : 1. There was no change in output.

Solution

Revised Standard Mix:

Material A 300 kgs. × $\frac{1}{2}$ = 150 kgs.

Material B 300 kgs. × $\frac{1}{2}$ = 150 kgs.

300 kgs.

Material Mix Variance = (Revised Standard Quantity – Actual Quantity) × Standard Price

Material A = (150 kgs. – 160 kgs.) × Rs. 12 = Rs. 120 (A)
Material B = (150 kgs. – 140 kgs.) × Rs. 10 = Rs. 100 (F)
Rs. 20 (A)

(*ii*) When the total weight (or total volume) of actual mix differs from the total weight (or total volume) of standard mix:

Material Mix Variance

$$= \left(\frac{\text{Total Weight of Actual Mix}}{\text{Total Weight of Standard Mix}} \times \text{Standard Cost of Standard Mix} \right) - \text{Standard Cost of Actual Mix}$$

Illustration 6

From the data given below, calculate the material price variance, the material usage variance and the material mix variance:

Raw Material	Standard	Actual
Material A	40 units @ Rs. 50 per unit	50 units @ Rs. 50 per unit
Material B	60 units @ Rs. 40 per unit	60 units @ Rs. 45 per unit

(*G.N.D.U., B.Com., 1974*)

Solution

Material Price Variance = (Standard Price – Actual Price) × Actual Quantity

Material A = (Rs. 50 – Rs. 50) × 50 units = 0

Material B = (Rs. 40 – Rs. 45) × 60 units = Rs. 300 (A)

Rs. 300 (A)

Material Usage Variance = (Standard Quantity – Actual Quantity) × Standard Price

Material A = (40 units – 50 units) × Rs. 50 = Rs. 500 (A)

Material B = (60 units – 60 units) × Rs. 40 = 0

Rs. 500 (A)

Material Mix Variance:

Total Volume of Standard Mix = 40 units + 60 units = 100 units

Total Volume of Actual Mix = 50 units + 60 units = 110 units

Since the total volume of standard mix differs from the total volume of actual mix, the Material Mix Variance shall be calculated by the following formula:

$$\left(\frac{\text{Total Weight of Actual Mix}}{\text{Total Weight of Standard Mix}} \times \text{Standard Cost of Standard Mix} \right) - \text{Standard Cost of Actual Mix}$$

	Standard Cost of Standard Mix	Standard Cost of Actual Mix
	Rs.	Rs.
Material A	40 units × Rs. 50 = 2,000	50 units × Rs. 50 = 2,500
Material B	60 units × Rs. 40 = 2,400	60 units × Rs. 40 = 2,400
	4,400	4,900

$$\text{Material Mix Variance} = \left(\frac{110}{100} \times \text{Rs. } 4{,}400\right) - \text{Rs. } 4{,}900$$

$$= \text{Rs. } 4{,}840 - \text{Rs. } 4{,}900 = \text{Rs. } 60 \text{ (Adverse)}$$

MATERIAL YIELD VARIANCE

It is that portion of direct material usage variance which is due to the difference between standard yield specified and the actual yield obtained. This variance denotes abnormal loss or abnormal saving of materials and arises in case of processing industries where materials are subjected to normal loss. If actual yield exceeds standard yield, the variance is favourable and vice versa. Material Yield Variance can be calculated as follows:

Material Yield Variance = (Actual Yield – Standard Yield) × Standard Rate per unit

$$\text{Standard Rate per unit} = \frac{\text{Standard Cost of Standard Mix}}{\text{Net Standard Output}}$$

Illustration 7

Calculate Material Yield Variance from the following particulars:

	Standard			Actual		
	Qty.	**Rate**	**Amount**	**Qty.**	**Rate**	**Amount**
	kgs.	**Rs.**	**Rs.**	**kgs.**	**Rs.**	**Rs.**
Material A	500	5.00	2,500	500	5.00	2,500
Material B	400	5.00	2,000	400	5.00	2,000
Material C	100	9.00	900	100	9.00	900
	1,000			1,000		
Less Normal Loss @ 10%	100		–	150		–
	900		5,400	850		5,400

Solution

Total Cost of Standard Input = Rs. 5,400
Standard Output (Normal Output) (units) = 900 kgs.
Standard Rate per unit = Rs. 5,400 ÷ 900 kgs.
= Rs. 6 per kg.
Standard Yield (1,000 kgs. – 100 kgs.) = 900 kgs.
Actual Yield (1,000 kgs. – 150 kgs.) = 850 kgs.
Material Yield Variance
= (Actual Output – Normal Output) × Standard Rate per Unit
= (850 kgs. – 900 kgs.) × Rs. 6
= Rs. 300 (Adverse)

Illustration 8

From the following data, calculate material yield variance:

	Standard Mix		Actual Mix	
	Units	Rate (Rs.)	Units	Rate (Rs.)
Material A	600	50.00	3,000	51.00
Material B	400	30.00	2,000	28.00

Standard loss is 10% of input and standard rate of scrap realisation is Rs. 6 per unit. Actual output is 4,400 units.

Solution

	Standard Mix	
	Units	Amount (Rs.)
Material A	600	30,000
Material B	400	12,000
	1,000	42,000
Less Standard Loss (10%)	100	600
Standard Output	900	41,400

$$\text{Standard Rate per unit} = \frac{\text{Rs.}41{,}400}{900 \text{ units}} = \text{Rs. } 46$$

Actual Mix: Material A	3,000 units
Material B	2,000 units
	5,000 units
Less Standard Loss on Actual Mix (10%)	500 units
Standard Yield on Actual Mix	4,500 units
Actual Yield	= 4,400 units

Material Yield Variance = (Actual Yield – Standard Yield) × Standard Rate per unit

= (4,400 units – 4,500 units) × Rs. 46

= Rs.4,600 (Adverse)

Illustration 9

The Standard Cost of a certain chemical mixture is:

40% Material 'A' @ Rs. 20 per kg.

60% Material 'B' @ Rs. 30 per kg.

Standard loss of 10% is expected in production.

During a period, there is used:

90 kgs. Material A at cost of Rs. 18 per kg.

110 kgs. Material B at a cost of Rs. 34 per kg.

The weight produced is 182 kgs. of good production. Calculate and present

(*i*) Material Cost Variance; (*ii*) Material Price Variance;

(*iii*) Material Mix Variance and (*iv*) Material Yield Variance.

[*I.C.W.A. Inter, G.N.D.U., B.Com., Delhi, B.Com.* (*Hons.*)]

Solution

Total quantity of Materials 'A' and 'B' used for 182 kgs. of output = 200 kgs.

Standard Cost of Material will be:

Material	Quantity (kgs.)	Price (Rs.)	Amount (Rs.)
A (40%)	80	20.00	1,600
B (60%)	120	30.00	3,600
	200		5,200
Less Normal Loss (10% of 200 kgs.)	20		–
Standard Yield	180		5,200

Actual Output is: 182 kgs.

$$\text{Standard Cost of Actual Output (182 kgs.)} = \text{Rs. } 5{,}200 \times \frac{182 \text{ kgs.}}{180 \text{ kgs.}}$$

$$= \text{Rs. } 5{,}257.78$$

Actual Cost of Material for Actual Output:

Material	Quantity (kgs.)	Price Rs.	Amount Rs.
A	90	18	1,620
B	110	34	3,740
	200		5,360

(*i*) Material Cost Variance = Standard Cost of Actual Output – Actual Cost of Actual Output
= Rs. 5,257.78 – Rs. 5,360
= Rs. 102.22 (A)

(*ii*) Material Price Variance = (Standard Price – Actual Price) × Actual Quantity
Material A = (Rs. 20 – Rs. 18) × 90 kgs. = Rs. 180 (F)
Material B = (Rs. 30 – Rs. 34) × 110 kgs. = Rs. 440 (A)
Rs. 260 (A)

Material Usage Variance = (Standard Quantity for Actual Output – Actual Quantity for Actual Output) × Standard Price

$$\text{Material A} = \left(80 \text{ kgs.} \times \frac{182 \text{ kgs.}}{180 \text{ kgs.}} - 90 \text{ kgs.}\right) \times \text{Rs. } 20 = \text{Rs. } 182.22 \text{ (A)}$$

$$\text{Material B} = \left(120 \text{ kgs.} \times \frac{182 \text{ kgs.}}{180 \text{ kgs.}} - 110 \text{ kgs.}\right) \times \text{Rs. } 30 = \text{Rs. } 340.00 \text{ (F)}$$

Rs. 157.78 (F)

(*iii*) Material Mix Variance = (Revised Standard Quantity – Actual Quantity) × Standard Price

Material A = (80 kgs. – 90 kgs.) × Rs. 20 = Rs. 200 (A)
Material B = (120 kgs. – 110 kgs.) × Rs. 30 = Rs. 300 (F)
= Rs. 100 (F)

(*iv*) Material Yield Actual = (Standard Yield – Standard Yield) × Standard Cost per Unit of Output

$$= (182 \text{ kgs.} - 180 \text{ kgs.}) \times \frac{\text{Rs. } 5{,}200}{180 \text{ kgs.}}$$

= Rs. 57.78 (F)

Proof: Material Cost Variance = Material Price Variance + Material Mix Variance + Material Yield Variance

Rs. 102.22 (A) = Rs. 260 (A) + Rs. 100 (F) + 57.78 (F)

LABOUR VARIANCES

Labour Cost Variance: It represents the difference between the Standard Cost of direct labour and the Actual Cost of direct labour. This variance is defined as the difference between the standard direct labour cost specified for the level of activity achieved and the actual direct labour cost incurred. Direct labour cost variance is calculated as follows:

Labour Cost Variance = Standard Labour Cost – Actual Labour Cost

or LCV = SC – AC

or Labour Cost Variance = (Standard Hours × Standard Wage Rate) – (Actual Hours × Actual Wage Rate)

or LCV = (SH × SR) – (AH × AR)

Labour Cost Variance can be analysed as:

(*a*) Labour Rate Variance

(*b*) Labour Efficiency Variance.

Labour Rate Variance: It is also known as Rate of Pay Variance and represents that portion of labour cost variance which is due to the difference between the standard rate of pay or wages specified and the actual rate paid. Labour Rate Variance is calculated as follows:

Labour Rate Variance = (Standard Wage Rate – Actual Wage Rate) × Actual Hours

or LRV = (SR – AR) × AH

Reasons responsible for Labour Rate Variance: The principal reasons responsible for labour rate variance are:

(*i*) Changes in basic wage rates.

(*ii*) Changes in grades of workers employed.

(*iii*) Change in the method of wage payment.

(*iv*) Employment of new workers at lower rate.

(*v*) Unscheduled overtime of workers engaged.

Labour Efficiency Variance: It is that portion of Labour Cost Variance which is due to the difference between the standard labour hours specified for the level of activity achieved and the actual labour hours expended. It is calculated as follows:

Labour Efficiency Variance = (Standard Hours – Actual Hours) × Standard Wage Rate

or LEV = (SH – AH) × SR

Reasons responsible for labour efficiency variance:

The principal reasons responsible for labour efficiency variance are:

(*i*) Improper working conditions.
(*ii*) Defective plant, machinery and tools.
(*iii*) Inefficient Workers.
(*iv*) Slackness on the part of supervisory staff.
(*v*) Idle time.
(*vi*) Use of sub-standard materials.
(*vii*) Sub-standard workers.
(*viii*) Efficient and skilled workers.
(*ix*) Improved tools, plant and machinery.
(*x*) Low or high rate of labour turnover.
(*xi*) Use of materials of good quality.
(*xii*) Good working conditions.
(*xiii*) Efficient supervision.

Illustration 10

From the following data, calculate the Labour Cost Variance, Labour Rate Variance and Labour Efficiency Variance:

	Standard	Actual
No. of hours per unit	720	800
Wage Rate per hour	Rs. 1.50	Rs. 1.40

Solution

Labour Cost Variance = (Standard Hours × Standard Wage Rate) – (Actual Hours × Actual Wage Rate)
= (720 Hrs. × Rs. 1.50) – (800 Hrs. × Rs. 1.40)
= Rs. 1,080 – Rs. 1,120
= Rs. 40 (Adverse)

Labour Rate Variance = (Standard Wage Rate – Actual Wage Rate) × Actual Hours
= (Rs. 1.50 – Rs 1.40) × 800 Hrs.
= Rs. 80 (Favourable)

Labour Efficiency Variance = (Standard Hours – Actual Hours) × Standard Wage Rate
= (720 Hrs. – 800 Hrs.) × Rs. 1.50
= Rs. 120 (Adverse)

Proof: Labour Cost Variance = Labour Rate Variance + Labour Efficiency Variance

Rs. 40 (Adverse) = Rs. 80 (Favourable) + Rs. 120 (Adverse)

Illustration 11

Ths budgeted labour force for a certain process is:

		Rs.
Skilled Men	800 Hrs. @ Re. 1 per hour	800
Semi-skilled Men	1,600 Hrs. @ 90 paise per hour	1,440
	2,400	2,240

During a certain week, the actual labour force was:

	Rs.
Skilled Men 1,200 hours @ 90 paise per hour	1,080
Semi-skilled Men 1,800 hrs. @ 90 paise per hr.	1,620
	2,700

Calculate Labour Cost Variance, Labour Rate Variance and Labour Efficiency Variance. *(G.N.D.U., B.Com., 1984)*

Solution

Labour Cost Variance = (Standard Hours × Standard Wage Rate) – (Actual Hours × Actual Wage Rate)

Skilled Men = (800 hrs. × Re. 1) – (1,200 hrs. × Re. 0.90)
= Rs. 800 – Rs. 1,080 = 280 (A)

Semi-skilled Men = (1,600 hrs. × Re. 0.90) – (1,800 hrs. × Re. 0.90)
= Rs. 1,440 – Rs. 1,620 = 180 (A)

= 460 (A)

Labour Rate Variance = (Standard Wage Rate – Actual Wage Rate) × Actual Hours

Skilled Men = (Re. 1 – Re. 0.90) × 1,200 Hrs. = Rs. 120 (F)

Semi-skilled Men – (Re. 0.90 – Re. 0.90) × 1,800 Hrs. = 0

= Rs. 120 (F)

Labour Efficiency Variance = (Standard Hours – Actual Hours) × Standard Wage Rate

Skilled Men = (800 Hrs. – 1,200 Hrs.) × Re. 1 = Rs. 400 (A)

Semi-skilled Men = (1,600 Hrs. – 1,800 Hrs.) × Re. 0.90 = Rs. 180 (A)

Rs. 580 (A)

Proof: LCV = LRV + LEV

Rs. 460 (A) = Rs. 120 (F) + Rs. 580 (A)

(A) denotes 'Adverse' while (F) denotes 'Favourable'.

Labour Idle Time Variance: Labour Idle Time Variance is that portion of labour cost variance which arises due to abnormal idle time of workers. Production may be affected due to abnormal causes like strikes, break-down of machinery, power failure, shortage of materials etc. Labour idle time variance is calculated in order to show separately the effects of idle time arising due to abnormal causes. It should be remembered that labour idle time variance will always be adverse or unfavourable. Labour Idle Time Variance is calculated as follows:

Labour Idle Time Variance = Abnormal Idle Hours × Standard Hourly Wage Rate

If labour idle time variance is calculated, the Labour Cost Variance = Labour Rate Variance + Labour Efficiency Variance + Labour Idle Time Variance.

Illustration 12

Product 'A' is estimated to require 10 hours per unit. The standard wage rate is Rs. 2 per hour. During May, 2007, 1,000 units were produced. Actual time taken was 9,500 hours and the actual wage rate was Rs. 2.40 per hour. 100 labour hours were lost due to break-down of machinery. Calculate the various labour variances.

Solution

Standard Time per unit = 10 hours
Standard Time for actual production of 1,000 units = 10,000 hours
Actual Time Taken = 9,500 hours
(including abnormal idle time)

Labour Cost Variance = (Standard Hours x Standard Wage Rate) – (Actual Hours × Actual Wage Rate)
= (10,000 Hrs. × Rs. 2) – (9,500 Hrs × Rs. 2.40)
= Rs. 20,000 – Rs. 22,800 = Rs. 2,800 (A)

Labour Rate Variance = (Standard Wage Rate – Actual Wage Rate) × Actual Hours
= (Rs. 2 – Rs. 2.40) × 9,500 Hours
= Rs. 3,800 (A)

Labour Efficiency Variance = (Standard Hours – Actual Hours) × Standard Wage Rate
= (10,000 Hrs. – 9,400 Hrs.) × Rs. 2
= Rs. 1,200 (F)

Note: Actual time taken for calculating labour efficiency shall exclude the abnormal idle time.

Labour Idle Time Variance = Abnormal Idle Hours × Standard Hourly Wage Rate
= 100 Hrs. × Rs. 2 = Rs. 200 (A)

Proof: Labour Cost Variance = Labour Rate Variance + Labour Efficiency Variance + Labour Idle Time Variance

Rs. 2,800 (A) = Rs. 3,800 (A) + Rs. 1,200 (F) + Rs. 200 (A)

Labour Sub-Variances: Labour Efficiency Variance can be sub-divided into:

(*a*) Labour Mix Variance
(*b*) Labour Yield Variance.

Labour Mix Variance: It is that portion of labour efficiency variance which is due to the difference between the standard composition of labour specified and the actual composition of labour utilised. Labour mix variance is also known as 'Gang Composition Variance' and is similar to Material Mix Variance. Labour Mix Variance is calculated as follows:

(*i*) When there is no difference between the total hours of standard composition and the total hours of actual composition:

Labour Mix Variance = Standard Cost of Standard Composition – Standard Cost of Actual Composition

or

Labour Mix Variance = (Standard Hours – Actual Hours) × Standard Wage Rate

(*ii*) When there is a difference between the total hours of standard composition and total hours of actual composition:

$$\text{Labour Mix Variance} = \left(\frac{\text{Total Time of Actual Labour Composition}}{\text{Total Time of Standard Labour Composition}} \times \text{Standard Cost of Standard Labour Composition}\right) - \text{Standard Cost of Actual Labour Composition.}$$

Revision of Standard Composition of Labour

Sometimes, on account of the shortage of a particular category or grade of workers, the standard composition of labour is itself revised. In such a case, Labour Mix Variance is calculated by taking into account the Revised Standard Composition (or Revised Standard Mix) in place of Standard Composition.

Illustration 13

From the following data calculate:

(*a*) Labour Cost Variance
(*b*) Labour Price Variance
(*c*) Labour Efficiency Variance, and
(*d*) Labour Mix Variance.

	Standard		Actual	
	Hours	Wage Rate Rs.	Hours	Wage Rate Rs.
Skilled Workers	800	4.00	700	4.40
Unskilled Workers	400	2.00	500	1.80
	1,200		1,200	

Solution

(*a*) Labour Cost Variance = (Standard Hours × Standard Wage Rate) – (Actual Hours × Actual Wage Rate)

Skilled Workers = (800 Hrs. × Rs. 4) – (700 Hrs. × Rs. 4.40) = Rs. 120 (F)
Unskilled Workers = (400 Hrs. × Rs. 2) – (500 Hrs. × Rs. 1.80) = Rs. 100 (A)
MCV = Rs. 20 (F)

(*b*) Labour Rate Variance = (Standard Wage Rate – Actual Wage Rate) × Actual Hours

Skilled Workers = (Rs.4 – Rs.4.40) × 700 Hrs. = Rs. 280 (A)
Unskilled Workers = (Rs. 2 – Rs. 1.80) × 500 Hrs. = Rs. 100 (F)
LRV = Rs. 180 (A)

(*c*) Labour Efficiency Variance = (Standard Hours – Actual Hours) × Standard Wage Rate

Skilled Workers = (800 Hrs. – 700 Hrs.) × Rs. 4 = Rs. 400 (F)
Unskilled Workers = (400 Hrs. – 500 Hrs.) × Rs. 2 = Rs. 200 (A)
LEV = Rs. 200 (F)

	Standard Cost of Standard Labour Composition		Standard Cost of Actual Labour Composition	
		Rs.		Rs.
Skilled Workers	800 Hrs. × Rs. 4 =	3,200	700 Hrs. × Rs. 4 =	2,800
Unskilled Workers	400 Hrs. × Rs. 2 =	800	500 Hrs. × Rs. 2 =	1,000
	1,200	4,000	1,200	3,800

Labour Mix Variance = Standard Cost of Standard Composition – Standard Cost of Actual Composition.
= Rs. 4,000 – Rs. 3,800 = Rs. 200 (F)

Proof: LCV = LRV + LEV
Rs. 20 (F) = Rs. 180 (A) + Rs. 200 (F)

Labour Yield Variance: It is just like Material Yield Variance arising due to the difference between standard yield obtainable by actual time utilised on production and actual yield obtained. It is calculated as follows:

Labour Yield Variance = (Actual Yield – Standard Yield obtainable by Actual Time Utilised) × Standard Labour Cost per unit

Illustration 14

Calculate the labour variances from the following information:

Standard Wages:
Grade X : 90 Labourers @ Rs. 2 per hour
Grade Y : 60 Labourers @ Rs. 3 per hour

Actual Wages:
Grade X : 80 Labourers @ Rs. 2.50 per hour
Grade Y : 70 Labourers @ Rs. 2.00 per hour

Budgeted Hours: 1,000 Actual Hours : 900
Budgeted Gross Production : 5,000 units
Standard Loss : 20%
Actual Loss : 900 units. (*G.N.D.U., B.Com., 1981*)

Solution

	Standard			Actual		
	Hours	Rate	Amount (Rs.)	Hours	Rate	Amount (Rs.)
Grade X	90 × 1,000 = 90,000	2.00	1,80,000	80 × 900 = 72,000	2.50	1,80,000
Grade Y	60 × 1,000 = 60,000	3.00	1,80,000	70 × 900 = 63,000	2.00	1,26,000
	1,50,000		3,60,000	1,35,000		3,06,000

Budgeted Gross Output (Input) = 5,000 units
Less Normal Loss (20%) = 1,000 units
Standard Yield = 4,000 units

$$\text{Standard Labour Cost per unit} = \frac{\text{Total Standard Labour Cost}}{\text{Standard Yield}}$$

$$= \frac{\text{Rs. } 3{,}60{,}000}{4{,}000 \text{ units}} = \text{Rs. } 90 \text{ per unit}$$

Actual Output = 5,000 units – 900 units (Loss) = 4,100 units.
Standard Labour Cost for Actual Output = 4,100 units × Rs. 90 = Rs. 3,69,000

(*a*) Labour Cost Variance = Standard Labour Cost – Actual Labour Cost
= Rs. 3,69,000 – Rs. 3,06,000 = Rs. 63,000 (F)

(*b*) Labour Rate Variance = (Standard Wage Rate – Actual Wage Rate) × Actual Hours

Grade X = (Rs. 2 – Rs. 2.50) × 72,000 Hrs. = Rs. 36,000 (A)
Grade Y = (Rs. 3 – Rs. 2.00) × 63,000 Hrs. = Rs. 63,000 (F)
LRV = Rs. 27,000 (F)

(*c*) Labour Efficiency Variance = (Standard Hours for Actual Output – Actual Hours) × Standard Wage Rate.

$$\text{Grade X} = \left(\frac{90{,}000}{4{,}000} \times 4{,}100 - 72{,}000 \text{ Hrs.}\right) \times \text{Rs. } 2 = \text{Rs. } 40{,}500 \text{ (F)}$$

$$\text{Grade Y} = \left(\frac{60{,}000}{4{,}000} \times 4{,}100 - 63{,}000 \text{ Hrs.}\right) \times \text{Rs. } 3 = \text{Rs. } 4{,}500 \text{ (A)}$$

LEV = Rs. 36,000 (F)

(*d*) Labour Mix Variance = (Revised Standard Labour Hours – Actual Labour Hours) × Standard Wage Rate

Revised Standard Labour Hours

$$= \frac{\text{Total Time of Actual Workers}}{\text{Total Time of Standard Workers}} \times \text{Standard Labour Hours}$$

$$\text{Grade X} = \frac{1{,}35{,}000 \text{ Hrs.}}{1{,}50{,}000 \text{ Hrs.}} \times 90{,}000 \text{ Hrs.} = 81{,}000 \text{ Hrs.}$$

$$\text{Grade Y} = \frac{1{,}35{,}000 \text{ Hrs.}}{1{,}50{,}000 \text{ Hrs.}} \times 60{,}000 \text{ Hrs.} = 54{,}000 \text{ Hrs.}$$

Labour Mix Variance:

Grade X = (81,000 Hrs. – 72,000 Hrs.) × Rs. 2 = Rs. 18,000 (F)

Grade Y = (54,000 Hrs. – 63,000 Hrs.) × Rs. 3 = Rs. 27,000 (A)

LMV = Rs. 9,000 (A)

(*e*) Labour Yield Variance = (Actual Yield – Standard Yield obtainable by Actual Time Utilised) × Standard Labour Cost per unit

= (4,100 units – 3,600 units) × Rs. 90 = Rs. 45,000 (F)

Note: Standard Yield obtainable by Actual Time utilised has been calculated as follows:

$$= \frac{\text{Actual Labour Hours}}{\text{Standard Labour Hours}} \times \text{Standard Output}$$

$$= \frac{1{,}35{,}000 \text{ hrs.}}{1{,}50{,}000 \text{ hrs.}} \times 4{,}000 \text{ units} = 3{,}600 \text{ units.}$$

Proof: Labour Cost Variance = Labour Rate Variance + Labour Efficiency Variance

Rs. 63,000 (F) = Rs. 27,000 (F) + Rs. 36,000 (F)

Labour Efficiency Variance = Labour Mix Variance + Labour Yield Variance

Rs. 36,000 (F) = Rs. 9,000 (A) + Rs. 45,000 (F)

Wages Revision Variance

Sometimes in a manufacturing concern wage rates are increased or revised on account of an industrial award or settlement with trade unions. In such a case, a wages revision variance is calculated to show to the management, the effect of revision due to the above reasons. Wages Revision Variance is:

= Standard Labour Cost of Actual Output at Original Standard Rate – Standard Labour Cost of Actual Output at Revised Standard Rate.

Illustration 15

The original standard rate of pay in a factory was Rs. 2 per hour. Due to settlement with trade union, this rate of pay per hour is increased by 20%. During a particular period, 5,000 actual labour hours were worked whereas work done was equivalent to 4,400 hours. The actual labour cost was Rs. 15,000. Calculate labour variances.

Solution

Original Standard Labour rate per hour = Rs. 2

Current Standard Labour rate per hour = Rs. 2 + 20% of Rs. 2 = Rs. 2.40

(*a*) Labour Rate Variance = (Revised Standard Wage Rate – Actual Wage Rate) × Actual Hours

= (Rs. 2.40 – Rs. 3.00) × 5,000 hours

= Rs. 3,000 (Adverse)

$$\text{Actual Wage Rate} = \frac{\text{Actual Wages}}{\text{Actual Hours}} = \frac{\text{Rs. 15,000}}{\text{5,000 hrs.}} = \text{Rs. 3.00}$$

(*b*) Labour Efficiency Variance = (Standard Hours – Actual Hours) × Revised Standard Wage Rate
= (4,400 hrs. – 5,000 hrs.) × Rs. 2.40
= Rs. 1,440 (Adverse)

(*c*) Labour Revision Variance = Standard Labour Cost of Actual Output at original Standard Rate – Standard Labour Cost of Actual Output at Revised Standard Rate
= (4,400 hrs. × Rs. 2) – (4,400 hrs. × Rs. 2.40)
= Rs. 8,800 – Rs. 10,560
= Rs. 1,760 (Adverse)

(*d*) Total Labour Cost Variance = [Standard Hours × Standard Wage Rate (Original)] – (Actual Hours × Actual Wage Rate)
= (4,400 hrs. × Rs. 2) – (5,000 hrs. × Rs. 3.00)
= Rs. 8,800 – Rs. 15,000
= Rs. 6,200 (Adverse)

Illustration 16

Raja Industries produces only one article, the prime cost standards for which have been established as following:

	Per unit cost Rs.
Materials 5 lbs. @ Rs. 4.20	21
Labour 3 hours @ Rs. 3.00	9

The production schedule for the month of Jan., 2003 required completion of 5,000 pieces. However, 5,120 pieces were actually completed.

Purchases for the month of Jan., 2003 amounted to 30,000 lbs. of material at the total invoice price of Rs. 1,35,000. Production records for the month of Jan., 2003 showed the following actual results:

Material requisitioned and used : 25,700 lbs.

Direct Labour –15,150 hours – Rs. 48,480.

Calculate appropriate material and labour variances.

(*G.N.D.U., B.Com.* (*P*) *2008*)

Solution

Calculation of Standard Quantity of Material and Standard Labour Hours:

Actual output: 5,120 pieces

Standard Quantity per unit (piece) : 5 lbs.

Standard Quantity for actual output:

= 5,120 pieces × 5 lbs.
= 25,600 lbs.

Standard Labour Hours per unit (Piece) = 3 hours

Standard Labour Hours for Actual output
= 5,120 pieces × 3 hours
= 15,360 hours

Actual Quantity of material used = 25,700 lbs.

Actual Labour Hours = 15,150 hrs.

Actual Price of material per lb. = $\frac{\text{Rs. 1,35,000}}{\text{30,000 lbs.}}$ = Rs. 4.50

Actual Labour cost per hour = $\frac{\text{Rs. 48,480}}{\text{15,150 Hours}}$ = Rs. 3.20

Material Cost Variance = (Standard Quantity × Standard Price) – (Actual Quantity × Actual Price)
= (25,600 lbs. × Rs. 4.20) – (25,700 lbs. × Rs. 4.50)
= Rs. 1,07,520 – Rs. 1,15,650
= Rs. 8,130 (A)

Material Price Variance = (Standard Price – Actual Price) × Actual Quantity
= (Rs. 4.20 – Rs. 4.50) × 25,700 lbs.
= Rs. 0.30 × 25,700 lbs.
= Rs. 7,710 (A)

Material Usage Variance = (Standard Quantity – Actual Quantity) × Standard Price
= (25,600 lbs. – 25,700 lbs.) × Rs. 4.20
= 100 lbs. × Rs. 4.20
= Rs. 420 (A)

Labour Cost Variance = (Standard Hours × Standard Wage Rate) – (Actual Hours × Actual Wage Rate)
= (15,360 Hrs. × Rs. 3.00) – (15,150 Hrs. × Rs. 3.20)
= Rs. 46,080 – Rs. 48,480
= Rs. 2,400 (A)

Labour Rate Variance = (Standard Wage Rate – Actual Wage Rate) × Actual Hours
= (Rs. 3.00 – Rs. 3.20) × 15,150 Hrs.
= Rs. 3,030 (A)

Labour Efficiency Variance = (Standard Hours – Actual hours) × Standard Wage Rate
= (15,360 Hrs. – 15,150 Hrs.) × Rs. 3.00
= Rs. 630 (F)

Proof: (*i*) MCV = MPV + MUV
Rs. 8,130 (A) = Rs. 7,710 (A) + Rs. 420 (A)

(*ii*) LCV = LRV + LEV
Rs. 2,400 (A) = Rs. 3,030 (A) + Rs. 630 (F)

OVERHEAD VARIANCES

Overhead Variances are calculated for overheads comprising indirect material cost, indirect wages and indirect expenses. Overhead cost variance is the difference between the standard cost of overhead specified for the actual output and the actual cost of overhead incurred. Overhead cost variance arises due to over/under-absorption of overhead. In relation to the calculation of overhead variances, the use of the following terms is commonly made:

(*i*) Standard Overhead Rate per unit = $\frac{\text{Budgeted Overheads}}{\text{Budgeted Output}}$

(*ii*) Standard Overhead Rate per hour = $\frac{\text{Budgeted Overheads}}{\text{Budgeted Hours}}$

(*iii*) Standard Hours for Actual Output = $\frac{\text{Budgeted Hours}}{\text{Budgeted Output}} \times \text{Actual Output}$

(*iv*) Standard Output for Actual Time = $\frac{\text{Budgeted Output}}{\text{Budgeted Hours}} \times \text{Actual Hours.}$

(*v*) Recovered Overheads or Absorbed Overheads = Standard Overhead Rate per unit × Actual Output

or

= Standard Overhead Rate per hour × Standard Hours for Actual Output

(*vi*) Budgeted Overheads = Standard Overhead Rate per unit × Budgeted Output

or = Standard Overhead Rate per hour × Budgeted Hours.

(*vii*) Standard Overheads = Standard Overhead Rate per unit × Standard Output for Actual Time

or = Standard Overhead Rate per hour × Actual Hours

(*viii*) Actual Overheads = Actual Overhead Rate per unit × Actual Output

or = Actual Overhead Rate per hour × Actual Hours.

Calculation of Overhead Variances

Overhead Cost Variance which represents the difference between the standard cost of overhead specified for the actual output and the actual cost of overhead incurred, is calculated as follows:

Total Overhead Cost Variance = Standard Total Overheads – Actual Total Overheads

or = Actual Output × Standard Overhead Rate per unit – Actual Overhead

or = Standard Hours for Actual Output × Standard Overhead Rate per Hour – Actual Overhead

Overhead Cost Variance may be calculated for Variable Overhead Cost and Fixed Overhead Cost.

VARIABLE OVERHEAD VARIANCE

It represents the difference between the standard variable overhead cost allowed for the actual output achieved and the actual variable overhead cost. It is calculated as follows:

Variable Overhead Variance = Standard Variable Overheads – Actual Variable Overheads

or = Actual Output × Standard Variable Overhead Rate – Actual Variable Overheads

or = Standard Hours for Actual Output × Standard Variable Overhead Rate per hour – Actual Variable Overheads.

Analysis of Variable Overhead Variance

Variable Overhead Variance is divided into two parts:

(*i*) Variable Overhead Expenditure Variance
(*ii*) Variable Overhead Efficiency Variance

Variable Overhead Expenditure Variance

It is the difference between the standard variable overheads for the actual time and the actual variable overhead incurred. It is calculated as follows:

Variable Overhead Expenditure Variance = (Actual Hours Worked × Standard Variable Overheads Rate per hour) – Actual Variable Overheads.

or

= (Actual Production × Standard Variable Overheads Rate per unit) – Actual Variable Overheads.

Variable Overhead Efficiency Variance

It is the difference between the standard variable overheads for actual output and the standard variable overheads for actual time and is calculated as follows:

Variable Overheads Efficiency Variance = (Standard Time for Actual Production – Actual Time Worked) × Standard Variable Overheads Rate per hour

or = (Standard Variable Overheads Rate per unit × Actual Output). – (Standard Variable Overheads Rate per hour × Actual Hours)

Note: If in a given case, no information is available about standard hours and actual hours for actual output, the above analysis of Variable Overheads Variance into Variable Overheads Expenditure Variance and Variable Overheads Efficiency Variance shall not be made (since in such a case Standard Overhead Rate per hour cannot be calculated). In such a case the Variable Overheads Variance shall be Variable Overhead Expenditure Variance.

Illustration 17

From the following information, Calculate the Variable Overhead Expenditure Variance:

Standard Variable Overhead Rate per unit = Rs. 4
Actual Output = 15,000 units
Actual Overhead Incurred = Rs. 62,000

Solution

Variable Overhead Expenditure Variance = (Actual Output × Standard Variable Overheads Rate per unit) – Actual Variable Overheads
= (15,000 units × Rs. 4) – Rs. 62,000 = Rs. 2,000 (Adverse)

Illustration 18

From the information given below, calculate Variable Overheads Variances:

Actual Variable Overhead = Rs. 20,000
Budgeted Variable Overhead = Rs 24,000
Budgeted Production = 1,000 units
Actual Production = 900 units
Actual Hours = 400 hours
Standard Time for one unit = 30 minutes (or $\frac{1}{2}$ hour)

Solution

$$\text{Standard Variable Overhead per unit} = \frac{\text{Rs. } 24{,}000}{1{,}000 \text{ units}} = \text{Rs. } 24 \text{ per unit}$$

$$\text{Standard Variable Overhead per hour} = \frac{\text{Rs. } 24{,}000}{\frac{1}{2}\text{ hour} \times 1{,}000 \text{ units}} = \text{Rs. } 48 \text{ per hour}$$

Standard Variable Overhead for Actual Production (or Recovered Overheads)
= Standard Variable Overhead rate per unit × Actual Output
= Rs. 24 × 900 units = Rs. 21,600

Standard Variable Overheads for Actual Time (or Standard Overheads)
= Standard Variable Overhead Rate per hour × Actual Hours
= Rs. 48 × 400 Hours – Rs. 19,200

Calculation of Variances

(*a*) Variable Overhead Cost Variance = Standard Variable Overhead on Actual Production – Actual Variable Overhead
= Rs. 21,600 – Rs. 20,000 = Rs. 1,600 (F)

(*b*) Variable Overhead Expenditure Variance = (Actual Hours Worked × Standard Variable Overheads Rate per hour) – Actual Variable Overheads.
= (400 Hrs. × Rs. 48) – Rs. 20,000
= Rs. 19,200 – Rs. 20,000 = Rs. 800 (Adverse)

Variable Overhead Efficiency Variance = (Standard Variable Overheads Rate per unit × Actual Output) – (Standard Variable Overheads Rate per hour × Actual Hours)

= (Rs. 24 × 900 units) – (Rs. 48 × 400 hrs.)

= Rs. 21,600 – Rs. 19,200 = Rs. 2,400 (F)

Proof: Variable Overhead Cost Variance = Variable Overhead Expenditure Variance + Variable Overhead Efficiency Variance

Rs. 1,600 (F) = Rs. 800 (A) + Rs. 2,400 (F)

Fixed Overhead Variance: It represents the difference between the standard cost of fixed overheads allowed or absorbed (for actual output) and the actual cost of fixed overheads incurred. It is calculated as follows:

Fixed Overhead Cost Variance = Standard Fixed Overheads – Actual Fixed Overheads

or = (Actual Output × Standard Fixed Overhead Rate) – Actual Fixed Overheads

Fixed Overhead Cost Variance can be analysed as:

(*i*) Fixed Overhead Expenditure Variance

(*ii*) Fixed Overhead Volume Variance.

Fixed Overhead Expenditure Variance: It is that portion of Fixed Overhead Cost Variance which arises due to the difference between budgeted fixed overhead expenditure and the actual fixed overhead expenditure relating to a specified period and can be calculated as follows:

Fixed Overhead Expenditure Variance = Budgeted Fixed Overheads – Actual Fixed Overheads

Fixed Overhead Volume Variance: It is that portion of Overhead Cost Variance which arises due to the difference between the budgeted level of output and the actual level of output attained. It is calculated as follows:

Fixed Overhead Volume Variance = Recovered Fixed Overheads – Budgeted Fixed Overheads

or = Standard Fixed Overheads (for actual output) – Budgeted Fixed Overheads

Illustration 19

From the following data, calculate the various fixed overhead variances:

Standard Rate of Fixed Overhead	= Rs. 10 per unit
Budgeted Production for the month	: 5,000 units
Actual Production for the month	: 4,500 units
Actual Fixed Overhead for the month	: Rs. 47,500

Solution

Recovered Overheads = Standard Overhead Rate per unit × Actual Output

= Rs. 10 × 4,500 units = Rs. 45,000

Budgeted Overheads = Standard Overhead Rate per unit × Budgeted Output

= Rs. 10 × 5,000 units = Rs. 50,000

(*a*) Fixed Overhead Cost Variance = Recovered Fixed Overheads – Actual Fixed Overheads

= Rs. 45,000 – Rs. 47,500 = Rs. 2,500 (A)

(*b*) Fixed Overhead Expenditure Variance = Budgeted Fixed Overheads – Actual Fixed Overheads

= Rs. 50,000 – Rs. 47,500 = Rs. 2,500 (F)

(*c*) Fixed Overhead Volume Variance = Recovered Fixed Overheads – Budgeted Fixed Overheads

= Rs. 45,000 – Rs. 50,000 = Rs. 5,000 (A)

Proof: Fixed Overhead Cost Variance = Fixed Overhead Expenditure Variance + Fixed Overhead Volume Variance

Rs. 2,500 (A) = Rs. 2,500 (F) + Rs. 5,000 (A)

Sub-Variances of Fixed Overhead Volume Variance: The Fixed Overhead Volume Variance can be further analysed as follows:

(*i*) Fixed Overhead Efficiency Variance

(*ii*) Fixed Overhead Capacity Variance

(*iii*) Fixed Overhead Calender Variance.

Fixed Overhead Efficiency Variance: It is that portion of Fixed Overhead Volume Variance which is due to the difference between the budgeted efficiency of production and the actual efficiency attained. This variance reflects the increased or reduced output arising from efficiency above or below the standard which is expected. It is calculated as follows:

Fixed Overhead Efficiency Variance = Recovered Overheads – Standard Overheads.

If the amount of standard overheads is in excess of the recovered overheads, the variance is adverse and vice-versa.

Fixed Overhead Capacity Variance: It represents that portion of Fixed Overhead Volume Variance which is due to the difference between the budgeted capacity specified and the actual capacity attained. This variance will indicate whether the capacity of the manufacturing concern has been fully utilised or not. It is calculated as follows:

Fixed Overhead Capacity Variance = Standard Fixed Overhead Rate per unit × (Revised Budgeted units – Budgeted units)

or

= Standard Fixed Overhead Rate per hour × (Revised Budgeted Hours – Budgeted Hours)

or

= Standard Overheads – Budgeted Overheads.

Fixed Overhead Calender Variance: Fixed Overhead Calender Variance is that portion of Fixed Overhead Volume Variance which arises due to the difference between the number of working days in the budget period and the actual number of working days in the period to which the budget is applied. It is calculated as follows:

Fixed Overhead Calender Variance = Possible Overheads – Budgeted Overheads

Where, Possible Overheads = Standard Rate of Overhead per Hour × Possible Hours

Possible Hours = Standard Working Hours per day × Actual Number of Working days

If the amount of possible overheads is more than the budgeted overheads, the variance will be favourable and vice-versa.

Note: In case the Calender Variance is calculated separately, the capacity variance (after segregating Calender Variance) will be calculated by applying the following formula:

Overhead Capacity Variance (Revised) = Standard Overhead – Possible Overhead.

Illustration 20

From the following data calculate fixed overhead cost, overhead expenditure, overhead efficiency, overhead capacity and overhead volume variances;

	Budget	Actual
Fixed overhead for Jan., 2007	Rs. 20,000	Rs. 20,400
Units of Production in Jan., 2007	10,000	10,400
Standard Time for one unit	4 hours	
Actual Hours Worked	20,100	

Solution

(*i*) Standard Overhead Rate per unit = $\frac{\text{Rs. } 20{,}000}{10{,}000 \text{ units}}$ = Rs. 2 per unit

(*ii*) Standard Overhead Rate per hour = $\frac{\text{Rs. } 2}{4 \text{ hrs.}}$ = Rs. 0.50 per hour.

(*iii*) Standard Hours for Actual Production = 10,400 units × 4 hrs. = 41,600 hrs.

(*iv*) Standard Overheads for Actual Production = 41,600 hrs. × Re. 0.50 = Rs. 20,800

Variances:

(*a*) Overhead Cost Variance = Recovered Overhead – Actual Overhead
= Rs. 20,800 – Rs. 20,400
= Rs. 400 (F)

(*b*) Overhead Expenditure Variance = Budgeted Overhead – Actual Overhead
= Rs. 20,000 – Rs. 20,400
= Rs. 400 (A)

(*c*) Overhead Volume Variance = Recovered Overhead – Budgeted Overhead
= Rs 20,800 – Rs. 20,000 = Rs. 800 (F)

(*d*) Overhead Efficiency Variance = Recovered Overhead – Standard Overhead
= Rs. 20,800 – Rs. 20,100 = Rs. 700 (F)

(*e*) Overhead Capacity Variance = Standard Overhead – Budgeted Overhead
= Rs 20,100 - Rs. 20,000 = Rs. 100(F)

Proof: Overhead Cost Variance = Overhead Expenditure Variance + Overhead Efficiency Variance + Overhead Capacity Variance

Rs. 400 (F) = Rs. 400 (A) + Rs. 700 (F) + Rs. 100 (F)

Illustration 21

A manufacturing company operating a standard costing system had the following data in respect of January, 2007:

Actual Number of working days:	22
Actual man-hours worked during the month:	8,600
Units produced:	850
Actual Fixed Overhead Incurred:	Rs. 3,600

The following information is obtained from the company's budget and standard cost data:

Budgeted Number of working days per month:	20
Budgeted man-hours per month:	8,000
Standard man-hours per unit produced :	10
Standard Fixed overhead rate per man-hour:	Re. 0.50

Calculate the Fixed Overhead Cost Variances for the month.

Solution

(*i*) Standard Fixed Overhead per unit = 10 hrs. × Re. 0.50 = Rs. 5

(*ii*) Standard Fixed Overhead per hour = Re. 0.50

(*iii*) Standard Working Hours per day = $\frac{8{,}000}{20}$ = 400 hrs.

(*iv*) Standard hours for actual output = 10 × 850 = 8,500 hrs.

(*v*) Possible Hours = Standard Working hours per day × Actual Number of working days
= 400 × 22 days = 8,800 hrs.

(*vi*) Recovered Overheads = Standard Overhead Rate per hour × Standard hours for actual output
= Re. 0.50 × 8,500 hrs. = Rs. 4,250

(*vii*) Budgeted Overheads = Standard Rate per hour × Budgeted Hours
= Re. 0.50 × 8,000 hours = Rs. 4,000

(*viii*) Standard Overheads = Standard Rate per hour × Actual Hours
= Re. 0.50 × 8,600 hrs. = Rs. 4,300

(*ix*) Actual Overheads = Rs. 3,600 (given)

(*x*) Possible Overheads = Standard Rate per hour × Possible Hours
= Re. 0.50 × 8,800 hrs. = Rs. 4,400

Variances

(*a*) Overhead Cost Variance = Recovered Overheads – Actual Overheads
= Rs. 4,250 – Rs. 3,600 = Rs. 650 (F)

(*b*) Overhead Expenditure Variance = Budgeted Overheads – Actual Overheads
= Rs. 4,000 – Rs. 3,600 = Rs. 400 (F)

(*c*) Overhead Volume Variance = Recovered Overheads – Budgeted Overheads
= Rs. 4,250 – Rs. 4,000 = Rs. 250 (F)

(*d*) Overhead Efficiency Variance = Recovered Overheads – Standard Overheads
= Rs. 4,250 – Rs. 4,300 = Rs. 50 (A)

(*e*) Overhead Capacity Variance = Standard Overheads – Budgeted Overheads
= Rs. 4,300 – Rs. 4,000 = Rs. 300 (F)

(*i*) Overhead Calender Variance = Possible Overheads – Budgeted Overheads
= Rs. 4,400 – Rs. 4,000 = Rs. 400 (F)

(*ii*) Overhead Capacity Variance (Revised) = Standard Overheads – Possible Overheads
= Rs. 4,300 – Rs. 4,400 = Rs. 100 (A)

Proof: Overhead Cost Variance = Overhead Expenditure Variance + Overhead Volume Variance

Rs. 650 (F) = Rs. 400 (F) + Rs. 250 (F)

Overhead Volume Variance = Overhead Efficiency Variance + Overhead Capacity Variance (Revised) + Overhead Calender Variance

Rs. 250 (F) = Rs. 50 (A) + Rs. 100 (A) + Rs. 400 (F)

Illustration 22

The details regarding a food product manufactured by ABC Co., for the last one week are as follows:

Standard cost for one unit

	Rs.
Direct materials 10 units @ Rs. 1.50	15
Direct wages 5 hours @ Rs. 8	40
Production overheads 5 hours @ Rs. 10	50
	105

Actuals (for whole activity)

Direct materials	Rs. 6,435
Direct wages	Rs. 16,324

Analysis of variances:

Direct materials:

Price Rs. 585 (adverse)

Usage Rs. 375 (favourable)

Direct wages (labour):

Rate Rs. 636 (favourable)

Efficiency Rs. 360 (adverse)

Production overheads:

Expenditure Rs. 400 (favourable)

Volume Rs. 750 (favourable)

You are required to calculate

(*i*) actual output units;

(*ii*) actual price of material per unit;

(*iii*) actual wage rate per labour hour;

(*iv*) the amount of production overhead incurred; and

(*v*) the production overhead efficiency variance.

(*C.A. Inter May 1999*)

Solution

(*i*) Calculation of Actual Output Units:

Material Cost Variance = Material Price Variance + Material Usage Variance

= Rs. 585 (A) + Rs. 375 (F)

= Rs. 210 (A)

Material Cost Variance = (Standard Quantity × Standard Price)

– (Actual Quantity × Actual Price)

Rs. 210 (A) = (Standard Quantity × Rs. 1.50) –Rs. 6,435

6,435 –210 = Standard Quantity × Rs. 1.50

Standard Quantity = 6,225 / 1.50 = 4,150 units of material

Material Usage Variance = (Standard Quantity – Actual Quantity)

× Standard Price per unit of material

Rs. 375 (F) = (4,150 units – Actual Quantity) Rs. 1.50

Rs. 375 (F) = Rs. 6,225 – (Rs. 1.50 × Actual Quantity)

Rs. 1.50 × Actual Quantity = Rs. 6,225 – Rs. 375

Rs. 1.50 × Actual Quantity = Rs. 5,850

Actual Quantity = Rs. 5,850 / Rs. 1.50 = 3,900 units of materials

Rate of consumption of material per unit of output 10 units

Actual consumption of material = 3,900 units

Actual output = 3,900 units / 10 units = 390 units

(*ii*) Calculation of Actual Price of Material per unit

Material Cost Variance= (Standard Quantity × Standard Price)

– (Actual Quantity × Actual Price)

Rs. 210 (A) = (4,150 units × Rs. 1.50) – (3,900 units × Actual Price)

Rs. 210 (A) = Rs. 6,225 – (3,900 units × Actual Price)

3,900 units × Actual Price = Rs. 6,225 + Rs. 210

3,900 units × Actual Price = Rs. 6,435

Actual price = Rs. 6,435/3,900 = Rs. 1.65 per unit of material

(*iii*) Calculation of Actual Wage Rate per labour hour

Labour Efficiency Variance = (Standard time – Actual time) × Standard wage rate

Rs. 360 (A)= [(390 units × 5 hrs) – Actual time] × Rs. 8

Rs. 360 (A)= Rs. 15,600 – Actual time × Rs. 8

Actual Time × 8 = Rs. 15,600 + Rs.360

Actual Time = Rs. 15,960/8 = 1,995 hours

Labour Cost Variance = Labour Rate Variance + Labour Efficiency Variance
= Rs. 636 (F) + Rs. 360(A) = Rs. 276 (F)

Labour Cost Variance = (Standard Time × Standard Wage Rate) – (Actual Time × Actual Wage Rate)
= (390 units × 5 hrs × Rs. 8) – (1,995 hrs × Actual wage rate)

Rs. 276 (F) = Rs. 15,600 – (1,995 hrs. × Actual wage rate)

1,995 hrs. × Actual wage rate = Rs. 15,600 – Rs. 276

Actual wage rate = 15,324/1,995 = Rs. 7.68 per hour

(*iv*) Calculation of the Amount of Production Overhead Incurred

Overhead Cost Variance = Overhead Expenditure Variance + Overhead Volume Variance
= Rs. 400 (F) + Rs. 750 (F) = Rs. 1,150 (F)

Production Overhead Cost Variance = (Actual Output × Standard Overhead Rate) – Actual Overheads

Rs. 1,150 (F) = (390 units × Rs. 50) – Actual Overheads

Rs. 1,150 (F) = 19,500 – Actual Overheads

Actual Overheads = Rs. 19,500 – Rs.1,150 = Rs. 18,350

(*v*) Calculation of the Production Overhead Efficiency Variance

Standard Quantity of materials = 4,150 units

Rate of consumption of material per unit of output =10 units (of material)

Standard output = 4,150/10 = 415 units

Overhead Efficiency Variance = Recovered Overheads – Standard Overheads

= (390 units × Rs. 50) – (415 units × Rs. 50)

= Rs. 19,500 – Rs. 20,750 = Rs. 1,250 (F)

Illustration 23

A company manufacturing two products uses standard costing system. The following data relating to April, 2001 have been furnished to you:

Products	**A**	**B**
	Rs.	**Rs.**
Standard Cost per unit:		
Direct Materials	2	4
Direct Wages	8	6
Fixed Overheads	16	12
	26	22

Units processed/in Process:

Beginning of the month: All materials applied and 50% complete in respect of labour and overheads 4,000 12,000

End of the month: All materials applied and 80% complete in respect of labour and overheads 8,000 12,000

Units completed and transferred to warehouse during the month 16,000 20,000

You may use average cost method to analyse.

The following were the actual costs recorded during the month:

Direct materials purchased at standard price amount to Rs. 2,00,000 and actual cost of which is Rs. 2,20,000. Direct materials used for consumption at standard price amount to Rs. 1,75,000. Direct wages for actual hours worked at standard wage rate were Rs. 4,20,000 and at actual wage rates were Rs. 4,12,000. Fixed overheads budgeted were Rs. 8,25,000 and actual fixed overheads incurred were Rs. 8,50,000.

Required:

(*i*) Direct material price variance at the point of consumption and at the point of purchase.

(*ii*) Direct material usage variance.

(*iii*) Direct wage rate and efficiency variance.

(*iv*) Fixed overheads volume and expenditure variance.

(*v*) Standard cost of WIP at the end of the month.

(*C.A. Inter, May, 2000*)

Solution

Statement of Equivalent Production

Output		Equivalent Production			
Items	Units	Material		Labour & Overhead	
		Units	% of Comp.	Units	% of Comp.
Product A:					
Units completed	16,000	16,000	100%	16,000	100%
Closing work-in-progress	8,000	8,000	100%	6,400	80%
	24,000	24,000		22,400	
Product B:					
Units completed	20,000	20,000	100%	20,000	100%
Closing work-in-progress	12,000	12,000	100%	9,600	80%
	32,000	32,000		29,600	

Direct Materials:

	Product A	Product B	Total Rs.
Equivalent units	24,000	32,000	
Standard cost per unit	2	4	
Standard cost of standard requirements of material	48,000	1,28,000	1,76,000
Standard cost of actual quantity of materials used			1,75,000
Actual cost of actual quantity of materials used $\left(\frac{2,20,000}{2,00,000} \times \text{Rs. } 1,75,000\right)$			1,92,500

Direct labour:

	Product A	Product B	Total Rs.
Equivalent units	22,400	29,600	
Standard direct wage rate per unit	8	6	
Standard direct wages at standard rate	1,79,200	1,77,600	3,56,800
Direct wages for actual hours at standard rate			4,20,000
Actual direct wages			4,12,000

Fixed overheads:

	Product A	Product B	Total Rs.
Equivalent units	22,400	29,600	
Fixed overhead per unit	16	12	
Fixed overhead charged to production	3,58,400	3,55,200	7,13,600
Budgeted fixed overheads			8,25,000
Actual fixed overheads			8,50,000

Calculation of Variances

(*i*) Direct Material Price Variance (at the point of consumption):
= (Standard cost of actual quantity – Actual cost of actual quantity)
= Rs. 1,75,000 – Rs. 1,92,500 = Rs. 17,500 (A)
Direct Material Price Variance (at the point of purchase):
= (Standard cost of materials purchased – Actual cost of materials purchased)
= Rs. 2,00,000 – Rs. 2,20,000 = Rs. 20,000 (A)

(*ii*) Direct Material Usage Variance
= (Standard cost of standard quantity required
– Standard cost of actual quantity used)
= Rs. 1, 76,000 – Rs. 1,75,000 = Rs. 1,000 (F)

(*iii*) Direct Wage Rate Variance:
= (Standard wages for actual hours – Actual wages for actual hours)
Rs. 4, 20,000 – Rs. 4,12,000 = Rs. 8,000 (F)
Labour Efficiency Variance:
= (Standard wages for standard hours – Standard wages for actual hours)
= Rs. 3,56,800 – Rs. 4,20,000 = Rs. 63,200 (A)

(*iv*) Fixed Overhead Volume Variance:
= (Fixed overhead recovered – Budgeted fixed overhead)
= Rs. 7,13,600 – Rs. 8,25,000 = Rs. 1,11,400 (A)
Fixed Overhead Expenditure Variance:
= (Budgeted fixed overhead – Actual fixed overhead)
= Rs. 8, 25,000 – Rs. 8,50,000 = Rs. 25,000 (A)

(*v*) Valuation of closing work-in-progress:

	Product A		Product B	
	Material	Labour & overhead	Material	Labour & overhead
Equivalent units	8,000	6,400	12,000	9,600
Standard cost per unit	2	24	4	18
Value of work-in-progress	16,000	1,53,600	48,000	1,72,800
Total	Rs.1,69,600		Rs. 2,20,800	

SALES VARIANCES

Some business firms are interested in calculating only cost variances relating to materials, labour and overheads. These variances are of great importance to the business firms. But in order to enjoy the full advantage of standard costing system, many business firms also calculate sales variances. Cost variances are related to cost and affect the budgeted profit due to increase or decrease in actual costs. On the other hand, sales variances are concerned with sales revenue and any change in the selling prices or sales quantities affects the budgeted profit favourably or adversely.

Sales variances can be calculated by two methods:

(A) The Value or the Turnover Method.

(B) The Profit or the Margin Method.

The Value or the Turnover Method: Under this method variances are calculated with reference to their effect on sales or sales value. A change in sales may be due to:

(*i*) Change in selling price, *i.e.*, the actual selling price may be higher or lower than standard selling price; and/or (*ii*) Change in volume, *i.e.*, quantities of sales attained may be higher or lower than those budgeted or actual mixture of sales may be different from standard mixture of sales.

As such, sales variances can be analysed as follows:

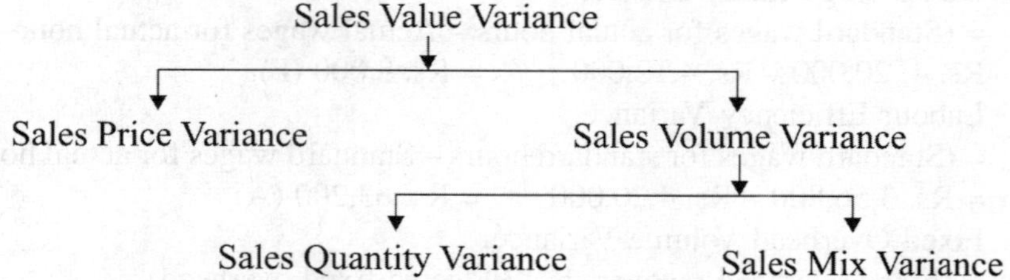

Sales Value Variance: Sales Value Variance is the difference between the actual sales and the budgeted sales. If the actual sales exceed the budgeted sales, the variance is favourable. But if the actual sales are less than the budgeted sales, the variance is treated as adverse or unfavourable. Sales Value Variance is calculated as follows:

Sales Value Variance =Actual Value of Sales – Budgeted Value of Sales.

Sales Price Variance: It is that portion of Sales Value Variance which arises due to the difference between the actual price and standard price of sales. If the actual price attained is more than the standard price, the variance shall be favourable and vice-versa. Sales Price Variance is calculated as follows:

Sales Price Variance = (Actual Sale Price – Standard Sale Price) × Actual Quantity Sold.

Sales Volume Variance: It is that portion of Sales Value Variance which arises due to the difference between the actual quantity sold and the standard quantity of sales. It is calculated as follows:

Sales Volume Variance = (Actual Quantity – Standard Quantity) × Standard Price.

Sales Quantity Variance: It is a sub-variance of Sales Volume Variance and represents that portion of sales volume variance which is due to the difference between standard value of actual sales at standard mix and the budgeted sales. It is calculated as follows:

Sales Quantity Variance = Standard Value of Revised Standard Mix – Budgeted Sales

or Sales Quantity Variance = (Revised Standard Mix – Standard Mix) × Standard Price

Sales Mix Variance: It is that portion of Sales Volume Variance which arises due to the difference between standard and actual composition of the sales mix. This variance arises only when the business firm deals in more than one product. It is calculated as follows:

Sales Mix Variance = Standard Sales Value of Actual Mix – Standard Sales Value of Revised Standard Mix.

Illustration 24

From the following Sales Budget and actual results attained, calculate the Sales Variances:

Products	Budget			Actual		
	Qty. (units)	Price Rs.	Value Rs.	Qty. (units)	Price Rs.	Value Rs.
A	2,500	5	12,500	3,300	6	19,800
B	1,500	10	15,000	1,200	9	10,800
C	1,000	15	15,000	1,500	14	21,000
	5,000		42,500	6,000		51,600

Solution

Before computing the Sales Variances, the following two calculations have to be made:

(*i*) Standard Value of the Actual Sales Mix *i.e.*, Actual Quantity sold at the Standard Price.

(*ii*) Standard Value of Revised Standard Sales Mix *i.e.*, Standard Ratio of Actual Sales at Standard Prices.

	Standard Value of Actual Sales Mix			Standard Value of Revised Standard Sales Mix		
Products	Qty. (units)	Price Rs.	Value Rs.	Qty (units)	Price Rs.	Value Rs.
A	3,300	5	16,500	3,000	5	15,000
B	1,200	10	12,000	1,800	10	18,000
C	1,500	15	22,500	1,200	15	18,000
	6,000		51,000	6,000		51,000

Revised Standard Sales Mix has been calculated as follows:

$$\text{Product A} = \frac{2{,}500}{5{,}000} \times 6{,}000 = 3{,}000 \text{ units}$$

$$\text{Product B} = \frac{1{,}500}{5{,}000} \times 6{,}000 = 1{,}800 \text{ units}$$

$$\text{Product C} = \frac{1{,}000}{5{,}000} \times 6{,}000 = 1{,}200 \text{ units}$$

Sales Value Variance = Actual Value of Sales – Budgeted Value of Sales

Product A = Rs. 19,800 – Rs. 12,500 = Rs. 7,300 (F)
Product B = Rs. 10,800 – Rs. 15,000 = Rs. 4,200 (A)
Product C = Rs. 21,000 – Rs. 15,000 = Rs. 6,000 (F)
= Rs. 9,100 (F)

Sales Price Variance = (Actual Sales Price – Standard Sales Price) × Actual Quantity

Product A = (Rs. 6 – Rs. 5) × 3,300 = Rs. 3,300 (F)
Product B = (Rs. 9 – Rs. 10) × 1,200 = Rs. 1,200 (A)
Product C = (Rs. 14 – Rs. 15) × 1,500 = Rs. 1,500 (A)
= Rs. 600 (F)

Sales Volume Variance = (Actual Quantity – Standard Quantity) × Standard Price

Product A = (3,300 – 2,500) × Rs. 5 = Rs. 4,000 (F)
Product B = (1,200 – 1,500) × Rs. 10 = Rs. 3,000 (A)
Product C = (1,500 – 1,000) × Rs. 15 = Rs. 7,500 (F)
= Rs. 8,500 (F)

Sales Mix Variance = Standard Sales Value of Actual Mix – Standard Sales Value of Revised Standard Mix
= Rs. 51,000 – Rs. 51,000 = 0

Sales Quantity Variance = Standard Sales Value of Revised Standard Mix – Budgeted Sales
= Rs. 51,000 – Rs. 42,500 = Rs. 8,500 (F)

Note: Calculation of Budgeted Sales (or Standard Sales)
Product A = 2,500 units × Rs. 5 = Rs. 12,500
Product B = 1,500 units × Rs. 10 = Rs. 15,000
Product C = 1,000 units × Rs. 15 = Rs. 15.000
= Rs. 42,500

The Profit or Margin Method: Under this method, sales variance analysis is made to measure the effect of deviations of actual from budgeted sales on profits. The variances to be calculated under this method may be given as follows:

Total Sales Margin Variance: It represents the difference between the actual margin from sales (valuing cost of sales at standard) and the budgeted margin and can be calculated as follows:

Total Sales Margin Variance = (Actual Sales – Standard Cost of Sales) – Budgeted Profit
or = Actual Profit – Budgeted Profit

Sales Margin Price Variance: It is that portion of the Total Margin Variance which is due to the difference between the standard price of the quantity of the sales effected and the actual price of those sales. Thus, it is the difference between the standard profit and the actual profit and is calculated as follows:

Sales Margin Price Variance = Actual Profit – (Actual Units Sold × Standard Profit per unit)
or = Actual Profit – Standard Profit

Sales Margin Volume Variance: It is that portion of Sales Margin Variance which is due to the difference between standard profit and budgeted profit and is calculated as follows:

Sales Margin Volume Variance = Standard Profit – Budgeted Profit

Sales Margin Quantity Variance: It is a part of Sales Margin Volume Variance and represents the difference between the budgeted profit and revised standard profit. It is calculated as follows:

Sales Margin Quantity Variance = Revised Standard Profit – Budgeted Profit

Sales Margin Mix Variance: It is a part of Sales Margin Volume Variance and arises due to the difference between standard profit and revised standard profit.

Illustration 25

Toshiba Toys Ltd has budgeted the following sales for the month of May:

Toy A = 900 units @ Rs 50 per unit
Toy B = 650 units @ Rs 100 per unit
Toy C = 1,200 units @ Rs 75 per unit

Actual sales were:

Toy A = 1,000 units @ Rs 55 per unit
Toy B = 700 units @ Rs 95 per unit
Toy C = 1,100 units @ Rs 78 per unit.

The costs per unit of A, B and C were Rs 45, Rs. 85 and Rs. 65 respectively. Compute the different variances and explain the difference between the budgeted and actual profit.

(*I.C.W.A., Final*)

Solution

Product	Quantity	Sales Price	Value	Cost of Sales Per unit	Amount	Profit Per unit	Amount
Budgeted							
		Rs.	Rs.	Rs.	Rs.	Rs.	Rs.
A	900	50	45,000	45	40,500	5	4,500
B	650	100	65,000	85	55,250	15	9,750
C	1,200	75	90,000	65	78,000	10	12,000
Total	2,750		2 ,00,000		1,73,750		26,250
Actual							
		Rs.	Rs.	Rs.	Rs.	Rs.	Rs.
A	1,000	55	55,000	45	45,000	10	10,000
B	700	95	66,500	85	59,500	10	7,000
C	1,100	78	85,800	65	71,500	13	14,300
Total	2,800		2,07,300		1,76,000		31,300

Standard sales and revised standard sales are computed as below:

Production	Sales Quantity	Price	Value	Cost Per unit	Amount	Profit Per unit	Amount
		Rs.	Rs.	Rs.	Rs.	Rs.	Rs.
A	1,000	50	50,000	45	45,000	5	5,000
B	700	100	70,000	85	59,500	15	10,500
C	1,100	75	82,500	65	71,500	10	11,000
Total	2,800		2,02,500		1, 76,000		26,500

Revised Standards

Product	Sales	Profit
	Rs.	Rs.
A	45,562	4,556
B	65,813	9,872
C	91,125	12,150
	2,02,500	26,578

Revised Standard Sales have been calculated as follows:

$$= \frac{\text{Budgeted Sales of the Product}}{\text{Total Budgeted Sales}} \times \text{Total Standard Sales}$$

$$\text{Product A} = \frac{45{,}000}{2{,}00{,}000} \times 2{,}02{,}500 = \text{Rs. } 45{,}562$$

$$\text{Product B} = \frac{65{,}000}{2{,}00{,}000} \times 2{,}02{,}500 = \text{Rs. } 65{,}813$$

$$\text{Product C} = \frac{90{,}000}{2{,}00{,}000} \times 2{,}02{,}500 = \text{Rs. } 91{,}125$$

Revised Standard Profit is computed as below:

*Budgeted profit percentage × Revised standard sales

$A = 45{,}562 \times 10\% = \text{Rs. } 4{,}556$

$B = 65{,}813 \times 15\% = \text{Rs. } 9{,}872$

$$C = 91{,}125 \times \frac{40}{3}\% = \text{Rs. } 12{,}150$$

*Budgeted Profit Percentage is calculated as follows:

$$A = \frac{4{,}500}{45{,}000} \times 100 = 10\%$$

$$B = \frac{9{,}750}{65{,}000} \times 100 = 15\%$$

$$C = \frac{12{,}000}{90{,}000} \times 100 = \frac{40}{3}\% = 13.33\%$$

Calculation of Variances:

Total Sales Margin Variance = Actual Profit – Budgeted Profit

						Rs.
A	=	10,000	–	4,500	=	5,500 (F)
B	=	7,000	–	9,750	=	2,750 (A)
C	=	14,300	–	12,000	=	2,300 (F)
Total		31,300		26,250	=	5,050 (F)

Sales Margin Price Variance = Actual Profit – Standard Profit

						Rs.
A	=	10,000	–	5,000	=	5,000 (F)
B	=	7,000	–	10,500	=	3,500 (A)
C	=	14,300	–	11,000	=	3,300 (F)
Total		31,300		26,500	=	4,800 (F)

Sales Margin Volume Variance = Standard Profit – Budgeted Profit

						Rs.
A	=	5,000	–	4,500	=	500 (F)
B	=	10,500	–	9,750	=	750 (F)
C	=	11,000	–	12,000	=	1,000 (A)
Total		26,500		26,250	=	250 (F)

Sales Margin Quantity Variance = Revised Standard Profit – Budgeted Profit

						Rs.
A	=	4,556	–	4,500	=	56 (F)
B	=	9,872	–	9,750	=	122 (F)
C	=	12,150	–	12,000	=	150 (F)
Total		26,578		26,250	=	328 (F)

Sales Margin Mix Variance = Standard Profit – Revised Standard Profit

						Rs.
A	=	5,000	–	4,556	=	444 (F)
B	=	10,500	–	9,872	=	628 (F)
C	=	11,000	–	12,150	=	1,150 (A)
Total		26,500		26,578	=	78 (A)

Proof:

Total Sales Margin Variance = Price Variance + Volume Variance

Rs. 5,050 (F) = Rs. 4,800 (F) + Rs. 250 (F)

Rs. 5,050 (F) = Rs. 5,050 (F)

Volume Variance = Quantity Variance + Mix Variance

Rs. 250 (F) = Rs. 328 (F) + Rs. 78 (A)

Rs. 250 (F) = Rs. 250 (F)

DISPOSITION OF VARIANCES

When standard costs are used by a business concern only as a statistical data and are not entered in the books of account, there is no problem as regards their disposal since no adjustments are required for variances in such a case. But in case, standard costs are incorporated into the accounting system through Work-in-Progress, Finished Goods and Cost of Goods Sold Accounts, there arises the need for adjustment and disposition of variances. There is no hard and fast rule regarding the disposition of variances nor there is any single way of dealing with them. The methods generally employed for disposition of variances may be given as follows:

(*i*) **Transfer to Costing Profit and Loss Account:** Under this method, variances are not treated as part of manufacturing costs and are transferred to Costing Profit and Loss Account at the end of the accounting period. Thus, the Work-in-Progress, Finished Goods and Cost of Goods Sold

Accounts are maintained at Standard Costs. This method assumes that Standard Cost represent correct or real costs and all forms of variances represent conditions of inefficiency, waste and below standard performance. This method has the advantage of prompt and uniform valuation of inventories and highlights the different variances separately to enable the management to pay due attention promptly and correctly.

(ii) **Allocation to various Stocks and Cost of Sales:** Under this method, variances are allocated to Finished Goods, Work-in-Progress and Cost of Goods Sold Accounts in proportion to the closing balances of each account. As a result of it, the inventories and cost of sales will appear in the books at actual cost. The allocation of all variances is not made in a uniform manner or to all accounts referred to above. For example, factory overhead variance may be allocated to all these accounts while office overhead variance may be allocated to Finished Goods and Cost of Goods Sold Accounts only. This method assumes that standard costs are only tools of control and do not represent the true or real costs.

(iii) **Transfer to Reserve:** The Variances arising due to seasonal factors may be transferred to a Reserve Account to be carried forward to the next accounting period as deferred 'debits' or 'credits'. This method is simple but can be applied to seasonal fluctuations only.

The first two methods of disposition of variances are simple to apply but the disposition should be made in the most logical way. In practice disposition of variances is affected by various factors like:

(*i*) Type of Variances *i.e.*, Material, Labour or Overhead,
(*ii*) Size of variance or amount involved,
(*iii*) Standard Cost Experience,
(*iv*) Causes for Variances, and
(*v*) Time of Variances etc.

All variances arising due to inaccuracy of standards or uncontrollable factors should be treated as part of costs and thus, should be allocated to Work-in-Progress, Finished Goods and Cost of Goods Sold on the basis of production (quantity or value) of that period. As against this, variances arising on account of controllable factors such as inefficiency, slackness, carelessness or idle time etc., should be transferred to Costing Profit and Loss Account.

OBJECTIVE TYPE QUESTIONS

A. Multiple Choice Questions

Select the correct answer:

(*a*) Difference between standard cost and actual cost is known as:

(*i*) Profit (*ii*) Loss
(*iii*) Wastage (*iv*) Variance.

(*b*) Excess of Actual Cost over Standard Cost is treated as:

(*i*) Favourable Variance (*ii*) Unfavourable Variance
(*iii*) Abnormal Effectives (*iv*) none of these.

(*c*) Standard quantity of material for one unit of output is 10 kgs. @ Rs. 8 per kg. Actual Output during a given period is 800 units. The standard quantity of raw material is:

(*i*) 8,000 kgs. (*ii*) 64,000 kgs.
(*iii*) 6,400 kgs. (*iv*) None of these

(*d*) Standard cost of material for a given quantity of output is Rs. 15,000 while the actual cost of material used is Rs. 16,200. The Material Cost Variance is:

(*i*) Rs. 16,200 (A) (*ii*) Rs. 15,000 (F)
(*iii*) Rs. 1,200 (A) (*iv*) Rs. 31,200 (A).

(*e*) For the purpose of Proof, Material Cost Variance is equal to:

(*i*) Material Price Variance + Material Usage Variance,
(*ii*) Material Price Variance +Material Yield Variance,
(*iii*) Material Mix Variance + Material Yield Variance,
(*iv*) Material Usage Variance + Material Mix Variance.

[**Ans.** (*a*) (*iv*); (*b*) (*ii*); (*c*) (*i*); (*d*) (*iii*); (*e*) (*i*)]

B. True/False Type Statements

State whether the following statements are True or False:

(*i*) Standard costing is more profitably employed in job order industries than in process type industries.

(*ii*) Standard costing cannot be used simultaneously with other methods like job costing.

(*iii*) Standard cost, once fixed, cannot be altered.

(*iv*) Pre-determined standards provide a yardstick for the measurement of efficiency.

(*v*) Standard costing aims at achieving maximum efficiency, hence standards should be based on ideal performance.

(*vi*) Standard costing is an ideal name given to the estimate making.

(*vii*) Fixing standards is the work of industrial engineers or the production people and not of cost accountant.

(*viii*) Material Cost Variance and Labour Cost Variance are always equal.

(*ix*) The total of Material Price Variance and Material Usage Variance should be equal to Material Cost Variance.

(*x*) Excess of Actual Cost over Standard Cost is treated as unfavourable variance.

(*xi*) While fixing standards, normal losses and wastages are taken into account.

(*xii*) Under the system of standard costing, there is no need for variance analysis.

(*xiii*) Variances are calculated for material, labour and overhead.

[**Ans.** (*i*) False; (*ii*) False; (*iii*) False; (*iv*) True; (*v*) False; (*vi*) False; (*vii*) False, (*viii*) False, (*ix*) True, (*x*) True, (*xi*) True, (*xii*) False, (*xiii*) True.]

C. Filling the Blanks

(*i*) Historical Costing uses post-period costs while standard costing uses .... costs.

(*ii*) Standard cost is a .... cost.

(*iii*) The drawbacks of .... have led to the developement of standard costing system.

(*iv*) Standard costing is more widely applied in .... industries.

(*v*) Three types of standards are ....

(*vi*) Standard costs for each product or service are recorded on .... card.

(*vii*) The .... is usually the co-ordinator of the standards committee.

(*viii*) The establishment of standard cost of direct material for each product will involve determination of standard quantity of material and ....

(*ix*) Basically there are two types of standards viz., (*a*) Basic standard, and ....

(*x*) The system of standard costing can't be introduced with advantage unless a well defined system of .... is in operation.

(*xi*) Standard Cost is a .... Cost.

(*xii*) Standard Costs when fixed are recorded on .... Card.

(*xiii*) Labour Cost Variance is sub-divided into .... Variance and .... Variance.

(*xiv*) Fixed Overhead Cost Variance is sub-divided into .... Variance and .... Variance.

(*xv*) When actual cost is less than the standard cost, it is known as .... Variance.

[**Ans.** (*i*) Pre-determined; (*ii*) Pre-determined; (*iii*) historical costing system; (*iv*) Process and Engineering Industries; (*v*) Current Standard, Basic Standard and Normal Standard; (*vi*) Standard Cost; (*vii*) Cost Accountant; (*viii*) Standard price of materials; (*ix*) Current Standard; (*x*) Budgetary Control; (*xi*) Pre-determined; (*xii*) Standard Cost; (*xiii*) Labour Rate, Labour efficiency; (*xiv*) Overhead Expenditure, Overhead Volume; (*xv*) Favourable.]

SHORT ANSWER TYPE QUESTIONS

1. What is meant by Standard Costing?
2. Distinguish between Standard Cost and Estimated Cost.
3. What is an ideal standard?
4. What are the limitations of Standard Costing?
5. What is meant by 'Standard Hour'? Give an example.
6. What is meant by 'Standard Cost Card'?
7. Distinguish between Basic Standard and Current Standard.
8. What do you mean by the term 'Variance'?
9. What is meant by 'Variance Analysis'?
10. What is the object of Variance Analysis?
11. Name the various Cost Variances.
12. What is Material Cost Variance?
13. Explain the meaning of Material Price Variance.
14. What is meant by Labour Rate Variance?
15. What is Labour Efficiency Variance? How is it calculated?
16. What is Overhead Expenditure Variance? How is it calculated?
17. Name the two methods of calculating Sales Variances.
18. State the reasons of Labour Efficiency Variance.
19. Write a brief note on Disposition of Variances.
20. State the reasons of Material Price Variance.

LONG ANSWER TYPE QUESTIONS

1. What is meant by Standard Costing? What are its advantages? Indicate in what type of industries this system is most suitable.
2. Explain the shortcomings of historical costing which are responsible for the emergence of standard costing system.
3. Distinguish between standard costing and budgetary control.
4. 'Standard costs today are basic for a proper managerial control of manufacturing operations.' Define standard cost and explain the above statement.
5. Describe the procedure of establishing standard costs within the divisions of material, labour and overhead costs.
6. There is a historical system of costing in operation in your company. Write a short report to the chief executive of the company recommending the introduction of standard costing system detailing the various advantages that would accrue.

7. What preliminaries are to be considered for installing a system of standard costing in an industry? Explain.

8. Discuss the advantages and disadvantages of standard costs and the conditions under which they may be adopted. (*G.N.D.U., B.Com., 2003*)

9. Outline the primary objects of Standard Costing. Describe briefly its uses under each of the following heads:
   (*a*) As measuring rod of performances.
   (*b*) As a basis of inventory valuation.
   (*c*) As an aid in preparing earnings budgets.
   (*d*) As a guide in fixing selling prices.

10. What is 'Variance Analysis'? Why is it called as a tool of management?

11. "The basic variances are Price and Usage Variance". Discuss this statement in relation to materials, labour and overheads indicating the main reasons for variations of actual costs when compared to standard costs.

12. State the reasons for each of the following variances:
    (*i*) Material Usage Variance,
    (*ii*) Material Mix Variance,
    (*iii*) Labour Efficiency Variance,
    (*iv*) Labour Rate Variance
    (*v*) Idle Time Variance.

13. Discuss the advantages and disadvantages of standard costing. What are the pre-requisites for the success of this system?(*G.N.D.U., B.Com., 2004*)

EXERCISES

1. (*a*) From the following, calculate Material Cost Variance:
   Standard Price = Rs. 14 per kg.
   Actual Price = Rs. 15 per kg.
   Standard Quantity = 600 kg.
   Actual Quantity = 500 kg. (*Madras, B.Com., March 1986*)

   (*b*) The following are the particulars regarding standard and the actual production of the Product X:
   Standard Quantity of Material per unit, 5 kg.
   Standard Price, Rs. 5 per kg.
   Actual Number of Units Produced, 400 units
   Actual Quantity of Material used, 2,200 kg.
   Price of material, Rs. 4.80 per kg.
   Calculate (*i*) Material Price, and (*ii*) Material Usage Variance
   (*G.N.D.U., B.Com. 2000; Madras, B.Com., May 1986*)

   [**Ans.** (*a*) MCV = Rs. 900 (Favourable)
   (*b*) MPV = Rs. 440 (Favourable); MUV = Rs. 1,000 (Adverse)]

2. (*a*) To manufacture a standard product, 10 units of materials are allowed at a standard price of Rs. 8 per unit. The actual production in a period was 10,000 products.

From the cost records, it is found that 1,05,000 units of materials were actually consumed and the price paid was 7.50 per unit.

Find out Materials Cost, Price and Quantity Variances.

[**Ans.** MCV = Rs. 12,500 (F), MPV = Rs. 52,500 (F)
MQV = Rs. 40,000 (A)]

(*b*) From the following calculate:

(*i*) Material Cost Variance
(*ii*) Material Usage Variance
(*iii*) Material Price Variance

Standard Quantity = 500 units
Actual Quantity = 520 units
Standard Price = Rs. 5 per unit
Actual Price = Rs. 5.50 per unit (*G.N.D.U., B.Com., 1996*)

[**Ans.** MCV Rs. 360 (A), MUV Rs. 100 (A), MPV Rs. 260 (A)]

3. A manufacturing concern which has adopted standard costing furnishes the following information:

Standard:

Material for 70 kg. Finished Products	100kg.
Price of Materials	Re. 1 per kg.

Actual:

Output	2, 10,000 kg.
Material used	2,80,000 kg.
Cost of materials	Rs. 2,52,000

Calculate:

(*a*) Material Usage Variance
(*b*) Material Price Variance
(*c*) Material Cost Variance

(*C.A., Inter; M.D.U., April 1984; G.N.D.U., B.Com. Hons., 1998*)

[**Ans.** (*a*) Rs. 20,000 (F)
(*b*) Rs. 28,000 (F)
(*c*) Rs. 48,000 (F)]

[**Hint:** (*i*) Standard quantity for actual output, 3,00,000 kgs.
(*ii*) Actual Price per kg., Re. 0.90.]

4. The Standard Cost Card for one unit of a product shows the following costs for material and labour:

Material – 4 pieces @ Rs. 5.00
Labour – 10 hours @ Rs. 1.50

5,700 units of the product were manufactured during the month of March, 2008 with the following material and labour costs

Material – 23,000 pieces @ Rs. 4.95

Labour – 56,800 hours @ Rs. 1.52

Calculate appropriate material and labour variances.

[B.Com. (Hons.), Delhi]

[**Ans.** (*i*) MCV Rs. 150 (F); MPV Rs. 1,150 (F); MQV Rs. 1,000 (A) (*ii*) LCV Rs. 836 (A); LRV Rs. 1,136 (A); LEV Rs. 300(F)]

5. (*a*) The following particulars are regarding the standard and the actual production of product X:

Standard quantity of material per unit – 5 kg

Standard price per kg. – Rs. 50

Actual number of units produced – 400.

Actual quantity of materials used – 2,200 kg.

Price of materials – Rs. 48 per kg.

Calculate:

(*i*) Material Price Variance

(*ii*) Material Usage Variance

(G.N.D.U., B.Com, 2001, Madurai)

[**Ans.** (*i*) Rs. 4,400 (F) (*ii*) Rs. 10,000 (A)]

(b) From the following information calculate:

(*i*) Labour Cost Variance, (*ii*) Labour Rate Variance, and (*ii*) Labour Efficiency Variance.

Actual Hours = 100 Standard Hours = 90

Standard Rate = Re. 1 per hour Actual Rate = Rs. 1.05 per hour.

(G.N.D.U., B.Com. 1997)

[**Ans.** LCV Rs. 15.00 (A), LRV Rs. 5.00 (A), LEV Rs. 10 (A)]

6. The standard costs on 'Material' and 'Labour' for the making of a unit of a certain product are estimated as under:

Material 80 kg. at Rs. 1.50 per kg.

Labour 18 hrs. at Rs. 1.25 per hour.

On completion of the production of a unit, it was found that 75 kgs. of material costing Rs. 1.75 per kg. has been consumed and that the time taken was 16 hours, the wage rate being 1.50 per hour.

You are required to calculate material and labour variances.

(B.Com., Delhi)

[**Ans.** MPV = Rs. 18.75 (A), MUV = Rs. 7.50 (F), LRV = Rs. 4 (A), LEV = Rs. 2.50 (F)]

7. Given that the cost standards for material consumptions are 40 kg. @ Rs. 10 per kg., compute the variances when actuals are:

(*a*) 48 kg. @ Rs. 10 per kg.
(*b*) 40 kg. @ Rs. 12 per kg.
(*c*) 48 kg. @ Rs. 12 per kg.
(*d*) 36 kg. for a total cost of Rs. 360.

(*C.A., Inter*)

[**Ans.** MPV – (*a*) nil, (*b*) Rs. 80 (A), (*c*) Rs. 96 (A), (*d*) nil;
MUV – (*a*) Rs. 80 (A), (*b*) nil, (*c*) Rs. 80 (A), (*d*) Rs. 40 (A)]

8. For a unit of product A, the Standard Data is given below:

Material	...5 kg. @ Rs. 40 per kg.	Rs. 200
Labour	...40 hrs. @ Re. 1.00 per hr.	Rs. 40
		Rs. 240

Actual Data:

Actual Production – 100 units	
Materials: 490 kg. @ Rs. 42 each = Rs. 20,580	
Labour 3,960 hrs. @ Rs. 1.10 per unit	4,356
	24,936

Calculate:

1. Material Cost Variance
2. Material Price Variance
3. Material Usage Variance
4. Labour Cost Variance
5. Labour Rate Variance
6. Labour Efficiency Variance (*M.Com., Bangalore*)

[**Ans.** 1. Rs. 580 (A), 2. Rs. 980 (A), 3. Rs. 400 (F),
4. Rs. 356 (A) 5. Rs. 396 (A), 6. Rs. 40 (F)]

9. From the following Data, calculate Material Mix Variance.

Materials	Standard Quantity	Actual Quantity	Price per unit (Rs.)
X	50	45	14
Y	40	35	12
Z	30	40	11

Due to shortage of X, it was decided to reduce its consumption by 10 and increase the consumption of Y and Z by 6 and 4 respectively.

(*B.Com., Calcutta*)

[**Ans.** Rs. 4 (A)]

10. The Standard Cost Card for a product shows as thus:

	Per Unit Rs.
Material Cost– 2 kg. @ Rs. 2.50 each	5.00
Wages– 2 hours @ 50 p. each	1.00

The actuals which have emerged from business operations are as follows:

Production	8,000 units

Materials Consumed–
16,500 kg. @ Rs. 2.40 each — Rs. 39,600
Wages Paid–
18,000 hours @ 40 p. each — Rs. 7,200

Calculate appropriate material and labour variances

[*B.Com. (Hons.) Delhi*]

[**Ans.** MPV Rs. 1,650 (F), MUV Rs. 1,250 (A), LRV Rs. 1,800 (F), LEV Rs. 1,000 (A)]

11. The Standard Material Cost to produce a tonne of chemical X is:

300 kg. of material A @ Rs. 10 per kg.
400 kg. of material B @ Rs. 5 per kg.
500 kg. of material C @ Rs. 6 per kg.

During a period, 100 tonnes of mixture X were produced from the usage of:

35 tonnes of material A at a cost of Rs. 9,000 per tonne.
42 tonnes of material B at a cost of Rs. 6,000 per tonne.
53 tonnes of material C at a cost of Rs 7,000 per tonne.

Calculate Price, Usage and Mix Variances.

[*I.C.W.A., Inter., B.Com. (Hons.), Delhi*]

[**Ans.** MPV Rs. 60,000 (A), MUV Rs. 78,000 (A); MMV Rs. 11,333 (A); MYV Rs. 66,667 (A)]

12. Compute Price, Usage and Mix Variances from the data given below:

	Standard			**Actual**		
	Quantity Kg.	**Unit Price**	**Total**	**Quantity Kg.**	**Unit Price**	**Total**
		Rs.	**Rs.**		**Rs.**	**Rs.**
Material A	6	1.50	9.00	5	2.40	12.00
Material B	2	3.50	7.00	1	6.00	6.00
Total	8	2.00	16.00	6	3.00	18.00

[**Ans.** Price Variance = Rs. 7 Unfav., Usage Variance = Rs. 5 Fav. and Mix Variance = Re. 1 Fav.]

13. Standard cost of a certain mixture of raw material in a process is:

70% material 'A' @ Rs. 50 per kg.
30% material 'B' @ Rs. 60 per kg.
Standard loss: 10% of input.

During a period, the following quantity of material has been used:

291 kgs. of material A @ Rs. 48 per kg.
109 kgs. of material B @ Rs. 65 per kg.
The actual output is 376 kgs.

Calculate:

(*i*) Material Cost Variance.

(*ii*) Material Price Variance.
(*iii*) Material Mix Variance.
(*iv*) Material Yield Variance
(*v*) Material Usage Variance.

[**Ans.** MCV Rs. 1,089.22 (F); MPV Rs. 37 (F); MMV Rs. 110 (F); MYV Rs. 942.22 (F); MUV Rs. 1052.22 (F)]

14. XYZ Ltd. has established the following standard mix for producing 9 gallons of product 'A':

	Rs.
5 gallons – Material X at Rs. 7 per gallon	35
3 gallons – Material Y at Rs. 5 per gallon	15
2 gallons – Material Z at Rs. 2 per gallon	4
	Rs. 54

A standard loss of 10% of input is expected to occur. Actual input was:

Material X – 53,000 gallons at Rs. 7 per gallon
Material Y – 28,000 gallons at Rs. 5.30 per gallon
Material Z – 19,000 gallons at Rs. 2.20 per gallon

Actual output for the period was 92,700 gallons. Calculate:

(*i*) Material Mix Variance,
(*ii*) Material Yield Variance. (*B.Com. Hons Delhi 1999*)

[**Ans.** MMV Rs. 9,000 (A); MYV Rs. 16,200 (F)]

15. The Standard mix of a product P is shown below:

Raw material X 30 units @ Rs. 2 each
Raw material Y 70 units @ Rs. 3 each

Standard loss is 10% of input. Actual mix is 34 units of X and 66 units of Y. Rates are the same. The actual loss is 15% of the input. Calculate the variances. (*I.C.S., Final*)

[**Ans.** Usage Variance = Rs. 11 Adverse; Mix Variance = Rs. 4 Fav; Yield Variance = Rs. 15 Adverse].

16. From the data given below compute Mix, Price and Usage Variances:

	Standard			**Actual**		
	Quantity Kg.	**Unit Price**	**Total**	**Quantity Kg.**	**Unit Price**	**Total**
		Rs.	**Rs.**		**Rs.**	**Rs.**
Material A	4	1.00	4.00	2	3.50	7.00
Material B	2	2.00	4.00	1	2.00	2.00
Material C	2	4.00	8.00	3	3.00	9.00
Total	8	2.00	16.00	6	3.00	18.00

(B.*Com. Hons. Delhi*)

[**Ans.** Mix Variance = Rs. 4 Adverse; Price Variance = Rs. 2 Adverse; Usage Variance = Rs. Nil].

17. The standard cost of a product is:

10 hours per unit at Rs 5 per hour. The actual data is:

Production 1,000 units

Hours taken

Production	10,400
Idle time	400
Total time	10,800 hours

Payments made Rs. 56,160 at Rs. 5.20 per hour. Calculate:

(*a*) Labour cost variance
(*b*) Labour efficiency variance
(*c*) Labour rate variance
(*d*) Idle time variance. *(B.Com., Meerut)*

[**Ans.** (*a*) Rs 6,160 (A), (*b*) Rs. 4,000 (A), (*c*) Rs 2,160 (A), (*d*) Rs 2,000 (A)]

18. For the following data, calculate:

(*a*) Labour cost variance
(*b*) Labour rate variance
(*c*) Labour efficiency variance.

	Deptt. A	Deptt. B
	Rs.	Rs.
Actual direct wages	2,000	1,800
Standard hours produced	8,000	6,000
Standard rate per hour	30 paise	35 paise
Actual hours worked	8,200	5,800

(I.C.W.A., Inter)

[**Ans.** Deptt. A (*a*) 400 (F), (*b*) 460 (F), (*c*) 60 (A)
Deptt. B (*a*) 300 (F), (*b*) 230 (F), (*c*) 70 (F)]

19. A gang of workers usually consists of 10 men, 5 women, and 5 boys paid at standard hourly rates of Rs. 1.25, Re. 0.80 and Rs 0.70 respectively. In a normal working week of 40 hours, the gang is expected to produce 1,000 units of output.

In a certain week, the gang consisted of 13 men, 4 women and 3 boys; actual hourly rates being Rs. 1.20, Re. 0.85 and Re. 0.65 respectively. Two hours were lost due to abnormal idle time and 960 units of output were produced.

Calculate appropriate labour variances. *(I.C.W.A., Adapted)*

[**Ans.** LCV Rs. 70 (A), LRV Rs. 24 (F), LEV Rs. 94 (A), LMV = Rs. 58.90 (A), LITV Rs. 43.10 (A), LREV Rs. 8 (F)]

20. In a factory section there are 80 workers and the average rate of wages per worker is Re. 0.50 per hour. Standard working hours per week are 45 and the standard performance is 6 units per hour.

During the four weeks in February, wages paid for 40 workers was Re. 0.50 per hour, for 15 workers Re. 0.60 per hour, and for 25 workers Re. 0.40 per hour.

The section did not work for 4 hours due to breakdown of machinery. Work out the labour rate variance for the Section for the 4 weeks.

[**Ans.** Labour rate variance = Rs. 180 Favourable].

(**Hints.** Standard wages for 80 workers @ 50 p. per hour for 4 weeks of 45 hours each $= 80 \times 4 \times 45 \times \frac{50}{100}$ = Rs. 7,200.

Actual Wages:

40 workers for 4 weeks of 45 hours each @ 50 p. per hour $= 40 \times 4 \times 45 \times \frac{50}{100}$ = Rs. 3,600

15 workers for 4 weeks of 45 hours each @ 60 p. per hour $= 15 \times 4 \times 45 \times \frac{60}{100}$ = Rs. 1,620

25 workers for 4 weeks of 45 hours each @ 40 p. per hour $= 25 \times 4 \times 45 \times \frac{40}{100}$ = Rs. 1,800

Rs. 7,020

[**Note.** Wages for 4 hours not worked due to breakdown of machinery will be paid].

21. From the particulars given below, compute: Material Price Variance, Material Usage Variance, Labour Rate Variance, Idle Time Variance and Labour Efficiency Variance with full working details.

One tonne of materials input yields a standard output of 1,00,000 units. The standard price of material is Rs. 20 per kg. Number of employees engaged is 200. The standard wage rate per employee per day is Rs. 6. The standard daily output per employee is 100 units. The actual quantity of material used is 10 tonnes and the actual price paid is Rs. 21 per kg. Actual output obtained is 9,00,000 units. Actual number of days worked is 50 and actual rate of wages paid is Rs. 6.50 per day. Idle time paid for and included in above time is 1/2 day.

(*C.A. Inter, May 1996*)

[**Ans.** MPV Rs. 10,000 (A); MUV Rs. 20,000 (A);
LRV Rs. 5,000 (A); ITV Rs. 5,400 (A); LEV Rs. 600 (A)]

22. The standard material input required for 1,000 kgs. of a finished product are given below:

Material	Quantity Kg.	Standard rate per kg. Rs.
P	450	20
Q	400	40
R	250	60
	1,100	
Standard loss	100	
Standard output	1,000	

Actual production in a period was 20,000 kgs. of finished product for which the actual quantities of material used and the prices paid thereof were as under:

Material	Quantity Kgs.	Actual rate per kg. Rs.
P	10,000	19
Q	8,500	42
R	4,500	65

Calculate (*i*) Material Cost Variance (*ii*) Material Price Variance (*iii*) Material Usage Variance (*iv*) Material Mix Variance (*v*) Material Yield Variance. (*I.C.W.A. Inter, June 1996*)

[**Ans.** MCV Rs. 39,500 (A); MPV Rs. 29,500 (A); MUV Rs. 10,000 (A); MMV Rs. 26,363 (F); MYV Rs. 36,363 (A)]

23. The standard output of 'X' is 25 units per hour in a manufacturing department of a company employing 100 workers. The standard wage rate per labour hour is Rs. 6.

In a 42 hours week, the department produced, 1,040 units of 'X' despite 5% of the time paid was lost due to abnormal reason. The hourly rate actually paid were Rs. 6.20, Rs. 6 and Rs. 5.70 respectively to 10, 30 and 60 workers. Compute relevant variances. (*C.A. Inter, May 1997*)

[**Ans.** LCV Rs. 432 (F); LEV Rs. 1,020 (F); LRV Rs. 672 (F); LITV Rs. 1,260 (A)]

24. Calculate variances from the standard for a particular month as disclosed from the following figures:

	Standard	In a Particular month
Number of workers employed	600	550
Average wages per worker per month	Rs. 250	Rs. 264
Number of working days in a month	25	24
Output in units	30,000	28,000

[**Ans.** Rate of Pay Variance = Rs. 13,200 Adverse; Efficiency Variance = Rs. 8,000 Favourable; Labour Cost Variance = Rs. 5,200 Adverse].

[**Hint.** Standard time for actual output of 28,000 units $= \frac{600 \times 25}{30,000} \times 28,000$

$= 14,000$ man days.

25. A contract job is scheduled to be completed in 30 weeks with a labour complement of 100 skilled operatives, 40 semi-skilled operatives and 60 unskilled operatives. The standard weekly wages of each type of operatives are-skilled Rs. 60, semi-skilled Rs. 36 and unskilled Rs. 24. The work is actually completed in 32 weeks with labour force of 80 skilled, 50 semi-skilled and 70 unskilled operatives and the actual weekly wages rates average Rs. 65 for skilled; Rs. 40 for semi-skilled and Rs. 20 for unskilled labour. Analyse the variances in the labour cost due to various reasons.

[**Ans.** Rate of Pay Variance = Rs. 10,240 Adverse;
Labour Efficiency Variance = Rs. 1,440 Favourable;
Labour Cost Variance = Rs. 8,800 Adverse].

26. The standard cost card for product 'Simco' reveals:

	Rs.
Standard materials –	
2 kg. of A Rs. 2 per kg.	4.00
1 kg. of B Rs. 6 per kg.	6.00
Direct labour (3 hours @ Rs. 6 per hour)	18.00
Variable Overhead (3 hours @ Rs. 4 per direct labour hour)	12.00
Total standard cost per unit	40.00

It is proposed to produce 10,000 units of 'Simco' in the month of March and budgeted cost based on the information contained in the standard cost card are as follows:

	Rs.
Direct materials –	
A 20,000 kg. @ Rs. 2 per kg.	40,000
B 10,000 kg. @ Rs. 6 per kg.	60,000
Direct labour (30,000 hours @ Rs. 6 per hour)	1,80,000
Variable overhead (30,000 hours @ Rs. 4 per direct labour hour)	1,20,000
	4,00,000

The actual results are:

Direct materials –	
A 19,000 kg. @ Rs. 2.20 per kg.	41,800
B 10,100 kg. @ Rs. 5.60 per kg.	56,560
Direct labour (28,500 hours @ Rs. 6.40 per hour)	1,82,400
Variable overheads	1,04,000
	3,84,760

Actual production was 9,000 units.
From the above information calculate the following variances:
Material : (*a*) price and usage
Labour : (*b*) wages rate and labour efficiency

Variable overhead: (*c*) total variable overhead variance and overhead expenditure variance.

(*G.N.D.U., B.Com., 2000*) (*B.Com. Hons., Delhi 1992*)

[**Ans.** (*a*) MPV Rs. 240 (F), MUV = Rs. 8,600 (A)
(*b*) LRV Rs. 11,400 (A), LEV Rs. 9,000 (A)
(*c*) TVOV Rs. 4,000 (F), OEV = Rs. 10,000 (F)]

27. S.V. Ltd. manufactures a simple product, the standard mix of which is:

Material A	60% at Rs. 20 per kg.
Material B	40% at Rs. 10 per kg.

Normal loss in production is 20% of input. Due to shortage of Material A, the standard mix was changed. Actual results for March, 2000 were:

Material A	105 kg. at Rs. 20 per kg.
Material B	95 kg. at Rs. 9 per kg.
Input	200 kg.
Loss	35 kg
Output	165 kg.

Calculate:

(*i*) Material Price Variance, (*ii*) Material Usage Variance, (*iii*) Material Mix Variance, (*iv*) Material Yield Variance.

(*B.Com. Hons. Delhi 1991*) (*G.N.D.U., B.Com., 2001*)

[**Ans.** (*i*) Rs. 95 (F); (*ii*) Rs. 2,050 (F); (*iii*) Rs. 150 (F); (*iv*) Rs. 100 (A)]

28. (*a*) Bellow Chemical Industries provide the following information from their record:

For making 10 kgs. of OMO, the standard material requirement is:

Material	**Quantity (Kgs.)**	**Rate per kg. (Rs.)**
X	8	6.00
Y	4	4.00

During December, 2009, 100 kgs. of OMO were produced. The actual consumption of material is as under:

Material	**Quantity (Kgs.)**	**Rate per kg. (Rs.)**
X	75	7.00
Y	50	5.00

Calculation required:

(*i*) Material Cost Variance
(*ii*) Material Price Variance
(*iii*) Material Usage Variance.

(*b*) From the following information compute Fixed Overhead Cost, Expenditure and Volume/Capacity Variances.

Normal capacity is 5,000 hours. Budgeted fixed overhead rate is Rs. 10 per standard hour. Actual level of capacity utilised is 4,400 standard hours. Actual fixed overheads Rs. 52,000.

(*B.Com Hons., Delhi 1991*)

[**Ans.** (*a*) (*i*) Rs. 135 (A); (*ii*) Rs. 125 (A) (*iii*) Rs. 10 (A); (*b*) FOC Rs. 8,000 (A) EV Rs. 2,000 (A), V/CV Rs. 6,000 (A)]

29. Mixers Ltd., is engaged in producing a 'standard mix' using 60 kgs. of chemical X and 40 kgs. of chemical Y. The standard loss of production is 30%. The standard price of X is Rs. 5 per kg. and of Y Rs. 10 per kg.

The actual mix and yield were as follows:

X 80 kgs. @ Rs. 4.50 per kg.

Y 70 kgs. @ Rs. 8.00 per kg.

Actual Yield: 115 kgs.

Calculate Direct Material Cost, Price, Usage Mix and Yield Variances.

[**Ans.** MCV = Rs. 230 (F), MPV = Rs. 180 (F) MUV = Rs. 50 (F) MMV = 450 (A), MYV = Rs. 100 (F)].

30. A company produces a single product from a single material. It operates a standard cost system and furnishes you the following information;

Particulars:	**Budgeted (Standard)**	**Actual**
Product units	8,000	6,000
Materials:		
Total quantity – kg.	16,000	13,000
Total amount – Rs.	32,000	27,300
Labour:		
Total hours	2,400	2,000
Total amount – Rs.	3,000	3,000
Variable overhead expenses:		
Total hours	2,400	2,000
Total amount – Rs.	2,400	2,000

You are required to compute the following variances:

(*a*) Material Price Variance

(*b*) Material Usage Variance

(*c*) Labour Rate Variance

(*d*) Labour Efficiency Variance

(*e*) Overhead Efficiency Variance

(*f*) Overhead Budget Variance. (*C.A., Inter; G.N.D.U. B.Com. April 1998*)

[**Ans.** (*a*) Rs. 1,300 (A), (*b*) Rs. 2,000 (A), (*c*) Rs. 500 (A), (*d*) Rs. 250 (A), (*e*) 200 (A), (*f*) Rs. 400 (A)]

(**Hint:** It is presumed that overheads are variable.

Budgeted overheads for actual output are = $\frac{2,400 \times 6,000}{8,000}$ = Rs. 1,800)

31. Calculate overhead variances from the following data:

	Standard	**Actual**
Fixed overheads (Rs.)	8,000	8,500
Variable overheads (Rs.)	12,000	11,200
Output in units	4,000	3,800

[**Ans.** Variable Overhead Variance Rs. 200 Fav; Fixed Overhead Variance Rs. 900 Adverse; Volume Variance Rs. 400 Adverse; Fixed Overhead Expenditure Variance Rs. 500 Adverse].

32. The following information was obtained from the records of a manufacturing unit using Standard Costing System:

	Standard	**Actual**
Production	4,000 units	3,800 units
Working Days	20	21
Fixed Overheads (Rs.)	40,000	39,000
Variable overhead (Rs.)	12,000	12,000

You are required to calculate the following Overhead Variances:

(*a*) Variable Overhead Variance
(*b*) Fixed Overhead Variance
(*i*) Expenditure Variance
(*ii*) Volume Variance
(*iii*) Efficiency Variance
(*iv*) Calender Variance

[**Ans.** (*a*) Rs. 600 Adverse; (*b*) Rs. 1,000 Adverse; (*i*) Rs. 1,000 Fav; (*ii*) Rs. 2,000 Adverse, (*iii*) Rs. 4,000 Adverse, (*iv*) Rs. 2,000 Fav.]

33. A manufacturer operating a standard costing system had the following data in respect of a month:

	Standard	**Actual**
Number of working days	25	27
Man hours per month	5,000	5,400
Output in units	500	525
Fixed Overheads (Rs.)	2,500	2,400

Calculate fixed overheads variance for the month.

[**Ans.** Total Fixed Overhead Variance Rs. 225 Favourable; Volume Variance Rs. 125 Favourable; Expense Variance Rs. 100 Favourable; Capacity Variance Nil; Calender Variance Rs. 200 Favourable; Efficiency Variance Rs. 75 Adverse].

34. From the following data, calculate:

(*a*) efficiency variance,
(*b*) capacity variance,
(*c*) calender variance,
(*d*) volume variance, and
(*e*) expenditure variance.

Item	Budgeted	Actual
No. of working days	20	22
Man hours per day	8,000	8,400
Output per man hour in units	1.0	0.9
Overheads (Rs.)	1,60,000	1,68,000

[**Ans.** (*a*) Rs. 18,480 Unfav; (*b*) Rs. 8,800 Fav; (*c*) Rs. 16,000 Fav; (*d*) Rs. 6,320 Fav; and (*e*) Rs. 8,000 Unfav].

35. Vimal Ltd. has furnished you the following information for the month of August, 2009:

	Budget	Actual
Output (units)	30,000	32,500
Hours	30,000	33,000
Fixed Overheads (Rs.)	45,000	50,000
Variable Overheads (Rs.)	60,000	68,000
Working days	25	26

You are required to calculate the various overhead variances.

(*G.N.D.U., B.Com., 2008*) (*C.A. Inter*)

[**Ans.** I Variable Overheads Variance = Rs. 3,000 (Adverse)]

II Fixed Overheads Variance:

(*i*) Expenditure Variance = Rs. 5,000 (Adverse)
(*ii*) Volume Variance = Rs. 3,750 (Favourable)
(*iii*) Total Variance = Rs. 1,250 (Adverse)
(*iv*) Capacity Variance = Rs. 2,700 (Favourable)
(*v*) Calender Variance = Rs. 1,800 (Favourable)
(*vi*) Efficiency Variance = Rs. 750 (Adverse)

36. The following data have been collected from the cost records of a unit for computing the various fixed overhead variances for a period:

Number of budgeted working days	25
Budgeted man-hours per day	6,000
Output (budgeted) per man-hour (in units)	1
Fixed overhead cost as budgeted	Rs. 1,50,000
Actual number of working days	27
Actual man-hours per day	6,300
Actual output per man-hour (in units)	0.9
Actual fixed overhead incurred	Rs. 1,56,000

Calculate Fixed Overhead Variances–

(*a*) Expenditure Variance, (*b*) Calendar Variance,
(*c*) Capacity Variance, (*d*) Efficiency Variance,
(*e*) Volume Variance, (*f*) Fixed Cost Variance.

(*I.C.W.A. Inter, Dec. 1995*)

[**Ans.** (*a*) Rs. 6,000 (A); (*b*) Rs. 12,000 (F); (*c*) Rs. 8,100 (F); (*d*) Rs. 17,010 (A); (*e*) Rs. 3,090 (F); (*f*) Rs. 2,910 (A)]

37. A company has a normal capacity of 120 machines, working 8 hours per day of 25 days in a month. The fixed overheads are budgeted at Rs. 1,44,000 per month. The standard time required to manufacture one unit of product is 4 hours.

In April, the company worked 24 days of 840 machine hours per day and produced 5,305 units of output. The actual fixed overheads were Rs. 1,42,000. Compute:

(*i*) Efficiency Variance (*ii*) Capacity Variance
(*iii*) Calendar Variance (*iv*) Expenditure Variance
(*v*) Volume Variance (*vi*) Total Fixed Overheads Variance.

(*C.A. Inter, May 1998*)

[**Ans.** (*i*) Rs. 6,360 (F); (*ii*) 17,280 (A); (*iii*) Rs. 5,760 (A); (*iv*) Rs. 2,000 (F); (*v*) Rs. 16,680 (A); (*vi*) Rs. 14,680 (A)]

38. Select the most appropriate answer:

Labour rate variance is computed by multiplying the:

(*a*) Standard labour rate with the difference between standard labour hours.

(*b*) Actual labour hours with the difference between standard labour hours and actual labour hours.

(*c*) Actual labour rate with the difference between standard labour hours and actual labour hours.

(*d*) None of the above. (*B.Com. Punjab, April 1993*)

[**Ans.** [(*d*)]

39. The following information is available from the cost records of a Company for February, 2008:

	Rs.
Materials purchased: 20,000 pieces	88,000
Materials consumed: 19,000 pieces	
Actual Wages paid	24,750
Factory Overheads Incurred	44,000
Factory Overheads Budgeted	40,000
Units produced	1,800

Standard Rates and Prices are:
Direct Material Rate Rs. 4 per piece.
Standard Input 10 pieces per unit.
Direct Labour Rate Rs. 4 per hour
Standard requirement 2.5 hours per unit
Overhead Rs. 8 per labour hour.
Required: (*a*) Show the Standard Cost Card.
(*b*) Compute all material, labour and overhead variances for February, 2008.

(*C.A. Inter*)

40. From the following information about sales, calculate:

(*a*) Total Sales Variance
(*b*) Sales Price Variance
(*c*) Sales Volume Variance
(*d*) Sales Mix Variance
(*e*) Sales Quantity Variance.

Product	Nos.	Standard Rate in Rs. per unit	Rs.	Nos.	Actual Rate in Rs. per unit	Rs.
A	5,000	5	25,000	6,000	6	36,000
B	4,000	6	24,000	5,000	5	25,000
C	3,000	7	21,000	4,000	8	32,000
	12,000		70,000	15,000		93,000

(*I.C.W.A., Inter Dec. 1984*)

[**Ans.** (*a*) Rs. 23,000 Favourable; (*b*) Rs. 5,000 Favourable; (*c*) Rs. 18,000 Favourable; (*d*) Rs. 500 Favourable; (*e*) Rs. 17,500 Favourable].

41. PH Ltd. furnishes the following information relating to budgeted sales and actual sales for April, 2009:

	Product	Sales Quantity (units)	Selling Price per unit Rs.
Budgeted sales:	A	1,200	15
	B	800	20
	C	2,000	40
		4,000	
Actual sales:	A	800	18
	B	880	20
	C	2,640	38
		4,320	

Calculate the following Variances:

(*i*) Sales Quantity Variance
(*ii*) Sales Mix Variance
(*iii*) Sales Price Variance
(*iv*) Total Sales Variance. (*C.A. Inter 1981*)

[**Ans.** (*i*) Rs. 19,380 (A), (*ii*) Rs. 40,580 (F), (*iii*) Rs. 2,880 (A), (*iv*) Rs. 18,320 (F)].

42. From the following particulars, calculate:

(*a*) Total sales margin variance.
(*b*) Sales margin variance due to selling price.
(*c*) Sales margin variance due to volume.

Product	Standard			Actual		
	Quantity	Cost per unit	Price per unit	Quantity	Cost per unit	Price per unit
X	3,000 units	Rs. 10	Rs. 12	3,200 units	Rs. 10.50	Rs. 13
Y	2,000 units	Rs. 15	Rs. 18	1,600 units	Rs. 14.00	Rs. 17

[**Ans.** (*a*) Rs. 800 Fav; (*b*) Rs. 1,600 Fav; (*c*) Rs. 800 Unfav.]

43. Ultra Modern Cassette Ltd., has budgeted the following sales for February, 2009:

Cassette A 1,100 units @ Rs. 50 per unit
Cassette B 950 units @ Rs. 100 per unit
Cassette C 1,250 units @ Rs. 80 per unit

As against this, the actual sales were:

Cassette A 1,300 units @ Rs. 55 per unit
Cassette B 1,000 units @ Rs. 95 per unit
Cassette C 1,200 units @ Rs. 78 per unit.

The cost per unit of cassette A, B and C was Rs. 45, Rs. 85 and Rs. 70 respectively.

Compute the different variances to explain the difference between the budgeted and actual profit.

(*C.S. Inter, June 1992*)

[**Ans.** Total Sales Margin Variance Rs. 350 (F); Sales Margin Variance due to Selling Price Rs. 900 (A); Sales Margin Variance due to volume Rs. 1,250 (F); Sales Margin Variance due to Sales quantity Rs. 1,955 (F); Sales Margin Variance due to Sales Mixture Rs. 705 (A); Actual Profit 32,600; Budgeted Profit Rs. 32,250].

44. Compute the following variances from the data given below:

(1) Total sales margin variance.
(2) Sales margin volume variance.
(3) Sales margin price variance.
(4) Sales margin quantity (Sub-volume) variance.

Product	Budgeted quantity units	Actual quantity units	Budgeted sale price per unit	Actual sale price per unit	Standard cost per unit
			Rs.	Rs.	Rs.
X	240	400	50	45	30
Y	160	200	25	20	15

(*C.A. Inter, May 1992*)

[**Ans.** (1) Rs. 600 Fav.; (2) Rs. 3,600 Fav.; (3) Rs. 3,000 Adverse; (4) Rs. 3,200 Fav.]

45. The budgeted and actual sales for a period in respect of three products are given below:

Budgeted Figures:

Products	Quantity	Price Rs.	Value Rs.
A	1,000	5	5,000
B	750	10	7,500
C	500	15	7,500
	2,250		20,000

Actual:

Products	Quantity	Price Rs.	Value Rs.
A	1,200	6	7,200
B	700	9	6,300
C	600	14	8,400
	2,500		21,900

Calculate Sales Variances. (*C.A. Inter, Nov. 1998*)

[**Ans.** SVV (value) Rs. 1,900 (F); SPV Rs. 100 (A); SVV (volume) Rs. 2,000 (F); SMV Rs. 222 (F); SQV Rs. 2,222 (F)]

46. In a certain period, results were as follows:

Output = 6,500 units: Wages paid Rs. 48,750 for 16,250 hours
Material Rs. 34,000 for 4,000 kgs.

Variances:

Labour Rate	Rs. 1,875 (Adverse)
Labour Efficiency	Rs. 1,275 (Favourable)
Labour Idle Time	Rs. 700 (Adverse)
Material Price	Rs. 1,850 (Favourable)
Material Usage	Rs. 1,200 (Favourable)

Calculate the Standard Prime Cost per unit. (*C.S. Inter Dec. 1999*)

[**Ans.** Rs. 13]

47. S. Ltd. operates a system of standard costing in respect of one of its products which is manufactured within a single cost centre. The following information is available:

For one unit of product the standard material input is 20 litres at a standard price of Rs. 2 per litre. The standard wage rate is Rs. 6 per hour and 5 hours are allowed in which to produce one unit. Fixed production overhead is absorbed at the rate of 100% of direct wages cost. During the month just ended the following occurred:

Actual price paid for material purchased Rs. 1.95 per litre
Total direct wages cost was Rs. 1,56,000
Fixed production overhead incurred was Rs. 1,58,000

Variances:	**Favourable**	**Adverse**
	Rs.	**Rs.**
Direct material price	8,000	–
Direct material usage	–	5,000
Direct labour rate	–	5,760
Direct labour efficiency	2,760	–
Fixed production overhead expenditure	–	8,000

Required:Calculate the following for the month

(*i*) Budgeted output in units.
(*ii*) Number of litres purchased.
(*iii*) Number of litres used above standard allowed.
(*iv*) Actual units produced.
(*v*) Actual hours worked.
(*vi*) Average actual wage rate per hour.

(*C.A.Inter Nov. 1995*)

[**Ans.** (*i*) 5,000 units; (*ii*) 1,60,000 Litres; (*iii*) 2,500 Litres; (*iv*) 5,100 units; (*v*) 25,040 Hrs.; (*vi*) Rs. 6.23]

21

Marginal Costing-I
(Variable Costing)

Profit planning, cost control and decision-making require the application of marginal costing technique in all the industries. Marginal costing is not a system of cost ascertainment but a special technique to deal with the effects on cost or profits, of changes in the volume or range of output and sales. Before discussing the meaning and features of marginal costing, it is necessary to know the meaning of marginal cost.

MARGINAL COST

The Institute of Cost and Management Accountants, London, has defined 'marginal cost' as "the amount at any given volume of output by which aggregate costs are changed if the volume of output is increased or decreased by one unit. In practice, this is measured by the total variable cost attributable to one unit." In this context, a unit may be a single unit, a batch of articles, an order, a stage of production capacity, a process or a department. Suppose the cost of production of 1,000 units is Rs. 6,000 and that of 1,001 units is Rs. 6,004, the marginal cost is Rs. 4. Marginal cost is the variable cost comprising the cost of direct materials consumed, direct wages paid and the variable overhead incurred for producing the additional unit.

MARGINAL COSTING

Marginal costing has been defined by the Institute of Cost and Management Accountants as "the ascertainment, by differentiating between fixed costs and variable costs, of marginal costs and of the effect on profit of changes in volume or type of output." Thus, marginal costing is not a system of ascertaining cost, such as process costing, job costing, operating costing etc., but a special technique which is concerned with the changes in costs resulting from changes in the volume or range of output. J. Batty has defined Marginal costing as "a technique of cost accounting which pays attention to the behaviour of costs with changes in the volume of output."[1] It is said to be super-imposed upon a system of job costing or process costing.

Features of Marginal Costing:

Marginal costing technique has the following main features:

1. Marginal costing is not a method of costing like process costing, job costing, operating costing etc., but a technique dealing with the effects of changes in the cost, volume, price, sales mix on the profits.
2. Marginal costing is concerned with marginal cost only. Under marginal costing technique, cost of production comprises of variable costs only. As such the valuation of the finished goods and work-in-progress is made on the basis of variable costs only.
3. Fixed costs do not form part of cost of production for the purposes of marginal costing. They are treated separately and may be charged wholly to the Profit and Loss Account for the accounting period.
4. The profitability of a product or department is ascertained in terms of 'Contribution' or 'Contribution Margin'. Contribution represents the difference between sales value and marginal cost of sales. The aggregate of contribution for all products is called 'fund'.
5. For marginal costing techniques prices of the various products are fixed by the manufacturing concerns on the basis of marginal cost and marginal contribution.

STEPS INVOLVED IN MARGINAL COSTING

The technique of marginal costing involves:

(*a*) differentiation between fixed costs and variable costs;

(*b*) ascertainment of marginal costs; and

(*c*) ascertaining the effect on profit due to changes in volume or type of output *i.e.*, the determination of cost-volume-profit relationship.

Differentiation between Fixed Costs and Variable Costs:

Marginal costing technique involves the segregation of all costs into fixed costs and variable costs. Costs may be divided into fixed costs, variable costs and semi-fixed or semi-variable costs. Fixed cost may be defined as a cost which tends to remain unaffected in aggregate by changes in the volume of output. Fixed costs are generally referred to as period costs as they are incurred on the basis of time and do not vary directly with volume or rate of output such as rent, rates, insurance premium etc. Variable cost may be defined as a cost which tends to change in aggregate in direct proportion to changes in output. Variable costs mainly depend on output and are sometimes referred to as direct costs. Examples of variable costs are direct material cost, direct wages, direct expenses

1. J.Batty, Standard Costing, 2nd Ed., p. 287

etc. Semi-variable cost or semi-fixed cost is a cost which is partly fixed and partly variable. It tends to change in aggregate with changes in volume of output but not directly in proportion to such changes. Examples of semi-variable costs are repairs and maintenance, cost of supervision etc.

DETERMINATION OF MARGINAL COST

Under the marginal costing technique only variable costs are applied to products. The cost of production is the marginal cost of production and the cost of sales is the marginal cost of sales. Marginal cost refers to the aggregate of prime cost and all variable overheads. Prime cost is the aggregate of direct material cost, direct wages and direct or chargeable expenses. 'All variable overheads' means variable overheads plus the variable portion of semi-variable overheads. Semi-variable overheads are partly fixed and partly variable, and require segregation into fixed and variable elements. The variable portion is added to variable overheads thus forming part of marginal cost whereas the fixed portion is added to fixed overheads and the total fixed overheads are treated as separate costs. These separate costs are related to time and hence known as 'period costs.'

The main problem to a cost accountant is to segregate the semi-variable overhead into fixed and variable elements. Segregation or separation of semi-variable overhead into fixed and variable elements can be done by adopting various methods such as Comparison Method, High and Low Points Method, Equation Method, Averages Method, Graphical Method or Least Squares Method. These methods have already been discussed in detail in chapter 8 on Overhead (1)

Cost-Volume-Profit Relationship

At this stage, we know that variable or marginal costs vary directly with production while fixed costs remain unchanged without any regard to the quantity of output. If this cost behaviour is related to sales revenue, it will show the cost-volume-profit relationship. This cost-volume-profit relationship actually represents the net effect of changes in cost, volume and price on the profits of the firm. Cost-volume-profit analysis is a device which is used to determine the usefulness of the profit planning process of the firm. Analysis of the cost-volume-profit relationship provides answers to questions such as:

(*a*) What should be the minimum level of sales to avoid losses?
(*b*) What should be the sales level to earn desired profits?
(*c*) What will be the effect of changes in costs, prices and volume on profits?
(*d*) What will be the effect of changes in sales-mix on profits?
(*e*) What will be the revised break-even point in case there is a change in costs, prices, volume or sales-mix?
(*f*) Which product is most profitable and which one is the least profitable?
(*g*) Should the sale of a product be discontinued? and so on.

ABSORPTION COSTING Vs. MARGINAL COSTING

Absorption costing is the traditional practice of charging all costs, variable as well as fixed to operations, processes or products. On the other hand, marginal costing is the technique of charging variable costs to operations, processes or products.

Under absorption costing, the stock of finished goods and work-in-progress is valued on the basis of total cost, comprising of fixed and variable costs. But, under marginal costing valuation of stock of finished goods and work-in-progress is made on the basis of variable cost only. Fixed cost is treated as a 'period cost' and is transferred to Profit & Loss Account.

Absorption costing technique involves the arbitrary apportionment of fixed costs which generally leads to under-and over-absorption of costs. On account of exclusion of fixed costs from marginal costing, the problem of arbitrary apportionment of overhead does not arise at all.

Under absorption costing technique, the various managerial decisions are taken with reference to 'profit' which represents the excess of sales value over total cost. But under marginal costing these decisions are based on 'contribution' or 'contribution margin' which represents the excess of sales value over marginal cost or variable cost.

The determination of 'profit' or 'income' under both absorption costing and marginal costing techniques can be illustrated by means of the following Profitability Statements–

Statement of Profitability

(Absorption Costing Technique)

	Products			
	A	**B**	**C**	**Total**
	(Rs.)	**(Rs.)**	**(Rs.)**	**(Rs.)**
(*a*) Sales	20,000	30,000	50,000	1,00,000
Direct Material	5,000	15,000	10,000	30,000
Direct Wages	6,000	4,500	5,000	15,500
Variable Factory Overhead	2,600	4,500	13,000	20,100
Variable Selling Overhead	1,400	3,000	10,000	14,400
Fixed Overhead	1,600	2,400	6,000	10,000
(*b*) Total Cost	16,600	29,400	44,000	90,000
Net Profit (*a*) – (*b*)	3,400	600	6,000	10,000

Statement of Profitability
(Marginal Costing Technique)

	Products			
	A	**B**	**C**	**Total**
	(Rs.)	**(Rs.)**	**(Rs.)**	**(Rs.)**
(*a*) Sales	20,000	30,000	50,000	1,00,000
Direct Material	5,000	15,000	10,000	30,000
Direct Wages	6,000	4,500	5,000	15,500
Variable Factory Overhead	2,600	4,500	13,000	20,100
Variable Selling Overhead	1,400	3,000	10,000	14,400
(*b*) Marginal Cost	15,000	27,000	38,000	80,000
Contribution (*a*) – (*b*)	5,000	3,000	12,000	20,000
Less Fixed Overhead				10,000
Net Profit				10,000

If we study the Statement of Profitability prepared under marginal costing technique, we will observe that:

Sales – Marginal Cost = Contribution.

Again, Fixed Cost + Profit = Contribution.

Similarly in case of loss:

Fixed Cost – Loss = Contribution.

Combining these two equations, we can get the fundamental marginal cost equation as follows:

Sales – Variable Cost = Fixed Cost ± Profit / Loss.

Or symbolically –

$S - V = F \pm P$

Where 'S' denotes : Sales

'V' denotes: Variable Cost or Marginal Cost

'F' denotes : Fixed Cost

'P' denotes : Profit

'– P' denotes : Loss.

This marginal cost equation is widely used in marginal costing problems since it plays an important role in profit projection. If in any given case, any three of the four factors or items (S, V, F and P) are known, the fourth can easily be found out with the help of the marginal cost equation.

Illustration 1

Following are the data relating to X Co. Ltd., for January, 2004:

Sales :	Rs. 1,00,000
Fixed Cost :	Rs. 25,000
Profit :	Rs. 15,000

Ascertain variable cost.

Solution

Marginal Cost equation is:

Sales – Variable Cost = Fixed Cost + Profit

Fixed Cost + Profit = Contribution

or

Rs. 25,000 (F) + Rs. 15,000 (P) = Rs. 40,000 (C)

Sales – Variable Cost = Contribution

or

Sales – Contribution = Variable Cost

or

Rs. 1,00,000 (S) – Rs. 40,000 (C) = Rs. 60,000 (V)

Hence : Variable Cost = Rs. 60,000.

Tools or Techniques of Marginal Costing

As we already know that marginal costing requires the ascertainment of the effects of changes in volume or type of output on profits or the cost-volume-profit analysis. The assessment of cost-volume-profit analysis requires the study of the following tools:

(*a*) Contribution
(*b*) P/V Ratio
(*c*) Break-even Point
(*d*) Margin of Safety
(*e*) Break-even Charts
(*f*) Profit Graph or Profit-Volume Graph

The last two tools are applied for the graphical presentation of cost-volume-profit relationship.

CONTRIBUTION

Contribution is the difference between sales and variable costs or marginal costs. It may also be defined as the excess of selling price over variable costs. Contribution is also known as 'Contribution Margin' and can be expressed as follows:

Contribution = Sales – Variable Costs

or

Contribution = Fixed Costs ± Profit/Loss.

The contribution or contribution margin of a product or process indicates the amount of sales revenue which is available towards fixed costs and profit. If variable cost of a certain product is Rs. 20,000, fixed cost Rs. 15,000 and selling price Rs. 40,000

Contribution = Selling Price – Variable Cost
= Rs. 40,000 – Rs. 20,000
= Rs. 20,000.

Advantages of Contribution

The knowledge of contribution margin is a valuable aid to management in the decision-making process. A few advantages resulting from the knowledge of contribution margin may be summarised as follows:

1. It helps in the determination of the profitability of various products, processes, departments etc.
2. Contribution helps the management in taking a decision on the proposal to introduce a new product in the market.
3. It assists in the fixation of the selling price of the product.
4. It helps the management in making 'buy or make decision'.
5. It assists in determining the break-even point.
6. It guides the management in the selection of the profitable sales-mix or the profitable method of production.
7. It also helps in determining whether it is worthwhile to continue a product among different products.

PROFIT/VOLUME RATIO OR CONTRIBUTION/SALES RATIO (P/V RATIO OR C/S RATIO)

The ratio (or percentage) of contribution to sales is known as Profit/Volume Ratio or Contribution/Sales Ratio. The P/V ratio denotes the amount of contribution per rupee (or hundredth) of sales revenue. P/V ratio may be expressed as:

$$\text{P/V Ratio} = \frac{\text{Sales} - \text{Variable Cost}}{\text{Sales}}$$

or

$$= \frac{\text{Contribution}}{\text{Sales}}$$

If expressed as a percentage:

$$\text{P/V Ratio} = \frac{\text{Contribution}}{\text{Sales}} \times 100$$

Assuming the sales price to be Rs. 40,000 and variable cost Rs. 30,000:

$$\text{P/V Ratio} = \frac{40{,}000 - 30{,}000}{40{,}000} \times 100$$

$$= \frac{10{,}000}{40{,}000} \times 100$$

$$= 25\%$$

P/V Ratio can also be calculated as follows:

$$\text{P/V Ratio} = \frac{\textbf{Change in Contribution in two periods}}{\textbf{Change in Sales in two periods}}$$

$$\text{or} = \frac{\textbf{Change in (F + P) in two periods}}{\textbf{Change in Sales in two periods}}$$

Where 'F' denotes Fixed Cost and 'P' denotes Profit.

And since fixed cost is constant or common in two periods.

$$\text{P/V Ratio} = \frac{\textbf{Change in Profits in two periods}}{\textbf{Change in Sales in two periods}}$$

A high P/V ratio denotes high profitability while a low P/V ratio is an indicator of low profitability. The basic property of P/V ratio is that it remains constant at various levels of sales activity since the variable costs change directly in proportion to changes in the volume of output. A change in the fixed costs does not affect the P/V ratio. The management always tries to increase the P/V ratio since by doing so the contribution margin towards meeting fixed costs and profits is increased. The P/V ratio can be increased by:

(*i*) increasing the selling price per unit; or

(*ii*) reducing the marginal cost per unit by new and improved methods of production ; or

(*iii*) selling more profitable products where relative contribution is larger, thereby improving the overall P/V ratio.

Uses of P/V Ratio

Profit/Volume ratio is one of the most important ratios to be taken care of in any business. P/V ratio helps the management in:

1. Ascertaining the relative profitability of different sections of the business such as sales area, product lines, methods of production etc.
2. Determining the break-even point i.e., the point of no profit and no loss.
3. Determining the amount of profit at a given volume of sales.
4. Calculating the volume of sales required to earn a desired amount of profit.
5. Calculating the volume of sales required to maintain the present amount of profit under the conditions of change in selling price.

Break-even Point

A break-even point may be defined as that point of sales volume at which there is neither a profit nor a loss. It is also known as the point of no profit no loss. Break-even occurs at the point at which total revenue is equal to total costs or total contribution is equal to total fixed costs.

Calculation of Break-even Point

The break-even point can be computed in terms of units, or in terms of money value (rupees etc.) of sales volume or as a percentage of estimated capacity.

(*a*) Break-even point in units

In case of single-product firm, the break-even point in terms of units will occur when the units sold create sufficient revenue to cover their total costs–fixed and variable. Each unit of product sold will cover its own variable cost and leave a remainder (known as contribution) to cover the fixed costs. The break-even point will occur when enough units have been sold so that the total contribution (Contribution per unit × Number of units sold) is equal to total fixed costs. The break-even point in terms of units can be determined by following formula:

$$\text{Break-even Point (in units)} = \frac{\text{Total Fixed Cost}}{\text{Selling Price per unit} - \text{Variable Cost per unit}}$$

or

$$= \frac{\text{Total Fixed Cost}}{\text{Contribution per unit}}$$

Illustration 2

From the following information in relation to a manufacturing concern, calculate the break-even point in units:

Output	:	3,000 units
Variable Cost per unit	:	Rs. 30
Selling Price per unit	:	Rs. 40
Total Fixed Cost	:	Rs. 15,000.

Solution

Contribution per unit = Selling Price per unit – Variable Cost per unit
= Rs. 40 – Rs. 30 = Rs. 10

$$\text{Break-even Point (in units)} = \frac{\text{Total Fixed Cost}}{\text{Contribution per unit}}$$

$$= \frac{\text{Rs.}15{,}000}{\text{Rs. }10} = 1{,}500 \text{ units}$$

At the sales level of 1,500 units, total contribution available will be Rs. 15,000 (1,500 units × Rs. 10) which is equal to total fixed costs. As such at the sales level of 1,500 units, there shall neither be profit nor loss.

(*b*) Break-even Point in rupees

The break-even for a single product firm can also be determined in terms of rupee value of sales volume. For calculating the break-even point for sales, the following formulae are applied:

(*i*) Break-even Point (for sales) $= \dfrac{\text{Total Fixed Cost}}{\text{Contribution per unit}} \times \text{Selling Price per unit}$

(*ii*) Break-even Point (for sales) $= \dfrac{\text{Total Fixed Cost}}{\text{Contribution per unit}} \times \text{Total sales}$

(*iii*) Break-even Point (for sales) $= \dfrac{\text{Total Fixed Cost}}{1 - \dfrac{\text{Variable Cost per unit}}{\text{Selling Price per unit}}}$

(*iv*) Break-even Point (for sales) $= \dfrac{\text{Total Fixed Cost}}{\text{P/V Ratio}}$

Continuing Illustration (2)

(*i*) Break-even Point (for sales) $= \dfrac{\text{Total Fixed Cost}}{\text{Contribution per unit}} \times \text{Selling Price per unit}$

$$= \frac{\text{Rs.}15{,}000}{\text{Rs.}10} \times \text{Rs. } 40$$

$$= \text{Rs. } 60{,}000$$

(*ii*) Break-even Point (for sales) $= \dfrac{\text{Total Fixed Cost}}{\text{Total Contribution}} \times \text{Total Sales}$

$$= \frac{\text{Rs.}15{,}000}{\text{Rs.}30{,}000} \times \text{Rs. } 1{,}20{,}000$$

$$= \text{Rs. } 60{,}000$$

Total sales = 3,000 units × Rs. 40 = Rs. 1,20,000
Total contribution = 3,000 units × Rs. 10 = Rs. 30,000

(*iii*) Break-even Point (for sales) $= \dfrac{\text{Total Fixed Cost}}{1 - \dfrac{\text{Variable Cost per unit}}{\text{Selling Price per unit}}}$

$$= \frac{\text{Rs.}15{,}000}{1 - \dfrac{30}{40}} = \frac{15{,}000}{\dfrac{10}{40}}$$

$$= \text{Rs. } 60{,}000$$

(*iv*) Break-even Point (for sales) $= \dfrac{\text{Total Fixed Cost}}{\text{P/V Ratio}} = \dfrac{15{,}000}{25\%}$

$$= 15{,}000 \times \frac{100}{25} = \text{Rs. } 60{,}000$$

Note: $$\text{P/V Ratio} = \frac{\text{Contribution}}{\text{Sales}} \times 100$$

$$= \frac{30{,}000}{1{,}20{,}000} \times 100 = 25\%$$

(*c*) Break-even Point as a percentage of Capacity

A number of business concerns are interested in ascertaining the break-down point as a percentage of estimated sales of capacity. It can be done by dividing the capacity sales by the break-even sales. For example, in illustration (2), if the firm has an estimated capacity of 5,000 units of the product, the firm breaks even at 30% of the capacity.

$$\left(\frac{1{,}500 \text{ units}}{5{,}000 \text{ units}} \times 100 \text{ or } \frac{\text{Rs. } 60{,}000}{\text{Rs. } 2{,}00{,}000} \times 100\right)$$

Direct calculation of the break-even point as a percentage of estimated capacity can be done if the total amount of contribution at estimated capacity is known, by applying the following formula:

$$\begin{array}{c}\text{Break-even Point}\\ \text{(as a percentage of capacity)}\end{array} = \frac{\text{Fixed Cost}}{\text{Total Contribution (at estimated capacity)}} \times 100$$

Continuing Illustration (2), where
Total Fixed Cost is Rs. 15,000
Total Contribution is Rs. 50,000
(at estimated capacity of 5,000 units)

$$\begin{array}{c}\text{Break-even Point}\\ \text{(as a percentage of capacity)}\end{array} = \frac{\text{Total Fixed Cost}}{\text{Total Contribution}} \times 100$$

$$= \frac{\text{Rs. } 15{,}000}{\text{Rs. } 50{,}000} \times 100 = 30\%$$

Assumptions of Break-Even Analysis:

The break-even analysis is based on the following assumptions:

1. All costs can be segregated into fixed and variable components.
2. Total fixed costs remain constant at all levels of production.
3. Total variable costs fluctuate directly in proportion to changes in volume of output but the variable cost per unit remains constant.
4. Selling price per unit remains constant and does not change with changes in volume or due to other factors.

5. The firm concerned is a single-product concern or if it is a multi-product concern, there is no change in the sales-mix.
6. The number of units produced and sold is the same so that there is no opening or closing stock.

Margin Of Safety (M.S.)

Every manufacturer is interested in knowing the extent by which he is above the break-even point, which is technically known as 'margin of safety'. Margin of safety may be defined as the excess of actual or budgeted sales over the break-even sales. The margin of safety can be ascertained as follows:

(*i*) Margin of Safety = Actual Sales (or Budgeted Sales) – Sales at Break-even Point.

or

(*ii*) $$\text{Margin of Safety} = \frac{\text{Profit}}{\text{P/V Ratio}}$$

The margin of safety, if expressed as a percentage of sales, will be:

$$\text{Margin of Safety Ratio} = \frac{\text{Actual Sales} - \text{Break-even Sales}}{\text{Actual Sales}} \times 100$$

Illustration 3

From the following data, calculate the P/V ratio, B.E.P., and Margin of Safety:

Sales		Rs. 80,000
Variable Costs	40,000	
Fixed Costs	24,000	64,000
Profit		16,000

Solution

(*a*) P/V Ratio
$$= \frac{\text{Sales} - \text{Variable Cost}}{\text{Sales}} \times 100$$
$$= \frac{\text{Rs. } 80{,}000 - \text{Rs. } 40{,}000}{\text{Rs. } 80{,}000} \times 100$$
$$= \frac{\text{Rs. } 40{,}000}{\text{Rs. } 80{,}000} \times 100 = 50\%$$

(*b*) Break-even Point (for sales)
$$= \frac{\text{Total Fixed Cost}}{\text{P / V Ratio}}$$
$$= \frac{\text{Rs. } 24{,}000}{50\%}$$
$$= \text{Rs. } 24{,}000 \times \frac{100}{50} = \text{Rs. } 48{,}000$$

(*c*) **Margin of Safety** = **Actual Sales – Sales at Break-even Point**

= **Rs. 80,000 – Rs. 48,000**

= **Rs. 32,000**

Alternatively:

$$\textbf{Margin of Safety} = \frac{\textbf{Total Fixed Cost}}{\textbf{P / V Ratio}}$$

$$= \frac{\textbf{Rs. 16,000}}{\textbf{50\%}}$$

$$= 16{,}000 \times \frac{100}{50} = 32{,}000$$

If it is desired to calculate Margin of Safety Ratio:

$$\textbf{Margin of Safety Ratio} = \frac{\textbf{Actual Sales – Break-even Sales}}{\textbf{Actual Sales}} \times 100$$

$$= \frac{\text{Rs. } 80{,}000 - \text{Rs. } 48{,}000}{\text{Rs. } 80{,}000} \times 100$$

$$= 40\%$$

The margin of safety shows the extent to which sales may fall before the firm suffers a loss. Larger the margin of safety, more safer is the firm. In times of depression when the demand for the firm's product is falling, a high margin of safety is particularly significant. In case of a firm having a low P/V ratio, the margin of safety is low. In case both the P/V ratio and margin of safety are low, management should explore the possibilities of increasing the selling price per unit without affecting sales volume adversely or by reducing the variable cost per unit by employing new improved methods of production.

Angle Of Incidence

In the break-even chart, angle of incidence is the angle formed by the sales line and total cost line at the break-even point. A large angle of incidence shows a high rate of profit being made while a small angle of incidence indicates a low rate of profit.

Additional Uses of the Formulae for Break-even Point

In addition to the calculation of the point at which a business firm breaks even, the above formulae can also be used for the following purposes:

(*i*) Calculation of Sales required to earn desired profits:

(*a*) Sales Required to earn desired profits (In terms of Number of Units) $= \dfrac{\text{Total Fixed Cost + Desired Profits}}{\text{Contribution per unit}}$

(*b*) Sales Required to earn desired profits (In terms of Sales Value) $= \dfrac{\text{Total Fixed Cost + Desired Profits}}{\text{P / V Ratio}}$

(*ii*) Calculation of profit at different levels of sales volume.

(*iii*) Ascertainment of missing figures.

These points can be understood with the help of the following illustrations:

Illustration 4

S.V. Ltd., gives you the following data

Present Sales	:	8,000 units
Fixed Cost	:	Rs. 6,000
Selling Price per unit	:	Rs. 6
Variable cost per unit	:	Rs. 4.50

You are required

(A) To calculate the number of units to be sold and the volume of sales required to earn a profit of (*i*) Rs. 9,000 and (*ii*) Rs. 24,000.

(B) To calculate the amount of profit when the actual sales are (*i*) Rs. 90,000 and (*ii*) Rs. 1,50,000.

Solution

Calculation of contribution:

	Rs.
Selling Price per unit	6.00
Less Variable Cost per unit	4.50
Contribution per unit	1.50

$$\text{P/V Ratio} = \frac{\text{Contribution}}{\text{Sales}} \times 100$$

$$= \frac{1.50}{6.00} \times 100 = 25\%$$

(A) Calculation of sales required to earn desired profit:

(*a*) $\text{No. of units} = \dfrac{\text{Total Fixed Cost + Desired Profit}}{\text{Contribution per unit}}$

(*b*) $\text{Sales Volume} = \dfrac{\text{Total Fixed Cost + Desired Profit}}{\text{P / V Ratio}}$

(*i*) Desired Profit of Rs. 9,000:

(*a*) No. of units $= \dfrac{\text{Rs. }6{,}000 + \text{Rs. }9{,}000}{\text{Rs. }1.50}$

$= \dfrac{\text{Rs. }15{,}000}{\text{Rs. }1.50} = 10{,}000 \text{ units}$

(*b*) Sales Volume $= \dfrac{\text{Rs. } 6{,}000 + \text{Rs. } 9{,}000}{25\%}$

$= \dfrac{\text{Rs. } 15{,}000}{25\%} = \text{Rs. } 60{,}000$

(*ii*) Desired profit of Rs. 24,000:

(*a*) No. of units $= \dfrac{\text{Rs. } 6{,}000 + \text{Rs. } 24{,}000}{\text{Rs. } 1.50}$

$= \dfrac{\text{Rs. } 30{,}000}{1.50} = \text{Rs. } 20{,}000 \text{ units}$

(*b*) Sales Volume $= \dfrac{\text{Rs. } 6{,}000 + \text{Rs. } 24{,}000}{25\%}$

$= \dfrac{\text{Rs. } 30{,}000}{25\%} = \text{Rs. } 1{,}20{,}000$

(B) Calculation of profit at given Volume of Sales:

Sales	Rs. 90,000	Rs. 1,50,000
Contribution	Rs. 90,000 × 25%	Rs. 1,50,000 × 25%
(Sales × P/V Ratio)		
	= Rs. 22,500	= Rs. 37,500
Profit	= Rs. 22,500 – Rs. 6,000	Rs. 37,500 – Rs. 6,000
(Contribution – Fixed Cost)		
	= Rs. 16,500	= Rs. 31,500

Illustration 5

S.V. Ltd., supplies you following information:

Break-even sales volume	:	Rs. 30,000
Profit	:	Rs. 1,500
Fixed Cost	:	Rs. 6,000

Calculate the amount of variable cost.

Solution

(*i*) Contribution = Total Fixed Cost + Profit
= Rs. 6,000 + Rs. 1,500
= Rs. 7,500

(*ii*) Actual sales:

Sales at B.E.P. $= \dfrac{\text{Fixed Cost}}{\text{Contribution}} \times \text{Sales}$

Rs. 30,000 $= \dfrac{6{,}000}{7{,}500} \times \text{Sales}$

Sales $= \dfrac{7{,}500}{6{,}000} \times 30{,}000 = \text{Rs. } 37{,}500$

(*iii*) Variable Cost:

Variable Cost = Sales – Contribution

= Rs. 37,500 – Rs. 7,500 = Rs. 30,000

Alternatively,

Calculation of variable cost can be made as follows:

$$\text{P/V Ratio} = \frac{\text{Contribution}}{\text{Sales}} \times 100 = \frac{7{,}500}{37{,}500} \times 100 = 20\%$$

If contribution is 20% of sales, variable cost is 80% of sales (since Sales – Contribution = Variable Cost).

Hence, Variable Cost = 80% of Rs. 37,500 = Rs. 30,000

Illustration 6

You are given the following data from the costing records of S.V. Ltd.,

Sales: 8,000 units @ Rs. 10 per unit
Break-even Point : 3,000 units
Fixed Cost : Rs. 6,000

Ascertain the amount of (*i*) Variable Cost and (*ii*) Profit.

Solution

(*i*) Calculation of Contribution per unit:

Given B.E.P. = 3,000 units

$$\text{Break-even Point (in units)} = \frac{\text{Total Fixed Cost}}{\text{Contribution per unit}}$$

$$\text{3,000 units} = \frac{\text{Rs. 6,000}}{\text{Contribution per unit}}$$

$$\text{Contribution per unit} = \frac{\text{Total Fixed Cost}}{\text{Break – even Point (in units)}} = \frac{\text{Rs. 6,000}}{\text{3,000 units}} = \text{Rs. 2}$$

(*ii*) Calculation of Variable Cost:

Variable cost per unit = Selling Price – Contribution

= Rs. 10 – Rs. 2

= Rs. 8 per unit

(*iii*) Calculation of Profit:

	Rs.
Sales (8,000 units @ 10 per unit)	80,000
Less Variable Cost (8,000 units × Rs. 8)	64,000
Total Contribution	16,000
Less Total Fixed Cost	6,000
Profit	10,000

Break-Even Chart

The computation of break-even point can also be presented graphically in the form of a break-even chart. A break-even chart is the graphic representation of the relationship between costs (marginal costs and fixed costs), sales volume and profit at various levels of activity. A break-even chart shows the following information at various levels of activity:

(*i*) Variable Costs, Fixed Costs and Total Costs
(*ii*) Sales Volume
(*iii*) Profit or loss
(*iv*) Break-even Point
(*v*) Margin of Safety.

Construction of Break-Even Chart:

First Method: Under this method, on *x*-axis is shown the volume of production or sales in units and on *y*-axis, costs and sales revenue are represented. Fixed cost line is drawn parallel to *x*-axis which shows that fixed cost remains constant at all levels. Variable cost line is shown above the fixed cost line. The point of intersection of total cost line and sales revenue line is the break-even point. This method can be explained by the following chart:

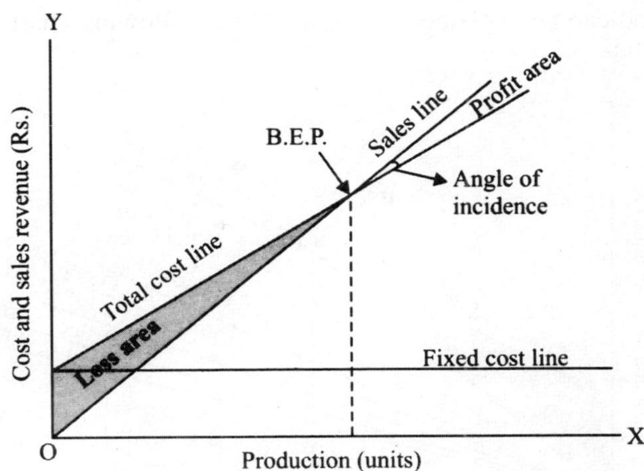

Second Method: Under this method on *x*-axis is represented the volume of production or sales in units and on *y*-axis variable costs, total costs and sales revenue are represented. Fixed cost line parallel to *x*-axis is not drawn. The point of intersection of total cost line and sales revenue line gives the break-even point. The break-even chart to explain this method can be given as follows:

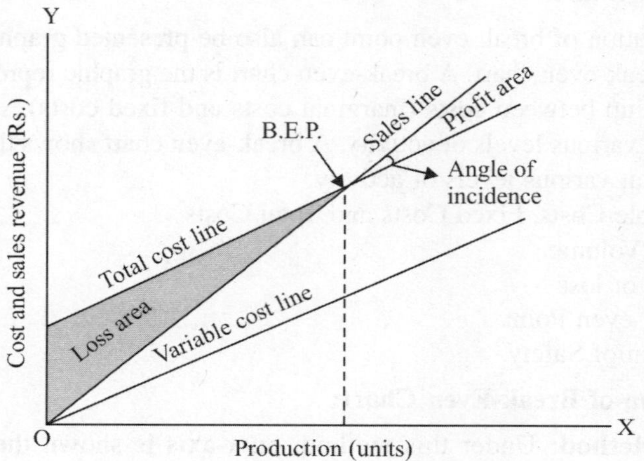

Third method: Under this method on *x*-axis is plotted the volume of production or sales in units and on *y*-axis various items of variable cost (*i.e.*, direct material cost, direct labour cost, variable factory, office and selling overhead), total cost and sales revenue are represented. The point where the lines of total cost and sales revenue intersect will give the break-even point. This method can be explained by means of the following chart:

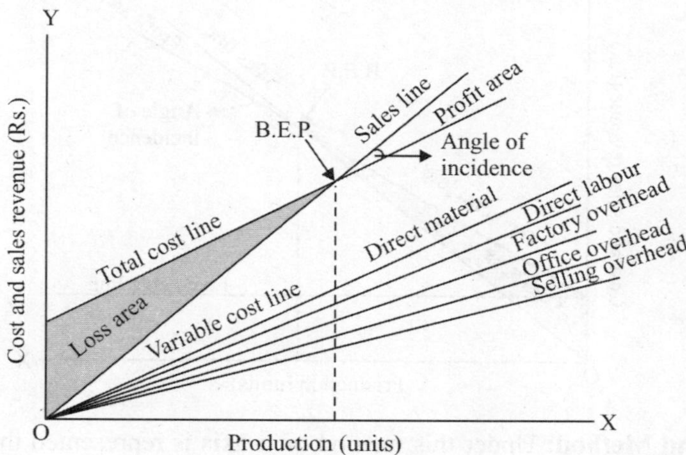

Contribution Break-even Chart

This is an alternate form of break-even chart and shows the amount of contribution at different levels of output. In this chart, variable cost is drawn first and fixed cost is super-imposed on the variable cost line. The gap between the variable cost line and sales revenue line shows contribution. It can be shown by means of the following figure:

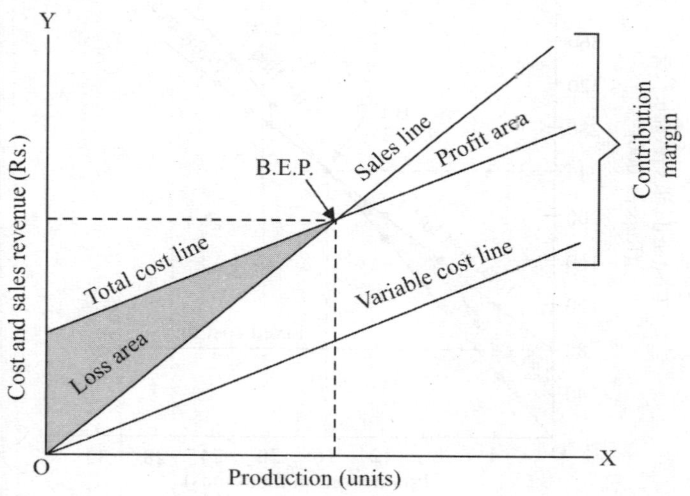

Illustration 7

From the following information, prepare a Break-even Chart and find out the Break-even Point:

	Rs.
Fixed Costs (Total)	80,000
Variable Cost per unit	10
Selling Price per unit	15
Budgeted Output	24,000 Units

Solution

Analytical Table

Output (units)	Fixed cost (Rs.)	Variable Cost (Rs.)	Total Cost (Rs.)	Sales Revenue (Rs.)
0	80,000	–	80,000	0
4,000	80,000	40,000	1,20,000	60,000
8,000	80,000	80,000	1,60,000	1,20,000
12,000	80,000	1,20,000	2,00,000	1,80,000
16,000	80,000	1,60,000	2,40,000	2,40,000
20,000	80,000	2,00,000	2,80,000	3,00,000
24,000	80,000	2,40,000	3,20,000	3,60,000

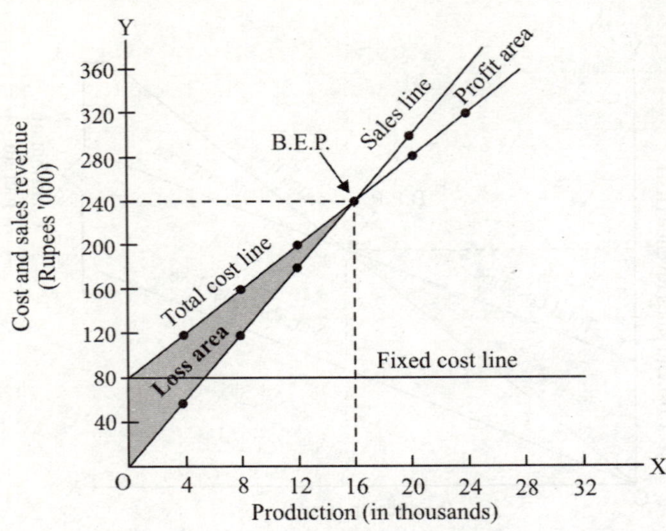

Verification:

(*i*) Contribution = Selling Price per unit – Variable Cost per unit
= Rs. 15 – Rs. 10 = Rs. 5

(*ii*) Break-even Point (in units) $= \dfrac{\text{Total Fixed Cost}}{\text{Contribution per unit}}$

$= \dfrac{\text{Rs. } 80{,}000}{\text{Rs. } 5}$

= 16,000 units.

(*iii*) Break-even Point (for sales Volume) $= \dfrac{\text{Total Fixed Cost}}{\text{Contribution per unit}} \times \text{Selling Price per unit}$

$= \dfrac{\text{Rs. } 80{,}000}{\text{Rs. } 5} \times \text{Rs. } 15 = \text{Rs. } 2{,}40{,}000$

Illustration 8

From the following data, plot a Break Even Chart showing:

(*a*) Break-Even Point (*b*) Margin of Safety and Profit

(*c*) Number of units to be sold for a profit of Rs. 2,000.

Selling Price	Rs. 5 per unit
Variable Cost	Rs. 3 per unit
Fixed Cost	Rs. 3,000
Total Number of units sold	2,000 units.

Show mathematical computations to verify your calculations.

(*H.P.,B.Com. 1994*)

Solution

Analytical Table

Output (units)	Fixed cost (Rs.)	Variable Cost (Rs.)	Total Cost (Rs.)	Sales Revenue (Rs.)
0	3,000	0	3,000	0
500	3,000	1,500	4,500	2,500
1,000	3,000	3,000	6,000	5,000
1,500	3,000	4,500	7,500	7,500
2,000	3,000	6,000	9,000	10,000
2,500	3,000	7,500	10,500	12,500
3,000	3,000	9,000	12,000	15,000

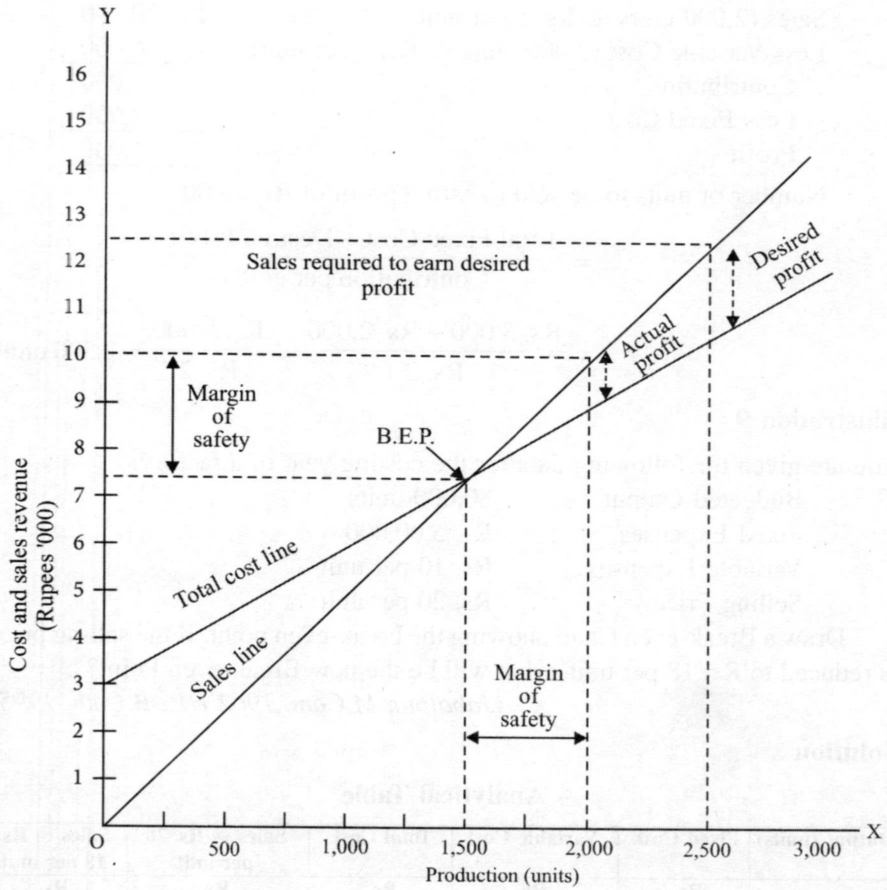

Verification:

(*i*) Contribution = Selling Price per unit – Variable Cost per unit
= Rs. 5 – Rs. 3
= Rs. 2

(*ii*) Break-even Point $= \dfrac{\text{Total Fixed Cost}}{\text{Contribution per unit}}$

$= \dfrac{\text{Rs. } 3{,}000}{\text{Rs. } 2} = 1{,}500 \text{ units}$

(*iii*) Margin of safety = Actual Sales – Sales at B. E. P.
= Rs. 10,000 – Rs. 7,500
= Rs. 2,500

(*iv*) Profit = Contribution – Fixed Cost

Sales (2,000 units @ Rs. 5 per unit)	Rs. 10,000
Less Variable Cost (2,000 units @ Rs. 3 per unit)	Rs. 6,000
Contribution	4,000
Less Fixed Cost	3,000
Profit	1,000

Number of units to be sold to earn a profit of Rs. 2,000

$= \dfrac{\text{Total Fixed Cost + Desired Profit}}{\text{Contribution per unit}}$

$= \dfrac{\text{Rs. } 3{,}000 + \text{Rs. } 2{,}000}{\text{Rs. } 2} = \dfrac{\text{Rs. } 5{,}000}{\text{Rs. } 2} = 2{,}500 \text{ units}$

Illustration 9

You are given the following data for the costing year of a factory:

Budgeted Output : 80,000 units
Fixed Expenses : Rs. 5,00,000
Variable Expenses : Rs. 10 per unit
Selling Price : Rs. 20 per unit

Draw a Break-even Chart showing the break-even point. If the selling price is reduced to Rs. 18 per unit, what will be the new Break-even Point?

(*Jabalpur, M.Com. 1962 HP., B.Com. 1995*)

Solution

Analytical Table

Output (units)	Fixed Cost	Variable Cost	Total Cost	Sales @ Rs. 20 per unit	Sales @ Rs. 18 per unit
	Rs.	Rs.	Rs.	Rs.	Rs.
0	5,00,000	0	5,00,000	0	0
20,000	5,00,000	2,00,000	7,00,000	4,00,000	3,60,000
40,000	5,00,000	4,00,000	9,00,000	8,00,000	7,20,000
60,000	5,00,000	6,00,000	11,00,000	12,00,000	10,80,000
80,000	5,00,000	8,00,000	13,00,000	16,00,000	14,40,000
1,00,000	5,00,000	10,00,000	15,00,000	20,00,000	18,00,000

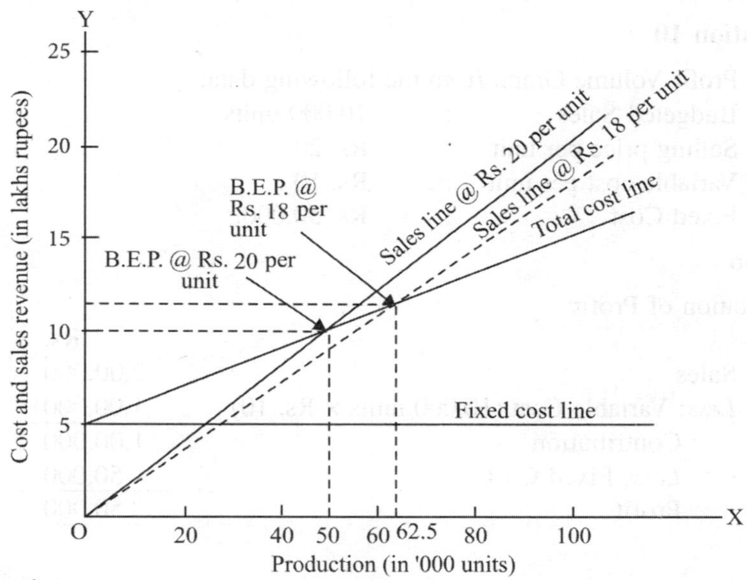

Verification:

Calculation of Break-even Point:

Contribution:		
Selling Price per unit	Rs. 20.00	Rs. 18.00
Less: Variable Cost per unit	Rs. 10.00	Rs. 10.00
Contribution per unit	Rs. 10.00	Rs. 8.00
Break-even Point (in units)	= Rs. 5,00,000 ÷ 10	= Rs. 5,00,000 ÷ 8
$\left(\frac{\text{Total Fixed Cost}}{\text{Contribution per Unit}}\right)$	= 50,000 units	= 62,500 units

PROFIT-VOLUME GRAPH

The profit-volume graph is an improved form of the break-even chart which shows clearly the relationship of profits to sales volume. The construction of the P/V graph involves the following steps:

(*i*) Profit-volume graph has two parts separated by the sales line.

(*ii*) The upper part of the graph *i.e.*, area above the horizontal-axis is the 'profit area' while the lower part or area below the horizontal-axis is the 'loss area'.

(*iii*) The fixed costs are marked on the lower part. The amount of fixed cost unrecovered is the loss incurred.

(*iv*) Profit line is drawn by joining fixed cost point and the sales line at the break-even point.

The amount of profit or loss can be determined by drawing a vertical line on the profit line from the assumed level of sales.

Illustration 10

Draw a Profit-Volume Graph from the following data:

Budgeted Sales	:	10,000 units
Selling price per unit	:	Rs. 20
Variable cost per unit	:	Rs. 10
Fixed Cost	:	Rs. 50,000.

Solution

Computation of Profit:

	Rs.
Sales	2,00,000
Less: Variable Cost (10,000 units × Rs. 10)	1,00,000
Contribution	1,00,000
Less: Fixed Cost	50,000
Profit	50,000

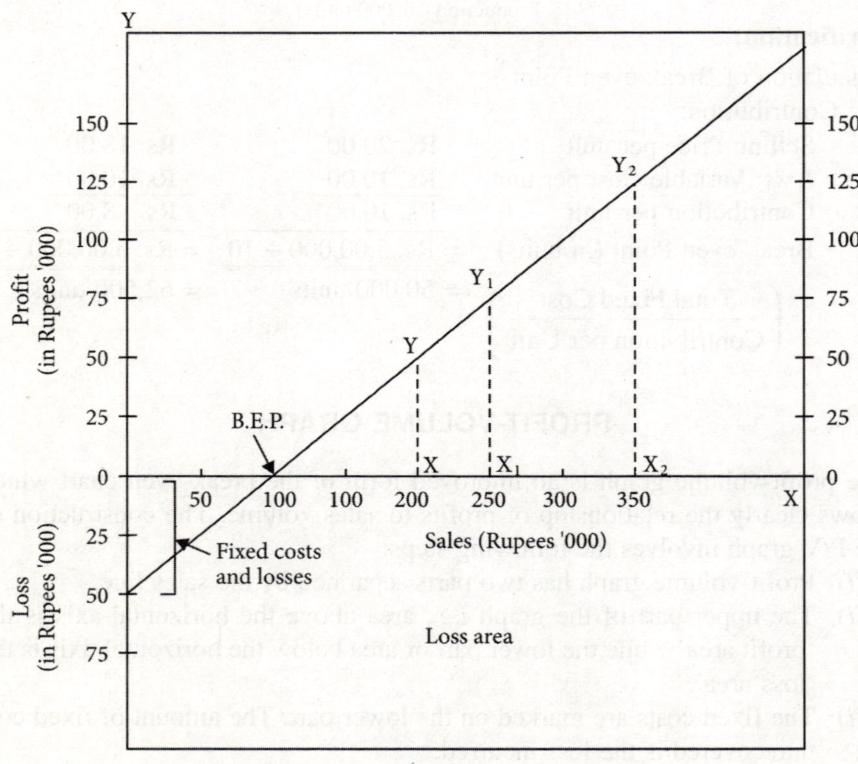

ADVANTAGES OF MARGINAL COSTING

Marginal costing technique is a very important tool in the hands of management as it helps and guides the management in solving a number of problems. The main uses of marginal costing may be given as follows:

1. **Simple Valuation of Stock:** Under marginal costing technique, the valuation of stocks of work-in-progress and finished goods is made on the basis of marginal cost (or variable cost) which is more simple and helps in ascertaining the profits accurately.
2. **Effective cost control:** Marginal costing involves the segregation of all costs into fixed and variable elements. Fixed costs are not treated as product costs but as period costs. The management, by concentrating more on controlling variable costs, can exercise effective cost control and ensure maximum profitability.
3. **No possibility of over-or under-absorption of overhead:** Under marginal costing, there is no question of under-absorption or over-absorption of fixed overhead since fixed overhead are not treated as product costs. It also simplifies the process of reconciliation of cost accounts and financial accounts.
4. **Ascertainment of Break-even Point:** Marginal costing technique helps in determining the level of production or sales at which a business firm breaks-even as a result of which it may plan its production at a level above the Break-even Point so as to earn profits.
5. **Ascertainment of the Comparative Profitability of various products:** Marginal costing technique, by showing the comparative profitability of various products manufactured by a manufacturing concern (by measuring the amount of Contribution and P/V Ratio), helps it in planning its future production and sales.
6. **Assistance in taking managerial decisions:** Marginal costing technique helps the management in taking a number of important business decisions such as:
   - *(i)* **Fixation of Selling Price:** Under normal conditions, selling price is fixed at a level which not only covers the total cost but also leaves some margin for profit. But under the conditions of trade depression, sale of production from surplus capacity etc., goods may be sold at a price below the total cost but not below the marginal cost. Thus, marginal cost is the guiding factor in the fixation of selling price of the products under abnormal market conditions.
   - *(ii)* **Buy or Make Decision:** Marginal costing helps the management in taking a decision as to whether a component or spare part should be manufactured in the factory or bought from outside supplier through the comparison of marginal cost and the market price.
   - *(iii)* **Determination of Profitable Sales-mix:** In case of a multi-product

concern selling various products in some pre-determined ratio, marginal costing technique helps in determining the most profitable sales-mix through the comparison of the total contribution available under the various alternatives of sales-mix.

(*iv*) **Determination of Profitable Method of Production:** In case of the availability of alternative methods of production for a particular product, marginal costing helps in determining the profitable method of production by making a comparison of the contribution available under various methods of production.

(*v*) **Problem of Limiting Factor:** Limiting factor or key factor refers to any factor which is likely to limit production or sale of a product e.g., shortage of material, labour, machine hours etc. In case of the presence of a limiting factor in a multi-product concern, marginal costing technique provides a guidance as to which line of production is least profitable and should be discontinued.

7. **Use with Standard Costing:** Marginal costing is simple to operate and can be combined with standard costing system for exercising cost control.
8. **Determination of Tender Price or Quotation Price:** Marginal costing helps in determining tender price or quotation price on scientific basis.

LIMITATIONS OF MARGINAL COSTING

Marginal costing suffers from the following limitations:

1. Marginal costing involves the segregation of all costs into fixed and variable elements but this segregation is very difficult in actual practice.
2. The calculation of variable costs and overhead is made on the basis of estimates and not on actuals. As such there is a possibility of under-recovery or over-recovery.
3. Marginal costing assumes that total fixed costs are constant at all levels of activity but this assumption is not always correct.
4. Under marginal costing technique, stocks of finished goods and work-in-progress are valued on the basis of variable costs only and the fixed costs are ignored as a result of which these are under -stated.
5. Under marginal costing technique, no consideration is given to the 'time factor' involved in production.
6. Marginal costing techniques cannot be applied to industries in which the value of work-in-progress is high in relation to turnover.

Illustration 11

From the following particulars, calculate variable cost:

Sales	Rs. 2,50,000
Fixed Cost	Rs. 75,000
Profit	Rs. 35,000

Solution

(*i*) Calculation of Contribution:

Contribution = Fixed Cost + Profit

= Rs. 75,000 + Rs. 35,000 = Rs. 1, 10,000

(*ii*) Calculation of Variable Cost:

Variable Cost = Sales – Contribution

= Rs. 2,50,000 – Rs. 1, 10,000 = Rs. 1,40,000

Illustration 12

Following particulars are given to you:

Sales	Rs. 5,00,000
Direct Materials	Rs. 1,20,000
Direct Wages	Rs. 1,00,000
Variable overhead	80% of direct wages
Profit	20% of sales

Calculate the amount of Fixed Cost.

Solution

Calculation of Variable Cost:

	Rs.
Direct Materials	1,20,000
Direct Wages	1,00,000
Variable Overhead (80% of wages)	80,000
Variable Cost	3,00,000

Calculation of Fixed Cost

	Rs.
Sales	5,00,000
Less Variable Cost	3,00,000
Contribution	2 ,00,000
Less Profit (20% on Sales)	1,00,000
Fixed Cost	1,00,000

Illustration 13

From the following data, find out:

(*a*) P/V Ratio (*b*) Break Even Point (*c*) Margin of Safety

Present Production and sales	:	10,000 units
Selling Price per unit	:	Rs. 200
Variable cost per unit	:	
Direct materials		Rs. 50
Direct wages		Rs. 25
Variable overhead		100% of direct wages
Fixed Cost		Rs. 4,00,000

Solution

		Rs.
Selling Price per unit		200
Less Variable cost:	Rs.	
Direct material	50	
Direct wages	25	
Variable overhead	25	100
Contribution per unit		100

(*a*) P/V Ratio $= \frac{\text{Contribution}}{\text{Sales}} \times 100$

$= \frac{100}{200} \times 100 = 50\%$

(*b*) Break-even Point (in units) $= \frac{\text{Total Fixed Cost}}{\text{Contribution per unit}}$

$= \frac{\text{Rs. } 4{,}00{,}000}{\text{Rs. } 100}$

$= 4{,}000$ units

Break-even point (for sales volume) $= \frac{\text{Total Fixed Cost}}{\text{Contribution per unit}} \times \text{Selling price per unit}$

$= \frac{\text{Rs. } 4{,}00{,}000}{\text{Rs. } 100} \times \text{Rs. } 200$

$=$ Rs. 8,00,000

(*c*) Margin of Safety = Actual Sales – Sales at B.E.P
= Rs. 20,00,000 – Rs. 8,00,000
= Rs. 12,00,000

Illustration 14

The following data are available from the records of S.T. Co. Ltd. for the year ended 31st March, 2007:

	Rs.
Sales	40,000
Variable Cost	20,000
Fixed Cost	12,000

You are required to:

(*a*) calculate the P/V ratio, B.E.P. and Margin of Safety at this level.
(*b*) calculate the effect of 10% increase in sales price.
(*c*) calculate the effect of 10% decrease in sales price.

Solution

(*a*) (*i*) P/V Ratio $= \dfrac{\text{Contribution}}{\text{Sales}} \times 100$

$= \dfrac{\text{Rs. } 40{,}000 - 20{,}000}{\text{Rs. } 40{,}000} \times 100$

$= \dfrac{\text{Rs. } 20{,}000}{\text{Rs. } 40{,}000} \times 100 = 50\%$

(*ii*) Break-even Point (for sales volume) $= \dfrac{\text{Total Fixed Cost}}{\text{P/V Ratio}}$

$= \dfrac{\text{Rs. } 12{,}000}{50\%}$

$= 12{,}000 \times \dfrac{100}{50}$

= Rs. 24,000

(*iii*) Margin of Safety = Actual Sales – Sales at B.E.P.
= Rs. 40,000 – Rs. 24,000
= Rs. 16,000

(*b*)

	Rs.
Given Sales	40,000
Add Increase @ 10% in Sales Price	4,000
Revised sales price	44,000
Less Variable cost	20,000
Contribution	24,000

(*i*) P/V Ratio $= \dfrac{\text{Contribution}}{\text{Sales}} \times 100$

$= \dfrac{\text{Rs. } 24{,}000}{\text{Rs. } 44{,}000} \times 100 = 54.55\% \left(\text{or } \dfrac{12}{22}\right)$

(*ii*) Break-even Point (for sales volume) $= \dfrac{\text{Total Fixed Cost}}{\text{P/V Ratio}}$

$= \dfrac{\text{Rs. } 12{,}000}{\frac{12}{22}} = \text{Rs.} 12{,}000 \times \dfrac{22}{12} = \text{Rs. } 22{,}000$

(*iii*) Margin of Safety = Total Sales – Sales at B.E.P.
= Rs. 44,000 – Rs. 22,000
= Rs. 22,000

(*c*)

	Rs.
Given Sales	40,000
Less Decrease @ 10% in Sales Price	4,000
Revised Sales Price	36,000
Less Variable cost	20,000
Contribution	16,000

(*i*) P/V Ratio $= \frac{\text{Contribution}}{\text{Sales}} \times 100$

$= \frac{\text{Rs. } 16{,}000}{\text{Rs. } 36{,}000} \times 100 = 44.44\% \left(\text{or } \frac{4}{9}\right)$

(*ii*) Break-even Point (for sales volume) $= \frac{\text{Total Fixed Cost}}{\text{P/V Ratio}}$

$= \frac{\text{Rs. } 12{,}000}{\frac{4}{9}} = \text{Rs. } 12{,}000 \times \frac{9}{4} = \text{Rs. } 27{,}000$

(*iii*) Margin of Safety = Total Sales – Sales at B.E.P.
= Rs. 36,000 – Rs. 27,000
= Rs. 9,000

Illustration 15

(*a*) From the following particulars find out the break-even point:

Variable cost per unit	Rs. 15
Fixed Expenses	Rs.54,000
Selling Price per unit	Rs. 20

(*b*) What should be the selling price per unit, if the break-even point is brought down to 6,000 units.

(*G.N.D.U, B.Com., 1996*)

Solution

	Rs.
(*a*) Selling Price per unit	20
Less Variable cost per unit	15
Contribution per unit	5

Break-even Point (in units) $= \frac{\text{Fixed Cost}}{\text{Contribution per unit}}$

$= \frac{\text{Rs. } 54{,}000}{\text{Rs. } 5}$

= 10,800 units

(*b*) If the Break-even Point is to be brought down to 6,000, it should provide a total contribution of Rs. 54,000 (*i.e.*, equal to fixed cost).

$$\text{Contribution per unit} = \frac{\text{Total Contribution}}{\text{Break -even Point (in units)}}$$

$$= \frac{\text{Rs. } 54{,}000}{6{,}000 \text{ units}} = \text{Rs. } 9$$

Selling Price per unit = Variable Cost per unit + Contribution per unit
= Rs. 15 + Rs. 9 = Rs. 24

Illustration 16

(*a*) Alcos Ltd. manufactures and sells four types of products under the brand names A, B, C and D respectively. The sales mix in value comprises $33\frac{1}{3}\%, 41\frac{2}{3}\%, 16\frac{2}{3}\%$, and $8\frac{1}{3}\%$ of A, B, C and D respectively. The total budgeted sales (100%) are Rs. 60,000 per month. Operating costs are:

Variable costs:

Product A : 60% of Selling Price
Product B : 68% of Selling Price
Product C : 80% of Selling Price
Product D : 40% of Selling Price

Fixed costs

Rs. 14,700 per month.

Calculate the break-even point for the products on an overall basis.

(*b*) It has been proposed to change the sales mix as follows, the sales per month remaining Rs. 60,000:

Product A	25%	Product B	40%
Product C	30%	Product D	5%

Assuming that the proposal is implemented, calculate the break-even point.

(*I.C.W.A. Final*)

Solution

	Products				Total
	A	B	C	D	
Sales Mix	$33\frac{1}{3}\%$	$41\frac{2}{3}\%$	$16\frac{2}{3}\%$	$8\frac{1}{3}\%$	100%
	Rs.	Rs.	Rs.	Rs.	Rs.
Sales	20,000	25,000	10,000	5,000	60,000
Variable Cost	12,000	17,000	8,000	2,000	39,000
Contribution	8,000	8,000	2,000	3,000	21,000

$$\text{Break-even Point} = \frac{\text{Fixed Cost}}{\text{Contribution}} \times \text{Sales}$$

$$= \frac{\text{Rs. } 14{,}700}{\text{Rs. } 21{,}000} \times 60{,}000 = \text{Rs. } 42{,}000$$

(*b*)

	Products				
	A	**B**	**C**	**D**	**Total**
Sales Mix	25%	40%	30%	5%	100%
	Rs.	Rs.	Rs.	Rs.	Rs.
Sales	15,000	24,000	18,000	3,000	60,000
Variable Cost	9,000	16,320	14,400	1,200	40,920
Contribution	6,000	7,680	3,600	1,800	19,080

$$\text{Break-even Point} = \frac{\text{Fixed Cost}}{\text{Contribution}} \times \text{Sales} = \frac{\text{Rs. } 14{,}700}{\text{Rs. } 19{,}080} \times 60{,}000$$

$= \text{Rs. } 46{,}226$ (Approximately).

Illustration 17

From the following data you are required to calculate break-even point and net sales value at this point:

		Rs.
Direct Material cost per unit		8
Direct Labour cost per unit		5
Fixed overheads		24,000
Variable overheads @ 60% on direct labour		
Selling Price per unit	25	
Trade discount	4%	

If sales are 15% and 20% above the break even volume, determine the net profits.

(*C.A. Inter*)

Solution

		Rs.
Selling Price per unit		25
Less Trade discount @ 4%		1
Net Selling Price		24
Less Variable Cost:		
Direct Material cost	8	
Direct wages	5	
Variable overheads	3	
(60% on wages)		16
Contribution per unit		8

$$\text{Break-even Point (for units)} = \frac{\text{Total Fixed Cost}}{\text{Contribution per unit}}$$

$$= \frac{\text{Rs. } 24{,}000}{\text{Rs. } 8} = 3{,}000 \text{ units}$$

$$\text{Break-even Point (for sales value)} = \frac{\text{Total Fixed Cost}}{\text{Contribution per unit}} \times \text{Selling Price per unit}$$

$$= \frac{\text{Rs. } 24{,}000}{\text{Rs. } 8} \times \text{Rs. } 24 = \text{Rs. } 72{,}000$$

Calculation of Profit on Revised Sales

	(i)	*(ii)*
Sales at B.E.P.	3,000 units	3,000 units
Add Increase	450 units (15%)	600 units (20%)
Revised Sales	3,450 units	3,600 units
	Rs.	Rs.
Total Contribution @ Rs. 8 per unit	27,600	28,800
Less Fixed Cost	24,000	24,000
Net Profit	3,600	4,800

Illustration 18

The ratio of variable cost to sales is given to be 70%. The break-even point occurs at 50% of capacity sales. Find out capacity sales when fixed costs are Rs. 90,000. Determine profit at 80% and 100% capacity sales.

Solution

Given: Ratio of Variable Cost to Sales = 70%
If Selling Price is assumed to be Rs. 100,
Variable cost will be = Rs. 70
and Contribution will be = Rs. 30

$$\text{Hence, P/V Ratio} = \frac{\text{Contribution}}{\text{Sales}} \times 100$$

$$= \frac{30}{100} \times 100 = 30\%$$

$$\text{Break-even Point (for sales value)} = \frac{\text{Total Fixed Cost}}{\text{P/V Ratio}}$$

$$= \frac{\text{Rs. } 90{,}000}{30\%} = 90{,}000 \times \frac{100}{30} = \text{Rs. } 3{,}00{,}000$$

Further, given that Break-even Point occurs at 50% of capacity sales.

$$\text{Hence capacity sales} = \text{Rs. } 3{,}00{,}000 \times \frac{100}{50}$$

$$= \text{Rs. } 6{,}00{,}000$$

Calculation of Profit at given Sales Volume

(*a*) Profit at 80% Capacity Sales

	Rs.
Sales (80% of Rs. 6,00,000)	4,80,000
Contribution (30% of Sales)	1,44,000
Less Fixed Cost	90,000
Profit	54,000

(*b*) Profit at 100% Capacity Sales

	Rs.
Capacity Sales	6,00,000
Total Contribution (30% of Sales)	1,80,000
Less Fixed Cost	90,000
Profit	90,000

Illustration 19

The following information is obtained from the books of Antimony Ltd., for 2005-06:

Sales	Rs. 2,00,000
Variable costs	Rs. 1,00,000
Fixed costs	Rs. 60,000

You are required to calculate:

(*a*) P/V Ratio and Break-even Point.

(*b*) The effect of 20% decrease in fixed costs and 10% increase in variable costs on (a) above.

(*c*) Percentage increase in production to earn the same amount of net profit as in 2005-06 if the selling price is reduced by 10%.

(G.N.D.U., B.Com.)

Solution

Calculation of Contribution and Profit for 2005-06

	Rs.
Sales	2,00,000
Less Variable Costs	1,00,000
Contribution	1,00,000
Less Fixed Costs	60,000
Profit	40,000

$$\text{P/V Ratio} = \frac{\text{Contribution}}{\text{Sales}} \times 100$$

$$= \frac{\text{Rs. } 1,00,000}{\text{Rs. } 2,00,000} \times 100 = 50\%$$

$$\text{Break-even Point} = \frac{\text{Fixed Cost}}{\text{P/V Ratio}}$$

$$= \frac{\text{Rs. } 60,000}{50\%} = \text{Rs. } 60,000 \times \frac{100}{50} = \text{Rs. } 1,20,000$$

(*b*) Effect of 20% decrease in fixed costs and 10% increase in variable costs:

Current Fixed Costs	Rs. 60,000
Less 20% decrease	Rs. 12,000
Revised Fixed Costs	48,000
Current Variable Costs	Rs. 1,00,000
Add 10% increase	Rs. 10,000
Revised Variable Costs	Rs. 1,10,000

$$\text{P/V Ratio} = \frac{\text{Sales} - \text{Variable Cost}}{\text{Sales}} \times 100$$

$$= \frac{\text{Rs. } 2,00,000 - \text{Rs. } 1,10,000}{\text{Rs. } 2,00,000} \times 100$$

$$= \frac{\text{Rs. } 90,000}{\text{Rs. } 2,00,000} \times 100 = 45\%$$

$$\text{Break-even Point} = \frac{\text{Fixed Cost}}{\text{P/V Ratio}}$$

$$= \frac{\text{Rs. } 48,000}{45\%} = 48,000 \times \frac{100}{45} = \text{Rs. } 1,06,667$$

(*c*)

Current Selling Price	Rs. 2,00,000
Less Reduction @ 10%	Rs. 20,000
New Selling Price	Rs. 1,80,000

$$\text{P/V Ratio} = \frac{\text{Sales} - \text{Variable Cost}}{\text{Sales}} \times 100$$

$$= \frac{\text{Rs. } 1,80,000 - \text{Rs. } 1,00,000}{\text{Rs. } 1,80,000} \times 100$$

$$= \frac{\text{Rs. } 80,000}{\text{Rs. } 1,80,000} \times 100 = 44.45\%$$

Sales required to earn desired profits $= \dfrac{\text{Fixed Cost + Desired Profit}}{\text{P/V Ratio}}$

$$= \frac{\text{Rs. } 60{,}000 + \text{Rs. } 40{,}000}{44.45\%}$$

$$= \frac{\text{Rs. } 1{,}00{,}000}{44.45} \times 100 = \text{Rs. } 2{,}24{,}972$$

Increase in sales = Rs. 2,24,972 – Rs. 2,00,000 = Rs. 24,972

Percentage of Increase $= \dfrac{24{,}972}{2{,}00{,}000} \times 100 = 12.48\%$

Illustration 20

The following information is obtained from A Co. Ltd., for the year 2005-06:

	Rs.
Sales	1,00,000
Variable Cost	60,000
Fixed Cost	30,000

(*a*) Find the P/V ratio, B.E.P. and margin of safety at this level.

(*b*) Calculate the effect of –

(*i*) 20% increase in selling price

(*ii*) 10% decrease in selling price;

(*iii*) 5% decrease in sales volume;

(*iv*) 10% decrease in fixed costs;

(*v*) 10% decrease in variable costs;

(*vi*) 20% increase in sales price accompanied by an increase of fixed overhead by Rs. 10,000;

(*vii*) 20% increase in sales price accompanied by 10% decrease in variable costs and 10% increase in fixed costs.

(*G.N.D.U., B.Com.*)

Solution

Profit/Volume Ratio:	Break-Even Point:	Margin of Safety:
$= \dfrac{\text{Contribution}}{\text{Sales}} \times 100$	$= \dfrac{\text{Fixed Cost}}{\text{P/V ratio}}$	$= \dfrac{\text{Profit}}{\text{P/V ratio}}$

(*a*) Existing circumstances:

$= \dfrac{40{,}000}{1{,}00{,}000} \times 100$	$= \dfrac{30{,}000}{40\%}$	$= \dfrac{10{,}000}{40\%}$
= 40%	= Rs. 75,000	= 25,000

(*b*) (*i*) 20% increase in selling price:

$= \frac{60,000}{1,20,000} \times 100$ $= \frac{30,000}{50\%}$ $= \frac{30,000}{50\%}$

= 50% = Rs. 60,000 = Rs. 60,000

(*ii*) 10% decrease in selling price:

$= \frac{30,000}{90,000} \times 100$ $= \frac{30,000}{33\frac{1}{3}\%}$ $= \frac{0}{33\frac{1}{3}\%}$

$= 33\frac{1}{3}\%$ = Rs. 90,000 = 0

(*iii*) 5% decrease in sales volume (*i.e.*, 5% decrease in level of activity)

$= \frac{38,000}{95,000} \times 100$ $= \frac{30,000}{40\%}$ $= \frac{8,000}{40\%}$

= 40% = Rs. 75,000 = Rs. 20,000

(*iv*) 10% decrease in fixed costs:

$= \frac{40,000}{1,00,000} \times 100$ $= \frac{27,000}{40\%}$ $= \frac{13,000}{40\%}$

= 40% = Rs. 67,500 = Rs. 32,500

(*v*) 10% decrease in variable costs:

$= \frac{46,000}{1,00,000} \times 100$ $= \frac{30,000}{46\%}$ $= \frac{16,000}{46\%}$

= 46% = Rs. 65,217 = Rs. 34,783

(*vi*) 20% increase in selling price and increase of fixed overhead by Rs. 10,000:

$= \frac{60,000}{1,20,000} \times 100$ $= \frac{40,000}{50\%}$ $= \frac{20,000}{50\%}$

= 50% = Rs. 80,000 = 40,000

(*vii*) 20 % increase in sales price, 10 % increase in fixed costs and 10 % decrease in variable costs

$= \frac{66,000}{1,20,000} \times 100$ $= \frac{33,000}{55\%}$ $= \frac{33,000}{55\%}$

= 55% = Rs. 60,000 = Rs. 60,000

Illustration 21

An analysis of costs of Shammitex Ltd., led to the following information:

	Variable Cost (% of sales)	Fixed cost Rs.
Direct Materials	33.6	–
Direct Labour	28.4	–
Factory Overhead	11.6	1,66,700
Distribution Expenses	3.3	63,400
General and Administration Expenses	1.1	99,900

Budgeted sales for the next year are Rs. 20,00,000. You are required to determine:

(*i*) the break-even sales volume,

(*ii*) the profit at the budgeted sales volume,

(*iii*) the profit, if actual sales -

(*a*) drop by 12½% (*b*) increase by 10%

(*iv*) sales to generate a profit of Rs. 2,20,000. (*G.N.D.U., B.Com. 1976*)

(*C.A Inter*)

Solution

Calculation of Percentage of Variable Cost on Sales

	% on sales
Direct Material	33.6
Direct Labour	28.4
Factory Overhead	11.6
Distribution Expenses	3.3
General and Administration Expenses	1.1
Total Variable Cost	78.0

Calculation of Contribution and Profit on Budgeted Sales

		Rs.
Budgeted Sales		20,00,000
Less Variable Costs (78 % of sales)		15,60,000
Contribution		4,40,000
Less Fixed Costs		
Factory Overhead	1,66,700	
Distribution Expenses	63,400	
General and Administration Expenses	99,900	3,30,000
Profit on Budgeted Sales		1,10,000

$$\text{P/V Ratio} = \frac{\text{Contribution}}{\text{Sales}} \times 100 = \frac{\text{Rs. } 4,40,000}{\text{Rs. } 20,00,000} \times 100 = 22\%$$

$$\text{Break-even Point} = \frac{\text{Fixed Cost}}{\text{P/V Ratio}} = \frac{\text{Rs. } 3,30,000}{22\%} = \text{Rs. } 3,30,000 \times \frac{100}{22}$$

$$= \text{Rs. } 15,00,000$$

Calculation of Profit on Revised Sales:

(*a*) If actual sales drop by 12½%

	Rs.
Budgeted Sales	20,00,000
Less Decrease @ 12½%	2,50,000
Revised Sales	17,50,000
Contribution (@ 22% on Sales)	3,85,000
Less Fixed Costs	3,30,000
Profit	55,000

(*b*) If actual sales increase by 10%

	Rs.
Budgeted Sales	20,00,000
Add Increase @ 10%	2,00,000
Revised Sales	22,00,000
Contribution (@ 22% on sales)	4,84,000
Less Fixed Costs	3,30,000
Profit	1,54,000

Calculation of sales required to generate a profit of Rs. 2,20,000:

$$\text{Sales required to earn desired profits} = \frac{\text{Fixed Cost + Desired Profit}}{\text{P/V Ratio}}$$

$$= \frac{\text{Rs. } 3,30,000 + \text{Rs. } 2,20,000}{22\%}$$

$$= \frac{\text{Rs. } 5,50,000}{22\%}$$

$$= 5,50,000 \times \frac{100}{22}$$

$$= \text{Rs. } 25,00,000$$

Illustration 22

Sales and profit during two periods for a company were as follows:

	Sales	Profit
	Rs.	Rs.
Period I	9,00,000	90,000
Period II	11,00,000	1,30,000

You are required to find out:

(*i*) P/V Ratio.

(*ii*) Fixed cost.

(*iii*) Break-even Point.

(*iv*) Profit at an estimated sales of Rs. 15,00,000

(*v*) Sales required to earn a profit of Rs. 2,00,000

Solution

	Sales	Profit
	Rs.	Rs.
Period I	9,00,000	90,000
Period II	11,00,000	1,30,000
Change	2,00,000	40,000

$$\text{P/V Ratio} = \frac{\text{Change in contribution in two periods}}{\text{Change in sales in two periods}}$$

$$\text{or} = \frac{\text{Change in Fixed Cost + Profit in two periods (or F+P)}}{\text{Change in Sales in two periods}}$$

or (Since Fixed Costs in two periods are constant) $= \frac{\text{Change in Profit in two periods}}{\text{Change in Sales in two periods}}$

$$= \frac{\text{Rs. }40,000}{\text{Rs. }2,00,000} = \frac{1}{5} \text{ or } 20\%$$

Calculation of Fixed Cost:

	Period I	Period II
	Rs.	Rs.
Sales	9,00,000	11,00,000
Total Contribution (20% of sales) (or Sales × P/V Ratio)	1,80,000	2,20,000
Less Profit	90,000	1,30,000
Fixed cost	90,000	90,000

Calculation of Break-even Point:

$$\text{Break-even Point} = \frac{\text{Fixed Cost}}{\text{P/V ratio}}$$

$$= \frac{\text{Rs. }90,000}{20\%} = 90,000 \times \frac{100}{20} = 4,50,000$$

Calculation of profit at given amount of sales volume:

	Rs.
Sales	15,00,000
Total Contribution (Sales × P/V Ratio) (Rs. 15,00,000 × 20%)	3,00,000
Less Fixed Cost	90,000
Profit	2,10,000

Calculation of sales required to earn a profit of Rs. 2,00,000

$$\text{Sales required to earn desired profits} = \frac{\text{Fixed Cost + Desired Profit}}{\text{P/V Ratio}}$$

$$= \frac{\text{Rs. 90,000 + Rs. 2,00,000}}{20\%}$$

$$= 2{,}90{,}000 \times \frac{100}{20} = \text{Rs. } 14{,}50{,}000$$

Illustration 23

The following information relates to production and sales of an article for January and February:

	January	February
	Rs.	Rs.
Sales	38,000	65,000
Profit	–	3,000
Loss	2,400	–

Calculate:

(*i*) Break-even sales volume;
(*ii*) Profit or loss at Rs. 46,000 sales;
(*iii*) Sales to earn a profit of Rs. 5,000. (*G.N.D.U., B.Com. 1976, 2001*)

Solution

	Sales	Profit/Loss
	Rs.	Rs.
January	38,000	(–) 2,400 (Loss)
February	65,000	3,000
Change or Increase in February over January	27,000	5,400

Calculation of P/V Ratio:

$$\text{P/V Ratio} = \frac{\text{Change in contribution in two periods}}{\text{Change in sales in two periods}}$$

$$\text{or} = \frac{\text{Change in F + P in two periods}}{\text{Change in Sales in two periods}}$$

$$\text{or (Since Fixed Costs are constant in two periods)} = \frac{\text{Change in Profit in two periods}}{\text{Change in Sales in two periods}}$$

$$\text{or} = \frac{\text{Rs. } 5{,}400}{\text{Rs. } 27{,}000} = \frac{1}{5} \text{ or } 20\%$$

Calculation of Fixed Cost:

	January Rs.	February Rs.
Sales	38,000	65,000
Total Contribution (Sales × P/V Ratio)	38,000 × 20% = Rs. 7,600	65,000 × 20% = Rs. 13,000
Add Loss or Less Profit	Rs. 2,400	Rs. 3,000
Fixed Cost	Rs. 10,000	Rs. 10,000

Calculation of Break-even Point:

$$\text{Break-even Point} = \frac{\text{Fixed Cost}}{\text{P / V ratio}}$$

$$= \frac{\text{Rs.}10{,}000}{20\%} = 10{,}000 \times \frac{100}{20} = \text{Rs. } 50{,}000$$

Calculation of Profit or loss at given sales volume:

Sales	Rs. 46,000
Total Contribution (Sales × P/V Ratio) (46,000 × 20%)	= Rs. 9,200
Less Fixed Cost	Rs. 10,000
Loss	(–) 800

Calculation of Sales required to earn a profit of Rs. 5,000:

$$\text{Sales required to earn desired profits} = \frac{\text{Fixed Cost + Desired Profit}}{\text{P/V Ratio}}$$

$$= \frac{\text{Rs. } 10{,}000 + \text{Rs. } 5{,}000}{20\%}$$

$$= \text{Rs.}15{,}000 \times \frac{100}{20} = \text{Rs, } 75{,}000$$

Illustration 24

There are two similar plants under the same management. The management desires to merge these two plants. The following particulars are available:

	Factory I	Factory II
Capacity operation	100%	60%
Sales	Rs. 300 1acs	Rs. 120 1acs
Variable costs	Rs. 220 lacs	Rs. 90 lacs
Fixed costs	Rs. 40 lacs	Rs. 20 lacs

You are required to calculate:

(*a*) What would be the capacity of the merged plant to be operated for the purposes of Break-even, and

(*b*) What would be the profitability on working at 75% of the merged capacity.

(*C.A. Final*)

Solution

Calculation of Contribution of Merged Plant:

	Factory I	Factory II	Merged Plant
Capacity	100%	100%	100%
	Rs.	Rs.	Rs.
Sales	300 lacs	200 lacs	500 lacs
		$\left(120 \times \frac{100}{60}\right)$	
Variable Costs	220 lacs	150 lacs	370 lacs
		$\left(90 \times \frac{100}{60}\right)$	
Contribution	80 lacs	50 lacs	130 lacs
Fixed Costs	40 lacs	20 lacs	60 lacs.

Notes: (*i*) In case of merger, both plants shall be merged to the full extent.

(*ii*) Sales and Variable Costs of Factory II at 100% capacity (under merger) will increase proportionately.

(*iii*) Fixed Costs of Factory II at 100% capacity shall be the same as that at 60%.

Calculation of P/V Ratio and Break-even Point of Merged Plant:

$$\text{P/V Ratio} = \frac{\text{Contribution}}{\text{Sales}} \times 100$$

$$= \frac{\text{Rs. } 130 \text{ lacs}}{\text{Rs. } 500 \text{ lacs}} \times 100 = 26\%$$

$$\text{Break-even Point} = \frac{\text{Fixed Cost}}{\text{P / V ratio}}$$

$$= \frac{\text{Rs. } 60 \text{ lacs}}{26\%} = \text{Rs. } 60 \text{ lacs} \times \frac{100}{26}$$

$$= \text{Rs. } 230.769 \text{ lacs}$$

$$\text{Capacity of the Merged Plant at Break-even Point} = \frac{\text{Sales at B. E. P.}}{\text{Sales at } 100\% \text{ capacity}} \times 100$$

$$= \frac{\text{Rs. } 230.769 \text{ lacs}}{\text{Rs. } 500 \text{ lacs}} \times 100$$

$$= 46.15\% \text{ (approx.)}$$

Calculation of Profitability of Plant at 75% Capacity

Sales (at 75% capacity)	Rs. 375 lacs
Contribution (Sales × P/V Ratio) (Rs. 375 lacs × 26%)	Rs. 97.5 lacs
Less Fixed Cost	Rs. 60.00 lacs
Profit	Rs. 37.5 lacs

$$\text{Rate of Profitability} = \frac{\text{Profit}}{\text{Sales}} \times 100 = \frac{\text{Rs. 37.5 lacs}}{\text{Rs. 375 lacs}} \times 100 = 10\%$$

Illustration 25

The following summarised information regarding manufacturing and sale operations of Nitlesh Co. Ltd., and Mithlesh Co. Ltd. has been extracted from their books:

		Nitlesh Co. Ltd.	Mithlesh Co. Ltd.
		Rs.	Rs.
Sales		1,00,000	1,00,000
Costs:	Fixed	30,000	50,000
	Variable	50,000	30,000
Profit		20,000	20,000

You are required to:

(*a*) calculate the break-even point of each business;

(*b*) compute 'Margin of Safety'; and

(*c*) state which business is likely to earn higher profits under conditions of–

(*i*) heavy demand for the product

(*ii*) low demand for the product. (*Punjabi, B.Com. 1971*)

Solution

Calculation of Contribution and P/V Ratio

	Nitlesh Co. Ltd.	Mithlesh Co. Ltd.
	Rs.	Rs.
Sales	1,00,000	1,00,000
Less Variable Cost	50,000	30,000
Contribution	50,000	70,000

P/V Ratio $= \frac{\text{Rs. 50,000}}{\text{Rs. 1,00,000}} \times 100 = \frac{\text{Rs. 70,000}}{\text{Rs. 1,00,000}} \times 100$

$\left(\frac{\text{Contribution}}{\text{Sales}} \times 100\right)$ $= 50\%$ $= 70\%$

Break-even Point $= \frac{\text{Rs. 30,000}}{50\%}$ $= \frac{\text{Rs. 50,000}}{70\%}$

$\left(\frac{\text{Fixed Cost}}{\text{P/V Ratio}}\right)$

	= Rs. 60,000	= Rs. 71,429
(*b*) Margin of Safety	$= \dfrac{\text{Rs. } 20{,}000}{50\%}$	$= \dfrac{\text{Rs. } 20{,}000}{70\%}$
$\left(\dfrac{\text{Profit}}{\text{P/V Ratio}}\right)$	= Rs. 40,000	= Rs. 28,571

(*c*) (*i*) **In case of heavy demand for the product:** Mithlesh Co. Ltd. will earn higher profits as it has a P/V ratio higher than that of Nitlesh Co. Ltd. and its fixed costs being higher than that of Nitlesh Co. Ltd., are not fully employed.

(*ii*) **In case of low demand for the product:** Nitlesh Co. Ltd. will do better as its fixed costs are limited and B.E.P. is lower (attainable earlier than that in case of Mithlesh Co. Ltd.). Nitlesh Co. Ltd. will start giving profits earlier.

Illustration 26

The Young Hotel has annual fixed costs applicable to rooms of Rs. 15,00,000 for a 300 room hotel with average daily room rates of Rs. 40 and average variable costs of Rs. 6 for each room rented. The Hotel operates 365 days per year. It is subject to an income tax rate of 30 percent.

It is required to:

(*i*) Calculate the number of rooms the Hotel must rent to earn a net income after taxes of Rs. 10,00,000 and

(*ii*) Compute the break-even point in terms of number of rooms rented.

(*Delhi, B.Com. Hons. 1982*)

Solution

Calculation of contribution per room per day

	Rs.
Average daily rate of one room	40
Average daily variable cost for one room	6
Contribution	34

	Rs.
Let us assume that Profit before tax	100
Income tax @ 30%	30
Profit after Tax (Rs. 100 – 30)	70
Desired Profit after tax	10,00,000

So, Profit before tax $= 10{,}00{,}000 \times \dfrac{100}{70}$

or $= \dfrac{1{,}00{,}00{,}000}{7}$

No. of rooms to be rented to earn desired profit of $\frac{1,00,00,000}{7}$

$$= \frac{\text{Fixed Cost + Desired Profit}}{\text{Contribution per room}}$$

$$= \frac{\text{Rs.}15,00,000 + \left(\frac{1,00,00,000}{7}\right)}{\text{Rs. }34} = 86,134 \text{ Rooms}$$

Break-even Point (in terms of number of rooms rented) $= \frac{\text{Fixed Cost}}{\text{Contribution per room}} = \frac{\text{Rs.}15,00,000}{\text{Rs.}34}$

$= 44,118$ Room

Illustration 27

Calculate from the following data (*i*) the value of the output at which the business breaks even and (*ii*) the percentage of capacity at which it breaks even:

	Budget for 2006-07 Based on 100% Capacity Rs.	Estimated Shut-down Expenditure Rs.
Direct Wages	2,09,964	–
Direct Materials	2,44,552	–
Works Expenses	1,81,820	93,528
Selling and Distribution Expenses	61,188	40,188
Administrative Expenses	30,000	20,508
Net Sales	8,40,000	–

(*C.A. Final*)

Solution

Budgeted costs for 2006-07
(at 100% Capacity)

	Total costs	**Shut-down Expenditure (or fixed costs)**	**Variable costs**
	Rs.	**Rs.**	**Rs.**
Direct materials	2,44,552	–	2,44,552
Direct wages	2,09,964	–	2,09,964
Works Expenses	1,81,820	93,528	88,292
Administration Expenses	30,000	20,508	9,492
Selling & Distribution Expenses	61,188	40,188	21,000
Total	7,27,524	1,54,224	5,73,300
Profit	1,12,476		
Sales	8,40,000		

Note: Total Cost – Shut Down Cost = Variable Cost

Calculation of contribution:

	Rs.
Sales	8,40,000
Less Variable Cost	5,73,300
Contribution	2,66,700

$$\text{P/V Ratio} = \frac{\text{Contribution}}{\text{Sales}} \times 100$$

$$= \frac{\text{Rs. } 2{,}66{,}700}{\text{Rs.} 8{,}40{,}000} \times 100 = 31.75\%$$

$$\begin{array}{c}\text{Break-even Point} \\ \text{(Sales Value)}\end{array} = \frac{\text{Total Fixed Cost}}{\text{P/V Ratio}}$$

$$= \frac{\text{Rs. } 1{,}54{,}224}{31.75\%}$$

$$= \text{Rs. } 1{,}54{,}224 \times \frac{100}{31.75} = \text{Rs. } 4{,}85{,}745$$

$$\% \text{ of Capacity at Break-even Point} = \frac{\text{Sales at B. E. P.}}{\text{Sales at 100\% Capacity}} \times 100$$

$$= \frac{4{,}85{,}745}{\text{Rs. } 8{,}40{,}000} \times 100 = 57.83\%$$

Illustration 28

A firm manufactures product X whose selling price is Rs. 10 per unit. The firm has the capacity to produce 10,000 units. The variable costs are Rs. 2.50 per unit. Fixed costs are estimated at Rs. 30,000 upto the capacity utilisation level of 50%; Rs. 36,000 above that level but Rs. 42,000 if the level of capacity utilisation is 80% or above.

(*a*) What is the break-even point?

(*b*) What will be the operating profits of the firm, if the levels of capacity utilisation are 70%, 80% and 90% respectively?

(*c*) What is level of activity at which the firm can make an operating profit of Rs. 18,000?

(*d*) What is the margin of safety, if the firm manufactures and sells only 6,000 units in a year due to market constraints?

(*e*) Management of the firm is advised that, if the selling price is reduced to Rs. 9 per unit, sales will go up from 7,000 units to 7,500 units. Is it worthwhile to reduce the selling price?

(*f*) Management of the firm is also advised that sale of 7,500 units at the present selling price can also be achieved, if a sum of Rs. 5,000 is spent on advertisement. Which alternative–reducing the selling price to Rs. 9 per unit or spending Rs. 5,000 on advertisement–will generate more profit? (*I.C.W.A. Inter, Dec. 1995*)

Solution

(a) Break-even Point (units) $= \dfrac{\text{Total Fixed Cost}}{\text{Contribution per unit}}$

$= \dfrac{30{,}000}{10 - 2.50} = \dfrac{30{,}000}{7.50} = 4{,}000$ units

Break-even Point in Rs. $= 4{,}000 \times 10 = \text{Rs. } 40{,}000$

Break-even Point in % capacity $= \dfrac{4{,}000 \text{ units}}{10{,}000 \text{ units}} \times 100 = 40\%$

(*b*) Computation of Operating Profits

	At 70%	At 80%	At 90%
Sales (units)	7,000	8,000	9,000
	Rs.	Rs.	Rs.
Sales @ Rs. 10 each	70,000	80,000	90,000
Less: Variable Cost @ Rs. 2.50	17,500	20,000	22,500
Contribution	52,500	60,000	67,500
Less: Fixed cost	36,000	42,000	42,000
Profit	16,500	18,000	25,500

(*c*) Sales required $= \dfrac{\text{Fixed Cost + Profit}}{\text{Contribution per unit}}$

$= \dfrac{30{,}000 + 18{,}000}{7.50}$

$= \dfrac{48{,}000}{7.50} = 6{,}400$ units (or 64% capacity)

At a capacity of 64%, fixed cost is Rs. 36,000

Thus: Required Sales $= \dfrac{36{,}000 + 18{,}000}{\text{Rs. } 7.50}$

= 7,200 Units or 72% Capacity

(*d*) Margin of Safety = Sales – Sales at B.E. point.

= (6,000 × Rs 10) – Rs. 40,000

= Rs. 20,000

		Rs.
(*e*) Sales 7,500 units @ Rs. 9		67,500
Less: Variable cost (7,500 units @ Rs. 2.50)		18,750
Contribution		48,750
Less: Fixed cost		36,000
Profit		12,750

Profit at 70% capacity is Rs. 16,500 as computed in part (*b*) above. It is thus not worthwhile to reduce the selling price to Rs. 9 per unit, because it results in reduction in profit by Rs. 3,750 (*i.e.*, Rs. 16,500 – 12,750).

(*f*) Sales at Rs. 10 per unit		Rs. 75,000
Less: Variable cost @ Rs. 2.50 each		18,750
Contribution		56,250
Less: Fixed cost	36,000	
Advertisement	5,000	41,000
Profit		15,250

Spending Rs. 5,000 on advertisement results in profit of Rs. 15,250 while reducing selling price to Rs. 9 results in profit of Rs. 12,750 [as calculated in part (*e*)]. Thus spending more on advertisement will generate more profit.

Illustration 29

On the basis of the following data, work out the expected profits, capacity utilisation (in %), break-even point and margins of safety (in terms of quantity and value in both the cases) for the year 2004-05 and 2005-06:

	2004-05	2005-06
Production capacity (in units)	2 lakhs	3 lakhs
Production/sales (in units)	1.8 lakhs	2.25 lakhs
Selling price per unit	Rs. 6	Rs. 6.50
Variable cost per unit	Rs. 3	Rs. 3.30
Fixed expenses (including depreciation)	Rs. 3 lakhs	Rs. 5.12 lakhs

(*I.C.W. A. Inter*)

Solution

	2004-05	2005-06
Capacity utilisation (%)	$\frac{1.8 \text{ lakhs}}{2 \text{ lakhs}} = 90\%$	$\frac{2.25 \text{ lakhs}}{3 \text{ lakhs}} = 75\%$
Break-even Point (in units)		
$\left(\frac{\text{Fixed Cost}}{\text{S} - \text{V}}\right)$	$= \frac{\text{Rs. } 3,00,000}{\text{Rs. } 6 - 3}$	$= \frac{\text{Rs. } 5,12,000}{\text{Rs. } 6.50 - 3.30}$
	= 1,00,000 units	1,60,000 units
Break-even Point (in Rs.)	1,00,000 × Rs. 6	1,60,000 × Rs. 6.50
	= Rs. 6,00,000	= Rs. 10,40,000

Margin of safety (units)	1,80,000 – 1,00,000	2,25,000 – 1,60,000
(Sales units – B.E. quantity)	= 80,000 units	= 65,000 units
Margin of Safety (in Rupees)	= 80,000 units×Rs. 6	= 65,000 units × Rs. 6.50
	= Rs. 4,80,000	= Rs. 4,22,500

Calculation of Expected Profit	Rs.	Rs.
Sales (Actual Quantity × Selling Price)	10,80,000	14,62,500
Less: Variable Cost (Units × V.C.per unit)	5,40,000	7,42,500
Contribution	5,40,000	7,20,000
Less: Fixed Cost	3,00,000	5,12,000
Profit	2,40,000	2,08,000

Illustration 30

A company has three factories situated in North, East and South with its Head Office in Mumbai. The management has received the following report on the operations of each factory for a period:

(Rs. '000)

	Sales		Profit	
	Actual	Over/(Under) Budget	Actual	Over/(Under) Budget
North	1,100	(400)	135	(180)
East	1,450	150	210	90
South	1,200	(200)	330	(110)

Calculate for each factory and the company as a whole for the period:

(*i*) the fixed costs.

(*ii*) break-even sales. (*C.A. Inter, Nov., 1996*)

Solution

	Sales	Profit
North – Actual	1,100	135
Add: Under-budgeted	400	180
Budgeted	1,500	315

$$\text{P/V Ratio} = \frac{\text{Difference in profit}}{\text{Difference in sales}}$$

$$= \frac{315-135}{1{,}500-1{,}100}\times 100 = \frac{180}{400}\times 100 = 45\%$$

	Sales	Profit
East – Actual	1,450	210
Less: Over-budgeted	150	90
Budgeted	1,300	120

$$\text{P/V Ratio} = \frac{90}{150}\times 100 = 60\%$$

South – Actual	1,200	330
Add: Under-budgeted	200	110
Budgeted	1,400	440

$$\text{P/V Ratio} = \frac{110}{200} \times 100 = 55\%$$

Calculation of Fixed Cost

Fixed Cost = (Actual Sales × P/V Ratio) – Profit

		(Rs. '000)
North	= (1,100 × 45%) – 135	= 360
East	= (1,450 × 60%) – 210	= 660
South	= (1,200 × 55%) – 330	= 330
	Total Fixed Cost	1,350

Calculation of Break-even Sales (in Rs. '000)

$$\text{B.E. sales} = \frac{\text{Fixed Cost}}{\text{P/V Ratio}}$$

$$\text{North} = \frac{360}{45\%} = 800$$

$$\text{East} = \frac{660}{60\%} = 1{,}100$$

$$\text{South} = \frac{330}{55\%} = 600$$

2,500

OBJECTIVE TYPE QUESTIONS

A. Multiple Choice Questions

Choose the correct answer:

(*a*) Under marginal costing technique, marginal cost is equal to:
- (*i*) Fixed Cost + Variable Cost
- (*ii*) Direct Material Cost + Direct Wages + Direct Expenses
- (*iii*) Prime Cost + Variable Overhead
- (*iv*) Factory Overhead + Office Overhead + Selling and Distribution Overhead.

(*b*) Marginal costing technique follows the following basis of classification of costs:
- (*i*) Behaviour-wise (*ii*) Element-wise
- (*iii*) Function-wise (*iv*) Identifiability-wise

(*c*) 'Contribution Margin' is equal to:

(*i*) Fixed cost – Variable cost (*ii*) Sales – Variable cost
(*iii*) Sales – Fixed cost (*iv*) Sales – Profit

(*d*) Variable Cost:

(*i*) Remains fixed in total
(*ii*) Varies per unit
(*iii*) Remains fixed per unit
(*iv*) Neither increases nor decreases.

(*e*) If sales are Rs. 1,00,000 and variable costs are Rs. 60,000, P/V Ratio is:

(*i*) 40% (*ii*) 60% (*iii*) 20% (*iv*) 10

(*f*) If sales are Rs. 80,000 and variable cost to sales is 70%, contribution is:

(*i*) Rs. 56,000 (*ii*) Rs. 24,000
(*iii*) Rs. 70,000 (*iv*) Rs. 30,000

(*g*) Break-even Point is:

(*i*) $\frac{\text{Profit}}{\text{P/V Ratio}}$ (*ii*) $\frac{\text{Total Variable Cost}}{\text{P/V Ratio}}$

(*iii*) $\frac{\text{Sales}}{\text{P/V Ratio}}$ (*iv*) $\frac{\text{Total Fixed Cost}}{\text{P/V Ratio}}$

(*h*) Margin of safety is:

(*i*) Actual Sales – Sales at Break-even Point
(*ii*) Sales – Contribution
(*iii*) Sales – Fixed Cost
(*iv*) Fixed Cost + Variable Cost

(*i*) P/V Ratio will increase if:

(*i*) there is an increase in fixed cost;
(*ii*) there is a decrease in fixed cost;
(*iii*) there is a decrease in variable cost per unit;
(*iv*) there is a decrease in selling price per unit.

[**Ans.** (*a*) (*iii*), (*b*) (*i*), (*c*) (*ii*), (*d*) (*iii*), (*e*) (*i*), (*f*) (*ii*), (*g*) (*iv*), (*h*) (*i*), (*i*) (*iii*)]

B. True/ False statements

State whether the following statements are 'true' or 'false':

(*a*) Marginal costing follows the behaviour-wise classification of costs.

(*b*) Marginal cost is the aggregate of Prime cost and fixed overhead

(*c*) Marginal cost is the aggregate of Prime cost and variable overhead.

(*d*) Contribution is the excess of sales over variable cost.

(*e*) At Break-even Point, Contribution available is equal to total fixed cost.

(*f*) P/V Ratio remains constant at all levels of activity.

(*g*) P/V Ratio can be increased by increasing the selling price per unit.

(*h*) Break-even Point = $\frac{\text{Profit}}{\text{P/V Ratio}}$

(*i*) Margin of Safety = $\frac{\text{Profit}}{\text{P/V Ratio}}$

(*i*) P/V Ratio = $\frac{\text{Sales} - \text{Contribution}}{\text{Sales}}$

(*k*) Contribution per unit = $\frac{\text{Total Contribution}}{\text{Total No. of Units Sold}}$

(*l*) Marginal costing and absorption costing are the same.

(*m*) Contribution = Sales × P/V Ratio.

[**Ans. True:** (*a*), (*c*), (*d*), (*e*), (*J*), (*g*), (*i*), (*f*), (*k*), (*m*) **False:** (*b*), (*h*), (*l*)]

C. Filling the blanks

Fill in the blanks:

(*a*) Marginal cost is the .... of sales over contribution.

(*b*) Profit/Volume Ratio is the ratio of .... to sales.

(*c*) Marginal costing technique takes into account the .... classification of costs.

(*d*) If Variable Cost to Sales Ratio is 60%, P/V Ratio is .... %.

(*e*) When Total Fixed cost is Rs. 1,00,000, Contribution per unit is Rs. 20, Break-even Point shall be .... units.

(*f*) ....+ Variable Overhead = Marginal Cost.

(*g*) When Sales are Rs. 2,00,000 and Variable Cost is Rs. 1,60,000, P/V Ratio will be ....%

(*h*) Variable cost per unit is ....

[**Ans.** (*a*) Excess, (*b*) Contribution (*c*) Behaviour-wise (*d*) 40, (*e*) 5,000 (*f*) Prime Cost (*g*) 20 (*h*) Fixed.]

SHORT ANSWER TYPE QUESTIONS

1. What is marginal costing?

2. What is marginal cost?

3. What is Break-even Analysis?

4. What is meant by P/V Ratio?
5. Give the meaning of Break-even Point.
6. Define Contribution.
7. What are the assumptions of Break-even Analysis?
8. Give the formula for calculating:
   (*a*) P/V Ratio
   (*b*) Break-even Point.
   (*c*) Margin of Safety.
   (*d*) Variable Cost to Sales Ratio.
   (*e*) No. of units to be sold to earn desired profits.
   (*f*) Sales volume required to earn desired profits.
9. What is the basis of valuation of stock under marginal costing and absorption costing?

LONG ANSWER TYPE QUESTIONS

1. What is Marginal Costing? Discuss its advantages and limitations.
2. What is Contribution? What are its advantages?
3. What is Profit/Volume Ratio? How would you calculate it?
4. Define Break-even Analysis. What are the uses and assumptions of such analysis?
5. What is Break-even Point? How is it computed? Illustrate your answer.
6. Write notes on:
   (*a*) Margin of Safety.
   (*b*) Break-even Point.
   (*c*) Marginal Cost.
   (*d*) Angle of Incidence.
   (*e*) Contribution. (*Punjabi, B.Com, 1983 K.U., B.Com, 1994*)
7. What are the underlying assumptions in Break-even Analysis? Enumerate at least six factors. (*C.A. Inter 1983*)
8. What is Break-Even Chart? How is it drawn?
9. Define Marginal Costing and explain its main features and useful contribution to the management in decision-making. (*Punjab, B.Com., 1984*)
10. State what do you mean by the technique of marginal costing and control. (*G.N.D.U., B.Com., 1995*)
11. Define marginal cost. Discuss the importance of classifying expenses into variable and fixed. Give two examples of each. (*M.D.U., B.Com. 1981, I.C.W.A. Final*)

12. What elements are included in marginal cost? How is contribution related to profit? Mention two advantages that management can obtain from knowing the contribution from its units. *(I.C.W.A. Inter 1990)*

13. What is Marginal Costing? How is control exercised on costs through Marginal Costing Technique? *(C.A. Inter 1978, 1989)*

14. Explain the role of 'Contribution' in profit maximisation. *(Madras, B.Com, 1983)*

15. Discuss the importance of the following terms in relation to Marginal Costing:

(*a*) Key Factor.

(*b*) Break-even Point.

(*c*) P/V Ratio.

(*d*) Margin of Safety. *(H.P., B.Com., 1984, Punjabi, B.Com., 1985)*

16. What do you understand by the term Break-even Point? Why should it be calculated ? *(Delhi, B.Com. (Hons) 1980)*

17. Draw a break-even chart with a few illustrative figures. Explain the cost-volume-profit relationship. How would a change in selling price affect the above? *(Punjabi, B.Com., 1982)*

18. Distinguish between absorption costing and marginal costing. Under what circumstances can selling price be reduced to marginal cost? *(I.C.W.A, Inter)*

19. Explain the term 'Marginal Costing' and discuss its advantages. *(G.N.D.U., B.Com. 1997)*

20. Define Profit-Volume Ratio and explain its significance. In what ways can the Profit Volume Ratio be improved upon? *(G.N.D.U., B.Com.1997)*

EXERCISES

1. From the following information, find out Variable Cost:

Sales	Rs. 1,00,000
Fixed Cost	Rs. 30,000
Profit	Rs. 14,000

[**Ans.** Rs. 56,000]

2. S.V Ltd., gives you the following data

Sales	Rs. 3,00,000
Direct Materials	Rs. 90,000
Direct Wages	Rs. 75,000
Direct Expenses	Rs. 5,000

Profit @ 20% on Sales.

Calculate Fixed Cost. [**Ans.** Rs. 70,000]

3. From the following data, prepare a statement showing the Total Contribution and Profit:

	Product A	Product B
	Rs.	Rs.
Sales	3,00,000	2,00,000
Direct Materials	80,000	60,000
Direct Wages	60,000	40,000
Variable Expenses	20,000	10,000
Fixed Expenses (Total) Rs.	1,20,000	

[**Ans.** Contribution Rs. 2,30,000, Profit Rs. 1,10,000]

4. From the data given below, find out
   (*i*) Variable Cost (*ii*) Contribution (*iii*) Profit.

	Rs.
Sales	1,20,000
Direct Materials	45,000
Direct Wages	27,000
Factory Overhead	
Fixed	15,000
Variable	4,500
General Overhead	
Fixed	9,000
Variable	1,500

[**Ans.** (*i*) Rs. 78,000 (*ii*) Rs. 42,000 (*iii*) Rs. 18,000]

5. Calculate P/V Ratio from the following:

Sales	Rs. 1,00,000
Variable Cost	Rs. 70,000
Fixed Cost	Rs. 15,000

[**Ans.** 30%]

6. Calculate Break - even Point (in units)

Sales 1,000 units	@ Rs. 100 per unit
Variable Cost	Rs. 60,000
Fixed Cost	Rs. 28,000

[**Ans.** 700 units]

7. X Y Co. Ltd. supplies you the following information:

Sales	Rs. 2,00,000
Fixed Cost	Rs. 90,000
Variable Cost	Rs. 1,25,000

Ascertain how much the value of sales must be increased for the company to break-even.

[**Ans.** Rs. 40,000]

8. From the following particulars calculate the Break-even Point:

Sales	Rs. 1,30,000
Units Sold	10,000
Fixed Cost	Rs. 40,000
Variable Costs	
Materials	Rs. 30,000
Labour	Rs. 30,000
Overhead	Rs. 20,000

[**Ans.** 8,000 units Rs. 1,04,000]

9. (*a*) You are given the following data

Selling Price per unit	Rs. 300
Variable Cost per unit	Rs. 200
Fixed Costs	Rs. 50,000

Calculate P/V Ratio and B.E.P.

[**Ans.** P/V Ratio $33\frac{1}{3}\%$ B.E.P. 500 units]

(*b*) Find out Sales and Variable Cost from the following:

Fixed Cost	= Rs. 4,000
Profit	= Rs. 1,000
Break-even Point	= Rs. 20,000

(*G.N.D.U., B.Com., 1997*)

[**Ans.** P/V Ratio = 20%; Sales = Rs. 25,000; Variable Cost = Rs. 20,000]

10. From the following information, calculate P/V Ratio, Break-even Point and Margin of Safety:

Fixed Costs	Rs. 1,80,000
Variable Cost per unit	Rs. 2
Selling Price per unit	Rs. 20
Present Output and Sales :	15,000 units

[**Ans.** P/V Ratio 90%, B.E.P. 10,000 units M.S. Rs. 1,00,000]

11. (*a*) From the following particulars, draw a Break-Even Chart and find out the B.E.P.

Variable Cost per unit	Rs. 30
Fixed Expenses	Rs. 1,00,000
Selling Price per unit	Rs. 50

(*b*) What should be the selling price per unit if the break-even point is to be brought down to 4,000 units.

(*c*) If the present volume of sales is Rs. 4,00,000, what is the margin of safety on the basis of the data given in (*a*) above.

[**Ans.** (*a*) 5,000 units or Rs. 2,50,000, (*b*) Rs. 55, (*c*) Rs. 1,50,000]

12. Prepare a statement showing Marginal Cost and Contribution from the following particulars:

	Per unit Rs.
Material	30
Labour	25
Chargeable Expenses	5
Variable Overhead	10
Fixed Overhead (Total)	Rs. 15,000
Selling Price (Rs. 100 per unit)	Rs. 1,00,000

[**Ans.** Marginal Cost Rs. 70, Contribution Rs. 30 per unit]

13. Calculate (*i*) Contribution and (*ii*) P/V Ratio from the following figures:

	Rs.
Materials	40,000
Wages	24,000
Overhead:	
Variable (@ Rs. 2.50 per unit)	10,000
Fixed	6,000
Selling Price	1,00,000

[**Ans.** Contribution Rs. 26,000; P/V Ratio 26%]

14. A company budgets for a production of 1,50,000 units, the variable cost per unit is Rs. 14 and fixed cost is Rs. 2 per unit. The company fixes its selling price to fetch a profit of 15% on cost.

(*i*) What is the break-even point?

(*ii*) What is the profit-volume ratio?

(*iii*) If it reduces its selling price by 5%, how does the revised selling price affect the break-even point and the profit-volume ratio?

(*G.N.D.U., B.Com., 1995*)

[**Ans.** (*i*) B.E.P. 68,182 units, (*ii*) P/V Ratio 23.91%, (*iii*) B.E.P. 86,207 units P/V Ratio 19.91%]

15. From the following particulars find out the selling price per unit if the Break-even Point is to be brought down to 9,000 units:

Variable cost per unit	Rs. 75
Fixed cost	Rs. 2,70,000
Selling price per unit	Rs. 100

[**Ans.** Selling Price Rs. 105]

16. From the following information, calculate the Break-even Point and turnover required to earn a profit of Rs. 30,000:

Fixed Overhead	Rs. 21,000
Variable Costs	Rs. 2 per unit
Selling price	Rs. 5 per unit

If the company is earning a profit of Rs. 30,000, express the margin of safety available to it.

[**Ans.** B.E.P. 7,000 units, Required Sales Rs. 85,000, M.S. Rs. 50,000]

17. A company had incurred fixed expenses of Rs. 4,50,000, with sales of Rs. 15,00,000 and earned a profit of Rs. 3,00,000 during the first half year. In the second half, it suffered a loss of Rs. 1,50,000.

Calculate:

(*i*) The profit-volume ratio, break-even point and margin of safety for the first half-year.

(*ii*) Expected sales volume for the second half-year assuming that selling price and fixed expenses remained unchanged during the second half year.

(*iii*) The break-even point and margin of safety for the whole year.

(C.A.Inter 1996)

[**Ans.** (*i*) 50% Rs. 9,00,000 Rs. 6,00,000 (*ii*) Rs. 6,00,000 (*iii*) Rs. 18,00,000 Rs. 3,00,000]

18. From the following find out:

(*a*) Break-even Point (*b*) P/V Ratio (*c*) Profit for the sales of Rs. 3,00,000 (*d*) Margin of safety from the sales of Rs. 3,00,000 (*e*) Required sales to earn a profit of Rs. 70,000 (*f*) Additional sales required to cover an increase of Rs. 3,000 p.a. in sales manager's salary:

	Rs.
Sales	2,00,000
Less Variable costs and over heads	1,50,000
Gross profit	50,000
Fixed overhead	15,000
Net Profit	35,000

(H.P., B.Com, 1994, 1995)

[**Ans.** (*a*) Rs. 60,000, (*b*) 25%, (*c*) Rs. 60,000, (*d*) Rs. 2,40,000, (*e*) Rs. 3,40,000, (*f*) Rs. 2,12,000]

19. You are given the following information

	Rs.
Fixed Cost	4,000
Break-even Sales	20,000
Profit	1,000
Selling Price per unit	20

Calculate: (*a*) Sales and variable cost,

(*b*) New Break-even point, if selling price is reduced by 10%.

(G.N.D.U., B.Com. April 1998)

[**Ans.** (*a*) Rs. 25,000 and Rs. 20,000; Variable Cost per unit = Rs. 16 (*b*) 2,000 units]

20. An analysis of costs of Sullival Mfg. Co., led to the following information:

	Variable Cost (% of sales)	Fixed costs (Rs.)
Direct Materials	32.8	–
Direct Labour	28.4	–
Factory Overhead	12.6	1,89,900
Distribution Overhead	4.1	58,400
General and Administrative Expenses	1.1	66,700

Budgeted sales for the next year are Rs. 18,50,000.

You are required to determine:

(*i*) the profit at the budgeted sales volume.

(*ii*) the break-even sales volume.

(*iii*) the profit, if actual sales

(*a*) drop by 10% (*b*) increase by 5% from budgeted sales.

[**Ans.** (*i*) Rs. 73,500 (*ii*) Rs. 15,00,000 (*iii*) Rs. 34,650 Rs. 92,925]

21. The total cost and profits during two periods were as follows

	Period I Rs.	Period II Rs.
Total Cost	4,50,000	6,50,000
Profits	50,000	1,10,000

Calculate (*a*) P/V Ratio (*b*) Break-even sales (*c*) Sales required to earn a profit of Rs. 1,25,000 (*d*) Profit earned when sales are Rs. 3,50,000.

(*H.P., B.Com., 1994 Sept.*)

[**Ans.** (*a*) $\frac{3}{13}$, (*b*) Rs. 2,83,335, (*c*) Rs. 8,25,002, (*d*) Rs. 15,384]

22. ABC Ltd., places before you the follwing trading results:

Year	Sales Rs.	Profit Rs.
2001	42,88,000	3,20,000
2002	47,98,000	4,22,000

Find out:

(*a*) P/V Ratio (*b*) Fixed Costs and Break Even Point (*c*) Amount of Profit when sales are Rs 70,00,000 (*d*) Sales when desired profit is Rs. 6,00,000 (*e*) Margin of Safety at a profit of Rs. 4,74,750. (*H.P.U., B.Com, 1993*)

[**Ans.** (*a*) 20% (*b*) Rs. 5,73,600 Rs. 26,88,000 (*c*) Rs. 8,62,400 (*d*) Rs. 56,88,000 (*e*) Rs. 23,73,750.]

23. The following information relates to a furniture maker:

(*a*) Number of sofa sets made 26

(*b*) Price per sofa set Rs. 1,250

(*c*) Prime cost per sofa set Rs. 675

(*d*) Variable overhead: one-third of Prime cost

(*e*) Fixed Overhead Rs. 35,000

Find out

(*i*) What should be the level of output in the next year to attain B.E.P.?

(*ii*) What should be quoted as the price per sofa set for this year so that profit per set is 20 % of variable cost? (H.P., *B.Com., 1995 Sept.*)

[**Ans.** (*i*) 100 sofa sets, (*ii*) Rs. 2,426.15]

24. S.V. Ltd., a multi-product company furnishes you the following data relating to the year 2007-08:

	First Half of the Year	Second Half of the Year
	Rs.	Rs.
Sales	45,000	50,000
Total cost	40,000	43,000

Assuming that there is no change in prices and variable costs and that the fixed expenses are incurred equally in the two half year periods, calculate for the year 2007-08 (*i*) The Profit/Volume Ratio (*ii*) Fixed Expenses (*iii*) Break-even sales (iv) Percentage of Margin of Safety.

[**Ans.** (*i*) 40% (*ii*) Rs. 26,000 (*iii*) Rs. 65,000 (*iv*) 31.58%]

25. The Reliable Company furnishes you the following information:

	Sales	Profit/Loss
	Rs.	Rs.
Period I	2,00,000	(–) 20,000 (Loss)
Period II	4,00,000	80,000

You are required to compute:

(*i*) P/V Ratio (*ii*) Fixed cost (*iii*) Break-even sales volume (*iv*) Profit or loss at a sales volume of Rs. 3,00,000 (*v*) the amount of sales required to earn a profit of Rs. 1,50,000.

[**Ans.** (*i*) P/V Ratio 50% (*ii*) Rs. 1,20,000 (*iii*) Rs. 2,40,000 (*iv*) Rs. 30,000 (*v*) Rs. 5,40,000]

26. The following information relates to a factory for different capacity levels of production:

	Capacity Levels of Production		
	60%	70%	80%
Production in units	6,000	7,000	8,000
	Rs.	Rs.	Rs.
Raw Materials	2,40,000	2,80,000	3,20,000
Direct Wages	1,80,000	2,10,000	2,40,000
Production Overhead	1,26,000	1,32,000	1,38,000
Total Cost	5,46,000	6,22,000	6,98,000
Profit	54,000	78,000	1,02,000
Sales	6,00,000	7,00,000	8,00,000

Calculation Break-even Sales Volume. (*G.N.D.U., B.Com., 1977*)

[**Ans.** P/V Ratio 24% B.E.P. Rs. 3,75,000]

27 Two businesses AB Ltd., and C.D. Ltd., sell the same type of product in the same type of market. Their budgeted Profit and Loss Accounts for the year ending 31st March, are as follows

		AB Ltd.		C.D. Ltd.
		Rs.		Rs.
Sales		1,50,000		1,50,000
Less: Variable Costs	1,20,000		1,00,000	
Fixed Costs	15,000	1,35,000	35,000	1,35,000
		15,000		15,000

You are required to: (*a*) Calculate Break-even point for each business, and (*b*) state which business is likely to earn greater profits in conditions of (*i*) heavy demand for the product; (*ii*) low demand for the product.

(*I.C.W.A. Inter*)

[**Ans.** (*a*) 20 % 33 1/3% (*b*) (*i*) C.D. Ltd., (*ii*) AB Ltd.)

28. The ratio of Variable Cost to Sales is 60%. Break-even point occurs at 80% of capacity sales. Calculate the capacity sales. Fixed costs are Rs. 2,00,000. Calculate profit at 90% and 100% of capacity sales.

(*M.D.U., B.Com., 1995*)

[**Ans.** Capacity sales Rs. 6,25,000; Profit at 90% Rs. 25,000; Profit at100% Rs.50,000)

29. The Profit/Volume ratio of a company is 50% and its margin of safety is 40%. You are required to work out the break-even point and the net profit if sales volume is Rs. 50 Lakhs.

(*B.Com. Delhi 1999*)

[**Ans.** B.E.P. Rs. 30 lakhs Profit Rs. 10 lakhs)

30. A Ltd. maintains a margin of safety of 37.5% with an overall contribution to sales ratio of 40%. Its fixed costs amount to Rs. 5 lakhs.

Calculate the following:

(*i*) Break-even sales;

(*ii*) Total sales;

(*iii*) Total variable costs;

(*iv*) Current profit;

(*v*) New "Margin of Safety" if the sales volume is increased by $7\frac{1}{2}\%$.

(*I.C.W.A. Inter. Dec. 1998*)

[**Ans.** (*i*), Rs. 12.50 lakhs (*ii*) Rs. 20 lakhs (*iii*) Rs. 12 lakhs (*iv*) Rs. 3 lakhs (*v*) Rs. 9 lakhs)

31. A single product company sells its product at Rs. 60 per unit. In 2006 company operated at margin of safety of 40%. The fixed costs amounted to Rs. 3,60,000 and the variable cost ratio to sales was 80%.

In 2007 it is estimated that the variable cost will go up by 10% and the fixed costs will increase by 5%. Find the selling price required to be fixed in 2007 to earn the same P/V ratio as in 2006.

Assuming the same selling price of Rs. 60 per unit in 2007 find the number of units required to be produced and sold to earn the same profit as in 2006.

(*C.A. Inter, May 1998*)

[**Ans.** 85,833 units]

32. A company earned a profit of Rs. 30,000 during the year 2005-06. If the marginal cost and selling price of a product are Rs. 8 and Rs. 10 per unit respectively, find out the amount of 'Margin of Safety'.

[**Ans.** Rs. 1,50,000]

33. Two firms A & Co. and B & Co. sell the same type of product in the same market. Their budgeted Profit & Loss Accounts for the year ending 31st March, 2008 are as follows:

	A & Co.		B & Co.	
	Rs.	Rs.	Rs.	Rs.
Sales		5,00,000		6,00,000
Variable costs	4,00,000		4,00,000	
Fixed Costs	30,000	4,30,000	70,000	4,70,000
Net Profit		70,000		1,30,000

Required:

1. Calculate at which sales volume both the firms will earn equal profit.
2. State which firm is likely to earn greater profit in condition of:
   (*i*) heavy demand for the product
   (*ii*) low demand for the product.

(*C.A. Inter, Nov. 1995*)

[**Ans.** (1) Rs. 3,00,000 (2) (*i*) B & Co. (*ii*) A & Co.]

34. The following costs and sales of a manufacturing company for the first half and second half of 2002-03 are given:

	First half	Second half
	Rs.	Rs.
Sales	24,00,000	30,00,000
Total Costs	21,80,000	26,00,000

You are asked to determine:

(*i*) Contribution/Sales Ratio of the firm.
(*ii*) Annual fixed costs.
(*ii*) Break-even point.
(*iv*) Margin of safety as percentage of sales.

(*I.C.W.A. Inter June, 1999*)

[**Ans.** (*i*) 30%, (*ii*) Rs. 10,00,000 (*iii*) Rs. 33,33,333 (*iv*) 38.27%]

35. (*a*) If margin of safety is Rs. 2,40,000 (40% of sales) P/V ratio is 30% of AB Ltd., calculate its (*i*) Break even sales, and (*ii*) Amount of profit on sales of Rs. 9,00,000.

(*b*) X Ltd. has earned a contribution of Rs. 2,00,000 and net profit of Rs. 1,50,000 on sales of Rs. 8,00,000. What is its margin of safety?

(*C.A. Inter, May 1997*)

[**Ans.** (*a*) (*i*) B.E.P. Rs. 3,60,000 (*ii*) Rs. 1,62,000 (*b*) Rs. 6,00,000]

36. Following figures relate to a company manufacturing varied range of products:

1st year	Sales Rs. 1,50,000	Profit Rs. 4,000
2 nd year	Sales Rs. 1,90,000	Profit Rs. 11,500

Calculate:

(*a*) P/V Ratio

(*b*) Profit on Sales of Rs. 1,20,000

(*c*) Sales required to earn a profit of Rs. 20,000.

(*d*) Margin of safety in 2nd year.

(*e*) Variable cost in 1st year. (*M.D.U., B.Com, 1994*)

[**Ans.** (*a*) 18.75%, (*b*) Loss Rs. 1,625, (*c*) Rs. 2,35,333.33, (*d*) Rs. 61,333.33, (*e*) Rs. 1,21,875]

37. Calculate the Break-even Point, P/V Ratio, Margin of safety and Profit on sale in the following case:

Fixed cost for the year Rs. 80,000

Variable Cost per unit for a single product made Rs. 4.

Estimated sales for the period are valued at Rs. 2,00,000. The number of units involved coincides with the expected volume of output. Each unit is sold at Rs. 20. Also calculate the profit when the sales are Rs. 3,00,000 and find out the sales to earn a profit of 10% on sales.

(*M.D.U., B.Com., 1993*)

[**Ans.** P/V Ratio 80%, B.E.P. 5,000 units; M.S. Rs. 1 ,00,000 Profit at a sale of Rs. 3,00,000 = Rs. 1,60,000; Sales to earn desired profit Rs. 1, 14,286]

38. The following information is obtained from Dixcy Co. Ltd.,

	Rs.
Sales	20,000
Variable costs	10,000
Fixed costs	6,000

(*a*) Find out the P/V Ratio, Break-even Point and Margin of Safety at this level.

(*b*) Calculate the effect of:

(*i*) 20% decrease in fixed costs;

(*ii*) 10% increase in fixed costs;

(*iii*) 10% decrease in variable costs;

(*iv*) 10% increase in selling price;

(*v*) 10% increase in selling price with an increase of fixed costs by Rs. 1,200;

(*vi*) 10% decrease in sales price;

(*vii*) 10% decrease in sales price accompanied by 10% decrease in variable costs.

[**Ans.**

		P/V Ratio	B.E.P.	Margin of Safety
(*a*)		50%	Rs. 12,000	Rs. 8,000
(*b*)	(*i*)	50%	Rs. 9,600	Rs. 10,400
	(*ii*)	50%	Rs. 13,200	Rs. 6,800
	(*iii*)	55%	Rs. 10,909	Rs. 9,091
	(*iv*)	54.55%	Rs. 11,000	Rs. 11,000
	(*v*)	54.55%	Rs. 13,200	Rs. 8,800
	(*vi*)	44.44%	Rs. 13,500	Rs. 4,500
	(*vii*)	50%	Rs. 12,000	Rs. 6,000]

39. Production costs of O.P. Ltd., are as follows:

	Level of Activity		
	60%	70%	80%
Output in units	1,200	1,400	1,600
	Rs.	Rs.	Rs.
Direct Material	24,000	28,000	32,000
Direct Labour	7,200	8,400	9,600
Factory Overhead	12,800	13,600	14,400
Total Cost	44,000	50,000	56,000
Sales	60,000	70,000	80,000

Calculate Break-even Sales Volume. [**Ans.** Rs. 20,000]

40. Prepare Income Statements under Absorption Costing and under Marginal Costing from the following information relating to the year 2002-2003.

Opening stock = 1,000 units valued at Rs. 70,000 including variable cost of Rs. 50 per unit.

Fixed cost = Rs. 1,20,000

Variable cost = Rs. 60 per unit

Production = 10,000 units

Sales = 7,000 units @ Rs. 100 per unit.

(*B.Com. Hons. Delhi 1998*)

[**Ans.** Profit: Absorption Costing Rs. 1,98,000;
Marginal Costing Rs. 1,70,000)

41. Your company has a production capacity of 2,00,000 units per year. Normal capacity utilisation is reckoned as 90%. Standard variable production costs are Rs. 11 per unit. The Fixed Costs are Rs. 3,60,000 per year. Variable Selling Costs are Rs. 3 per unit and fixed selling costs are Rs. 2,70,000 per year. The unit selling price is Rs. 20. In the year just ended on 31st March 2008, the production was 1,60,000 units and sales were 1,50,000 units. The closing inventory on 31.3.08 was 20,000 units. The actual variable production costs for the year were Rs. 35,000 higher than the standard.

(*i*) Calculate the profit for the year

(*a*) by the absorption costing method, and

(*b*) by the marginal costing method.

(*ii*) Explain the difference in the profits. (*C.A. Inter, Nov. 1983*)

[**Ans.** (*i*) (*a*) Rs. 2,64,375, (*b*) Rs. 2,39,118]

42. The particulars of two plants producing an identical product with the same selling price are as under:

	Plant A	Plant B
Capacity utilisation	70%	60%
	(Rs. Lacs)	(Rs. Lacs)
Sales	150	90
Variable costs	105	75
Fixed costs	30	20

It has been decided to merge Plant 'B' with Plant 'A'. The additional fixed expenses involved in the merger amount to Rs. 2 lacs.

Required:

(*i*) Find the break-even point of Plant 'A' and Plant 'B' before merger and the break-even point of the merged plant.

(*ii*) Find the capacity utilisation of the integrated plant required to earn a profit of Rs. 18 lacs. (*C.A. Inter, May 1993*)

[**Ans.** (*i*) A-Rs. 100 Lacs, B-Rs. 120 Lacs, and A & B Rs. 212.16 Lacs (*ii*) 78.40 %)

43. A, B and C are three similar plants under the same management who wants them to be merged for better operation. The details are as under:

Plant	A	B	C
Capacity Operated	100%	70%	50%
	Rs. (in Lakhs)	Rs. (in Lakhs)	Rs. (in Lakhs)
Turnover	300	280	150
Variable cost	200	210	75
Fixed Cost	70	50	62

Find out:

(*i*) the capacity of the merged plant for break-even.

(*ii*) the profit at 75% capacity of the merged plant.

(*iii*) the turnover from the merged plant to give a profit of Rs. 28 lakhs. (*C.A. Inter, May* 1986)

[**Ans.** (*i*) 52%, (*ii*) Rs. 80.5 lakhs and (*iii*) Rs. 600 lakhs.]

44. The following data relate to a manufacturing company:
Plant capacity : 4,00,000 units per annum
Present utilisation : 40%
Actuals for the year 2008 were:

Selling Price	Rs. 50 per unit
Materials Cost	Rs. 20 per unit
Variable Manufacturing Costs	Rs. 15 per unit
Fixed Costs	Rs. 27 Lakhs

In order to improve capacity utilisation the following proposals are considered:
Reduce Selling Price by 10%.
Spend additionally Rs. 3 lakhs on Sales Promotion.
How many units should be made and sold in order to earn a profit of Rs. 5 lakhs per year? [**Ans.** 3,50,000 units.]

45. A company budgets for a production of 1,50,000 units. The variable cost per unit is Rs. 14 and the fixed cost is Rs. 2 per unit. The company fixes its selling price to fetch a profit of 15% on cost.

(*a*) What is the break-even point?
(*b*) What is the profit-volume ratio?
(*c*) If it reduces its selling price by 5% how does the revised selling price affect the break-even point and the profit-volume ratio?
(*d*) If a profit increase of 10% is desired more than the budget, what should be the sale at the reduced prices?

(*H.P.U., B.Com. 1996; C.A. Inter, May 1984*)
[**Ans.** (*a*) 68, 182 units; (*b*) 23.91%;
(*c*) BEP -86,207 units and P/V Ratio 19.90% and (*d*) Rs. 34,96,000.]

46. The Laila Shoe Company sells five different styles of ladies chappals with identical purchase costs and selling price. The company is trying to find out the profitability of opening another store, which will have the following expenses and revenues:

	Per Pair Rs.
Selling Price	30.00
Variable Cost	19.50
Salesmen's Commission	1.50
Total Variable Cost	21.00

Annual fixed expenses are:

	Rs.
Rent	60,000
Salaries	2,00,000
Advertising	80,000
Other Fixed Expenses	20,000
	3,60,000

Required:

(*a*) Calculate the annual break-even point in units and in value. Also determine the profit or loss if 35,000 pairs of chappals are sold.

(*b*) The sales commissions are proposed to be discontinued, but instead a fixed amount of Rs. 90,000 is to be incurred in fixed salaries. A reduction in selling price of 5% is also proposed. What will be the break-even point in units?

(*c*) It is proposed to pay the store manager 50 paise per pair as further commission. The selling price is also proposed to be increased by 5%. What would be the break-even point in units?

(*d*) Refer to the original data. If the store manager were to be paid 30 paise commission on each pair of chappal sold in excess of the break even point, what would be the store's net profit if 50,000 pairs were sold?

Note: Consider each part of the question separately.

(*C.A. Inter, Nov. 1990*)

[**Ans.** (*a*) 40,000 pairs; (*b*) 50,000 pairs; (*c*) 36,000 pairs; (*d*) Profit Rs. 87,000]

47. Frazer Ltd., manufactures and sells a product, the selling price and raw material cost of which have remained unchanged during the past two years. The following are the relevant data:

Particulars	Year 1	Year 2
Quantity sold (Kgs.)	100	150
	Rs.	Rs.
Sales value	20,000	?
Raw Material	10,000	?
Direct Wages	3,000	?
Factory Overheads	5,000	5,700
Profit	2,000	2,550

During year 2, direct wage rates increased by 50% but there was a saving of Rs. 300 in fixed factory overheads. Required:

What quantity (in Kgs) the company should have produced and sold in year 2 in order to maintain the same amount of net profit per kg. as it earned during year 1?

(*C.A. Inter*) [**Ans.** 180 Kg.]

48. A Japanese soft drink company is planning to establish a subsidiary in India to produce mineral water.

Based on the estimated annual sales of 40,000 bottles of the mineral water, cost studies produced the following estimates for the Indian subsidiary:

	Total Annual Costs Rs.	Percent of Total Annual Cost which is variable
Material	2,10,000	100%
Labour	1,50,000	80%
Factory Overheads	92,000	60%
Administration Expenses	40,000	35%

The Indian production will be sold by manufacturer's representatives who will receive a commission of 8% of the sale price. No portion of the Japanese office expenses is to be allocated to the Indian subsidiary.

Required to:

(*i*) Compute the sale price per bottle to enable the management to realise an estimated 10% profit on sale proceeds in India.

(*ii*) Calculate the break-even point in Rupee sales as also in number of bottles for the Indian subsidiary on the assumption that the sale price is Rs. 14 per bottle.

(*C.A. Inter, May 1992*)

[**Ans.** (*i*) Rs. 15, (*ii*) Rs. 4,48,000]

49. Kalyan University conducts a special course on "Computer Applications" for a month during summer. For this purpose it invites applications from graduates. An entrance test is given to the candidates by whom application is made. The Entrance test consists of four objective type of Examinations and is spread over four days, one examination per day. Each candidate is charged a fee of Rs. 50 for taking up the entrance test. The following data was gathered for the past two years:

Kalyan University

Statement of Net Revenue from the Entrance Test for the course on "Computer Applications":

	2005 Rs.	2006 Rs.
Gross Revenue (Fees collected):	1,00,000	1,50,000
Cost:		
Valuation	40,000	60,000
Question Booklets	20,000	30,000
Hall Rent at Rs. 2,000 per day	8,000	8,000
Honorarium to Chief Administrator	6,000	6,000
Supervision Charges (one Supervisor for every 100 candidates at the rate of Rs. 50 per day)	4,000	6,000
General Administration Expenses.	6,000	6,000
Total Cost	84,000	1,16,000
Net Revenue	16,000	34,000

You are required to compute:

(*a*) The budgeted net revenue if 4,000 candidates take up the entrance test in 2007.

(*b*) The break-even number of candidates.

(*c*) The number of candidates to be enrolled if the net income desired is Rs. 20,000.

(*C.A. Inter, Nov. 1987*)

[**Ans.** (*a*) Rs. 52,000; (*b*) 1,112 candidates and (*c*) 2,223 Candidates]

50. Show the calculation of B.E.P. by means of P/V Graph from the following data:

Units produced and sold	20,000
Selling Price per unit	Rs. 25
Variable cost per unit	Rs. 15
Total Fixed Cost	Rs. 1,80,000

[**Ans.** B.E.P. 18,000 units]

51. The following figures relate to one year's working at 100% capacity level in a manufacturing business:

	Rs.
Fixed overhead	30,000
Variable overhead	50,000
Direct wages	40,000
Direct materials	1,00,000
Sales	2,50,000

Represent the above figures on a break-even chart and determine from the chart the Break-even Point. Verify your result by calculations.
(H.P., *B.Com 1986 Punjabi, B.Com. 1984 Delhi, B.Com. (Hons.) 1980*)

[**Ans.** B.E.P. Rs. 1,25, 000]

52. Draw a Break-even chart using the following information and show the B.E.P.:

Fixed Expenses (Total)	Rs. 40,000
Variable Cost per unit	Rs. 15
Selling Price per unit	Rs. 20

[**Ans.** B.E.P. 8,000 units]

53. XY Ltd. supplies you the following data:

	Rs.
Selling Price per unit	80
Variable Cost per unit	
Direct Material	25
Direct Wages	15
Variable Overhead	10
Total Fixed Cost	90,000

Draw a break-even chart and show the Break-even Point. What shall be the Break-even Point if the selling price is reduced to Rs. 70 per unit?

[**Ans.** B.E.P. 3,000 units. Revised B.E.P. 4,500 units.]

54. Following are the data taken from the records of a concern manufacturing a special part ZED.

Selling price per unit	Rs. 20
Direct material cost per unit	Rs. 5
Direct labour cost per unit	Rs. 3
Variable overhead cost per unit.	Rs. 2

Budgeted level of output and sales 80,000 units

Budgeted recovery rate of fixed overhead cost per unit Rs. 5

You are required to:

(*a*) Draw a break-even chart showing the break-even point.

(*b*) In the same chart show the impact on break-even point:

(1) If selling price per unit is increased by 30% and

(2) If selling price per unit is decreased by 10%.

Note: Assume a scale of 1" = 20,000 units for "X" axis and 1" = Rs. 4,00,000 for "Y" axis.

Working should form part of the answer.

(*C.A. Inter, May 1993*)

[**Ans.** (*a*) 40,000 units (*b*) (1) 25,000 units (2) 50,000 units.]

55. Two competing companies HERO Ltd. and ZERO Ltd. sell the same type of product in the same market. Their forecasted Profit and loss accounts for the year ending December, 2009 are as follows:

	HERO Ltd.		ZERO Ltd.	
	Rs.	Rs.	Rs.	Rs.
Sales		5,00,000		5,00,000
Less: Variable				
Cost of Sales	4,00,000		3,00,000	
Fixed Cost	50,000	4,50,000	1,50,000	4,50,000
Forcasted Net Profit before tax		50,000		50,000

You are required to state which company is likely to earn greater profits in conditions of:

(*a*) low demand, and

(*b*) high demand.

(*I.C.W.A. Inter, Dec. 1990*)

[**Ans.** (*a*) HERO Ltd. : (*b*) ZERO Ltd.].

22

Marginal Costing-II
(Variable Costing)

APPLICATION OF MARGINAL COSTING TECHNIQUES TO MANAGERIAL DECISION-MAKING

One of the basic functions of management is to make decisions. Decision-making process generally involves selecting a course of action from among various alternatives. Some of the important areas where marginal costing techniques are generally applied, can be given as follows:

1. Selection of a Profitable Sales mix or Profitable Product mix:

In case of a multi-product concern, there may arise a problem of the selection of the suitable or profitable sales mix *i.e.*, the determination of the ratio in which various products are produced and sold. For the purpose of determining the profitable sales mix, the amount of contribution available under each alternative of sales mix is to be considered and the sales mix giving maximum total contribution will be selected. But the various problems arising out of change in the sales mix e.g., limiting factors etc., must be properly considered.

Illustration 1

ABC Ltd., engaged in the manufacture of the two products 'A' and 'B' gives you the following information:

	Product A	**Product B**
	Rs.	**Rs.**
Selling Price per unit	60	100
Direct materials per unit	20	25
Direct wages per unit @ Re. 0.50 per hour	10	15
Variable overhead	100% of direct wages	
Fixed overhead	Rs. 10,000 per annum	
Maximum capacity	1,000 units	

Show the contribution of each of the products A and B and recommend which of the following sales mix should be adopted:

(*a*) 300 units of product A and 600 units of product B;
(*b*) 450 units of product A and 450 units of product B;
(*c*) 600 units of product A and 300 units of product B.

Solution

Statement of Marginal Cost

	Product A	Product B
	Rs.	Rs.
Direct Materials	20.00	25.00
Direct Wages	10.00	15.00
Variable Overhead		
(100% of direct wages)	10.00	15.00
Marginal Cost	40.00	55.00
Selling Price	60.00	100.00
Contribution per unit	20.00	45.00

Calculation of Total Contribution

Sales alternative (*a*): 300 units of 'A' and 600 units of 'B'

Contribution:		Rs.
Product A: 300 units × Rs. 20	=	6,000
Product B: 600 units × Rs. 45	=	27,000
Total Contribution		33,000
Less Fixed Overhead		10,000
Profit		23,000

Sales alternative (*b*): 450 units of 'A' and 450 units of 'B'

Contribution:		Rs.
Product A: 450 units × Rs. 20	=	9,000
Product B: 450 units × Rs. 45	=	20,250
Total Contribution		29,250
Less Fixed Overhead		10,000
Profit		19,250

Sales alternative (*c*): 600 units 'A' and 300 units of 'B'

Contribution:		Rs.
Product A: 600 units × Rs. 20	=	12,000
Product B: 300 units × Rs. 45	=	13,500
Total Contribution		25,500
Less Fixed Overhead		10,000
Profit		15,500

Hence sales mix under alternative (*a*) is more profitable as it gives maximum total contribution and profit.

Illustration 2

A farmer asks your recommendation for optimal mix of production for the coming year. The current data are given below:

Items produced

		A	B	C	D
Area Occupied (Acres)		25	20	30	25
Yield per acre (Tonnes)		10	8	9	12
Sale Price per Tonne	(Rs.)	1,000	1,250	1,500	1,350
Variable Cost per acre:					
Material	(Rs.)	700	600	950	900
Labour	(Rs.)	2,000	2,500	3,000	3,700
Variable Overhead	(Rs.)	2,000	2,000	2,000	2,000

	Rs.
Fixed Overhead:	
Cultivation and Growing	1,00,000
Harvesting and Transport	2,40,000
Land Revenue	90,000
Administration	1,10,000
	5,40,000

The land which is being used for producing items A and B can be used for either items but not for items C and D. The land which is being used for producing items C and D can be used for either items but not for items A and B.

In order to provide adequate market service, the farmer must produce each year atleast 40 tonnes each of A and B and 36 tonnes each of C and D. You are required to calculate the following:

(*a*) The profit for the current year; and

(*b*) The profit for the production mix which you would recommend.

(C.S. Inter, December 1996)

Solution

(*a*) Statement of Profitability for the current year

	Item A	Item B	Item C	Item D
Area Occupied (Acres)	25	20	30	25
Yield per Acre (Tonnes)	10	8	9	12
Total Yield (Tonnes)	250	160	270	300
	Rs.	Rs.	Rs.	Rs.
Total Sales Value	2,50,000	2,00,000	4,05,000	4,05,000
Variable Cost:				
Material	17,500	12,000	28,500	22,500
Labour	50,000	50,000	90,000	92,500
Variable Overhead	50,000	40,000	60,000	50,000
Total Variable Cost	1,17,500	1,02,000	1,78,500	1,65,000
Contribution (Sales-Variable Cost)	1,32,500	98,000	2,26,500	2,40,000

		Rs.
Contribution:	A	1,32,500
	B	98,000
	C	2,26,500
	D	2,40,000
Total Contribution		6,97,000
Less Total Fixed Cost		5,40,000
Profit for the current year		1,57,000

(b) Calculation of Contribution per Acre of Area Occupied:

	Item A	Item B	Item C	Item D
Total Contribution	Rs. 1,32,500	Rs. 98,000	Rs. 2,26,500	Rs. 2,40,000
Total Area Occupied (Acres)	25	20	30	25
Contribution per Acre =	Rs. 1,32,500 / 25	Rs. 98,000 / 20	Rs. 2,26,500 / 30	Rs. 2,40,000 / 25
	Rs. 5,300	Rs. 4,900	Rs. 7,550	Rs. 9,600

It is given that land which is being used for producing items A and B can be used for either items but not for items C and D. Similarly, the land which is being used for producing items C and D can be used for either items but not for items A and B. Out of items A and B, item A is more profitable but atleast 40 tonnes of item B (on 5 acres of land *i.e.*, 40 ÷ 8) are to produced to provide adequate market service. The remaining area of 40 acres (25 + 20 – 5 acres used for item B) is to be used for producing 400 tonnes of item A (*i.e.*, 40 acres × 10 tonnes).

Out of items C and D, item D is more profitable but atleast 36 tonnes of item C have to be produced to provide adequate market service on an area of 4 acres (36 tonnes ÷ 9 tonnes per acre). The remaining area of 51 acres (30 + 25 – 4 acres) can be used to produce 612 tonnes of item D.

Hence, the recommended production mix and profit for the coming year would be as follows:

Product	Output (Tonnes)	Area (Acres)	Contribution
			Rs.
(*i*) A	400	40	2,12,000 (40 × 5,300)
(*ii*) B	40	5	24,500 (5 × 4,900)
(*iii*) C	36	4	30,200 (4 × 7,550)
(*iv*) D	612	51	4,89,600 (51 × 9,600)
		Total Contribution	7,56,300
		Less Total Fixed Cost	5,40,000
		Profit	2,16,300

2. Problem of Limiting Factors:

Limiting factor (also known as 'key factor') is a factor which limits production and/or sales and thus prevents the manufacturing concern from earning unlimited profits. The limiting factors or key factors may be shortage of raw material, shortage of skilled labour and machine capacity, market for sales etc. In case of the existence of a key factor, a problem may arise as to which product should be pushed more in order to maximise profits. Selection of the profitable product shall be made on the basis of the contribution per unit of limiting factor. The profitability of a product with reference to limiting factor can be assessed as follows:

$$\text{Profitability} = \frac{\text{Contribution per unit}}{\text{Limiting Factor per unit}}$$

The higher the contribution per unit of limiting factor, the more profitable is the product and vice versa.

Illustration 3

In a factory producing two different kinds of articles, the limiting factor is the availability of labour. From the following information, show which product is more profitable:

	Product A Cost per unit Rs. P.	**Product B Cost per unit Rs. P.**
Materials	5.00	5.00
Labour:		
6 Hours @ Re. 0.50	3.00	
3 Hours @ Re. 0.50		1.50
Overheads:		
Fixed (50% of labour)	1.50	0.75
Variable	1.50	1.50
Total Cost	11.00	8.75
Selling Price	14.00	11.00
Profit	3.00	2.25
Total Production for the month (units)	500	600

Maximum capacity per month is 4,800 hours.

Give proof in support of your answer. (*G.N.D.U., B.Com.*)

Solution

Statement of Profitability

	Product A Rs. P.	**Product B Rs. P.**
Materials	5.00	5.00
Labour	3.00	1.50
Variable Overhead	1.50	1.50
Marginal Cost per unit	9.50	8.00
Selling Price per unit	14.00	11.00
Contribution per unit	4.50	3.00
No. of Labour Hours per unit (Limiting Factor)	6	3
Contribution per Labour Hour	$= \frac{\text{Rs. } 4.50}{6 \text{ Hrs.}}$ = Re. 0.75	$= \frac{\text{Rs. } 3.00}{3 \text{ Hrs.}}$ = Re. 1

Product B is more profitable as it gives higher contribution per labour hour (limiting factor).

Proof:

		Product A		Product B
Maximum capacity per month		4,800 Hrs.		4,800 Hrs.
Maximum capacity (in units)	=	$\frac{4{,}800 \text{ Hrs.}}{6 \text{ Hrs.}}$	=	$\frac{4{,}800 \text{ Hrs.}}{3 \text{ Hrs.}}$
$\left(\frac{\text{Total Hours}}{\text{Hours Per unit}}\right)$		= 800 units		= 1,600 units

Statement of Cost and Profit

	Rs.	Rs.
Materials	4,000	8,000
Labour (@ Re. 0.50 per labour hour for 4,800 hrs.)	2,400	2,400
Overhead:		
Fixed (50 % of labour)	1,200	1,200
Variable	1,200	2,400
Total cost	8,800	14,000
Profit	2,400	3,600
Sales	11,200	17,600

Illustration 4

The following particulars are extracted from the records of a company:

Per unit

	Product A	Product B
Selling Price per unit	Rs.100	Rs.120
Consumption of Materials	2 kgs.	3 kgs.
Material Cost	Rs. 10	Rs. 15
Direct Wages	Rs. 15	Rs. 10
Direct Expenses	Rs. 5	Rs. 6
Overhead Expenses:		
Fixed	Rs. 5	Rs. 10
Variable	Rs. 15	Rs. 20

Direct wages per hour is Rs. 5.

(*a*) Comment on the profitability of each product when raw material is in short supply.

(*b*) Assuming raw material as the key factor, availability of which is 10,000 kgs. and the maximum sales potential of each product being 3,500 units, find out the product-mix which will yield the maximum profit.

Solution

(a) Statement of Marginal Cost

	A	B	Product A Rs.	Product B Rs.
Selling Price per unit			100	120
Less Marginal Cost				
Direct Material	10	15		
Direct Wages	15	10		
Direct Expenses	5	6		
Variable Overhead	15	20	45	51
Contribution per unit			55	69

	Product A	Product B
Consumption of Raw Material per unit (Limiting Factor)	2 kgs.	3 kgs.

$$\text{Contribution per Kg. of Raw Material} = \frac{\text{Rs. } 55}{2 \text{ kgs.}} = \frac{\text{Rs. } 69}{3 \text{ kgs.}}$$

$$= \text{Rs. } 27.50 \qquad = \text{Rs. } 23.00$$

Product 'A' is more profitable as it gives higher rate of contribution per unit of limiting factor.

(*b*) For the purpose of determining the most profitable sales mix, the product preference shall be the same as in (*a*) above subject to the condition that maximum sales potential (or maximum demand) for each of the two products is 3,500 units. As such, 3,500 units of more profitable product will be produced first. The balance of raw materials then available will be utilitsed for the production of less profitable product.

Thus, the most profitable sales mix would be:

Product	Units	Raw Materials per unit (Kg.)	Total Raw Material Required (Kgs.)
A	3,500	2	7,000
B	1,000 (3,000 Kgs ÷ 3 Kgs)	3	3,000
	4,500		10,000

3. Make or Buy Decisions:

Sometimes a manufacturer has to decide as to whether a certain component or spare part should be manufactured in the factory (having unused installed capacity) or bought from the market. In taking such a 'make or buy' decision, the marginal cost of the component or spare part should be compared with the market price. If the marginal cost is lower than the market price, the component or spare part should be manufactured in the factory itself. However, the manufacturer must take into consideration any increase in fixed costs or any limiting factor which may arise if the production is undertaken in the factory. If the purchase price is lower than the marginal cost and provided regular supply and proper quality of the component are guaranteed by outside supplier, it should be purchased from outside supplier.

Illustration 5

A radio manufacturing company finds that while it costs Rs. 6.25 each to make a component X–2370, the same is available in the market at Rs. 5.75, with an assurance of continued supply. The break-down of cost is:

Direct materials	Rs. 2.75 each
Direct labour	Rs. 1.75 each
Other variables	Re. 0.50 each
Depreciation and other fixed cost	Rs. 1.25 each
Total	Rs. 6.25 each

(*a*) Should you make or buy?

(*b*) What would be your decision if the supplier offers the component at Rs. 4.85 each?

(*I.C.W.A., Inter*)

Solution

Calculation of Marginal Cost of Component X – 2370

	Per unit
	Rs. P.
Direct Material	2.75
Direct Labour	1.75
Other Variables	0.50
Marginal Cost	5.00

(*a*) Since the marginal cost per unit of Rs. 5 is lower than the market price of Rs. 5.75, it is recommended to manufacture the component in the factory.

(*b*) Since the purchase price of Rs. 4.85 is lower than the marginal cost, the component should be bought from outside supplier provided proper quality and regular supply are guaranteed.

4. Diversification of Production:

Sometimes a manufacturer may intend to add a new product to the existing product or products to utilise the idle capacity, to capture a new market or for some other purpose. In such a case, the manufacturer or management is interested in knowing the profitability of the new product before its production can be undertaken. It is advisable to undertake the production of the new product if it is capable of contributing something towards fixed costs and profit after meeting out its variable cost of sales. Fixed costs are not to be considered on the assumption that the new product can be manufactured by existing resources without incurring any additional fixed costs.

But if the introduction of a new product involves some specific or identifiable fixed costs (which arise due to the new product), these should be deducted from the contribution of the new product before making any decision.

Illustration 6

The following data are available in respect of product 'A' manufactured by SK Ltd.:

	Rs.
Sales	2,50,000
Direct materials	1,00,000
Direct wages	50,000
Variable overhead	25,000
Fixed overhead	50,000

The compnay now proposes to introduce a new product 'B' so that sales may be increased by Rs. 50,000. There will be no increase in fixed costs and the estimated variable costs of the product 'B' are:

	Rs.
Direct Materials	24,000
Direct Wages	11,000
Overhead	7,000

Advise whether product B will be profitable or not.

Solution

Calculation of Existing Profitablility

	(Product A) Rs.
Direct Materials	1,00,000
Direct Wages	50,000
Variable Overhead	25,000
Marginal Cost	1,75,000
Sales	2,50,000
Total Contribution	75,000
Less Fixed Costs	50,000
Profit	25,000

Statement of Marginal Cost under proposed position

	Product A Rs.	Product B Rs.	Total Rs.
Direct Materials	1,00,000	24,000	1,24,000
Direct Wages	50,000	11,000	61,000
Variable Overhead	25,000	7,000	32,000
Marginal Cost	1,75,000	42,000	2,17,000
Sales	2,50,000	50,000	3,00,000
Contribution	75,000	8,000	83,000
Less Fixed Overhead			50,000
Profit			33,000

Assuming that spare capacity cannot be used for any other purpose (except for producing product 'B'), it is advisable to undertake the production of product 'B' which shall give a contribution of Rs. 8,000 towards fixed costs and profit.

5. Fixation of Selling price

Marginal costing techniques assist the management in the fixation of the selling price of different products. Marginal cost of a product is the guiding factor in the fixation of selling price. Generally, the selling price of a product is fixed at a level which not only covers the marginal cost but also contributes something towards fixed costs. Hence, under normal circumstances for a long period, the fixation of selling price is done on the basis of the total cost of sales (*i.e.*, by adding some margin of profit to the total cost).

But in times of cut-throat competition, trade depression, in accepting additional orders for utilising unused capacity and in exploring foreign markets, the manufacturer may be ready to sell his products at a price below total cost but not at a price below marginal cost. For fixing the price at a level below total cost of sales, the manufacturer shall take into account the overall profitability or P/V Ratio of the business concern. Thus, the fixation of selling price becomes easy where marginal cost, overall P/V Ratio and the level of profits expected, are known. In case of exports to foreign markets, the effect of various direct and indirect benefits such as cash compensatory assistance, subsidies, import entitlements and other special favours or benefits from the Government should also be taken into account.

Further, pricing at or below marginal costs may be considered desirable for a shorter period under certain special circumstances given below:

(*i*) To introduce a new product in the market or to popularise it.
(*ii*) To drive out weaker competitors from the market.
(*iii*) To maintain production in order to avoid retrenchment of employees.
(*iv*) To keep the plant and machinery in gear.
(*v*) To avoid the loss of future markets.
(*vi*) To sell the goods of perishable nature.
(*vii*) To push up the sales of other conjoined profitable products.

Illustration 7

B Co. Ltd., has an overall P/V Ratio of 60%. If the variable cost of a product is Rs. 20, what will be its selling price?

Solution

Overall P/V Ratio of the company = 60%

$$\text{P/V Ratio} = \frac{\text{Contribution}}{\text{Sales}} = \frac{\text{Sales} - \text{Variable cost}}{\text{Sales}}$$

If selling price is assumed to be 100

Contribution = 60
Variable Cost = 100 – 60 = 40
Thus, when variable cost is 40, selling price = 100

When variable cost is 1 selling price will be $= \frac{100}{40}$

When variable cost is 20, selling price will be $= \frac{100}{40} \times 20 =$ Rs. 50.

Export Market vs. Home Market:

A firm engaged in supplying goods in the home market and having surplus production capacity, may think of utilising it to meet export orders at a price lower than that prevailing in the home market. Such a decision is made only when the local sale is earning a profit *i.e.,* when its fixed costs have already been recovered by the local sales. In such cases, if the export price is more than the marginal cost, it is advisable to enter the export market. Any reduction in the selling price in the local market to utilise the surplus capacity may adversely affect the normal local sales.

However dumping in the export market at a lower price even below marginal cost in order to capture future market, has no adverse effect on local sales.

Illustration 8

Indo-British Compnay has a capacity to produce 5,000 articles but actually produces only 2,000 articles for home market at the following costs:

	Rs.
Materials	40,000
Wages	36,000
Factory Overheads:	
Fixed	12,000
Variable	20,000
Administration overhead (Fixed)	18,000
Selling and Distribution overhead:	
Fixed	10,000
Variable	16,000
	1,52,000

The home market can consume only 2,000 articles at a selling price of Rs. 80 per article. An additional order for the supply of 3,000 articles is received from a foreign customer at Rs. 65 per article. Should this order be accepted or not?

(*M.Com., Calcutta Univ.*)

Solution

Calculation of Present Profitability

		Rs.
Sales (2,000 Articles @ Rs. 80 per article)		1,60,000
Less Marginal Cost:		
Materials	40,000	
Wages	36,000	
Variable Overheads:		
Factory	20,000	
Selling and Distribution	16,000	1,12,000
Contribution		48,000
Less Fixed overheads:		
Factory	12,000	
Office	18,000	
Selling & Distribution	10,000	40,000
Profit		8,000

Since there is a profit of Rs. 8,000 at the existing level of 2,000 articles sold in the home market, the fixed costs are fully recovered.

Calculation of contribution from additional order of 3,000 articles

	Per Article	3,000 Articles
	Rs.	Rs.
Material	20	60,000
Wages	18	54,000
Variable overhead:		
Factory	10	30,000
Selling and Distribution	8	24,000
Marginal Cost	56	1,68,000
Sales	65	1,95,000
Contribution	9	27,000

The acceptance of this additional order from a foreign customer will provide an additional contribution of Rs. 27,000 towards profits (since fixed costs are already covered). As such it is advisable to accept the order.

Illustration 9

A company manufactures annually 10,000 units of a product at a cost of Rs. 4 per unit and there is a home market for entire production @ Rs. 4.25 per unit in 2001. However, in 2002 there is a fall in the demand in the home market, which can now consume 10,000 units only @ Rs. 3.72 per unit. The analysis of the cost per 10,000 units is:

	Rs.
Materials	15,000
Wages	11,000
Fixed overheads	8,000
Variable overheads	6,000

Foreign market can consume 20,000 units if offered @ Rs. 3.55 per unit. It is given that for additional 10,000 units of the product (over initial 10,000 units) the fixed overheads will increase by 10%.

Is it worthwhile to capture the foreign market?

(G.N.D.U., B.Com. 2003), (G.N.D.U., B.Com. Prof. 2008)

Solution

Statement of profitability

	Year 2001	Year 2002		
	Home Market	Home Market	Foreign Market	Total
No. of units sold	10,000	10,000	20,000	30,000
	Rs.	Rs.	Rs.	Rs.
Sales	42,500	37,200	71,000	1,08,200
Marginal Costs:				
Materials	15,000	15,000	30,000	45,000
Wages	11,000	11,000	22,000	33,000
Variable overheads	6,000	6,000	12,000	18,000
	32,000	32,000	64,000	96,000
Contribution (Sales-Marginal Cost)	10,500	5,200	7,000	12,200
Less Fixed Cost	8,000	8,000	1,600	9,600
Profit/loss	2,500	(–)2,800	5,400	2,600

The company should enter the foreign market to sell additional 20,000 units @ Rs. 3.55 per unit, since it will lead to an increase of Rs. 100 in the amount of present profit.

Illustration 10

A firm having a capacity of 15,000 units per annum produces 10,000 units which are consumed in the home market at Rs. 25 per unit. The cost per unit is as under:

	Rs. P.
Materials	8.00
Labour	6.00
Fixed Factory Expenses	2.00
Variable Factory Expenses	1.50
Office Expenses	1.00
Fixed Selling Expenses	0.50
Variable Selling Expenses	1.00
Total	20.00

(*i*) A foreign customer is interested in the product but he is willing is buy only 5,000 units and that too at a price of Rs. 18 per unit. Do you recommend the firm to accept the order?

(*ii*) What will be your advice if in the above case:

(*a*) the new customer is not foreign.

(*b*) the price offered is Rs. 15 per unit.

(*c*) The foreign customer is unwilling to buy less than 8,000 units, the price per unit being Rs.22.

Solution

(*i*) Calculation of Marginal Cost per unit

	Rs. P.
Materials	8.00
Labour	6.00
Variable Factory Expenses	1.50
Variable Sellling Expenses	1.00
Marginal Cost	16.50

Contribution per unit = Selling Price – Marginal Cost
= Rs. 25 – Rs. 16.50
= Rs. 8.50

		Rs.
Present Profitabilitiy:		
Total Contribution (10,000 Units × Rs. 8.50)		85,000
Less Fixed Expenses		
Factory	20,000	
Office	10,000	
Selling	5,000	35,000
Total Profit		50,000

As such total fixed costs are already covered.

	Rs.
Price per unit offered by foreign customer for 5,000 units	18.00
Marginal cost	16.50
Contribution	1.50

Acceptance of the order from foreign customer will increase the total profit by Rs.7,500 (5,000 units × Rs. 1.50). As such it is recommended that the order should be accepted since the price offered is in excess of the marginal cost.

(*ii*) (*a*) If customer is not foreign and the price offered is Rs. 18, the offer should not be accepted (even though the price offered is in excess of the marginal cost). The local customer after purchasing the product at Rs. 18, may offer the same in the local market at a price below Rs. 25 which will adversely affect the local market of the firm.

(*b*) If the price offered is Rs. 15 per unit, the offer should be rejected since the price offered is less than the marginal cost.

(*c*) If the foreign customer is unwilling to buy less than 8,000 units (at Rs. 22), the selling price in the local market may be increased by such amount so as to bring down the local demand of the product to 7,000 units (to spare 8,000 units for foreign customer). Suppose, the selling price in local market is increased to Rs. 30 per unit, the position of profitability will be as follows:

	Rs.
Sales: 7,000 units @ Rs. 30 per unit (local market)	2,10,000
8,000 units @ Rs. 22 per unit (foreign market)	1,76,000
Total sales	3,86,000
Less Total Variable cost (15,000 units × Rs. 16.50)	2,47,500
Contribution	1,38,500
Less Fixed cost	35,000
Profit	1,03,500

6. Alternative Methods of Manufacture:

Sometimes a manufacturer is faced with the problem of the application of alternative methods of manufacture *i.e.*, whether machine work or hand work, employment of hand-driven machine or power-driven machine or employment of one machine or another machine etc. For the purpose of selecting the method of production to be adopted, a comparison of the amount of contribution available under different methods of manufacture shall be made. The alternative providing the maximum contribution per unit shall be considered to be more profitable. However, the limiting factor, if any, involved in the method of production, must be given proper consideration.

Illustration 11

Product 'X' can be manufactured either by Machine No. 1 or by Machine No. 2. Machine No. 1 can produce 10 units of 'X' per hour and Machine No. 2, 20 units per hour. Total machine hours available are 3,000 hours per annum. Taking into account the following comparative costs and selling price, determine the profitable method of manufacture:

	Per unit of Product 'X'	
	Machine No. 1	**Machine No. 2**
	Rs.	**Rs.**
Direct materials	30	30
Direct wages	15	18
Overhead:		
Variable	18	21
Fixed	5	5
Total Cost	68	74
Selling Price	90	90

Solution

Statement of Profitability

			Machine No. 1	Machine No. 2
Total Machine Hours Available			3,000 per annum	3,000 per annum
Output per hour			10 units	20 units
Total Output per annum			30,000 units (3,000 × 10)	60,000 units (3,000 × 20)
			Rs.	Rs.
Selling Price per unit			90	90
Less Marginal Cost per unit				
	No. 1	No. 2		
Direct Materials	30	30		
Direct Wages	15	18		
Variable Overhead	18	21	63	69
Contribution per unit			27	21
Hourly Contribution			= Rs. 27 × 10 units	= Rs. 21 × 20 units
			= Rs. 270	= Rs. 420
Total Annual Contribution			= 3,000 hours × Rs. 270	= 3,000 hours × Rs. 420
			= Rs. 8,10,000	= Rs. 12,60,000

Production by Machine No. 2 shall be more profitable as it gives higher rate of contribution per hour.

7. Operate or Shut down Decision:

In case of a multi-product concern, it may be found that the production of some of its products is being carried on at a loss. Under such a position, the production of non-profitable products shall have to be discontinued. But if the choice is out of two or more products, the decision shall be taken with reference to the amount of contribution or P/V Ratio of these products. Production of the product giving the least amount of contribution or least P/V Ratio should be discontinued on the assumption that production capacity thus freed can be used to produce other profitable products.

Illustration 12

The following information is supplied to you about products:

	Per unit		
	A	B	C
	Rs. P.	Rs. P.	Rs. P.
Materials	10.00	11.00	13.00
Wages	5.00	6.00	8.00
Expenses			
Fixed	3.00	3.60	4.80
Variable	2.00	2.50	3.00
Total Cost	20.00	23.10	28.80
Profit	2.00	1.90	1.20
Selling Price	22.00	25.00	30.00

(*i*) The firm wishes to give up one of the products. Which product should be given up, assuming that the plant and labour thus freed can be used to produce the other products?

(*ii*) Will it make any difference to you answer if you are told that the time required to produce the three products is 4 hours, 6 hours, and 8 hours respectively.

Solution

Statement of Profitability

	Product A	Product B	Product C
	Rs. P.	Rs. P.	Rs. P.
Materials	10.00	11.00	13.00
Wages	5.00	6.00	8.00
Variable Expenses	2.00	2.50	3.00
Variable cost per unit	17.00	19.50	24.00
Selling Price per unit	22.00	25.00	30.00
Contribution per unit	5.00	5.50	6.00
P/V Ratio $\left(\frac{\text{Contribution}}{\text{Sales}} \times 100\right)$	$= \frac{5}{22} \times 100$ = 22.7%	$= \frac{5.50}{25} \times 100$ = 22%	$= \frac{6}{30} \times 100$ = 20%

Since the selling prices of three products are not equal, the decision regarding giving up the production of one of the products is to be taken with reference to the P/V Ratio available. Since product C shows the least P/V Ratio, it is advisable to give up its production.

(*ii*) Since the time required to produce the products is given, it shall be treated as limiting factor and the decision is to be taken with reference to the amount of contribution per unit of limiting factor (*i.e.*, per hour).

	Product A	Product B	Product C
Contribution per unit	Rs. 5.00	Rs. 5.50	Rs. 6.00
Time required per unit	4 hrs.	6 hrs.	8 hrs.
Contribution per hour	$= \frac{\text{Rs. 5}}{\text{4 hrs.}}$	$= \frac{\text{Rs. 5.50}}{\text{6 hrs.}}$	$= \frac{\text{Rs. 6}}{\text{8 hrs.}}$
	= Rs. 1.25	= Re. 0.916	= Re. 0.75

Production of product 'C' should be discontinced as it gives least amount of contribution per hour.

8. Maintaining a Desired Level of Profit:

Sometimes the management may be interested in maintaining a desired level of profits under the conditions of a change in the sales price. The volume of sales required to earn a desired level of profits can be ascertained by applying marginal costing techniques. For ascertaining the sales required to earn a desired level of profits, the following formulae are applied:

(*i*) Number of Units to be sold to earn Desired Profits =

$$\frac{\text{Total Fixed Cost + Desired Profits}}{\text{Contribution per unit}}$$

(*ii*) Sales Value required to earn Desired Profits =

$$\frac{\text{Total Fixed Cost + Desired Profits}}{\text{P/V Ratio}}$$

Illustration 13

A company produces and markets industrial containers and packing cases. Due to competition, the company proposes to reduce the selling price. If the present level of profit is to be maintained, indicate the number of units to be sold if the proposed reduction in selling price is:

(*a*) 5%; (*b*) 10 %; and (*c*) 15%.

The following additional information is available:

	Rs.	Rs.
Present Sales Turnover (30,000 units)		3,00,000
Variable Cost (30,000 units)	1,80,000	
Fixed Cost	70,000	2,50,000
Net Profit		50,000

(*G.N.D.U., B.Com., C.A. Inter*)

Solution

Calculation of Contribution

	Present Conditions	Anticipated Conditions (Reduction in Selling Price)		
		5% Reduction	10% Reduction	15% Reduction
	Rs.	Rs.	Rs.	Rs.
Selling price per unit	10.00	9.50	9.00	8.50
Less Variable cost per unit $\left(\frac{\text{Rs. 1,80,000}}{\text{30,000 units}}\right)$	6.00	6.00	6.00	6.00
Contribution per unit	4.00	3.50	3.00	2.50

Number of units to be sold to earn desired profits =

$$\frac{\text{Total Fixed Cost + Desired Profits}}{\text{Contribution Per unit}}$$

(*i*) Under Present Conditions = $\frac{\text{Rs. 70,000 + Rs. 50,000}}{\text{Rs. 4}}$ = 30,000 units

(*ii*) At a Price Reduction of 5% = $\frac{\text{Rs. 70,000 + Rs. 50,000}}{\text{Rs. 3.50}}$ = 34,286 units (*iii*) At a Price Reduction of 10% = $\frac{\text{Rs. } 70{,}000 + \text{Rs. } 50{,}000}{\text{Rs. } 3}$ = 40,000 units

(*iv*) At a Price Reduction of 15% = $\frac{\text{Rs. } 70{,}000 + \text{Rs. } 50{,}000}{\text{Rs. } 2.50}$ = 48,000 units.

9. Alternative Courses of Action:

Sometimes the management has to select a course of action from amongst various alternative courses. Each course of action has its own merits and limitations. The course of action to be selected should ensure maximum profit to the business concern. The appraisal of the various courses of action available is possible through the analysis of contribution. The course of action ensuring highest contribution is generally adopted by the management.

Illustration 14

Quality Products Ltd., manufactures and markets a single product. The following data are available:

	Rs. per unit
Materials	16
Conversion costs (variable)	12
Dealer's Margin	4
Selling Price	40

Fixed cost: Rs. 5 lakhs
Present Sales: 90,000 units
Capacity utilisation: 60 percent.

There is acute competition. Extra efforts are necessary to sell. Suggestions have been made for increasing sales:

(*a*) By reducing the sales price by 5 per cent.
(*b*) By increasing dealer's margin by 25 per cent on the existing rate.

Which of these two suggestions you would recommend if the company desires to maintain the present profit. Give reasons.

(*Delhi University, B.Com. Hons. 1982, C.A. Final*)

Solution

Statement of Profitability (90,000 units)

	Per unit	Total
Marginal Cost:	**Rs.**	**Rs.**
Materials	16	14,40,000
Conversion Cost	12	10,80,000
Dealer's Margin	4	3,60,000
Total Marginal Cost	32	28,80,000
Sales	40	36,00,000
Contribution	8	7,20,000
Less Total Fixed Cost		5,00,000
Total Profit		2,20,000

Ascertainment of the effect of various suggestions:

Suggestion (*a*)

Revised Selling Price (Rs. 40 – 5% of Rs. 40) = Rs. 38

Dealer's Margin at existing rate of 10% on sales (since it is variable) = Rs. 3.80

Suggestion (*b*)

Selling Price (no change) = Rs. 40

Dealer's Margin (Existing rate Rs. 4 + 25 % of Rs. 4) = Rs. 5

Statement of Revised Profitability

	Suggestion (*a*)	Suggestion (*b*)
	Rs.	Rs.
Materials	16.00	16.00
Conversion Cost	12.00	12.00
Dealer's Margin	3.80	5.00
Variable Cost per unit	31.80	33.00
Selling Price per unit	38.00	40.00
Contribution per unit	6.20	7.00

Sales (in units) to maintain the existing profitability of Rs. 2,20,000:

$$\text{Required Sales (in units)} = \frac{\text{Total Fixed Cost + Desired Profit}}{\text{Contribution per unit}}$$

$$\text{As per suggestion } (a) = \frac{\text{Rs. } 5{,}00{,}000 + \text{Rs. } 2{,}20{,}000}{\text{Rs. } 6.20}$$

= 1,16,129 units

$$\text{As per suggestion } (b) = \frac{\text{Rs. } 5{,}00{,}000 + \text{Rs. } 2{,}20{,}000}{\text{Rs. } 7}$$

= 1,02, 857 units

The company should adopt suggestion (*b*) since it ensures the present profitability of Rs. 2,20,000 at a lower level of production activity of 1,02,857 units as compared to 1,16,129 units under suggestion (*a*). It is given that competition is acute.

10. Profit Planning:

Profit planning is one of the important functions of management. It relates to the attainment of maximum profit. Profit planning requires the management to have the proper knowledge of the inter-relationship of selling prices, sales volume, variable costs and fixed costs. Marginal costing helps the management in ascertaining the profit position at the various levels of operation through the technique of cost-volume-profit analysis. Thus, the management can plan its operations at the optimum level where profits are maximum.

Illustration 15

Ambitious Enterprises is currently working at 50% capacity and produces 10,000 units.

At 60% working, raw material cost increases by 2% and selling price falls by 2%. At 80% working, raw material cost increases by 5% and selling price falls by 5%.

At 50% capacity working, the product costs Rs. 180 per unit and is sold at Rs. 200 per unit.

The cost of Rs. 180 is made up as follows:

Material	Rs. 100
Wages	Rs. 30
Factory overheads	Rs. 30 (40% Fixed)
Administration overheads	Rs. 20 (50% Fixed)

Prepare a Marginal Cost Statement showing the estimated profit of the business when it is operated at 60 percent and 80 percent capacity.

(Delhi University, B. Com. (Hons.), 1979)

Solution

Statement of Marginal Cost

	50% Capacity 10,000 units	60% Capacity 12,000 units	80% Capacity 16,000 units
	Rs.	Rs.	Rs.
Materials	10,00,000	12,24,000	16,80,000
Wages	3,00,000	3,60,000	4,80,000
Variable Overheads			
Factory	1,80,000	2,16,000	2,88,000
Adminsitration	1,00,000	1,20,000	1,60,000
Total Marginal Cost	15,80,000	19,20,000	26,08,000
Sales	20,00,000	23,52,000	30,40,000
	(10,000 × Rs. 200)	(12,000 × Rs. 196)	(16,000 × Rs. 190)
Total Contribution	4,20,000	4,32,000	4,32,000
Less Fixed Cost	2,20,000	2,20,000	2,20,000
Profit	2,00,000	2,12,000	2,12,000

Calculation of Variable and Fixed Overheads at 50 percent capacity

	Factory Overhead	Administration Overhead
	Rs.	Rs.
Total Overhead (10,000 units)	3,00,000	2,00,000
Less Fixed Overhead	1,20,000	1,00,000
	(40%)	(50%)
Variable Overhead	1,80,000	1,00,000

Variable Overhead per unit $= \frac{\text{Rs. } 1,80,000}{10,000 \text{ units}} = \text{Rs. } 18$; $= \frac{\text{Rs. } 1,00,000}{10,000 \text{ units}} = \text{Rs. } 10$

11. Appraisal of Performance:

Cost accounting deals with costs and profits of each department, product, branch etc., of the business separately. Marginal costing being a technique of cost accounting, presents the comparative profitability of each part or segment of the business to the management in an analysed form. Thus, the management can know the efficiency or inefficiency of each segment of the business and can plan in such a way that the profits made by an efficient segment of the business are not eaten away by some inefficient segment.

Illustration 16

The management of a company considers that product Y, one of its three main lines, is not profitable as the other two with the result that no particular efforts are being made to push its sales. The selling prices and cost of the three products are:

Products	Selling Price	Direct Material	Direct Labour Deptt. A	Direct Labour Deptt. B	Direct Labour Deptt. C
	Rs.	Rs.	Rs.	Rs.	Rs.
X	68	10	8	2	2
Y	58	6	2	8	2
Z	64	8	2	2	8

Overhead rates for each department per rupee of Direct Labour are as follows:

	Deptt. A	Deptt. B	Deptt. C
	Rs.	Rs.	Rs.
Variable Overhead	1.20	0.40	1.00
Fixed Overhead	1.20	2.00	1.40
Total	2.40	2.40	2.40

What advice would you give the management about the profitability of product Y. Give reasons. *(I.C.W.A., Final)*

Solution

Calculation of overheads chargeable to the various products:

Variable Overhead:

	Product X	Product Y	Product Z
Deptt. A	8 × 1.20 = 9.60	2 × 1.20 = 2.40	2 × 1.20 = 2.40
Deptt. B	2 × 0.40 = 0.80	8 × 0.40 = 3.20	2 × 0.40 = 0.80
Deptt. C	2 × 1.00 = 2.00	2 × 1.00 = 2.00	8 × 1.00 = 8.00
Total	12.40	7.60	11.20

Fixed Overhead:

	Product X	Product Y	Product Z
Deptt. A	8 × 1.20 = 9.60	2 × 1.20 = 2.40	2 × 1.20 = 2.40
Deptt. B	2 × 2.00 = 4.00	8 × 2.00 = 16.00	2 × 2.00 = 4.00
Deptt. C	2 × 1.40 = 2.80	2 × 1.40 = 2.80	8 × 1.40 = 11.20
Total	16.40	21.20	17.60

Statement of Comparative Cost and Profit

	Product X	Product Y	Product Z
	Rs. P.	Rs. P.	Rs. P.
Direct Materials	10.00	6.00	8.00
Direct Wages	12.00	12.00	12.00
Variable Overhead	12.40	7.60	11.20
Marginal Cost per unit	34.40	25.60	31.20
Selling Price per unit	68.00	58.00	64.00
Contribution per unit	33.60	32.40	32.80
Fixed Overhead per unit	16.40	21.20	17.60
Profit	17.20	11.20	15.20
P/V Ratio = $\left(\frac{\text{Contribution}}{\text{Sales}} \times 100\right)$	$\frac{33.60}{68.00} \times 100$ = 49.41%	$\frac{32.40}{58} \times 100$ = 55.86%	$\frac{32.80}{64} \times 100$ = 51.25%

Although the profit per unit of product Y is lower, it has the highest P/V Ratio indicating highest profitability. As such the management should try to push up the sales of product Y.

TYPICAL PROBLEMS

Problem 1

An industrial concern which has no costing system appointed a Cost Accountant. After installing a system of collection of cost data, the Cost Accountant observed that out of the three products which are produced independent of each other, loss is being incurred in product B. He immediately decides to advise management to discontinue manufacture of this product supported by the following tabulation:

	Product A	Product B	Product C
	Rs.	Rs.	Rs.
Sales	1,00,000	65,000	4,90,000
Variable Manufacturing Cost	52,000	26,000	1,40,000
Fixed Manufacturing Overhead (apportioned)	6,500	19,000	1,05,000
Variable Selling and Distribution Cost	18,000	17,000	18,000
Fixed Selling and Distribution Cost	4,600	4,600	4,000
Total	81,100	66,600	2,67,000
Net Profit	18,900	–	2,23,000
Net Loss	–	1,600	–

Do you agree with the Cost Accountant's conclusion? Argue with your views on the basis of data.

(I.C.W.A., Inter)

Solution

Statement of Profitability

	Products		
	A	**B**	**C**
	Rs.	**Rs.**	**Rs.**
Sales	1,00,000	65,000	4,90,000
Variable Cost:			
Manufacturing Cost	52,000	26,000	1,40,000
Selling and Distribution Cost	18,000	17,000	18,000
Marginal Cost.	70,000	43,000	1,58,000
Contribution (Sales – Marginal Cost)	30,000	22,000	3,32,000
Fixed Costs:			
Manufacturing Cost	6,500	19,000	1,05,000
Selling and Distribution Cost	4,600	4,600	4,000
Total Fixed Cost	11,100	23,600	1,09,000
Profit/Loss (Contribution – Fixed cost)	18,900	(–) 1,600	2,23,000
(*i*) P/V Ratio	30%	34%	67.8%
(*ii*) Ratio of Fixed Cost to Variable Cost			
(*a*) Manufacturing Cost	12.5%	73.1%	75%
(*b*) Selling and Distribution	25.5%	27.1%	22%
(*iii*) Ratio of Selling and Distribution Cost to Sales	22.6%	33.2%	4.5%

Conclusion

(*i*) Product B appears unprofitable because of arbitrary apportionment of fixed overhead. It is burdened with 73.1% fixed manufacturing overhead of its variable cost which is six times that of product A.

(*ii*) Product B is no less profitable than product A as P/V Ratio of B is 34% which is more than that of A.

(*iii*) Although sales of B are much less than A and C, it is burdened with the same amount of selling and distribution costs.

(*iv*) By discontinuing product B, the contribution of Rs. 22,000 made by it will not be available, hence the fixed cots of Rs. 23,600 apportioned to it will be a loss as the surplus capacity cannot be utilised for the manufacture of other products.

Problem 2

Dimple Shoe Store currently stocks three lines of ladies shoes. Dimple is considering dropping one line of shoes and adding two more. From the data given, decide whether or not Dimple should make this change. Give reasons.

Fixed cost is Rs. 3,00,000

Shoes presently stocked

Type	Selling Price	Variable Cost per pair	Sales Value (per year)
	Rs.	Rs.	Rs.
Flat	100	60	3,00,000
Jaya	160	120	1,00,000
Nalini	200	120	6,00,000

Shoes Stocked if Proposal is Accepted

Type	Selling Price	Variable Cost per pair	Expected Sales (per year)
	Rs.	Rs.	Rs.
Flat	100	60	2,50,000
Nalini	200	120	6,00,000
Meena	160	80	1,00,000
Shammi	60	30	50,000

(*C.A., Final*)

Solution

Statement of Present Profitability

Type	Contribution per unit. (S – V)	P/V Ratio $\left(\frac{C}{S} \times 100\right)$	Total Contribution (Sales × P/V ratio)
	Rs.		Rs.
Flat	40	$\frac{40}{100} \times 100 = 40\%$	3,00,000 × 40% = 1,20,000
Jaya	40	$\frac{40}{160} \times 100 = 25\%$	1,00,000 × 25% = 25,000
Nalini	80	$\frac{80}{200} \times 100 = 40\%$	6,00,000 + 40% = 2,40,000
		Total Contribution	3,85,000
		Less : Fixed cost	3,00,000
		Profit	85,000

Statement of Profitability under Proposed Conditions

Type	Contribution per unit. (S – V)	P/V Ratio $\left(\frac{C}{S} \times 100\right)$	Total Contribution (Sales × P/V ratio)
	Rs.		Rs.
Flat	40	$\frac{40}{100} \times 100 = 40\%$	2,50,000 × 40% = 1,00,000
Nalini	80	$\frac{80}{200} \times 100 = 40\%$	6,00,000 × 40% = 2,40,000
Meena	80	$\frac{80}{160} \times 100 = 50\%$	1,00,000 × 50% = 50,000
Shammi	30	$\frac{30}{60} \times 100 = 50\%$	50,000 × 50% = 25,000
		Total Contribution	4,15,000
		Less : Fixed cost	3,00,000
		Profit	1,15,000

The proposal should be accepted as it increases the profitability by Rs. 30,000 (*i.e.*, Rs. 1,15,000 – 85,000). The improvement in profitability is due to the higher P/V Ratio of new types to be introduced as against lower P/V Ratio of type to be discarded.

Problem 3

'A' Limited manufactures three different products and the following information has been collected from the books of accounts:

	Products		
	S	**T**	**Y**
Sales mix	35%	35%	30%
Selling price (Rs.)	30	40	20
Variable cost (Rs.)	15	20	12
Total fixed costs:	Rs. 1,80,000		
Total sales:	Rs. 6,40,000		

The compnay has currently under discussion, a proposal to discontinue the manufacture of product Y and replace it with product M, when the following results are anticipated:

	Products		
	S	**T**	**M**
Sales mix	50%	25%	25%
Selling price (Rs.)	30	40	30
Variable cost (Rs.)	15	20	15
Total fixed costs:	Rs. 1,80,000		
Total sales:	Rs. 6,40,000		

Will you advise the compnay to change over to production of M? Give reasons for your answer. (*C.A. Final, May 1983*)

Solution

Analysis of the Existing Position

	Products		
	S	**T**	**Y**
Selling Price (Rs.)	30	40	20
Variable Cost (Rs.)	15	20	12
Contribution (Rs.)	15	20	8
P/V Ratio (*i.e.*, C/S)	15/30 or, 50%	20/40 or, 50%	8/20 or, 40%
Sales mix	35%	35%	30%
Contribution per rupee of Sales mix (P/V Ratio × Sales mix)	17.5%	17.5%	12%

Total Contribution per rupee of Sales mix

= 17.5% + 17.5% + 12% = 47%

Present Total Sales = Rs. 6,40,000

Total Contribution = S × P/V Ratio = Rs. 6,40,000 × 47%

= Rs. 3,00,800

Present profit (*i.e.*, C – F) = Rs. 3,00,800 – 1,80,000 = Rs. 1,20,800

$$\text{Present BEP Sales} = \frac{F}{P/V\ Ratio} = \frac{Rs.1,80,000}{47\%}$$

= Rs. 3,83,000

Analysis of Proposed Position

	Products		
	S	**T**	**M**
Selling Price (Rs.)	30	40	30
Variable Cost (Rs.)	15	20	15
Contribution (Rs.)	15	20	15
P/V ratio (*i.e.*, C/S)	15/30 or, 50%	20/40 or, 50%	15/30 or, 50%
Sales mix	50%	25%	25%
Contribution per rupee of Sales mix (P/V Ratio × Sales mix)	25%	12.5%	12.5%

Total Contribution per rupee of Sales mix

= 25% + 12.5% + 12.5% = 50%

Proposed Total Sales = Rs. 6,40,000

Total Contribution = S × P/V Ratio = Rs. 6,40,000 × 50%

= Rs. 3,20,000

Profit (*i.e.*, C – F) = Rs. 3,20,000 – 1,80,000

= Rs. 1,40,000

$$\text{B.E.P. Sales} = \frac{F}{P/V\,\text{Ratio}} = \frac{\text{Rs.}1,80,000}{50\%}$$

= Rs. 3,60,000

Advice:

The proposal to replace product Y with product M is acceptable due to the following factors:

(*i*) There is an increase in profit by Rs. 19,200, and

(*ii*) Break-even point shifts to a lower level, with the result that the company can start earning profit earlier and there arises a larger margin of safety.

Problem 4

Garden Products Limited manufactures the "Rainpour" garden spray. The accounts of the Company for the year 2009 are expected to reveal profit of Rs. 14,00,000 from the manufacture of "Rainpour"after charging fixed costs of Rs. 10,00,000. The "Rainpour" is sold for Rs. 50 per unit and has variable unit cost of Rs. 20.

Market sensitivity tests suggest the following responses to price changes.

Alternative	Selling price reduced by	Quantity sold increased by
A	5%	10%
B	7%	20%
C	10%	25%

Evaluate these alternatives and state which alternative, on profitability consideration, should be adopted for the forthcoming year, assuming cost structure unchanged from 2009.

(*C.S., May 1982*)

Solution

Statement of Evaluation of Alternative Price Changes

Alternative	% age Reduction in Selling Price	Decreace in Amount	Revised Contribution per unit*	% age Increase in Sales quantity	Increase in units Sold*	Revised Sales Quantity	Contribution from Revised Sales Quantity
		Rs.	Rs.				Rs.
A	5%	2.50	27.50	10%	8,000	88,000	24,20,000
B	7%	3.50	26.50	20%	16,000	96,000	25,44,000
C	10%	5.00	25.00	25%	20,000	1,00,000	25,00,000

(* See working notes)

Conclusion:

From profitability consideration only, alternative B is the best one, as it yields the largest amount of contribution. Fixed costs being Rs. 10,00,000, it yields a profit of Rs. 15,44,000 which is highest of all the alternatives.

Working Notes:

1. Existing contribution per unit = S – V = Rs. 50 – Rs. 20 = Rs. 30
2. *Ascertainment of Units sold*:

Existing contribution = Fixed cost + Profit
= Rs. 10,00,000 + 14,00,000
= Rs. 24,00,000

Units sold (at present) = Total Contribution ÷ Contribution per unit
= Rs. 24,00,000 ÷ 30 = 80,000 units.

Problem 5

A review, made by the top management of Sweat and Struggle Ltd., which makes only one product, of the result of the first quarter of the year revealed the following:

Sales	... (Units)	10,000
Loss	... Rs.	10,000
Fixed Cost (For the year Rs. 1,20,000)	... Rs.	30,000
Variable Cost per unit	... Rs.	8

The Finance Manager who feels perturbed suggests that the company should at least break-even in the second quarter with a drive for increased sales. Towards this, company should introduce a better packing which will increase the cost by Re. 0.50 per unit.

The Sales Manager has an alternate proposal. For the second quarter, additional sales promotion expenses can be increased to the extent of Rs. 5,000 and a profit of Rs. 5,000 can be aimed at the period with increased sales.

The Production Manager feels otherwise. To improve the demand, the selling price per unit has to be reduced by 3%. As a result, the sales volume can be increased to attain a profit level of Rs. 4,000 for the quarter.

The Managing Director asks you as a Cost Accountant to evaluate these proposals and calculate the additional sales volume that would be required in each case, in order to help him take a decision. (*C.A. Inter, 1985*)

Solution

Calculation of the existing Sales Price (*i.e.*, in first quarter)

Contribution = Fixed Cost – Loss
= Rs. 30,000 – 10,000 = Rs. 20,000

Contribution per unit = Rs. 20,000 ÷ 10,000 units.
= Rs. 2

Variable cost per unit = Rs. 8

So, Sales Price = Contribution + Variable Cost
= Rs. 2 + Rs. 8 = Rs. 10

Evaluation of Alternate Proposals (For Second Quarter)

A. Finance Manager's Proposal

Revised Variable Cost per unit = Existing Variable Cost + Packing Expenses
= Rs. 8 + Re. 0.50
= Rs. 8.50

Selling Price per unit (Unchanged) = Rs. 10

So, Contribution per unit = Rs. 10 – Rs. 8.50
= Rs. 1.50

$$\text{B.E.P. (Units)} = \frac{\text{Fixed Cost}}{\text{Contribution per unit}}$$

$$= \frac{\text{Rs. } 30{,}000}{1.50}$$

= 20,000 Units

Hence, additional 10,000 units have to be sold to break-even.

B. Sales Manager's Proposal

Revised Fixed Cost (Including Sales Promotion) = Rs. 30,000 + Rs. 5,000 = Rs. 35,000

Desired Profit = Rs. 5,000

Contribution per unit (Unchanged) = Rs. 2

$$\text{No. of units required to be sold to earn desired profits} = \frac{\text{Fixed Cost + Desired Profit}}{\text{Contribution per unit}}$$

$$= \frac{\text{Rs. } 35{,}000 + \text{Rs. } 5{,}000}{\text{Rs. } 2}$$

= 20,000 units.

Hence, additional 10,000 units have to be sold to earn a profit of Rs. 5,000.

C. Production Manager's proposal

Revised Sales Price per unit = Rs. 10 – 3% of Rs. 10
= Rs. 9.70

Variable Cost per unit (Unchanged) = Rs. 8

Contribution per unit = Rs. 9.70 – Rs. 8 = Rs. 1.70

Fixed Cost (Unchanged) = Rs. 30,000

Desired profit = Rs. 4,000

$$\text{Sales (in units)} = \frac{\text{Fixed Cost + Desired Profit}}{\text{Contribution per unit}}$$

$$= \frac{\text{Rs. } 30{,}000 + \text{Rs. } 4{,}000}{\text{Rs. } 1.70}$$

= 20,000 units

Hence, additional 10,000 units have to be sold to have a profit of Rs. 4,000.

Conclusions:

1. All the three proposals require additional sales of 10,000 units. So, evaluation requires some other basis.
2. Finance Manager's proposal does not yield any profit as compared to other proposals yielding profit. So, Finance Manager's proposal may be rejected.
3. Sales Manager's proposal yields a profit of Rs. 5,000, but it requires additional expense. Production Manager's proposal does not require any additional expense. It requires a decrease in sales price and yields a profit of Rs. 4,000
4. Though Production Manager's proposal yields less profit than Sales Manager's proposal, yet the former is more practical since it does not require any additional investment in promotion expenses. Sales Manager's proposal can also be accepted if he has solid ground to anticipate the increase in the sales figure.

LONG ANSWER TYPE QUESTIONS

1. What is Marginal costing? How does it help in managerial decision-making process?

2. Discuss the role of contribution in marginal costing and its relevance to decisions relating to fixation of selling prices. Enumerate the circumstances which might justify the fixation of selling prices equal to or below marginal cost. *(I.C.W.A. Inter)*

3. "The technique of marginal costing can be a valuable aid to management." Discuss. *(B.Com. Hons. Delhi)*

4. State the costing data required for:
   (*i*) determining the profitable sales mix
   (*ii*) determining the priority of various products, and
   (*iii*) make or buy decisions.

5. It has been said that "marginal costs are used primarily in guiding decisions yet to be made." Explain the above statement by choosing two examples with illustrative figures. (*C.A. Final*)

6. Mention five areas of business activity that frequently require managerial decision as to policy. How cost analysis is helpful in decision making in these areas?

7. Give applications of marginal costing in decision making.
(*G.N.D.U., B.Com., 2008*)

8. Write Notes on:
   (*i*) Profitable Sales Mix
   (*ii*) Limiting Factors
   (*iii*) Profitable Methods of Production
   (*iv*) Buy or Make Decision
   (*v*) Operate or shut-down decision.

EXERCISES

1. Given the following information, you are required to:
   (*a*) Calculate and present the marginal product cost and contribution per unit.
   (*b*) State which of the alternative sales mixes you would recommend to management and why:

Per unit		
Selling Price	X	Rs. 500
	Y	Rs. 400
Direct Materials	X	Rs. 160
	Y	Rs. 120
Direct Wages	X	24 hours at Rs. 5 per hour per unit
	Y	16 hours at Rs. 5 per hour per unit
Fixed Overhead		Rs. 15,000
Variable overhead		150% of direct wages

Alternative sales mix:
(*i*) 250 units of X and 250 units of Y. (*ii*) Nil units of X and 400 units of Y. (*iii*) 400 units of X and 100 units of Y.
(*G.N.D.U., B.Com. April 1984*)

[**Ans.** Marginal product cost per unit: X, Rs. 460; Y, Rs. 320 Contribution per unit: X, Rs. 40, Y Rs. 80. Net profit: Sales Mix (*i*) Rs. 15,000; Sales Mix (*ii*) Rs. 17,000; Sales Mix (*iii*) Rs. 9,000; Alternative sales mix (*ii*) is the best]

2. The Directors of Vibhu Ltd., are considering a suitable sales mix for the next period. There are the four alternatives available:

Mix 1	450 units of product P and 300 units of Q.
Mix 2	900 units of Product P only
Mix 3	600 units of Product Q only
Mix 4	600 units of Product P and 200 units of Q.

You are provided with the following information:

	Product P	**Product Q**
Direct Labour @ Rs. 5 per hour	2 hours	3 hours
Direct Material (Rs.)	20	25
Variable overheads (100% of direct labour)		
Selling price (Rs.)	60	100
Fixed expenses (total) (Rs.)	10,000	

[**Ans.** Mix 3 is recommended]

[**Hint:** Total Contribution: Mix, 1, Rs. 22,500; Mix 2, Rs. 18,000; Mix 3, Rs. 27,000; Mix 4, Rs. 21,000]

3. A manufacturer with an overall (inter-changeable among the products) capacity of one lakh machine hours, has been so far producing a standard mix of 15,000 units of product A and 10,000 units of products B and C each. The total expenditure exclusive of fixed charges is found to be Rs. 2.09 lakhs and the cost ratio among the products approximates 1 : 1.5 : 1.75 respectively per unit. When the unit selling prices are Rs. 6.25 for A, Rs. 7.50 for B and Rs. 10.50 for C, he incurs a loss. He desires to change the sales mix as under:

	Mix I	**Mix II**	**Mix III**
A	18,000	15,000	22,000
B	12,000	6,000	8,000
C	7,000	13,000	8,000

As a Cost Accountant which mix do you recommend? Assume that fixed cost is Rs. 2 per unit.

[**Ans.** Sales mix III is recommended as it shows a profit of Rs. 300. Sales mix I shows a loss of Rs. 6,300 and sales mix II shows a loss of Rs. 450]

4. A manufacturing compnay produces and sells three produces P, Q and R. It has an available machine hour capacity of one lakh hours, inter-changeable among the three products. Presently, the compnay produces and sells 20,000 units of P and 15,000 units each of Q and R. The unit selling prices of the three products are Rs. 25, Rs. 32 and Rs. 42 for P, Q and R respectively. With this price structure and the aforesaid sales-mix, the company is incurring loss. The total expenditure, exclusive of fixed charges (presently~Rs. 5 per unit), is Rs. 13.75 lakhs. The unit cost ratio amongst the products P, Q and R is 4:6:7. Since the company desires to improve its profitablility without changing its cost and price structures, it has been considering the following three mixes so as to be within its total available capacity:

Produts	Mix I (in units)	Mix II (in units)	Mix III (in units)
P	25,000	20,000	30,000
Q	15,000	12,000	5,000
R	10,000	18,000	15,000

You are required to compute the quantum of loss now incurred and advise the most profitable mix which could be considered by the company.

(I.C.W.A. Inter, Dec. 1995)

[Ans. Mix III]

5. Given the following information, you are required to:

(*a*) Calculate the marginal product cost and contribution per unit.

(*b*) State which of the alternative sales mixes you would recommend to management and why.

	Per unit X	Per unit Y
Selling price	Rs. 25	Rs. 20
Direct materials	8	6
Direct wages	24 hours at 25 paise per hour.	16 hours at 25 paise per hour.

Fixed overhead – Rs. 750

Variable overhead – 150% of direct wages.

Alternative sales mix:

(*i*) 250 units of X and 250 units of Y

(*ii*) Nil units of X and 400 units of Y

(*iii*) 400 units of X and 100 units of Y *(I.C.W.A., Inter Adapted)*

[Ans. Sales mix (*ii*) is the most profitable.]

6. Calculate the effect of change in the sales mix from the following data.

	A	B	C	D	Total
Sales (Rs.)	40,000	50,000	20,000	10,000	1,20,000
Variable cost (Rs.)	24,000	34,000	16,000	4,000	78,000
Fixed cost (Rs.)	–	–	–	–	29,400
Sales mix changed to	30,000	44,000	40,000	6,000	1,20,000

(Columns A–D under the heading **Products**.)

(I.C.W.A. Final)

[Ans. The new sales mix will reduce profit by Rs. 4,320]

7. A Company produces three products. The cost data are as under:

Products		A	B	C
Direct materials		Rs. 64	152	117
Direct labour:				
Dept.	**Rate per hour Rs.**	**Hrs.**	**Hrs.**	**Hrs.**
1	5	18	10	20
2	6	5	4	7
3	4	10	5	20
Variable overheads Rs.		16	9	21
Fixed overheads		Rs. 4,00,000 per annum		

The budget was prepared at a time when the market was sluggish. The budgeted quantities and selling prices are as under:

Product	Budgeted Qty.	Selling Price (Rs.)/Unit
A	9,750	270
B	7,800	280
C	7,800	400

Later the market improved and the sales quantities could be increased by 20% for product A and 25% each for products B and C. The sales manager confirmed that the increased quantities could be achieved at the prices originally budgeted. The production manager stated that the output cannot be increased beyond the budgeted level due to limitation of direct labour hours in Department 2.

Required:

(*i*) Present a statement of budgeted profitability.

(*ii*) Set optimal product mix and calculate the optimal profit.

(*C.A. Inter, May 1998*)

[**Ans.** (*i*) Budgeted Profit Rs. 3,99,500; (*ii*) 11,700 units of A, 9,750 units of B, 5,272 units of C; Optimal Profit Rs. 4,06,430]

8. XYZ Ltd. which produces three products furnishes you the following data for the year 2009:

	Products		
	A	**B**	**C**
Selling price per unit (Rs.)	100	75	50
Profit/Volume Ratio	10%	20%	40%
Maximum sales potential (units)	40,000	25,000	10,000
Raw material content as percentage of variable costs	50%	50%	50%

The fixed expenses are estimated at Rs. 6,80,000. The company uses a single raw material in all the three products. Raw material is in short supply and the company has a quota for the supply of raw materials of the value of Rs. 18,00,000 for the year 2009 for the manufacture of its products to meet its sales demand.
You are required to (*i*) set a product mix which will give the maximum overall profit keeping the short supply of raw material in view; (*ii*) compute the maximum profit.

(*B.Com. Hons Delhi*)

[**Ans.** (*i*) 10,000 units of C, 25,000 units of B and 20,000 units of A; (*ii*) Rs. 95,000]

9. From the following data, show which product you would recommend for manufacture in a factory, TIME being the Key factor.

	Per Unit of Product A	Per Unit of Product B
	Rs.	Rs.
Direct Material	24	14
Direct labour at Rs. 1 per hour	2	3
Variable Overhead at Rs. 2 per hour	4	6
Selling Price	100	110
Standard Time to produce	– 2 hours	– 3 hours

(*G.N.D.U., B.Com.*)

[**Ans.** Product A is more profitable]

[**Hint:** Contribution per hour: A, Rs. 35; B, Rs. 29]

10. A company manufactures and markets three products A, B and C. All the three products are made from the same set of machines. Production is limited by machine capacity. From data given below indicate priorities for products A, B and C with a view to maximise profits.

	Products A	B	C
	Rs.	Rs.	Rs.
Raw Material cost per unit	2.25	3.25	4.25
Direct labour cost per unit	0.50	0.50	0.50
Other variable cost per unit	0.30	0.45	0.71
Selling price per unit	5.00	6.00	7.00
Standard machine time required per unit	39 mts.	20 mts.	28 mts.

In the following year, the company faces extreme shortage of raw materials. It is noted that 3 kg. 4 kg. and 5 kg. of raw materials are required to produce one unit of A, B and C respectively. How would products' priorities change?

(*I.C.W.A., Inter 1977*)

[**Ans.** *Key factor*	*Priority for Products*
Machine Capacity	B, C and A
Materials Supply	A, B and C]

[**Hint:** Contribution per minute of machine A : Re. 0.05; B : Re. 0.09: C: Re. 0.055. Contribution per kg. of materials A: Re. 0.65; B: Re.0.45; C: Re. 0.31]

11. A company manufactures and markets three products X,Y and Z. All the three products are made from the same set of machines. Production is limited by machine capacity. From the data given below, indicate priorities for products X, Y and Z with a view to maximising profits:

	Products		
	X	**Y**	**Z**
Raw material cost per unit (Rs.)	11.25	16.25	21.25
Direct labour cost per unit (Rs.)	2.50	2.50	2.50
Other variable cost per unit (Rs.)	1.50	2.25	3.55
Selling price per unit (Rs.)	25.00	30.00	35.00
Standard machine time required per unit (in minutes)	39	20	28

(*C.A. Inter, May 1996*)

[**Ans.** Priority X – III, Y –II, Z – I]

12. (*a*) The following particulars are taken from the records of a company engaged in manufacturing two products, A and B, from a certain material:

	Product A (per unit) Rs.	**Product B (per unit) Rs.**
Sales	2,500	5,000
Material cost (Rs. 50 per kg.)	500	1,250
Direct labour (Rs. 30 per hour)	750	1,500
Variable overhead	250	500

Total Fixed overhead: Rs. 10,00,000

Comment on the profitability of each product when:

(*i*) Total sales in value is limited.

(*ii*) Raw material is in short supply.

(*iii*) Production capacity is the limiting factor.

(*iv*) Total availability of raw materials is 20,000 kg. and maximum sales potential of each product is 1,000 units, find the product mix to yield maximum profits.

(*b*) The Profit Volume Ratio of X Ltd. is 50% and the Margin of Safety is 40%. You are required to calculate the net profit if the sales volume is Rs 10,00,000.

(*C.A. Inter, Nov. 1998*)

[**Ans.** (*a*) Product A in all cases (*i*) (*ii*) (*iii*) and (*iv*); (*b*) Rs. 20,000]

13. You are given the following data:

Per Unit	**Product A** **Rs.**	**Product B** **Rs.**
Direct materials	40	35
Direct labour @ Rs. 5 per hour	20	25
Variable overheads @ 60% of direct labour	12	15
Selling price	180	200

Total Labour hours available are 40,000

Which product would you recommend to be manufactured in the factory (*i*) If time is the key factor, and (*ii*) if Sales is the key factor. Give reason in support of your answer.

[**Ans.** (*i*) Product A, on the basis of contribution per hour.
(*ii*) Product B, on the basis of P/V ratio.]

[**Hint**: (*a*) Contribution per labour hour: Product A, Rs. 27
Product B, Rs. 25
Labour hours per product : Product A, Rs. 20 ÷ 5 = 4 hrs.
Product B, Rs. 25 ÷ 5 = 5 hrs.
(*b*) Ratio of Contribution to Sales
(*i.e.*, P/V Ratio) Product A, 60
Product B, 62.5 %].

14. Auto Parts Ltd., has an annual production of 90,000 units for a motor component. The component's cost structure is as below:

	Rs.		
Material	270	per	unit
Labour (25% fixed)	180	per	unit
Expenses:			
Variable	90	per	unit
Fixed	135	per	unit
Total	675	per	unit

The purchase manager has an offer from a supplier who is willing to supply the component at Rs. 540. Should the component be purchased and production stopped? What will be your answer if the offer is made at Rs. 450 per unit?

[**Ans.** Marginal Cost Rs. 495 (*a*) The offer should be rejected (*b*) The offer should be accepted assuming that capacity spared can be diverted to some other profitable use.]

15. X Y Ltd., is manufacturing three household products A, B and C, and selling them in a competitive market. Details of current demand, selling price and cost structure are given below:

	A	**B**	**C**
Expected Demand (units)	10,000	12,000	20,000
Selling price per unit (Rs.)	20	16	10
Variable cost per unit (Rs.) –			
Direct material (Rs. 10/kg.)	6	4	2
Direct labour (Rs. 15/hr.)	3	3	1.50
Variable overheads	2	1	1
Fixed overhead per unit (Rs.)	5	4	2

The company is frequently affected by acute scarcity of raw material and high labour turnover. During the next period it is expected to have one of the following situations:

(*a*) Raw materials available will be only 12,100 kg.

(*b*) Direct labour hours available will be only 5,000 hrs.

(*c*) It may be possible to increase sales of any one product by 25% without any additional fixed costs but by spending Rs. 20,000 on advertisement. There will be no shortage of materials or labour.

Suggest the best production plan in each case and the resultant net profit that the compnay would earn according to your suggestion.

(*I.C.W.A., Inter, June 1998*)

[**Ans.** Profit: (*a*) Rs. 1, 17,500, (*b*) Rs. 1,02,000, (*c*) Rs. 1,65,000]

16. The Fast Bicycles Ltd., manufactures a number of cycle parts. The cost per unit of part No. 845 is as follows:

	Rs.
Materials	3.00
Labour (25% Fixed)	2.00
Expenses	
Variable	1.00
Fixed	1.50
Total	7.50

The company is informed by an outside firm that the part can be supplied by it @ Rs. 6 per unit, quality and regular supplies guaranteed. The present consumption and production is 50,000 units per annum.

Do you recommend that production be stopped and the part purchased ? Will your answer be different if the men and plant required for making part No. 845 can be used to turn out a defence item for which a price of Rs. 4.25 is offered, materials being supplied by the Government?

[**Ans.** (*a*) Production should not be stopped as the marginal cost is less than the purchase price.

(*b*) Production of part No. 845 should be stopped and Govt. offer accepted

Price offered	Rs. 4.25
Variable cost (Wages + Variable Exp.)	Rs. 2.50
Contribution	Rs. 1.75
Extra Price paid	0.50
Net Saving	1.25]

17. A car manufacturing company purchases a meter from the market. The normal intake is 1,00,000 meters per year. The price paid is Rs. 25 each. A proposal is being considered to make the meters internally. The cost department has provided the following data:

	Rs.
Material per meter	16.00
Labour per meter	5.00

The company recovers overheads at 60% of labour cost. Besides, machinery will be required costing Rs. 2,00,000, its life being 4,00,000 meters in terms of production units. Power will cost Re. 0.40 per meter. Should the proposal to manufacture the meters instead of buying them be accepted? Comment.

[**Ans.** The proposal be accepted].

[**Hint: 1.** Marginal cost of manufacture, Rs. 24.90 per meter including depreciation charge Re. 0.50.)

2. Depreciation is considered variable, as machinery is to be specially bought.]

18. S.K. Co. Ltd. has an overall P/V ratio of 60%. If the marginal cost of a certain product is assessed as Rs. 12, what will be the selling price?

[**Ans.** Rs. 30]

19. A company follows the flexible budgeting system and the position at 70% level of production is as follows:

Production - 40,000 units	Rs.
Direct wages	60,000
Direct materials	80,000
Overhead:	
Fixed	84,000
Variable	42,000
	2,66,000

The selling price per unit is Rs. 8.65.

In the present market conditions there is hardly any chance for selling more locally. A special export order for 8,000 units @ 6.50 per unit, is received. (*a*) Would it be prudent for the company to accept the order at this price? (*b*) What is the price beyond which it would be profitable to accept this order?

(*C.A. Final*)

[**Ans.** (*a*) The sale of additional 8,000 units will give an additional profit of Rs. 15,600. (*b*) Rs. 4.55 *i.e.*, the marginal cost.]

20. Sterling Industries Ltd., manufactures a product 'Z' by making and assembling three components A, B and C. The components are made in a machine shop using three identical machines each of which can make any of the three components. However the total capacity of the three machines is only 12,000 machine-hours per month and is just sufficient to meet the current demand. Labour for assembling is available according to requirements. Further details are given below:

Components	Machine-hours required per unit	Variable cost per unit	Market price at which the component can be purchased, if required
A	4	Rs. 48	Rs. 64
B	5	60	75
C	6	80	110
Assembling	–	30 (per unit Z)	–

Fixed cost per month amounts to Rs. 50,000. Product 'Z' is sold at Rs. 300 per unit. From next month onwards, the company expects the demand for 'Z' to rise by 25%. As the machine capacity is limited, the company wants to meet the increase in demand by buying such number of components A, B or C which is most profitable.

You are asked to find out the following:

(*a*) Current demand and profit made by the company.

(*b*) Which component and how many units of the same, should be bought from the market to meet the increase in demand?

(*c*) Profit, made by the company, if suggestion in (*b*) is accepted.

(*I.C.W.A. Inter, Dec. 1998*)

[**Ans.** (*a*) Rs. 15,000; (*b*) 600 units of B; (*c*) Rs. 23,000]

21. Welsch Industries Limited produces 10,000 units per annum, by employing 50% of the factory capacity. The selling price of the unit is Rs. 5, and the total costs were:

	Rs.
Material	10,000
Wages	20,000
Fixed overhead	10,000
Variable overhead	4,000
	44,000

Variable overhead maintains a constant ratio to the number of units produced. The company accepts an order for additional 10,000 units at a selling price of Rs. 3.875 each. The increased volume of purchases reduces the material prices by 2½%, wage rates remain constant, but due to employment of new workers there is a drop in labour efficiency of 5% on all production.

Prapare a statement showing the variation of net profits resulting from the acceptance of the order.

(I.C.W.A. Inter)

[**Ans.** Additional order gives Rs. 3,145 as additional profit and thus the offer should be accepted.]

22. Comment on the profitability of the following two products.

	Production cost per unit	
	Product A	**Product B**
	Rs.	**Rs.**
Materials	200	150
Wages	100	200
Fixed overhead	350	100
Variable overhead	150	200
Profit	200	350
Selling price	1,000	1,000
Output per week	200 units	100 units

(I.C.W.A., Final)

[**Ans.** Product A is more profitable as contribution and total profit of A are more than that of B.]

23. The management of a company desires to an export order for 1,000 units per month @ Rs. 7 per unit. Its position is as follows:

Production Capacity	4,000 units per month
Present Sales	3,000 units per month
Selling price	Rs. 10 per unit
Total Cost	Rs. 8 per unit
Fixed cost (total)	Rs. 6,000 per month
Additional shipping expenses	Rs. 400

Do you advise the proposal to be accepted?

(H.P.U., B.Com. 1993)

[**Ans.** Contribution on export order Re. 0.60. Should be accepted]

24. XYZ Co. manufactures lathes of Captain brand and sells them at Rs. 36,500 each made up as follows:

	Rs.
Direct materials	16,000
Direct labour	2,000
Factory variable overhead	5,000
Fixed overhead	3,000
Depreciation	2,000
Selling variable overheads	500
Royalty	1,000
Profit	2,000
Total	31,500
Central excise duty	2,000
Sales tax	3,000
Selling price	36,500

There is enough idle capacity.

(*a*) A firm in Africa has offered to buy 10 lathes at Rs. 28,500 each. Should the company be interested in the business?

(*b*) It has also decided to sell five such lathes to an engineering company under the same management at bare cost. What price should be charged?

(*I.C.W. A., Inter*)

[**Ans.** (*a*) Offer should be accepted presuming sales tax and excise duty are exempted. (*b*) Rs. 29,500 (*i.e.*, marginal cost + excise duty + sales tax)]

25. The operating statement of a company is as follows:

				Rs.
Sales (80,000 units @ Rs. 15 each)				12,00,000
Costs:				
		Rs.	Rs.	
Variable:	Materials	2,40,000		
	Labour	3,20,000		
	Overheads	1,60,000	7,20,000	
Fixed			3,20,000	10,40,000
Profit				1,60,000

The plant capacity is 1,00,000 units. A customer from the U.S.A. is desirous of buying 20,000 units at a net price of Rs. 10 per unit. Advise the producer whether or not the offer should be accepted. Will your advice be different if the customer is a local one?

(*M.Com., Calcutta*)

[**Ans.** Offer from a customer from U.S.A. should be accepted as it is above the marginal cost. However, offer from a local customer should be accepted only when price discrimination is possible.]

26. A toy manufacturing company presents the following information for the year 2009:

	Rs.
Material cost	1,20,000
Labour cost	2,40,000
Fixed overhead	1,20,000
Variable overhead	60,000
Units produced – 12,000	
Selling price per unit	50

The available capacity is a production of 20,000 units per year. The firm has an offer for the purchase of 5,000 additional units at a price of Rs. 40 per unit. It is expected that by accepting this offer there will be a saving of Re. 1 per unit in material cost on all units produced, the fixed overhead will increase by Rs. 35,000 and the overall efficiency will drop by 2% on all production. Draft a report to management giving your recommendations as to whether this offer should be accepted.

[**Ans.** The offer should be accepted.]

27. A company produces and sells 10,000 units of product 'T' per month at Rs. 20 each. Marginal cost per unit is Rs. 12 and fixed cost is Rs. 30,000 per month. It is proposed to reduce the selling price by 20%. Find out the additional sales required to earn the same amount of profit as before.

[**Ans.** 10,000 units]

28. The price structure of a cycle made by the Cycle Co. Ltd., is as follows:

	Per cycle Rs.
Materials	60
Labour	20
Variable overheads	20
	100
Fixed overheads	50
Profit	50
	200

This is based on the manufacture of one lakh cycles per annum.

The company expects that due to competition they will have to reduce selling price, but they want to keep the total profits intact. What level of production will have to be reached, i.e., how many cycles will have to be made to get the same amount of profits, if:

(*a*) the selling price is reduced by 10%

(*b*) the selling price is reduced by 20%? (*I.C.W.A., Inter*)

(**Ans.** (*a*) 1,25,000 cycles : (*b*) 1,66,667 cycles).

$$\left(\textbf{Hint:} \text{ Cycles to be sold} = \frac{\text{F + Desired P}}{\text{C per unit}}\right)$$

29. The Everest Snow Company manufactures and sells direct to consumers 10,000 jars of 'Everest Snow' per month at Rs. 1.25 per jar. The company's normal production capacity is 20,000 jars of snow per month. An analysis of cost for 10,000 jars shows:

	Rs.
Direct Material	1,000
Direct labour	2,475
Power	140
Miscellaneous supplies	430
Jars	600
Fixed expenses of manufacturing, selling and administration	7,955
Total	12,600

The company has received offer for the export under a different brand name of 1,20,000 jars of snow at 10,000 per month at 75 paise a jar. Write a report on the advisability or otherwise of accepting the offer.

(*I.C.W.A., Final*)

[**Ans.** The offer should be accepted. Additional contribution Rs. 2,855
Net Profit from 20,000 jars (including exports), Rs. 2,755]

(**Hint:** Loss on the existing 10,000 jars, Rs. 100)

30. M/s Arvind & Co. are producing and selling fancy footwears only in Indian market. The cost break-up is as follows:

	Per pair Rs.
Raw materials	30.00
Labour	15.00
Packing, labelling	3.00
Factory expenses	5.00
Administrative expenses	2.00
	55.00
Profit added	17.00
Sale price	72.00

A foreign stockist has offered to purchase footwear at a competitive price. The senior partner has suggested a price of either Rs. 55 or Rs. 65 per pair for foreign customer. A junior partner thinks to quote a lower price based on marginal costing analysis.

You are requested to determine the lowest price that can be quoted, stating the assumptions you have taken.

[**Ans.** Marginal cost: Rs. 50; Lowest Price to be quoted Rs. 50
plus any special costs on packing etc.]

(**Hint:** *Assumptions:* (*i*) Factory expenses are fixed to the extent of Rs. 3. (*ii*) Adm. expenses are all fixed. (*iii*) No rise in fixed cost.)

31. A well-managed company makes seven products in equal volume. The cost sheet of product No. 7 is as follows:

	Rs.
Direct material	57.00
Direct Labour	23.00
Direct Charges	9.00
Manager's Salary (1/7)	8.00
Sales Commission	5.00
Total Cost per unit	102.00

The selling price is Rs. 95 per unit. Would you advise the discontinuance of this line? Give the theoretical basis. (*C.A. Inter*)

[**Ans.** Discontinuance not advised]

[**Hint:** 1. Manager's salary is a fixed cost.
2. Total variable cost Rs. 94 and contribution Re. 1 per unit towards fixed costs]

32. A mechanical toy factory presents the following information for the year 2009:

	Rs.
Material cost	1,20,000
Labour cost	2,40,000
Fixed overheads	1,20,000
Variable overheads	60,000
Units produced	15,000
Selling price per unit	40

The available capacity is a production of 20,000 units per year. The firm has an offer for the purchase of 5,000 additional units at a price of Rs. 30 per unit. It is expected that by accepting this offer, there will be a saving of Re. 1 per unit in material cost on all units manufactured; the fixed overheads will increase by Rs. 20,000 and the overall efficiency will drop by 3% on all production.

Prepare a statement showing the variation of net profits resulting from the acceptance of the order. (*Punjab, B.Com. 1981*)

[**Ans.** Increase in net Profit Rs. 103]

33. Production Costs of Dixcy Creation Ltd. are as follows:

	Level of Activity		
	60%	**70%**	**80%**
Output (in units)	1,200	1,400	1,600
Costs (in Rs.)			
Direct Materials	24,000	28,000	32,000
Direct Labour	7,200	8,400	9,600
Factory Overheads	12,800	13,600	14,400
Works Cost	44,000	50,000	56,000

A proposal to increase production to 90% level of activity is under the consideration of management. The proposal is not expected to involve any increase in fixed factory overheads.

Prepare a statement showing the prime cost, total marginal cost and total factory cost at 90% level of activity.

(*Delhi, B.Com. Hons. 1976*)

[**Ans.** At 90% level Activity: Prime Cost Rs. 46,800; Marginal Cost Rs. 54,000; Total Factory Cost Rs. 62,000]

[**Hint:** 1. For every 10% level of activity, variable (*i.e.*, incremental) factory overheads are Rs. 800.

2. Fixed factory overheads Rs. 8,000.

For example: At 60% level, variable overheads $\left(\frac{800}{100}\times 60\right)=$ Rs. 4,800. Fixed Overheads (balance) = Rs. 8,000 and so on for 70%, 80%, and 90% level of activity]

34. A factory engaged in manufacturing plastic buckets is working at 40% capacity and produces 10,000 buckets per annum.

The present cost break-up for one bucket is as under:

	Rs.
Material	10
Labour Cost	3
Overheads	5 (60% fixed)

The selling price is Rs. 20 per bucket.

If it is decided to work the factory at 50% capacity, the selling price falls by 3%. At 90% capacity, the selling price falls by 5%, accompanied by a similar fall in the prices of material.

You are required to calculate the profit at 50% and 90% capacities, and also calculate break-even-point for the same capacity production.

(*C.A. Inter*)

[**Ans.** Capacities:	50%	90%
Net Profit (Rs.)	25,000	71,250
B.E.P. (Units)	6,818	6,667]

35. For the production of a product, either of Machine – 003 and Machine – 051 can be used. Total machine hours available per annum are 4,500. You are given the following data for the machines. Assess their profitability.

	Per Unit of product A	
	Machine – 003	Machine – 051
	Rs.	Rs.
Direct Materials	30	30
Direct labour	15	19
Overheads		
Fixed	4.50	4.50
Variable	18.00	21.50
Total cost	67.50	75.00
Selling Price	90	90
Output per hour	10 units	20 units

[**Ans.** Production by machine – 051 is more profitable.]

[**Hints:** 1. Contribution per unit
Machine – 003 Rs. 27; Machine – 051 Rs. 19.50
2. Contribution per hour (multiplying by units per hour)
Machine – 003 Rs. 270; Machine – 051 Rs. 390]
(*i.e.*, 27 × 10) (*i.e.*, 19.50 × 20)

36. From the cost records of a company, for a specific period for product X, the information given in the first column is extracted, the second column can be ignored since it is only one of the projections of an assistant; but it may be useful to you:

	This period actuals	One of the future projections
Sales, in units	10,000	20,000
Profit (Loss)in Rs.	(10,000)	10,000
Fixed cost in Rs.	30,000	30,000
Variable cost per unit in Rs.	8	8

On the basis of the first column, determine:

(*a*) What increased sales volume is required to cover an extra attractive packaging cost of Re. 0.50 per unit, to increase the sales at the existing sale price, to yield zero profit?

(*b*) What increased sales volume is required at the present sale price, to cover an additional publicity expense of Rs. 5,000 for that period while yielding a profit of Rs. 5,000 ?

(*c*) What increased sales volume is required to reach a profit of Rs. 4,000, while reducing the selling price by 3% per unit?

(*C.A., Final*)

[**Ans.** (*a*) B.E. Point 20,000 units. (*b*) 20,000 units, (*c*) 20,000 units.]

37. Atlantic Company has a capacity of producing 1,00,000 units of product 'T' in a month. The Sales Manager reports that the following schedule of sale price is possible at different levels of production:

Volume of Production	Selling price per unit (Re.)
60%	0.90
70%	0.90
80%	0.75
90%	0.67
100%	0.61

The variable cost of manufacture between these levels is Rs. 0.15 per unit and the fixed costs Rs. 40,000. At what volume of production will the profit be maximum? (*I.C.W.A., adapted*)

[**Ans.** at 70%]

38. East and West Enterprises is currently working at 50% capacity and produces 10,000 units. Estimate the profits of the company when it works at 60% and 70% capacity.

At 60% capacity, the raw material cost increases by 2% and the selling price falls by 3%. At 70% capacity the raw material cost increases by 4% and the selling price falls by 5%.

At 50% capacity working, the product costs Rs. 180 per unit and is sold Rs. 200 per unit.

The unit cost of Rs. 180 is made up as follows:

Material	Rs. 100
Wages	Rs. 30
Factory overhead	Rs. 20 (40% fixed)
Administration overhead	Rs. 30 (50% fixed)

(*Punjab, B.Com., April 1982*)

[**Ans.** Profit at 60% Rs. 1,90,000; 70% Rs. 1,76,000]

39. AB Co. Ltd., has capacity to produce 1,00,000 units of a product every month. Its works cost at varying levels of production is as under:

Level	Works cost per unit (Rs.)
10%	400
20%	390
30%	380
40%	370
50%	360
60%	350
70%	340
80%	330
90%	320
100%	310

Its fixed administration expenses amount to Rs. 1,50,000 and fixed marketing expenses amount to Rs.2,50,000 per month respectively. The. variable distribution cost amounts to Rs. 30 per unit.

It can market 100% of its output at Rs. 500 per unit provided it incurs the following further expenditure:

(*a*) it gives gift items costing Rs. 20 per unit of sale;

(*b*) it has lucky draws every month giving the first prize of Rs. 50,000; 2nd prize of Rs. 25,000, 3rd prize of Rs. 10,000 and three consolation prizes of Rs. 5,000 each to customers buying the product.

(*c*) it spends Rs. 1,00,000 on refreshments served every month to its customers;

(*d*) it sponsors a television programme every week at a cost of Rs. 20,00,000 per month.

It can market 30% of its output at Rs. 550 per unit without incurring any of the expenses referred to in (*a*) to (*d*) above.

Advise the company on its course of action. Show the supporting cost sheets.

(*C.A. Inter, Nov. 1998*)

[**Ans.** Company should produce and sell 1,00,000 units (100%) to earn higher profits]

40. A company produces a single product which is sold by it presently in the domestic market at Rs. 75 per unit. The present production and sale is 40,000 units per month representing 50% of the capacity available. The cost data of the product are as under:

Variable costs per unit Rs. 50.

Fixed costs per month Rs.10 Lakhs.

To improve the profitability, the management has three proposals on hand as under:

(*a*) to accept an export supply order for 30,000 units per month at a reduced price of Rs. 60 per unit, incurring additional variable costs of Rs. 5 per unit towards export packing, duties etc.

(*b*) to increase the domestic market sales by selling to a domestic chain stores 30,000 units at Rs. 55 per unit, retaining the exisiting sales at the existing price.

(*c*) to reduce the selling price for the increased domestic sale as advised by the sales department as under:

Reduced selling price per unit by Rs.	Increase in sales expected (in units)
5	10,000
8	30,000
11	35,000

Prepare a table to present the result of the above proposals and give your comments and advice on the proposals.

(*I.C.W.A., Inter, June 1996*)

[**Ans.** Proposal (*c*) is more profitable]

41. A company produces 30,000 units of product A and 20,000 units of product B per annum. The sales value and costs of the two products are as follows

Sales value	7,60,000
Direct material	1,40,000
Direct labour	1,90,000
Factory overheads	1,90,000
Administrative and selling overheads	1,20,000

50% of factory overheads are variable and 50% of administrative and selling overheads are fixed. The selling price of A is Rs. 12 per unit and B is Rs. 20 per unit.

The direct material and labour ratio for product A is 2 : 3 and for B is 4 : 5. For both the products, the selling price is 400% of direct labour. The factory overheads are charged in the ratio of direct labour and administrative and selling overheads are recovered at a flat rate of Rs. 2 per unit of A and Rs. 3 per unit of B.

Due to fall in demand of the above products, the company has a plan to diversify and make product C using 40% capacity. It has been estimated that for C direct materials and direct labour will be Rs. 2.50 and Rs. 3 per unit respectively. Other variable cost will be same as applicable to product A. The selling price of product C is Rs. 14 per unit and production will be 30,000 units.

Assuming 60% capacity is used for manufacture of A and B, calculate

(*a*) present costs and profit.

(*b*) cost and profit after diversification, and

(*c*) give your recommendation as to whether to diversify or not.

(*I.C.W.A. Inter, June 1999*)

[**Ans.** (*a*) Profit Rs. 1,20,000; (*b*) Profit Rs. 1,55,000; (*c*) Diversification recommended]

23

Differential Cost Analysis

MEANING OF DIFFERENTIAL COST ANALYSIS

In the decision making process, the management always makes a comparison of two or more alternatives. These decisions may relate to making or buying alternatives, replacement of an existing machinery with new machinery, exploring new markets, determination of most profitable product mix or sales mix etc. In order to select the best alternative, a conscious management compares the relevant costs of available alternatives with the respective revenues. The best alternative is one which ensures maximum profits or minimum loss. Differential cost analysis is quite helpful in making the analysis of costs involved in the various alternatives.

The Institute of Cost and Management Accountants has defined 'differential cost' as "The increases or decreases in total costs or the changes in specific elements of costs that result from any variations in operations". These variations in operations may be due to changes in the level of activity, changes in the sales mix, changes in sales price, make or buy decision etc. Thus, differential cost is the difference in cost between one alternative and another and can be obtained by subtracting the cost of one alternative from the cost of the other alternative. With reference to level of output, differential cost is the difference in total costs for two levels of output.

But it should be remembered that in making a choice out of two or more alternatives, mere differential cost is not the only consideration. The decision has to be made in the light of the differential revenue i.e., the difference in revenue (increase or decrease) between the two alternatives. This point can be made clear with the help of the following example:

Statement of Differential Costs and Revenues

	Alternative I	Alternative II	Differential Costs and Revenues
	Rs.	Rs.	Rs.
Sales	1,40,000	2,00,000	60,000
Costs:			
Direct Materials	30,000	40,000	10,000
Direct Wages	24,000	40,000	16,000
Variable Overheads	6,000	8,000	2,000
Total Marginal Cost	60,000	88,000	28,000
Fixed Cost	40,000	48,000	8,000
Total Cost	1,00,000	1,36,000	36,000

	Rs
Increase in Revenue	60,000
Increase in Differential Cost	36,000
Increase in Profit	24,000

From the above example, it is clear that alternative II is more profitable and should be adopted as the increase in revenue involved in it is more than the increase in cost.

Increase in cost or revenue is also known as Incremental Cost/Incremental Revenue while decrease in cost or revenue may also be referred to as Decremental Cost/Decremental Revenue. Differential costs do not form part of the accounting records but may be incorporated in the budgets.

MAIN FEATURES OF DIFFERENTIAL COST ANALYSIS

The important features of differential cost analysis may be given as follows:

(*i*) Differential cost analysis does not form the part of the accounting records although it can be incorporated in the budgeting process while preparing flexible budgets showing budgeted costs at various levels of activity.

(*ii*) Differential cost analysis takes into consideration the total differential costs and not the per unit cost.

(*iii*) Differential costs are measured from a common base point which may be the present level of production or the present course of action being followed in the business concern.

(*iv*) Differential cost analysis takes into consideration the costs which are relevant to the decisions. Costs which are not relevant to the decisions, are not considered.

(*v*) Differential cost analysis takes into account the total costs. If fixed costs also change under various alternatives, these shall be included in differential costs.

(*vi*) Differential costs are treated as future costs since these are related to a future course of action or future level of activity (production).

(*vii*) Under differential cost analysis, total differential revenues are compared with total differential costs. The alternative showing the maximum difference between incremental revenue and incremental cost, is considered to be more profitable and recommended for adoption.

DIFFERENTIAL COST ANALYSIS AND MARGINAL COSTING

Generally the terms, 'differential cost analysis' and `marginal costing' are used interchangeably since both these techniques are similar in some respects. But there is some basic difference between these two terms.

Similarities between Differential Cost Analysis and Marginal Costing:

(*i*) Both differential cost analysis and marginal costing are the techniques of analysing and presenting costs for specific purposes.

(*ii*) Both these techniques are based on the classification of costs into fixed and variable costs. When fixed costs do not change, the differential cost and the marginal cost is the same.

(*iii*) Both these techniques are used for providing data to the management for use in decision making and formulating business policies.

DISSIMILARITIES BETWEEN DIFFERENTIAL COST ANALYSIS AND MARGINAL COSTING

(*i*) Differential cost analysis includes fixed costs if fixed costs change with changes in operations, but marginal costing technique excludes fixed costs.

(*ii*) Marginal costing techniques may be incorporated in the accounting system while differential costs are worked out separately for reporting to management for use in decision making process and cannot form part of accounting system.

(*iii*) Differential cost analysis is used when there is a comparison between two or more alternative courses of action but marginal costing technique can be used independently for making evaluation of performance through contribution margin and Profit/Volume Ratio.

(*iv*) Under differential cost analysis the desirability of any alternative course of action (*i.e.,* whether it should be adopted or not) is determined by comparing incremental revenues and incremental costs. Under marginal costing, the desirability or profitability of any alternative is determined with the help of contribution and P/V Ratio.

Applications of Differential Cost Analysis:

The technique of differential cost analysis is applied to take a number of valuable policy decisions involving alternative choices. Such decisions include the following:

(*i*) Acceptance of an additional order at a price below the existing price of the product.
(*ii*) Determination of the optimum level of production.
(*iii*) Introduction of a new product or new product line.
(*iv*) Exploring new markets.
(*v*) Replacement of an existing machinery or equipment by a new one.
(*vi*) Evaluation of make or buy alternatives.
(*vii*) Further processing of a product.

Illustration 1

A company is at present working at 90% of its capacity and producing 13,500 units per annum. It operates flexible budgetary control system. The following figures are obtained from its budget:

	90%	100%
Sales	Rs.15,00,000	16,00,000
Fixed Expenses	Rs. 3,00,500	3,00,500
Semi- fixed Expenses	Rs. 97,500	1,00,500
Variable Expenses	Rs. 1,45,000	1,49,500
Units made	13,500	15,000

Labour and material cost per unit are constant under present conditions. Profit margin is 10 percent.

(*a*) You are required to determine the differential cost of producing 1,500 units by increasing capacity to 100 percent.

(*b*) What would you recommend for an export-price for these 1,500 units taking into account that overseas prices are much lower than indigenous prices ?

[*Part (a) G.N.D. U., B. Com., 1997, I.C.W.A., Final; Delhi, B.Com. 1983*]

Solution

Calculation of cost of material and labour

Capacity (Existing)		90%
		Rs.
Sales		15,00,000
Less Profit @ 10%		1,50,000
Cost of Goods Sold		13,50,000
Less overheads:		
Fixed	3,00,500	
Semi-Fixed	97,500	
Variable	1,45,000	5,43,000
Cost of Material and Labour		8,07,000

Cost of Material and labour at 90% capacity Rs. 8,07,000

Hence cost of Material and Labour at 100% capacity $= 8,07,000 \times \frac{100}{90}$

$= 8,96,667$

Statement of Differential Cost

	90% Capacity 13,500 units	100% Capacity 15,000 units	Differential Cost
	Rs.	Rs.	Rs.
Material and Wages.	8,07,000	8,96,667	89,667
Variable Expenses.	1,45,000	1,49,500	4,500
Fixed Expenses.	3,00,500	3,00,500	–
Semi-fixed Expenses	97,500	1,00,500	3,000
	13,50,000	14,47,167	97,167

(*a*) Differential cost for increasing capacity to 100% = Rs. 97,167

(*b*) Cost Price per unit = $\frac{\text{Rs. } 97{,}167}{1{,}500 \text{ units}}$ = Rs. 64.78 per unit

Price recommended for export purpose: Any price above Rs. 64.78 per unit.

Illustration 2

A company has a capacity of producing 1,00,000 units of a certain product in a month. The sales department reports that the following schedule of sale prices is possible:

Volume of Production	Selling Price per Unit
	Rs. P.
60%	0.90
70%	0.80
80%	0.75
90%	0.67
100%	0.61

The variable cost of manufacture between these levels is 15 paise per unit and fixed cost Rs. 40,000. Prepare a statement showing incremental revenue and differential cost of each stage. At which volume of production will the profit be maximum?

Solution

Statement of Differential Cost Analysis

Capacity	Units	Variable Cost	Fixed Cost	Total Cost	Differential Cost	Sales	Incremental Revenue
		Rs.	Rs.	Rs.	Rs.	Rs.	Rs.
60%	60,000	9,000	40,000	49,000	–	54,000	–
70%	70,000	10,500	40,000	50,500	1,500	56,000	2,000
80%	80,000	12,000	40,000	52,000	1,500	60,000	4,000
90%	90,000	13,500	40,000	53,500	1,500	60,300	300
100%	1,00,000	15,000	40,000	55,000	1,500	61,000	700

At 80% capacity, the amount of profit is maximum. It is due to the fact that upto this level, incremental revenue is more than differential cost. After 80% capacity level, differential cost exceeds incremental revenue thereby resulting in a loss.

Illustration 3

The management of a company is thinking whether it should drop one item from the product line and replace it with another. Given below are present cost and output data:

Product	Price Rs.	Variable costs per unit Rs.	Percentage of Sales
Book Shelfs	60	40	30%
Tables	100	60	20%
Beds	200	120	50%
	Total Fixed Costs per year		Rs. 7,50,000
	Sales		Rs. 25,00,000

The change under consideration consists in dropping the line of tables and adding the line of cabinets.

If this drop and change is made, the manufacturer forecasts the following cost and output data:

Product	Price	Variable costs per unit Rs.	Percentage of Sales Rs.
Book Shelfs	60	40	50%
Cabinets	160	60	10%
Beds	200	120	40%
Total Fixed Costs per year	Rs. 7,50,000		
Sales	Rs. 26,00,000		

Is this proposal to be accepted? Comment.

(*Calcutta, M.Com.*)

Solution

Statement of Differential Cost Analysis

	Existing Situation				Proposed Situation			
	Book Shelfs	Tables	Beds	Total	Book Shelfs	Cabinets	Beds	Total
	Rs.	Rs.	Rs.	Rs.	Rs.	Rs.	Rs.	Rs.
Sales	7,50,000	5,00,000	12,50,000	25,00,000	13,00,000	2,60,000	10,40,000	26,00,000
Less: Variable Costs	5,00,000	3,00,000	7,50,000	15,50,000	8,66,667	97,500	6,24,000	15,88,167
	2,50,000	2,00,000	5,00,000	9,50,000	4,33,333	1,62,500	4,16,000	10,11,833
Less: Fixed Cost				7,50,000				7,50,000
Profit				2,00,000				2,61,833

The replacement of line of tables by the line of cabinets improves the profit position. Therefore, the proposal should be accepted.

Note: Calculation of variable cost has been made as follows:

(*i*) Sales of Book shelfs = Rs. 25,00,000 × 30% = Rs. 7,50,000

$$\text{Variable cost} = 7,50,000 \times \frac{40}{60} = \text{Rs. } 5,00,000$$

(*ii*) Sales of Tables : Rs. 25,00,000 × 20% = Rs. 5,00,000

$$\text{Variable cost} = 5,00,000 \times \frac{60}{100} = \text{Rs. } 3,00,000$$

(*iii*) Sales of Beds = Rs. 25,00,000 × 50% = 12,50,000

$$\text{Variable cost} = \text{Rs. } 12,50,000 \times \frac{120}{200} = \text{Rs. } 7,50,000$$

Calculation of variable cost under the proposed situation has been made on the same lines.

OBJECTIVE TYPE QUESTIONS

A. Multiple Choice Questions

Select the correct answer:

(*a*) Difference between the costs of two alternatives is known as:
 (*i*) Differential cost. (*ii*) Marginal cost.
 (*iii*) Opportunity cost. (*iv*) Variable cost.

(*b*) The technique of differential cost is adopted:
 (*i*) to ascertain marginal cost.
 (*ii*) to ascertain the cost per unit.
 (*iii*) to make choice between two or more alternative courses of action.
 (*iv*) to ascertain the P/V ratio.

(*c*) Differential cost analysis is relevant to the following decisions:
 (*i*) Fixation of selling Price.
 (*ii*) Adding or dropping a product line.
 (*iii*) Determining the amount of sales required to earn desired profits.
 (*iv*) Calculating the Break-even Point.

[**Ans.** (*a*) (*i*), (*b*) (*iii*), (*c*) (*ii*)]

B. True/false Type Statements

State whether the following statements are True or False:

(*a*) Differential costs and marginal costs are synonyms.

(*b*) Differential cost analysis deals with total costs.

(*c*) Differential cost analysis involves the calculation of per unit cost.

(*d*) Differential cost analysis is relevant for making choice between two alternatives.

(*e*) Contribution Margin and Incremental Revenue carry the same meaning.

(*f*) Differential costing is a method of ascertaining cost of products and services.

(*g*) Differential cost analysis takes into account those costs which are relevant to decision.

[**Ans.** (*a*) False, (*b*) True, (*c*) False, (*d*) True, (*e*) False, (*f*) False, (*g*) True.]

C. Filling the Blanks

Fill in the blanks:

(*a*) The technique of differential cost analysis is based on the classification of costs into ....

(*b*) Differential cost is obtained by .... the cost of one alternative from the cost of other alternative.

(*c*) Differential cost analysis is a .... of cost .... and presentation.

(*d*) Differential cost analysis also .... fixed costs.

[**Ans.** (*a*) fixed and variable, (*b*) subtracting, (*c*) technique, analysis, (*d*) includes]

SHORT ANSWER TYPE QUESTIONS

1. What is meant by Differential costs?
2. Name the problems to which differential cost analysis is applicable.
3. Give two similarities between Differential cost analysis and Marginal costing.
4. Give any two points of difference between differential costing and marginal costing.

LONG ANSWER TYPE QUESTIONS

1. What is meant by differential cost analysis? How does it differ from marginal costing?
2. What is meant by differential cost analysis? Explain the essential features and points of similarity and difference between differential cost analysis and marginal costing.

   (*Calicut, B.Com. 1981*) (*Andhra, B.Com.*)
3. What do you understand by Differential Cost Analysis? Explain (*a*) the essential features of differential costing, and (*b*) its practical application.

   (*Andhra, B.Com.*)

4. In making any decision, the businessman has to ask himself whether his proposal will add more to the total revenue than to total cost. If it does, he will proceed with the proposal in question, otherwise he will not. Explain.

(*Meerut University, M. Com.*)

EXERCISES

1. In a factory, the rated capacity is 30,000 units. The following data is supplied:

	Output upto 15,000 units	From 15,001-25,000 units	From 25,001-30,000 units
	Rs.	Rs.	Rs.
Fixed Cost	15,000	16,000	19,500
Variable cost per unit	3	3	3.25
Sales revenue per unit	4	3.80	3.80

What is the most profitable level of output? (M.*Com, Adapted*)

[**Ans.** 25,000 units]

2. A company has a capacity of producing 50,000 units of a certain product in a month. The sales department reports that the following schedule of selling prices is possible:

Volume of sales (% capacity)	**Unit selling price Rs.**
50%	2.00
60%	1.90
70%	1.85
80%	1.80
90%	1.70
100%	1.60

The variable cost of manufacture between the above levels is Re 1 per unit and the total amount of fixed cost is Rs. 20,000 p.m. at 100% capacity level.

Prepare a statement showing incremental revenue and differential cost at each of the above levels of production and sales. At which level the profit will be maximum? (*M.Com,. Bombay*)

[**Ans.** 80%]

3. A practising Chartered Accountant now spends Re. 0.90 per km. on taxi fare for his client's work. He is considering two other alternatives, the purchase of a new small car or an old bigger car. The estimated cost figures are:

Items	**New Small Car**	**Old Bigger Car**
	Rs.	**Rs.**
Purchase price	35,000	20,000
Sale price, after 5 years	19,000	12,000
Repairs and servicing per annum	1,000	1,200
Taxes and Insurance per annum	1,700	700
Petrol consumption, per litre	10 km.	7 km.
Petrol price, per litre	3.50	3.50

He estimates that he does 10,000 km. annually. Which of the three alternatives will be cheaper? If his practice expands and he has to do 19,000 km. per annum, what should be his decision? At how many km. per annum will the cost of the two cars break-even and why? Ignore interest and income tax. (*C.A. Inter*)

[**Ans.** For the present practice, old bigger car is the cheapest. When practice expands, new small car will be the cheapest. Break-even point 16,000 km.]

4. Volume of output of a product to be manufactured and sold may be 1,000, 2,000 or 3,000 units. When the above units of the product are sold, the selling prices per unit are estimated to be Rs. 50, Rs. 45 and Rs. 40 respectively. The material and labour cost per unit are Rs.12 and Rs. 10 respectively. Variable production overheads are 75% of wages. Other variable overheads are Rs. 6 per unit. Fixed costs are the same for all volumes.

Apply the differential cost analysis to determine the most profitable volume of output. (*M.Com., Bombay*)

[**Ans.** 2,000 units]

5. X Ltd., having installed capacity of 1,00,000 units of a product, is currently operating at 70% utilization. At current levels of input prices, the FOB unit costs (after credit for applicable export incentives) work out as follows:

Capacity utilization	**FOB unit costs**
Percent	**Rs.**
70	97
80	92
90	87
100	82

The company has received three foreign offers from different sources as under:

Source A 5,000 units at Rs. 55 per unit FOB.
Source B 10,000 units at Rs. 52 per unit FOB.
Source C 10,000 units at Rs. 51 per unit FOB.

Advise the company as to whether any or all the export order should be accepted or not. (*C.A. Final*)

[**Ans.** Accept the offers. Profit: A - Rs. 10,000 (Loss) B - Nil C - Rs. 90,000]

6. A company is currently working at 80% capacity. The Profit and Loss Account shows the following:

			Rs. in lakhs
Sales			640
Less:	Cost of sales:		
	Direct material	200	
	Direct expenses	80	
	Variable overhead	40	
	Fixed overhead	260	580
	Profit		60

The managing director is discussing an offer from Middle East, of a quantity which will require 50 per cent capacity of the factory. The price is 10 per cent less than the current price in the local market. Order cannot be split. You are asked to find out the most profitable alternative. The factory capacity can be augmented by 10 per cent by adding facilities at an increase of Rs. 40 lakhs in fixed cost. (*I.C.W.A., Final*)

[**Ans.** Offer from Middle East should be accepted]

7. A manufacturing concern sells one of its products under the brand name 'Utility' at Rs. 3.50 each, the cost of which is Rs. 3.00 each. After further processing, which entails additional material and labour costs of Rs. 2.50 and Rs. 2.00 per number respectively, 'Utility' is converted into another product 'Ace' which is sold at Rs. 8.00 each. The concern at present produces per day 600 numbers of the two products for which 2,500 labour hours are utilised.

The factory overheads have been budgeted as under:

Labour hours		2,000	2,500	3,000	3,500
Factory overheads	Rs.	700	800	900	1,000

The following alternative proposals have been put forth for varying the sales mix.

(*a*) To process the entire quantity of 'Utility' so as to convert it into 600 numbers of 'Ace'. This will need an additional 500 labour hours.

(*b*) To continue the present level of output of 'Utility' but double the production of 'Ace'.

You are required to work out the incremental profit/loss involved in each of the two proposals and to offer your suggestions. (*I.C.W.A., Final*)

[**Ans.** Proposal (*a*) increases loss by Rs. 100, and Proposal (*b*) reduces loss by Rs. 100. Hence, Proposal (*b*) should be accepted.]

(**Hint**. It is assumed that total hours worked for proposal (*b*) are 3,500).

8. The present volume of sales in a factory is 80,000 units per year and the management has recently installed modern plants to increase the volume up to maximum limit of half a million units annually. The present selling price is Rs. 15 per unit.

In addition to the present level, six alternative levels of output with equal increments in annual output level reaching up to a maximum limit are contemplated. The reduction in the selling price is expected to be Re. 1 at each higher level of sale.

The present variable costs and semi-variable costs amount to Rs. 4,00,000 and Rs. 2,30,000 respectively. Fixed costs which at present amount to Rs. 2,00,000 are not expected to increase for any of the alternative levels contemplated. The variable costs and semi-variable costs at the six projected levels of output are calculated to be as follows:

Variable cost (Rs.): 7,50,000; 11,00,000; 15,00,000; 17,50,000; 20,50,000; 25,00,000.

Semi-variable cost (Rs.): 2,30,000; 2,60,000; 2,60,000; 2,80,000; 2,80,000; 3,20,000.

Tabulate the above data and show total costs, incremental costs, total and incremental sales income at various output levels. Offer your recommendations as to the most advantageous level of sales volume.

(M.Com., Calcutta)

[**Ans.** Most Profitable Sales Volume – 4,30,000 units at Rs. 10 per unit]

9. An enthusiastic marketing manager suggests to his managing director that only if he is permitted to reduce the selling price of a product by 20%, he would be able to achieve a 30% increase in sales volume. The managing director, finding that the sales volume increase exceeds in percentage the extent of requested reduction in price, gives the clearance. You are given the following information:

Present Selling Price per unit	Rs. 7.50
Present volume of sales	2,00,000 Nos.
Total variable costs	Rs. 10,50,000
Total fixed costs	Rs. 3,60,000

Assuming no changes in the costs pattern in the coming period.

(*a*) Examine the consequences of the managing director's decision assuming that 30% increase in sales is realised.

(*b*) At what volume of sales can the present quantum of profits be sustained, after effecting the price reduction.

(C.A. Final)

[**Ans.** (*a*) By reducing selling price by 20%, there is a loss of Rs. 1,65,000 in spite of increase in sales volume.

(*b*) 6,00,000 Nos. need to be sold out to earn the present profit of Rs. 90,000.]

24

Cost Control Accounts and Integrated Accounts

The main object of cost accounting is the ascertainment of cost already incurred and requires the maintenance of a set of accounts to record all transactions relating to costs. As in financial accounts, in cost accounts also, recording of transactions is done on the basis of double entry system. Moreover, both financial accounts and cost accounts are written up on the basis of same basic documents. But the Accounting Department is interested in personal accounts, real accounts and nominal accounts, whereas the Costing Department is particularly interested in nominal accounts and to some extent, in real accounts since it is concerned with the income and expenditure of the business. Thus, nominal accounts and real accounts are given detailed treatment in cost accounts. Basically there are two methods of keeping cost-books of accounts:

1. Independent Accounts and
2. Integrated Accounts.

Under the first method, two separate sets of account books are maintained to record cost and financial data while under the second method only one integrated ledger containing both financial and cost records is maintained.

In a business using cost control accounts, the Costing Department maintains independent or non-integrated accounts. Costing books, in such a case, consist of four principal ledgers, namely Cost Ledger, Stores Ledger, Stock Ledger and Work-in-Progress Ledger. In small concerns, these ledgers may be kept in a bound book while in big concerns loose leaf or card ledgers are convenient.

Cost Ledgers

1. **Stores Ledger:** Stores Ledger consists of accounts of individual items of raw materials, components and consumable stores. Entries into the Stores Ledger are made from basic documents such as Good Received Notes, Material Return Notes, Transfer Notes and Material Requisition Slips.
2. **Finished Goods Ledger:** It is also known as Stock Ledger and consists of item-wise accounts in respect of finished stock intended for sale. Entries into the Finished Goods Ledger are made on the basis of Shop Delivery

Notes, Sales Return Notes and Requisition for Sales Orders or some special issues.

3. **Work-in-Progress Ledger:** This Ledger consists of individual accounts for each job under execution and each product under production and costs incurred therefor during the period. Work-in-Progress Ledger is also known as Job Ledger.
4. **Cost Ledger:** This is the principal ledger of the Costing Department to which above mentioned three ledgers serve as subsidiary ledgers. Cost Ledger contains three control accounts to represent the Stores, Stock and Work-in-Progress Ledgers. In addition, it contains General Ledger Control Account, Wages Control Account and Overhead Control Accounts.

CONTROL ACCOUNTS

In a business where subsidiary ledgers such as Stores Ledger, Work-in-Progress Ledger, Finished Goods Ledger etc., are employed, the Cost Ledger is made self balanced with the use of Control Accounts. Control Accounts are the total accounts maintained in the Cost Ledger, each representing a Subsidiary Ledger in which individual accounts are maintained. The details of the transactions are recorded in the subsidiary ledgers and their totals are posted in the Control Accounts at the end of the accounting period. As a result of it, the total balance in the Control Accounts and total of individual balances in the subsidiary ledger accounts should agree.

The preparation of Control Accounts:

(*i*) provides a summary of a number of individual accounts.
(*ii*) provides consolidated information regarding pending jobs, value of materials in hand etc.
(*iii*) facilitates the preparation of final accounts.
(*iv*) facilitates the reconciliation of cost accounts with financial accounts.

The following is the list of important Control Accounts to be prepared in the Cost Ledger:

(*i*) **General Ledger Adjustment Account:** This account is also known as 'Cost Ledger Control Account' or 'Financial Ledger Adjustment Account' and is maintained to make the cost ledger self-balancing. All items of income and expenditure, which have been extracted from financial books are posted to this account. In fact, this account represents the personal accounts shown in the financial books. It should be noted that no entry should be made direct from the financial books to cost books. Entries must be passed only through the General Ledger Adjustment Account or Cost Ledger Control Account.

(*ii*) **Stores Ledger Control Account:** This account deals with all transactions which involve the receipts and issues of materials. The balance of Stores Ledger Control Account should agree with the total of the balances of individual accounts prepared in the Stores Ledger. The purchases of materials for specific jobs are not recorded in the Stores Ledger Control Account. These are debited to the Work-in-Progress Control Account.

(*iii*) **Wages Control Account:** This account deals with the total amount of wages paid. It is debited with the gross wages (paid and accrued). The amount of direct wages is transferred to Work-in-Progress Ledger Control Account while the amount of indirect wages is transferred to Factory, Administration and Selling and Distribution Overhead Control Accounts.

(*iv*) **Work-in-Progress Ledger Control Account:** This account represents total work-in-progress at any time. This account is debited with the opening balance of work-in-progress, production costs incurred during the period in the form of direct material, direct wages, direct expenses and works overhead recovered and credited with the value of the finished goods completed and transferred. The balance on this account will reveal the total value of jobs/works which are in progress.

(*v*) **Stock Ledger Control Account:** This account represents the total value of finished goods in stock. This account is debited with the value of the opening stock of finished goods, the value of the finished goods transferred from Work-in-Progress Ledger Control Account and the amount of administration overhead recovered, if any. It is credited with the cost of goods sold leaving the balance of finished goods in hand at end.

(*vi*) **Cost of Sales Account:** This account shows the total selling and distribution overheads recovered, which together with the cost of finished goods sold, represent the cost of sales.

(*vii*) **Production Overhead Control Account or Factory Overhead Control Account:** This account deals with production overhead or factory overhead. This account is debited with indirect material cost, indirect wages and indirect expenses and is credited with the amount of overheads absorbed and transferred to Work-in-Progress Ledger Control Account. The balance of this account representing under-absorbed or over-absorbed overheads is transferred to Costing Profit and Loss Account.

(*viii*) **Administration Overhead Control Account:** This account is debited with the total amount of office and administration overhead and credited with the amount of overheads absorbed by finished goods. The balance in the account representing over-absorbed or under-absorbed amount of overhead, is transferred to Costing Profit and Loss Account. If the administration overheads are excluded from costs, the entire amount of this account is transferred to Costing Profit and Loss account.

(*ix*) **Selling and Distribution Overhead Control Account:** This account is debited with the amount of selling and distribution overheads incurred and credited with the amount of overheads absorbed. The balance in the account representing under-absorbed or over-absorbed overheads, is transferred to Costing Profit and Loss Account.

(*x*) **Costing Profit and Loss Account:** This account is debited with the cost of sales, abnormal losses and under-absorbed overheads and is credited with the sale value of goods sold, abnormal gains and profits and over-absorbed overheads. The balance of the Costing Profit and Loss Account represents costing profit or loss which is transferred to Cost Ledger Control Account.

ACCOUNTING ENTRIES

The important journal entries for posting into Control Accounts are as follows:

1. Material purchased for store:	Debit Stores Ledger Control Account Credit Cost Ledger Control Account
2. Materials Purchased specifically for jobs:	Debit Work-in-Progress Control Account Credit Cost Ledger Control Account
3. Return of Materials to Suppliers:	Debit Cost Ledger Control Account Credit Stores Ledger Control Account
4. Issue of materials and stores for production to Jobs:	Debit Work-in-Progress Control Account Credit Stores Ledger Control Account
5. Return of Materials from Production to Stores:	Debit Stores Ledger Control Account Credit Work-in-Progress Control Account
6. Payment of direct wages:	Debit Wages Control Account Credit Cost Ledger Control Account
7. Allocation of Wages to production:	Debit Work-in-Progress Control Account Credit Wages Control Acccount
8. Payment of Factory Expenses: (Actual)	Debit Factory Overhead Control Account Credit Cost Ledger Control Account
9. Payment of Office Expenses: (Actual)	Debit Office Overhead Control Account Credit Cost Ledger Control Account
10. Payment of Selling Expenses: (Actual)	Debit Selling Overhead Control Account Credit Cost Ledger Control Account
11. Allocation of Factory Expenses:	Debit Work-in-Progress Control Account Credit Factory Overhead Control Account
12. Normal Wastage of Stores and Normal Idle Time:	Debit Factory Overhead Control Account Credit Stores Ledger Control Account Credit Wages Control Account

13. Abnormal Wastage of stores and Abnormal Idle Time:	Debit Costing Profit and Loss Account Credit Stores Ledger Control Account Credit Wages Control Account
14. Allocation of Office Expenses	Debit Work-in-Progress Control Account Credit Office Overhead Control Account
15. Completed Jobs and Products passed to Finished Stock:	Debit Stock Ledger Control Account Credit Work-in-Progress Control Account
16. Cost of Goods Sold:	Debit Cost of Sales Account Credit Stock Ledger Control Account
17. Sales of goods:	Debit Cost Ledger Control Account Credit Cost of Sales Account
18. Allocation of Selling Expenses:	Debit Cost of Sales Account Credit Selling Overhead Control Account
19. Profit on Sales:	Debit Cost of Sales Account Credit Costing Profit and Loss Account (Reverse the above noted entry in case of Loss)
20. Works Overhead Chargeable to Incomplete Jobs:	Debit Works Overhead Suspense Account Credit Works Overhead Control Account
21. Office Overhead Chargeable to Incomplete Jobs:	Debit Office Overhead Suspense Account Credit Office Overhead Control Account
22. Over-recovery of Expenses in cost accounts:	Debit Factroy Overhead Control Account Debit Office Overhead Control Account Debit Selling Overhead Control Account Credit Costing and Profit & Loss Account (Reverse the above noted entry in case of under-absorption or under-recovery of overhead)
23. Final Profit as per Costing Profit & Loss Account:	Debit Costing Profit and Loss Account Crebit Cost Ledger Control Account.

Illustration 1

From the following information obtained from costing records and financial books of A.B. Manufacturing Co., you are required to pass the necessary entries in the Cost Journal (assuming that a system of maintaining Cost Control Accounts prevails in the concern):

	Rs.
Purchases of Stores	80,000
Carriage Inwards	1,000
Stores Issued	76,000
Productive Wages Paid	60,000
Indirect Wages Paid	20,000
Works Overhead	69,000
Materials used for repairs in the factory	600
Cost of Finished Jobs	2,20,000

Solution

Cost Journal

	Particulars		Debit Amount	Credit Amount
			Rs.	Rs.
1.	Stores Ledger Control A/c To Cost Ledger Control A/c (Being the purchases of stores)	Dr.	80,000	80,000
2	Stores Ledger Control A/c To Cost Ledger Control A/c (Being the amount of carriage inward paid)	Dr.	1,000	1,000
3.	Work-in-Progress Ledger Control A/c To Stores Ledger Control A/c (Being the amount of Stores issued to jobs)	Dr.	76,000	76,000
4.	Wages Control A/c To Cost Ledger Control A/c (Being the amount of Productive Wages and Indirect Wages Paid)	Dr.	80,000	80,000
5.	Work-in-Progress Ledger Control A/c To Wages Control A/c (Being the amount of Direct Wages allocated to jobs)	Dr.	60,000	60,000
6.	Works Overhead Control A/c To Wages Control A/c (Being the amount of indirect wages allocated to works overhead)	Dr.	20,000	20,000
7.	Works Overhead Control A/c To Cost Ledger Control A/c (Being the amount of works overhead other than indirect wages incurred)	Dr.	69,000	69,000
8.	Works Overhead Control A/c To Stores Ledger Control A/c (Being the cost of materials used for repairs in the factory)	Dr.	600	600
9.	Work-in-Progress Ledger Control A/c To Works Overhead Control A/c (Being the recovery of works overhead)	Dr.	89,600	89,600
10.	Finished Goods Ledger Control A/c To Work-in-Progress Ledger Control A/c (Being the cost of completed jobs transferred from Work-in-Progress Ledger Control A/c)	Dr.	2,20,000	2,20,000

LEDGER ACCOUNTS

Ledger accounts have been explained with the help of the following illustrations:

Illustration 2

The cost ledger of Bharat Motors Ltd., showed the following balances as at 1st April, 2002:

	Rs.	Rs.
Stores Ledger Control Account	3,600	
Work-in-Progress Control Account	2,000	
Finished Goods Ledger Control Account	400	
Cost Ledger Control Account		6,000
	6,000	6,000

Further balances resulting from operations for the year ended 31st March, 2003, were:

	Rs.
Materials purchased for stores	12,000
Materials purchased for special jobs	400
Materials returned to suppliers	200
Issue of materials for production	10,260
Materials issued for Service Order No. 1	120
Materials issued for Work Order No. 2	240
Balances at the end:	
Stores Ledger	2,400
Finished Goods Ledger	1,800
Wages paid to direct workers	7,200
Wages paid to indirect workers	1,200
Wages allocated to production	5,000
Wages allocated to Service Order No. 1	600
Wages allocated to Work Order No. 2	400
Abnormal Losses:	
Materials	80
Time	660
Works Expenses	5,000
Office Expenses	4,000
Selling Expenses	3,000
Materials returned from production	400
Depreciation of productive assets	1,000
Sales	30,000
Cost of Finished Goods Transferred	19,800
Selling Expenses Recovered	4,400

Allocation of Expenses:

	Works Rs.	Office Rs.
Completed Jobs	3,000	2,000
Incomplete Jobs	1,000	1,200
Service Order No. 1	400	
Work Order No. 2	200	

Show Ledger Accounts in the Cost Ledger and also prepare a Trial Balance.

Solution

Cost Ledger

Cost Ledger Control Account

Date	Particulars	Rs.	Date	Particulars	Rs.
2003 March 31	To Stores Ledger Control Arc	200	2002 April1	By Balance b/d	6,000
			2003 March 31	By Stores Ledger Control A/c	12,000
	To Cost of Sales A/c (Sales)	30,000	"	By Work-in-Progress Control A/c	400
			"	By Wages Control A/c	7,200
	To Work Order No. 2 A/c	840		By Works Overhead Control A/c (Indirect Wages)	1,200
			"	By Works Overhead Control A/c	5,000
			"	By Office Overhead Control A/c	4,000
			"	By Selling Overhead Control A/c	3,000
			"	By Works Overhead Control A/c (Depreciation)	1,000
March 31	To Balance c/d	8,860	"	By Costing Profit and Loss A/c	100
		39,900			39,900
			2003 April 1	By Balance b/d	8,860

Stores Ledger Control Account

Date	Particulars	Rs.	Date	Particulars	Rs.
2002 April 1	To Balance b/d	3,600	2003 March 31	By Work-in-Progress Control A/c (Issue for Prod.)	10,260
2003 March 31	To Cost Ledger Control A/c	12,000	"	By Service Order No. 1 A/c	120
	ToWork-in-Progress Control A/c (Materials returned from Production)	400	"	By Work Order No. 2 A/c	240
			"	By Cost Ledger Control A/c. (Materials returned to Suppliers)	200
			"	By Costing Profit & Loss A/c (Abnormal Loss)	80
				By Works Overhead Control A/c (Normal Loss Balancing Figure)	2,700
			"	By Balance c/d	2,400
		16,000			16,000
2003 April 1	To Balance b/d	2,400			

Work-in-Progress Control Account

		Rs.			Rs.
2002			2003		
April 1	To Balance b/d	2,000	March 31	By Stores Ledger Control A/c	400
2003	To Stores Ledger		”	By Finished Goods	
March 31	Control A/c	10,260		Ledger Control A/c	19,800
”	To Cost Ledger				
	Control A/c	400			
”	To Wages Control A/c	5,000			
”	To Works Overhead				
	Control A/c	3,000			
”	To Office Overhead				
	Control A/c	2,000	March 31	By Balance c/d	2,460
		22,660			22,660
2003					
April1	To Balance b/d	2,460			

Wages Control Account

		Rs.			Rs.
2003			2003		
March	To Cost Ledger	7,200	March	By Work-in-Progress	5,000
31	Control A/c		31	Control A/c	
				By Service Order No. 1 A/c	600
				By Work Order No. 2 A/c	400
				By Costing Profit and	
				Loss A/c (Abnormal Loss)	660
				By Works Overhead	
				Control A/c (Balance	540
				being normal idle time)	
		7,200			7,200

Finished Goods Ledger Control Account

		Rs.			Rs.
2002			2003		
April 1	To Balance b/d	400	March 31	By Cost of Sales A/c	18,400
2003	To Work-in-Progress			(Cost of Goods Sold)	
March 31	Control A/c	19,800	”	By Balance c/d	1,800
		20,200			20,200
2003					
April 1	To Balance b/d	1,800			

Service Order No. 1 Account

		Rs.			Rs.
2003			2003		
March	To Stores Ledger		March 31	By Works Overhead	1,120
31	Control A/c	120		Control A/c	
”	To Wages Control A/c	600			
”	To Works Overhead	400			
	Control A/c				
		1,120			1,120

Work Order No. 2 Account

		Rs.			Rs.
2003			2003		
March	To Stores Ledger		March	By Cost Ledger	840
31	Control A/c	240	31	Control A/c	
”	To Wages Control A/c	400			
”	To Works Overhead				
	Control A/c	200			
		840			840

Works Overhead Control Account

2003		Rs.	2003		Rs.
March 31	To Cost Ledger Control A/c:		March 31	By Work-in-Progress Control A/c	3,000
	Indirect Wages	1,200			
	Works Expenses	5,000			
	Depreciation	1,000	"	By Service Order No. 1 A/c	400
	To Service Order No. I A/c	1,120	"	By Work Order No. 2 A/c	200
"	To Wages Control A/c (Normal idle time)	540	"	By Works Overhead Suspense A/c (Incomplete Jobs)	1,000
"	To Stores Ledger Control A/c (Normal Loss)	2,700	"	By Costing Profit and Loss A/c (Under-recovery)	6,960
		11,560			11,560

Works Overhead Suspense Account

2003		Rs.	2003		Rs.
March 31	To Works Overhead Control A/c	1,000	March 31	By Balance c/d	1,000
		1,000			1,000
2003 April 1	To Balance b/d	1,000			

Office Overhead Control A/c

2003		Rs.	2003		Rs.
March 31	To Cost Ledger Control A/c	4,000	March 31	By Work-in-Progress Control A/c (Completed Jobs)	2.000
			"	By Office Overhead Suspense A/c (Incomplete Jobs)	1,200
			"	By Costing Profit and Loss A/c (Under-recovery)	800
		4,000			4,000

Office Overhead Suspense Account

2003		Rs.	2003		Rs.
March 31	To Office Overhead Control A/c	1,200	March 31	By Balance c/d	1,200
		1,200			1,200
2003 April 1	To Balance b/d	1,200			

Selling Overhead Control Account

2003		Rs.	2003		Rs.
March 31	To Cost Ledger Control A/c	3,000	March 31	By Cost of Sales A/c	4,400
"	To Costing Profit and Loss A/c (Over-recovery)	1,400			
		4,400			4,400

Cost of Sales Account

2003		Rs.	2003		Rs.
March 31	To Finished Goods Ledger Control A/c	18,400	March 31	By Sales	30,000
	To Selling Overhead Control A/c	4,400			
	To Costing Profit and Loss A/c	7,200			
		30,000			30,000

Costing Profit and Loss Account

2003		Rs.	2003		Rs.
March 31	To Stores Ledger Control A/c (Abnormal Loss)	80	March 31	By Cost of Sales A/c	7,200
”	To Wages Control A/c (Abnormal idle time)	660		By Selling Overhead Control A/c (Over-recovery)	1,400
”	To Works Overhead Control A/c (Under-recovery)	6,960			
”	To Office Overhead Control A/c (Under-recovery)	800			
”	To Cost Ledger Control A/c	100			
		8,600			8,600

Trial Balance as on March 31, 2003

	Rs.	Rs.
Cost Ledger Control A/c		8,860
Stores Ledger Control A/c	2,400	
Work-in-Progress Control A/c	2,460	
Finished Goods Ledger Control A/c	1,800	
Works Overhead Suspense A/c	1,000	
Office Overhead Suspense A/c	1,200	
	8,860	8,860

Illustration 3

The following balances are given in the Cost Ledger of M/s X Ltd. as on 1st April, 2002.

	Dr. Rs.	Cr. Rs.
Stores Ledger Control Account	12,000	–
Stock Ledger Control Account	25,000	–
Work-in-Progress Ledger Control A/c	8,000	–
Works Overhead Control A/c	16,000	–
Administration Overhead Control Account	10,000	–
Selling and Distribution Overhead Control A/c	19,000	–
General Ledger Adjustment Account	–	90,000
	90,000	90,000

The following transactions took place during the year ended on 31st March, 2003:

	Rs.
Purchase of Materials	25,000
Materials issued to Production	20,000
Materials issued for repairs	1,000
Materials returned to vendor	2,000
Materials returns to store from production	3,000
Material lost by fire	1,000
Wages paid to direct labour	18,000
Wages paid to indirect labour	5,000
Direct wages charged to production	16,000
Works Expenses	12,000
Works overhead allocated to production	15,000
Goods finished during the year (at cost)	46,000
Administration Expenses	9,000
Administration overheads allocated to production	8,000
Finished goods sold (at cost)	49,000
Selling and Distribution Expenses	15,000
Selling and Distribution overheads allocated to production sold	20,000
Sales	80,000

Prepare the necessary accounts in Cost Ledger and a Trial Balance as on 31st March, 2003 from the above transactions.

Solution

Stores Ledger Control Account

Particulars	Amount	Particulars	Amount
	Rs.		Rs.
To Balance b/d	12,000	By Work-in-Progress Ledger Control Account	20,000
To General Ledger Adjustment Account	25,000	By Works Overhead Control Account	1,000
To Work-in-Progress Ledger Control (Returns to store)	3,000	By General Ledger Adjustment Account	2,000
		By Costing Profit and Loss A/c	1,000
		By Balance c/d	16,000
	40,000		40,000

Wages Control Account

Particulars	Amount	Particulars	Amount
	Rs.		Rs.
To General Ledger Adjustment Account	18,000	By Work-in-Progress Ledger Control A/c	16,000
		By Balance c/d	2,000
	18,000		18,000

Works Overhead Control Account

Particulars	Amount	Particulars	Amount
	Rs.		Rs.
To Balance b/d	16,000	By Work-in-Progress Ledger Control Account	15,000
To Stores Ledger Control A/c	1,000		
To General Ledger Adjustment Account	5,000		
To General Ledger Adjustment Account	12,000	By Balance c/d	19,000
	34,000		34,000

Administration Overhead Control Account

Particulars	Amount	Particulars	Amount
	Rs.		Rs.
To Balance b/d	10,000	By Stock Ledger Control A/c	8,000
To General Ledger Adjustment Account	9,000	By Balance c/d	11,000
	19,000		19,000

Selling and Distribution Overhead Control Account

Particulars	Amount	Particulars	Amount
	Rs.		Rs.
To Balance b/d	19,000	By Cost of Goods Sold A/c	20,000
To General Ledger Adjustment Account	15,000	By Balance c/d	14,000
	34,000		34,000

Work-in-Progress Ledger Control Account

Particulars	Amount	Particulars	Amount
	Rs.		Rs.
To Balance b/d	8,000	By Stock Ledger Control A/c	46,000
To Stores Ledger Control Account	20,000	By Stores Ledger Control A/c	3,000
To Wages Control A/c	16,000		
To Works Overhead Control A/c	15,000	By Balance c/d	10,000
	59,000		59,000

Stock Ledger Control Account

Particulars	Amount	Particulars	Amount
	Rs.		Rs.
To Balance b/d	25,000	By Cost of Goods Sold A/c	49,000
To Administration Overhead Control Account	8,000		
To Work-in-Progress Ledger Control Account	46,000	By Balance c/d	30,000
	79,000		79,000

Cost of Goods Sold Account

Particulars	Amount	Particulars	Amount
	Rs.		Rs.
To Stock Ledger Control A/c	49,000	By General Ledger Adjustment A/c	80,000
To Selling and Distribution Overhead Control A/c	20,000		
To Costing Profit & Loss A/c	11,000		
	80,000		80,000

General Ledger Adjustment Account

Particulars	Amount	Particulars	Amount
	Rs.		Rs.
To Stores Ledger Control A/c	2,000	By Balance b/d	90,000
To Cost of Goods Sold A/c	80,000	By Stores Ledger Control A/c	25,000
		By Wages Control A/c	18,000
		By Works Overhead Control A/c	5,000
		By Works Overhead Control A/c	12,000
		By Administration Overhead Control A/c	9,000
		By Selling and Distribution Overhead Control A/c	15,000
		By Costing Profit and Loss A/c	10,000
To Balance c/d	1,02,000		
	1,84,000		1,84,000

Costing Profit & Loss Account

Particulars	Amount	Particulars	Amount
	Rs.		Rs.
To Stores Ledger Control A/c	1,000	By Cost of Goods Sold A/c	11,000
To General Ledger Ajustment A/c	10,000		
	11,000		11,000

Trial Balance as on 31st March 2003

Particulars	Dr. (Rs.)	Cr. (Rs.)
Stores Ledger Control A/c	16,000	—
Stock Ledger Control A/c	30,000	—
Work-in-Progress Ledger Control A/c	10,000	—
Wages Control A/c	2,000	—
Works Overhead Control A/c	19,000	—
Administration Overhead Control A/c	11,000	—
Selling & Distribution Overhead Control A/c	14,000	—
General Ledger Adjustment A/c	—	1 ,02,000
	1,02,000	1,02,000

Advantages of Cost Ledger or Cost Control Accounts:

The main advantages of maintaining Cost Ledger are as follows:

(*i*) In case of a large business concern, it becomes difficult to keep a track of all transactions. Cost control accounts provide a systematic summary of masses of detailed information recorded in subsidiary records. Thus cost control accounts provide invaluable data to the management in formulating business policies.

(*ii*) Cost control accounts help in preparing the Costing Profit and Loss Account promptly as a result of which the management is in a position to know the results of the operations of the firm.

(*iii*) Cost Control Accounts involve the use of the internal check system which helps in detecting errors and ensuring accuracy of costing records.

(*iv*) Cost Control Accounts help in maintaining the secrecy of cost data if cost accounts have not been maintained on integrated basis.

(*v*) Cost Control Accounts help in making the reconciliation of costing profit or loss with that of financial books.

INTEGRATED ACCOUNTS

Generally cost and financial accounts are maintained separately in a business concern. But sometimes, with a view to ensure economy, both cost and financial accounts are merged into one common set of books. It is known as Integrated System of Accounting. Integral or Integrated System of Accounting is a system whereby cost and financial accounts are maintained in the same set of books and the integrated accounts will provide full data required for costing as well as for financial accounting purposes. The integrated system of accounting eliminates the necessity of preparing Cost Ledger and of reconciling cost and financial books.

Preliminaries to be considered while introducing Integrated Accounting System:

The following principles shall be taken into consideration while designing Integrated Accounting System:

(*i*) First of all the degree of integration should be determined. In some concerns, integration is done upto the stage of prime cost or factory cost while in others, integration of full records is done.

(*ii*) The degree of integration will determine the classification of expenditure. The classification of the expenditure shall be made according to functions, for example, office expenses, selling expenses, etc.

(*iii*) Various Subsidiary Ledgers and Control Accounts to be maintained in the main ledger for carrying out the scheme of integration are as follows:

Subsidiary Ledgers	Control Accounts
(*a*) Sales Ledger (for accounts of customers)	Sales Ledger Control Account
(*b*) Purchases Ledger (for accounts of suppliers)	Purchases Ledger Control Account
(*c*) Stores Ledger (for accounts of individual items of stores and materials)	Stores Ledger Control Account
(*d*) Stock Ledger (for accounts of items of individual finished goods)	Stock Ledger Control Account
(*e*) Job Ledger (for accounts of individual jobs)	Work-in-Progress Control Account
(*f*) Expenses Ledger (for accounts of expenses to be kept separately for Factory, Office and Selling expenses)	Works Overhead Control Account Office Overhead Control Account Selling Overhead Control Account

(*iv*) Full particulars of items posted to the Control Accounts are supplied to the Cost Office at regular intervals. These details are analysed and tabulated by Cost Office in accordance with the system of costing in use.

(*v*) The extent of the details to be recorded in the ledger depends upon circumstances but attempts should be made to keep it to the minimum. But full details and complete information regarding each department, process or job are, however given in the tabulations prepared by the Cost Office.

Advantages of Integrated Accounts:

The various advantages of integrated accounts may be given as follows:

(*i*) Under the integral accounting system only one set of accounts is maintained. There is only one Profit and Loss Account. As such there is no need of reconciliation of Cost and Financial Accounts.

(*ii*) Under integral accounting system, duplication of accounting work is avoided which leads to saving in cost.

(*iii*) The cost data are obtained promptly as cost accounts are posted directly from the books of original entry.

(*iv*) The integrated accounting system helps in co-ordinating functions of various sections of Accounts Department

(*v*) The correctness of the cost data is automatically checked under the integral accounting. As such this system provides reliable data to the management for making decisions.

Journal Entries:

Items	Financial Books	Cost Books	Integrated Books
1. Purchase of Materials	Purchases A/c Dr. To Creditors	Stores Ledger Control A/c Dr. To Cost Ledger Control A/c	Stores Ledger Control A/c To Creditors
2. Wages Paid in Cash	Wages A/c Dr. To Cash A/c	Wages Control A/c Dr. To Cost Ledger Control A/c	Wages Control A/c Dr. To Cash A/c
3. Issue of Materials for production	No entry	Work-in-Progress Control A/c Dr. To Stores Ledger Control A/c	Work-in-Progress Control A/c Dr. To Stores Ledger Control A/c
4. Allocation of Wages to Production	No entry	Work-in-Progress Control A/c Dr. To Wages Control A/c	Work-in-Progress Control A/c Dr. To Wages Control A/c

5. Works Expenses Incurred	Individual Expenses A/c Dr. To Cash A/c To Expenses Outstanding A/c	Works Overhead Control A/c Dr. To Cost Ledger Control A/c	Works Overhead Control A/c Dr. To Cash A/c To Expenses Outstanding A/c
6. Works Expenses charged to production	No entry	Work-in-Progress Control A/c Dr. To Works Overhead Control A/c	Work-in-Progress Control A/c Dr. ToWorks Overhead Control A/c
7. Job Completed	No entry	Finished Goods Ledger Control A/c Dr. To Work-in-Progress Control A/c	Finished Goods Ledger Control A/c Dr. ToWork-in-Progess Control A/c
8. Sales	Debtors Dr. To Sales A/c	Cost Ledger Control A/c Dr. To Sales A/c	Debtors Dr. To Sales A/c
9. Interest paid	Interest A/c Dr. To Cash A/c	No entry	Interest A/c Dr. To Cash A/c
10. Abnormal Idle Time	No entry	Costing Profit and Loss A/c Dr. To Wages Control A/c	Costing Profit and Loss A/c Dr. To Wages Control A/c

Illustration 4

Journalise the following transactions assuming cost and financial accounts are integrated:

	Rs.		Rs.
Raw Material Purchased	1,00,000	Selling and Distribtuion Costs	10,000
Direct Materials issued to production	75,000	Finished Product (at Cost)	1,00,000
Wages paid (30% indirect)	60,000	Sales	1,50,000
Wages charged to Production	50,000	Closing Stock	Nil
Manufacturing Expenses incurred	42,000	Receipts from debtors	35,000
Manufacturing Overheads charged to Production	46,000	Payment to creditors	55,000

Solution

Journal Entries

Particulars		Dr. Rs.	Cr. Rs.
Stores Ledger Control A/c	...Dr.	1,00,000	
To Bought Ledger Control A/c			1,00,000
(Being raw materials purchased)			
Work-in-Progress Ledger Control A/c	...Dr.	75,000	
To Stores Ledger Control A/c			75,000
(Being material issued to production)			
Wages Control A/c	... Dr.	42,000	
Factory Overheads Control A/c	... Dr.	18,000	
To Bank A/c			60,000
(Wages paid)			
Work-in-Progress Ledger Control A/c	... Dr.	50,000	
To Wages Control A/c			35,000
To Factory Overheads Control A/c			15,000
(Being allocation of wages to production)			
Factory Overheads Control A/c	... Dr.	42,000	
To Bank A/c			42,000
(Being the manufacturing expenses incurred)			
Work-in-Progress Ledger Control A/c	...Dr.	46,000	
To Factory Overheads Control A/c			46,000
(Overheads charged to production)			
Selling and Distribution Overheads Control A/c	... Dr	10,000	
To Bank A/c			10,000
(Selling and Distribution Cost incurred)			
Finished Stock Ledger Control A/c	...Dr.	1,00,000	
To Work-in-Progress Ledger Control A/c			1,00,000
(Cost of Production of Completed units)			
Cost of Sales A/c	...Dr.	1,10,000	
To Finished Stock Ledger Control A/c			1,00,000
To Selling and Distribution Overheads Control A/c			10,000
(Cost of products sold)			
Sales Ledger Control A/c	...Dr.	1,50,000	
To Sales A/c			1,50,000
(Being the amount of Sales)			
Bank A/c	...Dr.	35,000	
To Sales Ledger Control A/c			35,000
(Amount received from debtors)			
Bought Ledger Control A/c	... Dr.	55,000	
To Bank A/c			55,000
(Amount paid to creditors)			

PROBLEM RELATING TO VALUATION OF STOCKS

Under the integrated accounting system, there normally arises the problem of valuation of stock. The values of stocks appearing in cost accounts and financial accounts are generally different from each other. The valuation of stocks per cost accounts is considered to be more reliable and hence included in the integrated accounts. But in order to serve the purpose of Final Accounts at the end of the year, Stock Adjustment Accounts may be prepared which will record the difference in the valuation of stock as per two sets of books. The treatment can be explained with the help of the following example:

Example:

The stock valuations of Dixcy Creation Ltd., as per cost and financial accounts are shown below:

	Cost Accounts	**Financial Accounts**
	Rs.	**Rs.**
Raw Material	40,000	38,000
Work-in-Progress	30,000	28,500
Finished Goods	50,000	47,000

If the company decides to integrate its accounts, integrated accounts will show the following:

Debit:

	Rs.
Raw Material	40,000
Work-in-Progress	30,000
Finished Goods	50,000

Credit:

	Rs.
Raw Material Adjustment	2,000
Work-in-Progress Adjustment	1,500
Finished Goods Adjustment	3,000

INTEGRATED ACCOUNTING SYSTEM

For the purpose of integrating cost and financial accounts, the following traditional systems are in use:

(*i*) The Double Entry Method

(*ii*) The Third Entry Method

The Third Entry Method differs from the Double Entry Method in the sense that under this Method (*i.e.*, Third Entry Method) a Cost Control Account is prepared with memorandum column. Further, Wages Control and Overhead Control Accounts are not made and entries relating to these accounts are passed through Cost Control Account. In other words, the various items of cost are collected in the Cost Control Account. Thereafter, a third entry analysis sheet is prepared showing direct and indirect costs of production and these items are then transferred from the Cost Control Account to Work-in-Progress Account. These methods can be explained with the help of the following illustrations:

Illustration 5

The following are some of the transactions taken from an integrated ledger:

	Rs.	Rs.
Materials issued		
Direct	12,800	
Indirect (Production)	1,200	
		14,000
Wages Paid:		
Direct	6,000	
Indirect:		
Production	2,200	
Administration	3,200	
Selling & Distribution	2,400	
		13,800
Expenses Incurred:		
Direct	400	
Production	3,000	
Administration	2,400	
Selling & Distribution	1,200	
		7,000
Prepaid Expenses (Administration)		200
Wages accrued (Production)		20
Depreciation of Plant		400
Overheads recovered:	Rs.	
Production	6,880	
Administration	5,400	
Selling and Distribution	2,520	

Prepare a third-entry analysis sheet and show how the cost control account will appear in the integrated ledger.

Solution

Third Entry Analysis Sheet

Particulars	Production		Administration	Selling and Distribution
	Direct	Indirect		
	Rs.	Rs.	Rs.	Rs.
Materials	12,800	1,200	–	
Wages	6,000	2,200	3,200	2,400
Expenses	400	3,000	2,400	1,200
Wages Accrued	–	20	–	–
Depreciation of Plant	–	400	–	–
	19,200	6,820	5,600	3,600
Less: Prepaid Expenses	–	–	200	–
Cost/Overheads Incurred	19,200	6,820	5,400	3,600
Cost/Overheads Recovered	19.200	6,880	5,400	2,520
Over/(–) under-recovery	–	60	–	(–)1,080

Cost Control Account

Dr. Cr.

		Rs.			Rs.
To Stores Ledger Control A/c:			By Prepaid Expenses A/c (Administration)		200
Direct	12,800		By Work-in-Progress A/c		
Indirect	1,200	14,000	Direct	19,200	
To Bank (Wages)		13,800	Recovered	6,880	26,080
To Bank (Expenses)		7,000	By Finished Stock A/c (Administration Overhead)		5,400
To Wages Accrued A/c		20	By Cost of Sales A/c (Selling and Distribution overhead)		2,520
To Depreciation Provision A/c		400	By Overhead Adjustment A/c (under-recovery)		1,080
To Overhead Adjustment A/c (over-recovery)		60			
		35,280			35,280

When detailed analysis of expenditure concerning a number of departments or cost centres is available, the third entry method is to be preferred to the double entry method; otherwise, the use of double entry system may seem to be satisfactory.

Illustration 6

Bhushan Manufacturing Co. Ltd., had the following balances in its Integrated Ledger on 1st April, 2008:

	Dr Rs.	Cr Rs.
Stores Ledger Control A/c	5,400	
Work-in-Progress Ledger Control A/c	5,100	
Finished Goods Ledger Control A/c	3,900	
Cash at Bank	3,000	
Creditors Control A/c		2,400
Fixed Assets A/c	16,500	
Debtors Control A/c	3,600	
Share Capital A/c		24,000
Depreciation Provision A/c		1,500
Profit and Loss A/c		9,600
	37,500	37,500

Transactions for the year ended 31st March, 2009 were as follows:

	Rs.	Rs.
Wages		
Direct	15,000	
Indirect	2,500	17,500
Materials Purchased on Credit		30,000
Materials issued to:		
Production	30,500	
Repair Order	500	
		31,000
Goods finished during the year, at cost		64,000

Sales (on credit)		89,500
Goods sold during the year at cost		66,500
Production Overhead Recovered		14,500
Administration Expenses Recovered		4,000
Selling and Distribution Expenses Recovered		5,000
Overhead Expenses Incurred (paid by cheque)		
Production	12,000	
Administration	3,600	
Selling and Distribution	5,000	
		20,600
Depreciation (Production) for the period		400
Payment to Creditors		30,300
Payment from Debtors		87,000

You are required to write up the accounts in the Integrated Ledger and take out a Trial Balance on the basis of:

(*a*) Double Entry Method.

(*b*) Third Entry Method.

Solution

Bhushan Manufacturing Co. Ltd.,
Stores Ledger Control Account

	Rs.		Rs.
To Balance b/d	5,400	By Work-in-Progress Ledger Control A/c	30,500
To Creditors Control A/c	30,000	By Production Overhead Control A/c	500
		By Balance c/d	4,400
	35,400		35,400

Work-in-Progress Ledger Control Account

	Rs.		Rs.
To Balance b/d	5,100	By Finished Goods Ledger Control A/c	64,000
To Stores Ledger Control A/c	30,500	By Balance c/d	1,100
To Wages Control A/c	15,000		
To Production Overhead Control A/c	14,500		
	65,100		65,100

Wages Control Account

	Rs.		Rs.
To Bank A/c	17,500	By Work-in-Progress Ledger Control A/c	15,000
		By Production Overhead Control A/c	2,500
	17,500		17,500

Production Overhead Control Account

	Rs.		Rs.
To Stores Ledger Control A/c	500	By Work-in-Progress Ledger Control A/c	14,500
To Wages Control A/c	2,500	By Costing Profit and Loss A/c	900
To Bank A/c	12,000		
To Depreciation Provision A/c	400		
	15,400		15,400

Depreciation Provision Account

	Rs.		Rs.
To Balance c/d	1,900	By Balance b/d	1,500
		By Production Overhead Control A/c	400
	1,900		1,900

Administration Overhead Control Account

	Rs.		Rs.
To Bank A/c	3,600	By Finished Goods Ledger Control A/c	4,000
To Costing Profit and Loss A/c	400		
	4,000		4,000

Selling and Distribution Overhead Control Account

	Rs.		Rs.
To Bank A/c	5,000	By Cost of Sales A/c	5,000
	5,000		5,000

Finished Goods Ledger Control Account

	Rs.		Rs.
To Balance b/d	3,900	By Cost of Sales A/c	66,500
To Work-in-Progress Ledger Control A/c	64,000		
To Administration Overhead Control A/c	4,000	By Balance c/d	5,400
	71,900		71,900

Cost of Sales Account

	Rs.		Rs.
To Finished Goods Ledger Control A/c	66,500	By Sales A/c (transferred)	71,500
To Selling and Distribution Overhead Control A/c	5,000		
	71,500		7 1.500

Sales Account

	Rs.		Rs.
To Cost of Sales A/c	71,500	By Debtors Control A/c	89,500
To Costing Profit and Loss A/c	18,000		
	89,500		89,500

Costing Profit and Loss Account

	Rs.		Rs.
To Production Overhead Control A/c	900	By Sales A/c	18,000
To Net Profit	17,500	By Administration Overhead Control A/c	400
	18,400		18,400

Profit and Loss Account

	Rs.		Rs.
To Balance c/d	27,100	By Balance b/d	9,600
		By Costing Profit and Loss A/c (Net Profit)	17,500
	27,100		27,100

Debtors Control Account

	Rs.		Rs.
To Balance b/d	3,600	By Bank A/c	87,000
To Sales A/c	89,500	By Balance c/d	6,100
	93,100		93,100

Creditors Control Account

	Rs.		Rs.
To Bank A/c	30,300	By Balance b/d	2,400
To Balance c/d	2,100	By Stores Ledger Control A/c	30,000
	32,400		32,400

Bank Account

	Rs.		Rs.
To Balance b/d	3,000	By Wages Control A/c	17,500
To Debtors Control A/c	87,000	By Creditors Control A/c	30,300
		By Production Overhead Control A/c	12,000
		By Administration Overhead Control A/c	3,600
		By Selling and Distribution Overhead Control A/c	5,000
		By Balance c/d	21,600
	90,000		90,000

Fixed Assets Account

	Rs.		Rs.
To Balance b/d	16,500	By Balance c/d	16,500
	16,500		16,500

Share Capital Account

	Rs.		Rs.
To Balance c/d	24,000	By Balance b/d	24,000
	24,000		24,000

Bhushan Manufacturing Company Ltd.
Trial Balance
As on 31st March, 2009

Particulars	Dr. Rs.	Cr. Rs.
Stores Ledger Control Account	4,400	
Work-in-progress Ledger Control Account	1,100	
Finished Goods Ledger Control Account	5,400	
Bank Account	21,600	
Fixed Assets Account	16,500	
Debtors Control Account	6,100	
Creditors Control Account		2,100
Share Capital Account		24,000
Depreciation Provision Account		1,900
Profit & Loss Account		27,100
	55,100	55,100

(b) Third Entry Method:

Stores Ledger Control Account

	Rs.		Rs.
To Balance b/d	5,400	By Cost Ledger Control A/c (Issued to Production)	30,500
To Creditors Control A/c	30,000	By Cost Ledger Control A/c (Issued to Repair Order)	500
		By Balance c/d	4,400
	35,400		35,400

Work-in-Progress Ledger Control A/c

		Rs.		Rs.
To Balance b/d		5,100	By Finished Goods Ledger Control A/c	64,000
To Cost Ledger Control A/c:				
Direct Cost	45,500		By Balance c/d	1,100
Indirect Cost	14,500	60,000		
		65,100		65,100

Bank Account

	Rs.			Rs.
To Balance b/d	3,000	By Cost Ledger Control A/c :		
To Debtors Control A/c	87,000	Direct Wages	15,000	
		Indirect Wages	2,500	
		Production Expenses	12,000	
		Administration Expenses	3,600	
		Selling and Distribution Expenses	5,000	
				38,100
		By Creditors Control A/c		30,300
		By Balance c/d		21,600
	90,000			90,000

Depreciation Provision Account

	Rs.		Rs.
To Balance c/d	1,900	By Balance b/d	1,500
		By Cost Ledger Control Account A/c	400
	1,900		1,900

Cost Ledger Control Account

		Rs.			Rs.
To Bank A/c:			By Work-in-Progress Ledger Control A/c:		
Direct Wages	15,000		Direct Cost	45,500	
Indirect Wages	2,500		Indirect cost	14,500	60,000
Production Expenses	12,000		By Finished goods Ledger Control A/c (Admn. Overhead Recovered)		4,000
Administration Expenses	3,600				
Selling and Distribution Expenses	5,000	38,100	By Cost of Sales Account (Selling and Distribution Overhead recovered)		5,000
To Stores Ledger Control A/c:			By Overhead Adjustment A/c (Under-recovery of Production Overhead)		900
Direct Material	30,500				
Indirect Material	500	31,000			
To Depreciation Provision A/c		400			
To Overhead Adjustment A/c (Over-recovery of Admn. Overhead)		400			
		69,900			69,900

Third Entry Analysis Sheet

Particulars	Production		Administration Overhead	Selling and Distribution Overhead
	Direct	Indirect		
	Rs.	Rs.	Rs.	Rs.
Material	30,500	500	–	–
Wages	15,000	2,500	–	–
Overhead	–	12,000	3,600	5,000
Depreciation	–	400	–	–
Cost/Overhead Incurred	45,500	15,400	3,600	5,000
Cost/Overhead Recovered	45,500	14,500	4,000	5,000
Over/Under- (+) (–) Recovery of Overhead	Nil	(–) 900	(+) 400	Nil

OBJECTIVE TYPE QUESTIONS

A. Multiple Choice Questions:

Select the Correct Answer in each of the following:

(*a*) Which of the following accounts makes the Cost Ledger Self-Balanced:

(*i*) Costing Profit and Loss Account
(*ii*) Stores Ledger Account
(*iii*) Overhead Ledger Account
(*iv*) Cost Ledger Control Account

(*b*) Which of the following is the principal ledger under control accounting:

(*i*) Stores Ledger
(*ii*) Work-in-Progress Ledger
(*iii*) Finished Goods Ledger
(*iv*) Cost Ledger

(*c*) Costing Profit and Loss Account does not record:

(*i*) Balance of Cost of Sales Account:
(*ii*) Balance of Stores Ledger Control Account
(*iii*) Sales value of goods sold
(*iv*) Balance of Overhead Adjustment Account

(*d*) Journal Entry for purchases of materials for stores under cost control accounting system is:

(*i*) Stores Ledger Control Account Dr. To Cost Ledger Control Account
(*ii*) Work-in-Progress Ledger Control Account Dr.
To Cost Ledger Control Account
(*iii*) Cost Ledger Control A/c Dr.
To Stores Ledger Control A/c
(*iv*) Stores Ledger Control A/c Dr.
To Work-in-Progress Ledger Control A/c

(*e*) Journal entry for absorption of factory overhead under Cost Control Accounting System is:

(*i*) Factory Overhead Control Account Dr.
To Cost Ledger Control Account
(*ii*) Cost Ledger Control Account Dr.
To Factory Overhead Control Account
(*iii*) Work-in-Progress Ledger Control Account Dr.
To Factory Overhead Control account
(*iv*) Factory Overhead Control Account Dr.
To Work-in-Progress Ledger Control Account

(*f*) Under Integrated Accounting System, journal entry for payment of wages in cash is:

(*i*) Wages A/c Dr.
To Cash A/c

(*ii*) Wages Control Account Dr.
To Cost Ledger Control Account

(*iii*) Cost Ledger Control Account Dr. To Wages Control Account

(*iv*) Wages Control Account Dr. To Cash Account

(*g*) Journal entry for works overhead incurred in integrated books is:

(*i*) Factory Overhead Account Dr.
To Cash Account

(*ii*) Factory Overhead Control Account Dr.
To Cash Account

(*iii*) Factory Overhead Control Account Dr.
To Cost Ledger Control Account

(*iv*) Cost Ledger Control Account Dr.
To Factory Overhead Control Account

[**Ans.** (*a*) (*iv*), (*b*) (*iv*), (*c*) (*ii*), (*d*) (*i*), (*e*) (*iii*), (*f*) (*iv*), (*g*) (*ii*)]

B. True/False Type Statements

State whether the following statements are true or false:

(*a*) Stock Ledger contains the accounts of all items of finished goods.

(*b*) Cost Control accounts are prepared on the basis of double entry system.

(*c*) The purpose of Cost Control Accounts is to control the cost.

(*d*) Integrated Accounts eliminate the necessity of operating cost ledger control accounts.

(*e*) Under Integrated Accounts, there is no need of reconciliation of cost and financial accounts.

(*f*) Under Integrated Accounts, no accounts are opened for debtors and creditors.

(*g*) Cost Ledger Control Account makes the cost ledger self-balancing.

(*h*) The balance in Costing Profit and Loss Account represents under or over-absorption of overheads.

[**Ans.** (*a*) True, (*b*) True, (*c*) False, (*d*) True, (*e*) True, (*f*) False, (*g*) True, (*h*) False.]

C. Filling the Blank

Fill in the Blanks:

(*a*) Work-in-Progress Ledger contains the accounts of all the .... which are under................... .

(*b*) All the transactions relating to materials are recorded through.............. .

(*c*) The net balance of .... represents net profit or net loss.

(*d*) Under integrated system, the accounting entry for payment of wages is to debit.................. and to credit cash.

(*e*) The two traditional systems of accounting for integration of cost and financial accounts are the .... and ....

[**Ans.** (*a*) Jobs, Execution, (*b*) Stores Ledger Control A/c, (*c*) Costing Profit and Loss A/c, (*d*) Wages Control A/c, (*e*) Double Entry Method, the Third Entry Method]

SHORT ANSWER TYPE QUESTIONS

1. What is Cost Control System?
2. What is Cost Ledger?
3. What is Stores Ledger?
4. What is Stock Ledger?
5. What is Integrated Accounting?

LONG ANSWER TYPE QUESTIONS

1. What do you mean by Cost Control Accounts? Explain the various Cost Control Accounts.
2. What are Control Accounts? Describe their advantages.
   (*Delhi, B.Com.*)
3. What is Integrated Accounting? State its advantages.
4. What do you understand by Integrated Accounts? What are the principles involved? State the advantages of integrated accounts.
   (*C.A. Inter*)

EXERCISES

1. From the following figures ascertained from costing records and financial books of a factory, you are required to pass the necessary entries in the cost journal (Assume that a system of maintaining control accounts prevails in the organisation):

	Rs.
Purchases (stores)	4,00,000
Carriage on Purchases	5,000
Stores Issued	3,80,000
Productive Wages	3,00,000
Unproductive Wages	1,00,000
Works Overhead	3,45,000
Materials used in repairs in the factory	3,000
Cost of finished jobs	11,00,000

(C.A., Inter)

2. From the following figures ascertained from costing records and financial books, you are required to pass necessary entries in Cost Journal (assume that a system of maintaining control accounts prevails in the organisation):

	Rs.
Purchases	78,000
Carriage Inward	1,000
Stores Issued	72,000
Productive Wages	65,000
Unproductive Wages	22,000
Works Oncost	61,000
Materials used in repairs	500
Cost of completed jobs	2,50,000

3. The balances in the Cost Ledger of a manufacturing concern on April 1, 2005 were:

	Rs.	**Rs.**
Stores Ledger Control Account	3,500	
Work-in-Progress Control A/c	6,400	
Finished Stock Ledger Control A/c	1,000	
Cost Ledger Control Account		10,900
	10,900	10,900

The following data are supplied for the year ended 31st March, 2006:

	Rs.
Purchase of materials	20,000
Materials Issued to Production	18,600
Direct Wages	30,000
Manufacturing Expenses	17,300
Selling Expenses	2,700
Manufacturing Expenses Recovered	17,220
Goods Finished	64,870
Selling Expenses Recovered	2,750

Goods Sold at Cost	63,520
Sales	75,500

You are required to show the accounts in the Cost Ledger for the year ended 31st March, 2006, to prepare the Costing Profit and Loss Account and extract a Trial Balance.

[**Ans.** Closing stock of stores Rs. 4,900; Closing stock of work-in-progress Rs. 7,350; Closing stock of Finished Goods Rs. 2,350; Cost of Sales Rs. 66,270; Profit on Sales Rs. 9,230; Costing Profit Rs. 9,200; Total of Trial Balance Rs. 14,600]

4. From the following information gathered from the Cost records of an industrial unit prepare:

(*i*) A Work-in-Progress Control Account,

(*ii*) A Cost of Sales Account and

(*iii*) A Costing Profit and Loss Account.

Opening Balances:	**Rs.**	**Rs.**
Work-in-Progress	3,800	
Materials	22,000	
Finished Stock	17,000	
		42,800
Materials Purchased		58,000
Direct Labour Wages		21,000
Electricity Charges		20,000
Factory Overheads Expenses–Incurred		27,000
Factory Overheads Expenses applied to Production		26,000
Selling, Distribution and Administration Expenses		28,000
Selling, Distribution and Administration Expenses Charged to Finished stock sold.		29,000
Sales		1,86,000
Closing Balances		
Work-in-progress	2,500	
Materials	15,000	
Finished Stock	32,000	
		49,500

[**Ans.** Materials issued to production Rs. 65,000; Profit Rs. 38,700; Total of Cost Ledger Control Rs. 2,35,500]

5. The following balances are given in the Cost Ledger of a manufacturer as on 1st April, 2008:

	Dr. Rs.	Cr. Rs.
Stores Ledger Control Account	25,000	–
Stock Ledger Control Account	35,000	–
Work-in-Progress Ledger Control Account	12,000	–
Works Overheads Control Account	28,000	–
Administration Overheads Control Account	20,000	
Selling and Distribution Overheads Control Account	30,000	–
Cost Ledger Control Account	–	1,50,000
	1,50,000	1,50,000

The following transactions took place during the year ended on 31st March, 2008:

	Rs.
Wages paid	40,000
Direct wages charged to production	25,000
Indirect wages charged to production	10,000
Materials purchased	50,000
Materials issued to production	35,000
Materials issued for repairs	10,000
Materials returned to vendor	5,000
Materials returned to store from production	6,000
Materials lost by fire	8,000
Works Expenses	20,000
Works overhead allocated to production	25,000
Administration Expenses	15,000
Administration Overheads allocated to production	12,000
Goods finished during the year	70,000
Selling and Distribution Expenses	18,000
Selling and Distribution Overheads allocated to production	20,000
Finished goods sold	60,000
Sales	1,00,000

Prepare necessary accounts in Cost Ledger and a trial balance as on 31st March, 2009 from the above transactions.

[**Ans.** Closing Stock of Stores Ledger Rs. 23,000; Closing Stock of W.I.P. Rs. 21,000 Closing Stock of Finished Goods Rs. 57,000; Cost of Sales Rs. 80,000; Profit on Sales Rs. 20,000 Costing Profit Rs. 12,000; Total of T.B. Rs. 2,00,000]

6. Journalise the following transactions assuming that cost and financial accounts are integrated:

Raw Materials purchased	1,20,000
Direct Materials issued to Production	90,000
Wages Paid (30% Indirect)	72,000
Wages charged to Production	50,400
Manufacturing Expenses Incurred	57,000
Manufacturing overheads charged to production	55,200
Selling and Distribution costs	12,000
Finished product at cost	1,20,000
Sales	1,74,000
Receipts from customers	41,400
Paid to creditors	66,000
Closing Stock	Nil

7. The following are some of the transactions of Anu Enterprises Ltd.'s Integrated Ledger:

	Rs.	Rs.
Material Issued:		
Direct	30,800	
Indirect (works)	3,600	34,400
Wages Paid:		
Direct	14,000	
Indirect:		
Production	4,000	
Administration	7,000	
Selling and Distribution	5,000	30,000
Expenses Incurred:		
Direct	1,400	
Indirect:		
Production	5,400	
Administration	4,000	
Selling and Distribution	3,000	13,800
Prepaid Expenses (Administration)	800	
Accrued Wages (Production)	80	
Depreciation of Plant	3,600	
Overheads Recovered:		
Production	Rs. 46,200 (Direct)	Rs. 17,080 (Indirect)
Administration	Rs. 10,200	
Selling and Distribution	Rs. 7,000	

Prepare a third entry analysis sheet and show how the Cost Control Account will appear in the Integrated Ledger.

8. Beta Manufacturing Co. has the following balances in its Integrated Ledger as on 1st April, 2008:

	Dr. Rs.	Cr. RS.
Stores Ledger Control Account	18,000	–
Work-in-Progress Ledger Control A/c	17,000	–
Finished Goods Ledger Control A/c	13,000	–
Cash and Bank	10,000	–
Creditors Control Account	–	8,000
Fixed Assets Account	55,000	–
Debtors Control A/c	12,000	–
Share Capital Account	–	80,000
Depreciation Provision Account	–	5,000
Profit and Loss Account	–	32,000
	1,25,000	1,25,000

Transactions for the year ended 31st March, 2009 were as below:

	Rs.	Rs.
Wages:		
Direct	87,000	
Indirect	5,000	92,000
Material Purchased on Credit		1,00,000
Material Issued to:		
Production	1,10,000	
Repair Orders	2,000	1,12,000
Goods finished during the year at cost		2,15,000
Sales (on credit)		3,00,000
Goods sold during the year at cost		2,20,000
Production Overhead Cost Recovered		48,000
Overhead Expenses Incurred (paid by Cheque):		
Production	40,000	
Administration	12,000	
Selling and Distribution	14,000	66,000
Depreciation (Production) for the year		1,300
Payment to creditors		1,01,000
Payments from customers		2,90,000
Rates Prepaid (Included in works overheads paid)		300

It is the practice of the company to write off Administration Overhead to Profit & Loss Account.

You are required to write up the accounts in the Integrated Ledger and take out a Trial Balance when the system of accounting is:

(1) The Double Entry Method.

(2) The Third Entry Method.

25

Uniform Costing and Inter-firm Comparison

MEANING OF UNIFORM COSTING

Uniform costing is not a separate method of costing like job costing or process costing. It is a technique of uniform application of the principles of a costing method agreed upon and adopted by all or majority of the undertakings in a particular line of industry. The Institute of Cost and Management Accountants, U.K., has defined Uniform Costing as "the use by several undertakings of the same costing principles and/or practices." Thus, uniform costing is a system of costing under which several units of the same industry adopt the common principles and procedures of costing. Normally the principles and methods adopted for compilation, analysis, apportionment and absorption of overhead differ from one undertaking to the other in the same industry, but the adoption of a common or uniform pattern by different units in the industry facilitates comparison of cost, cost control and cost reduction.

Objects of Uniform Costing:

The main objects of uniform costing are:

(*i*) To provide reliable data for making inter-unit comparisons of cost performances;

(*ii*) To assist the comparison of cost of production and production efficiencies of different units of the industry;

(*iii*) To eliminate unhealthy competition among the different units of an industry;

(*iv*) To ensure that the product prices are common and based on authentic data;

(*v*) To determine a common policy for the various units of an industry on the basis of cost data of each unit;

(*vi*) To maintain and stabilise demand for the products of an industry by exercising proper control on production;

(*vii*) To encourage exchange of ideas among different units in the industry;

(*viii*) To encourage and extend the areas of research and development in matters concerning production and sales;

(*ix*) To improve production capacity and labour efficiency;

(*x*) To control costs and set up Standards common to different units;

(*xi*) To regulate production, administration, selling and distribution costs and to exercise control on fixed costs;

(*xii*) To ensure reasonable price to customers and profit to manufacturers.

Requisites for Installation of Uniform Costing:

The main requisites for installation of uniform costing are as follows:

1. **Mutual Relationship:** There should be mutual trust, confidence and co-operation among all the member units participating in the plan of uniform costing. There should be free exchange of ideas among the member units. Large sized manufacturing concerns should help the small sized concerns by passing on their knowledge regarding achievements, innovations, improvements etc. Under uniform costing, there is no place for the sense of competition among the member units.
2. **Levelling of Costing Systems:** Normally, the manufacturing units before joining the uniform costing plan, might be having different cost structures. The difference in cost structure may arise due to difference in size of units, their organisational structure, methods of production, methods of costing, techniques of costing etc. Uniform costing plan requires the elimination of differences in cost structure and promoting common-ness. For this purpose, it is necessary that member units should be placed in different categories (on the basis of their size, organisational structure and methods of production)and should be made to adopt different uniform costing systems suitable to their respective categories. For this purpose, a Uniform Cost Manual may be prepared for the guidance of member units.
3. **Points of Uniformity:** In installing the uniform costing system for an industry, uniformity should be introduced both in the methods of measuring production and of collecting the costs. This will require laying down the principles and practices to be followed in respect of the following:
   (*i*) The stages at which the production should be measured, particularly in case of industries following process costing.
   (*ii*) Determination of the cost unit or the method of measuring output.
   (*iii*) Determination of cost centre.
   (*iv*) Classification and grouping of expenses under each element of cost.
   (*v*) The source document or records from which the expenses should be collected and the time intervals at which they should be accumulated.

(*vi*) The principle to be applied in making distinction between direct material and indirect material, direct labour and indirect labour.
(*vii*) Method and technique of costing.
(*viii*) Basis for the allocation, apportionment and absorption of overhead.
(*ix*) Basis for distribution of service department cost to production departments.
(*x*) Determination of the method and rate of depreciation.
(*xi*) Items to be excluded from costs.
(*xii*) Treatment of defective work, spoilage, waste, overtime, fringe benefits, etc.
(*xiii*) Method for the pricing out of materials.
(*xiv*) Method for the valuation of stock.
(*xv*) Notional expenses to be considered.
(*xvi*) Recording of cost data and presentation of information.

Uniform Cost Manual:

Uniform Cost Manual is a document which contains detailed instructions to be followed by different units of an industry adopting uniform costing for the purpose of determining and controlling costs. It is a formal document defining the recommended cost plans, policies and other relevant matters necessary for the effective operation of uniform costing system. The uniform cost manual helps the member units in verifying the adherence to uniform costing plan and correctness of the steps taken by them to achieve uniformity.

Applicability of Uniform Costing:

Uniform costing can be applied in the following types of undertakings:

(*a*) **Undertakings Manufacturing Identical Products:** The manufacturing concerns producing identical products or commodities can adopt uniform costing since the nature of their business is the same.

(*b*) **Undertakings Carrying on Similar Operations:** The business concerns engaged in providing similar type of service or facility e.g., transport undertakings, gas companies, electricity companies etc., can adopt uniform costing technique.

(*c*) **Members of the Same Trade Association:** The business concerns engaged in the same industry, although not manufacturing identical products, enjoying the membership of the same trade association, may adopt uniform costing. It will enable them to study the cost structure and getting fixed reasonable prices for their products and services.

Advantages of Uniform Costing:

The main advantages of uniform costing are as follows:

(*i*) Uniform costing helps in the installation of an ideal costing system.

(*ii*) Standard norms of operations are set for the industry as a whole. Every member unit can evaluate its performance against these standard norms and strive for betterment.

(iii) It helps in eliminating cut throat competition in the line of industry and ensures stability.

(*iv*) Small sized undertakings can enjoy the benefits of research and development programmes carried on by large sized undertakings since relevant information is passed on by the latter to the former.

(*v*) It creates cost consciousness among the member units and thus leads to economy and efficiency.

(*vi*) It assists in making effective cost control.

(*vii*) It provides a suitable basis for making inter-firm comparison.

(*viii*) Prices based on uniform costing are reliable from the view point of customers. It helps in improving relationship between industry and customers.

(*ix*) Uniform costing, by making available reliable cost data for the industry as a whole, guides the Government in making suitable State Policy.

(*x*) Uniform Costing technique also assists the Wage Boards in fixing minimum wages and fair wages for the workers of the industry.

Disadvantages of Uniform Costing:

Uniform costing technique has the following limitations:

(*i*) This technique assumes that all the undertakings in the industry are identical, which is not possible.

(*ii*) Uniform costing system requires the adoption of a common basis of allocation and apportionment of costs. It is very difficult to find out a common basis of allocation and apportionment of costs.

(*iii*) Uniform costing involves the mutual exchange of information among member units. Sometimes, the member units may not provide secret information and data to the common pool. Thus, mutual trust among member units may be missing after some time.

(*iv*) The installation of uniform costing system is quite expensive and the medium and small sized units are not in a position to adopt it.

(*v*) Uniform costing encourages monopolistic trend in the industry. Monopolistic trends have their own economic and social evils.

Inter-firm Comparison:

Inter-firm comparison refers to a technique of comparing the costs and profits of different firms or units in an industry which have joined to exchange information on a voluntary basis for their mutual benefit. It involves the comparison of the results of the different firms *inter se* so that efficiencies and inefficiencies may be located and profitability may be judged. Thus, it is a type of standard used for performance evaluation and cost-benefit-analysis. For the purpose of inter-firm comparison, data regarding cost, prices, profits etc., of different undertakings are put in the form of consolidated statements and are provided to all the member units so that they can make a comparative assessment of their achievements and weaknesses with those of others. This comparison is possible only if the various undertakings have been using uniform costing. Thus, inter-firm comparison is based on uniform costing.

Objects of Inter-firm Comparison:

The main objectives of inter-firm comparison may be given as follows:

(*i*) **To Improve Efficiency:** Inter-firm comparison enables each member unit to improve its efficiency after knowing its weaknesses and inefficiencies through comparison of its performance with other member firms.

(*ii*) **To Affect Economy:** Inter-firm comparison aims at affecting economy by locating the inefficiencies or weaknesses and eliminating them.

(*iii*) **To Maximise Profitability:** Inter-firm comparison also aims at improving profitability through the measurement of adequacy of profits.

Requirements of Inter-firm Comparison:

The success of inter-firm comparison basically depends on the efficient operation of uniform costing system which requires uniformity in costing principles and procedures. The implementation of inter-firm comparison scheme must take into consideration the following points:

1. **Central Organisation:** A Central Organisation is required for the collection and analysis of data, provided by the member units, for making a comparative study and for the dissemination of the results of study. For this purpose a trade association may be formed. Sometimes, these functions may be performed by a holding company.
2. **Nature of Information to be collected:** The nature and extent of the information to be collected shall depend on the needs of the management, comparative value of the information and the efficiency of the Central Organisation responsible for the collection of data. Although no standard list of information to be collected can be given, the following are the general matters on which information may be collected:

   (*i*) Costs and cost structure

   (*ii*) Consumption of raw materials.

   (*iii*) Wastage of raw materials.

   (*iv*) Methods and techniques employed in production.

   (*v*) Labour utilisation and labour efficiency.

   (*vi*) Machine utilisation and machine efficiency.

   (*vii*) Capital Employed and Return on Capital Employed.

   (*viii*) Liquidity of the Organisation.

   (*ix*) Reserves and Appropriation of Profits.

   (*x*) Accounts Receivable and Accounts Payable.

3. **Collection and Presentation of Information:** The responsibility for collection and presentation of information lies with the Central Organisation. It collects information from members at fixed intervals in the prescribed form. Information may also be collected through questionnaire sent to the members. Since much of the information relates to the final accounts of the member units, collection of information is done at the end of the accounting year when final accounts are prepared. The data collected are edited, classified and presented in a consolidated form for use strictly by member units only. The information regarding profitability, efficiency and productivity etc., is presented in the consolidated report in the form of ratios and not absolute figures. The report also includes standards and variances to enable the assessment of individual performance by the members.

Advantages of Inter-firm Comparison:

Inter-firm comparison is considered to be the part of uniform costing, giving to the member units all the advantages of uniform costing. The specific advantages of inter-firm comparison can be given as follows:

(*i*) Inter-firm comparison provides an overall view of the industry as a whole to its members. The Central Organisation provides information regarding present position, progress made and future prospects of the industry enabling the member units to plan accordingly.

(*ii*) A firm can know the points of efficiencies and inefficiencies in relation to other firms through inter-firm comparison and can take steps to improve in respect of the points of its weaknesses. It helps the management in controlling costs.

(*iii*) Inter-firm comparison enables the member units to maintain secrecy. All the firms are known by their code numbers (and not by their specific names) and the data are presented in the form of ratios. As such a firm knowing its code number can easily ascertain its position in relation to other firms.

(*iv*) Expert know-how and guidance of the Central Organisation is made available to the member units through its reports, magazines and journals etc. It also makes available to the members the information relating to the results of research conducted by it in various fields of the industry which can be used for the development of the member units.

(*v*) Inter-firm comparison is helpful in avoiding cut-throat competition among the member units.

(*vi*) It is helpful in improving the quality and quantity of output and in reducing the cost of production which ultimately benefits both the industry and the society.

Limitations of Inter-firm Comparison:

Inter-firm comparison system has the following limitations:

(*i*) If the data for the purpose of inter-firm comparison are not properly collected, the conclusions drawn by the Central Organisation and the member units would be misleading. Right decisions cannot be taken on the basis of such conclusions.

(*ii*) The member units, sometimes, hesitate to supply such data which are considered secret. The misleading information supplied by them may not be useful for the inter-firm comparison.

(*iii*) Difference in the nature and size of the member units may make the operation of inter-firm comparison difficult.

(iv) In the absence of a Central Organisation, the scheme of inter-firm comparison cannot be operated properly.

OBJECTIVE TYPE QUESTIONS

1. Select the correct alternative in the given statements:

(*i*) Uniform costing is a

(*a*) System of costing.

(*b*) Technique of costing.

(*c*) Method of costing.

(*ii*) Uniform costing

(a) Does not remove cut throat competition among the member units.

(*b*) Removes cut throat competition and develops healthy competition among member units.

(*iii*) Inter-firm comparison can be made

(*a*) Without following uniform costing.

(*b*) By adopting uniform costing only.

(*c*) By following any other method of costing.

[**Ans.** (*i*) (*a*) (*ii*) (*b*) (*iii*) (*b*)]

2. Which of the following statements are True/ False.

(*i*) The main objective of uniform costing is to maximise profits.

(*ii*) Uniform costing may lead to monopolistic conditions within the industry leading to increase in prices and customers may suffer.

(*iii*) The success of uniform costing depends upon the mutual confidence and trust among the participating members.

(*iv*) Uniform costing does not help free exchange of ideas among the participating members.

(*v*) Uniform cost manual is a booklet or formal document which lays down detailed instructions with regard to cost principles, plans and procedures to be followed.

[**Ans.** (*i*) True, (*ii*) True, (*iii*) True, (*iv*) False, (*v*) True.]

3. Fill in the blanks by appropriate words

(*i*) The system of uniform costing can be applied successfully only when two or more units want to follow the same ....

(*ii*) By adopting uniform costing techniques, free exchange of information leads to considerable cost reduction and .... of the product.

(*iii*) The success of uniform costing depends upon mutual .... and......... among the participating members.

(*iv*) Inter-firm comparison depends upon successful implementation of ....

(*v*) Inter-firm comparison creates .... among the participating firms and they are cautious in respect of all the levels of management.

[**Ans.** (*i*) costing principles & practices, (*ii*) Improvement in the quality (*iii*) Trust, confidence (*iv*) Uniform costing system (*v*) Cost consciousness.]

SHORT ANSWER TYPE QUESIONS

1. What is meant by the term uniform costing?
2. What is meant by the term Inter-firm comparison?
3. What is meant by uniform cost manual?
4. What are the objectives of 'inter-firm comparison'?

LONG ANSWER TYPE QUESTIONS

1. Define the term 'uniform costing'. Give its advantages and limitations.
2. What are the pre-requisites to be considered while introducing the system of uniform costing in an industry?
3. What is uniform cost accounting system? What are the items on which you would seek uniformity so far as overheads are concerned in uniform cost accounting system.
4. What do you mean by inter-firm comparison? Give its advantages and limitations.
5. "A scheme of inter-firm comparison combines the advantages of a uniform costing system and benefits arising out of the use of ratios". Discuss.

6. You have been retained to advise on the introduction of a system of inter-firm comparison for a number of units in an industry. What are the essential points you would take care of to start with? Design your answer under the following heads:
   (*a*) The nature and extent of information to be collected.
   (*b*) The organisation to be set up for this purpose.
   (*c*) The method of collection, analysis and presentation of information.
7. Discuss the scope and application of uniform costing methods and their usefulness especially in the context of the economy of our country. Assume that you are advising a Trade Association in this regard in the interest of its member firms and outline your views and suggestions.

26

Cost Audit

MEANING

'Audit' may be described as a systematic examination of the books, vouchers and records of a business to enable the auditor to satisfy himself and to report whether the accounts thereof are properly drawn up so as to exhibit a true and fair view of the state of affairs of the business. Initially, the scope of audit was limited to the verification of the transactions of financial nature but in the recent times, it has been extended to other fields also. Cost audit is one of them. Cost audit is concerned with the verification of the correctness of the cost records or cost accounts maintained in a business concern.

The Institute of Cost & Works Accountants of India defines 'cost audit' as "an audit of efficiency of minute details of expenditure while the work is in progress and not a post-mortem examination .... Financial audit is a 'fait accompli'. Cost Audit is mainly a preventive measure, a guide for management policy and decision, in addition to being a barometer of performance". The Institute of Cost and Management Accountants, U.K., has defined 'Cost Audit' as "the verification of the correctness of cost accounts and a check on the adherence to the cost accounting plan". According to Smith and Day ..."By the term 'Cost-Audit' is meant the detailed checking of the costing system, techniques and accounts to verify their correctness and to ensure adherence to the objective of cost accounting". In the words of R.W. Dobson ... "Cost Audit is the verification of the correctness of cost accounts and of the adherence to the cost accountancy plans".

On the basis of the analysis of the above definitions, it can be said that cost audit is the detailed checking as well as the verification of the correctness of costing techniques, systems and cost accounts. In any manufacturing concern or in a service organisation, it is generally felt necessary to compute the correct cost of products or services so as to charge the customers correctly. For this purpose, cost accounts or costing records are maintained. But, only the maintenance of cost accounts is not sufficient. In order to ascertain the true and accurate cost of products and services, it is necessary to ensure that these records are accurate and correct. As such there is a need to get the costing records properly audited and checked by a properly qualified and trained professional.

OBJECTS OF COST AUDIT

The main objects of cost audit are:

(*i*) To verify that the cost accounting records (or costing books) are accurate.

(*ii*) To certify that costing principles have been fully adhered to in maintaining cost accounts.

(*iii*) To find out whether the pre-determined cost accounting procedures and processes have been strictly followed by the management.

(*iv*) To detect errors and frauds, which might have been committed intentionally or otherwise in preparing cost accounts.

(*v*) To check whether each item of expenditure involved into the relevant components of goods manufactured has been properly incurred.

(*vi*) To see how far the existing practices of cost records are helpful for the management to take decisions.

(*vii*) To disclose the deficiencies or inefficiencies in the use of material, labour and machines with a view to assist the management.

(*viii*) To assist the external auditor in conducting detailed checking by reducing the volume of audit work through the use of internal cost audit system.

(*ix*) To exercise moral check on the cost accounting staff and to attain efficiency in cost accounting systems and procedures.

SCOPE OF COST AUDIT

The scope of audit has two important aspects viz.,

(*i*) Propriety Audit.

(*ii*) Efficiency Audit.

Propriety Audit: This aspect of audit is concerned with actions and plans of management which affect the finance and expenditure of the business concern. Under this aspect, the cost auditor is required to ensure that an item of expenditure is sanctioned or approved by the proper authority. It is done with the help of documents and vouchers. In addition, the cost auditor has to ensure that the item of expenditure is proper and reasonable on the grounds of propriety. Thus, the cost auditor has to report:

(*a*) Whether or not the planned expenditure could give optimum results.

(*b*) Whether or not the size or channels of investment were designed to produce the best results.

(*c*) Whether the return from investment in certain channels could be bettered by some alternative plan of action.

Efficiency Audit : This aspect of cost audit is concerned with the evaluation of performances. It covers the verification of the facts that the expenditure has been incurred according to the plan and the results obtained have also been according to the plan. It covers the examination of the plan prepared in the form of budgets (financial and functional) and the comparison of the actual performance with the budgeted performance and analysing the reasons for variances. Thus, efficiency audit ensures that:

(*a*) every rupee invested in capital or in other fields gives the optimum return; and

(*b*) investment in different spheres of the business has been so balanced that it gives maximum results.

Therefore, the cost auditor plays the role both as consultant and financial adviser. He assists the Chief Executive of the business concern in judging the soundness of the financial plans and performances by co-ordinating the results of actions of heads of various departments.

DISTINCTION BETWEEN COST AUDIT AND FINANCIAL AUDIT

It is difficult to make a distinction between cost audit and financial audit from the practical point of view though in principle the difference does exist. The main points of distinction between cost audit and financial audit may be summarised as follows:

1. Audit of the financial accounts is compulsory under the provisions of the Companies Act while cost audit is not compulsory except in the case of companies carrying on manufacturing or mining business which have been specifically required to maintain cost accounts under Section 209 (1) (d) and get them audited under Section 233.
2. The main object of the financial audit is to see whether the accounts of the business have been properly maintained and whether the Profit and Loss Account and Balance Sheet exhibit a true and fair position of the state of affairs while in case of cost audit the auditor has to examine whether the expenditure involved has been wisely incurred or not and to find out the cost of manufacture of each unit of articles.
3. In case of financial audit, the auditor has to examine the financial accounts such as capital, debtors, creditors, assets, liabilities, expenses and income etc., and he does not go into the details of cost records but the cost auditor has to go into the details of cost records to detect errors and manipulation in cost accounts.
4. In respect of closing stock, the financial auditor has to see whether it has been correctly valued for the purpose of inclusion in Balance Sheet while the cost auditor has to see whether the stock is excessive or otherwise keeping in view the needs of the manufacturing concern.

5. In case of financial audit, the auditor examines the financial aspect of accounts while the cost auditor is concerned with the cost aspect of accounts.
6. The financial auditor has to certify the arithmetical accuracy of the transactions in proper books of accounts relating to cash receipts and payments, purchases and sales and assets and liabilities while the cost auditor has to certify the facts relating to the utilisation of material, labour and other services.

FUNCTIONS AND AREAS OF COST AUDIT

The functions and areas of cost audit as given in the booklet named "Cost Audit, its Significance" issued by the Institute of Cost and Works Accountants of India may be summarised as follows:

(*i*) Inventory

The Cost Auditor will examine, *inter alia,* the following:

(*a*) Is the size of inventory adequate or excessive compared with the production programme?
(*b*) Is the provisioning drill most economical?
(*c*) Does it ensure optimum order size?
(*d*) Does it take into account the storage cost on the one hand, and carrying cost on the other?
(*e*) Does it take note of lead-time of the various items or group of items?
(*f*) Does the receipt and issue system cause any bottleneck in production?
(*g*) Does it involve too many forms and too much paper work?
(*h*) Is there any room for reduction of inventory cost consistent with production needs?
(*i*) Is there inventory as per the priced store ledger and as certified by the management physically correct?
(*j*) Is the same amount of attention and care given to moneys translated into material things like raw materials, stores and supplies of all kinds as is given to liquid cash?
(*k*) Does the issue of raw materials make the production in accordance with the standard or schedule or otherwise, or covered by authorised schedule?
(*l*) Is the expenditure of consumable stores within the standard? If not, why not?

(*ii*) Opening and Closing Stock

(1) The Cost Auditor will see, *inter alia,* the following:
    (*a*) that the opening stock is not unduly large compared with the volume of production during the year;

(*b*) that the opening stock against various jobs does really represent the actual physical stock in the production shop and is not merely an accounting figure;

(*c*) that the responsibility of the Shop-Foreman-in-charge of the stock held in the production shop is clear and properly documented; that he maintains proper record of actual consumption vis-a-vis the actual withdrawal from the stock.

2. Valuation and correct indication of closing stock in the Trading and Profit and Loss Account and in Balance Sheet is important. The Cost Auditor will examine and certify, *inter alia,*

(*a*) that the physical verification is correctly carried out;

(*b*) that the valuation is correct with reference to the actual cost of production and recognised policy for valuation;

(*c*) that the volume of closing stock is commensurate with the volume of production and that it does not reflect any failure or bottleneck in Sales Budget or Production Budget;

(*d*) that the volume of unmoved stores is not abnormal in comparison with the normal rate of yearly consumption. The Cost Auditor will recommend disposal of such unmoved stores with consequent release of capital unnecessarily locked up to the advantage of the financial resources of the concern.

(*iii*) Stores Issue Procedure

The Cost Auditor will see, *inter alia*:

(*a*) that withdrawal of materials from stores by production shop is scientific or covered by authorised schedule and permits receipts to be located;

(*b*) that there is no possibility of loss or pilferage of stock lying in the production sections;

(*c*) that surplus materials and scraps arising in production shops are returned to stores correctly and without delay for which necessary credit is given to unit cost of production. If transferred to other jobs, proper transfer voucher has been prepared and copies sent to the accounts, stores, etc.

(*iv*) Work-in-Progress

The Cost Auditor will ensure, *inter alia*, the following:

(*a*) that the Work-in-Progress has been physically verified and that it agrees with the balance in the incomplete cost cards;

(*b*) that the valuation of the Work-in-Progress is correct with reference to the stage of completion of each job or process and the value booked in the job cost cards or process cost sheet;

(*c*) that there is no over-valuation or under-valuation of opening or closing Work-in-Progress, thereby artificially pushing up or down net profits or net assets as the case may be;

(*d*) that the volume and value of Work-in-Progress is not disproportionate compared with the finished out-turn.

(*v*) Labour

(*a*) Proper utilisation of labour and increase in productivity are now receiving greater attention. Several productivity teams have emphasised great importance of higher productivity. It is, therefore, essential to assess performance efficiency of labour and compare it with the standard performance, so that labour utilisation could be progressively improved. Labour force in Indian industries is generally very high compared to similar types of industries in other developed countries. Our aim should be to reach that level, though necessarily not immediately but over a period. A study of this nature would give an idea where inefficiency lies so that timely and adequate steps could be taken to ensure maximum utilisation of labour and to reduce labour cost.

(*b*) Cost of labour is allocated to different jobs with reference to time or job cards.

(*vi*) Capacity Utilisation

The Cost Auditor will see, *inter alia*,

(*a*) that the idle capacity in any production shop or of transport facilities for distribution is not excessive;

(*b*) that production volume and overall machine time utilised are commensurate. In other words, the machine hours utilised have given the optimum out-turn.

(*vii*) Overheads

The Cost Auditor will see and certify, *inter alia*,

(*a*) that allocation of indirect expenditure over production, sales, and distribution is logical and correct;

(*b*) that compared with the volume of production in a production shop, the overhead charges are not excessive:

(*c*) that the actual indirect expenditure does not exceed budgets or standard expenditure significantly and that any variations are satisfactorily explained and accounted for;

(*d*) that the relation of indirect expenditure in keeping with the load on individual production shop is appropriate;

(*e*) that allocation of overheads between finished and unfinished products is in accordance with correct costing principles.

Capital Expenditure

The Cost Auditor will see and certify:

(*a*) that the purchase of new plant and machinery is duly authorised;

(*b*) that the capital expenditure has been regularly collected;

(*c*) that the actual progress of capital expenditure is according to the budget
(*d*) that the capital expenditure is profitable; and
(*e*) that the fixed assets and proper maintenance of plant records have been physically verified.

TYPES OF COST AUDIT

The following are the different types of cost audit:

1. **Cost Audit on behalf of Management:** Cost audit on behalf of management is a part of general internal control measure. Depending on the size of the organisation and the importance of cost accounts a separate Cost Audit Department is set up to ensure that the costing records are accurate and compiled correctly to facilitate cost ascertainment and cost control and to ascertain whether the cost procedures and routines *i.e.,* pricing of stores, allocation of overhead expenses etc., are being uniformly followed.
2. **Cost Audit on Behalf of a Customer:** Sometimes the contracts and orders are placed on 'Cost-Plus' basis. In such a case the price is based on cost plus an agreed margin of profit. The customer, in such a case, may get the cost accounts audited in order to establish the accuracy of cost.
3. **Cost Audit on behalf of Labour Tribunals:** Sometimes a Labour Tribunal may get the cost accounts of a manufacturing concern audited for deciding labour's claim for higher wages, bonus and share in profits, etc.
4. **Cost Audit on behalf of Government:** Government may get the cost accounts of a manufacturing concern audited for the following reasons:
   (*i*) for fixing fair prices of some commodities so as to prevent over profiteering;
   (*ii*) for providing protection to certain industries;
   (*iii*) for fixing the price of cost plus contracts given to private contractors.
5. **Cost Audit Under the Companies Act:** Under the Companies (Amendment) Act, 1965, two new amendments have been added to the Companies Act, 1956 in this respect, *i.e.,* Clause (*d*) to Sub-Sec. (1) of Secs. 209 and 233 B to Sec. 233 which have provided for the audit of Cost Accounts in certain cases. Section 209 (1) (*d*) provides that every company shall keep at its registered office proper books of accounts with respect to–

In the case of a company pertaining to any class of companies engaged in production, processing, manufacturing or mining activities, such particulars relating to utilisation of materials or labour or as to other items of cost as may be prescribed, if such class of companies is required by the Central Government to include such particulars in the books of account.

It would be observed that the cost audit can be ordered in case of those companies which are required to maintain Cost Accounts[1] under Sec. 209 (1) (*d*) cited above and which are engaged in production, processing, manufacturing or mining activities. More and more companies are now asked under Sec. 233B to get their Cost Accounts audited.

The Classes of Companies which are required to maintain cost records under section 209 (1) (*d*) of the Companies Act, 1956 are as follows:

S. No.	**Class of Companies**
1.	Cement
2.	Cycles
3.	Rubber tyres & tubes
4.	Caustic soda
5.	Room Air Conditioner
6.	Refrigerators
7.	Automobile Batteries
8.	Electric Lamps
9.	Electric Fans
10.	Electric Motors
11.	Motor Vehicles
12.	Tractors
13.	Aluminium
14.	Vanaspati
15.	Bulk Drugs
16.	Sugar
17.	Infant Milk Food
18.	Industrial Alcohol
19.	Jute Goods
20.	Paper
21.	Rayon
22.	Dyes
23.	Soda Ash
24.	Nylon
25.	Polyester
26.	Cotton Textiles
27.	Dry Battery Cell

1. The General Government in exercise of the powers conferred by Sub-Sec (1) of Sec. 642 read with clause (*b*) of Sub-Sec. (1) of Sec. 209 of the Companies Act, 1956 (1 of 1956), makes cost accounting record rules to bring about uniformity in the maintenance of Cost Accounts by companies to which such rules apply. Recently, the Central Government has made Cost Accounting Records (Dyes) Rules, 1976 (Vide Notification G.S.R. No. 605, dated 22nd April, 1976) and Cost Accounting Records (Rayon) Rules, 1976 (Vide Notification G.S.R. No. 606, dated 20th April, 1976) which have come into force on Ist May, 1976.

The Central Government has issued cost accounting records rules under Sec. 233 (*b*) and 209 (1) (*d*) for 35 industries so far (G.S.R. No. 909 (E) Dt. 7.9.88).

28. Sulphuric Acid
29. Steel Tubes & Pipes
30. Engineering Industries
    (*i*) Power driven pumps
    (*ii*) Diesel engines/Internal Combustion Engines
31. Electric cables & conductors
32. Bearings
33. Milk Food
34. Chemical Industries:
    (1) Ethylene
    (2) Ethylene Oxide
    (3) Ethylene Glycol
    (4) Diethylene Glycol
    (5) Polyethylene Glycol
    (6) Ethylene Dichloride
    (7) Propylene
    (8) Isopropanal
    (9) Acetone.
    (10) Diacetene Alcohol
    (11) Methyl Isobutyl Ketone
    (12) Butanol
    (13) Ethyl Hexanol
    (14) Butadiene
    (15) Benzene
    (16) Toluene
    (17) Synthetic Resins
35. Formulations.

(G.S.R. No. 909 (E) Dt. 7.9.88)

Where, in the opinion of the Central Government it is necessary so to do in relation to any company required under clause (*a*) of Sub-Sec (1) of Sec. 209 to include in its books of account the particulars referred to therein, the Central Government may, by order, direct that an audit of Cost Accounts of the company shall be conducted in such manner as may be specified in the order, by an auditor who shall be a Cost Accountant within the meaning of the Cost and Works Accountants Act, 1959. Provided that if the Central Government is of opinion that sufficient number of Cost Accountants within the meaning of the Cost and Works Accountants Act, 1959, are not available for conducting the audit of Cost Accounts of companies generally, that Government may, by notification in the Official Gazette, direct that, for such period as may be specified in the said notification, such Chartered Accountant within the meaning of the Chartered Accountants Act, 1949, as possesses the specified Qualifications, may also conduct the audit of the Cost Accounts of Companies and thereupon a Chartered Accountant possessing the prescribed qualifications may be appointed to audit the Cost Accounts of the company.

(Sec. 233 (B) (1)).

Appointment: An auditor under this Section shall be appointed by the Board of Directors of the Company in accordance with the provisions in sub-section (1B) of section 224 and with the previous approval of the Central Government.

(Sec. 233 (B) (2)).

Provided that before the appointment of any auditor is made by the Board, a written certificate shall be obtained by the Board from the auditor proposed to be so appointed to the effect that the appointment, if made, will be in accordance with the provisions of sub-section (1B) of section 224.

A firm of Cost Accountants can also be appointed as Cost Auditors now, if all the partners of the firm are practising as Cost Accountants and such a firm is constituted with the previous approval of the Central Government as required under Regulations of the Cost and Works Accountants Act, 1959.[2] The cost audit report shall be signed in such a case by any one of the partners for and on behalf of firm.

Additional Audit: An audit conducted by an auditor under this section shall be in addition to an audit conducted by an auditor appointed under Sec. 224.

(Sec. 233 (B) (3).)

Powers and Duties: An auditor shall have the same powers and duties in relation to an audit conducted bv him under this Section as an auditor of a company has under Sub-Sec (1) of Sec. 227 and such auditor shall make his report in triplicate[3] to the Central Government in such form and within such time as may be prescribed and shall also at the same time forward a copy of the report to the company.

(Sec. 233 (B) (4).)

Disqualifications: A person referred to in Sub-Sec. (3) or Sub-Sec. (4) of Sec. 226 shall not be appointed or re-appointed for conducting the audit of the cost accounts of a company.

(Sec. 233 (B) (5 a).)

A person appointed under Sec. 224, as an auditor of a company, shall not be appointed or re-appointed for conducting the audit of the cost accounts of that company.

(Sec. 233 (B) (5 b).)

If a person appointed for conducting the audit of Cost Accounts of company, becomes subject, after his appointment, to any of the disqualifications specified in clause (*a*) or clause (*b*) of this Sub-Sec., he shall on and from the date on which he becomes so subject, cease to conduct the audit of the Cost Accounts of the company.

Other Provisions

Upon receipt of an order under Sub-Sec. (1), it shall be the duty of the company to give all facilities and assistance to the person appointed for conducting the audit of the cost accounts of the company.

(Sec. 233 (B) (6).)

2. Letter No. 54/409/80 C.A.B. dated 19.11.83, Department of Company Affairs.
3. Notification No. G.S.R. 681 dated 3.8.82.

The company shall, within thirty days from the date of receipt of a copy of the report referred to in Sub-Sec. (4), furnish the Central Government with full information and explanations on every reservation or qualification contained in such report.

(Sec. 233 (B) (7).)

If, after considering the report referred to in Sub-Sec. (4) and the information and explanations furnished by the company under Sub-Sec. (7), the Central Government is of the opinion that any further information or explanation is necessary, the Government may call for such further information and explanation and thereupon the company shall furnish the same within such time as may be specified by that Government.

Sec. 233 (B) (8).)

On receipt of the report referred to in Sub-Sec. (4) and the information and explanations furnished by the company under Sub-Sec. (7) and Sub-Sec. (8) the Central Government may take such action on the report in accordance with the provisions of this Act or any other law for the time being in force, as it may consider necessary.

The Central Government may direct the company whose Cost Accounts have been audited under this Section to circulate to its members alongwith notice of the Annual General Meeting to be held for the first time after submission of such report, the whole or such portion of the said report as it may specify in this behalf.

(Sec. 233 (B) (10).)

If default is made in complying with the provisions of this section the company shall be liable to be punished with fine which may extend to fifty thousand rupees, and any officer of the company who is in default shall be liable to be punished with imprisonment for a term which may extend to three years, or with fine which may extend to fifty thousand rupees, or with both.

(Sec. 233 (B) (11).)

COST AUDIT REPORT

The Central Government has made the Cost Audit (Report) Rules, 1968 (subsequently amended in 1969 and 1971) which provide for the form of report and the time limit for submission of the report. These rules have been framed for the audit of accounts of companies producing cycles, cement, caustic soda, rubber tyres, etc. The Cost Auditor is expected to examine these rules for general guidance before he undertakes audit of such industries.

Under the Cost Audit (Report) Rules, 1968, (subsequently amended in 1969, 1971 and 1982) every auditor (hereinafter called the Cost Auditor) who conducts an audit of the cost accounting records of the company shall make a report to the Central Government in the form and in accordance with the procedure laid down in the Schedule annexed to these rules and at same time forward a copy of the report to the company within 120 days from the end of company's financial year to which the Cost Audit Report relates. To facilitate the cost audit, the company and every officer thereof have to make available to him within 90 days from the end of the financial year of the company, cost accounting records, Cost Statements and other books and papers that would be required for conducting the cost audit.

Since the time limit beyond 120 days cannot be extended, the Cost Auditor in certain cases where financial accounts have not been finalised, be able to reconcile the cost accounts with the financial accounts. In such cases, the Cost Auditor, if he thinks necessary, can submit a supplementary report but preferably before the date of the Annual General Meeting of the company.

If default is made by any Cost Auditor in complying with these provisions, he shall be punishable with fine which may extend to Rs. 5,000.

Speciman of Cost Audit Report

I/We*............having been appointed as auditor (s) under section 233-B of the Companies Act, 1956 (I of 1956) hereinafter referred to as the "Cost Auditor (*s*)" of Messrs ....Ltd. (hereinafter referred to as the company) have examined the books of accounts prescribed under clause (*d*) of sub-section (*i*) of Section 209 of the said Act and other relevant records for the year ended .... relating to**......... maintained by the company and report that,

(*a*) I/we* have obtained all the information and explanations which to the best of my/our* knowledge and belief were necessary for the purpose of this audit;

(*b*) proper cost accounting records as required under clause (*d*) of sub-section (1) of Section 209 of the Companies Act, 1956 (1 of 1956) have been kept by the company;

(*c*) proper returns adequate for the purpose of my/our* cost audit have been received from branches not visited by me/us*;

(*d*) The said books and records give the information required by the Companies Act, 1956 (1 of 1956) in the manner so required; and

(*e*) In my/our* opinion the company's cost accounting records have been properly kept so as give a true and fair view of the cost of production, processing, manufacturing or mining activities, as the case may be and marketing of the product under reference.

The matters contained in the Annexure to this report form part of this report which is also subject to my/our* observations made therein.

Dated this ....day of........ 20........ at...............................

Cost auditor (*s*)

---

* The inapplicable words may be deleted at all places in the report.

** Here specify the product under reference.

ANNEXURE TO THE COST AUDIT REPORT

1. General

(*i*) Name and address of the registered office of the company whose accounts are audited.

(*ii*) Name and address of the Cost Auditor.

(*iii*) Reference no. and date of Government Order under which the audit is conducted.

(*iv*) Date of the general meeting of the company in which the auditor under Section 233 B has been appointed.

(*v*) The company's financial year for which the audit report is rendered.

(*vi*) Date of incorporation of the company, and its 'status' (*i.e.,* whether it is a public company/private company which is a subsidiary company, etc.).

(*vii*) Location where accounts are maintained.

(*viii*) Location of factory/factories.

(*ix*) If there is any foreign technical collaboration for the product under reference, attach a copy of the collaboration agreement. If this is not possible, prepare a brief note indicating:

- (*a*) Name and address of the foreign collaborators.
- (*b*) Main terms of agreement.
- (*c*) Amount of Royalty/Technical aid fee payable and the basis of calculating the same.
- (*d*) Whether the technical collaborator has contributed to the share capital. If so, the paid-up value of shares so held.

(*x*) Licensed, installed and utilised capacities of the factory/factories for the product under reference.

(*xi*) Date of first commencement of commercial production of the product under reference. (If more than one factory under the same company produces the product under reference, particulars in respect of each may be given).

(*xii*) If the company is engaged in other activities besides the manufacture of the product under reference, give a brief note on the nature of such other activities.

2. Cost accounting system

Brief comment on the Cost Accounting system and its adequacy or otherwise to determine correctly the cost of the product under reference.

3. Financial position

(Relating to the product under reference if possible, otherwise for the company as a whole).

(*i*) Capital employed

Capital employed is defined as total assets at book values (excluding investments outside the business) minus current liabilities.

(*ii*) Net worth

Net worth *i.e.,* capital plus reserves or less capital losses, as the case may be. If there is any change in the composition of the net worth during the year, special mention may be made.

(*iii*) Profit before tax

Profit after providing for depreciation and all the other expenditure except interest on borrowings and debentures but before providing for taxes on income.

(*iv*) (*i*) Expenses to be specified

The amounts in respect of the following:

(*a*) Annual bonus to employees.
(*b*) Interest on borrowings and debentures, etc.
(*c*) Bad debts.
(*d*) Donations of all kinds.
(*e*) Retrenchment or other Compensation to employees, excluding premia on account of workmen's compensation, insurance.
(*f*) Lay-off wages.
(*g*) Expenditure on special exhibitions etc., other than normal trade advertisements.
(*h*) Commission based on profit to managerial personnel.
(*i*) Income tax and sur-tax.
(*j*) Any other item of expenditure the incidence of which is neither normal nor of a recurring nature.

(*ii*) Income to be specified

(*a*) Interest received on investments outside the business.
(*b*) Capital gains
(*c*) Any other income which is neither normal nor of a recurring nature.

(*v*) Ratios

(*a*) Profit arrived at as per 3 (*iii*) above expressed as a percentage of:
  (*i*) Capital employed as per 3 (*i*) above.
  (*ii*) Net sales.
(*b*) (*i*) Current assets expressed as a percentage of current liabilities.
  (*ii*) Net worth expressed as a percentage of long term borrowings and liabilities.
  (*iii*) Net worth expressed as a percentage of capital employed as per 3 (*i*) above.
(*c*) Cost of production as a percentage of
  (*i*) Capital employed as per 3 (*i*) above
  (*ii*) Working capital (*i.e.,* current* assets less current liabilities)

4. Production

(This information is to be given for each type of product under reference):

(*i*) Production in quantities

(*ii*) Indicate percentage of production of the product under reference in relation to installed capacity. If there is any shortfall in production as compared to the installed capacity, comment briefly as to the reason for the shortfall.

(*iii*) If there is any addition to the production during the year under review or in the immediately preceding two years, this may also be mentioned.

5. Process of manufacture

A brief note regarding the process of manufacture of the product under reference may be given.

***6. Raw materials**

(*i*) Show the cost of major raw materials consumed both in terms of quantity and value. Where the cost of transport etc., of raw materials is significant, specify the same separately.

(*ii*) (*a*) Consumption of major raw materials per unit of production compared with the standard requirements, if any.

(*b*) Explanation for variations, if any, in the consumption of major raw materials per unit of production as compared to the preceding two years.

(*iii*) Briefly comment on the method of accounting followed for recording the quantities and values of receipts, issues and balances of all materials directly used in production.

***7. Power and fuel**

Quantity, rate per unit and total cost separately for each major form of power and fuel used in production, e.g., coal, furnace oil, electricity etc. Compare the actual consumption per unit of production with the standards, if any. Speical features if any, may also be indicated.

***8. Wages and Salaries**

(*i*) Total wages and salaries paid for all categories of employees, separately in respect of each of the following:

(*a*) Direct labour costs on production.

(*b*) Indirect employee costs on production,

(*c*) Employee costs on administration.

(*d*) Employee costs on selling and distribution.

(*e*) Other employee costs, if any (specifying purpose).

(*J*) Total employee costs (Total of items (*a*) to (*e*) above).

(*ii*) Total man-days of direct labour available and actually worked for the year.

(*iii*) Average number of workers employed for the year.

(*iv*) Direct labour cost per unit of output of the product under reference (if more than one type of product, give information in respect of each).

(*v*) Brief explanations for variations in (*iv*) above, if any, as compared to the previous two years.

(*vi*) Comments on the incentive schemes, if any, with particular reference to its contributions towards increasing productivity and its effects on cost of production.

***9 Stores and Spare Parts**

(*i*) The expenditure per unit of output on stores, etc.

(*ii*) Discuss the system of stores accounting for recording receipts, issues and balances, both in quantities and values.

(*iii*) Indicate, if practicable, the proportion of closing inventory of stores representing items which have not moved for over 24 months.

10. Depreciation

(*i*) State the method of depreciation adopted by the company *e.g.*,straight line or diminishing balance etc. State whether the depreciation provided by the company is more or less than the amount of depreciation worked out in accordance with the provisions of sub-section (2) of Section 205 of the Companies Act, 1956.

(*ii*) State the basis of allocation of depreciation on common assets to the different departments.

(*iii*) Indicate the basis of charging depreciation to the cost of products.

11. Overheads

(*i*) Give separately the total amounts of the following overheads and break-up of items (*a*), (*b*) and (*c*) below:

(*a*) Factory Overheads.
(*b*) Administration Overheads.
(*c*) Selling and Distribution Overheads.
(*d*) Interest.
(*e*) Bonus to employees.
(*f*) Commission to Managerial Personnel.

State whether any amounts in respect of items (*d*), (*e*) or (*f*) have been included in the total amounts of items (*a*), and (*c*) and given the amounts so included, if any.

(*ii*) Indicate reasons for any significant variations in the expenditure incurred against the items included in overheads as compared with the previous two years.

(*iii*) State the basis of allocation of overheads to cost centres and of absorption to products. Give brief comments, if any, on the basis of allocation adopted by the company.

(*iv*) Cost of packing, if any, of the products under reference to be shown separately with details to the extent possible.

***12. Royalty/Technical Aid Payments**

State the total amounts of Royalty/ Technical Aid Fees payable for the year and the amount chargeable per unit of the product.

***13. Sales**

(*i*) Indicate the sales in quantities and net sales realisation of the products under reference showing the average sales realisation per unit (if more than one type of product is sold, information to be given in respect of each).

(*ii*) If product under reference is exported, indicate quantity exported, net realisation per unit, countries to which exported - details may be given. Indicate the profit/loss incurred in exports.

14. Abnormal Non-recurring Costs

If there were any abnormal features affecting production during the year e.g., strikes, lock-outs, major breakdowns in the plant, substantial power cuts, serious accidents etc., wherever practicable, briefly be mentioned indicating their effect on the cost of production.

15. Other Items

If there are any special expenses which have been directly allocated to products under reference, the total amount as also its incidence shall be shown.

16. Auditor's Observations and Conclusions

(*i*) The cost auditor may here report on

(*a*) Matters which appear to him to be clearly wrong in principle or apparently unjustifiable;

(*b*) Cases where the company's funds have been used in a negligent or inefficient manner;

(*c*) Factors which could have been controlled, but have not been done resulting in increase in the cost of production;

(*d*) Contracts or agreements, if any, between the company and other parties relating to selling, purchasing etc.

(*e*) (*i*) The adequacy or otherwise of budgetary control system, if any, in vogue in the company;

(*ii*) The scope and performance of internal audit, if any;

(*f*) Suggestions for improvement in performance, if any, e.g., by

1. Rectification of general imbalance in production facilities;
2. Full utilisation of installed capacity;
3. Concentration on areas offering scope for

(*i*) Cost reduction.

(*ii*) Increased productivity.

(*iii*) Key/limiting factors causing production bottlenecks.

4. Improved inventory policies

(*i*) The opinions expressed shall be based on verified data, reference to which shall be made here and shall, wherever practicable, be included after the company has been afforded an opportunity to comment on them.

(*ii*) Copies of the cost statements in respect of completed products as given in Schedule 11 of the notification issued under clause (*b*) of sub-section (1) of Section 209 of the Companies Act, 1956 duly completed, and audited shall be appended to the report.

Note: 1. *Figures to be given for the year under audit and to the extent practicable, for the two preceding years.

2. If the company has more than one factory producing the product under reference, details indicating in the annexure may be given separately for each factory, if such details are available.
3. If different varieties/types of product under reference are manufactured by the company, details of cost in respect of each shall be given.
4. The matters contained in the annexure shall be duly authenticated by the cost auditor.

Advantages of Cost Audit

Cost audit is beneficial to a variety of people like manufacturers, management, shareholders, government and society. These advantages can be given as follows:

Advantages to Cost Accountant:

1. It provides accurate and reliable costing data for presentation and improves the status of cost accountants.
2. If cost audit is undertaken by the external auditor, his varied experience helps the cost accountants in tackling complexities involved in applying cost methods. It also improves performance of cost accountant and the overall efficiency of his department.
3. Cost audit makes possible the reconciliation of cost accounts with the financial accounts, which is the most important requirement of a costing system.

Advantages to Management:

1. Cost audit is quite an important advantage to management for detecting frauds, errors and misappropriations in the organisation.
2. Audited cost accounts help in making comparison of the performance of two firms.
3. The process of managerial decision making is considerably improved as it is based on reliable cost reports and cost data.

4. Cost audit exercises a moral check on the employees which promotes honesty and improves their efficiency. It is also helpful in developing better understanding and liaison with the management. In this way the employer - employee relations improve further.
5. It is also helpful in reducing cost of production by checking wastages of materials, labour and overhead.
6. The cost audit can help the firm in determination of tender prices, especially for big contracts, where these are undertaken on cost plus basis.
7. By cost audit it is easy to find the measurement basis of the computation of profitability.

Advantages to Shareholders:

1. With the reduction in cost of production, the shareholders can get higher rate of dividend. Thus they always appreciate the adoption and efficient working of cost audit system.
2. Cost audit helps in making correct valuation of the Closing Stock. Thus, it assists in making the correct assessment of the position of the organisation.
3. It also helps in assessing the productivity of labour, materials and machines employed in the company.

   In a way cost audit reflects the levels of efficiency or inefficiency of management.

Advantages to the Government:

1. Cost audit, by keeping proper checks on uneconomic units, helps in increasing efficiency, decreasing prices and hence is helpful to Government.
2. Cost Audit ensures the provision of correct and reliable cost data for determining the cost of contracts under the system of 'cost plus contracts'.
3. It helps the Government in fixing the proper price of the commodities, if it is to be done by it.
4. It is helpful to government in improving the efficiency of weak and sick industrial concerns.
5. It helps in settlement of industrial disputes regarding payment of wages, bonus and tax assessment in government concerns.
6. It brings to lime light the cases of forgery and frauds in case of government companies.
7. It is helpful in determining the grant of various tariffs and protections to various industries, in the best interest of the public.

QUESTIONS

1. What do you understand by the term "Cost audit"? What are its main objects and advantages.
2. Discuss briefly the functions of "cost audit" in a manufacturing concern.
3. Enumurate briefly the provisions of Companies Act relating to Cost Audit.
4. How a cost auditor will verify the following items:
   (*i*) Materials.
   (*ii*) Labour,
   (*iii*) Work-in-progress,
   (*iv*) Overheads, and
   (*v*) Capital Expenditure.
5. How is Cost Audit different from Financial Audit?
6. Cost audit will help to maintain, among other things, the integrity of inventory valuation. Discuss the role of cost audit in this as well as in other fields.
7. Enumerate the arguments whereby you would try to convince the management that an internal auditor should be appointed to operate regularly in the cost department.
8. "Cost audit" is a necessity and not a luxury and is viewed as a barometer to measure the operational performance, the effectiveness of utilisation of resources and working results. Illustrate.
9. What is Cost Audit Report? Discuss its provisions briefly.
10. Briefly explain the various techniques of Cost Audit.
11. You have been required by a manufacturing company to conduct a periodical audit of their costing records. Write down the points that will receive your special attention in this behalf.

27

Cost Control, Cost Reduction, Value Analysis and Productivity

COST CONTROL

Modern management is becoming increasingly cost-conscious and is constantly in search of new ways of controlling costs and eliminating wastages. One of the basic objectives of cost accounting is to achieve cost control. It is not enough if costs are worked out and presented regularly to the management. The effectiveness of cost accounting is judged primarily from the extent to which it has been able to bring about a control over the manufacturing and other expenses.

The Terminology of Cost Accountancy of the Institute of Cost and Management Accountants, London, defines 'cost control' as "the guidance and regulation by executive action of the costs of operating an undertaking, particularly where such action is guided by cost accounting."

In cost control, the first step is to set up the target to be achieved, *i.e.*, the goal or objective to be attained. The cost control system guides the organisation to reach that goal. For this purpose, budgets or standards are used. These budgets or standards provide the yardstick against which actual costs and performances may be compared. If at any stage, it is noticed that the expenses are showing a trend away from the goal, resulting thereby in a variation from the target, the cost control systems help to regulate this trend and to eliminate the variations. This guidance and regulation is by executive action, *i.e.*, through an action taken by the executive who is responsible for the incurring of the expenditure. It should be clearly understood that a cost accountant by himself does not control the expenses. He merely assists in the control of expenses since an expenditure can be controlled only by the person who incurs the expenditure. The cost accountant brings to the notice of the executive concerned, the exact point on which an action is required of him for regulating the expenses. Thus, cost control is the guidance and regulation through an executive action and this executive action is exercised in respect of all the expenses incurred in operating an undertaking. Cost control comprises all procedures and measures by which the cost of carrying out an activity is kept under check and aims at ensuring that costs do not go beyond a certain level.

STEPS IN COST CONTROL

Efficient organisation and operation of cost control system involves the following steps:

1. Setting up the targets.
2. Measurement of the actuals.
3. Comparison of actuals with the targets to ascertain variances.
4. Analysis of variances (between the targets and the actuals) to their causes.
5. Taking such corrective actions as are necessary to eliminate the variations.

TOOLS AND TECHNIQUES OF COST CONTROL

Cost control can be exercised by adopting the following tools and techniques:

(*a*) Material control
(*b*) Labour control
(*c*) Overhead control
(*d*) Budgetary control
(*e*) Standard costing
(*f*) Capital expenditure control.

MAKING COST CONTROL A SUCCESS

In order to carry out cost control system efficiently so as to obtain the required results, there are certain basic measures which should be adopted. These measures may be given as follows:

1. The targets for performance of work as well as the costs to be incurred for the purpose should be laid down for each area of responsibility as far as practicable. It would enable to locate the exact person responsible for a given state of affairs. The powers, responsibilities and obligations of each executive in the organisation should be clearly defined.
2. The target should always be fixed up in consultation with the individual responsible for attaining the target. The impression should never be created that the target is purely a result of some calculations in the accounting department. Further, the targets should be 'attainable' and not merely 'ideal'. If the targets are not attainable even in the best of circumstances, a certain amount of frustration will be created in the minds of the persons concerned and the whole object of the cost control will thereby get defeated.
3. The targets fixed in an undertaking should not be treated as permanent. They should be reviewed whenever necessary and should be revised when conditions change.

4. Collection of costs should be made by each area of responsibility and reports thereon should be drawn up similarly. These reports should clearly indicate in monetary terms the effect of efficiency or inefficiency shown by each section or department.
5. The reports should be presented sufficiently in time for necessary action to be taken. Belated presentation of reports will only give statistical information and cannot be helpful in taking an action.
6. Utmost care should be exercised while making a judgement about the efficiency or inefficiency of various persons on the basis of the reports. A single report is likely to be misleading under certain circumstances and hence a number of reports should be considered together.
7. A proper and thorough enquiry into factors leading to exceptionally good or bad performance should be made and appropriate remedial action should be taken. The main objective should be to locate and remove the factors leading to wastage and losses rather than to punish people. If there is too much emphasis on punishment, it is possible that figures will be cooked and the truth hidden.
8. A good performance should attract immediate reward and consistently bad performance should attract the necessary dis-incentive. It should also cover those whose task is to prepare reports.

COST REDUCTION

Whereas cost control aims at reducing the actuals to the targets, cost reduction aims at reducing the targets themselves. In other words, the aim of cost reduction is to see whether there is any possibility in bringing about a saving in the cost incurred – materials, labour, overheads etc. According to the Terminology of Cost Accountancy of the Institute of Cost and Management Accountants, London, "Cost reduction is to be understood as the achievement of real and permanent reduction in the unit costs of goods manufactured without impairing their suitability for the use intended." It, therefore, follows that:

(*i*) the reduction must be a real one in the course of manufacture of goods or services rendered through increase in productivity;

(*ii*) the reduction must be a permanent one. Reduction in cost due to windfalls, reduction in taxes due to change in government policy or any other fortuitous receipts do not fall within the purview of cost reduction;

(*iii*) the reduction should not be at the cost of essential characteristics and quality of the products or services rendered.

Thus, the term 'cost reduction' denotes real or genuine savings in production, administration, selling and distribution costs brought about by the elimination of wasteful and non-essential elements from the design of the product and from the techniques and practices carried out in connection therewith. The necessity for cost reduction arises when profit margin has to be increased without an increase in the sales turnover i.e., for the same volume of sales, the cost of sales should be reduced.

COST CONTROL AND COST REDUCTION

Cost control and cost reduction are considered to be two efficient tools of management. But these tools differ from each other in respect of the following:

1. Firstly, cost control represents efforts made towards achieving a target while cost reduction represents achievement in reduction of cost.
2. Cost control assumes the existence of certain standards which are not subject to challenge while cost reduction, on the other hand, assumes the existence of concealed potential savings in the standards set for control and these standards are subject to constant challenge.
3. Cost control implies setting up of standards and maintaining the performance according to the standards while cost reduction is not concerned with the maintenance of performance according to set standards.
4. Cost control is said to be preventive function acting within the framework of some target or standard. Cost reduction, on the other hand, is considered to be corrective function by continuous process of analysis of costs, functions etc.

ADVANTAGES OF COST REDUCTION

The main advantages of cost reduction may be summarised as follows:

1. Cost reduction increases the profits of an undertaking which ultimately provides a basis for more dividends to shareholders, higher rate of bonus to staff and retention of more profits for ploughing back in business.
2. Due to increase in profits, management may spend more in providing amenities to workers. It will ensure more cordial relationship between management and workers and reduce the labour turnover.
3. Increased profitability of the undertaking due to cost reduction adds to its goodwill.
4. Reduction in the unit cost indicates better productivity and efficiency. The efficiency of a firm may benefit the members of the industry as a whole.
5. Higher profitability will ensure increased revenue to the government by way of taxation..
6. Cost reduction may lead to lower export prices resulting in higher total exports.

TOOLS AND TECHNIQUES OF COST REDUCTION

The tools and techniques of cost reduction include the following:

(*a*) Standard Costing
(*b*) Budgetary Control
(*c*) Inventory Control
(*d*) Production Planning and Control
(*e*) Statistical Quality Control
(*f*) Standardisation and Simplification
(*g*) Operational Research
(*h*) Value Analysis
(*i*) Automation
(*j*) Design Improvement
(*k*) Market Research
(*l*) Job evaluation and merit-rating.

AREAS OF COST REDUCTION

The scope of cost reduction is very wide and it is not practicable to develop fully the areas in which cost reduction may be applied. Any area wherein costs are incurred has the scope for cost reduction and it should not be thought that there is no scope for cost reduction in any particular area. However, the following areas have the largest scope of cost reduction:

1. Product Design

The design of the product provides the maximum scope for cost reduction. Since product design is the first step in production, cost reduction effected at this stage is likely to benefit throughout the manufacturing life of the product. Possibilities in the reduction of cost should be investigated, both, while improving existing design or introducing new designs. Cost reduction in product design can be effected in the following manner:

(*a*) Materials Cost: Cheaper substitutes, higher yield, lesser investment in inventory, lower storage cost etc.
(*b*) Labour Cost: Higher productivity, reduced time of operation etc.
(*c*) Tools and Equipment: Reduction in the cost of tools, jigs and other equipment.
(*d*) Standardisation and simplification leading to increased productivity and reduced cost.
(*e*) Shape and weight resulting in reduced transport cost, etc.

2. Factory Organisation and Production Methods

Cost reduction can be effected to a great extent by improving factory organisation and production methods in the form of clear-cut lines of authority and responsibility, well defined channels of communications, co-ordination and co-operation between various executives, new manufacturing techniques, new processes, new production methods etc.

3. Administration

Cost reduction in administration can be effected by re-organising the office, scrutinising the effectiveness of existing staff, introducing mechanical and electronic aids in office routines, modifying internal and external communication systems etc.

4. Marketing

In the area of marketing, cost reduction can be effected by improving the methods of remuneration of salesmen, re-arranging territorial responsibilities of sales representatives, improving the current methods of advertising, improving product design and production quality so as to reduce after sales service, economising channels of distribution, improving packing etc.

5. Finance

Cost reduction in relation to finance may be effected by securing capital at economical cost, employing capital to give maximum return and eliminating over and under-capitalisation and wasteful use of capital etc.

VALUE ANALYSIS OR VALUE ENGINEERING

Cost reduction in an organisation can be achieved through the following channels:

(*i*) By economising expenditure or increasing productivity; or
(*ii*) By improving the use value and esteem value of products.

Value analysis is a scientific approach to cost reduction by increasing the use value in a product. Value analysis (or, value engineering as it is sometimes called) is a systematic analysis and evaluation of the techniques and functions in the various spheres of an organisation with a view to explore channels of performance improvement so that the value in the particular product or service can be bettered. It enables the maximum possible value to be achieved for a given cost. Thus, value analysis is a technique which is used to analyse all aspects of an existing product or service to determine the minimum cost necessary for specific functional requirements. The basic idea under this technique is to weigh cost against value.

The terms 'value analysis' and 'value engineering' are often used interchangeably since both have many identical steps in their working procedure. Yet there is fundamental difference between the two on account of the areas of their application. While value analysis can be applied to any type of cost, value engineering is applicable mainly to direct cost, *i.e.*, direct material, direct labour etc. Value engineering is generally applied before a product is born and is in the design and development stage and value analysis is applied to existing products due to dropping sales.

VALUE

The term 'value' is very important in relation to value analysis and is used in a wide sense. In order to understand clearly the principles and procedure of value analysis, it is necessary to know the various types of value. It is used in different senses for different persons and at different times and places. For a designer, value means the quality of the product designed ; for the salesmen, it means the price which it can fetch in the market ; and for management, 'value' would be the return on capital employed. An industrial product may have four types of value.

1. Use Value

'Use value' refers to the characteristics and features which make a product useful so that it can provide useful service for which it is intended. A watch, for example, is meant to indicate time; if it gives correct time, it gives its full value. Thus, use value is the measure of the quality of performance of a product. Use value may be classified as,

(*a*) Primary use value,

(*b*) Secondary use value, and

(*c*) Auxiliary use value.

The attributes of a product which are necessary for its performance may be treated as having primary use value. For instance, in a motor cycle, the engine and the handle may be considered to be primary use value because in their absence, the motor cycle cannot be made to run. The mud-guards are also necessary for the protection of the engine and other parts but the motor cycle can be run even without these. Such items carry secondary use value. Items such as speed meter, miles meter, fuel meter etc., which make the control and operation of motor cycle better but are not very essential, are treated as having auxiliary use value.

2. Esteem Value

There may be certain features or properties of a product which do not contribute to its utility or performance but make it more attractive or esteemable so as to induce the cutomers to buy it. A rich customer may prefer a gold watch for its esteem value although a watch made of steel could serve the purpose of keeping time equally well.

Certain features of a product may have use as well as esteem value both of which may be important. A piece of highly polished furniture will not only look better but will also last longer, thus combining esteem value with use value.

3. Cost Value

Cost value refers to the value measured in terms of cost. It is the total cost required to produce an item. If an item is manufactured in own factory, cost value is denoted by its cost of production but in case it is purchased from outside, it is denoted by its purchase price.

4. Exchange value

Exchange value means features of a product facilitating its exchange for something else. The exchange value of a product is equivalent to its sale value.

Relationship between Value, Function and Cost

Value of an item is closely related to its function or purpose, viz., quality, elegance, prestige etc. Value is the ratio of worth (or, function) to the price (or, cost) of an item. The relationship between value, function and cost may be expressed as:

$$\text{Value} = \frac{\text{Function (or, Worth)}}{\text{Cost (or, Price)}}$$

There are three ways in which the value of an item can be improved or enhanced:

(*i*) by reducing cost, function remaining constant, or
(*ii*) by improving function, cost remaining constant, or
(*iii*) by improving function and reducing cost.

PROCEDURE OF VALUE ANALYSIS

Work relating to value analysis is a specialised job and is to be carried on by experts in various disciplines. Systematic operation of value analysis involves the following procedure:

1. Scope of the Problem

At the first stage, it has to be determined whether the product has full use value and esteem value, and if not, in what respects it is lacking so as to plan action on those lines.

2. Collection of Relevant Information

Under this step a careful study of the characteristics and all the uses made of the product by the customers, costs of production, selling and distribution, competitive and substitute products, manufacturing methods etc., is to be made.

3. Assessment of Various Alternatives

At the third stage, a careful study of the various alternatives which are available for cost reduction and giving best value of the product to the customer, should be made.

4. Development

The best alternative proposed by the experts is reviewed by the top management and necessary authority for its development granted.

5. Implementation

After the final proposal is accepted for implementation, production drawings and models are prepared and production is started on the proposed lines.

6. Follow-up Action

It involves the ascertainment as to whether the proposals implemented have achieved the reduction in costs that were planned.

QUESTIONNAIRE IN VALUE ANALYSIS

The value analysis team consists of design, production control, purchasing and distribution staff besides cost or management accountant. While collecting information, the particular questions that the value analyst is to ask himself are:

(*a*) Does its use contribute to value?
(*b*) Is the price proportionate to performance, utility and value?
(*c*) Does it need all its features and characteristics?
(*d*) Is any better substitute available?
(*e*) How much would that cost?
(*f*) Can a standard part be used instead of specially made one?
(*g*) Is it designed to proper tooling considerations?
(*h*) Can it be made cheaper?
(*i*) Is there any scope of reducing labour operations?
(*j*) Can the manufacturing operations be standardised and simplified?

The above queries are only illustrative and are, by no means, comprehensive. There may be so many other questions which may be raised by the analyst relevant for his analysis.

ADVANTAGES OF VALUE ANALYSIS

The main advantages of the technique of value analysis are as follows:

(*a*) Value analysis is the most effective tool of cost reduction which ultimately leads to improvement in profitability.
(*b*) Value analysis ensures improved productivity through the continuous process of search for improvement in all fields.
(*c*) It helps in obtaining maximum production from limited resources of capital, time, space etc.
(*d*) As value analysis makes a close study of a product in order to determine the features which would give the highest satisfaction to customers, the manufacture of most suitable products is ensured.

(*e*) It helps in maintaining the desired quality of products.

(*f*) Value analysis creates the proper atmosphere for increased efficiency by a continuing search for improvement.

(*g*) It is a specialised job involving the utilisation of the talents of a team of persons drawn from the various sectors of the business. This has the effect of integrating the various management functions and infusing a spirit of co-operation and raising the morale.

(*h*) It helps in creating work interest by making the full use of the creative ability and other qualifications of the staff.

PRODUCTIVITY

Productivity, in modern times, is referred to as 'key to prosperity' and is being used as a synonym for progress. Productivity is an economic concept and is an index of efficiency showing the effectiveness of the individual or combined factors used in producing goods or services. According to International Labour Organisation, "In the broadest concept, productivity may be taken to constitute the ratio of available goods and services to the potential resources of the group, community or the country." According to Mayadeo & S.B. Karmakar, "Productivity is the ratio between the production of a given commodity measured by volume and one or more of the corresponding input factors also measured by volume." In the words of M. Banerjee, "The word productivity usually means the ratio between the output of wealth in the form of goods and services and input of resources used up in that output."

From the above mentioned definitions, it is clear that productivity refers to measurable relationships between well-defined output and input. Input means the diverse resources employed in a business, i.e., raw materials, labour, capital, building, plant and machinery, components etc., and output means the end product. Productivity aims at the maximisation of output by the most economic use of input and elimination and minimisation of wastage.

Production and Productivity

The term 'productivity' must not be confused with 'production'. There is a clear line of demarcation between the two. Production relates to volume, value and quantum of goods and services produced during a given period of time by a worker, enterprise or an economy. It is the resultant of various factors of production combined together. On the other hand, productivity studies and reviews the volume, value of quantity of production in relation to the input or resources utilised in the production of goods and services. It is the ratio between input and output *i.e.*, various factors of production (input) and the resulting therefrom of products and services (output).

Production is an absolute concept whereas productivity is a relative term. Production is absolute in the sense that it relates to the volume, value and quantity of goods produced during a specified period of time, whereas productivity of inputs can be increased and is directly related to the efficiency of resources utilised for production. An increase in production does not necessarily mean increase in productivity.

Productivity and Efficiency

The terms 'productivity' and 'efficiency' are also distinct from each other. Efficiency relates to inherent competence *i.e.*, capability of a given input or production unit to produce under given conditions of work, whereas productivity refers to actual production results shown by an input or production line under given conditions during a given time at given costs or input. It may be pointed out that productivity may be increased without actually increasing efficiency. Similarly, efficiency of an individual input can be increased without increasing the productivity. A worker may be quite efficient, yet he may not be able to increase his productivity due to improper inputs of work provided to him. But still an inter-relationship can be established between productivity and efficiency. Higher productivity on account of the best utilisation of the available inputs of production leads to higher efficiency.

Measurement of Productivity

Theoretically, it is very easy to understand the concept of productivity, but it is not very easy to measure it on account of the following reasons:

(*i*) **Total or over-all productivity:** Although it is comparatively easy to measure total productivity, this measurement will not be of much importance on account of the fact that an increase in productivity of one factor may be counter-balanced by another. As such, the real position cannot be known.

(*ii*) **Inter-dependence of factoral productivities:** Productivity of various factors is inter-dependent and not independent. As such the productivity of one factor may be affected by the productivity of another factor, e.g., the productivity of labour affected by inferior quality of material and defective tools.

(*iii*) **General disagreement as to the measurement of output and input:** In a multi-product concern, where a variety of goods are manufactured, it may be difficult to measure the productivity of the whole concern due to the differences in the volume of individual products, quality and disparate degree of sub-contracting. Further, in case of fluctuation in the price level, the productivity measured in terms of monetary value may not represent the true position.

In order to overcome the above difficulties, both the productivity of individual factors and the over-all productivity of the business should be measured at regular intervals. In case of multi-product concern, the output may be expressed in terms of standard hours. The general productivity may be expressed as,

$$\text{Productivity} = \frac{\text{Output}}{\text{Input}} = \frac{\text{Out Cost + Value Added}}{\text{Total Cost}}$$

$$= \frac{\text{Gross Income}}{\text{Gross Expenditure}}$$

The factoral productivity can be measured as follows:

Labour Productivity

In a concern where most of the work is done by manual labour, measurement of labour productivity is of utmost importance. For measurement of labour productivity, both direct and indirect factory labour should be considered. The usual measures of labour productivity are as follows:

(*a*) In terms of hours

(*i*) $\text{Productivity} = \frac{\text{Production in Standard Hours}}{\text{Possible (or, actual) man hours}}$

(*ii*) $\text{Lost Time Percentage} = \frac{\text{Man hours lost}}{\text{Possible (or, actual) man hours}} \times 100$

(*b*) In terms of money

By any one of the following ratios:

(*i*) $\frac{\text{Sales value or cost of output}}{\text{Number of workers}}$

(*ii*) $\frac{\text{Direct wages}}{\text{Sales value}}$

(*iii*) $\frac{\text{Indirect wages}}{\text{Direct wages}}$

(*iv*) $\frac{\text{Direct wages}}{\text{Number of units}}$

Increase in labour productivity is possible through increased efficiency of labour, reduction of idle time, improvment in working conditions of labour and adoption of effective labour welfare schemes.

Material Productivity

In case of a new product, a good design may be helpful in reducing the wastage and excess usage of material. In case of an existing product or at the operation stage, higher productivity can be achieved by using minimum material through skilled workmanship, efficient and adequate machine tools and efficient and quality purchases. The material productivity can be measured by using the following ratios:

(*i*) $\frac{\text{Material cost}}{\text{Number of units produced}}$

(*ii*) $\frac{\text{Direct material cost}}{\text{Production cost}}$

(*iii*) $\frac{\text{Indirect material cost}}{\text{Direct material cost}}$

(*iv*) $\frac{\text{Direct material consumed}}{\text{Sales}}$

(*v*) $\frac{\text{Direct material consumed}}{\text{Number of employees}}$

(*vi*) $\frac{\text{Waste or scrap}}{\text{Total material consumed}}$

The purchase efficiency of material can be measured by using any of the following ratios:

(*i*) $\frac{\text{Actual purchase price}}{\text{Budgeted purchase price}}$

(*ii*) $\frac{\text{Purchases in the current period}}{\text{Purchases in the previous period}}$

(*iii*) $\frac{\text{Purchases return}}{\text{Total purchases}}$

(*iv*) $\frac{\text{Purchase cost or trade discount earned}}{\text{Total purchases}}$

Machine productivity

In a factory where most of the work is done with the help of machines due to its highly technical nature, the capacity utilisation of machinery is considered to be more important than the proper utilisation of other factors of production. The productivity of the machinery can be measured by using any of the following ratios:

(*i*) Machine utilisation = $\frac{\text{Output in standard hours}}{\text{Planned (or, actual) machine hours}}$

(*ii*) Activity percentage = $\frac{\text{Actual machine hours}}{\text{Planned machine hours}} \times 100$

(*iii*) Lost time percentage = $\frac{\text{Machine hours lost}}{\text{Planned machine hours}} \times 100$

Productivity of power and services

For ensuring higher productivity, effective utilisation of power and other services is very essential. The productivity of power and other services can be measured by using the following ratios:

(*i*) $\dfrac{\text{Horse-power utilised}}{\text{Number of hours worked}}$

(*ii*) $\dfrac{\text{Maintenance cost (or, other services)}}{\text{Number of hours worked}}$

Selling, distribution and administration productivity

The following ratios may be used to measure the selling, distribution and administration productivity:

(*i*) $\dfrac{\text{Selling, distribution or administration costs}}{\text{Total sales}}$

(*ii*) $\dfrac{\text{Salesmen's salaries, commission, etc.}}{\text{Total sales}}$

(*iii*) $\dfrac{\text{Advertising costs}}{\text{Total sales}}$

Over-all productivity

Over-all productivity of the business concern can be measured by using the following ratio:

$$\text{Return on capital employed} = \frac{\text{Profit}}{\text{Capital employed}}$$

$$= \frac{\text{Profit}}{\text{Sales}} \times \frac{\text{Sales}}{\text{Capital employed}}$$

Both profit to sales and sales to capital employed indicate the efficiency in selling as they indicate the profit earning capacity.

Benefits of productivity

Following benefits can be derived from increased productivity:

1. It ensures effective utilisation of available resources thereby increasing total volume of production and decreasing cost of production.
2. It reduces the price of goods to be sold and better quality products are provided to consumers.
3. It ensures increased wages to workers thereby raising their standard of living.
4. It leads to lesser overhead costs.

5. It leads to higher profits to entrepreneur which can be re-invested in meeting future financial needs of the concern.
6. It is considerably helpful in increasing exports.
7. It leads to higher per capita income.

Factors affecting productivity

The various factors which affect the productivity may be given as follows:

(*a*) **Technological factors:** These are the most important factors influencing industrial productivity now-a-days. Various factors viz., degree of mechanisation, technical know-how, proper layout of plant and quality of raw materials used substantially affect productivity of an industrial concern. Other factors which can be included in this category of factors are equipment and machine design, production processes to be undertaken and application of scientific management techniques. These factors have positive impact on productivity.

(*b*) **Performance of workers:** Human factor occupies an important place in any industrial undertaking. The success of a business enterprise largely depends upon the performance of its labour force. The concern may have top class machines, right type of material, appropriate layout and other requirements, but it cannot achieve the desired production results unless the work force is willing to work and possesses proper ability to perform their jobs.

(*c*) **Adequate finance:** Finance plays an important role in enhancing total production and productivity of an undertaking. Desired changes in productivity cannot be ensured without adequate finance. If adequate finance is available, introduction of latest and up-to-date techniques of production and innovations for carrying out production operations can be possible.

(*d*) **Government regulations:** Various government policies and regulations viz., financial, administrative, taxation, trade and tariff policies also affect industrial productivity. The government policies should be framed in such a manner as to provide favourable and healthy working conditions to industries.

(*e*) **Natural factors:** These include mainly geographical, climatic and physical factors and their impact on productivity. In case of some of the industries, these have lesser influence while in the case of others they have more influence. The climatic factors also affect the productivity of workers.

(*f*) **Managerial factors:** Application of scientific management techniques and latest innovations in the field of management have positive impact on productivity. In this modern era of large scale production and cut-throat competition, necessity of applying latest managerial techniques becomes more imperative in order to increase productivity.

IMPROVEMENT OF PRODUCTIVITY

Productivity can be improved by applying the following methods:

1. Provision of incentives to workers

Labour productivity can be increased to a great extent by providing various wage and non-wage incentives to the workers. Wage incentives comprise increased wage rates, bonus, allowance etc., while non-wage incentives are workers' participation in management, job security, appreciation for their work etc.

2. Provision of adequate health, safety and welfare measures

The provision of adequate health, safety and welfare measures will assist in improving the working conditions in the factory which will ultimately lead to lesser accidents and improvement in over-all productivity and efficiency of workers.

3. Application of scientific management

Scientific management techniques and practices including the application of work, time and motion studies will lead to savings in time and most effective utilisation of available resources and removal of wastage and inefficiency which will assist in enhancing the productivity of workers and machines.

4. Application of simplification, standardisation and specialisation

Process of simplification, standardisation and specialisation have positive impact on productivity. Work is carried out systematically and in the most effective manner thereby considerably reducing production costs and enhancing productivity.

5. Scientific selection and training of workers

Scientific selection, placement and training are greatly helpful in increasing productivity of the workers. Scientific selection ensures the selection of the right type of workers for a particular job.

6. Application of cost, quality and production control

Different techniques of cost, quality and production control are very helpful in increasing productivity.

7. Industrial research

Constant industrial research and experimentation bring about new methods and techniques of production which are greatly helpful in increasing industrial productivity and total production.

8. Proper plant layout

The layout of machines and equipment should be in such a manner which ensures smooth and unrestricted flow of production operations and processes. The proper plant layout ensures lesser degree of work stoppage thereby increasing total volume of production and productivity.

9. Effective material handling and internal transport

An effective and efficient system of material control and internal transport is immensely helpful in enhancing productivity.

OBJECTIVE TYPE QUESTIONS

A. Multiple Choice Questions

Select the correct answer in each of the following cases:

1. Cost reduction is achieved through

(*a*) Value analysis (*b*) Economic batch quantity
(*c*) Inventory control (*d*) Production planning and control
(*e*) All of the above.

2. A fountain pen with a gold nib has more

(*a*) Use value (*b*) Esteem value
(*c*) Use as well as esteem value.

3. Value analysis mainly aims at increasing the

(*a*) Use value (*b*) Esteem value
(*c*) Cost value (*d*) Exchange value
(*e*) All of these

4. The most important field where cost reduction may be attempted is the

(*a*) Improvement in organisation (*b*) Purchase procedure
(*c*) Product design (*d*) Better factory layout.

5. Labour productivity may be measured by

(*a*) Total labour hours/Total output
(*b*) Total output/Total man-hours
(*c*) Actual labour time/Standard labour time
(*d*) All of these.

[**Ans.** 1. (*a*); 2. (*c*); 3. (a) 4. (*c*); 5. (*b*).]

B. 'True/False' type questions

Indicate whether the following statements are 'True' or 'False':

1. Cost reduction is cost control.

2. Higher productivity always leads to larger production.

3. Budgetary control and standard costing are techniques of cost reduction.

4. Value analysis is mainly concerned with the esteem value of the product.

[**Ans.** 1. False; 2. False; 3. True; 4. False.]

C. Filling the blanks type questions

Fill in the blanks

1. Value analysis is a powerful tool of ....
2. Cost reduction is the .... reduction in the unit cost of goods manufactured or services rendered without impairing their suitability for the ....

[**Ans.** 1. Cost reduction; 2. Real; use intended.]

SHORT ANSWER TYPE QUESTIONS

Answer each of the following questions in four lines:

1. What is value analysis?
2. What is the purpose of value analysis?
3. Define cost reduction.
4. Is cost reduction and cost control the same thing?
5. What is the main point of difference between cost reduction and cost control?
6. What is productivity? How does it differ from production?

LONG ANSWER TYPE QUESTIONS

1. What is 'Cost Control'? How is it exercised? What are the essentials of an efficient system of cost control?
2. What is cost reduction? What are the areas of cost reduction? Give the advantages of cost reduction.
3. What is the difference between cost control and cost reduction? Enumerate some of the possibilities in reducing the cost of a product and outline a programme for cost reduction.
4. What is value? What is value analysis? Discuss how value analysis programme can be applied in a manufacturing organisation to bring down the cost of production.
5. Differentiate between 'production' and 'productivity'. Which would you prefer to improve in your organisation and why?
6. What is productivity? How can it be measured and improved?

28

Activity Based Costing (ABC System)

Pricing of products by any organisation is very important and is generally done with reference to the cost of products. But a number of business organisations are not interested in knowing how much it costs to make a product with precise accuracy. It is due to the fact that in these organisations pricing is based on factors other than cost e.g., what the customers or market will bear, nature of the product, nature of the customers, competitors' moves etc. A majority of the organisations, however, fix their price on the basis of cost and need to be able to determine it with reasonable accuracy. The traditional absorption costing systems aim at ascertaining the cost of products and services by tracing direct portion of the cost to the product and indirect portion of cost allocated through various cost centres.

There is a general belief that traditional absorption costing systems are not accurate enough to give adequate information for pricing purposes or other long-term management decision purposes. But it is also true that some traditional systems treat overheads in a detailed way and relate them to production cost centres as well as service cost centres. The overheads related to service cost centres are then spread over the production cost centres before absorption rates are calculated. Many organisations for the purpose of cost smoothing (sometimes referred to as, 'peanut-butter costing') use broad averages (or overhead rates based on direct costs, direct labour hours or machine hours) for spreading the cost of resources (overheads) uniformally to cost objects (e.g., products or services), when the individual products or services in fact, use these resources in a non-uniform way. These overhead rates assume that products which take longer time to make, generate more overheads and vice versa. This process of cost smoothing leads to under-costing or over-costing of products. The organisations which under-cost products may actually make sales that result in losses under the erroneous impression that these sales are profitable. But these sales bring in less revenues than the cost of the resources they use. On the other hand, the organisations which over-cost products, may over-price their products and lose market share to existing or new competitors.

Activity Based Costing (also known as ABC System) has been developed as a more modern absorption costing method to overcome the problems of under-costing and over-costing and to produce more accurate product costs.

Factors prompting the development of Activity Based Costing System:

ABC System has developed basically on account of the limitations of the traditional absorption costing system. The basic factors which have prompted the development of ABC System may be summarised as follows:

(*i*) The traditional basis of segregating costs into fixed and variable elements on the basis of their behaviour is generally considered to be unrealistic. It is due to the fact that with the growth of business, the costs have become more complex and complicated.

(*ii*) The traditional methods applied for absorbing overheads lay emphasis on the calculation and application of overhead recovery rates which are acceptable for the valuation of stocks for the purposes of routine financial reporting. The management does not find these traditional methods helpful in making complicated decisions related to product strategies.

(*iii*) The traditional absorption costing does not render any valuable assistance to multi-product concerns in making decisions regarding process technology, product-mix, product pricing etc.

(*iv*) The rapid development of automated production has led to growing overhead costs. According to an estimate, the normal overhead rate which was 200% to 300% of direct costs about 15 years ago, has gone upto 500% to 800%.

(*v*) The ever increasing and severe market competition due to globalisation has increased the necessity of more accurate product costs in order to avoid the disadvantages of under-costing and over-costing.

(*vi*) There has been an increase in tendency towards product diversification to secure economies of scope and increased market share requiring the ascertainment of more accurate product costs under the conditions of fast changing cost structure.

Activity Based Costing – Meaning:

Activity based costing should not be treated as an alternate to job costing or process costing but as one of the best tools for refining a costing system which provides better measurement of the non-uniformity in the use of an organisation's overhead resources for jobs, products and services. Activity based costing incorporates in its costing system the basic and vital role of different activities. ABC System refines costing system by focussing on individual activities as the fundamental cost objects. An activity is an event, task or unit of work with a specified purpose e.g., designing products, setting up machines, operating machines and distributing products. According to R. Cooper and R.S. Kaplan — "ABC Systems calculate the costs of individual activities and assign costs to cost objects such as products and services on the basis of the activities undertaken to produce each product or service."[1] In traditional absorption

[1] R. Cooper and R.S. Kaplan – The Design of Cost Management System – Edition 1999.

costing, overheads are first assigned or related to cost centres, (production and service centres)and then to cost objects i.e., products or services. But in Activity Based Costing System, overheads are related or assigned to activities or grouped into cost pools before they are related to cost objects i.e., products or services. Thus, ABC System uses activities instead of functional departments (Cost Centres) for absorbing overheads. The basic feature of functional departments is that they tend to include a series of different activities causing different costs that behave in different ways. Further, the activities also tend to run across functions. For example, the procurement or purchase of materials is made on the basis of a requisition note sent by a manufacturing department or stores. The purchase requisition note is not raised in the purchasing department where most of the costs relating to procurement or purchase are incurred. Activity costs tend to behave in a similar manner to each other i.e., they have the same cost driver or the factor causing a change in the cost of an activity. Thus, it is believed that activity based costing helps in presenting a more realistic picture of the behaviour of costs.

Features of Activity Based Costing System

The main features of ABC System may be summarised as follows:

(*i*) ABC System is a tool for refining a costing system.

(*ii*) It involves the creation of smaller cost pools linked to the different activities.

(*iii*) Cost collection is made on the basis of a measurement of activity performed by each activity-cost pool. For example–set up hours may be taken as a measure of set up activity and cubic feet of packages moved as a measure of distribution activity.

(*iv*) Costs in each cost pool have a cause and effect relationship with the cost-allocation base over a period of time.

(*v*) Some of the costs in a cost pool can also be traced directly to products which leads to improvement in cost accuracy since no assumption is made about the cause and effect relationship between the cost pool and the cost-allocation base.

Important Terms in Activity Based Costing:

The operation of the ABC System involves the use of the following terms:

Cost Object: It refers to an item for which cost measurement is required e.g., a product, a service or a customer.

Cost Driver: A cost driver is any factor or force that causes a change in the cost of an activity. Cost driver may be divided into two parts:

(*a*) Resource Cost Driver and (*b*) Activity Cost Driver.

A resource cost driver is a measure of the quantity of resources consumed by an activity. It is used to assign the cost of a resource to an activity or cost pool.

An Activity cost driver is a measure of the frequency and intensity of demand, placed on activities by cost objects. It is used to assign activity costs to cost objects.

The cost drivers for various business functions i.e., production, marketing, research and development etc., are given below:

Business Functions	Cost Driver
1. Production	Number of Units
	Number of Set-ups.
2. Marketing	Number of Sales Personnel
	Number of Sales Orders
3. Research & Development	Number of research projects
	Personnel hours spent on a project
	Technical complexities of projects
4. Customer Service	Number of service calls
	Number of products serviced
	Hours spent on servicing products.

Steps/Stages in Activity Based Costing

The different steps or stages in ABC System can be given as follows:

1. **Identifying the chosen cost objects:** The cost objects of any organisation are the products or services and the goal is to first calculate the total cost of manufacturing and distributing these products and then their unit cost.
2. **Identifying the different activities within the organisation:** After the identification of the cost objects, the main activities which are being performed in the organisation have to identified. Usually the number of activities over cost centres in ABC will be much more as compared to traditional overhead system. The exact number will depend on how the management sub-divides the organisation's activities.
3. **Identifying the direct costs of products:** The direct costs of products / objects may comprise direct materials cost, direct labour cost and direct expenses. Classification of as many of the total costs as direct costs as is economically feasible, should be made. It reduces the amount of costs classified as indirect.
4. **Relating the overhead to the activities:** After identifying the organisation's activities, the various items of overhead are related to activities, both support and primary, that caused them. As a result of relating the items of overhead to various activities, 'Cost Pools' or 'Cost Buckets' are created. It is done by using resource cost drivers that reflect causality.
5. **Spreading the support activities across the primary activities:** The spreading of support activities (i.e., the activities which support or assist manufacturing) across the primary activities (correlated to the number

of units produced) is done on some suitable base, which reflects the use of the support activity. The base is the cost driver and is the measure of how the support activities are used.

6. **Determining the Activities Cost Drivers:** The determination of the activity cost drivers is done in order to relate the overheads collected in cost pools to the cost objects or products. It is done on the basis of the factor that drives the consumption of the activities.
7. **Calculating the Activity Cost Driver Rates:** The activity cost driver rates for each activity are calculated in the way in which overhead absorption rates would be calculated under the traditional system. It can be presented as follows:

$$\text{Activity Cost Driver Rate} = \frac{\text{Total Cost of Activity}}{\text{Activity Driver}}$$

   These activity cost driver rates are to be used for ascertaining the amount of overhead chargeable to various cost objects or products.
8. **Computing the Total Costs of Products or Cost Objects:** The total costs of the products shall be computed by adding all direct and indirect costs assigned to them. The amount of overhead chargeable to a product or cost object shall be calculated by multiplying the activity cost driver rates by different amounts of each activity that each product/other cost object consumes.

Need or Objects of Activities Based Costing:

ABC System is needed by an organisation for the purpose of accurate product costing in cases where–

(*i*) Production overhead costs are high in comparison to the various direct costs;

(*ii*) Product range of the organisation is highly diverse;

(*iii*) Overhead resources used by various products are very different in amounts;

(*iv*) Volume or quantity of production is not primary driving force for the consumption of overhead resources.

Illustration

Jumbo Auto Ltd., produces three products 'P', 'Q' and 'R', for which the standard costs and quantities per unit are as follows:

Products	P	Q	R
Output (units)	5,000	15,000	22,500
Direct Material per unit (Rs.)	100	80	60
Direct Wages per unit (Rs.)	60	80	100
Labour Hours per unit	3	4	5
Machine Hours per unit	4	4	7
No. of Purchase Requisitions	600	900	1,000
No. of Set-ups	140	110	150

Production Overhead split by departments:

Department A	Rs. 5,50,000
Department B	Rs. 7,50,000
	13,00,000

Department 'A' is labour intensive while Department 'B' is machine intensive.

Total labour hours in Department A = 55,000
Total machine hours in Department B = 1,50,000

Production overhead split by activity:

	Rs.
Receiving/Inspecting	7,00,000
Production Scheduling/Machine Set-up	6,00,000
	13,00,000

No. of batches received/inspected = 2,500
No of batches for scheduling and set-up = 400

You are required to:

(*i*) Prepare Product Cost Statement under traditional Absorption Costing and Activity Based Costing Method.

(*ii*) Compare the results under two methods.

Solution

Traditional Absorption Costing:

Calculation of overhead absorption rates:

$$\text{Department 'A'} = \frac{\text{Rs. } 5{,}50{,}000}{55{,}000 \text{ Labour Hours}}$$

$$= \text{Rs. } 10 \text{ per labour hour}$$

$$\text{Department 'B'} = \frac{\text{Rs. } 7{,}50{,}000}{1{,}50{,}000 \text{ Machine Hours}}$$

$$= \text{Rs. } 5 \text{ per machine hour.}$$

Product Cost Statement

	P	Q	R
	Rs.	Rs.	Rs.
Direct Materials	100	80	60
Direct Wages	60	80	100
Production Overheads:			
Department A	30	40	50
	(3 hrs. × Rs. 10)	(4 hrs. × Rs. 10)	(5 hrs. × Rs. 10)
Department B	20	20	35
	(4 hrs. × Rs. 5)	(4 hrs. × Rs. 5)	(7 hrs. × Rs. 5)
Total Cost Per Unit	210	220	245

Activity Based Costing:

Calculation of Cost Driver Rates:

(*i*) Receiving/Inspecting $= \dfrac{\text{Rs. 7,00,000}}{\text{2,500 (No. of Batches received/inspected)}}$

= Rs. 280 per requisition.

(*ii*) Production Scheduling/Machine Sets-up

$= \dfrac{\text{Rs. 6,00,000}}{\text{400 (No. of batches for scheduling)}}$

= Rs. 1,500 per set-up.

Product Cost Statement

	Product P	Product Q	Product R
	Rs.	Rs.	Rs.
Direct Materials	100	80	60
Direct Wages	60	80	100
Production Overheads:			
(*i*) Receiving	33.60	16.80	12.44
(*ii*) Production Scheduling	42.00	11.00	10.00
Total Cost per Unit	235.60	187.80	182.44

Note: Calculation of Overhead Per Unit.

Receiving :

Product P = Rs. 280 × 600 ÷ 5,000 = Rs. 33.60

Product Q = Rs. 280 × 900 ÷ 15,000 = Rs. 16.80

Product R = Rs. 280 × 1,000 ÷ 22,500 = Rs. 12.44

Production Scheduling

Product P = Rs. 1,500 × 140 ÷ 5,000 = Rs. 42.00

Product Q = Rs. 1,500 × 110 ÷ 15,000 = Rs. 11.00

Product R = Rs. 1,500 × 150 ÷ 22,500 = Rs. 10.00

From the above analysis, it is clear that Traditional Absorption Costing Method and Activity Based Costing Method show different cost results. Under traditional absorption costing method, Product 'R' is more expensive while under activity based costing method Product 'P' is more expensive. If we assume that Activity Based Costing is more accurate (which may or may not be possible), under traditional absorption costing method, product 'R' would be over-priced while product 'P' would be under-priced as a result of which sales for product 'R' would be less and sales for product 'P' would be more leading to a loss to the company.

Advantages of Activity Based Costing System:

ABC System is helpful for an organisation in a number of ways. These are:

(*i*) It helps in the ascertainment of more accurate cost information for the product and services.

(*ii*) It assists in overcoming the problems of over-costing and under-costing as a result of which the management can make more judicious pricing policies.

(*iii*) The analysis of the overhead costs with reference to activities is considered to be more realistic.

(*iv*) ABC system is very helpful in making the evaluation of new process technologies in multi-product concerns.

(*v*) It helps the management in taking better decisions relating to product strategies, product designs, product-mix and marketing.

(*vi*) This system makes available a systematic report on the resource spending as well as on resource consumption.

But the ABC System suffers from the following limitations:

(*i*) This system is more time-consuming due to the fact that the number of activities to which the overhead resources of an organisation have to be related, is very large.

(*ii*) It involves high cost of operation and can be used only by large organisations. It is not suitable for small scale units.

(*iii*) In some cases, the establishment of cause and effect relationship between Cost Driver and Costs may not be a simple affair.

QUESTIONS

1. Discuss the various limitations of traditional Absorption Costing System which have prompted the development of Activity Based Costing.

2. What do you mean by Activity Based Costing? What are its main features and need?

3. What is Activity Based Costing? Discuss the various steps or stages involved in ABC System.

4. Discuss the meaning and features of Activity Based Costing. What are its uses and limitations.

5. Write notes on:

(*i*) ABC System.

(*ii*) Cost Object.

(*iii*) Cost Driver.

EXERCISES

1. XY Co. Ltd., provides you the following information relating to its products 'R' and 'S'.

	Product 'R'	**Product 'S'**
Yearly Output	3,000 units	30,000 units
No. of Machine Hours per unit	4	4
No. of Labour hours per unit	8	8
Total Machine hours	12,000	1,20,000
Total Labour hours	24,000	2,40,000
No. of Purchase orders	240	480
No. of Set-ups	120	180

The overhead cost of the activities has been as under:

Volume related	3,30,000
Purchase related	3,60,000
Set-up related	6,30,000
	13,20,000

You are required to show the allocation of overhead costs of these activities to the products:

(*i*) On traditional absorption costing method and

(*ii*) On activity based costing method.

[Ans.	Product R	Product S
Traditional Method	Rs. 1,20,000	Rs. 12,00,000
ABC Method	Rs. 4,02,000	Rs, 9,18,000]

2. A company produces three products A, B and C for which the standard costs and quantities per unit are as follows:

Products	**A**	**B**	**C**
Quantity produced	10,000	20,000	30,000
Direct material/per unit (Rs.)	50	40	30
Direct Labour/per unit (Rs.)	30	40	50
Labour hours/per unit	3	4	5
Machine hours/per unit	4	4	7
No. of purchase requisitions	1,200	1,800	2,000
No. of set-ups	240	260	300

Production overhead split by departments – Department 1 = Rs. 11,00,000
– Department 2 = Rs.15,00,000

Department l is labour intensive and Department 2 is machine intensive.

Total labour hours in Department 1= 1,83,333

Total machine hours in Department 2 = 5,00,000

Production overhead split by activity – Receiving/inspecting	Rs. 14,00,000
– Production scheduling/machine set-up	Rs 12,00,000
	Rs. 26,00,000

Number of batches received/inspected = 5,000

Number of batches for scheduling and set-up = 800

You are required to:

(*i*) Prepare Product Cost Statement under traditional absorption costing andActivity Based Costing Method.

(*ii*) Compare the results under two methods.

[Ans. Total cost per unit

Products	**A**	**B**	**C**
Traditional Method	Rs. 110	Rs. 116	Rs. 131
ABC Method	Rs. 150	Rs. 125	Rs. 114]